Chapter Title	Focus Company Used as Main Illustration	Focus Company Logo	Type of Organization
12. Financial and Cost-Volume-Profit Models	Fairfield Blues, Inc.		Owner of minor league baseball team
13. Cost Management and Decision Making	Bootstrap Industries		Non-profit company providing jobs
14. Strategic Issues in Making Investment Decisions	Shade Tree Roasters		Sells organic coffees, teas, and specialty items
15. Budgeting and Financial Planning	Collegiate Apparel Company		Small manufacturer of college T-shirts
16. Standard Costing, Variance Analysis, and Kaizen Costing	Koala Camp Gear Company		Manufacturer of camping tents
17. Flexible Budgets, Overhead Cost Management, and Activity-Based Budgeting	Koala Camp Gear Company		Manufacturer of camping tents
18. Organizational Design, Responsibility Accounting, and Evaluation of Divisional Performance	Outback Outfitters, Ltd.		Large retailer of camping equipment and apparel
19. Transfer Pricing	Outback Outfitters, Ltd.		Large retailer of camping equipment and apparel
20. Strategy, Balanced Scorecards, and Incentive Systems	Valley Commercial Bank		Independent, five-branch bank

Cost Management

Strategies for Business Decisions

Third Edition

Cost Management

Strategies for Business Decisions

Ronald W. Hilton
Cornell University

Michael W. Maher
University of California, Davis

Frank H. Selto
University of Colorado at Boulder

McGraw-Hill
Irwin

Boston   Burr Ridge, IL   Dubuque, IA   Madison, WI   New York   San Francisco   St. Louis
Bangkok   Bogotá   Caracas   Kuala Lumpur   Lisbon   London   Madrid   Mexico City
Milan   Montreal   New Delhi   Santiago   Seoul   Singapore   Sydney   Taipei   Toronto

To my wife, Meg, and to our sons, Tim and Brad.

Ronald W. Hilton

To my family: my wife Miriam, my daughters Krista and Andrea, and my father Bill, who have taught me just about everything worth knowing.

Michael W. Maher

To my parents, Frank and Dorothy Selto, who taught me the value of love, hard work, and integrity. To my wife, Linda, and sons, Michael and Mark, who inspire and support me. To my first accounting teachers, Bill Bruns and Gary Sundem, who surprised me by demonstrating that accounting can be fun, useful, and intellectually challenging and that an academic career can be immensely rewarding. Finally, to my students, who every semester teach me something significant.

Frank H. Selto

ABOUT THE AUTHORS

Ronald W. Hilton is a Professor of Accounting at Cornell University. With bachelor's and master's degrees in accounting from The Pennsylvania State University, he received his Ph.D. from The Ohio State University.

A Cornell faculty member since 1977, Professor Hilton also has taught accounting at Ohio State and the University of Florida, where he held the position of Walter J. Matherly Professor of Accounting. Prior to pursuing his doctoral studies, Hilton worked for Peat, Marwick, Mitchell and Company and served as an officer in the United States Air Force.

Professor Hilton is a member of the Institute of Management Accountants and has been active in the American Accounting Association. He has served as associate editor of *The Accounting Review* and as a member of its editorial board. Hilton also has served on the editorial board of the *Journal of Management Accounting Research*. He has been a member of the resident faculties of both the Doctoral Consortium and the New Faculty Consortium sponsored by the American Accounting Association.

With wide-ranging research interests, Hilton has published articles in many journals, including the *Journal of Accounting Research, The Accounting Review, Management Science, Decision Sciences, The Journal of Economic Behavior and Organization, Contemporary Accounting Research,* and the *Journal of Mathematical Psychology*. He also has published a monograph in the AAA *Studies in Accounting Research* series, and he is the author of *Managerial Accounting: Creating Value in a Dynamic Business Environment,* and is a co-author of *Budgeting: Profit Planning and Control,* and *Cost Accounting: Concepts and Managerial Applications*. Professor Hilton's current research interests focus on contemporary cost management systems and international issues in managerial accounting. In recent years, he has toured manufacturing facilities and consulted with practicing managerial accountants in North America, Europe, Asia, and Australia.

Michael W. Maher A Professor of Management at the University of California–Davis, Professor Maher previously taught at the University of Michigan, the University of Chicago, and the University of Washington. He also worked on the audit staff at Arthur Andersen & Co. and was a self-employed financial consultant for small businesses. He received his BBA from Gonzaga University (which named him Distinguished Alumnus in 1989) and his MBA and Ph.D. from the University of Washington, and he earned the CPA from the state of Washington.

Professor Maher was president of the Management Accounting Section of the American Accounting Association and has served on the editorial boards of *The Accounting Review, Accounting Horizons, Journal of Management Accounting Research,* and *Management Accounting*. Co-author of two leading textbooks, *Principles of Accounting* and *Managerial Accounting*, Maher has co-authored several additional books and monographs, including *Internal Controls in U.S. Corporations* and *Management Incentive Compensation Plans*, and published articles in many journals, including *Management Accounting, The Journal of Accountancy, The Accounting Review, Journal of Accounting Research, Financial Executive,* and *The Wall Street Journal*.

For his research on internal controls, Professor Maher was awarded the American Accounting Association's Competitive Manuscript Award and the AICPA Notable Contribution to Literature Award. He also has received the award for the Outstanding Tax Manuscript, and from the students at the University of California's Graduate School of Management, he has received the Annual Outstanding Teacher Award three times and a special award for outstanding service twice. Maher's current research includes studies of the efficacy of online education, health care costs, and corporate corruption.

Frank H. Selto Professor Selto has been on the faculty at the University of Colorado at Boulder since 1985, where he has taught accounting at the undergraduate and graduate levels and served as Division Chair of Accounting and Information Systems. He served as a research fellow for six years at the University of Melbourne. Selto has taught at the University of Denver, the University of Colorado at Denver, and the University of Washington. He holds MBA and Ph.D. degrees in accounting from the University of Washington and BS and MS degrees in mechanical engineering from Gonzaga University and the University of Utah, respectively. Prior to earning his MBA and Ph.D. degrees, he worked as a mechanical engineer and served as an officer in the US Army Corps of Engineers.

Active in the American Accounting Association and its Management Accounting Section, Professor Selto was the editor of the Education Research section of *The Accounting Review* and has served on the editorial boards of *The Accounting Review, Journal of Management Accounting Research, Management Accounting Research,* and *Accounting Horizons*. A researcher of management accounting and management control, Selto has published articles in the *Journal of Accounting Research, Accounting, Organizations & Society, Journal of Cost Management* and *Journal of Management Accounting Research*, one of which was recognized as a Notable Contribution to the Management Accounting Literature.

Hilton/Maher/Selto

Cost Management.

The front view of the Louvre Museum in Paris presents a striking juxtaposition. The museum itself is a Renaissance palace, while the entrance is a modernist glass pyramid. The dramatic combination of these two styles shows how contemporary ideas can provide new perspectives on classic principles.

For this reason, we have chosen the entrance of the Louvre as the cover of *Cost Management: Strategies for Business Decisions*, by Ronald Hilton, Michael Maher, and Frank Selto. This image—the combination of the classic and the cutting-edge—encapsulates the authors' mission and vision.

Accountants, financial analysts, and consultants must measure costs, as they always have, but it is vital today that they also identify, analyze, and design opportunities and methods for improving costs and performance. Tomorrow's managers must actively manage costs to deliver more value.

The text is user friendly, does a good job of presenting and explaining the material, and makes cost accounting interesting—no easy feat! — Scott Butterfield, University of Colorado at Colorado Springs

Where Tradition and Innovation Converge

Focus Companies.

The concepts and applications explored in each chapter are developed in the context of a realistic focus company, based closely on the practices and experiences of an actual organization. Ronald Hilton pioneered this approach in his Managerial Accounting textbook, and Hilton/Maher/Selto's integration of focus companies and real world examples is unmatched by any other cost accounting book.

I find these very effective. I think the focus companies are really a great way to motivate the students to look at some very challenging material. — John Haverty, St. Joseph's University

Balance.

Cost Management features a balance of manufacturing, service, government, mature, and start-up focus companies to demonstrate that cost management concerns are universally applicable. Today's students will work in a wide variety of business environments and will benefit from exposure to the diverse examples used by Hilton/Maher/Selto.

Contemporary.

The authors combine value chain, activity-based costing, activity-based management, value-added analyses, and economic value added to build a logical and easily communicated view of cost management, one that is highly relevant to business today. Because the field of cost management is evolving daily, the authors incorporate current research throughout the book in Research Insights boxes.

I have always believed that good research should support what we do in the classroom. This is achieved with the "Research Insight" sections. — Douglas Clinton, Northern Illinois University

Decision-Making Focus.

Concepts are presented in a decision-making context, so students learn how they can use cost information to make better business decisions. Each chapter begins with Cost Management Challenges, which engage students and ask them to take a proactive approach to mastering chapter concepts, while numerous You're the Decision Maker applications actively involve the students in problem-solving. Accompanying focus company sites on the book's CD and Online Learning Center give students an opportunity to perform further analyses and make more decisions based on extensive simulated data.

The Decision Maker boxes connect the course content to the "real world" for students, which increases their perceptions of the course's relevance. I believe this emphasis is very valuable. — Laurie Burney McWhorter, University of North Carolina at Charlotte

How Does *Cost Management: Strategies for Business Decisions* Motivate Students?

To help students learn the principles of cost management and appreciate their importance in contemporary business, Cost Management includes a wide range of pedagogical features.

Learning Objectives

These appear at the beginning of every chapter and are re-visited in the margin where they are first addressed. Each end-of-chapter exercise, problem or case references its learning objective.

Photos

Photos add to the realism of the topics and in Cost Management are carefully chosen for pedagogical value. Photos from real organizations show operational concepts and cost management practices to engage students and emphasize key points.

Chapter 3

Cost Accumulation for Job-Shop and Batch Production Operations

After completing this chapter, you should be able to:

1. Explain the differences in job-order, process, and operation costing.

2. Explain how costs flow through the manufacturing accounts.

_____ jobs or products using a

_____ entries to record job

5. Use a predetermined overhead rate to assign indirect resource costs to production jobs.

6. Explain how to measure production costs under actual, normal, and standard costing systems.

7. Discuss the role of job-order costing in service organizations.

8. Understand how companies manage long-term projects and their costs.

...antity to the production line is a ...incurred for each pro...

Designing a product using this computer-ai...

This book is more focused on decision making and providing discussion within real business context. — Huey-Lian Sun, Morgan State University

Interweaving the theoretical concepts into the focus company makes the concepts more memorable and understandable. Students typically remember a good story. The focus companies assist the instructor in becoming a storyteller. — Linda Maurer, Fontbonne University

The Focus Company illustrations are critical to keeping my students interested in the chapter content. — Alexander Sannella, Rutgers University at Newark

Focus Companies

Each chapter is built around a focus company whose story continues through the chapter. These diverse companies include enough background to add realism to the presentation and stimulate student interest in the topic. They represent manufacturing, retail, not-for-profit, and service firms and are listed on the front endpapers of the text.

- Every chapter begins with a company document highlighting a business challenge facing the organization featured in the chapter.

- Each time the focus company is presented in the chapter, its logo is shown so the student sees its application to the text topic.

Spreadsheet Exhibits

Many of the exhibits are Excel spreadsheets used to make students comfortable with this widely used analytical tool and emphasize its use in cost management. Spreadsheets are also used in the end-of-chapter material.

Cost-Management Challenges

(Solutions are on page 116.)

1. **What** factors should a cost-management analyst consider when designing a product-costing system?

2. **What** features should a job-order costing system have, and how can they be developed?

3. **How** can cost-management analysts use job-cost information to support planning and decision-making activities?

Glass Creations
2819 Pelican Drive
Madeira Beach, Florida 33708

January 30

Ms. Grace Riley
Gulf Coast Aquarium
Tampa, Florida

Dear Ms. Riley:

We have completed the estimates for the two stained glass doors you are planning for the aquarium's main entry portico. Our designer has developed sketches for some beautiful stained glass panels for the doors following the guidelines you gave us during our meeting in November. Each door has six stained glass panels, featuring a variety of marine species, from dolphins and whales to starfish and sea horses. The panel designs are, as you requested, very colorful. I think you will be pleased with them.

We have carefully estimated the costs of the doors, which cover the materials, design talent, glass workers' labor, and applied overhead, which is based on the projected labor time required for the job. As per our previous discussions, our price for your nonprofit organization will be cost plus a modest 10 percent profit margin.

I will call you next week to set up a meeting so that we can go over the design sketches and the projected job-cost figures. Naturally, we will be happy to make any modifications that you wish. Thank you for allowing us to make a contribution to your aquarium project.

Sincerely,

Jeremiah Jacobson

Jeremiah Jacobson

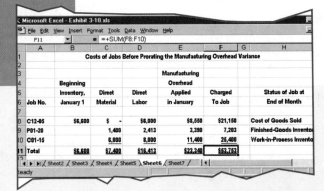

How Does *Cost Management* Prepare Students to Make Decisions that Influence Company Performance?

REAL WORLD EXAMPLES

Cost Management Challenges

Each chapter begins with this unique feature that focuses students on the key content of the chapter. This feature challenges students to answer questions the cost manager must answer.

You're the Decision Maker

Each chapter actively involves the student in problem solving by posing strategic questions at key points in the chapter. These aren't quizzes or examples. They expand the text by asking students to apply the knowledge gained in the chapter to realistic conditions. They actively engage the student in the decisions the focus company face.

Cost Management in Practice

This feature highlights the cost management practices of real companies.

Research Insight

We believe an effective way to demonstrate the value of research to cost managers is to include short descriptions of research studies that address important cost management issues. This feature incorporates research that has been replicated and applied successfully.

Cost Management Challenges

(Solutions are on page 23)

↓ Chapters begin with a company document that introduces issues to be discussed in the chapter. These companies are fictional, but based on practices of real companies.

1. What should a cost-management analyst do when the demands of the job conflict with personal or professional ethical standards?

2. How does a cost-management analyst contribute to strategic decision makin

EMAIL MEMORANDUM

To: Melanie DelVal, Chief Financial Officer
    Jackie Lin, Vice President, Marketing
From: Frank Barnes, President and CEO
Subject: URGENT: New product idea
Attachment: Newproduct.doc (145 KB)

Jackie and Melanie: I am still at the Data Communication Conference in Boston. I just met with our largest European customer, who gave me an intriguing idea for a new Internet-based data communication product. I ha attached my preliminary description of the new product's goals, objective functions, and operating requirements that are based on the customer's emerging needs

d Rates

d overhead rate on a quarterly basis de for the year:

Estimated Direct-Labor Hours	Quarterly Predetermined Overhead Rate
2,000	?
3,500	?
4,000	?
2,500	?
12,000	

You're the Decision Maker 3.1

neron window, requires the following

ply chain management. An organiza-
ormation into and out of the organiza-
supply chains to reduce costs and

re than $65 million over an 18-month
ram to collaborate with retailers about
ve greater integration within its opera-
lations."
ram (ARP) to ship products from its
ters from which stores are restocked.
inventory positions and sales data to
d on this information. Campbell Soun

Cost Management in Practice 3.1

nizations could focus on improving
nformation). Most IT improvements
g computing speed to deliver more
ialists are sometimes providing the
s competitive environment. To build
bout external competitors, changes
ost managers and IT specialists is to
understand the capability of "tech-

Research Insight 3.1

How Does *Cost Management* Reinforce Learning?

SUCCESSFUL LEARNING BEGINS WITH PRACTICE

There is no shortcut to learning accounting. Students must practice to master basic accounting concepts. The text includes a prodigious supply of practice materials, exercises and problems.

End-of-Chapter Material

Hilton/Maher/Selto's Cost Management is known for its comprehensive and reliable end-of-chapter material. Each chapter includes an extensive selection of assignment material including Review, Critical Analysis, Exercises, Problems and Cases. Numerous adapted CMA and CPA problems are included to prepare students for the CPA exam.

Every chapter in the text includes problems and cases exploring
• Ethical issues
• International matters
• Group work
• Internet use
• Communication skills

I think your textbook does a great job of using Excel illustrations and providing some substantive Excel problems to assign.
—John Haverty, St. Joseph's University

Excel Spreadsheets

• Build Your Own Spreadsheet. One or more of the exercises and problems in each chapter include an option for students to build a spreadsheet to solve the problem's requirements. Students are also asked to use the spreadsheet to determine the effect on the solutions if various parameters in the problem are changed. This is critical in helping students develop the spreadsheet skills necessary for graduation and on the new CPA exam.

• Excel templates. Many exercises and problems can be solved using the Excel templates contained on the text's Online Learning Center. An Excel logo appears next to these problems for easy identification.

g. Build your own spreadsheet. Build an Excel spreads spreadsheet to determine the new value for the total assigned to job 52 in November, and the actual facto following input parameters changes by the amount ir each parameter change independently.)
1. Estimated overhead costs for the year are as foll

Machine hours	50,0
Unit-level overhead	$400,0
Facility-level overhead	210,0

Nocando Manufacturing, 300 hours
Ianhattan Consultants bills clients at
ars were worked in January with 200
curred and assigned to clients on the
, some overhead was not assigned to
nistrative costs. All transactions were

Problem 3.49
Job Costs in a S
Organization
(LO 2, 3, 5, 7)

mhhe.com/hilton3e

WHAT'S NEW IN THE THIRD EDITION

Revisions to Cost Management are in response to extensive feedback from instructors and student reviews, comments and suggestions.

Overall Revisions

- The material in Chapter 21 has been condensed and incorporated into other chapters, primarily Chapters 18 and 20. The new edition has 20 chapters instead of 21.

- A new Build Your Own Spreadsheet feature appears in one or more exercises or problems in each chapter. Students are asked to build a spreadsheet to solve the problem's requirements, and then are asked to use their spreadsheet to solve the same requirements when key parameters in the problem are changed.

- In recognition of the need to address ethical issues in accounting, many of the chapters highlight ethical issues that arise in the context of cost management.

- Many of the popular Cost Management in Practice and Research Insight boxes have been replaced or revised to ensure that the third edition is up-to-date and relevant.

- Many of the exercises, problems and cases have been revised, with new numbers or additional requirements. The third edition also contains many new problems.

Chapter 1

Expanded coverage of basic ethical behavior, standards, and codes.

Explained strategic decision making, threats to competitive advantages, and cost management's support role.

De-emphasized benchmarking and accounts-receivable analysis.

Focused on benefit-cost and variance analysis as fundamental cost-management analysis tools.

Chapter 2

Content divided into two sections, which can be covered independently. Section I covers cost management and product-costing systems. Section II covers absorption, variable and throughput costing.

Emphasized tie-ins between cost management and organizational strategy.

Added coverage of ethical issues involving the intentional overproduction of inventory to reduce unit costs and boost current income under absorption costing.

Added discussion of direct labor as a variable or a committed, and largely fixed, cost.

Chapter 3

Revised and updated end-of-chapter material.

Chapter 4

Revised assignments to demonstrate limitations of traditional costing methods.

Added new research insight addressing the performance of companies that installed ABC.

Chapter 5

Consolidated discussion of target costing. (Previously discussed in Chapters 5 and 12.)

Chapter 6

Simplified discussion of distribution costs.

Revised discussion of customer sales analysis to make it more clear.

Chapter 7

Revised discussion of JIT manufacturing to make the discussion more clear.

Expanded discussion of quality to tie it to corporate integrity.

Added new chapter summary.

Chapter 8

Improved presentation of exhibits to make the computations more clear.

Added demonstration of cost flows for abnormal spoilage.

Chapter 9

Updated Cost Management in Practice.

I think your approach to Activity Based Costing is terrific and is one of the really strong aspects of this book.
— John Haverty, St. Joseph's University

Chapter 10

Updated Cost Management in Practice.

Revised end-of-chapter material.

Chapter 11

Revised cost management challenges.

Integrated simple and multiple regression discussions.

Added a five-step regression-analysis process.

Moved high-low method to separate section after simple regression.

Added basic choice among multiple regression models based on economic plausibility and adjusted R-square.

Simplified discussion of account analysis.

Added discussion of how regression works to Appendix A.

Moved learning curve estimation and use to Appendix B.

Chapter 12

Moved material on managing scarce resources and Theory of Constraints to an Appendix.

Updated and added new end-of-chapter material.

Chapter 13

Improved introduction and motivation for focus company.

Deleted duplicate coverage of target costing, which is covered in Chapter 4.

Improved coverage of lifecycle costs; added numerical example.

Improved discussion of outsourcing, relevant costs, and long-term impacts of decisions.

Improved cost management challenges and chapter summary.

Chapter 14

Added new focus on strategic investments, including effects of external events and competitors' actions.

Emphasized modeling external events and competitors' actions.

Introduced real option value (ROV) analysis, not available in any competing text.

Revised end-of-chapter materials with extensive Excel solution support.

Chapter 15

Added new research insights covering CAM-I's beyond budgeting and other new developments in budgeting.

Chapter 16

Added material on the ethical issues surrounding employees' reluctance to share cost-saving ideas.

Chapter 17

Updated and revised end-of-chapter material.

Chapter 18

Added material using investment center performance measures to provide managerial incentives. (Moved from Chapter 21.)

Chapter 19

Added new Research Insight.

Updated and revised end-of-chapter material.

Chapter 20

Combined balanced scorecard and incentive topics to create capstone chapter.

Provided critical appraisal of balanced scorecards.

Eliminated quantified scorecards.

Focused on ethical issues of incentive systems.

Moved theories of motivation (expectancy, goal-setting, and agency) to an appendix.

(Quote about chapter 2) Excellent presentation of absorption and variable costing.
— Scott Butterfield, University of Colorado at Colorado Springs

(Quote about chapter 7) This is one of the best and most comprehensive chapters that I have ever seen in the area of quality.
— Robert Zelin, Minnesota State University at Mankato

(Quote about chapter 14) Due Diligence is extremely important yet not covered in texts—great section.
— Margaret O'Reilly-Allen, Rider University

SUPPLEMENTS

Hilton/Maher/Selto's Cost Management provides materials that supply yo with superior classroom support to bring out the best in your students.

Instructor Supplements

Instructor's Resource Manual
(Available on the Online Learning Center (OLC) and Instructors Resource CD)

This comprehensive manual includes detailed chapter outlines with teaching tips and suggestions for alternate ways to present the text material. It was prepared by Roger Doost of Clemson University.

Solutions Manual
(Available on the OLC and Instructor Resource CD)

Prepared by the authors and carefully reviewed for accuracy, the manual contains complete solutions to all the text's end-of-chapter assignments.

Overall, I believe that this is the best Cost Management text on the market.
— Alexander Sannella, Rutgers University at Newark

Test Bank
(Available on the Instructor's Resource CD)

This test bank in Word format contains true/false, multiple-choice questions, essay, and short problems requiring analysis and interpretation. Each test item is coded for level of difficulty and tied to a learning objective. It was prepared by Kathleen Sevigny of Bridgewater State College and Karen Tabak of Maryville University.

Computerized Test Bank
(Available on the Instructor's Resource CD)

This test bank utilizes McGraw-Hill's EZ Test testing software to quickly create customized exams. This user-friendly program allows instructors to sort questions by format, edit existing questions or add new ones. It also can scramble questions for multiple versions of the same test.

The text is clearly superior to other books in the managerial/cost accounting market.
— Richard Kelsey, Nova Southeastern University

PowerPoint Slides
(Available on the OLC and Instructor's Resource CD)

These slides illustrate key chapter topics. They were prepared by Jon A. Booker and Charles W. Caldwell of Tennessee Technological University and Susan Galbreath of David Lipscomb University.

Instructor Resource CD-ROM
ISBN 007283014X

This CD includes electronic versions of the Instructor's Manual, Solutions Manual, Test Bank, as well as PowerPoint slides, video clips, exhibits in the text, and Excel templates and solutions.

Online Learning Center (OLC)
www.mhhe.com/hilton3e

See page xviii for details.

Student Supplements

Study Guide
ISBN 0072830093

This invaluable guide incorporates many of the accounting skills essential to student success. Each chapter contains an overview of the main topics, chapter study suggestions, and review and self test questions. It was prepared by Janice Mereba of North Carolina A&T State University.

You're The
Decision Maker CD

This CD includes simulated Internet sites for six of the Focus Companies found in the textbook. The visually rich sites are based on and extend the "You're the Decision Maker" activities and include management interviews, company background, and cost information data on spreadsheets. Students are asked to make decisions based on the information in the text and found on the "company site." These activities reinforce the importance of cost management and can be used for independent study or additional assignments by instructors. Students will be engaged by this unique opportunity to act as a cost manager or consultant who is called upon to solve an important, real-world company challenge. These simulated sites were prepared by Frank Selto. This CD can be packaged with the text. PowerPoint slides are also included.

Check Figures
(Available on the Online Learning Center (OLC)

These provide key answers for selected problems in the text.

PowerPoint Slides
(Available on the Online Learning Center (OLC)

These slides cover the key concepts presented in each chapter.

Excel Templates
(Available on the Online Learning Center (OLC)

This software allows students to develop spreadsheet skills by using templates to solve selected assignments identified by an icon in the end-of-chapter material. These were developed by Peggy Hussey.

Online Learning Center (OLC)
www.mhhe.com/hilton3e
See the next page for details.

> *This web-based development is a new and unique concept. It gives students an active learning experience. They are immersed in the company as if they are an employee or consultant and solving its problems.*
> — Anwar Salimi, California State Polytechnic University at Pomona

A New Focus on Technology

Our technology resources help students and instructors focus on learning success. By using the Internet and multimedia students get book-specific help at their convenience.

Teaching aids make in-class presentations easy and stimulating. These aids give you more power than ever to teach your class the way you want.

Online Learning Center (OLC)

www.mhhe.com/hilton3e

More and more students are studying online. That's why we offer an Online Learning Center (OLC) that follows Cost Management chapter by chapter. It doesn't require any building or maintenance on your part. It's ready to go the moment you type in the URL. The OLC includes:

- You're The Decision Maker Activities
- Text Updates
- Excel Templates
- Glossary
- Chapter Objectives
- Interactive Quizzes
- PowerPoint slides
- Check Figures
- Key Term Flashcards
- Sample Study Guide chapter

For instructors, the book's password-protected OLC contains:
- Instructor's Manual
- Solutions Manual
- PowerPoint slides
- Excel templates and solutions
- You're the Decision Maker exercise solutions
- Transition Notes
- Text Updates

Instructors can pull all of this material into their PageOut course syllabus or use it as part of another online course management system.

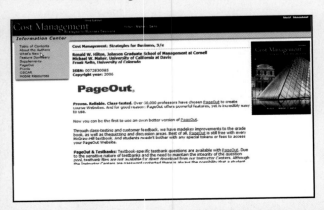

CPS Classroom Performance System

This is a revolutionary system that brings ultimate interactivity to the classroom. CPS is a wireless response system that gives you immediate feedback from every student in the class. CPS units include easy-to-use software for creating and delivering questions and assessments to your class. With CPS you can ask subjective and objective questions. Then every student simply responds with their individual, wireless response pad, providing instant results. CPS is the perfect tool for engaging students while gathering important assessment data.

Online Course Management
(WebCT, Blackboard, and eCollege)

We offer Cost Management content for complete online courses. You can customize the Online Learning Center content and author your own course materials. No matter which online course solution you choose, you can count on the highest level of support. Our specialists offer free training and answer any question you have through the life of your adoption.

Instructor Resource CD-ROM

This CD includes electronic versions of the Instructor's Manual, Solutions Manual, Test Bank, Computerized Test Bank, as well as PowerPoint slides, video clips, and all exhibits in the text in a PowerPoint format.

Excel Spreadsheets

One of the key features of Cost Management is the integration of Excel. Many of the problems on the new CPA exam require "simulations" using Excel-like software. Students need to be comfortable using spreadsheets to concentrate on the content of the problem. Beside "Build Your Own Spreadsheet" exercises, Cost Management also includes Excel templates to give students more practice in using this tool. The templates are on the Online Learning Center.

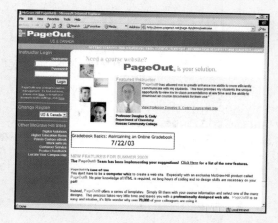

PageOut
McGraw-Hill's
Course Management System

Pageout is the easiest way to create a Website for your accounting course. Just fill in a series of boxes with plain English and click on one of our professional designs. In no time your course is online with a Website that contains your syllabus. If you need help, our team of specialists is ready to take your course materials and build a custom website to your specifications. To learn more visit www.pageout.net.

Knowledge Gateway

Knowledge Gateway is an all-purpose service and resource center for instructors teaching online. While training programs from WebCT and Blackboard will help teach you their software, only McGraw-Hill/Irwin has services to help you actually manage and teach your online course, as well as run and maintain the software. To see how these platforms can assist your online course, visit www.mhhe.com/solutions.

Acknowledgments

We have learned from long experience that the most useful comments challenge our assumptions and expose any weaknesses in our thought or exposition. The many reviewers, editors, and students who challenged us and held us to the highest standards have contributed to the success of this revision. The authors sincerely appreciate the efforts of the many people who have helped to improve this text. Our students continue to challenge us and insist that our text be at least as accessible as we are. Numerous professors in reviews and focus groups have thoroughly reviewed, criticized, and commented on the first and second editions. We have thoroughly digested that invaluable input and feedback, especially when some of it was harsh. In particular, we want to thank the following professors for their help in preparing the third edition.

REVIEWERS

Vidya Awasthi, *Seattle University*

K. R. Balachandran, *NYU - Stern*

Joyce Berg, *University of Iowa*

Joseph Berry, *Campbell University*

James Bierstaker, *University of Massachusetts at Boston*

Wayne Bremser, *Villanova University*

Scott Butterfield, *University of Colorado at Colorado Springs*

Douglas Clinton, *Northern Illinois University*

Robert Cooper, *Methodist College*

Alan Czyzewski, *Indiana State University*

Charles Davis, *Baylor University*

Robert Elmore, *Tennessee Tech University*

Michael Farina, *Cerritos College*

Tim Farmer, *University of Missouri at St. Louis*

Donald Gribbin, *Southern Illinois University*

Kay Guess, *St. Edward's University*

Nanette Hagood, *Spring Hill College*

Steven Hall, *University of Nebraska at Kearney*

Michael Haselkorn, *Bentley College*

John Haverty, *St. Joseph's University*

Thomas Hemmer, *University of Chicago*

Geoffrey Heriot, *Greenville Technology College*

Deborah Hughes Newell, *Union University*

Celina Jozsi, *University of South Florida at Tampa*

Sanford Kahn, *University of Cincinnati*

Richard Kelsey, *Nova Southeastern University*

David Keys, *Northern Illinois University*

Cindy Killian, *Wilkes Community College*

Chor Lau, *California State University at Los Angeles*

Lillie Lewis, *Southwest Tennessee Community College*

Suzanna Lowensohn, *Barry University*

Linda Maurer, *Fontbonne University*

Brian McGuire, *University of Southern Indiana*

Laurie McWhorter, *University of North Carolina at Charlotte*

Cheryl Mitchem, *Virginia State University*

Margaret O'Reilly-Allen, *Rider University*

Roy Regal, *University of Montana at Missoula*

Lawrence Roman, *Cuyahoga Community College*

Gerald Rosson, *Lynchburg College*

Anwar Salimi, *California State Polytechnic University at Pomona*

Alexander Sannella, *Rutgers University at Newark*

Gregory Sinclair, *California State University at Hayward*

Thomas Smith, *Fort Valley State University*

Soliman Soliman, *Tulane University*

Carol Springer, *Georgia State University*

John Stancil, *Florida Southern College*

Jane Stoneback, *Central Connecticut State University*

Huey-Lian Sun, *Morgan State University*

Kim Tan, *California State University at Stanislaus*

Michael Tyler, *Barry University*

Dan Viele, *Webtser University*

Robert Zelin, *Minnesota State University at Mankato*

Thomas Zeller, *Loyola University, Chicago*

The authors also express their appreciation to the many people who have contributed to the development of this textbook and gratefully acknowledge their valuable constructive criticism and many suggestions.

Karen Adamson, *Central Washington University*

Neil Adkins, *Marshall University*

Penne Ainsworth, *University of Wyoming*

Henry Anderson, *University of Central Florida*

Rowland Atiase, *University of Texas at Austin*

Jack Bailes, *Oregon State University*

Homer Bates, *University of North Florida*

James Bedingfield, *University of Maryland*

Margaret Boldt, *Murray State University*

Tom Buckoff, *North Dakota State University*

Marv Bouillon, *Iowa State University*

Annhenrie Campbell, *California State University, Stanislaus*

Dennis Caplan, *Columbia University*

Bill Carter, *University of Virginia*

John Chandler, *University of Illinois*

Gordon Chapman, *Eastern Washington University*

Kim Charland, *Kansas State University*

Al Chen, *North Carolina State University*

Ray Clanton, *University of Central Oklahoma*

Peter Clarke, *University College, Dublin*

Thomas Clausen, *Kansas State University*

Elizabeth Cole, *Old Dominion University*

John Core, *University of Pennsylvania*

Susan Crosson, *Santa Fe Community College*

Masako Darrough, *Baruch College*

Larry Ducharme, *University of Washington*

Michael Eames, *Santa Clara University*

Leslie Eldenburg, *University of Arizona*

James Emig, *Villanova University*

Neil Fargher, *University of Oregon*

Len Fertuck, *University of Toronto*

Michael Finch, *University of Maryland*

David Franz, *San Francisco State University*

Karen Frey, *Gettysburg College*

Ann Gabriel, *University of Notre Dame*

Jackson Gillespie, *University of Delaware*

Robert Greenberg, *Washington State University*

Dale Grinnell, *University of Vermont*

Daryl Guffey, *East Carolina University*

Rama Guttikonda, *Alabama State University*

Steven Hansen, *University of California, Los Angeles*

James Russell Hardin, *Pittsburg State University*

Rosalie Hallbauer, *Florida International University*

Ennis Hawkins, *Sam Houston State University*

Cynthia Heagy, *University of Houston, Clear Lake*

Leon Hoshower, *Ohio University*

Muhammed Hussein, *University of Connecticut*

Paul Hutchison, *University of North Texas*

Raffi Indjejikian, *University of Michigan*

Steven Jackson, *University of Tennessee, Martin*

Phillip Jagolinzer, *University of Southern Maine*

Holly Johnston, *Boston University*

Suresh Kalagnanam, *University of Saskatchewan*

Hussein Kandiel, *SUNY-Plattsburgh*

Robert Kee, *University of Alabama*

Il-Woon Kim, *University of Akron*

Lawrence Klein, *Bentley University*

Paul Koogler, *Southwest Texas State University*

Leon Korte, *University of South Dakota*

Stacy Kovar, *Kansas State University*

Leslie Kren, *University of Wisconsin, Milwaukee*

Ranjani Krishnan, *Michigan State University*

Robert Lin, *California State University, Hayward*

Danny Litt, *University of California, Los Angeles*

Jordan Lowe, *University of Nevada, Las Vegas*

Joan Luft, *Michigan State University*

Ron Marshall, *Michigan State University*

Annie McGown, *Texas A&M University*

Kevin McNelis, *New Mexico State University*

Bruce Miller, *University of California, Los Angeles*

David Morris, *North Georgia College*

Ann Murphy, *Metro State College-Denver*

Gordon Niemi, *Northwestern Michigan University*

Emeka Nwaeze, *Rutgers University*

Marilyn Okleshen, *Mankato State University*

Richard Ortman, *University of Nebraska at Omaha*

Guy Owings, *Pittsburgh State University*

Mary Ellen Oliverio, *Pace University*

Janet Papiernik, *Edinboro University of Pennsylvania*

Barbra Peck, *University of Illinois-Chicago*

David Platt, *University of Texas, Austin*

Peter Poznanski, *Cleveland State University*

Jenice Prather-Kinsey, *University of Missouri*

Claire Purvis, *California State University-San Bernardino*

Olga Quintana, *University of Miami*

Priscilla Reese, *Idaho State University*

Leslie Richeson, *Franklin and Marshall*

Diane Roberts, *University of San Francisco*

Hanno Roberts, *Norwegian School of Management*

Gerald Rosson, *Lynchburg College*

Jack Ruhl, *Western Michigan University*

Grant Russell, *University of Waterloo*

Jane Saly, *University of Minnesota*

Henry Schwarzbach, *University of Rhode Island*

Robert Seay, *Murray State University*

Ali Sedaghat, *Loyola College, Maryland*

Inshik Seol, *University of Massachusetts*

Doug Sharp, *Wichita State University*

Karl Sherman, *Lake Superior State University*

Jeffrey Shields, *Suffolk University*

Frank Shuman, *Utah State University*

Kenneth Sinclair, *Lehigh University*

Mark Soczek, *Washington University*

Lanny Solomon, *University of Missouri-Kansas City*

Parvez Sopariwala, *Grand Valley State University*

Carolyn Stokes, *Francis Marion University*

David Stout, *Villanova University*

Nathan Stuart, *University of Florida*

Cathy Sullivan, *James Madison University*

Paulette Tandy, *University of Nevada-Las Vegas*

Leslie Turner, *Northern Kentucky University*

Michael Ulinski, *Pace University*

Catherine Usoff, *Bentley College*

Bente Villadsen, *University of Michigan*

Gloria Vollmers, *University of Maine*

David Wallin, *The Ohio State University*

Timothy West, *Iowa State University*

Jackson White, *University of Arkansas*

Sally Widener, *Rice University*

Patrick Wilkie, *George Mason University*

Neil Wilner, *University of North Texas*

Jim Xie, *University of Alberta*

We thank Beth Woods and Cathleen Burns (University of Colorado at Boulder) for their thorough checking of the text for accuracy and completeness. We also acknowledge Lanny Solomon (University of Missouri) for his help with special topics.

Supplements are an important part of any textbook and we especially thank the people who helped prepare them. The Study Guide was prepared by Janice Mereba of North Carolina A&T State University. Excel templates developed by Peggy Hussey of Colorado Technical University. The Instructor's Manual was prepared by Roger Doost of Clemson University. Roger also developed the OnLine Quizzes on the text web site. The Test Bank was written by Kathleen Sevigny of Bridgewater State College and Karen Tabak of Maryville University. The PowerPoint Slides were done by Jon A. Booker and Charles W. Caldwell of Tennessee Technological University and Susan Galbreath of David Lipscomb University.

The authors acknowledge the Institute of Management Accountants for permission to use problems from the Certified Management Accountant (CMA) examinations. We also acknowledge the American Institute of Certified Public Accountants for permission to use problems from the Uniform CPA Examinations, Questions, and Unofficial Answers.

Finally, the authors express their gratitude to the many fine people at McGraw-Hill/Irwin who have so professionally guided this book through the development and publication processes. In particular we acknowledge Steve DeLancey, Gail Korosa, Christine Vaughan, Matthew Baldwin, Debra Sylvester, Lori Kramer, Elizabeth Mavitz, Marc Chernoff, and Carol Loreth.

Ronald W. Hilton
Michael W. Maher
Frank H. Selto

Brief Contents

Contents

Part One

Setting the Strategic Foundation
The Importance of Analyzing and
Managing Costs   *1*

3 Cost Accumulation for Job-Shop and Batch Production Operations 86

PART TWO
Activity-Based Management 135

4 Activity-Based Costing Systems 136

PART THREE

*Process Costing
and Cost Allocation   291*

8   Process-Costing Systems   292

9   Joint-Process Costing   332

10   Managing and Allocating Support-Service Costs   362

Part Four

Planning and Decision Making   407

11   Cost Estimation   408

12   Financial and Cost-Volume-Profit Models   458

13   Cost Management and Decision Making   506

14   Strategic Issues in Making Investment Decisions   552

15 Budgeting and Financial Planning 594

Part Five
Evaluating and Managing Performance
Creating and Managing Value-Added
Effort *645*

18   **Organizational Design, Responsibility Accounting, and Evaluation of Divisional Performance   742**

20 Strategy, Balanced Scorecards, and Incentive Systems   818

19 Transfer Pricing   788

Cost Management

Strategies for Business Decisions

Setting the Strategic Foundation

The Importance of Analyzing and Managing Costs

◀ **A Look at This Part**

The first part describes how cost management supports strategic decision making. Part One introduces cost management, strategic management of the value chain, cost system design, and measurement of product costs. It sets the foundation for managing costs to meet strategic goals.

▼ **A Look Ahead**

The second part explores the activity-based approach to cost management as a highly effective tool to achieve the strategic goal of more value at lower cost. Part Two explains and applies activity-based costing, activity-based management, customer profitability, and management of internal processes.

Chapter 1

Cost Management and Strategic Decision Making

Evaluating Opportunities and Leading Change

After completing this chapter, you should be able to:

1. Understand how cost management supports strategic planning and decision making.

2. Understand the importance of ethical behavior and decision making.

3. Describe and understand steps in strategic decision making.

4. Apply benefit-cost and variance analysis to help evaluate an organization's strategic plans.

Learning Objectives appear at the beginning of each chapter and are repeated in the margin of the text where they are addressed. Also, each end-of-chapter assignment lists its learning objective.

Cost *Management* Challenges

(Solutions are on page 23)

1. **What** should a cost-management analyst do when the demands of the job conflict with personal or professional ethical standards?

2. **How** does a cost-management analyst contribute to strategic decision making?

3. **How** should a cost-management analyst prepare information for strategic decision making?

- Cost Management Challenges ask you to think about the key content in the chapter. Suggested solutions are at the end of the chapter.

- Chapters begin with a company document that introduces issues to be discussed in the chapter. These companies are fictional, but based on practices of real companies.

EMAIL MEMORANDUM

To: Melanie DelVal, Chief Financial Officer
            Jackie Lin, Vice President, Marketing
From: Frank Barnes, President and CEO
Subject: URGENT: New product idea
Attachment: Newproduct.doc (145 KB)

Jackie and Melanie: I am still at the Data Communication Conference in Boston. I just met with our largest European customer, who gave me an intriguing idea for a new Internet-based data communication product. I have attached my preliminary description of the new product's goals, objectives, functions, and operating requirements that are based on the customer's emerging needs. Please review this description. Review it with Engineering and Manufacturing and get back to me this evening with your critique and alternative solutions. This looks good to me now, but please be critical and prepare me for my lunch meeting tomorrow with the customer. I will be at my hotel after 10 PM waiting for your call.

Frank

EMAIL MEMORANDUM

To: Frank Barnes, President and CEO
CC: Jackie Lin, Vice President, Marketing
From: Melanie DelVal, Chief Financial Officer
Subject: RE: New product idea
Attachment: Newproduct-v2.doc (387 KB)

Frank: Good morning. Here are the revised product descriptions that we promised in our phone call last night. Engineering and Manufacturing were so excited by the idea that they joined us for the all-nighter. We think we have done another good job anticipating where the data communications market is going, and our preliminary analyses indicate technical feasibility and profitability for several alternative product solutions. We do not want to give away the ideas or even signal to competitors what we are planning. However, we believe that we do not have the resources for testing products of this scope in the field. A partnership with the customer to develop the product might protect the idea and might be an excellent marketing and development strategy. We are ready to debate the alternatives, and are eager for your return. Good luck with the customer.

Jackie and Melanie

Evaluation of Opportunities at Pursuit Data

' Real companies are
highlighted in blue.

Pursuit Data, Inc., a small data-communication company, uses cost management to support its strategy of innovation and high growth. The data-communication industry changes rapidly, and competition is fierce among agile companies, such as Brocade Communications Systems, Cisco Systems, Inrange Technologies, and McDATA Corp. Companies in this industry (and other evolving industries) compete on the basis of superior ideas and technology, marketing, service, and cost management. Cost-management analysts must understand their company's strategy, technology, customers, and marketing and must develop innovative ways to improve quality and cost.

A decade ago, an engineering manager, Frank Barnes, and a marketing director, Jackie Lin, worked for a large, multinational technology company. Barnes and Lin observed that their employer was not providing data-communication products and services that met the needs of small, fast-growing companies. Their employer focused, instead, on the data-communication needs of large companies.

This two-person team saw a potentially lucrative data communication market and left to form Pursuit Data. The company's mission was to provide quick, flexible, and reliable data-communication devices and services to small companies with good growth potential. An early realization for Pursuit Data's founders was the importance of managing costs. One of their first professional hires was an experienced cost management analyst, Melanie DelVal, who joined the company as chief financial officer (CFO).

Career Perspectives   An organization's chief financial officer (CFO) is responsible for managing the firm's financial resources and the financial personnel. Increasingly, CFOs also manage human and information resources. CFOs typically are trained in accounting and finance as undergraduates or as graduate students and often are professionally certified (for example, certified public accountant, certified management accountant, or certified financial manager). Several professional organizations that can provide information about financial management careers and certification include the Financial Executives Institute (www.feiaz.org), American Institute of CPAs (www.aicpa.org), Institute of Management Accountants (United States) (www.ima.net), Society of Management Accountants (Canada) (www.cma-canada.org), Institute of Chartered Accountants (Australia) (www.icaa.org.au), and Institute of Chartered Management Accountants (Great Britain).

The Institute of Management Accountants (United States) recently completed a study of the current and future work activities and competencies of financial managers, which can be found at www.ima.net/pracana. This study indicates that the role of financial managers in many companies is changing to focus on, among other things, customer profitability, process improvement, performance evaluation, and strategic planning. The most important qualities needed include a strong work ethic, understanding the business, and problem-solving, interpersonal, and listening skills. The modern financial and cost manager is hardly the stereotypical image of a cost accountant but of a successful business consultant. The stereotyped cost accountant, who is complete with green eyeshade and calculator and who records the financial data about events from a distance, is a relic of the past in many companies. It is likely that no one at these companies even has the title "cost accountant." A more common title is "financial analyst" or "internal business consultant," and a few companies use the term "cost-management analyst," which we prefer. These titles and the tasks they represent demonstrate a dramatic evolution in accountants' jobs from preparers of reports to proactive managers and consultants. More evidence of the change in the field can be found by reviewing the topics (and authors) of articles in *Emerging Practices in Cost Management* (edited by J. B. Edwards) and by noting the conclusions of the study completed by several PricewaterhouseCoopers employees (T. Walther, H. Johansson, J. Dunleavy, and E. Hjelm, *Reinventing the CFO: Moving from Financial Management to Strategic Management*). (Full citations to references are in the Bibliography.)

Pursuit Data's products include fiber-optic, data-communication switches that route incoming and outgoing data to the right users via the Internet or internal networks. Pursuit Data also provides other products, including software solutions to data sharing and communication, and services (consulting on data communication and reporting) to optimize the use of its switches and software. Pursuit Data currently has more than 300 full-time employees and has tripled its sales from products and services in the past four years. Because data-communication needs are growing rapidly, Pursuit Data believes its market and profitability also will grow.[1]

Strategic Role of Cost Management

Pursuit Data's strategy of innovation and high growth in the data-communication industry is challenged by competition from nearly every corner of the world. To meet this competition, the company must be constantly aware of its strengths, weaknesses, opportunities, and threats. Because the company is small, it cannot afford major mistakes in its products, services, or customers. CFO DelVal and her team of analysts develop financial and nonfinancial information about alternative opportunities and uses of resources to help Pursuit Data make decisions consistent with its goal of earning long-term, competitive profits.

LO I Understand how cost management supports strategic planning and decision making.

Characteristics of Cost Management

Cost management is important to organizations because it is more than measuring and reporting costs that have occurred. Cost management is focused on the future impacts of current or proposed decisions. **Cost management** is a *philosophy,* an *attitude,* and a *set of techniques* to create more value at lower cost.

Philosophy.   First, cost management is a *philosophy* of improvement because it promotes the idea of continually finding ways to help organizations make the right decisions to create more *customer value* at lower cost.[2] Efficient companies (such as Pursuit Data) provide products that customers want by using the minimum of the organization's scarce resources while continuously seeking to improve value and costs.

Attitude.   Second, cost management represents a proactive *attitude* that all costs of products and operations result from management decisions. In other words, *costs do not just happen.* Therefore, cost management analysts do not simply document decisions and record costs. Instead, they are active partners in management decisions to develop and improve products and improve efficiency.

Techniques.   Third, cost management is a set of reliable techniques that use diverse performance measures to assess the impacts of decisions. These techniques may be used individually to support a specific decision or together to support the overall management of the organization. A **cost-management system** is the set of cost-management techniques that function together to support the organization's goals and activities.

The focus of this text is to demonstrate how the cost-management philosophy, attitude, and techniques work together. They combine to develop measures of value, costs, quality, time, and profits that allow managers to evaluate and predict the impacts of their decisions. Many chapters in this text focus on specific techniques to measure the impacts of decisions on costs. This reflects organizations' strong historical and continuing interest in controlling costs. However, the text also focuses on measuring causes or drivers of costs, such as management decisions about capacity, technology, quality, learning, and customers, among others. All of these factors are integral to a well-designed strategy, and all affect costs and profitability.[3]

` Key Terms are bolded and are listed at the end of the chapter. They also are in the Glossary at the end of the text.

---

[1] The firm's founders and employees own 90 percent of the corporation's stock. An investment firm that specializes in supporting small high-technology companies owns the other 10 percent. The current owners hope to publicly sell shares of the firm in the next several years to obtain additional capital for the firm and liquidity for the owners.

[2] Customers demonstrate value by the prices they are willing to pay. Constituents of nonprofit organizations express value by supporting preferred organizations with donations of money, time, and other resources. Constituents of government organizations express value preferences by voting, lobbying, or supporting political candidates.

[3] Readers should know that cost management fits within the larger scope of *management control systems,* which can be defined as "anything that management does to control, direct, or evaluate the organization's people and activities." Several excellent management control systems texts exist, but these do not provide detailed coverage of cost management.

Characteristics of Cost-Management Analysts

LO2 Understand the importance of ethical behavior and decision making.

Cost-management analysts bring a philosophy, an attitude, and techniques to the table that help create more value at lower cost.

Pursuit Data has computerized most of the cost accountant's data-intensive, recording work. The company also redesigned its information system to make data widely available throughout the company. Because of changes in information technology and increased competition, most organizations now need cost-management analysts with integrity and broad knowledge of the business who work well in cross-functional teams more than they need cost accountants who measure and report costs of past operations.

Cost-management teams transform cost accounting and other data into information for decisions that support strategies, improve products and services, and the use of resources and that systematically reduce costs. These analysts are the most reliable sources of information on the impacts of planned and actual management decisions at Pursuit Data. This reliable information is especially important for effective strategic decision making in a rapidly changing, globally competitive industry such as data communication.

Ethical Standards.   Cost-management analysts must maintain high standards of ethical behavior because they can control the information on which strategic decisions are based and justified. Unethical behavior can lead to wasted resources, lost time, ruined reputations, and perhaps legal penalties for all involved. Individuals can be pressured to misstate information or results regarding strategic decisions because of:

- *Bias from personal commitment to a decision.* This bias can be caused by a manager's unwillingness to look sufficiently far ahead or admit that a strategy might be a failure. The manager will continue to be pressured to misstate information, unwilling to face the fact that a failing strategy should be terminated.
- *Fear of loss of prestige, position, or compensation from a failed strategy.* The pressures to succeed or not admit failure can be very strong in any type of organization. Some organizations have an "up or out" advancement policy that rewards only managers who continue to succeed financially. A manager might give in to the temptation to misstate strategic information or might force analysts to do so, perhaps rationalizing that it is only to buy a little time until the market or the industry turns around. This dangerous practice usually leads to continued misstatements that ultimately cannot be sustained.
- *Greed and intentional behavior to defraud an organization or its stakeholders.* Some people seek opportunities to defraud others. Trust is very important in business, but it has been and will be abused. No contract can be written to anticipate every contingency, natural or criminal. The best defenses against fraud are to work with people who have earned trust and to use an effective system of controls. As former President Ronald Reagan used to say, "Trust but verify." When markets inevitably turn down or when predicted events do not occur, powerful managers have pressured analysts to misstate information in order to sustain their image and income.

Unfortunately, these practices are too widespread to ignore. Cost management analysts must be vigilant to undue pressures to misstate information.

Codes of Ethics.   Pursuit Data and many other organizations have ethical codes that describe approved and prohibited practices. These ethical codes educate and support employees who want to behave ethically but either would not know what to do or might be pressured to act unethically. The codes also form grounds for termination of employees who violate them. Pursuit Data has learned from the sad experiences of others that condoning ethical violations is prohibitively costly in the long run. Thus, the company has fully supported employees who adhere to the code and has dismissed several employees, including one in a management position, who violated it.

Regulators have allowed self-regulation of industries and professions that have shown strong enforcement of their own codes of ethics and business practices. A successful legal defense against alleged wrongdoing might be based on the fact that employees followed the company's or industry's code of ethics. The accounting scandals of recent years, despite the existence of accountants' ethical codes, have seriously harmed the public's image of the accounting profession and business in general. Note that the famous financial fraud at Enron was uncovered partly because one determined financial executive refused to participate in continued misstatements. More regulation and legal scrutiny are the natural but unfortunate result of these scandals.

Pursuit Data's ethical code advertises the company's ethical policy to future employees and can help attract the right employees. Prospective employees who want to work for an ethical company will be attracted to Pursuit Data, and those who do not will find other places to work.

Although many organizations have ethical codes, cost-management analysts also can subscribe to the code of ethics developed by Institute of Management Accountants (IMA). This code stresses the importance of integrity, competence and completeness of analyses, and full disclosure of both favorable and unfavorable information to management (see Appendix A to this chapter).

Ethical Considerations

Competitive and personal pressures sometimes tempt individuals to act unethically to gain an advantage. Put yourself in the place of CFO DelVal and describe how you would respond to each of the following independent situations.

a. An acquaintance who is a technical employee of a close competitor calls you at home to say, "You know that I have wanted to work for Pursuit Data for several years, and I am calling to explore options. I have been working on a new data communication product that I think you will find interesting. I just put some of my cost projections on your front porch. Please call me back when you've had a chance to look at them."

b. You have received a "cold call" from a company that specializes in competitive intelligence, which the salesperson describes as periodic updates on market conditions and competitors' actions and gathering timely information about specific competitors. You are offered a steeply discounted three-month trial without future obligations unless you agree that the information is valuable.

c. Your staff's initial analysis of a new product indicates possibly higher costs and more uncertainty about future demand for the product than expected. If the combination of higher costs and lower demand actually occur, the product will be a financial failure. In private conversation, the manager of the new product argues that the company's future could depend on getting this product quickly to market, and you agree. The manager urges you to not distribute the pessimistic analysis but to wait until his group can develop the product further and its costs are better understood.

(Solutions begin on page 23.)

You're the Decision Maker 1.1

You're the Decision Maker scenarios get you involved in the decisions that the focus company needs to make. Suggested solutions are at the end of the chapter.

Strategic Decision Making

An organization's **strategy** can be described as its overall plan or policy to achieve its goals. To develop a strategy, managers answer two basic questions: (1) where do we want to go? and (2) how do we want to get there?[4] One cost management role is to provide "financial reality" to the answers to these questions and to the development of a successful strategy by focusing the organization on providing more value at lower cost.

LO3 Describe and understand steps in strategic decision making.

---

[4] Kathleen Eisenhardt, "Strategy as Strategic Decision Making."

Strategic decision making determines "where" and "how" by choosing and implementing actions that will affect an organization's future abilities to achieve its goals. For example, strategic decisions might include launching an innovative product line to meet an emerging market or organizing to be the lowest-cost producer of an existing product. Some have argued that observed strategic decision making, which informs us about how these decisions are made, really is taking actions to implement past decisions or rationalizing past decisions that have been implemented. We take an explicitly *intentional* view of strategic decision making. In other words, we will describe what we believe strategic decision makers intend to do although implementations might falter.[5] Recent research shows that the way organizations answer the two strategic questions separates success from mediocrity or failure. We will follow Pursuit Data's decision making to understand how it has continued to be successful in its highly competitive industry.

"Where Do We Want to Go?"

Pursuit Data's answer to the first question is a strategy to achieve high growth and profitability by making innovative data communication products for growing markets and customers that themselves have high growth potential. This strategy can be successful if Pursuit Data quickly develops innovative products that capture shares of growing markets, but it will be successful only if the company develops products and serves customers profitably. It is sadly possible to be innovative, to grow rapidly, and to go bankrupt. Pursuit Data's strategy is important in technology, science, and fashion-driven industries, but it is not the only successful one for all organizations and industries. Furthermore, organizations and industries have life cycles, and certain strategies can be more appropriate at different times and for different parts of the organization.

Before examining how Pursuit Data can reach its destination, we first discuss four major types of strategic destinations, or "missions." Exhibit 1–1 shows four common types of strategic missions along the important dimensions of rewards and risk: build, hold, harvest, and divest.

Rewards for profit-seeking firms generally mean financial incentives in the form of profits, cash flow, and stock price appreciation, although many profit-seeking firms also seek nonfinancial rewards such as improved social responsibility. Governmental and nonprofit organizations might seek rewards such as improved health care and improved environmental quality. Risks, on the other hand, can be defined as the possible variations in incentives, which might turn out to be very high or very low. High-risk strategies might offer very high rewards, but they also can result in very low or negative returns. Conversely, the possible rewards for low-risk strategies might have very little variation but are usually also low. For example, investors who kept large stock investments in 2000 hoped for continuing the very high returns of previous years, but the dot.com bubble burst and losses resulted. Conversely, investors who kept or switched to money-market investments in 2000 were not expecting high returns, but their low positive returns were better than the losses many suffered when the market bubble burst.

The build strategy requires the organization to achieve high rates of sales growth. An organization pursues the build strategy by identifying new markets and customers with high growth potential. For example, Pursuit Data, which follows this strategy, seeks new data communications opportunities by working closely with key customers who have large, novel communication problems that seem likely to emerge in other organizations. By quickly finding solutions to these problems, Pursuit Data can be the first to offer them to others. Being first—and being right about the problem and the solution—means that Pursuit Data can attract new customers, capture a large share of a new, growing market, and earn high rewards. The build strategy is risky because the potentially high rewards will attract competitors who also want to be first and right. If Pursuit Data is late or wrong, the company could quickly lose its customers, reputation, and investment in new products and services.

---

[5] For a scholarly discussion of these points, see John Hendry, "Strategic Decision Making, Discourse, and Strategy as Social Practice."

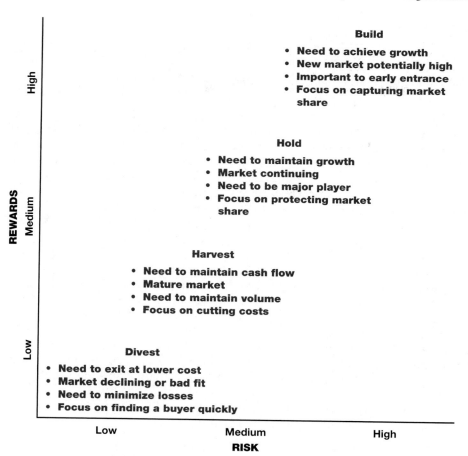

Exhibit 1–1

Major Categories of
Strategic Missions

The hold strategy means that the organization needs to maintain its current rate of growth, which generally reflects the overall market growth for a continuing market. For example, an automobile retailer that pursues a hold strategy works to maintain its retail sales growth at a rate that is at least equal to the regional population growth. To thrive with this strategy, an organization usually must be a major competitor so that activities by other major competitors do not threaten its survival. The organization must guard its market share to maintain steady growth. This strategy is less risky than the build strategy because the firm understands its market and competitors fairly well. Rewards are also lower because competition drives down profits.

A firm that follows a harvest strategy needs to maintain its cash flow, so some call this the "cash cow" strategy. Firms that follow the harvest strategy usually operate in mature markets, which no longer experience much growth and might be on the verge of decline. Sometimes larger firms control harvest *business units* (somewhat autonomous divisions) that provide cash to fund new build business units. Harvest firms need to maintain sales volume while cutting costs, particularly in anticipation of declining sales. Lower risks and rewards are more typical in harvest firms than in either hold or build firms, but harvest firms can perform valuable functions as sources of internally generated cash.

Sometimes, or at the end of an organization's life cycle, the best strategy is to divest, and the organization needs to exit the business at the lowest cost. The divest strategy can result from a realization that a business unit is a bad fit with the rest of the organization, as, for example, when Quaker Oats determined that its purchase of the Snapple beverage business had been a mistake. In other situations, an organization might have reached the end of its life, and liquidation is the best course of action. As another example, Montgomery Ward was a major U.S. retailer for many decades but reached a time when it could no longer compete, and it was liquidated. Although rewards can be low in a divest strategy, the risks of continuing operations can be substantial. The more quickly a buyer can be found, the better, because each day of failed operations raises the possibility of having to abandon resources before they can be sold to others.

"How Do We Want to Get There?"

Successful strategic decision making involves choosing the destination and the best route to it. A myriad of possible routes to a destination exist, and it is easy to take a wrong turn along the way. Finding the best route can be more successful when managers (1) understand sources and threats to competitive advantages and (2) use effective decision-making techniques.

Sources of competitive advantages.   Organizations such as Pursuit Data face fierce competition and seek a **competitive advantage,** which is a resource, process, or value chain that enables the organization to provide more value, perhaps at lower cost, than its competitors. A competitive resource might be extremely talented employees or control of natural resources. A **process** is a related set of tasks, manual or automated, that transforms inputs into identifiable outputs. A competitive process can be the innovative use of a proprietary database of customers' buying habits or a patented process to produce a valuable chemical, which are costly or difficult to imitate.

A **value chain** is the relation of an organization's processes that links ideas, resources, suppliers, and customers; a competitive value chain does so in a superior way. Decisions to change all or parts of the value chain are usually strategic because they affect the organization's ability to meet its goals. Exhibit 1–2 shows a generic value chain that links all major processes that most organizations perform in some way.

The value chain begins by obtaining physical and human resources and ends by providing products or services that customers value. Each part of the value chain describes a process that an organization performs, and each process in the chain should focus on improving customer value. The value chain also shows that managers must decide how to apply the organization's valuable (and scarce) physical and human resources to each linked process. The complete value chain includes the following processes, which are exemplified by Pursuit Data:

Research and development (R&D).   Pursuit Data has extensive R&D operations to develop innovative telecommunication devices and software applications.

Design.   Pursuit Data incorporates its new telecommunication ideas into the designs of innovative communications hardware and software.

Supply.   Pursuit Data has strong relations with its external suppliers who work closely with it to control the quality and timing of supply shipments. Some external

Exhibit 1–2

The Value Chain—Sources of Competitive Advantage

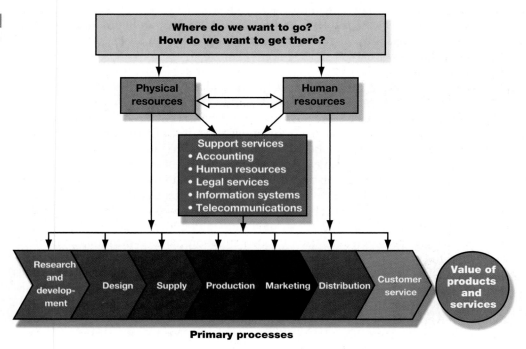

suppliers have become part of Pursuit Data's **extended value chain,** which encompasses the ways companies obtain their resources and distribute their products and services, possibly using the services of other organizations.

Production. Pursuit Data assembles its own fiber-optic devices and writes its own software applications.

Marketing. Pursuit Data successfully markets its products and services using both traditional, face-to-face presentations and Internet-based information (for example, websites) and solicitations.

Distribution. Pursuit Data contracts with land-based delivery companies for local and regional deliveries and with air-delivery companies that can deliver products anywhere in the world.

Customer service. Pursuit Data guarantees the performance of its products and services and moves quickly to resolve customer problems or complaints.

Support services. Some companies would not identify support functions, such as accounting, human resources, legal services, information systems, and telecommunications, as critical parts of the value chain. However, Pursuit Data recognizes that these are important processes that it must perform, either by itself or by *outsourcing* the work to firms that specialize in these services.

In general, a resource, a process, or an entire value chain can be a continued source of competitive advantage if it is valuable, rare, difficult to imitate, and without substitutes. Otherwise, these items would be freely available to competitors; all competitors could have them; and they could not provide any unique advantages. Organizations can find competitive advantages either by (1) creating new knowledge, which relies on supporting human innovation and experimentation, or (2) imitating others' ideas and implementing them in a superior way. Either creation or imitation can provide advantages, but sometimes the outcomes are unintentional. For example, the recorded music industry (firms, artists, and musicians) relies heavily on profiting from controlling the distribution of new music. However, Internet-based music trading practices can easily and cheaply distribute recorded music. These superior distribution practices have all but eliminated the profits from producing and selling recorded music, threatening the entire industry and its artists.

Michael Porter[6] identified three basic ways to use resources, processes, and value chains to create competitive advantages based on (1) low-cost production, (2) product differentiation, or (3) market focus. Becoming the low-cost producer requires making investments to reduce operating costs to earn higher profits at market prices or lowering prices to attract more customers. Differentiating products means providing goods with superior features that command premium prices and that competitors cannot copy. Organizations also can narrow or broaden their market focus to serve either the

---

Outsourcing the Value Chain

Research on outsourcing components of the value chain has identified several characteristics of firms and their operations that could lead to more outsourcing. Firms now focus their resources on those parts of the value chain that are most important to their goals and outsource other operations. Some observers predict that, in 10 to 20 years, many firms will have outsourced every part of the value chain except the few key components that are unique and sources of competitive advantage. Information services (information technology, Internet services) and traditional support services (legal, logistics, human resources, payroll, accounting transactions, and tax) are most likely to be outsourced: Companies seeking to reduce costs or gain access to specialized information (information technology, foreign markets) are more likely to outsource parts of the value chain. Because outsourcing can result in loss of control and internal expertise, trust and reliable measurement of outsourcing performance are essential. Providing outsourced services is one of the fastest growing businesses in the world. *Source: S. Widener and F. Selto, "Management Control Systems and Boundaries of the Firm."*

Research Insight 1.1

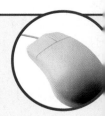

Research Insights provide research findings relevant to the chapter topics.

---

[6] Michael Porter, *Competitive Advantage.*

special needs of select (niche) customers or the broad needs of a wider (mass) market. The narrow approach requires detailed information about specific customers and an ability to customize products to meet their needs. The broad approach necessitates understanding marketwide needs and trends. Exhibit 1–3 displays the sources of competitive advantages and threats to those advantages, which we discuss next.

Threats to competitive advantages.   The nature of competition means that competitors continually try to outperform each other. Therefore, no competitive advantage lasts forever. Michael Porter identifies five competitive forces that describe the sources of threats to competitive advantages. These forces determine how long a competitive advantage can last.

n   The first force refers to the combined basis, intensity, breadth, and competence of *existing competitors,* who vie for the same customers and market share. Most of Pursuit Data's competitors are trying hard to identify new problems and solutions, but a few attempt to copy Pursuit's solutions in a less costly way. Pursuit protects its innovations with copyrights and patents, but skillful imitators can find legal ways to produce similar products.

n   The second force involves the difficulty and likelihood of entry to the market by *new competitors,* who are attracted by success and high profits. Pursuit Data maintains close relations with its customers and guards its patents and highly paid scientists and engineers, all of which would be costly and difficult for newcomers to imitate or hire.

n   The third force reflects the demand and stability of *customers,* whose needs and financial stability also are affected by competitive forces and can change overnight. Pursuit Data manages its relations with customers closely so that the company knows about their critical needs and changes as quickly as possible.

Exhibit 1–3   Competitive Advantages, Sources and Threats

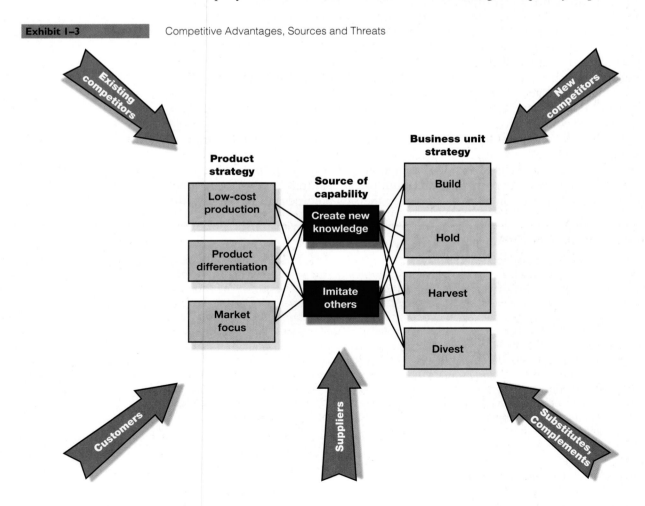

n   The fourth force refers to the reliability, quality, and breadth of *suppliers,* who also face competitive forces and can change their focus or experience difficulties. For a while, Pursuit Data cultivated close relations with just a few suppliers to facilitate on-time deliveries of high-quality goods. When one supplier unexpectedly declared bankruptcy, Pursuit expanded its set of suppliers and used improved technology to manage its relations with them.

n   The fifth force includes the availability and likelihood of *substitute* or *complementary* products, technologies, and services that can render current advantages obsolete. Pursuit Data made its first big advance in the industry when it correctly predicted that optical data-communication switches would quickly replace copper-wire switches. The company knows that technological breakthroughs are the rule in its industry and invests in R&D and in smaller, highly innovative firms that might be the sources of these breakthroughs. Complementary improvements in data storage devices also drive Pursuit Data's R&D and sales.

Formulation of Strategic Action Plans

Pursuit uses an eight-step process that other successful organizations also employ to implement strategic plans, such as the launch of an innovative product line consistent with its build strategy.

Eight Elements of Leading and Managing Change

Kotter has identified elements in a process for implementing change.[7] The following sections identify these elements and Pursuit Data's implementation of them.

Step 1. Identify a Need for Change.   Sometimes external threats force organizations to change, and at times unforeseen opportunities make change attractive. Consistently successful managers and organizations always expect and anticipate change and always look for opportunities to improve. Importantly, they also assess the impact of not changing. Research indicates that thriving firms keep moving, not aimlessly but always to create competitive advantages.[8] Some managers say they find opportunities by "measuring everything" and continually evaluating trends and changes in their performance and the performance of their customers and competitors. A **performance measure** is an indicator that allows an organization to determine the level of performance according to a critical attribute (for example, profit, quality) and to compare performance to expectations (see the next section of this chapter).

Providing the right measures of performance for making these evaluations is a primary role of cost management and a primary focus of this text. (See Appendix B of this chapter for a preview of the remaining text chapters.) Frequent face-to-face meetings that develop and use the appropriate performance measures also allow managers to identify alternative actions, debate them objectively, and identify opportunities and threats quickly and accurately.

The opening email messages between Pursuit Data's top managers show that they quickly identify opportunities for change consistent with the firm's strategy. Furthermore, they usually generate multiple, alternative actions to meet those opportunities and count on debates among informed team members to choose the best course of action.

Step 2. Create a Team to Lead and Manage the Change.   Teams have replaced individual decision makers in many organizations, including Pursuit Data. A few years ago, different people and functions within organizations performed separate parts of cost management but did not communicate effectively with each other. These people usually operated in separate functional roles that often impeded cooperation among functional areas. Functional roles usually are narrowly defined jobs that focus on specific types of activities, such as accounting or manufacturing. Persons restricted to functional roles

---

[7] This process is adapted from John P. Kotter, "Why Transformation Efforts Fail."

[8] S. L. Brown and K. M. Eisenhardt, *Competing on the Edge: Strategy as Structured Chaos.*

The development of the Hewlett-Packard Deskjet printer involved teams from manufacturing, accounting, marketing, and finance. By their interaction, the team lowered costs and speeded development, providing H-P a competitive market advantage.

often were most interested in parts of business issues that fit their own expertise. In some companies, people operating in these different functional areas rarely spoke with each other, and their actions were not necessarily consistent with organizational goals.

People from different training and backgrounds at Pursuit Data work in small, cross-functional, diverse teams to make decisions, such as developing new products. They are assigned to specific departments such as accounting, engineering, or marketing, but they spend most of their time and efforts in team activities. Cost management is an integral part of a cross-functional and innovative approach to management decision making. Anyone who is preparing to become a cost-management analyst must be ready to work in cross-functional teams in which critical skills are leadership and effective communication. Most successful organizations have learned to create cross-functional, diverse teams that are more likely to be innovative in their solutions and discovery of opportunities.

Step 3. Create a Vision of the Change and a Strategy for Achieving the Vision.   Pursuit's strategy is to provide innovative telecommunication services and products to high-growth customers. This vision is widely shared within the company because its employees are frequently involved in team decisions and are accustomed to open but disciplined debates about choosing the best route to their "build" strategy. It seems natural to employees to question and debate whether new products and processes are consistent with the company's overall strategy. It is very difficult to predict financial outcomes of alternative decisions, but teams create alternative scenarios of future outcomes that reflect their understanding of the impacts of internal and external events on achieving the organization's goals.

Step 4. Communicate the Vision and Strategy for Change and Have the Change Team Be a Role Model.   Pursuit constantly communicates its vision and strategy and encourages input from employees. Team members are well suited and trained to gather employees' input and include it in their analyses and recommendations. Giving credit for others' suggestions increases the chances that they will participate again in the future. An important behavior to model is to fearlessly compare planned and actual outcomes, which encourages learning and improved decision making.

Step 5. Encourage Innovation and Remove Obstacles to Change.   Diverse teams almost guarantee innovations. CEO Barnes reserves the right to make final decisions, but he gives authority to the diverse teams to develop new product opportunities. Top managers eliminate any political or "turf" issues that might derail or delay new product decisions by emphasizing common goals and refusing to accept obvious turf-based arguments for or against an idea.

Cost Management in Practice
1.1

Actual cost management practices are highlighted in these boxes.

Team Selection

Selecting the right form of team is crucial to organizational success. Peter Drucker, the eminent management consultant, observes that there are only three types of teams. He uses sports and music analogies to describe them. The first team type is similar to a doubles tennis pair or a jazz combo. The team is small, and although each player has a primary position, each adjusts to the actions, strengths, and weaknesses of the others. This type of team is most likely to create dramatic innovations and is becoming very popular in high-technology firms. The second team type is similar to a soccer team (football to the world outside the United States) or orchestra. Each soccer or orchestra player has specific responsibilities, but they all play in unison—moving up and down the field as the flow of the game dictates. The strength of this type of team is its ability to execute plans flexibly, and it is common in larger firms that practice "mass customization"—preparing variations of basic products and services to meet customers' specific needs. The third team type is the baseball team on which each player has a fixed position and role and usually plays independently of other players (music from this type of team would not be pleasant listening). The strength of this type of team is its development of individual expertise, but its greatest weakness is its inflexibility. This team type is disappearing because it has not been capable of responding quickly in today's rapidly changing environment. See P. Drucker, *Managing in a Time of Great Change.*

Step 6. Ensure that Short-Term Achievements Are Frequent and Obvious. Analyzing the new product proposal is an example of an effort that could have an obvious impact on the company. Pursuit's approach to new product development is to break its large problems into smaller ones that teams can analyze and solve in a short amount of time. To keep the decision making on schedule, Pursuit also requires each team to commit to a schedule that can be changed but only after management approval. Even projects that do not meet their original objectives are treated as successes because the company learns why something did not work. This is valuable information that helps to prevent future failures.

Step 7. Use Successes to Create Opportunities for Improvement in the Entire Organization. By making sequential parts of the process visible, the company can point to many examples of employee contributions to significant improvements in products and processes. Pursuit Data uses this practice to make future improvements even more likely and, importantly, encourage employees to recommend improvements even if they are small.

Step 8. Reinforce a Culture of More Improvement, Better Leadership, and More Effective Management. The climate of striving for improvements permeates Pursuit Data. Employees know that opportunities for improvement always exist and that managers take their recommendations seriously. Treating occasional failures as opportunities for learning rather than reasons for assigning blame is important for motivating team members to be creative and honest in their appraisals.

Evaluation of Plans and Outcomes

Some plans that seemed wonderful on paper or in the team meeting room fail to meet expectations. Others greatly exceed expectations. The success of an individual plan is important, but understanding why and how a plan or project failed or succeeded can help organizations learn to make better future decisions. Two levels of analysis are important to evaluating the success or failure of a plan. The first level is **operational performance analysis,** which measures whether the performance of current operations is consistent with expectations. The second level is **strategic performance analysis,** which measures whether a strategic decision has met expectations. Generally, operational performance analysis considers performance measures within relatively short time periods (for example, days, weeks, or months), but strategic performance analysis can consider years of performance. For example, a particular plan might not meet current operational performance expectations (for example, this month's lower-than-expected profit from a new product), but longer term performance can indicate that the strategic decision was correct (for instance, with the exception of this month, a new product's performance in the past year has met or exceeded expectations).

LO 4 Apply benefit-cost and variance analysis to help evaluate an organization's strategic plans.

Another distinction between operational and strategic performance is the level of the results that are analyzed. For example, an operational performance measure could reflect the quality of parts made in a particular department, but a strategic performance measure could reflect the reputation of quality for an entire product line or company.

Benefit-Cost Analysis

We will analyze a recently completed new product from Pursuit Data's past to illustrate the important practice of comparing plans to actual results. This type of comparison can be used to evaluate either operational or strategic performance. A Pursuit Data analyst based her reasoning on benefit-cost analysis of pertinent information about the product's performance. **Benefit-cost analysis** measures the effects of a plan by comparing its expected benefits and costs, which can be *quantitative* and *qualitative*. **Quantitative information** is expressed in dollars or other quantities relating to size, frequency, and so on. **Qualitative information** is descriptive and based on characteristics or perceptions, such as relative desirability, rather than quantities.

An organization must be concerned with both the quantitative and qualitative costs and benefits. In some cases (for example, concerns about employee morale and customer perception of service quality), qualitative information can outweigh quantitative information (such as, cost savings) in making a decision. For example, a company might find an opportunity to reduce its costs in the short run, but doing so would violate its strategy. The company must weigh qualitative factors against the quantitative benefits and costs. The initial analysis of the new product was based on the quantitative and qualitative information shown in Exhibit 1–4, which shows that the company expected the product to recover its costs of development and production within two years. The company also expected normal sales growth, completion time, quality, and customer satisfaction. Furthermore, Pursuit Data expected that anticipated layoffs might adversely affect overall employee morale.

Benefit and Cost Variances

After several years of experience with the new product, analysts compared the earlier expectations with actual results, as shown in Exhibit 1–5. The differences between a plan's actual and expected quantities are called **variances.** Because few predictions

---

Exhibit 1–4   Expected Benefits and Costs Two Years after Introducing a New Product

Expected Benefits of New Product	Expected Amount	Qualitative Comments and Explanations
Sales	$1,500,000	Based on estimated customer demand and annual sales growth
Personnel cost savings	80,000	Process improvements indicate fewer personnel required to service customers after sale
Total financial benefits	$1,580,000	
Annual sales growth (percent)	20%	Normal sales growth for this type of product
Time to completion (months)	15	Normal completion time for product of this complexity
Product quality (number of defects)	2	Normal number of defects detected by customers for this type of product
Customer satisfaction (score out of 100)	95	Normal satisfaction for this type of product and related services

Expected Costs of New Product	Expected Amount	Qualitative Comments and Explanations
Development costs	$ 300,000	Based on product complexity and time to completion
Production costs	600,000	Based on estimates from design plans and similar products
Service costs	130,000	Normal service costs for this type of product
Total financial costs	1,030,000	
Net financial benefits	$ 550,000	Product expected to recover costs of development and production within this time frame
Effects of personnel reductions		Personnel layoffs could cause morale problems and higher than desired turnover of other personnel

Exhibit 1–5   Benefits and Costs of Introducing a New Product

Benefits of New Product	Expected Amount	Actual Amount	Variance	Qualitative Comments and Explanations
Sales to date	$1,500,000	$1,200,000	$(300,000)	Sales lower than expected because of competition and lower product quality
Personnel cost savings to date	80,000	60,000	(20,000)	One fewer person laid off to meet higher than expected service calls
Total financial benefits to date	$1,580,000	$1,260,000	(320,000)	
Annual sales growth (percent)	20%	17%	–3%	Sales growth lower because of stronger competition and lower product quality than expected
Time to completion (months)	15	12	(3)	Product release date accelerated to meet competition
Product quality (number of defects)	2	23	21	Higher than expected defects caused by skipped quality testing to meet accelerated release date
Customer satisfaction (score out of 100)	95	89	(6)	Lower customer satisfaction because of increased defects and extensive calls for customer service

Costs of New Product	Expected Amount	Actual Amount	Variance	Qualitative Comments and Explanations
Development costs	$ 300,000	$ 360,000	$ 60,000	Higher costs because of accelerated development schedule
Production costs to date	600,000	500,000	(100,000)	Lower costs because of lower production volume
Service costs to date	130,000	155,000	25,000	Higher costs because of lower quality and more service calls
Total financial costs to date	1,030,000	1,015,000	(15,000)	
Net financial benefits to date	$ 550,000	$ 245,000	$(305,000)	
Effects of personnel reductions				Adverse effects observed on remaining personnel but moderated by keeping one more person than expected to correct customer-detected defects

are perfect, some variances are normal. Managers can evaluate the quantitative aspects of this type of comparison by considering the causes of the exceptionally large variances. These explanations are shown in the qualitative section of Exhibit 1–5.

CFO DelVal's review of the analysis in Exhibit 1–5 told her that the original plan was faulty, and she recommended a complete review of the new product and its development process. Her reasons were that (1) revenues were lower than expected by $300,000, which was mostly attributable to an inaccurate assessment of the competition and lower product quality, and (2) most of the lower cost realized was attributable to lower product volume. In fact, other costs—development and service costs—were higher than expected and attributable to lower product quality. The lower product quality itself probably was the result of the decision to rush the product's development to meet a competitive threat, but that backfired. The loss of customer satisfaction probably contributed to lower than expected sales growth and could have affected the sales of other products. This latter result might have had a much greater adverse impact on the company than any other factor. Although adverse effects on personnel morale were lower than expected, the reason again was the poor quality that necessitated keeping more personnel than planned.

Although it might be difficult to admit that a decision of this magnitude had been wrong, DelVal urged the company to learn from the mistake. The results of learning from this painful review were renewed commitments to improving the product development process and to enhancing the quality of the company's products. Years of hard work and close contact with customers were necessary to overcome the adverse effects of that early decision on Pursuit Data's reputation. That mistake was not repeated, and the new product development process emerged stronger than ever. As a result, Pursuit Data's reputation for innovation and quality is unmatched in the industry.

You're the Decision Maker 1.2

Benefit-Cost Analysis of Introducing a New Product

Refer to the information in Exhibit 1–5.

a. Explain how you think Pursuit Data compared the expected costs and benefits in the analysis even though some are quantitative but others are qualitative.

b. Is it possible that the qualitative or nonquantified costs or benefits of this decision could be more important than those that are quantified? Explain with an example from Exhibit 1–5.

c. Explain the possible linkages among development time, sales, product quality, and customer satisfaction that are reflected in Exhibit 1–5.

d. If personnel are laid off or dismissed to realize cost savings, does Pursuit Data have any ethical obligations to those employees? Could the way that Pursuit Data treats those employees affect retained or future employees? Explain.

(Solutions begin on page 23.)

Chapter Summary

This first chapter has two purposes. One is to explain what cost management is, and the second is to illustrate how cost management supports strategic decision making. Of paramount importance is supporting and encouraging ethical decision making, not just because it is the right thing to do, but also because it is the most effective and efficient way to do business in the long run.

Strategic decisions are among the most important ones an organization makes because they determine the organization's future activities and performance. Strategic decisions include finding opportunities and responding to threats to competitive advantages as well as selecting the organization's destination and the best route to that destination.

Cost management is (1) a *philosophy* of seeking increased customer value at reduced cost, (2) an *attitude* that management decisions cause all costs, and (3) a reliable set of *techniques* that increase value and reduce cost. To provide information, interpretations, and analyses of alternative courses of action that managers are contemplating, cost-management analysts need broad knowledge of the organization's activities and the ways those activities interact. Benefit-cost analysis is a common and powerful technique, particularly when used to compute variances between expected and actual benefits and costs.

Cost-management analysts are valued members of the management team because they understand how managing the organization's value chain affects cost, quality, and customer value. They also are trusted sources of objective information. Companies use cost-management teams to evaluate alternative uses of resources. Successfully managing change requires an understanding that its management will affect the success not only of a particular change but also of future changes. Successful companies often use a formal process to lead and manage change, such as Kotter's eight-step process.

Appendix A to Chapter One

Institute of Management Accountants: Standards of Ethical Conduct for Management Accountants

Management accountants have an obligation to the organizations they serve, their profession, the public, and themselves to maintain the highest standards of ethical conduct. In recognition of this obligation, the IMA has promulgated the following standards of ethical conduct for management accountants; adherence to them is integral to achieving the objectives of management accounting. Management accountants shall not commit acts contrary to these standards, nor shall they condone the commission of such acts by others within their organizations.

Competence

Management accountants have a responsibility to:

- Maintain an appropriate level of professional competence by ongoing development of their knowledge and skills.
- Perform their professional duties in accordance with relevant laws, regulations, and technical standards.
- Prepare complete and clear reports and recommendations after appropriate analyses of relevant and reliable information.

Confidentiality

Management accountants have a responsibility to:

- Refrain from disclosing confidential information acquired in the course of their work except when authorized, unless legally obligated to do so.
- Inform subordinates as appropriate regarding the confidentiality of information acquired in the course of their work and monitor their activities to assure the maintenance of that confidentiality.
- Refrain from using or appearing to use confidential information acquired in the course of their work for unethical or illegal advantage either personally or through third parties.

Integrity

Management accountants have a responsibility to:

- Avoid actual or apparent conflicts of interest and advise all appropriate parties of any potential conflict.
- Refrain from engaging in any activity that would prejudice their ability to carry out their duties ethically.
- Refuse any gift, favor, or hospitality that would influence or would appear to influence their actions.
- Refrain from either actively or passively subverting the attainment of the organization's legitimate and ethical objectives.
- Recognize and communicate professional limitations or other constraints that would preclude responsible judgment or successful performance of an activity.

n   Communicate unfavorable as well as favorable information and professional judgments or opinions.

n   Refrain from engaging in or supporting any activity that would discredit the profession.

Objectivity

Management accountants have a responsibility to:

n   Communicate information fairly and objectively.

n   Disclose fully all relevant information that could reasonably be expected to influence an intended user's understanding of the reports, comments, and recommendations presented.

Source: National Association of Accountants, *Statement No. 1B*, "Statements on Management Accounting: Objectives of Management Accounting" (New York, June 17, 1982). These standards are reprinted with the permission of the Institute of Management Accountants.

Appendix B to Chapter One

Preview of the Remaining *Cost Management* Chapters

The primary purpose of the field of cost management is to help organizations provide more value at lower cost. The purpose of this textbook is to demonstrate how cost-management analysts use traditional and new techniques to do just that in many different types of organizations. All chapters use realistic focus companies to illustrate common decisions and the cost-management tools that support them. What follows is a brief preview of the text. Note that instructors might choose to reorder or skip topics to fit their specific courses.

Chapter 2: Product Costing Systems: Concepts and Design Issues

This chapter introduces cost systems and concepts, which this and all subsequent chapters use extensively.

Chapter 3: Cost Accumulation for Job-Shop and Batch Production Operations

The use of a product-costing system called *job-order costing* (or *job costing*) designed for organizations that produce unique products, services, and custom orders is the focus of this chapter. The job-order costing system helps such companies measure the cost of the resources used in the production process to help management better manage those resources and their costs.

Chapter 4: Activity-Based Costing Systems

This chapter illustrates the activity basis for measuring and analyzing costs; this costing approach is known as *activity-based costing*. ABC measures the costs of resources used to perform activities and builds the costs of products and services by accumulating the activities performed and their costs.

Chapter 5: Activity-Based Management

By identifying value-added and non-value-added activities (as well as activity costs discussed in Chapter 4), this chapter focuses on ways a company can use ABM to find opportunities to improve its process efficiency.

Chapter 6: Managing Customer Profitability

Chapter 6 reflects the increasing importance of managing customer profitability and relations, particularly in firms that implement a focused-market strategy. This approach, which often is activity based, is nearly universal in some industries (for example, banking), and its application is increasing in nearly every economic sector.

Chapter 7: Managing Quality and Time to Create Value

The chapter discusses how analysts increasingly measure and interpret nonfinancial indicators of internal performance that complement financial, cost-based measures. The most important of these operational areas of performance are quality, productivity, capacity, and time.

Chapter 8: Process-Costing Systems

Chapter 8 describes how an organization that produces similar items in a continuous process accounts for its costs of production. Process costing is a straightforward and effective cost system for this type of company.

Chapter 9: Joint-Process Costing

Some companies produce multiple products from common inputs and must decide which products to sell after joint products appear (split-off) or after further processing. After the companies determine the appropriate products, they can allocate production costs using one of several acceptable joint-costing methods.

Chapter 10: Managing and Allocating Support-Service Costs

Organizations' allocation of the costs of support services to production departments for many legitimate reasons is a chapter focus. Although all cost allocations are arbitrary, they can be useful for promoting organizational goals if done carefully. The chapter demonstrates that cost allocations are particularly important in government and service organizations that typically have not used services available in the market.

Chapter 11: Cost Estimation

Prior chapters assume the knowledge of cost drivers, and this chapter demonstrates how to identify those drivers and estimate cost relationships using linear regression, account analysis, and the engineering method.

Chapter 12: Financial and Cost-Volume-Profit Models

This chapter focuses on the principles and applications of financial modeling. Simple models assume that product volume is the primary driver of costs and revenues. More complex models introduce multiple drivers. The chapter gives direct guidance on building and using spreadsheet models and modeling the effects of uncertainty.

Chapter 13: Cost Management and Decision Making

Chapter 13 uses an explicit decision-making framework to present consistent approaches to making common business decisions. The chapter uses target costing, decision trees, and cost-benefit analysis to evaluate both quantitative and qualitative information. The chapter presents a common structure for making decisions about new technology, outsourcing, products and services, and pricing special orders.

Chapter 14: Strategic Issues in Making Long-Term Capital Investment Decisions

The focus of this chapter is strategic issues, discounted cash flow (DCF) analysis, real option value analysis, sources of information, sensitivity analysis, relevance of nonfinancial information, due diligence, project approval processes, and follow-up to the decision.

Chapter 15: Budgeting and Financial Planning

The chapter discusses the role of budgeting in the strategic planning process and the development of the master budget. In addition to discussing the steps in preparing a master budget, the chapter provides extensive coverage of sales forecasting, behavioral issues in budgeting, and contemporary topics such as the international aspects of budgeting, e-budgeting, and ethics.

Chapter 16: Standard Costing, Variance Analysis, and *Kaizen Costing*

Standard-costing systems, cost-variance analysis, and the cost-reduction process known as *kaizen costing* are the focus of this chapter. Coverage includes the standard-setting process, use of standard costing in nonmanufacturing settings, determination of the significance of variances, behavioral effects of standard costing, impact of information technology, and changing role of standard costing in today's manufacturing environment.

Chapter 17: Flexible Budgets, Overhead Cost Management, and Activity-Based Budgeting

This chapter focuses on the use of flexible budgeting and standard costing in the management and control of overhead costs, as well as the use of activity-based flexible budgets. The chapter emphasizes the interpretation of standard and activity-based flexible budgets, overhead variances, the choice of activity measures, and performance reporting.

Chapter 18: Organizational Design, Responsibility Accounting, and Evaluation of Divisional Performance

This chapter discusses responsibility accounting, performance reporting, and investment center performance measures, which include return on investment, residual income, and economic value added. The chapter includes extensive coverage of organizational design issues, behavioral effects of responsibility accounting systems, and implementation issues in divisional performance measurement.

Chapter 19: Transfer Pricing

Focus of this chapter includes the role and purpose of transfer pricing. It explores several approaches to setting transfer prices with ample coverage of incentive problems in transfer pricing and the international implications of transfer pricing systems.

Chapter 20: Performance Measurement Systems

The final chapter of the text can serve as a capstone topic because all issues of cost management and performance measurement are its focus. The chapter covers the use of multiple performance measures for various operations. These include measures of performance that are lead indicators of the company's strategic success (or failure). Some organizations combine these lead indicators of performance into a performance measurement model, commonly known as the *balanced scorecard*. The chapter covers theoretical and practical issues of motivating employees with performance evaluation and incentive systems.

Key Terms

For each term's definition, refer to the indicated page or turn to the glossary at the end of the text.

benefit-cost analysis, 16
competitive advantage, 10
cost-management system, 5
cost management, 5
extended value chain, 11

operational performance analysis, 15
performance measure, 13
process, 10

qualitative information, 16
quantitative information, 16
strategic decision making, 8
strategic performance analysis, 15

strategy, 7
value chain, 10
variances, 16

Meeting the Cost Management Challenges

I. What should a cost-management analyst do when the demands of the job conflict with personal or professional ethical standards?

A conflict between the demands of a job and a person's ethical standards can be one of the most stressful career experiences. Job-related stress caused by this conflict can result in physical and mental ailments, such as headaches, backaches, sleeplessness, anxiety, withdrawal, and inability to concentrate or perform the job. The effects of these ailments can be debilitating and dangerous to a person's long-term health. Furthermore, reaction to the situation can affect job security, reputation, and exposure to legal actions. Clearly, an ethical conflict is nothing to treat lightly. No two situations are identical, but these are some guidelines that can help if you experience a conflict between your job and your ethics:

a. Get clarification about the task your superior has given you. Perhaps you have misunderstood the task or request. If not, consider the following steps.

b. Do not react hastily unless an imminent threat to health or safety exists.

c. Seek advice from an ombudsperson or a trusted, experienced co-worker who can help you understand the conflict and suggest actions you might take.

d. Raise your concerns with appropriate internal authorities, such as a superior a level or more above your boss, the internal audit staff, or audit committee members.

e. Quit your job. Even in difficult economic times, no job is worth sacrificing your health or reputation.

f. Do not leak information to the media or other external parties until you have received sound legal advice about your legal status and whistle-blower protections.

2. How does a cost-management analyst contribute to strategic decision making?

One of the greatest aids a cost-management analyst offers to strategic decision making is providing financial and operational reality to the feasibility and impacts of proposed decisions. Although no forecasts are 100 percent accurate and no one expects them to be, challenging the validity of future costs and benefits and identifying all relevant costs and benefits allows managers to make better decisions. Analysts have more credibility if they challenge their analyses as well as those of others. Finding the strengths and weaknesses of plans is a sure but sometimes uncomfortable way to test plans. Exposing and correcting weaknesses in plans before they are executed is far less costly than finding out later from customers and competitors when real damage has been done or significant opportunities have been missed.

3. How should a cost-management analyst prepare information for strategic decision making?

Cost-management information for strategic decision making is forward looking and identifies future costs, benefits, strengths, weaknesses, and opportunities. Sometimes these can be quantified as in forecasted income or net cash flow statements. Qualitative aspects of decisions also can be critically important so an analyst does decision makers a disservice by not clearly stating qualitative factors also. Furthermore, analysts should anticipate that inexperienced managers might not question quantitative forecasts and analyses. Therefore, analysts should provide "what if" and "scenario" analyses that demonstrate the ranges of possible outcomes and the sensitivity of forecasts to assumptions about the organization's plans and competitors' actions. (These issues are explored in depth in Chapters 12 through 14.)

Solutions to You're the Decision Maker

1.1 Ethical Considerations, p. 7

a. This person sounds like trouble with a capital "T." First, he or she appears to be offering proprietary information. Accepting it would be the same as accepting a stolen stereo or worse. Second, why would you ever consider hiring such an unethical, mercenary person? You should expect the same behavior in the future. Most certainly, you should not call this person but should call your company's security department to remove the information from your porch immediately. Consider whether you should identify whom you believe left the information because you might expose yourself to legal actions if that person has been duped or set up by another.

b. Competitive intelligence (CI) is a growing activity and field of work. At one end of the spectrum is theft of proprietary information or illegal corporate espionage. The other end is legal but uninteresting rehashing of readily available public information. Neither of the extremes is worth purchasing. In between can lie insightful gathering and analyses of public but obscure information that can be quite valuable and difficult for most organizations to duplicate. After assuring yourself of the legality of the company's practices and conferring with your co-executives, you might well consider this trial offer by giving the CI company specific objectives for its information and analysis activities.

c. If the manager is asking you to bury the pessimistic analysis until the project has been approved, you clearly would be acting unethically. Instead, you should report all relevant analyses and indicate the likelihood of both good and bad news. On the other hand, if the manager is asking for deferral of the decision until you can analyze more information, you might want to consider this to prevent a mistaken denial of a good project. You and other executives must balance the value of waiting for more information against the value of acting now.

1.2 Benefit-Cost Analysis of Introducing a New Product, p.18

a. Probably the best decision-making environment exists when cost-management analysts clearly communicate the confidence they have in their measurements and team members discuss the importance of all costs and benefits. Identifying quantified and nonquantified costs and benefits is a good first step. The next step is to use your preliminary analysis to begin a discussion within the team about the reasonableness of the estimates and whether the nonquantified items are important. Starting with a preliminary analysis usually is better than starting a team meeting with a "blank sheet." On the other hand, you need to be careful because some team members who are less quantitatively inclined might not think to challenge your preliminary figures or ask "what if" questions but could treat these estimates as the unshakable truth. Although the estimates might be reasonable first guesses, they could be quite inaccurate. All team members need to challenge and ultimately feel comfortable with what the numbers do and do not say.

b. Not all costs and benefits can be measured easily or with enough accuracy to justify attaching dollar values to them. Some cost-management analysts believe that people pay attention only to measurable costs and benefits, so they might argue the value of trying to measure all of them. On the other hand, others believe that attaching highly inaccurate dollar figures to some costs or benefits reduces the confidence that managers have in all numbers. Therefore, some nonquantified or qualitative costs or benefits might be more important than the quantified ones and can lead to proper decisions that contradict the numbers.

   Measures of the future costs and benefits will be somewhat subjective because the future is uncertain, and specific measures depend on assumptions about future changes (organizational structure, market demand, technological change, etc.). Organizations usually rely on accountants, financial analysts, or cost-management analysts to develop these measures. They base their measures on their understanding of the way the organization has acquired and used resources in the past and the way changes will affect the resources needed. They rely on information from their own organization and from sources outside that help them predict the effects of changes. This is a complex topic that is covered in more detail in subsequent chapters of this text.

c. Everything really is connected. For example, the accelerated development and production schedule might have caused lower quality because critical steps were skipped or abbreviated. Lower product quality probably is responsible for lower customer satisfaction and a resulting loss of current sales. Importantly, Pursuit Data might lose future sales opportunities, making the company more vulnerable to competitors. Loss of good customers can outweigh the net benefits getting products to market quickly.

d. Outsourcing and downsizing decisions often result in costs that the organization might not recognize. If reassigned employees need training, they will not be fully productive for some time. These costs must be considered. Most large organizations have formal severance policies that specify the terms of dismissal (e.g., notice, pay, benefits). The organization usually is legally obligated to live up to these terms. Do organizations have ethical obligations that extend beyond their legal obligations? One point of view is that employees joined the organization knowing what its severance policy is and should not expect more than it specifies. In fact, if managers give more, they might be betraying their responsibility to owners and other contributors because they are the ones paying the cost of the additional severance benefits, perhaps unknowingly. Another view is that, depending on the economic climate and the availability of jobs, the organization might "owe" loyal employees assistance in finding other employment. A more pragmatic perspective is that the organization can enhance its reputation with potential employees and reduce morale problems with retained employees by treating its dismissed employees generously. Thus, it could be in the best interests of the organization (and its owners) to provide more than the contractually agreed-on severance benefits.

Review Questions

1.1 Review and define each of the chapter's key terms.

1.2 What is the primary objective of cost management?

1.3 What is the concept of the value chain, and why is it important for cost management?

1.4 What is strategic decision making? Give examples of several strategic decisions.

1.5 What are some cost management techniques that help make better management decisions?

1.6 What are cross-functional teams, and why are they important?

1.7 How do companies use benefit-cost analysis to make important decisions?

1.8 How does outsourcing affect an organization's value chain?

1.9 What is the value of ethical standards to individuals? To an organization? To society?

1.10 How does a code of ethics differ from personal ethical standards?

1.11 How do the strategic missions of build, hold, harvest, and divest differ?

1.12 How do organizations create and maintain competitive advantages?

1.13 What is the difference between quantitative information and qualitative information?

1.14 What are the eight steps of leading and managing change?

Critical Analysis

1.15 "Cost accounting and cost management really are the same functions and operations." Do you agree or disagree? Explain.

1.16 Peter Drucker, the famous management consultant, has said, "Every three years, an organization should challenge every product, every service, every policy, every distribution channel with the question: If we were not in it already, would we be going into it now?" Why is this question important? How can cost managers help pose and answer this question?

1.17 Assume that you are a vice president of the largest department store in the region. The store president has called you in to give you a challenging assignment: "Though we are the largest store, only 10 percent of the region's residents are our customers. Find out why the other 90 percent are not." Why could this be a critically important assignment? How would you organize a team to find the answers?

1.18 Refer to Exhibit 1–4. How could Pursuit Data determine whether it has a competitive advantage in new product development? What would it mean to employees of Pursuit Data if it does or does not have an advantage?

1.19 A recent survey by KPMG, one of the world's largest business services firms, determined that 88 percent of other large U.S. companies have outsourced at least some parts of their value chains or support services. One of the most commonly outsourced services is income tax reporting. Assume that you are a cost-management analyst of a large company. How would you determine whether to outsource tax services? How might this trend in outsourcing tax services affect individuals interested in careers in the taxation field?

1.20 "If every manager minimizes the cost of the process he or she supervises, overall costs of the company will decrease." Do you think this would be a wise strategy? Why or why not?

1.21 Some years ago, General Motors installed industrial robots worth billions of dollars in its automobile assembly lines, believing that the robots would increase the efficiency of its manufacturing processes and improve profitability. In fact, General Motors lost many billions of dollars more despite the fact that it was able to make automobiles more quickly using the robots. What reasons can you think of to explain this paradox?

1.22 For many years, department stores prospered because they enhanced the process of shopping, which for many people was a break from the routine of housework and child care and was an opportunity to obtain information about available products and services. What changes have occurred in recent years that might explain the rise in shopping in "virtual stores" via the Internet? What do these changes imply for the retail processes of traditional department stores?

1.23 "I understand the possible value of strategic planning, but I really consider it to be a luxury. I am doing all that I can just to keep the doors open and meet the next payroll." What advice would you offer this harried CEO of a small manufacturing company?

1.24 One of your fellow classmates remarks, "I thought this was an accounting class. If I wanted to study strategic decision making, I would take a management class. When do we get to crunch numbers?" How would you explain the importance to accounting students of understanding strategic decision making?

Exercises

Exercises, problems, and cases include the learning objective they cover. Logos indicating whether the question focuses on ethics, group work, communication skills, or Internet research. A spreadsheet logo indicates that an Excel template is available on the website for that problem.

Review the IMA analysis of management accounting practice (www.imanet.org) and prepare a memo or visual presentation (instructor's choice) that explains one of the following:

a. The most important personal attributes of successful financial managers.

b. The most important competencies for entry-level financial managers.

c. The financial management activities that will increase the most in the future.

d. The four quotations from in-person interviews that you find most interesting.

Exercise 1.25
Characteristics of Successful Cost Management Analysts
(LO 1)

New Zealand recently transformed many of its government agencies into private corporations. This is a difficult process that many developing and former communist and socialist countries have been implementing. Match the following general techniques of cost management with the management decisions in these new corporations that were most likely to be assisted by using the techniques.

Exercise 1.26
Cost Management Techniques
(LO 1)

Cost Management Technique	**Management Decision**
a. Learning about how operations work	_____ The design of incentive bonuses of up to 12 percent of salary by Electricity Corporations (ECNZ) for middle managers based on meeting difficult profit goals
b. Organizing resources into efficient activities and operations	_____ The use of seminars called "What If I Owned the Business?" by Television Corporation (TVNZ) to introduce staff to issues of competition
c. Measuring actual and expected costs of activities, products, and services	_____ ECNZ's decision to restructure into four major operating divisions: Production, Marketing, Power Transmission, and Construction
d. Identifying profitable products, services, customers, and distribution	_____ The decision by Coal Corporation (CoalCorp) to evaluate every job currently performed to determine which is essential to the goal of profitability
e. Identifying opportunities for improvements in the value of products and services	_____ TVNZ's new focus on estimating the costs of television programming and production
f. Communicating effectively	_____ The decision by Public Works Corporation (WORKS) to sell its poorly performing Property and Computing Services divisions
g. Motivating and evaluating personnel	_____ TVNZ's analysis of the programming and advertising practices of its new commercial rival, TV3.

[Adapted from B. Spicer et al., *Transforming Government Enterprise.*]

Exercise 1.27
Teamwork
(LO 1)

Select the decision-making team that most likely would be best for each of the following operations or decisions. Explain your choices.

Type of Team

a.   Individual (no team)

b.   Small doubles tennis team whose members have special skills that complement each other's strengths and weaknesses

c.   Large soccer team whose members have assignments but work closely together

d.   Large swimming team whose members have individual responsibilities and normally do not interact but share in team outcomes

Operation or Decision

_____Word processing center of a large university where most of the work is preparing exams, copying articles, and preparing promotional materials

_____Development of a new business curriculum to meet specific educational needs

_____Design of advertising campaign to counter a rival's new product announcement

_____Development of a new video game for PlayStation

_____Writing a new cost-management textbook

_____Completion of a complex project with a short, rigid deadline

_____Completing an application to graduate school

_____Competing in a collegiate intramural volleyball league

Exercise 1.28
Strategic Decision
Making
(LO 1, 3)

Review the elements of strategic missions in Exhibit 1–1. Assume that you are managing a small business that sells coffee, espresso, and possibly various other drinks in a university's engineering center. Consider the possibility that the business mission could be any of the four basic types. First, for each mission, describe several decisions you must make. Second, try to arrange these decisions in roughly the order you must make them, from the earliest to the latest or ongoing decisions. Third, describe the information you will need to make these decisions.

Exercise 1.29
Strategic Decisions
(LO 1, 3)

Two of the world's largest soft drink companies are PepsiCo and Coca-Cola. Find their most recent annual reports in either your library or on the Internet (look, for example, at the companies' Websites or the Securities and Exchange Commission's EDGAR site, www.sec.gov). From the presidents' letters, identify and list similarities and differences in these two competitors' declared strategies. (*Hint:* Describe and contrast each company's value chain.)

Exercise 1.30
Benefit-Cost Analysis
(LO 4)

Quantorus Corporation manufactures disk drives for computers by assembling parts and components from hundreds of suppliers. Cost-management analysts have been analyzing costs to produce disk drives and have determined that a large proportion of the cost is caused by detecting and replacing faulty components received from suppliers. Most faulty components currently cannot be detected until they are assembled into products that then fail performance tests. Following are estimated annual costs of three alternative decisions to manage this aspect of operations.

Alternatives for Supply of Disk Drive Components	Cost per Year (US$ thousands)
1. Continue current supply and assembly operations—detect and replace faulty components	$2,331
2. Thoroughly inspect incoming components before they are assembled	$1,708
3. Develop close relationships with a few selected suppliers that will guarantee the performance of all components	$1,387

Required

a.   Describe and explain other possible costs and benefits of each alternative.

b.   How do you think cost-management analysts might have developed these cost estimates?

c.   Which alternative do you recommend? Why?

Exercise 1.31
Cost Management
Support
(LO 1)

Find a recent article in a professional magazine, such as *Strategic Finance, Management Accounting (UK), Journal of Cost Management,* or *Harvard Business Review,* that describes accounting and finance support of strategic decision making at a specific organization.

Required

a. Prepare an outline of the article that identifies the following:

  ▨ The definition of *strategic decision making* used in this article.

  ▨ The strategic "problem" or opportunity that motivated the decision making.

  ▨ Areas of operations where this organization focused its strategic efforts.

  ▨ Sources of information to support this organization's strategic decision making.

  ▨ Whether strategic decision making was a success, and how "success" was defined and measured.

b. Present your own evaluation of the success of this strategic decision-making support.

Match the following operations with appropriate elements of an organization's value chain.

Exercise 1.32
Value Chain Analysis
(LO 4)

Value-Chain Element	**Operation or Decision**
a. Research and development	____Dell Computer's replies to customers' questions via email
b. Design	
c. Supply	____Electronic ordering link between Container Industries, Inc., and a division of DuPont Corp. that supplies raw plastic pellets to Container Industries
d. Production	
e. Marketing	____Purchase by 3-Squared, Inc. of McData Corp. to acquire its data communications technology
f. Distribution	
g. Customer service	____Pickup of StorageTek Corp.'s packaged disk drives by United Parcel Service for delivery to customers
	____Development of animation for Yahoo! home pages
	____RCA's outsourcing of the assembly of its portable CD players to a company in Mexico
	____Updating Canterbury New Zealand's electronic Internet catalog of sport and casual clothing

Problems

Vasco Corporation is considering outsourcing its accounts receivable function, a support service in the finance department. Vasco's cost management analyst expects annual benefits that include personnel cost savings of $121,000, facilities savings of $90,000, other support service cost savings of $60,000, and no loss of service quality. The analyst also estimated annual costs of the decision to include the contract cost to DeGama, Inc. of $160,000, severance costs of dismissed personnel of $20,000, and contract administration costs of $12,000.

Problem 1.33
Benefit-Cost Analysis
(LO 4)

Required

a. Based on the quantifiable benefits and costs of the decision, would you recommend that Vasco should outsource its accounts receivable function? What qualitative factors should Vasco also consider?

b. Vasco did outsource the accounts receivable function and measured actual benefits to include personnel cost savings of $82,000, facilities cost savings of $100,000, suport service cost savings of $70,000. Actual costs included $160,000 for the outsourced service, $30,000 for training costs, and $13,000 for contract administration. Furthermore, customer billing complaints were lower than in previous years; sales growth was lower; and employee turnover in other support service areas was higher. Prepare an analysis similar to Exhibit 1–5.

c. On balance, do you agree with the outsourcing decision? Why or why not?

Consider the following data on last year's accounting operations that were obtained by Clean Air Systems, Inc. (CAS), from an industry trade association that gathers and reports data from all members of the association anonymously.

Problem 1.34
Benefit-Cost Analysis
(LO 4)

Accounting operation	CAS Cost per Year	CAS Cost per Transaction	Association Cost per Transaction
Accounts receivable	$50,000	$12.00	$8.00
General ledger...............................	23,000	7.00	4.00
Accounts payable	35,000	9.00	5.00
Payroll	20,000	6.00	2.50
Credit & collections	9,000	11.00	6.00

Required

a.   How many of each type of transaction did CAS perform that year?

b.   In every case, the association average cost per transaction was less than CAS's cost. How might other companies operating in the same industry have lower accounting transaction costs?

c.   If CAS could process accounts receivable transactions at the association's average cost, how much would it save each year at the same levels of transactions?

d.   Security Detection Devices Corporation (SDDC) is a comparably sized competitor of CAS and has the same number of accounting transactions per year as CAS. SDDC, however, processes each accounting transaction for 20 percent less than the association average. What total cost advantage does SDDC have over CAS just in the area of accounting costs per year? What is the importance to CAS of knowing this cost advantage?

e.   Why do many companies compare their performance against their own industry and the best in the world?

Problem 1.35
Benefit-Cost Analysis:
Outsourcing
(LO 4)

Great Basin Oil Company, Inc., is a large oil and gas producer headquartered in Utah. Historically, most of its operations have been in the continental United States. However, in the past decade, Great Basin expanded its operations to 14 foreign locations where it operates alone or in conjunction with foreign companies or governments. Great Basin currently maintains a large department of 73 highly trained tax specialists who report to the chief financial officer and assist with planning for the tax impacts of management decisions for domestic and foreign operations. The tax department also prepares its many, complex tax returns. Great Basin is considering eliminating its internal tax department and outsourcing all of its tax planning and tax return preparation to a large international business services firm. A cost management team has prepared the following preliminary calculations:

Great Basin Tax Operation	Current costs
Information systems	$ 900,000
Tax planning	1,200,000
Tax return preparation.................................	2,000,000

Required

a.   What is the most that Great Basin Oil Company should pay for tax services from an external provider if all but the information systems costs could be saved?

b.   What considerations in addition to cost should be important to Great Basin' decision to outsource its tax services?

c.   Evaluate a business services company's offer to provide tax planning and return preparation services for $3 million per year. This offer is contingent, however, on Great Basin' acceptance of another offer from the business services company to improve Great Basin' tax information systems at a one-time cost of $1.5 million. This improvement should reduce annual costs of the information system by $300,000 per year for the next five years and greatly improve the accuracy and responsiveness of the system. (Ignore the time value of money.)

Problem 1.36
Ethical Issue
(LO 3)

Paul Martinez recently joined Toxic, Inc., as assistant controller. Toxic processes chemicals to use in fertilizers. During his first month on the job, Martinez spent most of his time getting better acquainted with those responsible for plant operations. In response to his questions as to the procedure for disposing of chemicals, the plant supervisor responded that Martinez was not involved in the disposal of waste and would be wise to ignore the issue. Of course, this just drove him to investigate the matter further. He soon discovered that Toxic was dumping toxic waste in a nearby public landfill late at night. He also learned that several members of management appeared to be involved in arranging for this dumping. He was unable, however, to determine whether his superior, the controller, was involved. Martinez considered three possible courses of action. He could discuss the matter with the controller, anonymously release the information to the local newspaper, or discuss the situation with an outside member of the board of directors whom he knows personally.

Required

a.   Does Martinez have an ethical responsibility to take a course of action? Why or why not?

b.   What course of action do you recommend? Why?

[CMA adapted]

Andover Division is part of a large corporation. It normally sells to outside customers but, on occasion, sells to another division of its corporation. When it sells internally, corporate policy states that the price must be cost plus 25 percent. Andover received an order from Baltimore Division for 4,000 units. Andover's planned output for the year had been 23,000 units before Baltimore's order, but its capacity is 30,000 units per year. The costs for producing the planned 23,000 units follow:

Problem 1.37
Benefit-Cost Analysis:
Internal Orders
(LO 4)

	Total	Per Unit
Materials	$ 30,000	$ 1.30
Labor	120,000	5.22
Other manufacturing costs	85,000	3.70
Total costs	$235,000	$10.22

Based on these data, Andover's controller, who was new to the corporation, calculated that the unit price for Baltimore's order should be $12.77 ($10.22 × 125 percent, rounded). After producing and shipping the 4,000 units, Andover sent Baltimore an invoice for $51,080. Shortly thereafter, Andover received a note from Baltimore's buyer stating that this invoice was not in accordance with company policy. Because Andover would incur the labor and "other" costs regardless of whether it accepted Baltimore's order, the unit cost should have been only $1.30 to cover Andover's materials costs. The price paid would be $1.63 ($1.30 × 125 percent, rounded) per unit, and the total payment to Andover should be $6,522.

Required

a.   What are the costs and benefits of internally "sourcing" products and services? Which can be quantified and which cannot?

b.   If the corporation asked you to review the current intercompany policy, what policy would you recommend? Why? (*Note:* You need not limit yourself to Baltimore Division's calculation or to current policy.)

Aroma Coffee, Inc., operates a small coffee shop in the downtown area. Its profits have been declining, and management is planning to expand and add ice cream to the menu. The annual ice cream sales are expected to increase revenue by $30,000. The cost to purchase ice cream and cones from the manufacturer is $15,000. The present manager will supervise the coffee shop and ice cream shop. Due to expansion, however, the labor costs and utilities would increase by 30 percent. Rent and other costs will increase by 25 percent.

Problem 1.38
Benefit-Cost Analysis:
Add a Product Line
(LO 4)

AROMA COFFEE, INC.
Annual Income Statement
Before Expansion

Sales revenue	$55,000
Costs	
Food	16,000
Labor	12,000
Utilities	3,000
Rent	6,000
Other costs	3,000
Manager's salary	20,000
Total costs	$60,000
Operating profit (loss)	$ (5,000)

Required

a.   Should management open the ice cream shop? Show an analysis of the costs and benefits of adding ice cream.

b.   ***Build your own spreadsheet.*** Create a spreadsheet model of this problem and analyze the decision to expand if you learn that Baskin-Robbins will open an ice cream store down the block. Aroma's ice cream sales could drop by one-third. Use the following hints.

These problems provide practice in building your own spreadsheets. Use the Hints here to build spreadsheets in future chapters.

Hint 1: Follow these steps to build a flexible spreadsheet (also see Chapter 12):

1. Place all facts, assumptions, and estimates in a "data input" section of the spreadsheet. For example, place each number used in the spreadsheet in a separate, labeled cell. This is the only place you should enter any numbers.

2. Write the relations among the spreadsheet's numbers (or "parameters") as algebraic formulas using the numbers' cell addresses (not the numbers themselves) in a separate section of the spreadsheet. For example, expected total revenues could be calculated with a formula containing the cell addresses of current revenue + expected revenue from the expansion (e.g., = B3 + C3).

3. Steps 1 and 2 allow the spreadsheet to easily and flexibly reflect any changes you make in the parameters, such as the expected sales level, which appear only in the data input section.

Hint 2: You must make assumptions about how the possible drop in ice cream sales will affect revenues and costs. Make these assumptions explicit in the data input section and in the formulas. For example, enter the possible drop in sales, $-1/3$, in the data input section and use that number in any formulas related to sales.

The following spreadsheet fragment illustrates these hints, but you should feel free to structure the income statement in the way that you prefer.

	A	B	C	D	E
1	Aroma Coffee, Inc.				
2	Data Input	Current Operations	Ice Cream Expansion	Impact of Competitor*	
3	Sales revenue	$55,000	$30,000	−0.3333333	
4	Other data............				
5					
6	Annual Income Statement	Current Operations	Ice Cream Expansion	Total	
7	Sales revenue	=B3	=C3*(1 + D3)	=B7 + C7	
8	Other calculations.............				
9					
10					

*Because 1/3 is not an even decimal, the number in D3 was created by a formula, = −1/3, to generate the most accurate measure.

Problem 1.39
Benefit-Cost Analysis:
Add a Project
(LO 4)

Change Management Corp. is a consulting firm that helps companies adapt organizational structures to current industry trends. Recently, one of its officers was approached by a representative of a high-tech research firm that offered a six-month contract to Change Management for some help in reorganizing the company. Change Management reported the following costs and revenues during the past year.

CHANGE MANAGEMENT CORP.
Annual Income Statement

Sales revenue......................................	$1,500,000
Costs	
Labor	700,000
Equipment lease..............................	104,000
Rent	120,000
Supplies	60,000
Officers' salaries	400,000
Other costs	50,000
Total costs	$1,434,000
Operating profit	$ 66,000

If Change Management decides to take the six-month contract to help the company reorganize, it will hire two part-time consultants at $150,000 (salaries and benefits) and add support staff at a cost of $25,000. Equipment lease will increase by 12 percent because the company must buy certain computer equipment. Supplies and other costs will increase by an estimated 15 percent. The existing building has space for the new consultant. In addition, management believes that no new officers will be necessary for this work and that officers' salaries will not change.

Required

a. What costs would be incurred as a result of taking the contract?

b. If the contract will pay $200,000 for the six months, should Change Management accept it?

c. What considerations, other than costs, are necessary before making this decision?

Cases

You have recently been hired as a new cost-management analyst by Corporate Express, the world's largest supplier of office supplies to large corporations. Corporate Express takes orders from its customers via the Internet, processes those orders with office supply manufacturers, and delivers the supplies to the corporate employees who ordered them. Corporate Express' customers do not need to hire anyone whose job is to order, receive, or distribute supplies, nor do customers need supplies inventories or warehouses. Large customers (such as Coca-Cola and Hewlett-Packard) save millions of dollars per year by outsourcing their office supply tasks to Corporate Express.

Case 1.40
Analyze Strategic
Decision
(LO 1, 3, 4)

The vice president of marketing is concerned that the company's policy to serve only large companies does not fit its strategic goals. She believes it might be worthwhile to offer limited services to small, rapidly growing businesses because they could graduate to the full line of services offered to large companies. As a first step, the VP has asked you to analyze the costs and benefits of serving small and large customers.

You have developed the following information:

Annual Average Data	One Large Company	One Small Company
Number of orders per year	2,000	200
Sales value of supplies per order in dollars	$1,000	$600
Cost of supplies to Corporate Express as a percent of sales	80%	75%
Processing cost per order	$25	$25
Delivery cost per order as a percent of sales	8%	8%
Cost to create and maintain Internet access per customer per year	$3,000	$3,000

Required

a.   Compute the annual profit generated from an average large or small company.

b.   Would it be worthwhile to add 10 small customers to replace one large customer? Why or why not?

c.   If other characteristics of small firms differ from those of large ones, would this change your evaluation? Give an example.

d.   Do you recommend that Corporate Express consider this business alternative further?

e.   *Build your own spreadsheet.* Create a spreadsheet to solve the numerical portions of this case. What would your recommendation be if the sales value of supplies per order of a typical small customer increased to $700? to $800? Explain.

Many companies use the services of *internal auditors,* who perform various investigative and consulting tasks within organizations, such as reviewing divisional financial statements and making recommendations to improve operating performance (e.g., improving quality and customer service). In the past, this has provided both career paths for professional internal auditors and valuable training for new managers, who benefit from seeing firsthand many of the company's operations. In recent years, however, many companies have begun to outsource their internal auditing services.

Case 1.41
Analyze Support
Services in the Value
Chain
(LO 1, 2, 4)

Consider this recent discussion between the new chief financial officer (CFO) and the long-time director of internal auditing (DIA) at Jeans 'R Us, a large manufacturer of casual and fashion denim clothing, which has experienced serious declines in profitability.

CFO: We need to look very hard at all of our support services and consider whether we can afford them. We need to talk seriously because I think that outsourcing internal auditing will save the company millions of dollars. In our current situation, we need to save costs wherever we can.

DIA: I think you are being shortsighted. I believe our staff can provide the best possible service to management because it understands our business. An external provider of internal audit services just will not appreciate the unique aspects of our business and our culture.

CFO: I understand that internal audit has had a long tradition here, but based on our budget constraints, I think we have no choice but to use an outside service. The service provider we are considering has a worldwide staff with wide-ranging expertise that we can utilize. You know that many of our manufacturing plants are foreign operations and require the auditors to be fluent in speaking and writing the local language and to understand the local culture. Furthermore, all of our data communications rely on information technology that changes every year. To keep internal auditing staff with these talents at Jeans 'R Us will just be too costly. And what about all of the travel expenses in the internal audit department?

>   ***DIA:*** I'm sorry, but you don't appreciate that internal audit is a strength of the company that has been built over the years by a trust between the internal auditors and the operational and financial management. You cannot replace that level of trust and understanding with outsourced internal auditors whose only loyalty is to the fee they will collect. Internal audit is a "partner" promoting valuable improvements, and top management has always supported it in that way. If you outsource internal audit, you will change the climate of cooperation and trust and free flow of information that you need. In the long run, you will end up paying a lot more for inferior service. Outsourcing internal audit will be a serious mistake. If you insist on this approach, I will go straight to the board of directors. By the way, you know that internal audit reports to the board each year on whether it can rely on the company's financial statements.

Required

a.   Describe the possible costs and benefits of outsourcing internal auditing at Jeans 'R Us.

b.   What pressures are motivating the arguments of both the CFO and the DIA?

c.   How do you interpret the DIA's last comment?

d.   Can you recommend a course of action that might satisfy the CFO, DIA, and board of directors?

Case 1.42
Cost Management
Support of Strategy
(LO 1, 3, 4)

Boeing Company is the world's largest manufacturer of commercial jet airplanes. To meet growing demand, Boeing in 1997 decided to more than double its rate of production from approximately 17 to more than 40 planes per month. In March 1999, Boeing reported that this increase in production, which normally would be considered a fortunate turnaround, unfortunately could have cost the airplane manufacturer more than $2.6 billion in 1997–1998 for unnecessary costs. Unexpected delays and disruptions caused these extra costs. Financial analysts on Wall Street predicted that Boeing's production problems would persist for nearly a year longer (which proved to be true) as the company struggled to "ramp up" its production level. The next day, after the reports from Boeing and financial analysts, Boeing's common stock declined 7.6 percent, or $4.12 per share.

Required

Hint: Access information about Boeing Company at the SECs EDGAR website (www.sec.gov/edgar.shtml).

a.   If this event were announced today and Boeing's common stock lost $4.12 per share, approximately how much total (before-tax) wealth would Boeing's common shareholders lose today?

b.   Describe Boeing's value chain in general terms, as described in the firm's Form 10-K.

c.   What parts of Boeing's value chain would be affected by doubling its production operations?

d.   Explain how Boeing's decision to quickly double its production level actually could reduce its profitability.

e.   Cost-management support of management's decision to double output might have saved Boeing and its stockholders a lot of money (and prevented some unflattering publicity). Describe in general terms what support operations you might have anticipated to support Boeing's doubling of production.

Case 1.43
Cost Management
Support and Ethics of
Strategic Decisions
(LO 1, 2)

Interview with Jamie O'Connell, president, CEO, and cofounder of Datacom, Inc., a leading designer and manufacturer of storage area network (SAN) switching devices.[9]

>   ***Author:*** How did you decide to drop other products and direct Datacom's resources toward the design and manufacture of these behind-the-scenes network switches? This was a major strategic decision, wasn't it?
>
>   ***O'Connell:*** This was a huge decision. We have staked the future of the company on it, but let's be clear about strategic decision making at Datacom. Before we made this decision, we— and I do mean all of us at Datacom—spent months understanding our strengths and weaknesses, our competitors' strengths and weaknesses, our customers' future needs, our business partners, and the future of data-network technology. *I* did not make this decision, *we* made the decision to focus on these very important, high-value switches.
>
>   ***Author:*** Is it really possible to involve everyone? Can you trust everyone with the responsibility of this kind of decision?

---

[9] Datacom is the disguised name of a real company, with approximately 200 employees and $200 million sales. SANs are high-capacity, high-speed configurations of data-storage devices, such as disk drives, that are accessible to computer networks through Datacom's fiber-optic switches.

O'Connell: Yes, yes, and yes. Of course it takes time, but who knows our capabilities and customers better than our own employees? And anyone who won't take responsibility for shaping the future of this company should look for another job. In this competitive and dynamic industry, we need the help and input of everyone. This decision affects every employee, stockholder, business partner, their families, and the community. True, the ultimate decision was up to the board of directors and me, but we could not and did not make this decision in a vacuum. That would have been irresponsible.

Author: Can you talk a bit about the role of cost management personnel and the information that supported this decision?

O'Connell: One of the great strengths of our company is a finance group that understands the company's business and technology. I think that is essential in a technology-driven company of our size. Not only that, they truly understand cost management and how to effectively support our strategic decision making. These are not your typical green eyeshade bean counters. The CFO, in particular, brings what I call the "reality of finance" to our analysis of the future of data-storage technology. Most of us are engineers by background, and we tend to focus on the technology more than the business. We would not have made our decision to focus on SAN switches so confidently and responsibly without the daily use of cost management insight and information. We might not have predicted the future of technology and the market perfectly, but we understood beforehand, as well as we could, our alternatives and their impacts on this company and its stakeholders. This was vital, strategic information. Without it, we might as well be playing the lottery with the company's resources. Current events are proving that we chose correctly, and we are positioned to be worldwide leaders in this rapidly growing market.

Required

a.   CEO O'Connell of Datacom, Inc., referred to various elements of making strategic decisions. How can cost-management information support each of these elements?

b.   What quantitative and nonquantitative costs and benefits might be relevant to Datacom's strategic decisions?

c.   How can organizations choose which processes to perform and which to outsource to business partners?

Chapter 2

Product Costing Systems: Concepts and Design Issues

After completing this chapter, you should be able to:

1. Explain the role of product costs, period costs, and expenses in financial statements.

2. Prepare an income statement and a schedule of cost of goods manufactured and sold.

3. List the components of manufacturing cost, and diagram their flow through a production process.

4. Explain how unit-level, variable, and fixed costs differ.

5. Distinguish between the costs of resources used and those of resources supplied.

6. Understand the concepts of opportunity cost, sunk cost, committed cost, direct cost, and indirect cost.

7. Prepare income statements using absorption, variable, and throughput costing.

8. Reconcile income under absorption and variable costing.

9. Discuss the advantages and disadvantages of absorption, variable, and throughput costing.

10. Discuss the ethical issues concerning the intentional overproduction of inventory.

Cost *Management* Challenges

(Solutions are on page 67.)

1. **What** are the significant inputs to a production process, and how do cost managers track the flow of costs through the process?

2. **How** can alternative methods to calculate product costs create different incentives?

3. **How** should cost-management analysts measure costs for internal decision making?

EMAIL MEMORANDUM

Memorandum

To: Jack Canfield
         Director of Cost Management

From: Maria Perez
         President

CC: Anne Harrison
         Vice President of Manufacturing

         Jorge Gonzalez
         Vice President of Marketing and Sales

Re: Projections of operating income for the new plant

Jack: The new plant in central Pennsylvania will be on line soon to manufacture our new ScholarPak product. Since we're focusing on a single product line there in the beginning, I'm requesting that you prepare separate operating income statements for this plant for each of the first three years of operations. That will enable us to see how the new product line is doing.

As you know, we compete effectively by being a low-cost producer of quality backpacks, and we cannot let our cost structure change from what has been successful for us in the past. In particular, we have to watch our committed costs. Our competitors surely will take advantage if our costs increase and we try to raise prices.

Please give these issues some thought, and we'll discuss them at our next Monday morning meeting.

SECTION I. COST-MANAGEMENT AND PRODUCT-COSTING SYSTEMS[1]

The explosion in technology we are experiencing, coupled with increasing world-wide competition, is forcing organizations to produce high-quality goods and services and to provide outstanding customer service, and to do so either at the lowest possible cost or in a distinctive way that others cannot imitate. Success in this highly competitive environment demands that a company have a highly effective cost-management system. The role that cost management plays in helping organizations to maintain a competitive advantage is to help create more value at lower cost by efficiently managing an organization's value chain of activities, processes, and functions. These are some examples:

- In formulating its strategy, Southwest Airlines' management team considers the cost savings from being a low-cost, no-frills airline and the benefits of partnering with others in the travel industry to increase the value of its no-frills approach.

- The Boeing Company uses cost-management techniques to better understand and control the costs of aircraft production, which includes managing the costs of using many suppliers of outsourced services and products.

- Whirlpool found through its cost-management system that some of its products cost much more and others much less to produce than management previously had realized. These discoveries led to critical decisions about which products to produce, outsource, or drop.

- AT&T uses cost-management information to help management make better decisions about the services it provides. On the basis of this information, it has extended its value chain to include providing products and services for many forms of communication in ways that others cannot easily imitate (e.g., cable access to the Internet).

- Cost management techniques at Hewlett-Packard help its engineers to design products for ease of manufacturability and reduce the development time of new products, which creates a competitive advantage by being first in the market.

- Blue Cross/Blue Shield uses cost-management data to better understand the cost of its services. With this information, the company can make decisions about which services to offer and how to price them.

This list could be many times longer, but as these examples show, cost-management information helps organizations in various ways to be successful in achieving their goals. In each case, these organizations are using cost-management information to identify the activities and processes they can perform better than their competitors and to build competitive advantages.

The Role of Cost Management at CollegePak Company

The email memorandum from CollegePak Company's president to the director of cost management requests operating income statements for a new product line, and discusses CollegePak's cost commitments. These are routine issues for a company's cost-management team. This chapter explores these and other aspects of the vital role of cost management in today's business environment. Before continuing the discussion, however, let's first find out about the chapter's focus company, CollegePak.

---

[1] To facilitate course design by instructors, this chapter is formally divided into two sections, which can be assigned independently. Section I, which covers the fundamentals of product costing systems and their role in cost management, should be covered immediately after Chapter 1. Section I lays important terminological and conceptual groundwork for subsequent chapters. Section II covers absorption, variable, and throughput costing systems. Section II also can be covered at this point, or some instructors may prefer to delay its coverage until later when students have developed a deeper cost management background.

CollegePak Company manufactures backpacks sold to college and high school students through college bookstores and other traditional retail outlets. Although the company started by focusing on the college market, which explains the name CollegePak, it has expanded into the high school market and now is considering an entry into the middle school and elementary school markets as well. The company operates a single production facility located in Trenton, New Jersey. CollegePak's market covers all regions of the United States, and the company has recently entered the European market. The family-owned company has been in business for 22 years, and its annual sales are now $4.5 million. CollegePak has been profitable every year since its founding by Gustavo Perez, who turned over the company's reins to his daughter, Maria, four years ago. Both credit the company's success to four factors: a reliable, durable, functional product; a successful marketing approach that focuses directly on the collegiate and scholastic markets; an outstanding group of employees from the top management team to the machine operators' helpers; and a strong commitment to sound cost-management practices. As Gustavo has said more than once, "You can't be successful in business unless you understand what it costs you to make your product. Then you must manage that cost diligently to consistently deliver value to customers at a price they will pay." CollegePak's current president echoes her father's sentiment, adding that "we have an outstanding cost-management team. It has pulled us out of the fire many a time by finding ways to create value at lower cost."

CollegePak's value chain in Exhibit 2–1 depicts its internal processes: product design, purchasing and material handling, production, marketing, distribution, and customer service. Notice, however, that the value chain also shows the *upstream suppliers* on which CollegePak relies for raw materials, energy and various services as well as the *downstream distributors* through which CollegePak sells its backpacks. One service firm in CollegePak's upstream value chain is Eastern Market Research Associates, a consulting company that CollegePak uses for various market-research studies that fall outside the scope of the company's small marketing team's expertise. On the downstream end of the value chain is University Outfitters, one of CollegePak's oldest retail customers. Although a few companies perform nearly all of their value-chain activities, CollegePak, like most companies,

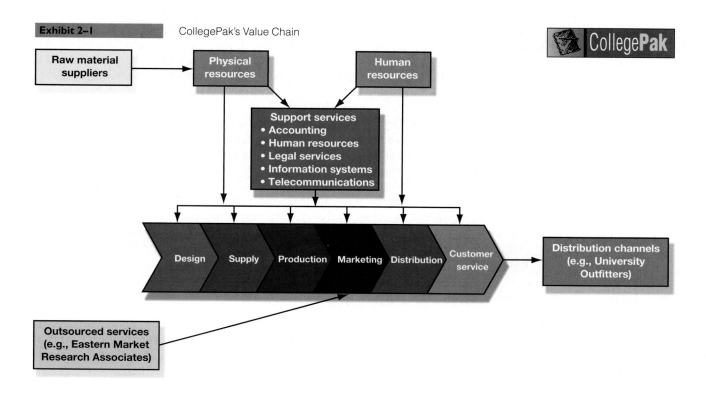

Exhibit 2–1 CollegePak's Value Chain

has decided to outsource some services to others who can do them more efficiently. Unlike some of its competitors, CollegePak would not outsource its manufacturing processes because design and control of costs and quality are what it does best. Maintaining that aspect of competitive advantage does not just happen, however, and CollegePak must work hard to control costs.

The Meaning of Cost

LO 1 Explain the role of product costs, period costs, and expenses in financial statements.

An important first step in studying cost management is to gain an understanding of the various types of costs incurred by organizations and how they actively manage those costs. At the most basic level, a **cost** can be defined as the sacrifice made, usually measured by the resources given up, to achieve a particular purpose. If we look more carefully, however, we find that the word *cost* can have different meanings depending on the context in which it is used. In addition, cost data classified and recorded in a particular way for one purpose could be inappropriate for another use. For example, the costs incurred to produce gasoline last year are important in measuring British Petroleum's income for the year, but those costs might not be useful in planning the company's refinery operations for the next year if the cost of oil has changed significantly or if the methods to produce gasoline have improved. The important point is that different cost concepts, classifications, and measures are used for different purposes. Understanding these differences enables the cost-management analyst to provide appropriate cost data to the managers who need it.

Product Costs, Period Costs, and Expenses

An important issue in both cost management and external financial reporting is the timing with which the costs to acquire assets or services are recognized as expenses. An **expense** is the cost incurred when an asset is used up or sold for the purpose of generating revenue. The terms *product cost* and *period cost* are used to describe the events that cause their conversion into expenses.

A **product cost** is a cost assigned to goods that were either purchased or manufactured for resale; it is used to value the inventory of manufactured goods or merchandise until the goods are sold. In the period of the sale, the product costs are recognized as an expense called **costs of goods sold.** The product cost of merchandise inventory acquired by a retailer or wholesaler for resale consists of the purchase cost of the inventory plus any shipping charges. The product cost of manufactured inventory includes all costs incurred in its manufacture. For example, the labor cost of a production employee at Intel is included as a product cost of the microchips manufactured. Another term for product cost is **inventoriable cost** since product costs are stored as the cost of inventory until the goods are sold. See Exhibit 2–2, which illustrates the relationship between product costs and cost-of-goods-sold expense.

Any cost that is not a product cost is a **period cost.** These costs are identified with the period of time in which they are incurred rather than with units of purchased or produced goods. Period costs are recognized as expenses during the time period in which they are incurred. (Thus, period costs are *not* included in the cost of inventory.) For financial reporting by manufacturing, retail, and service-industry firms, all research and development as well as selling and administrative costs are treated as period costs. As we will see later in this chapter and throughout the text, however, this distinction does not have to be true for internal, cost-management information. Exhibit 2–3 illustrates the nature of period costs.

Costs Reported in Financial Statements

LO 2 Prepare an income statement and a schedule of cost of goods manufactured and sold.

Financial statements provide an important means of communicating about an organization's operations to people both inside and outside of the organization. Internal uses of such information include decision making, planning, and cost management. Creditors, investors, governmental agencies, and other interested parties are external users of financial statements.

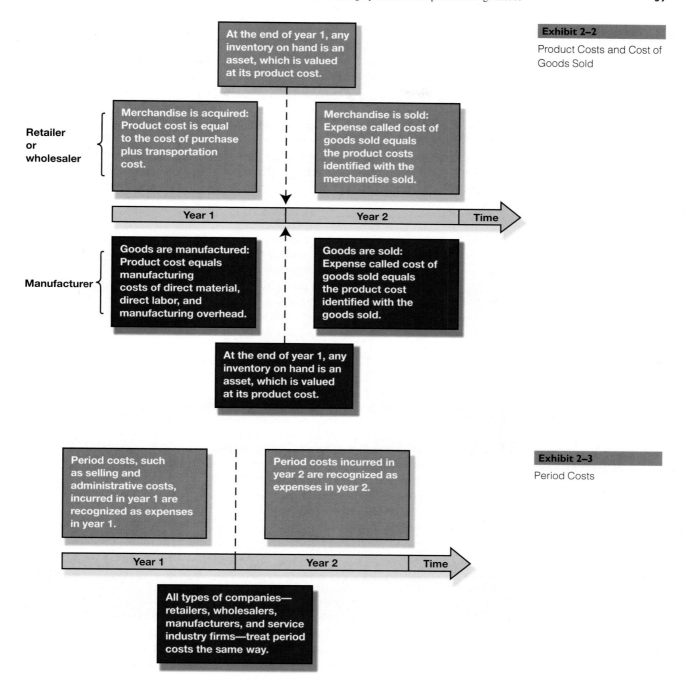

Exhibit 2–2

Product Costs and Cost of Goods Sold

At the end of year 1, any inventory on hand is an asset, which is valued at its product cost.

Retailer or wholesaler

Merchandise is acquired: Product cost is equal to the cost of purchase plus transportation cost.

Merchandise is sold: Expense called cost of goods sold equals the product costs identified with the merchandise sold.

Year 1   Year 2   Time

Manufacturer

Goods are manufactured: Product cost equals manufacturing costs of direct material, direct labor, and manufacturing overhead.

Goods are sold: Expense called cost of goods sold equals the product cost identified with the goods sold.

At the end of year 1, any inventory on hand is an asset, which is valued at its product cost.

Exhibit 2–3

Period Costs

Period costs, such as selling and administrative costs, incurred in year 1 are recognized as expenses in year 1.

Period costs incurred in year 2 are recognized as expenses in year 2.

Year 1   Year 2   Time

All types of companies— retailers, wholesalers, manufacturers, and service industry firms—treat period costs the same way.

Before returning to CollegePak, let's briefly consider the role of costs in the financial statements of service-industry firms and retailers. The reason for this digression is that the financial statements of these types of firms are simpler than those of manufacturing companies such as CollegePak. After discussing these simpler cases, we will examine CollegePak's statements. Two organizations in CollegePak's value chain are a management consulting company, Eastern Market Research Associates (EMRA), and a retailer specializing in merchandise for college students, University Outfitters. CollegePak's management has engaged EMRA to do specialized research on the market for backpacks such as those CollegePak manufactures. This important market-research effort is too specialized and extensive to be accomplished in-house by CollegePak's own marketing personnel, so management has outsourced it to EMRA. On the downstream end of CollegePak's value chain, University Outfitters is one of the oldest distribution channels for its products.

Service Firms

Service firms provide customers a product that is consumed as it is produced. Thus, service firms do not carry inventories of produced goods. For example, management consulting firms provide a variety of services to improve their clients' business processes. Labor costs tend to be the most significant cost category for most service organizations. The costs associated with EMRA are reported in the income statement in Exhibit 2–4. The costs of its services include the cost of billable hours, which are the hours billed to clients, plus other charges. (For example, the cost of billable hours includes the cost of compensation for the consultants who provide the service; the other charges might include the cost of specialized software purchased to meet the client's needs). Costs that are not part of services billable to clients are included in selling and administrative costs.

Retail Companies

Retail and wholesale companies, including supermarkets, clothing stores, furniture stores, and motorcycle distributors, sell tangible products that can be inventoried. The income statement for these companies includes revenue and cost items such as those for service companies, but it also includes the expense *cost of goods sold* to track the tangible goods they buy and sell.

University Outfitters is a retail company that sells a variety of merchandise typically needed by college students, such as books, paper, sportswear, and CollegePak's backpacks. The company's *income statement* and *schedule of cost of goods sold* are shown in Exhibit 2–5, which illustrates the computation of the cost

---

Exhibit 2–4

Income Statement for a Service Industry Firm

EASTERN MARKET RESEARCH ASSOCIATES Income Statement For the Year Ended December 31, 20x2	
Sales revenue	$1,000,000
Cost of consulting services sold	600,000
Gross margin	$ 400,000
Selling and administrative expenses	290,000
Operating profit	$ 110,000

Exhibit 2–5

Income Statement and Schedule of Cost of Goods Sold for a Retailer

UNIVERSITY OUTFITTERS Income Statement For the Year Ended December 31, 20x2		
Sales revenue		$1,000,000
Cost of goods sold		530,000
Gross margin		$ 470,000
Selling and administrative expenses		200,000
Operating profit		$ 270,000

UNIVERSITY OUTFITTERS Schedule of Cost of Goods Sold For the Year Ended December 31, 20x2		
Beginning inventory		$ 100,000
Cost of goods purchased:		
Merchandise cost	$600,000	
Transportation-in costs	30,000	
Total cost of goods purchased		630,000
Cost of goods available for sale		$ 730,000
Less: Cost of goods in ending inventory		200,000
Cost of goods sold		$ 530,000

Cost management plays an important role in many types of organizations. The financial statements of service-industry firms, retailers, and manufacturing companies use cost information.

of goods sold on the income statement; the schedule shows the following information for University Outfitters:

■ The $100,000 beginning inventory on January 1, 20x2, represents the cost of the books, paper, apparel, backpacks, and other merchandise on hand at the beginning of the year.

■ The company's total cost of goods purchased was $630,000.

■ Based on this information, University Outfitters had merchandise costing $730,000 available for sale. This is the cost of the goods that the company *could have sold.*

■ At year-end, the company subtracted the value of its merchandise inventory on hand costing $200,000 to arrive at the cost of merchandise sold, $530,000.

The income statement summarizes University Outfitters' operating performance with the following information:

■ *Sales revenue.*

■ *Cost of goods sold*, which comes from the schedule of cost of goods sold.

■ The gross margin (the difference between sales revenue and cost of goods sold) is $470,000 ($470,000 = $1,000,000 sales revenue − $530,000 cost of goods sold). If you were University Outfitters' general manager, you would know that, on average, every $1 of sales gave you $.47 to cover selling and administrative costs and earn a profit.

■ *Marketing and administrative costs.*

■ *Operating profit.*

The term *cost of goods sold* is intended to be self-descriptive. It includes only the costs to obtain the goods that were sold. It does not include the costs of *selling* them, such as the salaries of the sales personnel, which are selling costs, or the salaries of the top managers, which are administrative costs.

Manufacturing Companies

A manufacturing company such as CollegePak has a more complex income statement than do service or retail companies. Whereas the retailer *purchases* the goods for sale, the manufacturer *makes* them. CollegePak purchases materials (for example, fabric and thread), hires employees to convert the materials into finished products, and then offers the products for sale. These additional activities add to the complexity of CollegePak's cost structure and financial reports.

As the email memorandum at the beginning of the chapter noted, CollegePak's strategy is to be a low-cost producer of quality backpacks. The company enjoys some regional and even national name recognition, which helps to boost its sales. Even so,

LO 3 List the components of manufacturing cost, and diagram their flow through a production process.

CollegePak must carefully manage its costs to compete successfully. To execute this low-cost strategy, it is critical that CollegePak have a cost system that can collect cost information about the backpacks the firm manufactures. What then are the manufacturing costs that CollegePak incurs? These are the three major categories of manufacturing costs.

■ **Direct materials** are resources such as raw materials, parts, and components that one can feasibly observe being used to make a specific product. The term "feasibly observe" means that the cost of observing the use of the resource is less than the benefit of doing so. For example, observing the use of fabric, thread, buckles, and other fasteners that CollegePak uses to make backpacks is easy; therefore, the costs of these resources are all direct material costs. Materials that one cannot feasibly identify with making a specific product (that is, it is too costly to observe the various uses of these resources) are discussed later.

   The seemingly interchangeable use of the terms *raw material* and *direct material* is somewhat confusing. However, there is a difference in their meanings. *Before* material enters the production process, it is called *raw* material. *After* it enters production, it becomes *direct* material. Thus, the cost of raw material *used* in production equals the direct-material cost.

■ **Direct labor** is the cost of compensating employees who transform direct material into a finished product. The cost of fringe benefits for direct-labor personnel, such as employer-paid health-insurance premiums, workers' compensation, and the employer's pension contribution, are also included in direct-labor cost. These costs are just as much a part of the employees' compensation as are their regular wages, and CollegePak includes them in direct-labor cost. Although conceptually correct, this treatment of fringe benefits is not always used by other companies. Some companies classify all fringe-benefit costs as *manufacturing overhead,* which is defined next.

■ **Manufacturing overhead** includes all other costs of transforming materials into a finished product, which one cannot feasibly observe being used to make specific products, but are necessary for the production process. Some examples of manufacturing overhead follow.

   Indirect-material cost includes all materials that either (1) are not a part of the finished product but are necessary to manufacture it or (2) are part of the finished product but are insignificant in cost. ("Insignificant in cost" means that the cost of collecting information about the use of these materials exceeds the value of the information collected.) Some examples include lubricants for CollegePak's production machinery and cleaning materials, repair parts, and lightbulbs for the production plant.

   Indirect-labor cost consists of the wages of production employees who do not work directly on the product yet are required for the manufacturing facility's operation. These employees include supervisors, maintenance workers, purchasing managers, and material-handling employees. (When labor is only a small part of total manufacturing costs, some companies classify *all* labor as overhead because observing the way labor is used is too costly. Most companies, including CollegePak, do not follow this practice.)

   Manufacturing overhead also includes *other manufacturing costs,* such as depreciation on the factory building and equipment, insurance on the factory building and equipment, heat, light, power, and similar expenses incurred to keep the manufacturing facility operating. In today's manufacturing environment, managing manufacturing overhead costs is becoming more and more important as they comprise an increasing part of companies' cost structures. As a manager at DaimlerChrysler noted, when you put in a robot to perform an operation that was previously performed by a person, you increase overhead and decrease direct labor. Why does overhead increase in this scenario? If the setup, depreciation, and operating costs of the robotic equipment, as well as the salaries of the technicians who program and maintain it, cannot be tied to specific products, these costs are part of manufacturing overhead. These overhead costs, which sometimes are ignored in decisions to automate processes, can result in total costs that exceed cost savings from replacing direct labor. For example, a major auto manufacturer once automated one of its assembly plants only to find that its total costs were higher than before, and it could not assemble enough additional cars to justify the increased cost.[2]

Support (or **service**) **departments** do not work directly on a product but are necessary to operate the production process. Support departments represent a significant source of manufacturing overhead costs, and include supplier relations, machine maintenance, production scheduling, engineering, purchasing, material handling, and quality assurance. Notice that many of the indirect-labor employees mentioned earlier actually work in a support department. Recall from Chapter 1 that many organizations perceive that the activities of some support departments do not add to their competitive advantages and have outsourced them. The costs of these outsourced activities used for production also should be counted as part of overhead costs.

Other manufacturing overhead costs include overtime premiums and the cost of idle time. An **overtime premium** is the extra hourly compensation paid to an employee who works beyond the time normally allowed by regulation or labor contracts. Suppose, for example, that an employee's regular hourly wage rate is $12 and that he or she receives time and a half ($18) for each overtime hour. The $6 of *additional* compensation per hour is the overtime premium. **Idle time** is time that an employee does not spend productively because of events such as equipment breakdowns or new setups of production runs. Idle time is an unavoidable feature of most manufacturing processes. The costs of employees' overtime premiums and idle time are classified as overhead so that they can be spread across all products rather than being associated with a particular product or batch of products.

Although we use the term *manufacturing overhead* in this book, other synonyms used in practice are *burden, factory overhead, factory expense*, and simply *overhead*.

Prime costs and conversion costs. In manufacturing companies, you are likely to encounter the following two categories of costs: prime and conversion. **Prime costs** are direct costs, namely the costs of direct material and direct labor. **Conversion costs** are the costs incurred to convert direct material into the final product, namely, costs for direct labor and manufacturing overhead.

Nonmanufacturing costs. Nonmanufacturing costs include selling and administrative costs, which are not used to produce products. CollegePak also incurs selling costs to obtain customer orders and provide finished products to customers. **Selling costs** include costs such as sales commissions, sales personnel salaries, and the sales departments' building occupancy costs. CollegePak also incurs **administrative costs,** which are the costs incurred to manage the organization and provide staff support, including executive and clerical salaries; costs for legal, computing, and accounting services; and building space for administrative personnel.

Nonmanufacturing costs are period costs for financial reporting purposes and thus are expensed in the period incurred. For managerial purposes, however, managers often want to see nonmanufacturing costs associated with specific products. For example, managers at PepsiCo assign the cost of advertising and promotion for Diet Pepsi to that specific product so that they can measure its total cost. Chapter 4 discusses activity-based costing, which is a method to observe how most, if not all,

---

[2] Chapter 5, "Activity-Based Management," covers the redesign of processes to generate more value at lower cost.

costs of the value chain are used to manufacture products (or serve customers and provide services).

Sometimes distinguishing between manufacturing costs and nonmanufacturing costs is conceptually difficult. For example, are the salaries of staff who handle factory payrolls manufacturing or nonmanufacturing costs? What about the rent for offices for the manufacturing vice president? Some of these costs have no clear-cut classification, so companies usually set their own guidelines and follow them consistently.

Stages of Production and the Flow of Costs

Suppose that we are able to tour CollegePak's Trenton production facility. We would encounter the following stages of production:

- We would see *raw material* that has not yet been put into production (e.g., bolts of fabric). **Raw material** is material that has not yet been entered into production.
- Next we would find *work in process,* which refers to partially completed products being worked on. **Work in process** refers to partially completed products.
- Finally, somewhere past the end of the production process, perhaps in the shipping area, we would find *finished goods.* **Finished goods** are products ready for sale.

Manufacturing organizations use **cost-accounting systems** to measure their use of resources in these three production stages. These systems have three major categories of inventory accounts, one category for each of these three production stages: *raw-material inventory, work-in-process inventory, and finished-goods inventory.*

Each inventory account typically has a beginning inventory amount, additions and withdrawals during the period, and an ending inventory based on what is still on hand at the end of the period. Those costs added to inventory accounts are called *inventoriable costs.*

A simplified version of the production process at CollegePak's Trenton plant reviews how this works. It is a traditional manufacturer that produces products, places them in inventory, and then seeks to sell those products. Exhibit 2–6 shows the stages of production from the receipt of raw material through manufacturing to the storage of finished goods. CollegePak's Raw Material Receiving Work Center receives its fabric. The employees in this department are responsible for checking each order to ensure that it meets quality specifications and that the goods received are those ordered.[3]

When the production process begins, the Cutting Work Center cuts and seals the edges of the fabric pieces needed for the main part of each backpack in the production batch and the various small pieces of fabric used for the front and side pockets on each backpack. Then the Cutting Work Center sends the pieces to the Sewing Work Center, which sews them together to form the backpacks in the production lot. Both the cutting and sewing operations are semiautomated with significant touch (i.e., direct) labor involved.

Next the Sewing Work Center sends the backpacks to the Finishing Work Center, which adds the straps, buckles, snaps, zippers, and the CollegePak label, as well as any other trim items, such as the logo of the college or university where the backpacks will be sold. Then the backpacks transfer to the Quality Assurance Work Center, where they are inspected for fabric, sewing, or other flaws. Note that the partially completed products in the Cutting, Sewing, Finishing, or Quality Assurance Work Centers are part of work in process. The costs associated with any product still in these work centers at the end of an accounting period is included in Work-in-Process Inventory.

---

[3] Chapter 7, "Managing Quality and Time to Create Value," discusses different production processes that can be more efficient than CollegePak's approach. Chapter 7 also discusses ways that many companies ensure the quality of incoming materials by partnering with suppliers. Effectively, they outsource this value-chain activity to suppliers.

After Quality Assurance inspects the backpacks, the products become finished goods inventory. The Finished Goods/Shipping Work Center stores the finished goods, packages them for shipment, and ships them to various retailers, who are CollegePak's customers. The costs of any products that are finished but have not yet been sold to customers are included in the Finished-Goods Inventory account at the end of an accounting period.

Income Statement and Schedule of Cost of Goods Manufactured and Sold

Given CollegePak's strategy of being a low-cost manufacturer of quality backpacks, how will the company's management assess the firm's success? Companies use *lead measures,* such as rates of defective product, market share, and introductions of new products, to assess contemporaneous actions that will ultimately affect the firm's financial success. (Subsequent chapters will cover such measures in detail.) Companies also use *lag measures,* such as net income, to assess the company's current financial success, which largely results from past actions. CollegePak's income statement for the most recent year, shown in Exhibit 2–7, is a typical income statement for a manufacturer. The income statement shows that CollegePak generated sales revenue of $4,500,000, had costs of goods sold of $2,810,000, and incurred selling and administrative expenses of $1,440,000 for the year.

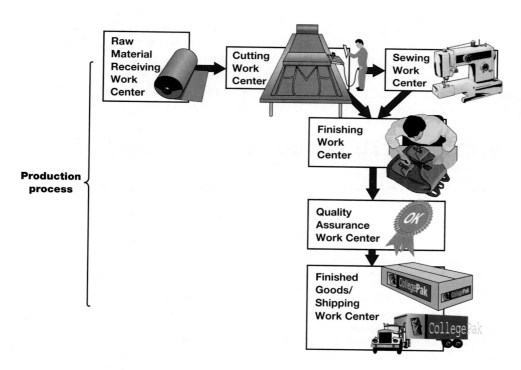

Production process

Exhibit 2–6

CollegePak's Production Stages

COLLEGEPAK		
Income Statement		
For the Year Ended December 31, 20x2		
Sales revenue	$4,500,000	
Cost of goods sold (see Ex. 2–8)...................................	2,810,000	
Gross margin..	$1,690,000	
Less: Selling and administrative expenses	1,440,000	
Operating profit before taxes	$ 250,000	

Exhibit 2–7

Income Statement for a Manufacturer

Now let's consider how to derive the cost-of-goods-sold amount on CollegePak's income statement. The cost management group in a manufacturing company usually uses the cost accounting system to provide management with a schedule of cost of goods manufactured and sold, such as the one shown in Exhibit 2–8 for CollegePak. This schedule reflects the costs of the goods manufactured and sold during a *period* of time, and its result, cost of goods sold, is shown on the income statement for that period. Thus, like the income statement, this schedule is prepared for a *period* of time.

Direct material.   Let's focus on the amount for direct material on CollegePak's schedule of cost of goods manufactured and sold, lines 7 through 12 in Exhibit 2–8.

- The company's raw-material inventory on hand January 1, $200,000, is added to the $800,000 of raw material purchased during the year. This yields the raw material available for use during the year, $1,000,000.
- Deducting the ending inventory on December 31, $150,000, the cost of direct material put into production during the year was $850,000.

Work in process.   Now let's turn our attention to the work in process on CollegePak's schedule of cost of goods manufactured and sold. The Work-in-Process Inventory account had a beginning balance on January 1 of $350,000, as shown in Exhibit 2–8.

- Exhibit 2–8 also shows the following: Costs incurred during the year for direct material were $850,000 (see the calculations given above for direct material); direct-labor cost was $700,000, and manufacturing overhead was $1,850,000. The sum of direct material, direct labor, and manufacturing overhead costs incurred, $3,400,000, is the total manufacturing cost incurred during the year. Managers in production and operations give careful attention to these costs. CollegePak knows that it must manage these costs effectively on a daily basis to be competitive.
- Next we add the beginning work-in-process inventory cost to the total manufacturing cost to obtain the total cost of work in process during the year. This is a measure

Exhibit 2–8

CollegePak: Schedule of Cost of Goods Manufactured and Sold

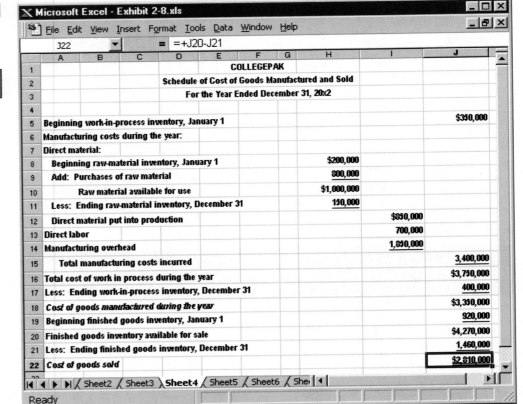

of the costs of resources purchased in a previous year that have gone into production during the year. Some of these costs were in the work in process inventory on hand at the beginning of the year (the beginning inventory), but CollegePak incurred much of the cost during the current year (the total manufacturing costs).

▨ At year-end, the cost of the Work-in-Process Inventory account is subtracted to arrive at the cost of goods manufactured during the year. This amount represents the cost of the good backpacks finished during the year.

Finished goods. After inspection, Quality Assurance transfers the good work finished and inspected during the period to the finished-goods storage area before shipment to customers. (Under a just-in-time inventory and production-management system, goods are shipped to customers directly from the production line, so no finished-goods inventory exists. CollegePak maintains a finished goods inventory, however.) The Finished-Goods Inventory account appears as follows on the financial statements:

▨ Exhibit 2–8 shows that CollegePak had $920,000 of finished goods inventory on hand at the beginning of the year (January 1). From the discussion about work in process, we know that CollegePak completed $3,350,000, which was transferred to finished-goods inventory. Therefore, CollegePak had $4,270,000 of finished-goods inventory available for sale in total.

▨ Of the $4,270,000 available, CollegePak had $1,460,000 of finished goods still on hand at the end of the year. That means that the cost of goods sold was $2,810,000 ($4,270,000 available − $1,460,000 in ending inventory).

Schedule of cost of goods manufactured and sold. As part of its internal reporting system, CollegePak prepares a schedule of cost of goods manufactured and sold. This report is only for managerial use; it rarely appears in external financial statements. Cost-management analysts typically prepare this schedule to summarize and report manufacturing costs for managers' use. Some companies have experimented with preparing these reports for production employees and supervisors, who in some cases have found them effective communication devices. For example, management at CollegePak might use its schedule of cost of goods manufactured and sold to communicate the magnitude of manufacturing overhead or work-in-process inventory to stimulate creative ideas from employees for more effectively managing these amounts. Most important, CollegePak can use existing production costs as a basis for evaluating changes in its value chain, such as processes that it can decide to retain or outsource. These types of decisions are discussed in detail in later chapters of this text.

Flow of Manufacturing Costs

The following diagram summarizes the types of manufacturing costs and their flow through the manufacturing accounts. The detailed process used to record these cost flows will be covered in detail in Chapter 3, along with some important conceptual issues about cost-system design. Moreover, some of the more controversial issues involved in determining the amounts to be entered into Work-in-Process Inventory as product costs will be explored later in this chapter. For now, let's just note that the basic flow of costs in a manufacturing operation is very simple, as the diagram shows. As we will see, however, determining the *amounts* that flow through the accounts can be far less straightforward.

Production Costs in the Service Industry

Firms in the service industry and many nonprofit organizations also engage in production. What distinguishes these organizations from manufacturers is that the producer cannot inventory a service, whereas a manufacturer can store its finished goods. Businesses such as Hyatt Hotels, Allstate Insurance, American Airlines, and the New York Yankees, produce services. Similarly, nonprofit service organizations, such as Habitat for Humanity or New York's Metropolitan Opera, are engaged in service production. Service firms can use the same cost classifications that manufacturing companies do, although this practice is less common. For example, an airline produces air-transportation services. Direct materials for flights include jet fuel and food and beverages. Direct labor for flights is provided by the flight crew. Overhead includes amortization of leased aircraft, depreciation of baggage-handling equipment, and insurance.

Managing the costs of value-chain activities is important in service firms and nonprofit organizations for the same reasons it is in manufacturing firms. These activities can signal opportunities for improvement, can be the basis of competitive advantage, and can create more value for the organization at lower cost. Pricing bank and insurance services, setting enrollment targets in universities, and determining cost reimbursements in hospitals involves cost analysis. As service and nonprofit organizations occupy an ever-increasing role in our economy, applying cost-management methods to their activities assumes ever-greater importance.

Cost-Management Concepts: Different Costs for Different Purposes

An understanding of cost concepts is absolutely critical to cost management. Moreover, different perspectives on costs are important in different managerial situations. In making a decision about flight routes, for example, Air France needs information about the additional costs it would incur if it adds another flight on the Paris-to-New York route. For cost-control purposes, Hertz needs information about both the expected cost of operating its national reservations center and the actual costs incurred in running the center. In deciding whether to expand its operations by adding branches in upper Manhattan, Citibank needs information about the costs and benefits of doing so as well as the costs and benefits of alternative uses for its available resources. The phrase "different costs for different purposes" often is used to convey the notion that different characteristics of costs can be important to understand in a variety of managerial circumstances. This section explores some key cost terms and concepts used in cost management. We use these concepts throughout the book as we explore various issues in contemporary cost-management systems.

Cost Drivers

To implement its strategy of being a low-cost manufacturer of quality backpacks, CollegePak's management needs a firm understanding of the company's activities and how those activities result in costs. One of the most important cost concepts is the way a cost changes in relation to changes in the organization's activity. **Activity** is any discrete task that an organization undertakes to make or deliver a good or service. The number of computers manufactured by Dell, the number of days of patient care provided by the Mayo Clinic, and the number of loans issued by Citibank are all measures of output activity. The activities that cause costs to be incurred are called "cost drivers."

A **cost driver** is a characteristic of an activity or event that causes that activity or event to incur costs. In most organizations, costs respond to widely differing cost drivers. For example, at CollegePak, among the cost drivers for the cost of labor in the Cutting Work Center is the quantity of backpacks manufactured and the number and shapes of the fabric pieces in each backpack. (These are *not* the only cost drivers, but we defer a complete discussion of cost-driver analysis to Chapter 4, where we discuss the cost-management tool *activity-based costing*.) In contrast, the cost of machine setup labor is driven by, among other things, the number of production runs. The cost of material-handling labor is driven by material-related factors such as the quantity and cost of raw material used, the number of parts in various products, and the number of raw-material shipments received. (Again, we defer the discussion of other cost drivers to Chapter 4.) Thus, lumping all manufacturing labor costs together and saying that they are driven by the quantity of products manufactured is an over-simplification. In state-of-the-art cost-management systems, cost-management analysts carefully separate various types of costs into different groupings called *cost pools* and identify the most appropriate cost driver for each cost pool.

The cost driver and cost pool concepts are important aspects of many topics discussed in subsequent chapters and are particularly central to Chapter 4, which introduces activity-based costing. The examples in Exhibit 2–9 illustrate the identification of cost drivers in both the manufacturing and service sectors.

Cost Behavior

Any organization produces and distributes its services or products by engaging in various activities. Costs do not just happen; they are the result of decisions about the number and nature of activities that the firm undertakes and the levels of those activities. To be able to make informed decisions, plan operations, and evaluate performance, management must first know which activities cause costs to be incurred and how changes in activity levels affect the various costs incurred by the firm. "Cost behavior" refers to the way in which costs respond to changes in decisions and activity.

LO 4 Explain how unit-level, variable, and fixed costs differ.

Chapter 11 discusses cost behavior and the methods used to estimate costs in considerable detail. At this juncture, however, we need to explore the two most fundamental types of cost behavior before continuing the discussion of how product and service costs are managed.

Fixed versus variable costs.   Suppose that management is contemplating a change in the volume of an activity. Managers might ask questions such as these:

- *A production manager at Toyota Corporation.* How much will our costs decrease if we cut the volume of production by 1,000 automobiles per month?
- *A manager of Marriott Corporation's campus food service.* How much will our costs increase if we serve 200 more meals per day?
- *The president of your college or university.* How much will costs increase if the number of students enrolled increases by 10 percent?

This type of question recently arose at CollegePak Company. The production manager, in pursuit of the firm's low-cost/high-quality strategy, asked the cost management team how much quality assurance costs would increase if the number of inspections increased by 5 percent.

To answer questions such as these, the managers need to know which costs are *variable costs,* and which are *fixed costs.* **Variable costs** change in total in proportion to a change in the activity volume. **Fixed costs** remain unchanged in total as the volume of activity changes. (*Note:* Both variable costs and fixed costs can change, however, if an organization makes changes in *decisions* about which resources to acquire and how to use them in productive processes. Again, we will have more to say about this issue throughout the text.)

Cost	Examples of Cost Drivers
Cost of food served at Philadelphia Children's Hospital	Number of days of patient care
Fuel costs at Federal Express	Number of tons of cargo transported; distance flown
Cost of handling insurance claims at State Farm Insurance	Number of claims processed
Cost of material handling at Ford Motor Company	Number of material moves, weight of material handled, type of material handled
Cost of taking customer orders at Microsoft	Number of customer orders

Exhibit 2–9

Cost Drivers

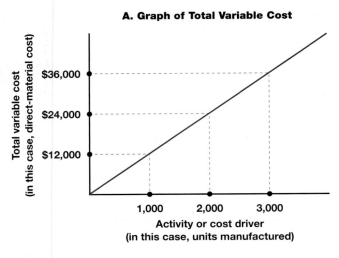

Exhibits 2–10 and 2–11 depict variable cost behavior and fixed cost behavior, respectively. Notice in these exhibits that production volume is on the horizontal axis, and cost (variable or fixed, total and unit, measured in dollars) are on the vertical axis. Exhibit 2–10, which focuses on variable costs, shows CollegePak's total direct-material cost across a range of production activity levels, assuming that direct material costs $12 for each unit manufactured.

Total variable costs increase in direct proportion to changes in volume. Thus, if volume doubles, say from 1,000 to 2,000 units, total variable costs also double, but the unit variable cost remains constant at $12.

Exhibit 2–11 depicts CollegePak's fixed manufacturing overhead cost assumed to be $300,000 per year. Notice that total fixed cost in Panel A remains constant at a particular level and does not increase as volume increases. As Panel B shows, however, the fixed cost *per unit* declines as volume increases.

Variable manufacturing costs typically include costs for direct material, various manufacturing overhead items (for example, electricity used to power production equipment), and some types of direct labor. Portions of certain nonmanufacturing costs, such as distribution costs and sales commissions, typically vary with respect to output volume. However, much manufacturing overhead and many nonmanufacturing costs typically are fixed with respect to output volume.

Direct labor traditionally has been considered a variable cost. Today, however, the production process at many firms is very capital intensive. In a setting in which a fixed amount of labor is needed only to keep machines operating, direct labor is probably best considered a fixed cost. (We will explore this issue more later in the chapter.) For a retailer, such as University Outfitters, variable costs include the cost of the merchandise and some selling and administrative costs. All of a retailer's product costs are variable. For manufacturers, a portion of the product cost is fixed. For service organizations, variable costs typically include compensation for some types of direct labor (such as temporary employees) as well as costs for office supplies, photocopying, and printing.

The identification of a cost as fixed or variable is valid only within a specific range of output volume. For example, suppose that the manager of an Outback Steakhouse restaurant in a shopping complex increased its capacity from 150 to 250 seats, requiring an increase in the costs of rent and supervision. Although these costs are usually considered to be fixed, they change when the decision to increase seating capacity moves output activity beyond a specific range. This range within which the *total* fixed costs and *unit* variable costs do not change is called the *relevant range*. The **relevant range** is the range of activity over which the company expects to operate and over which assumed cost patterns are reasonably accurate.

Variable Costs and Unit-Level Costs

The term "variable cost" is a traditional term in cost-accounting and cost-management practice. Use of this term *assumes* that we are discussing a cost that varies in total in direct proportion to output activity, which typically is measured in terms of the number of units of product manufactured or service produced. As contemporary cost-management systems have developed in both theory and practice, however, cost managers have realized the importance of being very careful about using this term because costs can vary in total in relationship to many different cost drivers, not just

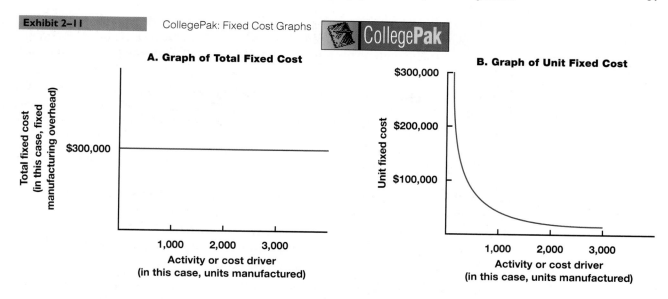

Exhibit 2–11 CollegePak: Fixed Cost Graphs

the number of units produced. For example, consider the cost of setting up a cutting machine at CollegePak's Trenton plant. (Setting up a machine involves making detailed adjustments so that it performs the desired operation.) The machine must be set up for each production run, which typically consists of several hundred backpacks of a particular size and style. Suppose that the production run, or "batch," is for 500 DesignerPaks, one of CollegePak's most popular product lines. The direct-material cost for these backpacks is incurred for every unit because every backpack requires fabric, thread, and various fasteners. Thus, direct-material cost is variable, in the traditional sense, because it varies in total with the number of units produced. The 500 DesignerPaks in this production run require twice as much direct material as 250 DesignerPaks would have required.

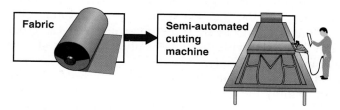

What about the cost of setting up the cutting machine? How many times does this need to be done? Of course, it is just once for this 500-unit batch of DesignerPaks. So, *using traditional terminology,* we classify direct material as a variable cost since it varies in total with the number of backpacks manufactured, but we classify the setup cost of the cutting machine as a fixed cost since it remains constant across all 500 DesignerPaks in the batch.

Now think carefully about this. Taking a slightly different perspective, we could say that *both* the direct-material cost and the setup cost are variable costs, but *they are variable with respect to two different cost drivers.* Direct-material cost is variable with respect to the cost driver, number of units produced, which is the traditional meaning for the term "variable cost." The setup cost for the cutting machine also is variable, however, but it is variable *with respect to the number of batches.* It is true that the setup operation does not have to be done for every *unit* produced, but it does have to be done for every *batch* produced.[4]

---

[4] For a familiar analogy, suppose that you and your friend decide to make some cookies. You want to make chocolate chip cookies, but your friend is partial to peanut butter. Being the convivial pair that you are, you decide to compromise and make a batch of each. What type of cost do the ingredients represent? Their cost will vary in proportion to the number of cookies of each type that you make. Therefore, their cost is variable with respect to the number of units produced. But what about (the cost of) your time required to clean up the mixer after each batch? This operation needs to be performed only once per batch, so it is variable with respect to the number of batches produced, not the number of cookies produced.

Now we have identified a terminological problem. What does it mean to say that a particular cost is variable or fixed? The classification of a cost as variable requires us to ask, Variable with respect to what? or, better yet, *Variable with respect to what cost driver(s)?*

Cost hierarchy. Contemporary cost-management systems have overcome this terminological problem with the concept of a *cost hierarchy.* The hierarchy can have many different levels; a relatively simple hierarchy includes the following five types of costs.

1. **Unit-level costs** are incurred for every unit of product manufactured or service produced.
2. **Batch-level costs** are incurred for every batch of product or service produced.
3. **Product-level costs** are incurred for each line of product or service.
4. **Customer-level costs** are incurred for specific customers.
5. **Facility-level** (or **general-operations-level**) **costs** are incurred to maintain the organization's overall facility and infrastructure.

See Exhibit 2–12 for some examples of these types of costs for CollegePak. We will explore and use the concept of a cost hierarchy in much greater detail in Chapter 4, which discusses activity-based costing. For our purposes here, it is sufficient simply to realize that when the term "variable cost" is used, it is crucial to ask the question, Variable with respect to what cost driver? In general, if variable cost is used without any further explanation, it is most likely used in the traditional sense (i.e., variable with respect to the number of units of product or service produced).

Cost of Resources Used versus Resources Supplied

LO 5 Distinguish between the costs of resources used and those of resources supplied.

Another important issue in thinking about variable and fixed costs involves the utilization of productive capacity. An organization's productive capacity is limited by things such as the overall size of the production facilities, the number and speed of production machines, and the size and skills of its workforce. The most limiting aspects of the production process are sometimes referred to as production "bottlenecks." (Chapters 4 and 7 provide discussions of the use of productive capacity and production bottlenecks, respectively.)

At CollegePak's Trenton plant, the company employs skilled workers who are highly trained in running the production machinery. Making and selling more or fewer backpacks will use more or fewer resources and will cause the *costs of using* these resources to go up or down. For example, making more backpacks will use more skilled labor; we know this because the use of skilled labor easily can be traced to the additional products manufactured. However, making or selling more or fewer products and services might not cause the costs of *supplying* these resources to go up or down. CollegePak pays skilled employees for *at least* 40 hours per week even if the demand for backpacks is not sufficient to keep them busy for that many hours.

Exhibit 2–12	Cost Hierarchy	Examples of Costs at Each Level
CollegePak's Cost Hierarchy	Unit-level costs	Costs for direct material, such as fabric; electricity to run the production equipment
	Batch-level costs	Setup costs for production runs; material-handling costs incurred to deliver batch quantities of raw material to the production area.
	Product-level costs	Design costs for a line of backpacks, such as the DesignerPak, which specifies aspects such as size, color, number of pockets
	Customer-level costs	Costs to obtain licenses of university logos, which CollegePak sews onto some lines of backpacks
	Facility-level costs	Production manager's salary, depreciation on the plant, and insurance on the facility and equipment

Therefore, the costs of *using* skilled employees to make backpacks could vary with the number of products manufactured, but the costs of *supplying* (paying the wages and benefits for) skilled employees would not vary unless CollegePak decides to hire or lay off production workers as the demand requires.

Failing to distinguish between the cost of *supplying* (e.g., spending for) resources and the cost of *using* resources has caused much confusion and controversy among cost managers, accountants, financial analysts, and engineers. We need to be clear about this, and we identify as unit-level costs those costs incurred for resources that are *both supplied and used* to produce units of a product or service. The term "variable cost" will be used in its traditional sense to refer to the cost of a resource whose *use* varies with the number of units of product manufactured or service provided. Note that all unit-level costs are variable costs, but not all variable costs are unit-level costs.

The electricity and welding material used by robotic welders represent *unit-level* costs, since these costs are incurred for every unit produced.

A digression: The pizza business.   To focus our thoughts on this issue, let's briefly digress to consider a familiar scenario. Suppose that you have just taken a job at the nearby college pizza shop making pizzas. (You know, the one just down the street where you go with your friends after an exam to celebrate, or before studying for the exam to fortify yourself, or when you should be studying for the exam because, well, eating pizza is more fun than studying.) You work the 8:00 to 10:00 PM shift three evenings a week, Monday, Wednesday, and Friday. In addition

Moving materials in batch quantity to the production line is a *batch-level* cost, because it is incurred for each production batch.

Designing a product using this computer-aided design software represents a *product-level* cost.

Special packaging for a particular customer constitutes a *customer-level* cost.

The depreciation and insurance on this refinery represent *facility-level* costs.

to the obvious fringe benefit of getting to scarf the occasional slice of pizza with your favorite toppings, you receive a wage of $7 an hour. So each evening that you work, you make $14.

After a brief training session and a little experience, you can make a pizza in 5 minutes. This includes picking up a premeasured lump of pizza dough, patting it out, twirling it ostentatiously over your head a few times, putting it down, covering it with pizza sauce, applying the cheese and other toppings, and tossing it in the oven. (The difference in time required to apply the toppings on a plain cheese pizza or one with "the works" is negligible.) You have one 20-minute break during your 2-hour shift, so on a busy evening, you could make as many as 20 pies (100 minutes available ÷ 5 minutes per pizza).

Now suppose that during the first week of October, you experience very different levels of demand on the three evening shifts. Monday-night football causes a steady demand for pizzas, and you make and sell 20 pies that evening. Wednesday evening is pretty slow, and you make just 10 pies. Friday evening, which normally is very busy, is unusually slow because of a pep rally held that evening before the next day's big game against your school's arch rival, the Fighting Piglets. You make just 1 pie.

Now we must calculate the cost of your labor for a pizza during each of your three shifts. One fairly simple answer is to divide your labor cost per shift by the number of pizzas you made in each shift, as follows:

Shift	Your Labor Cost	Pizzas Made	Cost per Pizza
Monday	$14.00	20	$ .70
Wednesday	14.00	10	1.40
Friday	14.00	1	$14.00

Let's stop and think about this. Does this analysis make any sense? Most accountants and managers would argue that it does not make much sense to say that Monday's pizzas cost $.70 each for your labor, Wednesday's cost $1.40 each, and the one you made Friday evening cost $14.00! This result highlights the problem of confusing the cost of a resource *supplied* with the cost of a resource *used*. The cost of your labor *supplied* during each shift was $14.00, but the cost of your labor *used* varied from shift to shift due to widely different demand levels. Many cost managers would argue that the cost of your labor *used* should be computed as shown in the middle column of the following table.

(a) Shift	(b) Cost of Your Labor Supplied (2 hours × $7.00 per hour)	(c) Cost of Your Labor Used ($.70 × number of pizzas made*)	(d) Cost of Your Labor Used per Pizza	(e) Cost of Unused Capacity ($14.00 − cost of labor used)
Monday	$14.00	$14.00 ($.70 × 20)	$.70 ($14.00 ÷ 20)	$ .00
Wednesday	14.00	7.00 ($.70 × 10)	$.70 ($7.00 ÷ 10)	7.00
Friday	14.00	.70 ($.70 × 1)	$.70 ($.70 ÷ 1)	13.30

*$.70 = $14.00 per shift ÷ 20 pizzas, at capacity production.

The moral of the story is that it is very important to distinguish between the cost of resources used and the cost of resources supplied. This distinction can affect the decisions that managers make about the organization's operations. This issue will reappear later in this chapter as we explore some controversial issues in determining product costs.

Committed Costs, Opportunity Costs, and Sunk Costs

LO 6 Understand the concepts of opportunity cost, sunk cost, committed cost, direct cost, and indirect cost.

For many years, accountants have used the term "fixed costs" for production or nonproduction costs that do not vary with production or sales volumes, such as costs of salaries, rent, depreciation, and property taxes. However, decisions cause costs— costs do not just happen—and an organization makes many more decisions than just those related to production volume. No resource decisions are irreversible. All future costs, therefore, are variable with respect to some decision, so no future cost really can be fixed. It might be costly to change a resource cost in the future (e.g., renegotiate or nullify a resource contract), but it can be changed.

Committed costs.   A **committed cost** is a cost for which management has taken actions that result in some level of commitment to incur the cost. This term reflects the fact that the organization has committed to a certain level and type of resource spending, but it can change that commitment (at some further cost, perhaps). In most organizations, labor cost is a committed cost and cannot be changed easily because of contractual obligations, company policy, or its critical importance. Other committed costs could include lease obligations, licenses, and various taxes. In contrast, "discretionary costs," such as some costs for advertising, remodeling, or charitable giving, could be changed quickly and easily. This is a difference of degree; that is, both committed and discretionary costs can be changed, but changing committed costs is more difficult.

When labor is a committed cost, as for many unionized companies or organizations with strong employment policies, making more or fewer units of product might not affect the cost to supply labor positively or negatively. If this is so, spending for labor resources is not different from spending for other physical capacity resources. In organizations where this is true of other resources as well, the only unit-level cost of products and services that varies proportionately with the number of units produced could be the cost of parts and materials. Under these conditions, the cost to supply all other resources would not vary with the number of units produced.

Opportunity costs.   Think for a moment about the cost of your college education. Certainly, the cash outflows for tuition, books, and fees are important costs. We often call these "outlay costs." Cash is not the only resource that many college students sacrifice, however; they also sacrifice their time to get a college education. This sacrifice of time is an **opportunity cost,** which is the forgone benefit that could have been realized from the best alternative use of a resource. For example, many of you gave up jobs to take the time to earn a college degree. The forgone income is part of the cost of getting a college degree and is the forgone benefit that could have been realized from an alternative use of a scarce resource—time. Of course, no one can ever know all opportunities possible at any moment. Hence, some opportunity costs are undoubtedly not considered. Accounting systems typically record outlay costs but not opportunity costs. Unfortunately, managers sometimes incorrectly ignore or downplay opportunity costs in making decisions. One way you can add value to your organization is to remind your managerial colleagues of the opportunity costs that they might have ignored in making decisions.

Sunk costs.   Most organizations have made payments in the past to acquire resources that they now control. These resources include equipment, buildings, and purchased technology or knowledge. Should you consider the costs of these resources when making production decisions? That is, should the past payments for these resources be part of the costs of future products and services? The correct answer is no; past payments for resources are *sunk costs;* they cannot be undone. **Sunk costs** are past payments for resources that cannot be changed by any current or future decision. Just as with any other resource, only the *opportunity cost* of these already acquired resources should be counted as part of the cost of future products and services. If these resources have no alternative use or value (that is, they cannot even be sold to others), how much you paid for them does not matter; their opportunity costs are zero.

This fact leads to a common behavioral problem. Managers sometimes have a tendency to consider sunk costs when making a decision although they were incurred in the past and cannot be affected by a current or future decision. In some cases, managers are unwilling to admit that payments for unproductive resources have been wasted, so they continue to value the resources at their book value unless they are required to write these assets down to a lower value. Cost-management personnel can assist their management colleagues in this area by ensuring that they do not inappropriately consider sunk costs when they analyze decision alternatives. (This issue will be addressed more extensively in Chapter 13, which covers cost management and decision making.)

**Research
Insight
2.1**

Direct Labor: Variable or Committed Cost?

Are direct-labor costs variable or committed costs? The answer as with many questions, is "it depends." The factors it depends on are the ability and willingness of a company's management to continually fine-tune the size of its workforce. If labor contracts make it difficult to lay off workers during an economic downturn or if top management adopts a policy of maintaining a stable workforce, direct-labor costs will tend to be largely fixed (or step-fixed). However, if management can *and is willing to* reduce the labor force when activity declines, then labor cost will be a variable (or step-variable) cost. The current trend in many companies seems to be toward adjusting the workforce to conform to current needs.

By relying more on part-time workers and daily call-ins, cross-training and frequently moving employees to new jobs, and shortening the workweek, Nestlé, Lincoln Electric, and Hilton Hotels are moving toward direct-labor costs that are much more variable than in the past. Other companies trending toward a "just-in-time workforce" are Wal-Mart, Taco Bell, Starbucks, and U-Haul, among others. This is "all part of the larger development in corporate America of transforming labor from a fixed to a more flexible cost." Consider two cases in point.

"Nestlé's prepared foods unit has built an in-house roster of part-time workers in Cherokee County, South Carolina, who stick by the telephone to hear if they should report on a given day to assemble frozen chicken dinners." The head of human resources for the prepared-foods division says demand for its Lean Cuisine glazed-chicken entrees and Stouffers creamed-spinach side dishes is fairly steady. The company still hires some people full-time. But the Nestlé executive says it is still hard to predict labor needs because schedules for producing certain meals vary, and each product requires a different number of people to make. "We don't need the same number of people every day," he says. "They work as we need them." Lincoln Electric Co. shifts salaried workers to hourly clerical jobs, paying them a different wage for each assignment. The Cleveland-based manufacturer of welding and cutting parts says that, for nearly 60 years, it has guaranteed long-term employment for all of its workers who have worked steadily for three years in its U.S. operations. The flip side is that employees have to be willing to change their job assignments, depending on the type and volume of orders Lincoln receives. *Sources: M. Conlin, "The Big Squeeze on Workers," and "The Software Says You're Just Average"; C. Ansberry, "In the News Workplace, Jobs Morph to Suit Rapid Change of Pace"; and J. Eig, "Do Part-Time Workers Hold Key to When the Recession Breaks?"*

Traceability of Resources

Another useful dimension of resources is the ease with which the cost of a resource can be traced to a decision or set of decisions. Cost managers sometimes ask, "If we make this particular decision, what resources must we obtain or use, and what will they cost?" The acquisition and use of all resources is caused by management decisions, but the ease of tracing the costs of these resources to specific decisions is important for analyzing the cost effects to those decisions of the organization.

Direct costs. Sometimes seeing how specific decisions have caused the acquisition and use of specific resources is easy. A **direct cost** of a cost object is traceable to that cost object. These decisions are directly responsible for those resources, and their costs are called the *direct costs* of those decisions. For example, CollegePak's decision to produce a new line of backpacks would cause the use of the materials necessary to make them. Making more backpacks causes the use of more materials. Likewise, the decision to open a sales office in Boston creates the use of specific physical and human resources necessary to staff it. Seldom, however, is tracing *all* resources to *all* decisions easy.

Indirect costs. An **indirect cost** of a cost object is not feasibly traceable to that cost object. Resources that are difficult to trace to specific management decisions are the *indirect costs* of those decisions. Other common names for indirect costs are "overhead, common costs," and "burden," although these sometimes convey a derogatory image (e.g., unproductive or unnecessary).

CollegePak hired Jorge Gonzales as vice president of marketing and sales; that hiring decision is directly responsible for recruiting and paying for this human resource. Although Gonzales manages all of CollegePak's sales operations, tracing any of his cost to the decision to open the Boston sales office is not easy. Thus, he could be classified as an indirect resource of the Boston office. CollegePak hired Anne Harrison, vice president of manufacturing, to manage its manufacturing processes, but she does not

You're the Decision Maker 2.1

Relevant Costs for a Decision

Suppose that CollegePak received a special order for a product it does not usually produce, a special gift bag to be handed out to the delegates at a political convention. Suppose also that CollegePak currently has excess production capacity, and so management is considering the acceptance of the special order.

Production of the special order would require 8,000 yards of the fabric Stylex. CollegePak no longer uses this particular type of fabric for any of its current products, but it does have 8,000 yards of it on hand from previous years. The Stylex could be sold to a wholesaler for $14,500; its book value is $2.00 per yard. CollegePak could buy new Stylex for $2.40 per yard.

The special order also requires 1,000 yards of a fabric called Duraban, a material regularly used by CollegePak in its stock products. The current stock of Duraban is 8,000 yards, at a book value of $8.10 per yard. If the special order is accepted, CollegePak will be forced to restock Duraban earlier than expected at a predicted cost of $8.70 per yard. Without the special order, the purchasing manager predicts that the price will be $8.30 when the regular restocking takes place. Any order of Duraban must be in the amount of 5,000 yards.

a. What is the relevant cost of the Stylex for the purpose of analyzing this special-order decision?

b. Discuss each Stylex cost figure with regard to its relevance to the decision.

c. What is the relevant cost of the Duraban?

d. Discuss each Duraban cost figure with regard to its relevance to the decision.

(Solutions begin on page 67.)

actually manufacture a single backpack herself. Thus, although she is necessary to support production, CollegePak uses this human resource to indirectly support the manufacture of its products. Thus, Harrison's salary is an indirect cost of manufacturing.

The distinction between direct and indirect costs is not restricted to human resources. For example, CollegePak's administrative team in its Trenton facility manages the company and manufactures its products in the same large building using the same computer network. How much of the building and computer network resources are used for administration? How much is used for manufacturing each backpack? Tracing these resources directly to decisions about either administration or manufacturing, let alone to manufacturing specific products, is not easy. Thus, the costs associated with the building and computer network would be considered an indirect cost for both administration and manufacturing.

To summarize, any cost that can be directly related to a *cost object* is a direct cost of that cost object. A **cost object** is any entity to which a cost is assigned, for example, a decision, a unit of inventory, a department, or a product line. Those costs that cannot be directly related to a cost object are indirect costs. Cost-management analysts use the terms "direct cost" and "indirect cost" much as a nonaccountant might expect, but the fact that a cost might be direct to one cost object and indirect to another could be a source of confusion. For example, the salary of a supervisor in a manufacturing department is a direct cost of that department but an indirect cost of the individual products the department produces. Therefore, when someone refers to a cost as being either direct or indirect, you should immediately ask, "Direct or indirect with respect to what cost object? Units produced? A department? A division?" (When we use *direct* and *indirect* to describe labor and materials, the cost object is the unit being produced.) See Exhibit 2–13 for several examples of direct and indirect costs.

Cost	Classification as Direct or Indirect
Salary of a Harley-Davidson plant manager	Direct cost of the plant; indirect cost of each department in the plant
Advertising for a particular Ramada Inn in Cleveland, Ohio	Direct cost of that hotel; indirect cost of that hotel's Food and Beverage Department
Salary of the U.S. Secretary of the Interior	Direct cost of the Interior Department; indirect cost of Yosemite National Park

Exhibit 2–13

Direct and Indirect Costs

SECTION II. INCOME-REPORTING EFFECTS OF ALTERNATIVE PRODUCT-COSTING SYSTEMS

LO 7 Prepare income statements using absorption, variable, and throughput costing.

Operating income is a key measure used to evaluate the performance of both entire companies and segments of them. Managers watch the bottom line as they make the decisions that determine the future of their companies. The product-costing method used, however, can significantly affect a manufacturing company's reported income. This section explores three alternative product-costing methods. It begins by comparing the two traditional methods, absorption costing and variable costing. Then it examines a method that is more recent in origin, throughput costing.

What Costs Should Be Considered Product Costs?

As discussed earlier, the typical product-costing system applies manufacturing overhead, direct material, and direct labor to Work-in-Process Inventory as a product cost. When the manufactured goods are finished, these product costs flow from Work-in-Process Inventory into Finished-Goods Inventory. Finally, during the accounting period when the goods are sold, the product costs flow from Finished-Goods Inventory into Cost of Goods Sold, an expense account. The following diagram summarizes this flow of costs:

Since the costs of production are stored in inventory accounts until the related goods are sold, these costs are said to be "inventoriable costs." This section addresses whether *all* costs added to the manufacturing inventory accounts in the preceding diagram should be treated properly as product costs or whether *some* of them more properly should be considered period costs.[5]

Fixed Manufacturing Overhead: The Key

One type of product-costing system includes direct material, direct labor, and *both* variable and fixed manufacturing overhead in the product costs that flow through the manufacturing accounts. This approach to product costing is *absorption* or *full costing*. **Absorption** (or **full**) **costing** applies all manufacturing-overhead costs to manufactured goods along with direct-material and direct-labor costs. An alternative approach to product costing is *variable* or *direct costing*. **Variable** (or **direct**) **costing**) applies only variable manufacturing overhead to manufactured goods as a product cost along with direct material and direct labor costs.[6]

See Exhibit 2–14 for a summary of the distinction between absorption and variable costing. Notice that the distinction involves the *timing* at which fixed manufacturing overhead becomes an expense. Eventually, fixed overhead is expensed under both product-costing systems. Variable costing considers fixed overhead a period expense and expenses it *immediately*, as it is incurred. Absorption costing, however, *inventories* fixed overhead with the other product costs (i.e., for direct material, direct labor, and variable overhead) until the accounting period during which the manufactured goods are sold.

---

[5] If you wish to review the discussion of product costs and period costs earlier in the chapter, see pages 38 and 39.

[6] Here we use the term "variable cost" in its traditional meaning (i.e., those costs that vary in total in proportion to the volume of output activity). The term "fixed cost" also is used in its traditional sense (i.e., those costs that do not vary in total with respect to the volume of output, within the relevant range).

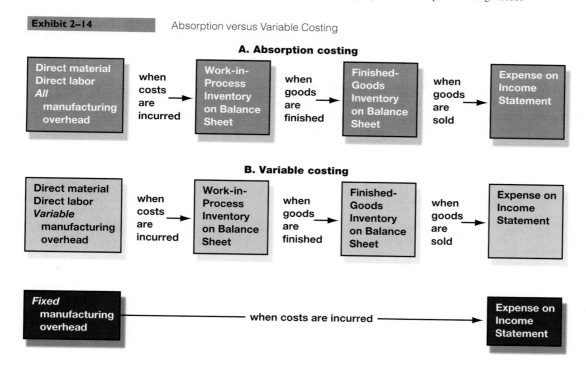

Exhibit 2–14   Absorption versus Variable Costing

Illustration of Absorption and Variable Costing

To illustrate the income effects of absorption and variable costing, we return to the discussion of CollegePak. After several years of success with its Trenton, New Jersey operations, the company built a new plant in central Pennsylvania. (Recall the email memorandum at the beginning of the chapter.) The new plant was built to manufacture a new line of backpacks to be sold under the brand name ScholarPak, and marketed primarily in Europe. CollegePak's president wanted to watch the new product line's performance closely so she asked that separate income statements be generated for the Pennsylvania plant's operations.

See Exhibit 2–15 for cost, production, and sales data for the first three years of the Pennsylvania plant's operations and Exhibit 2–16 for comparative income statements for the first three years using both absorption and variable costing.

Absorption-Costing Income Statements

Examine the absorption-costing income statement in the upper half of Exhibit 2–16. Two features of these income statements are highlighted in the left-hand margin. First, notice that the cost of goods sold expense for each year is determined by multiplying the year's sales by the absorption-manufacturing cost per unit, $36. Included in the $36 cost per unit is the fixed manufacturing-overhead cost of $12 per unit. Second, notice that on the absorption-costing income statement, the only period expenses are the selling and administrative expenses. There is no deduction of fixed-overhead costs as a lump-sum period expense at the bottom of each income statement. As mentioned, fixed manufacturing-overhead costs are included in cost of goods sold on these absorption-costing income statements.

Variable-Costing Income Statements

Now examine the income statement based on variable costing in the lower half of Exhibit 2–16. Notice that its format and that of the absorption-costing statement are different. The format of the variable-costing statements highlights the separation of variable and fixed costs. The variable-costing statement also highlights an amount

Exhibit 2–15

Basic Data for Illustration:
Pennsylvania Plant of
CollegePak Company

	Year 1	Year 2	Year 3
Production and inventory data			
Planned production (in units)	25,000	25,000	25,000
Finished-goods inventory (in units), January 1	0	0	7,500
Actual production (in units)	25,000	25,000	25,000
Sales (in units)	25,000	17,500	32,500
Finished-goods inventory (in units), December 31	0	7,500	0
Revenue and cost data, all three years			
Sales price per unit			$48
Manufacturing costs per unit			
Direct material			$12
Direct labor			8
Variable manufacturing overhead			4
Total variable cost per unit			$24

Used only under absorption costing:

Fixed manufacturing overhead:

$$\frac{\text{Annual fixed overhead}}{\text{Annual production}} = \frac{\$300,000}{25,000} = 12$$

Total absorption cost per unit			$36
Variable selling and administrative cost per unit			$ 4
Fixed selling and administrative cost per year			$50,000

Exhibit 2–16

Income Statements under
Absorption and Variable
Costing

COLLEGEPAK COMPANY
Absorption-Costing Income Statement
Pennsylvania Plant

		Year 1	Year 2	Year 3
1	Sales revenue (at $48 per unit)	$1,200,000	$840,000	$1,560,000
	Less: Cost of goods sold (at absorption cost of $36 per unit)	900,000	630,000	1,170,000
	Gross margin	$ 300,000	$210,000	$ 390,000
	Less: Selling and administrative expenses:			
2 No	Variable (at $4 per unit)	100,000	70,000	130,000
fixed	Fixed	50,000	50,000	50,000
overhead	Operating income	$ 150,000	$ 90,000	$ 210,000

COLLEGEPAK COMPANY
Variable-Costing Income Statement
Pennsylvania Plant

		Year 1	Year 2	Year 3
	Sales revenue (at $48 per unit)	$1,200,000	$840,000	$1,560,000
	Less: Variable expenses:			
1	Variable manufacturing costs (at variable cost of $24 per unit)	600,000	420,000	780,000
	Variable selling and administrative costs (at $4 per unit)	100,000	70,000	130,000
	Contribution margin	$ 500,000	$350,000	$ 650,000
	Less: Fixed expenses:			
2	Fixed manufacturing overhead	300,000	300,000	300,000
	Fixed selling and administrative expenses	50,000	50,000	50,000
	Operating income	$ 150,000	$ 0	$ 300,000

called the **contribution margin,** which is is the amount of sales revenue remaining, after covering all variable costs, to contribute toward covering fixed cost and profit. The contribution margin, as its name implies, is the amount of sales revenue left *after* covering all variable costs to *contribute* to covering fixed cost and profit. (This contribution-margin concept is discussed extensively in Chapters 12 and 13.)

Let's focus on the same two aspects of the variable-costing statements that we discussed for the absorption-costing statements. First, the manufacturing expenses subtracted from sales revenue each year include only the variable costs, which amount to $24 per unit. Second, fixed manufacturing overhead is subtracted as a lump-sum period expense at the bottom of each year's income statement.

Reconciliation of Income under Absorption and Variable Costing

Examination of Exhibit 2–16 reveals that the operating income reported under absorption and variable costing is sometimes different. Although it is the same for the two product-costing methods in year 1, it is different in years 2 and 3. Let's figure out why these results occur.

LO 8 Reconcile income under absorption and variable costing.

No change in inventory.   Year 1 had no change in inventory over the course of the year. Beginning and ending inventories are the same because actual production and sales are the same. Think about the implications of the stable inventory level for the treatment of fixed manufacturing overhead. On the variable-costing statement, the $300,000 of fixed manufacturing overhead incurred during year 1 is an expense in year 1. Absorption costing, however, applies fixed manufacturing overhead to production at the rate of $12 per unit. Since all units produced in year 1 also were sold in year 1, all fixed manufacturing-overhead cost flowed through the inventory accounts into Cost of Goods Sold. Thus, the entire $300,000 of fixed manufacturing overhead is an expense of year 1 under both variable and absorption costing.

The year 1 column of Exhibit 2–17 reconciles that year's income reported under absorption and variable costing. The reconciliation focuses on the two places in the income statements where differences occur for absorption and variable costing. The blue numbers in the left-hand margin of Exhibit 2–17 correspond to the blue numbers in the left-hand margin of the income statement in Exhibit 2–16.

Increase in inventory.   In year 2, inventory increased from zero on January 1 to 7,500 units on December 31. The increase in inventory was the result of production exceeding sales. Under variable costing, the $300,000 of fixed overhead cost incurred is an expense of year 2, just as it was in year 1. Under absorption costing, however, only a portion of the year 2 fixed manufacturing overhead is expensed in year 2. Since the fixed overhead is inventoried under absorption costing, some of this cost *remains in inventory* at the end of year 2.

		Year 1	Year 2	Year 3
1	Cost of goods sold under absorption costing	$900,000	$630,000	$1,170,000
	Variable manufacturing costs under variable costing	600,000	420,000	780,000
	Subtotal	$300,000	$210,000	$ 390,000
2	Fixed manufacturing overhead as a period expense under variable costing	300,000	300,000	300,000
	Total	$ 0	$ (90,000)	$ 90,000
	Operating income under variable costing	$150,000	$ 0	$ 300,000
	Operating income under absorption costing	150,000	90,000	210,000
	Difference in operating income	$ 0	$ (90,000)	$ 90,000

Exhibit 2–17

Reconciliation of Income under Absorption and Variable Costing: Pennsylvania Plant, CollegePak Company

The year 2 column of Exhibit 2–17 reconciles that year's income reported under absorption and variable costing. As before, the reconciliation focuses on the two places in the income statements where differences for absorption and variable costing occur.

Decrease in inventory.   In year 3, inventory decreased from 7,500 units to zero. Sales during the year exceeded production. As in years 1 and 2, under variable costing, the $300,000 of fixed manufacturing overhead incurred in year 3 is an expense of year 3. Under absorption costing, however, *more than* $300,000 of fixed overhead is an expense in year 3 because some of the fixed overhead incurred during the prior year, which was inventoried then, is now an expense of year 3 when the goods are sold.

The year 3 column of Exhibit 2–17 reconciles that year's income using absorption and variable costing. Once again, the blue numbers on the left-hand side of Exhibit 2–17 correspond to those on the left-hand side of the income statement in Exhibit 2–16.

Shortcut to reconciling income.   When inventory increases or decreases during the year, reported income differs under absorption and variable costing. This results from the fixed overhead that is inventoried under absorption costing but expensed immediately under variable costing. The following formula can be used to compute the difference in the amount of fixed overhead expensed in a given time period under the two product-costing methods. (An important assumption underlying this formula is that fixed overhead remains the same for the two accounting periods.)

$$\begin{matrix} \text{Difference in fixed} \\ \text{overhead expensed} \\ \text{under absorption} \\ \text{and variable costing} \end{matrix} = \begin{matrix} \text{Change in} \\ \text{inventory} \\ \text{in units} \end{matrix} \times \begin{matrix} \text{Fixed-overhead} \\ \text{rate per unit} \end{matrix}$$

As the following table shows, this difference in the amount of fixed overhead expensed explains the difference in reported income under absorption and variable costing.

Year	Change in Inventory (in units)		Fixed-Overhead Rate		Difference in Fixed Overhead Expensed		Absorption-Costing Income Minus Variable-Costing Income
Year 1	0	×	$12	=	0	=	0
Year 2	7,500 increase	×	12	=	$ 90,000	=	$ 90,000
Year 3	7,500 decrease	×	12	=	(90,000)	=	(90,000)

Length of time period.   The discrepancies between absorption-costing and variable-costing income in Exhibit 2–16 occur because of the changes in inventory levels during years 2 and 3. Production and sales commonly differ over the course of a week, month, or year. Therefore, the income measured for those time periods often differs for absorption and variable costing. This discrepancy is likely to be smaller over longer time periods. Over the course of a decade, for example, CollegePak cannot sell much more or less than it produces. Thus, the income amounts under the two product-costing methods, when added together over a lengthy time period, will be approximately equal under absorption and variable costing.

Notice that in Exhibit 2–17 the *total* income over the three-year period is $450,000 under *both* absorption and variable costing. This results from the fact that CollegePak's Pennsylvania plant produced and sold the same total number of units over the three-year period.

Evaluation of Absorption and Variable Costing

LO 9 Discuss the advantages and disadvantages of absorption, variable, and throughput costing.

Some managers find absorption costing to be nonintuitive and confusing and prefer to use variable costing for internal income reporting. Variable costing dovetails much more closely than absorption costing with any operational analyses that require a separation between fixed and variable costs. Later chapters detail these types of analyses; they include such value-chain decisions as adding a production process and outsourcing a service.

Product-cost information. Product costs computed under absorption costing could be more accurate measures of the use of production resources than those computed under variable costing because absorption costs recognize and contain fixed, indirect production costs. However, just as the overall average cost could misstate product costs by allocating indirect production costs, absorption costs could misstate the use of indirect production resources. It is possible that CollegePak's various product lines use indirect production resources to a different degree. Absorption costing also ignores each product line's differential use of nonproduction resources. Thus, absorption costing actually could distort the costs to provide products and services if they represent greatly different levels of support from indirect resources. For example, one product line might need much more design support than another, but allocations unrelated to resource usage obscure this difference.[7]

Pricing decisions. Many managers prefer to use absorption-costing data in cost-based pricing decisions. They argue that fixed manufacturing overhead is a necessary cost incurred in the production process. To exclude this fixed cost from the inventoried cost of a product, as variable costing does, is to understate the product's cost. For this reason, many companies that use cost-based pricing base their prices on absorption-costing data.

Proponents of variable costing argue that a product's variable cost provides a better basis for making the pricing decision. They note that any price above a product's variable cost makes a positive contribution to covering fixed cost and profit.

Unit costs under absorption costing can be misleading for decision making. When fixed costs are allocated to each unit, as they are under absorption costing, the *fixed* costs could appear as though they are *variable*. For example, allocating some of the factory insurance cost to each unit of product results in including insurance as part of the "unit cost" even though the total insurance cost does not increase with the manufacturer of another unit of product. Therefore, cost data that include unitized fixed costs could be misleading if used incorrectly. Later chapters cover this issue in detail.

Absorption versus Variable Costing in the Financial Services Industry

Cost Management in Practice 2.1

American National Bank in Chicago offers a check-processing service for small banks in the area. Small banks accumulate their day's checks and send them to American National, which presents them to the banks on which they are drawn. The major variable costs of this service are those for processing the checks and outside vendor charges, such as the use of the Federal Reserve clearinghouse for checks drawn on certain banks. In addition, fixed indirect costs are added to the variable costs of each product line. The sum of variable and fixed costs are full costs that cover all costs of running the bank, including general and administrative costs.

Several other financial institutions also offer this service. Although American National relies on its excellent reputation for quality service to justify charging a higher price than its competitors, it nevertheless has dropped its prices in recent years to avoid losing customers. At one point, its prices were less than 80 percent of the unit costs charged to the product line. Although it appeared that the bank could not justify continuing to offer the service based on a comparison of prices and full costs, several executives were not convinced that the full absorption-cost numbers developed for monthly financial reporting purposes were appropriate for the decision about whether to drop this service. Consequently, these executives decided to analyze which costs and revenues would change from dropping the service.

Their analysis indicated that few, if any, of the indirect costs allocated to the product line would be saved by dropping this service. Furthermore, some of the processing costs included depreciation and other costs that would not be cash savings if the service were discontinued. Their analysis indicated that the bank could lose several million dollars in contribution to fixed cost and profit by dropping the service. Based on this analysis, the bank decided against dropping the service. *Source: Based on an author's research.*

---

[7] Chapter 4, which covers activity-based costing, addresses this concern about traditional absorption-costing systems.

Definition of an asset.   Another controversy about absorption and variable costing hinges on the definition of an asset. An *asset* is a thing of value owned by an organization with future service potential. Under generally accepted accounting principles, assets are valued at their cost. Because fixed costs represent part of the cost of production, advocates of absorption costing argue that inventory (an asset) should be valued at its full (absorption) cost of production. Moreover, they argue that these costs have future service potential since the inventory can be sold in the future to generate sales revenue.

Proponents of variable costing argue that the fixed-cost component of a product's absorption-costing value has no future service potential. Their reasoning is that the fixed manufacturing-overhead costs incurred during the current period will not prevent these costs from being incurred again in the next period. Fixed-overhead costs will be incurred every period regardless of production levels. In contrast, the incurrence of variable costs in manufacturing a product allows the firm to avoid incurring these costs again.

To illustrate, let's return to the information detailed in Exhibits 2–15 and 2–16. The Pennsylvania plant produced 7,500 more units in year 2 than it sold. It carried these units in inventory until they were sold. CollegePak will never again have to incur the costs of the direct material, direct labor, and variable overhead incurred in year 2 to produce those particular products, yet it must incur approximately $300,000 of fixed-overhead costs every year although the firm has the 7,500 units from year 2 in inventory.

Use of both costing methods.   In the age of computerized accounting systems, it is straightforward for a company to prepare income statements under both absorption and variable costing. Since absorption-costing statements generally are used for external reporting, managers need to review the effects of their decisions on financial reports to outsiders, yet it is difficult to deny the benefit of variable-costing income reporting as a method for dovetailing with operational analyses. Preparation of both absorption-costing and variable-costing data for internal management use is perhaps the best solution to the controversy.

JIT manufacturing environment.   Most manufacturing firms now strive to minimize inventories because they do not create value but use valuable resources. As shown in the year 1 example for the Pennslvania plant, when inventories are zero or very small, differences between absorption- and variable-costing operating income also are small.

In a just-in-time inventory and production-management system, companies keep all inventories very low. Since finished-goods inventories are minimal, inventory changes little from period to period. Thus, in a JIT environment, the *income differences* under absorption and variable costing generally are insignificant. Note, however, that absorption- and variable-costing income statements provide different information about the costs incurred in the production process even if net income is not significantly different. In other words, the "bottom line" is not the only important number on an income statement. (Chapter 7 covers the cost-management implications of JIT systems in detail.)

Throughput Costing

In recent years, some managers have been advocating *throughput costing* as an alternative to either absorption or variable costing. **Throughput costing** assigns *only* the unit-level *spending* for direct costs as the cost of products or services. Advocates of throughput costing argue that adding any other indirect, past, or committed costs to product cost creates improper incentives to drive down the average cost per unit by making more products than can be used or sold. Since these other costs are committed, making more units with the same level of resource spending arithmetically reduces the average cost per unit and makes the production process appear to be more efficient. Throughput costing avoids that incentive because the cost per unit depends only on unit-level *spending* (e.g., costs of materials), not how many units are made.[8]

---

[8] This statement ignores possible effects of gaining or losing purchase discounts on purchases by changing production levels. These effects usually are small, but they would be considered a benefit or cost of changing purchasing levels.

Using throughput costing means that cost-management analysts must distinguish between (1) spending for resources caused by the decision to produce different levels of products and services and (2) the use of resources that the organization has committed to supply regardless of the level of products and services provided. (Chapter 4 covers this important distinction in the context of activity-based costing.)

Suppose that CollegePak's cost-management team decided that only direct materials qualified as a throughput cost. This implies that CollegePak's management has *committed,* at least for the time being, to provide *all* other resources (i.e., direct labor and all manufacturing-support costs included in manufacturing overhead) regardless of how many backpacks CollegePak produces. Throughput costing considers all other indirect, discretionary, committed, or past spending for resources to be operating costs of the period (i.e., *period costs*).[9] Under throughput costing, then, CollegePak's income statements for the three years in our illustration would appear as in Exhibit 2–18. Notice that all costs other than the throughput cost (only direct materials in this illustration) are considered to be operating costs of the period.

Overproduction of Inventory: An Ethical Issue

A comparison of the reported income under throughput costing (Exhibit 2–18) with the reported income under either variable or absorption costing (Exhibit 2–16) reveals substantial differences in the "bottom line" under the three methods for each year. Proponents of throughput costing argue that this method alone eliminates the incentive to produce excess inventory simply to reduce unit costs by spreading *committed* resource costs (i.e., direct labor and variable- and fixed-manufacturing overhead) across more units. The incentive for such overproduction disappears under throughput costing because all nonthroughput costs (direct labor and manufacturing overhead in our illustration) are expenses of the period regardless of how many units are produced.

LO 10 Discuss the ethical isues concerning the intentional overproduction of inventory.

---

[9] Note that in some cases, an organization might pay for its labor force or other resources such as energy consumption on an hourly or piece-rate basis, depending on how many units of product it makes. Because these resources are supplied and used on an hourly or piece-rate basis, these would be unit-level costs and, therefore, product costs under throughput costing.

COLLEGEPAK COMPANY Throughput-Costing Income Statement Pennsylvania Plant			
	Year 1	Year 2	Year 3
Sales revenue (at $48 per unit)	$1,200,000	$840,000	$1,560,000
Less: Cost of goods sold (at throughput cost: direct-material cost)*	300,000	210,000	390,000
Throughput	$ 900,000	$630,000	$1,170,000
Less: Operating costs:			
Direct labor[†]	$ 200,000	$200,000	$ 200,000
Variable manufacturing overhead[‡]	100,000	100,000	100,000
Fixed manufacturing overhead[‡]	300,000	300,000	300,000
Variable selling and administrative costs[§]	100,000	70,000	130,000
Fixed selling and administrative costs[§]	50,000	50,000	50,000
Total operating costs	$ 750,000	$720,000	$ 780,000
Operating income	$ 150,000	$ (90,000)	$ 390,000

Exhibit 2–18

Income Statements under Throughput Costing

* Standard direct-material cost per unit of $12 multiplied by sales volume in units.

[†] Assumes that management has committed to direct labor sufficient to produce the planned annual production volume of 25,000 units; direct-labor cost is *used* at a rate of $8 per unit produced. (See Exhibit 2–15.)

[‡] Assumes management has committed to support resources sufficient to produce the planned annual production volume of 25,000 units; variable-overhead cost is *used* at a rate of $4 per unit produced. Fixed overhead is $300,000 per year. (See Exhibit 2–15.)

[§] Variable selling and administrative costs *used* amount to $4 per unit sold. Fixed selling and administrative costs are $50,000 per year. (See Exhibit 2–15.)

It is worthwhile to note that variable costing also eliminates the incentive to overproduce inventory *if all* throughput costs also happen to be variable costs. If, for example, direct labor can be adjusted to meet short-term needs, it will be a throughput cost rather than a committed cost. Thus, if direct labor and variable overhead can be adjusted rather than committed for the long term, variable and throughput costing will yield the same income results.

Finally, a word about the ethics involved in this situation. Most managers and accountants believe it would be unethical for a manager to intentionally overproduce inventory just to reduce unit costs and temporarily boost reported income.[10]

---

[10] See case 2.76 for an exploration of this ethical issue.

Chapter Summary

Cost management helps an organization's management create more value at lower cost by efficiently managing the organization's value chain of activities, processes, and functions. *Cost-management information* is used in a variety of roles to help organizations be successful in achieving their goals. An important first step in studying cost management is to gain an understanding of the various types of costs that organizations incur and the way that the organizations actively manage those costs. At the most basic level, a *cost* is defined as the sacrifice made, usually measured by the resources given up, to achieve a particular purpose.

Financial statements provide an important means of communication about an organization's operations to people both inside and outside the organization. Internal uses of such information include decision making, planning, and cost management. External uses of financial statements are made by creditors, investors, governmental agencies, and other interested parties. A manufacturing company has a more complex income statement than do service or retail companies. Whereas the retailer purchases goods for sale, the manufacturer makes them. The three major categories of manufacturing costs are direct material, direct labor, and manufacturing overhead, which includes all other costs of transforming materials into a finished product. Cost managers track the flow of production costs using three accounts: *Work-in-Process Inventory, Finished-Goods Inventory,* and *Cost of Goods Sold;* the latter is an expense on the income statement.

An understanding of *cost concepts* is absolutely critical to cost management. Moreover, the ability to view different managerial situations from the appropriate perspective is important. Among the more important cost concepts is *cost behavior,* which refers to the way in which costs respond to changes in decisions and activity. *Variable costs* are the costs of resources used that change in total in direct proportion with a change in volume of activity. Contemporary cost-management systems have expanded the notion of a variable cost with the concept of a cost hierarchy, which more explicitly describes the way in which a cost varies. *Fixed costs* remain unchanged in total as the volume of activity changes. Other important cost concepts include *product and period costs, direct and indirect costs,* and the distinction between the cost of *resources supplied* and *resources used.*

Absorption and variable costing are two alternative product-costing systems, which differ in their treatment of fixed manufacturing overhead. *Absorption (or full) costing* applies fixed overhead to produced goods as a product cost. Therefore, the fixed-overhead cost remains in inventory until the goods are sold. *Variable (or direct) costing* applies fixed overhead as a period cost that is expensed during the period when it is incurred. *Absorption costing* is required for external reporting and tax purposes. However, variable costing is more consistent with operational decision analyses, which require a separation of fixed and variable costs.

Some accountants and managers advocate *throughput costing,* in which only throughput costs are inventoried as product costs. They argue that throughput costing reduces the incentive for management to produce excess inventory simply for the purpose of spreading committed (nonthroughput) costs across a larger number of units produced.

Key Terms

For each term's definition, refer to the indicated page or turn to the glossary at the end of the text.

absorption (full) costing, 58	committed cost, 55	cost-accounting system, 44	customer-level costs, 52
activity, 48	contribution margin, 61	cost driver, 48	direct costs, 56
administrative costs, 43	conversion costs, 43	cost object, 57	direct labor, 42
batch-level costs, 52	cost, 38	cost of goods sold, 38	direct materials, 42

Meeting the Cost Management Challenges

1.   What are the significant inputs to a production process, and how do cost managers track the flow of costs through the process?

The significant inputs to a production process are direct material, direct labor, and manufacturing overhead. Manufacturing overhead consists of indirect material, indirect labor, and other manufacturing costs, such as utilities and depreciation on the plant and equipment. Cost managers track the flow of costs for these inputs using three accounts: Work-in-Process Inventory, Finished-Goods Inventory, and Cost of Goods Sold. Production costs are entered into Work-in-Process Inventory as they are incurred. When the products are finished, their production costs are transferred from Work-in-Process Inventory to Finished-Goods Inventory. Finally, when the goods are sold, their production costs are transferred from Finished-Goods Inventory to Cost of Goods Sold, which is an expense on the income statement.

2.   How can alternative methods to calculate product costs create different incentives?

If managers of manufacturing companies are rewarded on the basis of profits (this is very common), the way that product costs are calculated can affect incentives to produce more parts, assemblies, and products than can be sold. Specifically, variable costing and absorption costing add costs of *resources used* to products without considering whether *spending* to supply resources is affected. Levels of spending for some resources might be unaffected by how those resources are used (e.g., salaries or rent). Making more units with the same capacity reduces the average cost of products produced. Since the costs of products are held in inventory until the products are sold, these costs also can be "hidden" in inventory.

Under throughput costing, only spending for resources is counted as costs of products, and all other costs are expensed. Average product costs cannot be reduced and profits increased merely by making more products than can be sold. Therefore, proponents argue, throughput costing alone aligns the financial incentives of managers with the objective of using resources wisely.

3.   How should cost-management analysts measure costs for internal decision making?

Although the previous discussion indicates that the answer should be straightforward (i.e., use throughput costing), this actually is a difficult question to answer outside the context of a specific organization. Most organizations are required to use absorption costing for financial and tax reporting. Therefore, the decision to use a different costing method internally depends on whether the benefits (i.e., making better operating decisions) outweigh the costs of an additional costing system. Although it might seem intuitively obvious that managers should make better decisions using throughput costing, remarkably little reliable research indicates that better decisions really result. The lack of research might be attributed to the newness of throughput costing and the reluctance of organizations that have successfully employed it to give away a source of competitive advantage. It also might be that using absorption costing is beneficial in complex organizations because it ensures that indirect costs are not forgotten in production and pricing decisions. It also could be that the costs of using additional internal information are higher than the benefits. Although improvements in costing practices are always possible and should be explored, asserting that all firms using absorption costing for internal purposes are making a mistake is not necessarily accurate.

Solutions to You're the Decision Maker

2.1   Relevant Costs for a Decision   p. 57

a.   The relevant cost of the stylex to be used in producing the special order is the $14,500 sales value that the company will forgo if it uses the material. This is an example of an opportunity cost.

b.   **1.** $14,500 sales value; discussed in (a).

   2. $16,000 book value (8,000 yards × $2 per yard); irrelevant since the book value is a sunk cost.

   3. $19,200 current purchase cost (8,000 yards × $2.40 per yard); irrelevant since the company will not be buying any stylex.

c.   The relevant cost of duraban is calculated as follows:

Cost of replacing the 1,000 yards to be used in the special order (1,000 yards × $8.70)	$ 8,700
Additional cost incurred on the next order of duraban as a result of having to place the order early* [4,000 yards × ($8.70 − $8.30)]	1,600
Total relevant cost	$10,300

*This cost would not be incurred if the special order were not accepted.

d.   **1.** $64,800 book value (8,000 yards × $8.10 per yard); irrelevant, since it is a sunk cost.

2. Cost of the 1,000 yards to be used in the special order; relevant, as shown in (c).

3. $8.70 price if the next order is placed early; relevant since this is the cost of replacing the used Duraban.

4. $8.30 price if the next order is placed on time; relevant because an additional 4,000 yards in the next order will be purchased at a $.40 per yard premium ($8.70 price − $8.30 price).

Review Questions

2.1 What is the difference between the meanings of the terms *cost* and *expense*?

2.2 What is the difference between product costs and period costs?

2.3 Is cost of goods sold an expense? Explain.

2.4 What are the three categories of product cost in a manufacturing operation? Describe each element briefly.

2.5 What does the term *variable cost* mean?

2.6 What does the term *fixed cost* mean?

2.7 Distinguish among material resources, conversion resources, and operating resources.

2.8 Distinguish between production and nonproduction resources. Give examples of each.

2.9 Explain the concept of traceability and the way it is used to classify resources as direct or indirect.

2.10 Is a resource always either direct or indirect? Explain.

2.11 What is a unit-level cost? How does it differ from an average cost? How does it differ from a variable cost?

2.12 Define and give an example of each of the following costs:

   a. Opportunity cost   *d.* Period cost

   b. Outlay cost   *e.* Direct cost

   c. Product cost   *f.* Indirect cost

2.13 Is a committed cost the same as a fixed cost? Explain.

2.14 How does throughput costing differ from variable or absorption costing?

2.15 What are the differences among throughput, contribution margin, and gross margin on an income statement?

2.16 Explain how absorption costing can create an incentive to make more products than can be sold.

2.17 Timing is the key in distinguishing between absorption, variable, and throughput costing. Explain this statement.

2.18 When inventory increases, is absorption-costing or variable-costing income higher? Why?

2.19 Do throughput, variable, and absorption costing result in significantly different income measures in a JIT setting? Why?

Critical Analysis

2.20 Evaluate this statement: Issues of product costing are irrelevant for service organizations since they cannot build up inventories of services, and all costs for providing services are expensed in the period they are used. Service firms effectively use throughput costing.

2.21 Evaluate this statement: Issues of product costing are unimportant for virtual organizations that outsource their production operations.

2.22 Prepare a diagram that illustrates how the following resources—headquarters, facilities, division managers, information systems personnel—can be considered both direct and indirect in a company that has four operating divisions, each of which provides multiple services.

2.23 Respond to this comment from an economist friend: You cost-management analysts use an overabundance of cost terms to cover up the fact that you really do not understand opportunity costs. You create jobs for yourselves based on unintelligible jargon. Not that that's a bad thing.

2.24 Respond to this observation: So, there really is no fundamental difference between tracing costs and allocating costs. The only difference is the degree of accuracy with which you want to trace costs.

2.25 A colleague challenges you: What do you mean that there is no such thing as a *fixed cost?* Pick up any microeconomics or cost-accounting book, and you will see the term used all the time. We have lots of fixed costs in our organization, don't we? What about your salary and the depreciation of your computer? Why do you want to replace *fixed cost* with *committed cost?*

2.26 Individually or as a group, prepare written arguments for and against the following proposition. (Be prepared to present your arguments.) The company needs to use absorption costing for financial and tax reporting. We make so many products in so many places that it would be too expensive to develop a separate accounting system based on throughput costing in addition to the system we are required to have. The way to keep divisions from making more than they can sell is to charge them interest on any inventories they maintain. If divisions want to tie up the company's resources in inventory, then they should pay the company at least the interest it could be earning if the treasurer had the same amount of cash.

2.27 Explain how making more products than can be sold in a period can increase the organization's operating income. Is this a sustainable tactic to increase operating income? Would this happen in a service company, or is it an issue only in manufacturing companies? Explain.

2.28 Respond to this comment: Your analysis of last month's financial performance demonstrates that it really doesn't matter whether we use throughput, variable, or absorption costing. All the costs are accounted for; you've just put them in different places. I can't see what real difference this analysis makes. Isn't this just a bean-counting exercise?

2.29 Evaluate this criticism of the financial management of processes: All this emphasis on operating income, regardless of how you measure it, contributes to our continuing, short-term outlook. If we focus only on operating income, managers will do whatever they can to increase that measure, regardless of long-term impacts. This is what is wrong with modern business. We need to look beyond this period's operating income and focus on the long-term.

2.30   In general, how would you expect a company's balance sheet at any particular date to be different under absorption and variable costing?

2.31   The term *direct costing* is a misnomer. *Variable costing* is a better term for this product-costing method. Do you agree or disagree? Why?

2.32   Prime costs are always direct costs, and overhead costs are always indirect. What is your opinion of this statement?

Exercises

The following items appeared in the records of Herget Corporation, for the last year:

Sales revenue	$2,036,000
Supervisory and indirect labor	127,000
Supplies and indirect materials	14,000
Work-in-process inventory, January 1	135,000
Work-in-process inventory, December 31	142,000
Administrative costs	304,000
Depreciation, manufacturing	103,000
Direct labor	482,000
Finished-goods inventory, January 1	160,000
Finished-goods inventory, December 31	147,000
Heat, light, and power (plant)	87,000
Marketing costs	272,000
Miscellaneous manufacturing costs	12,000
Plant maintenance and repairs	74,000
Raw-material purchases	313,000
Raw-material inventory, January 1	102,000
Raw-material inventory, December 31	81,000

Exercise 2.33
Income Statement;
Schedule of Cost of
Goods Sold
(LO 1, 2)

Required

a.   Prepare an income statement with a supporting schedule of cost of goods sold.

b.   *Build your own spreadsheet.* Build an Excel spreadsheet to complete requirement (a). Use the spreadsheet to determine the new values for cost of goods sold and operating income if each of the following input parameters changes by the amount indicated. (Unless otherwise stated, treat each parameter change independently.)

1.   Direct labor increases by 10 percent.

2.   Manufacturing overhead cost decreases by 10 percent.

3.   Selling, general, and administration costs increase by 5 percent.

4.   Sales revenue decreases by 4 percent.

5.   All of the changes listed in (1)–(4) occur simultaneously.

Read two articles by Mishelle Conlin in *BusinessWeek:* "The Big Squeeze on Workers," May 13, 2002, pages 96 and 97, and "The Software Says You're Just Average," February 25, 2002, page 126.

Exercise 2.34
Direct Labor: Variable or
Fixed Cost
(LO 4)

Required

As a group, discuss whether direct labor is a fixed or a variable cost. What are the pros and cons of management treatment of direct labor as a variable cost? Are there ethical issues here?

Indicate whether each of the following costs incurred in a manufacturing operation are fixed or variable (F or V) and whether they are period costs or product costs (P or R) under absorption costing.

a.   Sales commissions.

b.   Office rent for sales personnel.

c.   Salaries for sales supervisors.

d.   Office rental for cost-management staff.

Exercise 2.35
Basic Concepts
(LO 1, 4)

e.   Administrative office heating and air conditioning.

f.   Transportation-in costs on materials purchased.

g.   Assembly-line workers' wages.

h.   Property taxes on office buildings for administrative staff.

i.   Salaries of the company's top executives.

j.   Overtime pay for assembly workers.

Exercise 2.36
Basic Concepts
(LO 1, 3, 4)

Indicate whether each of the following costs incurred in a manufacturing operation is included in prime costs (P), conversion costs (C), or both (B).

a.   Assembly-line worker's salary.

b.   Direct material used in production.

c.   Indirect material used in production.

d.   Factory heating and air conditioning.

e.   Production supervisor's salary.

f.   Transportation-in costs on materials purchased.

Exercise 2.37
Basic Concepts
(LO 1, 4)

Indicate whether each of the following costs incurred in a manufacturing operation is fixed or variable (F or V) and whether it is a period cost or product cost (P or R) under absorption costing.

a.   Utilities in cost-management analysts' office.   **d.**   Power to operate factory equipment.

b.   Factory security personnel.   **e.**   Depreciation on furniture for company executives.

c.   Factory heating and air conditioning.

Exercise 2.38
Statements for a
Merchandising Company
(LO 1, 2)

CompuTech sells computers. On January 1 of this year, it had a beginning merchandise inventory of $500,000, including transportation-in costs. It purchased $2,600,000 of merchandise, had $260,000 of transportation-in costs, and had marketing and administrative costs of $1,600,000 during the year. The ending inventory of merchandise on December 31 of this year was $300,000, including transportation-in costs. Revenue was $5,000,000 for the year.

Required

a.   Prepare an income statement with a supporting schedule of cost of goods sold.

b.   *Build your own spreadsheet.* Build an Excel spreadsheet to solve (a). Use your spreadsheet to determine the new values for the gross margin and operating income if each of the following input parameters changes by the amount indicated. (Unless otherwise indicated, treat each parameter change independently.)

   1. Purchases (invoice cost) increase by 5 percent.

   2. Purchases (transportation cost) decrease by 10 percent.

   3. Marketing and administrative costs increase by 2 percent.

   4. All of the changes listed in (1)–(3) occur simultaneously.

Exercise 2.39
Statements for a
Manufacturing Company
(LO 1, 2)

The following balances appeared in the accounts of Hasegawa Machine Tool Company during the current year. (y denotes *yen*, the Japanese national currency.)

	January 1	December 31
Finished-goods inventory	146,000y	150,000y
Work-in-process inventory	362,000y	354,000y
Raw-material inventory	328,000y	366,000y

During the year, 1,732,000y of direct material was used in production, and the year's cost of goods sold was 6,000,000y.

Required

Prepare a schedule of cost of goods sold, and fill in the following missing data.

a.   Cost of raw material purchased during the year.

b.   Cost of goods manufactured during the year.

c.   Total manufacturing costs incurred during the year.

The following information appears in Cleveland Cable Company's records for last year:

Sales revenue	$420,800
Administrative costs	88,600
Manufacturing building depreciation	54,000
Indirect materials and supplies	12,600
Sales commissions	30,400
Raw-material inventory, January 1	36,800
Direct labor	71,200
Raw-material inventory, December 31	38,000
Finished-goods inventory, January 1	21,800
Finished-goods inventory, December 31	18,000
Raw-material purchases	44,600
Work-in-process inventory, December 31	26,200
Supervisory and indirect labor	28,800
Property taxes, manufacturing plant	16,800
Plant utilities and power	47,000
Work-in-process inventory, January 1	30,800

Exercise 2.40
Statements for a
Manufacturing Company
(LO 1, 2)

Required

Prepare an income statement with a supporting schedule of cost of goods sold.

The following information appears in Tallehasse Toy Company's records for last year:

Sales revenue	$97,200
Administrative costs	21,550
Manufacturing building depreciation	12,500
Indirect materials and supplies	2,150
Sales commissions	7,100
Raw-material inventory, January 1	8,200
Direct labor	16,300
Raw-material inventory, December 31	9,000
Finished-goods inventory, January 1	4,450
Finished-goods inventory, December 31	4,050
Raw-material purchases	10,150
Work-in-process inventory, December 31	5,550
Supervisory and indirect labor	6,200
Property taxes, manufacturing plant	3,700
Plant utilities and power	10,750
Work-in-process inventory, January 1	6,600

Exercise 2.41
Statements for a
Manufacturing Company
(LO 1, 2)

Required

Prepare an income statement with a supporting schedule of cost of goods sold.

Zodiac Company manufactured 1,000 units of product last year and identified the following costs associated with the manufacturing activity (variable costs are indicated with V, fixed costs with F):

Direct material used (V)	$ 70,400
Direct labor (V)	133,000
Supervisory salaries (F)	62,200
Indirect materials and supplies (V)	16,000
Plant utilities (other than power to run plant equipment) (F)	19,200
Power to run plant equipment (V)	14,200
Depreciation on plant and equipment (straight-line, time basis) (F)	9,600
Property taxes on building (F)	13,000

Exercise 2.42
Cost Behavior for
Decision Making
(LO 4, 5, 6)

Required

Unit variable costs and total fixed costs are expected to remain unchanged next year. Calculate the unit cost and the total cost if 1,400 units are produced next year.

Exercise 2.43
Cost Behavior
(LO 4)

Refer to the information in the preceding exercise.

Required

Construct graphs of total fixed and variable costs.

Exercise 2.44
Variable and Absorption
Costing; Comparison of
Operating Profit
(LO 7)

mhhe.com/hilton3e

Minnesota Mustard Company produces a specialty mustard product, which it sells over the Internet for $21.50 per case. The company produced 120,000 units (cases) and sold 104,000 units last year. There were no beginning inventories or ending work-in-process inventories last year. Manufacturing costs and selling and administrative costs for last year follow:

Direct material	$780,000
Direct labor	450,000
Manufacturing overhead (unit level; variable)	180,000
Manufacturing overhead (facility level; fixed)	180,000
Selling and administrative (unit level; variable)	140,000
Selling and administrative (facility level; fixed)	120,000

Required

a. Compute the unit product (manufacturing) cost using variable costing.
b. Compute the operating profit using variable costing.
c. Compute the operating profit using absorption costing.

Exercise 2.45
Straightforward Exercise
on Absorption versus
Variable Costing
(LO 7, 8)

mhhe.com/hilton3e

New Jersey Catsup Company produces catsup, which it sells exclusively to fast-food restaurants in five-gallon containers, which sell for $15 each and have the following variable costs:

Direct material	$5
Direct labor	2
Variable overhead	3

Budgeted fixed overhead in 20x0 was $300,000. Actual production totaled 150,000 five-gallon containers, of which 125,000 were sold. The company incurred the following selling and administrative expenses:

Fixed	$50,000 for the year
Variable	$1 per container sold

Required

a. Compute the standard product cost per container of catsup under (1) absorption costing and (2) variable costing.
b. Prepare income statements for 20x0 using (1) absorption costing and (2) variable costing.
c. Reconcile the income reported under the two methods by listing the two key places where the income statements differ.
d. Reconcile the income reported under the two methods using the shortcut method.

Exercise 2.46
Comparison of Variable
and Absorption Costing
(LO 7, 8)

The following questions are based on Pittsburgh Pickle Corporation. The company's gourmet pickles are sold to restaurants for $12 per unit (one jar). Of the 100,000 units produced, 80,000 were sold during year 1; all ending inventory was in finished-goods inventory. The company had no inventory at the beginning of the year.

Direct material (unit-level or variable cost)	$240,000
Direct labor (unit-level or variable cost)	160,000
Manufacturing overhead (unit-level or variable cost)	80,000
Manufacturing overhead (facility-level or fixed cost)	240,000
Selling and administrative (unit-level or variable cost)	80,000
Selling and administrative (facility-level or fixed cost)	128,000

Required

a.   In presenting inventory on the balance sheet at December 31, what is the unit cost under absorption costing?

b.   In presenting inventory on a variable-costing balance sheet, what is the unit cost?

c.   What is the operating profit using variable costing?

d.   What is the operating profit using absorption costing?

e.   What is the cost of the ending inventory using absorption costing?

f.   What is the cost of the ending inventory under variable costing?

[CPA adapted]

Superior Lawn Equipment Company manufactures lawn mowers with a unit variable cost of $200. The mowers sell for $450 each. Budgeted fixed manufacturing overhead for the most recent year was $2,200,000. Planned and actual production for the year were the same.

Exercise 2.47
Difference in Income under Absorption and Variable Costing
(LO 7, 8)

Required

Under each of the following conditions, state (a) whether income is higher under variable or absorption costing and (b) the amount of the difference in reported income under the two methods. Treat each condition as an independent case.

1. Production	....	11,000 units
Sales	....	9,000 units
2. Production	....	10,000 units
Sales	....	10,000 units
3. Production	....	20,000 units
Sales	....	23,000 units

Compute throughput product cost of goods sold, throughput, and operating income from the following data for each month.

Exercise 2.48
Throughput Costing
(LO 7)

mhhe.com/hilton3e

	Month 1	Month 2	Month 3
Beginning inventory, in units	0	0	100
Units produced	500	600	400
Units sold	500	500	500
Sales	$50,000	$50,000	$50,000
Material cost	10,000	12,000	8,000
Direct conversion cost used	12,000	14,400	9,600
Indirect conversion cost	8,000	5,600	10,400
Indirect operating cost	16,000	16,000	16,000

Refer to the data in the preceding exercise. Compute variable cost of goods sold, contribution margin, and operating income. Why is operating income different from one month to the next?

Exercise 2.49
Variable Costing
(LO 8)

Refer to the data in Exercise 2.48. Compute absorption cost of goods sold, gross margin, and operating income. Why is operating income different from one month to the next?

Exercise 2.50
Absorption Costing
(LO 8)

Philadelphia Security Systems, Inc., uses the following unit costs for one of the products it manufactures:

Exercise 2.51
Comparison of Income Amounts under Absorption and Variable Costing
(LO 7, 9)

Direct material	$164.00
Direct labor	70.80
Manufacturing overhead (based on planned production of 5,000 units):	
Variable	31.20
Fixed	28.00
Selling and administrative costs (based on 6,500 units sold):	
Variable	20.80
Fixed	14.00

This year, 1,500 units were in beginning finished-goods inventory, 5,000 units were produced, and 6,500 units were sold at $400 per unit. The beginning inventory was valued at $266 per unit using variable costing and at $294 per unit using absorption costing. There was no beginning or ending work-in-process inventory.

Required

a.   Prepare an income statement for the year using variable costing and a contribution-margin format.

b.   Would reported operating profits be more, less, or the same if absorption costing were used? Support your conclusions with an income statement using absorption costing.

Exercise 2.52
Absorption, Variable, and
Throughput Costing
(LO 7, 8, 9)

Information taken from Laramie Lumber Company's records for the most recent year is as follows:

Direct material used	$290,000
Direct labor	100,000
Variable manufacturing overhead	50,000
Fixed manufacturing overhead	80,000
Variable selling and administrative costs	40,000
Fixed selling and administrative costs	20,000

Required

a.   Assuming that Laramie Lumber Company uses variable costing, compute the inventoriable costs for the year.

b.   Compute the year's inventoriable costs using absorption costing.

c.   Now assume that the company uses throughput costing and has *committed* to spending for direct labor, variable overhead, and fixed overhead in the amounts given in the problem. Under this scenario, compute the company's inventoriable cost for the year.

[CMA adapted]

Exercise 2.53
Absorption, Variable, and
Throughput Costing
(LO 7, 8, 9)

Pandora Pillow Company's planned production for the year just ended was 10,000 units. This production level was achieved, but it sold only 9,000 units. Other data follow:

Direct material used	$40,000
Direct labor incurred	20,000
Fixed manufacturing overhead	25,000
Variable manufacturing overhead	12,000
Fixed selling and administrative expenses	30,000
Variable selling and administrative expenses	4,500
Finished-goods inventory, January 1	None

There were no work-in-process inventories at the beginning or end of the year.

Required

a.   What would be Pandora Pillow Company's finished-goods inventory cost on December 31 under the variable-costing method?

b.   Which costing method, absorption or variable costing, would show a higher operating income for the year? By what amount?

c.   Suppose that Pandora Pillow Company uses throughput costing, and the cost of direct material is its only unit-level cost. What would be the company's finished-goods inventory on December 31?

[CPA adapted]

Exercise 2.54
Internet Search
(LO 7, 9)

Search the Internet for at least one example of an actual organization that uses throughput or variable costing (preferably not a university class or consultant's homepage). (*Hint:* Begin by using a search engine to find sites with the key words "variable cost" or "throughput." Prepare a memorandum to your instructor that describes:

a.   The organization—its name, industry, size, profitability, strategy, etc.

b.   The way that the organization uses variable or throughput costing

c.   Any costs or benefits the organization discloses about using variable or throughput costing

Problems

Each of the following columns is independent and for a different company. Use the data given, which refer to one year for each company, to find the unknown account balances.

Problem 2.55
Unknown Account
Balances
(LO 1, 2, 3)

Account	Company 1	2	3
Sales revenue	$1,088,000	$69,600	$3,359,900
Raw-material inventory, January 1	24,600	8,000	45,000
Raw-material inventory, December 31	20,000	12,400	(d)
Work-in-process inventory, January 1	11,600	12,560	(e)
Work-in-process inventory, December 31	12,000	12,560	85,200
Finished-goods inventory, January 1	254,200	2,800	334,480
Finished-goods inventory, December 31	(a)	4,600	367,400
Purchases of raw material	262,000	(c)	248,400
Cost of goods manufactured during the year	679,200	58,000	1,518,220
Total manufacturing costs	679,600	58,000	1,526,800
Cost of goods sold	760,000	56,200	(f)
Gross margin	328,000	13,400	1,874,600
Direct labor	173,000	23,200	(g)
Direct material used	(b)	15,000	234,200
Manufacturing overhead	240,000	19,800	430,600

You have been appointed manager of an operating division of Tucson Technology, Inc., a manufacturer of products using the latest developments in microprocessor technology. Your division manufactures the chip assembly, CH-1. On January 1 of this year, you invested $1 million in automated processing equipment for the chip assembly. At that time, your expected income statement for this year was as follows:

Problem 2.56
Impact of a Decision on
Income Statements
(LO 4, 5, 6)

Sales revenue	$1,600,000
Operating costs:	
Variable (cash expenditures)	$ 200,000
Fixed (cash expenditures)	750,000
Equipment depreciation	150,000
Other depreciation	125,000
Total operating costs	$1,225,000
Operating profit (before taxes)	$ 375,000

On November 15 of this year, a sales representative for Osaka Machine Company approaches you. Osaka wants to rent to your division a new assembly machine that would be installed on December 31 for an annual rental charge of $230,000. The new equipment would enable you to increase your division's annual revenue by 10 percent. The more efficient machine would decrease fixed cash expenditures by 5 percent. You will have to write off the cost of the automated processing equipment this year because it has no salvage value. Equipment depreciation shown on the income statement is for the automated processing equipment.

Your bonus is determined as a percentage of your division's operating profit before taxes. Equipment losses are included in the bonus and operating profit computation.

Ignore taxes and any effects on operations on the day of installation of the new machine. Assume that the data given in your expected income statement are the actual amounts for this year and next year if you keep the current equipment.

Required

a. What is the difference in this year's divisional operating profit if the new machine is rented and installed on December 31 of this year?

b. What would be the effect on next year's divisional operating profit if the new machine is rented and installed on December 31 of this year?

c. Would you rent the new equipment? Why or why not?

Problem 2.57
Schedules of Cost of
Goods Manufactured
and Sold; Income
Statement
(LO 1, 2, 3)

The following data refer to Metro Fashions Company for the year 20x2:

Work-in-process inventory, December 31	$ 30,000
Work-in-process inventory, January 1	40,000
Selling and administrative expenses	150,000
Income tax expense	90,000
Purchases of raw material	180,000
Raw-material Inventory, December 31	25,000
Raw-material Inventory, January 1	40,000
Direct labor	200,000
Utilities: plant	40,000
Depreciation: plant and equipment	60,000
Finished-goods inventory, December 31	50,000
Finished-goods inventory, January 1	20,000
Indirect material	10,000
Indirect labor	15,000
Other manufacturing overhead	80,000
Sales revenue	950,000

Required

a. Prepare Metro Fashions' schedule of cost of goods manufactured for the year.

b. Prepare Metro Fashions' schedule of cost of goods sold for the year.

c. Prepare Metro Fashions' income statement for the year.

Problem 2.58
Fixed and Variable
Costs; Forecasting
(LO 4)

Kingston Electronics Corporation incurred the following costs during 20x1. The company sold all of its products manufactured during the year.

Direct material	$3,000,000
Direct labor	2,200,000
Manufacturing overhead:	
Utilities (primarily electricity)	140,000
Depreciation on plant and equipment	230,000
Insurance	160,000
Supervisory salaries	300,000
Property taxes	210,000
Selling costs:	
Advertising	195,000
Sales commissions	90,000
Administrative costs:	
Salaries of top management and staff	372,000
Office supplies	40,000
Depreciation on building and equipment	80,000

During 20x1, the company operated at about half of its capacity due to a slowdown in the economy. Prospects for 20x2 are slightly better. The marketing manager forecasts a 20 percent growth in sales over the 20x1 level.

Required

Categorize each of the preceding costs as most likely variable or fixed. Forecast the 20x2 amount for each cost item.

Problem 2.59
Characteristics of Costs
(LO 4, 6)

The following terms are used to describe various characteristics of costs.

1. *Opportunity cost*
2. *Out-of-pocket cost*
3. *Sunk cost*
4. *Prime cost*
5. *Conversion cost*
6. *Average cost*

Required

Choose one of the terms to characterize each of the following amounts.

a. The cost to build an automated assembly line in a factory was $800,000 when the line was installed three years ago.

b. The management of a high-rise office building using 2,500 square feet of space in the building for its own management functions but could be rented for $250,000.

c. The direct-material and direct-labor cost incurred by a mass customizer such as Dell Computer to produce its most popular line of laptop computers.

d. The cost of feeding 500 children in a public school cafeteria is $800 per day, or $1.60 per child per day.

e. The cost of merchandise inventory purchased two years ago, which is now obsolete.

f. The cost of direct labor and manufacturing overhead incurred in producing frozen, microwavable pizzas.

g. The $1,000 cost of offering a computer workshop for a group of 20 students, or $50 per student.

Albany Alloys, Inc. incurs a variable cost of $40 per pound for direct material to produce a special alloy used in manufacturing aircraft.

Problem 2.60
Variable Costs;
Graphical and Tabular
Analyses
(LO 4)

Required

a. Draw a graph of the firm's direct material cost, showing the total cost at the following production levels: 10,000 pounds, 20,000 pounds, and 30,000 pounds.

b. Prepare a table that shows the unit cost and total cost of direct material at the following production levels: 1 pound, 10 pounds, and 1,000 pounds.

Airway Comfort Corporation manufactures a special fabric used to upholster the seats in small aircraft. The company's annual fixed production cost is $100,000.

Problem 2.61
Fixed Costs; Graphical
and Tabular Analyses
(LO 4)

Required

a. Graph the company's fixed production cost showing the total cost at the following production levels of upholstery fabric: 10,000 yards, 20,000 yards, 30,000 yards, and 40,000 yards.

b. Prepare a table that shows the unit cost and the total cost for the firm's fixed production costs at the following production levels: 1 yard, 10 yards, 10,000 yards, and 40,000 yards.

c. Prepare a graph that shows the unit cost for the company's fixed production cost at the following production levels: 10,000 yards, 20,000 yards, 30,000 yards, and 40,000 yards.

The following data appeared in Tuscaloosa Tile Company's records on December 31 of last year:

Problem 2.62
Reconstructed Financial
Statements
(LO 1, 2, 3)

Direct material used	$191,050
Work-in-process inventory, December 31	12,300
Raw-material inventory, December 31	42,500
Raw-material purchased during the year	180,000
Finished-goods inventory, December 31	45,000
Indirect labor	16,000
Direct labor	200,000
Plant heat, light, and power	18,600
Building depreciation (7/9 is for manufacturing)	40,500
Administrative salaries	25,700
Miscellaneous factory cost	15,950
Selling costs	18,500
Maintenance on factory machines	6,050
Insurance on factory equipment	9,500
Distribution costs	800
Taxes on manufacturing property	6,550
Legal fees on customer complaint	4,100

On January 1, at the beginning of last year, the Finished-Goods Inventory account had a balance of $40,000, and the Work-in-Process Inventory account had a balance of $12,950. Sales revenue during the year was $812,500.

Required

Prepare a schedule of cost of goods sold and an income statement.

Problem 2.63
Unknown Account
Balances
(LO 1, 2, 3)

Each of the following columns is independent and for a different company. Use the data given, which refer to one year for each example, to find the unknown account balances.

Account	Company 1	2	3
Raw-material inventory, January 1	(a)	$ 3,500	$ 16,000
Raw-material inventory, December 31	$ 3,600	2,900	14,100
Work-in-process inventory, January 1	2,700	6,720	82,400
Work-in-process inventory, December 31	3,800	3,100	76,730
Finished-goods inventory, January 1	1,900	(d)	17,200
Finished-goods inventory, December 31	300	4,400	28,400
Purchases of raw materials	16,100	12,000	64,200
Cost of goods manufactured during the year	(b)	27,220	313,770
Total manufacturing costs	55,550	23,600	308,100
Cost of goods sold	56,050	27,200	302,570
Gross margin	(c)	16,400	641,280
Direct labor	26,450	3,800	124,700
Direct material used	15,300	(e)	66,100
Manufacturing overhead	13,800	7,200	(g)
Sales revenue	103,300	(f)	943,850

Problem 2.64
Cost Concepts
(LO 3, 4, 5, 6)

The following data pertain to the photon gismo manufactured by Gizmos R Us, Inc.:

Sales price	$160 per unit
Fixed costs:	
Selling and administrative	$20,000 per period
Manufacturing overhead	$15,000 per period
Variable costs:	
Selling and administrative	$5 per unit
Manufacturing overhead	$30 per unit
Direct labor (manufacturing)	$10 per unit
Direct material (manufacturing)	$40 per unit
Number of units produced and sold during the period	1,000 units

Required

a.   How much is the variable *manufacturing cost* per unit?

b.   How much is the *variable cost* per unit?

c.   How much is the *full absorption cost* per unit?

d.   How much is the *prime cost* per unit?

e.   How much is the *conversion cost* per unit?

f.   How much is the *profit margin* per unit?

g.   How much is the *contribution margin* per unit?

h.   How much is the *gross margin* per unit?

i.   If the number of units increases from 1,000 to 1,100, which is within the company's relevant range of activity, will the *fixed manufacturing cost* per unit decrease, increase, or stay the same? Why?

Problem 2.65
Cost Concepts
(LO 1, 3)

Items (a) through (e) are based on the following data pertaining to Atlantic Company's manufacturing operations:

Inventories	November 1	November 30
Raw material	$ 9,000	$ 7,500
Work in process	4,500	3,000
Finished goods	$13,500	$18,000

Additional information for the month of November:

Raw material purchased	$21,000
Direct-labor costs	15,000
Manufacturing overhead	20,000

Required

Calculate the following amounts for the month of November:

a.   Prime costs

b.   Conversion costs

c.   Total manufacturing costs

d.   Cost of goods manufactured

e.   Cost of goods sold

[CPA adapted]

Florida Fruits, Inc., agreed to sell 40,000 cases of Fang, a dehydrated fruit drink, to NASA for use on space flights at "cost plus 10 percent." The company operates a manufacturing plant that can produce 120,000 cases per year, but it normally produces 80,000. The costs to produce 80,000 cases are as follows:

Problem 2.66
Cost Data for Managerial Purposes
(LO 4, 5, 6)

	Total	Per Case
Direct material	$ 960,000	$12.00
Direct labor	1,520,000	19.00
Supplies and other costs that vary with production	640,000	8.00
Costs that do not vary with production	440,000	5.50
Variable selling costs	160,000	2.00
Administrative costs (all fixed)	160,000	2.00
Total	$3,880,000	$48.50

Based on these data, company management expects to receive $53.35 (that is, $48.50 × 110 percent) per case for those sold on this contract. After completing 10,000 cases, the company sent a bill (invoice) to the government for $533,500 (that is, 10,000 cases at $53.35 per case).

The president of the company received a call from a NASA representative, who stated that the per-case cost should be as follows:

Material	$12
Labor	19
Supplies and other costs that vary with production	8
Total	$39

Therefore, the price per case should be $42.90 (that is, $39 × 110 percent). NASA ignored selling costs because the contract bypassed the usual sales channels.

Required

What price would you recommend? Why? Write a memo to management explaining your reasoning. (*Note:* You need not limit yourself to the costs selected by the company or by the NASA representative.)

You have been given the following information concerning Eclipse Corporation, which manufactures the ever-popular cosmic gismo.

Problem 2.67
Variable-Costing Operating Profit and Reconciliation with Absorption Costing
(LO 7, 8, 9)

▨   *Sales:* 10,000 units per year at a price of $46 per unit

▨   *Production:* 15,000 units in year 1; 5,000 units in year 2

▨   *Beginning inventory:* None in year 1

▨   *Variable (unit-level) cost:* $5 per unit

▨   *Facility-level production costs for the year:* $225,000, all fixed

▨   *Ending finished-goods inventory in year 1:* One-third of that year's production

▨   *Annual facility-level selling and administrative costs:* $140,000, all fixed

Required

a.   Prepare absorption-costing income statements for year 1, year 2, and the two years taken together.

b.   Prepare variable-costing income statements for year 1, year 2, and the two years taken together.

c.   Write a short report to management that reconciles absorption-costing operating profit to variable-costing operating profit for year 1 and year 2.

Problem 2.68
Variable-Costing
Operating Profit versus
Absorption-Costing
Operating Profit
(LO 7, 8, 9)

Huron Fabricating Company (HFC) employs an absorption-costing system for external reporting and internal management purposes. The latest annual income statement follows:

Sales revenue		$415,000
Cost of goods sold:		
Beginning finished-goods inventory	$ 22,000*	
Cost of goods manufactured	315,000	
Ending finished-goods inventory	(86,000)†	
Cost of goods sold		251,000
Gross margin		$164,000
Selling costs		83,000
Administrative costs		49,800
Operating profit before taxes		$ 31,200

*Includes $9,900 variable costs.
†Includes $60,200 variable costs.

Management is somewhat concerned that although HFC is showing adequate income, it is short of cash to meet operating costs. The following information has been provided to assist management with its evaluation of the situation:

Schedule of Cost of Goods Manufactured

Direct material:		
Beginning inventory	$ 16,000	
Purchases	62,000	
Ending inventory	(22,000)	$ 56,000
Direct labor		125,100
Manufacturing overhead:		
Variable		39,400
Fixed (including depreciation of $30,000)		94,500
Cost of goods manufactured		$315,000

There are no work-in-process inventories. Management reports that it is pleased that this year's manufacturing costs are 70 percent variable compared to last year's costs when they were only 45 percent variable. Although 80 percent of the selling costs are variable, only 40 percent of the administrative costs are considered variable. The company uses the first-in, first-out (FIFO) inventory method.

Required

a. Prepare a variable-costing income statement for the year.

b. Write a short report to management that explains why the company might be experiencing a cash-flow shortage despite the adequate income shown in its absorption-costing income statement.

c. *Build your own spreadsheet.* Build an Excel spreadsheet to solve (a) and (b). Use your spreadsheet to determine the new values for the contribution margin and variable-costing operating profit if each of the following input parameters changes by the amound indicated. (Unless otherwise indicated, treat each parameter change independently.)

1. Direct labor increases by 5 percent.

2. Raw material purchases decrease by 2 percent.

3. Fixed manufacturing overhead increases by 10 percent.

4. All of the changes listed in (1)–(3) occur simultaneously.

Problem 2.69
Absorption and Variable
Costing; Incomplete
Records
(LO 7, 8, 9)

On December 31 of last year, a fire destroyed the bulk of the accounting records of Ozark Company, a small, one-product manufacturing firm. In addition, the chief accountant mysteriously disappeared. You have the task to reconstruct last year's records. The general manager has said that the accountant had been experimenting with both absorption costing and variable costing.

The records are a mess, but you have gathered the following data for last year:

Operating profit, absorption-costing basis	$ 60,000
Notes receivable from chief accountant	14,000
Contribution margin	180,000
Raw-material purchases	175,000
Actual selling and administrative costs (all fixed)	21,000
Gross margin	81,000
Sales	450,000
Actual fixed manufacturing costs incurred	66,000
Actual variable manufacturing costs per unit for last year and for units in beginning finished-goods inventory on January 1 of last year	3

The company had no beginning or ending work-in-process inventories. You also learn that the absorption cost per unit in last year's beginning finished-goods inventory is the same as the absorption cost per unit for units produced during the year.

Required

a.   Prepare a comparative income statement on an absorption-costing and a variable-costing basis.

b.   At a meeting with the board of directors, the following questions were raised:

   1. How many units did we sell last year?

   2. How many units did we produce last year?

   3. What were the unit production costs last year under both absorption and variable costing? Write a short report responding to these questions.

c.   Reconcile the operating profit under variable costing with that under absorption costing, showing the exact source of the difference.

Toronto Tool Corporation (TTC) manufactures small electric hand tools in Toronto, Ontario. The firm uses a standard absorption-costing system for internal reporting purposes; however, the company is considering using variable costing. Data regarding TTC's planned and actual operations for 20x0 follow:

Problem 2.70
Variable versus
Absorption Costing; JIT
(LO 7, 8, 9)

	Planned Activity	Actual Activity
Beginning finished-goods inventory in units	35,000	35,000
Sales in units	140,000	125,000
Production in units	140,000	130,000

	Budgeted Costs		
	Per Unit	**Total**	**Actual Costs**
Direct material	$12.00	$1,680,000	$1,560,000
Direct labor	9.00	1,260,000	1,170,000
Variable manufacturing overhead	4.00	560,000	520,000
Fixed manufacturing overhead	5.00	700,000	715,000
Variable selling expenses	8.00	1,120,000	1,000,000
Fixed selling expenses	7.00	980,000	980,000
Variable administrative expenses	2.00	280,000	250,000
Fixed administrative expenses	3.00	420,000	425,000
Total	$50.00	$7,000,000	$6,620,000

The budgeted per-unit cost figures were based on TTC producing and selling 140,000 units in 20x0. TTC uses a predetermined overhead rate for applying manufacturing overhead to its product. A total manufacturing-overhead rate of $9 per unit was employed for absorption-costing purposes in 20x0. Any overapplied or underapplied manufacturing overhead is closed to the Cost of Goods Sold account at the end of the year. The 20x0 beginning finished-goods inventory for absorption-costing purposes was valued at the prior year's budgeted unit manufacturing cost, which was the same as the 20x0 budgeted unit manufacturing cost. There are no work-in-process inventories at either the beginning or the end of the year. The planned and actual unit selling price for 20x0 was $70 per unit.

Required

Was TTC's 20x0 income higher under absorption costing or variable costing? Why? Compute the following amounts.

a.   The value of TTC's 20x0 ending finished-goods inventory under absorption costing.

b.   The value of TTC's 20x0 ending finished-goods inventory under variable costing.

c.   The difference between TTC's 20x0 reported income calculated under absorption costing and calculated under variable costing.

d.   Suppose that TTC had introduced a JIT production and inventory-management system at the
beginning of 20x0.

   1.   What would likely be different about the scenario as described in the problem?

   2.   Would reported income under variable and absorption costing differ by the magnitude you
found in requirement (c)? Explain.

[CMA adapted]

Problem 2.71
Comparison of
Absorption and Variable
Costing; Actual Costing
(LO 2, 3, 4)

mhhe.com/hilton3e

Ticonderoga Toner Company (TTC) manufactures toner used in photocopy machines. The company's
product is sold by the jug at $50 per unit. TTC uses an actual costing system, which means that the
actual costs of direct material, direct labor, and manufacturing overhead are entered into work-in-
process inventory. The actual application rate for manufacturing overhead is computed each year; actual
manufacturing overhead is divided by actual production (in units) to compute the application rate.
Information for TTC's first two years of operations is as follows:

	Year 1	Year 2
Sales (in units)	2,500	2,500
Production (in units)	3,000	2,000
Production costs:		
Variable manufacturing costs	$21,000	$14,000
Fixed manufacturing overhead	42,000	42,000
Selling and administrative costs:		
Variable	25,000	25,000
Fixed	20,000	20,000

Required

Ticonderoga Toner Company had no beginning or ending work-in-process inventories for either
year.

a.   Prepare operating income statements for both years based on absorption costing.

b.   Prepare operating income statements for both years based on variable costing.

c.   Prepare a numerical reconciliation of the difference in income reported under the two costing
methods used in requirements (1) and (2).

d.   Reconcile TTC's income reported under absorption and variable costing, during each year, by
comparing the following two amounts on each income statement.

   ▪ Cost of goods sold
   ▪ Fixed cost (expensed as a period expense)

e.   What was TTC's total income across both years under absorption costing and under variable costing? Comment on this result.

Problem 2.72
Comparison of Variable
and Absorption Costing:
Profit Performance
Analysis
(LO 7, 8, 9)

Miami Enterprises released the following figures from its records for the past two years:

	Year 1	Year 2
Sales (units)	250,000	250,000
Production (units)	250,000	344,000
Selling price per unit	$40	$40
Variable manufacturing cost per unit	$24	$24
Annual committed manufacturing cost	$860,000	$860,000
Variable selling and administrative costs per unit sold	$2.40	$2.40
Committed selling and administrative costs	$840,000	$840,000
Beginning inventory	$0	?

Required

a. Prepare income statements for both years using absorption costing.

b. Prepare income statements for both years using variable costing.

c. Comment on the two operating profit figures. Write a brief report explaining why the operating profits are different, if they are.

The following questions are based on Laredo Leather Corporation, which produces belts that sell for $12 per unit. Of the 100,000 units produced, 80,000 were sold during the year. All ending inventory was in finished-goods inventory. Laredo had no inventory at the beginning of the year.

Problem 2.73
Comparison of Variable and Absorption Costing
(LO 7, 8)

Direct material (unit-level cost)	$240,000
Direct labor (unit-level cost)	160,000
Factory overhead (unit-level cost)	80,000
Factory overhead (capacity cost)	240,000
Selling and administrative (unit-level cost)	80,000
Selling and administrative (capacity cost)	128,000

Required

a. In presenting inventory on the balance sheet at December 31, what is the unit cost under absorption costing?

b. In presenting inventory on a variable-costing balance sheet, what is the unit cost?

c. What is the operating profit using variable costing?

d. What is the operating profit using absorption costing?

e. What is the ending inventory (dollar amount) using absorption costing?

f. What is the ending inventory (dollar amount) under variable costing?

[CPA adapted]

Alexander Corporation, which uses throughput costing, just completed its first year of operations. Planned and actual production equaled 10,000 units, and sales totaled 9,600 units at $72 per unit. Cost data for the year are as follows:

Problem 2.74
Throughput Costing, Absorption Costing, and Variable Costing
(LO 7, 8)

Direct material (per unit)	$	12
Conversion cost:		
Direct labor		45,000
Variable manufacturing overhead		65,000
Fixed manufacturing overhead		220,000
Selling and administrative costs:		
Variable (per unit)		8
Fixed		118,000

The company classifies only direct material as a throughput cost.

Required

a. Compute the company's total cost for the year assuming that variable manufacturing costs are driven by the number of units produced and that variable selling and administrative costs are driven by the number of units sold.

b. How much of this cost would be held in year-end inventory under (1) absorption costing, (2) variable costing, and (3) throughput costing?

c. How much of the company's total cost for the year would be included as an expense on the period's income statement under (1) absorption costing, (2) variable costing, and (3) throughput costing?

d. Prepare the company's throughput-costing income statement.

Cases

Case 2.75
Inventory Turnover
(LO I)

Campus Bookstore is a profit-making organization that reports to the Student Council. Martha Wailua, a part-time student employee, noticed that the managers at the bookstore seemed unconcerned about the costs of carrying large inventories. For example, several times a year the manager of the general merchandise department (one of six departments) bought large quantities of merchandise (clothing, gift items, etc.) with the university and sports team logos to get quantity discounts. The general merchandise manager also had argued successfully for more warehouse space for the merchandise, for which the bookstore pays rent to the university. Inevitably, several months later, the manager marks down the unsold merchandise to purchase cost or less to make room for the next purchase. This seemed very inefficient to Wailua, and she began to analyze the bookstore's purchases and sales for the past year. She gathered the following data.

Department	Cost of Goods Sold	Average Inventory	Percent of Warehouse Space	Average Number of Days Items Were Purchased in Advance of Sale
New textbooks	$ 5,730,972	$ 840,475	25%	63
Used textbooks........................	1,258,007	180,600	12	37
Trade books	563,686	370,500	10	86
Supplies	662,560	251,700	8	71
General merchandise...............	883,251	640,600	25	94
Computers	2,246,600	402,000	20	28
Total store	$11,345,076	$2,685,875	100%	66.3

Required

a.   Compute inventory turnover ratios (i.e., cost of goods sold ÷ average inventory) for each department and the bookstore as a whole. What would these ratios tell Wailua about the management of inventories at Campus Bookstore? Is it reasonable to compare these ratios across departments? Why or why not?

b.   A privately owned store in the university commercial area sells licensed (general) merchandise with the university's logo and reported to Wailua that its inventory turnover ratio for the past year was 5.30. Is that a legitimate benchmark for Campus Bookstore? Why or why not?

c.   What are the benefits and costs to the bookstore of its methods for purchasing and inventory?

d.   What information would Wailua need to place a dollar figure on all of those costs?

e.   Wailua has learned that the manager of the General Merchandise Department is a close personal friend of the bookstore manager and receives incentive prizes from suppliers for ordering large quantities of merchandise. What are her ethical responsibilities?

Case 2.76
"I Enjoy Challenges";
Effect of Changes in
Production and Costing
Method on Operating
Profit
(LO 7, 8, 9, 10)

(This classic case is based on an actual company's experience.) Brassinni Company uses an actual absorption cost system to apply all production costs to units produced. The plant has a maximum production capacity of 40 million units but produced and sold only 10 million units during year 1. There were no beginning or ending inventories. Brassinni Company's income statement for year 1 follows:

BRASSINNI COMPANY
Income Statement
For the Year Ending December 31, Year 1

Sales (10,000,000 units at $6)...		$ 60,000,000
Cost of goods sold:		
Direct costs, material, and labor		
(10,000,000 at $2)	$20,000,000	
Manufacturing overhead	48,000,000	
Cost of goods sold		68,000,000
Gross margin...		$ (8,000,000)
Selling and administrative costs		10,000,000
Operating profit (loss)		$(18,000,000)

The board of directors is concerned about the $18 million loss. A consultant approached the board with the following offer: "I agree to become president for no fixed salary. But I insist on a year-end bonus of 10 percent of operating profit (before considering the bonus)." The board of directors agreed to these terms and hired the consultant as Brassinni's new president.

The new president promptly stepped up production to an annual rate of 30 million units. Sales for year 2 remained at 10 million units. The resulting Brassinni Company absorption-costing income statement for year 2 follows:

BRASSINNI COMPANY
Income Statement
For the Year Ending December 31, Year 2

Sales (10,000,000 units at $6)		$60,000,000
Cost of goods sold:		
Cost of goods manufactured:		
Direct costs, material, and labor		
(30,000,000 at $2)	$ 60,000,000	
Manufacturing overhead	48,000,000	
Total cost of goods manufactured	$108,000,000	
Less: Ending inventory:		
Variable (20,000,000 at $2)	$ 40,000,000	
Indirect (20/30 × $48,000,000)	32,000,000	
Total ending inventory	$ 72,000,000	
Cost of goods sold		36,000,000
Gross margin		$24,000,000
Selling and administrative costs		10,000,000
Operating profit before bonus		$14,000,000
Bonus		1,400,000
Operating profit after bonus		$12,600,000

The day after the statement was verified, the president took his check for $1,400,000 and resigned to take a job with another corporation. He remarked, "I enjoy challenges. Now that Brassinni Company is in the black, I'd prefer tackling another challenging situation." (His contract with his new employer is similar to the one he had with Brassinni Company.)

Required

a. Step back, and look at this overal situation. In general, what do you think is going on here? More specifically, how would you evaluate the company's year 2 performance?

b. Using variable costing, what would operating profit be for year 1? For year 2? (Assume that all selling and administrative costs are committed and unchanged.) Compare those results with the absorption-costing statements.

c. Comment on any ethical issues you see in this scenario.

Cotierre imports designer clothing manufactured by subcontractors in Mexico. Clothing is a seasonal product. The goods must be ready for sale prior to the start of the season. Any goods left over at the end of the season usually must be sold at steep discounts. The company prepares a dress design and selects fabrics approximately six months before a given season. It receives these goods and distributes them at the start of the season. Based on past experience, the company estimates that 60 percent of a particular lot of dresses will be unsold at the end of the season and will be marked down to one-half of the initial retail price. Even with the markdown, a substantial number of dresses will remain unsold and will be returned to Cotierre and destroyed. Although a large number of dresses must be discounted or destroyed, the company needs to place a minimum order of 1,000 dresses to have a sufficient selection of styles and sizes to market the design.

Recently, the company placed an order for 1,000 dresses of a particular design for $25,000 plus import duties of $5,000 and a $7 commission for each dress sold at retail, regardless of the price. Return mailing and disposing of each unsold dress cost $3 after the end of the markdown period.

Case 2.77
Absorption and Variable Costing; Import Decisions
(LO 7, 8, 9)

Required

a. Use absorption costing to compute the cost of each dress in this lot of dresses.

b. Suppose that the company sells 30 percent of the dresses in this lot for $75 each during the first accounting period. Using absorption costing, what is the value of the ending inventory? What is the operating profit or loss for the period, assuming no other transactions and that the season has not ended, so that the number of dresses subject to markdown or to be returned is unknown?

c. During the second period, 10 percent of the 1,000 dresses were sold at full price, and 30 percent were sold at the half-price markdown. The remaining dresses were returned and disposed of. Using absorption costing, what is the operating profit or loss for the period, assuming no other transactions?

d. Suggest a method to account for these dresses that would more closely relate revenues and costs.

Chapter 3

Cost Accumulation for Job-Shop and Batch Production Operations

After completing this chapter, you should be able to:

1. Explain the differences in job-order, process, and operation costing.

2. Explain how costs flow through the manufacturing accounts.

3. Assign costs to production jobs or products using a job-order costing system.

4. Prepare accounting journal entries to record job costs.

5. Use a predetermined overhead rate to assign indirect resource costs to production jobs.

6. Explain how to measure production costs under actual, normal, and standard costing systems.

7. Discuss the role of job-order costing in service organizations.

8. Understand how companies manage long-term projects and their costs.

Cost-Management Challenges

(Solutions are on page 116.)

1. **What** factors should a cost-management analyst consider when designing a product-costing system?

2. **What** features should a job-order costing system have, and how can they be developed?

3. **How** can cost-management analysts use job-cost information to support planning and decision-making activities?

Glass Creations
2819 Pelican Drive
Madeira Beach, Florida 33708

January 30

Ms. Grace Riley
Gulf Coast Aquarium
Tampa, Florida

Dear Ms. Riley:

We have completed the estimates for the two stained glass doors you are planning for the aquarium's main entry portico. Our designer has developed sketches for some beautiful stained glass panels for the doors following the guidelines you gave us during our meeting in November. Each door has six stained glass panels, featuring a variety of marine species, from dolphins and whales to starfish and sea horses. The panel designs are, as you requested, very colorful. I think you will be pleased with them.

We have carefully estimated the costs of the doors, which cover the materials, design talent, glass workers' labor, and applied overhead, which is based on the projected labor time required for the job. As per our previous discussions, our price for your nonprofit organization will be cost plus a modest 10 percent profit margin.

I will call you next week to set up a meeting so that we can go over the design sketches and the projected job-cost figures. Naturally, we will be happy to make any modifications that you wish. Thank you for allowing us to make a contribution to your aquarium project.

Sincerely,

Jeremiah Jacobson

Jeremiah Jacobson

Glass Creations creates and markets stained glass windows, doors, and free-standing pieces for private homes, businesses, and other organizations. The small, family-run business is located in Madeira Beach, Florida, a barrier island community on the Gulf Coast in the Tampa/St. Petersburg area. Jeremiah and Anita Jacobson, who studied fine arts in college, founded the business 15 years ago. Both are involved in the design and creation of the stained glass pieces. In addition, Glass Creations' employees include one other designer, several highly skilled glass workers, a framing technician, and various office personnel. Tom Nakagawa, a certified management accountant, provides support to the firm in purchasing, production scheduling, accounting, and cost management.

Almost from its inception, Glass Creations has been a successful business, with sales and profit growing, at least modestly, almost every year. The Jacobsons can now boast the placement of their leaded, glazed, etched, and stained glass creations in almost every state in the United States and several foreign countries. The couple's most famous piece, "Calm Over Calamity," depicts a Native American lad of about 10 years standing calmly only a few feet away from a very menacing grizzly bear. The piece stands some 12 feet high and contains several hundred pieces of stained glass. It was commissioned by a commercial bank in Vancouver, British Columbia, where it is permanently installed in the lobby. As the correspondence on the preceding page indicates, Glass Creations is currently developing the design and cost estimate for two elaborate stained glass doors to be installed in the new Gulf Coast Aquarium.

Glass Creations designs and creates stained glass windows, doors, and other pieces in the firm's Madeira Beach glass studio. Roughly 75 percent of the firm's sales are for single, unique pieces, most of which are commissioned by private homeowners and businesses. They sell for prices ranging from $350 for a simple, relatively small piece, to tens of thousands of dollars for large, complex pieces. Glass Creations has produced stained glass pieces for all types of religious organizations, but the vast majority of its products are secular in nature. The remainder of Glass Creations' products are its windows, which are produced in small batches and sold as stock items at arts festivals, on the firm's website, or through catalogues of specialized building materials. Among the firm's stock windows are the pelican window, the blue heron window, and the dolphin window. Each unit in a batch of these types of window uses the same basic design with minor modifications from batch to batch. Moreover, the units within a batch typically are somewhat different because of the different glass colors used.

Although Glass Creations has been profitable throughout its life as a business, its owners recently became concerned because several large window manufacturers have begun to produce glazed, etched, and stained glass windows for private homes. These companies employ more mechanization than Glass Creations' artists use, and they produce stock windows in larger batches, thus driving down the costs. The Jacobsons are now concerned that these larger competitors might satisfy enough of the consumer demand for stained glass and other artistic windows to adversely affect Glass Creations' business. Although this has not been a problem yet, it is a cause for concern. Anita worries that consumers will not recognize or perhaps fail to properly appreciate the difference between a mass-produced window and one made by a skilled glass worker in a studio. As Jeremiah recently said, "Anita and I are in this business because we love what we do. It's a really satisfying medium in which to work. But we do have to make a living. We have several employees and lots of bills to pay, not to mention providing for a secure retirement."

The owners must make some important marketing and strategic decisions to thrive in this potentially more competitive environment. For example, they must decide whether Glass Creations should compete with the large window manufacturers for the stock artistic window market or should concentrate on the custom design market. They must also determine how best to use the typically slow months of December and January. Should they aggressively seek more custom design work or use this period to produce stock windows for inventory to be sold later in the spring and summer months when arts festivals are in full swing and the home building industry picks up?

During their first decade as the owners of a small business, the Jacobsons focused exclusively on the artistic side of their enterprise. They were artists, after all, not businesspeople. However, they became increasingly aware of their problem related to the seemingly total unpredictability of the cost (and, by implication, the profit) on large, custom glass pieces. Sometimes Glass Creations bid too high on a job and lost it. Other times it bid too low and got the job but lost money on it. As Jeremiah said in frustration, "The profit margins on our various jobs were all over the map. We'd just never know what to expect." That frustration, coupled with several lean years of the "starving artist" syndrome, led the owners to hire Tom Nakagawa, a college friend who had majored in business, to support their operations in a number of important business functions. The owners were becoming frustrated by spending too much time ordering materials, making estimates, and so on, and not getting enough time in the studio. They needed Nakagawa to help develop a sound costing system and help manage costs. He installed a simple product-costing system for Glass Creations, which gave the Jacobsons a much better idea of the costs of their jobs, which in turn helped them make better cost estimates for prospective jobs.

As the Jacobsons learned, a key element in deciding which products to offer is understanding the company's product costs. For example, Glass Creations has many opportunities to bid on commissioned pieces. Should it bid on every design? How much should it bid on the pieces for which it competes? This chapter explores a cost-accounting system called "job-order costing" (or simply "job costing"), which traces costs in organizations such as Glass Creations. This chapter discusses job-order costing using Glass Creations' business. The methods illustrated apply, however, to all types of organizations—manufacturing, service, nonprofit, and government—for which job-order costing is appropriate.

Choice among Product-Costing Systems

Cost-management analysts could ask themselves and the managers with whom they work a number of questions regarding the nature of the information needed to support their organization's decision making. Answers to these questions have direct implications for designing a **product-costing system,** which accumulates the costs of a production process and assigns them to the products or services that constitute the organization's output. One question of direct interest for the Jacobsons to consider for Glass Creations' cost-system design is the following: Are specific costs of each product and product line necessary, or are average costs across products adequate?

LO 1 Explain the differences in job-order, process, and operation costing.

As cost-management analysts develop answers to this question, a certain type of costing system usually appears to be most appropriate. The most common types of product-costing systems include *job-order costing* and *process costing,* as well as their hybrid, *operation costing.* In addition, other important variations of costing systems can be implemented in conjunction with job-order, process, or operation costing. We address these other cost-system design variations later in this chapter.

Evaluating Major Types of Product-Costing Systems

Job-order costing treats each individual job as the unit of output and assigns costs to it as it uses resources. A job can be a single, unique product, such as Glass Creations' piece "Calm Over Calamity," a custom home, a super tanker, a feature film, or an architectural design. Alternatively, a job can be a relatively small batch of identical or very similar products, such as Glass Creations' dolphin window that is produced in batches of about 20 to 25 units, or batches of printed wedding invitations, high-quality furniture, or heavy construction equipment. Job-order costing creates and maintains separate records or accounts for each job. Job-order costing is appropriate for the following types of production processes:

- Each unit or batch of products is distinct and clearly distinguishable from other products.
- Each unit is of relatively high value, which makes the benefits of separately assigning production costs worth the cost of doing so.

■ Each unit or batch of products is often priced differently, frequently in accordance with a bidding process.

■ Each unit or batch of products can feasibly have its direct costs traced.

Glass Creations and other producers of unique jobs can see important benefits of tracing resource costs to each job that justify the expenses of doing so. Job-order costing is useful for the following purposes:

■ *Identifying types of jobs* that are likely to be most profitable so that the organization can specify the scope and scale of its operations.

■ *Providing data to predict costs of future jobs* so that the organization chooses appropriate jobs on the basis of the resources needed and their expected profitability.

■ *Managing the costs of current jobs* to ensure that they stay within expectations and to provide early warning if costs will exceed expectations.

■ *Renegotiating job contracts* before introducing any significant changes in jobs that will affect resources, costs, or profits.

■ *Reporting actual financial results* of the period's operations to demonstrate the organization's efficiency to external parties such as creditors and stockholders.

Managers use their knowledge of the cost of past jobs to estimate the costs of prospective jobs. Accurate cost estimates on future jobs help them prepare competitive bids. The Jacobsons know that if Glass Creations bids too high on a commissioned job, it will not be awarded the job and if the bid is too low, the company could lose money on the job. Artists working on commissioned pieces, construction contractors, and other businesspeople who bid on jobs must have reliable estimates of the costs of prospective jobs to prepare bids that are low enough to win but high enough to make a profit.[1]

Managers compare actual job costs to the estimated (*budgeted*) job costs to help manage them. A contractor once noted that if she did not have job-cost information, she could have experienced huge cost overruns without anticipating it. For example, on one job she estimated the cost of lumber at a certain level. Then a hurricane hit the southeastern United States, causing lumber prices to double. She did not realize that the lumber shipped to the job was at the higher posthurricane prices until she got the job cost information. Based on this information, she redesigned the job to use less lumber where it was not essential.

Managers can use job-cost information to renegotiate contracts with customers. Glass Creations has found that jobs often turn out differently than the customer originally specified. Sometimes these changes are inexpensive, and the company does the extra work as part of good customer service. Other times the changes are expensive, and the customer and the firm need to negotiate who will bear their cost. Reliable cost information helps management know (1) whether the changes are expensive or inexpensive and (2) what the changes cost so that the commissioned price or bid can be renegotiated.

To summarize, job-order costing is important for both pricing and cost management. Businesses must be able to estimate costs accurately if they are to be competitive and profitable.

Widespread use of job-order costing.   Many companies that produce customized products and services use job-order costing. Examples include Morrison-Knudsen, the worldwide construction company; The Boeing Company, the large commercial airplane manufacturer and defense contractor; Mayo Clinic, the world-renowned hospital where the jobs are "cases"; New Line Cinema, the producer of jobs such as the movie *Lord of the Rings: Return of the King;* Accenture and Deloitte-Touche, worldwide business-services firms, whose jobs often are called "clients"; and McGraw-Hill, the publisher of this and other leading textbooks.

---

[1] Economists sometimes refer to the "winner's curse," which means that if you bid low enough to get the job, you could well have bid too low to make a profit.

Job-Order Costing	Operation Costing	Process Costing
NASA Mars rover mission	Toyota's automobiles	British Petroleum's gasoline
New Line Cinema's *Lord of the Rings* Trilogy, by Peter Jackson	H & R Block's tax returns	Quaker Oats' oatmeal
A custom home built by American Homes	Woolrich's sweaters	Levi's jeans
Steinway's pianos	Wilson's basketballs	Intel's computer chips
Microsoft's tax return	Dell's computers	Georgia Pacific's lumber
A heart transplant at the Mayo Clinic	Eddie Bauer's shirts	Olympic Stains' paints
Installation of multiple, high-end photocopiers and related business-systems equipment by Xerox in a new office building	Xerox's mid-range photocopiers for light use by small business and individuals	Xerox's photocopier paper

Exhibit 3–1

Examples of Job-Order, Operation, and Process Costing

Process costing.   In contrast, **process costing,** discussed in depth in Chapter 8, treats all units processed during a time period as the output to be costed and does not separate and record costs for each unit produced. The next time you have a bottle of Coke or Pepsi, consider whether the bottler tracked the cost of the specific bottle you are drinking. Not likely! It would be prohibitively costly to do so and without benefit since the bottler would not expect any cost variation among bottles of the same soft drink. Process costing is appropriate for the following types of production processes:

- Units of output that are relatively homogeneous and indistinguishable from one another.
- Individual product units that are typically of relatively low value.
- Individual product units for which it is not feasible to trace direct costs.

Companies that use continuous processes (such as bottling beverages, manufacturing chemicals, grinding flour, refining oil, and processing credit-card transactions) to produce many identical units of product or service use process costing.

Operation costing.   Another product costing method is *operation costing.* Also covered in Chapter 8, **operation costing** is a hybrid of job-order and process costing used when companies produce large batches of similar products in which significantly different types of materials are used. Examples include shirts made from different fabrics such as cotton and wool and basketballs covered with real or simulated leather. As output becomes more unique and separately identifiable, job costing becomes more appropriate. Conversely, as separate units of output become indistinguishable, process costing is more appropriate. An organization where output falls somewhere between the two extremes might use operation costing.

Some organizations use job-order costing for their unique projects and process costing for their continuous processes. A large homebuilder, such as American Homes, might use process costing for its many standardized homes and job-order costing for its more expensive, semicustom homes. Honeywell, Inc., a high-tech company, uses process costing for most of its furnace thermostats but job-order costing for specialized defense and space contracting work. See Exhibit 3–1 for examples of products and services best suited to job-order costing, operation costing, and process costing.

Basic Cost-Flow Model

As your previous accounting courses probably discussed, all cost-accounting systems rely on a basic cost-flow model, which is a periodic accounting framework for recording the costs of jobs (or processes). The basic cost-flow model is an inventory model or equation since it measures resources acquired to produce products or services that

LO 2 Explain how costs flow through the manufacturing accounts.

have not yet been sold. This model applies to all of an organization's physical resources. The basic cost-flow equation follows:

$$\underset{\text{BB}}{\underset{\text{beginning balance}}{\text{Job cost}}} + \underset{\text{TI}}{\underset{\text{transfers in}}{\text{Resource}}} - \underset{\text{TO}}{\underset{\text{transfers out}}{\text{Resource}}} = \underset{\text{EB}}{\underset{\text{ending balance}}{\text{Job cost}}}$$

Cost Flows and Jobs

The cost-flow model assigns costs of resources used to complete jobs according to the cost-flow equation, as explained here:

- At any time, every active job has a beginning balance (BB) measuring the cost of resources used on the job to date. The beginning balance might be zero if the job so far is only an idea. (Although one could argue that human resources have been used to generate the idea, the beginning balance still is zero.)
- Resources used or transferred in (TI) during a particular time period also are assigned to measure resource usage. The time period for recording costs can be of any length to suit decision-making needs.
- Transfers out (TO) record the accumulated costs of products or services transferred to another process in the organization, completed and stored, or sent to the customer. Transfers out ordinarily are the costs of good products suitable for further processing or sale but also can include the costs of defective products that must be reworked or scrapped. (We defer discussion of costs of defective or scrapped products until Chapter 8).
- The ending balance (EB) for the job is a residual that can be found by the simple algebra of the cost-flow equation:

$$EB = BB + TI - TO$$

You use this same model when you periodically update your checking account. Alternatively, if you use a debit or ATM card, the bank's system perpetually updates your account balance. Similarly, inventory systems either periodically or perpetually update inventory balances, depending on the need and technology used.

The ending balance, EB, also can be determined by (1) physically observing the number of units of product or service completed and (2) costing them using an appropriate cost-driver rate. If all of the model's components do not balance the cost-flow equation, evidence indicates an unintentional error, wasted resources, or, perhaps, theft or fraud. One of the best features of the basic cost-flow model is its use as a powerful tool for controlling the use of all physical resources. By making the misuse of physical resources difficult, the cost-flow model becomes a *control mechanism,* which is a policy or procedure that helps the organization ensure that its goals and objectives are met. (This topic is discussed in Chapters 18 and 20, which cover responsibility accounting and performance evaluation, respectively.)

Simple cost-flow examples.   Examine the examples in Exhibit 3–2, and observe how to use the cost-flow equation to solve for the missing inventory element in each column:

Cost-Flow Equation (BB + TI − TO = EB)

B1: BB + $8,000 − $11,000 = $16,000
  BB = $16,000 − $8,000 + $11,000
  BB = $19,000
C2: $4,000 + TI − $61,000 = $3,000
  TI = $3,000 − $4,000 + $61,000
  TI = $60,000

D3: $5,000 + $8,000 − TO = $7,000
  −TO = $7,000 − $5,000 − $8,000
  −TO = − $6,000
  TO = $6,000
E4: $3,000 + $55,000 − $48,000 = EB
  EB = $10,000

We are ready to add a slight complication to the basic cost-flow model by recognizing that most organizations use several types of inventory accounts to manage job costs. Most commonly, these additional accounts include Work-in-Process and Finished-Goods Inventories, which record

Exhibit 3–2

Cost-Flow Examples

X Microsoft Excel - Exhibit 3-2				
File Edit View Insert Format Tools Data Window Help				
E4 = EB = ?				
	A	B	C	D	E
1	Beginning balance	BB = ?	$4,000	$5,000	$3,000
2	Transfers-in	8,000	TI = ?	8,000	55,000
3	Transfers-out	11,000	61,000	TO = ?	48,000
4	Ending balance	16,000	3,000	7,000	EB = ?

costs as jobs are in process and when they have been completed, requiring cost flows to be managed and recorded in several related accounts. (Recall the discussion of the inventory accounts in Chapter 2.)

Managing and Using Cost-Flow Information

Companies such as Glass Creations that use job-order costing employ several accounts (or files) to track the costs of resources used on jobs. These accounts are the sources of data for product costing, estimating costs of future jobs, and financial reporting for both internal and external purposes. The Work-in-Process (WIP) Inventory account collects all costs of resources used on various jobs not yet completed. Each job also has its own job-cost record or subsidiary account. The **job-cost record** (*or* **file, card** *or* **sheet**) records the costs of all production-related resources used on the job to date.

The total cost in the Work-in-Process account is the sum of the costs in all active (but not completed) jobs, as recorded on their respective job-cost records. Similarly, the Finished-Goods Inventory account collects total costs of all completed jobs not yet sold to customers. The Cost of Goods Sold account records the costs of finished goods (or jobs) that have been sold during a specific period. The basic cost-flow model ties these accounts together as Exhibit 3–3 shows.

LO 3 Assign costs to production jobs or products using a job-order costing system.

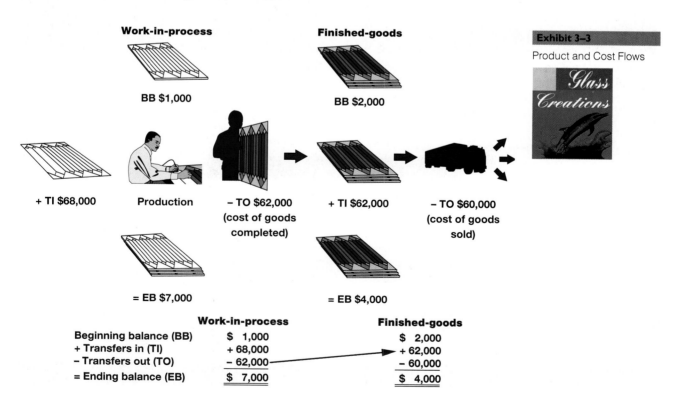

Exhibit 3–3

Product and Cost Flows

	Work-in-process	Finished-goods
Beginning balance (BB)	$ 1,000	$ 2,000
+ Transfers in (TI)	+ 68,000	+ 62,000
– Transfers out (TO)	– 62,000	– 60,000
= Ending balance (EB)	$ 7,000	$ 4,000

Transfers in (TI) to Work-in-Process Inventory include direct-material, direct-labor, and manufacturing-overhead costs. As jobs or products are completed, they and their accumulated costs are transferred out (TO) of the Work-in-Process Inventory account. This cost of completed goods becomes the transfers in (TI) to the next sequential process (if there are sequential production processes) and ultimately, as Exhibit 3–3 shows, to Finished-Goods Inventory. The transfers out of Finished-Goods Inventory become the transfers in to Cost of Goods Sold, which is an expense of the period.

The Process of Tracking Job-Order Costs

In job-shop or batch-production operations, managers estimate and manage costs by keeping separate cost records for each job. The primary cost document for a job is the "job-cost record" (also called a "job-cost file or sheet"). See Exhibit 3–4 for a print-out of the job-cost record for Glass Creations' job P01-20. [This job-numbering scheme denotes that this is the first batch of pelican windows during the current year (P01) and the quantity is 20 units]. Note that this record shows detailed calculations for the direct materials, direct labor, and manufacturing overhead charged to the job and that Nakagawa, Glass Creations' cost analyst, compared the actual costs accumulated for the job with the estimated costs to evaluate employee performance in man-

Exhibit 3–4   Job Cost Record

GLASS CREATIONS								

Job number: P01-20   **Stock number or name of customer:** PEL-100
Date started: January 8   **Date finished:** January 26
Description: Pelican window—quantity 20   **Job supervisor:** Brent Dean

Direct Materials			Direct Labor			Manufacturing Overhead		
Date	Requisition Identifier	Cost	Date	Employee Identifier	Cost	Date	Direct-Labor Hours × Overhead Rate	Cost
Jan 8	P01-20-A	$1,000	Jan 8	D01: 3 @ $21	$ 63	Jan 31	113 @ 30*	3,390
Jan 13	P01-20-B	400	Jan 12–18	G03: 60 @ $22	1,320			
Total		$1,400	Jan 12–18	G06: 40 @ $22	880			
			Jan 18	F02: 10 @ $15	150			
			Total	Total 113	$2,413			

*Predetermined overhead rate (explained later in chapter)

Total Job Cost
Direct materials... $1,400
Direct labor 2,413
Manufacturing overhead 3,390
Total $7,203

Transferred to Finished-Goods Inventory
Direct materials... $1,400
Direct labor 2,413
Manufacturing overhead 3,390
Total $7,203

Cost Comparison
Explain below any differences between estimated job cost and costs accumulated for job: None

aging costs. Any significant differences are noted on the job-cost record. The comparison also provides feedback on the accuracy of the cost estimates, which is important for future pricing decisions.

Product-Costing System Design Issues

Three design aspects of Glass Creations' product-costing system are noteworthy at this juncture. First, as noted previously, the company uses *job-order costing.* It is an appropriate method for Glass Creations because the firm's products are relatively heterogeneous, and many of them are custom jobs. Second, Glass Creations uses *absorption costing,* which was explained in detail in Chapter 2. Thus, the manufacturing overhead shown on the job-cost record in Exhibit 3–4 includes both variable and fixed overhead as product costs. Third, Glass Creations uses a *normal costing system,* which assigns actual costs of direct material and direct labor to each production job but *applies* (or allocates) the manufacturing overhead using a *predetermined overhead rate* based on a cost driver. This third design aspect of Glass Creations' product-costing system (i.e., normal costing and the use of a predetermined overhead rate) is explored in more detail later in the chapter. For now, it is important to realize only that these three terms (job-order, absorption, and normal costing) describe the type of product-costing system employed by Glass Creations.

Recording Job-Order Costs

Most companies with job-shop or batch-production environments follow the basic job-order costing steps presented in this section. We show the journal entries to record the costs incurred by Glass Creations in January, a typically slow month. Several employees take their vacations then, and during the current year, the studio worked on only three jobs.

In a job-order costing system, Work-in-Process Inventory is a *control account* because it is supported by cost records in the subsidiary ledger. Costs associated with each job are recorded on a job-cost record as shown in Exhibit 3–4. Thus, job-cost records serve as *subsidiary ledgers* to the Work-in-Process Inventory account. This enables management to identify the costs for a particular job by reviewing its job-cost record.

One of Glass Creations' jobs, C12-05, in process on January 1, had been started during December of the preceding year. [The different job number used for custom jobs (C) denotes that this custom job, was started on December 5 (12-05).] After some additional work, it was completed and installed for the customer in January. Glass Creations' second job, P01-20, was started on January 8 and moved to finished-goods inventory on January 26. On January 31, it awaited shipment to various customers. Its costs are presented on the job cost record in Exhibit 3–4. The third job, C01-15 (a custom job started on January 15), was still in process on January 31. Therefore, the following is the status for each of these production jobs on January 31.

Job	Status on January 31
C12-05	Sold
P01-20	Finished but not sold
C01-15	In process

Beginning inventories. Exhibit 3–5 shows the beginning balances in the Raw-Material Inventory and Work-in-Process Inventory accounts. Raw-Material Inventory on January 1 was $5,000. Beginning Work-in-Process Inventory on January 1 consisted of only job C12-05, which had incurred the following costs during December of the previous year:

Direct material	$1,400
Direct labor	2,200
Manufacturing overhead applied	3,000
Total	$6,600

So the balance in the Work-in-Process Inventory account on January 1 was $6,600.

Exhibit 3–5

Cost Flows through the
Manufacturing Accounts:
Direct Material

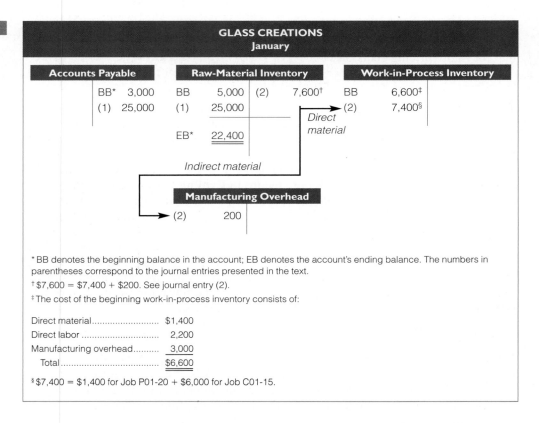

Notice the difference between the Raw-Material Inventory, $5,000, that has not yet been entered into production, and the direct-material component of beginning Work-in-Process Inventory, $1,400. The $1,400 amount has already been sent to production.[2] These beginning balances are shown in Exhibit 3–5. There was no beginning Finished-Goods Inventory on January 1.

Direct material.   In January, Glass Creations purchased $25,000 of raw material. This purchase anticipated the Gulf Coast Aquarium job mentioned in the letter at the beginning of the chapter and was made somewhat early to take advantage of an exceptionally favorable price for glass. This purchase was recorded as follows:

(1)	Raw-Material Inventory	25,000	
	Accounts Payable		25,000

When raw material is needed for a production job, the job supervisor, one of the owners, or one of the other skilled glass workers requisitions it using a **material requisition form.** This is the source document for the entry transferring the cost of a raw material from Raw-Material Inventory to the Work-in-Process Inventory account and to the job-cost record for the production job. No materials were requisitioned for job C12-05 in January. Job P01-20 had requisitions for raw material totaling $1,400 (see Exhibit 3–4). The journal entry to record this transfer of the cost of raw material follows:

(2a)	Work-in-Process Inventory	1,400	
	Raw-Material Inventory		1,400

To record the requisition of raw material and its entry into production.

---

[2] Recall from Chapter 2 the seemingly interchangeable use of the terms "raw material" and "direct material." As noted, the meaning of these terms is different. *Before* materials are entered into the production process, they are called *raw* materials. *After* they enter production, they become either *direct* materials or *indirect* materials. Thus, the cost of raw material *used* equals the direct-material cost plus the indirect-material cost.

Raw material of $6,000 was requisitioned for Job C01-15 and recorded in entry (2b). The raw-material classification is also used for indirect materials and supplies. These costs are not assigned to specific jobs but are charged to the Manufacturing Overhead account. For Glass Creations, the $200 of indirect material requisitioned in January was also recorded in entry (2b), as follows:

Production of stained glass windows by skilled artists is a painstaking job that entails significant direct labor and support services such as purchasing and material handling for the delicate glass pieces.

(2b)   Work-in-Process Inventory........ 6,000
        Manufacturing Overhead   200
           Raw-Material Inventory   6,200

To record direct-material cost of $6,000 assigned to job C01-15 and indirect material costs of $200 charged to Manufacturing Overhead.

Journal entries (2a) and (2b) are combined into one journal entry (journal entry 2) in Exhibit 3–5. Notice that Exhibit 3–5 also includes the ending raw-material inventory, which can be found as follows:

Beginning inventory	+	Purchases	−	Requisitions	=	Ending inventory
$5,000	+	$25,000	−	$7,600	=	$22,400

Direct labor.   Production employees are usually paid an hourly rate and account for their time each day on time records, which now are generally computerized. These records account for the hours spent on each production job during the day. The company's total cost includes the employee's gross pay plus the employer's share of Social Security and employment taxes, the employer's contribution to pension and insurance plans, and any other benefits that the company pays for the employee. In general, these costs range from 15 to 70 percent of the wage rate, depending on a company's benefit plan. Companies generally add their benefit costs to the wage rate when assigning costs to production jobs.

Glass Creations' cost-management analyst recorded accumulated costs of $22,413 for production employees during January. Of the $22,413 total, $16,413 was attributed to direct-labor costs, including employee benefits and taxes. The $16,413 is charged (debited) to Work-in-Process Inventory and assigned to the specific jobs worked on during the period. Based on the time records, the jobs were charged direct-labor costs as follows: job C12-05, $6,000 in January (for 285 direct-labor hours of differing wage rates); job P01-20, $2,413 (for 113 direct-labor hours) as indicated in the job-cost record in Exhibit 3–4; and job C01-15, $8,000 (for 380 direct-labor hours, also of differing wage rates). Since design costs are easily traceable to specific jobs, they are included in direct labor. Moreover, design costs for existing stock windows are minimal.

The remaining $6,000 (of the $22,413 discussed earlier) is indirect labor and is charged to Manufacturing Overhead. Recall from Chapter 2 that indirect labor is the cost of compensating employees such as supervisory, custodial, maintenance, security, and material-handling personnel, as well as idle time and overtime premiums paid to direct-labor employees. Glass Creations is a small firm, of course, and its employees perform a variety of activities. Sometimes an employee works directly on a specific job (classified as direct labor) and sometimes does work unrelated to any particular job, such as general cleanup of the glass studio (classified as indirect labor). This is typical for small companies.

Exhibit 3–6

Cost Flows through the
Manufacturing Accounts:
Direct Labor

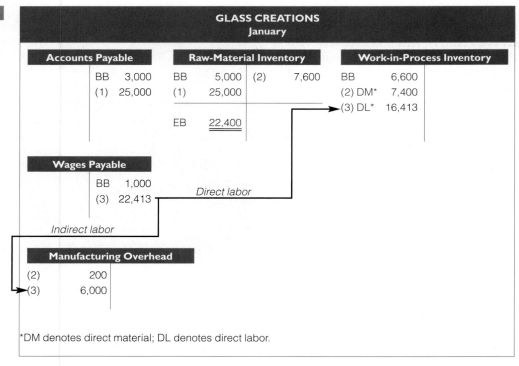

*DM denotes direct material; DL denotes direct labor.

The following entry records Glass Creations' labor costs in January:

(3)   Work-in-Process Inventory..................................... 16,413
       Manufacturing Overhead....................................... 6,000
          Wages Payable 22,413

To record direct-labor costs of $16,413 assigned to production jobs and indirect
labor costs of $6,000 charged to Manufacturing Overhead.

The flow of labor costs through the manufacturing accounts is shown in Exhibit 3–6.

Manufacturing overhead.   Accounting for manufacturing overhead is less straight-forward than for direct labor and direct material. Manufacturing overhead is a hetero-geneous pool of indirect costs. These costs are assigned to individual production jobs based on an overhead rate calculated with respect to a cost driver, such as machine or direct-labor hours.[3] We address the process of establishing this overhead rate in the next section. At this point, however, note that Glass Creations' approach to assigning overhead is the simplest such system possible. We will explore *activity-based costing* (ABC), a more elaborate approach, in Chapter 4. As you will see then, the ABC approach provides more accurate cost information but is also more costly to imple-ment and use.

At Glass Creations, indirect manufacturing costs, including costs such as indirect material, indirect labor, electricity, and insurance, are accumulated in the Manufacturing Overhead account. Glass Creations uses absorption costing, dis-cussed in Chapter 2, so it treats *all* manufacturing overhead (variable and fixed) as a product cost. In large manufacturing companies, each department typically has its own Manufacturing Overhead account so each department manager can be held accountable for that department's overhead costs. This helps top management evalu-

---

[3]The concept of *cost driver* was introduced and defined in Chapter 2 and will be explored in more depth in Chapter 4.

ate how well department managers are managing their overhead and support department costs. Then these departmental overhead accounts are combined into one account, simply called *Manufacturing Overhead.*

In January, Glass Creations charged indirect-material costs of $200 and indirect labor costs of $6,000 to the Manufacturing Overhead account as shown earlier in entries (2) and (3). Utilities and other overhead costs credited to Accounts Payable were $12,000. The $700 portion of prepaid insurance applicable to the period is also included in the actual overhead amount, as is depreciation of $6,000. These items total $18,700 and represent the actual overhead incurred during the period, in addition to indirect material and indirect labor.

The journal entry to record manufacturing overhead follows:

(4)	Manufacturing Overhead	18,700	
	Accounts Payable		12,000
	Prepaid Expenses		700
	Accumulated Depreciation		6,000

To record actual manufacturing overhead costs other than indirect labor and indirect materials.

The entry is labeled (4) in the manufacturing account diagram in Exhibit 3–7.

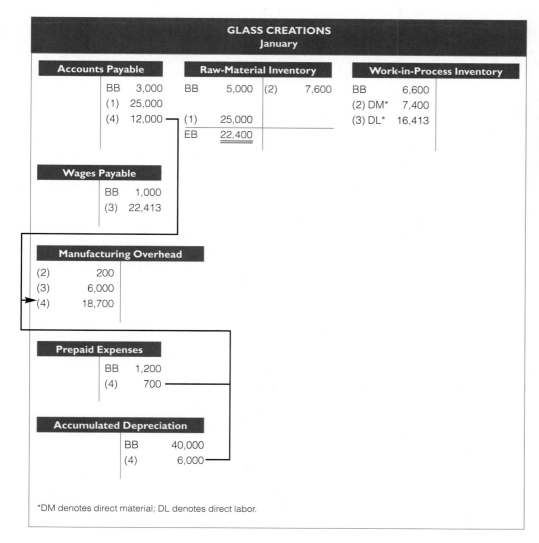

GLASS CREATIONS
January

Accounts Payable	
	BB 3,000
	(1) 25,000
	(4) 12,000

Raw-Material Inventory	
BB 5,000	(2) 7,600
(1) 25,000	
EB 22,400	

Work-in-Process Inventory	
BB 6,600	
(2) DM* 7,400	
(3) DL* 16,413	

Wages Payable	
	BB 1,000
	(3) 22,413

Manufacturing Overhead	
(2) 200	
(3) 6,000	
(4) 18,700	

Prepaid Expenses	
BB 1,200	
(4) 700	

Accumulated Depreciation	
BB 40,000	
(4) 6,000	

*DM denotes direct material; DL denotes direct labor.

Exhibit 3–7

Cost Flows through the Manufacturing Accounts: Manufacturing Overhead

Use of Predetermined Overhead Rates

LO 5 Use a predetermined overhead rate to assign indirect resource costs to production jobs.

Companies have traditionally used predetermined overhead rates to assign manufacturing overhead to individual production jobs. A **predetermined overhead rate** is the budgeted manufacturing overhead divided by the budgeted level of the cost driver. The predetermined overhead rate usually is established before the year in which it is to be used and remains the same for the entire year. By using a predetermined overhead rate, a company *normalizes* (i.e., smooths out) overhead applied to various production jobs. Over time, manufacturing overhead costs can be quite erratic. Preventive maintenance costs often are higher in months when activity is low. Utility costs in cold climates are higher in the winter than in the summer; the opposite is true in warm climates. If *actual* overhead costs were assigned to production jobs, more overhead would be assigned in some months than in other months. In addition, a company might not know its actual overhead costs until the end of an accounting period. Management can prepare financial statements and use product cost data for cost-management and decision-making purposes based on a reliable estimate of product costs by using predetermined overhead rates.

Because predetermined overhead rates *normalize* the application of manufacturing overhead to jobs, the resulting product costs are called "normal costs;" this product costing method is called a *normal costing system*. A **normal costing system** assigns to production jobs the actual cost of direct material, actual cost of direct labor, and applied manufacturing overhead, which is calculated by multiplying the predetermined overhead rate by the actual amount of the cost driver. Predetermined overhead rates can be established by following a five-step approach:

Step 1. *Identify the costs to be included as indirect costs.* Glass Creations has developed a detailed list of cost items included as manufacturing overhead. The total of these costs represents the company's total manufacturing overhead.

Step 2. *Establish the costs for each cost item identified in step 1.* Budgeted (i.e., estimated) annual manufacturing-overhead costs for Glass Creations total $360,000 based on last year's actual manufacturing overhead adjusted for anticipated changes this year. (We discuss the budgeting process in detail in Chapter 15.)

Step 3. *Select the cost driver(s).* Operating personnel at Glass Creations have determined that the number of direct-labor hours is the best cost driver to use for manufacturing overhead costs. That is, manufacturing overhead costs are highly correlated with the number of direct-labor hours used.

Glass Creations uses only a single, volume-related cost driver for its overhead application. Activity-based costing uses multiple cost drivers to assign indirect production costs to products (as well as other cost objects; see Chapter 4). This approach results in much more accurate cost assignments but is also considerably more costly to implement and use.

Step 4. *Estimate the amount of the cost-driver rate.* Glass Creations' practical production capacity, given its artistic talent and size, is estimated to be 12,000 direct-labor hours during the year. ("Practical capacity" refers to the level of activity that can reasonably be expected under normal operating conditions, allowing for scheduled machine maintenance.)

To be most useful for describing resource supply and usage, the quantity estimate of the cost driver should be based on the practical capacity of the firm's resources to perform activities. Manufacturing firms often have more objective data on machine-based process capacities, but their estimates of human-based process capacities can be quite subjective. "Subjective" does not mean random, capricious, or useless, however, but based on sound judgment and experience. These decisions are better than random guesses or making decisions based on no information. Glass Creations' estimates are based on experience, but they still could be the least objective data in this product-costing analysis. This subjectivity is common in many companies, particularly small ones.

Step 5.   *Compute the predetermined overhead rate.* This calculation follows:

$$\text{Predetermined overhead rate} = \frac{\text{Budgeted manufacturing overhead for the year}}{\text{Budgeted direct-labor hours for the year}}$$

$$= \frac{\$360,000}{12,000 \text{ direct-labor hours}} = \$30 \text{ per direct-labor hour}$$

In January, Glass Creations used its predetermined overhead rate to apply manufacturing overhead to individual production jobs as follows:

	Actual Direct-Labor Hours (DLH) Used in January		Predetermined Overhead Rate		Manufacturing Overhead Applied
Job C12-05	285	×	$30 per DLH	=	$ 8,550
Job P01-20	113	×	$30 per DLH	=	3,390
Job C01-15	380	×	$30 per DLH	=	11,400
Total	778		$30 per DLH	=	$23,340

Glass Creations' entry to record the application of manufacturing overhead to jobs using the predetermined overhead rate follows. The flow of these applied overhead costs through the manufacturing accounts is illustrated in Exhibit 3–8.

(5)	Work-in-Process Inventory	23,340	
	Manufacturing Overhead		23,340
	To record the application of manufacturing overhead to production jobs.		

Limitation of direct labor as a cost driver.   In traditional product-costing systems, like the one used by Glass Creations, the most common volume-related cost drivers are direct-labor hours and direct-labor cost. However, there is a trend away from using direct labor as the overhead application base. Many production processes are becoming increasingly automated through the use of robotics and computer-integrated manufacturing systems. Increased automation brings two results. First, manufacturing-overhead costs represent a larger proportion of total production costs. Second, direct labor decreases in importance as a productive input. As direct labor declines in importance as a productive input, it becomes less appropriate as a cost driver. For this reason, many firms have switched to machine hours, process time, or throughput time as cost drivers that better reflect the pattern of overhead cost incurrence. **Throughput (or cycle) time** is the average time required to convert raw materials into finished goods ready to be shipped to customers. It includes the time required for activities such as material handling, production processing, inspecting, and packaging.

Many companies not only have moved away from direct labor as a cost driver but also have abandoned the idea of using *any* single, volume-related cost driver. Many of them use multiple, departmental predetermined overhead rates. For example, a manufacturer's assembly department might use direct-labor hours as a cost driver, its machining department might use machine hours, and its material-handling department might use pounds of raw material moved. Still other organizations have adopted activity-based costing (ABC), which identifies the key activities they engage in and uses multiple cost drivers associated with these activities. ABC is the topic of Chapter 4.

For Glass Creations' simple, labor-intensive production process, direct labor is probably an appropriate cost driver, particularly when viewed from a cost-benefit perspective. The benefits associated with the increased information accuracy from a more elaborate product-costing system would not likely exceed the additional costs to generate the information for a company such as Glass Creations.

Manufacturing overhead account: A summary.   Exhibit 3–9 summarizes the accounting procedures used for manufacturing overhead. The left side of the Manufacturing Overhead account accumulates *actual overhead* costs as they are incurred throughout the accounting period. The actual costs incurred for indirect material, indirect labor, factory and equipment depreciation, utilities, property taxes, and insurance are recorded as additions to the left (debit) side of the account.

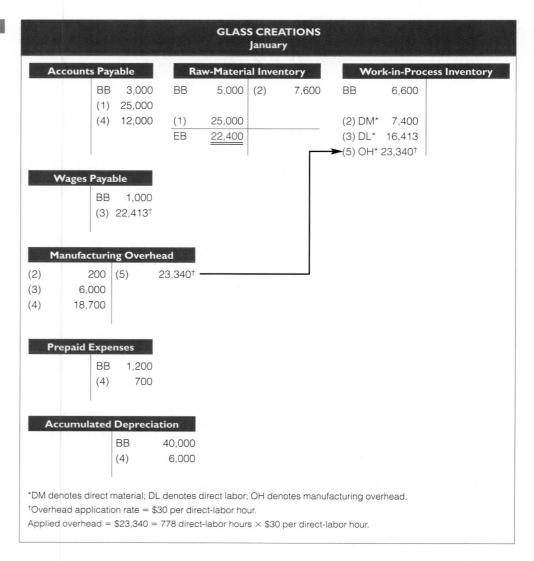

Exhibit 3–8

Cost Flows through the Manufacturing Accounts: Actual and Applied Manufacturing Overhead

The right (credit) side of the Manufacturing Overhead account is used to record *overhead applied* to Work-in-Process Inventory.

The left side of the Manufacturing Overhead account accumulates *actual* overhead costs, and the right side *applies* overhead costs using the predetermined overhead rate, which is based on *estimated* overhead costs. The estimates used to calculate the predetermined overhead rate generally prove to be incorrect to some degree. Consequently, a nonzero balance (usually relatively small) generally is left in the Manufacturing Overhead account at year-end; its disposition is covered later in the chapter.

Transfers to Finished-Goods Inventory.   When jobs are transferred from production to finished goods, an entry is made to transfer the costs of the jobs from the Work-in-Process Inventory account to the Finished-Goods Inventory account. For example, Glass Creations completed jobs C12-05 and P01-20 in January and transferred them to finished-goods inventory. The journal entry is as follows:

(6)	Finished-Goods Inventory.................................	28,353	
	Work-in-Process Inventory		28,353

To transfer completed jobs to finished-goods ($21,150 for job C12-05 and $7,203 for job P01-20, as shown in the job cost record in Exhibit 3–4).

Notice that the amount transferred includes costs incurred in both the current and previous periods. For example, the transfer for job C12-05 includes $6,600 from

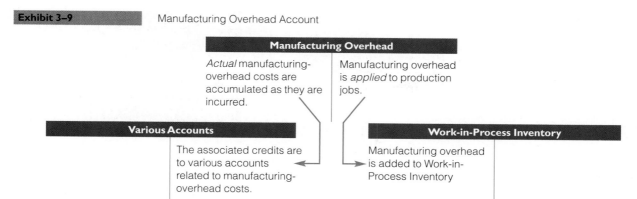

Exhibit 3–9   Manufacturing Overhead Account

beginning Work-in-Process Inventory and $14,550 of costs incurred in January to complete the job ($6,000 of direct labor and $8,550 of applied overhead, which was computed as 285 direct-labor hours to finish the job in January × $30 per direct-labor hour).

Transfers to Cost of Goods Sold.   When finished goods are sold, their production cost is transferred from Finished-Goods Inventory to Cost of Goods Sold, which is an expense account. For example, Glass Creations sold job C12-05 in January for a total of $33,000, the commissioned price for this custom job. The profit on this job, $11,850, although enormous relative to the job cost of $21,150, is not far out of line for high-end, commissioned works of art. Nevertheless, this is one of Glass Creations' most profitable jobs ever. The journal entries recording this transaction are as follows:

(7)	Cost of Goods Sold	21,150	
	Finished-Goods Inventory		21,150
	Accounts Receivable	33,000	
	Sales Revenue		33,000

To transfer finished-goods inventory to cost of goods sold and to record the corresponding sales revenue. [*Note:* Job C12-05 was the only one sold in January.]

Overhead variance.   The Manufacturing Overhead account is a temporary account, so it is "closed" at the end of an accounting period. *Closing* an account means that its balance is transferred to some other account, leaving a zero balance in the closed account at the end of the accounting period. You might recall from your study of financial accounting that this is the way that revenue and expense accounts are treated. That is, they are closed to the Income Summary account at the end of the accounting period, which leaves them with a zero balance. Usually this closing process is not performed until the end of the year when the books are closed. For illustrative purposes, however, let's assume that Glass Creations closes its Manufacturing Overhead account each month.

   Applied overhead, calculated by multiplying the predetermined overhead rate by the actual amount of the cost driver, is the amount of manufacturing overhead assigned to Work-in-Process Inventory as a product cost. **Actual overhead** is the amount of manufacturing overhead actually incurred during an accounting period. Under normal costing, the *actual* manufacturing overhead (recorded in the left side of the Manufacturing Overhead account) is unlikely to equal the amount of overhead *applied* (based on budgeted overhead and recorded on the right side of the account). The difference between the applied-overhead and the actual overhead amounts is the **overhead variance.** When actual overhead exceeds applied overhead, we say that overhead was *underapplied,* and the amount of the overhead variance equals **underapplied overhead.** In the opposite case, the variance equals **overapplied overhead.**

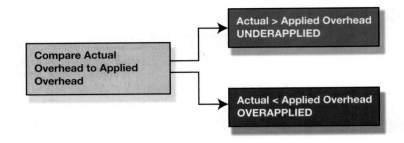

During January, Glass Creations credited $23,340 to Manufacturing Overhead (as *applied* manufacturing overhead, based on the budget), and debited $24,900 to Manufacturing Overhead (*actual* overhead).[4] The $1,560 difference is the *overhead variance,* in this case *underapplied overhead.* We explain the process used to dispose of (i.e., close) this overhead variance later in the chapter.

What does it mean to say that Glass Creations has *underapplied* overhead in January? Recall that it applies overhead at the predetermined rate of $30 per direct-labor hour based on *budgeted* manufacturing overhead and *budgeted* direct-labor hours for the year. Since these are *estimates,* they typically are inaccurate, at least to some extent. To say that Glass Creations underapplied overhead in January means that the pre-determined rate of $30 per direct-labor hour proved to be too low to apply enough overhead to Work-in-Process Inventory to equal January's actual manufacturing-overhead cost of $24,900. Thus, $24,900 in overhead costs were actually incurred in January, but only $23,340 was applied. Hence, the term "underapplied overhead." In most instances, these underapplied or overapplied amounts tend to be relatively small and, thus, usually do not reflect gross inaccuracies in the predetermined overhead rate.

How to report the manufacturing overhead variance to management.   At year-end the manufacturing overhead variance is either (1) closed to Cost of Goods Sold, or (2) prorated (i.e., allocated) to Work-in-Process Inventory, Finished-Goods Inventory, and Cost of Goods Sold. Thus, **proration** of the overhead variance assigns proportionate amounts of it to Work-in-Process Inventory, Finished-Goods Inventory, and Cost of Goods Sold. The Excel spreadsheet in Exhibit 3–10 recaps the costs of January's three production jobs before proration.

Method 1: Prorate the overhead variance.   If the variance is prorated to Work-in-Process Inventory, Finished-Goods Inventory, and Cost of Goods Sold, the cost of each job is adjusted to approximate its actual cost. The status and cost of each of Glass Creations' jobs before prorating the overhead variance are shown in Exhibit 3–10. The variance is prorated so that each account and job bear a share of the $1,560 manufacturing-overhead variance. This share is proportional to the overhead applied to the account during the month as shown in the Excel spreadsheet in Exhibit 3–11.

---

[4] Applied overhead:

$23,340 = 778 direct-labor hours used in January × $30 per direct-labor hour

Actual overhead:

Indirect material	$ 200
Indirect labor	6,000
Insurance	700
Depreciation	6,000
Utilities and other overhead	12,000
Total..	$24,900

X Microsoft Excel - Exhibit 3-10.xls

File Edit View Insert Format Tools Data Window Help

F11   = =+SUM(F8:F10)

Costs of Jobs Before Prorating the Manufacturing Overhead Variance

Job No.	Beginning Inventory, January 1	Direct Material	Direct Labor	Manufacturing Overhead Applied in January	Charged To Job	Status of Job at End of Month
C12-05	$6,600	$ -	$6,000	$8,550	$21,150	Cost of Goods Sold
P01-20		1,400	2,413	3,390	7,203	Finished-Goods Inventory
C01-15		6,000	8,000	11,400	25,400	Work-in-Process Inventory
Total	$6,600	$7,400	$16,413	$23,340	$53,753	

Sheet2 Sheet3 Sheet4 Sheet5 **Sheet6** Sheet7

Ready

Exhibit 3-10

Glass Creations: Cost of Jobs Before Prorating the Manufacturing Overhead Variance

X Microsoft Excel - Exhibit 3-11.xls

File Edit View Insert Format Tools Data Window Help

H12   = =SUM(H9:H11)

Prorating the Overhead Variance

Job No.	Account	Manufacturing Overhead Applied in January[a]	Percentage of Total Overhead Applied in January[b]		Overhead Variance to be Prorated		Prorated Variance[c]
C12-05	Cost of Goods Sold	$8,550	36.63%	x	$1,560	=	$ 571.43
P01-20	Finished-Goods Inventory	3,390	14.52%	x	1,560	=	226.51
C01-15	Work-in-Process Inventory	11,400	48.85%	x	1,560	=	762.06
Total		$23,340	100.00%				$ 1,560.00

[a]From Exhibit 3-10.

[b]Column C amount / $23,340; rounded. For example, the formula for cell D9 is as follows: C9 / 23,340

[c]Rounded to nearest cent.

Sheet2 Sheet3 Sheet4 Sheet5 Sheet6 **Sheet7**

Ready

Exhibit 3-11

Glass Creations: Prorating the Overhead Variance

The following entry prorates the overhead variance and closes the Manufacturing Overhead account at the end of January.

Cost of Goods Sold	571.43	
Finished-Goods Inventory	226.51	
Work-in-Process Inventory	762.06	
Manufacturing Overhead		1,560.00

A small number of firms that are required to do so under the rules specified by the *Cost Accounting Standards Board (CASB)* prorate the overhead variance. This federal agency was chartered by Congress in 1970 to develop cost-accounting standards for large government contractors. Congress discontinued the agency in 1980 and recreated it in 1990. Its standards apply to significant government contracts and have the force of federal law.

Method 2: Close the overhead variance to Cost of Goods Sold.   Most companies, including Glass Creations, do not prorate the manufacturing-overhead variance to Work-in-Process Inventory, Finished-Goods Inventory, and Cost of Goods Sold, but close the entire variance to Cost of Goods Sold as in the following journal entry:

Cost of Goods Sold	1,560	
Manufacturing Overhead		1,560

In a company with many types of products and inventories, proration can be complicated. If the amounts to be prorated are immaterial relative to operating income or do not affect managerial decisions, proration might not be necessary. The difference in net income between prorating the variance and assigning it to Cost of Goods Sold is a matter of timing. Any difference between actual and applied overhead eventually is expensed, even if a company prorates. Prorating the overhead variance merely defers expensing the portion allocated to Work-in-Process and Finished-Goods Inventory until the products are sold. For managerial purposes, one must ask how useful it is to revalue work-in-process and finished-goods inventories to their actual cost. A large overhead variance could affect some cost-management, performance-evaluation, pricing, and other decisions, but if the variance is small, proration is probably not worthwhile.

However the variance is disposed of, the key managerial issue is to understand the causes of the difference between actual and applied overhead. Management might need to revise overhead rates, impose new cost-management procedures, or take other action.

Summary of Job-Cost Flows

The flow of all manufacturing costs from purchasing raw materials to selling the finished product appears in Exhibit 3–12. Notice that Glass Creations' schedule of cost of goods manufactured and sold (Exhibit 3–13) presents the data from the manufacturing accounts in Exhibit 3–12. It might be helpful to cross-reference each item in the schedule in Exhibit 3–13 to the accounts in Exhibit 3–12. Exhibit 3–13 also presents Glass Creations' income statement for January.

Selling and Administrative Costs

Selling and administrative costs do not flow through the inventory accounts because they are period costs, not product costs, and are expensed during the period incurred. Glass Creations' selling and administrative expenses (all on account) amounted to $8,000 in January. The entry to record these expenses follows:

Selling and Administrative Expenses	8,000	
Accounts Payable		8,000
To record selling and administrative expenses incurred in January.		

Notice that these expenses appear on the income statement in Exhibit 3–13.

Meaning of the Overhead Variance

The $1,560 manufacturing-overhead variance discussed in the preceding section appears in the schedule of cost of goods manufactured and sold in Exhibit 3–13 as underapplied manufacturing overhead. As explained in the preceding section, a common method for disposing of the overhead variance is to close it to Cost of Goods Sold. Glass Creations uses this method, and the result of closing January's underapplied overhead amount of $1,560 is to adjust Cost of Goods Sold upward by $1,560, as shown in Exhibit 3–13.

Why does actual overhead typically differ from applied overhead? Remember that applied overhead is based on a predetermined overhead rate based on budgeted amounts for both manufacturing overhead and the cost driver (in this case, direct-

Exhibit 3–12   Summary of Job Costs

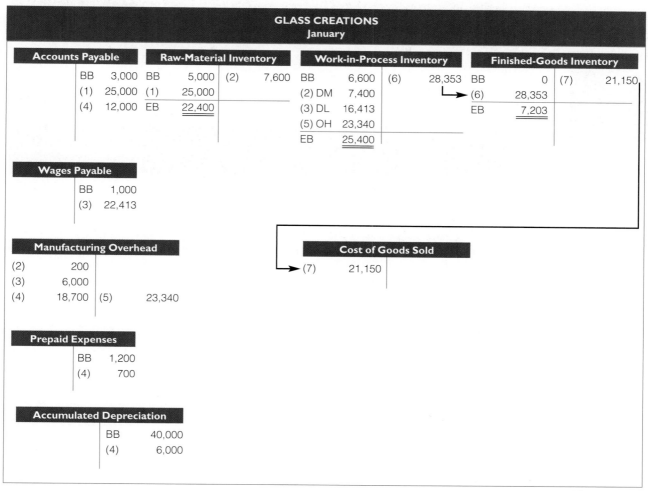

GLASS CREATIONS
January

Accounts Payable			Raw-Material Inventory				Work-in-Process Inventory				Finished-Goods Inventory			
BB	3,000	BB	5,000	(2)	7,600	BB	6,600	(6)	28,353	BB	0	(7)	21,150
(1)	25,000	(1)	25,000			(2) DM	7,400			(6)	28,353		
(4)	12,000	EB	22,400			(3) DL	16,413			EB	7,203		
						(5) OH	23,340						
						EB	25,400						

Wages Payable	
BB	1,000
(3)	22,413

Manufacturing Overhead					Cost of Goods Sold	
(2)	200				(7)	21,150
(3)	6,000					
(4)	18,700	(5)	23,340			

Prepaid Expenses	
BB	1,200
(4)	700

Accumulated Depreciation	
BB	40,000
(4)	6,000

labor hours) using the five-step approach outlined earlier to establish the predetermined rate. Glass Creations *budgeted* $360,000 of total manufacturing overhead costs and 12,000 direct-labor hours. Thus, for every direct-labor hour used, $30 in manufacturing overhead is *applied* to Work-in-Process Inventory. Since this application of overhead is based on budgeted amounts, applied overhead typically does not equal actual overhead during any accounting period (unless, of course, the budgeted amounts happen to be the same as the actual amounts).

Difference between Actual, Normal, and Standard Costing

Suppose that Glass Creations had used actual overhead costs rather than a predetermined overhead rate to compute job costs. Then management would have waited until the actual overhead costs were known and then assigned them to jobs based on the actual number of direct-labor hours worked. At the end of January, management would know that the actual overhead cost amounted to $24,900 and would assign this cost to jobs based on the actual direct-labor hours (DLH) worked on each job, as follows:

LO 6 Explain how to measure production costs under actual, normal, and standard costing systems.

$$\frac{\text{Actual manufacturing overhead costs}}{\text{Actual direct-labor hours used}} = \frac{\$24,900}{778 \text{ DLH}} = \$32.01 \text{ per DLH*}$$

*Rounded

GLASS CREATIONS **Income Statement** For the Month of January		
Sales revenue		$33,000
Less: Cost of goods sold (see following schedule)		22,710
Gross margin		$10,290
Less: Selling and administrative expenses.....................................		8,000
Operating income		$ 2,290

GLASS CREATIONS **Schedule of Cost of Goods Manufactured and Sold** For the Month of January			
Beginning work-in-process inventory, January 1			$ 6,600
Manufacturing costs during the month:			
Direct material:			
Beginning raw-material inventory, January 1...........................	$ 5,000		
Add: Purchases	25,000		
Raw material available for use	$30,000		
Less: Ending raw-material inventory, January 31	22,400		
Total raw material used	$ 7,600		
Less: Indirect material used...	200		
Direct material entered into production		$ 7,400	
Direct labor		16,413	
Manufacturing overhead applied		23,340	
Total manufacturing costs incurred			47,153
Total cost of work in process...			$53,753
Less: Work-in-process inventory, January 31			25,400
Cost of goods manufactured..			$28,353
Add: Beginning finished-goods inventory January 1			0
Less: Ending finished-goods inventory, January 31			7,203
Cost of goods sold (unadjusted)..			$21,150
Add: Underapplied overhead*			1,560
Cost of goods sold (adjusted for underapplied overhead)			$22,710

*Glass Creations closes underapplied or overapplied overhead to Cost of Goods Sold.

The actual manufacturing overhead applied to each job in January is computed as follows:

	Direct-Labor Hours Used		Actual Overhead Rate		Manufacturing Overhead Applied
Job C12-05	285	×	$32.01	=	$ 9,122.85
Job P01-20.....................................	113	×	32.01	=	3,617.13
Job C01-15	380	×	32.01	=	12,163.80
Total	778	×	32.01	=	$ 24,903.78*

*Differs from the actual overhead amount of $24,900 because of rounding error in the $32.01 rate.

Actual costing assigns only the actual costs of both direct and indirect resources (i.e., direct material, direct labor, and manufacturing overhead) to the products. **Standard costing** uses a predetermined (or standard) rate for both direct and indirect costs to assign manufacturing costs to products. (Compare this to the normal-costing approach used by Glass Creations, which uses a predetermined rate for indirect costs only.) The following display compares actual, normal, and standard costing.

	Actual Costing	**Normal Costing**	**Standard Costing**
Direct costs	Actual rate × Actual inputs	Actual rate × Actual inputs	Predetermined rate × Standard allowed inputs
Indirect costs	Actual rate × Actual inputs	Predetermined rate × Actual inputs	Predetermined rate × Standard allowed inputs

To summarize, organizations can choose among these three methods for assigning costs to production jobs. They may use *actual costing,* which assigns direct-resource costs to jobs as they are used and assigns the costs of indirect resources when the actual amounts spent on these resources are known, usually at the end of each accounting period. The advantage to actual costing is that the measurement of job costs is accurate. The disadvantage is that the cost information is not timely since it is available only at the end of the accounting period.

When organizations need continuous or interim cost reports or early warning information on the cost status of jobs, they use *standard* or *normal costing,* which assign indirect resource costs as they are used before the amounts actually spent are known. Thus, standard and normal costing require the use of *estimates* of cost-driver rates.

Normal costing bases cost-driver rates on past spending for indirect resources and could be appropriate when business conditions are relatively stable. However, even under stable conditions, spending for indirect resources can vary from one period to the next. For example, preventive maintenance activities often are higher in months when activity is low. By using average resource spending, a company normalizes the costs of work in different periods. Organizations that use normal costing expect differences between average (i.e., normalized) and actual resource spending to average out over time. Companies engaged in cost-plus contracts often use normal costing, including The Boeing Company and Rockwell International, which use it for their government defense-contract work.

An advantage of the standard-costing system, in addition to relatively stable product costs, is that the standard cost provides a benchmark against which the actual production cost can be compared. The resulting variances between actual and standard costs provide valuable cost-management information to use in controlling costs. Many manufacturing companies use standard-costing systems as a cost-management tool. (Chapters 16 and 17 discuss standard costing and cost variance analysis in detail.)

Normal Costing and Predetermined Overhead Rates

You're the Decision Maker 3.1

Suppose that Glass Creations computed its predetermined overhead rate on a quarterly basis instead of annually. The following projections have been made for the year:

	Estimated Manufacturing Overhead	Estimated Direct-Labor Hours	Quarterly Predetermined Overhead Rate
First quarter	$ 50,000	2,000	?
Second quarter	122,500	3,500	?
Third quarter	100,000	4,000	?
Fourth quarter	87,500	2,500	?
Total	$360,000	12,000	

One of Glass Creations' most popular products, the blue heron window, requires the following *direct* inputs:

Direct material	$100 per unit
Direct labor (@$22 per hour)	5 hrs per unit
Direct labor (@$15 per hour)	1 hr per unit

a. Calculate the quarterly predetermined overhead rate for each quarter.

b. Determine the cost of one blue heron window if it is manufactured in February versus October.

c. Suppose that the company's pricing policy calls for a 20 percent markup over cost. Calculate the price to charge for one blue heron window in February versus October.

d. Calculate the predetermined overhead rate if it is calculated annually.

e. Based on your answer to part (d), what is the cost per unit if it is manufactured in February? In October?

f. What is the price per heron window if the predetermined overhead rate is calculated annually?

g. What do you recommend to Glass Creations for its product costing system? Quarterly or annual predetermined overhead rates? Explain.

(Solutions begin on page 117.)

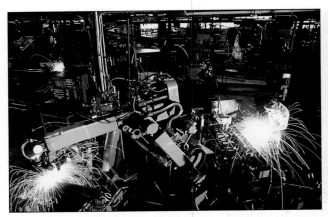

Deere and Company carefully tracks the costs of the resources used to manufacture its equipment.

In the health care industry, patient cases are similar to "jobs" in that treatment costs are carefully tracked by patient and by diagnosis.

Choice of Cost Driver for Overhead Application

Our illustration used direct-labor hours as the cost driver to apply overhead to jobs at Glass Creations. Organizations use a variety of cost drivers to apply overhead to products, including the number of machine hours, the number of direct-labor hours, and the amount of direct-labor cost on each job. The choice of cost drivers for applying overhead is an important and complex topic and is discussed in more detail in Chapter 4.

Job-Order Costing in Service Organizations

LO 7 Discuss the role of job-order costing in service organizations.

Job operations frequently are used in service organizations, such as architectural firms, consulting firms, moving companies, and consulting firms. The job-order costing process is basically the same in both service and manufacturing organizations except that service firms generally use fewer direct materials than manufacturing firms do.

An architectural firm, for example, is very interested in the profitability of each job (referred to as a "client"). Bids to obtain or retain a client typically are based on projected costs estimated using actual results for comparable jobs. Job-order costing, therefore, provides management the information necessary to assess job profitability and to use historical cost data to estimate costs for bidding purposes. (Many firms use an even more sophisticated approach, called *customer profitability analysis* to assess the profitability of each customer or client; see Chapter 6).

Application of Job-Order Costing to the Value Chain

Glass Creations' value chain, shown in Exhibit 3–14, includes its important business functions of design, purchasing and material handling, production, marketing, distribution, and customer service. (The value chain for most manufacturers begins with research and development, but this is not a relevant function for Glass Creations.) Notice that the *design* and *production* components are highlighted to reflect the fact that the design and creation (or production) of stained glass and other artistic glass pieces are the primary functions of Glass Creations. These two functions, above all others, distinguish it from its competitors. Nevertheless, the other functions in the value chain are not completely unimportant. Securing the stained glass and channeled lead strips used to create each piece is important, too. Finding the right sources of supply at the best possible prices is a key element in helping Glass Creations to be profitable. Marketing the studio's windows, doors, and other artistic pieces is important as well. The firm has done limited advertising but doing more is being considered as competition in the business increases. Distribution channels are similarly

Exhibit 3–14

Glass Creations' Value
Chain

important for Glass Creations. The studio relies on arts festivals, builders' catalogues, and their own website as its primary distribution channels. Customer service is not a major element of Glass Creations' value chain because problems with the studio's glass pieces after they are sold or installed are rare. For most companies, however, this is a key element of the value chain. Think, for example, about your last automobile purchase. Have you been satisfied with the dealership's service department? If not, would that affect your next automobile purchase decision?

Now what, you might ask, does this discussion have to do with job-order costing? The point is that traditional product-costing systems, and job-order costing systems in particular, have tended to emphasize the production component of the value chain to the relative exclusion of the other components. Most of our discussion of Glass Creations' job-order costing system focused on the actual production costs for its stained glass pieces. Little was said about measuring or managing the costs of design, purchasing, marketing, and so forth, yet all of these functions are important contributors to the firm's profitability.

What is needed to overcome this deficiency is a broader focus on *all* of the *activities* in the organization's value chain. Then the costing system can be built on those activities by measuring the costs of the resources they use and associating those costs with various cost objects, including the organization's product or service output. Activity-based costing (covered in Chapter 4) is better suited to this value-chain perspective than are traditional approaches to product costing like Glass Creations' system.

Supply Chain Management

A key aspect of optimizing a company's value chain is *supply chain management.* An organization's *supply chain* is the flow of all goods, services, and information into and out of the organization. Two examples of the way companies manage their supply chains to reduce costs and improve services follow.

Procter & Gamble (P&G) saved its retail customers more than $65 million over an 18-month period, primarily by using an automatic replenishment program to collaborate with retailers about restocking their inventories. The program "helps P&G achieve greater integration within its operations, and closer customer linkages have enhanced trade relations."

"Cambell Soup uses an automatic replenishment program (ARP) to ship products from its manufacturing plant warehouses to retailer distribution centers from which stores are restocked. Every weekday morning retail customers send their current inventory positions and sales data to Campbell Soup via electronic data interchange (EDI). Based on this information, Campbell Soup then sends out resupply shipments to the retail distribution centers." *Source: Noah P. Barsky and Alexander E. Ellinger, "Unleashing the Value in the Supply Chain." (Full citations to references are in the Bibliography.)*

Cost Management in Practice 3.1

Job and Project Management

Managing jobs and projects requires attention to quality, customer satisfaction, costs, and adherence to schedules. When jobs fall behind schedule or costs become higher than expected, some individuals might be tempted to compromise quality or even to cheat. Neither behavior is usually successful for, in the long run, reputations for quality and honesty generate more opportunities than shortsighted opportunism does. This section discusses the methods for tracking and ensuring successful project management and the aspects of behavior sometimes associated with jobs.

LO 8 Understand how companies manage long-term projects and their costs.

Exhibit 3–15

Project Percentage of
Completion Charts

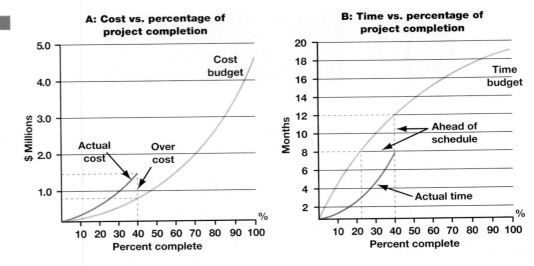

Project Management

Complex jobs (for example, bridges, shopping centers, and complicated lawsuits) often take months or years to complete and require the work of many different departments, divisions, or subcontractors. These projects, unlike short jobs that can be evaluated relatively quickly (typically within a reporting period), are more difficult to evaluate. Consider the job of painting a small house. The painter might estimate the costs and bid on the job accordingly. A week later, when the job is complete, the painter can compare estimated costs to actual costs and evaluate the job's profitability. In contrast, consider a contractor building a hospital, which will take more than two years to complete. The contractor must find a way not only to bid on the project but also to evaluate it at critical intervals to update and anticipate the cost and timing changes.

Project cost and time budgets.   The contractor of a long-term project must first establish a budget of costs to be incurred throughout the project at various stages of completion. The stage of completion usually appears in reports as a percentage of completion for the entire project or as the completion of certain critical steps in the project. Then, as the project progresses, the contractor evaluates two critical areas: (1) the budgeted cost of work completed to date versus the actual cost of work completed to date and (2) the budgeted percentage or stage of completion since the project began versus the actual percentage or stage of completion. The two graphs in Exhibit 3–15 are examples of useful information for evaluating the progress of project costs and schedules.

Exhibit 3–15 shows that the project is 40 percent complete (the horizontal axes of panels A and B). The budget line indicates that, for this stage of completion, costs should be $ .9 million, as shown in panel A. The actual cost line indicates, however, that actual costs were $1.4 million. Thus, at the 40 percent stage of completion, the project has a cost overrun of $500,000.

Although we know that cost overruns have occurred, we do not know whether the project is on schedule. Panel B of Exhibit 3–15 shows that the project should be 23 percent complete by month 8. Because the contractor is 40 percent complete by month 8, the project is approximately four months ahead of schedule. The trade-off of earlier completion for a higher cost might be acceptable to the customer. Given the complex nature of projects, however, revising budgeted costs and budgeted percentages or stages of completion throughout the project to reflect these changes might be desirable. (Most major projects require changes due to their inherent uncertainty.) Thus, the graphs in Exhibit 3–15 need updating to reflect revised cost and time budgets to allow managers to evaluate the project by comparing actual results against the revised budget, which reflects current expectations.

Exhibit 3–16 Gantt Chart for Building a Custom Home

Job RR6—Gantt Chart

		May				June				July				August				Sept.				Oct.				Nov.			
Weeks from start		1	2	3	4	5	6	7	8	9	10	11	12	13	14	15	16	17	18	19	20	21	22	23	24	25	26	27	28
Major activity																													
1. Testing and permits	Plan																												
	Actual																												
2. Excavation	Plan																												
	Actual																												
3. Utilities	Plan																												
	Actual																												
4. Concrete	Plan																												
	Actual																												
5. Framing	Plan																												
	Actual																												
6. Mechanical	Plan																												
	Actual																												
7. Masonry	Plan																												
	Actual																												
8. Finish	Plan																												
	Actual																												

Project scheduling.   Many companies engaged in large, complex projects use a project scheduling aid called a **"Gantt chart"** (named after its developer, Henry Gantt). A **Gantt chart** depicts the stages required to complete a project and the sequence in which the stages are to be performed. A Gantt chart for building a custom home is shown in Exhibit 3–16; it shows the eight major construction activities (corresponding to the home builder's job-costing system) and reflects planned and actual start-and-finish dates by week for the project's duration. The colored bars describe the original building plan by each activity. For example, the builder planned to start the permitting process in the first week of May and complete that activity by the end of the third week. The actual completion of each activity is shown in the gray bars below the plan. As shown, the permitting activity took two weeks longer than expected, which delayed excavation because it could not commence without the proper permits. Because many building activities are sequential, the permitting delay affected the entire building plan. The chart shows that the project finished only one week later than planned. More important, the builder was able to notify the customer about the delay early and to manage the building process so that only a week was lost. The Gantt chart allowed the builder to visualize what to expect and what to modify over the life of the project soon enough to favorably affect its cost and timing.

Job-Cost and Project Improprieties: An Ethical Issue

Organizations occasionally have been criticized for improprieties in assigning costs to jobs, in some cases resulting in criminal proceedings, ruined careers, large fines, or prison terms. For example, major defense contractors have been caught overstating the cost of their jobs. Several universities have overstated the costs of research projects (which are jobs for costing purposes) to be reimbursed by the government. Improprieties in job costing generally result from one or more of the following actions: misstating the stage of completion, charging costs to the wrong jobs or categories, or simply misrepresenting the cost.

Misstating the stage of completion.   Management needs to know the stage of completion of projects to evaluate performance and control costs. If the expenditures on a job are 90 percent of the amount budgeted but the job is only 70 percent complete, management needs to know as soon as possible that the job will require higher costs than estimated. Job supervisors who report the stage of completion of their jobs are in positions to affect managers' decisions based on how realistic the supervisors' estimates are. Some contracts allow for partial payments to contractors based on the percentage of the project's completion. An unethical contractor might overstate the actual percentage of completion to receive unauthorized payments.

Charging costs to the wrong job.   To avoid the appearance of cost overruns on a specific job, supervisors sometimes are tempted to encourage employees to charge its costs to other jobs that are not in danger of cost overruns. At a minimum, this practice misleads managers who rely on accurate cost information for pricing, cost control, and other decisions. It also can cheat the organization or people paying for a job on a cost-plus-a-fee basis if the actual job costs based on resource usage do not total as much as claimed.

Misrepresenting the cost of a job.   What about the problem of misrepresenting the actual costs of a job? Sometimes managers know a job's correct costs but intentionally deceive a customer to obtain a higher payment. Sometimes deceiving a banker to obtain a larger loan for the job by overstating its expected cost is possible. One way to combat these potential problems is to insist on audits of the job's financial records to avoid such deception. Government auditors generally work on-site at defense contractors, universities, and other organizations that have large government contracts.

Preventing improprieties by understanding contracts.   Intentional misrepresentation is not the same as agreeing to a contract that is favorable to your interests. Contracts and agreements for jobs usually result from negotiating and bargaining, and each side strives for favorable terms. Naivete in contracting could be the cause of disappointment (and learning the hard way), but lack of understanding of terms and conditions is not usually grounds to recover damages or nullify contracts.

Especially in the context of job-order costing, it is important for parties who agree to the terms for reimbursement of job costs that the definition of costs and method of tracing them are clearly described. For example, agreeing to reimburse a contractor for simply "the costs of construction" is unwise without clarifying the nature and scope of eligible costs. With that liberal terminology, one would expect the contractor to interpret the costs of construction broadly. This might be acceptable to both parties, but getting a clear agreement before signing is wise. In fact, references to "cost" as a basis for reimbursement, performance, or allocations of profit should be clarified for any contract or agreement. For example, a general partner might sell limited partnerships to others who share the profits of the partnership after the general partner's costs have been covered. Without clarification about what costs are allowed to be charged to the partnership, the general partner could be tempted to allocate as many costs as possible from his or her related activities to it.

Most project contractors have learned over the years that it is far better for the job, the customer, and their reputation if:

- The contractor and the customer clearly agree on what the project's contract covers and what it does not.
- Both parties agree to all changes before the contractor executes them.
- Both parties resolve disputes amicably and without resort to legal proceedings if at all possible.

These stipulations are not always attainable, which is why contractors and sophisticated customers have capable lawyers.

Exhibit 3–17									

Excerpt from Cost and Profit Table

	Direct Material		Direct Labor		Manufacturing Overhead		Profit	
Job No.	*Estimate*	**Actual**	*Estimate*	**Actual**	*Estimate*	**Applied**	*Estimate*	**Actual**
C12-05	$1,520	$1,400	$7,900	$8,200	$11,100	$11,550	$12,480	$11,850
P01-20	1,400	1,400	2,413	2,413	3,390	3,390	1,440	Unsold

Use of Job-Order Costing Information for Planning and Decision Making

In Glass Creations' case, Tom Nakagawa used the job-cost information to analyze the relative profitability of two types of jobs, stock and commissioned glass pieces. He made a comprehensive list of every job undertaken in the past five years, the period during which the costing system had been in place. He prepared a cost and profit table, from which two entries are shown in Exhibit 3–17.

The job-costing system gave Glass Creations' owners information allowing them to plan the costs of both types of new work. The job-cost information showed that stock items are less profitable than custom (commissioned) jobs in most cases. Moreover, custom jobs generally are relatively low-risk jobs since a buyer already has commissioned the piece. Unfortunately, not enough commissioned work is available during a typical year to keep the glass studio busy, given its current size and talent staffing.

The Jacobsons considered using the slow months of December and January to build an inventory of stock windows to sell in the busier spring and summer months. However, Nakagawa's analysis indicated that Glass Creations would be forced to rent space in another building to store the window inventory, to insure it, and to provide security for it. All things considered, it became apparent that building stock windows for inventory was not the best strategy. The owners concluded that the best way to increase their productivity during the slow winter months was to seek to increase their commissioned business by advertising and attending more arts festivals, which are good places to gain exposure for their products. If they are able to increase their commissioned work, they will solve two problems simultaneously. First, they will increase the productivity in the studio in the December–January period. Second, they will reduce their reliance on the stock window business, thereby minimizing the effect of potentially losing that type of business to their new competitors. This evolving strategy would not have been possible without the information provided by Glass Creations' job-order costing system.

Information Technology and Job-Cost Information

The information technology (IT) efforts of many organizations could focus on improving the quality of "inside" information (e.g., improved job-cost information). Most IT improvements take advantage of declining computing costs and increasing computing speed to deliver more data to more people, but as Peter Drucker argues, IT specialists are sometimes providing the wrong "data" and ignoring the right "information" for today's competitive environment. To build wealth and value, today's managers need more information about external competitors, changes in markets, and profitable opportunities. The challenge for cost managers and IT specialists is to understand the need for information as well as they currently understand the capability of "technology."
Source: P. Drucker, "The Next Information Revolution."

Research Insight 3.1

Chapter Summary

Cost-management analysts work closely with their management colleagues to design cost-management systems to support their organization's decision making. An important component of a cost-management system is the product-costing system, which accumulates the costs of a production process and assigns them to the products that constitute the organization's output. The most common types of product-costing systems include job-order costing, process costing, and operation costing.

Job-order costing treats each individual job as a unit of output and assigns costs to it as resources are used. A *job* may be a single, unique product or a relatively small batch of identical or very similar products. Job-order costing is useful for identifying types of jobs likely to be most profitable, providing data to predict costs of future jobs, managing the costs of current jobs, renegotiating job contracts, and financial reporting of actual results of the period's operations.

Process costing (see Chapter 8) treats all units processed during a period as its output and does not separate and record costs for each unit produced. *Operation costing* (also covered in Chapter 8) is a hybrid of job-order and process costing used when companies produce batches of similar products with significantly different types of materials.

Companies using job-order costing employ several accounts (or files) to track the costs of resources used on jobs. These accounts are the sources of data for product costing, estimating costs of future jobs, and financial reporting for both internal and external purposes. The Work-in-Process Inventory account collects all costs of resources used on various jobs that have not been completed. Each job also has its own job-cost record on which the costs of all production-related resources used on that job to date are reported.

Companies have traditionally used *predetermined overhead* rates to assign manufacturing overhead to individual production jobs. The predetermined overhead rate is usually established before the year in which it is to be used and remains the same for the entire year. Predetermined overhead rates normalize (i.e., smooth out) the application of manufacturing overhead to jobs. Thus, the resulting product costs are called "normal costs," and this product-costing method is called "normal costing."

The Manufacturing Overhead account records both *actual overhead* and the *overhead applied* to Work-in-Process Inventory. Under normal costing, the actual manufacturing overhead is unlikely to equal the amount of overhead applied, which is based on budgeted overhead. The difference between the actual and the applied manufacturing overhead amounts is the *overhead variance* referred to as *overapplied* or *underapplied overhead*. At year-end, the manufacturing overhead variance is either (1) prorated (i.e., allocated) to Work-in-Process Inventory, Finished-Goods Inventory, and Cost of Goods Sold or (2) closed to Cost of Goods Sold.

Alternatives to *normal costing* include actual costing and standard costing. *Actual costing* assigns only the actual costs of both direct and indirect resources (i.e., direct material, direct labor, and manufacturing overhead) to the products. *Standard costing* uses predetermined (or standard) rates for both direct and indirect costs to assign manufacturing costs to products.

Managing jobs and projects requires attention to quality, customer satisfaction, costs, and adherence to schedules. Among the tools used in project management are *project percentage of completion charts* and *Gantt charts*. Organizations occasionally have been criticized for the following improprieties in assigning costs to jobs: misstating the percentage of completion, charging costs to the wrong job, and misrepresenting the job costs. In the context of job-order costing, parties who agree to the terms for reimbursement of job costs should require the definition and method of tracing of costs to be clearly described before signing a contract.

Job-order costing systems are indispensable for reporting and controlling costs of jobs, particularly when the jobs are numerous and complex. Job-order costing systems also provide valuable information as feedback for decision making and planning future operations.

Key Terms

For each term's definition, refer to the indicated page or turn to the glossary at the end of the text.

Meeting the Cost Management Challenges

I.   What factors should a cost-management analyst consider when designing a product-costing system?

Designers of cost systems must evaluate the trade-offs of the costs of designing and operating the system itself and the expected value of the information it provides. No organization would implement a cost system that measured every resource and activity cost with 100 percent accuracy (if that could be defined), instantaneously, and for every authorized decision maker. Cost-management analysts must design and implement a system that supports the organization's most important decisions well, usually within a development and operating budget. This often means that relatively fewer important decisions are supported by less accurate or timely information. The cost system itself should not consume more resources than the savings to be gained by using it to make better decisions.

2. What features should a job-order costing system have, and how can they be developed?

As jobs become more unique and individually important to the organization, the job-cost system should more precisely trace or assign costs to jobs. The method of measuring job costs also should differ, depending on the relative importance of easily traced, direct job costs versus less easily assigned, indirect costs. The costs of major activities must be assigned using predetermined cost-driver rates, which could be difficult to measure. The complexity of resources, activities, cost-driver rates, and products or services jointly determines the complexity and cost of the

job-costing system. Thus, a job-costing system should trace direct costs to jobs and assign indirect costs as accurately as necessary to support management decisions.

3. How can cost-management analysts use job-cost information to support planning and decision-making activities?

Understanding what drives the costs of jobs—the various activities that are performed to design and complete jobs—is critical to planning the use of resources and making decisions about which jobs to seek. This is particularly true when the nature of jobs (i.e., necessary activities to perform them) varies greatly. Job-costing systems should provide information on (a) the completion of past jobs and (b) cost-driver rates. Both types of information should be useful to decision makers who must plan how to organize resources for current jobs and how to bid for future jobs.

Solutions to You're the Decision Maker

3.1 Normal-Costing and Predetermined Overhead Rates   p. 109

a.

Quarter	Predetermined Overhead Rate	Calculations
1	$25 per DLH	$ 50,000 ÷ 2,000
2	35 per DLH	$122,500 ÷ 3,500
3	25 per DLH	$100,000 ÷ 4,000
4	35 per DLH	$ 87,500 ÷ 2,500

b.

	February	October
Direct material	$100	$100
Direct labor ($22 × 5) + ($15 × 1)	125	125
Manufacturing overhead:		
6 hrs × $25 per hr.	150	
6 hrs × $35 per hr.		210
Total cost	$375	$435

c.

	February	October
Total cost	$375	$435
Markup (20%)	75	87
Price	$450	$522

d.

$$\text{Predetermined rate} = \frac{\text{Annual budgeted manufacturing overhead}}{\text{Annual budgeted direct-labor hours}}$$
$$= \$360,000/12,000$$
$$= \$30 \text{ per direct-labor hour}$$

e.

	February	October
Direct material	$100	$100
Direct labor ($22 × 5) + ($15 × 1)	125	125
Manufacturing overhead (6 hr. × $30)	180	180
Total cost	$405	$405

f.

Total cost	$405
Markup (20%)	81
Price	$486

g. Glass Creations' use of quarterly overhead rates might *undercost* and *underprice* the blue heron window in February and *overcost* and *overprice* it in October. For this reason, the use of a predetermined overhead rate calculated annually rather than quarterly is preferable. This is the essence of normal costing (i.e., smoothing out fluctuations in the overhead rate and reported product costs over a reasonably long period of time, in this case, one year).

Review Questions

3.1 What is a product-costing system and what does it do?

3.2 What are the characteristics of the following three product-costing methods: (a) job-order costing, (b) process costing, and (c) operation costing? Give an example of a product or service that would be accounted for by each method.

3.3 What is each component of the basic cost-flow model? Describe each component.

3.4 Describe the basic cost-flow model as an algebraic equation.

3.5 Distinguish between work-in-process, finished-goods, and cost of goods sold.

3.6 Explain how to measure the costs of a product using normal costing, actual costing, and standard costing.

3.7 How are the events "complete a job," "sell a job," and "end the accounting period" different and how are inventory accounts affected by these events?

3.8 How does job-order costing differ for service organizations and manufacturing organizations?

3.9 How can overhead be over- or underapplied?

3.10 Does it matter how the overhead variance is disposed? Explain.

3.11   Describe several ways in which job costing can be misused.

3.12   Is job-order costing information sufficient to support management decisions? Why or why not?

3.13   What are the characteristics of companies likely to use a job-order costing system?

3.14   Why is the use of direct-labor as a cost driver for manufacturing overhead declining?

3.15   What are the purposes of the following documents: (a) material requisition form, (b) labor time record, and (c) job-cost record.

3.16   Explain the benefits of using a predetermined overhead rate instead of an actual overhead rate.

3.17   Describe one advantage and one disadvantage of prorating overapplied or underapplied overhead.

Critical Analysis

3.18   Would a dentist, an architect, a landscaper, and a lawyer use job-order costing or process costing? Explain.

3.19   An employee of Doughties Foods overstated inventories to make periodic profits higher. Using the basic cost-flow model, explain how overstating inventories could increase profits. If the employee did this a second and a third time, use the basic cost-flow model to show what the effect would be. How could this misrepresentation be detected?

3.20   Interview the manager of a construction company (for example, a company that does house construction, remodeling, landscaping, or street or highway construction) about how it bids on prospective jobs. Does it use cost information from former jobs similar to prospective ones, for example? Does it have a specialist in cost estimation to project the costs of prospective jobs? Write a report to your instructor summarizing the results of your interview.

3.21   Interview the manager of a campus print shop or a print shop in the local area about how the company bids on prospective jobs. Does it use cost information from former jobs similar to prospective ones, for example? Does it have a specialist in cost estimation to project costs of prospective jobs? Write a report to your instructor summarizing the results of your interview.

3.22   A co-worker states, I don't know why we spent so much money on that new job-costing system. I can do everything we need on a simple spreadsheet. If the CFO had listened to me, we could have saved a lot of money. Would it have been desirable to follow your co-worker's advice? Why or why not?

3.23   Your manager tries to persuade you that all of the overhead variance should be charged to Cost of Goods Sold. This is appealing to you since you have hundreds of jobs and many overhead accounts to reconcile, and this is the least fun part of your job. Why should you consider this argument with caution?

3.24   How might job-order costing for a homebuilder be similar to and differ from that used by a consulting firm?

3.25   A government contractor had a contract with NASA, to build a space shuttle. Under this contract, all costs of development and construction are to be reimbursed and the contractor is to be guaranteed a specific profit. At the same time, the contractor had a fixed-fee contract with the U.S. Air Force to build fighter planes, which limited total reimbursement to the contractor to a fixed amount. The Air Force contract had a cost overrun that the contractor transferred to the NASA contract. Explain how this might have been accomplished and why the contractor might have thought it was desirable.

3.26   Motion picture contracts often offer some participants residual profits, which are shares of profits computed after all costs of production have been covered. Sometimes blockbuster movies never pay residual profits because they do not fully recover their costs, which could include up-front payments to movie stars and producers. If you sold your novel to a producer in exchange for residual profits that never materialized, yet the stars and producers made millions of dollars, is there anything wrong or unethical about this?

Exercises

Exercise 3.27
Basic Cost-Flow Model
(LO 2)

A small building-supply company, Quality Lumber, experienced the following events during the year:

- Incurred $250,000 in selling costs.
- Purchased $800,000 of building material.
- Paid $20,000 for vehicles and transportation resources.
- Incurred $400,000 of general and administrative costs.
- Took a periodic inventory at year-end and learned that building material costing $250,000 was on hand. This compared with a beginning inventory of $300,000 on January 1.
- Determined that sales revenue during the year was $2,000,000.

All costs incurred were added to the appropriate accounts. All sales were for cash.

Required

Give the amounts for the following items in Quality Lumber's Building-Material Inventory account:

a. Beginning balance (BB).

b. Transfers in (TI).

c. Ending balance (EB).

d. Transfers out (TO).

Assume that the following events occurred at a division of American Homes, Inc., a large homebuilder, for the current year.

1. Purchased $270 million in building material.

2. Incurred construction labor costs of $156 million.

3. Determined that general and administrative overhead was $246 million.

4. Transferred 70 percent of the materials purchased to jobs (work) in process.

5. Completed work on 60 percent of the jobs in process. Costs are assigned equally across all work in process.

The inventory accounts have no beginning balances. All costs incurred were debited to the appropriate accounts and credited to Accounts Payable.

Exercise 3.28
Basic Cost-Flow Model
(LO 2)

Required

Give the amounts for the following items in the Work-in-Process account:

a. Transfers in (TI).

b. Transfers out (TO).

c. Ending balance (EB).

Fill in the missing items for the following inventories:

Exercise 3.29
Basic Cost-Flow Model
(LO 2)

	(A)	(B)	(C)
Beginning balance	$136,000	$ 56,800	$312,000
Ending balance	?	49,600	256,000
Transferred in	128,000	?	560,000
Transferred out	152,000	176,000	?

	(D)	(E)	(F)
Beginning balance	$ 34,000	$ 14,200	$ 78,000
Ending balance	?	12,400	64,000
Transferred in	32,000	?	140,000
Transferred out	38,000	44,000	?

Fill in the missing items for the following inventories:

Exercise 3.30
Basic Cost-Flow Model
(LO 2)

	(A)	(B)	(C)
Beginning balance	$ 5,000	$?	$ 12,000
Ending balance	?	16,000	12,000
Transferred in	75,000	45,000	56,000
Transferred out	79,000	52,000	?

	(D)	(E)	(F)
Beginning balance	$170,000	$ 71,000	$390,000
Ending balance	?	62,000	320,000
Transferred in	160,000	?	700,000
Transferred out	190,000	220,000	?

The following T-accounts represent data from a division of Northeast Metals Company's accounting records. Find the missing amounts represented by the letters. (*Hint:* Rearrange accounts to conform with the flow of costs.)

Exercise 3.31
Basic Cost-Flow Model
(LO 2, 3)

Finished-Goods Inventory		
BB	23,000	
	(c)	(d)
EB	(f)	

Raw-Material Inventory			
BB	(a)		
Purchases	9,000	TO	10,500
EB	3,750		

Cost of Goods Sold	
41,000	

Work-in-Process Inventory		
BB	3,000	
Material	(b)	
Labor	8,500	
Overhead	(e)	29,300
EB	4,850	

Exercise 3.32
Basic Cost-Flow Model
(LO 2, 3)

The following T-accounts represent data from a division of New England Fashion's accounting records. Find the missing amounts represented by the letters. (*Hint:* Rearrange accounts to conform with flow of costs.)

Cost of Goods Sold	
123,000	

Finished-Goods Inventory		
BB	69,600	
	(c)	(d)
EB	(f)	

Work-in-Process Inventory		
BB	9,000	
Material	(b)	
Labor	25,500	
Overhead	(e)	87,900
EB	14,550	

Raw-Material Inventory			
BB	(a)		
Purchases	27,000	TO	31,500
EB	11,250		

Exercise 3.33
Assignment of Costs
to Jobs
(LO 2, 3, 4, 5)

Danby Hardwoods, a custom manufacturer of furniture, uses job-order costing. The following transactions to support job 402 for a custom meeting room set—a large table plus 16 chairs—occurred in January:

a.   Purchased $10,000 of materials.
b.   Issued $500 of supplies from raw-material inventory.
c.   Purchased $7,000 of raw material.
d.   Paid for the raw material purchased in transaction (a).
e.   Issued $8,500 in raw material to the production department.
f.   Incurred production labor costs of $12,500, which were credited to Payroll Payable.
g.   Paid $23,250 cash for utilities, power, equipment maintenance, and miscellaneous items for the manufacturing plant.
h.   Applied overhead on the basis of 185 percent of $8,500 in material costs.
i.   Recognized depreciation on manufacturing property, plant, and equipment of $6,250.

Required
Prepare journal entries to record these transactions.

Exercise 3.34
Assignment of Costs
to Jobs
(LO 2, 3, 4, 5)

Refer to the data in the preceding exercise. The following balances appeared in the accounts of Danby Hardwoods for January before closing temporary accounts:

	Beginning	Ending
Material inventory	$18,525	
Work-in-process inventory	4,125	
Finished-goods inventory	20,750	$17,900
Cost of goods sold	32,925	

Required

Prepare T-accounts to show the flow of costs during the period from raw-material inventory purchases through cost of goods sold.

Partially completed T-accounts and additional information for Circle-T Company for the month of May follow:

Exercise 3.35
Costs Traced to Jobs
(LO 2, 3, 4, 5)

Raw-Material Inventory		
BB	2,000	
	8,000	6,400

Work-in-Process Inventory		
BB	4,000	
Labor	6,000	

Finished-Goods Inventory		
BB	6,000	
	12,000	8,000

Cost of Goods Sold	

Manufacturing Overhead	
5,200	

Additional Information

- Labor wage rate was $24 per hour.
- Overhead is applied at 80 percent of direct-material cost.
- During the month, sales revenue was $18,000, and selling and administrative costs were $3,200.

Required

a. What was the amount of direct material issued to production during May?
b. What was the amount of manufacturing overhead applied to production during May?
c. What was the cost of products completed during May?
d. What was the balance of the Work-in-Process Inventory account at the end of May?
e. What was the manufacturing-overhead variance during May?
f. What was the operating profit for May?

Maritza Corporation, located in Buenos Aires, Argentina, manufactures cutlery. Management estimates manufacturing overhead to be 44,000p and direct-labor costs to be 80,000p for year 1. The actual manufacturing labor costs were 20,000p for job 1, 30,000p for job 2, and 40,000p for job 3 during year 1; the actual manufacturing overhead was 52,000p. Manufacturing overhead is applied to jobs on the basis of direct-labor costs using a predetermined rate. (p denotes the peso, Argentina's national currency. Several countries use the peso as their monetary unit. On the day this exercise was written, Argentina's peso was worth 1.003 U.S. dollars.)

Exercise 3.36
Predetermined Cost-Driver Rate
(LO 3, 5)

Required

a. How much manufacturing overhead (in Argentina's peso) was assigned to each job during year 1?
b. What was the manufacturing overhead variance for year 1?

Paige Printing uses a job-order costing system. The following debits (credits) appeared in the Work-in-Process account for May:

Exercise 3.37
Overhead Application Using a Predetermined Rate
(LO 3, 5)

	Description	Debits	Credits
May 1	Balance	$ 5,000	
Entire month	Direct material	30,000	
Entire month	Direct labor	20,000	
Entire month	Factory overhead	16,000	
Entire month	To finished goods		$60,000

Paige Printing applies overhead to production at a predetermined rate of 80 percent based on direct labor cost. Job 75, the only job still in process at the end of May, has been charged with direct labor of $2,500.

Required

What was the cost of direct material charged to job 75?

[CPA adapted]

Exercise 3.38
Overhead Variance
Calculation
(LO 3, 5)

Reimel Furniture Co. uses a predetermined cost-driver rate based on direct-labor hours. For October, Reimel's budgeted overhead was $900,000 based on budgeted activity of 100,000 direct-labor hours. Actual overhead amounted to $975,000 with actual direct-labor hours totaling 110,000.

Required

How much was overhead overapplied or underapplied?

[CPA adapted]

Exercise 3.39
Under- or Overapplied
Overhead Prorated
(LO 3, 5)

Refer to the information in the preceding exercise. Prorate the overhead variance as follows:

Work-in-process inventory	10%
Finished-goods inventory	25
Cost of goods sold	65

Exercise 3.40
Closing the Overhead
Variance
(LO 3, 5)

Refer to the information in exercise 3.38. Prepare an entry to close the overhead variance into cost of goods sold.

Exercise 3.41
Predetermined
Overhead Rate
(LO 3, 5)

Kitchen Craft Company manufactures one product and accounts for costs using a job-order costing system. You have obtained the following information from the corporation's books and records for the year ended December 31, year 1:

▨   Total manufacturing cost during last year was $500,000 based on actual direct material, actual direct labor, and manufacturing overhead applied on the basis of actual direct-labor dollars.

▨   Manufacturing overhead was applied to work in process at 75 percent of direct-labor dollars. Applied manufacturing overhead for the year was 33 percent of the total manufacturing cost during the year.

Required

Compute actual direct material, actual direct labor, and applied manufacturing overhead. (*Hint:* The total of these costs is $500,000.)

Exercise 3.42
Job Costs for a Service
Organization
(LO 3, 5)

At the beginning of the month, Melody Corporation had two jobs in process that had the following costs assigned from previous months:

Job No.	Direct Labor	Applied Overhead
X-10	$1,280	?
Y-12	840	?

During the month, jobs X-10 and Y-12 were completed but not billed to customers. The completion costs for X-10 required $1,400 in direct labor. For Y-12, $4,000 in direct labor was used.

During the month, a new job, Z-14, was started but not finished; it was the only new job. Total direct-labor costs for all jobs amounted to $8,240 for the month. Overhead in this company refers to the cost of work that is not directly traced to particular jobs, including copying, printing, and travel costs to meet with clients. Overhead is applied at a rate of 50 percent of direct-labor costs for this and previous periods. Actual overhead for the month was $4,000.

Required

a.   What are the costs of jobs X-10 and Y-12 at (1) the beginning of the month and (2) when completed?

b.   What is the cost of job Z-14 at the end of the month?

c.   How much was the manufacturing overhead variance for the month?

Exercise 3.43
Job Costing in a Service
Organization
(LO 3, 7)

For September, Twiddle & Company worked 600 hours for client A and 1,400 hours for client B. Twiddle bills clients at the rate of $140 per hour; labor cost for its audit staff is $70 per hour. The total number of hours worked in September was 2,000, and overhead costs were $20,000. Overhead is applied to clients at $12 per labor hour. In addition, Twiddle had $84,000 in selling and administrative costs. All transactions are on account. All services were billed.

Required

a.   Show labor and overhead cost flows through T-accounts.

b.   Prepare an income statement for the company for September.

Read "General Mills Boosts Target for Savings Project to $1 Billion," *The Wall Street Journal,* February 14, 2003, page B4, by Patricia Callahan.

Exercise 3.44
Supply Chain
Management
(LO 1)

Required

How is General Mills using supply-chain management to achieve its goal of $1 billion in savings over 10 years? In particular, how is the company saving $1.5 million annually on its cake mix line?

Visit the website of a film producer, such as Warner Brothers (www.warnerbros.com), MGM (www.mgm.com), or Walt Disney Studios (www.disney.com).

Exercise 3.45
Job-Order Costing for
Feature Film Production;
Internet
(LO 1)

Required

Read about one of the company's recent (or upcoming) film releases. Then discuss why job-order costing is or is not an appropriate costing method for feature film production.

Problems

Kalamazoo Quality Instruments produces sensitive heat-measurement devices in three manufacturing stages: (1) meter assembly, (2) case assembly, and (3) testing. The company has a large backlog of orders and had no beginning inventories because all units in production last year were sold by the end of the year. At the start of this year, the firm received an order for 4,000 devices.

Problem 3.46
Cost Flows
(LO 2, 3, 5)

- The company purchased $260,000 of materials on account. Meter assembly used $210,000 of the materials in production, case assembly used $40,000, and testing used $10,000.

- Production labor costs of $640,000 were incurred. These costs were assigned as follows: meter assembly, $200,000; case assembly, $350,000; and testing, $90,000.

- Overhead costs of $1,040,000 were charged to departments based on materials used [($210,000/$260,000) × $1,040,000] to meter assembly, for example.

- Ninety percent of the costs charged to meter assembly were transferred to case assembly during the period; 95 percent of the costs charged to case assembly (including the costs transferred in from meter assembly) were transferred to testing. All costs charged to testing were transferred to finished goods, and all finished units were delivered to the buyer.

Required

Use T-accounts to show the flow of costs for this order.

Borealis Corporation uses a job-order costing system for its production costs. A predetermined cost-driver rate based on machine hours is used to apply facility-level overhead to individual jobs. An estimate of overhead costs at different volumes was prepared for the current year as follows:

Problem 3.47
Analysis of Overhead
Using a Predetermined
Rate (LO 2, 3, 5)

Machine hours	50,000	60,000	70,000
Unit-level overhead costs	$350,000	$420,000	$490,000
Facility-level overhead costs	216,000	216,000	216,000
Total overhead	$566,000	$636,000	$706,000

The expected volume is 60,000 machine hours for the entire year. The following information is for November, when jobs 50 and 51 were completed:

Inventories, November 1		
Raw materials and supplies	$ 10,500	
Work in process (job 50)	54,000	
Finished goods	112,500	
Purchases of raw materials and supplies		
Raw materials	$135,000	
Supplies	15,000	
Materials and supplies requisitioned for production		
Job 50	$ 45,000	
Job 51	37,500	
Job 52	25,500	
Supplies	6,000	
Subtotal	$114,000	

Job	Production Machine Hours (MH)	Direct-Labor Hours (DLH)
Job 50	3,500 MH	2,000 DLH
Job 51	3,000 MH	3,000 DLH
Job 52	2,000 MH	3,500 DLH

Labor costs:

Production labor wages (all hours @ $8)	$ 68,000
Support labor wages (4,000 hours)	17,000
Supervisory salaries	36,000
Subtotal	$121,000

Building occupancy costs (heat, light, depreciation, etc.):

Factory facilities	$ 6,500
Sales and administrative offices	2,500
Subtotal	$ 9,000

Factory equipment costs:

Power	$ 4,000
Repairs and maintenance	1,500
Other	2,500
Subtotal	$ 8,000

Required

a.   Compute the predetermined cost-driver rate (combined unit and facility) to use to apply overhead to individual jobs during the year.

   [*Note:* Without prejudice to your answer to requirement (a), assume that the predetermined cost-driver rate is $9 per machine hour. Use this amount in answering requirements (b) through (e).]

b.   Compute the total cost of job 50 when it is finished.

c.   Compute the overhead costs applied to job 52 during November.

d.   Compute the total amount of overhead applied to jobs during November.

e.   Compute the actual factory overhead incurred during November.

f.   At the end of the year, Borealis Corporation had the following account balances:

Overapplied overhead	$ 1,000
Cost of goods sold	980,000
Work-in-process inventory	38,000
Finished-goods inventory	82,000

   What is the most common treatment of the overapplied overhead, assuming that it is not material?

g.   *Build your own spreadsheet.* Build an Excel spreadsheet to solve requirements (a)–(f). Use your spreadsheet to determine the new value for the total cost of job 50 when finished, the overhead cost assigned to job 52 in November, and the actual factory overhead in November, if each of the following input parameters changes by the amount indicated. (Unless otherwise indicated, treat each parameter change independently.)

   1.   Estimated overhead costs for the year are as follows for the indicated levels of machine hours.

Machine hours	50,000	60,000	70,000
Unit-level overhead	$400,000	$480,000	$560,000
Facility-level overhead	210,000	210,000	210,000

   2.   The production labor wage rate is $10 per hour.

   3.   The actual cost of power for the factory equipment was $6,500.

   4.   All of the changes listed in (1)–(3) occur simultaneously.

   [CMA adapted]

Problem 3.48
Job Costing in a Service Organization
(LO 2, 3, 5, 7)

Corner Cleaners has five employees and a president, Marty Stuart. Stuart and one of the five employees manage all the marketing and administrative duties. The remaining four employees work directly on operations. Corner Cleaners has four service departments: dry cleaning, coin washing and drying, special cleaning, and repairs. A time report is marked, and records are kept to monitor the time each employee spends working in each department. When business is slow, there is idle time, which is marked on the time record. (Some idle time is necessary because Corner Cleaners promises 60-minute service, and it must have reserve labor available to accommodate fluctuating peak demand periods throughout the day and the week.)

Some of the November operating data are as follows:

	Idle Time	Dry Cleaning	Coin Washing and Drying	Special Cleaning	Repairs
Sales revenue		$4,625	$5,250	$2,000	$625
Direct labor (in hours)	25	320	80	125	90
Overhead traceable to departments:					
Cleaning compounds		$ 500	$ 250	$ 400	$ 0
Supplies		125	200	175	140
Electric usage		250	625	100	25
Rent		200	500	90	10

Additional Information

▨ Each of the four employees working in the operating departments makes $8 per hour.

▨ The fifth employee, who helps manage marketing and administrative duties, earns $1,500 per month, and Stuart earns $2,000 per month.

▨ Indirect overhead (i.e., overhead that is not traceable to departments) amounted to $512 and is assigned to departments based on direct-labor hours used. Because of the idle hours, some overhead will not be assigned to a department.

▨ In addition to salaries paid, marketing costs for such items as advertising and special promotions totaled $400.

▨ In addition to salaries, other administrative costs were $150.

▨ All sales transactions are in cash; all other transactions are on account.

Required

Corner Cleaners' management wants to know whether each department is contributing to the company's profit. Prepare an income statement for November that shows the revenue and cost of services for each department. Write a short report to management about departmental profitability. No inventories were kept.

During January, Manhattan Consultants worked 1,000 hours for Nocando Manufacturing, 300 hours for Sails, Inc., and 500 hours for Original John's Restaurants. Manhattan Consultants bills clients at $80 an hour; its labor costs are $30 an hour. A total of 2,000 hours were worked in January with 200 hours not billable to clients. Overhead costs of $30,000 were incurred and assigned to clients on the basis of direct-labor hours. Because 200 hours were not billable, some overhead was not assigned to jobs. Manhattan Consultants had $25,000 in marketing and administrative costs. All transactions were on account.

Problem 3.49
Job Costs in a Service Organization
(LO 2, 3, 5, 7)

mhhe.com/hilton3e

Required

a. What are the revenue and cost per client?
b. Prepare an income statement for January.

The following transactions occurred at Arrow Space, Inc., a small defense contractor that uses job costing:

a. Purchased $71,600 in raw material on account.

b. Issued $2,000 in supplies (indirect material) from raw-material inventory to the production department.

c. Paid for the raw material purchased in (a).

d. Issued $34,000 in raw material to the production department.

e. Incurred wage costs of $56,000, which were debited to Payroll, a temporary account. Of this amount, $18,000 was withheld for payroll taxes and credited to Payroll Taxes Payable. The remaining $38,000 was paid in cash to the employees. See transactions (f) and (g) for additional information about the Payroll account.

f. Recognized $28,000 in fringe benefit costs, incurred as a result of the wages paid in (e). This $28,000 was debited to Payroll and credited to Fringe Benefits Payable.

Problem 3.50
Assignment of Costs Using Predetermined Cost-Driver Rate
(LO 2, 3, 5)

g.   Analyzed the Payroll account and determined that 40 percent represented production labor; 40 percent manufacturing support (overhead) labor; and 20 percent administrative and marketing costs.

h.   Paid for utilities, power, equipment maintenance, and other overhead items for the manufacturing plant totaling $43,200.

i.   Recognized depreciation of $21,000 on manufacturing property, plant, and equipment.

j.   Applied manufacturing overhead on the basis of 400 percent of *production* labor costs.

Required

Prepare T-accounts to show the flow of costs during the period. The following balances appeared in Arrow Space's accounts before closing temporary accounts:

	Beginning	Ending
Raw-material inventory	$74,100	?
Work-in-process inventory	16,500	?
Finished-goods inventory	83,000	$ 66,400
Cost of goods sold	0	131,700

Problem 3.51
Cost Estimation
Using Alternative
Cost-Driver Rates
(LO 2, 3, 5)

Refer to the information in the preceding problem. Arrow Space, Inc., has determined that 65 percent of its manufacturing overhead spending is related to jobs' use of material, and 35 percent is related to jobs' use of production labor.

Required

a.   Based on information in this problem and the preceding problem, calculate cost-driver rates using actual material cost and production labor costs as possible cost-driver bases.

b.   Arrow Space, Inc., is considering bidding on two jobs with the following budgeted characteristics:

Job	A	B
Direct-material cost:	$40,000	$30,000
Production labor cost	20,000	30,000

Estimate the costs of these two jobs using (1) the original cost-driver rate of 400 percent of production labor and (2) the cost-driver rates derived in requirement (a).

c.   What are the possible outcomes if bids for the two jobs are based on the original cost-driver rate but resource costs are actually *used* in accordance with the new cost-driver rates?

Problem 3.52
Cost Flows through
Accounts
(LO 2, 3, 5)

You are employed by the management consulting group Business Solutions, Inc., which Leevies Pants, Inc., has asked to help in improving its job-costing system. Leevies employed 20 full-time workers at $8 per hour. Since beginning operations last year, it had priced the various jobs by marking up the sum of direct-labor and direct-material costs by 20 percent. Despite operating at capacity, however, last year's performance was a great disappointment to the managers. In total, 10 jobs were accepted and completed, incurring the following total costs:

Direct material	$103,540
Direct labor	400,000
Manufacturing overhead	104,000

Of the $104,000 manufacturing overhead, 30 percent was unit level and 70 percent was facility level. This year Leevies expects to operate at the same activity level as last year, and overhead costs and the wage rate are not expected to change. For the first quarter of this year, Leevies had just completed two jobs and was beginning the third. The costs incurred follow:

Jobs	Material	Production Labor	Overhead
81	$13,720	$49,000	$13,390
82	9,300	31,240	11,570
83	9,400	19,760	2,160
Total factory overhead			27,120
Total selling and administrative costs	11,200		

In the first quarter of this year, 40 percent of selling and administrative costs were job level and 60 percent were facility level. Leevies has told you that jobs 81 and 82 were sold for $91,000 and $61,000, respectively. All over- or underapplied overhead for the quarter is expected to be expensed on the income statement.

Required

a. Begin your analysis by presenting in T-accounts the absorption, *actual* manufacturing cost flows for the three jobs in the first quarter of this year.

b. Using last year's costs and direct-labor hours as this year's estimate, calculate predetermined cost-driver rates for unit-level overhead as a percentage of direct-material cost and facility-level overhead as a percentage of direct-labor cost.

c. Present in T-accounts the absorption, *normal* manufacturing cost flows for the three jobs in the first quarter of this year. Use the cost-driver rates derived in requirement (b).

d. Prepare income statements for the first quarter of this year under the following costing systems:

   1. Absorption, actual.

   2. Absorption, normal.

e. Prepare a short presentation to demonstrate and explain whether the choice of method in requirement (d) makes a difference.

Superior Staging, Inc. assembles light and sound equipment for installation in various entertainment facilities. An inventory of material and equipment is on hand at all times so that installation could start as quickly as possible. Special equipment has been ordered as required. On September 1, the Materials and Equipment Inventory account had a $48,000 balance. The Work-in-Process Inventory account is maintained to record the costs of installation work not yet complete. There were two such jobs on September 1, with the following costs:

Problem 3.53
Flow of Costs to Jobs;
Journal Entries
(LO 2, 3, 4, 5)

	Memphis Country Music Hall Job 106	Starlight Theater Job 111
Material and equipment	$32,000	$95,000
Technician labor	6,500	9,700
Overhead (applied)	4,800	14,250

Overhead has been applied at 15 percent of the costs of material and equipment installed. During September, two new installations were begun. Additional work was done on jobs 106 and 111, with the latter completed and billed to Starlight Theater. Details on the costs incurred on jobs during September follow:

Job	106	111	115	116
Material and equipment	$3,200	$14,200	$17,000	$6,200
Technician labor (on account)	1,800	1,200	3,100	900

Other Period Events

▪ Received $25,000 payment on job 111, which was delivered to the customer.

▪ Purchased material and equipment for $18,700.

▪ Billed Starlight Theater $175,000 and received payment for $100,000 of that amount.

▪ Determined that payroll for support personnel totaled $1,300.

▪ Issued supplies and incidental installation material for current jobs costing $310.

▪ Recorded overhead and advertising costs for the installation operation as follows (all cash except equipment depreciation):

Advertising and promotion campaign	$1,200
Electrical inspections	400
Telephone and other miscellaneous	650
Equipment depreciation	900
Property taxes	1,100
Showroom and storage area rental	1,350
Truck and delivery cost	640

Required

a. Prepare journal entries to record the flow of costs for the installation operation during September.

b. Calculate the amount of over- or underapplied overhead for the month. This amount is closed to Cost of Goods Sold.

c. Determine inventory balances for Material and Equipment Inventory and Work-in-Process Inventory.

Problem 3.54
Cost-Driver Rates
(LO 2, 3, 5)

Rosado Pasta Company prepares, packages, and distributes six frozen pasta entrees in two different container sizes. It prepares the different pastas and different sizes in large batches. It uses a normal job-order costing system. Manufacturing overhead is assigned to batches by a predetermined rate on the basis of machine hours. The company incurred manufacturing-overhead costs during two recent years (adjusted for changes using current prices and wage rates) as follows:

	20x5	20x6
Machine hours worked	1,380,000	1,080,000
Manufacturing-overhead costs incurred:		
Power..	$ 2,208,000	$ 1,728,000
Heat and light	552,000	552,000
Support (indirect) labor	11,040,000	8,640,000
Employee benefits...	4,140,000	3,240,000
Supplies..	2,760,000	2,160,000
Supervision	2,865,000	2,625,000
Depreciation	7,930,000	7,930,000
Property taxes and insurance	3,005,000	3,005,000
Total manufacturing-overhead costs.................................	$34,500,000	$29,880,000

Rosado Pasta expects to operate at a level of 1.15 million machine hours in 20x7.

Required
Using the data from the two previous years, write a report to management that shows the cost-driver rate used to assign manufacturing overhead to its products. Prepare a memo explaining whether it is advisable for Rosado Pasta to use an average cost-driver rate for all jobs.

[CMA adapted]

Problem 3.55
Journal Entries in
Job-Order Costing
(LO 2, 3, 4, 5)

eXcel
mhhe.com/hilton3e

Plattsburg Pump, Inc. manufactures bilge pumps for small boats. It uses a job-order costing system. Normal costing is used, and manufacturing overhead is applied on the basis of machine hours. Estimated manufacturing overhead for the year is $1,464,000, and management expects that 73,200 machine hours will be used.

Required
a.   Calculate the company's predetermined overhead rate for the year.
b.   Prepare journal entries to record the following events, which occurred during April.
    1.   Purchased pump impellers from Marion Corporation for $7,850 on account.
    2.   Processed requisition from the Gauge Department supervisor for 300 pounds of clear plastic. The material cost $ .60 per pound when it was purchased.
    3.   Processed the Testing Department's requisition for 300 feet of electrical wire, which is considered an indirect material. The wire cost $ .10 per foot when it was purchased.
    4.   Paid on electric utility bill of $800 in cash.
    5.   Incurred direct-labor costs of $75,000 in April.
    6.   Recorded April's insurance cost of $1,800 for insurance on the cars driven by sales personnel. The policy had been prepaid in March.
    7.   Purchased metal tubing costing $3,000 on account.
    8.   Made cash payment of $1,700 on outstanding accounts payable.
    9.   Incurred indirect-labor costs of $21,000 during April.
    10.   Recorded depreciation of $7,000 on equipment for April.
    11.   Finished job G22 during April at a total cost of $1,100.
    12.   Used 7,000 machine hours during April.
    13.   Made sales on account for April of $181,000. The April cost of goods sold was $139,000.

Problem 3.56
Missing Data; Cost
Flows; Income Statement
(LO 2, 3, 5)

A hysterical I. M. Dunce corners you in the hallway 30 minutes before accounting class. "Help me, help me!" I. M. pleads. "I woke up this morning and discovered that my pet German Shepherds Fifo and Lifo ate my homework, and these shredded pieces are all that I have left!" Being a kind and generous soul, you willingly declare, "There's no need to fear! I'm a real whiz at accounting and will be glad to help you." A relieved I. M. Dunce hands you the following torn homework remnants.

Page 1

Direct-labor hours used	125
Direct-labor rate per hour	$ 15
Raw material purchased	5,250
Raw material beginning inventory	1,400

Page 2

Manufacturing overhead (actual equals applied)	$ 750
Beginning work-in-process inventory	1,500
Cost of goods manufactured	8,000
Ending finished-goods inventory	3,000

Page 3

Job remaining in ending work-in-process inventory:	
Direct labor	$ 500
Direct material	1,300
Overhead ($2 per direct-labor hour)	200
Ending work-in-process inventory	$ 2,000
Total revenue	$13,500
Gross margin	4,000
Marketing and administrative costs	
Operating profit	1,000

Required

a. Prepare T-accounts to show the flow of costs and determine each of the following:
 1. Selling and administrative costs.
 2. Cost of goods sold.
 3. Beginning finished-goods inventory.
 4. Direct material used.
 5. Ending raw-material inventory.
b. Prepare an income statement.

On June 1, two jobs were in process at Top Notch Painters, Inc. Details of the jobs follow:

Problem 3.57
Job Costs in a Service Company
(LO 2, 3, 5, 7)

Job No.	Direct Material	Direct Labor
P-20	$174	$64
P-43	32	84

Material inventory (for example, paint and sandpaper) on June 1 totaled $920, and $116 in material was purchased during the month. Indirect material of $16 was withdrawn from material inventory. On June 1, finished-goods inventory consisted of two jobs: P-12, costing $392, and P-26, costing $158. Both jobs were transferred to Cost of Goods Sold during the month.

Also during June, jobs P-20 and P-43 were completed. To complete job P-20 required an additional $68 in direct labor. The completion costs for job P-43 included $108 in direct material and $200 in direct labor.

Job P-45 was started during the period but was not finished. A total of $314 of direct material was used (excluding the $16 indirect material) during the period, and total direct-labor costs during the month amounted to $408. Manufacturing overhead has been estimated at 150 percent of direct-labor costs, and this relationship has been the same for the past few years.

Required

Compute the costs of jobs P-20 and P-43 and the balances in the June 30 inventory accounts.

Problem 3.58
Missing Data; Cost Flows
(LO 2, 3, 5)

A disastrous fire struck the only manufacturing plant of Badomen Equipment, Inc., on December 1. All work-in-process inventory was destroyed, but a few records were salvaged from the wreckage and the company's headquarters. The insurance company has stated that it will pay the cost of the lost inventory if adequate documentation can be supplied. The insurable value of work-in-process inventory consists of direct material, direct labor, and applied manufacturing overhead.

The following information about the plant appears on the October financial statements:

Accounts payable (raw material suppliers) on October 31	$ 21,600
Acutal manufacturing overhead incurred through October 31	184,900
Payroll payable on October 31	0
Withholding and other payroll liabilities on October 31	9,700
Applied manufacturing overhead through October 31	179,600
Raw-material inventory, October 31	49,000
Work-in-process inventory, October 31	86,200
Finished-goods inventory, October 31	32,000
Cost of goods sold through October 31	$348,600

A count of the inventories on hand November 30 shows the following:

Raw-material inventory	$43,000
Work-in-process inventory	?
Finished-goods inventory	37,500

The accounts payable clerk tells you that outstanding bills to suppliers totaled $50,100 and that cash payments of $37,900 were made to them during the month. The payroll clerk informs you that the payroll costs last month for the manufacturing section included $82,400 of which $14,700 was indirect labor.

At the end of November, the following balances were available:

Actual manufacturing overhead incurred through November 30	$217,000
Cost of goods sold through November 30	396,600

Recall that each month there is only one requisition for indirect material. Among the fragments of paper, you located the following information:

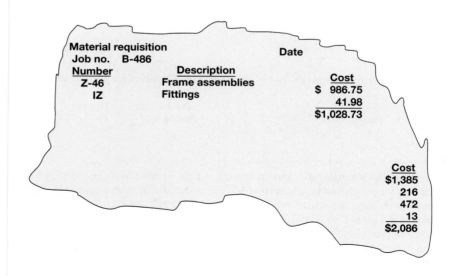

You also learn that the overhead during the month was overapplied by $1,200.

Required

Determine the cost of the work-in-process inventory lost in the disaster.

Portsmouth Printing, Inc., is a rapidly growing company that has not been profitable despite increases in sales. It has hired you as a consultant to find ways to improve the situation. You believe that the problem results from poor cost control and inaccurate cost estimation on jobs. To gather data for your investigation, you turn to the accounting system and find that it is almost nonexistent. However, you piece together the following information for April:

▨ Production
1. Completed job 101.
2. Started and completed job 102.
3. Started job 103.

▨ Inventory values:
1. Work-in-process inventory:

> March 31: Job 101
>
> Direct material .... $ 2,000
> Labor (960 hours × $10) 9,600
>
> April 30: Job 103
>
> Direct material .... $ 1,600
> Labor (1,040 hours × $10).............. 10,400

2. Each job in work-in-process inventory was exactly 50 percent completed as to labor hours; however, all direct material necessary to do the entire job was charged to each job as soon as it was started.
3. There were no raw-material inventories or finished-goods inventories at either March 31 or April 30.

▨ Actual manufacturing overhead was $20,000.

▨ Cost of goods sold (before adjustment for over- or underapplied overhead):

> Job 101:
>
> Direct material .... $ 2,000
> Labor .... ?
> Overhead .... ?
> Total $30,800
>
> Job 102:
>
> Direct material .... ?
> Labor .... ?
> Overhead .... ?
> Total .... ?

▨ Overhead was applied to jobs using a predetermined rate per labor dollar that has been used since the company began operations.

▨ All raw materials were purchased for cash and charged directly to Work-in-Process Inventory when purchased. Raw material purchased in April amounted to $4,600.

▨ Direct-labor costs charged to jobs in April totaled $32,000. All labor costs were the same per hour for April for all laborers.

Required

Write a report to management to show the following:

a. The cost elements (direct material, labor, and overhead) of cost of goods sold before adjustment for over- or underapplied overhead for each job sold.

b. The value of each cost element (direct material, labor, and overhead) for each job in work-in-process inventory at April 30.

c. Over- or underapplied overhead for April.

Problem 3.60
Gantt Chart
(LO 8)

Prepare a Gantt chart for the following business plan. Use one week as the incremental time interval.

a. Select a cross-functional planning team, duration two weeks.

b. Hold twice-weekly meetings until the plan is implemented.

c. Identify products or services to meet market needs, consistent with the organization's mission, six weeks, which can begin as soon as the team is assembled.

d. Select team information needs and technology, two weeks; can begin as soon as the team is assembled.

e. Select production technology, two weeks; can begin two weeks before the product or service is finalized.

f. Determine advertising, promotion, and distribution needs and methods, four weeks; can begin two weeks before the product or service is finalized.

g. Set the selling price and allowable (target) product or service cost, one week; can begin when the product or service is finalized.

h. Prepare budgeted sales, cost, and profitability forecasts, two weeks; can begin one week before the product or service is finalized.

i. Design the product or service to meet customer needs, sales price, and allowable cost, six weeks; can begin after sales price and allowable cost are determined.

j. Develop prototype product or service, four weeks; can begin three weeks after beginning design phase.

k. Test market the product or service, four weeks; can begin after the prototype is complete.

l. Present business plan and prototype to executive committee, one week; can begin after test marketing is complete.

Problem 3.61
Gantt Chart
(LO 8)

Prepare a Gantt chart for the following construction project for which you have plans and financing. Use one week as the incremental time interval.

a. Find a suitable location, duration five weeks.

b. Hire a construction team, duration two weeks; can begin after the site is found.

c. Obtain necessary permits, duration two weeks; can begin one week prior to finding the site.

d. Order and receive building materials, duration one week; can begin at any time.

e. Construct building, duration eight weeks; can begin after the permits are obtained.

f. Add actual activities after learning that finding the site will take seven weeks and permits will take three weeks.

Problem 3.62
Job Costing and Ethics
(LO 6, 7)

Marcella Garcia, an accountant for a consulting firm, had just received the monthly cost reports for the two jobs she supervises: one for Arrow Space, Inc., and one for the US government. She immediately called her boss after reading the figures for the Arrow Space job.

"We're going to be way over budget on the Arrow Space contract," she informed her boss. "The job is only about three-fourths complete, but we've spent all the money that we had budgeted for the entire job."

"You'd better watch these job costs more carefully in the future," her boss advised. "Meanwhile, charge the rest of the costs needed to complete the Arrow Space job to the government job. The government won't notice the extra costs. Besides, we get reimbursed for costs on the government job, so we won't lose any money because of this problem you have with the Arrow Space contract."

Required

a. What should Garcia do?

b. Does it matter that Garcia's company is reimbursed for costs on the US government contract? Explain.

Case

Hollywood accounting can be every bit as creative as a good movie script. At least, that is what some lawyers and journalists seem to be telling us. According to news reports, the hit movie *Forrest Gump,* which won "best picture" honors at the Academy Awards, claimed a worldwide theatrical gross of $661 million in the first 18 months after its release. That amount excludes videocassette and soundtrack revenues, nor does it include licensing fees on *Forrest Gump* products such as wristwatches, ping-pong paddles, and shrimp cookbooks. Yet, according to Paramount Studios, the film project lost $62 million on a box office gross of $382 million during its first year.

Forrest Gump is one of a string of hit movies to report a loss. Other losers include *Batman, Rain Man, Dick Tracy, Ghostbusters, Alien, On Golden Pond, Fatal Attraction,* and *Coming to America.* Each of these motion pictures grossed well over $100 million, but in each case, costs were reportedly higher than revenues.

How can the studios be losing so much money on their most successful projects? Sometimes what is referred to as a loss is not really a loss at all. Typically, profits are calculated based on contracts between the studios and the film's "net profit participants." In a typical net profit participation contract, "profit" is gross studio revenues after deducting:

- "Negative costs"—production costs and payments to "gross participants" (who receive a percentage of gross studio revenues).
- Studio overhead (some of which is allocated to the film as a percentage of the gross revenue).
- Promotion and distribution costs.
- Advertising overhead (which is computed as a percentage of promotion and distribution costs).
- A distribution fee paid directly to the studio.
- Interest on the unrecovered costs (losses), whether or not the film was financed with debt.

The net profit participation contract is not the same as profit or loss for the motion picture, which is accounted for as a project or job. Net profit participation is a contract for compensation between the studio and certain individuals.

Winston Groom, the author of *Forrest Gump,* retained an attorney to obtain a share of the profits from the film, although Paramount reported a loss. Groom was paid $350,000 for the movie rights to the book and is entitled to 3 percent of the film's net profits. Paramount says it expects *Forrest Gump* to eventually show a profit and has advanced Groom $250,000 against his net profit participation.

At issue in the lawsuit is the way the studios calculate net profit. Critics argue that some of the costs (such as the distribution fee), are not really costs at all; instead, they are studio profits disguised as costs. Overhead allocations, such as studio overhead and advertising overhead, are based on arbitrary allocations, which, some have argued, are much higher than the actual overhead costs that are assignable to the film. In addition, whether the net profit participants should lose compensation because of cost overruns is questionable; they are largely under the control of the director, the stars, and the studio.

Will Paramount ever report a profit for *Forrest Gump?* That depends on how you define "profit" and whose perspective you take. Actor Tom Hanks and director Robert Zemeckis have already made more than $20 million each, including a share of the gross. But from the point of view of the net profit participants (e.g., Winston Groom), the film might never show a profit.

Required

Examine the net profit participant statement of profit and loss on page 134.

a. What amount of box office gross revenues is required before *Forrest Gump* earns a profit according to the net profit participation contract?

b. What amount of box office gross revenues is required before *Forrest Gump* earns a profit for Paramount?

c. Is Paramount's calculation of net profit fair to the net profit participants?

Net Profit Participant Statement of Profit and Loss
Forrest Gump
During Its First Year of Release (in millions)

Box office gross revenues		$382
Less: Amount retained by movie theaters (50%)		191
Studio's gross revenues..		$191
Less: Negative costs:		
Production costs	$ 66.8	
Gross profit participation (director, actors, 16% of studio gross revenues)	30.6	
Studio's overhead (15% of negative costs)	14.6	
Promotion and distribution costs	67.2	
Advertising overhead (10% of promotion and distribution cost)	6.7	
Distribution fee (32% of studio gross revenue)	61.1	
Total operating costs	$ 247.0	
Operating profit (loss)		(56)
Less: Financing costs (3% above prime on operating loss, assume amount is fixed).........		6
Net profit (loss) for distribution to net profit participants		$ (62)

[Adapted from *Forrest Gump—Accountant,* a case by G. Pfeiffer, R. Capettini, and G. Whittenburg.]

Activity-Based Management

◀ **A Look Back**

Part One introduced cost management. It discussed managing the value chain, cost system design, and measuring product costs.

▼ **A Look at This Part**

Part Two builds cost management tools to help understand production processes. The topics in this part are recent innovations in the field of cost management. Chapter 4 discusses activity-based costing. Chapter 5 discusses activity-based management. Chapter 6 discusses customer profitability analysis. Chapter 7 discusses the management of quality and time to create value.

▶ **A Look Ahead**

Part Three discusses process costing and cost allocation.

Chapter 4

Activity-Based Costing Systems

After completing this chapter, you should be able to:

1. Describe how traditional costing could lead to undercosting and overcosting products.

2. Discuss the four steps used in an activity-based costing system.

3. Identify five different levels of resources and activities used in production processes.

4. Estimate the cost of activities and calculate a cost-driver rate.

5. Assign activity costs to goods and services.

6. Analyze the profitability of products and customers.

7. Apply activity-based costing to service and merchandising companies.

8. Distinguish between ABC unit-level costing and ABC full costing of goods and services (Appendix).

Cost-*Management* Challenges

(Solutions are on page 159.)

1. **How** did activity-based cost information help PMI, Inc.?

2. **What** data and knowledge are necessary to support the development of activity-based information?

3. **Is** activity-based information always better than traditional costing information?

PMI Precision Molding, Inc.

The following is the transcript of a recent conference call between David Peterson, North American vice president of logistics for MegaBurger Corporation, and the executive staff of Precision Molding, Inc. (PMI). MegaBurger Corporation is one of the world's largest fast-food restaurant chains. PMI is a small company that specializes in plastic-injection molding. Melody Fairchild, president and chief executive officer of PMI, responds to Mr. Peterson's comments and questions.

David Peterson, MegaBurger: Good morning, Melody. Thank you for getting your staff together on such short notice.

Melody Fairchild, PMI: My pleasure. Let me introduce you to the rest of the team. Chad Norris is vice president of manufacturing, Alex Lewis is chief financial officer, and Michael Chia is our vice president of logistics.

David Peterson, MegaBurger: Hello, all. Thanks for joining us. Let me outline what we are proposing. We need someone to supply promotional novelty toys, such as action figures and movie tie-ins, to one of our regions, and we believe PMI can do the job. You have a good reputation for quality products, ethical business practices, and community service. PMI is the type of company with which we like to be associated.

We want you and our current supplier in the region to submit bids for this business. Quite frankly, we've been disappointed with our current supplier's business practices, and we're prepared to offer you the business if you show that PMI can supply a quality product with on-time delivery and at a reasonable price.

Melody Fairchild, PMI: David, our record for quality and on-time delivery is superb. I believe you've already checked with our current customers to verify that. We're confident that we can exceed your expectations. Before we submit a bid to you, we need to know details about products and distribution to fully evaluate this opportunity.

David Peterson, MegaBurger: Melody, you should be receiving a fax with product and delivery specifications. This includes our expected sales and distribution, and, as you know, this is very sensitive information. Before we send this, I must have your agreement that this information stays within PMI.

Melody Fairchild, PMI: Agreed. When do you need our response?

David Peterson, MegaBurger: We need your bid within 90 days. I'll be out of the country for the next few weeks, so please contact my assistant if you need more information. Any questions now?

Melody Fairchild, PMI: No, this is clear. We just received your fax. If we have any questions about it, I'll be in touch. Have a safe trip.

PMI Background

"What an opportunity! Can we win this business? Can we profitably supply novelty toys to MegaBurger? I don't know at this time, but we'd better figure it out!" Fairchild exclaimed to her executive team as she hung up the phone.

The small novelty toys are more complex than any product PMI has made. MegaBurger also has very high expectations for quality and on-time deliveries. Winning this bid could mean a large increase in PMI's sales and create future opportunities to partner with MegaBurger, which is a global giant. Fairchild was eager to expand PMI's customer base because she believed the company was too dependent on just two customers. However, she knew that if PMI did not evaluate this opportunity realistically, the company could suffer large losses on the MegaBurger business. Such a mistake could mean disaster for the company's employees and stockholders.

PMI's Competitive Situation

PMI, Inc., founded in 1981, had become one of the dominant manufacturers of plastic-injection-molded products in its geographical region. It emphasized consistent quality, quick order turnaround, reliable distribution, and reasonable prices, with a high level of service. PMI outsourced certain parts of its value chain to suppliers and machine shops that have been reliable business partners since the early 1980s. Melody Fairchild, the chief executive officer (CEO), believes that decisions such as selective outsourcing have allowed the company to focus on its primary competitive advantages, which are careful design, quality production, and a high level of customer service.

PMI was a small company that, although profitable, could ill afford to make mistakes by doing unprofitable work. PMI's management knew that it must accurately measure the costs of its current processes and apply those costs to current and future products. To prepare its bid for the MegaBurger business, PMI had to have good estimates of the costs to produce the novelty toys. Management needed accurate cost information so it could propose a product price that would ensure the business's profitability. Companies that submit low-price bids to prospective customers often find to their dismay that they have won an unprofitable bid because the prices that they charged were below their costs.

PMI's Products and Processes

We need some background information. PMI's current plastic products range from relatively simple items, such as reusable 1- and 4-liter beverage containers for a national discount retail chain, to complex products, such as plastic baby carriers and strollers. The simple beverage containers require blowing liquefied plastic into a mold, sometimes combining it with different colors for different types of drinks (e.g., green for ginger ale). The more complicated baby-care products, which are under exclusive contract for an international firm, have multiple, complex parts that require complicated molds and precise control over colors, injec-

Workers inspect the quality of plastic containers.

tion pressures, and temperatures. PMI's ability to make these complex products attracted MegaBurger's attention.

The company purchases small plastic pellets that are heated to make liquid plastic, which is put through a process known as "injection molding" that molds the plastic into the desired shapes. See Exhibit 4–1 for the steps involved in the production process:

■ Purge or clean the system before each production run to prevent contamination by dirt or leftover plastic and color.

■ Set up the machine to ensure that order data are recorded properly and that machine settings are correct for the product.

■ Begin the production run to verify production data and ensure that the machine is operating properly; then start the full-scale operation of the run.

■ Perform the actual production run.

■ Remove products from the mold and visually inspect them to ensure that they meet visual quality standards.

■ Recycle defective products to reduce waste and prevent defective products from reaching customers.

■ Place good products in inventory in preparation for delivery to customers.

■ End the production run so that the machinery and work area are left in a safe, clean condition.

PMI's Costing-System Options

PMI could use a simple cost system, such as the ones discussed in Chapter 3, or a more complex cost system, such as the one discussed in this chapter. In choosing among alternative cost systems, PMI managers must assess the costs and benefits of their choice. The simpler system requires less effort and time but provides less accurate cost estimates. The more complex system requires more effort and time but provides more accurate cost estimates. In general, company managers will weigh the benefits of more accurate cost estimates against the time and effort required to obtain them.

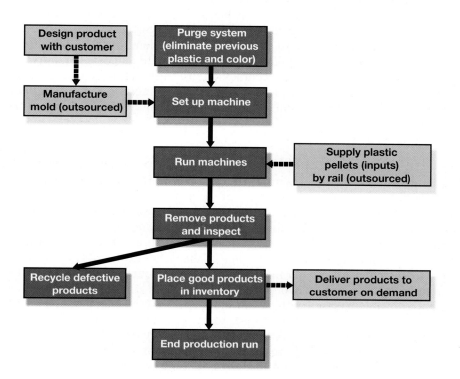

Exhibit 4–1

Injection-Molding Process at PMI

PMI's Costing-System Team

Melody Fairchild, the CEO, knew that reliable cost-management information would be critically important to PMI as it prepared the bid for the MegaBurger business. Accordingly, she asked her chief financial officer (CFO), Alex Lewis, to form the best team possible to prepare the bid for MegaBurger. He already had three top-notch employees in mind. These included a recently hired finance employee, who had just received her MBA with top honors, and a production supervisor with 20 years of experience in the industry, mostly with other companies. The final team member was an employee who worked in product design and did a good deal of consulting with customers who had several years of experience with the company. Lewis realized that the team also would need information from other company employees in all areas, including human resources and information technology, although these people would not be part of the formal team.

The team formed by Lewis discussed different costing-system alternatives with the company's accounting personnel. The team's goal was to find an accounting system to measure the costs of existing products as accurately as possible. The team planned to use this information to estimate the costs of the novelty toys to produce for MegaBurger. Team members knew that MegaBurger's novelty toys would require many of the same activities already being used for existing PMI products. Thus, members believed that using historical data and adjusting these data for differences, such as differences in the costs of materials, would be appropriate for estimating the costs of the MegaBurger toys.

Traditional Costing System

The traditional cost system that many companies use does not trace indirect costs, such as supervisors' salaries and utilities, directly to the product. Instead, using a traditional cost system, companies allocate indirect costs to the product using an allocation base such as direct-labor hours or machine hours. We discussed this type of cost system in Chapter 3.

The advantage of a traditional cost system is its simplicity. However, the saying "you get what you pay for," is appropriate here. The resulting cost data are typically not as accurate as those that more complex and expensive cost systems provide.

Nevertheless, a traditional cost system can be sufficient to meet managers' cost-information requirements, particularly if the level of indirect costs is relatively low compared to direct costs and if the accuracy of cost information is not critical to the company's success. Managers of organizations using a traditional cost system might decide that the costs to implement a more complex cost system are higher than its potential benefits.

Undercosting and Overcosting Products: Cost of Dinner Example

LO 1 Describe how traditional costing could lead to undercosting and overcosting products.

Suppose that you go to dinner with a friend to celebrate the end of finals week at school. You order an entrée ($8) and a cup of specialty coffee ($3). Your friend orders an appetizer ($6), a salad ($5), an entrée ($10), and dessert with coffee ($8). You agree to split the bill at the end of the evening, which means each of you will pay $20 (excluding the tip!). Is this $20 a fair cost of your meal? It is not; your meal was overcosted because you simply took an average of the entire cost of the two dinners. If you were to track the cost of your meal more precisely, your cost would be $11 ($3 + $8), and the cost to your friend would be $29.

A similar problem arises with a traditional cost system. Many companies have found that this system tends to assign costs to products based on an arbitrarily developed average rather than the actual resource usage. As a result, products that are more complex to build and consume more resources (for example, more inspections, machine setups, materials) are not necessarily assigned their fair share of costs.

Instead, many of these complex products' costs could be unfairly assigned to simpler products. Thus, the complex products are undercosted, and the simple products are overcosted. Note the similarity of this problem and the shared dinner bill. Using a simple average of the total meal cost overcosted your simple meal and undercosted your friend's more complex meal.

Refining a Traditional Costing System

Clearly, the traditional costing system has a number of weaknesses, including the problem of undercosting and overcosting products as mentioned. A refined costing system allows for more accurate costing of goods and services. Three key points should be made with respect to refining a traditional costing system.

1. Trace as many costs directly to the good or service as possible, as long as the cost of doing so does not outweigh the benefit. For example, when you and your friend split the dinner tab, you could easily have traced all costs to each of you, thereby resulting in a more accurate assignment of costs.

2. Categorize indirect costs, which are not easily traced to the product, into cost pools. **Cost pools** are groups of individual cost items; costs with similar cost drivers or allocation bases are grouped together. Ideally, match the costs with allocation bases or cost drivers that have a cause-and-effect relationship with the cost. For example, group together all indirect costs driven by machine usage, such as those for machine maintenance and the energy to run the machines.

   Continue this categorization until all indirect costs have been appropriately grouped into pools. Most companies do not allocate some of the administrative costs of running the business to products because these costs are peripheral to the company's production activity.

3. Use cost allocation to assign indirect costs to products. In general, **cost allocation** is the process of assigning indirect costs to products or organizational units (e.g., departments). Select an appropriate cost-allocation base for each cost pool established in item 2. Ideally, the allocation base has a causal relationship to the cost pool, so if a particular cost pool has costs driven by machine usage, the amount of time the machine is used (e.g., minutes or hours) is an appropriate cost-allocation base.

Activity-Based Costing System

Activity-based costing is a commonly used approach to improve a traditional costing system. **Activity-based costing,** or **ABC,** is a costing method that first assigns costs to activities and then to goods and services based on how much each good or service uses the activities. As defined in Chapter 2, an *activity* is any discrete task that an organization undertakes to make or deliver a good or service. To reduce the cost of goods and services, managers must modify the activities required to produce the goods and services.

LO 2 Discuss the four steps used in an activity-based costing system.

An increasing number of companies around the world are using ABC systems. To name a few, American Airlines, Hewlett-Packard, DaimlerChrysler, and the United States Postal Service use or have used it. As noted in Cost Management in Practice 4.1, a survey of 177 companies in the United Kingdom indicated that 37.8 percent of the companies surveyed were using or considering using ABC. Results from this study and similar ones in developed economies around the world indicate that ABC is not a passing fad. A majority of companies still use traditional costing methods such as those discussed in Chapter 3, but the use of ABC appears to be increasing.

Note that ABC is used to establish product costs primarily for decision-making purposes, such as whether to continue offering a product, not for inventory valuation for external reporting.

Cost Management in Practice 4.1

Use of Activity-Based Costing

Activity-based costing has maintained a high profile as a cost-management innovation for two decades. Enough time has passed to assess whether it is a passing fad. Studies of company practices indicate that a large number of companies, as well as some organizations in the public sector, are using ABC.

Some companies have tried ABC and dropped it. Reasons for this include its implementation cost. In the case of a Hewlett-Packard division that one of the authors studied, management obtained a great deal of information from ABC, restructured activities as a result, and no longer had the problems that ABC had uncovered. ABC had served its purpose and was no longer needed.

A recent survey of practices in the United Kingdom indicated that 37.8 percent of the companies that provided usable responses were using ABC or were considering using it. The study reported these results:

ABC Adoption Status	Number of Companies in Study	Percent of Companies in Study
Currently using it	31	17.5%
Currently considering using it	36	20.3
Considered but rejected it	27	15.3
Had not considered using it	83	46.9
Total	177	100.0%

Although ABC has its roots in manufacturing companies, the study found that the financial services companies surveyed were more likely to use ABC than were manufacturing companies. *Source: J. Innes, F. Mitchell, and D. Sinclair, "Activity-Based Costing in the U.K.'s Largest Companies." (Full citations to references are in the Bibliography.)*

Four steps are used to determine the cost of goods and services using ABC. The following briefly summarizes those four steps. Much of this chapter is devoted to discussing them in detail.

Step 1:   *Identify and classify the activities related to the company's products.* Activities in all areas of the value chain (product design, production, marketing, distribution, etc.) must be included. People identify the activities that a company performs to produce a product to prepare an **activity dictionary,** a list of activities performed by an organization to produce its products. The activity dictionary can be obtained in a number of different ways, including interviews with the employees who perform the activities. As activities are identified, they are classified as unit level, batch level, product level, customer level, or facility level. We discuss these classifications shortly.

Step 2:   *Estimate the cost of activities identified in step 1.* Estimate the costs of specific activities that cause costs. These costs are for both *human resources,* such as employee labor for production and machine maintenance, and *physical resources,* such as the cost of machinery and building occupancy. Information must include employee data from personnel interviews and financial data from the accounting department. Then calculate the total cost of each activity.

Step 3:   *Calculate a cost-driver rate for each activity.* The activity cost data from step 2 is used to calculate a cost-driver rate that the company can use for assigning activity costs to goods and services. This rate should use a base that has some causal link to the cost. For example, costs of running a production machine are likely caused by the number of hours it is run. Thus, choosing a rate for this activity based on machine hours is wise.

Step 4:   *Assign activity costs to products.* The cost-driver rates prepared in step 3 are used to assign activity costs to goods and services. For example, if a particular product uses 1.5 machine hours in production and the rate from step 3 is $50 per hour, the product is assigned $75 based on its machine usage.

Upon completing these four steps, a company can calculate the costs to provide existing goods and services, which can be used to better understand the profitability of each. The activity-based costing data also could be used to estimate the cost of future products.

After discussing the costing-system alternatives, PMI's team decided to use an activity-based costing (ABC) system and at this point became known as the "ABC team," which we shall use in this chapter. First, the team would use ABC to identify the cost of existing products and then it would adjust this cost information as necessary to estimate the cost to produce the MegaBurger products.

Step 1: Identify and Classify Activities Related to Products

Bakery Example

How would you identify the activities performed to produce goods and services? Imagine for the moment that you own a bakery that makes and sells a variety of cookies. You simply list all activities required to make them. The major categories of activities include purchasing the materials, mixing the dough, forming the cookies, baking, performing quality control through taste tests, and packaging or displaying the cookies. (Performing quality control should be one of the more desirable activities.) Your activity list might have many details. For example, the baking activity might include subactivities such as warming the oven, watching the cookies to prevent burning, washing the pans, and cleaning the oven.

LO 3 Identify five different levels of resources and activities used in production processes.

Five-Level Hierarchy of Resources and Activities

Analyzing all resources and activities needed to produce and support a company's products and services is made easier by recognizing that these resources and activities support different levels of the company, which are described here. Examples are based on the bakery business.

1. **Unit-level resources and activities** are resources acquired and activities performed specifically for individual units of product or service. *Unit-level resources* could include materials, parts, and components and perhaps labor and energy resources if they are acquired for each unit of output. *Unit-level activities* could include work efforts that transform the resources into individual products and services. Unit-level resources and activities are directly traceable to units of output.

    In our bakery example, the materials (e.g., dough, chocolate chips) for cookies are unit-level resources because each cookie produced requires them. At PMI, the materials used to make products were unit-level resources.

2. **Batch-level resources and activities** are the resources acquired and the activities performed to make a group, or batch, of similar products. *Batch-level activities* usually include the work performed to set up the production machinery to produce a certain batch (i.e., group) of products or to

Bakery products are made in batches.

test quality control for a batch of product. *Batch-level resources* include the expenditure of labor to set up and test machines. Batch-level resources and activities are directly traceable to certain batches but are indirect to the individual units produced.

We return to the bakery example. Mixing the cookie dough for each batch of cookies, placing the batch in the oven, and testing for quality control when the batch comes out of the oven (or even before it goes into the oven) are included in this category because these are required to make a batch of cookies but are indirect activities of one particular cookie.

3. **Product-level resources and activities** are the resources acquired and the activities performed to produce and sell a specific good or service. *Product-level resources* could include specialized equipment, software, and personnel that would not be needed except to provide that particular product. *Product-level activities* could include the design or advertisement of a particular product. Product-level resources and activities are directly traceable to specific goods or services but are indirectly related to batches or individual units produced.

    Assume that our bakery produces several different types of cookies (peanut butter, chocolate chip, etc.). Developing or purchasing the recipe for each type of cookie is in this category since a recipe is required for each cookie type (product) produced. Furthermore, if a special mixing machine were required for a particular type of cookie (e.g., cream-filled bran cookies), the cost of that particular mixing machine is a product-level resource.

4. **Customer-level resources and activities** are the resources acquired and the activities performed to serve specific customers. *Customer-level resources* could include specialized equipment, software, and personnel dedicated to serving specific customers. *Customer-level activities* could include consulting with customers and making special distribution arrangements for specific customer requirements (e.g., using an air-freight service instead of normal ground service because of a particular customer's needs).

    Suppose that a customer at our bakery asked us to produce 1,000 cookies in the shape of its company logo for which we had to design a special mold. The special mold is a customer-level resource because only this customer requires it.

5. **Facility-level resources and activities** are the resources acquired and the activities performed to provide the general capacity to produce goods and services. *Facility-level resources* could include land, buildings, and, in some cases, the labor force, which some companies maintain without laying people off despite changes in products, customers, batches, and units of output. *Facility-level activities* could include the activities of plant or store managers, research and development, and companywide advertising versus product-specific advertising.

    Facility-level resources and activities are directly related to the scale, scope, and location of operations but are indirectly related to customers, products, batches, or individual units produced. The cost of the space leased by our bakery is in this category.

    Ford Motor Company's advertising of the Ford Explorer is in the product-level category. If Ford sponsors a public television program to promote the company's brand name, however, this advertising is in the facility-level category.

Classification Objectives

The objectives of classifying resources and activities into the five categories are to create (1) accurate descriptions of how the organization performs its work and (2) the ability to trace the cost of resources acquired and activities performed to goods and services produced.

Methods for Identifying and Classifying Activities

Organizations generate their activity lists in a variety of ways, including these:

Top-down approach. Some organizations use ABC teams of people at the middle-management level or above. The primary advantage to this top-down approach is that generating the activity dictionary is quick and inexpensive. A large consumer products company used this approach to develop activity dictionaries for many of its operations.[1] A business unit of American Express developed a variation of this approach by slightly modifying a predefined (or boiler plate) activity dictionary based on years of experience with each business unit's processes.[2]

Interview or participative approach. This approach relies on the inclusion of operating employees on the team and/or interviews with them. For example, PMI's ABC team would interview production personnel to identify and understand the activities involved to produce the product. This approach is likely to generate a more accurate activity dictionary than is the top-down approach. People doing jobs usually know more about their jobs than their supervisors do.

One danger associated with the interview or participative approach, however, is that employees might not disclose their activities truthfully if they are concerned about the possible effects of giving higher-level management specific information about what they actually do. Another danger is that employees might not recall their work processes accurately.

Recycling approach. Reusing documentation of processes developed for other purposes is possible. (That is, "Don't reinvent the wheel.") Many companies, for example, have sought and achieved ISO 9000 certification, which requires thorough documentation of their processes.[3] Recycling this documentation into an activity dictionary can be relatively straightforward.

PMI's Activity List

We now return to PMI to describe how the ABC team performed step 1 of the ABC process, identifying and classifying activities related to the company's products.

The ABC team decided to start to establish a list of its activities using the recycling approach because the company had recently identified activities in the production process while preparing for ISO 9000 certification. The team rejected the top-down approach not only because information was already available but also because team members believed that input from all levels of the organization (including production personnel) was needed.

See Exhibit 4–2 for the information for ISO 9000 certification used to list PMI's activities. The ABC team organized this list according to the categories just discussed (unit, batch, etc.). Exhibit 4–2 includes only major categories of PMI's total list to keep the list short; note that Exhibit 4–2 refers to "detailed subactivities omitted" in several places.

The first digit in the left column of the activity dictionary or list in Exhibit 4–2 is the most general activity (e.g., 1.), and the third digit represents the most detailed

---

[1] F. Selto, "Implementing Activity-Based Management." (Full citations to references are in the Bibliography.)

[2] D. Carlson and S. M. Young, "Activity-Based Total Quality Management at American Express." A company executive claimed that approximately 200 to 300 activities are sufficient to describe all of the processes of medium-size (less than 1,000 employees) organizations.

[3] The International Organization of Standardization (ISO) based in Geneva administers ISO 9000 certification of companies who either desire or are required by customers to certify the quality of their processes. Many books, articles, and Internet sites are devoted to this certification. Go to *www.isonet.com.*

Exhibit 4–2

PMI, Inc., Activity and
Resource List

Activity/Resource	
Number	**Description**
1.	**Unit Level**
1.1	Acquire and use materials for containers
1.1.1	Medium-grade plastic pellets
1.1.2	Colors
1.2	Acquire and use materials for baby-care products
1.2.1	High-grade plastic pellets
1.2.2	Fasteners
1.2.3	Colors
2.	**Batch Level**
2.1	Set up manually controlled injection-molding machines
2.1.1	Set up manually controlled injection-molding machines (detailed subactivities omitted)
2.1.2	Perform quality control of batches of products produced on manually controlled machines
2.2	Set up computer-controlled injection-molding machines
2.2.1	Set up computer-controlled injection-molding machine (detailed subactivities omitted)
2.2.2	Perform quality control of batches of product produced on computer-controlled machines
3.	**Product Level**
3.1	Design and manufacture molds (outsourced)
3.2	Use manually controlled injection-molding machines
3.2.1	Machine depreciation
3.2.2	Machine maintenance
3.2.3	Machine operation–labor
3.3	Use computer-controlled injection-molding machines (detailed subactivities omitted)
4.	**Customer Level**
4.1	Consult with customers
4.2	Provide warehousing for customers
5.	**Facility Level**
5.1	Manage workers
5.2	Use main building
5.2.1	Lease building
5.2.2	Use utilities
5.2.3	Maintain building

activity shown. Everything listed under activity 1 refers to unit-level activities and resources; everything listed under activity 2 refers to batch-level activities and resources, and so forth for activities 3 through 5. Activity/Resource 1.2.2 refers to the materials fasteners, which is part of activity 1.2, acquire and use materials for baby-care products, which are part of activity 1, "unit-level" activities.

As you will note, the activity is actually the *acquisition* of the material and its *use* in producing the product. At PMI, the activities' acquisition and use of the materials to produce the product can be stated in the amount paid for the materials, the cost of inspecting and storing them, and other costs related to acquiring them and getting them ready to be used in the production process.

In interviewing production workers, PMI's ABC team asked a question such as, What do you do to prepare to produce a batch of beverage containers? A production-line employee might respond, "I set these dials and insert the specified colors every time we start a new batch of beverage containers."

Developing the Activity List

You're the Decision Maker 4.1

Refer to Exhibit 4–2 and the preceding discussion. Put yourself in the role as a member of the ABC team preparing PMI's list of activities.

a. If you were developing PMI's activity list, would you regard the list in Exhibit 4–2 as complete (not considering the subactivities omitted)? Do certain types of activities seem to be missing? Explain.

b. Suppose that people are reluctant to acknowledge that they perform some types of unproductive activities. How should a company's management deal with this problem?

(Solutions begin on page 160.)

Step 2: Estimate the Cost of Activities

The next step in the ABC process is to estimate the cost of the activities that were identified in step 1. PMI's ABC team proceeded by asking all employees to indicate how much time they spent on each activity in an average week and then identified the physical resources that supported various activities.

LO 4 Estimate the cost of activities and calculate a cost-driver rate.

PMI's Use of the Employee Activity Data Sheet

The employee activity data sheet completed by Margaret Smythe appears as Exhibit 4–3. Before completing this activity data sheet, Ms. Smythe indicated which detailed activities from the list in Exhibit 4–2 that she performed. Using the data Ms. Smythe provided, the ABC team customized a blank sheet for her by filling in her department, name, title, and the list of activities she had identified. The team emailed the customized sheet to Ms. Smythe, who added her estimates of the number of hours per typical week that she spent on each activity. After adding this information, she emailed the sheet back to the team, which computed the cost of her time on activities (multiplying Ms. Smythe's hours by the hourly salary and benefits; $30 per hour). The ABC team collected data from all of PMI's employees or from the employees' supervisors in the same way.

Activity Data Sheet Combined with Accounting Information

For each activity, the ABC team combined the information collected from employees with data from the accounting and other records. For example, for the activity "provide warehousing for customers" (4.2), the team collected data about the costs to lease warehouse space and insure the products in the warehouse, and about employee time spent performing warehousing activities (e.g., moving products from place to place).

Exhibit 4–3

Employee Activity Data Sheet

Name	Margaret Smythe		
Title	Supervisor		
Wages and benefits per hour $30			
Activity Number	Activity Description	Hours per Week	Cost
2.2.1	Set up computer-controlled machine	20	$ 600
2.2.2	Perform quality control of batches of product produced on computer-controlled machines	6	180
4.1	Consult with customers	8	240
5.1	Manage workers	6	180
	Total hours	40	$1,200

Step 3: Calculate a Cost-Driver Rate for the Activity

Cost-Driver Rates: Bakery Example

A **cost-driver rate** is the estimated cost of resource consumption per unit of the cost-driver for each activity. A **cost driver** is a characteristic of an activity or event that causes that activity or event to cause costs.[4] A **cost-driver base** is the base used to trace or assign costs to activities.

Using the bakery as an example, what drives (or causes) the cost of performing maintenance on the mixing machines? An appropriate cost-driver base might be the number of batches produced (the more batches produced, the more maintenance costs incurred). This rate is calculated by dividing the activity cost by the estimated level of activity in the cost-driver base. For example, if the bakery spends $4,800 per year on activities related to maintaining the mixing machine and produces 400 batches of cookies each year, the cost-driver rate is $12 per batch.

An appropriate cost-driver base should:

- Logically have a cause-and-effect relationship with the activity and its costs.
- Be measurable.
- Predict or explain the activity's use of resources with reasonable accuracy.
- Be based on the resource's practical capacity to support activities.

Practical Capacity Note

This last point requires some explanation. Imagine that a warehouse has 1,000 square feet of capacity for storage. If its cost is $1,000, the cost-driver rate is $1 per square foot ($1,000 ÷ 1,000 square feet).

Now suppose that only 800 square feet of the warehouse is used to store product A with the remaining 200 (1,000 − 800) square feet unused. Analysts should assign $800 ($1 per square foot × 800 square feet) to Product A and $200 ($1 per square foot × 200 square feet) to "unused capacity." (Recall our discussion in Chapter 2 that distinguished between resources used—the 800 square feet in this example—and unused capacity— the 200 square feet in this example.) The total resources supplied equal 1,000 square feet, but the cost of only the 800 square feet used by product A should be assigned to it.

Assignment of Cost-Driver Rates to PMI's Activities

PMI's ABC team gathered the activity-cost information from all staff as described previously. Then the team decided to use the cost drivers shown in Exhibit 4–4. To simplify the presentation, we condense the activity list in Exhibit 4–2 according to common cost drivers as shown in Exhibit 4–4. This allows us to work with fewer categories of activities in assigning costs to goods and services for product-costing purposes. For example, the unit-level for materials for baby-care products condenses the individual items—high-grade plastic, fasteners, and colors—into one category that we call "materials for baby-care products."

The following explains the cost driver for the five cost-driver rates in Exhibit 4–4.

1. *Unit level.* The cost of materials to make both types of products is driven by the number of units produced. In effect, the materials costs vary with the volume of output.
2. *Batch level.* Batches are groups of the same units. For example, a batch of baby-care products could be 100 identical baby seats; a batch of containers could be 1,000 green 1-liter ginger ale bottles with particular lettering. Each batch of units

---

[4] Often in the ABC literature, authors refer to "cost drivers" when they mean the bases used to trace or assign costs. We use the term "cost drivers" to mean the decisions managers make about the structure and use of resources that drive costs. This is consistent with the economics and strategy literature that gave birth to ABC. See M. Porter, *Competitive Advantage*. To avoid confusion with the economic basis for ABC, we use the term "cost-driver base" to mean the base used to trace or assign costs. Another term for the base used to trace costs is "activity base."

Activities Resources	Cost-Driver Bases	Exhibit 4—4
1. Unit Level		Activity List and Cost-Driver Bases
1.1 Acquire and use materials for containers	Number of units of beverage containers produced	**PMI**
1.2 Acquire and use materials for baby-care products	Number of units of baby-care products produced	
2. Batch Level		
2.1 Set up manually controlled machines	Number of batches of beverage containers	
2.1.1 Do the setup		
2.1.2 Perform quality control of batches of products produced on manually controlled machines		
2.2 Set up computer-controlled machines	Number of batches of baby-care products	
3. Product Level		
3.1 Design and manufacture molds (outsourced)	Number of molds required for each product type	
3.2 Use manually controlled machines	Number of different product types (i.e., containers)	
3.3 Use computer-controlled machines	Number of different product types (i.e., baby-care products)	
4. Customer Level		
4.1 Consult with customers	Number of consultations	
4.2 Provide warehousing for customers	Number of cubic feet	
5. Facility Level		
5.1 Manage workers	Amount of salaries and benefits of production workers	
5.2 Use main building	Number of square feet of each product's usage	

requires the machines to be set up according to design specifications, just as building a house requires following the architect's design specifications. The costs of setting up the machines and of performing quality-control inspections on batches are driven by the number of batches produced. Nearly all of PMI's batch-level costs are labor costs.

3. *Product level.* Activity 3.1, design and manufacture molds, refers to the molds used in machines to shape the liquefied plastic as desired. This activity comprises designing and making the molds and remaking them to satisfy changing customer requirements. PMI outsources this activity to a company that specializes in these activities for plastic products. The outside company owns the mold and leases it to PMI.

   The cost of activities 3.2 and 3.3 are the depreciation, maintenance, and operating costs from using the machines. These operating costs include costs for energy, the labor to operate the manually controlled machines, and a small amount of labor to maintain both the manually controlled and computer-controlled machines.

4. *Customer level.* Activity 4.1, consult with customers, refers to customer consultations about orders, changes in orders, and complaints. The cost of these consultations is composed almost entirely of labor costs. Activity 4.2, provide warehousing for customers, refers to leasing the warehouse space and using personnel to move items in and out of it and to provide its security.

5. *Facility level.* Activity 5.1 refers to the management of production workers. Activity 5.2 refers to the use of the main factory building to produce either containers or baby-care products. Occupancy costs include the lease of the building space, the cost of heating and lighting it, insurance and taxes on it and its contents, and maintenance.

Exhibit 4–5	Computing Predetermined Cost-Driver Rates for a Typical Month

(A) Activity/Resource	(B) Cost-Driver Base	(C) Activity Cost	(D) Activity Volume	(E) Predetermined Cost Driver Rate (C) ÷ (D)
1. Unit Level				
1.1 Acquire and use materials for containers	Units of beverage containers produced	$40,000	1,000,000 units	$.04 per unit
1.2 Acquire and use materials for baby-care products	Units of baby-care products produced	$80,000	8,000 units	$10 per unit
2. Batch Level				
2.1 Set up manually controlled machines	Number of batches of beverage containers	$ 3,000	10 batches	$300 per batch
2.2 Set up computer-controlled machines	Number of batches of baby-care products	$12,000	20 batches	$600 per batch
3. Product Level				
3.1 Design and manufacture molds	Number of molds required for each product type	$ 5,000	5 molds	$1,000 per mold
3.2 Use manually controlled machines	Product type (i.e., containers)	$15,000	1 product type	$15,000 for containers per month
3.3 Use computer-controlled machines	Product type (i.e., baby-care products)	$40,000	1 product type	$40,000 for baby-care products per month
4. Customer Level				
4.1 Consult with customers	Number of consultations	$ 4,000	40 consultations	$100 per consultation
4.2 Provide warehousing for customers	Number of cubic feet	$ 2,000	10,000 cubic feet	$.20 per cubic foot
5. Facility Level				
5.1 Manage workers	Salaries and benefits of production workers	$ 3,000	$15,000 production labor costs	20% of production labor cost
5.2 Use main building	Square feet of each product's usage	$48,000	16,000 sq. ft.	$3 per sq. ft.

PMI

Sources of information in this exhibit:

Column (A) activities are from Exhibits 4–2 and 4–4.

Column (B) cost-driver bases are from Exhibit 4–4.

Column (C), the total costs in a typical month for each activity, was developed by the ABC team from reviewing accounting records, interviewing operating personnel, and collecting employee activity data sheets such as that in Exhibit 4–3.

Column (D), the activity volume for each cost-driver base, was developed by the ABC team from interviewing operating personnel and reviewing various records.

Column (E), the predetermined cost-driver rate, is, as indicated, Column (C) divided by Column (D) and is the cost per unit of activity for each cost-driver base.

See Exhibit 4–5 for the information the ABC team used to compute the predetermined cost-driver rates. Note that the numbers are calculated for a typical month. The ABC team wanted to derive cost-driver rates that would be generally useful and not affected by large variations in a particular month (e.g., utilities costs). Many companies develop cost-driver rates for a typical or "average" month.

The method that the ABC team used to calculate cost-driver rates is the same method used to develop predetermined overhead rates that you learned in Chapter 3. By using these predetermined rates, the ABC team saved the time and effort of computing cost-driver rates for every month. The predetermined cost-driver rates computed for a typical month might not be exactly the same as those for a specific month, say October, but they are likely to be very close to the actual rates. Many companies

You're the Decision Maker 4.2

Using Cost-Driver Rates

Review Exhibit 4–5 and the preceding discussion.

a. Does the cost-driver rate for activity 1.1 have the same meaning as the one for activity 2.1? Explain.

b. Suppose that you are PMI's CEO and decide to stop providing warehousing services for customers. Would PMI really save the $2,000 per month for activity 4.2? Why or why not?

c. What other factors would you consider in deciding whether to stop providing warehousing services?

(Solutions begin on page 160.)

are willing to sacrifice a little accuracy to avoid computing actual cost-driver rates every month. (Most companies compute predetermined rates once or twice per year.) PMI's chief financial officer, Alex Lewis, was willing to give up a little accuracy to save time and effort by computing predetermined rates just once a year instead of every month.

Few companies assign *all* of their costs to products. For example, companies generally do not assign the chief executive's salary or other administrative costs to products. An allocation of such costs to products is likely arbitrary and does not reflect a particular product's use of resources. As is common practice, PMI's ABC team did not assign administration costs to the products.

Furthermore, PMI appropriately did not assign the cost of unused capacity to products. Unused main building capacity and employee time paid for but not used in production was not charged to products.

Before discussing step 4, we should note that many companies stop at this point and use the information obtained from steps 1 through 3 to identify their cost activities. These companies then focus on the more costly activities and modify processes to reduce or eliminate them. PMI used step 4 in the ABC process, however, to assign activity costs to products.

Step 4: Assign Activity Costs to Products

Bakery Example

Recall the bakery example in which we established a cost-driver rate for maintenance of the mixing machine. This rate is used to assign mixing-machine maintenance costs to batches of cookies at a rate of $12 per batch. If the bakery makes 10 batches of chocolate chip cookies in a month, it assigns $120 to chocolate chip cookies for mixing-machine maintenance for that month.

LO 5 Assign activity costs to goods and services.

PMI Example

See Exhibit 4–6 for the way that PMI's ABC team determined the cost of products for the month of October. Exhibit 4–6 applies the *cost-driver rates for a typical month* from Exhibit 4–5 to the *actual cost-driver volumes* for October.

Column (A) of Exhibit 4–6 shows the activities that we have been discussing. Column (B) shows the cost-driver rate that is related to a particular activity. We derived these rates in Exhibit 4–5. We have omitted listing the cost drivers for each activity to simplify the presentation. Recall that we present these cost drivers in Exhibit 4–5 if you want to review them.

Column (C) presents the actual cost-driver volumes for the month of October. Note that these differ somewhat from the typical month volumes shown in Exhibit 4–5. Columns (D) and (E) present the product costs for each of the two products—containers and baby-care products. Columns (D) and (E) show the total ABC costs for October computed using predetermined cost-driver rates and actual cost-driver

Exhibit 4–6   Assigning Costs to Products for the Month of October

(A) Activity/Resource	(B) Predetermined Cost-Driver Rate (from Exhibit 4–5)	(C) Actual Activity Volume in October	(D) Cost of Products [column (B) × column (C)] Containers	(E) Baby Care
1. Unit Level				
1.1 Acquire and use materials for containers	$.04 per unit	1,200,000 units	$48,000	NA
1.2 Acquire and use materials for baby-care products	$10 per unit	7,000 units	NA	$ 70,000
2. Batch Level				
2.1 Set up manually controlled machines	$300 per batch	12 batches	$ 3,600	NA
2.2 Set up computer-controlled machines	$600 per batch	16 batches	NA	$ 9,600
3. Product Level				
3.1 Design and manufacture of molds				
Containers	$1,000 per mold	1 mold	$ 1,000	NA
Baby-care products	$1,000 per mold	4 molds	NA	$ 4,000
3.2 Use manually controlled machines	$15,000 for product type	1 product type	$15,000	NA
3.3 Use computer-controlled machines	$40,000 for product type	1 product type	NA	$ 40,000
4. Customer Level				
4.1 Consult with customers				
Containers	$100 per consultation	2 consultations	$ 200	NA
Baby-care products	$100 per consultation	40 consultations	NA	$ 4,000
4.2 Provide warehousing for customers				
Containers	$.20 per cu. ft.	8,000 cu. ft.	$ 1,600	NA
Baby-care products	$.20 per cu. ft.	2,000 cu. ft.	NA	$ 400
5. Facility Level				
5.1 Manage workers				
Containers	20% of the production labor costs	$ 4,000	$ 800	NA
Baby-care products	20% of the production labor costs	$10,000	NA	$ 2,000
5.2 Use main building				
Containers	$3 per sq. ft.	5,000 sq. ft.	$15,000	NA
Baby-care products	$3 per sq. ft.	7,000 sq. ft.	NA	$ 21,000

Total costs traced to products in October, by product type $85,200 $151,000

Total costs traced to products in October   → $236,200 ←

ABC costs per unit (total ABC costs ÷ product volume)

(1,200,000 containers and 7,000 units of baby-care products)

$85,200 ÷ 1,200,000 $151,000 ÷ 7,000 units

= $.071 per unit   = $21.57 per unit

Sources of information in this exhibit:

Column (A) activities are from Exhibits 4–2, 4–4, and 4–5.

Column (B) cost-driver rates are from Exhibit 4–5.

Column (C), the actual cost-driver volume for the month of October, was collected by the ABC team by interviewing operating personnel and from company records. The cost-driver volume in October is a bit different from that in a "typical" month, which is to be expected in ABC analyses.

Columns (D) and (E), the cost of each product, was computed by multiplying the cost-driver rate in column (B) by the actual cost-driver volume in October in column (C). Column (D) and column (E) show the product cost for containers and baby-care products, respectively.

volumes for October. The unit costs for the two products are computed using the total ABC costs for the month and the monthly production volumes from the top of Column (C):

Containers $85,200 ÷ 1,200,000 units = $.071 per unit

Baby-Care Products $151,000 ÷ 7,000 units = $21.57 per unit

Note the term "costs traced to products" where the amounts in Exhibit 4–6 are totaled. The ABC team appropriately excluded from the exhibit amounts of certain costs, including particular administrative costs of running the company that were not directly related to production (e.g., the salaries of the CEO and CFO) and the cost of unused parts of the main building because that space was not used to produce either product.

Product and Customer Profitability

The information presented in Exhibit 4–6 is important in measuring both product and customer profitability. It is central to managing products and customers and deciding whether to drop either products or customers.

LO 6 Analyze the profitability of products and customers.

Product Profitability

See Exhibit 4–7 for a profitability report for PMI's two products sold during October. Assume that the average selling price for containers and baby-care products was $.10 and $22.00 per unit, respectively. The costs traced to products in Exhibit 4–7 come from Exhibit 4–6. For example, the product-level costs in Exhibit 4–7 are the sum of the product-level costs in Exhibit 4–6 ($16,000 for containers in Exhibit 4–7 = $1,000 + $15,000 for product-level costs in Exhibit 4–6).

Note that the "costs not traced to products" at the bottom of Exhibit 4–7 are the general and administrative costs and unused main building space mentioned earlier that the ABC team did not trace to products.

PMI's management was pleased with the ABC team's work but was disappointed with the results for October. Ms. Fairchild stated, "The good news is that we are in the black; the bad news is that we are *barely* in the black. Our operating income was only $5,400 on total revenue of $274,000—a return on sales of about 2 percent. The industry average is about 10 percent return on sales, so we are behind our peers. Clearly, we have work to do to improve those operating income numbers."

	Containers	Baby Care	Total
Revenues:			
Containers (1,200,000 × $.10)	$120,000		$120,000
Baby-care products (7,000 × $22.00)		$154,000	154,000
Total revenue			$274,000
Costs traced to products (from Exhibit 4–6):			
Unit level	$ 48,000	$ 70,000	$118,000
Batch level	3,600	9,600	13,200
Product level	16,000	44,000	60,000
Customer level	1,800	4,400	6,200
Facility level	15,800	23,000	38,800
Total costs traced to products	$ 85,200	$151,000	$236,200
Revenues minus costs traced to products	$ 34,800	$ 3,000	37,800
Costs not traced to products			32,400
Operating income			$ 5,400

Exhibit 4–7

ABC Profitability Reports for October

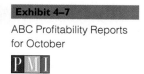

	(A)	(B)	(C)	(D)
	Containers		Baby-Care Products	
	Traditional	ABC	Traditional	ABC
Revenues	$120,000	$120,000	$154,000	$154,000
Costs traced to products:				
Materials*	48,000	48,000	70,000	70,000
Labor and overhead†	48,000	37,200	70,000	81,000
Revenues minus costs traced to products	$ 24,000	$ 34,800	$ 14,000	$ 3,000

Note: These costs exclude costs not traced to products.

*These are the unit-level costs for materials reported in Exhibit 4–7.

†The traditional labor and overhead are simply assumed to be 100 percent of materials costs. The activity-based costing labor and overhead costs are the sums of the batch-level, product-level, customer-level, and facility-level costs traced to products as reported in Exhibit 4–7. Do not assume that the *total* labor and overhead costs assigned to products are the same for the ABC and traditional cost systems because the two systems have such different approaches to assigning costs.

Mr. Lewis added, "The ABC team's work has enabled us to pinpoint some of the problems. Look at the baby-care products. Revenue minus costs traced to products is only $3,000 *before considering costs that have not been traced to products.* The container business looks good to me, but we are in trouble with baby-care products. They require complex machinery and frequent quality-control checks, which are costly."

Ms. Fairchild commented, "I've been reading literature on activity-based costing, which states that highly complex business often turns out to be more costly than people thought and low-complexity business turns out to be less expensive. We seem to have that situation here. The low-complexity container business is clearly profitable, but the more complex baby-care products business is marginal, *at best!* I'm pleased that we are learning about this now before we are in real financial trouble."

As this conversation suggested, the ABC results surprised management. Before developing the ABC information, the company had assumed that all labor and overhead traceable to products were 100 percent of each product's materials costs. The information comparing the traditional and ABC results in Exhibit 4–8 was a real eye-opener for PMI's management. See the exhibit for the results of the traditional costing approach in columns (A) and (C), and the ABC amounts in columns (B) and (D).

Armed with this information, Fairchild decided to meet with Elizabeth Forney, vice president of marketing to discuss the problem. Forney indicated that the $22 market price per unit was relatively low for the baby-care products and was expected to increase within the next six months. Fairchild and Forney decided to keep producing baby-care products and to monitor the relation between their selling price and costs over the next several months.

Customer Profitability

Customer costing analyzes the costs of activities to serve specific customers. **Customer profitability analysis** identifies the costs and benefits of serving specific customers or customer types to improve an organization's overall profitability.[5] The same activity-based information used to analyze products can be used to measure major customers' contributions to profit.

Some companies are surprised to learn that 10 to 20 percent of their customers generate 80 to 90 percent of their total profit and that some customers actually cause losses. (See the extensive discussion in Chapter 6.) Some customers require so much

---

[5] Chapter 6 discusses customer profitability analysis in more detail.

service (placing many small orders, for example) that the cost of resources used to serve them (including order processing, setups, and shipping) exceeds the revenue they provide. Customer profitability analysis identifies the most profitable customers so that the company can ensure that they remain customers. Knowing which customers are unprofitable also allows the company either to work with them to reduce the costs they cause or to decide not to continue serving them.

In PMI's case, since beverage containers and baby-care products are sold to separate, individual customers, Exhibit 4–7 can also be used as a customer profitability report. It shows that the customer purchasing containers generates a higher level of profitability than the customer purchasing baby-care products.

Estimation of Costs of New Products Using ABC

Activity-based costing information for existing products can be helpful for estimating the costs of new products if the activities used to make these new products are similar to those used to make the existing ones.

MegaBurger Novelty Toy Decision

The team at PMI compiled the cost data using ABC and then met with Fairchild to discuss the results. She first asked whether the MegaBurger business would be profitable.

To answer Ms. Fairchild's questions, Lewis and his team matched MegaBurger's product specifications to the activity list and cost drivers for existing products (Exhibits 4–5 and 4–6). The team then decided that producing novelty toys would be similar to making complex baby-care products with several notable exceptions:

- PMI must use a higher grade of plastic and more colors although smaller amounts of both per unit for the toys.
- The product molds for the toys must be more precise. A small error or blemish would be very noticeable in such a small product that children (and collectors) look at very carefully.
- PMI would have more consultations with customers for the toys.
- MegaBurger expects its toy suppliers to warehouse the products and ship them directly to its restaurants on demand. This is similar to the baby-care company's requirements except that the MegaBurger project requires complex inventory controls and distribution to many locations. PMI would have to lease additional warehouse space to meet MegaBurger's needs.
- More production space is required for the toys. Some space could be obtained in an adjacent building, and the remainder could be obtained from the presently unused space.

PMI's application of the cost information from activity-based costing to assess the product profitability of one of MegaBurger's products is shown in Exhibit 4–9. PMI's ABC team started with the cost-driver rates for the baby-care product in Column B and then adjusted those rates to reflect what it thought the cost-driver rates should be for the MegaBurger product (Column C). Column D presents the adjusted cost-driver rates. Column E shows the cost-driver volume expected for 20,000 units per month. (Each "unit" contains eight novelty toys.) Column F shows each activity's expected cost. Work through this exhibit to see how PMI adjusted its activity-based cost information for existing products (column B) to obtain estimated costs of the new product (column F).

PMI's analysis indicated that the estimated revenues on the MegaBurger job would exceed estimated costs by $18,600 per month as shown at the bottom of Column G. On the basis of the analysis reported in Exhibit 4–9, Fairchild decided that the company had the knowledge and technical capability to be a reliable supplier for MegaBurger. Based on the team's analysis, PMI was able to keep its existing products and still submit a successful and profitable bid to MegaBurger. Ms. Fairchild, Mr. Lewis, and the ABC team were all excited about the prospect of landing a big contract with MegaBurger.

Exhibit 4–9   Application of ABC Cost Information to Estimate New Product Costs

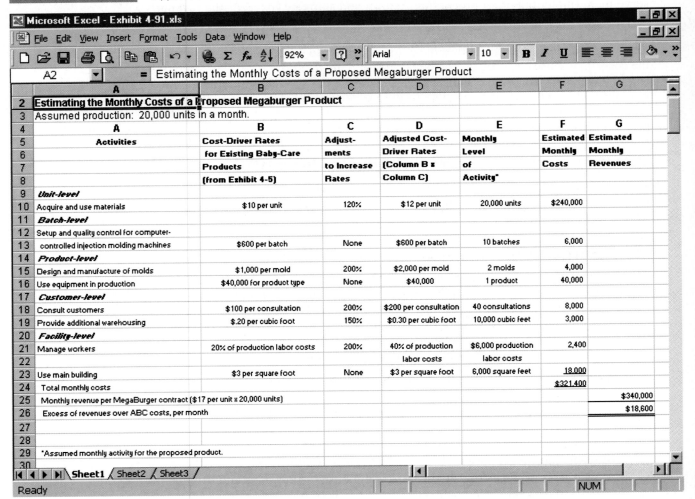

Microsoft Excel - Exhibit 4-91.xls

File Edit View Insert Format Tools Data Window Help

A2   = Estimating the Monthly Costs of a Proposed Megaburger Product

	A	B	C	D	E	F	G
2	**Estimating the Monthly Costs of a Proposed Megaburger Product**						
3	Assumed production: 20,000 units in a month.						
4	**A**	**B**	**C**	**D**	**E**	**F**	**G**
5	**Activities**	**Cost-Driver Rates**	**Adjust-**	**Adjusted Cost-**	**Monthly**	**Estimated**	**Estimated**
6		**for Existing Baby-Care**	**ments**	**Driver Rates**	**Level**	**Monthly**	**Monthly**
7		**Products**	**to Increase**	**(Column B x**	**of**	**Costs**	**Revenues**
8		**(from Exhibit 4-5)**	**Rates**	**Column C)**	**Activity***		
9	*Unit-level*						
10	Acquire and use materials	$10 per unit	120%	$12 per unit	20,000 units	$240,000	
11	*Batch-level*						
12	Setup and quality control for computer-						
13	controlled injection molding machines	$600 per batch	None	$600 per batch	10 batches	6,000	
14	*Product-level*						
15	Design and manufacture of molds	$1,000 per mold	200%	$2,000 per mold	2 molds	4,000	
16	Use equipment in production	$40,000 for product type	None	$40,000	1 product	40,000	
17	*Customer-level*						
18	Consult customers	$100 per consultation	200%	$200 per consultation	40 consultations	8,000	
19	Provide additional warehousing	$.20 per cubic foot	150%	$0.30 per cubic foot	10,000 cubic feet	3,000	
20	*Facility-level*						
21	Manage workers	20% of production labor costs	200%	40% of production	$6,000 production	2,400	
22				labor costs	labor costs		
23	Use main building	$3 per square foot	None	$3 per square foot	6,000 square feet	18,000	
24	Total monthly costs					$321,400	
25	Monthly revenue per MegaBurger contract ($17 per unit x 20,000 units)						$340,000
26	Excess of revenues over ABC costs, per month						$18,600
27							
28							
29	*Assumed monthly activity for the proposed product.						
30							

Sheet1 / Sheet2 / Sheet3 /

Ready   NUM

You're the Decision Maker 4.3

Making Product Decisions

Consider the information in Exhibit 4–6. Assume the role of an analyst who will recommend whether to produce a new product line. Assume that PMI obtains sufficient additional capacity to offer a third product line that has the following characteristics per month:

- Uses the same amount of medium-grade plastic and colors per unit as beverage containers and requires two molds.
- Is made on a new injection-molding machine that costs $20,000 per month to use.
- Produces 100,000 units in 15 batches each month.
- Ships products to customers directly from production (no warehousing). However, 2,000 square feet of space for production are needed at a cost of $3 per square foot.
- Provides three customer consultations per month.
- Incurs production labor costs of $4,500. The cost-driver rate for the activity manage workers is 20 percent of production labor costs.

Any cost items not specifically listed are the same per month as for the beverage containers reported in Exhibit 4–6.

a. Estimate the costs of this product using activity-based costing.

b. What additional information would you need before deciding whether to recommend this product?

(Solutions begin on page 160.)

Activity-Based Costing in Service and Merchandising Companies

Many service and merchandising companies also have benefited from using an ABC system. For example, the United States Postal Service used ABC to decide whether to use debit cards, credit cards, checks, cash, or a combination as payment for postal transactions. ABC results indicated that for the same transaction size, debit cards were slightly less costly and credit cards were only slightly more costly than cash. The Postal Service's customers can use debit and credit cards as well as cash partly as a result of its analysis using ABC.

LO 7 Apply activity-based costing to service and merchandising companies.

Service and merchandising organizations (including nonprofit and governmental organizations) implement ABC as described earlier in this chapter; no changes are necessary. Any organization—manufacturing, merchandising, or service—must follow these four steps presented earlier in the chapter and briefly reviewed here for a service organization.

Step 1. *Identify and classify the activities related to the company's products.* A bank can identify activities such as processing ATM transactions, processing car loans, opening customer checking accounts, and maintaining investment accounts. As activities are identified, they are classified as unit-level, batch-level, product-level, customer-level, or facility-level activities.

Step 2. *Estimate the cost of activities identified in step 1.* A bank could estimate the cost of employee time spent processing ATM transactions and ATM machine maintenance costs to the activity processing ATM transactions.

Step 3. *Calculate a cost-driver rate for each activity.* With the activity cost data from step 2, the bank then can calculate a cost-driver rate that will allow the company to assign activity costs to goods and services. This rate's base should have some causal link to the cost. For example, the cost associated with running an ATM machine is likely caused by the number of transactions it processes. Thus, the rate for this activity could be based on the number of transactions.

Step 4. *Assign activity costs to products.* The bank then uses the cost-driver rates identified in step 3 to assign activity costs to goods and services. For example, if a particular customer uses an ATM machine eight times a month and the rate per ATM transaction from step 3 is \$.50, \$4.00 in costs are assigned to the customer (\$.50 × 8).

Costs and Benefits of Using Activity-Based Costing

This chapter's discussion of activity-based costing implies that implementing it adds value to an organization. This is likely to be true for companies that have complex production processes producing many different products or services in highly competitive markets. This is the reason that companies such as Hewlett-Packard, DaimlerChrysler, and IBM implemented ABC.

We should remember, however, that implementing ABC is costly. Costs include those to develop and implement the system, to provide additional record keeping, to change the computer system, and to hire consultants. Therefore, managers must choose carefully when to implement an ABC system. Several "red flags" indicate problems with an organization's costing system and the likely need to refine it. Some of these problems are as follow:

- Indirect costs are significant in proportion to direct costs and are allocated to goods and services using one or two cost pools (and therefore one or two cost-driver rates).
- Goods and services are complex and require many different processes and inputs.
- Standard high-volume goods and services show losses or small profits while complex low-volume goods and services show significant profits.
- Different departments within the company believe that the costs identified for producing goods and providing services (as calculated by accounting) are not accurate and often are misleading.

- The company loses bids it thought were priced relatively low and wins those it thought were priced relatively high.
- The company has not changed its costing system in spite of major changes it has made to its operations.

Although all companies should not implement an ABC system, a firm that experiences several of these problems should seriously consider adopting it.

Research Insight 4.1

Does ABC Improve Firm Performance?

The ultimate test of ABC in for-profit companies is whether it increases profits, not whether it provides more precise cost measures. Professors Kennedy and Affleck-Graves set out to find whether companies that adopted ABC had better financial performance than comparable companies that did not adopt ABC. In their study of companies in the United Kingdom, they found that the companies that adopted ABC significantly outperformed the companies that had not adopted ABC over the three years after implementing it. *(Source: T. Kennedy and J. Affleck-Graves, "The Impact of Activity-Based Costing Techniques on Firm Performance,"* Journal of Management Accounting Research.*)*

Chapter Summary

The theme of this book is that managers' decisions drive an organization's costs. To manage costs, managers and employees must understand how those decisions affect the efficiency of work being accomplished. Activity-based costing traces the costs of resources to activities, which are the basic elements of an organization's work. By learning what activities the organization uses to produce goods and services, managers can trace the organization's costs to the products via the activities performed. We trace these costs using these steps:

1. Identify and classify the activities related to the company's products.
2. Estimate the cost of the activities identified in step 1.
3. Calculate a cost-driver rate for each activity.
4. Assign activity costs to products.

ABC can provide data related to a company's processes. These data can be used in various ways to benefit the company. It can identify expensive and inefficient processes that could have been unnoticed in the past. The company can then change these processes to make them more efficient, often reducing their costs and increasing customer satisfaction. ABC data also can be used to establish more accurate cost information for goods and services.

Appendix to Chapter Four

Unit-Level ABC Costing

LO 8 Distinguish between ABC unit-level costing, and ABC full costing of goods and services.

This chapter discussed the **ABC full costing** method, which assigns as many costs as possible to products. Exhibit 4–6 reports the results of assigning costs to production using ABC full-costing.

An alternative to this approach is **ABC unit-level costing** which assigns only the costs of unit-level resources to products. Exhibit 4–10 shows how ABC unit-level costs are computed using the data in Exhibit 4–6.

Cost management analysts have different opinions about the choice between ABC unit-level costing and ABC full costing. We have presented both ideas here so that you will be able to understand their differences when making management decisions.

Note that in Exhibit 4–10 only the unit-level costs—materials—are assigned to units. All other resources, called "higher-level resources," are not assigned. These higher-level resources are batch-level, product-level, customer-level, and facility-level resources. Higher-level resources are tied to higher-level activities but not to unit-level activities in this example.

	Containers	Baby-Care Products	
			Exhibit 4–10
Units produced	1,200,000	7,000	ABC Unit-Level Costing Report
Unit-level resources: Materials	$48,000	$70,000	
Cost per unit ($48,000 ÷ 1,200,000 units; $70,000 ÷ 7,000 units)	$ .04	$ 10.00	
Higher-level resources: Sum of resources used for batch-level, product-level, customer-level, and facility-level activities*	$37,200	$81,000	

*These amounts are the totals of the batch-level, product-level, customer-level, and facility-level amounts presented in Exhibit 4–6.

The concept of ABC unit-level costing is to assign only the costs clearly and certainly driven by specific units to these units. Materials used to make products certainly qualify for this assignment.

Cost Differences

The following compares ABC unit-level costing and ABC full costing:

	Containers	Baby-Care Products
ABC unit-level costing cost per unit (Ex. 4–10)	$.04 per unit	$10.00 per unit
ABC full costing per unit (bottom of Ex. 4–6)	$.071 per unit	$21.57 per unit

The per-unit cost for each product using each method differs dramatically because they are based on different concepts. The full-costing approach says, in effect, that a firm has costs because it produces units; therefore, all costs related to the production (and sale) of the units should be assigned to units.

The unit-costing approach says, however, that resources supplied for higher-level activities, such as batch-level and product-level activities, are not caused by the production and sale of each unit. Therefore, these higher-level resources should not be applied to the units.

Key Terms

For each term's definition, refer to the indicated page or turn to the glossary at the end of the text.

ABC full costing*, 158
ABC unit-level costing*, 158
activity-based costing (ABC), 141
activity dictionary, 142

batch-level resources and activities, 143
cost allocation, 141
cost driver, 148
cost-driver base, 148
cost-driver rate, 148

cost pools, 141
customer costing, 154
customer-level resources and activities, 144
customer profitability analysis, 154

facility-level resources and activities, 144
product-level resources and activities, 144
unit-level resources and activities, 143

*Terms appear in the chapter Appendix.

Meeting the Cost Management Challenges

I. How did activity-based cost information help PMI, Inc.?

Activity-based cost information provides more accurate information about the costs of existing products, which PMI's management used to decide whether to continue supplying particular products (e.g., the baby-care products). (See Exhibits 4–6 and

4–7.) The ABC information showed that the traditional costing system was "undercosting" baby-care products and "overcosting" beverage containers. (See Exhibit 4–8.) The ABC information also helped PMI estimate the cost of the new products for the MegaBurger contract, which would use most of the same activities (at different cost-driver rates, however) as do existing baby-care products. (See Exhibit 4–9.)

2. **What** data and knowledge are necessary to support the development of activity-based information?

An organization needs the following data: (1) a list of its activities categorized according to the five levels (unit, batch, product, customer, and facility), (2) the cost of each of its activities, (3) the costs per unit of activity (cost-driver rates), and (4) the costs of goods and services (after assigning activity costs to them).

3. **Is** activity-based information always better than traditional costing information?

It is not. Organizations must determine whether the decision-making value of ABC information exceeds the costs to develop and maintain it. For example, organizations whose goods and services use resources in relatively similar ways might have activity-based costs similar to those obtained by using traditional costing approaches. In this case, the decision-making value would be unaffected by more complex (and costly) ABC estimates of costs. However, activity-based information can be used to support decisions about process improvements. Any organization faced with competition based on price could benefit from process improvements that increase customer value while reducing process costs. This important use of activity-based information is one of the topics of Chapter 5.

Solutions to You're the Decision Maker

4.1 Developing the Activity List p. 147

a. Aside from a reasonable level of detail (which is missing for many types of activities), the list includes few activities that might indicate process inefficiencies. For example, employees could have idle time when machines need repair or during a break in production (due to excess capacity). All employees are not likely to be productively employed every hour for which they are paid. While they might be uneasy about admitting unplanned breaks and idle time, they should realize that these activities exist in most organizations. Including them in the activity list improves the analysis of the organization's work.

b. To answer the question, management or high-level staff might estimate how much time and resources are spent on the omitted activities. This is a questionable practice, however, because of its top-down nature. Upper-level managers or staff are unlikely to be able to identify these problem areas with much precision, and a blanket assumption that they exist throughout the organization could do more harm to employee relations than good. It is preferable for individuals who do the actual work to identify these unproductive activities and help the organization to minimize them. As noted in part (a), employees might not want to recognize them because they might be "blamed" for the unproductivity. The organization should promote honesty by not assigning blame but by encouraging and rewarding employees to identify and fix problems. Many firms do this by implementing a "suggestions for improvement program."

4.2 Using Cost-Driver Rates p.151

a. The cost-driver rates have different meanings. The cost-driver rate for activity 1.1 is a unit-level activity for the acquisition and use of materials and, therefore, is easily traced to each unit of product 1. However, the cost-driver rate for activity 2.1 is a batch-level activity not easily traced to particular units but more easily traced to batches of product.

b. PMI might save this amount but only if eliminating the activity really eliminates the need for the resource (i.e., the warehouse).

c. Although eliminating this service could save money, it also could result in losing a customer. If so, then eliminating it could lose benefits that are far greater than the costs that would be saved.

4.3 Making Product Decisions p. 156

a.

Activity Level	Activity Volume	Cost-Driver Rate	Total Cost
Unit—Materials	100,000 units	$ .04	$ 4,000
Batch	15	300	4,500
Product—Molds	2	1,000	2,000
Product—Equipment	1 product	20,000	20,000
Customer—Consultations	3	100	300
Facility—Employee management	Production labor costs are $4,500	20%	900
Facility—Use building	2,000 sq. ft.	$3 per sq. ft.	6,000
Total costs			$37,700

b. The selling price and additional information regarding whether PMI is at practical capacity for all levels of resources prior to making this new product could be helpful. If it is not, PMI might devote unused resource capacity to this new product. For example, PMI could have unused building space to use for the new product. If that were the case, PMI would not have to spend as much as indicated by the costs computed in part (a).

Review Questions

4.1 Review and define each of the chapter's key terms.

4.2 What factors should managers assess in choosing among alternative costing systems?

4.3 How are indirect costs allocated to products using traditional costing systems?

4.4 What are the three key points with respect to refining a traditional costing system?

4.5 What is the ideal relation between allocation bases (cost drivers) and costs?

   a. Simple

   b. Cause and effect

   c. Complex

   d. What top management wants

4.6 Why do few companies allocate the general and administrative costs of the business to products?

4.7 Is it true that activity-based costing first assigns costs to products and then to activities?

4.8 Fill in the missing words: An activity is any discrete ____ that an organization ____ to make or deliver a ____ or service.

4.9 Organizations that use or have used activity-based costing include the following:

   a. United States Postal Service.

   b. American Airlines.

   c. Hewlett-Packard.

   d. (a), (b), and (c).

   e. (b) and (c).

4.10 Briefly describe the four steps in measuring the costs of goods and services.

4.11 Briefly describe the five levels of resources and activities.

4.12 Fill in the blanks. An activity list (or dictionary) is a ____ of ____ performed by an organization to produce its product.

4.13 Describe how to calculate the cost of an activity.

4.14 Why is employee participation in identifying activities important?

4.15 Describe how to calculate the activity-based cost of a product.

4.16 Why would organizations compute cost-driver rates for a "typical" month instead of for each month of the year?

4.17 "I work for an airline. ABC is irrelevant to my company because we do not manufacture things." Discuss the validity of this statement.

4.18 What "red flags" indicate that companies have problems with their costing systems?

4.19 Is there any fundamental difference in applying ABC to goods versus services? Explain.

4.20 What conditions are necessary for using activity-based costs of existing services for estimating costs of new services to be valid?

Critical Analysis

4.21 Explain why overcosting and undercosting products occur with traditional costing systems.

4.22 Why might a company adopt activity-based costing, then stop using it, but consider that its adoption had been a success?

4.23 In developing an activity list, why might employees not want to reveal realistic information about time spent on their activities?

4.24 What criteria should management use to decide whether to assign general and administrative costs to products?

4.25 Why would each of the following be important to the success of activity-based costing:

   a. Top management's support.

   b. Other companies' successes and failures with it.

   c. Sufficient time to gather and analyze the data.

4.26 Professor John Shank has said that the use of contribution margins to select products is "a snare, a trap, and a delusion" because a firm will never drop a product that has a positive contribution margin for fear of losing even a small amount of profit.[6] Explain the meaning of this argument. How might the use of activity-based costing (unit level or full cost) improve the product selection process?

4.27 It has been suggested[7] that ABC should be used to measure the costs of "people-intensive" processes but not "machine-intensive" processes. People-intensive processes have adaptable resources, employee-paced work flows, and salary-oriented costs. Examples include engineering and customer service. Machine-intensive processes have machine-paced work flows, depreciation-oriented costs, and employee tasks that depend on technology. Examples include automated painting and robotic assembly. Contrast how ABC and throughput costing treat these types of processes. Make an argument either for or against this proposition.

4.28 Some believe that universities are among the organizations most resistant to change. However, some universities are beginning to analyze the profitability of their major departments and colleges by applying ABC concepts. Develop an exhibit similar to Exhibit 4–4 that shows major university activities and resources (without numbers, of course). How difficult would it be to trace university resource costs to these activities?

4.29 Evaluate this comment: "Historical costs are only the starting point for predicting future costs. . . . Many types of costs, such as inventory, book value of equipment, and allocation of fixed [higher-level resource] costs are not relevant for decision making."[8]

4.30 One implication of ABC systems could be that using fewer cost-driver bases reduces consumption of resources, which reduces costs. Therefore, this logic continues, managers should seek to reduce the number of cost-driver bases

---

[6] Quoted in R. Kee, "Integrating Activity-Based Costing with the Theory of Constraints to Enhance Production-Related Decision Making."

[7] R. Campbell, P. Brewer, and T. Mills, "Designing an Information System Using Activity-Based Costing and the Theory of Constraints."

[8] L. Boyd, "Cost Information: The Use of Cost Information for Making Operating Decisions."

used. A prominent critic of ABC has stated that activity-based prescriptions for improved competitiveness usually entail steps that lead to doing less of what should not be done in the first place. "[F]ocus on reducing variation and lead time in the work itself, and costs will take care of themselves . . . get busy with the improvement process."[9] Can these views be reconciled? Explain.

Exercises

Exercise 4.31
Cost-Driver Identification
(LO 2)

Place the following activities involved in a university's admission process in chronological order and match each to its most likely cost driver. (Cost-driver bases may be used more than once.)

Activities	**Possible Cost-Driver Bases**
1. Processing applications	a. Number of acceptances
2. Enrolling students	b. Number of applications
3. Receiving applications	c. Number of inquiries
4. Receiving and responding to student inquiries	
5. Accepting students	

Exercise 4.32
Cost-Driver Identification
(LO 2)

Volkswagen Canada developed ABC costs of the wheel-building process at one of its plants.[10] The process involves melting aluminum, pouring the melted aluminum into molds (casting), testing, finishing/polishing, painting, and packaging wheels.

Required
Match each activity with its most likely cost-driver base. (Cost-driver bases may be used more than once.)

Activities	**Possible Cost-Driver Bases**
1. Melting aluminum	a. Number of wheels
2. Casting aluminum	b. Number of setups
3. X-ray testing	c. Number of casting hours
4. Drilling bolt holes	d. Number of kilograms melted
5. Finishing surfaces	
6. Chrome plating	
7. Painting	
8. Packaging	
9. Setting up machines	
10. Shipping	

Exercise 4.33
Different Levels of
Activities and Resources
(LO 3)

Match each of the following resources and activities with the most likely activity level.

Resource and Description	**Activity Level**
1. Production management—salaries and support for managers	a. Unit
2. Marketing research—salaries and support for marketing research to identify new product opportunities	b. Batch
	c. Product
3. Labor—hourly as needed to meet production levels	d. Customer
4. Setup labor—set up equipment and software for production runs	e. Facility
5. Utilities—electrical power for operating computing equipment used by setup workers	
6. Legal department—salaries and facilities to support legal staff who prepare contracts for each customer	
7. Equipment—equipment specifically designed to produce one product line	

---

[9] H. T. Johnson, "It's Time to Stop Overselling Activity-Based Concepts: Start Focusing on Total Customer Satisfaction Instead."

[10] Adapted from J. Gurowka, "ABC, ABM, and the Volkswagen Saga."

8. Materials—purchased for product manufacturing
9. Supplies—purchased to support customer-service representatives
10. Software—programs to control computerized equipment; revised for each batch of product

---

Match each of the following activities and resources with the most likely activity level for a social services agency.

Resources and Activities

1. Case workers—personnel who interview and service clients by type of service (child, homeless, and elderly citizen)
2. Supplies—materials for office personnel
3. Library—regulations, research, and court documents to support child, homeless, and elderly citizen services
4. Information technology—desktop and mobile computing equipment and personnel to develop and maintain information system
5. Management—salaries and support for administrators
6. Building—offices of employees
7. Automobiles—transportation for caseworkers to meet clients
8. Utilities—building's electrical power, natural gas, phone, and sanitation services

Activity Level

a. Unit
b. Product
c. Facility

Exercise 4.34
Different Levels of Activities and Resources
(LO 3)

Match each of the following activities to the most likely activity level for a bank. Suggest a feasible cost-driver base for each, and explain why you think that your chosen cost-driver bases are feasible.

Activity

1. Sales calls—existing commercial customers
2. Sales calls—new commercial customers
3. Commercial loan negotiation
4. Commercial loan review
5. Customer file maintenance
6. Community involvement
7. Employee relations
8. Commercial loan customer service
9. Consumer loan customer service
10. Consumer loan review
11. Consumer deposit/withdrawal processing
12. Commercial deposit/withdrawal processing
13. Advertising particular products

Activity Level

a. Unit
b. Batch
c. Product
d. Customer
e. Facility

Exercise 4.35
Different Activity and Resource Levels
(LO 3)

Syno Corporation produces two types of flat-screen televisions. The standard televisions are designed for durability. The company recently began producing the higher-quality, high-grade model to appeal to dedicated watchers. Since the introduction of the high-grade product, profits have steadily declined. Management believes that the accounting system might not be accurately allocating costs to products, particularly since sales of the high-grade product have been increasing.

Management has asked you to investigate the cost allocation problem. You find that manufacturing overhead is currently assigned to products based on the direct-labor costs in the products. For your investigation, you have data from last month. Last month's manufacturing overhead was $2,200,000 based on the production of 3,200 standard units and 1,000 high-grade units. Direct-labor and direct-material costs were as follows:

Exercise 4.36
Limitations of Traditional Costing Methods
(LO 1, 4, 5, 6)

	Standard	High-Grade	Total
Direct labor	$1,740,000	$ 660,000	$2,400,000
Direct material	1,250,000	1,140,000	2,390,000

Management believes that overhead costs are caused by three cost drivers. The cost drivers and their costs for last month were as follows:

			Activity Level		
Cost Driver		**Costs Assigned**	**Standard**	**High Grade**	**Total**
Number of production runs		$1,000,000	40	10	50
Quality tests performed		900,000	12	18	30
Shipping orders processed		300,000	100	50	150
Total overhead		$2,200,000			

Required

a. How much of the overhead will be assigned to each product if these three cost drivers are used to allocate overhead? What is the total cost per unit produced for each product?

b. How much of the overhead was assigned to each product if direct-labor cost had been used to allocate overhead? What is the total cost per unit produced for each product?

c. How might the results from using activity-based costing in requirement (a) help management understand Syno's declining profits?

Exercise 4.37
Activity-Based Costing in a Service Environment
(LO 4, 5, 6, 7)

Green Garden Care, Inc., is a lawn and garden care service. It originally specialized in serving small residential clients but recently started contracting for work on office building grounds. Since Glenn Greenthumb (owner) believes that commercial lawn care is more profitable, he is considering dropping residential services altogether.

Employees worked a total of 20,000 hours last year, 13,000 on residential jobs and 7,000 on commercial jobs. Wages amounted to $9 per hour for all work done. Materials are included in overhead. All overhead is allocated on the basis of labor-hours worked, which also is the basis for customer charges. Glenn can charge $22 per hour for residential work but only $19 per hour for commercial work.

Required

a. If overhead for the year was $62,000, what were the profits of commercial and residential service using labor-hours as the allocation base?

b. Overhead consists of costs of transportation, equipment use, and supplies, which can be traced to the following activities:

			Activity Level	
Activity	**Cost Driver**	**Cost**	**Commercial**	**Residential**
Transportation	Number of clients serviced	$ 8,000	15	45
Equipment use	Equipment hours	18,000	3,500	2,100
Supplies	Area serviced in square yards	36,000	130,000	70,000
Total overhead		$62,000		

Recalculate profits for commercial and residential services based on these activity bases.

c. What recommendations do you have for management regarding the profitability of these two types of services?

d. *Build your own spreadsheet.* Prepare a spreadsheet to answer (a) and (b).

Exercise 4.38
Limitations of Traditional Costing Methods
(LO 1, 4, 5, 6)

Reclite, Inc., produces headlamps for campers, hikers, and other people who want the convenience of a light at night without carrying a flashlight. It currently allocates overhead costs using direct-labor hours, but the controller has recommended an activity-based costing system using the following data:

			Activity Level	
Activity	**Cost Driver**	**Cost**	**Product A**	**Product B**
Production setup	Number of setups	$50,000	10	15
Materials handling and requisition	Number of parts	15,000	18	36
Packaging and shipping	Number of units shipped	30,000	45,000	75,000
Total overhead		$95,000		

Required

a. Compute the amount of overhead to be allocated to each product under activity-based costing.

b. Compute the amount of overhead to be allocated to each product using direct-labor hours as the allocation base. Assume that the number of direct-labor hours required to assemble each unit is 0.5.

per unit of Product A and 1.0 per unit of Product B. The company produced 45,000 units of Product A and 75,000 units of Product B.

c.   Should the company follow the controller's recommendations?

Eisner & Associates provides consulting and tax preparation services to its clients. It charges a $100 fee per hour for each service. The firm's revenues and costs for the year are shown in the following income statement:

Exercise 4.39
Activity-Based Costing versus Traditional Costing
(LO 3, 4, 5, 6, 7)

	Tax	Consulting	Total
Revenue	$130,000	$270,000	$400,000
Expenses:			
Secretarial support			80,000
Supplies			72,000
Computer costs, etc.			40,000
Profit before direct labor costs			$208,000

The firm uses ABC and the following cost drivers:

		Activity Level	
Overhead Cost	Cost Driver	Tax Preparation	Consulting
Secretarial support	Number of clients	72	48
Supplies	Transactions with clients	200	300
Computer costs	Computer hours	1,000	600

Required

a.   Complete the income statement using activity-based costing and the firm's three cost drivers.

b.   Recompute the income statement using direct-labor hours as the only allocation base: 1,300 hours for tax; 2,700 hours for consulting.

c.   How might the firm's decisions be altered if it were to allocate all overhead costs using direct-labor hours?

d.   Under what circumstances would the labor-based allocation and activity-based costing (using the three cost drivers) result in similar profit results?

e.   *Build your own spreadsheet.* Develop a spreadsheet to answer (a) and (b).

Problems

Assume that you manage a business that provides services to both state government agencies and private organizations. Contracts for both groups are awarded on the basis of competitive bids. Your contracts with government agencies provide for reimbursement of costs plus a set percentage markup above cost for negotiated levels of service. Your contracts with private organizations are based on fees for levels of service. The relative profitability of the two types of contracts based on average cost information using hypothetical numbers follows:

Problem 4.40
Comparison of Traditional Costing and Activity-Based Costing: Service Organization
(LO 1, 7)

Costs and Revenues	Government Contract	Private Contract	Total
Costs	$2,000	$2,000	$4,000
Revenues:			
Cost × 140%	2,800	NA	2,800
Negotiated fee	NA	3,000	3,000
Profit	$ 800	$1,000	$1,800

You recently completed an ABC analysis that indicates that government contracts are much less costly than estimated previously:

Costs and Revenues	Government Contract	Private Contract	Total
ABC costs	$1,000	$3,000	$4,000
Revenues			
Cost × 140%	1,400	NA	1,400
Negotiated fee	NA	3,000	3,000
Profit	$ 400	$ 0	$ 400

Required

If you used the preceding ABC analysis for contracting, overall profitability would be much less. How should you use this information?

Problem 4.41
Limitations of Traditional
Costing Methods
(LO 1, 4, 5)

Import Glass & Crystal Company manufactures three types of glassware: unleaded glass, low-lead crystal, and high-lead crystal. Glass quality increases with higher lead content, which allows for more detailed cutting and etching. Unleaded glass production is highly automated, but cutting and etching crystal products require a varying degree of labor, depending on the pattern's intricacy. Import Glass & Crystal applies all indirect costs according to a predetermined rate based on direct-labor hours. A consultant recently suggested that the company switch to an activity-based costing system and prepared the following cost estimates for year 5 for the recommended cost drivers:

Activity	Recommended Cost Driver	Estimated Costs	Estimated Cost-Driver Units
Order processing	Number of orders	$ 15,000	150 orders
Production setup	Number of production runs	60,000	50 runs
Material handling	Number of pounds of materials used	100,000	80,000 pounds
Machine depreciation and maintenance	Number of machine hours	80,000	8,000 hours
Quality control	Number of inspections	20,000	30 inspections
Packing	Number of units	40,000	320,000 units
Total estimated overhead		$315,000	

In addition, management estimated 5,000 direct-labor hours for year 5.

Assume that the following activities occurred in January of year 5:

	Unleaded Glass	Low-Lead Crystal	High-Lead Crystal
Number of units produced	20,000	8,000	3,000
Direct-material costs	$13,000	$8,000	$5,000
Direct-labor hours	150	150	200
Number of orders	4	3	2
Number of production runs	1	1	2
Number of pounds of material used	5,000	2,000	1,000
Number of machine hours	580	140	80
Number of inspections	1	1	1
Number of units shipped	20,000	8,000	3,000

Actual direct-labor costs were $15 per hour.

Required

a. (1) Compute a predetermined overhead rate for year 5 for each cost driver using the estimated costs and estimated cost-driver units prepared by the consultant. (2) Also compute a predetermined overhead rate for year 5 using direct-labor hours as the allocation base.

b. Compute the production costs for each product for January using direct-labor hours as the allocation base and the predetermined overhead rate computed in requirement (a,2).

c. Compute the production costs for each product for January using the cost drivers recommended by the consultant and the predetermined rates computed in requirement (a,1). (*Note:* Do not assume that total overhead applied to products in January will be the same for activity-based costing as it was for the labor-hour-based allocation.)

d. Management has seen your numbers and wants to know how you account for the discrepancy between the product costs using direct-labor hours as the allocation base and the product costs using activity-based costing. Write a brief response to management.

Problem 4.42
Limitations of Traditional
Costing Methods
(LO 1, 4, 5)

Sparkle Company makes three types of sunglasses: Stars, Surfs, and Fashions. Sparkle presently applies overhead using a predetermined rate based on direct-labor hours. A group of company employees recommended that Sparkle switch to activity-based costing and identified the following activities, cost drivers, estimated costs, and estimated cost-driver units for year 2 for each activity center.

Activity	Recommended Cost Driver	Estimated Costs	Estimated Cost-Driver Units
Production setup	Number of production runs	$ 60,000	200 runs
Order processing	Number of orders	100,000	200 orders
Material handling	Number of pounds of material	40,000	8,000 pounds
Equipment depreciation and maintenance	Number of machine hours	120,000	10,000 hours
Quality management	Number of inspections	100,000	40 inspections
Packing and shipping	Number of units shipped	80,000	20,000 units
		$500,000	

In addition, management estimated 2,000 direct-labor hours for year 2.

Assume that the following activities occurred in February of year 2:

	Stars	Surfs	Fashions
Number of units produced	1,000	500	400
Direct material costs	$4,000	$2,500	$2,000
Direct-labor hours	100	120	110
Number of orders	8	8	4
Number of production runs	4	8	16
Number of pounds of material	400	200	200
Number of machine hours	500	300	300
Number of inspections	2	2	2
Number of units shipped	1,000	500	300

Direct-labor costs were $20 per hour.

Required

a. (1) Compute a predetermined overhead rate for year 2 for each cost driver recommended by the employees. (2) Also compute a predetermined overhead rate using direct-labor hours as the allocation base.

b. Compute the production costs for each product for February using direct-labor hours as the allocation base and the predetermined rate computed in requirement (a,2).

c. Compute the production costs for each product for February using the cost drivers recommended by the employees and the predetermined rates computed in requirement (a,1). (*Note:* Do not assume that total overhead applied to products in February will be the same for activity-based costing as it was for the labor-hour-based allocation.)

d. Management has seen your numbers and wants to know how you account for the discrepancy between the product costs using direct-labor hours as the allocation base and the product costs using activity-based costing. Write a brief response to management.

Cannonball Corporation manufactures three bicycle models: racing, mountain, and children's. The racing model, the Aerolight, is made of a titanium-aluminum alloy. The mountain bike, the Summit, is made of aluminum. The steel-framed children's bike is the Spinner. Because of the different materials used, production processes differ significantly among models in terms of machine types and time requirements. Once parts have been produced, however, assembly time per unit required for each bike type is similar. For this reason, Cannonball allocates overhead on the basis of machine hours. Last year, the company produced 1,000 Aerolights, 2,000 Summits, and 5,000 Spinners and had the following revenues and expenses:

Problem 4.43
Limitations of Traditional Costing Methods
(LO 1, 4, 5, 6)

CANNONBALL CORPORATION

Income Statement

	Aerolight	Summit	Spinner	Total
Sales	$380,000	$560,000	$475,000	$1,415,000
Direct costs:				
Direct material	150,000	240,000	200,000	590,000
Direct labor	14,400	24,000	54,000	92,400

CANNONBALL CORPORATION
Income Statement

	Aerolight	Summit	Spinner	Total
Variable overhead:				
Machine setup	_____	_____	_____	26,000
Order processing	_____	_____	_____	64,000
Warehousing costs...................................	_____	_____	_____	93,000
Energy to run machines	_____	_____	_____	42,000
Shipping..	_____	_____	_____	36,000
Contribution margin	_____	_____	_____	471,600
Fixed overhead:				
Plant administration................................				88,000
Other fixed overhead				140,000
Gross profit				$ 243,600

Cannonball's CFO hired a consultant to recommend cost allocation bases. The consultant recommended the following:

Activity	Cost Driver	Activity Level		
		Aerolight	Summit	Spinner
1. Machine setup	Number of production runs	11	17	22
2. Sales-order processing	Number of sales orders received	400	600	600
3. Warehousing costs	Number of units held in inventory	200	200	400
4. Energy	Number of machine hours	10,000	16,000	24,000
5. Shipping	Number of units shipped	1,000	4,000	10,000

The consultant found no basis for allocating the plant administration and other fixed overhead costs and recommended that they not be allocated to products.

Required

a. Using machine hours to allocate production overhead, complete the income statement for Cannonball Corp. (See activity 4 for machine hours.) Do not attempt to allocate plant administration or other fixed overhead.

b. Complete the income statement using the bases recommended by the consultant.

c. How might ABC help Cannonball's management make better decisions?

d. After hearing the consultant's recommendations, the CFO decided to adopt ABC but expressed concern about not allocating some overhead (plant administration and other fixed overhead) to the products. In the CFO's view, "Products have to bear a fair share of all overhead or we won't be covering all of our costs." How would you respond to this comment?

Problem 4.44
Benefits of Activity-Based Costing
(LO 1, 6)

Many companies recognize that their cost systems are inadequate for today's global market. Managers in companies selling multiple products are making important product decisions based on distorted cost information, because many cost systems are designed to focus on inventory valuation.

Required

If management should decide to implement an ABC system, what benefits should it expect?

[CMA adapted]

Problem 4.45
Benefits of Activity-Based Costing
(LO 1, 5)

Security, Inc., has just completed a major change in its method to inspect its product. Previously, 10 inspectors examined the product after each major process. The salaries of these inspectors were charged as direct labor to the operation or job. To improve efficiency, Security's production manager recently bought a computerized quality-control system consisting of a microcomputer, 15 video cameras, peripheral hardware, and software. The cameras are placed at key points in the production process, take pictures of the product, and compare these pictures with a known "good" image supplied by a quality-control engineer. This new system allows Security to replace the 10 quality control inspectors with only two quality-control engineers.

The company president is concerned. She was told that the production process is now more efficient, yet she notices a large increase in the factory overhead rate. The computation of the rate before and after automation follows:

	Before	After
Estimated overhead	$1,900,000	$2,100,000
Estimated direct labor	$1,000,000	$ 700,000
Predetermined overhead rate	190%	300%

Required

Prepare a report that states how an ABC system might benefit Security, Inc. and alleviate the president's concern.

[CMA adapted]

The ABC team at Sky Enterprises, a surveillance company, is attempting to complete a table similar to the one in Exhibit 4-6 except that it is for just one product, Sky Spi. The team has pieced together the following data:

Unit-level actual activity (hours of surveillance) is unknown; predetermined cost-driver rate is $10,000 per unit; total unit cost assigned to the product in November is $14,000,000.

Batch-level activity is 4 (satellite launches); cost of batches assigned to the product is $5,000,000 (predetermined cost driver rate is unknown).

Product-level activity is 1 product; predetermined cost-driver rate is $1,000,000.

Customer-level activity is 100 customers; predetermined cost-driver rate is $50,000 per customer.

Facility-level activity is 50,000 square feet; predetermined cost-driver rate is $500 per square foot.

Problem 4.46
Cost-Driver Rate
Computation and Cost
Assignment to Services:
Missing Information
(LO 4, 5, 7)

mhhe.com/hilton3e

Required

Prepare a table similar to Exhibit 4–6. You must provide missing data. Label the table column headings as follows: Activity/Resource, Predetermined Cost-Driver Rate, Actual Activity Volume: November, and Cost of Sky Spi: November. All activity levels are for the month of November.

The ABC team at Spear, Inc., a concert-planning company, is attempting to complete a table similar to the one in Exhibit 4–6 except that it is for just one product, Brit Ni. The team has pieced together the following data:

Unit-level actual activity (number of concerts times number of band members) is 120; predetermined cost-driver rate is unknown; total unit cost assigned to the product in March is $480,000.

Batch-level activity is 12 concerts ("batches" of music); cost of batches assigned to the product is $600,000 (predetermined cost driver rate is unknown).

Product-level activity is 1 product; predetermined cost-driver rate is $100,000.

Customer-level activity (number of consultations with customers) is unknown; predetermined cost-driver rate is $250 per consultation; total customer-level cost assigned to the product in March is $25,000.

Facility-level activity is 5,000 hours of management and high-level staff support; cost of management and staff support assigned to the product in March is $400,000 (predetermined cost-driver rate is unknown).

Problem 4.47
Cost-Driver Rate
Computation and Cost
Assignment to Services:
Missing Information
(LO 4, 5, 7)

Required

Prepare a table similar to Exhibit 4–6. You must provide the missing data. Label the table column headings as follows: Activity/Resource, Predetermined Cost-Driver Rate; Actual Activity Volume: March, Cost of Brit Ni: March. All activity levels are for the month of March.

The ABC team at Social Services is attempting to complete a table similar to the one in Exhibit 4–6 except that it is for just one product, Consultation Sessions. The team has pieced together the following data:

Unit-level activity is 10,000 hours; predetermined cost-driver rate is $50 per hour.

There are no batch-level activities.

Product-level activity is 1 product; predetermined cost-driver rate is $100,000.

Customer-level activity is 4,000 clients; predetermined cost driver rate is $100 per client.

Facility-level activity is 1,000 square feet; total facility cost assigned to the product in January is $3,000. (Predetermined cost-driver rate is unknown.)

Problem 4.48
Cost-Driver Rate and
Computation Cost
Assignment to Services:
Missing Information
(LO 4, 5, 7)

Required

Prepare a table similar to Exhibit 4–6. You must provide the missing data. Label the table column headings as follows: Activity/Resource, Predetermined Cost-Driver Rate, Actual Activity Volume: January, Cost of Consultation Sessions: January. All activity levels are for the month of January.

Problem 4.49
Product Profitability
(LO 1, 2, 4, 5, 6)

An ABC team at Drugs 'R Us, a pharmaceutical company, identified these data for a typical month:

Activity/Resource	Cost-Driver Base	Activity Cost in a Typical Month	Activity Volume in a Typical Month
1. Unit Level			
1.1 Acquire and use material for Product A	Number of units produced	$ 60,000	1,000,000 units
1.2 Acquire and use direct labor for Product A	Number of direct-labor hours worked	20,000	2,000 direct-labor hours
1.3 Acquire and use material for Product B	Number of units produced	80,000	800,000 units
1.4 Acquire and use direct labor for Product B	Number of direct-labor hours worked	30,000	2,000 direct-labor hours
2. Batch Level			
2.1 Quality control	Number of batches	30,000	100 batches
3. Product Level			
3.1 Provide product-level advertising	Number of promotions	100,000	100 promotions
3.2 Provide product-level records	Number of products	20,000	2 products
4. Customer Level			
4.1 Take customer product orders	Number of customer orders	40,000	2,000 customer orders
4.2 Deal with customer complaints	Number of complaints	20,000	1,000 complaints
5. Facility Level			
5.1 Supervise direct labor	Amount of direct-labor costs	10,000	$50,000 for activities 1.2 and 1.4 (supervision costs = 20% of direct labor costs.)
5.2 Use main building	Number of square feet	40,000	10,000 square feet

The company's management wants you to compute the total cost and unit cost of each product for the month of July, which had the following level of activities:

		Product A	Product B
1.1 and 1.3	Material	800,000 units	900,000 units
1.2 and 1.4	Direct labor	1,600 hours	2,100 hours
2.1	Quality control—batches	50 batches	40 batches
3.1	Advertising projects—promotions	50 promotions	40 promotions
3.2	Products recorded	1 product	1 product
4.1	Customer orders	800 customer orders	900 customer orders
4.2	Customer complaints	600 complaints	300 complaints
5.1	Direct-labor supervision	$16,000	$31,500
5.2	Main building use	6,000 sq. ft.	3,000 sq. ft.

Required

a. Compute the cost-driver rate for each cost-driver base.

b. Use ABC to compute the cost of each of the two products given the activity level for the month of July. Compute both the total cost and unit cost for each product for the month of July.

c. Assume that the company's traditional costing system had assigned overhead costs at a rate of $.10 per unit of output plus $20.00 per direct-labor hour. Overhead costs are the sum of the batch-level, product-level, customer-level, and facility-level costs. Using this traditional costing approach, compute the cost of each product (including material and direct-labor costs) given the activity level for the month of July. Compute both the total cost and unit cost for each product for the month of July.

d. Do the unit costs of the two products computed under ABC and traditional costing systems differ significantly? If so, what causes the differences?

Refer to problem 4.49. You have just discovered that the product manager of product A has been less than honest in reporting the number of direct-labor hours used. In checking the payroll records, you discover that 2,000 direct-labor hours ($20,000 direct-labor costs) actually were used in July to produce Product A, not 1,600 hours as the product manager reported.

Required

a. Using this new information, recompute the total and unit costs for product A for July using both the activity-based and traditional costing systems.

b. Does this new information significantly affect the cost numbers using either traditional or ABC systems?

c. Does this new information affect the cost computations for product B using either the activity-based or traditional costing systems?

d. Why might the product manager of product A have understated the number of direct-labor hours used to produce it?

Problem 4.50
Information Misreported: Traditional versus Activity-Based Costing
(LO 1, 2, 4, 5, 6)

Refer to problem 4.49. The company's management wants to compare the unit-based cost of each product to its full cost.

Required

a. Compute the total costs of each product for the month of July using the unit-based cost approach described in the chapter Appendix.

b. Repeat requirement (a), but compute the unit cost of each product [divide your results in requirement (a) by the number of units produced in July].

c. Write a brief memo that explains the differences in results between this problem and problem 4.49.

Problem 4.51
Unit-Based and ABC Full-Costing Comparison (Appendix)
(LO 8)

An ABC team at Happy Surgeries, an outpatient surgery center that performs 25 different types of surgeries, identified the data shown below for a typical month (excluding costs of surgeons and anesthesiologists). The ABC team learned that surgeries are not performed in batches, so there are no batch-level activities or resources.

Problem 4.52
Product Profitability in a Service Organization
(LO 1, 2, 4, 5, 6, 7)

Activity/Resource	Cost-Driver Base	Activity Cost in a Typical Month	Activity Volume in a Typical Month
1. Unit Level			
1.1 Acquire and use medical supplies	Number of surgeries	$ 80,000	2,000
1.2 Acquire and use surgical nursing staff	Number of hours of surgery	180,000	2,400
1.3 Clean operating room and set up for surgeries	Number of surgeries	100,000	2,000
1.4 Provide recovery room care	Number of hours of patient time in recovery room	120,000	4,000
2. Product Level			
2.1 Maintain information for each type of surgery performed	Number of types of surgeries performed	40,000	20
2.2 Provide special equipment for eye surgeries	Number of types of eye surgery	50,000	1
2.3 Provide hip and knee replacement parts	Number of hip and knee replacements	400,000	50
3. Customer Level			
3.1 Conduct presurgery visit with patient	Number of presurgery patient visits	80,000	4,000
3.2 Make postsurgery calls to patients	Number of calls	30,000	6,000
3.3 Do patients' postsurgery visits	Number of postsurgery visits	50,000	1,000

Activity/Resource	Cost-Driver Base	Activity Cost in a Typical Month	Activity Volume in a Typical Month
4. Facility Level			
4.1 Provide supervision	Cost amount of activities 1.2, 1.3, and 1.4	60,000	$400,000 for activities 1.2, 1.3, and 1.4 (Supervision costs = 15% of the costs of activities 1.2, 1.3 and 1.4.)
4.2 Use operating rooms	Number of hours of use	720,000	2,400
4.3 Use recovery rooms	Number of patient hours in recovery room	200,000	4,000

Happy Surgery's management wants you to compute the total cost and unit cost of 2 of their 25 different products, eye surgery and hip replacement, for the month of March. The activity levels for the month of March follow:

		Eye Surgery	Hip Replacement
1.1	Use medical supplies	50 surgeries	20 surgeries
1.2	Use surgical nursing staff	80 hours of surgery	50 hours of surgery
1.3	Clean operating room and set up for surgeries	50 surgeries	20 surgeries
1.4	Provide recovery room care	100 hours of patient time in the recovery room	80 hours of patient time in the recovery room
2.1	Maintain information for each type of surgery performed	1 type of surgery	1 type of surgery
2.2	Provide special equipment for eye surgeries	1 type of eye surgery	NA
2.3	Provide parts for hip and knee replacement	NA	20 parts (1 per surgery)
3.1	Conduct presurgery visit with patient	80 visits	40 visits
3.2	Make postsurgery calls	120 calls	60 calls
3.3	Do patients' postsurgery visits	50 visits	25 visits
4.1	Provide supervision	See cost of activities 1.2, 1.3, and 1.4.	See cost of activities 1.2, 1.3, and 1.4.
4.2	Use operating rooms	80 hours	50 hours
4.3	Use recovery rooms	100 hours	80 hours

Required

a.   Compute the cost-driver rate for each cost-driver base.

b.   Using ABC, compute the cost of each product, eye surgery and hip replacement, given the activity level for the month of March. Compute both the total cost and unit cost for each product for the month of March.

c.   Assume that the company's traditional costing system had assigned product-level, customer-level, and facility-level costs to surgeries amounting to $815 per surgery. Using this traditional costing approach, compute the cost of eye surgery and hip replacement given the activity level for the month of March. Be sure to add unit-level costs to the $815 per surgery. Compute both the total cost and unit cost for each product for the month of March.

d.   Comparing the ABC and traditional costing systems, do the unit costs of the two products differ significantly? If so, what causes the differences?

Problem 4.53
Information Misreported: Traditional versus Activity-Based Costing
(LO 1, 2, 4, 5, 6, 7)

Refer to problem 4.52. You have just discovered an error in data reporting for eye surgeries. The number of eye surgeries during March was 60, not 50. The extra eye surgeries had been misclassified as colonoscopies.

Required

a.   Using this new information, recompute the total and unit costs for eye surgeries in March using both ABC and traditional costing systems.

b.   Does this new information significantly affect the cost numbers using either traditional costing or ABC systems?

c.   Does this new information affect the cost computations for hip replacement surgeries using either ABC or traditional costing systems?

Refer to problem 4.52. Management of Happy Surgeries wants to compare the unit-based cost of eye surgery and hip replacement to its full cost.

Required

a.   Compute the total costs of each product for the month of March using the unit-based cost approach described in the chapter appendix.

b.   Repeat requirement (a) but compute the unit cost of eye surgery and hip replacement [divide your results in requirement (a) by the number of units produced in March].

c.   Write a brief memo that explains the differences in results between this problem and problem 4.52.

Problem 4.54
Comparison of Unit-Based and ABC Full Costing (Appendix)
(LO 8)

An ABC team at Sporti Gus, a sporting goods store, identified the following data. These amounts exclude the cost of the merchandise itself.

Problem 4.55
Product Profitability in a Merchandising Company: Traditional versus Activity-Based Costing
(LO 1, 2, 4, 5, 6, 7)

Activity/Resource	Cost-Driver Base	Activity Cost in a Typical Month	Activity Volume in a Typical Month
1. Unit Level			
1.1 Sell goods	Units sold	$23,000	10,000
2. Batch Level			
2.1 Process purchases	Number of purchase orders	6,000	200
3. Product Level			
3.1 Provide product-level advertising	Number of promotions	30,000	200
3.2 Provide product-inventory record-keeping	Number of products	3,000	600
4. Customer Level			
4.1 Accept customer returns	Number of returns	12,000	800
5. Facility Level			
5.1 Supervise sales personnel	Cost of sales personnel	4,000	$23,000 for activity 1.1 (supervision costs = 17.39% of activity 1.1 costs.)
5.2 Use building	Square feet of shelf space used by merchandise	32,000	8,000

Sporti Gus' management wants you to compute the total cost and unit cost of two products for the month of June, which had the following level of activities:

		Tennis Rackets	Fishing Rods
1.1	Units sold	20	10
2.1	Process purchases	0.25 (1 of 4 items purchased in one purchase order)	1.5 (part of three separate purchase orders)
3.1	Provide product-level advertising	2 promotions	4.5 promotions (part of 12 promotions)
3.2	Provide product-inventory record-keeping	1 product	1 product
4.1	Accept customer returns	6 returns	2 returns
5.1	Supervise sales personnel	See your computations for activity 1.1	See your computations for activity 1.1
5.2	Use building	80 sq. ft.	60 sq. ft.

Required

a.   Compute the cost-driver rates for each cost-driver base.

b.   Using ABC, compute the cost of each product given the activity level for the month of June. Compute both the total cost and unit cost for each product for the month of June.

c.   Assume that the company's traditional costing system had assigned the batch-level, product-level, customer-level, and facility-level costs at a rate of $8.70 per unit sold. Using this traditional costing approach, compute the cost of each product given the activity level for the month of June. Be sure to add the unit-level costs to the $8.70 per unit sold. Compute both the total cost and unit cost for each product for the month of June.

d. Comparing ABC and traditional costing systems, do the unit costs of the two products differ significantly? If so, what causes the differences?

Problem 4.56
Information Misreported:
Traditional versus
Activity-Based Costing
(LO 1, 2, 4, 5, 6, 7)

Refer to problem 4.55. You have just discovered an error in counting the sales of fishing rods. Sporti Gus actually sold only 8 fishing rods, not 10 (the other two sales were actually rifles).

Required

a. Using this new information, recompute the total and unit costs for fishing rods for June using both the ABC and traditional costing systems.

b. Does this new information significantly affect the cost numbers using either traditional costing or ABC systems?

c. Does this new information affect the cost computations for tennis rackets using either the activity-based or traditional costing systems?

Problem 4.57
Activity Analysis
(LO 2, 3, 4)

mhhe.com/hilton3e

Intellig provides the following data for a one-week period for the assembly of circuit boards used by two different computer manufacturers (A and B):

   ▨   Material costs used and supplied for 3,500 units of board A produced and shipped, $40,000; 2,000 units of board B produced and shipped, $40,000.

   ▨   Batch setup labor cost used for five batches of board A, $1,000; two batches of board B, $600.

   ▨   Batch setup materials used and supplied for seven batches, $4,200.

   ▨   Labor supplied (a unit-level cost) for production of both boards, $14,000; usage based on number of manually assembled parts: eight parts for each board A, 16 parts for each board B.

   ▨   Facility-level equipment for both products, $25,000, allocated 60 percent to Product A and 40 percent to Product B.

   ▨   Packaging and shipping provided on a per-unit basis, $10,500 shipping, $7,000 for materials, and $14,000 for labor.

   ▨   Custodial and security service (facility-level cost) for the manufacturing area, $3,000 allocated 50 percent to Product A and 50 percent to Product B.

Required
Prepare an exhibit similar to Exhibit 4–5 using the preceding information.

Problem 4.58
Profitability Analysis
(LO 5, 6)

Refer to problem 4.57.

Required

a. Compute the total and per-unit costs using a format similar to the one in Exhibit 4–6.

b. Intellig receives a sales price of $30 each for board A and $30 each for board B. Prepare a profitability report similar to the one in Exhibit 4–7. Should Intellig discontinue either product? Why or why not?

Problem 4.59
Activity Analysis in a
Service Organization
(LO 2, 3, 4, 7)

Marketing Solutions is a regional provider of telemarketing surveys and sales for non-profit organizations. The basic unit of service is a completed survey or sales call. Assume that all telemarketing labor is paid hourly. Supervisory labor is salaried. The following are data from a recent month:

   ▨   Hourly telemarketing labor to complete 22,000 surveys and 90,000 calls, $176,000; completed surveys take 8 minutes each; sales calls 3 minutes each.

   ▨   Long-distance phone charges for 10 percent of surveys, $7,000.

   ▨   Preparation of scripts for surveys, $5,000, and sales pitches for calls, $4,000.

   ▨   Training telemarketing labor to conduct surveys, $13,200.

   ▨   Automated dialing equipment that serves all calls, $10,000.

   ▨   Occupancy costs, $12,000.

   ▨   Two supervisors, $9,600.

   ▨   Human Resources Department, $5,200.

Allocate automated dialing equipment, occupancy costs, supervisors, and human resources costs 50 percent to surveys and 50 percent to telemarketing calls.

Required
Prepare a table similar to the one in Exhibit 4–6 using the preceding data.

Refer to the previous problem.

Required

a. Compute the total per-unit costs as these costs were computed in Exhibit 4–6.

b. Marketing Solutions is paid $5 per completed survey and $2 per completed sales call. Prepare a profitability report similar to the one in Exhibit 4–7. Should Marketing Solutions discontinue either service? Why or why not?

Problem 4.60
Profitability Analysis
(LO 5, 6, 7)

Search your library or the Internet for a recent article on an organization's experiences using activity-based costing.

Required

Prepare a short report that includes:

a. A description of the organization (economic sector, size, international scope, etc.).

b. The reasons the organization used ABC.

c. The operations that were the focus of the analysis.

d. The impact(s) of ABC on organizational performance.

Problem 4.61
Research Report
(LO 1–7)

ABC in its modern form was developed largely in the United Kingdom and United States. As a result, ABC might reflect certain cultural norms about business management that are common to these countries but are not worldwide practice. At least one article has contrasted US and French approaches to business that could account for relatively fewer applications of ABC in France than in either the United States or United Kingdom. These factors allegedly include the language, opening of the European Union, preexistence of a complex French full-cost method, management style, class and corporate barriers, and contractual basis for performance evaluation in the United States versus importance of honor and rank in France.

Problem 4.62
International Issues
(LO 1–7)

Required

As an individual or (ideally, an internationally diverse) group project, evaluate how these factors could affect the adoption of ABC. If internationally diverse group members are available, contrast US/UK characteristics with those of another country.

Cases

Insurance companies and the federal government are restricting reimbursements to health care facilities and causing these facilities to seek cost reductions and more accurate tracing of costs without reducing the quality of care. Marian Rodriguez, the administrator of Community Hospital, is exploring whether ABC can be applied to her hospital's operations. She is meeting with your consulting team to seek your advice and to determine whether to hire you to lead an ABC pilot project that, if successful, could be extended to the rest of the hospital.

Case 4.63
Activity-Based Costing in Health Care
(LO 1–7)

Rodriquez: "I'm not too sure whether ABC is right for our situation, but I believe I should explore it at least. I think ABC is primarily for manufacturing companies, but there might be legitimate parallels between a hospital and a factory."

You: (Provide a brief response to these concerns that might encourage Rodriquez to hire you.)

Rodriquez: "That seems reasonable, though I'm not sure that we want to tell our board of directors and the general public that Community Hospital will be run like a factory. That's not the image we want to project. Nonetheless, I think we should proceed. I suggest that you analyze a typical nursing station and show me what analyses you can produce from an ABC perspective."

You work with nursing staff and the administrator's office to gather the following information:

Nursing Activity	Personnel	Annual Cost
Providing supervision	1	$ 70,000
Delivering nursing care	5	250,000
Cleaning, changing linens and garments	3	60,000
Total annual costs		$380,000
Total patient days (one patient in the hospital for one full day)		2,000
Average nursing cost per patient day		$190

All patients receive approximately the same level of cleaning and changing linens and garments, but the level of nursing care varies. Nursing staff suggested that patient days should be weighted by the level of care required. Using this input, you categorized the patients served by this nursing station in the past year as follows. Weights approximate the intensity of care needed.

Nursing Care Level	Number of Patients	Patient Days	Weight	Weighted Patient Days
Level 1 (needs typical nursing care)	300	600	1	600
Level 2 (needs more than typical nursing care but not intensive care)	300	900	2	1,800
Level 3 (needs most intensive nursing care)	100	500	4	2,000
Totals	700	2,000		4,400

Required

Prepare a report in memorandum form that explains the following:

a. The objective of your ABC analysis.
b. The reason that the average cost per patient day is misleading.
c. The sources of your data and the feasibility of collecting them in the future.
d. The confidence you have in that data to support your analysis and conclusions.
e. The method of tracing operating costs of the nursing station to its activities.
f. The calculations of activity costs per unit and examples of nursing station costs of different patients.
g. The implications of your analysis for managing Community Hospital's nursing stations.

Case 4.64
Choice of Cost System
(LO 1–7)

Huge Company's tooling business unit (TBU) manufactures metal and carbon-fiber parts for the company's major products. TBU's principal focus in recent years has been to schedule its resources properly, but its manager is concerned that the current method of costing the unit's work is causing other business units to send it work that does not use TBU's strengths to the company's overall advantage. TBU computes a combined labor and overhead cost per labor hour and charges each job based on the number of labor hours used. This labor-based charge is added to materials cost to calculate the total job cost.

TBU works for internal customers exclusively, and there is no consideration to allow it to seek outside work. Other business units are allowed to use external suppliers, however, and are encouraged but not required to use TBU, which has 19 work centers, each of which uses computer-controlled machines and processes.

TBU uses two basic types of machines: (1) 6 multi-axis (M) machines, which allow complex parts to be rotated in multiple directions while being completed without removing the part and (2) 13 single-axis (S) machines, which are used for parts that do not have to be rotated more than once to be completed. The M machines were just purchased to replace 6 (S) machines. They are three times as expensive to operate as (S) machines. Each machine is considered a work center and is available 6,000 hours (three shifts) per year.

TBU's employees are highly skilled and are among Huge Company's highest paid hourly workers. They are qualified to work on either type of machine and any type of job. As a practical matter, employees tend to work on machines and jobs that interest them most, but TBU management encourages workers to diversify their efforts. TBU employees are available 2,000 hours per year.

Stainless steel (SS) and aluminum (A) parts are machined from metal stock. Carbon fiber (CF) parts are made by laminating carbon fiber and plastic resins. Carbon-fiber materials are much more expensive and require more labor.

Last year's labor cost and overhead (which includes the costs of management and equipment but excludes materials costs) follow:

Labor (1,000 employees)	$ 90,000,000
Overhead	
Equipment (19 work centers)	190,000,000*
Management and engineering	20,000,000
Total	$300,000,000

*Based on 19 (S) machines.

The following are the data for and characteristics of five representative jobs:

Job	Equipment	Machine Hours	Materials Type	Weight (kg)	Materials Cost	Labor Hours
1	M	7.50	SS	300	$ 30,000	22.50
2	S	10.00	CF	200	100,000	160.00
3	M	8.75	A	350	28,000	21.00
4	S	12.50	A	500	40,000	120.00
5	S	5.00	SS	200	20,000	60.00

Required

a. Compute the costs of each job using the current cost system.

b. Recommend an alternative cost system that recognizes additional differences among jobs.

c. Recompute the job costs using your alternative cost system.

d. Explain differences in decision making at TBU.

e. Identify TBU's internal customers that might be influenced by the use of the alternative cost system.

Chapter 5

Activity-Based Management

After completing this chapter, you should be able to:

1. Understand the key steps of an activity-based management system.

2. Demonstrate how to use activity-based costing for target costing.

3. Identify and measure the costs of activities that add value or do not add value in organizations.

4. Use the elements of an activity-based management system to help identify opportunities for process improvements.

5. Evaluate capacity utilization by identifying resources supplied and resources used.

6. Understand methods of and problems related to implementing activity-based costing and management.

Cost-*Management* Challenges

(Solutions are on page 197.)

1. **Is** implementing activity-based costing enough to improve efficiency? Can cost management analysts measure costs more accurately using it and, by doing so, ensure that the organization will meet its efficiency goals?

2. **Do** the numbers "speak for themselves"? Does the cost management analyst's responsibility end with making recommendations for improvements?

3. **How** do you know that activity-based cost-management methods are worthwhile?

PMI Precision Molding, Inc.

The scene is a meeting of the executive committee of Precision Molding, Inc. (PMI), including Melody Fairchild, chief executive officer; Chad Norris, vice president of manufacturing; and Elizabeth Forney, vice president of marketing. The meeting occurred one year after PMI began supplying MegaBurger Corporation with promotional plastic toys. MegaBurger is one of the world's largest fast-food chains, and PMI is a leading supplier of plastic products in its geographical region.

Melody Fairchild (CEO): We need to decide whether to continue supplying toys to MegaBurger. This business was somewhat profitable last year but not at the level we would like. We must increase our income on the MegaBurger business, or continuing it is simply not worth our effort.

Chad Norris (Manufacturing): We've already shown that we're capable of meeting MegaBurger's quality standards, but we need to work closely with our production personnel to make the process more efficient to reduce costs. My gut feeling is that we can do it, but *everyone* will have to work hard.

Elizabeth Forney (Marketing): As you know, this industry is a small world. Given our success with MegaBurger last year, a dozen other companies have invited us to consider bidding on their business. The reputation of being a MegaBurger supplier is already creating new business opportunities for us.

Melody Fairchild (CEO): I agree with Elizabeth that the potential for new business is terrific, but let's focus on MegaBurger for now.

Chad, I want you to work closely with the ABC team that we established last year when we first considered bidding for the MegaBurger job. That team should recommend improvements in the production processes necessary to reduce costs.

Thanks for your input, and good luck to all of us.

Importance of Activity-Based Information to PMI's Success

LO 1 Understand the key steps of an activity-based management system.

We return to our focus company of Chapter 4, Precision Molding, Inc. (PMI). This manufacturer of plastic containers and baby-care products supplied plastic promotional novelty toys to all MegaBurger restaurants in the region last year. The products, although small, are more complex than PMI's other products, and MegaBurger has very high expectations for quality and on-time deliveries. Delivering these products successfully last year resulted in a large increase in sales and the near certainty of continued business with MegaBurger. Although PMI met MegaBurger's quality standards and on-time delivery expectations, PMI has not found MegaBurger's business to be sufficiently profitable.

To continue doing business with MegaBurger, PMI must increase its income; to do that, it must refine its processes. On the basis of the ABC team's analysis, the firm decided that it had the knowledge and technical capability to meet the company's profit goals with respect to the MegaBurger business.

As described in Chapter 4, *activity-based costing (ABC)* focuses on (1) understanding the way resources are used in current processes and (2) accurately measuring product costs using those processes. By itself, however, ABC does not result in the process improvements that might be necessary to achieve desired efficiency. Thus, ABC stops short of being a comprehensive cost-management system. This chapter continues to develop questions raised in Chapter 4 concerning how to build a cost-management system that increases the understanding of the uses of resources and that promotes process improvements. To illustrate these concepts, we discuss how PMI is able to submit a successful and profitable bid to MegaBurger for another year by using activity-based management for its existing processes.

Activity-based management (ABM) is used by management to evaluate the costs and values of process activities to identify opportunities for improved efficiency. ABM combines activity-based costing analysis and value-added analysis to make process improvements that improve customer value and reduce wasted resources.[1] ABM uses and builds on basic ABC analysis. Recall the four ABC steps discussed in Chapter 4:

Step 1.   Identify and classify the activities related to the company's products.
Step 2.   Estimate the cost of activities identified in step 1.
Step 3.   Calculate a cost-driver rate for the activity.
Step 4.   Assign activity costs to products.

ABM takes ABC a step further to include these steps:

- Identify activities as value added or non-value added.
- Score each activity as high or low value added as perceived by the customer.
- Identify opportunities to enhance value-added activities and to reduce or eliminate non-value-added activities.

Activity-Based Costing: Foundation of Process Improvement

Chapter 4 describes how PMI followed the four ABC steps to estimate the cost of the products to be produced for MegaBurger. It used this information to submit a successful bid for last year's business with MegaBurger. To obtain the needed information, Melody Fairchild, CEO, asked Alex Lewis, CFO, to create a cross-functional team to evaluate the MegaBurger offer. The team first matched MegaBurger's product and service specifications to the activities and cost-driver rates derived from

---

[1] ABM is a popular business approach to process redesign. Other process redesign business approaches include quality function deployment (QFD), which focuses on improving quality, and business process reengineering (BPR), which generally seeks radical changes to processes. Many believe that ABM is superior to QFD because it focuses on the concept of customer-based value, which is broader than quality. ABM has proved to be more enduring than BPR, probably because ABM embraces continuous improvement rather than BPR's radical change, which sounds more exciting but has proven more difficult to design and to implement. Engineering approaches to process redesign, which could be applied to business processes, often involve computer modeling and simulation of activities that can be described mathematically.

Exhibit 5–1	Application of ABC Cost Information to Estimate New Product Costs

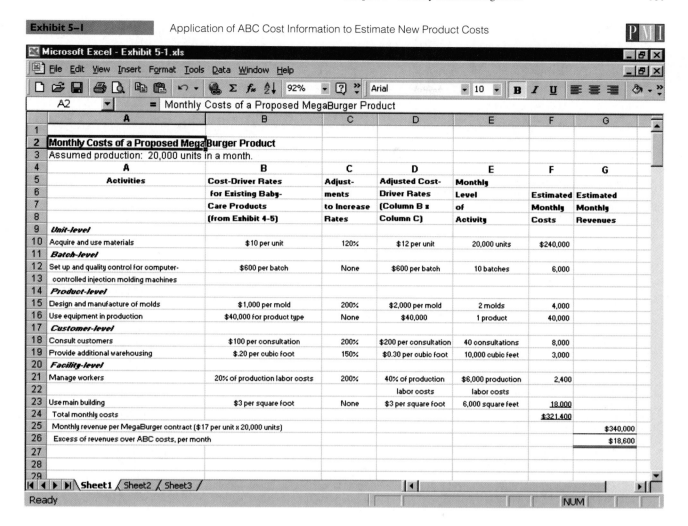

PMI's activity analysis of its current products. These activities and cost-driver rates are shown in columns A and B of Exhibit 5–1, which is reproduced from Exhibit 4–9 in Chapter 4.

Based on a review of MegaBurger's specifications, the ABC team determined that producing the toys would be similar to making complex baby-care products with several adjustments to improve product quality. Column C of Exhibit 5–1 indicates the adjustments necessary to accurately estimate the cost to produce the MegaBurger products as calculated in columns D, E, and F.

The data in Exhibit 5–1 came from the previous year before PMI actually produced any products for MegaBurger. After producing the MegaBurger products for a year, the ABC team had the new task of considering those results and confirming that the estimates had been accurate. However, the team also realized that process improvements had to be made to enable the company to continue doing business with MegaBurger.

Combination of ABC and Target Costing

At this point, PMI's goal was to modify the information obtained last year after considering the firm's first-year results with MegaBurger and as a starting point to decide whether to continue producing toys for it. Revenues from sales to MegaBurger are relatively easy to forecast because of the nature of the contract.

PMI will estimate the toys' **target cost,** which is the highest cost of a good or service that meets both customer needs and company profit goals. The preliminary analysis shown in Exhibit 5–2 indicates that costs to produce toys for MegaBurger are too high to justify their continuation.

LO 2 Demonstrate how to use activity-based costing for target costing.

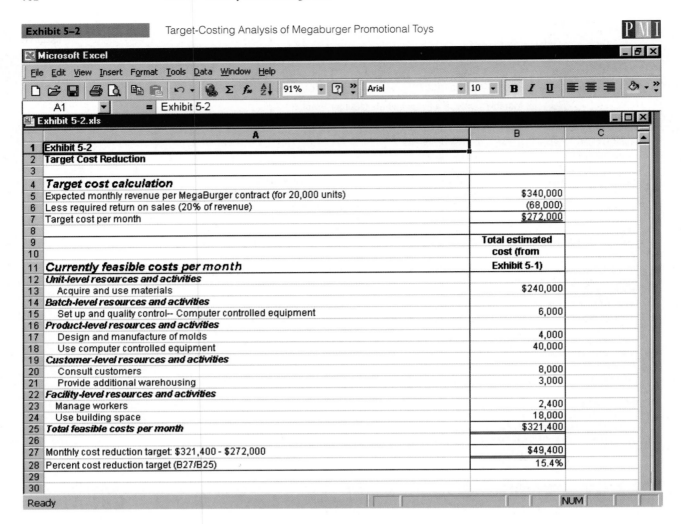

Exhibit 5–2   Target-Costing Analysis of Megaburger Promotional Toys   PMI

The sales price and order quantity shown at the top of column B of Exhibit 5–2 are based on MegaBurger's stated requirements discussed in Chapter 4 (price = $17 per unit, sales quantity = 20,000 units per month, each "unit" is a package of 8 novelty toys). PMI's management set a 20 percent return on sales (ROS) target for the MegaBurger business. This ROS might seem high, but recall that the product margins must cover PMI's administrative and other costs that have not been assigned to each product. Subtracting the required ROS from the expected monthly revenue gives a target cost of $272,000 per month, as shown near the top of column B in Exhibit 5–2. With monthly revenue of $340,000 and monthly costs of $272,000, PMI will generate a monthly product margin of $68,000.[2] (See computations at the top of column B in Exhibit 5–2.)

The ABC team used cost-driver base and rate information (from Exhibit 5–1) to compute the monthly costs for each level of resources and activities (see rows 13 through 25). The total cost—$321,400—shown in B25 is the currently feasible cost per month *without* improving the efficiency of PMI's production processes. A currently feasible cost is the cost of all current operations necessary to produce and deliver a product.

Subtracting the monthly total target cost of $272,000 (B7) from the currently feasible cost of $321,400 (B25) gives the cost reduction target of $49,400 (B27) for the month, which would represent an average cost reduction of 15.4 percent. The ABC

---

[2] The team was given these figures.

Using Target Costing

Review Exhibits 5–1 and 5–2.

a. Two ways for PMI to reduce costs are to seek a higher price from MegaBurger or accept a lower return on sales (ROS). What total revenue (sales-dollar) amount would justify the business without reducing costs or reducing the 20 percent return on sales? Alternatively, what (lower) return on sales would justify the business without reducing costs or increasing the total revenue? Would you recommend either of these alternatives? Why or why not?

b. Many cost-driver rates of the target-costing analysis in Exhibit 5–2 are taken directly from the original ABC analysis of existing products. Several cost-driver rates are notably different, however, to reflect the team's expectations of differences in the products. Do you think it is advisable to directly apply cost-driver rates from the experience of making existing products to new products? Why or why not?

c. *Team Focus.* Assume that you are PMI's customer-service manager and a member of its cross-functional team analyzing the MegaBurger toy cost information. If costs must be reduced to make PMI's profit goal feasible, does it make sense to recommend that all areas of the company find ways to reduce costs by 15.4 percent? Why or why not? As an alternative, does it make more sense to focus cost-reduction efforts on the largest costs?*

(Solutions begin on page 197.)

*This is the so-called Willie Sutton rule of cost reduction. Willie Sutton was a notorious bank robber, who after capture was asked why he robbed banks. He replied, "Because that's where the money is."

team believed that 15.4 percent would be difficult to achieve. Expressing discouragement, some team members thought PMI should forgo the MegaBurger business. Others regarded the findings in Exhibit 5–2 as tangible evidence that PMI needed to improve its processes to become more efficient. After much discussion, the team presented the cost reduction target to PMI's top management as an objective for the company to achieve by redesigning its production processes.

Importance of Customer-Perceived Value

Value-added activities enhance the value of products and services in the eyes of the customer while meeting the company's own goals. Note that customers could be either internal or external to the organization, but the ultimate test of customer value is the external customer's perception. **Non-value-added activities** are activities that do not contribute to customer-perceived value. Eliminating these activities by redesigning processes would not reduce customer value.

LO 3 Identify and measure the costs of activities that add value or do not add value in organizations.

PMI must improve processes to reduce costs. An appropriate place to start is to identify activities as value added or non-value added. The company's goal is to eliminate non-value-added activities while making value-added activities more efficient.

Eliminating Non-Value-Added Activities: Competitive Necessity

In a competitive environment, an organization should waste as few resources on non-value-added activities as possible because competitors are continuously striving to create more customer value at lower cost. For example, many banks recently eliminated most levels of approval for consumer and commercial loans because the multiple approval layers almost never affected the decision of granting the loans. The multiple approvals merely used scarce resources and delayed final approval, and the delays greatly annoyed customers. Those loan approval levels represented non-value-added activities because neither customers nor the bank realized value from them. By substituting information technology for multiple levels of manual assessments of loan applications, some banks now are able to advertise nearly instant loan decisions. These businesses seek to attract customers from less efficient banks by offering more value through faster loan decisions at lower cost because their process needs fewer approval levels.

Even in a less competitive environment, organizations have incentives to reduce non-value-added activities because they could apply the freed-up resources to value-added activities or distribute them to their employees and owners. Unless individuals in the organization derive benefits from the non-value-added activities, such as extra on-the-job perquisites, the organization might be better off using the resources for value-added activities. Organizations without non-value-added activities should be better able to compete than organizations that have allowed wasteful practices to become part of their culture.

Competition can appear unexpectedly.   An environment that is currently not competitive could become competitive quickly if, for example, competitors are able to copy superior products or technology or provide substitutes for them. RCA and other US television manufacturers, for example, virtually lost their hold on the US market in the face of effective, international competition from Japanese companies such as Sony and Hitachi, which offered lower-priced, higher-quality TVs. Some countries could and have rewritten regulations that guaranteed a market for some products and services to encourage competition and lower costs for citizens. Deregulation of many industries in the United States and elsewhere has been very difficult for firms that were not prepared to compete.

Sources of non-value-added activities.   All organizations have some non-value-added activities that can be reduced or eliminated. These are the most likely sources of the non-value-added activities:

- Producing to build up inventory.
- Waiting for processing.
- Spending time and effort to move products from place to place.
- Transporting workers to work sites.
- Producing defective products.

Identifying Value-Added Activities

The test for whether an activity adds customer value is met by answering two questions:

1. Would an external customer encourage the organization to do more of that activity?
2. Would the organization be more likely to reach its goal by performing that activity?

If both answers are yes, the activity adds value. If either answer is no, the activity adds no value and consumes scarce resources, perhaps unnecessarily. Answering these two questions also leads to two related questions:

1. How should an organization measure its value-added activities?
2. Who should be responsible for performing the measurement activity?

How should an organization measure its value-added activities?   The value-added/non-value-added dichotomy is important, but it could be too restrictive. Some activities, such as delivering service on time, obviously add value, and the organization would benefit from enhancing those activities. Other activities, such as rewrite faulty software code or rework faulty products, obviously add no value because they should not have to be performed, and customers would not willingly pay for them. Although it might not be possible to entirely eliminate non-value-added activities such as these, organizations should identify them to truthfully portray the current state of processes and to motivate employees to eliminate or reduce these activities.

Other activities, which could be necessary because of current technology, policy, or regulatory requirements, might lie between these extremes, and identifying them as one extreme or the other could lead management to make incorrect decisions about whether to enhance or eliminate them. For example, customers probably do not care whether an organization spends its resources to file its periodic tax returns. This process obviously is necessary but customers would not rate it as highly value-added. Most would agree, however, that eliminating this process altogether would be a mistake.

Many companies identify the value of their activities on a scale from 1 to 5 or 1 to 10 with the higher end representing added value. The narrower the scale, the more likely the organization is to misclassify an activity because the categories might not fit well. The wider scale, however, could make distinguishing levels of value more difficult for individuals. Although practices vary, a five-point scale could provide the right amount of detail for measuring levels of value added in most cases. On a five-point scale, an activity that is necessary but does not add value from the customer's perspective could be rated 3 while obviously value-added or non-value-added activities would be rated as a 5 or 1, respectively.

The large number of assemblies awaiting processing is a sign of inefficient processes that generate excess inventory.

Who should perform the measurement activity?   Ideally, someone who is objective and knowledgeable about what customers value and what the organization must do to meet its goals should measure value. It is unlikely, however, that one person could measure value reliably and without bias—intentional or not. It might not be possible for even a group or team to do so without input from others, such as internal and external customers. The reasons are numerous:

1. *Everyone's knowledge is limited.* For example, the sales manager might believe he or she knows what customers want and are willing to pay for, but customers are diverse, and their preferences could change over time. Asking a single customer might not generate representative answers. Furthermore, external customers might not communicate their desires directly to the company; they just might shop elsewhere if they are not satisfied.

    Another possibility is that customers could have different values, and the organization would have to decide whether to satisfy only one or both types of customer. Some level of market research and knowledge is essential to understanding what customers value. This reinforces the benefit of using cross-functional teams.

2. *Everyone's responses are potentially biased.* The warehouse supervisor could argue that inventory management and warehousing are crucial to ensuring customer value. This might be due, in part, to the fact that providing and managing product inventories is part of the business routine. Because some current jobs involve managing inventory and the warehouse, the supervisor might be unwilling to jeopardize those jobs even though he or she is responsible to the management and stockholders. Thus, the supervisor could be tempted to provide misleading information that would protect employees' jobs. Alternatively, an upwardly mobile supervisor might tell cost managers what he or she thinks they want to hear: that jobs can be cut without harming processes. Although inventory and warehouse operations could seem necessary because of current processes, they are non-value-added activities unless they are performed at the request of customers.

At any rate, the customer could care very little whether the company even has an inventory. Instead, the customer just wants the product on time and with the expected quality.

In practice, cost management analysts or market researchers measure value-added activities using anything from a single person's beliefs to sophisticated surveys of internal and external customers. If the organization cannot justify expending many resources to measure its activities, the benefits of doing so might not be expected to be significant. If that is the case, the organization could be better off using its resources on more beneficial activities.

Performing PMI's Value-Added Analysis

 PMI used a different cross-functional team headed by the director of marketing research to measure value-added activities using small groups of internal and external customers. It used a five-point scale (5 = highest value, 1 = lowest value). Other teams, including the ABC team working on the MegaBurger bid, used this team's output to evaluate and improve existing processes.

A partial list and valuation of PMI's activities appears in Exhibit 5–3 for manually controlled injection molding for a typical month. This list formed the basis of the ABM analysis. The complete value-added analysis measures the costs and value of the activities in all parts of the organization's value chain. Although this can be a formidable task, it could be necessary if departments or processes depend on each other. That is, improving a process in one area might not be possible without considering its ties to other processes and areas. For example, improving the processing of customer orders could require changes in several functional areas such as marketing, engineer-

Exhibit 5–3   PMI's Activity List: Setup and Quality Control for Manually Controlled Machines for a Typical Month

		ABC Data			Value-Added Data
A Activity	**B** Activity Description	**C** Sub-activity Cost	**D** Sub-activity Cost	**E** Activity Cost	**F** Customer Value
2.1	Set up manually controlled machines			$3,000	
2.1.1	Set manually controlled injection-molding machine dials		$ 200		3
2.1.2	Perform quality control of batches produced on manually controlled machines		200		3
2.1.3	Observe start of production run		100		5
2.1.4	Remove pieces and inspect		300		3
2.1.5	Recycle defective pieces		100		1
2.1.6	Place good pieces in inventory		2,000		
2.1.6.1	Trim excess plastic	$500			1
2.1.6.2	Place trimmings in recycle bags	400			1
2.1.6.3	Place good piece in bin or box	200			3
2.1.6.4	Log out completed order	200			3
2.1.6.5	Move completed order to warehouse	500			2
2.1.6.6	Register completed order in inventory	200			2
2.1.7	End production run		100		3

ing, and accounting and in multiple production and distribution processes. Thus, a piecemeal approach to ABM that does not consider process interactions might not be feasible or successful if attempted.

Notice that PMI is using a large proportion of its resources on low-valued activities. If PMI could save these resources or redirect them to high-valued activities, it could either reduce its costs or greatly increase its effectiveness in generating customer value.

Looking at one activity within Exhibit 5–3, we can begin to see how this information might help PMI. Activity 2.1.6.5, move completed order to warehouse, is rated 2 on the customer value scale, indicating that this activity has little, if any, value as perceived by the customer. PMI can review this process to find a way to eliminate, or at least minimize, it. For example, perhaps the completed order immediately could be shipped to Megaburger rather than stored in a warehouse. PMI should review all activities that add little or no value (scores 1, 2, and 3) to find ways to minimize or eliminate them.

Tasks Required by Activity-Based Management

Activity-based management uses the information derived from activity and value-added analyses to identify opportunities for process improvements. The twin objectives of ABM are, first, to identify non-value-added activities to eliminate or at least reduce them and, second, to identify value-added activities to enhance them. The next ABM stage is to actually redesign processes to eliminate wasteful spending on non-value-added activities.

An organization is unlikely to simply eliminate wasteful activities without redesigning entire processes. This is similar to making across-the-board cost cuts, which reduce both value-added and non-value-added activities, without changing the required work. If the organization can eliminate non-value-added activities by redesigning processes, the resources that these activities waste could either be saved to reduce spending or applied to value-added activities to increase their effectiveness. Thus, simply eliminating non-value-added activities could create short-term benefits, and redesigning processes to eliminate the need for such activities can generate long-term benefits.

Detailed Activity Analysis

As an example of ABM, refer to Exhibit 5–3. The first activity level shown is the overall setup and quality control check of the manually controlled machines (activity 2.1). The next level is a subactivity, 2.1.1, set manually controlled injection-molding machine dials. Further down the list of activities is another level of subactivities in the shaded area of Exhibit 5–3 (activities 2.1.6.1 through 2.1.6.6).

Sorting activities by cost and value. The most direct use of the information presented in Exhibit 5–3 is simply to sort the activities by value and by cost. These rankings can clearly identify opportunities for improvement. Summing the costs of an activity, for example, 2.1, by adding the cost of all the activities rated from 1 to 5 as shown in column F of Exhibit 5–3 yields the summary information shown in Exhibit 5–4.

Using Value-Added Analysis

Review Exhibit 5–3.

a. Based on the information in Exhibit 5–3 for PMI, where would you start to evaluate potential improvements for existing activities?

b. Which three activities would you recommend eliminating and why?

(Solutions begin on page 197.)

You're the Decision Maker 5.2

Exhibit 5–4

Comparisons of Activity Values and Costs: PMI's Activity 2.1: Set Up Manually Controlled Machines

Customer Value	Sum of Activity Cost	Percentage
5 (highest value)	$ 100	3.3%
4	0	0.0
3	1,200	40.0
2	700	23.3
1 (lowest value)	1,000	33.3
Total	$3,000	100.0%*

Data come from Exhibit 5–3.
* Rounded.

This table indicates that activities rated 3 and lower consume about 97 percent of the resources. PMI's cost management analysts need to find out why these activities that consume so many resources are generating so little value for customers. A competitor that could eliminate these low-value-added activities would have a cost advantage over PMI, particularly if PMI's other production processes also consume so many resources but generate so little value.

This process seems to have great room for improvement. For example, if PMI could eliminate activities rated 1 by redesigning the process, the company's cost would decline by 33.3 percent.

Not surprisingly, analysis of PMI's other processes yielded similar information, which identified many opportunities for process improvement to increase the profitability of current products, including the MegaBurger novelty toys.

Identification of Process-Improvement Opportunities

LO 4 Use the elements of an activity-based management system to help identify opportunities for process improvements.

From the analysis just discussed, the production team learned that the company was spending a large proportion of cost on low-value activities. Team members closely observed several activities, among them the subactivity "place good pieces in inventory," which had no activities valued above "3," to find precisely where they could make improvements. The result of the analysis of this activity appears in Exhibit 5–5, which has time data before and after improvements.

Cost Management in Practice 5.1

Examples of Value-added and Non-value-added Activities

The concepts of value-added and non-value-added activities can vary across organizations, depending on the internal or external customers served. The following are examples of these activities from some of the many companies that have used ABM:

Company (Process)	Value-Added Activities	Non-Value-Added Activities
Pacific Bell* (accounts receivable)	Processing payments	Reprocessing payments to correct errors
Dayton Extruded Plastics* (manufacturing)	Extruding window frames	Setting up machines
Tektronix* (product development)	Making new products	Making engineering changes
Stockham Valves and Fittings* (manufacturing)	Improving tooling	Moving and storing products
US-WEST† (sales and marketing)	Making customer calls and quotes, taking orders	Processing orders
Weyerhaeuser‡ (payroll)	Paying employees accurately and on a timely basis	Making data entries

* P. Turney, "Activity-Based Management."
† S. Convey, "Eliminating Unproductive Activities and Processes."
‡ R. B. Pederson, "Weyerhaeuser: Streamlining Payroll."
(Full citations to references are in the Bibliography.)

Sub-Activity	Before Process Improvements Elapsed Time: 100-unit order	After Process Improvements Elapsed Time: 100-unit order
Trim excess plastic	83 min.	———
Place trimmings in recycle bags	60 min.	———
Place good piece in bin or box	25 min.	25 min.
Log out completed order	30 min.	15.1 min.
Move completed order to warehouse	60 min.	30 min.
Register completed order in inventory	28 min.	12.1 min.
Total elapsed time	**286 min.**	**82.2 min.**

Exhibit 5–5

Value-Added Analysis of Injection-Molding Process: Place Good Pieces in Inventory

Asking the Question, Why?

Anyone who has been around four-year-old children knows that they often repeatedly ask adults the question, Why? This is a rational process of exploration that adults have rediscovered in seeking to find why the performance of non-value-added activities persists in organizations. Asking why often enough (some believe that asking it five times in sequence is enough) most likely will identify the root cause of performing the activity. Identifying and changing that root cause almost always eliminates the need for a non-value-added activity and often leads to additional benefits because of linkages among processes.

In consultation with the mold supplier, the production team asked why employees needed to trim excess plastic from molded products. These reasons were identified:

1. The product's appearance and function require the removal of the excess.
2. Under high-injection pressure, plastic leaks from the edges of the mold.
3. High pressure is required to mold the products properly.
4. The design of the molds permits leakage.
5. The molds are based on old designs.

The company could rework or replace old molds with improved designs to eliminate the need to trim the excess plastic and recycle excess trim. This would reduce the labor time by 143 minutes and prevent loss of good material, which had been given to the recycler in exchange for its removal.

The team also examined record-keeping activities and persuaded Chad Norris, the vice president of manufacturing, to install a **bar-coding system,** which creates a unique bar code for each order and allows the company to mark and track all orders electronically. This benefited the entire

Bar-coding systems reduce non-value-added recording time.

company by eliminating non-value-added record-keeping activities and the need to correct recording errors.

PMI expected the bar-coding system to create resource savings for virtually all its orders. As a result of this and similar analyses, production teams were able to reduce the time of several processes dramatically while increasing product quality and customer service. PMI was able to offer more customer value while consuming fewer resources and to transfer that knowledge to the production of MegaBurger toys.

Identifying the Cost of Saved Resources

Operators of injection-molding machines at PMI, on average, earn $10 per hour (including benefits). Before process improvements, the cost of the activity "place good pieces in inventory" for a 100-unit baby-care order, was:

$$\text{(286 minutes} \div \text{60 minutes per hour)} \times \$10 \text{ per hour} = \$47.67$$

After process improvements, the cost of this activity was reduced to

$$\text{(82.2 minutes} \div \text{60 minutes per hour)} \times \$10 \text{ per hour} = \$13.70$$

This represents a savings of $33.97 (= $47.67 − $13.70) for every 100-unit order. The savings is 71.3 percent ($33.97 ÷ $47.67).

Capacity Utilization

LO 5 Evaluate capacity utilization by identifying resources supplied and resources used.

Organizations acquire resources to provide the capacity to produce a certain level of products or services. **Resources supplied** refers to the capacity that the organization makes available for use; their cost is measured by totaling the cost of all resources provided, whether used or not. However, most companies provide more resources than the process uses. **Resources used** are the resources actually used by the production processes.

In general, ABC estimates the cost of resources used for an activity by multiplying the cost-driver rate (step 3 of ABC) by the cost-driver volume (step 4 of ABC). Financial statements show resources supplied. **Unused capacity** is the difference between the resources supplied and the resources used.

To demonstrate this idea of resources used, resources supplied, and unused capacity, imagine that you have rented a storage unit for $100 per month. Your possessions take up 60 percent of the space in the storage unit. Resources supplied for storage total $100 per month, but the resources used are only 60 percent of the space. Therefore, we assign the cost of "resources used" to storage as $60 per month. We assign $40 ($100 resources supplied − $60 resources used) to "unused capacity," representing the 40 percent of the free space in the storage unit.

You assigned only $60 to the activity "storing my possessions," because your possessions require only 60 percent of the space. Because the resources supplied, or space provided, exceeds what you need, you have unused storage capacity. You could use this unused storage capacity to store more belongings, or you could sublease it to a friend (perhaps for more than the $40 that the unused capacity costs you).

The difference between resources used and resources supplied applies to any resource: peoples' time, equipment, and space, to name a few. Most employees have time when they do not have to serve customers, care for patients, or perform work activities. For example, PMI's production department that makes baby-care products has seven employees who collectively provide labor resources totaling 280 hours per week (*resources supplied*). On average, however, they utilize only 250.5 hours (*resources used*), and the remaining 29.5 hours are unassigned (*unused capacity*) that are available for use, just as the unused space in your storage unit is available for use.

Differences between resources supplied and resources used generally occur because managers have committed to supply a certain level of resources before using them. Knowing the difference between resources used and supplied helps managers to identify unused capacity, which helps them reduce it or use it in creative ways. Perhaps PMI's production workers could utilize the 29.5 hours of unassigned time to perform other productive functions, such as providing additional workforce training or designing improved factory floor layouts.

Activity-Based Reporting of Unused Resources

Notice that conventional management reports do not typically distinguish between resources used and resources supplied. Instead, cost-management reports (for internal reporting) generally focus on the *resources used,* or costs, of activities. (An example of resource use is the cost of the storage unit used.) Financial accounting reports (for external reporting) generally focus on the *resources supplied* to various parts of the organization. (An example of resource supply is the lease payment for the entire storage unit whether it is used or not.)

Information about both resource used and resource supplied is useful to managers. See Exhibit 5–6 for a reporting format that combines information about resource use and resource supply for Donovan Company. Note that column A categorizes costs into the cost hierarchies discussed in Chapter 4. Managers can see the amount of costs in each hierarchy and find ways to manage those resources effectively to reduce costs. For example, managers see that batch-level activities use $46,000 of resources (column B). If managers cut the number of batches in half, they might reduce the use of resources from $46,000 to $23,000.

The report shows managers the unused portion of the resources for each type of cost, perhaps the most important information provided. Consider setup costs as an example. Assume that the cost driver is hours of setup and the cost driver rate is $200 per hour. Based on the information in the income statement, $40,000 was spent on

A	B Resources Used	C Unused Capacity	D Resources Supplied
Sales			$360,000
Unit-level activity costs:			
Materials	$ 60,000	$ 0	$ 60,000
Energy	20,000	0	20,000
Short-term labor	7,000	1,000	8,000
Outside contracts	12,000	0	12,000
	$ 99,000	$ 1,000	$100,000
Batch-level activity costs:			
Setups	$ 28,000	$12,000	$ 40,000
Purchasing	18,000	2,000	20,000
	$ 46,000	$14,000	$ 60,000
Product-level activity costs:			
Parts management	$ 12,000	$ 2,000	$ 14,000
Marketing	28,000	2,000	30,000
Engineering	10,000	2,000	12,000
	$ 50,000	$ 6,000	$ 56,000
Customer-level activity costs:			
Customer service	$ 4,000	$ 4,000	$ 8,000
Facility-level activity costs:			
Long-term labor	$ 10,000	$ 4,000	$ 14,000
Depreciation (buildings)	24,000	16,000	40,000
Administrative	20,000	6,000	26,000
	$ 54,000	$26,000	$ 80,000
Total costs	$253,000	$51,000	$304,000
Operating profit			$ 56,000

Exhibit 5–6

Donovan Company: ABM Income Statement (January)

setups (column D). That represents 200 hours of setup capacity ($40,000 ÷ $200 per setup hour). However, the company used only 140 hours ($28,000 resources used ÷ $200 cost driver rate) during the month. The report shows managers that $12,000 (or 60 hours) of unused setup resources is available.

All other things equal, managers could have used perhaps as many as 60 additional hours of setup in January without increasing expenditures. In reality, managers know that some unused resources are a good thing. Having some unstructured time for ad hoc training, leisure, or thinking about ways to improve work and the work environment can boost morale and productivity.

Notice that some costs have more unused resources than others. The unit-related activity costs show little or no unused resources. These costs vary proportionately with output and often have little or no unused resources. Short-term labor, for example, is the cost of piecework labor or temporary help employed on an "as-needed" basis. In a college, a part-time lecturer hired for only one class is an example of short-term labor. Many of us have worked as short-term laborers during the summer in resorts, on farms, fighting forest fires, in retail stores, or providing delivery services.

Facility-related costs have unused resources unless the company operates at full capacity. Long-term labor resources are the costs of employing people who are not laid off during temporary fluctuations in production. In colleges, permanent faculty and staff are examples of long-term labor.

Implementation of Activity-Based Costing and Management

LO 6 Understand methods of and problems related to implementing activity-based costing and management.

Activity-based costing and activity-based management offer feasible ways to evaluate and improve process efficiency, and their benefits could well exceed their costs. Remember that ABC focuses on developing improved product or service costs given current processes. ABM, however, involves identifying opportunities for improving processes. Thus, although not all organizations might need improved product or service costs, most could benefit from process improvements.

Some ABC critics have faulted it for generating, in some cases, product costs that are not significantly different from traditional, functional costs. They argue, therefore, that ABC is too expensive for the benefits it offers. These same critics, however, usually do not consider the benefits of taking ABC to ABM and making significant process improvements. Some ABM advocates argue that ABC product costs are merely a by-product of ABM and process improvement efforts, which can be much more important to the organization's long-term success than knowing current product costs accurately. Activity-based techniques are conceptually appealing, but they are not trivial to implement.

Observers of ABC and ABM implementation have identified a number of factors that appear to influence whether it will be successful or unsuccessful. Research in this area is ongoing, so we must stress that this discussion is preliminary. It appears that not all companies that have considered ABC or ABM have implemented them fully or successfully. Some firms have tried ABC and apparently have found that the cost exceeded the expected benefits.[3]

Should All Organizations Adopt ABC and ABM?

It seems intuitive that companies facing the most price competition are most eager to consider ABC as a way to improve their cost measurement and to identify the most profitable products. Likewise, firms that produce many different, complex products from common facilities might obtain more benefits from ABC than firms that have simpler processes and product offerings.

---

[3] For a thorough discussion of ABC implementation, see S. W. Anderson and S. M. Young, *Implementing Management Innovations: Lessons Learned from Activity-Based Costing in the U.S. Automobile Industry.* (Full citations to references are in the Bibliography.)

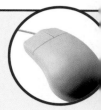

Research Insight 5.1

Comparison of Resource Use and Resource Supply in a Health Care Organization

In a study conducted in an outpatient surgery center of a large Midwestern US hospital, researchers compared the effect of a new anesthetic on the resources supplied and resources used to care for patients in the surgery center's recovery rooms. This new drug enabled patients to wake up faster after surgery. The pharmaceutical company producing the drug claimed that switching to it could reduce the cost of recovery-room nurses (the resource used) by 33 percent because patients would spend 33 percent less time in the recovery room. The study's research supported the company's claim that *resources used* would decrease by 33 percent. However, the researchers found that the effect of switching to the new drug would likely not decrease *resources supplied* by 33 percent.

Nurses were hired in shifts of one, four, or eight hours at the hospital. Reducing a patient's time from 60 minutes in the recovery room, for example, to 40 minutes reduced the use of the recovery room's nursing time by 20 minutes (33 percent); however, if the nurse was hired for an eight-hour shift, the hospital still paid the nurse for the full eight hours even if the patient went home early. In the end, the researchers concluded that the *resources supplied*—the amounts paid to recovery room nurses—would decrease in the range of 10 to 20 percent. Therefore, switching to the new drug would decrease the resources used (i.e., the cost of recovery-room nursing time) by 33 percent but would decrease resources supplied (i.e., amounts spent to pay recovery-room nurses) by only 10–20 percent. Because the decrease in resources used was greater than the decrease in resources supplied, the hospital would have increased its unused capacity in recovery room nursing time. This unused capacity would be available for other uses, such as improving patient care. *Source: M. W. Maher and M. L. Marais, "A Field Study on the Limitations of Activity-Based Costing When Resources Are Provided on a Joint and Indivisible Basis." For related articles, see E. Noreen, "Conditions under Which Activity-Based Costing Systems Provide Relevant Costs"; and R. Balakrishnan and N. S. Soderstrom, "The Cost of System Congestion: Evidence from the Health Care Sector."*

It might be no coincidence that modern ABC applications began in manufacturing firms facing new, intense competition from foreign firms in industries such as electronics, equipment, and automobile manufacturing. These industries also have pioneered ABM as a way to improve processes and profitability. As service and regulated firms have been exposed to more competition, they also have considered both ABC and ABM as solutions. Many recent applications have been in the service departments (purchasing, finance, administration, and distribution) of manufacturing firms. Financial service, pharmaceutical, and government contracting firms also report using activity-based methods.

Although not all firms have adopted or will adopt ABC or ABM, and some have backed away from it, these methods appear to have had a lasting impact on cost-management practices, particularly in multiproduct firms facing intense price competition.

Can You Be Sure That ABC and ABM Will Be Successful?

Determinants of successful ABC or ABM implementations are less obvious, perhaps, and research continues on this important issue. One thing seems clear: Spending significant effort on planning the project before the first item of data is collected is crucial. Most of the success of ABC or ABM could be attributed to good planning. Although planning does not guarantee success, the six Ps of planning have been validated in many ABC/ABM contexts: prior planning prevents particularly poor performance. Planning issues to consider include these:

- Intended scope of the ABC/ABM project.
- Resources necessary to plan and implement the project.
- Resistance to change.
- Information to be gathered.
- Analysis team's responsibility for information analysis and decision making.

Each of these issues is discussed in more detail.

Intended scope of the ABC/ABM project.   An early decision regarding ABC or ABM implementation centers on whether the project is intended to be a problem-solving tool used by cost management analysts or a more ambitious, organizationwide system. In either case, most observers agree that a small pilot project, which has a high chance for success, is the proper way to introduce ABC or ABM to an organization.

A **pilot project** is a limited-scope project intended to be a small-scale model of a larger, possibly systemwide, project. A general-use, or systemwide, project that has not been pilot tested has little hope of succeeding because the organization's complexities will overwhelm the learning and development that must take place first.

Translating the technical requirements of ABC and ABM into a feasible project for an actual organization should be done on a small scale first. Management must also anticipate the linkages across departments, groups, and processes as well as the data-gathering and reporting requirements of the full-scale implementation. For example, PMI created data-input worksheets with the same format for all teams and departments so the worksheets could be collected and combined electronically with minimum effort and chance for data-entry errors.

Resources necessary.   Virtually all observers of activity-based methods agree that any ABC or ABM project is a significant undertaking that requires sufficient management commitment, personnel and time, and technology resources.

Management commitment.   Unless management is committed to the effort and to implementing the pilot project recommendations, ABC or ABM is unlikely to have a significant impact on the organization. Gaining this commitment might mean that management analysts must educate top managers to appreciate the benefits and costs of the approach.

The challenge for cost management analysts is to communicate clearly and effectively what ABC/ABM can and cannot be expected to do. Overselling ABC or ABM as the cure for all of an organization's business problems is sure to lead to disappointment. These techniques can be valuable diagnostic and decision-making aids, but they do not replace careful decision making.

Personnel and time.   Knowledgeable observers estimate that significant ABC/ABM projects require a three- to four-person cross-functional team and at least four to six months of full-time effort. Unless the ABC/ABM project is intended only as a demonstration or for a very small company, it most likely cannot be completed successfully by one or two people on a part-time basis. Starving the project for time limits the team to considering only a few activities and might require it to take planning and data-analysis shortcuts that will lessen the confidence in its recommendations.

Technology resources.   Personal computer spreadsheets (as used throughout this book) are appropriate for applications in small companies, but they are difficult to use as systems for large organizations. If the intent is to develop an ABC/ABM system, most consultants argue that it is most efficient to begin with existing commercial software rather than develop in-house software that will be difficult to create and maintain. Consultants might be biased in this regard because, after all, selling their services and products is their business. Furthermore, some survey evidence indicates that successful ABC implementation does not depend on using either commercial software or consultants.

Resistance to change.   ABC and ABM analyses often indicate the opportunity and need for dramatic changes in organizations. Believing that everyone in the organization will agree with the need for the analyses or the recommendations that follow to revise processes is a mistake. Fear, distrust, and cynicism, which should be expected when jobs are affected, could motivate some of this resistance.

Preventing resistance.   Progressive organizations prevent or minimize resistance to change by (1) education and training, (2) widespread sponsorship and participation, and (3) incentives to encourage and reward change. Therefore, advance work is necessary to prepare personnel at all of the organization's levels for the analysis and changes that probably will result. It seems obvious, for example, that gaining affected employees' full participation will be difficult if they believe that ABC/ABM places their jobs in jeopardy (i.e., identifies them as non-value-added personnel). One recommended, bottom-up approach is to educate employees about the competitive necessity of ABC/ABM, give them a voice and influence in the analysis, and assure them that they will have meaningful jobs in the redesigned organization. Otherwise, it might be more effective to plan a top-down approach, using a team or a consultant to devise the solution and impose it on the organization.

In some organizations, employees might be suspicious of the advertised benefits of ABM because management could have implemented different initiatives that were unsuccessful or appeared to have adverse effects on the employees. Employees in these organizations might regard ABM as just the latest management fad and, if they resist long enough, the company will replace it with yet another attempt to change processes. In this situation, a pilot project that demonstrates objectively to suspicious employees what ABM can be expected to do might be imperative.

Effects of culture. Although this practice is somewhat controversial, some authors also recommend that companies with culturally diverse employees be especially sensitive to differences in various cultures, particularly with regard to the roles of individuals versus groups in promoting and accepting changes such as ABC and ABM. US and UK companies, in particular, have often been criticized for assuming that their management approaches will translate naturally to other cultures (perhaps because they have so much foreign investment in developing countries). For example, a bottom-up approach might not work at all in a culture in which employees regard criticizing existing processes as disloyal to the company. It might be more effective for international companies to encourage local solutions that might differ in approach from the most effective ones in the United States or Great Britain. There is much to learn about implementing ABC and ABM in international companies and those with employees from different cultures.[4]

Information to be gathered. ABC and ABM require information not normally available from an organization's information systems. Usually observation, interview, or survey of the organization's employees provide this information. An organization can use any of these methods, but unless the information about resources, activities, and uses of resources is reasonably accurate (e.g., reliable and unbiased), the analyses and recommendations based on the information will not be valid guides for changing processes. It is important to realize that perfect accuracy is neither attainable nor desirable since the costs to obtain perfect information are prohibitive. Nonetheless, concerns about obtaining accurate activity and resource information lead many organizations to hire either consultants or experienced employees to conduct this part of the analysis.

The approach that PMI used to obtain activity and resource use information (described in Chapter 4) is modeled on the experience of several large, successful companies (FirstData Corporation, Procter & Gamble, and SyBase Corporation). PMI used existing documentation (e.g., ISO 9000 information) to prepare the master activity list and surveyed and interviewed employees to measure the uses of resources to perform activities. This information probably was not perfectly accurate, but the CFO stated that he would rather be "approximately correct" (using reasonable ABC information) than "100 percent wrong" (using guesses or financial accounting information, which were the alternatives).

---

[4] For example, see P. Brewer, "National Culture and Activity-Based Costing Systems."

A complication related to gathering reliable information in any organization occurs when the jobs that must change the most are middle-management and staff support. Employees in these positions could be the most resistant to changes that require them to give up power and control. For example, one of PMI's recommendations, which is common at other companies, was that teams should be able to perform minor repairs and adjustments to equipment without having to wait for an engineer or technician. At first, this was resisted by staff personnel who feared they would first train employees to make the repairs and adjustments and then would watch their own jobs disappear. PMI overcame their resistance by redesigning staff jobs to focus more on improving designs and preventing equipment problems than on correcting designs and problems.

Analysis team's responsibility for information analysis and decision making. Although top managers ultimately have the responsibility for authorizing and effecting major changes, the study team is best prepared to analyze the data and make recommendations for several reasons. First, the team is intimately familiar with the data, its strengths, and its weaknesses. Second, empowering and requiring the team to make recommendations gives them control and accountability for the entire project and motivates them to gather and analyze the data carefully and consider a wide range of opportunities for change.

Whether the team should make its recommendations directly to top management depends on the organization's culture and needs. In some organizations, it could be important for the team to solicit and receive input from many individuals and departments before it issues its final recommendations to management. This allows the team to obtain even more information and to "float trial balloons" to gauge the effectiveness of its proposals. In other organizations, however, top management might need to impose major changes and be more involved in developing recommendations for change.

PMI's Decision to Keep MegaBurger as a Customer

 From our earlier discussion, it is clear that PMI decided to implement ABC and ABM. The ABC analysis performed in Chapter 4 provided an estimate of future product costs based on PMI's current processes. PMI's ABC team realized that although the first year's business with MegaBurger was profitable, the profits did not meet the company's target return on sales of 20 percent. Several weeks after the initial meeting regarding the MegaBurger contract, PMI's executive committee met to decide whether to bid on a second year's contract. The following is a transcript from this meeting with Melanie Fairchild (CEO), Alex Lewis (CFO and team leader), Chad Norris (VP of Manufacturing), Michael Chia (VP of Logistics), and Elizabeth Forney (VP of Marketing).

Fairchild: Hello, everybody. I know we are concerned about hitting the 20 percent target on the MegaBurger business. What is our plan of attack?

Lewis: Our team has done a tremendous amount of work to identify areas for potential cost savings. Its target-cost analysis shows that a 15.4 percent decrease in costs is necessary to meet the 20 percent return on sales target. The team believes that this is attainable. One example of potential savings is in our injection-molding process. We can redesign the molds currently used to reduce the need for trimming products as they come out of the mold.

Norris: Our manufacturing employees believe many processes can be improved in addition to the molds just mentioned by Alex. The manufacturing department is now offering a cash bonus to all employees who make a suggestion for a process improvement that is ultimately implemented. Not surprisingly, we have been flooded with ideas, many of which will reduce costs substantially.

Chia: Based on this information, I believe we have the capability to reach the 20 percent target. Let's move forward with MegaBurger.

Fairchild: I agree. Good work everyone! Based on your efforts, I think we can look forward to working with MegaBurger for another year and to hitting our target of 20 percent return on sales.

Chapter Summary

ABC provides important information about the uses of resources given current processes but stops short of identifying opportunities for decreasing costs and increasing value. Activity-based management (ABM) uses ABC information and perceived customer values to improve the organization's efficiency and consequently create more value at lower cost. Organizations should redesign processes to reduce or eliminate activities that add no value and either save those resources or reapply them to value-added activities. Implementing ABM (and ABC) could be difficult, but prior planning is essential to doing so effectively. Factors to be considered include the project's scope, necessary resources, resistance to change, information to be gathered, and the analysis team's responsibilities for information analysis and decision making.

Key Terms

For each term's definition, refer to the indicated page or turn to the glossary at the end of the text.

Activity-based management (ABM), 180

Bar-coding systems, 189

Non-value-added activities, 183

Pilot project, 194

Resources supplied, 190

Resources used, 190

Target cost, 181

Unused capacity, 190

Value-added activities, 183

Meeting the Cost Management Challenges

1. **Is** implementing activity-based costing enough to improve efficiency? Can cost management analysts measure costs more accurately using it and, by doing so, ensure that the organization will meet its efficiency goals?

Activity-based costing (ABC) usually is not enough for most organizations with inefficient processes. Measuring costs accurately with ABC allows organizations to understand their cost drivers and their processes consumption of scarce resources. Knowing what drives costs allows employees to manage cost drivers to reduce costs. Cost is only part of the efficiency picture, however; employees also must know which activities drive value as perceived by the customer. Minimizing something that customers value would likely not improve profitability. Therefore, ABC is a valuable first step, but improving efficiency and profitability also requires knowing the drivers of value. Activity-based management considers both cost and value and, therefore, is a more comprehensive guide to cost management.

2. **Do** the numbers "speak for themselves"? Does the cost management analyst's responsibility end with making recommendations for improvements?

Numbers rarely speak for themselves and typically require analysis and interpretation. Thus, it is just as important for cost management analysts to measure costs as it is for them to communicate the meaning of the cost data. Cost management analysts also need to communicate the reliability of their measurements and

the implications of possible errors in the data. In addition, making recommendations for improvement is important, but leading and implementing the required changes is even more important. Many good ideas never get beyond the idea stage because no one takes the lead to implement them.

3. **How** do you know that activity-based cost-management methods are worthwhile?

Perhaps one can never know for sure, but that is not unique to evaluating ABC or ABM. The effectiveness of any management technique or action is uncertain; that is the reason organizations need managers who can exercise professional judgment. Otherwise, all decisions could be programmed and left to mathematical decision rules. Cost management analysts can evaluate the prospective value of ABC and ABM on the basis of

- Prior personal experience or the experience of others in similar situations.
- Recommendations of trusted internal or external consultants.
- Results of a small, controlled pilot test in which the cost management analyst has evaluated processes before, during, and after applying ABC and ABM. The "before" conditions provide the basis of comparing cost, time, quality, and so on. The "during" observations yield knowledge of information needs, communication and implementation difficulties, and successful procedures. The "after" conditions permit an objective evaluation of improvements in areas such as cost and quality that could be expected in more complete implementations.

Solutions to You're the Decision Maker

5.1 Using Target Costing p. 183

a. The required higher price must yield a 20 percent return on sales (ROS) given the currently feasible cost. This new total revenue can be computed as follows (solving for "revenue"):

$$\text{Revenue} - (\text{ROS\%} \times \text{Revenue}) = \text{Currently feasible cost}$$

Inputting the known data:

$$\text{Revenue} - (0.20 \times \text{Revenue}) = \$321,400 \text{ (from Exhibit 5–2)}$$
$$0.80 \times \text{Revenue} = \$321,400$$
$$\text{Revenue} = \$321,400/0.80$$
$$\text{Revenue} = \$401,750$$

Thus, the total annual revenue of $401,750 is required to make 20 percent ROS given the currently feasible cost of $321,400. At 20,000 units per month, this equates to a $20.09 sales price per unit (versus the previous $17.00 sales price per unit in the original proposal).

If the alternative is to accept a lower ROS at MegaBurger's stated price, the equation is the same but solves for a different variable (ROS). The revenue of $340,000 appears in the information in Exhibit 5–2.

Revenue − (ROS × Revenue) = Currently feasible cost

Inputting the known data, and solving for ROS:

$$\$340,000 - (ROS \times \$340,000) = \$321,400$$
$$- (ROS \times \$340,000) = \$321,400 - \$340,000$$
$$(ROS \times \$340,000) = -\$321,400 + \$340,000$$
$$ROS = (\$340,000 - \$321,400) \div \$340,000$$
$$ROS = 0.055 = 5.5\%$$

MegaBurger is not likely to agree to paying a higher price for the product since it can choose from many suppliers. Accepting a lower ROS could be feasible in the short run to get the business, but if PMI really believes that a 20 percent return on sales is appropriate, it should agree to a lower ROS only if it can be sure that it can improve processes sufficiently and quickly to get a 20 percent ROS.

b. If products are sufficiently similar and will use similar processes, the cost-driver rates probably can be used at least as starting points for estimating the costs of new products. PMI's ABC team apparently compared the attributes of the new product with those of existing products and modified cost-driver rates as necessary. An organization should not blindly apply cost-driver rates from current products and processes, but they can provide a valid basis.

c. Managers might argue in favor of equal percentage, across-the-board cuts to "share the pain equitably." This approach is not likely to benefit the entire organization because it ignores the causes of waste—non-value-added activities—which might occur anywhere in the organization and dispro-

portionately in some areas. Scrutinizing only the highest-cost activities for opportunities to cut costs could be expedient but also could allow waste to persist in many smaller activities. Ideally, PMI should identify and try to reduce all non-value-added activities. In practice, many organizations undertake these cost-cutting exercises in times of crisis or short-lived opportunity and believe they cannot afford the time necessary to thoroughly investigate all processes. Thus, they tend to attack the highest-cost processes first. One wonders why organizations do not conduct these analyses without the motivation and time pressure of a crisis.

5.2   Using Value-Added Analysis   p. 187

a. A number of different approaches can be used. PMI could first look at activities with a cost above a certain dollar amount (for example, all items above $300) and then select the items that customers ranked as lowest values, or it could start with high-cost activities first, regardless of scores.

Most companies start with the high-cost activities first, thinking that the highest potential for cost savings is within these activities. Even if the customer value-added ranking is relatively high (that is, customers perceive an activity as value added), there might be room for making the process more efficient.

b. Answers will vary, depending on the approach used [see solution to part (a)]. If PMI starts with the lowest value scores first, regardless of the cost, the three activities (recycle defective pieces: $100; trim excess plastic: $500; place trimmings in recycle bags: $400) rated 1 are prime candidates for elimination.

Since value scores of 1 and 2 represent activities that add little (if any) value as perceived by the customer, PMI could start by examining the highest cost activities first within these value scores (trim excess plastic: $500 and move completed order to warehouse: $500).

Regardless of the proposed approach, PMI should remember that the goal is to minimize or eliminate all non-value-added activities and to make all value-added activities as efficient as possible.

Review Questions

5.1 What do ABC and ABM have in common, and how do they differ?

5.2 How can ABC and target costing be used together to motivate ABM?

5.3 What are alternatives to reducing process costs to meet target costs?

5.4 What are the advantages and disadvantages of using knowledge about current processes to evaluate future processes?

5.5 What are examples of value-added and non-value-added activities?

5.6 What is the relationship between non-value-added activities and waste?

5.7 Does eliminating non-value-added activities necessarily eliminate waste?

5.8 What are the questions to ask to determine whether an activity adds customer value?

5.9 How do organizations reduce spending by eliminating non-value-added activities? Is spending reduction the only result of eliminating non-value-added activities?

5.10 What is the difference between a pilot project and a systemwide project?

5.11 Why might individuals resist ABM?

5.12 Must ABM information be 100 percent accurate to be useful? Explain.

Critical Analysis

5.13 Is it fair to assume that all individuals in an organization welcome the opportunity to improve processes by eliminating non-value-added activities? Explain.

5.14 "The cost of repairing all these defective products is killing us. We should hire more highly qualified employees who won't make so many mistakes and who can figure out how to improve our processes so that mistakes are less likely." Write a memo explaining the trade-offs involved with this recommendation.

5.15 You have been hired as a consultant to improve a hospital's patient admission process. Assume that you could describe this process using 100 small activities or 10 broader activities. How would you decide how many activities to use?

5.16 "Come on, be serious. Some of these activities that you have identified as non-value-added just cannot be eliminated. We have to send monthly reports to corporate headquarters, and we need to file tax return information quarterly. This ABM analysis doesn't seem to work in the real world." Respond to this comment.

5.17 According to several writers, corporate America whacked away at labor costs throughout the 1990s. Corporations tamed unions and laid off millions of hourly workers, yet multitudes of US companies still cannot compete with their international rivals, and large operations such as AT&T, General Motors, and Du Pont are going through new rounds of restructuring. Why is competitiveness still so elusive for large US corporations? Prepare a written answer to this question.

5.18 Eastman Kodak Co. expected to save thousands of dollars a year when it laid off Maryellen Ford in a companywide downsizing. Within weeks, however, it was paying more for the same work. A local contractor that gets much of its work from Kodak snapped up Ms. Ford, a computer-aided designer and 17-year Kodak veteran. "I took the project I was working on and finished it here," she says. Instead of paying her $15 per hour plus benefits, Kodak now pays the contractor $65 per hour, and Ms. Ford earns $20 an hour (but gets no benefits). A Kodak spokesman acknowledges that the photography and imaging company has to outsource work during peak periods and adds, "There are a lot of challenges facing the company. People throughout the company are working a lot harder, but I'm not hearing that they're demoralized." He also says that by reducing staff, Kodak has saved money in computer equipment and workspace.[5] Explain what probably took place at Kodak. How would you determine whether Kodak has improved its efficiency by downsizing?

5.19 Explain the following comment: "Cost cutting has become the holy grail of corporate management, but what helps the financial statement up front can end up hurting it down the road."[6]

5.20 Connecticut Mutual Life Insurance offered a lucrative buyout plan to its 1,675 workers. About 900—more than twice the anticipated number—accepted forcing it to fill 400 vacated positions. Senior employees were the ones who left, and the company brought in new entrants at the lower end of the wage scale. The company estimates it will save $10.4 million per year.[7] What are the trade-offs and implications associated with this decision to restructure the workforce?

5.21 Your boss sent the following e-mail this morning: "Today I am announcing a 10 percent reduction in spending in every department, effective immediately. We must improve profitability, and this is the quickest way to improve the bottom line. I assure you that every department will share the pain equally. I am not asking anyone to work harder, but all of us will have to work smarter." Explain why the announced across-the-board cuts in resource spending might not improve but actually worsen profitability. How would this situation differ, if at all, in a governmental agency?

Exercises

Listed here are four activities that some students undertake to prepare for an exam.

1. Gather study materials.
2. Organize study materials.
3. Organize support materials.
4. Study.

Required

Create at least two subactivities for each of the four activities and assign a value score of 1 to 5 (5 having the highest value) to each subactivity.

Exercise 5.22
Activity Analysis
(LO 1)

Label the following steps as appropriate for ABC and for ABM. List them in the proper order starting with the ABC activities.

a. Calculate a cost-driver rate.
b. Score each activity as adding high or low value as perceived by the customer.
c. Assign activity costs to goods and services.
d. Identify opportunities to enhance value-added activities and to reduce or eliminate non-value-added activities.

Exercise 5.23
Steps in Activity-Based
Costing and Activity-
Based Management
(LO 1)

---

[5] For additional discussion of ABC/ABM implementation issues, see F. Selto, "Implementing Activity-Based Management"; and M. Shields and M. McEwen, "Implementing Activity-Based Costing Systems Successfully."

[6] "Call it Dumbsizing: Why Some Companies Regret Cost-Cutting," *The Wall Street Journal.*

[7] Ibid.

e. Identify and classify the activities related to the company's goods and services.

f. Identify activities as value added or non-value added.

g. Estimate the cost of activities.

Exercise 5.24
ABC and ABM Steps
(LO 1)

Describe the four steps of ABC and the three additional steps of ABM.

Exercise 5.25
Activity Analysis
(LO 1)

Loomis Distribution Company (LDC) is a distributor of soft drinks. It receives products from beverage manufacturers (e.g., Coca-Cola) and ships them to retail outlets (e.g., convenience stores and supermarkets).

Required

The following activities and subactivities of LDC's warehousing process (the receiving and shipping of goods) are *not* in logical order. Arrange them into a numbered, logical sequence (e.g., 1.0, 1.1, . . . , 2.0, 2.1, . . .).

Warehousing Activity	Warehousing Subactivity	Annual Time (hours)
Store beverages	Physically store products	1,400
Receive beverages	Identify where to locate product	700
Pack, mark, and prepare customer orders for shipping	Update inventory records when product received	200
	Unload vehicle	1,200
Ship customer orders	Check products for damage	500
	Return damaged products to supplier	300
	Compare products to purchase order	400
	Return incorrect products to supplier	300
	Package and label products by customer order	400
	Place orders on loading dock for shipment	300
	Load vehicle	1,400
	Prepare invoice and notification of shipment	500
	Retrieve products from storage	1,500
	Update inventory records when product shipped out	500

Exercise 5.26
Value-Added Analysis
(LO 3)

Consider the activities and subactivities in Exercise 5.25.

Required

Form small groups to rate each activity on a value-added scale from 1 to 5, with 5 being the most highly valued from an external customer's perspective.

Exercise 5.27
Value-Added Analysis
(LO 3)

Continue the analysis in Exercise 5.26. The hours spent on various activities are for a five-person warehousing team. Each team member earns on average $16 per hour (including benefits).

Required

What is the cost of each activity?

Exercise 5.28
Activity-Based
Management
(LO 4)

Continue Exercise 5.27.

Required

Calculate subtotals for each value-added score (1, 2, 3, 4, and 5). If the company could eliminate low-valued activities (by your definition), how much cost could it save?

Exercise 5.29
Activity Analysis
(LO 1)

Michigan Insurance, Inc. (MII), an insurer of small businesses, has a claims-processing department that receives, processes, and refers casualty and property loss claims to insurance adjusters for resolution. Approximately half of the claims arrive by standard mail; the other half are phoned in by policyholders.

Required

The following activities and subactivities of MII's claims process are *not* in a logical order. Arrange them into a numbered, logical sequence or process (e.g., 1.0, 1.1, . . . , 2.0, 2.1, . . .).

Claims-Processing Activity	Claims-Processing Subactivity	Annual Time (hours)
Receive claims	Take phone call..	1,000
Check information	Open mail	700
Analyze claim	Sort mail by claim type	200
Forward claim to adjuster	Refer phone call by claim type	800
	Verify completeness of information on written claim	900
	Compare coverage in policy to casualty or loss claim	800
	Log in claim	500
	Verify accuracy of policy information on written claim	1,000
	Return incorrect claims to policyholders	400
	Review incorrect claims with policyholders	500
	File multiple copies of claims	1,400
	Send claim and policy copy to adjuster	400
	Package copy of claim and policy for shipment to adjuster	500
	Log out claim	500

Consider the activities and subactivities in Exercise 5.29.

Required

Form small groups to rate each activity on a value-added scale from 1 to 5, with 5 being the most highly valued from an external customer's perspective.

Continue the analysis in Exercise 5.30. The hours spent on various activities are for a five-person claims-processing team. Each team member earns on average $20 per hour (including benefits).

Required

What is the cost of each activity?

Continue Exercise 5.31.

Required

a. Calculate subtotals for each value-added score (1, 2, 3, 4, and 5). If the company could eliminate low-valued activities (by your definition), how much could it save?

b. *Build your own spreadsheet.* Develop a spreadsheet to answer (a) based on data from Exercises 5.29–5.31.

Identify a non-value-added activity in your workplace or school.

Required

a. Identify the root cause of performing the non-value-added activity.

b. Does identifying the root cause suggest a way to eliminate the non-value-added activity?

c. What complications can you anticipate in making this change?

Review the information in Exhibit 5–2 for PMI. Assume that the sales price of $17 per unit remains the same but that the total units to be sold each month increases to 21,000 (from the original proposal of 20,000 units). (Assume that the only costs that will change are the costs driven by unit-level activities.)

Required

How much will this impact the monthly cost-reduction target

a. In dollars?

b. As a percent of currently feasible costs?

Exercise 5.35
Target Costing
(LO 2)

Review the information in Exhibit 5–2 for PMI. Assume that the total number of units to be sold each month remains the same but that the sales price increases to $18 per unit (from the original sales price of $17 per unit).

Required
How much will this impact the monthly cost-reduction target

a.   In dollars?
b.   As a percent of currently feasible costs?

Exercise 5.36
Target Costing
(LO 2)

Review the information in Exhibit 5–2 for PMI. After further discussion, PMI's management is willing to lower the required return on sales (ROS) to 16 percent (from the original 20 percent).

Required
How much will this impact the monthly cost-reduction target

a.   In dollars?
b.   As a percent of currently feasible costs?

Exercise 5.37
Resources Supplied
versus Resources Used
(LO 5)

Information about two activities for Northern Products, Inc., follows:

Resources Supplied		Cost-Driver Rate	Cost-Driver Volume
		Resources Used	
Energy	$7,300	$12 per machine hour	500 machine hours used
Marketing	5,500	25 per sales call	200 sales calls made

Required
Compute the unused capacity for each activity.

Exercise 5.38
Resources Supplied
versus Resources Used
(LO 5)

Information about two activities for Systems Integrators, Inc., follows:

Resources Supplied		Cost-Driver Rate	Cost-Driver Volume
		Resources Used	
Machine setups	$10,000	$200 per run	30 runs
Administrative	3,500	300 per job	11 jobs

Required
Compute the unused capacity for each activity.

Exercise 5.39
Resources Supplied
versus Resources Used
(LO 5)

Selected information about several activities for Quality Printing follows:

Resources Supplied		Cost-Driver Rate	Cost-Driver Volume
		Resources Used	
Material	$50,000	$ 5	10,000
Energy	7,000	15	400
Setups	3,500	50	60
Purchasing	3,000	40	70
Customer service	3,200	50	60
Long-term labor	12,000	40	250
Administrative	24,000	50	400

Required
a.   Compute the unused capacity for each activity.
b.   Write a short report stating why managers should know the difference between resources used and resources supplied. Give examples of how managers could use the preceding information on resources used and resources supplied.

Problems

Robert Lutz, when president and chief operating officer at the former Chrysler (now DaimlerChrysler), was determined to replace the company's old cost-management system with one that could report costs by process and could separate value-added from non-value-added activities. After reading an article about activity-based costing and activity-based management, Lutz decided this was the system for his company. As Chrysler introduced ABC/ABM, many employees at various levels resisted. The new system represented a threat by changing the existing power structure and revealing inefficient processes hidden by the old cost-management system.

Problem 5.40
Activity-Based Costing and Activity-Based Management
(LO 6)

Required

a. Write a short report explaining why you think the Chrysler employees opposed ABC/ABM.

b. Recommend steps to take to mitigate the resistance of employees to the new cost-management system.

Refer to the information in and format of Exhibit 5–2. PMI is considering producing one product similar to the MegaBurger novelty toys but for another customer. It will ship the product to the customer immediately upon completion. The estimates for this new product follow. Assume that PMI can add capacity as needed at costs comparable to those in Exhibit 5–2. PMI requires a 20 percent return on sales for new business.

Problem 5.41
Activity-Based Costing and Target Costing
(LO 2)

Number of units per month		18,000
Sales price per unit		$18.00
Product life		3 years
1.	Unit-level costs	
	1.1 Acquire and use materials	18,000 units per month; $12.00 per unit
2.	Batch-level costs	
	2.1 Set up manually controlled machines	10 batches per month; $600 per batch
3.	Product-level costs	
	3.1 Design and manufacture molds	2 molds for the 1 product (to last 3 years); $4,000 per mold per month
	3.2 Use manually controlled injection-molding machines	$40,000 per month
4.	Customer-level costs	
	4.1 Consult with customers	20 consultations per month, $200 each
	4.2 Provide warehousing for customers	None
5.	Facility-level costs	
	5.1 Manage workers	$3,000 per month
	5.2 Use building space	$15,000 per month

Required

a. Calculate the dollar and percentage target-cost reduction for the three-year life of the new product.

b. As the manager responsible for making the decision, would you recommend that the company produce this product? Explain.

Refer to the information and format of Exhibit 5–2. PMI is considering producing one product similar to the MegaBurger novelty toys but for another customer. It will ship the product to the customer immediately upon completion. The estimates for this new product follow. Assume that PMI's cost of capital recently increased significantly, resulting in a return on sales requirement of 30 percent for all new business.

Problem 5.42
Activity-Based and Target Costing
(LO 2)

Number of units per month		24,000
Sales price per unit		$16.00
Product life		3 years
1.	Unit-level costs	
	1.1 Acquire and use materials	24,000 units per month; $11 per unit
2.	Batch-level costs	
	2.1 Set up manually controlled machines	10 batches per month; $600 per batch

3.   Product-level costs

| 3.1 | Design and manufacture molds | 2 molds for the 1 product (to last 3 years); $3,000 per mold per month |
| 3.2 | Use manually controlled injection-molding machines | $40,000 per month |

4.   Customer-level costs

| 4.1 | Consult with customer | 20 consultations per month; $300 per consultation |
| 4.2 | Provide warehousing for customer | $0.30 per cubic foot per month; 8,000 cubic feet |

5.   Facility-level costs

| 5.1 | Manage workers | 30% of production labor costs; production labor costs are $8,000 per month |
| 5.2 | Use building space | $24,000 per month |

Required

a.   Calculate the dollar and percentage target-cost reduction for the three-year life of the new product.

b.   As the manager responsible for making the decision, would you recommend that PMI produce this product? Explain.

Problem 5.43
Activity-Based and
Target Costing
(LO 2)

Refer to the information in and format of Exhibit 5–2. PMI is considering producing one product that is similar to the MegaBurger novelty toys but for another customer. This product will be larger and more complex than the MegaBurger products, and it will be sold in retail toy stores throughout the world. The product will be shipped to the customer immediately upon completion. The estimates for this new product follow. PMI's cost of capital recently increased significantly, resulting in a return on sales requirement of 25 percent for all new business.

Number of units per month	15,000
Sales price per unit	$19.00
Product life	3 years

1.   Unit-level costs

| 1.1. | Acquire and use materials | 15,000 units per month; $9 per unit |

2.   Batch-level costs

| 2.1. | Setup and quality control for manually controlled machines | 10 batches per month; $800 per batch |

3.   Product-level costs

| 3.1. | Design and manufacture molds | 2 molds for the 1 product (to last 3 years); $3,000 per mold per month |
| 3.2. | Use manually controlled injection-molding machines | $40,000 per month |

4.   Customer-level costs

| 4.1 | Consult with customer | 10 consultations per month; $150 per consultation |
| 4.2 | Provide warehousing for customer | None |

5.   Facility-level costs

| 5.1 | Manage workers | $2,000 per month |
| 5.2 | Use building space | $15,000 per month |

Required

a.   Calculate the dollar and percentage target-cost reduction for the three-year life of the new product.

b.   As the manager responsible for making the decision, would you recommend that the company produce this new product for its customer? Explain.

Problem 5.44
Value-Added Analysis
(LO 3, 4)

You have been hired as a consultant for Whoopee, a company that designs websites. Whoopee has asked for your advice in assessing customers' perceptions of the value of its products. You collect the following information about Whoopee's design of a website for a small co-op grocery store.

Number	Activity Description	Cost	Value (5 = highest value)
1	**Marketing and design**		
1.1	Prepare contract with the customer (the grocery store)	$ 5,000	4
1.2	Perform marketing research for customer	8,000	5

Number	Activity Description	Cost	Value (5 = highest value)
1.3	Whoopee purchases hardware, software, and infrastructure for the customer's site	6,000	4
1.4	Program and construct site	10,000	5
1.5	Whoopee performs payroll services, personnel administration, and other management functions for itself	16,000	2
1.6	Whoopee provides office space for its workers	6,000	1

Required

a. Explain the sources of the customer values. Do you agree with all of the customer values? Why or why not?

b. Create a table similar to Exhibit 5–4 for these activities, and prepare a memo to Whoopee's management summarizing your results.

Team focus. Consider two types of restaurants, (1) a favorite place for students to go in the evening and (2) a place to have a meeting.

Problem 5.45
Value-Added Analysis
(LO 3, 4)

Required

a. Identify the activities to prepare a meal, serve a customer, and clean up after the meal has been served.

b. For each activity you list in requirement (a), assign a value from 1 (= no value to you as a customer) to 5 (= essential to you as a customer). For example, does your team consider it important to be greeted when you arrive, be provided clean tablecloths, and be served a salad versus serving yourself at a salad bar?

Consider two types of health care organizations, (1) a campus health care center where you will be treated for influenza and (2) a hospital where you will have major surgery.

Problem 5.46
Value-Added Analysis
(LO 3, 4)

Required

Form small groups to respond to the following items.

a. Identify the activities to serve a patient and clean up after the patient has been discharged.

b. For each activity you list in requirement (a), assign a value from 1 (= no value to you as a customer) to 5 (= essential to you as a customer). For example, does your team consider it important to be provided with valet parking, to be provided with a nicely decorated waiting room, or to be admitted quickly after you arrive?

Now that local phone service in the United States is open to competition, some telephone service providers have begun purchasing individual phone services at a discount from the traditional phone companies and reselling them to customers who have been denied service because of poor credit. (College students represent a large group of customers of the resold services.)

Cindy Hodge is considering starting such a nontraditional phone service company in Houston, Texas. The current competitive price in the area is $35 per month, and she currently generates a 20 percent (pretax) return on sales in her other businesses. She expects a turnover of 10% per month (10% of customers will leave to be replaced by an equal number of new customers). She has estimated the following activities as necessary to operate the business for an estimated 1,000 customers.

Problem 5.47
Activity-Based
Management and
Process Improvements
(LO 1, 4)

Activity	Cost
Advertising and promotion	$ 400 per month
Bill collecting	960 per month
Service installation	45 per new customer
Credit analysis	25 per new customer
Phone service purchase from Southwestern Bell	17 per customer per month
Building occupancy	1,000 per month
Equipment utilization	300 per month
Invoicing and billing	3 per customer per month
Business planning and analysis	1,600 per month

Required

Form small groups to respond to the following items.

a. Is this proposed business expected to meet Hodge's financial goal of achieving a 20 percent return on sales? What, if any, cost reductions are necessary?

b. Prepare a short presentation outlining process improvements you would recommend to make the business more profitable.

c. *Build your own spreadsheet.* Devleop a spreadsheet to answer (a) and (b).

[Adapted from C. Palmer, "Dial Tones for Deadbeats."]

Problem 5.48
ABM and Process
Improvements
(LO 1, 4)

Recruiting a medical technologist for a hospital laboratory is a multistep process that includes the following activities.

Recruitment Activity	Personnel	Hourly Rate	Hours Spent	Recruitment Cost
Review need to retain position	HR director*	$40	4	$ 160
Revise job description as needed	HR analyst	15	8	120
Assess labor trends and compensation	HR director	40	8	320
Prepare and post job advertisement	HR analyst	15	8	120
Screen applications, verify credentials	HR analyst	15	12	180
Schedule personal interviews	HR analyst	15	6	90
Conduct personal interviews	Lab director	60	12	720
	HR director	40	6	240
Select finalist and make offer	Lab director	60	2	120
	HR director	40	1	40
Process new employee paperwork	HR analyst	15	4	60
Pay relocation expenses for new employee as needed				1,000
Provide orientation and training for new employee	HR analyst	15	4	60
	Lab director	60	2	120
	Technician	30	40	1,200
Total recruitment cost				$4,550

*HR refers to the Human Resources Department.

Required

a. If the hospital did not need to replace a medical technician, would it save these recruitment costs? Explain.

b. The laboratory customers are physicians who request tests and patients who are tested. Which of these recruitment activities would customers regard as value-added or non-value-added? What is the ratio of the cost of non-value-added to value-added activities?

c. Write a report recommending improvements to increase the human resources department's proportion of value-added activities.

[Adapted from R. Stiles and S. Mick. "What Is the Cost of Controlling Quality? Activity-Based Accounting Offers an Answer."]

Problem 5.49
ABM Income Statement
(LO 5)

eXcel

Gavin Corporation manufactures automobile parts. Information regarding its resources for the month of March follows:

	Resources Used	Resources Supplied
Parts management	$ 3,000	$ 3,500
Energy	5,000	5,000
Quality Inspections	4,500	5,000
Long-term labor	2,500	3,500
Short-term labor	2,000	2,400

	Resources Used	Resources Supplied
Setups	7,000	10,000
Materials	15,000	15,000
Depreciation	6,000	10,000
Marketing	7,000	7,500
Customer service	1,000	2,000
Administrative services	5,000	7,000

In addition, Gavin spent $2,500 on 10 engineering changes with a cost driver of $250 per change and $3,000 on four outside contracts with a cost-driver rate of $750 per contract. There was no unused capacity for these two activities. Sales for March were $100,000.

Required

a. Prepare an activity-based income statement (similar to Exhibit 5–6).

b. Write a short report explaining why the ABM income statement provides better information to managers than a traditional income statement. Use Gavin Corporation information in your discussion.

Rio Vista Manufacturing, Inc., manufactures speedboats and canoes. Information regarding its resources for the month of August follows:

Problem 5.50
Activity-Based Management Income Statement
(LO 5)

	Resources Used	Resources Supplied
Marketing	$28,000	$30,000
Depreciation	24,000	40,000
Outside contracts	12,000	12,000
Materials	60,000	60,000
Setups	14,000	20,000
Energy	20,000	21,000
Parts management	15,000	16,000
Engineering changes	10,000	12,000
Short-term labor	7,000	7,000
Long-term labor	10,000	14,000
Administrative services	20,000	26,000

In addition, Rio Vista spent $22,000 on 800 quality inspections with a cost-driver rate of $25 per inspection, and it spent $8,000 on 200 customer service calls with a cost-driver rate of $30 per service call. Sales for August were $350,000.

Required

a. Prepare an activity-based income statement (similar to Exhibit 5–6).

b. Write a short report explaining why the ABM income statement provides better information to managers than a traditional income statement. Use information for Rio Vista in your discussion.

Cases

An alternative to using ABM to identify opportunities for process improvement is to use benchmarking information to identify where an organization falls short of competitors and best practices. At 2 percent of sales, Cummins Engine's overall accounting costs were twice as high as companies with world-class accounting functions, and the company was determined to improve. More detailed benchmarking information revealed that accounts payable costs and payroll costs were four and three times higher, respectively, than best practices. These areas seemed to offer the opportunity for great improvement. Cummins created a cross-functional team to analyze these transaction processes and make recommendations for improvement that would increase the quality of transaction processing and achieve best-practice costs (i.e., cost reductions of 75 percent).

Case 5.51
Reengineering the Accounting Function
(LO 4, 6)

Cummins Engine's top management was fully committed to the project. It provided resources to the project team that enabled it to educate Cummins' finance and operating personnel around the world about the project's methods and objectives. Management also committed to no forced layoffs of personnel whose jobs would be affected by resulting process changes.

In the early part of the project (the "baseline" phase), the team recognized that accounts payable, cash disbursement, and procurement processes should be integrated and located at a single site rather than at 50 sites within the United States alone, and that new software and hardware would be required. The team began with a pilot study, however, so that it could understand the complexities of the project before launching a worldwide implementation. The pilot study allowed the team to identify tangible objectives for the new system that included:

- Electronic data interchange (EDI).
- Linkage between procurement, accounts payable, and cash disbursement.
- Use of client-server technology.
- Outsourcing of non-value-added activities such as check printing.
- Improvement of process quality measures involving statistical quality-control techniques.
- Software compatible with Cummins' data architecture at a competitive price and with a user-friendly graphical interface.

Project implementation was phased in over a three-year period, with inflexible target dates for each phase and continuous communication with affected finance and operating personnel. The workforce in accounts payable was reduced by 80 percent, costs reached best-practice levels, and errors were reduced dramatically. (The workforce reduction occurred through attrition, assigning employees to other areas, and early retirement plans.)

Required

Form small groups to prepare a report that answers the following questions:

a. What are the differences between the activity-based management approach and the benchmarking approach used by Cummins Engine to identify opportunities for process improvement? What are the relative advantages and disadvantages of the benchmarking approach to identifying opportunities?

b. What interests, skills, and knowledge would be required for members of a project team such as the one at Cummins to analyze accounts payable?

c. What are specific steps that Cummins Engine took to ensure the success of the accounts payable project?

d. Does the Cummins project appear to be perfect, or can you recommend improvement(s) and/or identify area(s) of concern if you were to copy this approach at another organization?

[Adapted from T. Compton, L. Hoshower, and W. Draeger. "Reengineering Transaction Processing Systems at Cummins Engine."]

Case 5.52
Effects of Changing Cost Drivers
(LO 1)

TransGlobe Airways (TGA) is an embattled US airline fighting to gain market share from its much larger, traditional competitors, such as United Airlines, Delta, and American Airlines, as well as successful discount airlines such as Southwest Airlines. TGA's current share of the US market is approximately 5 percent. The executive vice president of marketing, Jack Moore, believes that TGA must improve its customer satisfaction before it can improve its competitiveness. Surveys of TGA's customers indicate that they are most dissatisfied with these areas:

- In-flight meal quality.
- Attitudes of ticket counter and in-flight personnel.
- Storage space for carry-on luggage.
- Legroom in the economy sections of TGA's airplanes.
- Charges for movies and drinks on long flights.
- First-class seating availability for frequent fliers who want to upgrade from economy.

In an executive committee meeting, Moore insists that TGA must begin immediately to retrain personnel to interact well with customers, offer better meals and free movies, and begin remodeling planes to increase first-class seating, legroom in economy, and storage space for carry-on luggage. He is confident that these measures will increase market share dramatically and lead to future profitability.

You are a cost management analyst with TGA whom the chief financial officer invited to attend this executive committee meeting and then asked to prepare estimates of the impacts of making changes to TGA's structural cost drivers. You recall reading a recent *Wall Street Journal* article which indicated that the most important reasons business travelers choose one airline over another are ticket prices and flight schedules.

Required

a. Prepare a brief, narrative analysis of the possible impacts of these structural changes on customer satisfaction, market share, and profitability.

b. Make alternative recommendations for improving TGA's profitability.

"ASP Business Plan Estimates 60 FTE to be Eliminated in Consolidations" trumpeted the headline in the *Silver & Gold Record,* the university's faculty and staff newsletter. Administrators scrambled to justify the $35 million project and reassure worried staff who faced the loss of 60 full-time equivalent (FTE) jobs. Faculty scoffed at yet another administrative boondoggle that would siphon scarce funds from the university's academic mission. Staff council leaders vowed to protect their colleagues who might be affected by the Administrative Streamlining Project (ASP). It has pitted faculty, staff, and administrators against each other as the university struggles to improve its administrative operations. The irony is that nearly everyone agrees that the university's administrative processes are outmoded and inefficient and that the accounting system is nearly useless as a management tool, but there is little agreement about how to proceed. Some question the basic premise of the change, however, that the university should become more like a business. A distinguished professor of comparative literature argued against the university's mimicking the business world's addiction to management fads:

Case 5.53
Activity-Based
Management in a
University
(LO 6)

> Let us not ask the university to transform itself overnight in response to the latest fads and fashions of the business world. Let us not encourage an easy experimental attitude toward our structure, aims, and ends. Let our reply to our critics be this: Relax the drive to create a world of conformity, but instead, sit back and enjoy the differences.

ASP is charged "with improving the University's human resources and financial management business practices by simplifying work, increasing information access, minimizing future administrative costs, and implementing enabling technologies." ASP is expected to be "the first step in a continuous improvement program by providing tools and education that will enable the University to continually change how it does business."

ASP proposes to consolidate the purchasing, accounts payable, payroll, and human resources functions for all of the University's four campuses into two central areas: (1) benefits/payroll and (2) procurement. The expected costs of ASP over its three-year implementation follow:

University personnel to manage and implement ASP	$11.74 million
PricewaterhouseCoopers, consultants	9.02 million
PeopleSoft software (human resources and finance)	4.32 million
Hardware and networks	3.79 million
Training costs for ASP staff, system staff, and users	2.03 million
Operating expenses	1.75 million
Contingencies	2.28 million
Total implementation cost	$34.93 million

The ASP plan predicts the following annual savings after implementation:

Elimination of redundant positions (60 FTE)	$2.63 million
Elimination of "shadow" personnel and budgeting systems	3.34 million
Reduction of data-entry requirements	1.13 million
Elimination of system reconciliation	0.26 million
Total annual savings	$7.36 million

Members of the University's staff council stood up for their colleagues who face being displaced from their current jobs as a result of ASP. The staff council reminded University officials that staff within the state personnel system have retention rights and can "bump" others from similar positions in the University based on seniority. University officials, including the president, have stressed that layoffs will be a last resort to deal with job reductions and that positions will be eliminated through attrition or reassignment to new jobs. The staff council noted that the ASP budget does not contain any money for retraining staff whom ASP would displace. The ASP director admitted as much but noted that the University had been informed that it needs to set aside money for retraining.

ASP has not identified which jobs to eliminate. Its director recognized the need to "adopt an appropriate strategy for consolidating the campus functions. We could bring up the system, get the offices running, and then consolidate them, or we could consolidate and then bring up the system." One staff council member heatedly announced the doubt that ASP could make the right decisions on which jobs to eliminate: "The ASP committee is all administrators, but ASP affects staff on every side. You need to get opinions from the people actually doing the work. Administrators often don't know what staff do."

Required

Form small groups to prepare a presentation that responds to the following items:

a.   Does the ASP objective seem consistent with the University's goals?

b.   Why might ASP's objective (not considering its methods) be controversial within the University?

c.   What ethical and management responsibilities does the administration have for the University's constituents?

d.   Discuss your confidence in the reliability of the cost and savings estimates. How critical are these estimates to the project's implementation and success in meeting its objective?

e.   Critique the apparent method being used to implement ASP. Is this implementation approach likely to be successful? Explain.

f.   Make recommendations to the University president and the ASP director for improving the implementation process.

[Adapted from *Silver & Gold Record*, March 12, 1998.]

Case 5.54
Banking Processes
(LO 4)

Ogden Bank has been in the consumer-lending business for more than 100 years. Competitors recently have taken a considerable portion of its market share. In addition, its remaining customers have complained that the bank's loan-approval process is too slow and that finding out the status of a loan application is difficult. The traditional procedure for consumer loan approval is summarized here:

- A loan applicant picks up a standard loan application at the bank, completes it, and mails it to the bank. A mail clerk delivers applications along with regular mail.

- The loan application is delivered to a loan-processing clerk, who logs it in, attaches a routing/status form to the front page, and files it in a folder of outstanding loan applications. At the end of the day or when the folder is full, the clerk delivers the contents to a credit analyst.

- The credit analyst enters data from the application into a computer program, records the results on the status form, and sends the application through interoffice mail to a consumer-lending specialist.

- The consumer-lending specialist approves or rejects the loan application and customizes the loan if necessary according to the particular applicant's needs. From here, all applications go to a pricing specialist via interoffice mail.

- The pricing specialist determines the appropriate interest rate to charge approved applicants by using a computer program written for this purpose. The rate is recorded on the status form of approved applications, which are forwarded to another clerical group.

- These clerks prepare letters informing applicants of the bank's decisions along with a note stating the loan terms of approved applications.

- After the legal department reviews all of this material, clerks mail the bank's decision to the applicants along with a promissory note to be signed and returned to those who are approved.

This process takes four weeks on average, during which time applicants could find alternative financing but could almost never determine the status of their application with Ogden Bank. The bank has engaged you to analyze its loan approval process and make recommendations for improvement.

Required

a. Prepare a brief memo explaining how Ogden Bank could benefit from using ABM and what steps and resources would be necessary to successfully implement it.

b. Suggest and explain at least three ways that Ogden Bank could reduce the cycle time of its loan-application process.

c. Suggest and explain at least three ways that Ogden Bank could improve its communication, internally and externally, about its processes and possible process changes.

[CMA adapted]

Chapter 6

Managing Customer Profitability

After completing this chapter, you should be able to:

1. Explain the value of analyzing customer profitability according to major customer type.

2. Organize and prepare customer profitability analyses and reports using activity-based analysis.

3. Identify alternative actions and recommend improvements for overall and customer profitability based on analyzing customer-related activities.

Cost-*Management* Challenges

(Solutions are on page 234.)

1. **How** can you determine in advance whether investments of time, effort, and information systems to prepare customer profitability information are worthwhile?

2. **How** can customer profitability analysis be more relevant for service and governmental organizations than for others?

3. **How** do you evaluate the trade-offs among the desires for relevant, accurate, and timely information?

4. **How** can cost-management analysts help an organization plan and execute changes in operations to deliver more customer value at lower cost?

5. **How** can you determine whether operational changes in customer service have been beneficial or harmful?

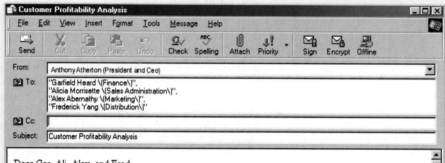

From: Anthony Atherton (President and Ceo)

To: "Garfield Heard \(Finance\)",
"Alicia Morrisette \(Sales Administration\)",
"Alex Abernathy \(Marketing\)",
"Frederick Yang \(Distribution\)"

Cc:

Subject: Customer Profitability Analysis

Dear Gar, Ali, Alex, and Fred,

As you know, the effects of our recent acquisition by London Pharmaceuticals continue to ripple through HealthWave. The best is yet to come, in my opinion. The purpose of this email is to formalise my request that you form a cost-management team to analyse our customer profitability.

I cannot stress the urgency of this request enough. I have reason to believe that our jobs and the future of HealthWave as an organization depend on this analysis.

We need to submit next year's budget to the corporate office in London in six months. That budget needs to clearly and convincingly explain how we will attain corporate's tough return-on-sales goals for next year and the following five years. I am convinced that our traditional product orientation obscures opportunities to improve our profitability. I also am convinced that we must focus on our customers to ensure both their satisfaction, which we always have done, and our profitability, which we need to improve. We need to understand who our customers are, what they want, and what they are willing to pay for. Furthermore, we need to understand which of our resources we apply to customers and whether all of our customers are profitable to us.

Thus, your first step is to analyse our customers and measure their profitability. I am calling the first meeting at 9:00 a.m. on Monday morning. Please clear your calendars for most of the day. I will attend the first meeting to underscore the importance of this project and to help set deliverables, but you will carry on as a team thereafter.

Thank you for your willingness to undertake this important task.

Tony

HealthWave, Ltd.

HealthWave, Ltd., is a wholesale-drug company headquartered in Auckland, New Zealand, with manufacturing, marketing, and sales operations throughout Australia and New Zealand (ANZ). A large UK firm, London Pharmaceuticals, recently purchased HealthWave from its stockholders with cash and an exchange of stock. HealthWave was an attractive acquisition because of its strong brand image, customer loyalty, ANZwide customer base, and skilled marketing and sales personnel.[1]

The London parent, however, has notified Anthony Atherton, HealthWave's CEO, that it expects a rapid increase in profitability. Its short-run objective for HealthWave is to increase the company's *return on sales* (ROS), which is operating income divided by sales, from its current 7.3 percent to 10 percent within a year. Furthermore, London expects steady improvement to at least 15 percent ROS within five years. London Pharmaceuticals regards this as a difficult but attainable objective, but at this point, HealthWave is certain only that it will be difficult.[2]

HealthWave's Products

HealthWave's three major product lines are nonprescription drugs, supplements, and herbal remedies. Nonprescription drugs include nonprescription headache, cold, and flu remedies such as aspirin, antihistamines, and cough syrup. Supplements include vitamin and mineral supplements, such as multivitamins, vitamin C, and zinc capsules. Herbal remedies include herbal products such as echinacea, spirulina, and St. John's wort. Profitability depends on maintaining the company's brand name, successful advertising, promotions, and customer service.

CEO Atherton formed a small, cross-functional cost-management team of talented and motivated people from the finance, sales, marketing, and distribution departments who tend to think "outside the box." He believed that their different perspectives and personalities were the right balance of individual talent and team orientation to find innovative and successful solutions to the company's profitability problem. Many jobs, including his perhaps, were at stake.

HealthWave's Customers

LO 1 Explain the value of analyzing customer profitability, according to major customer type.

HealthWave has three primary customer types: pharmacies, groceries, and herbal therapists. It serves pharmacies and groceries through sales representatives and herbal therapists through catalogue and mail-order sales. HealthWave currently has no e-commerce or Internet sales activities but recognizes the need to consider implementing them. HealthWave believes that competition based on customer service is changing, but its traditional focus on product profitability obscures changes in customer preferences.

Importance of Customer Profitability

Customer-profitability analysis identifies the costs and benefits of serving specific customers or customer types to improve an organization's overall profitability. It is a

---

[1] Also important was the unregulated nature of the ANZ market for over-the-counter medicines and herbal remedies in contrast to the European Union (EU) market where London Pharmaceuticals conducts most of its business. Most countries in the EU market classify over-the-counter and nonfood herbal products as medicines and strictly regulate their distribution and pricing. Similar to the situation in the United States, the ANZ area permits the sale of these nonprescription products, which include most of HealthWave's products. As a result, HealthWave can introduce new products quickly at relatively low cost unlike prescription drug companies, which must submit their new products to lengthy and often costly trials and reviews. On the other hand, HealthWave's profit margins are lower than those of prescription drug companies because patents or regulations do not protect its products.

[2] The analysis in this chapter relies, in part, on information in the Naturix-Bowen Case Study, The Boston Consulting Group. (Full citations to references are in the Bibliography.)

relatively new but increasingly popular cost-management tool, which has two primary objectives:

■ Measure customer profitability.
■ Identify effective and ineffective customer-related activities.

Measurement of Customer Profitability

The first objective of customer profitability analysis is to measure the profitability of existing customers or customer types. Most organizations measure profitability according to organizational boundaries (e.g., regions) or product line. These profit measures facilitate management of production-oriented operations. Operating profits, however, usually do not focus on sales or customer-service activities, which can constitute the majority of general and administrative operating costs.

Many organizations seek to increase market share and customer satisfaction without understanding the costs of doing so. Some organizations incur significant costs to satisfy customers but often do not know whether these efforts result in revenues that exceed their costs. Customer-profitability analysis seeks to perform cost-benefit analyses to identify profitable and unprofitable customers. This information helps the organization to ensure that it retains its profitable customers. It can either drop unprofitable customers or find ways to serve them profitably.

Some studies have found that only 20 percent of a company's customers contribute to profits; the remaining 80 percent generate losses. See Exhibit 6–1 for an example of customer profitability analysis that reflects the historical experience of many organizations that are just beginning to use this technique. The chart shows that a small percentage of customers generated significant profits and the majority generated small profits or significant losses. In this example, the top seven customers (20 percent of 34 total customers) contribute 155 percent of the total profit and more than half of the customers generate losses! The top 7 customers generate more than 100 percent of the profits because serving each at its levels of sales is much cheaper than serving the other 27 customers. This implies that this company is better off serving less than half of its customers.

Profit from top 7 customers	$ 381,147
Total company profit	245,941
Profit from top 7 customers	155.0%

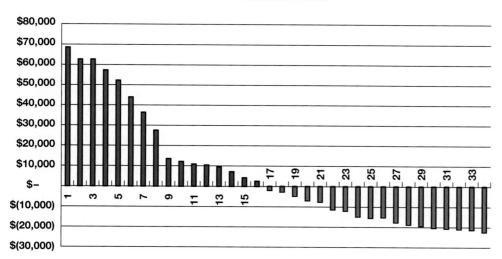

Customer Profit

Customers 1 to 34

Exhibit 6–1

Pareto Chart of Customer Profitability

Qualitative considerations.   The quantitative factors of customer profitability are important, but companies should not fail to consider qualitative reasons for retaining marginal or even unprofitable customers, including these:

- Status of being a supplier to a leading company, which can lead to referrals to similar ones.
- Potential for an unprofitable customer to become profitable by serving it more efficiently.
- Use of an unprofitable customer for entry into a new and profitable market by learning how to serve this market.
- Opportunity to receive transfers of knowledge from innovative but unprofitable companies about their cutting-edge needs or product applications.
- Ability to economize on customer-service activities for customers that partner with the organization or share processes with it.

Similarly, a company might *decline* to serve some profitable customers whose business practices or goals are inconsistent with its own. For example, many organizations decline to serve customers with poor environmental or human rights records. Conversely, companies might choose to serve unprofitable customers who promote goals they wish to support.

Companies concerned about social and environmental practices would want Ben & Jerry's as a customer because of its record in promoting those issues.

Identification of Effective and Ineffective Customer-Related Activities

The second objective of performing customer profitability analysis is to identify effective and ineffective customer-related activities. This analysis provides the information that organizations can use to decide which activities to enhance or eliminate that will increase total profitability, decrease or eliminate customer dissatisfaction, and clarify its view of what customers value and will pay for. Enhancing customer activities include simplifying cumbersome order processes, consolidating many small orders into fewer large ones, and teaching customers to minimize costs by eliminating numerous changes to their orders.

Many successful companies, such as Dell, Nike, Hewlett-Packard, Microsoft, General Electric, and FedEx, regularly use customer profitability analysis to manage customer relations activities. Banks, for example, compute the profitability of each account to identify those that are exceptionally profitable or unprofitable. It uses this information to support decisions to add or drop customers. This effort clearly requires intense use of information technology (large companies can spend millions of dollars for customer profitability analysis), and an understanding of the activities that drive customer profitability.

Many organizations also use activity-based costing approaches to measure the effectiveness of resources in serving customers,[3] as discussed in Chapters 4 and 5. Just as ABC can reveal product profitability, customer-profitability analysis can identify profitable or unprofitable customers. This information allows organizations to take appropriate actions to increase their profitability.

---

[3] For example, see C. Parry, "Hotels Plan Sector-Wide ABC Model."

Organizations that seek to implement customer profitability analysis must understand its customer-related cost and revenue drivers (see Chapters 4 and 11). Successful organizations recognize that sales-incentive systems, which traditionally have been based on revenue or product contribution margin, must encourage sales activities directed to profitable customers. (Chapter 20 covers incentive systems.)

HealthWave's Traditional Profitability Analysis by Product Line

HealthWave's financial accounting system prepares financial reports by major product line in contribution margin format, which reflects the company's historical product focus.[4] According to Exhibit 6–2, nonprescription products have the highest contribution margin ratio (48 percent), and herbal remedies have the lowest (31 percent). Furthermore, for the recently completed year, the ROS for nonprescription drugs (16.7 percent) exceeds the 10 percent target, but that for supplements and herbal remedy products does not [6.6 and (3.9) percent, respectively]. This ROS comparison could be misleading because it allocates general sales, and administrative costs on the basis of relative sales, a common practice. Only HealthWave's R&D costs are clearly traced to product lines, which also is common because R&D projects often are organized by product line. This traditional profit view is computationally correct but not particularly helpful for identifying opportunities for improving customer-related activities.

Let's start by measuring the magnitude of HealthWave's overall profitability problem. The new parent company assigned the profit objective of a 10 percent ROS for the first year after the acquisition. For now, assume that the next year's product-sales prices, costs, volume, and mix will remain the same. Exhibit 6–3 uses a target-profit approach,[5] applying information from the Total column of Exhibit 6–2. At the same level of sales (NZ$91,000,000), HealthWave must achieve a cost reduction of NZ$2,451,496 to meet this 10 percent goal (Exhibit 6–3). If sales do not increase

---

[4] Contribution margin (sales revenue less variable costs) is covered in Chapter 2.

[5] Target profit and cost analyses are described in more detail in Chapter 5. Briefly, the method computes a target profit based on required return on sales, which yields a target cost (Revenues − Target profit = Target cost). Comparing target cost to current cost results in a cost reduction target.

Exhibit 6–2   HealthWave's Product-Line Profitability (NZ$)

	Total	Nonprescription	Supplements	Herbal Remedies
Revenue	$91,000,000	$26,900,000	$44,260,000	$19,840,000
Variable cost of goods sold (CGS)	54,676,200	13,988,000	26,998,600	13,689,600
Contribution margin	$36,323,800	$12,912,000	$17,261,400	$ 6,150,400
Contribution margin ratio (Contribution margin ÷ Revenue)	39.9%	48%	39%	31%
Operating costs:				
Research and development (R&D)	1,200,000	—	480,000	720,000
General, Sales and Administrative (GS&A)*	28,475,296	8,417,423	13,849,633	6,208,240
Total operating costs	$29,675,296	$ 8,417,423	$14,329,633	$ 6,928,240
Operating income	$ 6,648,504	$ 4,494,577	$ 2,931,767	$ (777,840)
Return on sales	7.3%	16.7%	6.6%	(3.9%)

*Allocated on relative sales

Exhibit 6–3

HealthWave's Cost
Reduction Target (NZ$)

Target return on sales	10%
Current sales revenue (Exhibit 6–2)	$91,000,000
Target profit (0.10 × $91,000,000)	9,100,000
Target cost...	$81,900,000
Current costs (CGS + R&D + GS&A from Exhibit 6–2)........................	84,351,496
Target cost reduction..	$ 2,451,496

with the same level of resource use (one of several possible solutions to the problem), profit improvement must come from reducing costs, many of which are related to customer service.

The next objective of customer-profitability analysis is to identify customer-related actions that can improve the organization's overall profitability. To do so, the cost-management team gathered more information about HealthWave's customers and the services provided to them.

Research Insight 6.1

Customer Satisfaction and Profitability

An economic perspective of customer service predicts that if service is valued but freely offered, customers will demand more of it than they are willing to pay for. Many commercial firms attest that they are "customer focused" and seek to delight, not merely satisfy, customers. If their actions match their claims, can they do so profitably? In fact, maximizing customer satisfaction can be a recipe for unprofitable operations. On the other hand, some organizations identify more efficient ways to provide services, thus keeping customer satisfaction high and service costs low.

Interest in the drivers of customer profitability, particularly whether customer satisfaction leads to profitability, has stimulated considerable academic research that seeks objective evidence of a link between customer satisfaction and profitability. The evidence suggests that profits show a positive relation with, but decreasing marginal returns from, increases in customer satisfaction. As one study put it, "The customer is always right, but is it always worth it?" *Sources: For a partial list of relevant studies see E. W. Anderson, C. Fornell, and D. R. Lehmann, "Customer Satisfaction, Market Share and Profitability. Findings from Sweden"; R. D. Banker, G. Potter, and D. Srinivasan, "An Empirical Investigation of an Incentive Plan That Includes Nonfinancial Performance Measures"; C. D. Ittner and D. F. Larcker, "Are Non-Financial Measures Leading Indicators of Financial Performance? An Analysis of Customer Satisfaction"; and R. T. Rust and A. J. Zahorik, "Customer Satisfaction, Customer Retention, and Market Share." (Full citations to references are in the Bibliography.)*

Cost Management in Practice 6.1

Determinants of Service Quality

An increasing number of companies have made a deliberate decision to give some customers skimpy service because they believe that is all the business of these customers is worth. Information technology, particularly Internet-based commerce, permits the capture of detailed customer-related information to use for performing customer analyses and tailoring activities to customers. Companies use this information to segment their customers into an "A-list," which frequently buys premium products and services and are treated like royalty, and a "B-list" which tends to shop based on price and convenience.

These discriminating companies argue that premium customers' spending justifies the royal treatment. For example, the calls from Charles Schwab's top-rated clients, which have large asset accounts and trade frequently, are answered within a few seconds, but those from less valued customers might not be answered for 10 minutes or more. Similarly, after estimating that answering phone calls from investors costs $13 per call, Fidelity Investments now directs high-cost callers to its Web site or automated phone system for self-service.

Some critics argue that these customer-segmenting practices resemble invisible "redlining," a controversial form of customer discrimination that some laws prohibit. Some companies clearly are using customer profitability analysis to discriminate among customers, but others, such as Capital One Financial Corp and Walker Digital, are letting customers pay for their desired level of service by choosing among alternative products priced according to service levels. This approach increases customers' choices, which is the opposite of discrimination. *Source: D. Brady, "Why Service Stinks."*

Customer Sales Analysis

At its first meeting, the HealthWave cost-management team agreed to provide the CEO and executive staff for each customer an analysis of profitability including sales patterns and the customer-related activities. The team recognized the importance of structuring these analyses so that the company could develop more precise information in the future without reinventing the entire exercise. The team decided that it would:

LO 2 Organize and prepare customer profitability analyses and reports using activity-based analysis.

- Use existing information systems whenever feasible to generate customer-related revenues and costs.
- Obtain information from the most recent year to use as a baseline for predictions about future changes.
- Sample voluminous information (e.g., annual deliveries or orders) carefully.
- Use activity-based techniques (see Chapters 4 and 5) to analyze activities not reported by existing information systems.
- Focus on areas of customer-related activities most likely to yield large cost savings.

An obvious step in HealthWave's customer profitability analysis is to identify its customers and the activities the company performs to serve them. Like most organizations, HealthWave has up-to-date customer lists and can use its accounting, sales, and distribution records to calculate customer-level sales, which are an important part of the profit equation. These same records enable organizations, including HealthWave, to identify the way they use resources to serve customers. However, these companies must conduct additional investigations and revise their information systems to consistently provide *cost* information.

HealthWave Customer Profile

A **customer profile** categorizes individual or types of customers according to the major activities or factors that drive revenues and costs. For example, a bank might profile its customers by maintained account balances, number of transactions, types of services used, and risk, all of which can affect the bank's revenues and cost to serve customers. Presently, HealthWave does not sell to the general public but to three major customer types: pharmacies, groceries, and herbal therapists. These categories reflect HealthWave's major revenue and cost drivers. Its pharmacy, grocery, and herbal therapy customers are located throughout Australia and New Zealand. Grocery customers include approximately 1,500 independent grocers and 15,000 grocers served by four major grocery chain accounts. See Exhibit 6–4 for current customer-profile information.

Analysis of Customer Sales Patterns

The team sorted product-line revenues (reproduced in the top section of Exhibit 6–5 from Exhibit 6–2) by customer type: pharmacy, grocery, and herbal therapist. Next, the team inserted the contribution margin ratio in row 3 (also from Exhibit 6–2). Row 4 shows the cost of goods sold ratio, which is simply 100% minus the contribution margin ratio.

Analysis of a carefully selected, *representative sample* of last year's sales and distribution (shipping) data traced product sales to each customer type, as shown in rows 6 through 8 of Exhibit 6–5. For example, last year 78 percent of all *nonprescription drugs* were sold to pharmacies, 22 percent to grocery stores, and none to herbal therapists.

	Number of Separate Customer Accounts
Pharmacy customers	11,000
Independent grocery customers	1,500
Major grocery chain customers	4
Herbal therapists	800

Exhibit 6–4

HealthWave Customers by Type

HealthWave INC.

Exhibit 6-5   HealthWave Sales by Product Line and Customer (NZ$)

	A	B	C	D	E
1	**Product sales (Exhibit 6-2)**	**Total**	**Non-Prescription**	**Supplements**	**Herbal Remedies**
2	Product-line revenue	$ 91,000,000	$ 26,900,000	$ 44,260,000	$ 19,840,000
3	Contribution margin ratio		48.0%	39.0%	31.0%
4	Cost of goods sold ratio		52.0%	61.0%	69.0%
5	**Traced product sales to:**	**Total**	**Pharmacy**	**Grocery**	**Herbal therapists**
6	Sales of: Non-prescription drugs	100.0%	78.0%	22.0%	0.0%
7	Supplements	100.0%	8.0%	83.0%	9.0%
8	Herbal Remedies	100.0%	5.0%	34.0%	61.0%
9	**Traced customer revenues (C9=C2*C6+D2*C7+E2*C8)**	$ 91,000,000	$ 25,514,800	$ 49,399,400	$ 16,085,800
10	**Cost of goods sold (C10=C2*C6*C4+D2*C7*D4+E2*C8*E4)**	$ 54,676,200	$ 13,755,008	$ 30,140,662	$ 10,780,530
11	Contribution margin (C11=C9-C10)	$ 36,323,800	$ 11,759,792	$ 19,258,738	$ 5,305,270
12	Contribution margin ratio (C12=C11/C9)	39.9%	46.1%	39.0%	33.0%
13					

Cell C9 = =C2*C6+D2*C7+E2*C8

Sheet tabs: Exhibit 6-5 / Exhibit 6-6 / Basic analysis / Common size / Pareto charts

Applying estimated percentages of product-line sales provides a way to identify last year's customer-level revenues (row 9, Exhibit 6–5). See the spreadsheet formula bar for the calculations. Calculations for pharmacy customers follow:

Pharmacy revenue = ([78.0%] × Nonprescription revenue) + ([8.0%] × Supplements revenue) + ([5.0%] × Herbal remedy revenue)

Pharmacy revenue = (.78 × $26,900,000) + (.08 × $44,260,000)
+ (.05 × $19,840,000) = $25,514,800

Using last year's average contribution margin ratios by product line permitted a similar calculation for cost of goods sold (CGS) for each customer type (row 10, Exhibit 6–5). CGS calculations for pharmacy customers follow:

Pharmacy CGS = ([78.0%] × Nonprescription revenue) × [52.0%] CGS ratio + ([8.0%] × Supplements revenue) × [61.0%] CGS ratio + ([5.0%] × Herbal remedy revenue) × [69.0%] CGS ratio

Pharmacy CGS = (.78 × $26,900,000) × .52 + (.08 × $44,260,000) × .61
+ (.05 × $19,840,000) × .69 = $13,755,008

Because pharmacies purchase most of the nonprescription drugs (the most profitable product line in Exhibit 6–2), they have the highest contribution margin ratio (46.1 percent, C12 of Exhibit 6–5). Herbal therapists purchase the most herbal remedy products and have the lowest contribution margin ratio of all customers (33 percent, E12 of Exhibit 6–5). These facts might suggest that herbal therapists are less desirable customers; however, this conclusion is premature because Exhibit 6–5 traced only *manufacturing* costs to customers. To complete the analysis, we must analyze how HealthWave incurs costs to serve customers.

Sales and Administrative Cost Analysis

We now discuss the way that the cost-management analysis team analyzed other customer-related costs, including these:

- Selling costs
- Marketing costs
- Distribution costs
- General and administrative costs

Customer Selling Costs

Selling costs include the costs of all personnel, databases, equipment, and facilities devoted to supporting sales activities. Like many sales-oriented organizations, HealthWave's sales personnel were rewarded in part for the amount of sales revenue they generated. This reward system created an incentive to increase sales, which normally is good, but sales-only rewards do not recognize the costs to make these sales. Thus, sales personnel work to increase sales, but the increased revenues could be less than the costs to do so. HealthWave's customer profitability team began by sorting through the direct benefits and costs of selling activities. The team prepared Exhibit 6–6 based on their analyses.

Benefits and costs of direct sales. HealthWave organized its selling activities to independent groceries and pharmacies into six sales regions centered in the cities of Auckland, Adelaide, Brisbane, Melbourne, Perth, and Sydney. A separate group of its salespeople works in each sales area to call on and take orders from the pharmacies and independent grocers. A high-level account executive rather than salespeople serves each of the four major grocery chains. The team easily traced the use of these dedicated resources (row 7 in Exhibit 6–6) to pharmacy and grocery customers by multiplying the number of sales representatives and account managers (if any) by their average annual salaries. For example, the calculation of sales personnel cost traced to grocery customers follows:

$$\text{Grocery sales personnel cost} = (25 \text{ sales reps} \times \$42,000) + (4 \text{ major acct executives} \times \$200,000) = \underline{\text{NZ}\$1,850,000}$$

Interviews with independent pharmacy and grocery customers indicated that they greatly valued the sales personnel's knowledge of HealthWave's products and its customers' needs. They also valued the personal attention accorded by the sales force. Rows 9 and 10 indicate the percent of orders made by sales force and by telephone.

Benefits and costs of telephone-based ordering. Customers viewed HealthWave's telephone-based ordering system to be slow and difficult to access. They noted that competitive suppliers were introducing more convenient Internet-based or direct ordering systems that enable customers to easily place orders without the "clunkiness" of dealing with telephone operators. The team noted this as an issue for future consideration.

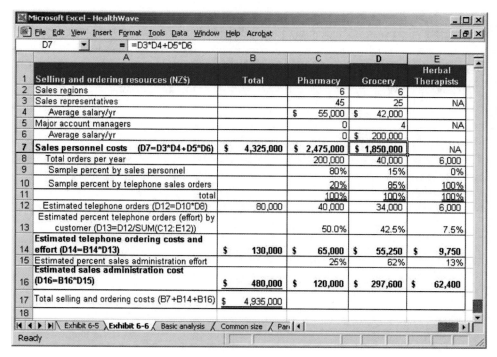

Exhibit 6–6

HealthWave's Analysis of Annual Selling Resources and Activities (NZ$)

	A	B	C	D	E
1	Selling and ordering resources (NZ$)	Total	Pharmacy	Grocery	Herbal Therapists
2	Sales regions		6	6	
3	Sales representatives		45	25	NA
4	Average salary/yr		$ 55,000	$ 42,000	
5	Major account managers		0	4	NA
6	Average salary/yr		0	$ 200,000	
7	Sales personnel costs (D7=D3*D4+D5*D6)	$ 4,325,000	$ 2,475,000	$ 1,850,000	NA
8	Total orders per year		200,000	40,000	6,000
9	Sample percent by sales personnel		80%	15%	0%
10	Sample percent by telephone sales orders		20%	85%	100%
11	total		100%	100%	100%
12	Estimated telephone orders (D12=D10*D8)	80,000	40,000	34,000	6,000
13	Estimated percent telephone orders (effort) by customer (D13=D12/SUM(C12:E12))		50.0%	42.5%	7.5%
14	Estimated telephone ordering costs and effort (D14=B14*D13)	$ 130,000	$ 65,000	$ 55,250	$ 9,750
15	Estimated percent sales administration effort		25%	62%	13%
16	Estimated sales administration cost (D16=B16*D15)	$ 480,000	$ 120,000	$ 297,600	$ 62,400
17	Total selling and ordering costs (B7+B14+B16)	$ 4,935,000			
18					

The accounting system could easily report telephone sales costs (cell B14 in Exhibit 6–6), but tracing these resources to each customer type was more difficult because the telephone sales order staff takes *all* herbal therapy customer orders as well as those placed by some pharmacy and grocery customers. The team decided to measure the telephone ordering effort by using the percentage of orders processed for each customer type. The large number of orders required the team to select a *random sample* of orders for each customer type to determine this information (rows 9 and 10 of Exhibit 6–6). The team multiplied these percentages (row 10) by the total number of orders from each customer type (row 8) to estimate the total number of telephone orders placed by customer type. This measures telephone ordering effort. The team then used the estimated percentage of telephone orders (row 13) to estimate the cost of telephone sales to apply to each customer type (row 14). For example, the team computed the telephone ordering costs for grocery customers as follows:

Grocery telephone ordering cost = 42.5% of telephone orders × $130,000 = $55,250

Benefits and costs of sales administration.   A sales administration staff also supports all sales activities (row 16 in Exhibit 6–6) by maintaining customer, product, and sales-order databases and the schedules and call records of salespeople. The staff also manages advertising placement, coordination of sales promotions, and distribution center activities in each sales area. Sales administration also coordinates the logistics among manufacturing facilities and the six sales regions. [Many organizations, however, have separate departments (and resources) to manage and provide the logistics and ordering activities.]

Because timeliness of information was paramount, the team decided to learn the way that sales administration staff support customers by interviewing most staff members. From these interviews the team estimated the percentages of service to each of the three customer types (row 15 of Exhibit 6–6) and then calculated the costs of serving each type of customer (row 16), as follows:

Grocery sales administration cost = 62% effort × $480,000 = $297,600

If this process later indicates costs that are disproportionate to sales, the team will focus on this area of customer service. Given the time constraint, however, this was the team's method of using ABC techniques.

Customer Marketing Costs

Marketing costs include the costs of personnel, databases, equipment, and facilities dedicated to providing market research, marketing strategy, and marketing plans. HealthWave has a marketing department to address its marketing needs in the six sales regions. This department designs advertising and promotion materials and campaigns and provides training and information support for sales personnel. It also

You're the Decision Maker 6.1

Customer Profitability

The effort and cost percentages in Exhibit 6–6 represent the data that support customer profitability analysis. Clearly, these data are not precise, could contain errors, and might not be actually relevant to decisions about *future* customer profitability.

a. Verify the estimated costs of sales personnel, telephone sales orders, and sales administration costs in Exhibit 6–6.

b. Evaluate the team's decisions concerning its methods of obtaining data for sales costs.

c. What is the average cost of processing a telephone sales order? Is this cost amount useful? Explain.

d. Because salespeople also take orders, should the analysis also consider the costs of the orders they take?

(Solutions begin on page 235.)

Exhibit 6–7	HealthWave's Marketing Activities (NZ$)			

Marketing Activities	Total	Pharmacy	Grocery	Herbal Therapist
1. Marketing management	100%	55%	35%	10%
Marketing management cost	$ 360,000	$ 198,000	$ 126,000	$ 36,000
2. Promotions and incentives	100%	44%	56%	0%
Promotion and incentive cost	$2,250,000	$ 990,000	$1,260,000	$ 0
3. Advertising	100%	50%	50%	0%
Advertising cost	$2,400,000	$1,200,000	$1,200,000	$ 0
4. Catalogue development	100%	0%	0%	100%
Catalogue development cost	$ 250,000	$ 0	$ 0	250,000
Total marketing costs	$5,260,000	$2,388,000	$2,586,000	$286,000

responds to customer needs forwarded from salespeople and major account executives. The results of the examination of marketing resources and activities are reported in Exhibit 6–7.

The cost management team interviewed marketing management staff members to estimate the percentage of their efforts devoted to each customer type (item 1 in Exhibit 6–7). Marketing personnel believed that the diversity of pharmacy customers and products requires spending relatively more time with this sector.

Promotion, advertising, and catalogue costs are committed to support marketing strategies. Using the past year's costs as baselines for its analysis, the team used carefully selected samples of product incentives and promotions to estimate the percentage of these marketing resources used by pharmacy and grocery customers (item 2 in Exhibit 6–7). The past year's advertising appeared to equally split between pharmacy and grocery customers (item 3 in Exhibit 6–7). The company's catalogue serves herbal therapists but neither pharmacy nor grocery customers (item 4 in Exhibit 6–7). Sample pharmacy calculations follow:

Pharmacy marketing management cost = 55% effort × $360,000 = $198,000

Pharmacy promotions cost = 44% promotions × $2,250,000 = $990,000

Pharmacy advertising cost = 50% effort × $2,400,000 = $1,200,000

Customer Distribution Costs

Distribution costs include the costs of packing, shipping, and delivering products or services to customers. HealthWave distributes products to customers using a company-owned, maintained, and operated fleet of trucks serving pharmacy and grocery customers and a private delivery service, PackageXpress serving herbal therapists. See Exhibit 6–8 for the results of the analysis of distribution resources and activities.

Benefits and costs of distribution by company truck fleet. HealthWave operates distribution centers near customers, so the company can respond quickly to customers' special orders. Interviews with independent pharmacy, grocery, and major account customers confirmed that they value HealthWave's shipping flexibility. Said one, "We know that HealthWave will respond to our emergencies quickly and accurately, and we really appreciate that they respond eagerly and cheerfully. The other suppliers act like they are doing us a huge favor, and they seem to resent the inconvenience. HealthWave understands customer satisfaction and service."

On average, company trucks deliver shipments bi-weekly to pharmacies and independent grocers. The cost-management team assigned truck-distribution costs on the basis of the percentage of deliveries to each customer type (item 1 of Exhibit 6–8).

| Exhibit 6–8 | HealthWave's Distribution Resources and Activities |

Distribution Resources	Total	Pharmacy	Grocery	Herbal Therapist
Major customer accounts	4	0	4	0
Independent customers	12,500	11,000	1,500	0
Sales/distribution regions	6	0	6	0
Deliveries per major customer account per year	52	0	52	0
Percent by company truck		0%	100%	0%
Deliveries per independent customer per year	52	26	26	0
Percent by company truck		100%	100%	0%
Deliveries by company truck	326,248	286,000	40,248	0
1. Analysis of truck distribution costs				
Percent of total deliveries by company truck (rounded)	100%	87.66%	12.34%	0.0%
Company truck distribution cost	**$ 8,080,000**	**$ 7,083,201**	**$ 996,799**	**NA**
2. Analysis of outsourced distribution costs				
Percent deliveries by PackageXpress		0%	0%	100%
PackageXpress cost as % of revenue		NA	NA	12%
Customer revenues (Ex. 6–5)		$25,514,800	$49,399,400	$16,085,800
Outsourced distribution cost	**1,930,296**	**0**	**0**	**1,930,296**
Total distribution costs	$10,010,296			

NA means "not applicable."

Example distribution cost calculations in Exhibit 6–8 for grocery and pharmacy customers follow.

$$\text{Grocery truck deliveries} = (4 \text{ major accts} \times 6 \text{ sales regions} \times 52 \text{ weekly deliveries}$$
$$\times 100\% \text{ by truck}) + (26 \text{ biweekly deliveries} \times 1,500$$
$$\text{independents} \times 100\% \text{ by truck}) = \underline{40,248 \text{ deliveries}}$$

$$\text{Pharmacy truck distribution cost} = 100\% \text{ by truck} \times 87.663\% \text{ total deliveries} \times \$8,080,000$$
$$= \underline{\$7,083,201}$$

Benefits and costs of distribution by PackageXpress.   The growth of HealthWave's catalogue business indicated a number of years ago that using the company's own fleet of trucks and drivers to deliver small shipments to widely scattered herbal therapists was prohibitively costly. Outsourcing herbal therapists' deliveries to PackageXpress greatly reduced the cost and increased the reliability and speed of sales deliveries to herbal therapists. Herbal therapists interviewed by the team expressed complete satisfaction with the cost, which they paid, and quality of this service.

HealthWave's contract with PackageXpress was based on a daily pickup of small, prepackaged shipments from HealthWave's regional distribution centers and no more than two-day delivery to herbal therapists within each sales region. The cost of this outsourced service to HealthWave is based on a negotiated fee to reserve the service availability and a fee based on weight and volume of shipments. The costs (and shipping fees charged to customers) have averaged 12 percent of the sales value of a shipment, which the team believed was a reasonable estimate for this analysis (item 2 in Exhibit 6–8).

$$\text{Herbal therapist courier distribution cost} = 100\% \text{ by courier} \times 12\% \text{ of revenue}$$
$$\times \$16,085,800 = \underline{\$1,930,296}$$

Customer General and Administration Costs

All operating costs must be covered by customer sales, and the remaining costs to be assigned to customers are research and development (R&D) and general and administrative costs. Exhibits 6–9 and 6–10 show the analyses of these other costs.

Costs and benefits of R&D.   R&D costs are committed annual costs driven by desired new product development goals. R&D projects almost always can be assigned to one of the three product groups. Although these costs are intended to generate future sales, the team chose the very conservative approach of allocating R&D costs to products by the year of spending. This decision resulted in no R&D cost assigned to nonprescription drugs, $480,000 to supplements, and $720,000 to herbal remedies. Furthermore, the team assigned these R&D costs to customers based on the percentage of product sales of each category last year (from Exhibit 6–5); see Exhibit 6–9.

The R&D cost calculation for pharmacy customers follows. You should verify similar calculations in Exhibit 6–9 for grocery customers and herbal therapists.

$$\text{Pharmacy R\&D cost} = (\$0 \text{ R\&D cost} \times 78\% \text{ nonprescription sales})$$
$$+ (\$480,000 \text{ R\&D cost} \times 8\% \text{ supplements sales}) + (\$720,000$$
$$\text{R\&D cost} \times 5\% \text{ herbal remedy sales}) = \$74,400$$

Exhibit 6–9   HealthWave's R&D Costs (NZ$)

Analysis of R&D Costs	Total	Non-prescription	Supplements	Herbal Remedies
R&D projects traced to products	100%	0%	40%	60%
R&D costs traced to products...	$ 1,200,000	0	$ 480,000	$720,000
		Pharmacy	**Grocery**	**Herbal Therapist**
Sales of Nonprescription drugs (Ex. 6–5)	100.0%	78.0%	22.0%	0.0%
Supplements...	100.0	8.0	83.0	9.0
Herbal remedies	100.0	5.0	34.0	61.0
R&D costs traced to customers	**$1,200,000**	**$74,400**	**$ 643,200**	**$482,400**

Exhibit 6–10   HealthWave's General and Administration Costs

Major Company Activities	Total	Manufacturing	Customer Service and General Administration	
Admin. efforts traced to activities	100%	30%	70%	
Admin. costs traced to activities	$ 8,270,000	$ 2,481,000	$ 5,789,000	
		Pharmacy	**Grocery**	**Herbal Therapist**
Analysis of customer service and general and administration support costs:				
Customer revenues (Ex. 6–5)	$91,000,000	$25,514,800	$49,399,400	$16,085,800
Customer revenues (rounded percentage)	100.00%	28.04%	54.29%	17.68%
Customer service and general and admin. cost	$ 5,789,000	$ 1,623,134	$ 3,142,562	$ 1,023,304
Analysis of manufacturing support costs:				
Customer cost of goods sold (Ex. 6–5)	$54,676,200	$13,755,008	$30,140,662	$10,780,530
Cost of goods sold (rounded percentage)	100.00%	25.16%	55.13%	19.72%
Manufacturing support activity cost	$ 2,481,000	$ 624,150	$ 1,367,670	$ 489,180
Total general and admin. costs traced to customers	**$ 8,270,000**	**$ 2,247,284**	**$ 4,510,232**	**$ 1,512,484**

You're the Decision Maker 6.2

Trade-offs between Accuracy and Timeliness

In its analysis of customer profitability, the HealthWave team clearly made trade-offs between the accuracy and the timeliness of cost-management information.

a. How might the diversity or complexity of pharmacy customers cause marketing managers to spend relatively more time serving this customer sector? Is it possible to test whether marketing managers actually spend more time serving pharmacy customers? If so, how?

b. What types of resources does HealthWave probably devote to its truck fleet? What costs and benefits should the company consider before deciding whether to retain the fleet or outsource all distribution?

c. The company fleet's costs are relatively high, and the team used an expedient activity base, the number of deliveries, to assign fleet distribution costs to customers. What possible inaccuracies might using this measure create? How might you assess whether the inaccuracies are relevant to the analysis?

d. The team decided to assign general and administrative costs related to customer service based on customer sales percentages. Do you think this was a justifiable assumption? What do you, as a member of the team, recommend knowing that the team was running out of time and concerned about completing the analysis on time?

(Solutions begin on page 235.)

Costs and benefits of general and administration activities. Presumably, all activities of a profit-seeking organization such as HealthWave are (or should be) performed to facilitate or support sales to customers. Because many general and administrative functions and activities are several steps removed from customer-related activities, tracing costs of these functions to customers is usually difficult.

When it was more than a month into its work, the team began its analysis of general and administrative costs—perhaps the most difficult cost to trace to customers because of their diverse activities (e.g., from human resources to tax compliance). The team asked the vice presidents of finance, marketing, and manufacturing to estimate the percentage of general and administrative efforts used to support each customer type. The vice presidents estimated that their percentage of general and administration effort spent was: 30 percent for manufacturing, 50 percent for customer activities, and 20 percent for general business activities (see Exhibit 6–10).

The team then decided to allocate the estimated manufacturing support cost based on the percentage of the cost of goods sold to each customer type (from Exhibit 6–5) and both customer and general and administration support costs based on the percentage of customer sales (also from Exhibit 6–5). Example calculations for pharmacy customers follow:

$$\text{Pharmacy administrative costs} = (\text{Customer service} + \text{General and admin. support costs})$$
$$\times \text{Percentage of sales} + \text{Manufacturing support costs}$$
$$\times \text{Percentage of CGS}$$
$$= \$5,789,000 \times .2803824 + \$2,481,000 \times .2515721$$
$$= \$1,623,134 + \$624,150 = \underline{\$2,247,284}$$

Customer Profitability Analysis

Conducting the type of analyses discussed for HealthWave results in a view of an organization's profitability by customer type that often generates information that differs from that previously available. HealthWave's historic product and functional orientation obscured the costs of selling to and serving customers, assuming that all customers were "average." For most organizations, however, this might not be true (recall Exhibit 6–1).

See Exhibits 6–11 and 6–12 for the cost-management analysis team's computations of HealthWave's customer profitability. Exhibit 6–11 combines all customer-oriented analyses into an income statement format, and Exhibit 6–12 displays customer profitability graphically. Exhibit 6–11 begins with customer-level revenues and cost of

Exhibit 6–11   HealthWave's Customer Profitability Statement

Customer Profitability	Total	Pharmacy	Grocery	Herbal Therapist
Revenue (Ex. 6–5)	$91,000,000	$25,514,800	$49,399,400	$16,085,800
Variable CGS	54,676,200	13,755,008	30,140,662	10,780,530
Contribution margin	$36,323,800	$11,759,792	$19,258,738	$ 5,305,270
Contribution margin ratio	39.9%	46.1%	39.0%	33.0%
Operating costs:				
Selling (Ex. 6–6):				
Sales personnel	$ 4,325,000	$ 2,475,000	$ 1,850,000	0
Telephone order system	130,000	65,000	55,250	$ 9,750
Sales administration	480,000	120,000	297,600	62,400
Total selling costs	$ 4,935,000	$ 2,660,000	$ 2,202,850	$ 72,150
Marketing (Ex. 6–7):				
Marketing management	360,000	198,000	126,000	36,000
Promotions and incentives	2,250,000	990,000	1,260,000	0
Advertising	2,400,000	1,200,000	1,200,000	0
Catalogue development	250,000	0	0	250,000
Total marketing costs	$ 5,260,000	$ 2,388,000	$ 2,586,000	$ 286,000
Distribution (Ex. 6–8):				
Company trucks	8,080,000	7,083,201	996,799	0
Courier service	1,930,296	0	0	1,930,296
Total distribution costs	$10,010,296	$ 7,083,201	$ 996,799	$ 1,930,296
Other operating costs:				
R&D (Ex. 6–9)	1,200,000	74,400	643,200	482,400
General and administrative support (Ex. 6–10)	8,270,000	2,247,284	4,510,232	1,512,484
Total operating costs	$29,675,296	$14,452,885	$10,939,081	$ 4,283,330
Operating income	$ 6,648,504	$ (2,693,093)	$ 8,319,657	$ 1,021,940
Return on sales	7.3%	(10.6%)	16.8%	6.4%

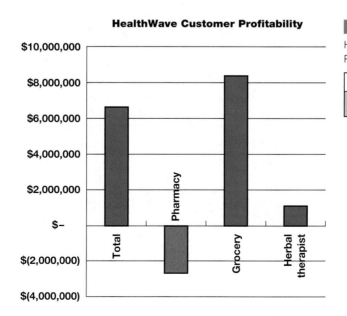

HealthWave Customer Profitability

Exhibit 6–12

HealthWave's Customer Profitability Chart

goods sold (Exhibit 6–5) and then adds customer-level selling costs (Exhibit 6–6), marketing costs (Exhibit 6–7), distribution costs (Exhibit 6–8), R&D costs (Exhibit 6–9), and general and administration costs (Exhibit 6–10). This "roll up" of the components of customer profitability results in the calculations of customer-level operating income and return on sales figures (bottom of Exhibit 6–11). Note that the total revenues, operating costs, and operating income are the same as in Exhibit 6–2, but the customer profitability analysis has sorted these income items by customer type.

Assuming that the cost-management analysis team's methods and estimates are reasonable, each type of customer clearly does not contribute equally to the company's overall profit. In particular, grocery customers already appear to exceed the long-term target return on sales (16.8% > 15%), whereas herbal therapists and especially pharmacy customers fail to meet even the short-term goal [6.4% and (10.6%), which are less than 10%]. Although herbal therapists are profitable, pharmacy customers generate a significant loss that itself is in excess of the target cost reduction (or profit enhancement) for the first year. This was surprising information to the HealthWave team. Although it believes that a recommendation to drop pharmacy customers just to meet the first-year target was inappropriate at the time, it could present the customer-profitability information in Exhibits 6–11 and 6–12 to help HealthWave identify areas for profit improvement previously that had not been apparent.

Identification of Alternative Actions and Choice of Appropriate One

Common-Size Profit Statements

LO 3 Identify alternative actions and recommend improvements for overall and customer profitability based on analyzing customer-related activities.

The absolute dollar amounts in Exhibit 6–11 indicate the profit or loss generated by customer type. As mentioned previously, some companies that are information-technology intensive can produce this information for every single customer; its most common use, however, is to identify which customers to encourage and which to drop or discourage (see Cost Management in Practice 6.1). Organizations also can use the information to identify opportunities to transform customer losses into customer profits. To highlight these opportunities, recasting the absolute dollar cost and profit amounts as percentages of revenues can be useful. **Common-size statements** are financial statements that express items as percentages of revenue.

Dividing the amount in each column in Exhibit 6–11 by its sales revenue reveals each amount as a percentage of revenue. See Exhibit 6–13 for the percentage of costs to revenues for each customer type. Review this exhibit and look for exceptionally large or small percentages of sales across the three types of customers.

Several amounts in Exhibit 6–13 are presented in bold. Look first at the Pharmacy column in the exhibit. Working from the bottom of Exhibit 6–13, the first exceptional figure is the negative 10.6 percent return on sales (ROS) for pharmacy customers, which we knew but now see must be related to the much higher relative operating costs estimated for pharmacy customers despite their higher contribution margin ratio. Operating costs for the pharmacy customer type are 56.7 percent of sales but average only 22.1 to 26.6 percent of sales for other customer types. Contributing to this much higher cost rate are higher distribution costs (27.8 percent of pharmacy sales compared to only 2 and 12 percent of sales for others) and selling costs (10.4 percent of sales compared to only 4.5 and 0.5 percent for others). HealthWave apparently serves its grocery and herbal therapists much more efficiently than its pharmacy customers. Can it solve the pharmacy customer-service problem?

Aided by the analysis of the information in Exhibit 6–13, the cost-management team identified four alternative courses of action to improve customer profitability and began to analyze the profit impact of each. The alternatives were:

- Continue the status quo; do nothing.
- Drop pharmacy customers.
- Increase the efficiency of serving pharmacy customers.
- Decrease operating activity costs for all customers.

Exhibit 6–13

HealthWave's Common-Size Customer Profitability Statement

HealthWave INC.

	Percentage (rounded)			
	Total	Pharmacy	Grocery	Herbal Therapist
Revenue	100.0%*	100.0%	100.0%	100.0%
CGS	60.1	53.9	61.0	67.0
Contribution margin	39.9%	46.1%	39.0%	33.0%
Operating costs:				
Selling:				
Sales personnel	4.8	**9.7**	3.7	0.0
Telephone order system	0.1	0.3	0.1	0.1
Administration	0.5	0.5	0.6	0.4
Total selling costs	5.4%	**10.4%**	4.5%	**0.5%**
Marketing:				
Marketing management	0.4	0.8	0.3	0.2
Promotions and incentives	2.5	3.9	2.6	0.0
Advertising	2.6	4.7	2.4	0.0
Catalogue development	0.3	0.0	0.0	1.6
Total marketing costs	5.8%	9.4%	5.2%	**1.8%**
Distribution:				
Company trucks	8.9	**27.8**	2.0	0.0
Courier service	2.1	0.0	0.0	12.0
Total distribution costs	11.0%	**27.8%**	**2.0%**	12.0%
Other operating costs:				
R&D costs	1.3	0.3	1.3	3.0
General and admin. costs	9.1	8.8	9.1	9.4
Total operating costs	32.6%	**56.7%**	22.1%	26.6%
Operating income	7.3%	**(10.6%)**	16.8%	6.4%

*Calculations use data from Exhibit 6–11.

Continue the Status Quo; Do Nothing

The team did not seriously consider recommending that HealthWave do nothing. Accepting the status quo surely would result in the failure to meet London Pharmaceutical's ROS targets. Furthermore, because competitors most likely also were looking closely at their customer-service operations, keeping the status quo surely would result in erosion of customer satisfaction and loyalty and increased losses. Understanding the implications of keeping the status quo was important motivation for seriously considering its alternatives. Because it was so close to the problem, the team was motivated and knew it must communicate that motivation when recommending changes to HealthWave management and employees. Keeping the status quo was unacceptable because choosing not to change would mean certain failure.

Drop Pharmacy Customers

A quick review of Exhibit 6–11 *implies* that dropping pharmacy customers also would eliminate the $2,693,093 loss attributed to this customer type. Eliminating this loss appears to provide more than the $2,451,496 cost reduction or profit enhancement needed to meet the target return on sales (see Exhibit 6–3). Certainly, HealthWave must ensure the secrecy of its investigation of whether it can save nearly $2.7 million by dropping pharmacy customers, or pharmacy customers might bolt to other suppliers.

The most certain outcome of dropping pharmacy customers is the loss of $11,759,792 in contribution margin from this customer type (see Exhibit 6–11). To avoid the estimated loss from pharmacy customers, however, HealthWave also has to save at least $14,452,885 (Exhibit 6–11) in operating costs that have been

HealthWave faces the difficult decision about whether to drop its unprofitable pharmacy customers. An alternative is to increase the efficiency of serving them.

assigned to this customer type. To properly address this issue, the team must use one of the major ABC principles presented in Chapter 4: Estimates of activity-based costs reflect the *uses* of resources, not necessarily the *acquisition* or *spending* for resources. Some customer-service costs are driven by unit-level or customer-level activities. Presumably, eliminating the customer activities and the capacity to provide them can save these costs, but facility-level decisions and activities drive other costs (e.g., general and administration costs), which do not depend directly on unit- or customer-level activities.

Let's assume that the team's estimates of customer-related operating costs are reasonably accurate measures of the costs of *using* customer-related resources. Does eliminating those pharmacy customer-related activities also eliminate the *spending* for the capacity to perform those activities? Furthermore, does eliminating pharmacy customers have adverse effects on the sale of goods or provision of services to other customers? The team really needs answers to these questions before correctly measuring the profit impact of dropping pharmacy customers. See the results of Exhibit 6–14 for the team's additional analysis, which focused on these elements related to pharmacy customers:

- Selling costs.
- Marketing costs.
- Distribution costs.
- Other costs.
- Elimination effects on other customers.

1. *Pharmacy-customer selling costs.* The costs to sell to independent pharmacies are much higher than those for the other customer types. The four major grocery accounts serve most grocery customers efficiently as a small telephone sales-order system does for herbal therapists. HealthWave's pharmacy customers, on the other hand, tend to be widely dispersed and have no major buying groups. Thus, serving them requires a relatively large dedicated sales force, which HealthWave can eliminate if it drops pharmacy customers, saving an estimated $2,475,000 annually.

   By dropping pharmacy customers, the team estimated that HealthWave could reduce its telephone sales-order system by one operator, saving $30,000 annually. Similarly, reducing sales and administration capacity by two employees reduces these costs, saving $65,000 annually. The team estimated that HealthWave would spend approximately 10 percent of the personnel cost savings on counseling and "outplacement" for terminated employees if they could be shifted to other areas. Thus, 90 percent of the cost savings probably could be realized in the short run. The team estimated no reductions in physical facilities or equipment related to sales and administration. Total annual selling cost savings were estimated to be:

Selling cost savings = .90 × ($2,475,000 + 30,000 + 65,000) = $2,313,000 (shown in Exhibit 6–14)

Drop Pharmacy Lost Revenue and Saved Cost	Customers
Lost revenue (Exhibit 6–11)	$(25,514,800)
Saved CGS (Exhibit 6–11)	13,755,008
Lost contribution margin	$(11,759,792)
Saved operating costs (see text):	
Selling and administration	2,313,000
Marketing	2,300,000
Distribution	5,666,561
General and administration	1,700,000
Total operating cost savings	$ 11,979,561
Increase in Profit (Operating cost savings − Lost contribution margin)	$ 219,769
Total sales without pharmacy ($91,000,000 − $25,514,800)	$ 65,485,200
Total profit without pharmacy ($6,648,504 + 219,769)	6,868,273
Revised return on sales (first year)	10.5%

Exhibit 6–14

Profit Effects of Dropping
Pharmacy Customers

2. *Pharmacy-customer marketing costs.* The vice president of marketing confirmed that dropping pharmacy customers would reduce the need for marketing management capacity by one manager and two support staff, saving $110,000 annually. Without pharmacy customers, HealthWave would have no need to offer pharmacy incentives and provide advertising, saving $2,190,000 annually. Total annual marketing cost savings will be:

    Marketing cost savings = $110,000 + 2,190,000 = $2,300,000 (shown in Exhibit 6–14)

3. *Pharmacy-customer distribution costs.* Most of the cost of HealthWave's truck fleet supports deliveries to pharmacy customers. Some fleet costs (e.g., the maintenance facility) cannot be reduced proportionately by fewer deliveries without pharmacy customers. Furthermore, an unknown percentage of fleet trips delivers to both pharmacy and independent grocery customers. Thus, HealthWave cannot reduce its fleet capacity by the full amount eliminated and maintain its desired level of service to independent grocery customers. Nonetheless, the team estimated that dropping pharmacy customers would save approximately 80 percent of the pharmacy-related distribution costs after outplacement and other shutdown costs, saving approximately $5,667,000 in the first year:

    Distribution cost savings = .80 × $7,083,201 = $5,666,561 (shown in Exhibit 6–14)

4. *Other Pharmacy-customer costs.* R&D costs are committed based on desired future product development. Although dropping pharmacy customers reduces the need for the *volume* of future products, the team was reluctant to recommend reducing R&D efforts because of the adverse impact on future revenues. The team believed that HealthWave could reduce general and administrative and customer-service support costs related to pharmacy customers, estimating cost savings of approximately $1,700,000 in the first year (including outplacement costs) by reducing general and administrative capacity. Note that general and administration cost is a large cost category; a closer look might identify even more cost-saving opportunities.

    General and administration cost savings = $1,700,000 (shown in Exhibit 6–14)

5. *Elimination effects on other customers.* The team anticipated other effects of dropping pharmacy customers, none of which could be quantified easily. Dropping pharmacy customers might adversely affect manufacturing efficiency,

particularly related to nonprescription drugs, 78 percent of which are sold to pharmacy customers. This might reduce grocery-customer contribution margins or make HealthWave products less competitive. Other adverse effects included employee morale which might decline and the loss of beneficial crossover product advertising and promotions. For example, product advertising and promotions that benefit the pharmacy customer segment sometimes also benefit grocery segment customers. On the other hand, marketing and administration efforts could focus more on grocery and herbal therapists and provide them more efficient service without the distraction of pharmacy customers.

Review the team's summary analysis of dropping pharmacy customers in Exhibit 6–14, which indicates that dropping pharmacy customers increases profitability by $219,769. Overall return on sales then increases to 10.5 percent for the first year. Although dropping pharmacy customers results in a loss of their contribution margin, the estimated cost savings and increase in profits are sufficient to increase the return on the reduced level of sales to more than the first-year 10 percent target. According to this analysis (and ignoring qualitative considerations), HealthWave would become a smaller but more profitable company without pharmacy customers. However, does this position it to meet the greater challenge of reaching future ROS targets?

Increase the Efficiency of Serving Pharmacy Customers

An alternative to dropping pharmacy customers is to improve the efficiency of serving them. The most prominent amounts in Exhibits 6–13 and 6–14 reflect distribution costs to pharmacy customers. The team had discovered that one reason for the higher percentage cost of pharmacy distribution is the greater dispersion of its customers (recall that four major association accounts served all but the 1,500 grocery customers efficiently). Herbal therapists were similarly dispersed, but through a contract with PackageXpress, the cost of shipping to them was only 12 percent of sales. Could HealthWave achieve the ROS target by eliminating the truck fleet serving pharmacy customers and totally outsourcing distribution? The team had to keep this very sensitive alternative secret to prevent other employees from learning about it prematurely.

See Exhibit 6–15 for the analysis of HealthWave's replacement of its fleet serving pharmacy customers with outsourced delivery at costs similar to those of its existing contract with PackageXpress (12 percent of sales value). Without considering other service improvements, the estimated distribution-cost savings [$2,604,785 = $5,666,561 − (.12 × $25,514,800)], when added to previous profits, would boost the revised profits sufficiently to meet the first-year target ROS (10.2% > 10%).

Although the effects on HealthWave affected personnel would be negative, outsourcing distribution was the team's preferred alternative. Unlike completely dropping pharmacy customers, outsourcing distribution to this customer type promised less disruption to customers and retained more future market opportunities.

Increasing the efficiency of sales activities to pharmacy customers is another likely source of profit improvement. The team did not believe that selling to pharmacy customers easily could be as efficient as selling to either grocery or herbal ther-

Exhibit 6–15
Profit Effects of Outsourcing Pharmacy Deliveries

Pharmacy Distribution Cost Savings:	
Pharmacy truck-fleet cost (Ex. 6–14)	$ 5,666,561
Outsourced delivery based on cost of pharmacy sales (.12 × $25,514,800)	3,061,776
Cost savings	$ 2,604,785
Effect on Profits:	
Total sales (Ex. 6–11)	$91,000,000
Revised profit with cost savings ($6,648,500 + $2,604,785)	$ 9,253,285
Revised return on sales	10.2%

Complications of Customer Service

In June 1999, Sun Microsystems, provider of Internet servers and software, learned an invaluable lesson in managing customer profitability. Sun's president received a call from the CEO of eBay (the online auction company) stating that eBay's Web site had been down for 22 hours because of a bug in its very expensive Sun server. Sun's costly crash-effort to revive the site revealed extensive problems related to eBay's installation and use of the server, which Sun had assumed were the customer's responsibilities. After this incident, Sun realized that the occurrence of these problems was imminent worldwide. Most of its dot-com customers were struggling with the complexities of installing and operating large Internet servers, and they expected a trouble-free, plug-and-play server. Their inattention to managing servers was sure to lead to outraged customers. Recognizing that the out-of-pocket costs and damaged reputation from these problems could be devastating to Sun, it quickly identified 14 important customer-related issues, placed a vice president in charge of managing each one, and dramatically overhauled its customer-sales and service activities to internalize and minimize the costs to prevent costly customer emergencies similar to the size that eBay had experienced. *Source: Peter Burrows. "Sun's Bid to Rule the Web."*

Cost Management in Practice 6.2

apists, but it suspected that improving sales activities to pharmacies might result in additional cost savings. Because this could require complicated organizational changes at HealthWave *and* for pharmacy customers, HealthWave would not realize these savings quickly. Furthermore, the team believed that improvements in activities supporting all customers might be necessary to meet long-term profit targets.

Decrease Operating Activity Costs for All Customers

Either of the two alternatives that focused on keeping pharmacy customers is likely to achieve profit improvements that would meet the first-year target. However, the team knew that it should make recommendations to help HealthWave to meet its long-term profit targets. Assume that HealthWave chooses to increase the efficiency of servicing pharmacy customers by outsourcing distribution. At last year's sales level of $91,000,000 plus cost savings from outsourcing pharmacy distribution, the company must improve profits by another $4,396,711 to meet the 15 percent long-term ROS target (see Exhibit 6–16). To achieve this profit improvement by decreasing operating activity costs would require a 16.2 percent reduction within five years.

The team realized that saving this amount from any single activity (e.g., cutting general and administrative costs by more than half) was unlikely. It expected that some profit increase would be achieved by sales growth if the company could keep cost increases low (e.g., by using ABC to manage costs). Some selling, ordering, and logistics activities were undoubtedly not value added and should be eliminated or improved. Perhaps moving many customer-related activities to the Internet would be cost effective and benefit relations with all customers. CEO Atherton and the executive committee decided to explore outsourcing pharmacy deliveries, to move aggressively to increase sales to profitable customers, and to improve the efficiencies of other customer services to meet long-run profit targets. As of this writing, the company is on track to meet its goals.

Total sales	$91,000,000
Long-term ROS target	15%
Target profit	$13,650,000
Total revenue at last year's sales level	$91,000,000
Variable CGS of last year's sales	54,676,200
Contribution margin	$36,323,800
Operating costs after possible distribution savings ($29,675,296 − $2,604,785)	27,070,511
Operating income	$ 9,253,289
Target profit improvement required ($13,650,000 − $9,253,289)	4,396,711
Improvement as a percent of operating costs ($4,396,711 ÷ $27,070,511)	16.2%

Exhibit 6–16

HealthWave's Long-Term Profit Target

Chapter Summary

Companies start assessing customer profitability by identifying quantitative and qualitative costs and benefits associated with all major resources and activities dedicated to serving customers. These profitability analyses include these elements:

- Obtain top management support for the analysis and implementing difficult action choices it recommends.
- Develop tangible objectives for the analysis (e.g., Exhibit 6–3).
- Obtain top management support to access the information needed to trace activities and resources to customers.
- Build customer profiles and trace sales to customers (e.g., Exhibits 6–4 and 6–5).
- Trace product selling, marketing, and distribution activities and resources to customers (e.g., Exhibits 6–5, 6–6, 6–7, and 6–8).
- Trace other resources to customers (Exhibits 6–9 and 6–10).
- Measure customer profitability (Exhibits 6–11, 6–12, and 6–13).
- Identify and measure the impact of alternative actions to improve customer profitability (Exhibits 6–14 and 6–15).
- Position the organization to continually improve long-term customer profitability.

Key Terms

For each term's definition, refer to the indicated page or turn to the glossary at the end of the text.

Common-size statements, 228   **Customer profile, 219**   **Customer-profitability analysis, 214**

Meeting the Cost Management Challenges

1. How can you determine in advance whether investments of time, effort, and information systems to prepare customer profitability information are worthwhile?

Other than relying on others' experience or consultants' assurances, determining the value of an investment in information to support customer profitability analysis is difficult. Many organizations approach customer profitability analysis by analyzing a segment of their operations first. This cautious approach allows them to assess the costs and benefits of obtaining information without investing in a full analysis, which can be very costly (millions of dollars for large organizations!).

2. How can customer profitability analysis be more relevant for service and governmental organizations than for others?

Various organizations employ different types of resources for different customer-service strategies at various costs. However, all types and sizes of organizations potentially can benefit from better understanding how they use scarce resources to serve different customers and customer types. Because service and government organizations use most of their resources to provide services (or they should), customer profitability analysis can be more important to their success than to other types of companies.

3. How do you evaluate the trade-offs among the desires for relevant, accurate, and timely information?

Few, if any, organizations have enough time and resources to obtain the information they really want to support their important decisions. Because traditional, product-line profitability information is largely irrelevant for customer profitability analysis, some

declare it to be completely irrelevant and inaccurate for that purpose. Trade-offs between relevance, accuracy, and timeliness almost always are necessary. The trade-off might be between (1) information that is only 50 percent accurate but 100 percent timely and relevant versus (2) information that is 100 percent accurate but too late to be useful. Analysts need to find trade-offs with which they feel comfortable given the importance of the decisions they are supporting. At a minimum, they must fully document and support the information they develop and use so that they and others can understand its limitations and make informed decisions about revising it.

4. How can cost-management analysts help an organization plan and execute changes in operations to deliver more customer value at lower cost?

Leading change is an important part of cost-management analysis. Significant resistance and opposition often accompany significant change; this is just human nature. Cost-management analysts should pay careful attention to the recommendations for leading change described in Chapter 1. Although there are no guarantees for seamless change, understanding the nature of change and the natural resistance to it and following a clear plan to lead it increases its chance of success.

5. How can you determine whether operational changes in customer service have been beneficial or harmful?

Another common human trait is unwillingness to reevaluate changes or investments that have been made. Often changes have been so difficult to implement that their lack of success is very disappointing and tends to reflect badly on those that led the change. Reevaluations or "postaudits" of an implemented change offer invaluable learning opportunities that should be part of every organization's culture. One strategy to ensure that postaudits occur is to enforce a policy requiring every major decision that involves a customer service change to include a scheduled postaudit.

Solutions to You're the Decision Maker

6.1 Customer Profitability p. 222

a. Costs rounded to the nearest $100.

	Pharmacy	Grocery	Herbal Therapist
Sales personnel cost	45 × $55,000 = $2,475,000	25 × $42,000 + 4 × $200,000 = $1,850,000	NA
Telephone sales order cost	.50 × $130,000 = $65,000	.425 × $130,000 = $55,250	.075 × $130,000 = $9,750
Sales administration cost	.25 × $480,000 = $120,000	.62 × $480,000 = $297,600	.13 × $480,000 = $62,400

b. The team's decision to calculate and assign costs of *sales personnel costs* seems straightforward, assuming that the costs reflect efforts. For example, no carryover in sales effort for grocery and pharmacy salespeople seems to exist. Assignment of *telephone sales order costs* apparently is accurate, but note that the number of orders reflects the volume of orders but not the complexity of each. A telephone order from one of the large grocery chain accounts is likely to be more complex and require more resources than one from an herbal therapist. Failure to consider complexity could lead to overestimates of the telephone sales order costs to serve customers with simple orders. Interviews with sales administration personnel are the basis of the assignment of *sales administration costs*. Time did not permit a formal observation of the use of these resources, which might have been more accurate. The failure to adjust Exhibit 6–6 or other exhibits for expected changes in cost, technology, organization, or service level is acceptable at this level of analysis.

c. The average cost for an operator to take an order placed by telephone is $1.625 ($130,000 ÷ 80,000), but this does not consider other related quantitative costs (e.g., the complexity of the order) or the qualitative factor of when the order was processed (during a slow or busy time), each of which could affect the cost of taking such orders. If the average cost does not consider these elements, it is less useful.

d. If the only analysis objective is to trace costs by type of customer, separate identification of the cost of salespersons taking orders is not necessary.

6.2 Trade-offs between Accuracy and Timeliness p. 226

a. Many people believe that the diversity and complexity of serving a customer are the most important cost drivers. HealthWave needs to identify what *marketing managers mean* by diversity or complexity. How do more complex customers use marketing managers' time? Is designing or administering marketing programs for pharmacies more complex than for groceries? Is communicating with pharmacies more difficult? Why? How? Perhaps dealing with the four major grocery accounts makes marketing management much simpler for the grocery customer type. Observations of how marketing management staff spends its time on randomly selected days can test this proposition.

b. The direct resources devoted to the fleet include the purchase and maintenance of the trucks, fuel, and garage and office facilities as well as the salaries, including benefits, of the drivers, dispatchers, and mechanics. Indirect resources likely include a percentage of marketing management, sales and administration, and general and administrative efforts. Before deciding whether to retain the fleet, HealthWave should consider the qualitative factors of the values of its flexible response to customer orders supplied by the fleet and the company identity provided by its logo on the trucks as well as the disruption caused by terminating employees and liquidating assets.

c. Distribution capacity is a matter of ability to do work or to carry weight (or volume) some distance. Doing so within some time period also is a factor because of the opportunity cost of delivery time. Assigning costs based only on the number of deliveries does not consider the distance of the deliveries or the weight of the shipments. The team's measure of distribution activity treats all as being the same. To the extent that the delivery work performed for different customers is diverse, the team's expedient measure misstates distribution costs across customers. You might assess whether the inaccuracies are relevant by obtaining information to determine whether many smaller deliveries over longer distances (serving pharmacy customers) consume more fleet resources than fewer larger ones over shorter distances (serving grocery customers).

d. Assigning general and administrative costs based on relative sales revenue certainly could be justified, but anyone reviewing the team's work would want assurance that this very large cost ($8,270,000) had been assigned accurately or at least in a way that does not materially affect any decisions based on the information. The team assigned marketing management costs more heavily to pharmacy customers based on interviews with marketing managers, which did not yield precise information, setting a disturbing precedent. You might ask the company's CEO for another week or so to refine estimates of assigned general and administrative costs. In this case, the trade-off of accuracy versus timeliness might tilt toward more accuracy.

Review Questions

6.1 Review and define each of the chapter's key terms.

6.2 How are product-line and customer profitability measures similar and different based on the discussions in this chapter.

6.3 Explain the point made by Exhibit 6–1.

6.4 List typical objectives of customer profitability analysis.

6.5 List and describe each major type of customer-related resource and the activities that drive their use, as illustrated by the analysis of HealthWave.

6.6 Describe the trade-offs analysts often must make when gathering and evaluating information about customer-related resources, activities, and costs.

6.7 Describe how customer profitability analysis can be related to ABC and ABM.

6.8 Describe typical qualitative factors to consider when evaluating alternatives to improve customer profitability.

6.9 Describe several types of improvements that an organization could make to increase its customer profitability.

6.10 How might you apply the recommendations in Chapter 1 for leading change when implementing customer-profitability improvements?

Critical Analysis

6.11 "There's no such thing as product profitability, only customer profitability." Discuss.

6.12 An Internet search of the key phrase "customer profitability" will result in thousands of "hits," many of which are Web sites of companies seeking to sell software or consulting services. If you were looking for assistance in designing and implementing customer profitability analysis, how could you discriminate among these competing sites?

6.13 Professor Johnson argues that ABC techniques have been oversold. Rather than focusing on reducing costs of production or serving customers, he argues, firms should strive to improve customer satisfaction because doing so will increase profitability more than cost cutting will.[6] Critically evaluate this argument.

6.14 A recent article lauded a major e-commerce supplier for its extraordinary commitments to product and service innovation and customer service. The article argued that these commitments are paying off by citing as proof higher than average contribution margins and growth in sales over the past three years. Evaluate this evidence of a payoff from R&D and customer service expenditures.[7]

6.15 Many financial services companies regularly offer credit cards to college students who have a low income and no credit history. On the face of it, this practice seems contrary to that used by many banks, such as Bank of America, to segment credit-card customers by income, risk, services, and profitability. Why do you think companies make these offers to college students?

6.16 Federal Express reportedly segments customers into "good," "bad," and "ugly" categories.[8] It gives good customers, who spend much and demand little service or marketing, preferential treatment; charges bad customers, who spend little but are expensive to serve, higher shipping charges; and it discourages ugly customers, who spend little with poor prospects of increases, from using its serv-

ices. Is this practice of segmenting and differential pricing evidence of illegal price discrimination by FedEx? Explain.

6.17 Deregulation of telecommunication in the United States has brought increased competition among long-distance telephone service providers, such as AT&T, Sprint, and MCI-Worldcom. Initially, these companies offered up to $50 to customers to switch to their service, but these offers now are rare. How do you explain this change in marketing and promotion?

6.18 A business publication reported across-the-board declines in customer satisfaction in the airline, banking, retailing, hotel, and telecommunication industries, yet most companies in these industries were profitable. How do you explain this apparent mismatch of customer satisfaction and profitability?

6.19 At your company's monthly marketing strategy meeting, the director of customer satisfaction happily reports that 80 percent of customers are at least "satisfied" and half of those are "delighted" with the company's products and services. This is good news because delighted customers are much more likely to be repeat customers. The director argues that with effort, it is possible to reach a customer satisfaction level of 90 percent by focusing on the 20 percent who are dissatisfied. Furthermore, a 50 percent overall delighted rating is within reach. Everyone turns to you for approval to attempt to achieve these higher goals. What is your response?

6.20 "Investing in customer profitability analysis will cost millions—and that's just to get started. I just can't justify that level of spending when our bottom line is so thin." "I challenge that expense-only thinking. The nature of business is spending money to make money. How else are we going to spend money that is more value added?" Evaluate this argument and develop criteria to judge whether to begin a major customer profitability analysis project.

---

[6] H. T. Johnson, "It's Time to Stop Overselling Activity-Based Concepts." Also see the rejoinder by R. S. Kaplan, "In Defense of Activity-Based Cost Management."

[7] P. Burrows, "Sun's Bid to Rule the Web."

[8] P. C. Judge, "Do You Know Who Your Most Profitable Customers Are?"

Exercises

An Internet search of the key phrase "customer profitability" results in thousands of "hits," many of which are Web sites of companies seeking to sell software or consulting services. Choose a sample of five of these Web sites and write a memo that evaluates the information they present and how well they present it.

Exercise 6.21
Customer Profitability
(LO 1)

Building a customer database can be expensive. Free information is available in the United States from the Census Bureau's Web site (*www.census.gov*). Visit this site (particularly the Economic Census link), and prepare a short report describing the type of information available that might be useful to start-up businesses.

Exercise 6.22
Customer Database
(LO 1)

Data mining and data warehousing techniques are potential tools to use to analyze customer profitability. Many companies have had disappointing results using them, however, despite great expense and effort in building data warehouses. Search the Internet for information about data mining and warehousing, and write a memo that makes recommendations for guiding a data warehouse project to deliver useful customer profitability information.

Exercise 6.23
Customer Data
Warehouse
(LO 1)

Daytona Company produces, sells, and distributes two products, A-7 and B-2, to two types of customers, urban and rural. Using the following information, prepare a customer profitability statement:

Exercise 6.24
Customer Profitability
(LO 2)

Daytona Product Profitability	Total	A-7	B-2
Contribution margin ratio	46.7%	40.0%	60.0%
Revenues	$9,000,000	$6,000,000	$3,000,000
Customer sales to:			
Sales of:		**Urban**	**Rural**
A-7	100%	70%	30%
B-2	100%	20%	80%
Operating costs traced to customers	$3,000,000	$2,200,000	$800,000

Refer to Exercise 6.24. Daytona desires to increase its return on sales to 25 percent. What amount of profit enhancement is required to meet this profitability target at the same level of sales?

Exercise 6.25
Return on Customer Sales
(LO 2)

LaBron sells two products, windshield wipers and sunshades, to two types of customers, grocery and auto parts stores. Using the following information, prepare a customer profitability statement:

Exercise 6.26
Customer Profitability
(LO 2)

mhhe.com/hilton3e

LaBron Product Profitability	Total	Sunshades	Windshield Wipers
Contribution margin ratio		70.0%	60.0%
Revenues	$11,000,000	$5,000,000	$6,000,000
Customer sales to:			
Sales of:		**Grocery**	**Auto Parts**
Windshield wipers	100%	50%	50%
Sunshades	100%	20%	80%
Operating costs traced to customers	$4,500,000	$2,200,000	$2,300,000

Refer to Exercise 6.26. LaBron desires to increase its return on sales to 30 percent. What amount of profit enhancement is required to meet this profitability target at the same level of sales?

Exercise 6.27
Return on Customer Sales
(LO 2)

Homeland Research Services (HRS) conducts personnel background checks and supplier reliability research for banks and manufacturers. Using the following information, prepare a customer profitability statement:

Exercise 6.28
Customer Profitability
(LO 2)

HRS Profitability	Total	Personnel Checks	Supplier Reliability
Contribution margin ratio	61.8%	65.0%	60.0%
Revenues	$11,000,000	$4,000,000	$7,000,000
Customer sales to:			
Sales of:		**Banks**	**Manufacturers**
Personnel checks	100%	75%	25%
Supplier reliability	100%	20%	80%
Operating costs traced to customers	$5,500,000	$1,400,000	$4,100,000

Exercise 6.29
Return on Customer Sales
(LO 2)

Refer to Exercise 6.28. HRS desires to increase its return on sales to 20 percent. What amount of profit enhancement is required to meet this profitability target at the same level of sales?

Exercise 6.30
Customer-Level Costs
(LO 2)

Carousel Shipping (CS) wishes to trace its distribution costs to each of its four customer types, alpha, beta, chili, and dog. CS delivers some shipments itself and outsources the delivery of others. Use the following information to estimate distribution costs per customer:

CS Customer Profitability	Total	Alpha	Beta	Chili	Dog
Shipments per year	121,400	40,000	16,600	57,000	7,800
Delivered by CS		80%	90%	25%	80%
Outsourced delivery		20%	10%	75%	20%
CS distribution costs	$6,700,000				
Outsourced shipment costs	120,000				
Total distribution costs	$6,820,000				

Exercise 6.31
Customer-Level Costs
(LO 2)

Outrageous Promotions (OP) is interested in tracing its promotion design costs to each of its three major customer types, groceries, drug stores, and discount stores. OP designs some promotions itself and outsources the other designs. Use the following information to estimate promotion design costs per customer:

OP Customer Profitability	Total	Groceries	Drug Stores	Discount Stores
Promotions per year	212	60	52	100
Designed by OP		85%	82%	95%
Outsourced design		15%	18%	5%
OP design costs	$ 112,000			
Outsourced design costs	27,000			
Total design costs by customer	$ 139,000			

Exercise 6.32
Customer-Level Costs
(LO 2)

mhhe.com/hilton3e

Castle Music seeks to trace its marketing costs to each of its two major customer types, record clubs and retail stores. It employs salespeople in all major world markets to serve retail stores. Account executives serve each of eight major record clubs in Europe and North America. In addition, a staff and a facility support marketing and promotions to all customers. Use the following information to trace marketing costs to customers:

Castle Music Marketing Cost Information and Effort	Total	Record Clubs	Retail Stores
Major account managers	8	8	0
Sales representatives	150	0	150
Average salary/year		$200,000	$32,000
Marketing staff support	100%	30%	70%
Marketing staff cost	$480,000		

Problems

Problem 6.33
Customer-Level Costs
(LO 2)

FirstCredit, Inc. (FCI) wishes to trace its service costs to each customer type, rated A, B, or C. A customers are believed to be the most profitable, Bs might become profitable, and Cs are unprofitable. FCI offers commercial loans, consumer loans, and credit cards. Its customer representatives sell services and manage customer accounts. In addition, a staff and a facility support marketing, promotions, and transactions for all customers at an annual cost of $400,000. Use the following additional information to trace service costs to customers:

FCI Service Cost Information	Total	A	B	C
Number of customers	3,500	1,000	2,000	500
Customer representatives	22	10	10	2
Average salary/year		$50,000	$40,000	$30,000
Support service staff effort	100%	60%	30%	10%
Support service staff cost	$400,000			

Beaujolais Financial Group (BFG) segments its customers into premium members, who purchase extensive services, and standard members, who purchase minimal services. It offers premium members a 10 percent discount on the total package of services purchased but requires standard members to pay full price. BFG devotes one full-time customer representative per 100 premium members and one per 1,000 standard members. Customer representatives receive salaries and a bonus of 1 percent of customer revenue (after 10 percent discount, if applicable). BFG estimates that it spends twice as much on total promotions for premium members to encourage their loyalty. General and administrative cost, which is *not* traced to customers, is $2,400,000 per year.

Problem 6.34
Customer Profitability
(LO 2, 3)

Customer Service Resources	Total	Premium	Standard
Number of customers..	125,000	45,000	80,000
Average sales salary/year		$35,000	$35,000
Promotion costs	$2,000,000		
Average revenue per customer (before discount)		$440	$50

Required

a. Estimate BFG's customer and overall profitability.

b. Write a short memo that critiques BFG's customer service policies and measurements.

c. *Build your own spreadsheet.* Develop a spreadsheet to answer requirement (a).

Lightwave Manufacturing Assembly, Inc., provides outsourced manufacturing assembly for electronic products companies. It currently has two major customers, MBI and TS, for which Lightwave assembles and delivers products on a just-in-time basis. Lightwave incurs annual warehousing and delivery costs solely to serve its customers. Warehousing costs are found to be proportional to the number of orders. Half of annual general and administrative costs are related to processing and managing customer orders; the remainder is not traced to customers.

Problem 6.35
Customer Profitability
(LO 2, 3)

Customer and Administrative Resources	Total	MBI	TS
Annual number of orders...	3,200	1,200	2,000
Average cost of goods sold per order...		$5,000	$2,000
Order price markup..		60%	60%
Average deliveries per order..		5	10
Warehousing costs per year	$1,000,000		
Delivery costs per year	3,100,000		
General administrative costs..	2,400,000		

Required

a. Estimate Lightwave's customer and overall profitability.

b. Write a short memo that critiques Lightwave's customer service policies and measurements.

c. *Build your own spreadsheet.* Develop a spreadsheet to answer requirement (a).

Bow House Architectural, Ltd. (BHA), produces commercial and residential architectural designs for national and regional construction firms. It submits designs in competitive bidding and considers the costs of unsuccessful designs as a cost of sales. Marketing efforts have focused on increasing sales of specific designs, but administrative efforts have focused on customer relations. Use this information to complete the following requirements:

Problem 6.36
Customer Profitability
(LO 2, 3)

Design Activities	Total	Residential	Commercial
Designs submitted	2,700	2,500	200
Designs sold..	2,100	2,000	100
Average direct cost per design (all)		$4,000	$25,000
Average markup..		100%	150%
Marketing effort	100%	20%	80%
Marketing cost	$2,400,000		

Customer Activities and Resources	Total	Regional	National
Traced sales of			
Residential designs	100%	60%	40%
Commercial designs..	100	20	80
Administrative effort	100	60	40
Administrative cost...	$3,000,000		

Required

a.   Estimate BHA's customer profitability for regional and national customers.

b.   Even if national design customers are less profitable than regional design customers why might BHA continue to seek them?

Problem 6.37
Customer Profitability
(LO 2, 3)

Concrete Constructors Corp. (CCC) is a subcontractor that specializes in installing concrete curbs, gutters, and driveways for commercial and residential development projects. It serves two types of customers, custom home builders and large general contractors. CCC obtains work from the general contractors via a competitive bidding process; its success rate has been 50 percent. It has long-term relationships with several custom home builders, and bidding with them has been 92 percent successful. Use this information to complete the following requirements. You must make judgments of how to assign bidding costs and whether to assign general and administrative costs.

Annual Activities and Resources	Total	Custom Home Builders	General Contractors
Bids submitted—residential	32	22	10
Bids submitted—commercial	13	3	10
Successful bids—residential	24	20	4
Successful bids—commercial	9	3	6
Success rate		92%	50%
Average direct cost of residential job		$10,500	$410,000
Average direct cost of commercial job		$45,000	$250,000
Average markup over cost		100%	50%
Contract management cost	$800,000		
Contract management effort	100%	20%	80%
General administration cost	$410,000		
Bidding cost	$630,000		

Required

a.   Estimate CCC's customer profitability.

b.   Do you have any reservations about the accuracy of this analysis? If so, discuss them.

Problem 6.38
Customer Profile
(LO 2)

Frederick Squab Brokerage (FSB) offers online securities trading and other services, such as financial planning and portfolio management. It is considering following the lead of competitors that segment their customers and focus marketing efforts. FSB believes that its customers can be segmented by the equally important attributes of account balance, trading frequency, and purchase of other services. These represent major uses of resources to serve customers and drivers of revenue. Following are the data from a random sample of 30 FSB customers.[9]

Random Sample of Customers			
Customer	Account Balance	Trades/Yr	Other Services
1	$29,396	135	0
2	85,679	30	1
3	11,027	41	6
4	50,512	31	0
5	20,960	164	13
6	17,674	13	11
7	18,026	10	3
8	32,546	49	11
9	13,738	172	4
10	4,370	20	2
11	42,881	135	1
12	23,988	38	8
13	35,950	24	6
14	26,398	12	0

---

[9] Note that for some companies, it is feasible to generate these data for millions of customers; sampling can be more efficient, especially in a textbook! (*Hint* to the instructor: The linked problems 6.38–6.41 are easier to answer if data are provided to students electronically.)

Random Sample of Customers

Customer	Account Balance	Trades/Yr	Other Services
15	28,470	11	19
16	42,749	92	0
17	604	14	1
18	54,789	120	2
19	86,367	171	17
20	22,192	3	1
21	17,517	40	8
22	72,023	171	3
23	23,609	52	5
24	25,076	8	1
25	65,984	59	16
26	50,003	107	4
27	897	6	0
28	3,455	47	10
29	51,743	138	9
30	31,791	30	3

Complete the following in small groups.

Required

a. Use this information to develop numerical scores for each customer attribute by classifying customers into no more than four categories within each attribute (e.g., scoring = 1, 2, 3, or 4). (*Hint:* Enter the data into a spreadsheet, such as Excel, and then plot each customer attribute and look for "natural" cutoffs for categories. *Note:* This is somewhat subjective but critically important to this type of analysis.)

b. Add individual attribute scores to obtain overall scores. Use overall scores to segment customers into no more than three categories (A = best, B = middle, and C = worst). You must judge where to make cutoffs here, too.

c. Express any concerns you have about this classification. How can you improve it or validate it?

Refer to the data and results of Problem 6.38. In small groups, complete the following.

Required

a. For each customer type (A, B, and C), estimate for the entire customer population the percentage of each type, average account balance, average number of trades, and average number of other services purchased. (*Hint:* This is easily done with Excel's Pivot Table function wizard [look under the Data menu].)

b. FSB charges customers for other services based on the extent and quality of services used. Interest on account balances and trading fees are the same for each customer type. Fill in the following table and estimate FSB's customer-level revenues.

Problem 6.39
Customer Activities and Revenues
(LO 2)

Customer Revenue Data	A	B	C
Customer sample percentages	?	?	?
Customer population (1,000,000)	?	?	?
Average account balance	?	?	?
Average annual trades	?	?	?
Average other services	?	?	?
Account revenue (spread)	2%	2%	2%
Trading fee per trade	$ 3	$ 3	$ 3
Other fees per service	$200	$100	$50

Refer to the data and results of Problems 6.38 and 6.39. In small groups, complete the following.

Problem 6.40
Customer Costs and Profitability
(LO 2)

Required

a. Use this additional information to estimate FSB's uses of resources to manage each customer service. Intensity of service means that FSB uses three times as many service resources to provide "other" services for A customers than for C customers.

Customer Cost Data	A	B	C
Intensity of service per unit of service:			
Account management per account	1	1	1
Trading management per trade	1	1	1
Other services management per service	3	2	1
General and administrative..	3	2	1
Service costs:			
Account management...$250,000,000			
Trading management	310,000,000		
Other services management	440,000,000		
General and administrative	360,000,000		

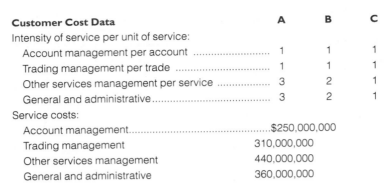

b.   Estimate overall and customer profitability.

Problem 6.41
Customer-Level
Improvements
(LO 3)

Refer to Problems 6.38–6.40. FSB has identified two alternatives to improve its overall profitability:

1.   Drop unprofitable customers; although this will lose those customers' margins, it will save 15 percent of overall committed management costs.

2.   Change fees to induce unprofitable customers to either leave or become more profitable and induce more customers to increase their revenue-generating activities. Marketing research indicates changes in the percentage of types of customers as follows. Other customer characteristics, service intensities, and costs remain unchanged.

Customer Revenue Data	Total	A	B	C
Customer sample 100.0%		45.0%	50.0%	5.0%
Account revenue (spread)	NA	1.5%	2.0%	3.0%
Trading fee per trade..........................	NA	$2.50	$3.00	$4.00
Other fees per service........................	NA	$180.00	$120.00	$150.00

In small groups, complete the requirements.

Required

a.   Measure the profit impact of each alternative.

b.   Prepare a report that makes and evaluates recommendations for profit improvement.

Cases

Case 6.42
Customer Profitability
(LO 1, 2, 3)

FirstBank of Rock Creek recently spent $400,000 to develop and implement a customer profitability analysis system that calculates the monthly profitability of each of its 40,000 customers.[10] This system also maintains extensive customer-level information about banking and demographic history. FirstBank offers the following services to its customers. (Note: Many customers use multiple services.)

Service	Average Annual Profit per Account
Checking account...	$ 50
Savings account	40
Safety deposit	20
Certificate of deposit account..	300
Consumer loan	400
Home equity line of credit	500

FirstBank plans to use its customer profitability information to identify opportunities to market and cross-sell other services, such as home equity lines of credit, to checking and savings account customers. In small groups, prepare a report or presentation that answers the requirements.

---

[10] Adapted from Peter Carroll and Madhu Tadikonda, "Customer Profitability: Irrelevant for Decisions?"; Claire Green, "Profitability Measurement for Small-Business Banking: A Strategic View"; and Gautam Bose and Erick Haskell, "Keeping the Ones with the 'Right Stuff.'"

Required

a. Explain what information you want from the customer profitability analysis system to identify checking and savings account customers most likely to be interested in other banking services.

b. Consider the following two checking-account customers with nearly equal and above average profitability. Does selling a home equity loan to each have equal expected profitability? Explain.

Annual Customer Information	Ms. Smith	Mr. Jones
Profit from checking account	$ 76	$ 76
Average checking account balance	$14,000	$900
Number of checks written	230	60
Number of ATM transactions	24	36
Number of returned checks	0	8
Overdraft fees paid	0	8

c. *Build your own spreadsheet:* Develop a spreadsheet to answer (b).

Corporate Express, the world's largest supplier of office supplies to major corporations, recently hired you as a new financial analyst. The company takes orders from its customers' employees via the Internet, processes them with office supply manufacturers, and delivers the supplies to the employees who ordered them. Its customers do not need to hire anyone to order, receive, or distribute supplies. Customers also do not need supplies inventories or warehouses. Large customers (like Coca-Cola and Hewlett-Packard) save millions of dollars per year by outsourcing their office supply tasks to Corporate Express.

Case 6.43
Customer Profitability
(LO 2, 3)

The vice president of marketing believes it is worthwhile to offer limited services to small, rapidly growing businesses because they could graduate to the full line of services offered to large companies. After analyzing the profitability of serving small and large customers, you have developed the following information for typical customers:

Annual Data	Representative Large Company (500 firms)
Average number of orders per year	2,000
Average sales value of supplies per order	$600
Average cost of supplies to Corporate Express as a percentage of sales	80%
Average processing cost per order	$40
Average delivery cost per order as a percentage of sales	5%
Average cost to maintain Internet access per customer per year	$ 2,000
Marketing management, average hours per customer	100
Marketing management, total annual cost (25 employees, 2,000 hours per year)	$ 1,250,000
Advertising and promotion, total annual cost	$ 2,000,000
Maintaining electronic catalogue, total annual cost	$ 4,000,000
General and administrative support, total annual cost	$28,000,000

You believe that small companies will place one-tenth as many orders per year as a large company and the amount of an average order will be approximately $500. Marketing management time is discretionary, but you estimate that 25 hours per year should be sufficient to manage a small company account. You are unsure how to trace advertising and promotion, electronic catalogue, and general and administrative costs but suggest allocating advertising and promotion on a per customer basis. Individually or in small groups, prepare a visual and verbal presentation that explains the required items.

Required

a. Compute the annual profit generated from an average large and small company.

b. If your analysis is correct, is it a worthwhile use of scarce capacity to add 10 small customers rather than one large customer? Why or why not?

c. Can you recommend possible ways to make small-customer business attractive to Corporate Express?

d. What improvements in tracing costs do you recommend?

e. *Build your own spreadsheet:* Develop a spreadsheet to answer (a).

Chapter 7

Managing Quality and Time to Create Value

After completing this chapter, you should be able to:

1. Evaluate the similarities and differences of total quality management and return-on-quality approaches to managing quality.

2. Measure and analyze the dimensions of quality with commonly used diagrams, charts, and reports.

3. Understand and explain the importance of managing process time.

4. Measure and manage productivity and capacity.

5. Evaluate how just-in-time methods create benefits by combining management of quality, time, productivity, and capacity.

6. Understand how to construct and use control charts (Appendix).

Cost-*Management* Challenges

(Solutions are on page 275.)

1. **Managing** quality seems to be a general management task, so what can cost-management analysts provide to improve this important activity?

2. **Is** there a conflict between meeting quality and time goals, or do these goals reinforce each other?

3. **How** should cost-management analysts choose among all available quality and time-management tools?

Dedication to quality and customer response time overcomes skeptical bankers

Fast-growing firm sets the pace in the customer service industry

By Harley Earl, Business Correspondent, Dissociated Press
Chicago: The concept of the company was revolutionary—some thought it audacious. The first loan officer to review Chicago-based TCSI's (Transformation Customer Services, Inc.) embryonic business proposal was less than diplomatic. Rhonda Cooper, the company's dynamic CEO, remembers his exact words as, "That is just about the craziest idea I have ever heard. There is no way that I would authorize lending you what you ask, even with your personal assets as collateral. I strongly believe that this is a flawed business concept. First of all, I cannot believe that any business would outsource its customer service representatives—its front-line with the customer—to anyone. Second, if they were to outsource customer service, why would they use you? You have no track record. You don't know their business, their customers, or their competitors. And that raises a third concern—what if you do know their competitors? How could any business be sure that sensitive customer information would not leak to the competition? I'm sorry, but you have come to the wrong place, Ms. Cooper. Have you considered a fast-food franchise?"

"I almost punched him out," a laughing Ms. Cooper recalls, still visibly affected by the banker's lack of vision.

Although that initial refusal hurt deeply, Ms. Cooper took away the message that her company would have to communicate clearly and demonstrate that TCSI would and could provide the highest quality service.

Ten years after that shaky start, Ms. Cooper's company provides services to many large and mid-sized companies in the US, Europe, and the Pacific Rim. TCSI has been one of the fastest growing service companies on the NASDAQ-AMEX exchange. Depending on the vagaries of the market, TCSI's common stock currently is worth nearly US$1 billion. Not bad for a startup that began in a renovated school annex with two employees, one phone line, and two personal computers.

TCSI employees and managers are relentless in their pursuit and maintenance of quality because a slip in quality of service could give competitors the opening they are looking for. "We have no intention of losing any of our valued clients to competitors or our competitive edge based on quality and customer response time," pledges Ms. Cooper. "We religiously measure and manage the quality of our personnel, processes, and services because we know that people pay attention to what gets measured and evaluated."

With a keen sense of irony, Ms. Cooper recently signed a contract to provide a full range of customer services for a large bank holding company that recently bought the very bank that had refused to loan her start-up capital 10 years ago. "I noticed that my original, would-be banker is no longer with the bank. Too bad, I would have liked to ask him how I could help him improve his customer service."

This chapter discusses the methods and measures that TCSI and other companies concerned about product and service quality use to stay ahead of the competition. The chapter describes eight important cost-management tools: histograms, control charts, run charts, cause-and-effect diagrams, scatter diagrams, flowcharts, Pareto charts, and cost-of-quality reports. They are presented as useful tools for monitoring process quality, time, productivity, and capacity and for preventing mistakes in meeting customer needs. The chapter also discusses the way that just-in-time methods combine concerns for managing quality, time, productivity, and capacity.

Many organizations use measures of quality, time, productivity, and capacity to evaluate performance. The measurement details presented in this chapter are very important to later chapters in this book that discuss uses of these measures.

Importance of Quality

You undoubtedly have experienced poor-quality service or defective merchandise and, as a result, might have decided never to deal with that particular organization again. As a result of poor quality, the company lost you as a customer, which concerns organizations and motivates them to provide quality products and services. Many chief financial officers (CFOs) believe that the most important changes in their companies' strategies in recent years have been to improve customer satisfaction and product quality. In today's globally competitive environment, improving quality is clearly a high priority for all organizations.

Cost Management in Practice 7.1

Effects of Quality

The effects of quality, good or bad, on the fortunes of companies are not limited to any economic sector or region. Silicon Graphics Inc., the computer company behind the dinosaurs of *Jurassic Park,* did not pay attention to the quality of its lower-end products and missed lucrative Internet opportunities taken over by high-quality, low-cost personal computers. The Warsaw (Poland) Marriott Hotel, in contrast, quickly recognized the importance of quality service in Poland's newly opened market and, by stressing quality in its hiring and training activities, is now rated by guests as among the top five in the international chain.

The Alexander Doll Co. has managed to keep top customers, such as FAO Schwartz, Disney, and Saks, and to grow, even in its high-cost New York location. "Our costs are offset by the benefits of producing here. Number one is that we are on hand every day to oversee and control the quality of the product. We can respond quickly to customers' needs," explained CEO Patricia Lewis. European winemakers, long used to world leadership, lost significant market share to North and South American and Australian competitors that offered higher-

quality wine at lower prices. European wine prices crashed in the 1990s as consumers worldwide reacted to their uneven quality. Some European winemakers took extended visits to American and Australian wineries to learn how to improve the quality of their products. The result of increased quality has been a resurgence of French and Italian wine sales. *Sources: R. D. Hof, "The Sad Saga of Silicon Graphics"; P. Simpson, "As Workers Turn into Risk-Takers . . . One Plant Really Turns on the Steam"; I. J. Dugan, "If They Can Make it There . . . ." (Full citations to references are in the Bibliography.)*

Costs of Improving Quality

Should organizations try to improve their quality—at any cost? Several years ago, that was the prevailing belief. However, there are now two somewhat competing approaches to improving product and service quality:

1. Total quality management.

2. Return on quality, a traditional view of quality that is reemerging.

LO 1 Evaluate the similarities and differences of total quality management and return-on-quality approaches to managing quality.

Total Quality Management (TQM)

Total quality management (TQM) is the view that improvements in quality, as defined by customers, always result in improved organizational performance because improving quality improves efficiency as problems are identified and eliminated. Furthermore, the quest for improved quality is never finished. TQM advocates, inspired by W. Edwards Deming, argue that customers seek the highest-quality products and services and are willing to pay a premium for them.[1] Thus, TQM advocates have claimed that "quality is free" or, more precisely, that improving quality more than pays its own way by creating higher profits. The TQM perspective assumes that quality can and should always be improved, with exceeding customers' quality expectations being the goal. Since customers define quality, customer satisfaction and product or service quality are closely linked. Quite naturally, adopters of TQM assume that increased customer satisfaction and product and service quality are the lead indicators of improved profits.

Return on Quality (ROQ)

Return on quality (ROQ) is the view that assumes a trade-off between the costs and benefits of improving quality. Although ROQ advocates believe quality is extremely important, they argue that the highest profits are obtained at an optimum quality level of products and services, which maximizes profits rather than quality.[2] The optimum quality level almost always is lower than the **maximum quality level,** which is total delight of the customer or zero defects, depending on one's definition of quality. Total delight occurs when a customer receives a product or service that far exceeds his or her expectations of quality. A **defect** is an attribute (tangible or intangible) that falls short of customer expectations. According to the ROQ view, at some point, the cost of improving quality must exceed the benefits of increased revenues. In other words, the ROQ approach argues that there can be too much quality, too few defects, and too much customer satisfaction because costs of improved quality could increase at a higher rate than revenues. Even if the ROQ approach is more profitable, however, it might not be the basis of an effective marketing campaign. Furthermore, ROQ might lead to complacency with current levels of quality, whereas TQM is relentless in its search for continuous improvement.

Exhibit 7–1 contrasts the TQM and ROQ views of quality. As the top graph shows, the TQM view implicitly assumes that the maximum profit is achieved at the maximum quality level because total revenues from increasing quality always should grow faster than total costs. ROQ, on the other hand, assumes that less-than-maximum quality maximizes profits. Regardless of the approach, the difference between total revenues and total costs represents profit. The bottom graph shows that ROQ

---

[1] For a classic discussion of quality, see W. E. Deming, *Automobile Magazine,* "A Seminal Thinker Takes a Detailed Look at the Quality of Quality."

[2] See R. Rust, A. Zahorik, and T. Keiningham, "Return on Quality (ROQ): Making Service Financially Accountable." ROQ also is similar to the notion of "reasonable assurance" in auditing—it might be uneconomical to detect all defects in financial reporting.

Exhibit 7–I

TQM versus ROQ Views of Quality

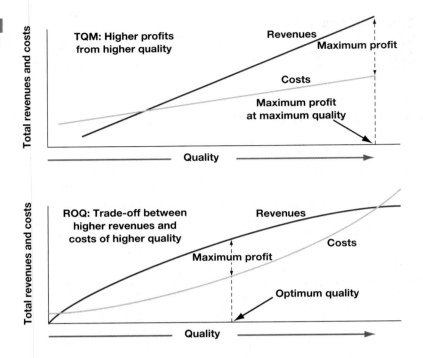

assumes that the total revenue and total cost lines converge at high levels of quality and even may cross, reducing profits. Accordingly, beyond the ROQ optimum level of quality, profits actually decline. Note that the TQM revenue and cost lines in Exhibit 7–1 might not be straight lines, but the difference between them is assumed to increase with increases in quality.

Comparison of the Views of Quality

The ROQ view of quality for many years was the traditional view, but the TQM movement eclipsed it in the 1980s as quality became a primary source of global competitive advantage. The ROQ view of quality and customer satisfaction has regained prominence in recent years as many companies have achieved parity in quality, and in response to observing the fate of some winners of prestigious quality awards. A number of companies that have strenuously and successfully improved quality and received prizes for their efforts have seen profits drop alarmingly, and some have been forced to declare bankruptcy. Improved quality might not have been the root cause of financial decline in these companies, but ROQ advocates point out that improved quality, indicated by quality awards, did not prevent failure in these companies and does not guarantee success in other companies.

Conflict between TQM and ROQ

At the extremes of the two views, TQM and ROQ do conflict because ROQ's "optimum" quality is usually less than TQM's "maximum" quality. Martin Freeman, CFO at TCSI, prefers a middle position:

> TCSI believes strongly in providing high-quality customer service and uses TQM tools to measure quality. But that does not mean TCSI would bankrupt the company to do *everything* service partners or their customers might want. If service partners are willing to pay for higher-quality service, the company will do its best to provide it, knowing that our competitors will be trying to do the same. On the other hand, we do not take out the calculator every time we consider a quality issue. Since quality service is our whole business, sometimes TCSI decides to increase quality to meet its goals and competition. TCSI pays attention to the numbers but also relies on judgment in the final analysis.

Return on Quality

The TQM vs. ROQ debate could be characterized as a difference in assumptions about the behavior of *marginal revenues* (the revenue earned from additional sales of products or services) and *marginal costs* from additional increases in quality. TQM argues that marginal revenues will exceed marginal costs, but ROQ argues that at some point the marginal cost of increasing quality will exceed the marginal revenues earned. Chris Ittner and David Larcker used survey data to find that a quality-oriented strategy and management participation in quality were associated with higher performance in a sample of North American, German, and Japanese auto and computer manufacturers. The bottom-line question for organizations and researchers is, Do firms that manage for higher quality *sustain* higher profits? This is an exceedingly difficult question to answer because a short-term increase in profits might not be sustained in the long term as competitors react with their own quality-related initiatives.

Some financial research supports this concern. One study found that many companies, once rated as excellent for quality, experienced below-average stock price returns just a few years later. This indicates that gains from quality must be sustained by continued efforts to outdo the competition; otherwise, competitors quickly catch up. Additionally, profits could be affected by many influences that are contemporaneous with quality efforts, such as other value-chain activities to develop new products, advertise, and reconfigure supplier and distributor relations. *Sources: C. Ittner and D. Larcker,* "Quality Strategy, Strategic Control Systems, and Organizational Performance"; *and P. Coy,* "Researching the Nitty-Gritty of Quality Control."

Research Insight 7.1

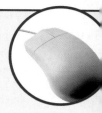

Dimensions of Quality

Customer-focused quality is a broad focus on meeting or exceeding customer expectations rather than a focus on only one of the dimensions of quality (as discussed later). TCSI measures its quality on two generally accepted quality dimensions: (1) *product* or *service attributes* and (2) *customer service* before and after the sale. TCSI believes that, to succeed in measuring and managing quality, it must understand customers' expectations on these two dimensions of quality.

Product and Service Attributes

A product's or service's attributes refer to its tangible and intangible features. Tangible features, in general, include performance, adherence to specifications, and functionality. Tangible features of TCSI's services include the following:

- Promptness of responses to customer inquiries.
- Accuracy of responses.
- Resolution of customer inquiries.
- Other criteria specific to each client.

Intangible features of products and services include reputation, taste, appearance, style, and appeal, which could be as important as tangible features to some customers. TCSI relies on its reputation for providing quality services as a major selling point to potential clients and a major factor in retaining current clients.

Customer Service before and after the Sale

Customers' perceptions of service before and after the sale influence whether they will become new customers and remain repeat customers. Customer service features include (among other activities):

- Provision of presale information.
- Proper treatment of customers by salespeople.
- On-time delivery to the customer after the product or service is ordered.
- Follow-up with customers after the sale.
- Timeliness and accuracy of resolution of questions and complaints.
- Warranty and repair services.

How Organizations Measure Quality

LO 2 Measure and analyze the dimensions of quality with commonly used diagrams, charts, and reports.

Determining customers' expectations and providing superior service are possible only if organizations are able to measure quality and provide helpful feedback to their members. To ensure that TCSI meets or exceeds customers' quality expectations on the two quality dimensions, the company first uses measures that indicate clients' and their customers' evaluations of service quality. Second, to measure the quality the company has delivered, TCSI also measures the satisfaction of clients and their customers with its services. TCSI uses measures similar to those used by other service and manufacturing companies that manage quality carefully.

How does TCSI know whether its quality is either sufficient or a problem? First, the company needs to identify indicators of customer-defined quality. If indicators show that the quality of products and services is deteriorating, the warning could, in turn, trigger an investigation to determine the cause so that the problem can be corrected before it becomes too large. Second, the company needs diagnostic information to suggest what the problem is and, perhaps, a way to solve it. We discuss each of these in turn.

Indicators of Quality

Organizations usually can measure tangible features of *products,* such as dimensions and functional performance, in time to correct faulty or substandard products before exposing them to customers. If the tangible features are important to customers, organizations can use these measures of the features as lead indicators of quality while manufacturing the product and before shipment.

Measuring tangible features of *services* in time to prevent problems is difficult because the service is not complete until the customer receives it. Therefore, service organizations often measure what they believe are lead indicators of service features. **Lead indicators** are measures that signal future outcomes of later operations. These include the capabilities of the personnel and technology that will provide the service.

Intangible features of products and services, such as appearance and appeal, generally occur after the customer receives the product or service. Measures of intangible features reflect customers' personal evaluations and must be obtained indirectly or by surveying current or potential customers.

Customer service features, such as treatment by salespeople and on-time delivery, are similar to intangible product or service features because they must be measured after the customer has had contact with the organization. Employees at TCSI (and other organizations) use several tools to measure lead indicators of quality, including histograms, run charts, and control charts.

Variation causes poor quality.   Quality experts believe that variation in process outcomes is a primary source of poor quality. Variability increases the chance for product and service attributes to disappoint customers. Most lead indicators of quality measure some form of variation in product or service attributes. For example, one of the attributes of TCSI's services that the company monitors is average length of time to resolve a customer complaint. TCSI believes that an optimum length of time exists; taking too much time frustrates the customer, but spending too little time increases the chance that the company will not understand and, therefore, will not react properly to the customer's true complaint.

Histograms.   A **histogram** is a chart that displays a frequency distribution, including the range and degree of concentration around an average value. A wider range, with less concentration, means more variation and increased likelihood that the customer received poor-quality service. Conversely, a narrower range, with tighter concentration, improves the likelihood that customers received good or high-quality service.

Exhibit 7–2 contrasts histograms of response times before and after improvements to TCSI's complaint resolution process. We discuss how cost-management analysts diagnosed the problem and worked with cross-functional teams to make

Exhibit 7–2   Histograms of Customer-Response Times, before and after Process Improvements

Panel A
Frequency before process improvements

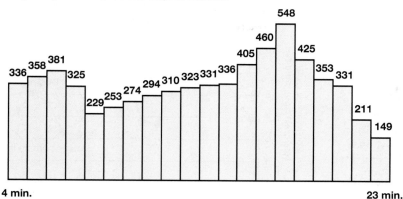

Panel B
Frequency after process improvements

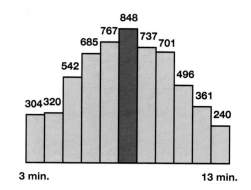

Customer response time:
average time = 13.52 min.
range = 4 to 23 min.

Customer response time:
average time = 7.95 min.
range = 3 to 13 min.

improvements later. Panel A of Exhibit 7–2 shows the range and concentration of response times during a week before improvements. Some variation is expected because not all complaints are the same. However, in response to customer satisfaction surveys, TCSI decided that response times varied too much, which led it to revise the process. Panel B reflects the effects of process improvements and shows a much tighter concentration (and lower average) of response times during a week after process improvements.

Because the distribution of response times is much tighter and centered around a lower average response time after process improvements, customers who call TCSI are more likely to have their problems resolved quickly and to be more satisfied with TCSI's service.

Run and control charts.   A **run chart** shows trends in variation in product or service attributes over time by reflecting measures of important quality features taken at defined points in time. Employees use run charts to identify persistent trends in important attributes that are adverse or beneficial to quality. Panel A of Exhibit 7–3 shows that TCSI's weekly, average customer-response time appears to be permanently lower after the company introduced process improvements in week 7. This chart reinforces the value of the decision to improve processes and provides some justification for more of the same effort.

A **control chart** also describes variation in product or service attributes over time by measuring important quality features. Additionally, it compares attributes to **upper** and **lower control limits,** which are the maximum- and minimum-desired levels of product or service features. A low level of variation in product or service features is desirable, but deviations that fall either above the upper control limit or below the lower control limit are unacceptable defects because the product or service will not perform reliably or customers will be disappointed by worse-than-expected intangible features.[3] Cost-management analysts usually prepare and analyze periodic charts such as those in Exhibit 7–3, but many organizations give individuals or teams direct responsibility for measuring product and service attributes as they perform their work so that they can detect any defects immediately and correct them before further processing or before shipping them to customers.

---

[3] The chapter Appendix presents an overview of technical details regarding the construction and use of control charts.

Exhibit 7–3   Run and Control Charts of Average Customer Response Time

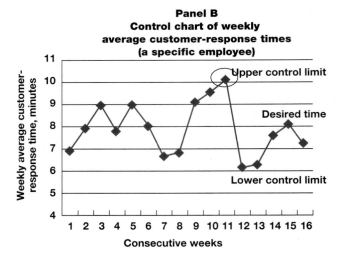

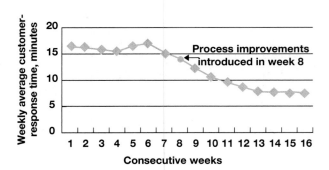

Organizations use summary control charts to distinguish between acceptable variations in quality and variations in performance that require further investigation. For example, TCSI evaluates each customer representative's average response time on a weekly basis. Employees whose average response times stray out of the acceptable region receive counseling or additional training. Employees whose performance is exceptionally good receive recognition for their work.

The control chart of one employee's weekly average response times (panel B of Exhibit 7–3) was within the control limits except during week 11 when the average time exceeded the upper control limit. The chart also shows that this employee's average times were trending toward the upper control limit during weeks 9 and 10. Although the average response time in week 9 does not look unusual by itself, the even higher time in week 10 signals a possible upward trend. Some organizations might intervene at this time even though the control limits have not been violated. By week 11, the employee had exceeded the upper limit, and the supervisor counseled the employee.

During counseling, the supervisor and employee discovered that the employee had become concerned about the reliability of the information supporting the new process improvements and was double-checking to be sure to give customers the right information. Upon investigation, the supervisor learned that the client had changed model numbers on several products but had not changed underlying product designs or information. This change, which had not been communicated to TCSI, was the cause of confusion. When customers called with problems, their products' model numbers did not match the documentation available to TCSI's employees. The succeeding weeks 12 and 13 show that the employee probably overcorrected and was tending toward the lower control limit before stabilizing (apparently) near the desired time.

Diagnostic Information

Lead indicator information identifies potential quality problems but usually does not diagnose their causes. Cost management analysts, often with team members from production and customer service, use a number of tools, including cause-and-effect diagrams, scatter diagrams, flow charts, and Pareto charts, to diagnose the causes of problems and to identify possible solutions.

Cause-and-effect diagrams.   Cause-and-effect analysis involves formulating diagnostic signals that identify potential causes of product or service defects. It first defines the defect, for example, *excessive and variable customer response time,* and

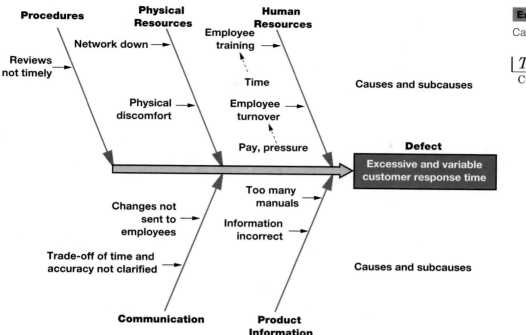

then the causes that could contribute to the problems. The potential causes of these problems in customer-response time can be deficiencies in:

- Human resources (e.g., inadequate training or staffing).
- Physical resources (e.g., insufficient capacity or availability).
- Procedures (e.g., inadequate or out of date).
- Information technology (e.g., unavailable or incorrect information).
- Communication (e.g., failure to communicate changes in procedures or objectives).

These causes often can be identified by asking the question, Why?, until the root cause of the problem is identified. As the causes are identified, the organization can develop and implement corrective measures.

TCSI's customers informed the company through customer satisfaction surveys that they were dissatisfied with both the length and variability of the time required to get a satisfactory response to their inquiries. TCSI was able to identify and correct causes of the problem by asking involved employees why response times were so long and variable. TCSI used a "fishbone," or Ishikawa, cause-and-effect diagram to analyze this problem. Exhibit 7–4 shows the information developed by a team of customer-service employees that answers the question. The defect, on the right of the diagram, was due to a number of related causes and subcauses, which are shown as "bones" on the diagram. For example, one of the causes identified by asking, Why?, was employee mistakes (Human Resources on the diagram). A second question— Why did employees make mistakes?—yielded two causes: employee training and employee turnover. A third—Why weren't employees properly trained?—yielded the cause (too little) time. A fourth—Why was employee turnover so high?—yielded the causes (too little) pay, (too much) pressure. TCSI researched each major bone of the diagram similarly to find causes of the defect.

Combining all information in Exhibit 7–4, the team determined that the most important root cause of the problem was complex product information that changed faster than employees could be trained to become familiar with it. TCSI's solution was to develop a centrally maintained, "intelligent" service database that allowed customer representatives to quickly diagnose and correct callers' service problems.

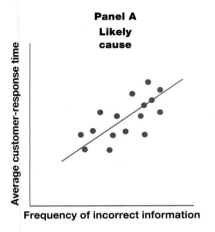

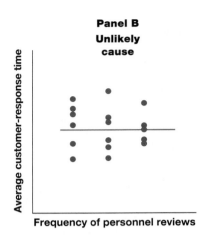

Exhibit 7–5

Scatter Diagrams

Transformation
Customer Services,Inc.

**Panel A
Likely
cause**

Average customer-response time

Frequency of incorrect information

**Panel B
Unlikely
cause**

Average customer-response time

Frequency of personnel reviews

TCSI's clients became responsible for entering changed and new product information directly into the database so the information that TCSI employees work with is always current.

The high cost of developing and maintaining this artificial-intelligence tool is justified by the large reduction in the time necessary to serve customers. In addition, the tool reduced stress and conflict in the workplace as well as employee turnover and discomfort. TCSI was able to find and develop a sophisticated information technology solution to its customer-response time problem. Furthermore, the company believed that this solution generated a positive return on quality (ROQ); that is, the benefits of increased sales from improved quality exceeded the costs of improving quality.

Scatter diagrams.   A **scatter diagram** is a plot of two measures that could be related. Such a plot helps analysts to diagnose the cause and effect between outcomes and the activities that might drive them. That is, changes in a value-added or non-value-added activity could cause or be associated with changes in a quality measure. Scatter diagrams are useful for diagnosing whether a suspected cause of a quality problem is really responsible. If plotted points hug a diagonal line, quality and other measures are more likely related. Knowing which of the two variables causes the other suggests a solution for the problem: change the cause to eliminate the problem. As panel A of Exhibit 7–5 shows, the quality measure, customer-response time, appears to be closely related to one suspected cause, frequency of incorrect information. Panel A indicates that as frequency of incorrect information increases, so does customer-response time. Thus, a reduction in the number of times TCSI's representatives received incorrect information resulted in a reduction in its customer-response time. Panel B, however, does not reflect any discernable relationship between customer-response time and another suspected cause of the problem, frequency of personnel reviews. The frequency of personnel reviews does not appear to affect customer-response time, which indicates that TCSI does not need to devote more resources to conducting frequent personnel reviews to reduce customer-response time. TCSI could have other reasons for frequent reviews, however.

A drawback to relying on scatter diagrams to diagnose causes of quality problems is that the organization must have sufficient reliable information on both quality measures and suspected causes. If sufficient data are not available, as is sometimes the case when processes or quality management efforts are new, the other diagnostic methods we discuss could be more helpful for identifying causes of quality problems.

Flowcharts.   A **flowchart** reflects cause-and-effect and sequential linkages among process activities. Knowing which activities cause or precede others in producing a product or offering a service can help diagnose where quality problems arise. Cost-management analysts also might prepare flowcharts to support systems analysis and auditing activities. The flowchart of the actual (not the ideal) customer-response process shown in Exhibit 7–6 helped the TCSI cost-management team discover that the root cause of excessive customer-response time resulted from working with

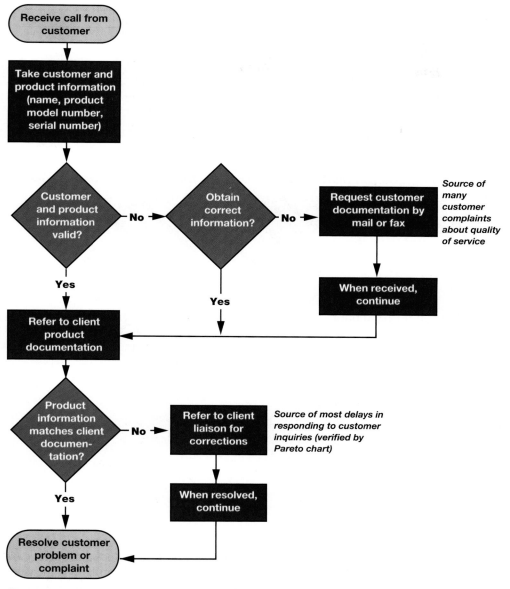

Exhibit 7–6

Customer Response
(to phone call) Activities
Flowchart

Transformation
Customer Services,Inc.

[Note: This last step has multiple activities depending on the nature
of problem or complaint, but a customer representative has
authority to resolve most issues.]

incorrect product information provided by the client. Comparing the actual process to an ideal process can highlight where improvements can be made. Identifying and eliminating non-value-added activities in processes often improves not only the efficiency of the process but also the quality of the product or service.

Pareto charts.   A **Pareto chart** (named after the Italian economist Wilfredo Pareto) prioritizes the causes of problems or defects as bars of varying height, in order of frequency or size. Pareto charts help analysis teams focus on the causes that could offer the greatest potential for improvement. Focusing on correcting the most frequent causes of quality problems, identified by Pareto charts, could show analysis teams where to focus initial efforts to make the most improvement in quality. Exhibit 7–7 is a Pareto chart for the causes of excessive customer-response time at TCSI before process improvements. This chart confirmed what customer representatives had told the analysis team: incorrect client information was responsible for most delays. Nonetheless, the Pareto chart identified other common causes of delays that TCSI also could correct, such as incorrect customer information and insufficient employee training.

Transformation
Customer Services,Inc.

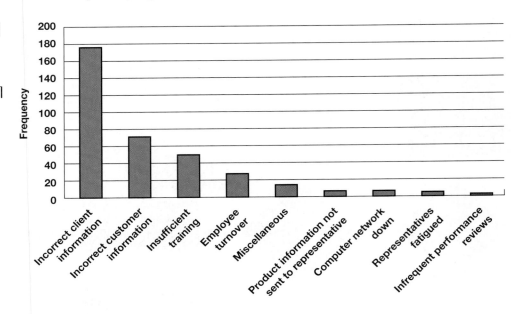

Organizations need both lead indicator and diagnostic information about activities to identify problems that require attention. However, most diagnostic information is expensive to collect, so cost management analysts might rely on lead indicators to signal the need to collect diagnostic information.

You're the Decision Maker 7.1

Using Diagnostic Quality Information

a. Do you think it is reasonable to delegate the responsibility for diagnosing quality problems to individuals in the departments where quality problems occur?

b. Would it always be better to use a cross-functional team (e.g., across departments or functions) to diagnose quality problems?

(Solutions begin on page 275.)

Customer Satisfaction

Customer satisfaction is the degree to which expectations of product attributes, customer service, and *price* have been or are expected to be met. Organizations measure customer satisfaction both as lead indicators of future sales and diagnostic tools to discover causes of unexpectedly low or high sales.

The most common methods of measuring customer satisfaction are phone or online surveys on which companies ask current or potential customers to rate attributes of products or services and customer service on a multiple-point scale. Many organizations outsource the actual measurement of customer satisfaction to benefit from both survey firms' expertise and the ability to generate more valid measures. TCSI market researchers, however, conduct their own customer satisfaction surveys because TCSI believes this is an area of its expertise. Other common measurement tools are to (1) ask focus groups of customers to evaluate real or proposed products or services and (2) use phantom, or unknown, shoppers, who really are employed by the agency evaluating the product or service and who report their experiences.

As an example of survey questions that TCSI asks clients and their customers, consider how clients and customers rate the *accuracy* of the customer services they have received from TCSI. Was it:

_____ Much better than expected?

_____ About as expected?

_____ Worse than expected?

By asking similar questions about all attributes of its services, TCSI is able to identify its strengths and problem areas as well as what clients and their customers really want. TCSI also uses customer satisfaction ratings to evaluate the performance of its employees and business units. Many organizations believe that strong links exist between meeting quality goals, customer satisfaction, and the organization's goals (e.g., profitability). These organizations might reinforce the importance of these linkages by tying customer satisfaction ratings to incentives for employees. Tying incentives to lead indicators of performance is covered in Chapter 21.

Trade-offs between Quality and Price

Market forces set competitive prices. Customers expect product or service attributes and customer service based on what is available at a comparable price from other sources. Customers buy the product or service that provides them the preferred mix of attributes, customer service, and price. If two products provide the same mix, for example, the customer most likely chooses the product with the lower price. Likewise, if an organization offers superior product attributes or customer service, it might be able to charge higher prices and/or increase its market share. Thus, trade-offs always are made among the various dimensions of a product's quality and its price. Decisions about the dimensions of quality are important cost and revenue drivers for any organization.

Costs of products and services are lead indicators of an organization's ability to meet market prices or offer competitive bid prices. Therefore, organizations that manage quality and the quality/price trade-off could also monitor costs and lead indicators of costs (e.g., changes in cost drivers).

Identifying Costs of Quality

The **costs of quality (COQ)** are the costs of activities to *control quality* and the costs of activities to correct *failure to control quality*. Costs to control quality are associated with lead indicators of imminent quality problems, and costs to correct failures could be lead indicators of future decreased sales.

COQ could be most valuable as a communication tool to inform employees at all levels of the magnitude and general sources of quality problems. Most organizations seek to spend most of their quality-improvement efforts on activities controlling quality rather than correcting quality failures. These organizations usually also have low total costs of quality. Organizations that spend most of their efforts on activities to correct quality failures usually have serious quality problems and excessive costs of quality.[4]

Controlling Quality

The two general activities to control quality are prevention activities and appraisal activities.

Prevention.   **Prevention** activities seek to prevent defects in the products or services being produced. Examples of prevention activities include the following:

- *Supplier certification.* Using only materials suppliers that can guarantee high quality.
- *Product design for manufacturability.* Designing products that can be made without defects.
- *Quality training.* Training employees to improve quality.
- *Quality evaluations.* Measuring or evaluating employees on their quality capabilities and performance to indicate or motivate improvements.
- *Process improvement.* Evaluating and improving processes to remove causes of defects.

---

[4] For examples of COQ reporting, see L. Carr, "Quality: Cost of Quality—Making It Work"; and S. Kalagnanam and E. M. Matsumura, "Quality: Costs of Quality in an Order Entry Department."

This TRW plant in Marshall, Illinois, manufactures air bag crash sensors. Workers become their own inspectors and are personally responsible for the quality of their outputs, an important component in total quality management.

TQM advocates argue that the most efficient use of quality resources is on prevention activities. Preventing defects, they argue, is the only value-added quality activity and the most profitable way to control quality. ROQ advocates agree that preventing defects is effective but also argue that preventing *all* defects could be prohibitively expensive. Some non-value-added quality activities in conjunction with activities that prevent defects could yield the most profitable level of quality.

Appraisal.   **Appraisal** activities (also called *detection* or *inspection* activities) inspect inputs and attributes of individual units of product or service to detect whether they conform to specifications or customer expectations and include the following:

- *Inspecting materials.* Inspecting production materials upon delivery.
- *Inspecting machines.* Ensuring that machines are operating properly within specifications.
- *Inspecting processes.* Manually inspecting the production process.
- *Performing automated inspection.* Using equipment to monitor the production process.
- *Employing statistical process control.* Using employees to inspect every unit for defects as they complete their productive activities (e.g., using control charts).
- *Sampling at end of process.* Inspecting the attributes of a sample of finished products to ensure quality.
- *Testing at end of process.* Testing the performance of all or a sample of finished products under the same or simulated conditions experienced by customers.
- *Field testing.* Testing products in use at customer sites.

Appraisal activities usually are recognized as non-value-added because customers do not pay for inspection—they pay for a high-quality product. Quality experts believe that appraisal activities can be avoided by placing more emphasis on preventing defects. To TQM advocates, an ideal process by design produces zero defects. ROQ advocates, as you can imagine, argue that this ideal process can, in fact, be unprofitable and that some small number of defects is optimal. Therefore, if preventing all defects is not feasible, some testing or appraisal is necessary. The earlier that testing can find defects, however, the lower the cost of defects is likely to be.

Failing to Control Quality

Failing to control quality causes internal failure and external failure activities. Organizations universally regard these as non-value-added activities.

Internal failure.   **Internal failure** activities are required to correct defective processes, products, and services that are detected before delivering them to customers. These include the following:

- *Disposing of scrap.* Recycling or dumping materials wasted in the production process.
- *Performing rework.* Correcting defects before the product or service is sold.
- *Reinspecting/Retesting.* Performing quality control testing after rework.
- *Delaying processes.* Reducing throughput because defective items are processed by scarce resources and must be scrapped or reworked—loss of irreplaceable scarce time.

Internal failures are non-value-added activities that can be quite costly—especially from lost processing time. Although this last internal failure activity can be the most costly, it is the most difficult to measure because it can affect future sales.

External failure.   **External failure** activities are required to correct defective products or services after they have been delivered to customers. They include:

- *Warranty repairs.* Repairing defective products.
- *Field replacements.* Replacing defective products at the customer's site.
- *Product liability settlements.* Responding to liabilities resulting from product failure.
- *Customer-complaint resolution.* Replacing products or services or adjusting billing to accommodate legitimate customer concerns about products or services received.
- *Restoration of reputation.* Engaging in marketing activities to improve the company's image tarnished from poor product quality.
- *Lost sales.* opportunity costs from decreases in sales resulting from poor-quality products (current and potential customers will go to competitors).

External failure activities could be the most costly because of their effects on the organization's reputation. Although the out-of-pocket costs of these activities can be large, they can be small compared to the opportunity costs of future sales. Because external failure costs have such harmful potential, TQM advocates argue that nearly every activity that would prevent an external failure is cost effective. This argument is difficult to refute because the opportunity costs of forgone sales can be very high but are difficult to measure objectively.

Measuring Costs of Quality

Organizations that use ABC and ABM have the activity-based information necessary to compile cost-of-quality information. The only additional step beyond ABM is classifying activities according to the cost-of-quality category, as described earlier. Simply sorting the activity-cost data by cost-of-quality classification yields the cost of the quality measures.

Reporting Costs of Quality

Organizations usually sort costs of quality by quality activity and express them as a percentage of sales. Some companies with serious quality problems might spend as much as 30 to 40 percent of sales on quality activities. Companies with excellent quality might spend much less than 10 percent of sales, and most of that cost is for prevention activities. In general, enhancing prevention activities should increase value while decreasing or eliminating the need for inspection, internal failure, and external failure activities.

An example of a quarterly COQ report prepared by cost management analysts for one of TCSI's business units appears in Exhibit 7–8. This report indicates that TCSI spent the most on prevention activities (e.g., value-added quality training and process evaluations). As is typical in companies with excellent quality, this was the largest amount spent on any of the four quality activity categories. More than half of the business unit's cost of quality was on non-value-added activities, as shown in Exhibit 7–9. CFO Freeman instructed the business unit manager to find ways to reverse that percentage while increasing quality of service.

TCSI believes that COQ information is not sufficient by itself to manage quality since it does not measure the quality of services delivered to customers or their satisfaction with services received. However, Freeman uses the COQ information prepared by his staff as one indication of the company's success in managing quality. He looks to see that COQ is less than 10 percent of sales in total and that most of the quality activities are for preventing mistakes, not correcting those that could have been avoided. Note that TCSI does not explicitly measure the opportunity cost of lost business; it uses qualitative measures of forgone sales from customer satisfaction surveys and measures of customer retention (repeat sales).

Exhibit 7–8

Cost-of-Quality Report
First Quarter

Transformation
Customer Services,Inc.

	Amounts		Percent of Sales
Sales..		$1,765,000	100%
Prevention activities:			
Training	$32,829		
Process evaluation...	21,886	$ 54,715	3.10%
Appraisal activities:			
Performance measurement	24,092		
Performance reviews	10,325	34,417	1.95%
Internal failure activities:			
Wasted time	3,883		
Revision of incorrect information	15,532	19,415	1.10%
External failure activities:			
Redoing customer service.................................	6,142		
Resolving complaints with TCSI service.............	9,213	15,355	0.87%
Total costs of quality		$ 123,902	7.02%

Exhibit 7–9

Relative Proportions of
Quality Costs at TCSI

Transformation
Customer Services,Inc.

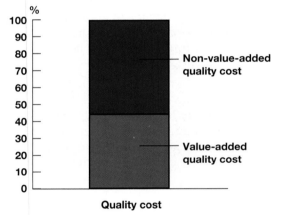

Note: Appraisal, internal failure, and external failure activities are regarded as non-value-added.

You're the Decision Maker 7.2

Evaluating the Cost of Quality

Some accountants ask this question about COQ: Are we really making a difference, or is COQ just another report? Evaluate these claims about the value of COQ.

a. COQ allows the organization to focus on the reduction or elimination of non-value-added costs of quality.

b. COQ is a better measure of performance than traditional operating income because costs of quality are not buried in FIFO cost of sales.

c. COQ provides a target (e.g., 4 percent of sales for total COQ) that really measures the progress of quality improvements in concrete terms. *Source: Adapted from S. Brinkman and M. Appelbaum, "The Quality Cost Report: It's Alive and Well at Gilroy Foods."*

(Solutions begin on page 275.)

Corporate Integrity and Quality

At a recent World Economic Forum, 1,500 corporate top execcutives were asked to indicate the most important measures of their companies' success. Less than 20 percent indicated that profitability was the most important measure. Another 27 percent said that quality of their products was the most important measure, and 24 percent stated that reputation and integrity of the companies' brands was most important.[5]

---

[5] "Two-faced Capitalism," *The Economist.*

Quality Awards and Certificates

Quality has become so important to success that currently many prestigious, internationally recognized awards are given to companies for quality by nearly every country and many professional organizations. For example, the **Malcolm Baldrige National Quality Award,** created by the United States Congress in 1987, recognizes US firms with outstanding records of quality improvement and quality management.[6] The **Deming Prize,** created in Japan by the Japanese Union of Scientists and Engineers long before the Baldrige Quality Award, is awarded to companies around the world that excel in quality improvement.[7]

The International Organization for Standardization, based in Europe, developed **ISO 9000,** which is a set of international standards for quality management. The ISO standards first gained popularity in Europe but are now global guidelines for the design, development, production, final inspection and testing, installation, and servicing of products, processes, and services. To be certified, a company must document its quality systems and pass a rigorous third-party audit of its manufacturing and customer-service processes.[8]

Organizations proudly display their quality awards and certificates as evidence of their commitment to product and service quality. Many organizations have adopted Baldrige or Deming prize criteria as their internal quality management guidelines even if they do not seek to win a prize for their efforts. TCSI, for example, has adopted criteria from both the Baldrige and Deming awards and has obtained ISO 9000 certification.

Importance of Managing Time in a Competitive Environment

TCSI and other successful organizations realize that competitive markets continuously demand shorter:

LO 3 Understand and explain the importance of managing process time.

- New product and service development time.
- Customer response time.
- Cycle time.

Accordingly, TCSI focuses on improving the three dimensions of time in all of its business units. This requires that all major business unit activities have time-measurement objectives. Improvements in response time can require simplifying and shortening work processes and almost always require improvements in quality. Poor quality, which requires inspection, testing, and rework, is a major cause of the excessive use of time. Eliminating the causes of poor quality, therefore, can shorten process time dramatically. Just-in-time management approaches simultaneously manage quality and time. Furthermore, some argue that quality and time are inextricably linked.

New Product (or Service) Development Time

New product (or **service**) **development time** is the period between the first consideration of a product and its initial sale to the customer. Firms that respond quickly to customer needs for new products and services can develop an advantage over competitors. For example, Honda and Toyota have identified US consumers' need for fuel-efficient cars. Early development has given Honda and Toyota a competitive advantage for several years. Likewise, TCSI was one of the first companies to recognize the market's need for outsourced customer services and continues to try to anticipate new market opportunities.

---

[6] See the Web site *www.quality.nist.gov* for details and recent winners.

[7] The Web site *www.deming.org/demingprize/index.html* describes the prize. Recent winners include Fuji Photo Optical Co. (*www.fujinon.co.jp*) and Lucent Technologies (*www.lucent.com*).

[8] A Web search on the keywords "ISO 9000" will overwhelm you with millions of "hits." View the ISO homepage at *www.iso.org.*

Exhibit 7–10

Customer-Response Time

Transformation
Customer Services, Inc.

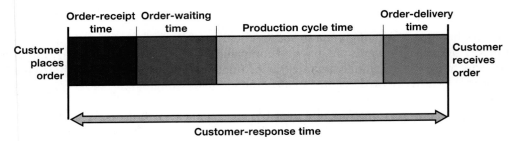

Order-receipt time   Order-waiting time   Production cycle time   Order-delivery time

Customer places order   Customer receives order

Customer-response time

Customer-Response Time and Cycle Time

Customer-response time is the amount of time between a customer's placing an order for a product or requesting service and delivering the product or service to the customer. The shorter the response time, the more competitive the company is on this dimension. The components of customer-response time appear in Exhibit 7–10. Improvements can be possible in all components. For example, many companies have reduced order-receipt time by incorporating electronic ordering (via wide area networks or the Internet). Electronic ordering also reduces chances for human errors in the ordering process. Organizations minimize order-waiting time by scheduling bottleneck resources carefully and by keeping some reserve capacity for unexpected but valuable orders. Companies also minimize order-delivery time by using overnight delivery services or, in the case of services, delivering them electronically. Most dramatic improvements in customer-response time could be made possible by eliminating non-value-added and poor-quality related activities in **production cycle time,** which is the elapsed time between starting and finishing a production process, including any time to correct mistakes.

Costs of Time

The old adage, "Time is money," has never been more true. Longer process times mean both higher out-of-pocket costs for human and physical resources and higher costs of forgone opportunities. In fact, time can be the scarcest resource of all. Individuals and organizations with good ideas can always obtain more money, but adding capacity and capability without improving processes and quality can perpetuate inefficiencies that reduce competitiveness. Attractive alternatives can be ignored because of insufficient time to analyze opportunities.

Some manufacturing companies allocate overhead costs to business units and products using cycle time as the cost-driver base although this allocation approach might not accurately measure the use of support resources or the opportunity costs of wasted time, it does get employees' attention. If evaluations and incentives are based on costs or profits, allocations based on cycle time also should motivate employees to improve processes to reduce cycle time. These organizations can use only costs or

---

Cost Management in Practice 7.2

Benefits of Managing Time

Many organizations report dramatic improvements in performance as a result of focusing on time management. For example, St. Joseph's Hospital near Atlanta redesigned its health care processes to reduce postsurgery hospital stays. As a result, quality of care increased, costs declined as much as one third for some procedures, and patients were more satisfied and healthier. The bottom line was that the hospital's profits rose 67 percent in one year.

Opel, the German subsidiary of General Motors, reduced non-value-added movement of parts and excess inventories and installed JIT parts delivery and a spirit of continuous improvement. One vital key was hiring and training workers who can work in creative, responsible teams. As these time- and quality-based methods have spread throughout the company, Opel has become one of the few European carmakers poised to compete effectively in Europe after import restrictions on Japanese cars expired. GM hopes that the lessons learned at Opel can be applied to its US operations. *Source: Authors' research.*

profits as the basis for performance evaluation since measured profits are improved with cycle time reductions, and cycle time can be reduced and revenues maintained or increased only by improving quality. Since some measures are lead indicators of quality, however, relying only on current profits to motivate employees could lead to myopic behavior, such as ignoring the future effects of current actions. Some organizations rely on multiple, nonfinancial measures (e.g., the balanced scorecard) that are lead indicators of future profits to motivate employees to improve all areas of performance, not just current profits.

Management of Process Productivity and Efficiency

Process efficiency—the ability to transform inputs into throughput at the lowest cost—depends on having all employees work toward a common goal. **Throughput** is the amount of goods and services produced and delivered to customers during a period of time measured in dollar terms or physical measures. Managers need to know how well they are managing the organization's processes and activities. Employees can help identify inefficient or wasteful processes and activities to make improvements that meet customers' needs at lower cost.

LO 4 Measure and manage productivity and capacity.

Organizations manage two types of processes: production and business. **Production processes** directly result in the production of products or services provided to external customers. Examples of production processes include Boeing's machining aluminum stock into airplane parts, DataPlay's manufacturing miniature hard drives for MP3 music players, and TCSI's providing outsourced customer services. **Business processes** support or enable production processes. Examples of business processes include the materials-ordering processes that Boeing uses to ensure that the correct aluminum stock is on hand at just the right time for machining.

Common measures of efficiency of both production and business processes include, in addition to quality:

- Productivity
- Cycle time
- Throughput time ratio

Exhibit 7–11 shows that measures of throughput and production cycle time are summary measures of efficiency, affected by quality and productivity. A low cycle time—from receipt of an order of a unit of existing product (or service) to its packaging and shipment (delivery) to the customer—and high throughput are possible only if processes are productive, and processes are productive only if they are of high quality.

Measuring Productivity

Many possible measures exist to determine productivity. **Productivity** is the ratio of the outcomes of a process divided by the amount of resources necessary to complete the process. **Total factor productivity** is the value of goods and services (measured as sales revenue) divided by the total cost to provide them. This diagnostic tool is especially useful when benchmarked against that of competitors. For example, as shown in Exhibit 7–12, TCSI compared its total factor productivity for a recent year to that of its competitors in the industry by dividing each company's total sales by its

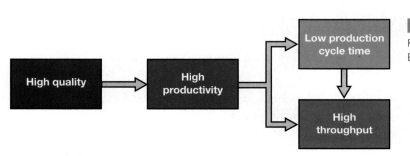

Exhibit 7–11

Relations among Process Efficiency Measures

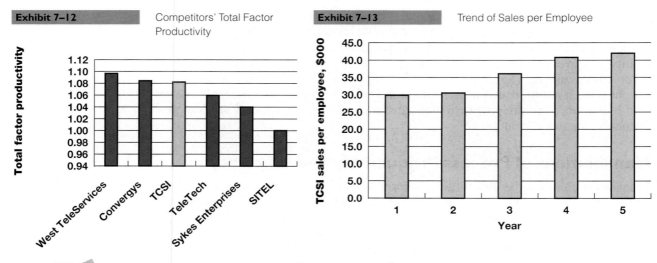

Exhibit 7–12   Competitors' Total Factor Productivity

Exhibit 7–13   Trend of Sales per Employee

Transformation
Customer Services, Inc.

total operating expenses. This type of information is freely available at Hoover's Online (www.hoovers.com). TCSI's total factor productivity is not the highest in the industry, and the company encourages employees to analyze all business and productive processes for ways to create more value at lower cost. Many employee suggestions for improvement (discussed earlier) focus on ways to reduce waste and improve the use of scarce resources.

More specific productivity measures compare outcomes valued by customers to the scarcest or most valuable resources used to achieve those outcomes, for example, sales revenue per employee. Last year, TCSI's sales revenue was $42,700 per employee. Is this good or bad? Productivity measures are meaningful only when compared over time or benchmarked against those of competitors. The historical trend of TCSI's sales revenue per employee shown in Exhibit 7–13 is increasing, which reflects improving sales productivity.

Measuring Cycle Time

Cycle time at TCSI includes the time elapsed from the start of a customer service call to its end. This definition of cycle time captures all processes that TCSI controls to deliver what customers expect: a quality service response in the shortest possible time.

In nearly all cases, customers and suppliers prefer short cycle times, which require a higher-quality product and fewer resources consumed by it. Therefore, low cycle times mean that organizations are delivering more customer value at lower cost, which is not possible without high quality and productive processes.

Average cycle time equals total processing time for all units divided by good units produced. To be most useful, average cycle time should include the average time necessary to complete and deliver all good units and dispose of units that have to be reworked or scrapped because of defects, which is non-value-added time.

Measuring Throughput Efficiency

Not all of the time a service or product spends in process is productive; that is, value is not added to it every minute of its cycle time. **Throughput efficiency** is the relation of throughput achieved to the resources used. The throughput time ratio measures throughput efficiency as follows:

Throughput time ratio = Value-added time ÷ Total processing time

In words, the throughput time ratio is the ratio of time spent adding customer value to products and services divided by total cycle time (also known as the "ratio of work content to lead time")

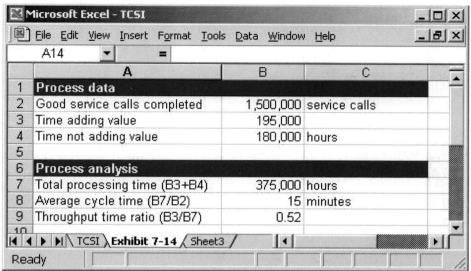

Exhibit 7–14

Analysis of Throughput Time

Transformation
Customer Services, Inc.

The highest possible value of this ratio is 1.00 or 100 percent, a theoretical ideal. Nonetheless, the closer an organization comes to a 100 percent throughput ratio, the more efficient its processes are, and the more quickly it can fill customers' orders. In some organizations, only 5 percent (or less) of its product or service cycle time is spent adding value; at least 95 percent of the time is wasted by waiting for processing or correcting mistakes. Efficient companies have achieved throughput time ratios of more than 50 percent by eliminating unnecessary delays and defects.

TCSI computes its throughput time ratio for service calls each week. See Exhibit 7–14 for a spreadsheet with data from a recent week. Value-adding time (cell B3: column B, row 3) includes receiving customers' calls, researching problems, giving advice, and ensuring that problems have been resolved. Time spent without adding customer value (B4) includes the time customers spend waiting on hold and for information as well as reworking defective or incomplete advice—activities that use scarce resources without creating anything for which customers are willing to pay. The average cycle time (B8) is the total processing time (B7) divided by the good service calls completed (units produced) during that time period (B2). A defective service call requires one or more return calls by the customer to resolve a problem. The throughput time ratio (B9) is the time spent adding value (B3) divided by total processing time (B7). Higher ratios (over time or across competitors) indicate better uses of the scarcest resource of all—time.

Managing Process Capacity

Process capacity is a measure of a process's *ability* to transform resources into valued products and services, usually expressed as a rate of processing inputs or generating outputs per time period. For example, the commuting capacity of a highway could be expressed in terms of the number of commuter vehicles entering the city per hour. Using this definition, one might incorrectly conclude that widening the highway or increasing its speed limit would increase the commuting capacity of vehicles in the city. This logic is flawed, however, because the perspective of capacity is too narrow. The capacity of the *entire* commuting process—or the manufacturing or service process—must be considered. Therefore, widening or increasing a highway's speed limit without providing for additional destination *parking* would not increase commuting capacity; instead of waiting on the highway, commuters will be looking for parking places. A process- or systemwide perspective is necessary to manage capacity.

Exhibit 7–15

Measures of Capacity

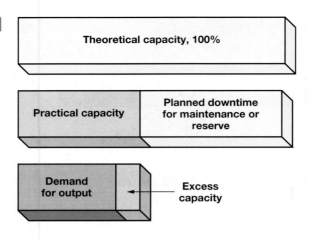

Measuring Capacity

Three common measures—theoretical, practical, and excess capacity—influence how organizations manage process capacity. The **theoretical capacity** of a process is the maximum possible rate of transformation of inputs into outputs if the process were fully used, with no downtime or unused capacity. Most organizations, however, operate processes at less than theoretical capacity (e.g., at 80 percent of theoretical capacity) for a number of reasons, including the following:

- Planned downtime usually is necessary for scheduled maintenance or improvements to equipment and procedures.
- Unplanned downtime caused by breakdowns in equipment or delays in supply of inputs can make it impossible to operate at theoretical capacity.
- Some capacity can be reserved for unforeseen needs and the ability to be flexible.
- Demand for the output of the process might be less than the theoretical capacity.

The **practical capacity** of a process is its *theoretical capacity* less planned downtime for scheduled maintenance or improvements. **Excess** (or **unused**) **capacity** is the amount (if any) by which practical capacity exceeds the demand for the output of the process. Note that organizations sometimes allow processes to operate in excess of practical capacity (i.e., at negative excess capacity) to meet urgent needs. In the long run, however, skipping maintenance and planned improvements will lead to breakdowns and reduced capacity. Exhibit 7–15 shows relations between measures of capacity for a process with theoretical and practical capacities in excess of demand. Persistent excess capacity indicates wasted resources; negative excess capacity can indicate lost opportunities.

Managing Quality + Time + Productivity + Capacity = JIT

LO 5 Evaluate how just-in-time methods create benefits by combining management of quality, time, productivity, and capacity.

Just-in-time (JIT) processes purchase, make, and deliver services and products just when needed. Organizations that use JIT find that it reduces, or potentially eliminates, inventory carrying costs. **Inventory carrying costs** are costs of receiving, handling, storing, and insuring inventory. JIT also requires high-quality processes. Defective products are incompatible with JIT because, in theory, no inventory is in reserve to keep production processes operating. Thus, defects trigger investigations of processes to eliminate their causes. Without wasteful efforts needed to correct defects, JIT processes also have short cycle times. The JIT philosophy—avoiding waste and non-value-added activities—is closely linked to activity-based management.[9] Thus, service organizations also apply JIT.

Think of JIT and the quality requirements for a course report. Suppose that you begin it just soon enough to complete it before it is due. If all goes as planned, you will finish printing the report just before class and hand it in on time. Fine—if all goes well.

Suppose, however, that your personal computer crashes while you are writing the report. This presents a major problem for you because you attempted to apply the JIT philosophy with a defective machine in your production process. Use of JIT forces

---

[9] Surveys show that manufacturing firms report improvements in cycle time and quality as a result of adopting JIT, particularly those that use batch and continuous flow processes (e.g., R. White, "An Empirical Assessment of JIT in U.S. Manufacturers," and M. Youssef, "Measuring the Intensity Level of JIT Activities and Its Impact on Quality").

you to think through all of the things that could go wrong and to correct them in advance of your report. If you use JIT to prepare course reports, you need to be sure that everything involved is reliable: your machine (or a backup), your transportation to deliver the product (your report), and your access to other resources, such as the library or the Internet. In short, to apply JIT, you cannot allow unreliable activities or defective resources in your process.

JIT Manufacturing

Service-based companies such as TCSI are ideally situated to implement the JIT philosophy because they can focus on improving quality and eliminating waste without the encumbrances of physical plants, inventories, and entrenched production processes. Manufacturing companies, however, also can gain from applying the JIT philosophy to their management of physical resources. For example, manufacturers should realize that customers do not care whether the manufacturer maintains inventories or has the largest, most efficient forklifts to move parts and materials from one manufacturing activity to the next. As far as customers are concerned, these are non-value-added activities that only waste resources and increase costs. Nor are customers interested in paying for the manufacturer to fix defective products. They prefer defect-free products, and if a competitor offers defect-free products at a lower cost, the customer has an obvious reason to buy elsewhere. Concerns for eliminating the waste caused by non-value-added activities and unnecessary defects converge in the solution offered by JIT manufacturing. We now compare the filling of the same order by a traditional manufacturer and a JIT manufacturer.

Traditional "push" manufacturing.   A traditional manufacturer begins the manufacturing cycle by forecasting total orders for a time period, say a month. Considering beginning and ending inventory levels yields the required production level. Based on the forecasted level of production and materials inventories, the manufacturer orders materials and then schedules production at each defined activity of the process. Thus, forecasting and scheduling activities push production through the process. For example, a traditional manufacturer of personal computers does the following:

- Forecasts sales (by model) well in advance of the start of production to accommodate purchasing and production lead times.
- Orders all components (circuit boards, disk drives, DVD or CD-ROM drives, processor chips, and so on).
- Prepares a production schedule and gives orders to all functional groups (motherboard assembly, storage device assembly, final assembly, etc.) to assemble the required number of parts, components, and computers.
- Upon receiving a customer order, ships products from finished goods inventory if the product is available, or if the product is not available, either places it on backorder status to be filled as soon as possible or expedites a special order.

Why is this approach to manufacturing possibly inefficient? First, it is driven by sales forecasting, which can be an inaccurate guide to production scheduling. Employees in every functional activity are motivated to meet production schedules regardless of overall sales. If sales are less than forecasted, the company invests too much in unused parts and unsold finished goods inventory, which consumes resources unnecessarily and can result in obsolete inventories. If sales are more than forecasted, the company must either backorder its sales, which could result in dissatisfied customers and lost sales, or rush orders for parts and expedite production beyond what was planned, which could greatly increase costs. Thus, pushing production through the company motivates adherence to production schedules and inhibits flexibility, regardless of the impact on throughput—the result of sales to customers.

Second, the traditional manufacturer usually does not balance the timing of receiving materials and of all production activities with capacity. Not considering capacity can result in a temporary, wasteful buildup of inventories if this is merely a matter of timing, or a permanent buildup of inventories if managers are covering their quality problems by ordering too many materials or overproducing. Thus, push production also can reduce the motivation to improve quality and can reinforce the motivation to overuse capacity.

JIT "pull" manufacturing.   Although a JIT manufacturer also uses long-term sales forecasting to determine its scale of operations and capacity, JIT production is "pulled" through the process by customer orders rather than pushed by a master production schedule. For example, consider how Dell Computer Corporation or Gateway pulls an order through its production process in a sequence almost the reverse of that of the traditional manufacturer:

- A customer places an order for a computer with specific features.
- The sales order triggers a production order.
- The production order triggers the ordering and assembly of individual components, which are started immediately and designated for the specific order.
- The requirements for components trigger orders to suppliers, which ship parts immediately.
- The customer receives the ordered computer approximately one week later.

A traditional manufacturer could be just as flexible to customer orders by forecasting sales perfectly, which is not possible, or by investing in large enough inventories to avoid all backorders, which could be prohibitively costly. Obviously, the JIT approach is flexible to customer needs and requires lower inventory levels than traditional methods—only as much as is necessary to process each order. JIT production is not trivial to design, implement, or manage, however.

Role of cost management.   The cost-management analyst can fill a valuable role by measuring the costs of excess inventories and costs of quality that traditional push production methods encourage. Often these costs have the most impact when they are benchmarked against more efficient competitors. Revealing these cost disadvantages could induce companies to consider adopting a JIT production approach. Consider the summary information in Exhibits 7–16 and 7–17 that contrast the production performance of a relatively traditional computer manufacturer, IBM with a more efficient competitor, Dell. Dell openly states that it has competitive advantages because of its flexible, JIT manufacturing approach.

Dell Computer assembles its products just in time to fill customer orders quickly, thus eliminating wasted effort and time. Dell's inventories are minimized because customer orders pull computers through its assembly processes.

Observe that Dell's employees generate more than twice the sales revenue per employee as do IBM's employees. This indicates that Dell uses human resources with greater effectiveness. Dell manages its costs more effectively; it has a much lower inventory level and a much higher inventory turnover ratio, reflecting more efficient production processes than IBM.

JIT Success Factors

How is the JIT manufacturer able to reliably produce and deliver its products? Manufacturers that

Exhibit 7–16 Inventory Management at Three Computer Manufacturers

Manufacturer Production Method	Dell JIT	IBM Traditional
Qualitative and quantitative data from recent Form 10-K filed with the Securities and Exchange Commission	"The Company's build-to-order manufacturing process is designed to allow the Company to quickly produce customized computer systems and to achieve rapid inventory turnover and reduced inventory levels, which lessens the Company's exposure to the risk of declining inventory values. This flexible manufacturing process also allows the Company to incorporate new technologies or components into its product offerings quickly."	"The company's businesses are characterized by rapid technological changes and corresponding shifts in customer demand, resulting in unpredictable product transitions and shortened life cycles. . . . In addition, from time to time the company may experience difficulties or delays in the development, production or marketing of new products and services."
Sales revenue	$12,327,000,000	$78,508,000,000
No. of employees	16,000	269,465
Sales per employee	$770,437	$291,347
Cost of goods sold	$9,605,000,000	$47,899,000,000
Inventories (year-end)	$233,000,000	$5,139,000,000
Inventory turnover*	41.2 times per year	9.3 times per year

*IBM's sales and cost of goods sold also include large sales of software and services, which lead to overstatement of IBM's inventory turnover ratio, which might be roughly half the calculated amount.

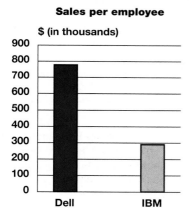

Sales per employee

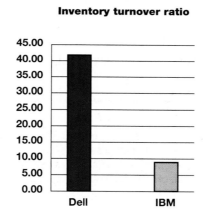

Inventory turnover ratio

Exhibit 7–17

Comparative Sales and Production Performance

apply JIT find that the following six factors are essential. Furthermore, all of them appear to be necessary; an organization probably cannot implement JIT successfully without implementing *all* of its components, at least to some degree.

1. *Commitment to quality.* All employees must be involved in the quality process. Defects cause delays and require buffer inventories. Employees must be able and motivated to take preventive actions. However, if defects occur, the sooner employees can detect a defect, the sooner they can correct it, minimizing lost time and resources.

2. *Creation of flexible capacity or predictable orders.* Short setup times and the ability to customize products is necessary to respond to unique orders. Mass-production can benefit from JIT if producers are able to stabilize orders through advance or long-term purchase agreements.

3. *Achievement of reliable supplier relations.* Suppliers must be reliable, providing on-time deliveries of high-quality materials. Unreliable suppliers necessitate buffer inventories. Developing strong supplier relationships often means reducing the number of suppliers, which also results in savings in support services that manage suppliers and orders.

4. *Development of smooth production flow.* Unbalanced production leads to delays at bottlenecks and the need for excess buffer inventories. Organizing production activities to respond to individual orders can mean configuring activities into "cells" that focus on completing a unique order rather than linear assembly lines best suited to producing large batches of identical items.

5. *Maintenance of a well-trained, motivated, flexible workforce.* In a production cell environment, workers must be well trained and cross-trained to use various machines and work on different areas of their production cell. Furthermore, they must be able and motivated to correct problems as they occur to keep the production process operating.

6. *Achievement and improvement of short cycle and customer-response times.* Short customer-response times enable companies to respond quickly to customer needs. Eliminating non-value-added time and activities results in shorter cycle times. For example, unnecessary paperwork or travel and movement of parts and assemblies waste time.

Organizations could benefit from JIT even if they cannot implement its components perfectly. In many areas of the world, for example, instantaneous resupply of materials is not possible, so many nearly JIT companies maintain some inventories. They still benefit from applying JIT principles to eliminate waste in other activities even though they still have inventories.

The cost-management analyst also fills a valuable role in JIT manufacturing organizations by identifying other areas for improvement and by monitoring performance in the preceding six components of JIT production using the same type of lead-indicator and diagnostic tools useful for managing quality. For example, measuring and reporting defects, causes of defects, cycle times, and employee capabilities support the management of both quality and time.

Research Insight 7.2

Benefits of JIT

Verifying average economic benefits derived from adopting JIT is difficult. The majority of self-reports are the apparent successes. Firms would be reluctant to disclose that they had failed at JIT.

A recent study using financial statement data demonstrates how difficult it is to isolate the effects of a single organizational factor such as JIT. The study did find that firms declaring that they had adopted JIT—though we do not know whether they adopted some or all of its components and how widely they adopted JIT—on average had significantly higher inventory turnover ratios afterward than did comparable firms that apparently did not adopt JIT. This confirms that JIT has a beneficial effect on the use of scarce resources.* However, this effect apparently did not extend to improvements in return on assets (ROA) because all firms in the study on average experienced declines in ROA.

Although the logic of JIT is compelling, we cannot be sure that adopting JIT results in improved profitability for all firms. More research is necessary to isolate contemporaneous and complementary effects. Some research on JIT processes indicates that firms do not and should not adopt management techniques in isolation, and it could be that the way firms bundle JIT with other techniques determines organizational performance. *Sources: R. Balakrishnan, T. Linsmeier, and M. Venkatachalam,* "Financial Benefits from JIT Adoption: Effects of Customer Concentration and Cost Structure"; *F. Selto, C. Renner, and S. M. Young,* "Assessing the Organizational Fit of a JIT Manufacturing System."

*This finding is supported by some studies, such as that by T. Billesbach and R. Hayen, "Long-Term Impact of Just-in-Time on Inventory Performance Measures," but not supported by others, such as that by S. Procter, "The Extent of JIT Manufacturing in the UK: Evidence from Aggregate Economic Data," which could not find evidence of average improvements in inventory turnover ratios that could be attributed to JIT.

Chapter Summary

Managers in all organizations understand that product quality is one of the critical success factors for organizations. Some managers adopt the total quality management (TQM) philosophy, which argues that organizations must constantly seek improved quality. Other managers have the return on quality (ROQ) view that there is a trade-off between cost and quality so that the best quality level might be less than total quality. These costs of quality include prevention, appraisal, internal failure, and external failure. Managers recognize trade-offs among these categories. For example, increased prevention resources can reduce internal and external failure costs.

On-time product delivery is also a critical success factor for organizations. Reducing the length of time between order and delivery of the product to the customer increases customer satisfaction. The just-in-time (JIT) philosophy is a natural fit with TQM and time management. With JIT, there is little or no room for product defects.

TCSI and other companies have been successful because they understand the informational and organizational requirements for managing quality, time, productivity, and capacity. These requirements include:[10]

1. *Employee responsibility and authority.* Employees, not just managers, should collect and use information to get feedback and solve problems.
2. *Lead indicator and diagnostic information.* Cost management information should be more detailed and focused on activities than that produced by traditional accounting systems. Instead of reporting just the cost of defects, for example, the information system should also report the types and causes of defects.
3. *Problem-solving information.* The information should include problem-solving information such as that coming from quality control charts. Financial reports would indicate a decline in revenues, for example, but not its causes. Control charts, however, could show an increase in customer complaints as a likely cause of the revenue decline.
4. *Timely information.* The information should be available quickly (for example, daily or "real time") so workers can get quick feedback.
5. *Appropriate evaluations and rewards.* Evaluations and rewards should be based on performing activities that lead to high quality and customer satisfaction. This reflects that you get what you reward.

Appendix to Chapter Seven

Construction and Use of Control Charts

Control charts display measures of important product or service attributes for individual items or for a sample of items to disclose attribute measures and variation in the production process. Organizations use control charts for several purposes, including process control, assurance sampling, and inspection activities. In most cases, control charts provide multiple benefits such as (1) causing employees to directly monitor the quality of their work, (2) detecting defects quickly and at the source, and (3) providing a common, objective means of communicating the quality of a process or product.

LO 6 Understand how to construct and use control charts.

Statistical Control

Organizations could base control charts on historical data of attributes achieved or on desired levels of the attributes. For example, historically, one of TCSI's customer service representative's response process times have averaged 7.95 minutes over the

---

[10] Adapted from Chris Ittner and David Larcker, "Total Quality Management and the Choice of Information and Reward Systems."

Week	Average Response Time
1	6.89
2	7.89
3	9.60
4	7.77
5	9.70
6	8.07
7	6.62
8	6.84
9	9.13
10	9.63
11	10.13
12	5.45
13	6.29
14	7.79
15	8.12
16	7.26

Statistical Control Parameters	
Overall mean	7.95 min.
Standard deviation (SD)	1.378 min.
2 SDs	2.755 min.
UCL = Mean + 2 SD	10.70 min.
LCL = Mean − 2 SD	5.19 min.

Target Control Parameters	
Target mean	7.50 min.
Target deviation	2.00 min.
UCL = Mean + 2.00	9.50 min.
LCL = Mean − 2.00	5.50 min.

past 16 weeks, as appears in Exhibit 7–18. Using this historical performance, TCSI could prepare a **statistical control chart,** which displays attributes, for example, customer-response times, against the historical parameters of the *mean* (7.95 minutes) and *variation.*[11] Variation usually is displayed as an interval based on the historical *range* of outcomes (high to low) or 2 or 3 *standard deviations* above and below the mean (e.g., between 10.70 and 5.19 minutes). Some experts recommend basing variation on range because it is easier to both compute for small samples and explain to employees than standard deviation. Because using the range to set the allowable interval requires access to special tables (available in all texts on quality control), we show intervals using standard deviation.

Target Control

Alternatively, TCSI could prepare a control chart based on specified or target levels of product attributes. For example, suppose that market and customer service research reveals that properly responding to a customer inquiry should take 7.5 minutes and that variation of plus or minus 2.0 minutes is within the range of acceptable service. In an ideal situation, the natural variation of a process is less than specified or target levels, but many quality problems result from natural process variation exceeding the target variation. Redesigning a process to reduce its natural variation can be more economical than imposing stricter target control levels that result in many defects, causing high levels of internal and external failure.

A control chart based on target-attribute parameters might classify a different set of outcomes as defects than would a statistical control chart. Exhibit 7–19 shows two sets of controls, statistical in blue and target in red. The horizontal lines in the middle of the chart reflect either the statistical (blue) or target (red) value of the attribute. The upper lines of the chart reflect the statistical (blue) or target (red) upper control limits (UCL). To give speedy customer service, customer-response times should not exceed the appropriate UCL level. The lower lines reflect the statistical (blue) or target (red) lower control limits (LCL). To fully consider the customer's inquiry, customer-response time should not fall below the appropriate LCL.[12]

---

[11] This form of control chart is called an $\bar{X}$ (X-bar) chart, since it is based on the historical mean, or *X*-bar. Many other forms of control chart are based on other statistical descriptions of historical or target attributes.

[12] Note that control limits do not have to be symmetrical. For example, an organization might believe that the consequences of exceeding an upper limit are worse than falling below a lower limit (or vice versa) and could set the UCL closer to the mean and the LCL farther from the mean (or vice versa).

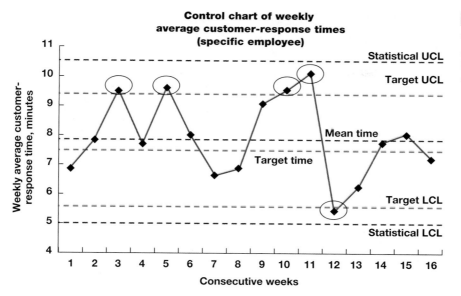

Exhibit 7–19

Control Chart of Weekly Average Customer-Response Times (specific employee)

The circled observations identify customer-response times that exceed or fall below *target* control limits. The statistical control limits, in contrast, do not identify any violations of control limits. Whether to use the tighter target limits rather than the looser statistical limits depends on the organization's estimates of the relative costs of:

- Intervening when a violation is detected (correctly or incorrectly) using tight limits. These costs include finding and correcting causes of defects, rework, delays, and even lost sales.

- Not intervening when a violation (from the customer's perspective) occurs but is not detected using loose limits. These costs include internal and external failures, which could be large.

Auditors face the same situation when deciding to perform additional auditing tests based on results of sampling transactions. For example, does a low level of confirmed account balances signal an out-of-control accounting system, or is this a chance occurrence? Considering the costs of making errors, auditors want to be able to assure users of the financial statements (and themselves!) that the financial statements fairly present the organization's status and performance.

Patterns of Variation

A process can be out of control (exhibiting undesirable variation) even if attribute measures do not violate control limits. Attribute measures could exhibit runs, cycles, extreme jumps, or concentrations at control limits, which can signal the need for intervention or opportunities for improvement. A **run** refers to sequential values above or below the mean or values sequentially increasing or decreasing. Based on an approximately 1 percent statistical probability of a run occurring by chance, a statistically out-of-control process can be identified using the following rules of thumb:[13]

- *Seven successive values* on the same side of the mean or target.
- *Four or more successive values* outside 1 standard deviation from the mean or target.
- *Two or more successive values* outside 2 standard deviations from the mean or target.

---

[13] A 1 percent chance can be too stringent; that is, the costs of not detecting an actual run can be high relative to the costs of intervening. Setting a less stringent criterion, say 5 or 10 percent, leads to fewer consecutive observations signaling a run.

Causes of runs include the following:

- Worker fatigue.
- Wear and deterioration of tools and equipment.
- Changes in environmental conditions.
- Accumulation of waste, scrap, and excess parts that cause congestion.
- Learning and improved use of resources.

The following can cause cyclical behavior:

- Recurring conditions (night/day, heat/cold).
- Rotation of employees, equipment, or suppliers.
- Rotation of testing and inspection.
- Periodic maintenance or training.

Causes of extreme jumps include these:

- Changes in tools, equipment, or setups.
- Change of employees.
- Changes or errors in testing or reporting procedures.

The following can cause values concentrated near control limits:

- Major differences in the quality of resources (human and physical).
- Mistakenly plotting outcomes from different processes on the same chart.

Benefits of Control Charts

Cost management analysts, industrial engineers, quality control specialists, managers, and employees in all types of organizations throughout the world have found that control charts are simple, versatile, and inexpensive tools for managing the quality of their products and services. If these charts are based on sound statistical evidence and compelling market research, control charts are reliable guides for controlling processes, preventing defects, and measuring quality performance.

Key Terms

For each term's definition, refer to the indicated page or turn to the glossary at the end of the text.

*In the chapter appendix

Meeting the Cost Management Challenges

1. **Managing** quality seems to be a general management task, so what can cost-management analysts provide to improve this important activity?

In our competitive economy, all members of organizations (private and government) need to be concerned about quality. There are several practical issues of managing and improving quality that can benefit from cost-management information. For example, some organizations have found it difficult to convince employees that they have a quality problem and that they therefore need to change practices and processes to improve quality. Cost-management analysts can demonstrate the magnitude of quality problems by benchmarking their organization's quality against internal quality goals and competitors' quality performance. They also can use the cost-of-quality report to identify and demonstrate any imbalance between costs of controlling or failing to control quality. Furthermore, because cost-management analysts can measure these effects of quality, they can have a strong and lasting impression on employees who now can see tangible evidence of the effects of quality and formulate clear quality goals. Reliable cost-management information can greatly reinforce an attitude of improving quality.

2. **Is** there a conflict between meeting quality and time goals, or do these goals reinforce each other?

If one were to look at each of these performance dimensions separately, they could conflict. For example, under the pressure to meet tight on-time delivery objectives, employees might cut corners on quality processes. Meeting the delivery schedule might achieve some short-term benefit, but at the cost of worsened customer satisfaction or external failure costs. This is a mistake that some companies have made in the past, but most organizations now realize that time and quality objectives can reinforce each other if companies pursue and reward them simultaneously. Mutual reinforcement is why JIT methods can be so successful—reducing process time is not possible without improvements in quality, and improving qual-

ity reduces process time by reducing testing, rework, and so on. Thus, it usually is shortsighted to try to improve process time without also improving quality, and vice versa.

3. **How** should cost-management analysts choose among all available quality and time-management tools?

There is no shortage of measures, charts, diagrams, and reports that cost-management analysts can use to study and communicate quality and time performance. Furthermore, there are many ways to present the information: text, tables, graphs, pictures, black-and-white, full color, and so on. Preparing too much quality and time information could be as mistaken as preparing too little. Individuals can process only so much information, and an *overload* of it can obscure or reduce the impact of any single piece of information. In other words, if presented with too much information, people just might "tune out" and put it all in the "circular file." Therefore, *cost-management analysts should find the most important quality and time information for the decisions facing their employees and the most salient way to communicate it.* Both are necessary.

For example, defects in certain product features could be the most important measures of quality in a particular situation. Cost-management analysts measure these accurately and in a timely manner but might try to communicate the information via computer spreadsheets filled to the margins with numbers. Since almost no one has the time to find the most important numbers to them among the mass of numbers presented, the quality message is lost. Although many people comprehend graphical information more easily than tabular data, no amount of effort spent on preparing fancy, full-color charts could make up for presenting the wrong quality or time data. To find the right combination of information and communication medium, cost-management analysts must first communicate with decision makers who will use the information by *listening to* what they need and by *seeking feedback* from them about the usefulness of cost-management information.

Solutions to You're the Decision Maker

7.1 Using Diagnostic Quality Information, p. 256

a. Diagnosing and improving quality cannot be divorced from the authority and responsibilities given to individuals and the way they are evaluated. In an ideal organization, individuals or groups would be able to objectively and thoroughly evaluate the causes of quality problems and act to eliminate them. Furthermore, they would be able to understand how their actions either to improve or not improve quality performance affect the rest of the organization. This is not always the case.

b. A cross-functional team can be better able to diagnose and correct quality problems than either individuals or a functional team. Both of these parties "might not see the forest for the trees" or, because of narrow evaluation criteria (e.g., this period's profits), might have incentives to hide rather than correct quality problems.

7.2 Evaluating the Cost of Quality, p. 260

a. COQ can be a valuable communication device by identifying the magnitude and types of quality problems. If this report is visible and regarded as reliable, it is hard to ignore, for example, the very high costs of activities to correct non-value-added internal and external failures. COQ does not, by itself, suggest ways to eliminate these activities, but it does make their impact on profits clear.

b. Profits are still an important goal of profit-seeking organizations, so profit reports cannot be ignored. However, costs of quality are buried in costs of sales and general overhead. Furthermore, if a company uses FIFO, it is possible that current costs of quality are hidden in inventories and will not affect profits until future periods. It is probably incorrect to say that COQ is "better" than traditional profits since they measure different areas of performance. It is likely that

COQ does add useful information about how the organization consumes resources, perhaps unnecessarily, to perpetuate quality problems.

c. Any numbers that become performance objectives have the appearance of being "concrete" or "hard" numbers. Some even believe that the true COQ objective is for total quality costs to be zero. What should the COQ objective be? ROQ advocates would say that some level of COQ is optimal and

that it can be driven too low. Perhaps the most defensible approach is to avoid hard COQ objectives since COQ is a result of quality activities, not a measure of quality itself. One should recognize that high levels of COQ are indicative of quality problems and that competition will require improvements—but this should already be known. Quality improvements come from understanding what customers want and meeting or exceeding their expectations.

Review Questions

7.1 Review and define each of the chapter's key terms.

7.2 Why is managing quality important?

7.3 Why is managing time important?

7.4 Why do advocates of TQM expect to earn higher profits?

7.5 What are the similarities and differences between TQM and ROQ?

7.6 What are the two dimensions of quality?

7.7 What is the major difference between tangible and intangible product features that affects management of quality?

7.8 How are process and product variations lead indicators of quality?

7.9 How do lead indicators of quality differ from diagnostic information about quality?

7.10 How does customer satisfaction differ from quality?

7.11 Is cost of quality a lead indicator or diagnostic information? Explain.

7.12 How do organizations make trade-offs among the four types of quality activities?

7.13 Is COQ more consistent with TQM or ROQ? Explain.

7.14 How are managing quality and managing time related?

7.15 Is JIT possible without high-quality processes? Explain.

7.16 What are some useful indicators of productivity? How are they measured?

7.17 What is cycle time? How is it measured?

7.18 What is throughput efficiency? How is it measured?

7.19 Explain the concept of process capacity. Use an example from the chapter to describe the capacity of a specific process.

7.20 What is the difference between theoretical and practical capacity? Why might an organization choose to operate processes at practical capacity rather than at theoretical capacity?

Critical Analysis

7.21 An engineer argues, "Quality means the product will perform faultlessly." A marketing manager retorts, "No, quality is whatever the customer says it is." Are these views conflicting? Explain.

7.22 You are discussing the importance of quality with a colleague. She says, "High quality may have been an important part of business competition in the 1980s and 1990s when quality varied across companies. Now, increasing quality is much less important than decreasing new product development time." Evaluate this comment.

7.23 Two years after Wallace Co. won the Malcolm Baldrige Quality Award, this small oil company filed for bankruptcy. Explain how this could have happened.

7.24 Contrast these statements. FedEx: "We're trying to isolate quality improvements that just don't add any value . . . to the customer." Hewlett-Packard: "Asking what quality is worth is like asking what my left lung is worth."

7.25 Consider your school's course-registration process. Why would goals to improve cycle time require improvements in quality?

7.26 In its marketing activities, United Airlines stresses the importance of on-time flight departures and dealing with customer complaints. Qantas Airlines stresses its safety record and in-flight service. Are both airlines concerned with quality? Explain.

7.27 Horace Mann Insurance Company sends a questionnaire to policyholders that have filed a claim. The questionnaire asks them whether they are satisfied with the way the claim has been handled. What useful information does Horace Mann Insurance obtain?

7.28 Why did students (in the 1960s) demand to evaluate university courses?

7.29 United Parcel Service (UPS) (www.ups.com) assumed that on-time delivery was the most important feature of its service and stressed (literally) its importance to UPS employees. UPS managers were confused as to why the company was not gaining market share even though customers rated the company's on-time delivery very high. Explain this apparently contrary result.

7.30 Motorola (www.motorola.com) has employed its Six Sigma approach to managing quality for many years. ("Six Sigma" refers to the probability of a defect occurring based on the area under a normal probability curve that is 6 standard deviations from the mean. This probability is .0000002 percent, or only 2 defects, per million events.) The company uses these six steps:

- Identify the product you create or the service you provide.
- Identify the customer(s) for your product or service and determine what they consider important.
- Identify what you need to satisfy the customer.
- Define the process for doing the work.
- Mistake-proof the process and eliminate wasted effort.
- Ensure continuous improvement by measuring, analyzing, and controlling the improved process.

Is Motorola's approach to quality more closely aligned with TQM or ROQ? Explain.

7.31 Consider the book in front of you. What are its tangible and intangible features? Are any more important than others? Can you rate these features according to a three-point scale? Is each feature:

1 = Much better than expected?

0 = About as expected?

−1 = Worse than expected?

Should the publisher and authors of the book be interested in your ratings?

7.32 What are the similarities and differences between TQM, ROQ, and COQ? Can an organization employ all three approaches to managing quality? Explain.

7.33 Allegheny Industries' top executives are evaluated on the basis of annual profits and earnings per share. Middle managers are evaluated on the basis of cycle time and product quality. Are these evaluations consistent? Does it matter? Explain.

7.34 Assume that a competitor of TCSI measures cycle time for only the products that pass through its processes without defects. Do you think this is necessarily a bad practice? What incentives might motivate such a practice?

7.35 Is it possible for a company to increase the throughput efficiency of one process to the point where an additional increase could reduce the company's overall profitability? If so, give an example.

7.36 Respond to this comment: "I think the way you have measured practical capacity is just an excuse to keep from trying to use our processes more efficiently. We should be trying to get as close to theoretical capacity as possible. Isn't that what is meant by 'continuous improvement'? Otherwise, aren't we wasting resources?"

7.37 Find a newspaper or magazine article about a recent transportation project (e.g., widening or adding a highway). Critically evaluate this project from a systemwide viewpoint, as discussed on p. 265.

Exercises

How do the Baldrige National Quality Award (www.quality.nist.gov), the Deming Prize (www.deming.org/demingprize/index.html), and ISO 9000 (www.iso.org) differ?

Exercise 7.38
Standards of Quality
(LO 1)

ZZK Industries manufactures zippers. The following table presents its financial information for one year:

Sales	$450,000
Material inspection	$13,000
Scrap	8,000
Employee training	13,000
Returned goods	3,000
Finished goods inspection	15,000
Processing customer complaints	6,000

Exercise 7.39
Costs of Quality
(LO 2)

Required

a. Classify these items into prevention, appraisal, internal failure, or external failure costs.

b. Prepare a cost-of-quality report for the year.

What are the most important customer-quality attributes for each of the following products or services?

a. Tuxedo for a bridegroom.

b. Microwave oven.

c. Accounting course at a university.

d. Cruise on a Princess ship.

e. Frozen dinner.

f. Tax return prepared by a professional.

Exercise 7.40
Quality According to the Customer
(LO 1)

What are the most important attributes of each of the following products or services?

a. Personal computer.

b. Television programming.

c. Meals in a fine restaurant.

d. Student study guides for an accounting text.

e. Running shoes.

f. Legal representation in traffic court.

Exercise 7.41
Quality According to the Customer
(LO 1)

What is the most important customer quality trade-off for each of the following products and services?

a. Personal computer.

b. Portable MP3 player.

Exercise 7.42
Quality According to the Customer
(LO 1)

c.   Checking account.
d.   Taxi ride through New York City.
e.   Personal clothing.

Exercise 7.43
Costs of Quality
(LO 2)

eXcel

mhhe.com/hilton3e

Vedral Industries manufactures computer printers. The following represents financial information for two years:

	Year 1	Year 2
Sales	$2,450,000	$2,200,000
Costs:		
Process inspection	16,500	18,800
Scrap	18,500	19,300
Quality training	198,000	130,000
Warranty repairs	43,000	48,000
Testing equipment	70,000	70,000
Customer complaints	28,000	34,000
Rework	170,000	185,000
Preventive maintenance	135,000	95,000
Materials inspection	65,000	48,000
Field testing	94,000	124,000

Required

a.   Classify these items into costs of prevention, appraisal, internal failure, or external failure activities.
b.   Calculate the ratio of the prevention, appraisal, internal failure, and external failure costs to sales for year 1 and year 2.
c.   Construct a cost-of-quality report for year 1 and year 2.

Exercise 7.44
Costs of Quality
(LO 2)

Owenborrogh Corporation manufactures air conditioners. The following represents its financial information for two years.

	Year 1	Year 2
Sales	$1,960,000	$1,760,000
Costs:		
Process inspection	13,200	15,000
Scrap	14,800	15,500
Quality training	158,000	105,000
Warranty repairs	34,000	38,000
Testing equipment	56,000	56,000
Customer complaints	22,500	27,200
Rework	136,000	148,000
Preventive maintenance	108,000	76,000
Materials inspection	52,000	38,000
Field testing	75,000	99,000

Required

a.   Classify these items into costs of prevention, appraisal, internal failure, or external failure activities.
b.   Calculate the ratio of the prevention, appraisal, internal failure, and external failure costs to sales for year 1 and year 2.
c.   Construct a cost-of-quality report for year 1 and year 2.

Exercise 7.45
Costs of Quality
(LO 2)

Ramirez Corporation manufactures refrigerators. The following represents its financial information for two years.

	Year 1	Year 2
Sales	$3,920,000	$3,520,000
Costs:		
Process inspection	26,400	30,000
Scrap	28,800	30,100

	Year 1	Year 2
Quality training	305,000	220,000
Warranty repairs	70,000	75,000
Testing equipment.......................	115,000	115,000
Customer complaints	44,500	54,200
Rework	272,000	195,000
Preventive maintenance	220,000	152,000
Materials inspection	105,000	75,000
Field testing.................................	150,000	200,000

Required

a.   Classify these items into costs of prevention, appraisal, internal failure, or external failure activities.

b.   Calculate the ratio of the prevention, appraisal, internal failure, and external failure costs to sales for year 1 and year 2.

c.   Construct a cost-of-quality report for year 1 and year 2.

The following are selected operating costs for Watson Products for last month.

Warranty claims	$ 476
Design engineering	600
Supplier evaluations	450
Lost contribution margins due to poor quality	300
Quality training...	500
Rework..	725
Equipment maintenance	1,154
Product testing	786
Product repair	695

Exercise 7.46
Cost of Quality
(LO 2)

Required

What is Watsons' total prevention and appraisal cost for last month?

[CMA adapted]

Prepare a run chart from the following, sequential weekly cycle-time data from the manufacture of computer tape storage devices. Use the historical mean of cycle time and a 2 standard-deviation upper and lower control limit. What does this chart indicate?

Exercise 7.47
Quality and Time Control
(Appendix)
(LO 2, 6)

mhhe.com/hilton3e

Week	Average Cycle Time in Hours
1	133.4
2	158.8
3	121.9
4	120.3
5	125.8
6	133.1
7	140.7
8	122.8
9	135.7
10	165.3
11	128.1
12	103.3
13	102.5
14	101.4
15	118.9
16	127.8
17	132.2
18	135.5

Prepare a quality control chart from the following sequential, monthly cycle-time data from the manufacture of computer library devices. The desired level of performance is 140. The upper control limit is 160, and the lower control limit is 120. What does this chart indicate?

Exercise 7.48
Quality and Time Control
(LO 2, 6)

Month	Average Cycle Time in Hours
January	124.0
February	175.0
March	147.5
April	97.0
May	153.2
June	132.0
July	228.0
August	152.0
September	172.0
October	112.0
November	138.0

Exercise 7.49
Quality Control
(LO 2, 6)

Prepare a quality control chart from the following sequential, weekly test data from the manufacture of computer tape storage devices. The desired level of performance is 1.5. The upper control limit is 2.1, and the lower control limit is 1.2. What does this chart indicate?

Week	Average Test Performance
36	1.7
37	1.7
38	1.7
39	1.6
40	1.6
41	2.2
42	1.4
43	1.4
44	2.0
45	2.1
46	1.2

Exercise 7.50
Quality Control
(Appendix)
(LO 6)

Prepare a quality control chart from the following sequential, weekly cycle-time data from the manufacture of computer-tape storage devices. Use the historical mean cycle time and a 2 standard-deviation upper and lower control limit. What does this chart indicate?

Week	Average Cycle Time in Hours
35	55
36	33
37	93
38	82
39	49
40	73
41	88
42	45
43	69
44	36
45	101
46	107
47	89
48	74
49	64
50	55
51	52
52	57

Exercise 7.51
Quality Control
(LO 2)

Prepare a Pareto chart using the following data on causes of adjustments to domestic and foreign customers' billings during the month of January. What does this chart indicate?

Causes of Defects	Frequency
Correction of incorrect prior adjustments	10
Miscellaneous	30

Causes of Defects	Frequency
Product did not perform	12
Product prices disputed	115
Product returned	15
Product shipped by wrong priority	70
Product shipped to wrong location	30
Shipments to foreign locations	64
Wrong product shipped	20

Prepare a Pareto chart using the following data on causes of defects during a week's manufacture of electronic circuit boards.

Exercise 7.52
Quality Control
(LO 2)

Causes of Defects	Frequency
Faulty board	6
Improper sequence of components	17
Incoming components	148
Incomplete solder	29
Mounting machine alignment	64
Operator error	23
Testing error	11

Required

Prepare a short presentation that explains what this chart indicates.

Canadian Seltzers has discovered a problem involving its mix of flavor to seltzer water that costs the company $3,000 in waste and $2,500 in lost business per period. There are two alternative solutions. The first is to lease a new mix regulator at a cost of $4,000 per period, which would save $2,000 in waste and $2,000 in lost business. The second alternative is to hire an additional employee to manually monitor the existing regulator at a cost of $2,500 per period, saving $1,500 in waste and $1,800 in lost business per period.

Exercise 7.53
Quality versus Cost
(LO 1)

Required

Prepare a memo that evaluates the two alternatives. Which alternative should Canadian choose?

Shaq, Inc. has discovered a problem involving the mix of limestone in its dry concrete mix that costs the company $5,000 in waste and $3,500 in lost business per period. There are two alternative solutions. The first is to lease a new mix regulator at a cost of $3,500 per period, which would save $3,500 in waste and $2,000 in lost business. The second alternative is to hire an additional employee to manually monitor the existing regulator at a cost of $3,000 per period, saving $2,500 in waste and $2,000 in lost business per period.

Exercise 7.54
Quality versus Cost
(LO 1)

Required

Prepare a memo that evaluates the two alternatives. Which alternative should Shaq choose?

Carlson Corporation has discovered a problem involving welding its bicycle frames that costs the company $3,000 in waste and $1,500 in lost business per period. There are two alternative solutions. The first is to lease a new automated welder at a cost of $3,500 per period, which would save $1,500 in waste and $1,000 in lost business. The second alternative is to hire an additional employee to manually weld the frames at a cost of $3,000 per period, which would save $2,500 in waste and $1,000 in lost business per period.

Exercise 7.55
Quality versus Cost
(LO 1)

Required

Form small groups and prepare an analysis of the two alternatives. Which alternative should Carlson choose?

Search the Internet for an example of a company that provides outsourced services or manufacturing activities on a just-in-time basis. As a potential client of that outsource provider, how would you evaluate whether to outsource your services or manufacturing activities to that company? How would you evaluate whether this outsourcing arrangement is beneficial to you?

Exercise 7.56
Managing Time
(LO 3)

Exercise 7.57
Managing Time
(LO 3)

Search your library or the Internet for a research study that investigates the costs and/or benefits of adopting JIT or other time-based process-management methods. Prepare a one-page summary that describes the study's objective, its source(s) of data, and its conclusion. Prepare two questions that, if you could, you would pose to the author(s) about the study.

Exercise 7.58
Productivity
(LO 5)

Consider the following information:

	Year 5	Year 4	Year 3	Year 2	Year I
Number of employees	22,230	24,400	24,100	22,000	21,800
Sales revenue ($ millions)	$2,843	$2,796	$2,669	$2,318	$1,993
Operating income ($ millions)	$468	$475	$530	$436	$303
Sales per employee	?	?	?	?	?
Total factor productivity	?	?	?	?	?

Required

a.   Using the preceding information, compute the productivity measures indicated by question marks. What appears to have happened?

b.   *Build your own spreadsheet.* Develop a spreadsheet to compute "sales per employee" and "total factor productivity."

Exercise 7.59
Cycle Time
(LO 5)

Consider the following information:

	January	February	March	April
Units completed	100	83	24	70
Processing time	145.3	145.3	170.4	158.4
Waiting time	2,579.5	2,477.8	1,782.7	1,525.7

Required

a.   Compute the average cycle time per unit and the throughput efficiencies for each month.

b.   *Build your own spreadsheet.* Develop a spreadsheet to answer requirement (a).

Problems

Problem 7.60
Capacity and Cycle Time
(LO 5)

Use the following data to supply information now represented by question marks. Practical capacities are 80 percent of theoretical capacities.

	A	B	C	D
Number of 40-hour shifts per week	2	3	1	2
Number of identical assembly lines	3	?	4	5
Available hours per week	?	600	?	?
Average cycle time per unit	3.5 hrs	9.5 hrs	?	?
Throughput time ratio	30%	?	40%	15%
Value-adding cycle time	?	1.9 hrs	?	?
Theoretical capacity in units	?	?	200	?
Practical capacity in units	?	?	?	1,600

Problem 7.61
Capacity and Cycle Time
(LO 5)

Use the following data to supply information now represented by question marks. Practical capacities are 80 percent of theoretical capacities.

	A	B	C	D
Number of 40-hour shifts per week	1	2	2	3
Number of identical assembly lines	4	?	7	5
Available hours per week	?	400	?	?
Average cycle time per unit	6.5 hrs	11.5 hrs	?	?
Throughput time ratio	50%	?	25%	15%
Value-adding cycle time	?	1.9 hrs	?	?
Theoretical capacity in units	?	?	700	?
Practical capacity in units	?	?	?	160

Individually or as a group with your classmates, interview the manager of a retail (or wholesale) store such as a music store, an automobile parts store, or the parts department of an appliance dealership. Ask the manager how items are ordered to replace those sold. For example, does he or she order based on observing inventory levels or place an order each time a customer buys an item? Does the manager appear to use just-in-time inventory? Write a brief report to your instructor summarizing the results of your interview.

Problem 7.62
Just-in-Time Process
(LO 5)

Individually or as a group with your classmates, interview the manager of a fast-food restaurant. Ask the manager how quality of service is measured and used to evaluate his or her performance. Write a brief report to your instructor summarizing the results of your interview.

Problem 7.63
Total Quality
Management **(LO 1)**

Individually or as a group with your classmates, observe an organization of your choice—wholesale, retail, or service. Prepare a short report illustrating examples of lead-indicator and diagnostic signals the organization uses or could use. How could it use quality management tools such as control charts, Pareto charts, and cause-and-effect analysis?

Problem 7.64
Identification of Quality
Control Problems
(LO 2)

Prepare a flowchart of the following medical appointment process at a Navy medical center.

Problem 7.65
Quality and Time Control
(LO 2, 3)

Prepare appointment book.

Open appointment book.

Is the appointment on shore or aboard ship?

If aboard ship, tell patient to call xxx-xxxx by 1500 hours (3 P.M.) to make own appointment for next working day.

If on shore, issue next available appointment to patient.

Remind patient to call 24 hours in advance to confirm appointment.

Did patient call 24 hours in advance?

If no, cancel appointment and give appointment to new patient.

If yes, give patient confirmation number.

    If yes, does patient show up for appointment?

        If yes, mark appointment book "patient showed."

           If no, mark appointment book "failure: Patient did not show."

               If no, place standby patient in appointment.

               If no, issue failure report to commanding officer.

Required

a. What is a defect in this process?

b. What does this flowchart indicate about possible sources of defects?

c. Can you recommend changes in the process to reduce defects?

Norsk Ferries operates daily round-trip voyages between Seattle and Vancouver using a fleet of three ferries, the *Sea Quill,* the *Neptune,* and the *Orcas.* The budgeted amount of fuel for each round trip is the average fuel usage, which over the last 12 months has been 150 gallons. Norsk has set the upper control limit at 180 gallons and the lower control limit at 130 gallons. The operations manager received the following report for round-trip fuel usage by the three ferries for the period:

Problem 7.66
Quality Control
(LO 2, 6)

Number of Gallons per Round-Trip

Trip	Sea Quill	Neptune	Orcas
1	156	155	146
2	141	141	156
3	146	144	167
4	152	161	156
5	156	138	183
6	161	170	177
7	167	149	189
8	186	159	171
9	173	152	176
10	179	140	185

Required

a.   Create quality control charts for round-trip fuel usage for each of the three ferries for the period. What inferences can you draw from them?

b.   Some managers propose that Norsk present its quality control charts in monetary terms rather than in physical amount (gallons) terms. What are the advantages and disadvantages of using monetary fuel costs rather than gallons in the quality control charts?

Problem 7.67
Inventory Management
(LO 5)

Consider the following annual information about three companies in the same manufacturing industry.

Company	A	B	C
Production method	JIT	JIT	Traditional
Sales revenue	$327,000,000	$584,000,000	$8,508,000,000
No. of employees	1,600	3,600	29,500
Cost of goods sold	$245,000,000	$414,000,000	$5,191,000,000
Inventories (average)	$5,700,000	$13,500,000	$763,000,000

Required

a.   Compare the three companies' uses of human and inventory resources using revenue per employee and inventory turnover measurers.

b.   Assume that you are a cost-management analyst employed by the least efficient user of inventories. At the request of the company CEO, prepare a short report that analyzes the relative cost advantages and outlines the types of costs and benefits that your company should expect by adopting JIT production.

Problem 7.68
Qualitative Evaluation
of JIT
(LO 5)

Toyota is credited with refining the practice of JIT. In Japan, it benefits greatly by having most of its suppliers in close proximity because suppliers are able to provide parts and materials almost instantaneously. A Fortune 500 manufacturing company in the center of the United States, which is separated by long distances from most suppliers, instituted JIT practices within local operations but found it necessary to maintain a large, computerized, central warehouse.

Required
Form small groups to consider the following:

a.   How could this company benefit from JIT even though it must maintain a costly inventory warehouse? Describe several examples of benefits this company could experience from its application of JIT.

b.   Prepare a short presentation that outlines a method for this company to determine whether the benefits from JIT outweigh the costs.

Problem 7.69
Quantitative and
Qualitative Evaluation
of JIT
(LO 5)

Your manufacturing company is considering adopting JIT production. You have gathered the following annual data, which you believe are relevant to the decision. For this analysis, ignore any initial investment costs necessary to start JIT.

▪   Average inventory will decline by $1,200,000, from $1,500,000 to $300,000.

▪   Current inventory handling, receiving, storing, and insuring costs are 12 percent of average inventory value plus $200,000. The committed portion will decline by $90,000 by transferring three employees to other work. Employee turnover in this area is approximately one-third per year. If any of these employees leaves the company, they will not be replaced.

▪   Annual costs of quality should change as follows:

   ▪   Prevention (additional training, improved supplier relations)—increase by $250,000.
   ▪   Inspection (employee time and testing equipment)—increase by $160,000.
   ▪   Internal failure (rework, delays)—decrease by $280,000.
   ▪   External failure (lost sales, warranty claims)—decrease by $210,000.

▪   Tooling and setup costs will increase by $140,000 per year.

▪   Opportunity cost of capital tied up in inventory is 10 percent per year.

Required

a. What is your estimate of the net annual quantifiable cost or benefit from your company's adopting JIT?

b. What qualitative factors should you consider before deciding this JIT issue?

Insurance companies spend considerable resources on processing claims (which results in a claim denial or payment to cover a loss). Short, accurate processing is desirable because both customers and the company benefit by resolving claims satisfactorily and by using minimum resources to do so. To improve its insurance claims processing, Global Insurance Company began a pilot project in its Northwest Region claims office to track the time to process each new automobile loss claim during a recent quarter. Processing time begins when a company representative receives a claim and ends when the final settlement is reached. Following are time data related to processing these claims at the company's Northwest Region.

Problem 7.70
Cycle Time and Throughput Efficiency
(LO 3)

Claim Processing Time Data

| | | | Average 8-Hour Days Spent in | | | | Average |
Days to Complete	Percent	Number	Processing by Adjusters	Waiting for Adjusters	Waiting for Information	Revisions and Corrections	Cycle Time in Days
0–10	4%	11,520	0.25	3.50	4.10	0.12	7.97
11–20	10	28,800	0.34	8.10	10.10	0.11	18.65
21–30	30	86,400	0.65	9.40	15.20	0.15	25.40
31–40	24	69,120	1.30	9.10	25.60	0.28	36.28
41–50	19	54,720	2.40	11.90	31.40	0.44	46.14
51–60	8	23,040	2.90	12.30	38.20	0.88	54.28
More than 60	5	14,400	3.10	11.50	49.70	2.60	66.90
Total	100%	288,000					

Required

a. Compute the overall average cycle time and throughput efficiency ratio in total and for each stage of processing for automobile loss claims during the quarter. (*Note:* These data can be easily analyzed with a computer spreadsheet.)

b. Comment on the apparent cause(s) of long cycle times and low throughput efficiencies.

c. What recommendation would you make to Global Insurance Company to improve its processing of automobile loss claims?

You are concerned that your company is understating its cycle time and throughput efficiency by measuring the cycle time for only those products completed without any defects. Products that are reworked or scrapped (because they cannot be made serviceable) are accounted for separately and removed from cycle time statistics. To understand the impact of this practice, you have decided to track the production of a typical product, Model DAD4700, over the course of four months. Sixteen different workgroups (each composed of approximately 7 to 10 employees) work on different stages of the product (and similar products). Three workgroups of 8 employees each do nothing but analyze and rework defective products (of all types) after the regular workgroups have completed them. You have gathered the following data on the DAD4700 over the past four months. (*Note:* These data can be more easily analyzed with spreadsheet software than by hand.)

Problem 7.71
Cycle Time and Quality
(LO 3)

Regular Workgroups	January	February	March	April
Units completed without rework	198	134	117	189
Assembly time for good units	1,809.70	1,293.60	1,105.60	1,714.20
Total cycle time for good units	4,994.70	4,791.05	3,397.06	2,891.13

Regular Workgroups	January	February	March	April
Units reworked successfully	10	8	5	13
Units scrapped	1	0	2	0
Rework time for all reworked units	57.20	43.20	54.60	48.60
Total rework cycle time	161.30	153.00	186.40	158.40

Required

a. Compute the average cycle time per unit and the throughput efficiency for good units produced by regular workgroups for each month and overall.

b. Compute the total cycle time and the throughput efficiency for units reworked successfully by rework workgroups for each month and overall. (*Hint:* Recall that these defective units were completed by regular workgroups first; an assumption is necessary.)

c. Compute the cycle times and the throughput efficiencies for each month for good and reworked products combined.

d. Prepare a group comment on the practice of computing separate cycle times and throughput efficiencies for good and reworked products.

e. What is your group's opinion about having separate workgroups perform all rework of defective products?

Problem 7.72
Capacity Management
(LO 4)

Rob Barkell, CFO of Monarch Electrical Corp., has asked you to estimate the benefits of changing the company's current production process to a design based on published data from a British electrical manufacturer. The British firm reported the following data for one of its circuit breaker assemblies. You have comparable information about the production of your Monarch's similar products (fourth column).

Production Item	Old British Circuit Breaker Process	New British Circuit Breaker Process	Monarch's Current Process
Average cost of parts and materials inventory	£24,300	£18,000	$110,000
Average cost of orders in process	£12,000	£375	$90,000
Cycle time per unit	20 hr.	35 min.	23 hr.
Number of employees	21	16	33
Production floor area..	109 sq. m.	30 sq. m.	1,000 sq. ft.
Output in units per day	330	345	420
Value-adding cycle time percentage	2%	63%	3%

Required

a. If Monarch copied the British firm's approach to managing its processes, what percentage of improvement in each production item could it expect? What new levels of each item could Monarch expect?

b. Is there a relationship between average work-in-process inventory and cycle time? Explain.

c. Monarch Electrical has a goal to earn a 20 percent before-tax return on all its resources. In other words, a resource costing $1,000 per year should earn $200 of profit annually before taxes. Prepare a memo to Barkell explaining that money tied up in inventory cannot be earning that return, so the 20 percent profit that is not earned is an opportunity cost of inventory. What is the opportunity cost of Monarch's inventory for this single product under current conditions? What is the dollar benefit of achieving reduced inventories by adopting the new production approach?

[Adapted from R. C. Barker, "Production Systems without MRP: A Lean Time-Based Design."]

Problem 7.73
Process Improvements
(LO 4)

Southern Cross Electrical, located in the state of Victoria, Australia, recently implemented changes to improve its manufacturing operations. Following are average process statistics before and after changes to one of the company's processes.

Item	Previous Process	Current Process	Percentage Change
Cost of orders in process	$ 5,568	$ 1,377	(75.3%)
Cycle time per unit	16 hr.	2 hr.	(87.5)
Labor time per unit..	4.45 min.	3.4 min.	(23.6)
Distance traveled in meters through the process...................	11.75 m.	5.5 m.	(53.2)
Floor area in meters used.......................................	36 sq. m.	12 sq. m.	(66.7)

Required

a. Explain how each of these changes could improve Southern Cross Electrical's profitability.

b. What are possible nonfinancial impacts of the process changes?

c. What decisions would Southern Cross Electrical's managers have to make for the company to benefit financially from these process improvements?

Cases

Billington Corporation makes bicycle frames in two processes, tube cutting and welding. The tube-cutting and welding processes have a practical capacity of 150,000 and 100,000 units per year, respectively. Committed costs of quality activities follow:

Case 7.74
Quality Improvement
(LO I)

Design of product and process costs	$220,000
Inspection and testing costs	85,000

The demand is very strong. Billington can sell all output it can produce at $180 per frame. It begins producing only 100,000 units in the tube-cutting department because of the capacity constraint on the welding process; any defective units it produces are scrapped. Of the 100,000 units started at the tube-cutting department, 1,000 units (1 percent) normally are scrapped. (Scrap is detected at the end of the tube-cutting operation.) Full costs, based on total manufacturing costs incurred through the tube-cutting operation, equal $105 per unit:

Direct materials (variable per unit)	$ 88
Direct manufacturing, setup, and materials handling labor	7
Equipment, rent, and other overhead (fixed for the year)	10
Full cost per unit	$105

The tube-cutting department sends its good units to the welding department. Unit-level manufacturing costs at the welding department are $43.50 per unit. Welders are very highly trained, and the welding department has no scrap. Therefore, Billington's total sales quantity equals the tube-cutting department's output. Billington's designers are considering several alternative improvements to reduce scrap in the tube-cutting department.

> *Alternative 1:* Leaving the process unchanged but starting enough units in the tube-cutting department so that the welding department can operate at practical capacity.
>
> *Alternative 2:* Using a different type of tubing that is more resistant to damage and would reduce scrap by 80 percent. It would increase the unit-level costs per unit in the tube-cutting department by $10 but would reduce costs in the welding department by $5.
>
> *Alternative 3:* Spending an additional amount on training to reduce scrap in the tube-cutting process.

Required

Form small groups to respond to each of the following items:

a. Which alternative—1 or 2—is more attractive financially?

b. How much would the company be willing to spend on training and how much would scrap have to be reduced to make alternative 3 as attractive as either alternative 1 or 2?

c. What other qualitative factors should Billington consider in making the decision?

d. *Build your own spreadsheet:* Develop a spreadsheet to answer the quantitative part of the analysis.

MBNA Corporation is one of the most successful banks in the world. Like traditional banks, MBNA takes deposits and makes loans, but it has no branch banks, no commercial loans, and only a small number of checking accounts. MBNA specializes in making loans to individuals through a credit card. Credit cards are commodities, but MBNA differentiates itself by the way it attracts and retains the highest-quality customers.

Case 7.75
Quality Management
(LO I)

Each of MBNA's 14.4 million customers on average carries an account balance that is more than $1,000 (45 percent) higher than the industry average, has average transactions that are $45 (47 percent) higher than the industry average, and has a loan default loss that is 40 percent lower than the industry average. Its customer retention rate is 97 percent, compared to the industry average of 89 percent.

One of the largest credit-card issuers in the world, MBNA states that through the use of advanced information technology, "We can control every aspect of our customer relationships and ensure consistency and quality in the delivery of our products. In 1997, MBNA's systems efficiently handled 12.5 billion on-line transactions, 120 million customer payments, 17 million requests for credit cards, and 192 million customer statements and letters." MBNA monitors 70 quality measures daily and evaluates its employees on 14 of them daily.

Required

In small groups or individually, respond to the following items:

a. How does MBNA Corporation define quality?

b. Examine MBNA's homepage and describe how the company attracts its customers.

c. What are the advantages and disadvantages of controlling variation and quality of services as closely as MBNA does?

d. Prepare a written evaluation of whether MBNA's approach to managing quality is desirable in all organizations.

[Adapted from the company's Web site, www.mbnainternational.com and various articles from *BusinessWeek*.]

Case 7.76

Analysis of Development Time in the Automobile Industry

(LO 3)

An analysis of the process of developing a new model automobile identified six major development activities, which together define a new model's product development lead time.

1. *Concept generation*—conducting marketing research and combining it with technical possibilities into a product concept to meet future market needs.

2. *Product planning*—translating the concept into product design, styling, and target costs.

3. *Advanced engineering*—conducting basic research to extend technical possibilities.

4. *Product engineering*—developing parts, components, and detailed, feasible designs.

5. *Process engineering*—translating product designs into manufacturing processes.

6. *Pilot run*—testing the manufacturability of the product and process performance.

The study also revealed significant differences in both the average overall product development lead time and the individual activities for high-volume automobile manufacturers in three major regions: the United States, Europe, and Japan. These differences appear in the following comparative Gantt charts, which show average time before the start of product sales for each major development activity.

Required

a. Describe the overall and specific development lead-time differences among the three types of manufacturers. What appear to be the most important differences in development lead time?

b. How can shorter development lead times result in competitive advantages for Japanese producers?

c. What factors other than lead time do you think are important for successful development of new products?

d. Explain how you would begin to analyze a typical US product development process with the objective of significantly reducing development lead time.

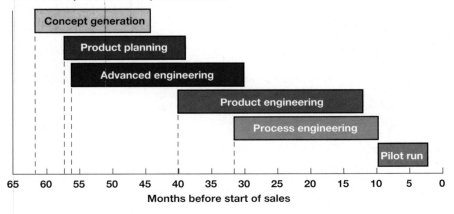

a. U.S. new product development lead time

b. European new product development lead time

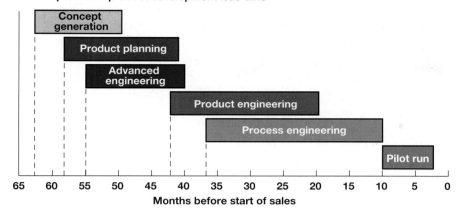

c. Japanese new product development lead time

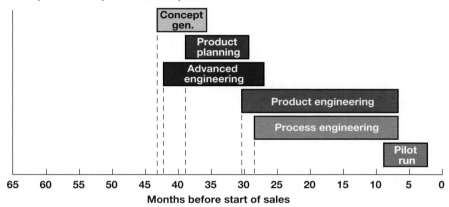

You are an analyst employed by a manufacturer that has traditionally produced large batches of identical items based on long-range sales forecasts. The company has maintained large buffer inventories to accommodate unforeseen fluctuations in demand and seemingly inevitable quality problems in the production process, which would result in significant rework and production delays without buffer inventory. Other members of the industry are adopting JIT production methods that are expensive to implement but are much more flexible and require fewer inventories to support production and sales. Your company is beginning to lose market share to its more flexible and efficient competitors.

Case 7.77
Qualitative and Quantitative Evaluation of JIT Production Costs and Benefits
(LO 5)

Required

a. Is the decision for the company to follow its competitors and adopt JIT production something that top management should make and announce to the company as a competitive necessity?

b. Assume that you have been appointed as the leader of a team that will analyze the costs and benefits of adopting JIT and make a recommendation to top management. What type of team do you prefer, and who should be its members?

c. Given the following representative data, what is your estimate of the net annual quantifiable cost or benefit from your company's adopting JIT? Use the format of Exhibit 1–2 of Chapter 1. (For this analysis, ignore any initial investment costs necessary to start JIT, although they can be quite large and must be considered for any final decision.)

  ▨   Average inventory will decline by $500,000, from $800,000 to $300,000.

  ▨   Current inventory carrying costs are estimated to be 15 percent of average inventory value plus $100,000. The variable portion will decline to 12 percent, and the committed portion used will decline to $60,000 by transferring an employee to other work.

- Costs of quality should change as follows:
- *Prevention* (additional training, improved supplier relations)—increase by $120,000.
- *Inspection* (employee time and testing equipment)—increase by $90,000.
- *Internal failure* (rework, delays)—decrease by $156,000.
- *External failure* (lost sales, warranty claims)—decrease by $185,000.
- Tooling and setup costs will increase by $80,000 per year.
- Opportunity cost of capital tied up in inventory is 10 percent per year.

d.   What qualitative factors should you, your team, and your company consider before deciding the JIT issue?

Process Costing and Cost Allocation

◀ **A Look Back**

Part II discusses cost-management tools to help understand production processes.

▼ **A Look at This Part**

Part III discusses several tried and true cost-accounting and management techniques. Chapter 8 discusses process costing. Chapter 9 discusses cost determination and management in joint processes. Chapter 10 discusses the allocation of support department costs to production departments.

▶ **A Look Ahead**

The next part discusses methods of developing and using cost information for decision making.

Chapter 8

Process-Costing Systems

After completing this chapter, you should be able to:

1. Recognize organizations that should use process costing and those that should use job costing.

2. Explain why process-costing information is useful.

3. Use the five-step costing method to assign process costs to products.

4. Assign process costs to products using weighted-average costing.

5. Account for costs transferred between processes.

6. Analyze and manage "normal" and "abnormal" spoilage.

7. Assign process costs to products using first-in, first-out (FIFO) costing (Appendix A).

8. Compare and contrast the results from weighted-average and FIFO costing (Appendix A).

9. Compare and contrast operation costing with job costing and process costing (Appendix B).

Cost-*Management* Challenges

(Solutions on page 320.)

1. **How** should Spirit Beverages measure the costs of products, services, and operations?

2. **How** should organizations recognize and measure the costs of spoilage and waste?

3. (Appendix A) **What** is the advantage of first-in, first-out (FIFO) process costing over weighted-average process costing?

Fernando Martinez, the newly hired chief financial officer of Spirit Beverages, sent the following email message to the company's other three senior executives, Sara Engle, chief executive officer; Nasreen Khan, vice-president of operations; and Jay Zhou, vice-president of marketing.

Date: Thurs 13 April 2006 14:38:39
To: Engle, Khan, Zhou
From: FM
Subject: Plans for developing a financial system

By now you have seen the poor results in last quarter's financial statements. I hope to develop a sound financial system within the next 60 days that will provide us the information needed to turn the situation around. Clearly, you all have done what is necessary to develop a quality product and a strong market. It's my task to improve cost management.

I would like to set a meeting at 10:00 (A.M.) on Friday, 21 April, to outline my plans. My initial thought is that we need to develop a good process-costing information system that fits our type of production process and will tell us our product costs. Knowing our product costs will help us to set prices, particularly for special deals and promotions, and to find ways to reduce costs. Once that basic process-costing system is in place, we can ascertain whether we need to go further, for example, to develop an activity-based costing system. As part of the initial process-costing system, we will get a better handle on whether spoilage in the production process is adding significantly to our costs. I suspect that it is.

Spirit Beverages, Inc., makes a sport drink, Spirit, a fortified soft drink that competes with Snapple and Gatorade, among others. Spirit Beverages is a closely held company managed by three people who had been college roommates. The company got off to a good start because of good marketing and a quality product, but its financial management system was virtually nonexistent. After three years of successful market growth, the company still had not made a profit. Rather than sell out to a big corporation, the three founders decided to bring in some financial talent, namely, a former auditor with Deloitte & Touche, Fernando Martinez, to try to turn success in marketing into profitable operations.

Introduction to Process Costing

LO 1 Recognize organizations that should use process costing and those that should use job costing.

Chapter 2 discussed issues in designing product-costing systems, and Chapter 3 dealt with product costing in organizations that produce jobs. This chapter focuses on process-costing methods.

As defined in Chapter 3, *process costing* treats all units processed during a time period as the output to be costed and does not separate and record costs for each unit produced. Organizations that produce products in a continuous-flow use process costing including Coca-Cola (cola concentrate), Sherwin-Williams (paint), Royal Dutch Shell (petrochemicals), and Kellogg (cereal).

Job shops record costs for specific jobs. In continuous-flow production, costs are first recorded for each department and then are assigned to the units (for example, gallons of cola concentrate) passing through the department. We show this distinction between job costing and process costing in Exhibit 8–1; note that at the bottom for

| **Exhibit 8–1** | Comparison of Job and Process Costing |

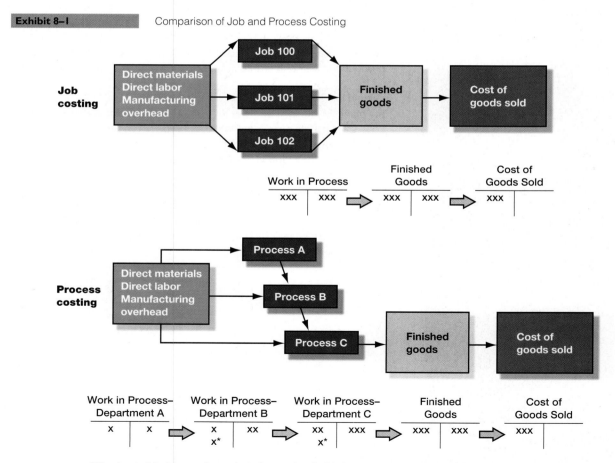

*Direct materials, labor and manufacturing overhead added in production in the department.

process costing, costs are added to the product as it passes through each department. (Although the illustration shows the product passing through each department sequentially, some products might skip departments in practice. In some cases, products could even recycle back through departments if the work was not done right the first time.)

Importance of Process Cost Information

Process costing is vitally important to companies in many ways.[1] The costs assigned to products are commonly used to help set prices, particularly in periods of severe competition or economic downturn. Product costs also are used to identify which products appear to be too costly and need to be redesigned or dropped. Managers use product costs to evaluate the efficiency of production operations. Costs assigned to products are used to determine inventory values for financial reporting.

LO 2 Explain why process-costing information is useful.

Assignment of Costs to Products

We discuss process costing using five examples, starting from the simplest situation and building to a more complex, realistic one. These examples are adaptable to all possible process-costing situations. These examples use just two categories of resource costs, direct materials and conversion costs, to keep the examples as simple as possible. Recall from Chapter 2 that *direct materials* are resources such as raw materials, parts, and components that one can feasibly observe being made into a specific product and that *conversion costs* include direct labor and manufacturing overhead. Conversion costs can apply to all levels of the cost hierarchy. For example, temporary labor is typically a unit-level conversion cost, and machine setup is an example of a batch-level conversion cost.

To present the five-step costing method to assign process costs to products, we use a number of examples from a simple scenario to more complex ones.

Example 1: Department with No Beginning or Ending WIP Inventory

We begin with a simple scenario: no beginning or ending work-in-process (WIP) inventory. This is common for companies that successfully use just-in-time production. Some companies schedule production so that they will have no inventory at the end of a day because work in process could deteriorate or spoil. (Consider a fast-food restaurant leaving partially completed hamburgers, french fries, and milkshakes overnight.)

LO 3 Use the five-step costing method to assign process costs to products.

Spirit Beverages produces a sports drink that it sells to retail stores (such as convenience stores and grocery stores). During October, the Blending Department, which had no beginning inventory, started 8,000 units (one "unit" is one four-pack of bottles). The following were the plant's manufacturing costs for October:

Direct materials	$16,000
Conversion costs	5,600
Total costs to be assigned	$21,600

All units placed into production in October were completed at the end of the month. The unit cost of goods completed is $2.70 (= $21,600 ÷ 8,000). Broken into components, manufacturing unit costs are as follows:

Direct materials ($16,000 ÷ 8,000)	$2.00
Conversion costs ($5,600 ÷ 8,000)	.70
Manufacturing unit cost of a completed unit	$2.70

---

[1] For examples of cost management in process companies, see "Targeting Costs in Process and Service Industries." (Full citations to references are in the Bibliography.)

As shown, process-costing systems do not track costs for each individual unit. Instead, they average the period's costs over its production. Consequently, managers should realize that if they have experienced large cost increases (or decreases) during the month, the average unit costs probably are out of line with the unit costs they face at the end of the month. In cases where costs changed a lot and quickly, managers should insist on weekly or even daily computations of unit costs.

Example 2: Department with Ending WIP Inventory

The facts for the second scenario are the same as for the first one except that at the end of October, only 6,000 of the 8,000 units started had been completed and transferred out of production. These 6,000 units were either sold or are in the finished goods warehouse at the end of October. All direct materials had been added to each of the 2,000 units still in process at the end of the month, but on average only 20 percent of the conversion costs had been incurred for the 2,000 units in ending WIP inventory. At the end of October, how should the Blending Department calculate the cost of (1) the 6,000 completed units and (2) the 2,000 units still in WIP inventory and not yet completed?

We assign costs to ending WIP inventory and to units completed (transferred out of WIP inventory) in five steps. These steps follow:

1. Summarize the flow of physical units.
2. Compute the equivalent number of units produced.
3. Summarize the total costs to be accounted for; these are the sums of the costs in beginning inventory and the costs incurred in the department during the period.
4. Compute costs per equivalent unit.
5. Assign costs to goods transferred out (completed) and to ending WIP inventory (not completed).

Step 1. Summarize the Flow of Physical Units

For *step 1,* summarize the flow of physical units, using the basic cost-flow model to help account for units:

$$\text{Beginning inventory} + \text{Transfers in} - \text{Transfers out} = \text{Ending inventory}$$

This example has no beginning inventory. Transfers in (or units started) total 8,000 units and transfers out (to finished goods) total 6,000 units. Thus, ending WIP inventory is 2,000 units (= 0 units of beginning inventory + 8,000 units started − 6,000 units transferred out).

Step 2. Compute the Equivalent Number of Units Produced

Step 2 requires us to understand the concept of **equivalent units,** which represent the amount of work actually performed on products not yet complete translated to the work required to complete an equal number of whole units. This concept is one of the keys to process costing. According to this concept, if two units were started at the beginning of a month and each was 50 percent finished at the end of the month, the work performed would be considered equivalent to the work performed to complete one whole unit. Thus, for process-costing purposes, the two half-finished units equal one equivalent unit. The equivalent unit concept is shown in Exhibit 8–2 using two half-full glasses of water.

Many organizations use the equivalent unit (EU) concept. For example, university administrators often count the number of students in a department in terms of *full-time equivalents.* Two half-time students are considered to be one full-time equivalent student.

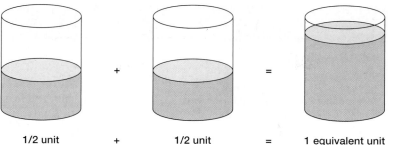

1/2 unit   +   1/2 unit   =   1 equivalent unit

Flow of Units	(Step 1) Physical Units	(Step 2) Equivalent Units	
		Direct Materials	Conversion Costs
Units to be accounted for:			
Beginning work-in-process inventory...............................	0		
Units started this period	8,000		
Total units to be accounted for	8,000		
Units accounted for:			
Completed and transferred out	6,000	6,000	6,000
In ending work-in-process inventory	2,000	2,000	400*
Total units accounted for	8,000	8,000	6,400
*2,000 units × 0.20 complete.			

Exhibit 8–3

Equivalent Units

SPIRIT

Beverages

Now we perform step 2 for Spirit Beverages. All direct materials have been added to each unit transferred out or in ending inventory. The units transferred out are fully complete with respect to conversion costs. Only 20 percent of the conversion costs have been applied to the units still in ending inventory. The following describes this situation:

■ EU for direct materials totaled 8,000 (6,000 completed and transferred out + 2,000 remaining in ending work-in-process inventory).

■ EU for conversion costs totaled 6,400 units [6,000 completed and transferred out + 400 remaining in work in process (= 2,000 × .20 complete for conversion costs)].

Exhibit 8–3 summarizes steps 1 and 2 for Spirit Beverages.

Note that direct materials are 100 percent complete with respect to ending WIP inventory in this example. In reality, direct materials might be added throughout the production process and therefore be partially complete for ending WIP inventory. If so, materials are treated the way that conversion costs are treated in this example.

Steps 3, 4, and 5. Cost Analysis

Steps 3, 4, and *5* provide managers the key cost information that appears in Exhibit 8–4 for Spirit Beverages.

■ Step 3 summarizes the costs to be accounted for. It shows no beginning WIP inventory. Current period costs are separated into direct materials and conversion costs.

■ Step 4 shows that total current period costs are divided by equivalent units to determine costs per equivalent unit. These unit costs are useful for managers in making pricing and other decisions such as whether to keep or drop products.

■ Step 5 shows costs assigned to units completed and transferred out and to units in ending WIP inventory. This information helps managers know how much money is tied up in inventory at the end of the period.

Exhibit 8–4

Production Costs

Flow of Costs	Total	Direct Materials	Conversion Costs
Costs to be accounted for (step 3):			
Costs in beginning work-in-process inventory	0	0	0
Current period costs	$21,600	$16,000	$5,600
Total costs to be accounted for	**$21,600**	**$16,000**	**$5,600**
Costs per equivalent unit (step 4)......................................		$ 2*	$0.875†
Costs accounted for (step 5):			
Costs assigned to units transferred out	$17,250	$12,000‡	$5,250§
Costs of ending inventory	4,350	4,000#	350**
Total costs accounted for...	**$21,600**	**$16,000**	**$5,600**

Computations:
* $2 = $16,000 ÷ 8,000 EU from Exhibit 8–3.
† $.875 = $5,600 ÷ 6,400 EU from Exhibit 8–3.
‡ $12,000 = $2 × 6,000 EU from Exhibit 8–3.
§ $5,250 = $.875 × 6,000 EU from Exhibit 8–3.
# $4,000 = $2 × 2,000 EU from Exhibit 8–3.
** $350 = $.875 × 400 EU from Exhibit 8–3.

Now that you have learned how to account for costs in a process-costing system under two relatively simple scenarios—one with no beginning or ending WIP inventory, and the other with ending WIP inventory but no beginning WIP inventory—we now discuss the more complex task of accounting for costs when both beginning *and* ending WIP inventory exists.

Example 3: Department with Beginning and Ending WIP Inventory

LO 4 Assign process costs to products using weighted-average costing.

Companies generally use one of two process-costing methods to assign costs to inventories when they have beginning inventory: first-in, first-out (FIFO) or weighted-average. You probably have heard these terms before in other accounting classes. The basic idea here is the same as those you learned there.

Weighted-average costing is an inventory method that combines the costs in beginning inventory with costs incurred during the period to compute unit costs. Many regard the weighted-average method as easier to learn and apply in practice, so we discuss it first. We present FIFO costing in Appendix A.

To illustrate accounting for process costing using weighted-average costing, let's use the Spirit Beverages example but change some facts, which are shown in panel A of Exhibit 8–5. It also shows a diagram of unit flows for the Blending Department for the month of December. These are the facts:

- The department had 2,000 units in beginning WIP inventory, which it finished during the month.
- Of the 12,000 units started in December, 8,000 were finished; the remaining partially completed 4,000 units were left in ending WIP inventory.

For weighted-average costing, we do not have to know which of the finished units were from beginning inventory and which were started and finished in the current period. This saves considerable time and effort both in textbook problems and in real-world applications.

Panel B of Exhibit 8–5 shows total costs as follows:

Beginning inventory	$ 3,000
Costs incurred in December	27,000

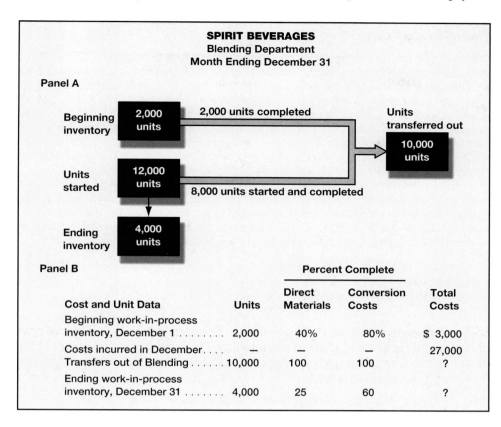

Exhibit 8–5

Data for Blending
Operation

Therefore, the Blending Department manager has $30,000 to account for in December (= $3,000 in beginning inventory + $27,000 in costs incurred during December).

Analysts now face two problems: (1) how much of the $30,000 should be assigned to the 10,000 units transferred out and (2) how much to the partially complete 4,000 units in the Blending Department's ending WIP inventory on December 31.

The Basic Idea: Applying the Basic Cost-Flow Model

The basic cost-flow model provides the underlying framework for solving how much of the cost incurred in the period should be assigned to units transferred out and to ending inventory.

> Beginning balance (BB) + Transfers in (TI) − Transfers out (TO) = Ending balance (EB)

The basic cost-flow model can also be stated as follows:

$$BB + TI = TO + EB$$

We know that BB equals $3,000 and TI equals $27,000. By following the five-step process outlined earlier in this chapter, we can determine how much of these costs should be assigned to units transferred out and how much to units in ending inventory.

Five Key Steps

Because this example is more complex than those earlier in the chapter, we discuss the five-step process in detail here.

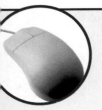

Environmental Costs

Chemical, paper, steel, oil, and other companies that produce in continuous processes often have significant environmental costs. Researchers have found that while such companies generally keep good records of such visible costs as fees for permits and the cost of maintaining pollution control equipment, they do not identify additional costs that are buried in overhead. Researchers of companies in the steel industry have found the additional "hidden" costs to be 10 times as much as the visible costs.* A controller in a small company that had pre-tax accounting income of $840,000 estimated the company's environmental costs to be $50,000. Upon further study, the company found the direct and indirect costs totaled $1,000,000, 20 times as much as the company controller had initially estimated.#

Accurate estimates of environmental costs enable managers to make good decisions that both benefit the environment and the bottom line. In the case of the small company just noted, an investment in environmental improvements seemed to be unprofitable when the most that could be saved appeared to be $50,000 per year. Realizing that hundreds of thousands of dollars could potentially be saved made it worthwhile to invest in environmental improvements.

* Joshi, S., R. Krishnan and L. Lave, "Estimating the Hidden Costs of Environmental Regulation." (Full citations to references are in the Bibliography.)
# T. Kunes, "A Green and Lean Workplace?"

Step 1: Summarize the flow of physical units. This step identifies the flow of physical units regardless of their stage of completion. This step has two parts: (1) identify units to be accounted for and (2) identify units accounted for. We identify these units for Spirit Beverages as follows:

Step 1a.	Units to be accounted for:	
	Units in beginning WIP inventory	2,000
	Units started this period	12,000
	Total units to be accounted for	14,000
Step 1b.	Units accounted for:	
	Units transferred out	10,000
	Units in ending WIP inventory	4,000
		14,000

Step 1 indicates that we must account for the costs of 14,000 units, of which 2,000 were in beginning inventory and 12,000 were started during December. Of those 14,000 units, 10,000 were transferred out and 4,000 remained in ending inventory at December 31. The following summarizes the flow of physical units in terms of the basic cost-flow model:

From 1a				From 1b		
BB	+	TI	=	TO	+	EB
2,000	+	12,000	=	10,000	+	4,000

Step 2: Compute the equivalent units produced. Some people find step 2 to be the most difficult part of process costing. We intend to make it as straightforward as possible.

Because Spirit Beverages' WIP inventories are at different stages of completion for direct materials and conversion costs, equivalent units must be calculated separately for direct materials and for conversion costs. Units transferred out are 100 percent completed (or they would not have been transferred out). Stages of completion for direct materials and conversion costs in ending inventory are given in panel B of Exhibit 8–5: Ending WIP inventory is 25 percent complete with respect to direct materials and 60 percent complete with respect to conversion costs.

Thus, equivalent units of work completed in December are computed as follows:

	Direct Materials	Conversion Costs
Units transferred out...	10,000	10,000
Units in ending WIP inventory:		
Materials (4,000 × .25)...	1,000	
Conversion costs (4,000 × .60)		2,400
Total equivalent units	11,000	12,400

Note that these numbers indicate the equivalent number of units *completed* during the month. In general, it is possible that almost all work was done in previous periods, but the finishing touches were applied this period. These numbers do not tell managers how much work was done in the period, but they do tell them the equivalent work *completed*. Of course, *we* know from the facts in this particular example that most of the work was done in December. However, the equivalent units of work completed based on the weighted-average method would not have told the manager how much of the work equivalently completed in December was actually done in December compared to how much was done in November (or previous months). This lack of information about production in December would be a problem for a manager who wants information about worker productivity.

Step 3: Summarize the total costs to be accounted for. Step 3 is easy. The total costs to be accounted for are those in beginning inventory plus those incurred during the period as shown in panel B of Exhibit 8–5. Assume that total costs are separated into direct materials and conversion costs as follows:

	Total Costs	Direct Materials	Conversion Costs
Costs to be accounted for:			
Costs in beginning WIP inventory	$ 3,000	$ 2,000	$1,000
Current period costs	27,000	20,000	7,000
Total costs to be accounted for	$30,000	$22,000	$8,000

This information indicates that $30,000 must be assigned either to products transferred out of the department or to ending WIP inventory.

Step 4: Compute costs per equivalent unit. Step 4 calculates costs per equivalent unit for direct materials (total costs = $22,000; equivalent units = 11,000) and conversion costs (total costs = $8,000; equivalent units = 12,400). The calculation is straightforward; simply divide total costs to be accounted for by the number of equivalent units for each cost category as shown:

	Direct Materials	Conversion Costs
Total costs to be accounted for (from step 3)	$22,000	$ 8,000
Number of equivalent units (from step 2)	11,000	12,400
Cost per equivalent unit	$ 2.00	$.64516

This cost information helps managers make pricing and other decisions.

Step 5: Assign costs to goods transferred out and to ending inventory. Now we have the data and computations needed to perform step 5 to complete the task: Assign the costs to be accounted for to goods transferred out and those in ending WIP inventory.

Exhibit 8–6

Cost Flows: Weighted
Average

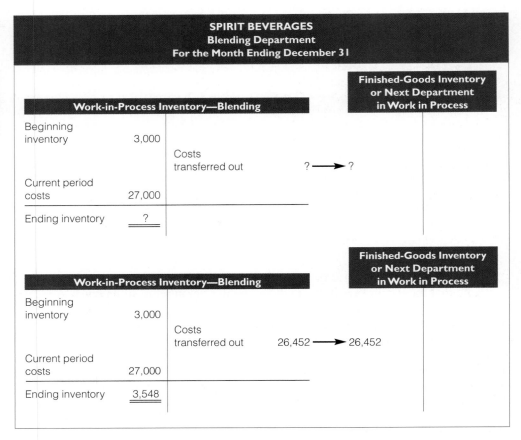

To perform step 5, we multiply the cost per equivalent unit (computed in step 4) by the number of equivalent units in ending WIP inventory and transferred out for the period shown in step 2.

Costs accounted for as follows:

Transferred out:	
Direct materials (10,000 units × $2)	$20,000
Conversion costs (10,000 units × $.64516)	6,452
Total transferred out	$26,452
Ending work in process, December 31:	
Direct materials (1,000 EU × $2)	$ 2,000
Conversion costs (2,400 EU × $.64516)	1,548
Total work in process	$ 3,548
Total costs accounted for	$30,000

How to check your work.   Note the following equality:

Total costs to be accounted for = Total costs accounted for
[step 3]   [step 5]

This equality must hold in every case (note that rounding can cause small discrepancies). Costs accounted for must equal costs to be accounted for because of the principle of the basic cost-flow model:

$$BB + TI = TO + EB$$

Costs to be accounted for represent the left side of the equation, $BB + TI$. The costs accounted for represent the right side of the equation, $TO + EB$.

How this looks in T-accounts.   Although the computations do not require T-accounts, you might find that understanding the big picture is easier if you see how costs flow through T-accounts. Exhibit 8–6 shows the flow of costs through the WIP Inventory

Exhibit 8–7

Production Cost Report:
Weighted Average

SPIRIT BEVERAGES
Blending Department
For the Month Ending December 31

Flow of Units	(Section 1) Physical Units	(Section 2) Equivalent Units	
		Direct Materials	Conversion Costs
Units to be accounted for:			
Beginning WIP inventory	2,000		
Units started this period	12,000		
Total units to be accounted for	**14,000**		
Units to be accounted for:			
Completed and transferred out	10,000	10,000	10,000
In ending WIP inventory	4,000	1,000*	2,400†
Total units accounted for	**14,000**	**11,000**	**12,400**

Flow of Costs	Costs (Sections 3 through 5)		
	Total	Direct Materials	Conversion Costs
Costs to be accounted for (section 3):			
Costs in beginning WIP inventory	$ 3,000	$ 2,000	$ 1,000
Current period costs	27,000	20,000	7,000
Total costs to be accounted for	**$30,000**	**$22,000**	**$ 8,000**
Costs per equivalent unit (section 4)		**$ 2.00‡**	**$.64516§**
Costs accounted for (section 5):			
Costs assigned to units transferred out	$26,452	$20,000#	$ 6,452**
Cost of ending WIP inventory	3,548	2,000††	1,548‡‡
Total costs accounted for	**$30,000**	**$22,000**	**$ 8,000**

Computations:

*Ending inventory is 25 percent complete. 1,000 EU = .25 × 4,000 units.

† Ending inventory is 60 percent complete. 2,400 EU = .60 × 4,000 units.

‡ $2.00 = $22,000 ÷ 11,000 EU

§ $.64516 = $8,000 ÷ 12,400 EU

$20,000 = 10,000 EU × $2 per EU

** $6,452 = 10,000 EU × $.64516 per EU

†† $2,000 = 1,000 EU × $2 per EU

‡‡ $1,548 = 2,400 EU × $.64516 per EU

T-account for the Blending Department. The top panel shows the T-account at the end of December after the costs incurred during the month were known but before completing the five steps to assign costs to ending inventory and transfers out. The bottom panel shows the T-account after completing step 5.

Managerial Use of the Production Cost Report

The **production cost report** summarizes the production and cost results for a period. Managers find it an important document for monitoring their flow. Using this report, managers can determine whether inventory levels are getting too high, costs are not low enough, or the number of units produced is too low.

Exhibit 8–7 presents a production cost report for the Blending Department of Spirit Beverages for December. Although it might look complex, you will soon see that this report simply includes the five steps for assigning costs to goods transferred out and to ending WIP inventory described earlier. To help relate the production cost report to those five steps, we present the report in five sections, each of which corresponds to a step.

Production Cost Report

Review Exhibit 8–7 and the preceding discussion.

a.   Why does Spirit Beverages use process costing rather than job costing?

b.   Why does the production cost report have separate columns for direct materials and conversion costs? Why not combine the data into one column to simplify the report?

(Solutions begin on page 320.)

Sections 1 and 2: Managing the Physical Flow of Units

Sections 1 and 2 of the production cost report correspond to steps 1 and 2 discussed above on pages 300 to 301. Section 1 summarizes the flow of physical units and shows 14,000 units to be accounted for, 10,000 as transfers out and 4,000 in ending inventory. Section 2 shows the equivalent number of units for direct materials and conversion costs separated into equivalent units transferred out and equivalent units remaining in WIP inventory.

Sections 3, 4, and 5: Managing Costs

Sections 3, 4, and 5 provide information about costs. Corresponding to step 3, section 3 shows the costs to be accounted for, $3,000 in beginning inventory and $27,000 incurred during December. Section 4 shows how we computed the cost per equivalent unit for direct materials ($2.00) and conversion costs ($.64516). Finally, section 5 shows the cost assignment performed in step 5 for direct materials and conversion costs. (Note that some rounding is inevitable. Do not be concerned if your numbers differ from ours by a few dollars.)

Example 4: Department with Costs Transferred in from Prior Departments

Accounting for Transferred-In Costs

LO 5 Account for costs transferred between processes.

Our discussion so far has assumed a single department. Products usually pass through a series of departments, however. As they pass from one department to another, their costs must follow.

Prior department costs, or *transferred-in costs,* are the costs of units transferred out of one department and into another. They are the manufacturing costs incurred in another department and transferred to a subsequent department in the manufacturing process. The costs of processing cereal at Kellogg is a prior department cost to its Packaging Department. Equivalent whole units are 100 percent complete in terms of prior department costs, so cost computations for prior department costs are relatively easy.

Let's go back to Spirit Beverages and change the assumptions to allow for prior department costs. Assume that the Blending Department's beginning WIP inventory came from another department. In this example, all facts remain the same as in the previous one except that we include additional costs from the prior department under a new column, Prior Department's Costs. This column includes the prior department's costs of $5,000 associated with beginning WIP inventory and current costs of $52,000 (for goods transferred in from the prior department during the month). All other costs and physical units remain the same as in our original example. The following data summary presents the new information in bold.

Exhibit 8–8 is a production cost report that summarizes these data. If you compare this report with the one in Exhibit 8–7, you'll see that Exhibit 8–8 is less complex than it looks. Notice that Exhibit 8–8 simply has the new column Prior Department to account for the goods transferred in from a prior department.

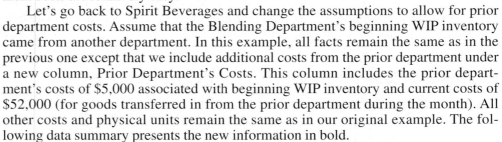

			Blending Department's Costs	
	Units	Prior Department's Costs	Direct Materials	Conversion Costs
Physical flow:				
Beginning inventory..............	2,000	**100% complete**	40% complete	80% complete
Ending inventory	4,000	**100% complete**	25% complete	60% complete
Units started **(transferred in)**	12,000	**100% complete**		
Started and completed	8,000	**100% complete**	100% complete	100% complete
Costs incurred:				
Beginning inventory.............................		**$ 5,000**	$ 2,000	$1,000
Current costs		**52,000**	20,000	7,000

Table title (above): **SPIRIT BEVERAGES** / Blending Department / For the Month Ending December 31

Responsibility for Costs Transferred in from Prior Departments

An important issue for performance evaluation is whether a department manager should be held accountable for all costs charged to the department. This usually is not the case; a department and its people are usually evaluated on the basis of costs that the department adds relative to the good output it produces. A prior department's costs are often excluded when comparing actual department costs with a standard or budget. We discuss this point more extensively in later chapters on performance evaluation, but we mention it here to emphasize that different information is needed for different purposes. Assigning costs to units for inventory valuation requires that the costs of all prior departments be included in the present department product cost calculations. However, assigning costs to departments for performance evaluation usually requires that costs from prior departments be excluded from the present department's costs.

Example 5: Department with Spoilage Costs

If you have ever worked on a project that you discarded and then started on a new one, you understand the concept of *spoilage*. From your experience, you understand that spoilage, whether a discarded term paper, meal, or college application, is costly. Sometimes it is a necessary part of doing the job right. Doing something that did not turn out right can be part of the learning experience. If you have learned to play a sport, to dance, or to play a musical instrument, you know that no matter how much instruction you get, at some point you just have to go out and learn from your mistakes.

LO 6 Analyze and manage "normal" and "abnormal" spoilage.

Spoilage represents goods that are damaged, do not meet specifications, or are otherwise not suitable for further processing or sale as good output. By measuring the costs of spoilage and the costs to reduce it (such as the costs to train employees, to use higher-quality materials, and to repair faulty equipment), managers are able to make informed decisions to improve quality and reduce costs.

Managers face these key problems concerning spoilage:

- Identifying whether it exists.
- Determining whether it can be eliminated, and if so, how. For example, spoilage can often be reduced by spending more time training employees.
- Deciding whether eliminating it is worthwhile. For example, is eliminating spoilage worth the cost of employee training?

Exhibit 8–8

Production Cost Report
with Prior Department
Costs: Weighted Average

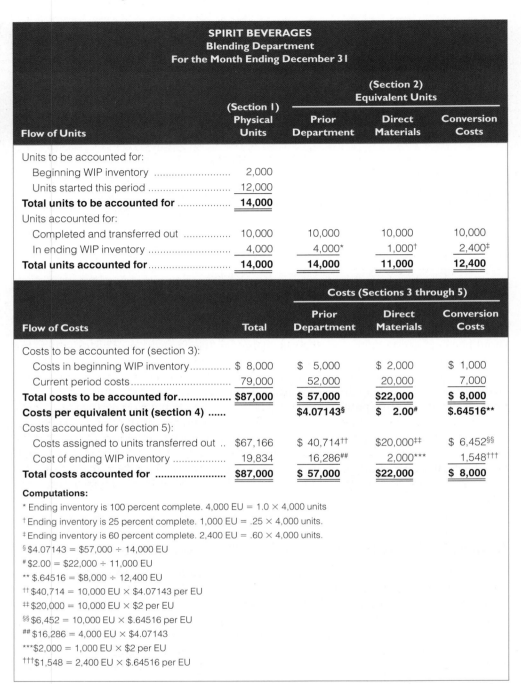

Flow of Units	(Section 1) Physical Units	(Section 2) Equivalent Units Prior Department	Direct Materials	Conversion Costs
Units to be accounted for:				
Beginning WIP inventory	2,000			
Units started this period	12,000			
Total units to be accounted for	**14,000**			
Units accounted for:				
Completed and transferred out	10,000	10,000	10,000	10,000
In ending WIP inventory	4,000	4,000*	1,000†	2,400‡
Total units accounted for	**14,000**	**14,000**	**11,000**	**12,400**

Flow of Costs	Total	Costs (Sections 3 through 5) Prior Department	Direct Materials	Conversion Costs
Costs to be accounted for (section 3):				
Costs in beginning WIP inventory	$ 8,000	$ 5,000	$ 2,000	$ 1,000
Current period costs	79,000	52,000	20,000	7,000
Total costs to be accounted for	**$87,000**	**$ 57,000**	**$22,000**	**$ 8,000**
Costs per equivalent unit (section 4)		$4.07143§	$ 2.00#	$.64516**
Costs accounted for (section 5):				
Costs assigned to units transferred out	$67,166	$ 40,714††	$20,000‡‡	$ 6,452§§
Cost of ending WIP inventory	19,834	16,286##	2,000***	1,548†††
Total costs accounted for	**$87,000**	**$ 57,000**	**$22,000**	**$ 8,000**

Computations:

* Ending inventory is 100 percent complete. 4,000 EU = 1.0 × 4,000 units

† Ending inventory is 25 percent complete. 1,000 EU = .25 × 4,000 units.

‡ Ending inventory is 60 percent complete. 2,400 EU = .60 × 4,000 units.

§ $4.07143 = $57,000 ÷ 14,000 EU

$2.00 = $22,000 ÷ 11,000 EU

** $.64516 = $8,000 ÷ 12,400 EU

†† $40,714 = 10,000 EU × $4.07143 per EU

‡‡ $20,000 = 10,000 EU × $2 per EU

§§ $6,452 = 10,000 EU × $.64516 per EU

$16,286 = 4,000 EU × $4.07143

*** $2,000 = 1,000 EU × $2 per EU

††† $1,548 = 2,400 EU × $.64516 per EU

Normal versus Abnormal Spoilage: Is Spoilage Ever Normal?

Lost units are goods that evaporate or otherwise disappear during a production process. **Normal spoilage** is a result of the regular operation of the production process (see the left half of Exhibit 8–9). Some managers might not consider this to be normal spoilage, however, and strive to eliminate all spoilage. **Abnormal spoilage** results from other than the usual course of operations of a process. It occurs if units are lost for unusual or abnormal reasons (see the right half of Exhibit 8–9). The debit for abnormal spoilage in the journal entry is made to an account such as Abnormal Spoilage, which writes off the costs as an expense for the period.

To illustrate the accounting for abnormal spoilage, assume that the managers of a Coca-Cola bottling plant discovered that it had received a shipment of defective plastic bottles. These bottles, which had already been filled with soft drink, had to be destroyed at a cost of $8,000. Thus, $8,000 must be taken out of the Work-in-Process Inventory account and charged to the expense account Abnormal Spoilage as follows:

Abnormal Spoilage Expense............................ 8,000

   Work-in-Process Inventory 8,000

Entry to account for abnormal spoilage that occurred during production.

Abnormal spoilage is an expense for the period and appears on the income statement. Managers watch the Abnormal Spoilage account closely to identify causes of spoilage and to prevent it from occurring in the future.

Companies that have a zero defects policy might treat *all* spoilage as abnormal. They probably would not consider the left half of Exhibit 8–9 to be normal. Cost Management in Practice 8.2, "Process Costing and Waste at Louisiana Pacific," discusses how and why the company changed its attitude toward "normal" waste.

Process Costing and Waste at Louisiana Pacific

Louisiana Pacific, one of the largest wood products firms, has operations throughout the Western Hemisphere. The company uses process costing for most of its many processes and is vitally concerned with the costs of its outputs, which include waste that it must treat before disposing of it. At one time, costs of waste disposal were not considered to be material and were counted as normal costs of products. However, higher costs caused by environmental concerns and regulations have motivated Louisiana Pacific to monitor costs of waste from its processes and to find ways to reduce those costs.

Its Chetwynd, British Columbia, mill, for example, utilizes a state-of-the-art mechanical pulping process and a zero-effluent discharge system to produce pulp for use in its paper processes or for sale to other paper manufacturers. Its Samoa, California, mill produces bleached and unbleached kraft pulp by a chlorine-free process, thereby eliminating environmentally dangerous dioxins. Louisiana Pacific decided to sell its Ketchikan, Alaska, Pulp Company subsidiary when the combination of low pulp prices, restricted access to raw timber, and greatly increased costs of reducing and treating its process waste made the plant unprofitable. *Source: Louisiana Pacific Form 10-K.*

Cost Management in Practice 8.2

Normal Spoilage

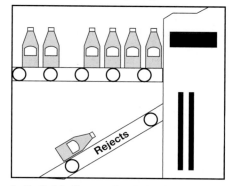

Abnormal Spoilage

In the left half, some bottled soft drinks are rejected because the bottling process did not sufficiently fill the bottles. Although not desirable, the company considers this "normal" spoilage. In the right half, an accident has created "abnormal" spoilage.

You're the Decision Maker 8.2

Analyzing Process Costs

Review Exhibit 8–10 and the preceding discussion.

a. Which parts of the production cost report do you think hold the most information about what the company needs to do to improve efficiency (and therefore, profitability)?

b. As a manager, what would you focus on to improve the profitability of Spirit Beverages?

(Solutions begin on page 320.)

Accounting for Spoilage Costs

Let's go back to example 3 for Spirit Beverages and recall the facts. It had beginning and ending WIP inventory for the month of December but no transfers in from other departments. It had 2,000 units in beginning WIP inventory, which were finished during the month of December. Of the 12,000 units that were started in December, 8,000 were finished, and the remaining 4,000 were left in ending WIP inventory. Total costs to be accounted for were calculated in Exhibit 8–7 and are repeated here.

	Total Costs	Direct Materials	Conversion Costs
Costs to be accounted for:			
Costs in beginning WIP inventory	$ 3,000	$ 2,000	$1,000
Current period costs	$27,000	$20,000	$7,000
Total costs to be accounted for	$30,000	$22,000	$8,000

Now we change the facts slightly; assume that of the 12,000 units started in December, 8,000 were finished, 3,500 were left in ending WIP inventory, and 500 were lost to spoilage. As in example 3, ending WIP inventory is 25 percent complete with respect to direct materials and 60 percent complete with respect to conversion costs.

To determine the cost of spoiled units, we must allocate all costs (beginning WIP inventory and current period costs) to Finished-Goods Inventory, Spoilage, and Ending WIP Inventory accounts. We learn that production people detect spoilage after 50 percent of conversion costs and 20 percent of materials costs have been applied.

Once again, we can use the five-step process (as displayed formally in a production cost report) to allocate costs. Exhibit 8–10 shows a production cost report for this example including spoilage. Note that the only difference between this report and a report without spoilage (Exhibit 8–7) is that equivalent units are calculated for spoiled units in steps 1 and 2, and costs are allocated to spoiled units in step 5.

Exhibit 8–10 indicates that spoiled goods cost $362 for the month of December. In general, the earlier spoilage can be detected in the process, the less costly it is to the company. If spoilage cannot be prevented, it should be detected as early as possible.

The $362 in spoilage costs is typically charged to an expense account when it is transferred out of WIP Inventory. The account most often used is Cost of Goods Sold. However, some companies prorate spoilage costs over inventory accounts (WIP and Finished Goods) and Cost of Goods Sold based on their respective account balances. As mentioned earlier, if the company deems the spoilage to be abnormal, it should use the expense account, Abnormal Spoilage.

Management of Spirit Beverages' Costs

At the beginning of the chapter, we saw that Fernando Martinez, the newly hired chief financial officer of Spirit Beverages, wanted to develop a good process-costing information system that would provide product cost information. This chapter has described the system that Martinez developed. He was pleased to see that the spoilage costs were low compared to his expectations—only $362 in the Blending Department for December compared to total costs of $30,000, according to Exhibit 8–10. Also, Martinez was pleased to see that the conversion costs per unit in the Blending Department were only $.6477 per unit. Most other companies in the industry experienced blending conversion costs in the range of $.65 to $.80 per unit.

| | | (Section 2) Equivalent Units | |
| | | | |

SPIRIT BEVERAGES
Blending Department
For the Month Ending December 31

Flow of Units	(Section 1) Physical Units	Direct Materials	Conversion Costs
Units to be accounted for:			
Beginning WIP inventory	2,000		
Units started this period	12,000		
Total units to account for	**14,000**		
Units accounted for:			
Good units completed and transferred out	10,000	10,000	10,000
Spoiled units transferred out	500	100‡	250§
Units in ending WIP inventory	3,500	875*	2,100†
Total units accounted for	**14,000**	**10,975**	**12,350**

Costs (Sections 3 through 5)

Flow of Costs	Total	Direct Materials	Conversion Costs
Costs to be accounted for (section 3):			
Costs in beginning WIP inventory	$ 3,000	$ 2,000	$ 1,000
Current period costs	27,000	20,000	7,000
Total costs to be accounted for	**$30,000**	**$ 22,000**	**$ 8,000**
Costs per equivalent unit (section 4)		**$2.00456#**	**$.64777****
Costs accounted for good units (section 5):			
Costs assigned to good units transferred out	$26,524	$ 20,046††	$ 6,478‡‡
Costs assigned to spoiled goods	362	200***	162†††
Cost of ending WIP inventory	3,114	1,754§§	1,360##
Total costs accounted for	$30,000	$ 22,000	$ 8,000

Computations:
‡ 100 EU = .20 × 500 units.
§ 250 EU = .50 × 500 units.
* Ending inventory is 25 percent complete. 875 EU = .25 × 3,500 units.
† Ending inventory is 60 percent complete. 2,100 EU = .60 × 3,500 units.
# $2.00456 = $22,000 ÷ 10,975 EU
** $.64777 = $8,000 ÷ 12,350 EU
†† $20,046 = 10,000 EU × $2.00456 per EU
‡‡ $6,478 = 10,000 EU × $.64777 per EU
*** $200 = 100 EU × $2.00456 per EU
††† $162 = 250 EU × $.64777 per EU
§§ $1,754 = 875 EU × $2.00456 per EU
$1,360 = 2,100 EU × $.64777 per EU

Exhibit 8–10

Production Cost Report with Spoilage: Weighted Average

SPIRIT Beverages

   Martinez was appalled at the direct materials costs, however. The cost, $2.00456 per Exhibit 8–10, was considerably higher than other companies in the industry who had direct materials costs ranging from $1.60 to $1.90 per unit. The cost information developed from the process costing system did not tell Martinez that he had to reduce product costs, but it told him to look into the causes of high direct materials costs.

Choice between Job and Process Costing

Job costing collects costs for each unit produced. For example, a print shop collects costs for each order, a defense contractor collects costs for each contract, and a custom home builder collects costs for each house. Process costing accumulates costs in a department for an accounting period (for example, a month) and then spreads them

Custom home builders generally use job costing to keep track of the costs of each house because each house is typically unique. Builders of tract houses might use process costing if all houses are the same.

evenly, or averages them, over all units produced that month. Process costing assumes that each unit produced is relatively uniform. Of course, process costing does not provide as much information as job costing because it does not record the cost of each unit produced. The choice of process- versus job-costing systems involves comparing the costs and benefits of each system. The production process being utilized is also a major factor in choosing a cost system.

Consider a home builder. Job costing accumulates costs for each house. It is not sufficient simply to record the amount of total lumber delivered to several houses, but records of the amount subsequently returned from each house must be kept. If laborers work on several houses, they must track their time spent on each house. Process costing, however, simply requires recording the total costs incurred on all jobs. For the home builder, process costing records the average cost of all houses built. A custom home builder probably uses job costing. A developer might consider each development a job but use process costing for each house within each development.

Under process costing, the actual cost incurred for a particular unit is not reported. If all units are homogeneous, this loss of information is most likely minimal. It probably is not important for Intel to know whether the cost of the 10,001st microprocessor chip is different from that of the 10,002nd, particularly if the unit cost is calculated primarily to value inventory for external financial reporting. Cost control and performance evaluation take place by department, not by unit produced, in process systems. For companies such as Intel that make homogeneous units, the additional benefits of job costing do not justify the additional record-keeping costs.

What if record-keeping costs were equal under job and process systems for the units in a product line? Then we would say that a job system is better because it provides all data that a process system does, and more. As a general rule, however, a job system is usually more costly than a process system. Thus, managers and accountants must decide whether knowing the actual cost of each unit, which is available in a job-costing system, is enough to justify additional record-keeping costs. Companies producing relatively large, heterogeneous items usually can justify the additional costs for the additional benefits of job costing.

Chapter Summary

Process costing is used when it is not possible or practical to identify costs with specific lots or batches of product. A process-costing system accumulates costs for each production department but does not maintain separate records of costs for each unit produced. When comparing job and process costing, companies generally find that job costing provides more data but has higher record-keeping costs. Managers and accountants must decide whether the additional data available under job costing justify these higher costs. For companies that produce relatively homogeneous units in a continuous process, cost-benefit analysis generally favors process costing.

The two most common process costing methods are weighted-average costing and first-in, first-out (FIFO) costing (discussed in Appendix A). The weighted-average method makes no distinction between beginning inventory and current period costs. As a result, its computations are simpler than those obtained using FIFO costing.

Process costing assigns costs to ending WIP inventory and units completed using five steps:

Step 1:   Summarize the flow of physical units.

Step 2:   Compute the equivalent number of units produced.

Step 3: Summarize the total costs to be accounted for.

Step 4: Compute costs per equivalent unit.

Step 5: Assign costs to goods transferred out (completed and to ending inventory and to spoiled units, if applicable).

Appendix A to Chapter Eight

Cost Assignment to Products Using First-In, First-Out Costing

A disadvantage of weighted-average costing is that it mixes current period costs with the costs of products in beginning inventory, making it impossible for managers to know how much it costs to make a product during the *current period.* **First-in, first-out (FIFO) costing** is an inventory method that identifies the first units completed as the first ones sold or transferred out. FIFO costing separates current period costs from those in beginning inventory and transfers out the costs in beginning inventory in a lump sum (assuming that the units in beginning inventory were completed during the current period) rather than mingling them with current period costs.

LO 7 Assign process costs to products using first-in, first-out (FIFO) costing.

FIFO gives managers more accurate information about the work done in the current period. Managers benefit from this separation of current period costs from those in beginning inventory because they can identify and manage current period costs.

If the production process is a FIFO process, the inventory numbers are more likely to reflect reality under FIFO costing than under weighted-average costing because the units in ending inventory are likely to have been produced in the current period. FIFO costing assigns current period costs to those units, but weighted-average costing mixes current and prior period costs in assigning a value to ending inventory.

Example 3: Department with Beginning and Ending WIP Inventory: FIFO

To illustrate accounting for process costing using FIFO, we use the data from example 3 for Spirit Beverages, which assumes beginning and ending WIP inventory (but no transfers in or spoilage). This allows for a comparison of FIFO and weighted-average costing and identification of the resulting differences. Recall the following facts:

	Units	Costs Direct Materials	Conversion Costs
Beginning WIP inventory	2,000	$ 2,000	$1,000
Started this period	12,000	20,000	7,000
Transferred out	10,000	?	?
Ending WIP inventory	4,000	?	?

Remember that Panel B of Exhibit 8–5 indicates that *beginning* WIP inventory is 40 percent complete for direct materials and 80 percent complete for conversion costs. *Ending* WIP inventory is 25 percent complete for direct materials and 60 percent complete for conversion costs.

Five key steps. The same five steps are used with FIFO costing as with the weighted-average costing approach and are displayed formally in a production cost report. Similarities and differences within each step are noted in the following discussion.

Step 1: Summarize the flow of physical units. This step identifies the flow of physical units regardless of their stage of completion and is the same for both FIFO and weighted-average costing. Section 1 of the production cost report in Exhibit 8–11 summarizes the flow of physical units, showing 14,000 units to be accounted for, 10,000 as transfers out of the Blending Department, and 4,000 units remaining in ending inventory.

Exhibit 8–11

Production Cost
Report: FIFO

SPIRIT Beverages

SPIRIT BEVERAGES
Blending Department
For the Month Ending December 31

Flow of Units	(Section 1) Physical Units	(Section 2) Equivalent Units Direct Materials	Conversion Costs
Units to be accounted for:			
Beginning WIP inventory	2,000		
Units started this period	12,000		
Total units to be accounted for	**14,000**		
Units accounted for:			
Units completed and transferred out			
Beginning WIP inventory....................................	2,000	1,200*	400†
Started and completed currently	8,000	8,000	8,000
Total..	10,000	9,200	8,400
Units in ending WIP inventory	4,000	1,000‡	2,400§
Total units accounted for.......................................	**14,000**	**10,200**	**10,800**

Flow of Costs	Costs (Sections 3 through 5) Total	Direct Materials	Conversion Costs
Costs to be accounted for (section 3):			
Costs in beginning WIP inventory..........................	$ 3,000	$ 2,000	$ 1,000
Current period costs..	27,000	20,000	7,000
Total costs to be accounted for...............................	**$30,000**	**$22,000**	**$ 8,000**
Costs per equivalent unit (section 4)		1.96078#	.64815**
Costs accounted for (section 5)			
Costs assigned to units transferred out:			
Costs from beginning WIP inventory..................	$ 3,000	$ 2,000	$ 1,000
Current costs added to complete beginning WIP inventory......................................	2,612	2,353††	259‡‡
Total costs from beginning WIP inventory	5,612	4,353	1,259
Current costs of units started and completed....	20,871	15,686§§	5,185##
Total costs transferred out..............................	26,483	20,039	6,444
Costs of ending WIP inventory	3,517	1,961***	1,556†††
Total costs accounted for	**$30,000**	**$22,000**	**$ 8,000**

Computations:

* 1,200 = 60% × 2,000. 60 percent of costs must be added to complete beginning WIP inventory.
† 400 = 20% × 2,000. 20 percent of costs must be added to complete beginning WIP inventory.
‡ Ending WIP inventory for direct materials is 25 percent complete.
§ Ending WIP inventory for conversion costs is 60 percent complete.
# $1.96078 = $20,000 ÷ 10,200 EU
** $.64815 = $7,000 ÷ 10,800 EU
†† $2,353 = 1,200 EU × $1.96078 per EU
‡‡ $259 = 400 EU × $.64815 per EU
§§ $15,686 = 8,000 EU × $1.96078 per EU
$5,185 = 8,000 EU × $.64815 per EU
*** $1,961 = 1,000 EU × $1.96078 per EU
††† $1,556 = 2,400 EU × $.64815 per EU

Step 2: Compute the equivalent number of units produced. FIFO costing and weighted-average costing compute equivalent units differently. Recall that FIFO costing separates what was in beginning inventory from what occurs this period. The FIFO equivalent unit computation is confined only to what was produced this period. Under FIFO, we compute equivalent units in three parts for both direct materials and conversion costs:

1. Equivalent units to complete beginning WIP inventory.
2. Equivalent units of goods started and completed during the current period.
3. Equivalent units of goods started during the period and still in ending WIP inventory.

Spirit Beverages had 2,000 units in beginning inventory that were 40 percent complete for direct materials and 80 percent complete for conversion costs at the beginning of the period. Completing the beginning inventory required 1,200 equivalent units for direct materials [(1.00 − .40) × 2,000 units], and 400 equivalent units for conversion costs [(1.00 − .80) × 2,000 units].

The units started and completed can be derived by examining the physical flow of units. Because 12,000 units were started and 4,000 of them remain in ending inventory, according to the FIFO method, the remaining 8,000 were completed. Thus, 8,000 units were started and completed. Another way to get the same result is to observe that of the 10,000 units completed during December, 2,000 came from beginning inventory (according to the FIFO method), so the remaining 8,000 units completed must have been started during December.

Either way one views the physical flow, the department started and completed 8,000 units. Because these 8,000 units were 100 percent complete when transferred out of the department, the units started and completed represent 8,000 equivalent units produced during the current period for both direct materials and conversion costs.

Finally, we determine the number of equivalent units of production in ending inventory.[2] Ending inventory of 4,000 units is 25 percent complete with respect to direct materials and 60 percent complete for conversion costs. Thus, ending WIP inventory has 1,000 equivalent units (.25 × 4,000) for direct materials and 2,400 equivalent units (.60 × 4,000) for conversion costs. These equivalent unit results appear in section 2 of the production cost report in Exhibit 8–11.

Note that the number of equivalent units under FIFO is less than or equal to the number under the weighted-average method because the FIFO computations refer to this period's production only. Weighted-average equivalent units consider all units in the department, whether produced in this period or a previous period. (If the department has no beginning inventory, the weighted-average and FIFO equivalent units are equal.)

Step 3: Summarize the total costs to be accounted for. The total costs to be accounted for under FIFO costing are the same as under weighted-average costing. Whatever our assumption about cost flows, we must account for *all* costs in the department (those in beginning inventory plus those incurred during the period). For Spirit Beverages, these costs are as follows:

	Total Costs	Direct Materials	Conversion Costs
Costs to be accounted for:			
Costs in beginning WIP inventory	$ 3,000	$ 2,000	$1,000
Current period costs	27,000	20,000	7,000
Total costs to be accounted for	$30,000	$22,000	$8,000

These costs are shown in section 3 of the production cost report in Exhibit 8–11.

Step 4: Compute costs per equivalent unit. Under FIFO, the costs per equivalent unit are confined to the costs incurred this period, $27,000, and the equivalent units produced this period, which were computed in step 2 (10,200 for direct materials and 10,800 for conversion costs). In formula form,

$$\text{Cost per equivalent unit} = \text{Current period costs} \div \text{Equivalent units of production this period}$$

---

[2] For our examples, units in ending inventory come from the current period production. Although it is unlikely, you could encounter cases in practice with inventory levels so high relative to current period production that some of the beginning inventory is still in ending inventory. In that case, you should keep separate the costs and units in ending inventory that come from beginning inventory. Having separated those costs and units, you can perform the computations described in the text for the current period costs.

Note that only current period costs are included in the numerator. The FIFO method excludes the beginning WIP costs from the cost per equivalent unit calculation. Instead, beginning WIP inventory is assumed to be completed during the period and transferred out to finished goods.

For Spirit Beverages, the cost per equivalent unit under FIFO is calculated here.

Direct Materials

$$\text{Cost per equivalent unit} = \$20,000 \div 10,200 \text{ equivalent units}$$
$$= \$1.96078 \text{ per equivalent unit}$$

Conversion Costs

$$\text{Cost per equivalent unit} = \$7,000 \div 10,800 \text{ equivalent units}$$
$$= \$.64815 \text{ per equivalent unit}$$

The cost per equivalent unit appears in section 4 of the production cost report.

Step 5: Assign costs to goods transferred out and to ending WIP inventory.   The cost of goods transferred out has the following components:

Costs in beginning WIP inventory (at beginning of period)	$ 3,000
Costs to complete beginning inventory	2,612
Costs of the 8,000 units started and completed this period	20,871
Costs of ending WIP inventory	3,517
Total costs accounted for	$30,000

These results appear in section 5 of the production cost report. Note that the costs to be accounted for in section 3, $30,000, equal the costs accounted for in section 5, $30,000.

Flow of costs through T-accounts.   Exhibit 8–12 shows the flow of costs through the WIP Inventory T-account for the Blending Department using FIFO. The top section shows the T-accounts as they appear before computing cost of goods transferred out

Exhibit 8–12

Cost Flows: FIFO

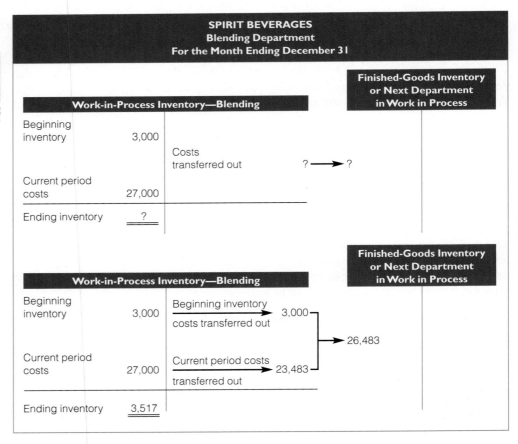

	Weighted-Average (from Exhibit 8–7)	FIFO (from Exhibit 8–11)
Equivalent unit costs:		
Direct materials	$ 2.00	$1.96078
Conversion costs	.64516	.64815
Cost of goods transferred out	26,452	26,483
Ending WIP inventory	3,548	3,517

Exhibit 8–13

Comparison of Weighted-Average and FIFO Costing

Step 1: Summarize the flow of physical units.

Step 2: Compute the number of equivalent units produced for direct materials and conversion costs.

> **Weighted average:** EU produced = Units transferred out + EU in ending WIP inventory

> **FIFO:** EU produced = EU to complete beginning WIP inventory + Units started and finished during the period + EU in ending WIP inventory

Step 3: Summarize the total costs to be accounted for.

> Total costs to be accounted for = Costs in beginning WIP inventory + Costs incurred this period

Step 4: Compute costs per equivalent unit.

Weighted average:

$$\frac{\text{Weighted-average}}{\text{unit cost}} = \frac{\text{Costs in beginning WIP inventory} + \text{Current period costs}}{\text{Units tranferred out} + \text{EU in ending WIP inventory}}$$

FIFO:

$$\frac{\text{Unit cost of}}{\text{current period work}} = \frac{\text{Current period costs}}{\text{EU of current work done}}$$

Step 5: Assign costs to goods transferred out and to ending WIP inventory.

> **Weighted average:** Using weighted average, the cost of goods transferred out equals the total units transferred out times the weighted-average unit cost computed in step 4.

> Using weighted average, the cost of goods in ending WIP inventory equals the equivalent units in ending WIP inventory times the weighted-average unit cost computed in step 4.

> **FIFO:** Using FIFO, the cost of goods transferred out equals the sum of the following three items:

> a. The costs already in beginning WIP inventory at the beginning of the period.

> b. The current period cost to complete beginning WIP inventory, which equals the equivalent units to complete beginning WIP inventory from step 2 times the current period unit cost computed for FIFO in step 4.

> c. The costs to start and complete units, calculated by multiplying the number of units started and finished from step 2 times the cost per equivalent unit computed for FIFO in step 4.

> Using FIFO, the cost of goods in ending WIP inventory equals the equivalent units in ending WIP inventory from step 2 times the cost per equivalent unit computed for FIFO in step 4.

Exhibit 8–14

Summary of Steps for Assigning Process Costs to Units

and ending WIP inventory amounts. (Note the question marks, which indicate unknown amounts.) After making the computations shown in the production cost report in Exhibit 8–11, we complete the T-accounts as shown in the bottom section of Illustration Exhibit 8–12. It is helpful to use T-accounts to keep the big picture in mind when working on detailed computations such as those reported in Exhibit 8–11.

Advantages and disadvantages of FIFO and weighted-average costing.   Weighted-average costing does not separate beginning inventory from current period activity. Unit costs are a weighted average of the two, whereas under FIFO costing, unit costs are based on current period activity only. FIFO is typically advantageous when the number of units in beginning WIP inventory is large relative to the number of units started during the period. If this is not the case, beginning WIP inventory has little influence on the average unit cost using the weighted-average approach.

Exhibit 8–13 compares the equivalent unit costs including direct materials conversion costs, cost of goods transferred out, and ending WIP inventory values under the two methods for Spirit Beverages. Although either weighted-average or FIFO

LO 8 Compare and contrast the results from weighted-average and FIFO costing.

SPIRIT BEVERAGES
Blending Department
For the Month Ending December 31

Flow of Units	(Section 1) Physical Units	(Section 2) Equivalent Units Prior Department Costs	Materials*	Conversion Costs*
Units to account for:				
Beginning work in process inventory	2,000			
Units started this period	12,000			
Total units to account for...........................	**14,000**			
Units accounted for:				
Units completed and transferred out:				
From beginning inventory	2,000	0†	1,200†	400†
Started and completed, currently	8,000	8,000	8,000	8,000
Units in ending WIP inventory...................	4,000	4,000	1,000	2,400
Total units accounted for...........................	**14,000**	**12,000**	**10,200**	**10,800**

Flow of Costs	Total Costs	Prior Department Costs	Materials*	Conversion Costs*
Costs to be accounted for (section 3):				
Costs in beginning WIP inventory..............	$ 8,000	$ 5,000	$ 2,000	$ 1,000
Current period costs...................................	79,000	52,000	20,000	7,000
Total costs to be accounted for..................	**$87,000**	**$ 57,000**	**$ 22,000**	**$ 8,000**
Cost per equivalent unit (section 4):				
Prior department costs ($52,000 ÷ 12,000)..		$4.33333		
Materials ($20,000 ÷ 10,200)			$1.96078	
Conversion costs ($7,000 ÷ 10,800)				$ .64815
Costs to be accounted for (section 5):				
Costs assigned to units transferred out:				
Costs from beginning WIP inventory......	$ 8,000	$ 5,000	$ 2,000	$ 1,000
Current costs added to complete beginning WIP inventory:				
Prior department costs	0	0		
Materials	2,353		2,353	
Conversion costs................................	259			259
Total costs to complete beginning inventory	2,612			
Costs of units started and completed:				
Prior department costs (8,000 × $4.33333)	34,667	34,667		
Materials	15,686		15,686	
Conversion costs	5,185			5,185
Total costs of units started and completed	55,538			
Total costs transferred out	66,150			
Costs assigned to ending WIP inventory:				
Prior department costs (4,000 × $4.33333)	17,333	17,333		
Materials	1,961		1,961	
Conversion costs................................	1,556			1,556
Total cost of ending WIP inventory	20,850			
Total costs accounted for	**$87,000**	**$ 57,000**	**$ 22,000**	**$ 8,000**

*See Exhibit 8–11 for calculations.
† EU required to complete beginning inventory.

costing is acceptable for assigning costs to inventories and cost of goods sold for external reporting, the weighted-average method has been criticized for masking current period costs. Thus, the unit costs reported for December using weighted-average costing are based not only on December's costs but also on the costs of previous periods that were in December's beginning inventory. For a company such as Phillips Petroleum, which experiences changing crude oil prices, managers' decisions require knowledge of current period costs. If computational and record-keeping costs are about the same under both FIFO and weighted average, FIFO costing is generally preferred.

Exhibit 8–14 summarizes the steps for assigning costs to units in process costing using FIFO and weighted-average costing. Notice how the steps correspond to the production cost report that management uses to monitor production unit and cost flows.

Example 4: Department with Costs Transferred in from Prior Departments: FIFO

Recall that example 4 in the chapter included goods transferred from a prior department. Exhibit 8–15 is a FIFO cost of production report using the data from example 4. This concludes our discussion of FIFO process costing.

Appendix B to Chapter Eight

Operation Costing

Operation costing is a hybrid of job-order and process costing, and is used when companies produce batches of similar products with significantly different types of material (see Exhibit 8–16). It is used for the manufacture of goods that have both common characteristics and some individual characteristics. An **operation** is a standardized method of making a product that is repeatedly performed. For example, an automobile assembly plant makes several models on the same assembly line. Each model has seat covers installed; installing them is an operation.

A company using operation costing typically uses different materials for products that pass through the same operation. Some automobiles have leather seats, others cloth seats. Whether the material is leather or cloth, the car passes through the same seat cover installation operation.

Companies such as Nike (shoes) and Volvo (automobiles) use operation costing. Van Heusen, a shirt maker, has a cutting operation and a stitching operation for each shirt, although the materials (cotton, wool, polyester) for each type of shirt can differ.

LO 9 Compare and contrast operation costing with job costing and process costing.

Product Costing in Operations

The key difference between operation costing, job costing, and process costing is that direct materials for each work order or batch passing through a particular operation are different although conversion costs (direct labor and manufacturing overhead) are the same.

Job Costing	Operation Costing	Process Costing
Job shops making customized products	Operations: Separate materials for each batch; common operations	Mass production in continuous processes

Exhibit 8–16

Comparison of Three Costing Methods

Exhibit 8–17

Overview of Operation Costing

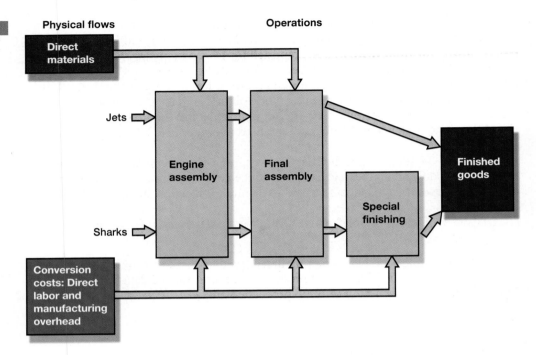

For example, assume that Yahonzi Motorcycle Company makes two models of motorcycles, Jets and Sharks. The Shark has a larger engine and generally more costly direct materials than the Jet. Exhibit 8–17 shows the flow of products through departments (assume that each department has one operation). Note that Jets pass through only the first two departments where operations are identical for both types of motorcycles but Sharks pass through all three departments. Direct materials costs are added to both models in Engine Assembly and Final Assembly, but none are added to Jets in Special Finishing. Conversion costs are added to Jets in the first two departments and to Sharks in all three departments. In principle, direct materials costs could be added in any operation. In this example, the direct materials costs per unit are higher for Sharks.

Illustration of Operation Costing

Assume that Yahonzi Motorcycle Company management gave the following production work order for the month of March. Each work order is also called a *batch*.

YAHONZI MOTORCYCLE COMPANY

	Work Order 101	Work Order 102
Number and model of motorcycles	1,000 Sharks	2,000 Jets
Direct materials:		
Engine parts	$150,000	$200,000
Motorcycle parts, other than engines	200,000	300,000
Conversion costs (direct labor and manufacturing overhead):		
Engine assembly	50,000	100,000
Final assembly	100,000	200,000
Special finishing	50,000	
Total costs	$550,000	$800,000

Note that the materials costs per unit are higher for Sharks than for Jets but the conversion costs per unit are the same for the two operations that both models pass through. For example, engine assembly conversion costs are $50 per motorcycle for both models ($50,000 ÷ 1,000 units for Sharks; $100,000 ÷ 2,000 units for Jets).

Exhibit 8–18 shows the flow of these costs through T-accounts to Finished Goods Inventory. In practice, direct labor and manufacturing overhead could be combined as they were in a Japanese motorcycle company that one of the authors studied.

Exhibit 8–18	Cost Flows through T-Accounts for Operation Costing

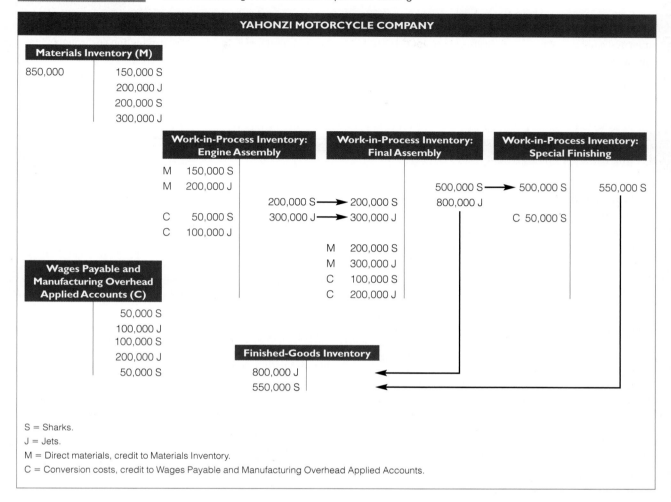

YAHONZI MOTORCYCLE COMPANY

S = Sharks.
J = Jets.
M = Direct materials, credit to Materials Inventory.
C = Conversion costs, credit to Wages Payable and Manufacturing Overhead Applied Accounts.

Direct labor and manufacturing overhead could be charged separately to production as well. In many companies, direct labor is such a small portion of the total product cost that the accountants classify direct labor as part of manufacturing overhead. For example, in numerous high-tech companies, such as Hewlett-Packard, direct labor is less than 5 percent of total manufacturing costs in many operations.

Comparison of Job Costing, Process Costing, and Operation Costing

We have now discussed how to account for product costs in three types of organizations: job shops, such as construction companies, that use job costing; organizations with continuous flow processing, such as soft drink syrup manufacturers, that use process costing; and companies with operations, such as automobile manufacturers, that use operation costing. Operation costing combines the aspect of job costing that assigns materials separately to jobs (also called *work orders* or *batches* in operation costing) with the aspect of process costing that assigns conversion costs equally to each operation. Thus, in our motorcycle example, Sharks and Jets had different per-unit materials costs but the same operations costs per unit for the two operations that both models passed through.

In practice, you are likely to encounter elements of all three production methods. You also will find that every company has its own unique costing method that does not precisely fit any textbook description. Having studied these three basic costing methods will enable you to learn the variations on the methods presented here.

Key Terms

For each term's definition, refer to the indicated page or turn to the glossary at the end of the text.

abnormal spoilage, 306

equivalent units, 296

first-in, first-out (FIFO) costing*, 311

lost units, 306

normal spoilage, 306

operation†, 317

prior department costs, 304

production cost report, 303

spoilage, 305

weighted-average costing, 298

*Term appears in Appendix A.

† Term appears in Appendix B.

Meeting the Cost Management Challenges

I.   How should Spirit Beverages measure the costs of products, services, and operations?

With numerous, undifferentiated outputs, attempting to measure the costs of individual items of output generally is not cost effective. In this case, organizations such as Spirit Beverages usually use process costing, which allows them to average costs across all units produced during a specific time period. An organization might operate numerous processes, however, each of which could have separate cost accounts so that employees can monitor and report cost information. If some individual processes are relatively unimportant, maintaining separate process accounts might not be necessary. In concept, process costing could be performed at the activity level, but organizations usually organize activities into processes or condensed activities. Within processes, organizations determine what number and types of cost categories to manage. The most common categories are materials and conversion costs, but organizations could use as many different material and conversion cost categories as they believe are necessary to generate the information they need and can justify.

2.   How should organizations recognize and measure the costs of spoilage and waste?

Nearly every process results in some outputs not fit for further processing or delivery to customers. All processes also gener-

ate waste from defective units that cannot be reworked or recycled to inefficient use of resources. Because competitive and regulatory (e.g., environmental) pressures are increasing for most organizations, it is advisable to measure spoilage and waste costs separately from costs of producing good output. High spoilage and waste costs indicate inefficient processes that do or could result in competitive disadvantages. Assuming that these costs can be computed reliably (this could be a problem with environmental waste costs), it is better to know the magnitude of the spoilage and waste problem so that it can be attacked in a cost-effective manner than to bury the cost in the costs of good output. These costs should be reported separately but internally to the organization (unless required by external parties).

3.   (Appendix A) What is the advantage of first-in, first-out (FIFO) process costing over weighted-average process costing?

FIFO separates the costs associated with products produced in a previous period from those produced in the current period. Weighted-average, on the other hand, mixes the costs of previous periods (which are in beginning WIP inventory) with current period production costs. FIFO gives managers more accurate information about current period costs.

Solutions to You're the Decision Maker

8.1   Production Cost Report   p. 304

a.   Job costing is used to track costs for each unit (or job) produced and for products that are somewhat unique, such as custom homes and landscaping projects. It is not cost effective to track costs for high-volume homogeneous products such as Spirit Beverage's sports drink. Instead, costs are tracked by process and an average cost is determined at the end of the period.

b.   Equivalent units and costs are calculated separately for direct materials and conversion costs because ending WIP inventory is typically at different stages of completion for each of these categories. Notice that ending WIP inventory for Spirit Beverages is 25 percent complete with respect to direct materials (i.e., 25 percent of the direct materials needed have been used) and 60 percent complete with respect to conversion costs (i.e., 60 percent of the activities required for conversion costs have been completed). The use

of two separate columns in the production cost report allows us to more accurately calculate the costs per equivalent units and assign costs to units transferred out and in ending WIP inventory.

8.2   Analyzing Process Costs   p. 308

a.   Reviewing costs related to spoiled units is important. Although the costs assigned to spoiled units are not substantial at this point, the company wants to prevent them from increasing in the future and would likely compare them to those of prior periods to review trends. Ending WIP inventory increased from 2,000 units last month to 3,500 units this month. Minimizing inventory levels is an effective way to reduce inventory costs; inventory can be monitored by reviewing this report. Finally, comparing the costs per equivalent unit for direct materials and conversion costs this month with prior months can help to evaluate the efficiency of production operations.

b. Several areas of improvement can help Spirit Beverages increase profitability. It can reduce ending WIP inventory levels, which minimizes inventory handling and storage costs (rent, labor, insurance, etc.). Direct materials represent approximately 73 percent of all costs to be accounted for.

Perhaps the company could negotiate a lower materials price with the current supplier or find a different supplier. The number of spoiled units, although not extremely high, should be reviewed, and processes modified to achieve lower spoilage rates.

Review Questions

8.1 Why are equivalent units computed for process costing?

8.2 A manufacturing company has records of its current activity in WIP inventory and its ending WIP inventory; however, the record of its beginning inventory has been lost. What data are needed to compute the beginning inventory? Express your answer in equation form.

8.3 (Appendix A) If costs change from one period to another, why do costs that are transferred out of one department under FIFO costing include units with two different costs?

8.4 (Appendix A) What is the distinction in equivalent units under the FIFO method and under the weighted-average method?

8.5 Do costs of a prior department behave similarly to costs of direct materials? Under what conditions are the costs similar? Why are they accounted for separately?

8.6 Assume that the number of units transferred out of a department is unknown. What is the formula to solve for units transferred out using the basic cost-flow model?

8.7 How does process costing treat spoiled units?

8.8 How are spoilage costs similar to underapplied overhead?

8.9 (Appendix A) What are the relative costs and benefits of weighted-average versus FIFO process costing?

8.10 (Appendix B) How is operation costing similar to, and different from, both job costing and process costing?

Critical Analysis

8.11 Management of a company that manufactures cereal is trying to decide whether to install a job or a process-costing system. The manufacturing vice president has stated that job costing gives the company the best control because it makes possible the assignment of costs to specific lots of goods. The controller, however, has stated that job costing requires too much record keeping. Would a process-costing system meet the manufacturing vice president's control objectives? Explain.

8.12 (Appendix A) A new member of the controller's staff in your company, a large producer of paper products, has just completed a report that urges the company to adopt the last-in, first-out (LIFO) method of process costing. The controller is concerned about the recommendation because the cost records are maintained on a FIFO basis. Indeed, the controller has not even heard of using LIFO for process-cost accounting. Form small groups to prepare a report addressing the following:

a. Would it be possible to use LIFO for process costing? What are the key issues? Would using it be desirable?

b. In your library or on the Internet (company home pages or the SEC's EDGAR database), obtain information on inventory policies of four paper manufacturers (e.g., MeadWestvaco, Weyerhaeuser, Simpson Paper). Describe how firms in this industry account for their process costs.

8.13 (Appendix A) Under which of the following conditions will the first-in, first-out (FIFO) method of process costing produce the same cost of goods manufactured as the weighted-average method?

a. When goods produced are homogeneous.

b. When there is no beginning inventory.

c. When beginning and ending inventories are each 50 percent complete.

d. None of these.

[CPA adapted]

8.14 An error was made in computing the percentage of completion of the ending WIP inventory for the current year. The error resulted in assigning a *lower percentage of completion* to each component of the inventory than actually was the case. Assume that there was no beginning inventory. What is the effect of this error on

a. The computation of total equivalent units? (understate or overstate?)

b. The computation of costs per equivalent unit? (understate or overstate?)

c. Costs assigned to cost of goods transferred out for the period? (understate or overstate?)

[CPA adapted]

8.15 In computing the cost per equivalent unit, the weighted-average method considers

a. Current costs only.

b. Current costs plus costs in beginning WIP inventory.

c. Current costs plus costs in ending WIP inventory.

d. Current costs less costs in beginning WIP inventory.

[CPA adapted]

8.16 (Appendix A) When using the FIFO method of process costing, total equivalent units produced for a given period equal the number of units

a. Started and completed during the period plus the number of units in beginning WIP plus the number of units in ending WIP.

b. In beginning WIP plus the number of units started during the period plus the number of units remaining in ending WIP times the percentage of work necessary to complete the items.

c. In beginning WIP times the percentage of work necessary to complete the items plus the number of units started and completed during the period plus the number of units started this period and remaining in ending WIP times the percentage of work necessary to complete the items.

d. Transferred out during the period plus the number of units remaining in ending WIP times the percentage of work necessary to complete the items.

e. None of these.

[CPA adapted]

8.17 One of your process supervisors said to you, "Well, you have to break eggs to make an omelet," as a reason for considering the period's spoilage as a normal cost of production. Is spoilage a normal cost of production? If so, why report it separately?

8.18 Explain how the concept of "normal spoilage" could impede quality improvements in processes. If you do not distinguish between normal and abnormal spoilage, how would you identify "unacceptable" spoilage?

8.19 Explain how an individual could manipulate reported earnings by misstating degrees of completion of ending WIP. Would it be easy to continue this manipulation for subsequent periods? Explain.

Exercises

Exercise 8.20
Equivalent Units Computation, Weighted-Average Method
(LO 4)

Nets, Inc., shows the following information concerning its work in process:

1. Beginning inventory, 2,000 partially complete units.
2. Transferred out, 9,000 units.
3. Ending inventory (materials, 10 percent complete; conversion costs, 20 percent complete).
4. Started this month, 12,000 units.

Required

a. Compute the number of equivalent units for materials using the weighted-average method.
b. Compute the number of equivalent units for conversion costs using the weighted-average method.

Exercise 8.21
Equivalent Units Computation, FIFO Method (Appendix A)
(LO 7)

Refer to the data in Exercise 8.20. Assume that beginning inventory is 20 percent complete with respect to materials and 15 percent complete with respect to conversion costs.

Required

a. Compute the number of equivalent units for materials using FIFO.
b. Compute the number of equivalent units for conversion costs using FIFO.

Exercise 8.22
Equivalent Units Computed, Weighted-Average Method
(LO 4)

Ben and Stiller Ice Cream Company shows the following information concerning the WIP at its plant:

1. Beginning inventory, partially complete.
2. Transferred out, 20,000 units.
3. Ending inventory, 10,000 units (materials, 20 percent complete; conversion costs, 10 percent complete).
4. Started this month, 25,000 units.

Required

a. Compute the number of equivalent units for materials using the weighted-average method.
b. Compute the number of equivalent units for conversion costs using the weighted-average method.

Exercise 8.23
Equivalent Units Computed, FIFO Method (Appendix A)
(LO 7)

Refer to the data in Exercise 8.22. Assume that beginning inventory is 55 percent complete with respect to materials and 70 percent complete with respect to conversion costs.

Required

a. Compute the number of equivalent units for materials using the FIFO method.
b. Compute the number of equivalent units for conversion costs using the FIFO method.

Exercise 8.24
Equivalent Units Computed, Weighted-Average Method
(LO 4)

Ron's Carefree Colas adds materials at the beginning of the process in Department A. The following information pertains to Department A's work in process during April:

	Units
Work in process, April 1 (60% complete as to conversion costs)	6,000
Started in April	40,000
Completed	30,000
Work in process, April 30 (40% complete as to conversion costs)	16,000

Required

a. Compute the number of equivalent units for materials using the weighted-average method.

b. Compute the number of equivalent units for conversion costs using the weighted-average method.

[CPA adapted]

Mikee's Cereals has a process-costing system using the FIFO cost-flow method. All materials are introduced at the beginning of the process in Department 1. The following information is available for the month of January:

	Units
Work in process, January 1 (40% complete as to conversion costs)	250
Started in January	1,000
Transferred to Department 2 during January	1,050
Work in process, January 31 (70% complete as to conversion costs)	200

Required

Compute the number of equivalent units of production for materials and conversion costs for the month of January.

[CPA adapted]

The following information pertains to Pete's Paint plant for the month of May:

	Number of Units	Cost of Materials
Beginning work in process	60,000	$13,200
Started in May	160,000	35,200
Units completed	170,000	
Ending work in process	50,000	

All materials are added at the beginning of the process.

Required

Using the weighted-average method, compute the cost per equivalent unit for materials.

[CPA adapted]

Department A is the first stage of Martinez Company's production cycle. The following information is available for conversion costs for the month of April:

	Units
Beginning work in process (60% complete)	40,000
Started in April	700,000
Completed in April and transferred to Department B	660,000
Ending work in process (20% complete)	80,000

Required

Using the FIFO method, compute the number of equivalent units for the conversion costs.

[CPA adapted]

Micro Chips uses the weighted-average method to account for its WIP inventories. The accounting records show the following information for a particular day:

Beginning WIP inventory:	
Direct materials	$ 488
Conversion costs	136
Current period costs in work in process:	
Direct materials	$5,720
Conversion costs	3,322

Quantity information is obtained from the manufacturing records and includes the following:

Beginning inventory .... 150 units (partially complete)
Current period units started .... 1,000 units
Ending inventory .... 300 units
   Percentage of completion:
      Direct materials........................ 40%
      Conversion costs 20%
Spoilage .... 100 units
   Percentage of completion:
      Direct materials........................ 100%
      Conversion costs 100%

Required

Compute the cost per equivalent unit for direct materials and conversion costs.

Exercise 8.29
Cost Assignment to Units
Transferred Out,
Spoilage, and Ending
Inventory, Weighted-
Average Method
(LO 4, 6)

Refer to the data in Exercise 8.28.

Required

Compute the cost of good units completed and transferred out, spoilage, and ending inventory using the weighted-average method.

Exercise 8.30
Cost per Equivalent Unit
(with Spoilage)
Computed, Weighted-
Average Method
(LO 4, 6)

Green Chemicals had beginning WIP inventory of $124,160 on October 1. Of this amount, $50,820 was the cost of direct materials, and $73,340 was for conversion costs. The 8,000 units in the beginning inventory were 30 percent complete with respect to both direct materials and conversion costs.

During October, 17,000 units were transferred out, 500 were spoiled, and 4,500 remained in the ending inventory. Spoiled units were 100 percent complete with respect to materials and 50 percent complete with respect to conversion costs. The units in the ending WIP inventory were 80 percent complete with respect to direct materials and 40 percent complete with respect to conversion costs. Costs incurred during the period amounted to $390,600 for direct materials and $504,640 for conversion costs.

Required

a. Compute the cost per equivalent unit for direct materials and for conversion costs using the weighted-average method.

b. *Build your own spreadsheet.* Develop a spreadsheet to answer (a).

Exercise 8.31
Cost Assignment to Units
Transferred Out,
Spoilage, and Ending
Inventory, Weighted-
Average Method
(LO 4, 6)

Refer to the data in Exercise 8.30.

Required

Compute the costs of good units completed and transferred out, spoilage, and ending inventory using the weighted-average method.

Exercise 8.32
Assign Costs to Products
Using Operation Costing
(Appendix B)
(LO 9)

The Charley-Davidson Company makes three types of motorcycles—dirt bikes, touring motorcycles, and racing motorcycles. The company had the following work orders for the month of September:

Customer	Order Quantity	Order Revenue
South	40 racing motorcycles, 40 dirt bikes	$90,000
Central	100 dirt bikes, 80 touring motorcycles	80,000
West	10 racing motorcycles, 100 dirt bikes	80,000

Direct materials costs are as follows:

Touring motorcycles.................... $200 per unit
Racing motorcycles .... 800 per unit
Dirt bikes .... 300 per unit

Conversion costs incurred in Work-in-Process—Basic Assembly = $100 per unit for all three types.

Conversion costs incurred in Work-in-Process—Special Assembly = $200 per unit for racing motorcycles and $40 per bike for dirt bikes. Touring motorcycles require no special assembly.

Required

a. Compute the product costs for September for each of the three types of motorcycles.

b. Show the flow of costs through T-accounts. Assume that all products are transferred to Finished Goods when completed, and then to Cost of Goods Sold when sold. All products in this exercise were sold in September. Use two work-in-process accounts: Work-in-Process—Basic Assembly and Work-in-Process—Special Assembly.

c. Taking into account the revenue from each customer's order and the direct materials and conversion costs required to produce the products for each order, compute customer profits for each order.

The Loafin' Leather Company makes three types of leather coats—the Brando, the Pitt, and the J. Dean. The company had the following work orders for the month of January:

Exercise 8.33
Assign Costs to Products-Operation Costing (Appendix B) **(LO 9)**

Customer	Order Quantity
N. Beach	30 units of the Pitt and 50 units of the Brando
Hoardstrum	100 units of the Brando and 80 units of the Pitt
Gop	100 units of the Brando, 30 units of the Pitt, and 60 units of the J. Dean

Direct materials costs for leather coats are as follows:

The Brando	$200 per unit
The Pitt	300 per unit
The J. Dean	500 per unit

Conversion costs incurred in Work-in-Process—Basic Assembly = $100 per unit for all three types of coats.

Conversion costs incurred in Work-in-Process—Special Finishing = $50 per unit for the Pitt and $40 per unit for the J. Dean. The Brando coat requires no special finishing.

Required

a. Compute the product costs for January for each of the three types of coats.

b. Show the flow of costs through T-accounts. Assume that all products are transferred to Finished Goods when completed, and then to Cost of Goods Sold when sold. All products in this exercise were sold in January. Use two work-in-process accounts: Work-in-Process—Basic Assembly and Work-in-Process—Special Finishing.

Problems

The following data are available for Rabbit Company for the month of February:

Problem 8.34
Production Cost Report (Beginning and Ending WIP Inventory), Weighted-Average Method **(LO 3, 4)**

	Units	Percentage Complete	Costs
Beginning WIP inventory, February	22,000		
Direct materials		75%	$ 4,200
Conversion costs		70	2,450
Units started in February	12,000		
Costs incurred in February:			
Direct materials			17,000
Conversion costs			16,800
Ending WIP inventory	6,000		
Direct materials		80	
Conversion costs		60	

Required

Use weighted-average process costing to

a.   Prepare a production cost report.

b.   Show the flow of costs through the WIP Inventory T-account.

Problem 8.35
Production Cost Report
(Beginning and Ending
WIP Inventory), FIFO
Method (Appendix A)
(LO 3, 7, 8)

mhhe.com/hilton3e

Refer to the data in Problem 8.34.

Required

Use FIFO process costing to

a.   Prepare a production cost report.

b.   Show the flow of costs through the WIP Inventory T-account.

c.   Prepare a short memo to Rabbit Company's CFO explaining whether you believe FIFO costing is better than weighted-average costing for the company.

Problem 8.36
Production Cost Report
(Beginning and Ending
WIP Inventory), Weighted-
Average Method
(LO 3, 4)

The following data are available for Travis Company for the month of July:

	Units	Percentage Complete	Costs
Beginning WIP inventory, July 15,000	15,000		
Direct materials...		60%	$ 8,800
Conversion costs		70	6,500
Units started in July	20,000		
Costs incurred in July:			
Direct materials...			13,500
Conversion costs			12,300
Ending WIP inventory	5,000		
Direct materials...		70	
Conversion costs		80	

Required

Use weighted-average process costing to

a.   Prepare a production cost report.

b.   Show the flow of costs through the WIP Inventory T-account.

c.   *Build your own spreadsheet.* Develop a spreadsheet to answer (a).

Problem 8.37
Production Cost Report
(Beginning and Ending
WIP Inventory),
Weighted-Average
Method
(LO 3, 4)

The following data are available for Needles Production Company for the month of December:

	Units	Percentage Complete	Costs
Beginning WIP inventory, December 20,000	20,000		
Direct materials...		80%	$20,000
Conversion costs		90	45,000
Units started in December	50,000		
Costs incurred in December:			
Direct materials...			27,000
Conversion costs			36,000
Ending WIP inventory	25,000		
Direct materials...		30	
Conversion costs		40	

Required

Use weighted-average process costing to

a.   Prepare a production cost report.

b.   Show the flow of costs through the WIP Inventory T-account.

Refer to the data in Problem 8.37.

Required

Use FIFO process costing to

a.   Prepare a production cost report.

b.   Show the flow of costs through the WIP Inventory T-account.

c.   Prepare a short memo to Needles Production Company's CFO explaining whether you believe
FIFO process costing would be worthwhile for the company.

Problem 8.38
Production Cost Report
(Beginning and Ending
WIP Inventory) FIFO
Method (Appendix A)
(LO 3, 7, 8)

For each of the following independent cases, determine the units or equivalent units requested (assuming weighted-average costing).

a.   In the beginning inventory, 4,100 units were 40 percent complete with respect to conversion costs.
During the period, 3,500 units were started. In the ending inventory, 3,250 units were 20 percent
complete with respect to conversion costs. How many units were transferred out?

b.   The beginning inventory consisted of 4,000 units with a direct materials cost of $14,200.
The equivalent units, including beginning WIP amounted to 18,000 units. Ending inventory
had 6,000 units that were 20 percent complete with respect to materials. The ending inventory
had a direct materials cost assigned of $4,500. What was the total materials cost incurred
this period?

c.   The WIP Inventory account had a beginning balance of $1,900 for conversion costs. During the
period, $18,100 in conversion costs were charged to WIP. Also during the period, $19,200 in costs
were transferred out. Beginning inventory had 400 units, and 4,800 units were transferred out during the period. How many equivalent units are in the ending inventory?

d.   During the period, 1,050 units were transferred into the department. The 1,600 units transferred
out were charged to the next department at an amount that included $3,360 for direct materials
costs. The ending inventory was 25 percent complete with respect to direct materials and had a
cost of $630 assigned to it. How many units are in the ending inventory?

Problem 8.39
Solving for Unknowns—
Weighted-Average
Method

Recycle Industries of Toronto recycles galvanized steel from automobile bodies in two processes:
shredding and degalvanizing. It processes galvanized steel auto bodies in the shredding process and
sends the shredded steel to the newly developed degalvanizing process which removes zinc by elec-
trolysis. Zinc, which has a relatively high value, is the principal product of the process. The company
transferred 6,000 metric tons of steel to the degalvanizing process this month. Neither process had
any spoilage.

Because the galvanized steel is homogeneous and shredded in a continuous process, the company
uses a process-costing accounting system to assign costs to it. The following information is available for
the degalvanizing process during the last year:

Problem 8.40
Production Cost Report
(Prior Department
Process Costs),
Weighted-Average
Method
(LO 3, 4, 5)

RECYCLE INDUSTRIES, INC.
Degalvanizing Process Last Year

		Shredding Process Costs	Degalvanizing Process	
	Units		Direct Materials	Conversion Costs ($Canadian)
Physical flow (metric tons):				
Beginning inventory	1,000	100% complete	60% complete	75% complete
Ending inventory	2,700	100% complete	80% complete	45% complete
Transferred in	6,000	100% complete		
Costs incurred ($Canadian):				
Beginning inventory		$ 7,100,000	$ 600,000	$ 420,000
Current costs		43,200,000	2,500,000	6,475,000

Required

a.   Prepare a production cost report using weighted-average costing.

b.   Show the flow of costs through the WIP Inventory T-account using weighted-average costing.

Problem 8.41
Production Cost Report
(Prior Department
Process Costs),
Weighted-Average
Method
(LO 3, 4, 5)

Dixie Corporation manufactures a child's car seat produced in three separate departments: Molding, Assembling, and Finishing. It uses the weighted-average process-costing method to account for costs of production. The following information was obtained for the Assembling Department for the month of June.

	Amount	Percentage Complete
WIP, June 1 (1,000 units):		
Prior department costs transferred in from the Molding Department	$32,000	100%
Costs added by the Assembling Department:		
Direct materials	$20,000	100
Direct labor	7,200	60
Manufacturing overhead	5,500	50
	$32,700	
Total WIP, June 1	$64,700	

During the month of June, the Molding Department transferred into the Assembling Department 5,000 units at a prior department cost of $160,000. The Assembling Department added the following $150,000 of costs:

Direct materials	$ 96,000
Conversion labor	36,000
Manufacturing overhead	18,000
	$150,000

The Assembling Department completed and transferred out 4,000 units to the Finishing Department. At June 30, 2,000 units were still in WIP. The degree of completion of WIP at June 30 was as follows:

Direct materials	90%
Direct labor	70
Manufacturing overhead	35

Required

a. Prepare a production cost report using weighted-average costing.

b. Management wants to decrease the costs of manufacturing the car seat. In particular, it has set the following per-unit targets for this product in the Assembling Department: materials, $20; labor, $10; and manufacturing overhead, $4.50. Has the Assembling Department achieved management's cost targets?

[CPA adapted]

Problem 8.42
Production Cost Report
(with Spoilage),
Weighted-Average
Method
(LO 3, 4, 6)

Nader Paints makes an environmentally sound paint. The following data are available for the month of April:

	Units	Percentage Complete	Costs
Beginning WIP inventory, April	11,000		
Direct materials		75%	$ 3,200
Conversion costs		70	1,450
Units started in April	6,000		
Costs incurred in April:			
Direct materials			16,000
Conversion costs			15,800
Ending WIP inventory	3,000		
Direct materials		80	
Conversion costs		60	
Spoilage	200		
Direct materials		100	
Conversion costs		100	

Required

a. Prepare a production cost report using weighted-average costing.

b. Show the flow of costs through the WIP Inventory T-account.

Outdoors Production, Inc., produces a sealant for wood decks. The following data are available for the month of April:

Problem 8.43
Production Cost Report
(with Spoilage),
Weighted-Average
Method
(LO 3, 4, 6)

	Units	Percentage Complete	Costs
Beginning WIP inventory, April	13,000		
Direct materials		70%	$ 6,500
Conversion costs		60	12,000
Units started in April	17,000		
Costs incurred in April:			
Direct materials			16,000
Conversion costs			15,800
Ending WIP inventory	6,000		
Direct materials		60	
Conversion costs		55	
Spoilage	1,500		
Direct materials		75	
Conversion costs		60	

Required

a. Prepare a production cost report using weighted-average costing.

b. Show the flow of costs through the WIP Inventory T-account.

Required

Answer each of the following questions regarding independent situations.

a. The following information is available for April (percents refer to conversion costs):

Problem 8.44
Equivalent Units
Computed, Weighted
Average
(LO 3)

mhhe.com/hilton3e

	Units
Work in process, April 1 (40% complete)	25,000
Started in April	120,000
Work in process, April 30 (30% complete)	12,500

Materials are added at the beginning of the process. Using the weighted-average costing method, what are the equivalent units of production for the month of April for materials? For conversion costs?

b. Second Department is the second stage of Hurley Company's production cycle. On May 1, beginning work in process contained 50,000 units, which were 80 percent complete as to conversion costs. During May, 320,000 units were transferred in from the first stage of the production cycle. On May 31, ending WIP in the Second Department contained 40,000 units, which were 90 percent complete as to conversion costs. Materials are added at the end of the process in the Second Department. Using the weighted-average costing method, how many equivalent units were produced during May?

[CPA adapted]

Cases

In the 1990s, the U.S. Government tightened the ban on timber sales from U.S. federal land. "For communities affected by federal timber, the outlook is dismal," observed an industry consultant in Oregon. In a related development, the British Columbia, Canada, government began implementing its Forest Practices Code, which has strict standards for logging activities and reforestation responsibilities. These developments unfavorably affected a number of U.S. wood and paper products companies that had relied heavily on timber sales from U.S. and B.C. public lands. They have experienced higher material costs and have had access to lower volumes of timber. Other companies, however, have benefited from the price increases caused by the ban on federal timber sales and increased restrictions on logging in British Columbia because they have either large private timberland elsewhere or long-term supply contracts with private timber owners.

Longview Fibre Co. of Longview, Washington, was one of the companies adversely affected by these developments. For several years after the imposition of these restrictions, the company suffered higher material costs for most of its products. Since Longview Fibre was at a disadvantage compared to

Case 8.45
Public Policy and
Process Costs
(LO 2, 3, 4)

its competitors with unaffected sources of raw materials, the company set a goal to significantly reduce its conversion costs. Following are the data that the company disclosed in one of its financial reports for each of its major product lines: timber products (logs and lumber), paper and paperboard, and container-board products (packaging).

LONGVIEW FIBRE CO
Consolidated Statement of Income (Unaudited)
For Six Months Ended April 30, Year 2

Net sales:

Timber products..	$ 79,045,000
Paper and paperboard	92,433,000
Container-board products	190,677,000
	362,155,000
Cost of products sold (all products)	329,748,000
Gross profit	$ 32,407,000
Selling, administrative, and general expenses	32,313,000
Operating profit	$ 94,000

Operating profit (loss) by product:

Timber products..	$ 37,309,000
Paper and paperboard	(11,842,000)
Container-board products	(25,373,000)
	$ 94,000

Inventories:	April 30, Year 2	October 31, Year 1
Finished goods	$ 25,445,000	$24,832,000
Work in process...	19,220,000	13,868,000
Raw materials and supplies	48,192,000	45,802,000
	$ 92,857,000	$84,502,000

Sales Quantity

Six months ended April 30, Year 2:

Timber products, board feet	144,000,000
Paper and paperboard, tons..........................	177,000
Container-board products, tons	255,000

Required

Work in small groups to develop solutions to the following requirements and then be prepared to present them to the class.

a.   Reconstruct the elements of the basic cost-flow model (BI + TI − TO = EI) for Finished Goods and Work-in-Process Inventories. (*Hint:* Work backward from cost of goods sold.)

b.   Compute the average process cost per unit sold of each of the three product lines for the period ending April 30, Year 2. [*Hint:* Work backward from operating profit (loss) for each product.] Assume that selling, general, and administrative costs were assigned to product lines on the basis of relative revenue.

c.   Average process costs per unit sold during the comparable period in year 1 follow:

Average Cost per Unit Sold	Year 1
Timber products, per board foot......................................	$ .23
Paper and paperboard, per ton	502.01
Container-board products, per ton	789.59

Compare the year 1 costs to the year 2 costs computed in part (b). During the year 2 period, the company's costs increased as follows: raw timber, 8 percent; wood chips used to make paper, 36 percent; and container board, 12 percent. From these data, does it appear that the company achieved its goal of reducing conversion costs? Describe a likely scenario that explains the company's changes in costs and year 2 profit performance.

[Adapted from "Splinters Everywhere," and Longview Fibre Co., Form 10-Q.]

Many companies use process costing for some products and job costing for others. The authors of a study of costing methods described a particular medium-sized manufacturing company as using process costing for its products sold to commercial customers and job costing for products sold to the government.[3] For the government products, each job represented a separate contract with the government, so the company's accountants carefully kept track of which costs should be assigned to each contract. For the commercial products, the company's managers appeared to believe that the averaging of costs across products was sufficient for decision-making and cost control.

Case 8.46
Choosing Between Job and Process Costing
(LO 1)

Required

Working in groups, identify several companies that would likely have both government and commercial (i.e., non-government) customers. Then identify which of these companies would likely use job costing for its products sold to the government. Write a brief report that explains why these companies would use job costing for products sold to the government.

Anderson Company is a mature firm that manufactures a variety of high-quality sports clothing for college and high school football programs throughout the country. During the last year, the company's profits declined. Anderson has been using cost information that was developed two years ago. To determine the causes for weakened earnings performance, Anderson's controller, Bill Rolland, has asked Amy Kimball, senior cost analyst, to investigate product costing at one of the company's largest plants in Lincoln, Nebraska.

Case 8.47
Spoilage Costs, Weighted-Average Method
(LO 3, 4, 6)

The Lincoln plant manufactures insulated warm-up jackets in a continuous, one-department process. The process first involves the partial assembly of jackets using materials packet 1 (liner, shell, hood, pocket linings, zippers), which consumes 70 percent of the conversion costs. At this point, partially complete jackets are inspected. Jackets that pass this inspection are finished with materials packet 2 (embroidered logos, numbers, and players' names). After the finishing process, the jackets are inspected again. Conversion costs are applied uniformly through the process, and the Lincoln plant uses the weighted-average process-costing method. Typical jackets cost $75 to produce and, based on desired return on sales, sell for $125 each in the competitive sports apparel market.

The following information for the most recent month was available to Kimball:

Units in beginning WIP inventory	560 jackets
Conversion costs	$4,506, 25% complete
Materials packet 1	$12,500
Units started	7,600 jackets
Units fully completed	6,600 jackets
Spoilage at first inspection	460 jackets
Spoilage at second inspection	200 jackets
Current costs applied during the month:	
Conversion costs	$278,400
Materials packet 1	$252,700
Materials packet 2	$74,120
Units in ending WIP inventory	900 jackets
Conversion costs	50% complete

Required

a. The Lincoln plant manager indicates to Kimball that all but 160 of the spoiled jackets at the first inspection point should be regarded as normal spoilage, and Rolland concurs. Discuss the accounting and management implications of separating spoilage into normal and abnormal spoilage.

b. Prepare a production cost report that analyzes the most recent month's process costs.

c. Given your analysis in requirement (b), what sales price is necessary to generate the desired return on sales? Alternatively, what total process-cost reduction is necessary to maintain the current sales price? What is your recommendation?

[CMA adapted]

---

[3] K. A. Timian and M. Fleming, "Toward Diversified Cost Accounting Systems."

Chapter 9

Joint-Process Costing

After completing this chapter, you should be able to:

1. Use cost-management information to increase the profits from using scarce resources of joint-production processes.

2. Use cost-management data in the sell-or-process-further decision.

3. Explain why organizations allocate joint costs.

4. Understand how to use the net-realizable-value and physical-measures joint-cost-allocation methods.

5. Know how to account for by-products.

6. Understand how to use the relative sales value at split-off and constant gross margin percentage methods of cost allocation (Appendix).

Cost-*Management* Challenges

(Solutions are on page 349.)

1. **How** do cost-management analysts anticipate and resolve potential conflicts between joint-product and process decision making and external reporting?

2. **If** joint-cost allocations are arbitrary, does that mean they are meaningless?

National
WOOD PRODUCTS

Address by Malcolm Fries, president and CEO of National Wood Products, Inc., to the company's management team. The setting is National Wood Products' annual, preliminary budget meeting where the company's top staff and division managers planned operations for the coming year. (National Wood Products, Inc., is a fictional company based on information from a number of wood-products firms, including Boise Cascade, International Paper, Longview Fibre, Louisiana Pacific, Pope & Talbot, and Weyerhaeuser.) National Wood Products has three major product lines: lumber, paper pulp, and paperboard (for packaging). The three products come from a standard source—softwood trees such as fir, hemlock, and pine. National Wood Products' customers are companies that use lumber, or that convert pulp into paper, or that produce packaging from paperboard. All of National Wood Products' customers can buy their lumber, pulp, or paperboard on the open, international market from the cheapest source.

"It looks like we are in for a rough year, and we have to be absolutely sure that we understand our costs and our capabilities. Each of us must make every decision count. We can't afford to waste any of our capacity on products that don't generate the most profit. In particular, we must produce more innovative products, such as specialty lumber, which takes advantage of our ability to dry "green" lumber. I don't need to tell you that the Board and industry analysts are watching us closely. We have to make smart, tough decisions. Let's get to work."

Joint Product Processes

WOOD PRODUCTS

Many companies that use natural resources face the problem of how to use cost information to manage processes that can produce different products but, perhaps, without the urgency faced by National Wood Products. As does NWP, companies such as Weyerhaeuser (wood), Shell Oil (petroleum and chemicals), Phelps Dodge (minerals), and ConAgra (meat) face the challenge of making informed decisions about these processes using cost information. A **joint process** simultaneously converts a common input into several outputs. For example, processing timber results *jointly* in lumber of various grades plus wood chips and sawdust that can be converted into paper pulp. Pulp can be sold or processed further into paperboard. As another example, processing crude oil can result *jointly* in gasoline of various grades, kerosene, jet fuel, asphalt, and/or petrochemicals. **Joint products** are the products that jointly result from processing a common input.

The Importance of Split Off

The **split-off point** is the point at which joint products appear in the production process. For example, literally, at the point of a saw blade, lumber appears. In refining oil, the split-off point occurs in a "cracking" process, which produces various petroleum products simultaneously. At split off, several types of products appear. A **final product** is one that is ready for sale without further processing. For example, National Wood Products sells specialty and standard lumber as final products. An **intermediate product** is a product that might require further processing before it is salable to the ultimate consumer, either by the producer or by another processor. Thus, an intermediate product might be a final product for one company (the producer) and input for another company that will process it further.

Joint costs are the costs to operate joint processes including the disposal of waste. Depending on the technology used, joint processes primarily use resources at the batch and facility levels. In most cases, companies set up the joint process to accommodate a specific type of input or to produce a specific type of output in a batch. Thus, an oil refiner might set up the refinery (a large, facility-level resource) to process a batch of crude oil of a particular grade and to produce specific petroleum products. National Wood Products sets up its sawmills to process logs and produce specific types and grades of lumber.

In practice, assigning joint costs to the various products for financial reporting and measuring product profitability involves a somewhat arbitrary cost *allocation* based on the quantities of outputs or the relative sales value of the joint products. Therefore, the sequence of decisions involved in the *management of joint processes requires, first, deciding which products to produce and, second, determining how to allocate joint-process costs.*

We now describe National Wood Products' joint-process decision making and costing and the importance of these managerial processes to the firm's profitability. Note that the decisions and methods described in this chapter are applicable to all joint processes.

One Input—More Than One Output

At National Wood Products' Georgia mill, raw timber (logs) is the common input to produce the following products:

1. Grade A Standard lumber, which is high quality with minor or no imperfections.
2. Grade B Standard lumber, which has imperfections but is acceptable for jobs that use rough lumber.
3. Grade A Specialty lumber, which is made by further processing Grade A Standard lumber by drying to eliminate the tendency of "green" lumber to warp.

Note that each log produces both Grade A and Grade B lumber. Management decides whether to process Grade A from Standard to Specialty with the drying process.

Exhibit 9–1
Measures of Process
Capacity

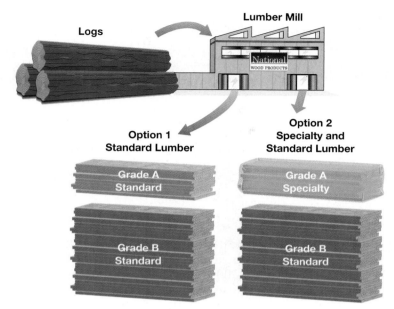

Exhibit 9–1 depicts the two alternatives that management can choose: (1) produce Grade A Standard and Grade B Standard or (2) produce Grade A Specialty and Grade B Standard.[1] The cost of the lumber and the cost of processing (e.g., sawing) up to the split-off point are joint costs. This split-off point is where the log has been sawed into lumber. Some of that lumber is Grade A and the rest is Grade B.

The Decision Challenge: Which Joint Products to Produce

The usual objective governing the production of joint products is to maximize profits, which clearly is an important objective for National Wood Products. In some situations, such as joint ventures among various parties that use the outputs of a process, contracts can specify the products to produce and the amounts.

LO 1 Use cost-management information to increase the profits from using scarce resources of joint-production processes.

Estimation of Profits from Joint Products

Using its best estimates of sales prices and production costs, National Wood Products makes decisions regarding how to use its mill capacity by going through these steps:

1. *Identify alternative sets and quantities of final products possible from the joint process.* From joint processing of logs, National Wood Products considers two sets of products, Grade A and Grade B Standard lumber—as final products.

2. *Forecast the sales price of each final product.* National Wood Products closely watches regional and international market prices and drivers of demand and prices, such as housing starts and monthly timber harvests reported by the Forest Products Association, an industry trade group. The company also seeks to establish long-term customer relationships and contracts to ensure predictable sales and prices.

3. *Estimate the costs (if any) required to further process joint products into salable products.* To produce Grade A Specialty lumber, National Wood Products incurs additional processing costs for drying the lumber.

4. *Choose the set of products with the overall maximum profit.*

---

[1] In practice, many more options for converting logs are available. Furthermore, in computer-controlled sawmills, each log can be evaluated and sawed to maximize the profit from alternative products based on current product prices.

You're the Decision Maker 9.1

Operate or Shut Down the Process?

The practical capacity of the Georgia mill is based on running one shift per day five days a week because of limited access to timber in that region. Negotiations to gain access to timber on Native American reservation land to replace reduced timber from U.S. federal land have not progressed satisfactorily (from the company's perspective).

a. A member of the corporate controller's staff has observed that the per-unit cost of lumber from the Georgia mill is higher than at mills running two shifts per day for six days a week. He suggests that the company should consider closing the Georgia mill because other mills are more efficient. Is there a sound basis for this recommendation? Explain.

b. As a member of the Georgia mill management team, how would you respond to the recommendation to close your mill? Consider both local and companywide issues.

(Solutions begin on page 349.)

Exhibit 9–2 shows the data to support joint-product decision making at National Wood Products' Georgia sawmill. The top line of Exhibit 9–2 shows the mill's monthly capacity to be 4,700 MBF (1,000 board feet with 1 board foot of lumber as a piece of lumber 1 foot square by 1 inch thick).

Just below the mill capacity is the forecasted sales prices of each of the three types of lumber. Below that are the alternative production quantities. National Wood Products can produce and sell either option 1 (all standard lumber) or option 2 (part specialty and part standard lumber). Option 2 was developed in response to the address by Malcolm Fries (president and CEO of National Wood Products) reported at the beginning of this chapter. Recall that he asked company employees to develop new product ideas. Plant employees at the company's Georgia plant developed the Grade A Specialty lumber as a new product.

Next are the joint costs to produce a total of 4,000 MBF for either option 1 or option 2. These joint costs, which total $1,400,000, include the cost of both obtaining the logs and cutting them into lumber. At this split-off point, the Georgia plant would have produced 1,000 MBF of Grade A Standard and 3,000 MBF of Grade B Standard lumber. To convert Grade A Standard lumber into Grade A Specialty lumber requires an additional cost of $100,000 to dry 1,000 MBF of Grade A Standard lumber.

Exhibit 9–3 diagrams the production process, showing the costs and revenues of the process and products. Exhibits 9–2 and 9–3 present important information referred to throughout the chapter. Be sure that you understand it before you continue.

Exhibit 9–2

National Wood Products, Inc., Georgia Mill

WOOD PRODUCTS

Mill capacity per month*	4,700 MBF†
Forecasted sales prices:	
Grade A Standard	$600 per MBF
Grade B Standard	400 per MBF
Grade A Specialty	900 per MBF
Alternative production quantities:	
Option 1:	
Grade A Standard	1,000 MBF
Grade B Standard	3,000 MBF
Option 2:	
Grade A Specialty	1,000 MBF
Grade B Standard	3,000 MBF
Joint costs to produce 4,000 MBF of Grade A and Grade B Standard lumber	$1,400,000 per month
Additional costs to convert Grade A Standard to Grade A Specialty ($100 per MBF)	100,000 per month

* Information is for a typical month.

† The abbreviation MBF refers to 1,000 board feet. One board foot is equivalent to a piece of lumber that is 1 foot square by 1 inch thick. MBF is a typical measure of volume in the US lumber industry. The international standard measure of lumber volume is cubic meters: 1 MBF = 2.4 cubic meters.

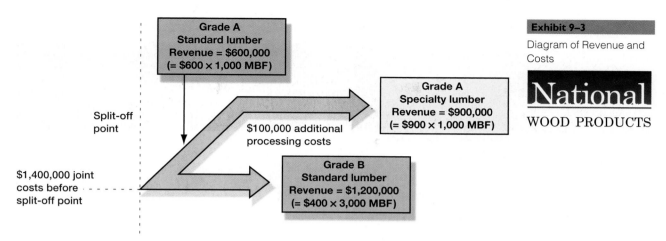

Exhibit 9–3
Diagram of Revenue and Costs

Decision to Sell Products at Split Off or Process Them Further

Many companies have opportunities to sell partly processed products at various production stages. The management team must decide whether selling the output at an intermediate stage or processing it further is more profitable. In such a "sell-or-process-further" decision, the relevant economic data to consider are (1) the potential additional revenue after further processing and (2) the additional costs to process further.

LO 2 Use cost-management data in the sell-or-process-further decision.

Profit Maximization of Joint-Product Processes

The **net realizable value (NRV)** is the measure of a product's contribution to profit after the split-off point and is computed as sales revenue minus additional processing costs. Computing the NRV of each set of products provides a comparison of each product's sales revenue to costs incurred *after* split off. It is important to note that any *allocation* of the mill's $1,400,000 joint-process costs among products is irrelevant to product decisions. Joint-process costs incurred *prior* to the split-off point are not affected by the decision to sell or process further after the split-off point. Only the revenues from selling or processing beyond the split-off point and any expenditures for additional processing are the relevant factors, regardless of the way the company allocates joint costs. It is ultimately necessary to measure whether the total NRV of the most profitable set of products exceeds the joint-process cost but only after selecting the best set of products.

Profit Analysis of Option 1: Grade A Standard Lumber

The profit analysis of the Georgia mill decision is in Exhibit 9–4. Expected quantities, prices, and further processing costs after the split off are based on the information of products from Exhibit 9–2. The exhibit shows that the total NRV for option 1 equals $1,800,000.

Profit Analysis of Option 2: Grade A Specialty Lumber and Grade B Standard Lumber

According to data in Exhibit 9–4, the total NRV of option 2 is $2,000,000, which is composed of the $800,000 NRV of Grade A Specialty lumber plus the $1,200,000 Grade B Standard lumber. Note that the additional processing of Grade A lumber to convert it from Standard to Specialty lumber cost $100,000 but added $300,000 to revenues from Grade A lumber.

Most Profitable Products

An analysis of Exhibit 9–4 indicates that the most profitable decision is to produce Grade A Specialty and Grade B Standard lumber (option 2). The NRV of this combination exceeds the NRV of option 1. Furthermore, the NRV of $2,000,000 per month for option 2 exceeds the joint-processing cost of $1,400,000 per month (from

| Exhibit 9–4 | Georgia Mill: Analysis of Alternatives for a Typical Month | | | | |

	A	B	C	D	E
	Quantity*	Price per Unit	Revenue (Column A × Column B)	Additional Processing Costs	Net Realizable Value of the split-off point (Column C − Column D)
Option 1: Produce Standard lumber:					
NRV, Grade A Standard lumber	1,000	$600	$ 600,000	$ 0	$ 600,000
NRV, Grade B Standard lumber	3,000	400	1,200,000	0	1,200,000
Total net realizable value for option 1					$1,800,000
Option 2: Produce Grade B Standard and Grade A Specialty lumber:					
NRV, Grade A Specialty lumber	1,000	$900	$ 900,000	$100,000	$ 800,000
NRV, Grade B Standard lumber	3,000	400	1,200,000	0	1,200,000
Total net realizable value for option 2					$2,000,000

Recommendation: Choose option 2 because it has the higher net realizable value.

* Quantity is expressed in thousand board feet (MBF). 1 unit = 1,000 board feet. One board foot of lumber is equivalent to 1 square foot of lumber that is 1 inch thick.

Exhibit 9–2), so the mill can operate profitably (assuming that general and administrative costs do not exceed $600,000, the difference between the best NRV and the joint-process cost).

Providing this type of accurate cost analysis is one of the most important contributions of cost-management analysts in organizations that use joint-production processes, but it is not their only contribution, as we see in the next section.

Reasons for Allocating Joint Costs

LO 3 Explain why organizations allocate joint costs.

None of the preceding analyses involved allocating any of the $1,400,000 joint cost to any product, but most companies allocate these costs. Why should cost-management analysts be overly concerned with allocating joint costs when such allocations appear to be completely arbitrary? Organizations allocate joint costs for many reasons, including measuring performance, estimating casualty losses, determining and responding to regulatory rates, and specifying and resolving contractual interests and obligations. Manufacturing companies are required to use joint-cost allocations for financial and tax reporting to value inventories and cost of goods sold. For example, valuing inventories and measuring reported income for specialty and standard lumber at National Wood Products' Georgia mill requires the allocation of joint-process costs to both products.

Realize that although there is no precise way to trace joint-process costs to joint products (as activity-based costing seeks to do in other production processes, for example), the results of allocating joint costs in different ways can be very important to management decision making. The following examples demonstrate that, although joint costs might be inexact, they should not be randomly determined. Cost-management analysts need to consider the decision-making implications of seemingly arbitrary joint-cost allocations.

Measuring Performance

Joint-cost allocations can serve as measures of some departmental or division costs when executive performance is evaluated. Many companies compensate executives and other employees, at least partly, on the basis of departmental or divisional earnings for the year, which could be based on allocated joint costs. For example, if one

Testing the Validity of the Analysis

Refer to Exhibits 9–2 and 9–4.

The analysis in Exhibit 9–4 is based on the company's best estimates of quantities, revenues, and costs, but actual amounts could differ. You have been asked to determine whether the recommendations could differ if these figures have errors.

a. Which figures in Exhibits 9–2 and 9–4 probably are most subject to error? Why?

b. Describe the concept of *materiality* in the context of the analysis in Exhibit 9–4.

c. Sensitivity analysis is a method of systematically testing whether a decision would change by changing one key figure in the analysis at a time and observing the change in expected outcomes. It is a way of asking "what-if" questions about changes in figures and measuring the effects. For example, *what if* economic troubles in Asia reduce the price for specialty lumber to $650 per MBF? Is the decision to produce lumber option 2 *sensitive* to this change in price?

d. What advice regarding the analysis would you give to managers of the Georgia mill to help them in their product planning for the year?

(Solutions begin on page 349.)

> **You're the Decision Maker 9.2**

division at National Wood Products is responsible for selling specialty lumber and another is responsible for selling standard lumber, the cost of processing logs could be allocated partly to the specialty lumber division and partly to the standard lumber division.[2] Both divisions have an interest in the way the costs are allocated because of the impacts on divisional profits. The company as a whole, however, must ensure that the divisions work together as a team to maximize overall profits.

Using any cost allocation as a performance measure raises the issue of fairness and could affect the use of resources or provide the incentive to manipulate the performance measure. Managers who are downstream from joint processes and are evaluated in part on the basis of allocated joint costs might feel that cost allocations are not fair since they cannot control the joint costs. An adverse effect of cost allocation occurs if managers mistakenly regard average joint costs per unit as unit-level or marginal costs and make improper product or service decisions based on this mistaken interpretation.

Estimating Casualty Losses

Joint-cost allocations can be useful in valuing inventory for insurance purposes. Should a casualty loss occur, the insurance company and the insured party must agree on the value of the lost goods. For example, suppose that a portion of the specialty lumber at National Wood Products was destroyed in a fire. From National Wood Product's perspective, the cost of the lumber destroyed should include a portion of the joint costs.

Determining and Responding to Regulated Rates

When companies are subject to rate (price) regulation, the allocation of joint costs can be a significant factor in the way regulators determine rates. Thus, the manner of allocating and using joint costs can be important cost drivers in utilities that depend on joint-cost allocations for pricing or reimbursement. The importance of joint-cost allocations continues in many industries, including telecommunications (see Cost Management in Practice 9.1). In some countries, however, utility rates have been partially or completely deregulated, so costs based in part on the allocation of the joint costs to produce energy or gas are becoming less important.

---

[2] Note also that if one division is in a higher income tax bracket than the other, the company might be motivated to use a joint-costing method that allocates as much cost to the division in the higher bracket as possible to increase its cost of goods sold and reduce its reported income. It is even possible that tax implications could change product choices.

Cost Management in Practice 9.1

Joint-Cost Allocations and the Telecommunications Industry

Anyone interested in exploiting his or her understanding of joint-cost allocations should look for work in the telecommunication industry! A large portion of telecommunication capacity is a facility-level resource that is analogous to a joint process, which is impossible to trace to any particular use of the resource. For example, customers or competing companies use network facilities to originate or terminate long-distance or local calls.

In the United States, *interstate* access rates are regulated by the Telecommunication Act of 1996. Federal courts have ruled that regulating *intrastate* access rates is up to individual states. Because access rates are based to a large degree on allocations of joint-capacity costs, numerous disputes have occurred among telecommunication companies competing for access to customers within specific states.

Joint-cost allocations of network costs, for example, were at the heart of a complaint by telecommunication giant AT&T against Ameritech (which was later acquired by SBC) in the State of Ohio. Because Ameritech owns the capacity (e.g., lines and networks) that other carriers must use in Ohio, overcharging (e.g., misuse of joint costing) allegedly allowed the local Ameritech company to squeeze out competition by allocating higher costs to competitors' use of capacity than to its own customers. MCI joined the fray charging that Ameritech was exploiting its monopoly position by charging competitors too much for the monthly and per-minute costs of access, which contain large amounts of allocated joint costs of Ameritech's operations. Ameritech's strategic joint-cost allocation had become the cost of doing business for AT&T and MCI. *Source:* "The First Report and Order Re Local Competition," FCC Common Carrier Docket 96–98, Part Two. Deposition by Mr. Dennis L. Ricca (MCI, Inc.) for the Ohio Public Utilities Commission. United States Court of Appeals for the Eighth Circuit Opinion No. 96-3321. (Full citations to references are in the Bibliography.)

Specifying and Resolving Contractual Interests and Obligations

Many contracts involve parties with potentially conflicting interests. For example, neither the insurance company nor the insured party wishes to pay any more or receive any less than is fair. Both buyers and sellers of contracted products or services are affected by pricing terms in the contract, and neither wishes to give the other an unfair advantage. Often prices for goods and services exchanged among contracting parties are based on costs, including allocated joint costs. Any cost-allocation method contains an element of arbitrariness or inexactness, although activity-based costing (discussed in Chapter 4) attempts to more accurately assign costs to products. Thus, specifying how to allocate costs in advance is advisable.

When joint costs are involved among contracting parties, a great potential for conflict exists because every joint-cost allocation is discretionary. By the nature of joint processes, determining exactly how much of joint process resources is used by any of the resulting joint products is impossible. Joint-cost allocation methods must be clearly stated in contracts before they are implemented. In that sense, the choice of the joint-cost allocation method is not arbitrary but is an integral part of the contract. To leave the definition of the joint-cost or other cost-allocation method ambiguous in a contract when the interests of either party can be affected is to invite dispute. On the other hand, cost-management analysts, by estimating the effects of joint-cost allocations and clearly spelling out how to allocate joint costs, contribute to informed negotiations and a smoothly functioning contractual arrangement.

Joint-Cost Implications in Contracts

Although properly described and implemented joint-cost allocations can be beneficial, as discussed, managers' lack of awareness of the discretionary nature of joint-cost allocation makes good business for lawyers and litigation support consultants who know something about accounting. In many cases, people or companies became involved in disputes because they did not consider the implications of joint costs in written or oral contracts. Disputes often arise over the application of the word *cost* in cost-sharing agreements. Consider these examples:

■ *Example 1.* Two companies, Tulsa Oil and Buffalo Energy, entered a joint venture to drill for oil and natural gas. Tulsa Oil wanted the oil from the well;

Buffalo Energy wanted the natural gas. The costs of exploration, drilling, pumping, and separating oil from natural gas are the joint costs shared by the two companies. Neither company would find the venture profitable alone, but, by sharing the costs, both companies find it profitable.

Joint ventures in oil and gas refining often require an allocation of joint costs to each of the business partners.

After 10 years without dispute, worldwide natural gas prices dropped substantially because of new discoveries and increased distribution of natural gas from Russia and neighboring countries. Buffalo Energy wanted out of the joint venture because selling natural gas from this venture was no longer profitable. Tulsa Oil wanted Buffalo Energy to continue sharing the costs of pumping and separating natural gas and oil, so it did not want Buffalo Energy to back out. Buffalo Energy ceased operations and stopped paying the costs of the joint venture: legal war broke out!

Example 2. Consider the State of Alaska's North Slope dispute with British Petroleum and Exxon Mobil over the joint costs of gas-processing plants. The oil companies paid the State of Alaska royalties amounting to one-eighth of the value of oil pumped off the North Slope. However, the oil companies reduced the royalty payment by a portion of joint costs incurred by certain gas-processing plants. These plants pumped a common input from underground and processed it into three joint products, two of which were then mostly pumped back into the ground because processing them further was not profitable. The single, retained joint product was oil.

How much of the joint cost of the gas-processing plant should be allocated to the oil? The oil companies wanted to allocate as much joint cost as possible to the oil to reduce their royalty payment to the state. Conversely, the state wanted to allocate as much as possible to the joint products that were pumped back into the ground.

After years of discussion and tens of millions of dollars of legal expense, the case was settled out of court just before going to trial. The resulting allocation was a compromise between the parties to the lawsuit.

Write contracts carefully. Those readers who become lawyers or litigation consultants are likely to work on legal cases involving joint costs because of their inherent arbitrariness. Legal cases involving oil and gas companies alone have hundreds of millions of dollars at stake. Accountants and cost-management analysts have an opportunity and a professional obligation to provide input to their organizations' contracts involving joint or indirect cost allocations. To minimize the incidence of such disputes, you should carefully word contracts to define the meaning, measurement, allocation, and sharing of *costs* and anticipate as many future events as possible that could affect the amount and measurement of costs. Although no contract can completely specify every contingency, above all avoid ambiguous phrases such as "share the costs of processing," which without careful elaboration invite trouble.

Joint Cost-Allocation Methods

The two major methods of allocating joint costs are (1) the net realizable value method and (2) the physical-measures method. Other methods, such as the sales value at split off and gross margin, are used much less frequently; they are discussed briefly in the chapter appendix.

LO 4 Understand how to use the net-realizable-value and physical-measures joint-cost-allocation methods.

Distinguishing between Main and By-Products

In practice, companies distinguish between main products and by-products before allocating joint costs because, by convention, joint costs are allocated only to main products. A **main product** is a joint output that generates a significant portion of the net realizable value (NRV) from the process. A **by-product** is the output from a joint-production process that is minor in quantity and/or NRV when compared to the main products. Kerosene, for example, is a by-product of gasoline production. You may have seen advertisements for carpet and cloth mill ends at bargain prices, which often are by-products of textile production. *By-products do not receive allocations of joint costs.* Suppose that as a by-product of cutting the bark off of logs, the Georgia mill also produces wood chips. Assume also that the NRV from the wood chips is considerably less than the NRV from either of the other two products. Therefore, National Wood Products considers the wood chips to be a by-product of lumber production.

Using the Net Realizable Value Method

The **net realizable value (NRV) method** allocates joint costs based on the net realizable value (NRV) of each *main product* at the split-off point. If the main products are to be sold at the split-off point without further processing, the market values or sales prices at split-off are used for this allocation base. If further processing is required, the NRV at the split-off point is computed by deducting those added processing costs from sales value. (If the added processing has not yet been done, then the added processing costs would be estimated.) Using the NRV method, joint costs are allocated to the main products in proportion to their NRVs at the split-off point.

From the previous analysis, assume that National Wood Products chose to produce Option 2; Grade A Specialty lumber and Grade B Standard lumber. The joint cost up to the split-off point is $1,400,000. Using the NRV method, this $1,400,000 joint cost is allocated based on the relative net realizable values of Grade A Specialty and Grade B Standard lumber.

According to Exhibit 9–4, the net realizable value of Grade A Specialty lumber was $800,000, or 40 percent of the total net realizable value of $2,000,000 for the option (.40 = $800,000 ÷ $2,000,000). The net realizable value of Grade B Standard lumber was $1,200,000, or 60 percent of the total net realizable value of $2,000,000 for the option (.60 = $1,200,000 ÷ $2,000,000).

Exhibit 9–5 shows the allocation of the $1,400,000 joint cost to each of the two products. Based on the net realizable values, 40 percent of the $1,400,000 joint cost is allocated to Grade A Specialty lumber and 60 percent is allocated to Grade B Standard lumber.

Exhibit 9–5

Joint Cost Allocations— NRV Method

	Grade A Specialty Lumber	Grade B Standard Lumber	Total
Sales revenue	$900,000	$1,200,000	$2,100,000
Less further processing costs	100,000	0	100,000
Net realizable value	$800,000	$1,200,000	$2,000,000
Proportionate share of net realizable value	40%	60%	100%
Allocated joint process costs	$560,000	$ 840,000	$1,400,000

Computations:

Proportional share of NRV:

Grade A Specialty lumber	40%	= $800,000 ÷ $2,000,000
Grade B Standard lumber	60%	= $1,200,000 ÷ $2,000,000
	100%	

Allocations of joint costs:

To Grade A Specialty lumber	$ 560,000 = 40% × $1,400,000
To Grade B Standard lumber	$ 840,000 = 60% × $1,400,000
	$1,400,000

	Grade A Specialty Lumber	Grade B Standard Lumber	Total
Sales revenues	$900,000	$1,200,000	$2,100,000
Less additional processing costs to point of marketability	100,000	0	100,000
NRV at split-off point	800,000	1,200,000	2,000,000
Allocation of joint costs:			
.40 × $1,400,000	560,000		1,400,000
.60 × $1,400,000		840,000	
Gross margin	$240,000	$360,000	$600,000
Gross margin as a percent of NRV at split-off point*	30%	30%	30%

* 30% = 240,000 ÷ $800,000; 30% = $360,000 ÷ $1,200,000; 30% = $600,000 ÷ $2,000,000

Exhibit 9–6

Gross margins: Net Realizable Value Method

National
WOOD PRODUCTS

	Grade A Specialty Lumber	Grade B Standard Lumber	Total
Quantity produced (MBF)	1,000	3,000	4,000
Proportionate share of physical quantity	25%	75%	100%
	(1,000 MBF ÷ 4,000 MBF)	(3,000 MBF ÷ 4,000 MBF)	
Allocated joint process costs	$350,000	$1,050,000	$1,400,000
	(25% × $1,400,000)	(75% × $1,400,000)	

Exhibit 9–7

Joint Cost Allocations: Physical-Measures Method

National
WOOD PRODUCTS

Exhibit 9–6 shows the equality of the gross margin percents, calculated as the relation between the gross margins and the NRVs at split-off. This equality is an important feature of the NRV method; namely, that it maintains the relative profitability of the products. Neither the Grade A Specialty nor the Grade B Standard lumber is advantaged or disadvantaged by the NRV method.

We have presented a typical method for allocating joint costs using the economic values of joint products. The Appendix to this chapter presents two alternative methods using economic values.

Using the Physical-Measures Method

The **physical-measures** (or **quantities**) **method** is a joint-cost allocation based on the relative volume, weight, energy content, or other physical measure of each joint product at the split-off point. Companies might prefer the physical-measures method when the prices of their output products are highly volatile or unpredictable. This method is sometimes used when significant processing occurs between the split-off point and the first sales opportunity, or when the market does not set product prices. The latter situation could arise when regulators set prices in regulated pricing situations or in cost-based contract situations, for example.

Many oil- and gas-producing companies allocate joint costs on the basis of the products' energy equivalents (BTU content). They use this method because the products are typically measured in different physical units (e.g., natural gas by thousands of cubic feet, oil by barrels), although oil and natural gas often are produced simultaneously from the same well.

Allocations. We return to the National Wood Products company example. The company produces lumber according to option 2—1,000 MBF of Grade A Specialty lumber and 3,000 MBF of Grade B Standard lumber. Using the physical measures method, cost-management analysts allocate 25% (1,000 ÷ 4,000 total MBF) of the joint process costs to Grade A Specialty lumber and 75% (3,000 ÷ 4,000 total MBF) of the joint-process costs to Grade B Standard lumber. Exhibit 9–7 shows the allocation of the

Gross Margins: Physical-Measures Method	Grade A Specialty Lumber	Grade B Standard Lumber	Total
Sales revenue	$900,000	$1,200,000	$2,100,000
Cost of goods sold			
Joint-cost allocations	$350,000	$1,050,000	$1,400,000
Further processing costs	100,000	0	100,000
Total cost of goods sold	$450,000	$1,050,000	$1,500,000
Gross margins: Physical-measures method	$450,000	$ 150,000	$ 600,000

$1,400,000 joint-process cost to each of the two products; $350,000 (25% × $1,400,000) to Grade A Specialty and $1,050,000 (75% × $1,400,000) to Grade B Standard lumber.

Gross margins.   The physical measures method does not allocate costs proportional to economic values, so the gross margins of joint products is not equal, as in the NRV method. Exhibit 9–8 shows that, in this example, Grade A Specialty lumber has a relatively high gross margin compared to Grade B Standard lumber. That is because the physical measures method allocates a relatively low proportion of joint costs to Grade A Specialty lumber.

It is wise not to rely too much on joint product margins or profits for decision making because such margin or profit computations are affected by the methods used to allocate joint costs. Clearly, if it were in the interest of a manager to make Grade A Specialty lumber appear profitable, then that manager would use the physical-measures method of joint-cost allocation. On the other hand, if a manager were interested in making Grade B Standard lumber appear to be as profitable as Grade A Specialty lumber, then that manager would use the NRV method. Of course, the combined profits of the two products would be the same whatever joint cost allocation method is used. But the relative profitability of joint products can be affected by which cost-allocation method is used.

Research Insight 9.1

Preference for Joint-Costing Methods

In practice, companies in similar industries allocate joint costs in a variety of ways, as a study of joint costing in the chemical and petrochemical industries in the United Kingdom indicates. The following table, which summarizes the study results, shows a variety in the preference for the method used. Accountants and managers might prefer different allocation methods in different situations. Alternatively, this variation in preference could reflect the inherently arbitrary nature of joint-cost allocation.

The study shows that some companies did not allocate joint costs at all. Many companies in the study used the net realizable value method, but even more companies used the physical-measures method. We can speculate that the physical-measures method seemed more objective and is more easily used than the NRV method.

Joint-Cost Allocations in Practice

	No Allocation	Net Realizable Value Method	Physical-Measures Method	Other Methods
Oil refining	7	0	0	2
Petrochemicals	1	5	4	0
Coal chemicals	0	1	6	4
Inorganic chemicals	1	2	2	3
Other companies in the chemicals industry	0	3	28	3
Total	9	11	40	12

Source: K. Slater and C. Wootton, A Study of Joint and By-Product Costing in the U.K.

Choosing among Joint-Cost Allocation Methods

The "jointness" of joint-production processes makes the separation of the portion of joint costs attributable to one product from another impossible on a cause-and-effect basis. As a result, allocating joint costs might be somewhat arbitrary. Since nearly any desired joint-cost allocation can be achieved by carefully choosing the method, it is important:

- Not to base product or service production decisions on gross margins (i.e., after joint-cost allocations) unless the choice is in response to regulatory opportunities (e.g., cost reimbursement from a governmental agency).

- To choose, when allowed, the joint-cost allocation method that maximizes regulated profits or cost reimbursements.

- To clearly define the way to allocate joint costs in contractual agreements among parties that share outputs and costs of joint processes. On the other hand, if contracts do not specify how to allocate joint costs, the party responsible for assigning costs to various products and parties can be expected to use the method that is personally most advantageous. As noted earlier, this lack of specificity can cause contentious negotiations beforehand or expensive litigation afterward.

Basics of Accounting for By-Products

By-products are by definition relatively minor products; hence, the method used to account for them is not likely to have a major effect on decisions or the financial statements for either internal or external reporting. Some companies make by-product accounting as easy as possible by simply expensing the by-products' separable (additional processing) costs in the period that they are incurred and then recording the total revenue from the by-products when they are sold.

LO 5 Know how to account for by-products.

Using this method, the accountants do not have to keep an inventory of the cost to process by-products or compute their net realizable value. Although this simple approach technically violates the matching principle—revenues and expenses should be matched in the same accounting period—this practice is acceptable if the amounts involved are immaterial.

Methods. Two typical methods of accounting for by-products that are sold at split-off are to (1) consider the by-product's NRV as "other revenue" or (2) deduct the by-product's NRV from the costs of main products. To understand these methods, assume that the Georgia mill chose lumber option 2 but sold wood chips at split off. Assume that, after selecting this option, the mill would have sold 1,500 metric tons of wood chips for $72,400 after additional processing (cleaning and drying) of $10,000, giving an NRV of $62,400.

Method 1: Treat the by-product's NRV as other revenue. Treating by-product NRV as other revenue is the simpler method. Since the by-product NRVs are small and the effects on income are immaterial, many companies use this approach. The by-product NRV is simply counted as other revenue, as shown:

Sales revenue	
Main products (Exhibit 9–6)	$2,100,000
Other revenue, by-products	62,400
Total revenue	$2,162,400
Cost of main products sold (Exhibit 9–6, $1,400,000 joint costs + $100,000 additional processing costs)	1,500,000
Gross margin	$ 662,400

Method 2: Deduct the NRV obtained from the sale of the by-products from the cost of the main products. This method can be slightly more complicated *if all main products produced are not sold* in the period that they are produced. The effect on gross

margin is the same as method 1, however, if all main products have been sold, as shown here:

Sales revenue (Exhibit 9–6)	$2,100,000
Cost of goods sold	
Cost of main products sold (Exhibit 9–6, $1,400,000 joint costs + $100,000 additional processing costs)	1,500,000
Less NRV of by-products	(62,400)
Adjusted cost of goods sold	1,437,600
Gross margin	$ 662,400

If all main products produced in the period have *not* been sold, the NRV of by-products should be prorated to the main product inventories and the cost of goods sold. These adjustments would be in proportion to the NRVs or physical measure of main products in those accounts, depending on the method used to allocate joint costs.[3] As one possibility, assume that at the end of the month, all Grade A Specialty lumber had been sold, but all Grade B Standard lumber was still in finished goods. The adjustments to the main product account costs based on the physical-measures method follow:

	Grade A Specialty Lumber	Grade B Standard Lumber	Total
Physical quantity	1,000 MBF	3,000 MBF	4,000 MBF
Proportionate share of quantity	25%	75%	100%
Allocation of by-product NRV	$15,600	$46,800	$62,400
	(.25 × $62,400)	(.75 × $62,400)	

Disposal of Scrap and Waste

Many companies have transformed waste into profitable products.

Our discussion so far has assumed that the by-product output has a positive net realizable value; that is, its sales value exceeds the costs of further processing. If an output's NRV is negative, it is usually considered scrap or waste and is disposed of legally at minimum cost. Keep in mind, however, that the cost of disposing of scrap or waste can be considerable, particularly if the disposal is harmful to the environment. The cost is usually estimated and counted as part of joint-processing costs (or manufacturing overhead in other processes) and allocated to products as part of joint costing. If scrap and waste are not disposed of properly, the company, its employees, and its directors can be subject to severe penalties.

In some cases, environmental regulations that discourage or prohibit dumping scrap or waste have motivated the creation of new products that can be sold profitably (or at lower cost than disposal). For example, years ago, lumber mills burned sawdust and tree bark or dumped it in rivers and landfills. Environmental regulations now prohibit these practices. In response,

---

[3] Another complication can arise under either method of accounting for by-products if the cost of processing them occurs in one period but they are not sold until the next period. In such a case, revenues might be recognized at the time of production, but companies could find it necessary to keep an inventory of the by-product processing costs in an Additional By-Product Cost account until the by-products themselves have been sold and cash has been received.

lumber companies asked, Why not process chips and sawdust into paper pulp and use bark for landscaping and mulch products? Alternatively, why not burn scrap to generate power for other operations? Thus, new sources of raw materials were created from what had been scrap and waste.

Another example to consider, according to the Recyclers' World (www.recycle.net), is the growth in recent years of the active industry to recycle scrap tires, which often sit in large, unsightly, and dangerous piles.[4] These tires have become the raw materials for many new products, including electricity produced by incinerating tires to pavement materials for hiking trails, streets, and highways produced by shredding tires.

---

[4] Piles of tires can catch fire from lightning strikes, support breeding of disease-carrying mosquitoes, and leach toxic chemicals into water supplies. Every automobile tire sold in most countries carries a fee that subsidizes proper disposal.

Chapter Summary

Joint processes simultaneously produce multiple outputs. Selling or processing these outputs further depends on the net realizable values (sales less further processing costs) of joint products. Product decisions should not be made, if at all possible, based on joint-cost allocations, which arise from the need to assign joint-process costs to two or more products manufactured from a common input. The usual objective of joint-cost allocation is to measure costs of the inputs for financial or contractual reporting. There is no exact way to trace joint costs to products, so arbitrary allocations might be necessary. On the other hand, joint-cost allocations might prove useful or strategically sound in some industries or situations where prices or revenues depend on discretionary choice of the allocation method. The two methods of joint-cost allocation distribute joint costs based on net realizable value (or *estimated* net realizable value) or the physical-measures method. Accounting for by-products seeks to accurately record transactions but at minimum effort and cost.

Appendix to Chapter Nine

Other Economic Value Methods

The chapter discussed the typical net realizable value (NRV) method for allocating joint costs. This appendix presents two other methods also based on the economic values of joint outputs: (1) the relative sales value at split-off method and (2) the constant gross margin percentage method.

LO 6 Understand how to use the relative sales value at split-off and constant gross margin percentage methods of cost allocation.

WOOD PRODUCTS

Relative Sales Value at Split-Off Method

The **relative sales value at split-off method** allocates joint costs based on the relative sales values of the joint products at their split-off point. This method does not consider additional processing costs after the split-off point. Recall that the revenues at the split-off point for National Wood Products' Georgia mill before additional processing were as follows:

Grade A lumber	$ 600,000
Grade B lumber	1,200,000

Given these values, one-third [$600,000 ÷ ($600,000 + $1,200,000)] of the joint costs would be allocated to Grade A lumber and two-thirds would be allocated to Grade B lumber. The allocated joint costs would be:

To Grade A lumber	.33 × $1,400,000 = $466,667
To Grade B lumber	.67 × $1,400,000 = $933,333

Note that the relative sales value method does not require knowing whether Grade A lumber will be processed into specialty lumber because it allocates joint costs based on *relative* values at the split-off point *before* any additional processing.

Exhibit 9–9

Joint Costs Allocated
Using the Constant Gross
Margin Percentage
Method

WOOD PRODUCTS

Panel A	Grade A Specialty Lumber	Grade B Standard Lumber	Total
Sales value	$900,000	$1,200,000	$2,100,000
Joint costs (step 3)	?	?	1,400,000
Additional processing costs	100,000	0	100,000
Gross margin (step 2)	?	?	$ 600,000
Gross margin percentage (step 1)	28.57143	28.57143	28.57143

Panel B			
Sales value	$900,000	$1,200,000	$2,100,000
Joint costs (step 3)*	542,857	857,143	1,400,000
Additional processing costs	100,000	0	100,000
Gross margin (step 2)†	$257,143	$ 342,857	$ 600,000
Gross margin percentage (step 1)	28.57143	28.57143	28.57143

*$542,857 = $900,000 − $100,000 − $257,143, etc.
†$257,143 = .2857143 × $900,000 sales value, etc.

Constant Gross Margin Percentage Method

The constant gross margin percentage method is another method of joint-cost allocation that is based on the economic values of joint products. The **constant gross margin percentage method** allocates joint costs to products in a way that the gross margin percentages as a percent of revenue are the same for each joint product. Three steps are required to use this method:

1. Compute the total gross margin percentage.
2. Use the total gross margin percentage calculated in step 1 to calculate the gross margin for each product (total gross margin percentage × sales value).
3. Deduct the additional processing costs from the total costs to calculate joint costs allocated to each product.

Using the data from the National Wood Products example, we can calculate the allocation of joint costs using the constant gross margin percentage method. Panel A of Exhibit 9–9 shows the data provided and the calculation of the total gross margin percentages (step 1). Panel A also indicates the amounts that remain to be calculated (denoted with a question mark). Panel B of Exhibit 9–9 shows the calculation of the gross margin dollar amount for each product (step 2). After the gross margin dollar amount has been calculated for each product, we can solve for the joint costs to be allocated to each product (step 3), which also is shown in panel B of Exhibit 9–9.

The constant gross margin percentage method is based on the same principle as the NRV method, except for one small difference. The NRV method results in gross margin percentages that are equal as a percent of the *net realizable values* of each joint product, whereas the constant gross margin method requires that gross margin percentages be equal as a percent of the *revenues* of each joint product.

Key Terms

For each term's definition, refer to the indicated page or turn to the glossary at the end of the text.

by-product, 342
constant gross margin
    percentage method,* 348
final product, 334
intermediate product, 334

joint costs, 334
joint process, 334
joint products, 334
main product, 342

net realizable value
    (NRV), 337
net realizable value (NRV)
    method, 342

physical-measures (or
    quantities) method, 343
relative sales value at split-
    off method,* 347
split-off point, 334

———
* Term appears in chapter Appendix.

Meeting the Cost Management Challenges

1. How do cost-management analysts anticipate and resolve potential conflicts between joint-product and process decision making and external reporting?

In some situations, joint-product decision making should be kept entirely separate from external reporting, such as when an organization sells its products in competitive markets and when joint-process costs are irrelevant to performance evaluations. Thus, measures of cost and profit for internal decision making should be more like throughput costing than absorption costing. That is, costs should reflect resource spending after the split off, and joint-process costs should be included in operating expenses. This should prevent managers from treating joint costs per unit as if they were unit-level costs and should enable them to make profit-maximizing decisions.

Separating joint-product decisions and costing when joint costs are integral parts of evaluations, contracts, and regulated prices is complicated and undesirable. Cost-management analysts must be especially sure that users of cost information, which includes joint-cost allocations, understand the meaning of this information for this more complex costing environment. When contracts are involved, all definitions (costs, sharing, allocation, reimbursement, etc.) must be clearly defined and agreed on in advance.

2. If joint-cost allocations are arbitrary, does that mean they are meaningless?

If joint-costs allocations truly are arbitrary [Webster's: not governed by principle, depending on whim, capricious], they can be dangerous if they are used as if they are based on causation (e.g., cost-driver bases) or deliberate intent. Managers who inappropriately rely on joint-cost information to make product decisions could be misled because joint costs do not behave like unit-level costs. Likewise, arbitrary, ill-defined joint-cost allocations in contracts are subject to dispute if one or more parties to the contract see an advantage to challenging another's interpretation. Therefore, joint-cost allocations can be arbitrary.

However, the word *arbitrary* has another meaning that is more benign and constructive [Webster's: left to discretion, not fixed by statute]. This meaning acknowledges that no joint-cost allocation method is based on higher (e.g., cost-driver) principles. Careful definition of terms and applications can guide certain types of decision making and cooperative ventures. Clearly, many firms, joint ventures, and industries rely on joint-cost allocations that are deliberate and not capricious. It is doubtful that these individuals and firms are being arbitrary in the pejorative sense but use their discretion to develop useful joint-cost mechanisms for sharing costs, profits, and efforts. Without these "arbitrary" arrangements, many business relationships might not proceed. There is a valuable role in these situations for cost-management analysts who understand how to craft useful joint-cost allocations.

Solutions to You're the Decision Maker

9.1   Operate or Shut Down the Process?   p. 336

a. High facility-level costs and low levels of production mean high average costs. In the long run, average costs must be surpassed by enough profit to justify the capital investment in the Georgia mill. The company should analyze and improve the mill's constraints on production (bottlenecks), which can be either internal or external. For example, the Georgia mill might have insufficient milling capacity (human or physical capital) to operate on a scale large enough to be more profitable. Alternatively, the mill's location could mean that the area does not have a sufficiently large market to support its capacity. Apparently, however, shortages of inputs (timber) are causing the mill to operate only one shift per day when other mills operate two or more shifts per day. Assuming that the mill is operating below capacity and there is ample opportunity to sell increased mill output profitably, the company needs to consider obtaining more input for the mill or putting the resources to a better use. This could mean closing the Georgia mill.

b. Let's assume that you prefer to continue working at the Georgia mill because of the good working conditions. You are, however, aware of the responsibility to external shareholders and creditors, and you have no intention of mislead-

ing your superiors. Your response to the possible closing of the mill should be factual and complete. Consideration of all the costs and benefits would include not only the mill's direct operating costs but also the opportunity costs of lost sales, lost goodwill, and lost skilled personnel. Other costs to consider are the costs of closing the mill, retraining employees for other jobs in the company, and offering severance packages to employees who are dismissed. You might be able to identify how the company could work with potential suppliers of timber to achieve mutual benefits—a fair price for timber, environmentally sensitive removal of timber, replanting trees, and regional income from mill employment and local purchases.

9.2   Testing the Validity of the Analysis   p. 338

a. The Georgia mill's products are commodities whose sales prices are set in very competitive markets. Thus, the revenue half of the data is subject to external forces that the company cannot control or forecast with complete accuracy. It is not unusual for some commodity prices to vary by 20 percent or more from year to year, depending on economic conditions. In contrast, production quantities—given timber quality and availability—are probably quite reliable estimates. Joint process and further processing costs also are likely to be known with confidence.

b. *Materiality* means the amount a figure must differ from what is expected before a decision maker would change his or her decision (e.g., the difference between the two alternatives, which is $200,000). The Georgia mill's product decision is based on the expected net realizable values of alternative product mixes. A material difference in any of the elements of NRV—sales and further processing costs—would cause the mill's managers to select a different lumber mix.

c. If the sales price for specialty lumber (only) drops as indicated, the product decision changes completely. Such a decline in price makes producing Grade A Standard lumber the more profitable option.

d. Managers who do not understand sensitivity analysis sometimes accept an initial analysis without asking sufficient "what-if" questions. Cost-management analysts should feel an obligation to subject important product analyses to thorough sensitivity analysis to determine which parameters are most material to product decisions. The sensitivity analysis at least should compute the effects of parameters at extreme values ("best-case" and "worst-case" levels) and most likely values—at first one at a time. Combining the worst-case or best-case values of each parameter results in the worst-case or best-case "scenarios." You should advise managers about which parameters are most sensitive so that they can take steps to minimize adverse effects. These actions include gaining more precise measures of parameters or negotiating long-term sales or supplier contracts to lock in quantities, prices, and costs.

Review Questions

9.1 What are the definitions of the key terms in this chapter?

9.2 What is the nature of a joint-production process?

9.3 How do joint products, intermediate products, and final products differ?

9.4 What are the similarities and differences between joint costs and indirect costs?

9.5 What are the steps to follow to make decisions about producing products from joint processes?

9.6 What could cause a difference between sales revenue and net realizable value?

9.7 What is the objective of joint-cost allocation?

9.8 Why might some accountants express a preference for the net realizable value method of joint-cost allocation over the physical-measures method?

9.9 When might a physical-measures method for allocation he preferred?

9.10 What is the basic difference between the allocation of joint costs to joint products and to by-products?

9.11 What is the condition under which an item should be treated as a by-product rather than as a joint product?

9.12 Why are joint costs irrelevant in the sell-or-process-further decision? What costs are important?

9.13 Under what conditions could the method of joint-cost allocation be important to product or service decisions?

9.14 How do joint products, by-products, and scrap differ?

Critical Analysis

9.15 The chapter indicated that joint costing is used to value inventory and report earnings. Explain at least two other situations when the method of joint-cost allocation could have an impact on decision making.

9.16 How is joint-cost allocation like prorating underapplied overhead?

9.17 Company A and Company B are negotiating the construction and operation of a plant that will produce joint products X and Y and by-product W, which has a positive net realizable value. Company A will use all of product X and operate the plant. Company B argues that it needs only 80 percent of product Y that will be produced. Company A has no use for the excess product Y, but a market for it exists. Prepare a written memo outlining the principles you recommend the companies use to negotiate the sharing of the plant's costs of production.

9.18 Bonzo Oil Co. and Crusty Petroleum, Inc., are entering a joint venture to construct and operate an oil refinery in a foreign country. This refinery will process crude oil in a joint process that results in multiple products, such as gasoline, jet fuel, asphalt, and petrochemicals that require further processing. The companies have determined to jointly create a corporation to operate the refinery and share its outputs and costs fairly. The joint venture will pay a royalty fee to the host country for each barrel of crude oil processed and will charge the costs of operations to Bonzo and Crusty. Ignore taxation, political issues, and technical processing considerations (all of which, by the way, are material).

Form small groups to design a costing system to allocate the costs of *receiving* crude oil, *refining* the crude oil, and *distributing* the products from the refinery that is both fair and informative to Bonzo and Crusty. Be prepared to present proposals in an open forum.

9.19 (continuation of 9.18) A year later, Bonzo Oil experienced a 25 percent decline in the sales of its products and no longer accepts its full shipments of the refinery outputs. Accordingly, Bonzo seeks to renegotiate the agreement based on the joint-costing system prepared previously. Form small groups, half representing Bonzo and half representing Crusty. Considering only your company's interests, prepare proposals to modify the joint-costing agreement. If possible, choose two representative groups to openly resolve their differences and develop a modified agreement.

9.20 Assume that your company operates a joint-production process that generates three main products and one by-product. If you allocate joint costs only for financial reporting, would you ever care whether you use the NRV or the physical-measures method? Explain.

9.21 Top management has decided that your division, which operates a joint-production process, no longer provides a competitive return and should be shut down and all assets liquidated. Prepare an outline of the costs and benefits (to all affected parties) of the decision to shut down and liquidate your division.

9.22 Respond to this comment: "Because joint-cost allocations are arbitrary, there is no rational argument for allocating joint costs except for complying with financial or tax reporting requirements."

9.23 Explain how production decisions based on expected gross margin per unit can be erroneous. Under what conditions could making production decisions this way be an acceptable practice?

9.24 Refer to Exhibit 9–4 as an example of the analysis of alternatives. Assume that changes in some figures cause the relative profitability of products to switch (e.g., a change in the price of Grade A Specialty from $900 to $650 per MBF). What do you recommend for (1) creating the framework (or *model*) for this analysis and (2) communicating the results of the analysis to decision makers?

Exercises

Search the Internet for a company that has joint costs. Prepare a short presentation that describes the nature of the organization (industry, products, services) and which of its costs are joint costs.

Exercise 9.25
Joint Costing
(LO 1, 3)

Glaxxo Company processes Chemical DX-1 through a joint-production process. The costs to process one batch of DX-1 are $100,000 for materials and $200,000 for conversion costs. This processing results in two outputs, Laudinium and Tranquil, that sell for a total of $500,000. The sales revenue from Laudinium amounts to $400,000 of the total. Joint-product Tranquil can be processed further and sold for $200,000 as T-Prime. Further processing costs for T-Prime are estimated to be $80,000 for the batch's production.

Exercise 9.26
Sell or Process Further
(LO 2)

Required
Which products should Glaxxo produce and sell?

Durango Mining Corporation operates an ore-processing plant. A typical batch of ore run through the plant yields three refined products: lead, copper, and manganese. At the split-off point, the intermediate products cannot be sold without further processing. The lead from a typical batch sells for $20,000 after incurring additional processing costs of $6,000. The copper is sold for $40,000 after additional processing costs of $5,000. The manganese yield sells for $30,000 but requires additional processing costs of $9,000. The cost of processing the raw ore, including its purchase, is $50,000 per batch.

Exercise 9.27
Sell or Process Further
(LO 2)

Required
Which products should Durango produce and sell?

Refer to Exercise 9.26.

Required
Using the net realizable value method, assign joint costs to Glaxxo's final products.

Exercise 9.28
Net Realizable Value Method
(LO 4)

Refer to Exercise 9.26. Assume that one batch of DX-1 produces 400 units of Laudinium and 100 units of T-Prime (after additional processing).

Exercise 9.29
Physical-Measures Method
(LO 4)

Required
Using the physical measures method, assign joint costs to final products.

Refer to Exercise 9.26.

Required
Allocate the joint costs using (1) the relative sales value at split off and (2) the constant gross margin percentage methods described in the chapter Appendix.

Exercise 9.30
Relative Sales Value at Split Off and Constant Gross Margin Methods (Appendix)
(LO 6)

Exercise 9.31
Estimated Net Realizable
Value Method
(LO 4)

Refer to Exercise 9.27.

Required

Use the net realizable value method to allocate Durango's joint-processing costs.

Exercise 9.32
Net Realizable Value
Method to Solve for
Unknowns
(LO 4)

Galway Products, Inc., manufactures Leprechauns and Shamrocks from a joint process using the raw material Green. In a recent month, Galway produced 4,000 Leprechauns having a sales value after the split-off point of $21,000. In the same month, it produced 2,000 Shamrocks having a sales value after split off of $14,000. The portion of the total joint product costs allocated to Leprechauns using the net realizable value method was $12,000.

Required

a. Compute the total joint-product costs before allocation.
b. *Build your own spreadsheet.* Develop a spreadsheet to answer (a).

[CPA adapted]

Exercise 9.33
Net Realizable Value
Method
(LO 1, 4)

Prepare a presentation that explains the following features of the net realizable value method.

a. Decision-making implications.
b. Steps to follow for allocating joint costs.
c. Major differences with the physical-quantities method.

Exercise 9.34
Comparison of Methods
(LO 4)

Each of these following situations should be considered independently of the others.

Required

a. Stiller Company manufactures products C and R from a joint process. The total joint costs are $120,000. The net realizable value at split off was $140,000 for 8,000 units of product C and $60,000 for 2,000 units of product R. Assuming that total joint costs are allocated using the net realizable value method, what were the joint costs allocated to product C?

b. Hackman Company manufactures products A and B from a joint process, which also yields a by-product, X. Hackman accounts for the revenues from its by-product sales as other revenue. Additional information follows:

	A	B	X	Total
Units produced...	9,000	15,000	6,000	30,000
Joint costs	?	?	?	$117,000
Sales value at split off..................................	$100,000	$100,000	$100,000	$300,000

Assuming that joint-product costs are allocated using the net realizable value method, what was the joint cost allocated to product B?

c. Damon Corp. manufactures products W, X, Y, and Z from a joint process. Additional information follows:

Product	Units Produced	Sales Value at Split Off	Further Processing Costs	Sales Values after Further Processing
W...	7,000	$ 70,000	$ 7,500	$ 90,000
X	5,000	60,000	6,000	70,000
Y	4,000	40,000	4,000	50,000
Z	4,000	30,000	3,500	32,000
	20,000	$200,000	$21,000	$242,000

Assuming that total joint costs of $80,000 were allocated using the net realizable value method, what joint costs were allocated to each product?

[CPA adapted]

The following questions are based on Costner Company, which manufactures products X, Y, and Z from a joint process. Joint-process costs were $80,000. Additional information is provided:

Exercise 9.35
Comparison of Methods
(LO 4)

			If Processed Further	
Product	**Units Produced**	**Sales Value at Split Off**	**Sales Values**	**Additional Costs**
X	12,000	$80,000	$110,000	$18,000
Y	10,000	70,000	90,000	14,000
Z	8,000	50,000	60,000	12,000

Required

a. Assuming that joint-product costs are allocated using the physical-measures (units produced) method, what were the total costs of product X (including $18,000 if processed further)?

b. Assuming that joint-product costs are allocated using the net realizable value method, what were the total costs of product Y (including the $14,000 if processed further)?

[CPA adapted]

Refer to Exercise 9.35.

Exercise 9.36
Relative Sales Value at
Split off and Constant
Gross Margin
Percentage Methods
(Appendix)
(LO 6)

Required

Allocate the joint costs using (1) the relative sales value at split-off method and (2) the constant gross margin percentage method described in the chapter Appendix.

Friendly Fertilizer Corporation uses organic materials to produce fertilizers for home gardens. Through its production processes, the company manufactures Nitro, a high nitrogen fertilizer, and Phospho, a high phosphorus fertilizer. A by-product of the process is methane, which is used to generate power for the company's operations. The fertilizers are sold either in bulk to nurseries or in individual packages to home gardeners. The company allocates the costs on the basis of the physical-measures method.

Exercise 9.37
Physical-Measures
Method with By-Product
(LO 4)

Last month, 275,000 units of input were processed at a total cost of $180,000. The output of the process consisted of 50,000 units of Nitro, 75,000 units of Phospho, and 150,000 units of methane. The by-product methane would have cost $4,000 had it been purchased from the local gas utility. This is considered to be its net realizable value, which is deducted from the joint processing costs of the main products.

Required

What share of the joint costs should be assigned to each main product using the physical-measures method?

Leather Products, Inc., processes cowhide to produce three outputs (leather, suede, dog chews). Leather and suede are considered main products, and dog chews are a by-product. During a recent month, the following events occurred:

Exercise 9.38
By-Products
(LO 4)

▨ Produced and sold 200 units of leather and 100 units of suede. Produced 25 units of dog chews.

▨ Recorded $140,000 sales revenue from leather and suede. The cost of sales before accounting for the by-product was $72,000.

▨ Incurred $100 to process the 25 units of dog chews to completion. These costs are charged as they are incurred against any by-product sales. (None of the by-products were in inventory at the end of the period.)

▨ Received $450 in revenue from the sale of the 25 units of dog chews.

Required

Prepare an analysis showing the sales revenue, other income, cost of goods sold, other relevant data, and gross margins that would be reported for each of the two methods of by-product accounting described in the text.

Exercise 9.39
By-Products
(LO 4)

The following questions are based on Seinfeld Corporation, which manufactures a product that gives rise to the by-product Castanza. The only cost associated with Castanza is the additional processing cost of $1 for each unit. Seinfeld accounts for Castanza sales first by deducting its separable costs from such sales and then by deducting this net amount from the cost of sales of the major product. (This is method 2 discussed in the text.) This year, 2,400 units of Castanza were produced; all were sold at $8 each.

Required

a.   Sales revenue and cost of goods sold from the main product were $400,000 and $200,000, respectively, for the year. What was the gross margin after considering the by-product sales and costs?

b.   If Seinfeld changes its method of accounting for Castanza sales by showing the net amount as other revenue, what would its gross margin be? Explain.

c.   If Seinfeld changes its method of accounting as indicated in requirement (b), what are the effects of the change on the company's profits?

[CPA adapted]

Problems

Problem 9.40
Sell or Process Further
(LO 1, 2)

Georgia Products, Inc., operates a sawmill facility. The company accounts for the bark chips that result from the primary sawing operation as a by-product. It sells the chips to another company at a price of $24 per hundred cubic feet. Normally, sales revenue from this bark is $1,800,000 per month. The customer loads and transports the bark at no cost to Georgia Products.

As an alternative, the company can rent equipment that will process the chips and bag them for sale as decorative garden mulch. Approximately 30 percent of the bark will be graded "large" and will sell for $64 per hundred cubic feet. About 60 percent will be graded "medium" and will sell for $32 per hundred cubic feet. The remainder will be sold as mulch for $8 per hundred cubic feet.

Costs of the equipment to process and bag the chips and the personnel to operate the equipment total $1,040,000 per month, regardless of the amount of bark processed.

Required

Assuming a typical month, prepare a memo to Georgia Products' management that demonstrates whether the company should sell the bark for $24 per hundred cubic feet or process it further.

Problem 9.41
Sell or Process Further
(LO 1, 2)

mhhe.com/hilton3e

O'Malley Corp. uses a joint process that costs $160,000 for inputs and processing per batch. Processing one batch results in the following joint outputs:

Product	Quantity	Sales Price at Split Off	Further Processing	Sales Price after Further Processing
X	1,000,000 liters	$.09 per liter	NA	NA
Y	500,000 liters	$.05 per liter	$20,000	$.10 per liter
Z	100,000 liters	NA	1,500	.02 per liter

O'Malley Corp. allocates joint costs on the basis of volume (liters) of output.

Required

a.   What is the first decision that O'Malley's management should make?

b.   Prepare a spreadsheet that analyzes the profitability of O'Malley's options.

c.   Compute the product costs for each main product in total and per unit for each option presented in requirement (b).

d.   How can your spreadsheet be used to demonstrate the effect of changes in sales prices or costs on O'Malley's decision to sell Product Y at split-off or process it further?

Problem 9.42
Net Realizable Value
Method
(LO 4, 5)

mhhe.com/hilton3e

Comfy Confections Company purchases cocoa beans and processes them into cocoa butter, a powder, and shells. The standard yield from processing each 100-pound sack of cocoa beans is 20 pounds of butter, 45 pounds of powder, and 35 pounds of shells. The powder can be sold for $.90 per pound and the butter for $1.10 per pound at the split-off point. The shells are disposed of at a cost of $2.00 per batch of 35 pounds of shells.

The cost of the cocoa beans is $15 per hundred pounds. Conversion resources to process each 100 pounds of beans up to the split-off point cost $37.

Required

Compute the joint cost allocated to cocoa butter and cocoa powder produced from 100 pounds of cocoa beans using the net realizable value method.

Refer to Problem 9.42.

Required

Use the physical-measures method to allocate joint costs.

Problem 9.43
Physical-Measures
Method
(LO 4)

Refer to Problem 9.42. Assume that the cocoa butter could be sold either at split off or after additional processing. The additional processing costs $.15 per pound, at which point the butter can be sold for $1.60 per pound.

Required

a. Should cocoa butter be sold at split off or processed further?
b. Assuming cocoa butter is processed further, allocate the joint costs using the net realizable value method.

Problem 9.44
Sell or Process Further
(LO 4)

Refer to Problems 9.42 and 9.44. In addition to possibly processing cocoa butter further, assume that the cocoa shells could be processed further at a cost of $3.00 per batch of 35 pounds and sold for $.05 per pound as garden mulch.

Required

a. Prepare a diagram that describes the possible sets of products and by-products.
b. Allocate the joint costs to the main products using the net realizable value method.

Problem 9.45
Sell or Process Further
(LO 4, 5)

mhhe.com/hilton3e

IMAC Company produces three products by a joint-production process. Raw materials are put into production in process A, and three products appear at the end of this process. Product X is immediately sold at the split-off point, with no further processing. Products Y and Z require further processing before they are sold. Product Y is processed in process B, and product Z is processed in process C. The company uses the (estimated) net realizable value method of allocating joint-production costs. Following is a summary of costs and other data for the quarter ended September 30.

No inventories were on hand at the beginning of the quarter or on July 1. No raw materials were on hand at September 30. All the units on hand at the end of the quarter were fully complete as to processing.

Problem 9.46
Net Realizable Value and
Effects of Processing
Further
(LO 2, 4)

Products	X	Y	Z
Pounds sold	40,000	118,000	140,000
Pounds on hand at September 30	100,000	0	80,000
Sales revenues	$ 30,000	$177,000	$274,400

Processes	A	B	C
Raw material cost	$112,000	$ 0	$ 0
Direct labor cost	48,000	80,900	191,750
Manufacturing overhead	20,000	21,100	73,250

Required

a. Assume that the entire output of product X could be processed further at an additional cost of $3 per pound and then sold for $5 per pound. What is the effect on operating profits if all product X output for the quarter had been processed and sold rather than all being sold at the split-off point?
b. Write a memo to management indicating whether the company should process product X further and why.
c. Determine the following amounts for each product: (1) net realizable value used for allocating joint costs, (2) joint costs allocated to each of the three products, (3) cost of goods sold, and (4) finished goods inventory costs, September 30.

Problem 9.47
Finding Missing Data:
Net Realizable Value
(LO 4)

Air Extracts, Inc., manufactures nitrogen, oxygen, and hydrogen from a joint process. Data on the process are as follows:

Product	Nitrogen	Oxygen	Hydrogen	Total
Units produced	8,000	4,000	2,000	14,000
Joint costs	$30,000*	$ (a)	$ (b)	$ 60,000
Sales value at split off	(c)	(d)	15,000	100,000

*This amount is the portion of the total joint cost of $60,000 that had been allocated to nitrogen.

The company uses the net realizable value method of joint-cost allocation.

Required
Determine the values for the lettered spaces.

[CPA adapted]

Problem 9.48
Joint-Cost Allocations
with By-Product
(LO 4, 5)

Exotic Aroma Company buys bulk flowers and processes them into perfumes in a two-stage process. Its highest-grade perfume, Seduction, and a residue that is processed into a medium-grade perfume, Romance, come from a certain mix of petals. In July, the company used 25,000 pounds of petals. The first stage is a joint process that reduces the petals to Seduction and the residue. This first stage had the following costs:

- $100,000 direct materials
- $200,000 conversion

The additional costs of producing Romance in the second (pressing) stage were as follows:

- $44,000 direct materials
- $180,000 conversion

For July, total production yielded 2,000 ounces of Seduction and 8,400 ounces of Romance. There was no beginning inventory on July 1, nor were there uncompleted units.

Packaging costs incurred for each product as completed were $120,000 for Seduction and $308,000 for Romance. The sales price per ounce is $180 for Seduction and $70 for Romance.

Required
a. Allocate joint costs using the net realizable value method. (Packaging and additional processing costs must be subtracted from revenue to compute net realizable values.)
b. Allocate the joint costs using the physical-measures method.
c. Management is concerned about the large disparity in allocation amounts using the physical-measures method versus the NRV method. Management has asked you to explain why this discrepancy occurred. Write a memo to management explaining it.
d. Assume that Exotic Aroma can sell the squeezed petals from the reduction process to greenhouses for fertilizer. In July, it sold 12,000 pounds of squeezed petals that were left over for $1.50 per pound. The squeezed petals are a by-product of reduction. Assume that the net realizable value of by-products reduces the joint costs of main products. Answer requirements (a) and (b) using this new information.

Problem 9.49
Joint Costing in a
Process-Costing
Context: Net Realizable
Value Method
(LO 4, 5)

Greek Company produces three products: Alpha, Beta, and Gamma. Alpha and Gamma are main products; Beta is a by-product of Alpha. Information on the past month's production processes follows:

- In process 1, 110,000 units of the raw material Rho are processed at a total cost of $290,000. After processing in process 1, 60 percent of the units are transferred to process 2, and 40 percent of the units (now unprocessed Gamma) are transferred to process 3.

- In process 2, the materials received from process 1 are processed at an additional cost of $76,000. Seventy percent of the units become Alpha and are transferred to process 4. The remaining 30 percent emerge as Beta and are sold at $4.20 per unit after additional processing. The additional processing costs to make Beta salable are $16,200.

■ In process 3, Gamma is processed at an additional cost of $330,000. A normal loss of units of Gamma occurs in this process. The loss equals 10 percent of the units processed. The remaining good output is then sold for $24 per unit.

■ In process 4, Alpha is processed at an additional cost of $32,960. After this processing, it can be sold for $10 per unit.

Required

a. Prepare a diagram to display Greek Company's revenues, costs, products, and processes.

b. Prepare a schedule showing the allocation of the $290,000 joint cost between Alpha and Gamma using the net realizable value approach. The net realizable value of by-products reduces the joint costs of the related main product (method 2 in the text).

[CPA adapted]

Harrison Corporation produces two joint products from its manufacturing operation. Product J sells for $41.50 per unit, and product M sells for $12 per unit at the split-off point. In a typical month, 38,000 units are processed; 30,000 units become product M and 8,000 units become product J after an additional $56,250 of processing costs are incurred.

The joint process has only unit-level costs. In a typical month, the conversion costs of the joint products amount to $114,075. Materials prices are volatile, and if they are too high, the company stops production. Harrison requires a minimum 20 percent return on sales.

Problem 9.50
Maximum Input Price:
Net Realizable Value
Method
(LO 1, 2)

Required

Management has asked you to determine the maximum price that the company should pay for the materials.

a. Calculate the maximum price that Harrison should pay for the materials.

b. Write a brief memo to management explaining how you arrived at your answer in requirement (a).

AMPHIB Corporation processes input Leonardo into three outputs: Michaelangelo, Raphael, and Donatello. At the split-off point, Michaelangelo results in 60 percent of the net realizable value, Raphael results in 30 percent, and Donatello accounts for the balance. The joint costs total $365,500. If Donatello is accounted for as a by-product, its net realizable value at split off of $37,600 is credited to the joint manufacturing costs.

Problem 9.51
Effect of By-Product
versus Joint-Cost
Accounting
(LO 4, 5)

Required

a. What are the allocated joint costs for the three outputs

   (1) If Donatello is accounted for as a main product?

   (2) If Donatello is accounted for as a by-product?

b. Management does not understand why no joint costs are allocated to Donatello when it is accounted for as a by-product. Write a brief memo explaining this.

Silicon Materials, Inc., processes silicon crystals into purified wafers and chips. Silicon crystals cost $60,000 per batch. The process involves slicing the crystals, which produces 45,000 wafers with a market value of $20,000 and 15,000 chips with a market value of $140,000. The cost of operating the heat process is $65,600.

Problem 9.52
Joint-Cost Allocation and
Product Profitability
(LO 1, 2, 4)

Required

a. If the costs of the crystal and the heat process are allocated on the basis of units of output, what cost would be assigned to each product?

b. If the costs of the crystal and the heat process are allocated on the basis of the net realizable value, what cost is assigned to each product?

c. How much profit or loss does the purified wafers product provide using the data in this problem and your analysis in requirement (a)? Is it really possible to determine which product is more profitable? Explain why or why not.

Problem 9.53
Joint-Cost Allocation and
Product Profitability
(LO 1, 2, 4)

Whitehall Corp. produces chemicals used in the cleaning industry. During the previous month, it incurred $300,000 of joint costs in producing 60,000 units of AM-12 and 40,000 units of BM-36. Whitehall allocates joint costs based on the number of units produced. Currently, AM-12 is sold at split off for $3.50 per unit. Flank Corp. has approached Whitehall to purchase all of the AM-12 monthly production after further processing, which will cost Whitehall $90,000 per month.

Required

a. What is the minimum sales price Whitehall should charge Flank for AM-12 after further processing?

b. Assume that Whitehall has agreed to sell AM-12 to Flank after further processing for $5.50 per unit. During the first month, Whitehall delivered 50,000 units to Flank and had 10,000 units remaining in inventory at the end of the month. What is the operating profit generated by sales of AM-12 during the first month, and what is the cost of processed AM-12 still in inventory at the end of the month?

[CMA adapted]

Cases

Case 9.54
Joint-Product Decision
Making and Joint-Cost
Allocation in a Risky
Venture
(LO 1, 2, 3, 4)

Honda imported the first automobile into the United States with a galvanized (zinc-coated) body. By the 1990s, nearly all automobile manufacturers in the world used galvanized metal to extend the life of vehicles. At the same time, the use of galvanized metal for appliances and structural applications, for example, increased.

Through obsolescence and recycling, a rapidly increasing amount of galvanized scrap exists. The zinc coating on this galvanized scrap causes pollution problems due to zinc contamination when the scrap is melted to produce new iron or steel. In conjunction with the University of California–Berkeley, Metal Recovery Technologies, Inc. (MRTI), is improving its doubly patented electrolytic process to strip pure zinc from galvanized scrap. The process originally was developed in 1991 with support from the Argonne National Laboratory and the U.S. Department of Energy. MRTI's process uses much less energy than other methods; produces two pure joint products, zinc and highest-quality, reusable ("black") steel; and prevents environmental damage from zinc and waste resulting from other methods.

The government and the company estimate that using this process to dezinc 5 million tons of galvanized scrap (the amount recycled in the United States each year) could

- Save 50 trillion BTUs of energy.
- Save $140 million in raw materials for U.S. iron and steel companies.
- Save $100 million in foreign exchange spending by reducing the need for zinc imports.
- Eliminate toxic zinc from waste streams.

In 1998 MRTI listed its stock on the Berlin Stock Exchange and received financing of $3 million from Geneva-based Zinc Investments, Inc. With the proceeds of stock sales and the Swiss financing, MRTI revamped its East Chicago, Indiana, plant to reach a commercial scale of 120,000 tons of galvanized scrap per year, which would result in expected revenues of $23 million per year (at 1998 prices) beginning in the year 1999. Clouding the future is the development-stage company's financial performance, which at December 31, 1997, included a net loss of $622,500, current assets of $61,619, and current liabilities of $7,295,282. MRTI's independent auditors raised questions about the company's ability to continue as a going concern, which could affect its ability to raise additional capital.

MRTI expects the following annual costs of operations for the commercialized process:

Material cost (galvanized steel scrap and sodium hydroxide)	$ 6,600,000
Conversion cost (labor, power, depreciation, and amortization)	12,500,000
General and administrative cost	1,800,000

The commercialized process, if successful, would separate and recover 100 percent of the steel and zinc from the galvanized scrap and regenerate the sodium hydroxide in the electrolytic solution. The typical proportion of steel and zinc in galvanized steel is 98 percent steel and 2 percent zinc. The 1998 per-ton market prices for black steel and recovered zinc were $170 and $1,200, respectively.

Required

Prepare group responses to each of the following items for presentation.

a.   If MRTI is successful in commercializing its electrolytic process, would the company be profitable?

b.   Market prices for nonprecious metals can fluctuate 20 percent per year. Would MRTI be profitable if the prices of the scrap it uses and of the metals it produces decline by 20 percent?

c.   Using the original data in the case, compare the profitability of the two joint products using the net realizable value and physical-measures methods.

d.   Under what conditions would MRTI have an incentive to use one method or the other to measure product profitability? What ethical responsibilities do MRTI's managers and auditors face?

[Adapted from "A Power-Pinching Way to Recycle Rust-Proof Steel"; and Recyclers' World (www.recycle.net).]

The weight of used tires in Europe was expected to reach 2.5 million tons by the end of 1999. Anne Forteza of IDE Environment argued that more intense retreading and recycling must replace the currently widespread practice of sending used tires to landfills. She estimated that approximately one-half of used tires is retreadable, but the balance is sent to landfills (36 percent), left on vehicles in scrap yards (30 percent), exported for incineration in the United States (8 percent), incinerated for power (22 percent), or incinerated for disposal (4 percent). Aside from power generation, the treatment of most nonretreadable tires is a waste of primary materials, an expensive disposal option, and a source of environmental pollution. Recently passed legislation in France requires alternative, environmentally sound solutions to dumping used tires. Costs of dumping used tires in landfills currently are US$220 per ton and are expected to rise dramatically in France and elsewhere if other European countries adopt similar legislation.

The Alpha Recyclage Project (ARP) was launched in France to demonstrate an economical and environmental treatment of nonretreadable tires. ARP will take large numbers of used tires at no cost if they contain the usual mix of retreadable tires (50 percent), sort them, sell suitable tires to retreaders for US$2 per tire, and treat the rest. ARP uses a cryogenic method to transform the waste tires into primary materials (30 percent fiber, 20 percent steel, and 50 percent reusable rubber pellets). The cryogenic method, which uses liquid nitrogen, is more expensive than mechanical grinding (the other currently feasible method) but is cleaner and results in a higher quality of rubber pellet.

Following are data regarding ARP's annual operations.

Case 9.55
Joint Products from
Recycling
(LO 1, 2, 4)

Weight of tires collected (average of 20 pounds per tire)	30,000 tons
Sold to retreaders @ US$2 each	15,000 tons
Cryogenic joint-process costs of recycled tires	$ 4,500,000
General and administrative costs	$ 1,900,000
Market price for scrap steel	$ 90 per ton
Market price for scrap fiber	$300 per ton
Market price for scrap rubber pellets	$ 45 per ton

Required

Prepare group responses to the following items for presentation.

a.   Is the ARP's process a viable process for disposing of used tires? Why or why not?

b.   ARP must report results of operations to the National Council of Car Professions (NCPA), which is sponsoring the project. ARP intends to report revenues and costs by major product.

Prepare an objective and factual report that shows the results of annual operation and explains them in a manner to persuade NCPA to continue to sponsor the project.

[Information taken from www.recycle.net]

Case 9.56
Effect of Cost Allocation on Pricing and Make-versus-Buy Decisions
(LO 1, 2, 4)

Ag-Coop is a large farm cooperative with a number of agriculture-related manufacturing and service divisions. As a cooperative, it pays no federal income taxes. It operates a fertilizer plant, which processes and mixes petrochemical compounds into three brands of agricultural fertilizer: Greenup, Maintane, and Winterizer. The three brands differ with respect to selling price and the proportional content of basic chemicals.

The Fertilizer Manufacturing Division transfers the completed product to the cooperative's Retail Sales Division at a price based on the cost of each type of fertilizer plus a markup. The Manufacturing Division is completely automated so that the only costs it incurs are for the petrochemical inputs plus automated conversion, which is committed for the coming period. The primary feedstock costs $1.50 per kilogram. Each 1,000 kilograms of feedstock can produce either of the following mixtures of fertilizer:

Output Schedules (in kilograms)	A	B
Greenup	500	600
Maintane	300	100
Winterizer	200	300

Production is limited to the monthly capacity of the dehydrator at 750,000 kilowatt-hours. The different chemical makeup of each brand of fertilizer requires different dehydrator use as follows:

Product	Kilowatt-Hour Usage per Kilogram
Greenup	32
Maintane	20
Winterizer	40

Monthly conversion costs are $81,250. The company is producing according to output schedule A. Joint-production costs including conversion are allocated to each product on the basis of weight.

The fertilizer is packed into 50-kilogram bags for sale in the cooperative's retail stores. The Manufacturing Division charges the retail stores its cost plus a markup. The sales price for each product charged by the cooperative's Retail Sales Division is as follows:

	Sales Price per Kilogram
Greenup	$10.50
Maintane	9.00
Winterizer	10.40

Selling expenses are 20 percent of the sales price.

The manager of the Retail Sales Division has complained that the prices charged are excessive and that she would prefer to purchase from another supplier. The Manufacturing Division manager argues that the processing mix was determined based on a careful analysis of the costs of each product compared to the prices charged by the Retail Sales Division.

Required

a. Assume that joint-production costs including conversion are allocated to each product on the basis of weight. What is the cost per kilogram of each product including conversion costs and the feedstock cost of $1.50 per kilogram, given the current production schedule?

b. Assume that joint-production costs including conversion are allocated to each product on the basis of net realizable value if it is sold through the cooperative's Retail Sales Division. What is the allocated cost per kilogram of each product, given the current production schedule?

c.   Assume that joint-production costs including conversion are allocated to each product on the basis of weight. Which of the two production schedules, A or B, produces the higher operating profit to the firm as a whole?

d.   Would your answer to requirement (c) be different if joint-production costs including committed overhead were allocated to each product on the basis of net realizable value? Explain.

e.   Can you recommend an approach to product planning that considers the organization's overall profitability and avoids the divisional controversy? What are the costs and benefits of your recommended approach?

[CMA adapted]

Chapter 10

Managing and Allocating Support-Service Costs

After completing this chapter, you should be able to:

1. Explain the importance of managing support-service costs and the reason these costs are allocated.

2. Understand how to choose cost pools and to separate the cost of resources supplied from the cost of resources used.

3. Understand how to choose appropriate allocation bases.

4. Allocate support-service department costs using the direct and step methods.

5. Evaluate the consequences of alternative cost allocations.

6. Allocate support-service department costs using the reciprocal method (Appendix).

Cost-Management Challenges

(Solutions are on page 389.)

1. **Cost** allocations are arbitrary. Does this mean that the way you decide to allocate costs is of no consequence to you or your organization?

2. **Choosing** a cost-allocation approach is always a judgment that is based on an evaluation of trade-offs. How can you be best prepared to evaluate the trade-offs and provide leadership if dramatic changes are needed?

3. **Some** cost-allocation approaches appear to be quite complex. How should you educate other managers to understand the complexities of the cost-allocation process?

City of Rock Creek

The scene is a meeting of Director of Finance Cindy Tukami and her budget staff who, under the guidance of the city manager, prepare the draft of the City of Rock Creek's budget for the next fiscal year. After it is approved by the city council, Tukami and her staff administer the budget. She had just presented the draft of next year's budget to an open city council meeting the week before. It had been a long, debate-filled meeting. The city's operating funds are not keeping pace with growing demands for services, so the city must make difficult trade-offs. The days since the meeting had been filled with angry phone calls and letters from citizens who felt the city was using the proposed budget to take funds away from valued programs.

"At times I think this budget process is hopelessly complex, and no matter what we do, someone is going to get angry," Tukami observed. "Who would think that something as ordinary as *cost allocations* would cause so many citizens to pack city council meetings, write angry letters to the editor of the local paper, and make us feel like public enemies instead of public servants?

"I know what we are doing is right, but we need to communicate better the whys and hows of what we are doing for the citizens of Rock Creek. They need to understand that we are trying to run an efficient city government, but even a lean government has staff and facilities that need to be paid for somehow.

"I thought our proposal for using an activity-based approach to allocating costs would be so obviously better than what we have been doing that we would get praise, not condemnation. I half-expected to get a medal," she chuckled ruefully.

Tukami was highly qualified for the technical aspects of her job, having her undergraduate degree in accounting from a good university and passing the CPA and CMA exams on the first try. But she was learning a difficult lesson in the art and politics of budgeting. Although a city's budget negotiations might be more open than most, cost-allocation issues can cause friction in nearly every organization—public or private, for-profit or nonprofit. In any organization, managing the process of cost allocation can be just as important as the allocations themselves.

Service-Cost Challenge

City of  **Rock Creek**

The goal of every organization should be to achieve the objectives that prompted its creation. Commercial firms are created to provide goods and services and earn at least a competitive profit. Nonprofit hospitals are created to provide superior health care for the community and at least cover their costs of operation. Cities are incorporated to provide essential services to their citizens within budgetary limits. Achieving these goals requires using scarce resources and making complex trade-offs among competing uses. Making these resource trade-offs requires reliable quantitative and qualitative cost-management information about relative costs and benefits of alternatives.

As discussed in earlier chapters, every organization must make cost-driver decisions that determine how to use its resources for productive processes that provide products and services directly to customers, clients, or citizens. The organization decides whether to perform all of the productive processes itself or to outsource some or part of them. In addition, organizations must decide how to support their productive processes, for example, by providing accounting, human resources, and legal support services. These support services could be provided by the organization's internal departments, or by outsourcing them to external providers.

Internal or Outsourced Support Services?

Some might argue that support services are a necessary part of every organization. But are they? Some organizations are outsourcing many of their internal support services. Companies commonly outsource traditional accounting functions such as payroll and accounts payable that require routine, straightforward procedures. Many companies also outsource their human resources, legal, tax, and internal auditing functions. Outsourcing has become a popular way to "right size" or "downsize" organizations. As a result, organizations that provide such services have become some of the fastest-growing industries in developed economies.

Whether to outsource any support service depends on the consideration of a combination of many quantitative and qualitative factors. Cost-management analysts most often are the professionals who prepare and analyze the information to support outsourcing decisions. This information includes the knowledge base required to perform a service, the sensitivity of information needed to perform a service, the relative costs of a service, and the difficulty in finding, managing, and keeping reliable, high-quality service providers.

Indian employees at a call center provide service support to international customers. The hiring frenzy in India is the flip side of the United States and Britain, where thousands of software and back-office jobs are being cut as companies take advantage of cheap communications offshore to drive down costs. The $3.6 billion industry in India is seen rocketing to $13.8 billion by 2007 with the number of jobs quadrupling to one million.

Knowledge base.   Complex or unique organizations might have distinct procedures and cultures that external service providers could have difficulty understanding and supporting. On the other hand, some support-service expertise could be too specialized for the organization to maintain itself. Consider, for example, the management of information technology in foreign countries. Organizations might see advantages to outsourcing these knowledge-based services to external service providers who have specialized expertise in these foreign countries and can provide benefits from economies of scale.

Sensitive information.   Some organizations compete on the basis of their knowledge of technology or complex market and political situations. These firms would be reluctant to outsource support services, such as internal auditing, that would allow outsiders to obtain their strategically important knowledge.

Relative costs.   Many organizations see the outsourcing of support services as a means to increase budget flexibility and reduce current and long-term costs (health care and pension costs, too). This puts great pressure on internal service departments either to provide comparable services at lower cost or to disappear.

Reliable service providers.   A less expensive outsourced service is not cost effective if its reliability and quality are low and adversely affect the organization's ability to meet its objectives. For example, many large firms have outsourced their customer-service departments to other companies (e.g., Teletech www.teletech.com). Customer service is a very sensitive function that, if poorly performed, can drive away customers and damage the company's reputation. A damaged reputation can be very difficult to repair.

Management of Internal Support-Service Costs

Customers accept products only if their value meets or exceeds the prices that they are charged. This provides a strong discipline to the organization's use of resources for producing products. But internal support-service departments function without such external discipline. How does the organization manage its support-service costs? There are several cost-based, management approaches, two of which are discussed here.

LO I Explain the importance of managing support-service costs and the reason these costs are allocated.

- *Charge internal customers nothing for support services and recover the costs of the services from general revenues.* The advantage to this approach is that it is simple and inexpensive to operate because there is no need either to measure or charge for support-service costs. Its disadvantage is that as long as internal customers perceive *any* positive value from free services, they may demand more without regard to the service costs to the organization. Thus, internal support-service departments could grow dramatically but inefficiently in response to high internal demand. There is no obvious signal to organization managers that they are using resources inefficiently to provide support services that few customers would want if they had to pay for them.

- *Charge the costs of support services provided to using departments and possibly recover the costs from these internal customers.* Because of problems with the first approach, most organizations use cost allocation—a systematic method of assigning the costs of resources to a department, product, or service when directly tracing costs is not possible—to charge support-service costs to internal customers. Many organizations also recover those costs from users in the form of actual payments or transfers of funds on the basis of the allocations. A user department or internal customer would accept support services only if the value of those services meets or exceeds their cost to the department. If user departments are required to utilize internal services, they might control spending for support services by demonstrating that the organization is spending too much for those services.

Exhibit 10–1

City of Rock Creek
Organization Chart

City of Rock Creek

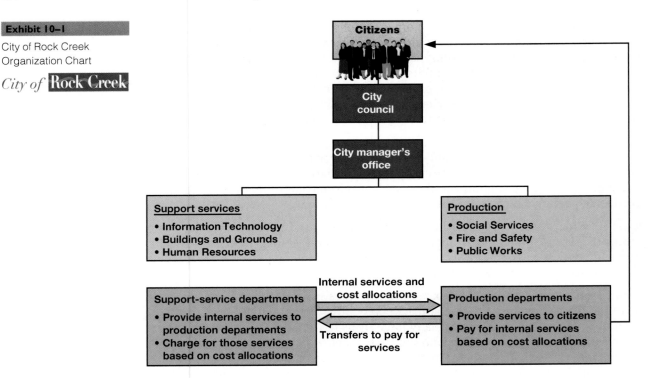

This second approach also has disadvantages. First, cost allocations are, by nature, arbitrary; they are, at best, *discretionary* and might not measure the uses of resources accurately. Second, if internal customers are required to use internal services, they might spend valuable time negotiating and lobbying over fair prices, which could be an inefficient process.

Poorly designed cost allocations can be the subject of disputes among departments and their constituents. Furthermore, cost allocations can create incentives to use or not use the services inappropriately if the allocated costs are not closely associated with the actual consumption of resources.

The issues of efficiency, fairness, and team building within private and public organizations are analogous to, although not as socially wrenching as, those that centrally managed countries recently faced. These countries, such as the People's Republic of China, relied on cost allocations in the past and are now experimenting with market mechanisms to measure the values of goods and services and to allocate resources. These countries are finding not only that market mechanisms are more efficient because they do not require a large bureaucracy of central planners (although they do require enforcement of contracts) but also that market solutions are challenging cultural concepts of fairness and cooperation.

Distinguishing between Support-Services and Production Departments

Tukami's staff had prepared the budget draft after coordinating the spending requests of all the city's departments. The city's organizational chart appears in Exhibit 10–1. This chart separates the two types of departments, production and support services.[1] **Production (or line) departments** provide services directly to customers or the public; for example, public works provides water, sewer, and flood control. **Support-service departments** (or **indirect departments**) provide support services to each other and to the production departments. Note that the Human Resources department

---

[1] In commercial firms, these types of departments might be called *direct* or *line departments* (or *divisions*) versus *support, indirect,* or *service departments* (or *divisions*).

Department	Cost*
Production department:	
P1. Social Services	$ 500,000
P2. Fire and Safety	270,000
P3. Public Works	185,000
Total production department costs	$ 955,000
Support-service department:	
S1. Information Technology	$ 36,000
S2. Buildings and Grounds	84,000
S3. Human Resources	25,000
Total support-service department costs	$ 145,000
Total costs	$1,100,000

*The amounts shown are costs (i.e., resources used), not expenditures (i.e., resources supplied).

Exhibit 10–2

City of Rock Creek: Costs for a Typical Month

City of Rock Creek

is considered a support service because it provides services to other city departments. Fire and Safety, however, is a production department because it provides a product to citizens. (Note that products can be goods or services. For a city, products are services.)

The City of Rock Creek actually has more departments than those shown here. The examples become unnecessarily complex and difficult to follow if we include all of the City's departments. You will learn just as much from this simple example without incurring the pain of struggling with a complex example.

Deciding Who Pays for Internal Support-Service Costs

Many production departments are supported by funds specifically designated for those purposes. For example, sales and property tax revenues, which citizens voted for, support the city library, parks, and recreation departments. These are analogous to the sales revenues that commercial organizations earn from selling products and services.

Support-service costs are the costs of the resources supplied by an organization to provide the support services. These costs include the costs of personnel and the equipment, facilities, and supplies these personnel need to provide the types and levels of support services that the organization desires. In a typical month, the City of Rock Creek spends $145,000 on support services (Exhibit 10–2).

In the City of Rock Creek, as in many private and public organizations, cost allocations measure the charges from support-service departments to production departments. As Tukami learned, making these transfers is not simply a technical or mechanical process, particularly if there is a change in the allocation method, which alters the amounts that production departments pay to support-service departments.

Reasons for Allocating Service Costs

Decision Making and Cost Allocations

Allocating costs to activities unavoidably is done on a somewhat arbitrary basis. Some critics of cost allocation interpret the word *arbitrary* to mean "unfounded" or "without justification." They argue, perhaps correctly, that this type of cost allocation can result in misleading information that causes poor decisions and, therefore, should be avoided. It is going too far, however, to argue that making decisions about support services, products, or direct services should never depend in *any* way on cost allocations.

As we discussed in earlier chapters, the cost-management issue is whether employees make better decisions with or without "deliberate, well-designed" cost allocations that reflect the use of resources.

Principles of Cost Allocation

a. Do you think it is a good idea for organizations to formally express principles of cost allocation? Would it be any more important in a public organization such as a municipality than in a private firm?

b. You are the manager of the Social Services Department (a production department with a budget of approximately $500,000 per month). How might you react if you found out that the Information Technology Department (a support-service department with a budget of approximately $36,000 per month) was increasing its budget by 50 percent over the next year?

c. Take the position of the city manager who is responsible for both support-service and production departments. Which of the four principles of cost allocation identified do you think is most important? How would you resolve disputes over cost allocations?

(Solutions begin on page 390.)

The City of Rock Creek recognizes that cost allocations are somewhat arbitrary but, like many organizations, has established cost-allocation principles intended to generate useful information for city employees and citizens:

> The city shall employ a cost-allocation system to identify the cost to provide services to the public and recover certain costs incurred by various departments in providing support services to other city departments. The system shall accomplish the following objectives:
> **a.** Equitable allocation of service costs to users.
> **b.** Provision of incentives for service providers to deliver products and services efficiently and effectively.
> **c.** Provision of a stable cost-allocation system to facilitate the organization's budgeting for charges and revenues.
> **d.** Promotion of customer confidence in and acceptance of the accuracy, reasonableness, and fairness of the charges they incur.

The city believes that these cost-allocation principles will create the atmosphere of a simulated market for services in which internal customers—those who use the internal services—will negotiate (or demand!) support-service cost allocations that are reasonable measures of the worth of those services. Thus, the allocation of service costs is especially important in nonmarket situations prevalent in both government and private organizations that have internal support-service departments.

Other Uses of Cost Allocations

Organizations might have cost-allocation requirements from both internal and external parties.

Required reporting. Tax regulations and external financial reporting require allocating manufacturing overhead to the units produced. This overhead often includes allocations of corporate or home-office expenses. Depreciation of long-term assets, which allocates the original cost of an asset over time periods, also is required. Many higher-level costs are allocated to products and services for regulatory purposes in public utilities.

Cost-based contracts. Some organizations work on a cost-basis or cost-plus basis. The federal government sometimes reimburses defense contractors for work done on a cost-plus (a profit) basis. Government agencies, foundations, and private industry reimburse universities for research on a cost-plus (an overhead-rate) basis. The U.S. government, for example, partially reimburses cities and counties for training personnel who administer federal Medicaid programs. Obtaining complete and proper levels of reimbursement requires allocating all allowed costs to the government contract, research work, or training activity.

Corporate Cost Allocation

An executive of Kmart, the retail giant, reported during an interview that "allocating corporate headquarters' costs to stores makes each store manager aware that these costs exist and must be covered by the individual stores for the company as a whole to be profitable." Surveys of corporate cost allocation found that the great majority of companies reported allocating common headquarters' costs to divisions. The studies indicated that a primary managerial reason for cost allocation was to give division managers incentives to generate sufficient division profits to cover all corporate costs. *Sources: G. W. Dean, M. P. Moye, and P. J. Blayney, Overhead Cost Allocation and Performance Evaluation Practices of Australian Manufacturers; and J. M. Fremgren and S. S. Liao, The Allocation of Corporate Indirect Costs. (Full citations to references are in the Bibliography.)*

Behavior influence. Managers often allocate costs to influence behavior. As mentioned, if costs of services are free to internal customers, you can expect the customers to demand these services as long as they perceive any benefit from them. Under this condition, you also can expect the size of service departments to attempt to grow almost without bounds to meet the demand for their services. On the other hand, allocating service costs to other departments for services provided gives managers of these other departments incentives to control their use of support services. For example, allocating

This Information Technology Department is a support-service department in a company.

the costs of the Information Technology Department to other city departments based on services provided causes those other department managers to request information technology service only when they believe that the service is worth at least as much as it will cost their departments to obtain it.

Cost-Management Implications for Internal Support Services

In the remainder of this chapter, we assume that in response to cost-management information about relative costs and benefits, the organization has decided both to provide internal support services using facility-level resources and allocate the costs of those resources to internal customers. These are important managerial decisions that can affect the organization's efficiency and ability to meet its goals. Once made, these decisions require implementation by cost-management analysts who use a systematic method to allocate support-service costs that also reinforces the organization's goals. We now consider alternative methods for allocating support-service costs.

Cost Allocation from Support-Service Departments to Internal Customers

As mentioned earlier, all cost allocations are at least somewhat arbitrary and cannot precisely link resource spending and resource use. For example, suppose that an organization allocates its human resources department spending (e.g., salaries, depreciation, and utilities) to internal customers proportionately based on the number of total full-time equivalent (FTE) employees in each department. What if a large department with mostly long-time employees needs less service from the human resources department than a smaller department that is hiring and training new employees and consumes much of the service department's time? If costs are allocated based on FTE, the larger department with established employees will be allocated a large share of the human resources department costs even though it uses little of that support-service resource. Likewise, the smaller department will pay only a small share of the cost even though it uses much of the resource. Is this cost allocation based on FTE fair? Will it cause unnecessary disputes? Does it motivate department managers to use human resources services properly? Does it result in the proper level and quality of human resource support services?

Allocating costs on the basis of FTE is easy because the necessary data are readily available. The allocations that result, however, might not accurately reflect the use of resources. But is it cost effective to obtain more accurate information that would allow cost allocations to more closely match the use of support services? Determining the proper basis for cost allocation can be very important, but this is not the only consideration to implementing a cost-allocation method that effectively supports the organization's goals. The process of allocating service costs systematically follows several steps, each of which can affect the success of cost allocations. The steps, which are explained in detail in subsequent sections, follow:

1. Identify the costs to be allocated to internal customers.
2. Choose the appropriate cost-allocation base(s) and rate(s).
3. Select and use a cost-allocation method.
4. Determine whether the cost allocations achieve the desired results; if they do not, begin the process again.

Step 1: Identify the Costs to Be Allocated to Internal Customers

LO 2 Understand how to choose cost pools and to separate the cost of resources supplied for the cost of resources used.

Typically, organizations separate support-service costs by department into separate *cost pools,* which are the budgeted or actual spending amounts for distinct sets of resources, as the City of Rock Creek has done. Using multiple cost pools facilitates the management of the different types of support services and should allow more accurate cost allocations to internal customers than using only one cost pool. As shown earlier, Rock Creek uses three support-service cost pools—Information Technology, Buildings and Grounds, and Human Resources—which correspond to the city's organizational structure and management responsibilities.

Support-service use. Organizations might implement multiple cost pools when the *uses* of the service resources have both facility- and unit-level components. For example, suppose that the Information Technology Department leases computer equipment and hires personnel based on the projected demand for services plus reserve capacity. Thus, these computing resources (acquired by facility-level spending) provide two types of services to the city's internal customers: (1) the reserve of capacity available and (2) the current use of capacity. Rock Creek could establish separate cost pools for each type of service.

Deciding how many cost pools to use involves another cost-benefit evaluation. If the organization designs cost pools carefully, using more cost pools should result in cost allocations that match resource use better than using fewer cost pools. This is effectively the message of activity-based costing, which provides better information about the use of service resources, resulting in better management decisions about support-service type, quantity, source, and payment. However, designing and maintaining a complex cost-allocation system with many cost pools can, itself, be very costly. Organizations would not willingly implement a complex cost-allocation system unless the benefits from its better decisions justify the costs required to set up and maintain the system.

For the purposes of this chapter, we assume that the City of Rock Creek maintains only three support-service cost pools, one for each support-service department. This level of complexity is sufficient to illustrate the methods and problems of cost allocation.

Telecommunications and Cost Allocations

The Telecommunications Act of 1996 deregulated much of the US telecommunications industry. Prior to the act, the Federal Communications Commission (FCC) regulated the way that companies allocated costs. The FCC particularly wanted to prevent companies from being reimbursed for costs that were "unfairly" allocated. With deregulation, the FCC got out of the cost allocation business. Deregulation and privatization of state-owned or socialized enterprises are having significant effects on cost-allocation practices around the world. *Sources: authors' research and Barry Spicer, David Emmanuel, and Michael Powell,* Transforming Government Enterprises.

Cost Management in Practice 10.1

Costs of resources used separated from the costs of resources supplied.   The purpose of cost allocation is to allocate support-service department costs to user departments based on some measure of the user departments' use of resources. As discussed in Chapter 5, the *use* of resources is not necessarily the same as the *supply* of resources. For example, you might spend $100 per month to acquire storage capacity for your belongings but use only 40 percent of the space. In that case, we distinguish between resources supplied (or money spent) of $100 per month, resources used of $40 per month (.40 × $100) and unused capacity of $60 per month ($100 resources supplied − $40 resources used).

Before allocating support-service department costs to user departments, we must first separate resources supplied from resources used. *Only resources used should be allocated to user departments* because users should be charged for services that they use. This argument states that users should not have to pay for the support-service departments' unused capacity.

In preparation for either an ABC or a traditional cost allocation, Tukami and her staff began by separating support-service department costs (resources used) from spending (resources supplied), with the following results:

Department	Resources Used	Resources Supplied	Unused Capacity
Information Technology	$36,000	$48,000	$12,000
Buildings and Grounds	84,000	90,000	6,000
Human Resources	25,000	27,000	2,000

Note that Tukami and her staff allocated to user departments only the amounts listed in the Resources Used column. The unused capacity information was included in various reports and was considered during budget negotiations. For example, the relatively large unused capacity in Information Technology existed because some user departments had outsourced these needs to outside companies or had hired information technology specialists to work in their own departments. These user departments no longer required Information Technology Department services. The unused capacity existed because the manager of the Information Technology Department had not fired people when other departments stopped using the department's services.

Step 2: Choose the Appropriate Cost-Allocation Base(s) and Rate(s)

Each cost pool should have its own appropriate cost-allocation base. **Cost allocation bases** are factors that cost management analysts use to assign indirect costs to cost objects. Ideally, a cost-allocation base reflects cause-and-effect relationships between resource spending and use, but determining these cause-and-effect relationships could be difficult or costly. In other words, finding a cost-allocation base that approximates cause-and-effect relationships is justified if the benefits from improved decisions exceed the costs of finding and using the base.

Recall that if an organization is able to accurately measure cause-and-effect relationships, it can *precisely trace* costs rather than *approximately allocate* them. If it

LO 3 Understand how to choose appropriate allocation bases.

cannot identify causal relationships between resource spending and use but still desires to allocate costs, it must use a less accurate cost-allocation base. The more closely the allocation base reflects a link between resource spending and use, the more useful allocated costs are likely to be for planning, decision making, and influencing behavior.[2]

Activity-based costing approach.   Applying the techniques of ABC (Chapter 4) is an effective way to generate accurate cost-allocation bases, which, to be consistent with Chapter 4, we call *cost-driver* bases to indicate their ABC origins. To summarize, this involves the following:

1. Identifying and measuring the *activities* demanded by internal customers that require support-service spending (e.g., hiring and training new employees) to obtain *cost-driver bases.*
2. Measuring each support-service department's resource spending by level (unit, batch, product, customer, facility).
3. Dividing support-service resource spending by appropriate cost-driver bases to derive *cost-driver rates.*

Using one of the cost-allocation methods discussed later, the organization could allocate support-service costs to internal customers by charging the cost-driver rate for each unit of activity, for example, $X for each new employee hired and trained.

Cindy Tukami applied ABC to measure cost-driver bases and, in her analysis, discovered that:

- Several of the support-service departments needed more capacity to offer expected levels of service.
- Several of the production departments had been greatly undercharged for the services they received, and several others had been overcharged.

These are common outcomes of changing to an ABC approach. Tukami was able to solve the technical problems of ABC, but her political problem in Rock Creek was that she chose to implement an ABC approach that seemed to her to be an obvious improvement without considering others' reactions.[3]

Many organizations have implemented an ABC approach to allocate service-department costs, and most have reported political as well as technical problems. Recall that organizations often design cost allocations explicitly to influence behavior, and individuals often resist unexplained changes. Therefore, successful cost-management analysts anticipate that changing cost-allocation bases might induce changes in behavior that also provoke complaints. We advise cost-management analysts to consider a way to effect change in organizations, even for something as mundane as changing cost allocations. We discuss Tukami's cost-driver base problems in more detail after discussing cost-allocation methods.

Cost Management in Practice 10.2

Use of ABC to Measure Costs

The use of ABC to measure the costs of internal services is increasing. One of the earliest (and best documented) reports comes from Weyerhaeuser, the international wood products firm (www.weyerhaeuser.com). Weyerhaeuser developed a comprehensive cost-allocation system based on the major activities demanded of its internal service divisions. As the product divisions use internal services, they are charged according to a reasonably simple but thorough set of cost-driver rates. These rates regulate demand for services and, since internal customers have a voice in setting the rates, force the internal service departments to provide high-quality, efficient services. *Source: H. Thomas Johnson and Dennis Loewe, "How Weyerhaeuser Manages Corporate Overhead Costs."*

---

[2] The important topic of cost estimation, which examines methods for measuring relationships between costs and activities, is the subject of Chapter 11, so we will not delve into this topic at this point.

[3] Tukami's City of Rock Creek analysis was nearly identical to the analyses presented in Chapter 4, so we do not discuss its technical details.

	Support-Service Cost	Typical Cost-Allocation Base
Labor related	Supervision	Number of employees, payroll dollars, or labor hours
	Personnel services	Number of employees
Equipment and technology related	Insurance on equipment	Value of equipment
	Taxes on equipment	Value of equipment
	Equipment depreciation...............	Hours of use or value of equipment
	Equipment maintenance	Number of machines or hours of use
Occupancy related..........	Building rental	Space occupied
	Building insurance	Space occupied
	Heat and air conditioning.............	Space or volume occupied
	Concession rental	Space occupied or desirability of location
	Interior building maintenance	Space occupied
Other service related	Materials handling	Quantity or value of materials
	Laundry	Weight of laundry processed
	Billing and accounting	Number of documents
	Indirect materials	Value of direct materials
	Dietary	Number of meals

Exhibit 10–3

Traditional Cost-Allocation Bases for Support-Service Costs

Allocation of support-service department costs.   Many organizations have found ABC too costly—either politically or financially—to implement or even consider. They have implemented simpler but probably less accurate approaches to choosing allocation bases and allocation rates. These organizations generally classify support-service costs and choose cost-allocation bases as Exhibit 10–3 shows for labor, equipment, occupancy, and other related costs.

Choice of reasonable and justifiable allocation bases.   If an ABC analysis is not possible or justified on a cost-benefit basis, the organization should choose allocation bases that at least seem reasonable and justifiable to internal customers. For example, prior to Tukami's ABC analysis, all support-service department costs were allocated using the following cost-allocation bases. Although these cost-allocation bases seem reasonable, the support-service departments provide a number of services that might not be related to these limited bases. This realization motivated Tukami to apply ABC.

Support-Service Department

Information Technology	Number of computers, including network servers
Buildings and Grounds.......................	Number of square feet in building
Human Resources	Number of newly hired employees (within one year)

Rock Creek's allocation bases. The (non-ABC) cost-allocation base amounts expected for each department appear in Exhibit 10–4. We use the data in this exhibit to demonstrate different cost-allocation methods as discussed in step 3.

Step 3: Select and Use a Cost-Allocation Method

This section describes two methods that allocate support-service costs: (1) the direct method and (2) the step method. These are the most commonly used methods by both private and public organizations. A third method, the reciprocal method, is more accurate than the two more common methods but is rarely used at this time. Because the reciprocal method could be used more in the future as cost-management analysts and their managers gain familiarity with it, we present it in the chapter Appendix.

We illustrate each method using Rock Creek's expected spending and allocation bases from Exhibit 10–4.

LO 4 Allocate support-service department costs using the direct and step methods.

Uses of Support-Service Department Services

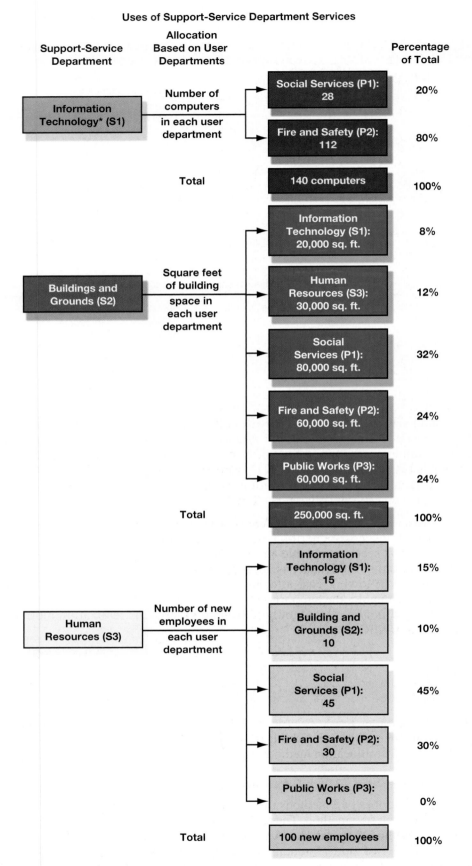

*The information Technology Department provides services to only two departments, Social Services and Fire and Safety. The other three departments—Buildings and Grounds, Human Resources, and Public Works—obtain information technology from outside companies.

Direct method.   The **direct method** of cost allocation charges the costs of support-service departments to internal customers *without making allocations among support-service departments.* All support-service cost allocations go directly to production departments.

Application of the direct method to Rock Creek.   Exhibit 10–5 describes the allocation of costs using the direct method for the City of Rock Creek. The direct method involves no allocations among the three support-service departments themselves. Thus, it ignores any support-service department relation to any other support-service department.

Allocation of Information Technology Department costs.   Tukami and her staff allocated the $36,000 monthly costs of the Information Technology Department based on the number of computers in the production departments. The Public Works, Human Resources, and Buildings and Grounds Departments had outsourced information technology to an outside company, so the Information Technology Department provided support services to only two production departments, Social Services, which had 28 computers and Fire and Safety which had 112 computers.

Using the direct method, the Information Technology Department costs are allocated 20 percent (28 ÷ 140) to Social Services because it had 28 of the 140 total computers and 80 percent (112 ÷ 140) to Fire and Safety which had 112 of them. (See Exhibit 10–4 for a summary of the percentages of Information Technology services used.) The allocation of costs are as follows:

Allocation of Buildings and Grounds Department costs.   Tukami and her staff allocated the $84,000 monthly costs of the Buildings and Grounds Department based on the number of square feet of building space used. (For purposes of this calculation, "building space" included parking areas, walkways, and other outdoor spaces immediately adjacent to buildings.) Because most of Buildings and Grounds' work was for repairs and maintenance, the size of the space was a relevant allocation base. Unlike Information Technology, Buildings and Grounds provided support services to all production departments and to the two other support-service departments, Information Technology and Human Resources.

Using the direct method of cost allocation, *none* of the Buildings and Grounds Department's costs are allocated to the other support-service departments, Information Technology and Human Resources. *All* of the Buildings and Grounds Department's monthly costs of $84,000 are allocated directly to the three production departments.

Note in Exhibit 10–4 that the five departments use a total of 250,000 square feet. Eliminating the two support-service departments leaves 200,000 square feet used by the three production departments.

Using the direct method, the Buildings and Grounds Department's costs are allocated 40 percent to Social Services (80,000 of the 200,000 square feet for the three production departments), 30 percent to Fire and Safety (60,000 square feet), and 30 percent to Public Works (60,000 square feet). The allocation of costs would be as follows:

$$.40 \times \$84,000 = \$33,600 \text{ — to} \rightarrow \boxed{\text{Social Services}}$$
$$\$84,000 \quad .30 \times \$84,000 = \$25,200 \text{ — to} \rightarrow \boxed{\text{Fire and Safety}}$$
$$.30 \times \$84,000 = \$25,200 \text{ — to} \rightarrow \boxed{\text{Public Works}}$$

Total costs allocated $\underline{\$84,000}$

Allocation of Human Resources Department costs.   Tukami and her staff allocated the $25,000 monthly Human Resources costs based on the number of new employees whom the production departments hired. The City of Rock Creek used new employees, defined as full-time or part-time employees hired within the last year, as the allocation base because most of Human Resources' costs were to advertise positions, hire and train employees, and conduct monthly performance reviews during a probation period following hiring. Departments that hired numerous employees consumed much of Human Resources' staff time. Furthermore, allocating costs to user departments based on "new employees" gave these departments incentives to reduce employee turnover. So new employees was a logical allocation base.

Using the direct method, *none* of the Human Resources Department's costs are allocated to the other support departments, Information Technology and Buildings and Grounds. *All* of the Human Resources Department's monthly costs of $25,000 are allocated directly to the three production departments. The percentage of services used, as reported in Exhibit 10–4, must be modified to eliminate the allocation bases for the support-service departments.

Note that in Exhibit 10–4 the three production and two support-service departments had a total of 100 new employees. Eliminating the two support-service departments leaves 75 employees hired by the three production departments.

Using the direct method, the Human Resources Department's costs are allocated 60 percent (45 ÷ 75) to Social Services because it had 45 of the 75 new employees and 40 percent (30 ÷ 75) to Fire and Safety because it had 30 of the 75 new employees. Public Works had no new employees, so it was allocated no Human Resources' costs. The allocation of costs is as follows:

$$.60 \times \$25,000 = \$15,000 \text{ — to} \rightarrow \boxed{\text{Social Services}}$$
$$\$25,000$$
$$.40 \times \$25,000 = \$10,000 \text{ — to} \rightarrow \boxed{\text{Fire and Safety}}$$

Total costs allocated $\underline{\$25,000}$

The direct method allocates support-service department costs based *only* on the relative amount of the cost-allocation base in each production department.

Because support costs are allocated directly, the order of allocation—which support cost is allocated first, second, and so on—does not affect the amounts allocated. We begin with the Information Technology Department, but we could have begun as easily with any of the others with the same results.

Summary of direct-method results.   We summarize the results of the direct method of support-service cost allocation for the City of Rock Creek in Exhibit 10–6. Panel A shows the percentages used in the cost allocation, and Panel B shows the costs allocated to the three production departments. The total charge to each production department for support services appears in columns (D) through (F) of Panel B. These figures are the proposed transfers from each production department to support-service departments and, if approved, would allow support-service departments to recover their costs.

Exhibit 10–6   Cost Allocations: Direct Method   *City of*

Panel A: Percentage of Support-Service Department Cost Allocated to User Departments Based on Text Discussion

		User (Production) Departments		
Support-Service Department	Support-Service Department Costs	Social Services	Fire and Safety	Public Works
Information Technology (S1)	$36,000	20%	80%	0%
Buildings and Grounds (S2)	84,000	40	30	30
Human Resources (S3)	25,000	60	40	0

Panel B: Direct Method of Cost Allocation

	Allocations from Support-Service Departments			Allocations to User (Production) Departments		
	(A) Information Technology	(B) Buildings and Grounds	(C) Human Resources	(D) Social Services	(E) Fire and Safety	(F) Public Works
Department costs before any interdepartment allocations (Exhibit 10–2)	$36,000	$84,000	$25,000	$500,000	$270,000	$185,000
Allocation of Information Technology; 20%, 80%, 0%*	(36,000)	NA†	NA†	7,200	28,800	0
Allocation of Buildings and Grounds; 40%, 30%, 30%*	NA†	(84,000)	NA†	33,600	25,200	25,200
Allocation of Human Resources; 60%, 40%, 0%*	NA†	NA†	(25,000)	15,000	10,000	0
Total department costs after allocations	$ 0	$ 0	$ 0	$555,800	$334,000	$210,200

* These percentages refer to the allocation percentages from Panel A. For example, 20% of Information Technology costs are allocated to Social Services (20% × $36,000 = $7,200).

† NA = not applicable. By definition for the direct method, once costs are allocated from a support-service department, no costs are allocated back to it.

Allocations of service costs in other organizations might not cause actual transfers of funds, but the cost allocations would be added to user departments' total overhead costs.

Limitations of the direct method.   Some people have criticized the direct method because it ignores the services that one support-service department provides to another. For example, Rock Creek's Human Resources Department hires and trains employees for other support-service departments as well as for production departments. If production departments are not vigilant, support-service departments could overserve each other and pass the costs to the production departments in the form of higher cost allocations. The step method of allocating support-service department costs attempts to remedy this problem by recognizing that support-service departments in fact render services to each other and use the organization's resources to do so.

Step method.   The **step method** of cost allocation allocates costs in steps. First, it allocates costs from the support-service department with the largest proportion of its total allocation base in other support-service departments to other support-service or production departments. Then it allocates costs from other support-service departments.

| Exhibit 10-7 | | Cost Allocations: Step Method | | | | | | *City of* Rock Creek  |

Panel A: Percentages of Support-Service Department Cost Allocated to User Departments Based on Text Discussion

Support-Service Department	Support-Service Department Cost	Departments					
		Human Resources	Buildings and Grounds	Information Technology	Social Services	Fire and Safety	Public Works
Human Resources	$25,000	(100)%*	10%	15%	45%	30%	0%
Buildings and Grounds†	84,000	NA‡	(100)	9%	37	27	27
Information Technology	36,000	NA	NA	(100)	20	80	0

Panel B: Step Method of Cost Allocation

	Support-Service Departments			Production Departments		
	Human Resources	Buildings and Grounds	Information Technology	Social Services	Fire and Safety	Public Works
Department costs before any interdepartment allocations	$ 25,000	$ 84,000	$ 36,000	$500,000	$270,000	$185,000
Allocation of Human Resources**	(25,000)	2,500	3,750	11,250	7,500	0
Allocation of Buildings and Grounds	NA‡	(86,500)	7,785	32,005	23,355	23,355
Allocation of Information Technology	NA	NA	(47,535)	9,507	38,028	0
Total department costs after allocations	$ 0	$ 0	$ 0	$552,762	$338,883	$208,355

* (100) means that 100 percent of the support-service department costs are being allocated to other departments.

† For ease of presentation, we have rounded the percentages, with the percentage allocated to Social Services rounded up to 37%.

‡ NA indicates "not applicable" because once costs have been allocated from a support-service department, no costs are allocated back to that support-service department.

** To derive cost allocations, multiply the percentages in Panel A by the support-service departmental costs before any interdepartmental allocations. For example, the allocation of $2,500 from Human Resources to Buildings and Grounds equals 10% from Panel A times $25,000 Human Resources costs before any interdepartmental allocations.

Unlike the direct method, the step method of cost allocation recognizes that some support-service departments provide services to other support services as well as to production departments. For example, Rock Creek's Human Resources Department provides the most services to the other support-services departments. Therefore, it is Rock Creek's most general service department. Using the step method, Rock Creek allocates Human Resources Department costs to all other departments first before allocating any other support-service costs.

Once the organization makes an allocation from a support-service department, no subsequent allocations are made back to that department. Thus, allocations from support-service departments are made in only one direction: from more general support services to less general support services and production departments.

Application of the step method to Rock Creek.   We show the flow of Rock Creek's support-service costs using the step method in Exhibit 10–7. We have ordered the support-service departments (top to bottom) from the most to least general. The step method allocates more general support-service department costs to less general support-service department costs. The most general support-service department is Human Resources because it allocates more of its costs to other support-service departments than does either of the other two support-service departments. To see that Human

Resources is the most general support-service department, recall the following uses of services among support-service departments (Exhibit 10–4):

- Information Technology provided no services to other support-service departments.

- Of its total services used, Buildings and Grounds provided 8 percent to Information Technology and 12 percent to Human Resources. Thus, the other two support-services departments used 20 percent of the Buildings and Grounds services.

- Of its total services used, Human Resources provided 15 percent to Information Technology and 10 percent to Buildings and Grounds. Thus, the other two support-services departments used 25 percent of the Human Resources' services.

Based on the fact that Human Resources provided relatively more of its services to other support-service departments than did either Information Technology or Buildings and Grounds, the other two support-service departments, it comes in first and allocates its costs to other departments first. Buildings and Grounds comes in second with 20 percent of its resources used by other support-service departments. The order of allocation for the step method is as follows:

Step Order	Support-Service Department
1	Human Resources
2	Buildings and Grounds
3	Information Technology

Allocation of Human Resources Department costs.   Using the step method, Tukami and her staff first allocate the Human Resources costs of $25,000 to all other departments. The percentages used in the allocation appear in panel A of Exhibit 10–7; they are simply the percentages of resources used (based on number of new employees in each department) presented in Exhibit 10–4.

The step method of allocation differs from the direct method by allocating costs to support-service and production departments whereas the direct method allocates costs directly to the production departments. Of course, Human Resources does not allocate any costs to itself. (We recommend that you take a minute to compare panel A of Exhibit 10–7 with panel A of Exhibit 10–6 to see how the direct and step methods differ.)

Using the step method, Tukami and her staff allocated the Human Resources costs as follows. Note that, according to Exhibit 10–4, Public Works had no new employees, so it was allocated no Human Resources costs. The allocation of costs to the other departments follows:

$25,000	.15 × $25,000 = $ 3,750 — to → Information Technology
	.10 × $25,000 = $ 2,500 — to → Buildings and Grounds
	.45 × $25,000 = $11,250 — to → Social Services
	.30 × $25,000 = $ 7,500 — to → Fire and Safety

Total costs allocated $25,000

We show this allocation in panel B of Exhibit 10–7.

After a support-service department's costs have been allocated to other departments, the step method allocates no other support-service department's costs back to itself. Therefore, having allocated Human Resource's costs to other departments, no costs are allocated back to it. (Later, we discuss a method that does allocate costs back and forth among support-service departments.)

Allocation of Buildings and Grounds Department costs.   Buildings and Grounds is second in the step method order, so its costs are allocated next. Having already allocated Human Resources' costs to other departments, its use of Buildings and Grounds resources are not considered in the Buildings and Grounds' allocation. Therefore, based on the number of building square feet for other departments but Human Resources (and Buildings and Grounds, itself, of course), Tukami and her staff calculated the following percentages of resource usage based on the data in Exhibit 10–4:

User Department	Building Space by User Department	Percentage of the Total
Information Technology	20,000 sq. ft.	9% (= 20,000/220,000)
Social Services	80,000	37
Fire and Safety	60,000	27
Public Works	60,000	27
Totals	220,000 sq. ft.	100%

These percentages appear in panel A of Exhibit 10–7. For ease of presentation, we have rounded the percentages, for example, the percentage allocated to Social Services is rounded up to 37 percent. If you do not use these rounded numbers, you will get slightly different cost allocations.

Recall that Buildings and Grounds' cost of resources used was $84,000 before allocating costs from any other support-service department. Tukami and her staff have already allocated $2,500 from Human Resources to Buildings and Grounds, so the Buildings and Grounds cost to be allocated equals $86,500, which is the total of $84,000 of Buildings and Grounds' own costs plus the $2,500 allocated to it from Human Resources.

Using the preceding percentages, the $86,500 is allocated as follows:

Total costs allocated	$86,500

Allocation of Information Technology Department costs. Finally, we allocate the Information Technology Department costs. Because the other two support-service departments' costs have already been allocated to other departments, no costs are allocated back to them. Therefore, Information Technology costs are allocated only to the production departments. (The City of Rock Creek's Information Technology Department charges nothing to the other support-service departments. Recall that the principle in the step method is that after a support-service department's costs have been allocated to other departments, no costs are allocated back to it.)

Information Technology costs are allocated based on the number of computers in the departments that it services. Information Technology services only Social Services and Fire and Safety (with 28 and 112 computers, respectively). Tukami and her staff calculated the following resource usage percentages based on the data in Exhibit 10–4. These percentages appear in Panel A of Exhibit 10–7.

User Department	Number of Computers	Percentage of the Total
Social Services	28	20%
Fire and Safety	112	80
Totals	140	100%

Recall that Information Technology's costs were $36,000 before receiving allocation from any other support-service department. Tukami and her staff had already allocated $3,750 from Human Resources plus $7,785 from Buildings and Grounds to Information Technology. This leaves $47,535 ($36,000 + $3,750 + $7,785) to allocate.

Using the preceding percentages, the $47,535 is allocated as follows:
See panel B of Exhibit 10–7 for this allocation.

$47,535 —— ⎡ .20 × $47,535 = $ 9,507 — to ➙ | Social Services |

⎣ .80 × $47,535 = $38,028 — to ➙ | Fire and Safety |

Total costs allocated $47,535

At this point, all support-service department costs have been allocated to production departments, and the cost-allocation process is complete.

Exhibit 10–8 compares step-method allocations with direct-method allocations. The differences in allocations do not seem large in absolute or relative terms, but some of the larger differences could represent adding or eliminating specific services. For example, if Rock Creek used the step method, Social Services would be charged $3,038 less per month for support services. Even this relatively modest cost-allocation difference could cause controversy when budgets are tight.

Limitations of the step method.   The step method might result in more reasonable allocations than the direct method because it recognizes that some service departments also use other service departments. The direct method ignores services among support-service departments. The step method is not necessarily better than the direct method, however. An organization that already uses the direct method could find switching methods uneconomical, particularly if the differences in cost allocations for the methods are small.

The City of Rock Creek uses the direct method because it is simpler. Other organizations also use the direct method because of its comparative simplicity. However, external parties require some organizations, such as many hospitals, to use the step method for cost reimbursement.

The step method does go part way in recognizing that support-service departments can benefit from using the resources of other support-service departments. However, as demonstrated, this use is recognized in only one direction. In fact, all of Rock Creek's support-service departments actually use services from each other. This means that they use **reciprocal services,** which are services provided among multiple support-service departments. If its support-service departments had relatively more reciprocal services, the city should consider using the *reciprocal method* of cost allocation to explicitly recognize reciprocal services. This method is defined and described in the Appendix to this chapter.

Tukami's accurate but politically incorrect ABC approach.   Tukami proposed to continue using the direct method for allocating support-service costs.[4] However, she created a controversy when she unveiled cost allocations based on ABC cost-driver

---

[4] She also considered ABC-step and ABC-reciprocal approaches, but for economy of discussion we do not discuss these.

Allocations to	Direct Method (Exhibit 10–6)	Step Method (Exhibit 10–7)	Differences Direct—Step
Social Services	$ 55,800	$ 52,762	$ 3,038
Fire and Safety	64,000	68,883	(4,883)
Public Works	25,200	23,355	1,845
Total allocated from support-service departments	$145,000	$145,000	$ 0

Exhibit 10–8

Comparison of Allocations Using the Direct and Step Methods

City of

Implementation of Changes in Cost-Allocation Approaches

Assume that Cindy Tukami has appointed you to head a team to review her ABC approach and develop a proposal to present to the city council no more than six months from now (with care, this can be a career-enhancing assignment). Develop a plan for preparing this proposal, including recommendations for team membership, division of duties, and an outline of the proposal. (Solutions begin on page 390.)

bases that reflect activities expected to be performed in the support-service departments for each production department. This was a radical departure from the simpler but less accurate cost-allocation bases that the city traditionally had used. Given the cost-management stance of this book, her approach seems appropriate. Tukami realized, however, that even ABC approaches cannot establish perfect causality.

The city manager and city council understood the inaccuracies and apparent inequities in the current allocation system and asked Tukami to study alternative cost-allocation bases for future years. They recommended that she present a new proposal for any changes well in advance of preparing the next budget so that the city could respond to comments from all affected departments and citizens.

Step 4: Determine Whether the Cost Allocations Achieve the Desired Results

LO 5 Evaluate the consequences of alternative cost allocations.

What is the most effective way for an organization to choose the method to allocate support-service costs? Discussions (or arguments) about the "best" approach to allocating support costs can waste valuable time and create dissension and lack of cooperation among departments. Clumsy implementation of new cost allocations is bound to create distrust because affected departments will suspect that the motive is to "steal" funds or profits. This could discredit the finance (or other responsible) department and cause relations among departments to worsen.

On the other hand, negotiations about cost allocations could increase information flow and cooperation if the negotiation process is open and all parties have an opportunity to participate and influence its outcome. An open evaluation of cost-allocation approaches would consider accuracy, effects on departments, and relation of costs and benefits.

Cost-allocation accuracy. One way to determine the best way to allocate costs is to examine how accurately each approach reflects the use of support-service resource costs by departments receiving these services. The direct method does not consider any interactions among service departments, whereas the step method considers some, and the reciprocal method is more thorough in this respect; see the chapter Appendix. Likewise, ABC cost-driver bases better reflect cause-and-effect relations between resource spending and use than do traditional cost-allocation bases.

Conceptually, combining ABC cost-driver bases and the reciprocal method should be the most accurate cost-allocation approach. Likewise, the combination of the direct method and traditional cost-allocation bases could be the least accurate reflection of resource spending, use, and provision of services. Other combinations lie somewhere between those extremes. Technical superiority or accuracy alone might influence the choice of approach. Accuracy, however, is only one consideration in choosing the appropriate approach for allocating support-service costs.

Cost-allocation effects. Another way to compare cost-allocation approaches is to examine the effects of alternative distributions of cost allocations to production (and support-service) departments, as shown in Exhibit 10–8. Cost allocations can have unintended behavioral effects. For example, consider the effects on department managers' performance evaluations that depend on their control of departmental costs.

Effects of distributions of costs. Both direct and step methods allocate the same total support-service cost for the City of Rock Creek, $145,000. Any differences between methods are in the amounts allocated to particular production departments. If the differences are large, alternative cost allocations could affect performance evaluations, decision making, and contracts.

Effects on performance evaluation.   If performance evaluations of department managers are based on their abilities to provide services and control costs, which cost-allocation method, direct or step, would they prefer? For example, consider Exhibit 10–8. Social Services and Public Works departments would prefer the step method, but Fire and Safety would prefer the direct method because of the effects on departmental costs.

Effects on decision making.   Cost-management analysts should consider the effects of cost-allocation differences on decision making in the affected departments. For example, the step method charges the Social Services Department $3,038 per month less than does the traditional direct method. Since this approximates the monthly cost of a counselor, the department head might regard this difference as important.

Except for the effects of the amounts of support-service costs allocated to production departments, the cost-driver or cost-allocation base itself could influence departmental decision making. For example, if Rock Creek allocates Human Resources Department costs on the basis of new employees, other department managers could perceive that they can reduce their costs (and transfers of funds to support services) by reducing the employee turnover. However, they *should* do this only if the benefits of reducing turnover exceeds the costs. This reasoning also applies to the use of other support services.

Effects on cost-plus contracts.   As noted earlier, many organizations sell products on a cost-plus basis in which the "plus" is a profit. Defense contractors, for example, traditionally have sold products to national governments on a cost-plus basis. Government agencies traditionally have reimbursed hospitals and nursing homes on a cost-plus basis for particular types of patients.

Cost-plus contracts give incentives to the supplier of the good or service to seek as much reimbursement as possible and, therefore, to allocate as much cost as possible to the product for which reimbursement is possible. For example, McLaren Construction Co. has contracts with both companies and the City of Rock Creek. For simplicity, assume that McLaren is deciding how to allocate $120,000 of support-service cost between two major contracts, Company A and City of Rock Creek. This $120,000 is a facility-level cost that cannot be directly traced to either contract. McLaren sells commercial jobs at a price set in the market, but the contract with Rock Creek was negotiated for cost plus a fixed profit. Thus, every dollar of overhead that can be allocated to the Rock Creek contract results in an additional dollar of revenue in cost reimbursement.

Suppose that McLaren is choosing between labor hours and construction-equipment hours as the two possible allocation bases. The relative use of labor hours and construction-equipment hours follows:

	Contract	
Possible Allocation Base	**Company A**	**Rock Creek**
Percentage of labor hours used	30%	70%
Percentage of construction-equipment hours used	60	40

Naturally, McLaren prefers to allocate the $120,000 using labor hours because it could seek $84,000 (.70 × $120,000) reimbursement from Rock Creek using labor hours but only $48,000 (.40 × $120,000) from the city using construction-equipment hours. McLaren would be $36,000 ($84,000 − $48,000) better off if it could use labor hours as the allocation base. Of course, Rock Creek would prefer construction-equipment hours for similar reasons. If the Rock Creek contract does not specify how costs should be allocated, McLaren ethically can choose the most advantageous approach.

Since the support-service costs cannot easily be directly attributed to a contract, allocation debates abound in cost-plus contracting. In such cases, specifying in the contract precisely how to define costs and how to make allocations is crucial. Thus, contracts and policies governing cost reimbursement try to clearly specify which costs and cost allocations are allowable.[5]

Cost-allocation costs and benefits.   A third consideration in the evolution of cost allocations is the relation of the costs and the benefits of setting up, administering, and maintaining the cost-allocation system. Cost-management analysts must realize that complex cost-allocation systems are not only difficult and costly to design but also are costly to maintain. For example, organizations that implement an ABC approach often find that the ABC information indicates where processes can be greatly improved (this is the topic of Chapter 5). Thus, after cost-management analysts lead and implement process improvements, they might recognize that the previous cost-driver base information is obsolete and requires revision. This can be a continual process of improvement, which is costly but justified if decisions and organizational performance also continue to improve.

If decisions or meeting organizational goals are unaffected by cost allocation type or improvements in the cost allocation used, however, it would be difficult to justify implementing a complex, expensive cost-allocation system. An unchanged or traditional direct approach could be quite adequate in this situation.

Finding the right allocation.   Since no absolutely precise allocation of support-service costs exists, an organization could experiment to find the right one. For example, administrators of a large university observed that its faculty and staff were using the university's Wide Area Telephone Service (WATS) so much that the lines were seldom free during the day. WATS allowed the university unlimited toll-free service within the United States. The monthly cost of the service was $10,000, which was fixed at this level for an agreed-upon overall volume of calls. The variable cost per call was zero.

University administrators learned that the average use on the WATS line was 50,000 minutes per month, so they allocated the $10,000 monthly charge to callers (that is, departments) at a rate of 20 cents per minute ($10,000 ÷ 50,000 minutes). After being charged for each use of WATS, department heads discouraged their faculty and staff from using it. Hence, the number of WATS minutes used dropped to 25,000 per month. The university increased the rate to 40 cents per minute ($10,000 ÷ 25,000). This decline in use and increase in charge continued until the internal cost allocation per minute exceeded the normal long-distance rates, and the use of WATS dropped almost to zero. The university's total telephone bill increased dramatically because it was paying for both the WATS monthly cost and normal long-distance charges.

University administrators subsequently compromised by charging a nominal fee of 10 cents per minute for WATS calls. According to the university's chief financial officer, "The 10 cents per minute charge made us aware that there was a cost to the WATS service, albeit a fixed cost per month. The charge was sufficiently low, however, so as not to discourage bona fide use of WATS."[6]

Ethical Issues

The inherent arbitrariness of cost allocation means that usually no clear-cut way to allocate costs exists. This arbitrariness can lead to difficult ethical choices for those responsible for allocating the costs. Consider again the allocation of costs in cost-

---

[5] For example, reimbursement by the U.S. federal government to other governmental bodies is covered by a lengthy, detailed document titled OMB Circular A-87. You can find information about these rules by searching on the Web for "Circular A-87" and "Cost Accounting Standards." Reimbursement to government contractors is covered by cost accounting standards.

[6] This example is based on Jerold L. Zimmerman, "The Costs and Benefits of Cost Allocations" (Full citations to references are in the Bibliography.) The solution to this problem is not necessarily to make WATS calls free. According to Zimmerman, the correct cost to charge users is "the cost imposed by forcing others who want to use the WATS line to either wait or place a regular call . . . this cost varies between zero (if no one is delayed) to, at most, the cost of a regular toll call if a user cannot use the WATS line" (p. 510). The necessary procedure to implement such a costing system is very difficult and costly. Zimmerman suggests that predetermined cost allocations could be a simplified way to approximate the results of the more complicated, theoretically correct system.

plus contracts. We have seen cases in which the contracts specified *manufacturing* cost plus a profit, yet the contractor added advertising, general and administrative, and similar costs to manufacturing overhead. This appears to be a violation of the contract terms, but the contractor argued that *full* manufacturing cost should include the allocations of these other costs.

Many lawsuits involving contract and tax disputes have arisen because people have allocated costs in inappropriate ways or contracts have been ambiguous. For example, a fast-growing county was sued by building contractors who argued that the total revenues collected by the county for building permits exceeded the costs to operate the county building department. Thus, the builders argued, the excess revenues amounted to an unfair tax on builders that the county used illegally to fund other programs and services. The county counterargued that permit revenues did not exceed the sum of both direct building department costs and costs allocated from county support services. After years of arguments and court appearances, the judge requested the opinions of outside experts on a reasonable cost-allocation approach and mediated the dispute.

Ethical Cost Allocations

Professor Mark Wolfson analyzes a classic example of the effects of ambiguous or unethical cost allocations in organizations structured as partnerships. General partners are responsible for conducting the work of the partnership, such as real estate development or oil and gas exploration, for the benefit of limited partners who share in the profits of the partnership. General managers also, however, can allocate their management costs to different partnerships that they manage to maximize their profits but perhaps at the expense of some limited partners. Wolfson finds that limited partners are willing to pay more to participate in partnerships managed by general partners with reputations for ethical cost allocations (and other practices). Therefore, general partners with reputations for ethical cost allocations earned higher returns, while less ethical general partners earned less. *Source: Mark Wolfson,* "Empirical Evidence of Incentive Problems and Their Mitigation in Oil and Gas Tax Shelter Programs."

Research Insight 10.2

Chapter Summary

Allocating service costs should reflect a cause-and-effect relationship between spending for support services and the services provided to internal customers. That is, cost allocations should measure the costs of support services provided. Tracing support-service spending directly to internal customers is usually difficult. Many organizations use reasonable, although not completely accurate, cost allocations based on allocation bases that reasonably describe the use of service resources.

The most common methods of allocating service costs are the direct and step methods. A currently less common method is the reciprocal-cost method (see the Appendix). Cost allocation is not a purely technical exercise since allocations can have both intended and unintended consequences. Therefore, choosing how to allocate costs should not be based solely on technical merits (e.g., recognizing reciprocal services). The way to allocate service costs depends more on the behavior of the departments and divisions that receive the allocations.

Appendix to Chapter Ten

Reciprocal Method

The step and direct methods omit the costs of support services consumed by one service department that were provided by other service departments. The reciprocal method of cost allocation addresses a technical limitation of the step method by making a reciprocal cost allocation when support-service departments provide reciprocal services, that is, they provide services to each other. The **reciprocal method** recognizes and allocates costs of all services provided by any support-service department, including those provided to other support-service departments. If allocation bases are reasonable, this

LO 6 Allocate support-service department costs using the reciprocal method.

method is the most accurate approach because it reflects the actual process by which services are exchanged among the organization's departments.

The reciprocal method expresses the total costs of each service and production department in equation form:[7]

$$\text{Total departmental costs} = \text{Direct costs of the department} + \text{Service costs to be allocated to the department}$$

This creates one equation for each department in which the unknown element is the total departmental cost. This set of equations (one equation for each unknown total department cost) is then solved simultaneously using matrix algebra.[8] As we shall demonstrate, solving all of the equations simultaneously accounts for all support-service department allocations, including reciprocal services provided by support-service departments to each other. This algebraic approach is also known as the *simultaneous solution method* because it solves a system of equations simultaneously.

For example, assume that the direct overhead costs of the departments at the City of Rock Creek are as follows:

Information Technology (S1) .... $ 36,000
Buildings and Grounds (S2)............................. 84,000
Human Resources (S3) 25,000
Social Services (P1)....................................... 500,000
Fire and Safety (P2) 270,000
Public Works (P3)... 185,000

Using the information in Exhibit 10–4, the total costs of the Social Services Department (P1) is expressed as follows:

$$\text{Total costs} = \text{Direct costs} + \text{Allocated costs}$$
$$P1 = \$500,000 + .20\,S1 + .32\,S2 + .45\,S3$$

Similar equations are constructed for each of the other production departments:

$$P2 = \$270,000 + .80\,S1 + .24\,S2 + .30\,S3$$
$$P3 = \$185,000 + .00\,S1 + .24\,S2 + .00\,S3$$

And for the service departments, the equations are

$$S1 = \$36,000 + .08\,S2 + .15\,S3$$
$$S2 = \$84,000 + .00\,S1 + .10\,S3$$
$$S3 = \$25,000 + .00\,S1 + .12\,S2$$

Now we have a set of equations that expresses the total cost of each department as a function of direct costs and allocated costs.

With the cost relationships written il equation form, the solution now can be found easily using the matrix invert function of a spreadsheet, such as Excel®. The matrix invert function uses inverse matrices, which are generally used to solve systems of mathematical equations involving several variables.

Setting the Equations in Matrix Form

When using matrix algebra to solve simultaneous equations, all coefficients need to be stated in the same terms. For instance,

$$\text{Total costs P1} = \$500,000 + .20\,S1 + .32\,S2 + .45\,S3$$

---

[7] The reciprocal method could include all costs of the department, including costs of production in the production departments. In our example, production departments do not provide any services. We are interested only in allocating support-service costs so we can ignore production costs without affecting the allocation results.

[8] The reader will recall from algebra class that solving two equations with two unknowns by algebraic substitution is relatively straightforward. However, using matrix algebra is preferred with more than two unknowns and equations.

should be restated as

$$\text{Total costs P1} = 1.00 \text{ P1(direct costs)} + .20 \text{ S1} + .32 \text{ S2} + .45 \text{ S3}$$

This process allows the information to be entered into a matrix on a spreadsheet, such as the one described next.

The following is based on using Excel to solve reciprocal-method cost allocations. The commands are shown in "quotes."

Step 1: Set up the parameter section.   The top section of Exhibit 10–9 (on page 388), titled Services, is the parameter section of the spreadsheet. This is the section on which the rest of the spreadsheet is calculated. It includes the matrix into which the percentage of services used and the amount of costs to be allocated will be entered.

Notice that all support-service and production departments are included in both the Performed By and Used By categories regardless whether they perform services for other departments. This creates a matrix with an equal number of rows and columns (remember that a matrix must have an equal number of rows and columns). The percentage of each department's use of another department's services and the amount of costs to be allocated to the user department are entered in the corresponding position.

For example, using the equation S1 = 1.00 S1(direct costs) + .08 S2 + .15 S3, we enter the amount of S2 services used by S1, 0.08, in cell C8; the amount of S3 services used by S1, 0.15, in cell D8; and (1.00) in cell B8 because all of S1 services were used by other departments. We entered 0.00 in cells E8, F8, and G8 because S1 used none of the production departments' services. Using the equation P1 = 1.00 P1(direct costs) + .20 S1 + .32 S2 + .45 S3, we enter .20 in cell B11, .32 in cell C11, .45 in cell D11, and 1.00 in cell E11 (because P1 used all of its own direct costs incurred), and 0.00 in F11 and G11.

The totals presented in row 14 represent the amount of costs remaining in each department after allocation. As you can see, the service departments retain none of their costs but allocate all of them to production departments when finished, but the production departments retain all of their costs. The costs to be allocated, entered in row 18, are entered under the department that incurred them.

Step 2: Set up the inverse matrix.   The middle section of Exhibit 10–9 Inverse Matrix, displays the output of the inverse matrix function of the spreadsheet. The output in this section is the same size as the parameter matrix and can be style formatted. Computer spreadsheets have commands that can be used to invert matrices (e.g., MINVERSE in Excel®).

The inverse matrix presents the percentage allocation of each department's costs to other departments. The negative percentages represent a service department's direct costs allocated to/from other service departments. They are negative because they will be reallocated to production departments.

You will notice that for departments S2 and S3, the total of the negative percentages is more than 100 because of the reciprocal nature of the allocations. The service departments allocate costs to other service departments, which are allocated back to them, bringing service departments' total costs to more than their direct costs. Therefore, there will be allocations out of the service departments in excess of 100 percent of their direct costs.

Step 3: Set up the cost allocation table.   The bottom section of Exhibit 10–9, Cost Allocation, presents the actual dollar amount of allocation to each department based on the inverse matrix and each department's direct costs. The amount calculated in each cell is the percentage in the corresponding inverse matrix cell multiplied by the direct cost in the same column. For instance, the cost allocated out of S1 $(36,000) equals the percentage allocated out of S1 represented in the inverse matrix (1.00) multiplied by S1 direct costs $36,000. Note that the percentages shown in the Inverse Matrix section are rounded for presentation purposes. However, unrounded numbers are used to calculate the cost allocations. Thus, when checking the math, notice that several amounts in the Cost Allocation section have rounding discrepancies.

Exhibit 10–9

Reciprocal Method
Spreadsheet

City of **Rock Creek**

	A	B	C	D	E	F	G	H
1								
2			*City of* **Rock Creek**					
3								
4	Services							
5		Performed by:						
6		S1	S2	S3	P1	P2	P3	
7	Used by:							
8	S1	(1.00)	0.08	0.15	0.00	0.00	0.00	
9	S2	0.00	(1.00)	0.10	0.00	0.00	0.00	
10	S3	0.00	0.12	(1.00)	0.00	0.00	0.00	
11	P1	0.20	0.32	0.45	1.00	0.00	0.00	
12	P2	0.80	0.24	0.30	0.00	1.00	0.00	
13	P3	0.00	0.24	0.00	0.00	0.00	1.00	
14		0.00	0.00	0.00	1.00	1.00	1.00	
15								
16								
17	Costs to Be Allocated:							
18		$36,000	$84,000	$25,000	$0	$0	$0	
19								
20								
21								
22	Inverse Matrix							
23		S1	S2	S3	P1	P2	P3	
24	S1	(1.00)	(0.099)	(0.16)	0.00	0.00	0.00	
25	S2	0.00	(1.012)	(0.101)	0.00	0.00	0.00	
26	S3	0.00	(0.121)	(1.012)	0.00	0.00	0.00	
27	P1	0.20	0.398	0.52	1.00	0.00	0.00	
28	P2	0.80	0.359	0.456	0.00	1.00	0.00	
29	P3	0.00	0.243	0.024	0.00	0.00	1.00	
30								
31	Cost Allocation							Total
32		From:						Allocated to Production
33		S1	S2	S3	P1	P2	P3	Departments
34	To:							
35	S1	$(36,000)	$(8,332)	$(3,998)	$0	$0	$0	
36	S2	$0	(85,020)	(2,530)	0	0	0	
37	S3	$0	(10,202)	(25,304)	0	0	0	
38	P1	$7,200	$33,464	$12,996	0	0	0	$53,660
39	P2	$28,800	$30,131	$11,397	0	0	0	$70,328
40	P3	$0	$20,405	$607	0	0	0	$21,012
41								$145,000
42								

Allocations to	Direct Method (Exhibit 10–6)	Step Method (Exhibit 10–8)	Reciprocal Method (Exhibit 10–9)
Social Services	$ 55,800	$ 52,762	$ 53,660
Fire and Safety	64,000	68,883	70,328
Public Works	25,200	23,355	21,012
Total allocated from support-service departments	$145,000	$145,000	$145,000

Exhibit 10–10

Comparing Direct, Step, and Reciprocal Cost Allocations

City of **Rock Creek**

The totals on the right of the bottom panel of the table show the total costs allocated to each department. Again, the totals for the service departments are negative because they do not remain in the department but are allocated out to the production departments. If you add these negative totals, you will find that they total more than the total service-department costs because some amounts are included twice. For example, the total cost of S1 (the sum of all amounts shown on line 35) includes the allocated costs from S2 and S3 plus all of the S1 direct costs, even though some of the direct costs are allocated to S2 and S3.

Department P1 was allocated $7,200 from S1 plus $33,464 from S2 plus $12,996 allocated from S3 for a total allocation of $53,660 from support-service departments.

Comparative cost allocations using the direct, step, and reciprocal methods appear in Exhibit 10–10. The allocations that result from the step and reciprocal methods are similar. If the City of Rock Creek wished to use a method that recognizes services among support-service departments, the finance department probably should use the reciprocal method since it is technically superior and actually easier to use since spreadsheets do most of the arithmetic. The reciprocal method could be more difficult to explain, however (some peoples' eyes glaze over on hearing the words "matrix" or "simultaneous equations").

Some organizations use the direct method if allocations are not dramatically different just because it is easier to explain to managers and internal customers than other methods. Cost-management analysts, however, should consider all issues raised at the end of this chapter regarding the choice among alternative cost-allocation approaches.

Key Terms

For each term's definition, refer to the indicated page or turn to the glossary at the end of the text.

cost-allocation bases, 371

direct method, 375

production (or line) departments, 366

reciprocal method*, 385

reciprocal services, 381

step method, 377

support-service costs, 367

support-service (or indirect) departments, 366

*Term appears in the chapter Appendix.

Meeting the Cost Management Challenges

1.   Cost allocations are arbitrary. Does this mean that the way you decide to allocate costs is of no consequence to you or your organization?

Some people use the word "arbitrary" to mean "capricious" or "without justification." If cost allocations in an organization truly are unrelated to either the use of resources or influencing desired behavior, it is difficult to justify any effort devoted to cost alloca-

tion. We think that the alternative definition meaning "discretionary" is more than a semantic difference; it reflects the deliberate intent to use cost allocations to achieve some goal. These include the legitimate purposes of managing support-service resources effectively, improved decision making, proper external reporting, faithfully executing of cost-based contracts, and influencing employee behavior. We do not mean to imply, however, that organizations can achieve these outcomes only by allocating costs. Employees might make some decisions better without cost-allocation information, (e.g., production or product-line decisions). We do mean that cost allocations, when considered necessary, should be made carefully and with an awareness of their effects and limitations.

2. **Choosing** a cost-allocation approach is always a judgment that is based on an evaluation of trade-offs. How can you be best prepared to evaluate the trade-offs and provide leadership if dramatic changes are needed?

Knowing the trade-offs you are likely to encounter and the limits to analysis is a good first step. The various trade-offs center around the value of more accurate cost-allocation information versus the cost of improved information. The most accurate cost allocations closely reflect the cause and effect between the desired or actual spending for resources and their use. We must realize, however, that we can never establish this causality with certainty and without measurement error. Therefore, cost-management analysts must judge how close is good enough because we can expect that, consistent with the law of diminishing marginal returns, making further improvements in accuracy costs increasingly more. At some point, the costs of more improvement will exceed the benefits. Armed with this realization, the next step is to identify the benefits and costs of cost allocation—generally and specifically, quantitatively and qualitatively. You might want to review the discussion of cost-benefit analysis in Chapter 1.

Benefits of more accurate cost allocations include better control and use of support services leading, for example, to better service levels, better operations, and less waste of resources. The costs of improved cost allocations include out-of-pocket and opportunity costs of information analysis and upkeep as well as the education of those who are affected by the allocations. Quantifying all of these costs and benefits could be difficult,

which is why judgment is necessary: to compare quantitative and qualitative information.

Education and communication are extremely important factors that determine the success of planned changes. If the decisions, evaluations, or behavior of individuals or departments is affected by cost allocations simply to announce a more accurate approach to cost allocation is foolish. The numbers almost never "speak for themselves." In real organizations where budgets and evaluations based on cost allocations matter, any unexplained or unjustified changes in cost allocations can provoke surprise, anger, and unproductive dissension. It is more effective to plan and execute these changes carefully so that affected parties understand why the change is necessary and how the change will affect them. You might want to review the steps for strategic decisionmaking in Chapter 1.

3. **Some** cost-allocation approaches appear to be quite complex. How should you educate other managers to understand the complexities of the cost-allocation process?

In this chapter we have first introduced the importance of cost allocations. Second, we illustrate the methods with simple examples and diagrams. We also contrast the effects of alternative methods so that it is clear that the distributions of costs can differ for each method. If we were addressing only users of cost-allocation information such as managers or executives, we would go no further in explaining how complex the methods become when applied to real organizations. They need to understand that the methods can differ and that you are fully aware of how to implement them. They do not need a great deal of detail, however. We have given you detailed applications because we believe that cost-management analysts need to know more than a simple example. You need to realize that applying cost-allocation methods is conceptually no different from analyzing the simple examples, but implementing them in real situations requires a careful, systematic approach to ensure accuracy and completeness.

Solutions to You're the Decision Maker

10.1   Principles of Cost Allocation   p. 368

a. Principles of cost allocation become more important as cost allocations become a larger part of an organization's total costs. Obviously, if most support services are outsourced, cost-allocation principles seem unnecessary. In this case, market transactions take the place of bureaucratic rules and principles. On the other hand, if most support services are internal and production departments bear the costs of those services via cost allocations, it is in the organization's interest to have clear cost-allocation principles and policies. Otherwise, managers will spend unproductive time mediating disputes over cost allocations.

Cost allocations might be more prevalent in public institutions because they seldom obtain or provide services through open markets (although this is changing throughout the world). Furthermore, since public organizations usually exist to provide goods and services that are not available via market transactions, monetary measures of their values are unavailable. Thus, cost allocations might be the predominant quantitative measures of services.

b. As the manager of a production department, you know that spending for support services can affect your department. First, you probably agree that information technology is important, but you might express surprise that you were not informed about this decision, which should have been discussed openly and fully as a major decision. Next, because departments like yours will pay for this increased support-service spending, you might wonder what services your department can expect in return. By challenging the budget increase, you are providing a control on support-service spending, but you also might wonder aloud whether your department might be better off if it could outsource information technology services. Furthermore, you might express concern about the unplanned effects on your budget and whether the city expects your department to reduce its spending to pay for increased support services, to increase fees charged to citizens, or to seek increased funding from tax revenues or state and federal grants. You also could express concern about whether the support-service departments are more concerned with their budgets than with providing reasonable charges for fair services to others. Note that these concerns are similar to those you would have as a department or division manager in a private corporation; sales from departments such as yours must cover spending for internal services.

c. As city manager, you must be concerned with the efficiency with which the city provides services to its citizens. That means ensuring that the city provides the type, quality, and quantity of services that citizens want and need within its budget and according to appropriate laws and regulations. Perhaps the most important principle is *provision of incen-* *tives for service providers to deliver products and services efficiently and effectively* because adhering to this principle will ensure that scarce city resources are supplied and used appropriately.

10.2 Implementation of Changes in Cost-Allocation Approaches p. 382

Before Tukami presents the proposal in six months, the finance department must repair the damage to the credibility of ABC as an approach that is consistent with the city's principles of cost allocation. One possible approach follows:

Steps for Leading Change	Possible ABC Plan
• Identify a need for change.	• Review Tukami's analyses to verify that previous cost allocations violate the city's cost-allocation principles and that ABC could improve cost allocations in significant ways.
• Create a team to lead and manage the change.	• Expand the team to include representatives from some of the support-service and production departments, taking care to add skilled, articulate team members but not so many that the team becomes too large to be efficient.
• Create a vision of the change and a strategy for achieving the vision.	• Stress the importance of city efficiency in all departments and that management decisions drive costs. Stress that both accurate cost allocations and process improvements are necessary to meet growing service expectations and the public's desire for lower taxes. Prepare a description of the benefits of an ABC approach, including:
	• Understanding how decisions affect how work is accomplished.
	• Learning what activities the organization uses to produce products and services.
	• Choosing the most profitable uses of scarce capacity.
	• Measuring the consumption of the organization's resources.
	• Guiding process improvements.
	• Steps in the analysis, adapted from Chapter 4, are to:
	1. Identify and classify the activities related to services.
	2. Estimate the cost of activities identified in step 1.
	3. Calculate a cost-driver rate for each activity.
	4. Assign activity costs to services.
• Communicate the vision and strategy for change and have the change team be a role model.	• Meet with all department managers to describe the need and proposal for revising cost allocations. Do not be defensive but be prepared to accept criticism and suggestions for improvement.
	• Have a similar meeting with the city manager and council.
• Encourage innovation and remove obstacles to change.	• Obtain approval from city and department managers to allow the team to develop best solutions.
• Ensure that short-term achievements are frequent and obvious.	• Consider beginning with a pilot project in one support-service department to demonstrate the approach and "work out the bugs."
• Use successes to create opportunities for improvement in the entire organization.	• Communicate the benefits of improvements and indicate how new knowledge about ABC approach can benefit the entire city management.
• Reinforce a culture of more improvement, better leadership, and more effective management.	• Apply the approach throughout the organization and let departments have continuing input to use and improve ABC information.

Review Questions

10.1 What factors would you consider when deciding whether to outsource a particular support service?

10.2 What are some costs of the cost-allocation process itself?

10.3 What are some benefits of cost allocation?

10.4 How should a manager decide whether to allocate costs?

10.5 What are some management uses of information based on allocated costs?

10.6 What are four broad categories of common costs and a typical basis for the allocation of costs in each category?

10.7 What are the similarities and differences of allocating service costs for the direct method and the step method (and the reciprocal method, if studied)?

10.8 What criterion should be used to determine the order of allocation from support-service departments when using the step method? Explain why.

Critical Analysis

10.9   Three students share a house. Having better things to do than clean house, they hire someone to come in and clean once each week. How should they share the costs of the housekeeper? One simple solution is to share the cost equally. Suppose, however, that one student's bedroom is twice as large as each of the other students' bedrooms. The second student has a small bedroom and uses the house only four days per week. The third student uses the house all week, has a small bedroom, and is generally acknowledged to be the cleanest of the three. Sharing the cost equally is simple, but is it fair? Form groups of three. Each should take the role of one of the roommates. Using the techniques of the chapter, develop a reasonable way to share housekeeping costs.

10.10   Respond to this comment: "Outsourcing is based on a market economy and, therefore, is the most efficient way to obtain a service."

10.11   Consider the following conversation between a self-styled cost-allocation expert and Joe, the manager of a diner.

Expert: Joe, you said you put in these peanuts because some people ask for them, but do you realize what this rack of peanuts is costing you?

Joe: It's not going to cost! It's going to be a profit. Sure, I had to pay $100 for a fancy rack to hold the bags, but the peanuts cost 24 cents a bag, and I sell 'em for 40 cents. Suppose I sell 50 bags a week to start. It'll take 12 1/2 weeks to cover the cost of the rack. After that I have a clear profit of 16 cents a bag. The more I sell, the more I make.

Expert: That is an antiquated and completely unrealistic approach, Joe. Fortunately, modern accounting procedures permit a more accurate picture that reveals the complexities involved.

Joe: Huh?

Expert: To be precise, those peanuts must be integrated into your entire operation and be allocated their appropriate share of business overhead. They must share a proportion of your expenditures for rent, heat, light, equipment depreciation, decorating, salaries for your waitresses, cook . . .

Joe: The cook? What's he got to do with the peanuts? He doesn't even know I have them.

Expert: Look, Joe, the cook is in the kitchen, the kitchen prepares the food, the food is what brings people in here, and the people ask to buy peanuts. That's why you must charge a portion of the cook's wages, as well as a part of your own salary, to peanut sales. This sheet contains a carefully calculated cost analysis, which indicates that the peanut operation should pay exactly $2,278 per year toward these general overhead costs.

Joe: The peanuts? $2,278 a year for overhead? Nuts! The peanuts salesman said I'd make money—put 'em on the end of the counter, he said, and get 16 cents a bag profit.

Expert   [with a sniff]: He's not an accountant. Do you actually know what the portion of the counter occupied by the peanut rack is worth to you?

Joe: Nothing. No stool there, just a dead spot at the end.

Expert: The modern cost picture permits no dead spots. Your counter contains 60 square feet, and your counter business grosses $60,000 a year. Consequently, the square foot of space occupied by the peanut rack is worth $1,000 per year. Since you have taken that area away from general counter use, you must charge the value of the space to the occupant.

Joe: [eagerly] Look! I have a better idea. Why don't I just throw the nuts out—put them in a trash can?

Expert: Can you afford it?

Joe: Sure. All I have is about 50 bags of peanuts—cost about 12 bucks—so I lose $100 on the rack, but I'm out of this nutsy business and no more grief.

Expert: [shaking head] Joe, it isn't quite that simple. You are in the peanut business! The minute you throw those peanuts out, you are adding $2,278 of annual overhead to the rest of your operation. Joe—be realistic—can you afford to do that?

Joe: [completely crushed]: It's unbelievable! Last week I was making money. Now I'm in trouble—just because I believed 50 bags of peanuts a week is easy.

Expert: [with raised eyebrow]: That is the object of modern cost studies, Joe—to dispel those false illusions.

Form small groups and develop a solution to Joe's problem. Be sure to consider appropriate cost allocations, if any, and the appropriate opportunity cost of counter space.

10.12   If support-service cost allocations are arbitrary and potentially misleading, should we assume that managers are foolish for using information about which services to provide based on allocated service costs?

10.13   One critic of cost allocation noted, "You can avoid the problem of arbitrary cost allocations by simply not allocating any higher-level resource service costs to lower-level uses of resources." Prepare a memo outlining the costs and benefits of this approach.

10.14   Explain how cost allocation in an organization could be both a technical and a political exercise.

10.15   (Appendix) What argument(s) could be given in support of the reciprocal method as the preferred method for allocating the costs of service departments?

10.16   Under what conditions are the results from using the direct method of allocations the same as those from the step method? Why?

10.17   Consider a company with two producing departments and one service department. The service department allocates its costs to the producing departments on the basis of the number of employees in each department. If the costs in the service department are fixed by policy for the coming period, what effect would the (unexpected) addition of employees in one production department have on the service costs allocated to the other? Comment on the reasonableness of the situation.

10.18   Prepare a short presentation to explain and comment on this argument: "Cost allocation can never provide an incentive to reduce service costs unless the amount allocated is tied to some controllable driver. Awareness of the service cost serves no purpose if the driver is not controllable."

10.19   The manager of an operating department just received a cost report and has made the following comment with respect to the costs allocated from one of the service departments: "This charge to my division does not seem right. The service center installed equipment with more capacity than our division requires. We seem to be allocated more costs in periods when other departments use less service capacity. We are paying for excess capacity of other departments when other departments cut their usage levels." Explain how this result occurred and how to solve this manager's problem.

Exercises

The Klingons and the Romulans own two adjacent tracts of land. Each tract has a surface area of 4,000 acres. During a recent shoot-out between the families, crude oil came bubbling to the surface where a phaser blast entered the ground. A petroleum geologist determined that an underground rock formation that extended under both tracts of land contained a substantial amount of oil. The formation was estimated at 800,000 acre feet of volume, of which 600,000 acre feet were under the Romulans' tract of land.

The Klingons and the Romulans received an offer to buy the mineral rights for $8.5 million provided that they can agree on how much of the purchase price should be allocated to each family.

Exercise 10.20
Alternative Allocation Bases
(LO 3)

Required

Form two groups to develop a solution to the allocation problem.

a.   As a Klingon, what basis would you recommend for allocating the purchase price? What arguments would you use to support your claim?

b.   As a Romulan, what basis would you recommend for allocating the purchase price? What arguments would you use to support your claim?

c.   Come together to find a joint solution to the allocation problem (not involving the use of phasers).

Powell Company has a TV station and a radio station that share the common costs of the company's AP wire service, which is $200,000 a year. You have the following information about the AP wire and the two stations:

Exercise 10.21
Alternative Service-Cost Allocation Bases
(LO 3)

Station	Wire Service Hours Used This Period	Hours of News Broadcasts
TV	300	100
Radio	450	460

Required

a.   What is the AP wire service cost charged to each station if wire service hours are used as an allocation base?

b.   What is the AP wire service cost charged to each station using hours of news broadcast as an allocation base?

c.   Which method allocates more costs to TV? Which method allocates more costs to radio? When and why would this matter?

Ray, Inc., operates a 120,000 square-foot supermarket. Each department in the store is charged a share of the cost of the building. The following information concerning two of the departments in the store is available.

Exercise 10.22
Alternative Allocation Bases
(LO 3)

Department	Meat	Dry Goods
Sales revenues	$250,000	$300,000
Cost of goods sold	85,000	90,000
Salaries and other direct expenses	55,000	70,000
Allocated administrative expenses	25,000	27,500
Operating profit before building occupancy costs	$ 85,000	$112,500
Area occupied (square feet)	10,000	30,000

Other departments use the other 80,000 square feet. The total building occupancy costs are $800,000 per year.

Required

a.   If area occupied is the basis for allocating building occupancy costs, what is the operating profit or loss for each of these two departments?

b.   Would you allocate based on something other than square feet if you learned that the dry goods department is located in a back corner of the store? Explain.

Exercise 10.23
Alternative Service-Cost Allocation Bases
(LO 3)

Quality Credit Company produces two styles of credit reports, standard and executive. The difference between the two is in the amount of background checking and data collection. The executive report uses more skilled personnel because additional interviews and analyses are performed. The relevant figures for the previous year follow.

Allocation Base	Standard Report	Executive Report
Data purchased...	$20,000	$30,000
Research hours	12,000	18,000
Interview hours	1,000	4,000
Number of reports	8,000	2,000

The company must allocate $1,600,000 in support-service costs to these two product lines.

Required

For each of the four potential allocation bases, determine the amount of support-service cost allocated to each type of report.

Exercise 10.24
Alternative Allocation Bases
(LO 3)

Refer to your calculations for exercise 10.23. Your supervisor wants to know the costs to prepare a standard report and an executive report, including the cost of data, labor (which costs $40 per hour), and support services.

Required

a.   Prepare four different answers to the question, "How much does it cost to produce?" for each type of report.

b.   Prepare a memo explaining to your supervisor why there are four different cost numbers for each report. Also indicate whether total costs are the same for Quality Credit Company regardless of the overhead allocation base used.

c.   What do you recommend?

Exercise 10.25
Cost Allocations: Direct Method
(LO 4)

All-Town Corporation has two production departments, P1 and P2, and two support-service departments, S1 and S2. Direct costs for each department and the percentage of service costs used by the various departments for the month of May are as follows:

Department	Direct Costs	Percentage of Services Used By			
		SI	S2	PI	P2
S1	$ 80,000		60%	20%	20%
S2	$100,000	20%		50%	30%
P1	160,000				
P2	140,000				

Required

a.   Compute the allocation of support-service department costs to producing departments using the direct method.

b.   *Build your own spreadsheet.* Develop a spreadsheet to answer (a).

Exercise 10.26
Service Department Costs Allocated First to Production Departments and Then to Jobs
(LO 4)

Refer to the facts in exercise 10.25. Assume that both P1 and P2 work on just two jobs, 10 and 11, during the month of May. Costs are allocated to jobs based on the number of labor hours in P1 and of machine hours in P2. The labor and machine hours worked in each department are as follows:

		PI	P2
Job 10	Labor hours	80	10
	Machine hours	10	20
Job 11	Labor hours	10	10
	Machine hours	10	90

Required

How much of the support-service department costs allocated to P1 and P2 in the direct method should be allocated to job 10? How much to job 11?

Ming, Inc., has two service departments (maintenance and general factory administration) and two production departments (cutting and assembly). Management has decided to allocate maintenance costs on the basis of the size of the area in each department and general factory administration costs on the basis of the number of labor hours worked by the employees in each of their respective departments.

Exercise 10.27
Cost Allocation: Direct Method
(LO 4)

The following data appear in the company records for the current period:

	General Factory Administration	Maintenance	Cutting	Assembly
Area occupied (square feet).........................	1,000	—	1,000	3,000
Labor hours	—	100	100	400
Direct labor costs (operating departments only)..	—	—	$3,000	$8,000
Service department direct costs	$20,000	$48,000	—	—

Required

Use the direct method to allocate the service department costs to the production departments.

Refer to the data for All-Town Corporation (exercise 10.25).

Exercise 10.28
Cost Allocation: Step Method
(LO 4)

Required

Use the step method to allocate the service costs, using:

a.   The order of allocation starting with S1.

b.   The allocations made in the reverse order (starting with S2).

mhhe.com/hilton3e

Refer to the data for Ming, Inc., in exercise 10.27.

Exercise 10.29
Cost Allocation: Step Method
(LO 4)

Required

Allocate the service department costs using the step method, starting with the maintenance department. How does using this method affect the allocation of costs compared to using the direct method?

Refer to the data for All-Town Corporation (exercises 10.25 and 10.28, part a).

Exercise 10.30
Cost Allocation Comparisons
(LO 5)

Required

Compare the results of the direct and step methods. Which method is better?

During the past month, the following costs were incurred in the three production departments and two service departments in the East Bay Company:

Exercise 10.31
Cost Allocation: Reciprocal Method
(Appendix)
(LO 6)

P1...$120,000
P2.. 312,500
P3.. 390,000
S1.. 67,000
S2.. 59,500

The use of services by other departments follows:

Service Departments	Percentages Used by Internal Customers				
	S1	S2	P1	P2	P3
S1	—	40%	30%	20%	10%
S2	10%	—	20	15	55

Required

Allocate service-department costs to P1, P2, and P3 using the reciprocal method, and present the total costs of P1, P2, and P3 after this allocation.

Exercise 10.32
Cost Allocation:
Reciprocal Method
(Appendix)
(LO 6)

Refer to the data for Ming, Inc., in exercise 10.27.

Required

Allocate the service-department costs using the reciprocal method.

Exercise 10.33
Evaluation of Cost-
Allocation Methods
(Appendix)
(LO 5)

Refer to exercises 10.27, 10.29, and 10.32 (Ming, Inc.).

Required

a. Which cost-allocation method do you think is best?

b. How much would it be worth to the company to use the best method compared to the worst of the three methods? (Numbers are not required in this answer.)

Exercist 10.34
Explain Differences in
Cost-Allocation Methods
(LO 5)

Form small groups and prepare a short visual presentation that Tukami could use to explain the advantages and disadvantages of using traditional cost-allocation bases and ABC cost-driver bases for allocating support-service costs at Rock Creek (in the chapter example).

Problems

Problem 10.35
Service Cost Allocation:
Direct Method
(LO 4)

Dual Division Corporation allocates service costs to its Alpha and Beta Divisions. During the past month, it incurred the following service costs:

Computing services	$254,000
Human resources	615,000
Custodial services	104,000

The following information concerning various activity measures and service uses by each of the divisions is available:

	Alpha	Beta
Area occupied	15,000 sq. ft.	40,000 sq. ft.
Payroll	$380,000	$170,000
Computer time	200 hr.	140 hr.
Computer storage	25 gigabytes	35 gigabytes
Equipment value	$175,000	$220,000
Operating profit, before allocations	$439,000	$522,000

Required

a. Allocate the service costs to the two divisions using the direct method and the most appropriate of these allocation bases. For computing services, use computer time only.

b. *Build your own spreadsheet.* Develop a spreadsheet to answer requirement (a).

Problem 10.36
Cost Allocation: Direct
Method
(LO 4)

mhhe.com/hilton3e

Selto & Company manufactures and sells T-shirts for advertising and promotional purposes. The company has two manufacturing operations, shirtmaking and printing. When the company receives an order for T-shirts, the shirtmaking department obtains the materials and colors requested and has the shirts made in the desired mix of sizes. It sends the completed shirts to the printing department where the custom labels or designs are prepared and silk-screened onto the shirts.

To support the manufacturing activity, the company has a building that houses the two manufacturing departments as well as the sales department, payroll department, and the design and patterns staff. To aid in cost control, the company accumulates the costs of these support functions in separate service departments: (1) building occupancy, (2) human resources, and (3) design and patterns.

During the current period, the direct costs incurred by each department are as follows:

Shirtmaking (P1)	$210,000
Printing (P2)	140,000
Sales (P3)	80,000
Building occupancy (S1)	45,000
Human resources (S2)	20,000
Design and patterns (S3)	10,000

Building occupancy costs are allocated on the basis of the number of square feet of each department. Human resources costs are allocated on the basis of the number of full-time equivalent employees. The design and pattern costs are charged to departments on the basis of the number of designs requested by each department. For the current period, the following table summarizes the usage of services by other service cost centers and other departments:

	S1	S2	S3	P1	P2	P3
Building occupancy (S1) (square feet)	—	8,100	3,900	27,000	36,000	6,000
Human resources (S2) (employees)	3	—	6	30	15	6
Design and patterns (S3) (designs)	—	—	—	15	40	5

Required

Using the direct method for service cost allocations, what are the total costs in each of the three "producing" departments?

Refer to the facts for problem 10.36.

Required

Compute the cost allocations and total costs in each production department using the step method. Which service costs should be allocated first? Second?

Problem 10.37
Cost Allocation: Step Method
(LO 4)

Chih-ling, Inc., has three service departments that support the production area. Outlined here is the budgeted support-service spending by department for the coming year.

Problem 10.38
Effects of Alternative Cost-Allocation Methods
(LO 4, 5)

Support-Service Departments	Budgeted Spending	Number of Employees
Receiving	$25,000	2
Repair	35,000	2
Tool	10,000	1

Production Departments		
Assembly		25
Bolting		12

The repair department supports the most support-service departments, followed by the tool department. Service costs are allocated to departments based on the number of employees.

Required

a.   Using the direct method of cost allocation, determine the amounts of support-service cost that will be allocated to each department.

b.   Using the step method of cost allocation, determine the amounts of support-service cost that will be allocated to each department.

c.   Do you believe that the method of cost allocation would matter to the support-service departments? To the production departments? Why?

[CMA adapted]

Micro Corporation's memory chip division manufactures two types of computer memory chips: The RAM-A chip is a commonly used chip for personal computer systems, and the RAM-B chip is used for specialized scientific applications. Unit-level materials costs for the RAM-A chip are 25 cents per unit and for the RAM-B are $1.12 per unit. The division's annual output is 32 million chips. Labor costs in the division total $625,000. Manufacturing overhead is composed of $1.2 million of corporate service cost allocated to the division on the basis of labor costs and $1.2 million of divisional overhead (supervision, materials handling and security, utilities, equipment costs and depreciation, etc.).

Problem 10.39
Choice of Appropriate Allocation Base
(LO 3)

The company's assembly process is highly automated. As a result, the primary function for direct labor is to set up a production run and to check equipment settings on a periodic basis. Yesterday the equipment was set up to run 1,600 RAM-B units. When that run was completed, equipment settings were changed, and 200,000 RAM-A units were produced. Part of the daily cost report follows:

	RAM-A	RAM-B
Units produced	200,000	1,600
Unit-level materials used	$ 25,000	$1,896
Labor used	$ 2,000	$1,200

Required

a. Recommend how to allocate the memory chip division's overhead (allocated and divisional) to the division's two products. What should influence your choice of allocation bases?

b. For yesterday's production run, what is the total manufacturing cost per unit for RAM-A and RAM-B using your recommended approach?

c. Compare your result in requirement (b) with another approach using a different cost-allocation base(s). Explain the source of the difference between full costs per unit for each product.

Problem 10.40
Step Method with Three Service Departments
(LO 1, 4)

Recycle Corporation refurbishes automobiles. It operates two production departments, mechanical repair and body work, and has three service departments for its plant: building occupancy, human resources, and equipment maintenance. Management is concerned that the costs of its service departments are getting too high. In particular, management would like to keep the costs of service departments under $500 per unit on average. You have been asked to allocate budgeted service department costs to the two production departments and compute the expected unit costs.

The company decided that building occupancy costs should be allocated on the basis of the number of square feet used by each production and service department. Human resources costs are allocated on the basis of the number of employees; equipment maintenance costs are allocated on the basis of the dollar value of the equipment in each department. The use of each basis by all departments during the current period follows:

	Used By				
Allocation Base	**Building Occupancy**	**Human Resources**	**Equipment Maintenance**	**Mechanical Repair**	**Body Work**
Building area, sq. ft.	5,000	15,000	10,000	180,000	45,000
Employees	9	5	6	35	50
Equipment value	$ 12,000	$240,000	$ 35,000	$ 624,000	$324,000
Budgeted departmental costs	$360,000	$500,000	$264,000	$1,350,000	$965,000

Required

a. Using the step method, determine the allocated costs and the total costs in each of the two producing departments. The allocation order is (1) building occupancy, (2) human resources, and (3) equipment maintenance.

b. Assume that 1,000 units were processed in each of the two producing departments during the current period. Did the company meet management's standards of keeping service department costs below $500 per unit?

Problem 10.41
Cost Allocation: Direct
Method
(LO 4)

Domino's Foods has a commissary that supplies food and other products to its restaurants. Its two support-service departments, purchasing (S1) and general administration (S2), support two direct-service departments, food products (P1) and supplies (P2). As an internal auditor, you are checking the company's procedures for cost allocation. You find the following cost-allocation results for June:

Costs Allocated to P1	Costs Allocated to P2
$40,000 from S1	$22,500 from S2
? from S2	? from S1

Total costs for the two support-service departments are $100,000. S2's services are provided as follows:

20 percent to S1
50 percent to P1
30 percent to P2

The direct method of allocating costs is used.

Required

a. What are the total support-service department costs (S1 + S2) allocated to P2?

b. Complete the following:

	To	
From	**P1**	**P2**
S1	$40,000	?
S2	?	$22,500

c. What were the proportions of S1's costs allocated to P1 and P2?

Minnesota Products Corporation is reviewing its operations to determine what additional energy-saving projects it might implement. The company's Utah plant has three service departments and two production departments. This plant has its own electric-generating facilities powered by natural gas wells that the company owns and that are located on the same property as the plant. The service departments are natural gas, electricity generation, and general administration. A summary of the use of services by other service departments as well as by the two production departments at the plant follows:

Problem 10.42
Cost Allocation: Step Method with Analysis and Decision Making
(LO 1, 4, 5)

	Services Provided To				
Services From	**Natural Gas (S1)**	**Electricity Generation (S2)**	**General Administration (S3)**	**Fertilizer (P1)**	**Additives (P2)**
Natural gas	—	40%	—	10%	50%
Electricity generation	10%	—	15%	45%	30%
General administration	10%	15%	—	40%	35%
Departmental costs	$70,000	$110,000	$48,000	$600,000	$440,000

The company currently allocates the costs of service departments to production departments using the step method. The local power company indicates it would charge $160,000 per year for the electricity now being generated by the company internally. Management rejected switching to the public utility on the grounds that its rates would cost more than the $110,000 cost of the present company-owned system.

Required

a.   Prepare for management an analysis of the costs of the company's own electric-generating operations. (Use the step method.) The order of allocation is S1, S2, and S3. Should Minnesota Products Corp. purchase or continue to make its own electricity?

b.   Indicate how your analysis would change if the company could realize $58,000 per year from the sale of the natural gas now used for electric generating. (Assume no selling costs.)

Refer to problem 10.42 and the data for Minnesota Products Corporation.

Problem 10.43
Cost-Allocation: Reciprocal Method (Appendix)
(LO 5)

Required

a.   Using the reciprocal method, compute the costs of electricity generation and the costs allocated to production.

b.   Explain the differences in costs for the two methods, step and reciprocal.

Biotech Company's promotion department is responsible for designing and developing all marketing campaign materials and related literature, pamphlets, and brochures. Management is reviewing the effectiveness of the promotion department to determine whether its services could be acquired more economically from an outside promotion agency. Management has received a summary of the promotion department's costs for the most recent year:

Problem 10.44
Cost Allocation and Decision Making
(LO 1, 4)

PROMOTION DEPARTMENT
Costs for the Year Ended November 30

Department costs	$128,750
Charges from other departments	33,460
Allocated share of general administrative overhead	22,125
Total costs	$184,335

Department costs can be traced directly to promotion department activities such as staff and clerical salaries, including related employee benefits, supplies, and so on. Charges from other departments represent the costs of services that other departments of Biotech provide at the promotion department's request. The company has developed a system to charge for such interdepartmental uses of services. For instance, the in-house printing department charges the promotion department for the promotional literature printed. All services provided to the promotion department by other Biotech departments are included in the charges from other departments. General and administrative overhead includes costs such as executive salaries and benefits, depreciation, heat, insurance, and property taxes. These costs are allocated to each department in proportion to the number of its employees.

Required

Prepare a report or visual presentation that explains the usefulness of the cost figures as presented for the promotion department as a basis to compare with a bid from an outside agency to provide the same type of activities that Biotech's promotion department now provides.

[CMA adapted]

Problem 10.45
Service Department Cost Allocation: Direct and Step Methods
(LO 4)

Doxolby Manufacturing Company has three support-service departments (general factory administration, factory maintenance, and factory cafeteria), and two production departments (fabrication and assembly). A summary of costs and other data for each department prior to allocation of service-department costs for the year ended June 30 follows:

	General Factory Admin.	Factory Maintenance	Factory Cafeteria	Fabrication	Assembly
Direct materials	0	$ 65,000	$ 91,000	$3,130,000	$ 950,000
Direct labor	$ 90,000	82,100	87,000	1,950,000	2,050,000
Manufacturing overhead	70,000	56,100	62,000	1,650,000	1,850,000
Total	$160,000	$203,200	$240,000	$6,730,000	$4,850,000
Direct labor hours	31,000	27,000	42,000	562,500	437,500
Number of employees	12	8	20	280	200
Square footage occupied	1,750	2,000	4,800	88,000	72,000

The costs of the service departments are allocated on the following bases: general factory administration department, direct labor hours; factory maintenance department, square feet occupied; and factory cafeteria, number of employees.

Required

Round all final calculations to the nearest dollar.

a.   Assume that Doxolby elects to distribute service department costs to production departments using the direct method. Compute the amount of factory maintenance department costs allocated to the fabrication department.

b.   Assume the same method of allocation as in requirement (a). Compute the amount of general factory administration department costs allocated to the assembly department.

c.   Assuming that Doxolby elects to distribute service department costs to other departments and using the step method (starting with factory cafeteria and then factory maintenance), compute the amount of factory cafeteria department costs allocated to the factory maintenance department.

d.   Assume the method of allocation as in requirement (c). Compute the amount of factory maintenance department costs allocated to factory cafeteria.

[CPA adapted]

Problem 10.46
Cost Allocations: Comparison of Single and Multiple Cost Pools
(LO 2)

SkyBlue Airlines operates a centralized computer center for the data-processing needs of its reservations, scheduling, maintenance, and accounting divisions. Costs associated with use of the computer are charged to the individual departments on the basis of time usage. Due to recent increased competition in the airline industry, the company has decided that it is necessary to more accurately allocate its costs to price its services competitively and profitably. During the current period, the use of data-processing services and the storage capacity required for each of the divisions was as follows (in thousands of seconds for time usage and in gigabytes for storage capacity):

Division	Time Usage	Storage Capacity
Reservations	2,500	1,500
Scheduling	1,700	600
Maintenance	6,300	210
Accounting	5,000	190

During this period, the cost of the computer center amounted to $7,050,000 for time usage and $5,000,000 for storage-related costs.

Required

a. Determine the computer service cost allocations to each division; you may round all decimals to three places. Use:

   (1) A single cost pool and rate based on time used.

   (2) Two cost pools and rates based on time used and capacity used.

b. Write an email memo to management (your instructor) explaining whether to use one or two cost pools and why.

Problem 10.47
Cost Allocation for Travel Reimbursement
(LO 4, 5)

Your company has a travel policy that reimburses employees for the "ordinary and necessary" costs of business travel. Employees often mix a business trip with pleasure either by extending the time at the destination or traveling from the business destination to a nearby resort or other personal destination. When this happens, an allocation must be made between the business and personal portions of the trip. However, the travel policy is unclear on the allocation method to use.

Consider this example. An employee obtained a first-class ticket for $2,640 and traveled the following itinerary:

From	To	Mileage	One-Way Regular Fare	Purpose
Washington, D.C.	Salt Lake City	1,839	$1,400	Business
Salt Lake City	Los Angeles	590	600	Personal
Los Angeles	Washington, D.C.	2,288	1,600	Return

Required

a. Form small groups to compute the business portion of the airfare and state the basis for the indicated allocation that is appropriate according to each of the following independent scenarios:

   (1) Based on the maximum reimbursement for the employee.

   (2) Based on the minimum cost to the company.

b. Prepare a short presentation to management explaining the method that you think should be used and why. What ethical issues do you perceive and how should they be resolved? You do not have to restrict your recommendation to either of the methods in requirement (a).

Cases

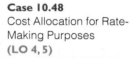

Case 10.48
Cost Allocation for Rate-Making Purposes
(LO 4, 5)

Allied Insurance Company asked the regulatory board for permission to increase the premiums of its insurance operations. Insurance premium rates in the jurisdiction in which Allied operates are designed to cover the operating costs and insurance claims. As a part of Allied's expenses, its agents earn commissions based on premium revenues. Premium revenues also are used to pay claims and to invest in securities.

Administrative expenses include the costs to manage the company's investments and investment services (e.g., retirement annuities). All administrative costs are charged against premium revenue. Allied claims that its insurance operations "just broke even" last year and that a rate increase is necessary. The following income statement (in millions) was submitted to support Allied's request:

Insurance income:	
Premium revenue	$300
Operating costs:	
Claims	205
Administrative	55
Sales commissions	40
Total operating costs	$300
Insurance profit (loss)	0
Investment income	35
Profits after Investment income	$ 35

Further investigation reveals that approximately 20 percent of the sales commissions might be considered related to investment activities. In addition, the investment division uses 30 percent of the support services. The state insurance commission (which sets insurance rates) believes that Allied's insurance activities should earn about 5 percent on its premium revenues.

Required

Form separate groups to prepare responses to the following:

a.   If you were a consumer group, how would you present Allied's income statement? (For example, how would you allocate administrative costs and sales commissions to the insurance income and investment income categories?) What ethical issues do you perceive as a consumer?

b.   If you were Allied's management, what arguments would you present in support of the cost allocations included in the income statement presented in the problem? What ethical issues do you perceive as management?

c.   Meet as opposing groups to resolve the allocation issue with the instructor acting as the mediator.

Case 10.49
University Instructional
Cost Study
(LO 1, 5)

Universities seek to understand their costs of offering services, which include the broad categories of instruction, research, and public service. The largest resource cost is for faculty and staff salaries, which are college- or departmental-level expenditures and, in the short run, do not vary with respect to instructional activities. Since university faculty provide most of the university's services, measuring the costs of the three types of service requires the allocation of faculty salaries. Likewise, expenditures for physical plant and libraries support all three types of service, which requires allocations of these costs.

The method and allocation bases used can affect a university's internal decisions about funding staffing in different colleges and departments and, for public and state universities, can affect decisions by state legislatures and governing boards for appropriations and tuition levels.

Many difficulties exist in developing these cost allocations, including these:

- Different sources of funding could restrict the use of funds. For example, nonstate-supported funds might specify that the funds be used to support research activities only.
- Faculty might teach classes in multiple disciplines.
- Faculty might have different assignments with respect to teaching, research, and public service.
- Different levels of classes (undergraduate, graduate, professional) might require different faculty and support resources.
- General administrative and library resources at the university, campus, college, and department levels provide support for all three types of services.

The Office of Planning and Analysis (OPA) of the University of Minnesota conducted an extensive analysis of the costs of instruction at each of the university's five campuses. One objective of the analysis was to measure the cost of instruction per full-year-equivalent (FYE) student in each department, college, and campus. A FYE student is the equivalent of one student taking a normal course load (30 semester credit hours) for a full academic year. The OPA followed these procedures for determining the instructional costs per FYE student:

1.   *Allocations of departmental resource costs.* Courses and FYE students taught were assigned by department according to course designation (e.g., accounting courses and FYE students taught in those courses were assigned to the accounting department). Instructors and their salaries were matched with courses taught. Faculty salaries (whole or part) were assigned to departments according to the designation of classes. Salaries were added to departmental administrative costs and allocated to FYE students by dividing total departmental costs by total FYE students taught.

2.   *Allocations of support-service costs.* Administrative and support-service costs at the university, campus, and college levels were allocated on the basis of departmental budgets before allocations using the step method. Graduate school administrative costs were allocated using the direct method on the basis of the number of graduate-level credit hours taught. Library costs were allocated directly to research, instruction, and public service based on historical percentages. Other service costs are allocated directly on the basis of FYE student enrollment. These departmental allocations also were divided by total number of FYE students taught.

A summary of results from the most recent OPA analysis at the college level follows:

Comparative Costs of Instruction, University of Minnesota

Campus	College	FYE Student	Departmental Cost per FYE Student	Allocated Cost per FYE Student	Total Cost per FYE Student
Twin Cities	Architecture	381	$ 6,914	$3,449	$10,363
	Biology	1,252	7,006	3,219	10,225
	Education	3,312	4,765	2,916	7,681
	Human ecology	892	5,996	3,325	9,321
	Liberal arts	12,480	4,883	2,621	7,504
	Natural resources	293	4,748	2,689	7,437
	Agriculture	1,185	5,870	3,685	9,555
	Business	2,175	9,059	3,191	12,250
	Dentistry	627	12,129	8,330	20,459
	General college	699	8,303	3,562	11,865
	Public affairs	193	12,501	3,980	16,481
	Engineering	6,627	7,702	3,392	11,094
	Law	801	9,365	2,567	11,932
	Medicine	4,063	15,554	4,422	19,976
	Nursing	368	10,198	4,665	14,863
	Pharmacy	377	15,328	5,040	20,368
	Public health	632	8,441	4,127	12,568
	ROTC	22	12,314	3,300	15,614
	Veterinary	545	14,859	4,991	19,850
	Total Twin Cities	36,924	7,646	3,325	10,971
Duluth	Achievement ctr	39	3,918	2,610	6,528
	Human services	1,107	4,198	2,804	7,002
	Liberal arts	2,071	3,046	2,466	5,512
	Science & engineering	1,970	4,780	2,284	7,064
	Medicine	212	22,944	6,964	29,908
	Business & economics	668	5,268	2,920	8,188
	Fine arts	611	4,498	2,673	7,171
	Total Duluth	6,678	4,740	2,836	7,576
Morris	Academic affairs	1,861	3,663	4,016	7,679
Crookston	Academic affairs	1,043	3,540	4,393	7,934

Required

a. Critique the allocation methods used by OPA to measure cost per FYE student at the college level.

b. A Minnesota state legislator at a recent budget hearing argued, "It is clear that the state could save significant funds by transferring programs from the Twin Cities campus to the Duluth campus. For example, every student in a business program that we transfer from the Twin Cities campus to Duluth would save the state $4,062. And every student in an engineering program that we transfer to Duluth would save nearly $4,030 per student. People are tired of paying high taxes to support inefficient programs. We need to be sure that taxpayers get the most for their money." What are the pros and cons of this argument?

c. How could the OPA figures be used to support higher-education decision making? In what ways are the figures presented either helpful or misleading?

[Adapted from the University of Minnesota's Instructional Cost Study]

Case 10.50
Federal Highway Cost-
Allocation Study
(LO 1, 2, 4, 5)

The U.S. Department of Transportation completed an extensive study of costs and uses of the federal highway system, the Federal Highway Cost Allocation Study (HCAS). This study led to recommendations for significant changes in user fees paid by private citizens (e.g., in fuel taxes) and commercial enterprises (e.g., licenses and fuel taxes paid by highway transportation companies). The costs of highway usage include their construction and repair due to traffic and weather damage. In a major departure from previous studies, the HCAS recommended including environmental impacts, safety, congestion, and noise caused by the federal highway system in the costs to be shared by highway users. Federal highway spending, not including mass transit, environmental impacts, and so on, amounted to approximately $27,102,000,000.

Vehicle miles traveled (VMT) on federal highways continued to be dominated by private automobile traffic as shown:

Passenger Vehicles	VMT Total (millions)	Number of Percentage	Vehicles	Percentage
Autos	1,818,461	67.5%	167,697,897	70.0%
Pickups/Vans	669,198	24.8	63,259,330	26.4
Buses	7,397	0.3	754,509	0.3
Single-unit trucks	83,100	3.1	5,970,431	2.5
Combination trucks	115,689	4.3	1,971,435	0.8
Total	2,693,845	100%	239,653,602	100%

Required

a. Compute highway spending costs per vehicle (by type) by allocating $27,102,000,000 highway spending on the basis of (1) the number of vehicles and (2) the vehicle miles traveled (VMT). Would inequities be created by either of these allocations? Explain.

b. The federal HCAS recommended the following cost pools and allocation bases:

Cost Pool*	Amount	Allocation Base
New construction and pavement replacement	$19.161 billion	VMTs weighted by passenger car equivalents (PCE)†
Bridge construction and replacement	3.757 billion	VMT
Highway enhancements	4.184 billion	VMT weighted by PCE
Mass transit	5.787 billion	VMT

*Not included in the previous total obligations.

†A passenger car equivalent (PCE) measures each type of vehicle's effects on highways compared to an automobile, pickup, or van. On average, a bus has a PCE of 4.0, a single-unit truck has a PCE of 5.4, and a combination truck has a PCE of 10.6. One mile driven by a bus, for example, has 4 times the effect as an automobile, pickup, or van.

Allocate the $27,102,000,000 highway costs to the types of vehicles using these cost pools and allocation bases. Compare them to allocations based on VMT alone.

[Adapted from a Federal Highway Cost Allocation Study.]

Case 10.51
WeCare Hospital: Cost-
Allocation, Step Method
(LO 4, 5)

The annual costs of hospital care under the Medicare program exceed $20 billion per year. In the Medicare legislation, the U.S. Congress mandated that reimbursement to hospitals be limited to the costs of treating Medicare patients. Ideally, neither non-Medicare patients nor hospitals would bear the costs of Medicare patients, nor would the government bear costs of non-Medicare patients. Given the large sums involved, it is not surprising that cost-reimbursement specialists, computer programs, publications, and other products and services provide hospital administrators the assistance needed to obtain an appropriate reimbursement for Medicare patient services.

Hospital departments can be divided into two categories: (1) revenue producing and (2) nonrevenue producing. This classification is simple but useful. The traditional accounting concepts associated with "service department cost allocation," while appropriate to this context, lead to a great deal of confusion in terminology since all of the hospital's departments are considered to be rendering services.

Costs of revenue-producing departments are charged to Medicare and non-Medicare patients on the basis of actual use of the departments. These costs are relatively simple to apportion. Costs of nonrevenue-producing departments are somewhat more difficult to apportion. The approach to finding the appropriate distribution of these costs begins with the establishment of a reasonable basis for allocating nonrevenue-producing department costs to revenue-producing departments. Statistical measures of the relationships between departments must be ascertained. The cost-allocation bases listed in Exhibit 10–11 were established as acceptable for cost-reimbursement purposes. The regulated order of allocation must be used for Medicare reimbursement.

A hospital then can use either the reciprocal method or the step method to solve the cost-allocation problem. If it uses the step method, the order of departments for allocation is the same as that by which the departments are listed in Exhibit 10–11. Thus, depreciation and maintenance, buildings, is allocated before depreciation, movable equipment. Cost centers must be established for each of these nonrevenue-producing costs that are relevant to a particular hospital's operations.

In the past year, WeCare Hospital reported the following departmental costs:

Nonrevenue producing:
Laundry and linen.. $ 250,000
Depreciation and maintenance, buildings 830,000
Employee health and welfare 375,000
Maintenance of personnel 210,000
Central supply 745,000
Revenue producing:
Operating room 1,450,000
Radiology 160,000
Laboratory 125,000
Patient rooms 2,800,000

Percentage usage of one department's services by another department follows:

| | To Nonrevenue Producing | | | | |
From	**Laundry and Linen**	**Depreciation and Maintenance, Buildings**	**Employee Health and Welfare**	**Maintenance of Personnel**	**Central Supply**
Laundry and linen	—	5%	10%	—	—
Depreciation and maintenance, buildings	10%	—	—	10%	—
Employee health and welfare	15	—	—	5%	3%
Maintenance of personnel.......................	—	—	—	—	12%
Central supply	10	—	—	8%	—

| | To Revenue Producing | | | |
From	**Operating Rooms**	**Radiology**	**Laboratory**	**Patient Rooms**
Laundry and linen	30%	10%	5%	40%
Depreciation and maintenance, buildings	5	2	2	71
Employee health and welfare	25	5	4	43
Maintenance of personnel	36	10	8	34
Central supply	9	4	3	66

The percentage usage of revenue-producing department services by Medicare and other patients follows:

	Medicare	**Other**
Operating rooms	25%	75%
Radiology	20	80
Laboratory..	28	72
Patient rooms...	36	64

Required

What is the amount of the reimbursement claim for Medicare services, using the step method of allocation? Use this order of allocation: (1) Depreciation and maintenance, buildings (2) employee health and welfare, (3) laundry and linen, (4) maintenance of personnel, and (5) central supply.

Exhibit 10–11

Bases for Allocating
Nonrevenue-Producing
Department Costs to
Revenue-Producing
Departments

Nonrevenue Cost Center	Basis for Allocation
Depreciation and maintenance, buildings	Square feet in each department
Depreciation, movable equipment	Dollar value of equipment in each department
Employee health and welfare	Gross salaries in each department
Administrative and general	Accumulated costs by department
Maintenance and repairs	Square feet in each department
Operation of plant	Square feet in each department
Laundry and linen	Pounds used in each department
Housekeeping	Hours of service to each department
Dietary	Meals served in each department
Maintenance of personnel	Number of departmental employees
Nursing administration	Hours of supervision in each department
Central supply	Costs of requisitions processed
Pharmacy	Costs of drug orders processed
Medical records	Hours worked for each department
Social service	Hours worked for each department
Nursing school	Assigned time by department
Intern/resident service	Assigned time by department

[Adapted from a case prepared by Ed Deakin.]

Planning and Decision Making

◀ **A Look Back**

Part Three discussed process costing and cost allocation.

▼ **A Look at This Part**

Part Four includes methods of developing and using cost information for decision making. Chapter 11 describes cost estimation methods. Chapter 12 shows how to develop financial and cost-volume-profit models. Chapter 13 discusses the use of cost information in short-term decision making. Chapter 14 discusses strategic issues in making capital-investment decisions. Chapter 15 covers financial planning and the development of budgets.

▶ **A Look Ahead**

Part Five discusses methods of measuring performance.

Chapter 11

Cost Estimation

After completing this chapter, you should be able to:

1. State the reasons that companies estimate relations between costs and cost drivers.

2. Recognize the following basic cost patterns: variable, fixed, step (semifixed), and mixed.

3. Use and interpret simple and multiple regression for cost estimation.

4. Use and interpret account analysis for cost estimation.

5. Use and interpret the engineering method for cost estimation.

6. Understand how regression works and identify potential statistical problems with regression analysis (Appendix A).

7. Estimate and use learning curve cost predictions (Appendix B).

Cost-Management Challenges

(Solutions are on page 443.)

1. **After** doing the multiple regression analysis, what additional information did Leah Cohen require to estimate costs using account analysis?

2. **Based** on information from the cost estimates and considering C.C. Catering's new strategy, will the company be successful in the future?

EMAIL MEMORANDUM

To: LMCohen@xxxxxx.com

From: JTChun@xxxxxx.com

Re: Future of C.C. Catering (and us)

Hi Leah:

I hope you enjoyed your trip to New Mexico while I was stuck doing the end-of-semester cleanup. It was quiet while you were gone, which gave me a chance to do some serious thinking about our future. I did some quick calculations that indicate we will not be profitable this year; close, but not quite. I am disappointed. I thought we would be in the black this year because of our solid revenue growth.

I think it's time to do some serious analysis of our costs. We should start by identifying cost drivers and estimating cost-driver rates. Do you remember that grouchy old Professor Maier who taught us that cost-driver rates indicate how activities consume costs? We need to know that information to manage our costs better. Also, we need better cost information to make some decisions that I've been thinking about. But more on that when we're both in the office.

Welcome back!

Jessie

After getting food poisoning from eating catered food at a luncheon for business honor students at their university, Jessie Chun and Leah Cohen decided to start their own company, a catering service, called C.C. Catering. With their contacts around the university and those of their families, who were heavily involved in community activities, Chun and Cohen believed that they could attract plenty of customers. Starting in the spring of their junior year in college, C.C. Catering provided Chun and Cohen with good part-time work. In fact, C.C. Catering eventually provided them with enough opportunity and fun that they turned down offers from several public accounting firms and industry to work full-time in the catering service. Three years later, revenues continue to grow, but Chun and Cohen are disappointed in the lack of profits.

C.C. Catering provides packaged sandwiches and salads in clear plastic containers (box lunches). The company provides food to numerous official university functions (e.g., administrative meetings), executive education and extension programs, university field trips, and business meetings in town.

Chun and Cohen take a small monthly management salary of $500 each, in addition to paying themselves $15 per hour for each hour worked to obtain customers, prepare meals, deliver meals, and perform other nonmanagement aspects of the operations. At present, both Chun and Cohen own minivans for delivering meals. The company reimburses them at $.30 per mile for deliveries. At the end of each fiscal year (June 30), they decide how much of the operating profit to put back into the business and share the rest 50-50. So far, that calculation has not been done because C.C. Catering has had no operating profit.

Chun and Cohen decide that it is now time to turn from growing their business to focusing on managing costs and creating profits. In addition, they face an opportunity to subcontract the meal preparation part of the business, and they are considering a strategic change in the business that would emphasize bigger jobs as their core business.

They begin a process of estimating costs for three purposes:

1. *Cost management.* What are the opportunities for reducing costs without reducing value to customers?
2. *Decision making.* How can they change their pricing policy to discourage particular customers and attract others? Should they subcontract the meal preparation part of the business?
3. *Strategic planning.* Is there a better customer mix and market niche than they currently have?

Cost Estimation

Cost estimation is the process of estimating the relations between costs and the cost drivers that cause those costs. For example, suppose you are trying to reduce your own personal transportation costs (that is, you are a personal cost-management analyst). You normally drive your car 15,000 miles per year, including commuting. If you use public transportation for commuting, you could reduce the annual mileage to 10,000 miles. How much would you save in automobile costs if you reduced driving by 5,000 miles per year?

The answer to that question is not easy because, as you know, some costs are related to the number of miles driven and others are not. Licensing costs are probably not related to the activity—miles driven—whereas fuel costs are. Repairs and depreciation costs are related to miles driven, but perhaps not proportionately.

Costs Do Not Just Happen

As we have emphasized throughout this book, costs do not just happen; they are caused by activities. The challenge for cost-management analysts is to identify the activities that cause costs, to estimate the relation between costs and their causes, and to manage the activities that cause those costs, as shown in Exhibit 11–1. This chapter deals with the middle part of the process shown in Exhibit 11–1, the relation between activities and costs.

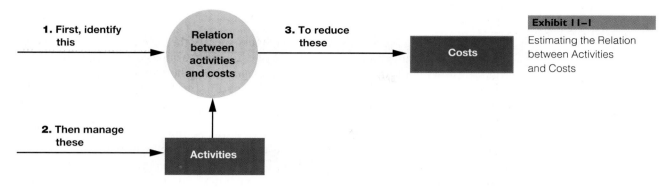

Exhibit 11–1

Estimating the Relation between Activities and Costs

Reasons for Estimating Costs

Organizations estimate costs primarily for three reasons:

1. To manage costs.
2. To make decisions.
3. To plan and set standards.

LO 1 State the reasons that companies estimate relations between costs and cost drivers.

Cost Management

As discussed in previous chapters, companies must manage costs to be successful. Many companies have gone out of business because they did not manage costs. Many factories have shut down because managers did not manage costs effectively. Some counties and cities have faced bankruptcy because of poor cost management.

For C.C. Catering, estimating the relation between costs and activities will help Chun and Cohen understand how to make the production process more efficient. If they find, for example, that the costs of delivering and setting up each catering job are high, then they should focus on ways to reduce delivery and setup costs. If such costs are not significant, then they should turn their attention to better opportunities for cost management.

Decision Making

In deciding among alternative actions, managers must know the costs that each alternative is likely to incur. These are examples of typical questions that require cost estimates for decision making:

■ University of Illinois administrators ask: "What will happen to total costs if we expand the student health center?" Decision: If estimated total costs do not increase much, the university expands the health center.

■ Managers at Accenture ask: "How much will it cost to perform the Department of Motor Vehicles information systems job?" Decision: If the cost of the job plus an adequate margin is below the price that Accenture can charge, then it does the job.

■ Managers of Starbucks ask: "How much will it cost for us to make display racks compared to the cost of buying them?" Decision: If it costs Starbucks less to buy the racks than to make them, then it buys them.

■ C.C. Catering currently prepares the meals that it sells. Chun and Cohen are considering outsourcing meal preparation to a local sandwich shop. To decide whether to outsource meal preparation, they should know the cost of preparing meals to compare with a meal preparation bid from the sandwich shop.

These are just a few of the numerous decisions that require the knowledge of the estimated costs of the alternatives being considered. Of course, cost comparison is not the only basis for decision making, but it is a major one—*the* major one in many instances. We discuss decision making in more detail in Chapters 12, 13, and 14.

Planning and Standard Setting

In planning an organization's future, managers specify the activities that they expect people in the organization to perform. Cost estimation assigns a cost to those activities. By knowing the costs of activities, managers know how much cost the organization will likely incur, which is helpful for preparing pro forma financial statements and estimating cash flows. Cost estimation also helps set standards for employee performance by estimating what the costs should be for performing particular activities.

At C.C. Catering, Chun and Cohen have estimated the costs of meal preparation to set standards. They use these standards to evaluate the performance of undergraduate students hired to help prepare meals. The main reason to consider outsourcing the meal preparation is that their best workers have graduated and taken jobs in public accounting and industry, leaving Chun and Cohen wondering what will happen to costs when they hire and train several new employees.

A Simple Model: One Cost Driver and Fixed/Variable Cost Behavior

LO 2 Recognize the following basic cost patterns: variable, fixed, step (semifixed), and mixed.

The two key issues in estimating the relation between costs and activities are (1) the number of cost drivers and (2) the cost behavior. The first issue, the number of cost drivers, refers to the number of factors that analysts believe cause costs. Analysts use only one cost driver in the simplest model. Our discussion of activity-based costing in previous chapters in this book assumes a more complex model with multiple cost drivers. In a Hewlett-Packard plant in Germany, for example, analysts used more than 100 cost drivers in their cost estimation.

The simplest cost behavior pattern is the breakdown of costs into fixed and variable components. You are already familiar with the term *variable costs*. You know that total variable costs change proportionately with total activity. The simple model of one cost driver assumes that costs separate simply into fixed and variable components, and costs increase linearly with the cost driver. In this simple model, analysts estimate the following cost equation:

$$TC = F + VX$$

where

TC	=	total costs
F	=	fixed costs that do not vary with the cost driver, but can vary with other management decisions
V	=	variable costs per cost driver unit = cost driver rate
X	=	the number of cost driver units

Exhibit 11–2 depicts this simple relation when the cost driver is miles driven for an automobile and the amounts are the monthly costs that we estimate for a particular automobile. This relation, in either algebraic or graphical form, is a *model,* which is a representation of reality.

This simple cost model of fixed and variable components misses other important types of cost behavior that we discuss later in the chapter. It also ignores the impact of other cost drivers on costs, as you know from our discussion of activity-based costing. Nevertheless, this simple model can be useful and sometimes can satisfy a cost-benefit test better than a more complex, albeit more accurate, cost model.

For example, suppose a company contemplates launching a new product for which managers have not fully worked out the product's specifications. The simple model could give managers a rough idea of whether it is worthwhile to proceed with more detailed specifications. For companies with simple operations, the simple model can capture the relation between costs and activities rather well. The manager of a taxicab company could find it sufficient to estimate the variable cost per mile driven, for example, or a retail store that pays commissions instead of salaries might find that more than 90 percent of its costs either vary proportionately with dollar sales or are fixed costs.

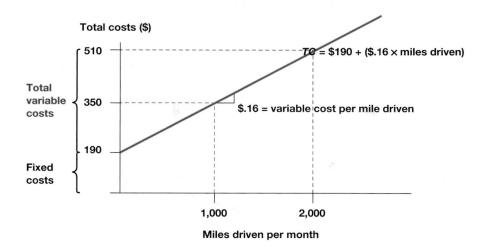

Exhibit 11–2
Simple Model:
Automobile Costs

This chapter discusses estimating costs for both simple and complex environments. That way you will be armed for whatever situation you encounter.

A More Complex Model: Multiple Cost Drivers and Complex Cost Behavior

Cost-Benefit Test

A more complex cost model has multiple cost drivers and more complex cost behavior than the simple model just described. As a manager or analyst, you choose how complex to make the cost estimation model. No "generally accepted rules" dictate how simple or complex to make the model, but good business sense says that you should apply a cost-benefit test to the choice of model complexity. Because you probably will not know what the costs and benefits of a particular cost estimation model are until you have estimated them, you are stuck with the task of attempting cost-benefit analysis before you have a good idea of either the costs or the benefits. Benefits can include improved accuracy and descriptiveness. Costs can be more difficult to predict, but they include the costs of measuring, gathering, *and* maintaining the data necessary for the analysis now and in the future. Avoid complexity just for the sake of complexity and simplicity just for the sake of simplicity. Common sense and experience (and this chapter) should guide you.

Step Costs

Costs follow many patterns in the real world. Unlike the simple model presented previously, some costs increase in steps and in curvilinear patterns as activity levels increase.[1]

Step costs appear as shown in Exhibit 11–3. A **step cost,** also called a **semifixed cost,** is a cost that increases in steps as the amount of the cost-driver volume increases. Many labor costs are step costs. In Exhibit 11–3, the costs are for delivery people for C.C. Catering. One delivery person can handle the delivery, setup, and cleanup for 50 meals in the two-hour period. In this example, the step increments are the number of delivery people for each two-hour food delivery period. The cost driver is the number of meals. If the number of meals to be delivered is less than 50, the company hires one

---

[1] For example, E. Noreen and N. Soderstrom, "Are Overhead Costs Strictly Proportional to Activity? Evidence from Hospital Service Departments," found that department overhead costs in a large sample of hospitals are not proportional to the activities in the departments. Their results imply that at least some overhead costs increase in steps and that at least some overhead costs are curvilinear. (Full citations to references are in the Bibliography.)

Exhibit 11–3

Step Costs: Costs of
Delivery Labor

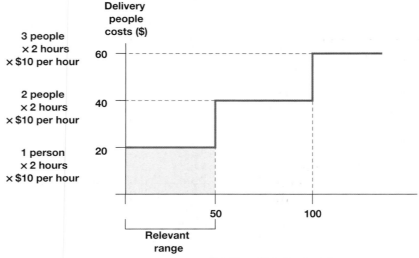

3 people
× 2 hours
× $10 per hour

2 people
× 2 hours
× $10 per hour

1 person
× 2 hours
× $10 per hour

Food servers can serve
more than one person, so
an increase in the number
of customers increases the
number of food servers in
steps.

delivery person for a two-hour period. If the number of meals is in the 51–100 range for a particular job, management increases the number of delivery people to two, and so forth as Exhibit 11–3 shows.

Step costs are common when people are hired in time increments, such as hourly, daily, or monthly. Examples include nurses in hospital departments where the number of nurses increases in steps as the number of patients increases; waiters and waitresses in restaurants; service personnel at rental car counters; and teachers at universities. In our experience, managers often ignore these steps, assuming that the step costs are either purely fixed or variable. Research shows, however, that managers can make erroneous decisions by treating step costs as variable costs.[2]

Relevant range. Managers also rely on the concept of relevant range to deal with step costs. Recall from Chapter 2 that the *relevant range* is the range over which the company expects to operate. Within this range, managers assume particular cost behavior patterns that are reasonably accurate. Such patterns would not necessarily be accurate outside the relevant range, however. For example, assume that C.C. Catering does not usually deliver more than 50 meals per job. Management could assume that 1 to 50 meals per job constitutes the relevant range, as shown in Exhibit 11–3. As long as a delivery person is needed at all, food delivery labor is a fixed cost. However, if the number of meals for a job increases to 75—outside the relevant range—then the assumption that food delivery labor is fixed and, therefore, does not vary with volume is no longer valid.

[2] See M. W. Maher and M. L. Marais. "A Field Study on the Limitations of Activity-Based Costing When Resources Are Provided on a Joint and Indivisible Basis."

Mixed Costs

Costs can also be **mixed costs,** which have both a fixed and variable component. Some utilities offer products (e.g., electricity, water) for a fixed cost up to a particular volume (which can be zero) after which they charge per unit. Exhibit 11–4 shows the mixed cost for C.C. Catering's cellular telephone plan that charges $40 per month for up to 600 minutes per month of airtime and then charges $.10 per minute for each minute used over 600. Compensation costs sometimes are mixed, as when a person earns a percentage bonus in addition to a salary for generating profits over a threshold.

Nonlinear Cost Behavior

The cost behavior patterns presented so far have been straight lines or sections of straight lines. Costs can also be curved. At C.C. Catering, for example, food costs are variable. Suppose the company receives a discount based on the volume of bread it buys, with the discount increasing as the volume purchased increases. Line A in Exhibit 11–5 represents variable costs that decrease per unit as volume per period increases.

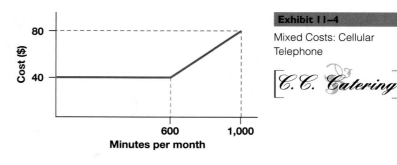

Exhibit 11–4

Mixed Costs: Cellular Telephone

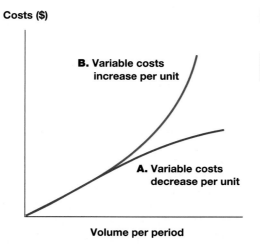

Exhibit 11–5

Nonlinear Cost Behavior

Line B represents variable costs that increase per unit as volume per period increases. An example of such a cost is the cost of energy in steel plants. If volume of steel production is low, companies use the most energy-efficient methods to produce steel. As volume per period increases, companies find it necessary to use less energy-efficient methods. Consequently, energy is a variable cost whose rate increases as the volume of steel production per period increases.

Cost-Estimation Methods

We now turn to the specific methods of cost estimation. Recall that C.C. Catering has grown to a level where Chun and Cohen want to measure costs for cost-management, decision-making, and planning purposes. We discuss three methods commonly used in practice:

1. Statistical methods (using regression analysis).
2. Account analysis.
3. Engineering estimates.

Results are likely to differ from method to method. Consequently, organizations often apply more than one approach to be able to compare and verify results. Managers and analysts who bear ultimate responsibility for all cost estimates frequently apply their own best judgment as a final step in the estimation process. Estimation methods, therefore, should be seen as ways to help management to arrive at the best estimates possible—not as the final answer themselves. The weaknesses of cost-estimation methods as well as their strengths require attention.

Statistical Cost Estimation Using Simple Regression Analysis

LO 3 Use and interpret simple and multiple regression for cost estimation.

This section discusses the use of regression analysis to estimate the relation between costs and cost drivers. **Regression analysis** is a statistical method used to create an equation relating independent (or X) variables to dependent (or Y) variables. Regression analysis uses data from the past to estimate relation between costs, which are the dependent variables, and activities, which are the independent variables and will be valid in the future. In particular, this technique will enable you to estimate the cost-driver rates that were given in examples in previous chapters.

The objective of cost estimation is to establish the existence of a cause-and-effect relationship between cost drivers and the cost to be estimated. These cost drivers are X terms or independent variables of a regression equation. **Independent variables** are the cost drivers that the analyst believes cause, or at least are correlated with, the dependent variable, costs. The cost to be estimated is the dependent variable, or the Y term. **Dependent variables** are caused by, or at least correlated with, independent variables. The distinction between dependent and independent variables should make sense because costs do not just happen, they *depend* on cost drivers. We refer to the Y term as TC because the Y variable is always some measure of total cost (TC) in our analyses. Depending on the context, TC can refer to the total costs of the organization, total overhead costs of the organization, or some other measure of total cost.

Regression analysis generates an equation or, visually, a line that best fits a set of data points. In addition, regression techniques provide information that helps a manager to ascertain how well the estimated regression equation describes the relation between costs and cost drivers.

Many moderately priced handheld calculators have regression capabilities. Computer spreadsheets such as Microsoft® Excel and Lotus 1-2-3® have regression capabilities. More powerful statistical packages such as Minitab, SAS, and SPSS are designed to run regressions. We leave descriptions of the computational details to statistics courses. Instead, we deal here with regression from the standpoint of accountants and managers who must use and interpret regression analyses. (Appendix A to this chapter discusses some of the more technical considerations that might interest those who might perform or use these analyses.)

Simple Model for Regression Analysis

Earlier in this chapter, we discussed the simple model with one cost driver. This model is a useful way to get a basic understanding about how to apply regression analysis to cost management. Later we shall discuss a more complex model.

As noted earlier in this chapter, in a simple model with one cost driver and costs divided simply into fixed and variable components, analysts estimate the following cost equation:

$$TC = F + VX$$

where

TC	=	total costs
F	=	fixed costs that do not vary with the cost driver
V	=	variable costs per unit for the cost driver
X	=	the independent variable, or cost driver

The regression model is called **simple regression** because it has only one independent variable.

Although regression programs accept any data for the Y and X terms, entering numbers that have no plausible relation will give you misleading estimates. The following are some relation between costs and cost drivers that make economic sense:

Costs (dependent variables)	Cost Drivers (independent variables)
Costs to operate an automobile	Number of miles driven
Costs to teach students	Number of students taught
Costs to operate C.C. Catering	Number of meals sold

As you can see, picking cost-activity relationships often just requires common sense.

Application of Simple Regression Analysis to C.C. Catering

Cohen and Chun followed five steps during their simple regression analysis to find an explanation of total costs. The steps were to:

1. Identify plausible cost drivers (*X* variables).
2. Gather relevant data.
3. Plot data in a scattergraph and correct data, if necessary.
4. Perform the regression analysis.
5. Interpret the regression results.

We now describe these steps.

Step 1: Identify a logical relation between costs and their drivers. The first, and perhaps most important, task is to identify the cost drivers. If an organization's structure, technology, processes, and supply markets have been stable, it is reasonable to use data from the past to estimate cost-driver rates. However, if the past relation is no longer valid, then it is necessary to adjust the cost-driver rates to reflect current conditions.

Over time, the cost-activity relation could change, making the past data inappropriate for estimating the future. This is a problem particularly for many high-tech companies and companies that have products with short life cycles.

Although the use of past data for future cost estimation has limitations, in many cases it is reliable. Using past data can be relatively inexpensive for analysts and managers because many data are available in the records. Cost estimations based on *past* data show *past* relationships between costs and activities. Past relations between costs and cost drivers can be a meaningful starting point for estimating the future relation between costs and activities as long as decision makers recognize the limitations of using past data, which might not reflect the future.

Cohen and Chun pooled their knowledge to identify several plausible cost drivers. They believed that the number of meals sold was the most important (all meals prepared are sold).

Relevant range of activity. As discussed earlier in this chapter, the limits within which a cost projection is valid represent the relevant range for that estimate. For example, if C.C. Catering has been producing between 1,000 and 4,000 meals per month, the relevant range of its cost estimates is valid between 1,000 and 4,000 meals. If C.C. Catering expects to produce between, say, 8,000 and 10,000 meals per month in the future, the cost estimates obtained from data for 1,000 to 4,000 meals might not be valid. We say that producing outside the 1,000 to 4,000 meal range is *outside the relevant range.*

Think of the problem of walking in winter on a lake that is frozen over. You have experience that the ice is thick enough to hold you between shoreline and 10 feet out from shoreline. That is the relevant range. When you get farther than 10 feet from shoreline, you are no longer in the relevant range. Your estimates of the relation between your weight and the ice thickness could no longer be accurate. In a similar way, managers might still use the cost estimates even though the company is operating outside the relevant range, but managers should be aware that they can be "walking on thin ice."

Step 2: Gather relevant data. For the second step of the analysis, Leah Cohen collected from company records the dataset that appears in Exhibit 11–6. (Recall that the first step was to describe plausible cost drivers.) These data are the total costs of operating the company and the number of meals sold each month for the past 16 months. It is important to note that these data were generated during an extended period of stable prices and consistent catering processes. Sometimes activities are greatly changed or new, and consistent cost and cost-driver data are not available. In these cases, analysts might feel uncomfortable using historical data to estimate future costs and use other cost estimation methods, which are described later in this chapter.

Although many specialized statistical software packages exist, Cohen entered the data into a Microsoft® Excel spreadsheet because she and Chun use Excel for financial modeling (see Chapter 12) and because it has convenient graphing and statistical analysis capabilities.

Step 3: Plot data in a scattergraph and correct data, if necessary.   After checking for data-entry errors, Cohen used Excel's chart "wizard," a step-by-step menu, for the third step to prepare a scattergraph with total costs as the *Y* variable and meals as the *X* variable. The **scattergraph** plots costs against activity levels and appears as Exhibit 11–7. Observe several things about this graph. First, note that the data lie in an upward-sloping pattern, scattered around a line that has been drawn through the data. This pattern suggests a positive relation between total costs and meals, as expected.

Second, note that none of the data points lie an unusual distance from the line. Some scatter is always expected (indeed, no scatter is suspect), but any points that lie much farther than others from the line indicate possible data-entry errors, measurement errors, or effects of other cost drivers that are not modeled in a simple regression. These data points, sometimes called *outliers,* should be investigated. The investigation might uncover errors that can be corrected, but, if the data are correct, they should not be discarded even if they appear to have a bad fit with the other data. Instead, the analyst should seek to find other causes or cost drivers of the data. A truly unusual event can cause unusual costs, such as a rare labor strike or a 100-year storm. This probably means that the unusual data point(s) should be removed from the dataset for simple regression analysis but not discarded. Analysts could learn about the impacts of uncontrollable events that can affect decision making about contracts, negotiations,

Exhibit 11–6

Input Data from Company Records

C.C. Catering

Month	Total Costs	Meals
Jan, last year	$ 6,720	1,280
Feb	6,640	2,021
Mar	7,270	1,620
Apr	12,600	2,830
May	11,570	3,630
Jun	8,400	2,383
Jul	10,880	2,460
Aug	10,180	2,640
Sep	13,050	3,620
Oct	9,200	2,840
Nov	8,400	1,937
Dec	8,000	1,650
Jan, this year	5,110	1,260
Feb	5,840	1,850
Mar	6,320	1,710
Apr	10,290	2,940

Exhibit 11–7

Scattergraph of Total Costs and Meals

C.C. Catering

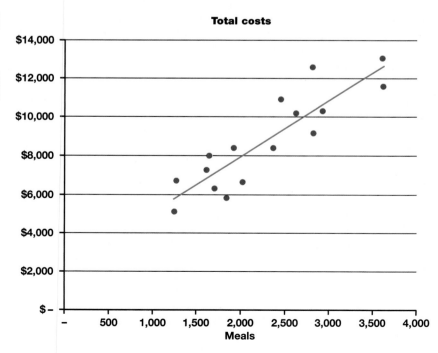

insurance coverage, and the like from these data. In the case of Exhibit 11–7, Cohen would have preferred that the data lie closer to the line but found no errors or evidence of unusual events.

Step 4: Perform the regression analysis.   Cohen completed the fourth step of the simple regression analysis by using Excel's data analysis tool. She selected the "regression" menu item, and with the regression wizard chose the column of total costs as the *Y* variable (dependent) and the column of meals as the *X* variable (independent). Exhibit 11–8 shows information that resulted from the regression output. (*Note:* This chapter's Appendix A presents more details about typical regression choices and regression output.) This abbreviated output contains the most important output details for this stage of our discussion.

Step 5: Interpret the regression results.   The fifth step of the analysis is the interpretation of the regression results. The first number of importance is labeled "R-square" of the regression, which is 0.7843. The **R-square** (R^2) is the proportion of the variation in the *Y* or dependent variable (total costs in Cohen's case) that is explained by the *X* or independent variable (the number of meals in Cohen's case). The R-square can vary between 0.00 and 1.00. An R-square value of 0.00 indicates no relation—none of the variance in *Y* is explained by *X*. However, a value of 1.00 indicates a perfect relation—100 percent of the variation in *Y* is explained by *X*. R-square usually lies between the extremes, and it measures how well the regression fits the data. Values close to 1.00 give the analyst confidence that he or she has found a reliable cost driver. Cohen believed that the R-square value of 0.7843 (78.43 percent) confirmed her belief that the number of meals sold drives total costs. Because R-square is not 1.00 (100 percent), she realized that other cost drivers probably exist. We describe her investigation of this possibility later.

The second set of important numbers in Exhibit 11–8 is labeled "independent variable" "coefficients" for "Intercept" and "Meals." These numbers, or coefficients, are the components of the linear cost equation sought by Cohen. Every straight line has an intercept and a slope. The coefficient for the intercept, $2,153.30, is where the line intersects the *Y* axis, as shown in Exhibit 11–9. Cohen reasonably

Dependent variable = Total costs	
Independent Variable	**Regression Coefficients**
Intercept	$2,153.30
Meals	$ 2.891
R-square	0.7843

Exhibit 11–8

Abbreviated and Reformatted Least Squares Regression Output

Exhibit 11–9

Scattergraph with Regression Line

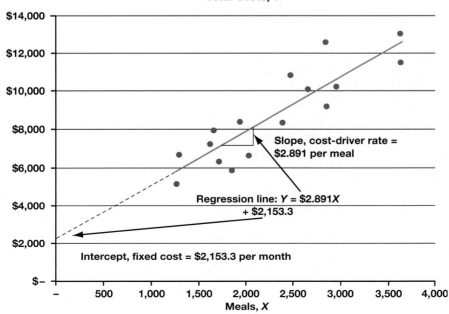

interpreted this figure as an estimate of monthly fixed costs. However, she realized that the intercept is measured at a level of zero meals sold, which is well outside the relevant range of data. Therefore, the safest interpretation of the intercept is that it is an estimate of the intercept *within* the relevant range (between 1,260 and 3,630 meals in Cohen's case). This estimate might not be reliable at meal levels much outside the relevant range. The coefficient for meals is the slope of the line, which measures the rate of change of Y with a single unit change of X (again, within the relevant range). One can interpret this figure, $2.891, as the meal cost-driver rate or the variable cost per meal sold.

C.C. Catering's cost estimation equation based on this regression result is:

Estimated total costs, Y = Intercept + Cost-driver rate × Level of activity, X
Estimated total costs = \$2,153.30 per month + \$2.891 × Number of meals sold

Next month, C.C. Catering expects to sell 3,000 meals. Estimated total costs are computed as follows:

Estimated total costs = \$2,153.30 per month + \$2.891 × 3,000 meals sold
Estimated total costs = \$10,826

Recall that these estimates of fixed and variable costs are reliable *only* within the relevant range and assume that the number of meals sold is the only cost driver. Both estimates might be measured inaccurately if other cost drivers exist. Cohen later made more precise estimates using more cost drivers. Nevertheless, her simple model provides enough information for a basic discussion of regression analysis. The simple model also is useful as a first approximation of the company's total cost-activity relations.

Use of the Regression Results

As noted at the beginning of this chapter, Chun and Cohen wish to use cost estimates for cost management, decision making, and planning. Starting with cost management, they want to estimate the cost of activities to identify which activities are costly. Costly activities get attention, but one must first know which ones are costly. The simple regression results shown in Exhibit 11–8 are not much help for cost management. After seeing the results, Chun turned to Cohen and said, "Well, we have an estimate of the variable cost per meal, but I don't see how we can use that information to become more efficient."

Cohen agreed, "Right, you are. This result just gives us a ballpark estimate of the variable cost of each meal without any of the detail that we need to manage costs. Still, it's comforting to know the variable cost estimate isn't more than we charge for meals. Then we would be in big trouble."

Cost estimation and computer analysis go hand in hand.

Cohen and Chun could use the cost estimate for decision making. They are considering outsourcing meal preparation to a local sandwich shop. To decide whether to do so, they want to know the cost of preparing meals to compare with a meal preparation bid from the sandwich shop.

Despite the limitations noted here, the simple regression estimate could be informative for particular decisions and for planning. Suppose that C.C. Catering plans to sell 3,000 meals next month at an average price of $4 per meal. Cohen and Chun would like to know how much profit the company would make.

The revenue estimate is \$12,000 (\$4 × 3,000 meals). The total cost estimates are based on the regression equation shown in Exhibit 11–8. The estimated costs for the month for 3,000 meals are:

$$\text{Estimated total costs} = \$2,153 + (\$2.891 \times 3,000 \text{ meals})$$
$$= \$10,826 \text{ (rounded)}$$

Therefore, they expect to show a profit (loss) of

$$\text{Operating profit (loss)} = \text{Total revenue} - \text{Total costs}$$
$$= \$12,000 - \$10,826$$
$$= \$1,174$$

Cohen and Chun use this information in their personal planning and in thinking about getting a bank loan to remodel their space. With good job prospects in industry and public accounting, they also ask themselves whether it is worthwhile to continue this company. Cohen asks, "Should we close up shop and get a 'paid' job?" Chun responds that the business provides them with some personal income from the \$15 per hour wage and \$500 per month management "salary" (both amounts are included in the preceding cost figures) plus income for the business that should influence the bank favorably. Nevertheless, they would like to find ways to be more efficient and increase profits. To do that, they know they will have to perform activity-based management, which will require a more sophisticated cost analysis than they have done so far (see Chapter 5).

High-Low Method

The **high-low method** estimates a cost function using only the costs and level of cost-driver activity from the highest and lowest levels of cost-driver activity. The high-low method is a simple "back of the envelope" way to get estimates of the slope and intercept of a straight line using just two points of data. Using the high-low method, one can either draw a straight line between the highest and lowest points to the Y axis or compute the slope and intercept mathematically using the formula for a straight line.

The high-low method has generally been replaced by the use of spreadsheets and regression analysis. Nevertheless, some people still use it, and it occasionally appears on professional examinations such as the CPA exam. We explain it here so you will not be caught unaware if you hear or read the term "high-low method." However, we regard it as inferior to the regression method because it uses only two data points.

Application of the High-Low Method to C.C. Catering

The following explains how to compute the cost function using the data from C.C. Catering. First, compute the slope of the straight line between the highest and lowest cost-driver level (i.e., number of meals) at C.C. Catering:

$$\text{Slope} = \text{(Cost at highest number of meals} - \text{Cost at lowest number of}$$
$$\text{meals)/(Highest number of meals} - \text{Lowest number of meals)}$$
$$= (\$11,570 \text{ in May, previous year} - \$5,110 \text{ in January, current}$$
$$\text{year)/(3,630 meals in May, previous year} - 1,260 \text{ meals in January,}$$
$$\text{current year)}$$
$$= \$2.73 \text{ per meal}$$

This compares with the estimate of \$2.89 (rounded) per meal in the regression results in Exhibits 11–8 and 11–9.

Second, compute the intercept by starting with the total cost at either the highest or lowest cost-driver level and then subtracting the estimated total variable cost at that activity:

$$\text{Intercept} = \text{Total cost at highest cost-driver level}$$
$$- \text{(Variable cost per unit} \times \text{Highest cost-driver level)}$$

or

$$\text{Intercept} = \text{Total cost at lowest cost-driver level}$$
$$- (\text{Variable cost per unit} \times \text{Lowest cost-driver level})$$

Using the highest cost-driver level, which is 3,630 meals sold in the previous May at a total cost of $11,570, subtract the total variable costs as follows:

$$\text{Intercept} = \$11,570 - (\$2.73 \times 3,630 \text{ meals sold})$$
$$= \$1,676 \text{ (rounded)}$$

Therefore, the high-low cost equation is:

$$\text{Total costs} = \$1,676 + (\$2.73 \times \text{Number of meals})$$

Comparing these high-low estimates to the estimated intercept in the regression results shown in Exhibit 11–8 of $2,153 (rounded) indicates that the estimated fixed costs are higher (and estimated variable costs per unit are lower) using the high-low method. We have more confidence in the regression results because regression incorporates all input data in the analysis whereas the high-low method incorporates only two points in the analysis.

Use of Multiple Regression Analysis to Estimate Cost-Driver Rates

Multiple regression is a regression equation with more than one independent variable. Using multiple regression analyses, company analysts might learn more about cost behavior than they do from simple regression. Furthermore, multiple regression has potentially greater explanatory power; that is, more of the variation in the dependent variable (total costs) can be explained by including more independent variables (cost drivers). Multiple regression requires gathering more data, which can be time consuming if the organization does not have a good information system.

Application of Multiple Regression Analysis to C.C. Catering

As noted earlier in this chapter, some organizations use many cost drivers. Analysts face a cost-benefit trade-off in choosing the number of cost drivers. More cost drivers require more data but probably provide better information. For example, as shown in Research Insight 11.1, researchers using multiple regression found that, for the compa-

---

Research Insight 11.1

Manufacturing Overhead Cost Drivers

Based on a study of 31 manufacturing plants in three industries—electronics, automobile components, and machinery—researchers used regression analysis to identify manufacturing overhead cost drivers. Their approach treated manufacturing overhead cost as the dependent variable and various cost drivers as the independent variables. Each plant was a separate data point, so there were 31 observations in total. The researchers' model had an adjusted R^2 of .78, indicating that the variation in the cost-driver activity levels explained 78 percent of the variation in manufacturing overhead costs.

Many accountants and managers believe that simple volume-based overhead cost drivers, such as machine hours and labor hours, do not fully capture the causes of overhead costs. They argue that other factors, such as the complexity of the production process, also cause overhead costs; consequently, activity-based costing is superior to traditional volume-based overhead allocation methods. These researchers found a strong relationship between overhead costs and both volume- and complexity-based cost drivers.

The researchers also found that plants implementing new manufacturing methods, namely, just-in-time production, total quality management, and the use of work teams for problem solving on the shop floor, had lower overhead costs than those that had not implemented these new manufacturing methods, all other things being equal. This result is particularly important as to whether improved quality increases or decreases costs. *Source: R. J. Banker, G. Potter, and R. G. Schroeder, "An Empirical Analysis of Manufacturing Overhead Cost Drivers." (Full citations to references are in the Bibliography.)*

nies studied, the volume of output and the complexity of operations increased costs, whereas introducing total quality management and other quality improvements reduced costs. These insights would be impossible to obtain from simple regression results.

Generally, we find diminishing marginal returns by using multiple cost drivers. At some point, the additional information from an additional cost driver is not worth the effort required to get the data. Furthermore, because of the phenomenon known as *information overload,* decision makers sometimes have trouble processing large amounts of data. Therefore, a limited number of cost drivers can prove to be an advantage by reducing the amount of information to consider.

The steps in performing multiple regression are the same as for simple regression, with an addition to the fifth step: Choose the best cost estimation model.

Step 1: Identify plausible cost drivers. After thinking carefully about C.C. Catering's production processes, its cost hierarchy, and the data that she could get from the company's records, Cohen decided to use the following cost drivers:

- *Unit-level: Units.* A unit is a meal sold. The cost related to meals sold includes materials such as the plastic meal containers and the food in each meal. Unit costs also include labor required to prepare meals.

- *Batch-level: Jobs (or batches).* If C.C. Catering takes an order for, say, 30 meals to be delivered to the dean of students' conference room for a lunch meeting, that order is one job. If the dean of students placed such an order six times in a month, C.C. Catering counts that as six different jobs.

- *Product-level: New products.* C.C. Catering sometimes changes its menu, deletes existing meals, and adds new ones to keep the menu fresh for existing customers and to attract new customers. For example, suppose the company adds a Thai noodle salad to its menu. It would incur the costs to experiment with various ingredients, develop a recipe that workers could easily follow in preparing the meal, and revise its menus and advertising copy.

- *Customer-level: New customers.* C.C. Catering conducts marketing to attract new customers. Once signed on, the company performs a credit check on the new customer, sets up billing files, and obtains delivery instructions for its drivers. Cohen decided that the activity—obtaining new customers—creates costs that should be estimated.

As an aside, take a minute to note that these cost drivers line up well with the activity-based cost (ABC) hierarchy from Chapter 4. That is, C.C. Catering has unit-level costs driven by the number of meals sold, batch-level costs driven by the number of jobs, product-related costs driven by the number of new products introduced, and customer-related costs driven by the number of new customers each month.

Question: Why has C.C. Catering not included a cost driver for facility-level costs? Answer: There was only one facility throughout this time period, so there would be no variance in that particular independent variable. Estimated facility-related costs are in the intercept of the regression equation.[3]

The cost drivers that you choose in practice might not line up well with the cost hierarchy, depending on the nature of the organization. For example, a service company such as Starbucks might not use a cost driver for the number of customers. Starbuck's customer-related costs from selling a drink are captured in the cost of selling that drink. So, cost drivers such as the number of units of a particular drink sold include customer-related costs. However, a utility company could have substantial customer-related costs because it collects information about usage, prepares bills, collects and deposits payments received, and maintains account records for each customer. A good place to start identifying cost drivers is to ask what drives the costs in the following five cost hierarchy levels: unit-level costs, batch-level costs, product-level costs, customer-level costs, and facility-level costs.

---

[3] The intercept also could include estimated costs of other omitted cost drivers. For simplicity, we consider the intercept to be an estimate of only facility-level costs.

Step 2: Gather relevant costs.   When estimating the costs for each cost driver, cost managers must collect total cost information for each time period, for example, total costs for each month. They also must collect information about the level of activity of each cost driver for each time period. To estimate the costs for each of its four cost drivers, C.C. Catering must collect the information shown in Exhibit 11–10. For the first month studied, which is January of the previous year, CC's records show one facility and the following costs and activities:

- Total costs of operations—$6,720.
- Meals—1,280.
- Different catering jobs—30.
- New products introduced—0.
- New customers—0.

Cohen obtained this information from the records for each month for 16 months beginning in January of the previous year and entered it into a regression software package (e.g., Microsoft Excel). The input data for the multiple regression appear in Exhibit 11–10. Comparing Exhibits 11–6 and 11–10, we see that the additional data required for the multiple regression approach were number of jobs, number of new products, and number of new customers. The total costs per month and number of meals per month already had been collected for the simple regression.

Step 3: Plot and correct the data if necessary.   To save space, we do not reproduce the three additional scattergraphs (total costs versus jobs, new products, and new customers). Cohen found no evidence of errors, and all the cost drivers show positive relations with total costs.

Step 4: Perform the regression analysis.   Cohen used Excel's regression wizard as before but selected multiple columns of X variables. (Note that in Excel, the columns of X variables must be contiguous.) She selected several combinations of cost drivers and compared the results in the next step.

Exhibit 11–10

Multiple Regression Results for C.C. Catering

Input Data from the Company's Records

| Month | Costs | Cost-Driver Volume | | | |
		Units (meals)	Jobs	New Products	New Customers
Jan, previous year	$ 6,720	1,280	30	0	0
Feb	6,640	2,021	28	0	0
Mar	7,270	1,620	38	0	0
Apr	12,600	2,830	32	2	6
May	11,570	3,630	40	2	6
Jun	8,400	2,383	28	1	2
Jul	10,880	2,460	38	1	6
Aug	10,180	2,640	31	2	7
Sep	13,050	3,620	30	2	5
Oct	9,200	2,840	40	0	3
Nov	8,400	1,937	38	1	4
Dec	8,000	1,650	30	0	4
Jan, current year	5,110	1,260	35	0	0
Feb	5,840	1,850	27	0	0
Mar	6,320	1,710	35	0	1
Apr	10,290	2,940	48	3	7

Step 5: Interpret the regression results and choose the best model. Cohen used the software to perform many multiple regressions. The first regression used all four cost-driver quantities for each month: numbers of meals, new customers, new products, and jobs. She tested other multiple regressions that used combinations of two or three cost drivers. Thankfully, the software does most of the work because the last analysis task is to choose among the many possible multiple regressions for the best model. Cohen and other analysts chose among multiple regressions using two criteria: economic sense and statistical superiority.

First, an acceptable model must make economic and intuitive sense, consistent with step 1 of the analysis. Consider the summary information from several of the multiple regressions as shown in Exhibit 11–11, which also displays the simple regression results for comparison. Multiple regression 1 contains all of the cost drivers, but not all of the X variable coefficients make economic sense. This multiple regression estimates fixed costs to be $4,974.60 per month, which is higher than the simple regression estimate, but this is not a cause for concern because we must look at the regression equation in its entirety. The estimated variable cost per meal is $1.763, which is lower than the simple regression, but this model has more cost drivers, so all the variation does not need to be explained by the number of meals.

Multiple regression 1 estimates the cost of each new customer to be $451.332, which we assume includes all customer-related costs. So far, we might wonder about the size of these coefficients, but they all have positive relations with total costs, which make economic sense. Now look at the negative coefficients for the numbers of new products and jobs. A naïve interpretation of these coefficients is that making new products and taking more jobs actually *reduces* costs by $5.019 per new product and $48.753 per job. It is difficult to tell an economically sensible story about these negative coefficients. As it turns out, the most likely explanation is a statistical problem with the X variables, which are supposed to be independent but which actually bring redundant information to the model (see Appendix A). The most straightforward solution is to omit the latter two variables and re-estimate the regression with the remaining X variables.

Multiple regression 2 is the re-estimated model with only meals and new customers as independent variables. Notice that the intercept coefficient is reduced to $3,414.40 per month because it does not have to compensate for the negative impacts of the omitted variables. the coefficients for meals and new customers remain positive and are nearly the same size as in the first multiple regression, $1.779 and $404.273, respectively. Cohen interpreted this stability as a good sign because these estimated cost-driver rates are not affected by other variables.

Second, the best model should make economic sense and should have superior statistical properties. As just discussed, multiple regression 2 makes economic sense. Note that R-square in Exhibit 11–11 is accompanied by adjusted R-square.

Exhibit 11–11

Multiple Regression Results (abbreviated and reformatted)

Dependent variable = Total costs

Independent Variables	Regression Coefficients		
	Simple	Multiple Regression 1	Multiple Regression 2
Intercept	$2,153.3	$ 4,974.6	$ 3,414.4
Meals	2.891	1.763	1.779
New customers		451.332	404.273
New products		−5.019	
Jobs		−48.753	
R-square	0.784	0.888	0.877
Adjusted R-square	0.769	0.847	0.858

You're the Decision Maker 11.1

Using Regression

Although the numbers of jobs and new products are not necessary to estimate costs, are they of no management value? Apply this to C.C. Catering.
(Solutions begin on page 443.)

Adjusted R-square serves the same purpose as the R-square presented in the earlier discussion of simple regression, but it assesses a statistical penalty for each added independent variable. Because it is more conservative, most analysts use adjusted R-square, not the R-square, to judge the statistical quality of a multiple regression. (Appendix A of this chapter considers other statistical criteria that analysts often use.) As it turns out, the adjusted R-square multiple regression 2 is the highest of all the multiple regressions that Cohen considered. Therefore, she judged multiple regression 2 as the best statistical description of C.C. Catering's total costs.

The results of multiple regression 2 can be written as the following equation:

$$\text{Estimated total costs} = \$3,414.40 \text{ per month}$$
$$+ \ \$1.779 \times \text{Meals sold}$$
$$+ \ \$404.273 \times \text{New customers}$$

Information regarding the numbers of new products or jobs is not necessary for estimated total costs. Estimated total costs for next month when activity expectations are 3,000 meals, two new customers, 30 jobs, and two new products are computed as follows:

$$\text{Estimated total costs} = \$3,414.40 \text{ per month}$$
$$+ \ \$1.779 \times 3,000 \text{ Meals sold}$$
$$+ \ \$404.273 \times 2 \text{ New customers}$$
$$\text{Estimated total costs} = \$9,559$$

We recommend that you answer the self-study question in You're the Decision Maker 11.1 to understand how to estimate costs using multiple regression results.

Cautionary Note about Using Regression

Regression analysis has an aura of scientific analysis about it. In fact, it is only as good as the thought process and the quality of the data that go into developing the model. Collecting appropriate data also is complicated by the following problems:

- *Insufficient data.* A good rule of thumb is to use at least 30 data points, but this often is impractical. See the next point.
- *Inconsistent data.* Organizations and processes change, and so do information systems. These changes can limit the amount of consistent data available.
- *Missing data.* Misplaced source documents or the failure to record a transaction can result in missing data.
- *Outliers.* Observations of extreme cost-activity relationships might unduly affect cost estimates. For example, a hurricane affected operations in a Florida company one August, resulting in high overhead due to one-time costs.
- *Allocated and discretionary costs.* Fixed costs are often allocated on a volume basis, resulting in costs that might appear to be variable. Discretionary costs also might be budgeted so that they appear variable (e.g., advertising expense budgeted as a percentage of revenue).
- *Inflation.* During periods of inflation, historical cost data do not accurately reflect future cost estimates.
- *Mismatched time periods.* The time periods for the dependent and independent variables might not match (e.g., running a machine in February and receiving and recording the energy bill in March).

Managers should be aware of problems in the data. No substitute exists for using experience to understand how costs and cost drivers are related.

Observe that if C.C. Catering had a formal ABC system, Chun and Cohen would not need to analyze total costs. Instead, they could use regression analysis for each of the activity cost accounts. Although many small companies use ABC for special analyses as Cohen has done here, few have formal ABC systems. In fact, Cohen could use her regression analysis as the basis for planning a more formal ABC system; the analysis has helped her identify important activity categories. Many large companies use systemwide information systems that can produce ABC account data that make regression analysis at the activity level feasible. Neither small nor large companies can perform regression analysis without a sufficient quality or quantity of data. In these cases, organizations turn to other cost-estimation methods. We now consider two of these: account analysis and engineering analysis.

Account Analysis Method

Sometimes analysts wish to estimate costs for activities that are new, greatly changed, or when the organization's information system does not allow objective classification of costs into activities. Many traditional information systems report costs by functions (e.g., administration, manufacturing, and marketing), but we know from Chapters 4 and 5 that activities often cut across functions. It might be possible to subjectively cut and sort many months of functional costs into activity accounts, but this can be a formidable task for even a small organization. When activity account information is available, **account analysis** estimates costs by measuring fixed and variable costs for each activity account. However, the benefits of doing this analysis for many months might not justify the costs, particularly if the effort is highly subjective. Fortunately, the method of account analysis can be useful for estimating costs with even a few observations of activity accounts.

The account analysis method follows three steps:

1. Identify the activity accounts (unit, batch, product, customer, and facility).
2. Gather cost and cost-driver amounts for each activity account for each time period.
3. Compute the average cost-driver rate for each activity account.

Note that each activity account might contain both fixed and variable costs, but usually insufficient account data exist to reliably separate these components. Thus, account analysis computes average costs per unit of activity, which might generate inaccurate cost estimates at activity levels far above or below the average. These estimates probably are better than no estimates at all, however.

Application of Account Analysis to C.C. Catering

Assume that Jessie Chun anticipated the possible value of estimating costs by activity account and for the past three months recorded operating costs into accounts consistent with five types of activities:

Activity Account	Cost Driver
Unit—meal preparation and serving	Meals sold
Batch—job management	Jobs
Product—new product development	New products
Customer—new customer management	New customers
Facility—general management and administration	Month

Any costs that could not be objectively classified otherwise were recorded as facility costs. Chun recorded the past three months of activity costs as objectively as possible, along with cost-driver amounts, and computed average cost-driver rates. Exhibit 11–12 presents this information.

LO 4 Use and interpret account analysis for cost estimation.

Exhibit 11–12

Activity Account Analysis

	Cost-Driver Amounts			
Month	Meals Sold	New Customers	Jobs	New Products
Feb	1,850	0	27	0
Mar	1,710	1	35	0
Apr	2,940	7	48	3
Total	6,500	8	110	3

	Activity Account Costs					
Month	Meal Preparation	New Customer Mgt.	Job Management	New Product Development	Facility	Total costs
Feb	$3,030	$ —	$ 650	$ —	$2,160	$ 5,840
Mar	2,250	240	1,200	—	2,630	6,320
Apr	3,945	1,560	1,400	525	2,860	10,290
Total	$9,225	$1,800	$3,250	$525	$7,650	$22,450

	Average Cost-Driver Rates				
	Meals Sold	New Customers	Jobs	New Products	Facility
Costs per unit of activity	$1.42	$225.00	$29.55	$175.00	$2,550.00

The cost estimation equation derived from the past three months of account analysis can be written as follows:

> Estimated total costs = $1.42 × Meals sold
> + $29.55 × Jobs + $175 × New products
> + $225 × New customers + $2,550 per month

Using this equation, costs for next month can be estimated as follows:

> Estimated total costs = $1.42 × 3,000 Meals sold
> + $29.55 × 30 Jobs + $175 × 2 New products
> + $225 × 2 New customers + $2,550 per month
> Estimated total costs = $ 8,494

Chun observed that this cost estimate was lower than those from either simple or multiple regression and wondered which to believe. She suspected that current costs and processes have changed over time, which makes the regression analyses suspect. Chun and Cohen decided to use yet another cost-estimation method, engineering analysis, before deciding how to estimate costs.

You're the Decision Maker

11.2

Using Account Analysis

Explain why the account analysis performed by Chun might be unreliable for estimating future costs. (Solutions begin on page 443.)

Engineering Method

Statistical methods and account analyses rely on data from the past. By contrast, the engineering method works with the present and future. Analysts make **engineering estimates** of costs, first by measuring the work involved in the activities that go into a product and then by assigning a cost to each of those activities. Analysts prepare a detailed step-by-step analysis of each activity required to make a product, together with the costs involved.

LO 5 Use and interpret the engineering method for cost estimation.

Analysts usually can obtain engineering estimates of the materials required for each unit of production from drawings and product specification records. Employees in the company's accounting and purchasing departments have data on the cost of materials that analysts can use to price the materials required to make a product. Analysts can perform time-and-motion studies or review labor time records to ascertain the time required to perform each step. Labor records also provide typical wage rates for various jobs. Coupling those wage rates plus benefits with the time required to perform activities gives the estimated labor cost.

Other costs are estimated similarly. For example, analysts can estimate the size and cost of a building based on area construction costs and space requirements. They can estimate the necessary number of supervisors and support personnel based on a direct labor-time estimate.

The engineering approach has an advantage over other cost estimation methods because it details each step required to perform an operation. Another advantage to this approach is that it does not require data from prior activities in the organization. Hence, it can be used to estimate costs for totally new activities and products.

The engineering approach can identify non-value-added activities. For example, if an engineering estimate indicates that 80,000 square feet of floor area are required for an assembly process but the company has been using 125,000 square feet, managers could find it beneficial to rearrange the plant to make floor space available for other uses. Or, if an engineering estimate indicates that the optimal production run is 1,000 units per setup but the company has been running only 100 units per setup, the managers might change production scheduling to get the optimal production run length.

A difficulty with the engineering approach is that it can be quite expensive to use because it analyzes each activity. Another consideration is that engineering estimates are often based on optimal conditions. Therefore, when evaluating performance, bidding on a contract, planning expected costs, or estimating costs for any other purpose, it is wise to consider that the actual work conditions will often be less than optimal.

Application of the Engineering Method to C.C. Catering

To use the engineering method for C.C. Catering, Chun estimated the following costs:

Unit costs. To estimate unit costs, Chun started with the materials required for a typical meal: a turkey sandwich, one apple, two oatmeal cookies, one piece of candy, one plastic container, and miscellaneous items such as napkins and plastic utensils. She considered waste; for example, she figured that 1 of 10 apples and 5 percent of turkey and bread would be wasted and that 1 of 40 plastic containers would be defective or ruined during production, and so forth. To estimate labor costs, she timed Cohen in preparing meals under ideal conditions. That was her estimate of the shortest time required to prepare meals. She also timed untrained workers to estimate the longest time for meal preparation. Considering these data, using her experience with the learning effects, and estimating how far along the learning curve the average workers were (see Appendix B), she estimated labor time per meal. She multiplied that by the sum of the average wage rate, payroll taxes, and benefits per hour to obtain the preparation cost per meal. To make her analysis comparable to Cohen's work with multiple regression and account analysis, she used input prices that were in effect on average over the previous 16 months. Based on this work, she estimated the cost per meal to be $1.88.

Job costs.   Job costs were mostly labor costs. Preparing a job included taking the order, shopping for food, instructing the meal preparation crew, delivering the meals to the customer's location, overseeing serving, and cleaning up. Some of these costs required cost allocation. For example, one of the employees did a shopping trip for four jobs. In this case, she allocated the costs equally to each job—one-fourth of the time and one-fourth of the mileage to each job. She estimated job costs to average $35.50 per job, considering the fact that job costs would be less for jobs having 50 or fewer meals and more for jobs having 51 to 100 meals, as we discussed in the section on step costs earlier in this chapter.

New-product costs.   New-product costs included labor to develop and test new meals for the menu, materials used to prepare new meals for testing (including those that were rejected), supervision and labor time to teach the meal preparation crew to prepare new meals, and the costs to print new menus. Chun's estimate of new product costs was $168 per new product.

New-customer costs.   New-customer costs included the costs of advertising time spent in marketing the company's products, time spent talking to prospective customers, and time spent in setting up a new customer's account in C.C. Catering's computer system. Chun estimated new customer costs to be $222 per new customer.

Facility costs.   To estimate facility costs, Chun included the base salaries that she and Cohen received, rent on the facilities, utilities, and other administrative costs. She estimated these costs to be $3,210 per month.

The engineering analysis cost-estimation equation can be written as follows:

$$\text{Estimated total costs} = \$1.88 \times \text{Meals sold}$$
$$+ \$35.50 \times \text{Jobs} + \$168 \times \text{New products}$$
$$+ \$222 \times \text{New customers} + \$3,210 \text{ per month}$$

Using this equation, estimated costs for next month can be computed as follows:

$$\text{Estimated total costs} = \$1.88 \times 3,000 \text{ Meals sold}$$
$$+ \$35.50 \times 30 \text{ Jobs} + \$168 \times 2 \text{ New products}$$
$$+ \$222 \times 2 \text{ New customers} + \$3,210 \text{ per month}$$
$$\text{Estimated total costs} = \$10,695$$

Comparison of the Methods and Estimates

Each cost-estimation method discussed has advantages and disadvantages. If one has the capability to work with statistical software packages and if relevant data are available, regression analysis is usually the least costly method. Account analysis requires breakdowns of cost data that are expensive to obtain. In contrast, regression requires only total cost data for each observation (i.e., each month for C.C. Catering), whereas account analysis requires the cost data to be divided into categories that correspond to the cost drivers (e.g., units, jobs, new products, new customers, and facility-level costs for C.C. Catering). Engineering estimates are costly because they require identifying and assigning a cost to each activity required to produce a product.

Relevance of Data Inputs

Regression and account analysis have a disadvantage because they rely on past data, which might not be a good basis for predicting the future. Engineering estimates, on the other hand, rely on anticipated activities and costs and therefore are likely to provide more relevant information. Each cost-estimation method might yield a different estimate of the costs that are likely to result from a particular management decision. This underscores the advantages of using multiple methods to arrive at a final estimate. By observing the range of cost estimates from different methods, management might be better able to decide whether to gather more data.

Costs and Benefits of More Sophisticated and Detailed Methods

Cost-management analysts must decide when the use of a more sophisticated and, therefore, more costly, cost estimation method is important. As with other managerial decisions, they should evaluate the costs and benefits of various cost-estimation techniques. If different estimates give about the same cost estimates, cost-management analysts might conclude that additional information gathering is not warranted and using the simplest method is justified.

Choice of Cost Equation

Sometimes analysts prepare several alternative cost-estimation equations. These alternatives could result from the use of alternative cost estimation methods: regression, account analysis, or engineering. Or they could result from the choice of several cost equations from using one method. For example, analysts frequently prepare several alternative cost equations using regression analysis by using various sets of independent variables. How should one select among several possible cost equations?

We recommend using the following criteria to select among alternative estimated cost equations.

- *Economic plausibility and relevance.* This is the most important criterion. The independent variables should be plausible. The cost equation should make sense. It is always possible to find some association among variables that are not logically related, enter data, and print out a sophisticated-looking result.[4] Be sure the cost drivers are reasonable causes of future costs and cost-driver rates are relevant for future activities.

- *Goodness of fit.* All other things equal, how well the variation in the independent variables explains variation in the dependent variables is important in regression analysis. R^2, or adjusted R^2, is one estimate of goodness of fit. For account analysis and engineering methods, which do not have an R^2, one typically uses good sense and judgment to assess goodness of fit.

- *Significance of the independent variables.* Are the independent variables significant? Appendix A to this chapter discusses a statistical test used in regression. For account analysis and engineering estimates, one uses good sense and judgment to assess the significance of independent variables. Good sense and good judgment are valuable characteristics of successful cost-management analysts.

Application of the Methods to C.C. Catering

When they were finished, Cohen and Chun compared the costs from each of the four estimation methods, which appear in Exhibit 11–13. Cohen remarked that the four methods gave different cost estimates for next month's total costs. "Doing all four methods gives us more information than had we done only one, but which should we use? Because we compute different total cost estimates, we need to find and resolve the sources of the differences before we decide which to believe."

---

[4] To make this point, we know of an analyst who performed a regression analysis with the telephone numbers of department heads as the independent variable and department costs as the dependent variable. This analyst reported the results, tongue-in-cheek, only to find that some managers took the results seriously.

Exhibit 11–13		Comparison of Estimated Cost-Driver Rates and Total Costs for Next Month (rounded)				

Cost Estimation Method	Unit Rate, per Meal	Batch Rate, per Job	Product Rate, per New Product	Customer Rate, per New Customer	Facility Rate, per Month	Estimated Total Cost, Next Month
Simple regression	$2.89				$2,153	$10,826
Multiple regression	1.79			$404.27	3,414	9,559
Account analysis	1.42	$29.55	$175.00	225.00	2,560	8,494
Engineering analysis	1.88	35.50	168.00	222.00	3,210	10,695

Chun noted, "The regression analyses were the easiest and the most objective, but they rely entirely on past data, which we thought were stable. Perhaps our costs and processes have changed more than we thought. Account analysis helped us to look at patterns of costs as we were able to construct them with our current accounting system, but we had to make some judgments about how to classify some costs, which regression analysis did more objectively. I like the way account analysis focuses on major activities, but I also suspect that the past three months had unusually low meal costs. If we had an ABC cost system, we probably could track all of our costs better over time. I'm not sure we can afford that yet, however.

"I think I like the process of the engineering analysis the best because it required me to work through exactly how the company prepares meals, manages jobs, develops new products, and so forth. I learned that we can do some things better. For example, I think we can cut down on meal costs by better training our employees, which also could reduce employee turnover and hiring costs."

Cohen said, "I agree with the value of engineering analysis, but I am surprised that the multiple regression analysis found that job management and new product development activities are redundant to new customer activities. I interpret this to mean that attracting new customers depends on our visibility from taking more jobs and by our reputation for developing new products to keep our menu fresh. I think we should take what we think is the best information from each cost-estimation method and use a hybrid approach to estimate future costs."

C.C. Catering's Hybrid Cost-Estimation Model

Chun and Cohen scrutinized the information in Exhibit 11–13 and debated the merits of each method's cost-driver rate estimates. Based on past information, the various cost estimates, and the expectations for improvements they would make during the next few months, they settled on the following estimates for next year's cost-driver rate estimates:

▪ *Unit rate: $1.80 per meal.* Cohen and Chun reasoned that the engineering estimate was a bit high considering the improvements they planned, but the account estimate was too low because it was based on unusually low costs during the past several months. The multiple regression estimate was nearly the same, which was partly coincidental, but it showed that the $1.80 per meal should be achievable.

▪ *Batch rate: $40 per job.* They hoped to improve their job management by being more efficient with orders and deliveries, which they felt should lead to cost savings. However, the estimate chosen was more than that from account analysis because they wanted employees to spend more time serving existing customers to improve customer satisfaction.

- *Product rate: $200 per new product.* Because Cohen and Chun realized the importance of new products to their business, they decided to spend a bit more on this activity than either account or engineering analysis estimated.

- *Customer rate: $200 per new customer.* They believed that job and new product activities contribute to attracting new customers, so both thought they could reduce the amount spent explicitly on acquiring new customers. The savings also could be used to manage jobs more carefully to increase customer loyalty.

- *Facility rate: $4,000 per month.* Improvements in meal preparation, job management, and new product development would require improvements in space, equipment, and training. Cohen and Chun planned to finance these improvements with a bank loan, and they were confident they could obtain a loan with favorable terms. The improvements and interest payments would increase monthly facility costs beyond any of the cost estimates.

The hybrid cost-estimation equation can be written as follows:

$$\text{Estimated total costs} = \$1.80 \times \text{Meals sold}$$
$$+ \$40.00 \times \text{Jobs} + \$200 \times \text{New products}$$
$$+ \$200 \times \text{New customers} + \$4,000 \text{ per month}$$

Because Cohen and Chun realized that all of these changes could not be implemented immediately, they did not use this equation to estimate next month's costs, but they did use it to estimate the next year's costs, as described next.

Use of the Results

Chun's and Cohen's comments and insights from comparing the cost-estimation results underscore the importance of using multiple methods to estimate costs. One should never blindly use only one method because each method can add unique information. Cohen and Chun found the cost-estimation process to be generally useful and, in some cases, surprising. They used the results to sharpen their cost estimations, strategic business planning, and personal career planning.

Forecasting

Cohen and Chun used their hybrid cost-estimation model to predict or forecast future costs based on expected future activities. This was a valuable exercise because it helped them quantify and organize both financial and physical resources to meet CCC's future needs.

Meal activities.   C.C. Catering had sold nearly 30,000 meals over the past year at $4.00 per meal. After some market research, Cohen and Chun decided to reduce the price to $3.80 per meal, which they believed would make them more competitive with lower-cost rivals. They believed that the price reduction could increase the number of meals sold to 40,000 meals for the year by attracting new customers and inducing existing customers to buy more. As mentioned previously, they expected to reduce costs by improving the efficiency of meal preparation. Considering all this, they estimated next year's meal activity costs to be $1.80 per meal $\times$ 35,000 meals = $63,000.

Job management activities.   Chun and Cohen expected the number of jobs to increase somewhat from last year because of lower meal prices and better job management. They estimated the number of jobs to be 500 over the next 12 months and the costs to be $40.00 per job $\times$ 500 jobs = $20,000.

New product development activities.   Cohen and Chun knew that new products are important to the business but that they could not introduce new products every month. They planned to develop new products during slower months and predicted they would introduce about 20 during the next 12 months. Estimated product costs were $200 per new product $\times$ 20 new products = $4,000.

New customer activities.   With the new pricing policy, better retention of existing customers, and an emphasis on developing customers who order more meals per job, they expected growth in their customer base. They estimated they would attract 60 new customers over the next year. Estimated customer activity costs would be $200 per new customer × 60 new customers = $12,000.

Facility activities.   Using their cost estimate of $4,000 per month, Cohen and Chun estimated facility costs to be $4,000 per month × 12 months = $48,000.

Altogether, Chun and Cohen estimated their revenues, costs, and profits for the next 12 months to be as follows:

Revenues (40,000 meals @ $3.80)	$152,000
Costs	
Meal activities (35,000 meals @ $1.80)	63,000
Job management activities (500 jobs @ $40)	20,000
New product development activities (20 new products @ $200)....	4,000
New customer activities (60 new customers @ $200)	12,000
Facility activities (12 months @ $4,000)	48,000
Total activity costs	147,000
Operating profit before tax...	$ 5,000

This modest profit is based on a 33.3 percent increase in meals sold that would strain their resources. Chun and Cohen worried whether they should rely on their cost estimates for such a major decision. They decided to experiment with the pricing decision to see whether they could develop customers who bought more per order. If they did not see growth in meals sold within several months—six months at the outside—Chun and Cohen decided they would terminate the experiment, return to their previous pricing policy, and consider whether catering is the career they wish to pursue.

Research Insight 11.2

Sticky Costs

Analysts usually expect that cost estimates apply to predicting costs when activities increase *or* decrease. However, an area of current research indicates that some costs can be "sticky;" that is, costs do not always increase or decrease proportionally over time with activity increases or decreases. This stickiness could be caused by a number of factors, including:

■ Nonlinear cost behavior, which results in more or less change in cost than a linear cost-estimation model would predict.

■ Large changes in activity, which violate the assumption that a linear model is reasonably accurate for predicting the effects of small changes in activity levels.

■ Large changes in activity, which managers find personally difficult or unpleasant to accommodate.

■ Capacity constraints, which are difficult to relax when activities push the limits of practical capacity.

■ Industry differences, which indicate the relative ease or difficulty of changing costs. For example, companies in an industry that requires large investments in equipment and machinery, such as manufacturing, might have stickier costs because management is less able to adjust resources than a firm, say, in the retailing industry, which has relatively less committed investment.

See these selected studies: M. Anderson, R. Banker, and S. Janikiraman, "Are Selling, General, and Administrative Costs Sticky?"; R. Balakrishnan, M. Peterson, and N. Soderstrom, "Does Capacity Utilization Affect the Stickiness of Cost?"; and C. Subramanium and M. Weidenmeir, "Additional Evidence on the Stickiness of Costs."

Problems with forecasting. Many factors can conspire to impede the accuracy of forecasting cost-driver activities and the costs they cause. These are some important factors that affect the forecasting ability of cost-estimation models:

- Changes in markets for inputs and products caused by new technologies, products, and competitors' actions.
- Changes in political climate, laws, and government regulations, which can restrict or open certain resources and markets.
- Weather and natural disasters, which can dramatically affect resources, costs, and schedules.
- Changes in processes and cost drivers, often as results of cost-management activities motivated by past cost estimation.
- Changes in activities that differ greatly from the immediate past or from the normal range of activities and that can affect the use or overuse of capacity.

Because they usually cannot avoid these factors, analysts often test the sensitivity of their forecasts to possible changes in these factors. This is known as *sensitivity* or *scenario analysis,* which is covered in Chapter 12.

Outsourcing Decision

At the beginning of this chapter, we noted that Cohen and Chun considered outsourcing by subcontracting the meal preparation to a local sandwich shop. The sandwich shop would purchase the food and prepare the meals, thus eliminating some of the costs for the job cost driver and nearly all of the costs for the meals cost driver. The sandwich shop offered to do this work for $2.50 per meal.

$[\mathscr{C}.\mathscr{C}.\ \mathscr{C}atering]$

Initially, Cohen and Chun thought the opportunity to outsource to be a good deal because they thought the cost per meal to be around $3. After going through the cost estimation exercise described in this chapter, however, they decided not to subcontract meal preparation to the sandwich shop. "We would save only $1.80 per meal at the unit level, and we would lose control over product quality," said Chun.

Cohen disagreed, "You haven't considered administrative opportunity costs of hiring and training food preparation people. Subcontracting meal preparation would free us to spend more time on marketing. Also, we could cut back on our rent and utilities because we would not need as much space." They agreed not to subcontract meal preparation at this time but to reconsider it in the future.

Costs and Benefits of Product Variety

Cohen and Chun also wondered about the costs and benefits of product variety. Companies with much product variety generally generate more revenue. However, research has shown that increasing product variety increases costs, even if volume does not increase. That is, product variety in itself is a cost driver. Chun commented, "I am intrigued by an article I found while doing a library search for publications on cost behavior. [See Cost Management in Practice 11.1.] According to the authors, carrying a wide range of products, or product variety, is known to affect costs. On the other hand, marketing studies show that increasing product variety increases revenues. What is not clear is whether the additional revenue from increasing product variety is enough to cover the related increase in costs."

"How does that apply to us?" Cohen asked.

"While we've had a lot of fun developing new meals and expanding our menu, we know from our cost estimation exercise that the cost of developing a new product is at least $200, maybe more. Do we gain enough additional revenue to justify those costs? The answer in the article that I read was no. I wonder what it would be for us," Chun asked.

Cohen laughed, "I think you are really hooked on cost estimation. I just hope I can get you back in the trenches for food prep."

Cost Management in Practice

II.I

Product Variety and Costs

Several studies have shown that cost drivers other than volume affect total costs.* These studies indicate that the greater the variety of products carried by a company, the higher the company's costs, all things being equal. However, greater variety of products can also increase revenue. Some of the reasons are that customers prefer one-stop shopping and are more likely to make impulse purchases if there are more products from which to choose. The question is whether the additional revenues from maintaining a broad product line justify the additional costs. That is, would a company have greater profits with a narrower product line implying lower costs and lower revenues? Or would it be better off with a broader product line implying higher costs and higher revenues?

Professors Ittner, Larcker, and Randall studied the question of whether it was profitable to maintain a broader product line after considering both the costs and revenues implied by a broader product line in a company that produces outdoor packs (e.g., bicycle packs).† They found that greater product variety increased the company's costs, a result consistent with studies of other companies. They found that greater product variety increased the company's revenues, also. Taking into account both increased revenues and increased costs, they found, "the revenue gains from higher sales volumes and broader product lines were offset by increased costs . . . on average, the firm offered greater product variety than optimal."‡ In short, the company could have been more profitable if it had offered less product variety. Of course, these findings are limited by the data available to the researchers and do not consider future benefits that might accrue to the company from having a broad product line today (e.g., dominance of the market might drive out competition). *Sources: *For example, see S. W. Anderson,* "Measuring the Impact of Product Mix Heterogeneity on Manufacturing Overhead Cost; *R. D. Banker, G. Potter, and R. G. Schroeder,* "An Empirical Analysis of Manufacturing Overhead Cost Drivers"; *and C. D. Ittner, D. F. Larcker, and T. Randall,* "The Activity-Based Cost Hierarchy, Production Policies and Firm Profitability."

†Ittner, Larcker, and Randall, "The Activity-Based Cost Hierarchy," pp. 143–162.

‡Ibid., p. 159.

Ethical Issues

Cost estimation results depend on the selection of cost drivers and on the data that are input. Analysts can manipulate the results by choosing particular cost drivers and by choosing particular data on which to do the estimates.

For an example of the effect of cost-driver selection, recall the simple and multiple regressions performed for C.C. Catering.

> **Simple regression: Total costs = $2.89 × Meals sold + $2,153 per month**
> **Multiple regression: Total costs = $1.79 × Meals sold + $404 × New customers**
>   **+ $3,414 per month**

In the simple regression, the cost-driver rate per meal is $2.89, whereas it is only $1.79 in the multiple regression. Suppose you are the manager of meals for C.C. Catering and are concerned that it will subcontract meal preparation to the local sandwich shop. Therefore, you want Cohen and Chun to believe you prepare meals at a lower cost than the sandwich shop. You would have incentives to choose cost drivers that make costs per meal appear low. In this case, you would choose the multiple regression over the simple regression. Although this is the better choice for statistical reasons, the point is that you might choose equations for self-serving reasons.

You might even find ways to further reduce the cost-driver rate below $1.79 by creatively selecting which months to include in the cost estimation. For example, reviewing the data input to the regression equation, suppose you find that meal costs were highest in three particular months. By omitting those months from the data, you could report a lower estimated cost per meal in your analysis. Of course, you would have to find a plausible reason to omit those months, but that seems possible.

Playing games with models and data to get desired results is not ethical unless two conditions are satisfied: (1) one fully discloses what one has done and (2) the user of the results completely understands the implications of what has been done. If both of those conditions are satisfied, the manipulation of the model or data to get desired results is pointless.

Chapter Summary

Cost estimation is the process of estimating the relation between costs and the cost drivers that cause those costs. Companies estimate costs for three purposes: to manage costs, to make decisions, and to plan and set standards. The simplest cost behavior pattern is the breakdown of costs into fixed and variable components. More complex cost patterns include step costs (also known as *semifixed costs*), mixed costs, and learning curves.

The three major methods of cost estimation are as follows: statistical methods using regression analysis, account analysis, and engineering estimates. Regression analysis is a statistical method used to relate independent variables (known as *cost drivers* in our application) to dependent variables (known as *costs* in our application). Simple regression has one independent variable; multiple regression has more than one independent variable. Using the account analysis method, an analyst separates costs from the accounting records into categories that correspond to the cost drivers. In the chapter example, that means the analyst separates monthly costs for C.C. Catering into unit-level costs, job-level costs, new-product costs, new-customer costs, and facilities-level costs.

Whereas regression and account analysis rely on past data, engineering estimates use data from current practices. Analysts (who are usually engineers) make engineering estimates by first measuring the work involved in the activities that go into a product and by then assigning a cost to each of those activities. Regression analysis usually requires fewer data than account analysis because it does not require costs to be divided into categories that correspond to cost drivers. Engineering estimates are probably the most costly method because they require time-consuming effort to identify activities and assign costs to them. Probably the most informative estimate of cost behavior results from using more than one of the methods because each has the potential to provide information that the others do not.

Appendix A to Chapter Eleven

Technical Notes on Regression

This appendix discusses technical issues that often arise when using regression analysis. The proper name for the technique used in this chapter is "least squares regression." You should not view Appendix A as a substitute for courses and books that deal with these issues in much more depth. The purpose here is to alert you to issues of concern. The old adage that a little knowledge is a dangerous thing applies in a big way to regression analysis. You should always consult an expert in statistics when using regression analysis (just as statisticians should consult cost experts when using costs in their statistical analyses). Teamwork pays.

LO 6 Understand how regression works and identify potential statistical problems with regression analysis.

How Least Squares Regression Works

Consider the scattergraph in Exhibit 11–14, which reflects the data from Exhibit 11–6 and regression results from Exhibit 11–8. First look at the horizontal line labeled Mean $Y = \$8,779$, which is the (rounded) average total cost for the 16 months of data.

Cohen and Chun could use the average as the estimate of total costs each month, but this ignores the expected cost-driver relation between total costs and meals served (or any other cost driver). If the relation between total costs and meals exists, CCC could use it to estimate total costs more accurately than simply using the average. For example, now look at the circled actual data point, $Y = \$12,600$ and $X =$

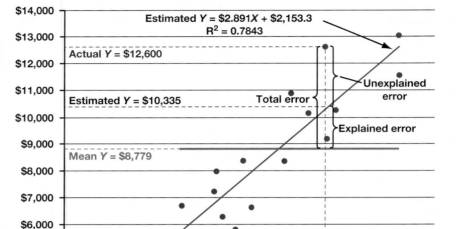

Exhibit 11–14

Scattergraph of Total
Costs and Meals

$\left[\mathscr{C}.\mathscr{C}.\ \mathscr{C}atering\right]$

2,830 meals. The total estimation error ("Total error" on the graph) from the average is $12,600 − $8,779, or $3,821, approximately a 30 percent error. Could the caterers estimate actual costs more accurately using the relation between total costs and meals?

Next look at the diagonal line labeled Estimated $Y = \$2.891X + \$2,153.3$, which is the least squares regression line that Cohen estimated earlier in the chapter. Notice how much closer this line is to the actual data point than the average cost. The line estimates total costs, $Y = \$10,335$. It has explained a large portion ("Explained error" on the graph) of the total error from the average. The remainder of the error ("Unexplained error" on the graph) is also called a "residual" and equals $12,600 − $10,335, or $2,265. This error indicates that the regression line does not estimate this actual total cost perfectly. This time, however, the error is much smaller—only about 18 percent. If the regression is a better description of the data than the average amount, the overall regression errors will be less than the errors from the average.

Least squares regression uses calculus to find the line [intercept and slope(s)] that minimizes the sum of the squared, unexplained estimation errors. Why squared errors? The reason is that the sum of the unsquared errors about the average is, by definition, equal to zero, and one could not improve on that. Squaring the errors makes them all positive and facilitates certain statistical statements about coefficients and the fit of the line to the data. Most statistics texts explain the mathematics of least squares regression in detail. We now turn to somewhat technical discussions about the statistical outcomes of least squares regression.

Confidence in the Coefficients

It is reasonable for managers to ask whether the coefficients of the independent variables are significantly different from zero. That is, do changes in the independent variables result in significant changes in the dependent variable? The **t-statistic** is used to test for the significance of the coefficients. This t is simply the coefficient divided by its standard error. The standard error is a measure of the uncertainty about the coefficient; the larger the standard error, the more the dispersion of coefficient values and the more uncertainty about its value.

Recall that for C.C. Catering, we estimated the relationship between the variation in the number of meals and the variation in total monthly costs in the simple regression. The coefficient was the cost-driver rate for meals. As you may recall, that cost-driver rate was $2.891. Although we did not report it in the text, the standard error of that coefficient was 0.405. Therefore, the t-statistic for the coefficient is:

$$t = \text{coefficient} \div \text{Standard error of the coefficient}$$
$$= \$2.891 \div \$0.405 = 7.134$$

where both figures are given by the computer output of the regression. As a rule of thumb, a t of 2.0 or better is usually considered statistically significant. With $t > 2.0$, analysts generally assume that the regression results are not due to chance. Clearly, the cost-driver rate, $2.891, is statistically significant.

Assumptions about the Residuals

The differences between the estimated Y values (found on the regression line) and the actual Y's are called estimation errors or *residuals*. If a residual is random, its expected value is zero for any observation. The three important assumptions about the residuals are that (1) they are normally distributed, (2) they are independent of each other, and (3) their variance is constant over the range of independent variables. Violation of these assumptions makes statistical inferences about regression estimates questionable (e.g., are the cost-driver rates statistically significant?).

We mention these assumptions because they are often violated for cost data. Consequently, you should be careful about the inferences you draw from regression analyses. You should consult statistics books for more information about how to deal with violations of the following assumptions.

Residuals are normally distributed. Drawing inferences about the estimated value Y (total costs in the text examples) or the cost-driver rates in the text examples requires the residuals to be normally distributed around the regression line. If residuals are normally distributed, the expected value for the residual is zero. If the residuals are not normally distributed, the residual for any observation may be statistically related to that for another observation.

Residuals are independent. A common condition in which residuals are not independent occurs when observations are related to each other over time. This is known as *serial correlation* or *autocorrelation*. Serial correlation does not affect the accuracy of the regression coefficients, but it affects the standard errors of the coefficients. This effect on the standard errors affects the t-statistics and significance tests discussed earlier. The presence of serial correlation might be tested using the Durbin-Watson statistic, which is provided by regression software packages such as SAS and SPSS (not Excel).

Variance of residuals is constant. The assumption of constant variance implies that the residuals are not affected by the level of the independent variable. For example, this means that the residuals are not systematically higher if the cost-driver volume is higher. Constant variance is known as *homoscedasticity*. Nonconstant variance is known as *heteroscedasticity*. (Try these words in a spelling bee.) As with serial correlation, heteroscedasticity does not affect the accuracy of the regression coefficients, but it affects the standard errors of the coefficients, which affects the t-statistics and confidence intervals discussed earlier.

For simple regressions, one can ascertain whether heteroscedasticity is present by plotting the residuals over different values of Y. If the scatter of residuals is not constant over these Y values, the residuals are likely to be heteroscedastic. In some cases, the problem can be cured by transforming the variables (X's and/or Y's) to their logarithms or square roots or by constructing a regression with a new set of variables.

Multicollinearity

If more than one predictor variable is used, as in multiple regression, the interpretation of the coefficients as variable costs is somewhat more hazardous. This was the problem in the multiple regression that used all of the cost-driver activities.

The following correlation matrix describes how the variables in Exhibit 11–10 are related to each other. The highlighted figures in the matrix show that meals, new products, and new customers are highly related (R > 0.7), which violates the assumption that the variables are independent.

Correlations (R) among variables	Meals	New customers	Jobs	New products	Total costs
Meals	1.000				
New customers	0.746	1.000			
Jobs	0.289	0.415	1.000		
New products	0.778	0.857	0.389	1.000	
Total costs	0.886	0.863	0.252	0.810	1.000

Including all cost-driver activities in a multiple regression often results in coefficients that do not make economic sense individually, as Exhibit 11–11 showed.

The overlapping or redundant explanatory power among the two predictors is referred to as **multicollinearity,** which is the high correlation between two or more independent variables in a multiple regression equation. It does not affect the Y estimate, but it does affect the interpretation of the contribution that each of the X's is making to the prediction of Y. With multicollinearity, one can still estimate total costs from the cost equation, but one must question the accuracy of the particular cost-driver rates.

Appendix B to Chapter Eleven

Learning Curves

LO 7 Estimate and use learning curve cost predictions.

A particular type of nonlinear cost behavior relates to the time required to learn to do a job. You may recall the first time that you used a spreadsheet program on a computer. While you might have been slow at first, your efficiency improved as you gained more experience. In practice, experience—or learning—obviously affects direct labor costs; therefore, it affects costs related to direct labor. For example, if the amount of labor required to do a job decreases because of the learning effect, the supervision of the labor to do the job also decreases.

The **learning phenomenon** is a systematic relation between the amount of experience in performing a task and the time required to perform it. This can occur when companies introduce new production methods, make new products (either goods or services), or hire new employees. For example, the effect of learning on the cost of aircraft manufacturing is well known. Manufacturers of products for the aerospace industry, such as General Electric and Boeing, write contracts that recognize the effect of learning by establishing a lower cost for the second item of an order than for the first, a lower cost for the third than for the second, and so forth.

The idea embodied in the learning phenomenon is that the greater the cumulative cost-driver activity, the greater the experience. The greater the experience, the lower the average number of labor hours required. The learning phenomenon partly explains why some firms seek to increase market share. They gain more cumulative experience and have lower average costs than competitors have.

Many companies have found a systematic mathematical relation within the learning phenomenon, which is expressed by the following equation:

$$Y = aX^b$$

where

Y = average number of labor hours per unit required for X units of cost-driver volume

a = number of labor hours required for the first cost-driver unit

X = cumulative number of cost-driver units

b = index of learning equal to the log of the learning rate divided by the log of 2. For example, an 80 percent cumulative learning rate for a doubling cumulative activity is common in practice. For an 80 percent cumulative learning rate, $b = -.322 = \log (.80)/\log (2)$

The **learning curve** is the mathematical or graphic model of the systematic relation between the amount of experience in performing a task and the time required to perform it. Assume that a company finds an 80 percent cumulative learning rate for producing Product A. This means that the average unit time required to prepare two units is 80 percent of the time required for one; the average unit time for four units is 80 percent of the average time required per unit for two units, and the average time required per unit for eight units is 80 percent of the average time for four units, and so on.

Suppose we apply an 80 percent cumulative learning rate to C.C. Catering for a new employee who is preparing meals. The number of labor minutes for this new meal-preparation employee at C.C. Catering appears in Exhibit 11–15. Assume the new employee prepares the first meal, one unit, in 1.25 direct labor minutes. Using the 80 percent cumulative learning rate, the *average* time per meal for two meals is estimated to be 1.00 minute (.80 learning rate × 1.25 minutes). If the average time per meal for two meals is one minute per meal, then the total time for both units (i.e., meals) must be 2.00 minutes.

Four meals would take an average of .80 minutes each (.80 learning rate × 1.00 minutes), or a total of 3.20 minutes according to the 80 percent cumulative learning curve. This means that a total of 1.20 minutes must be expended to produce the third and fourth meals. (1.20 minutes equals 3.20 minutes in total for four meals − 2.00 minutes in total for the first two meals.) As the labor minutes change, so do the costs affected by labor minutes.

Exhibit 11–16 presents the learning curve for meal preparation for a new employee at C.C. Catering. The curvilinear nature of the relation between activity volume (i.e., meals prepared) and labor minutes shows large initial learning effects that become increasingly smaller as employees learn how to prepare meals more efficiently.

Exhibit 11–15

Labor Minutes at
C.C. Catering

$\left[\mathscr{C.C.\ Catering} \right]$

	Number of Labor Minutes	
×	Per Meal—Average (Y)*	Total Time
1	1.25 minutes	1.25 minutes
2	1.00 (80% × 1.25)	2.00[†]
3	.878	2.634[†]
4	.80 (80% × 1.00)	3.20
. . .	. . .	. . .
8	.64 (80% × .80)	5.12

*Computations for Y using formula with exponent.

$Y_2 = 1.25 \times (2^{-.322}) = 1.00$

$Y_3 = 1.25 \times (3^{-.322}) = .878$

$Y_4 = 1.25 \times (4^{-.322}) = .80$

$Y_8 = 1.25 \times (8^{-.322}) = .64$

[†]2.00 = 2 units × 1.00 minute, 2.634 = 3 units × .878 minute, and so on.

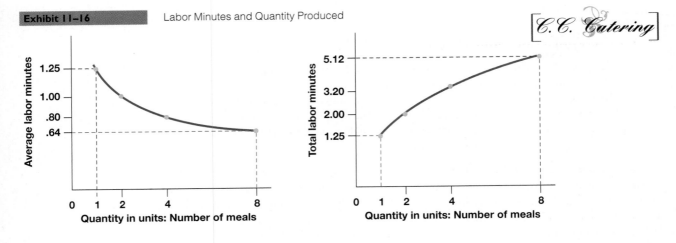

Exhibit 11–16   Labor Minutes and Quantity Produced

The learning function

$$Y = aX^b$$

is curvilinear, as shown in Exhibit 11–16. The function is linear when expressed in logarithmic form because taking the log of the learning function yields:

$$\log Y = \log a + b \log X$$

The function is linear when plotted on a log-log chart as shown in Exhibit 11–17. Thus, analysts often use simple regression to estimate the learning rate, *b,* after taking the log of each variable (*Y* and *X*). The percentage rate of learning, *L,* is found by solving the equation $b = \log (L) \div \log(2)$ for L.

Applications to Cost Management

The learning phenomenon applies to time; thus, it could affect any costs that are a function of time. The phenomenon affects most professional activities such as consulting, legal, medical, and engineering work, as well as any overhead costs related to labor time.

When estimating costs, decision makers should consider the potential impact of learning. The learning phenomenon can affect costs used in cost management, decision making, and performance evaluation. Failing to recognize learning effects can have some unexpected consequences, as shown in the following examples.

Decision making.   Assume that General Electric Company was considering the production of a new navigational device for NASA. NASA indicates it will pay $500,000 per unit for the device. General Electric engineers and cost management analysts estimate the cost to General Electric to produce the first four units of the device to be $600,000 per unit. At first, General Electric decided not to produce it because the unit cost exceeded the unit price. NASA assured General Electric that it would order 40 units of the device. After considering the learning phenomenon for the device, General Electric realized that the average cost per

Exhibit 11–17

Labor Minutes and Quantity Produced—Logarithmic Scales

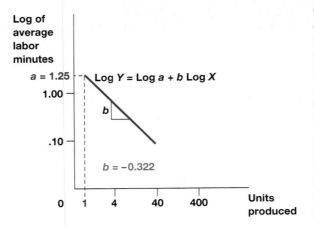

unit would drop to $400,000 for 40 units. For four units, the device was unprofitable. For 40 units, it was profitable because of the learning effect.

Performance evaluation.   Elite University (not its real name) has developed labor time and cost standards for some of its clerical activities that are subject to the learning curve phenomenon. Management observed that time spent on these activities systematically exceeded the standard. Upon investigating the problem, management found high personnel turnover, which meant that the activities were performed by inexperienced people. As a result, the university never experienced the expected benefits of the learning curve. After making changes in personnel policy, the university reduced turnover and staffed the jobs with more experienced people. The time spent on clerical activities no longer exceeded standards.

Key Terms

For each term's definition, refer to the indicated page or turn to the glossary at the end of the text.

account analysis, 427	independent variables, 416	multiple regression, 422	mixed costs, 415
cost estimation, 410	learning curve[†], 441	R-square, 419	simple regression, 416
dependent variables, 416	learning phenomenon[†], 440	regression analysis, 416	step (semifixed) costs, 413
engineering estimate, 429	multicollinearity[*], 440	scattergraph, 418	t-statistic[*], 438
high-low method, 421			

[*]Terms appear in Appendix A.

[†]Terms appear in Appendix B.

Meeting the Cost Management Challenges

1. **After** doing the multiple regression analysis, what additional information did Leah Cohen require to estimate costs using account analysis?

    Her account analysis required a breakdown of monthly costs into those related to each of the four cost drivers—units, jobs, new products, and new customers—and those related to facilities.

2. **Based** on information from the cost estimates and considering C.C. Catering's new strategy, will the company be successful in the future?

    Acknowledging that there is no objective answer to a question such as this, we believe they will be successful. They have survived the early difficult years of a new business and have developed a customer base in the process. They are thoughtful managers with a sensible strategy.

Solutions to You're the Decision Maker

11.1   Using Regression   p. 426

It is true that the best multiple regression equation uses only the numbers of meals sold and new customers as cost-driver activities to estimate total costs. The other activities do not appear to contribute information about total costs given the current relation among activities. Estimating costs is not the only management activity, however, so Cohen and Chun would be wise to continue to be concerned about all of its activities, including the numbers of jobs and new products that the company undertakes. They need to schedule, monitor, and evaluate their effectiveness and efficiency in performing all major activities if the business is to continue to succeed. If they mistakenly stopped managing these activi-

ties and concentrated only on the numbers of meals and new customers, you can bet that the previous synergistic relations among the business' activities would break down, and the company might fail.

11.2   Using Account Analysis   p. 428

Chun's account analysis was costly because C.C. Catering's accounting system was not designed to record costs by activity; that is, it was not an ABC system. Because Chun had to record activity costs manually, it was a costly effort that probably did not benefit from a thorough system design. She did what seemed to be reasonable in addition to all of the other activities she must perform, so her classifications of costs might be unreliably subjective. Additionally, she chose the most recent three months because that was as soon as she thought to do the task and did not have the time to recreate past months' activity costs. The choice of months was opportunistic but might not represent normal operations. In particular, the most recent months might have had lower meal preparation costs because of customer demands

for lower-cost meals or unusually low input prices. Although account analysis can be a useful exercise and can be a motivation to design and install a formal ABC system, without sufficient quality and quantity of activity cost data, the method is prone to errors caused by hasty analysis and selection of atypical time periods.

Review Questions

11.1 For what reasons do companies estimate the relationship between costs and cost drivers?

11.2 Which method of cost estimation is least based on company records?

11.3 True or false: The relevant range is usually the range of observations included in a data set for cost-estimation purposes.

11.4 Under what conditions is the engineering method preferred to other estimation methods?

11.5 What problems might you encounter if you simply enter data into a regression program to compute cost estimates?

11.6 When using cost-estimation methods based on past data, what are the trade-offs between gathering more and fewer data?

11.7 Give an example of a step cost other than the examples mentioned in the text.

11.8 (Appendix A) What is the purpose of the t-statistic?

11.9 (Appendix A) True or false: Violations of assumptions that residuals are independent and are homoscedastic means that the cost drivers are correlated.

Critical Analysis

11.10 The following costs are labeled fixed or variable according to a typical designation in accounting. Under which circumstances would any of these costs behave in a manner opposite to that listed?

    a. Direct labor—variable.

    b. Equipment depreciation—fixed.

    c. Utilities—variable.

    d. Supervisory salaries—fixed.

11.11 Discuss the objectivity/subjectivity trade-off that apparently is a key difference between multiple regression analysis and account analysis. Is one always more objective or subjective than the other? Explain.

11.12 An associate of yours states, "I would never use the results of regression because the past is a poor predictor of the future." How would you respond?

11.13 Explain the objection to using past data to estimate future costs. Is the past always irrelevant to predicting the future? Explain. How might you reasonably adjust cost-estimation results based on past data to estimate future costs?

11.14 (Appendix B) The fast-food restaurant McDonald's is known for high employee turnover, high quality, and low costs. Using your knowledge of the learning phenomenon, how does McDonald's get high quality and low costs when it has so much employee turnover?

11.15 Your colleague says, "I understand that multiple regression computes the best cost-driver rates for the production cost data we have. I also see how we can use those cost-driver rates to trace costs to products, similar to ABC analysis. However, aren't we still stuck with allocating the facility-level cost arbitrarily for absorption costing purposes? What have we gained by using multiple regression?" Respond.

11.16 Search the Internet for applications of simple or multiple regression analysis to business, economic, governmen-

tal, or scientific purposes. Describe five of the most interesting applications in a brief report.

11.17 A friend comes to you with the following problem. "I provided my boss a cost equation based on account analysis. He was unhappy with the results. He told me to do more work and not return until I had a lower cost estimate for one of the cost drivers—number of setups. My analysis covered the last 12 months, January through December of last year. I found that by including the 12 months before that, January through December of the year before last, I was able to get a lower estimated cost-driver rate for number of setups. My boss was happy with my new results. Do you think that what I did was unethical?" How would you respond?

11.18 After performing a regression analysis and giving the results to your boss, you discover an error in the data. Because of a formatting error, you understated costs by three digits. For example, $100 should have been $100,000. When you told your boss about the error, your boss said that the analysis had already been passed on to a top executive who was going to use it in a presentation to the board of directors tomorrow. Your boss does not want to tell the top executive about the error. Should you?

11.19 In doing cost analysis, you realize that there could be errors in the accounting records. For example, maintenance costs were recorded as zero in December. However, you know that maintenance was performed in December. You find that maintenance costs were about double the normal monthly amount in the next month, January. You suspect that maintenance costs were not recorded in December, the last month of the year, so the department's costs would appear to be below budget. The apparent error could affect regression analysis because you are using both December and January in your analysis. Should you report your concerns about the way maintenance costs were recorded? If so, to whom would you report your concerns?

11.20   Assume that you are performing multiple regression for an international company. What potential problems might you encounter when using data from multiple countries?

Exercises

Label each of the following graphs as to cost pattern: variable, fixed, step, mixed.

Exercise 11.21
Cost-Behavior Patterns
(LO 2)

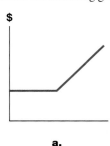

a.

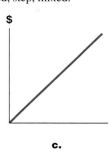

b.

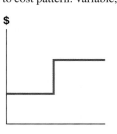

c.

d.

Select the following graph that best matches the description of each of the following cost items.

Exercise 11.22
Cost-Behavior Patterns
(LO 2)

a.   A telephone bill where the amount charged has two components: (1) a fixed amount for the first 60 minutes per month and (2) a variable cost for usage greater than 60 minutes per month. The horizontal axis is number of telephone minutes.

b.   Insurance on an automobile for which the insured pays a fixed amount for the first 10,000 miles per year, and then the rate increases in a step as the car is driven more than 10,000 miles per year. The horizontal axis is the number of miles driven per year.

c.   Wages paid to strawberry pickers paid $4 per crate picked. The horizontal axis is the number of crates of strawberries picked.

d.   The salary of a college professor who is paid the same salary regardless of the number of students taught. The horizontal axis is number of students taught.

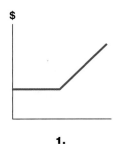

1.

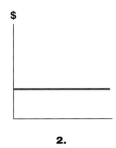

2.

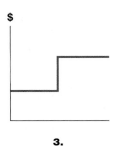

3.

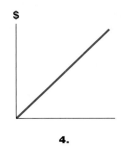

4.

Assume that General Electric, which manufactures high-technology instruments for spacecraft, is considering the sale of a navigational unit to a government agency in India that wishes to launch its own communications satellite. The government agency plans to purchase eight units for a total of $2,500,000, although it would also consider buying 16 units for a total of $4,000,000. General Electric requires a margin of 40 percent of sales to cover administrative costs, contribute to basic research, and make a profit. For example, the sale of eight units must cost no more than $1,500,000 to produce [(1.00 − .40) × $2,500,000]. General Electric has started a chart for this product assuming the production costs are subject to a 75 percent cumulative learning curve.

Exercise 11.23
Learning Curves
(Appendix B)
(LO 7)

Cumulative Number of Units Produced	Average Production Cost per Unit	Total Production Costs
1	$400,000	$400,000
2	300,000	600,000
4	?	?
8	?	?
16	?	?

Required

a.   Complete the chart by filling in the cost amounts for volumes of 4, 8, and 16 units.

b.   Should General Electric sell eight units? Should it sell 16 units?

Exercise 11.24
Learning Curves
(Appendix B)
(LO 7)

Assume that Whee, Cheatham, and Howe is an auditing firm that has found that its summer interns are subject to an 80 percent cumulative learning curve for one of its important tasks, proofreading financial statements. For one of its interns, Kim Down, the firm has started to analyze the relation between costs and financial statement proofreading.

Cumulative Number of Financial Statements Proofread	Average Time Spent per Financial Statement	Total Time Spent
1	30 hours	30 hours
2	24 hours	48 hours
4	?	?
8	?	?
16	?	?

Required

a.   Complete the chart by filling in the amounts for volumes of 4, 8, and 16 units.

b.   If Down is paid $30 per hour, how much will it cost, in total, for Down to proofread 8 financial statements?

Exercise 11.25
Learning Curves
(Appendix B)
(LO 7)

You have performed a simple regression analysis using the natural log (Ln) of cumulative production as the X-variable and the natural log of cumulative average cost as the Y, variable with the following results:

$$Ln\ Y = 5.2983 - 0.2345\ Ln\ X$$

Required

a.   Explain the meanings of the intercept and slope terms.

b.   Show how to find the percentage learning rate that this regression result implies.

Exercise 11.26
Simple Regression
(LO 3)

Aliens, Inc., has developed a regression equation to analyze the behavior of its maintenance costs (C) as a function of machine hours (MH). The following equation was developed using 30 months of data:

$$C = \$6,000 + \$5.25MH$$

Required

a.   Using this cost equation, what are the estimated total maintenance costs at an activity level of 500 machine hours?

b.   What problems might arise from using these data?

[CPA adapted]

Exercise 11.27
Simple Regression
(LO 3)

I. R. Esse Tax Consultants has developed a regression equation to analyze the behavior of its tax return preparation costs (C) as a function of the number of returns prepared (TR). The following equation was developed to estimate tax return preparation costs. Analysts used 24 observations of data for last year, one observation for each of its 24 offices:

$$C = \$112,000 + \$154TR$$

Required

a.   What is the estimated tax return preparation cost for an office that prepares 1,000 tax returns?

b.   What problems might arise from using these data?

[CPA adapted]

Exercise 11.28
Simple Regression
(LO 3)

Use the regression results for C.C. Catering in Exhibit 11–8.

Required

a.   What are the estimated total costs for a month in which 3,000 meals will be sold?

b.   What are the estimated committed costs for a month in which 3,000 meals will be sold?

c.   What are the estimated total variable costs for a month in which 3,000 meals will be sold?

d.   What might be a problem with using the results in Exhibit 11–8 if C.C. Catering plans to sell 7,000 meals in a month?

Use the regression results for C.C. Catering in Exhibit 11–8.

Required

a.   What are the estimated total costs for a month in which 2,200 meals will be sold?

b.   What are the estimated committed costs for a month in which 2,200 meals will be sold?

c.   What are the estimated total variable costs for a month in which 2,200 meals will be sold?

d.   What might be a problem with using the results in Exhibit 11–8 if C.C. Catering plans to sell 400 meals in a month?

Exercise 11.29
Simple Regression
(LO 3)

Use the regression results for C.C. Catering in Exhibit 11–8.

Required

a.   What are the estimated total costs for a month in which 2,100 meals will be sold?

b.   What are the estimated committed costs for a month in which 2,100 meals will be sold?

c.   What are the estimated total variable costs for a month in which 2,100 meals will be sold?

d.   What might be a problem with using the results in Exhibit 11–8 if C.C. Catering plans to sell 8,000 meals in a month?

Exercise 11.30
Simple Regression
(LO 3)

Use the best multiple regression results for C.C. Catering in Exhibit 11–11.

Required

What are the estimated total costs in a month in which there are:

> 2,000 meals sold
> 30 jobs
> 1 new product
> 2 new customers

Exercise 11.31
Multiple regression
(LO 3)

Use the best regression results for C.C. Catering in Exhibit 11–11:

Required

What are the estimated total costs in a month in which there are:

> 3,000 meals sold
> 40 jobs
> 4 new products
> 8 new customers

Exercise 11.32
Multiple Regression
(LO 3)

Fast Eddie's Limo Service operates a fleet of limousines. Management wants to estimate the fixed and variable costs per mile. A recent trade publication indicated that variable costs should be no more than $.25 per mile. To check his costs against those indicated in the trade journal, Fast Eddie collected the following data for his limousine fleet for last month:

Exercise 11.33
High-Low Method
(LO 3)

Limousine Number	Costs	Miles
1	$3,500	12,400
2	3,400	11,800
3	3,200	10,600
4	3,800	11,500
5	3,500	11,800
6	4,000	13,200
7	3,200	9,800
8	3,000	9,200
9	4,200	11,700
10	3,900	12,300

Required

a.   Use the high-low method to estimate the fixed and variable portions of overhead costs based on miles driven.

b.   What is the estimated total cost of driving one limousine 10,000 miles?

c.   Fast Eddie has heard that the high-low method has a major limitation compared to simple regression. What is it?

Exercise 11.34
Simple Regression
(LO 3)

Refer to the data for Fast Eddie's Limousine Service in Exercise 11.33.

Required

Build your own spreadsheet. Using miles as the cost driver, what are the simple regression results and estimated total cost for Fast Eddie's Limousine Service?

Exercise 11.35
High-Low
(LO 3)

mhhe.com/hilton3e

Feno Menn, the owner of Phenomeno's Pizza, wishes to estimate the committed and variable costs per pizza production. Feno collected the following data from the accounting records:

Month	Pizza Production Costs	Number of Pizzas Produced
1	$28,560	8,600
2	31,400	9,800
3	33,200	12,600
4	32,800	12,500
5	36,500	14,800
6	41,100	15,200
7	30,200	9,800
8	34,000	10,200
9	41,200	14,700
10	30,900	13,300

Required

a.   Use the high-low method to estimate the committed and variable portions of overhead costs based on number of pizzas produced.

b.   What is the estimated total variable cost for a month in which 4,000 pizzas are produced?

c.   Feno has heard that the high-low method has a major limitation compared to simple regression. What is it?

Exercise 11.36
Simple Regression
(LO 3)

Refer to the data for Phenomeno's Pizza in Exercise 11.35.

Required

Build your own spreadsheet. Using pizzas produced as the cost driver, what are the simple regression results for Phenomeno's Pizza?

Exercise 11.37
Interpretation of
Regression Results
(LO 3)

Customers 'R First Bank is planning to offer a new debit card for which it expects to charge $1 per transaction. The following cost estimates have been made assuming 1 million transactions during the first month that the card is used.

Direct labor $500,000 (the labor rate is $25 an hour × 20,000 estimated direct-labor hours)

Overhead costs have not yet been estimated for the new product, but 12 months of data on total production activities and overhead costs have been analyzed for similar products using simple linear regression. The following results were derived from the simple regression and provide the basis for overhead cost estimates for the new product:

SUMMARY OUTPUT
Dependent variable = Overhead costs

Regression Statistics	
R-square	0.8803
Standard error	6,175.0321
Observations	12

Independent Variable	**Coefficients**
Intercept	112,153.335
Direct labor hours	5.496

Required

a.   What percentage of the variation in overhead costs is explained by the independent variable?

b.   What is the total overhead cost for an estimated activity level of 20,000 direct-labor hours per month?

c.   Will the $1 per transaction charge cover the costs of direct labor and overhead, assuming one million transactions?

[CMA adapted]

The advertising manager of Leonine Company wants to know whether the company's advertising program is successful. The manager used a spreadsheet to estimate the relationship between number of advertisements (the independent variable) and sales dollars. Monthly data for the past two years were entered into the computer. The regression results indicated the following equation:

Exercise 11.38
Interpretation of
Regression Results
(LO 3)

SUMMARY OUTPUT
Dependent variable = Sales dollars

Regression Statistics	
R-square	0.5821
Standard error	12,162.4321
Observations	24

Independent Variable	**Coefficients**
Intercept	845,153.335
Advertisements	−503.496

These results might imply that the advertising was reducing sales. The manager was about to conclude that statistical methods were so much nonsense when you walked into the room.

Required

Help the manager. What might cause the negative relationship between advertising and sales?

Mimi's Dance Studio estimates studio (noninstruction) costs based on student hours of instruction, where 1 student receiving a private lesson for 1 hour is "1 student hour." Data were gathered for the past 24 months and entered into a regression program. The following output was obtained:

Exercise 11.39
Interpretation of
Regression Results
(LO 3)

SUMMARY OUTPUT
Dependent variable = Studio costs

Regression Statistics	
R-square	0.1609
Standard error	612.0926
Observations	24

Independent Variable	**Coefficients**
Intercept	1,451.784
Student hours	2.551

The company is planning to operate at a level of 250 student instruction hours per month during the coming year.

Required

a.   Use the regression output to write the cost equation.

b.   Based on the cost equation, compute the estimated studio cost per month for the coming year.

Farout Cards makes and produces greeting cards. Every month, it produces from 5 to 15 new products in batches. At the end of the month, the company destroys the master copy of all existing cards so that it produces new card products each month. The costs of designing the card, including design and art work, are product-level costs. The costs of materials, ink, and other printing costs are unit-level costs. The costs of setting up the production run are batch-level costs. All other costs are facility-level costs. Farout's accounting records report the following production costs for last December:

Exercise 11.40
Account Analysis
Method
(LO 4)

mhhe.com/hilton3e

Unit-level costs.................................	$24,000
Batch-level costs	8,000
Product-level costs..........................	18,000
Facility-level costs	25,000

Production was 100,000 units for 10 different new products produced in 100 batches.

Costs for this coming December are expected to increase over last December's costs as follows: the unit-level costs, 20 percent per unit; the batch-level costs, increase 10 percent per batch; the product-level costs, 10 percent per product; and the facility-level costs, 10 percent for the month.

Required

a. What is the unit-level cost per unit for last December?

b. What is the estimated unit-level cost per unit for this coming December?

c. What are the estimated facility-level costs for this coming December?

d. If Farout expects to produce 120,000 units for 12 new products in 100 batches this coming December, what will be its estimated total costs for the month?

Exercise 11.41
Account Analysis
Method
(LO 4)

Highland Music records and sells music. Every month, it produces several new products in batches. The costs of making the master CD, including hiring musicians and studio costs, are product-level costs. The costs of materials and packaging are unit-level costs. The costs of setting up the production run are batch-level costs. All other costs are facility-level costs. Highland Music's accounting records report the following production costs for January of this year:

Unit-level costs	$160,000
Batch-level costs	40,000
Product-level costs	180,000
Facility-level costs	50,000

Production was 50,000 units for eight new products, produced in 50 batches.

Costs for June of this year are expected to increase over the costs for January of this year as follows: the unit-level costs, 5 percent per unit; the batch-level costs, 4 percent per batch; the product-level costs, 4 percent per product; and the facility-level costs, 5 percent for the month.

Required

a. What are the unit-level cost per unit, the batch-level cost per batch, and the product-level cost per product for January of this year?

b. What are the estimated facility-level costs for June of this year?

c. If in June of this year, Highland Music expects to produce 60,000 units for 12 new products in 100 batches, what will be its estimated total costs for the month?

Exercise 11.42
Account Analysis
(LO 4)

Use the account analysis results for C.C. Catering in Exhibit 11–12.

Required

What are the estimated total costs in a month in which there are:

3,000 meals sold

30 jobs

4 new products

10 new customers

Exercise 11.43
Engineering Estimates
(LO 5)

Use the engineering cost estimates for C.C. Catering presented in Exhibit 11–13.

Required

What are the estimated total costs in a month in which there are:

3,500 meals sold

50 jobs

5 new products

8 new customers

Exercise 11.44
Interpretation of
Regression Data
(Appendix A)
(LO 6)

Unsafe Insurance Company needs to forecast its personnel department costs. The following output was obtained from a regression program used to estimate the department's costs as a function of the number of employees:

SUMMARY OUTPUT

Dependent variable = Personnel costs

Regression Statistics

R-square	0.7255
Standard error	612.0926
Observations	24

Independent Variable	Coefficients	Standard Error	T-Statistic
Intercept	8,421.441	2,687.979	3.133
Employees	492.703	164.949	2.987

Monthly data for the past two years were used to construct these estimates. Cost relationships are expected to be the same for the coming period.

Required

a. What are the estimated personnel costs for 4,200 employees?

b. (Appendix A) How confident are you that a significant cost-driver relation exists?

Problems

University Hospital has prepared a schedule of actual overhead costs for its blood test unit for the past year.

Problem 11.45
Methods of Cost Estimation: Account Analysis
(LO 3, 4)

	Activities			Overhead Costs							
Month	Tests	Technician Hours	Total Overhead	Supplies	Indirect Labor	Building Occupancy	Utilities	Equipment Cost	Equipment Maint.	Data Processing	Technical Support
1	4,034	1,644	$ 55,093	$ 2,210	$ 15,631	$ 16,300	$ 2,332	$ 12,800	$ 1,910	$ 2,710	$ 1,200
2	4,532	1,884	56,451	2,970	15,650	16,300	2,498	12,800	2,190	2,843	1,200
3	5,267	2,090	65,797	2,637	15,712	21,800	2,880	16,000	2,274	3,093	1,400
4	4,303	1,743	55,716	2,133	15,650	16,300	2,489	12,800	1,990	3,154	1,200
5	4,450	1,764	55,513	2,349	15,637	16,300	2,240	12,800	1,910	3,076	1,200
6	5,458	2,009	66,010	3,110	15,750	21,800	2,540	16,000	2,170	3,240	1,400
7	5,419	2,049	66,911	3,440	15,724	21,800	2,820	16,000	2,290	3,437	1,400
8	5,716	2,059	66,628	3,030	15,755	21,800	2,740	16,000	2,310	3,593	1,400
9	4,570	1,918	55,955	2,420	15,689	16,300	2,220	12,800	2,050	3,275	1,200
10	4,984	1,940	66,072	3,195	15,700	21,800	2,539	16,000	2,276	3,161	1,400
11	4,431	1,796	55,644	2,790	15,667	16,300	2,140	12,800	1,806	2,942	1,200
12	4,737	1,805	56,939	3,140	15,669	16,300	2,650	12,800	1,980	3,000	1,400
Total	57,901	22,701	$722,728	$33,424	$188,236	$223,100	$30,088	$169,600	$25,156	$37,523	$15,600

In the past, the overhead costs have been related to the number of tests. Following management instructions, data were gathered on past costs and past test levels and technician hours.

Required

Prepare a cost-estimation equation using the account analysis approach in which the only independent variable is the number of tests. (*Hint:* Make a scattergraph of each cost with tests as the *X* variable.)

Refer to the data in Problem 11.45.

Required

Use simple regression to estimate total overhead costs in months with 6,000 or 4,000 tests.

Problem 11.46
Simple Regression
(LO 3)

Refer to Problem 11.45.

Required

a. Use multiple regression to estimate monthly total overhead cost behavior.

b. As a group, decide which method you think is best to estimate costs: simple regression, multiple regression, or account analysis. Also recommend whether management should use just one method, any two of the methods, or all three methods. Consider both the costs and benefits of using multiple cost estimation methods in your recommendation. Have a member of your group write a short report to management that expresses your group's views.

Problem 11.47
Various Methods of Cost Estimation
(LO 3, 4)

Problem 11.48
Interpretation of
Regression Results:
Simple Regression
(LO 3, 4)

Your company, Local Express Services, makes special deliveries to real estate and law firms. It is estimating its costs for the coming period.

The controller's office estimated overhead costs at $9,000 per month for fixed costs and $12 per delivery for variable costs. Your nemesis on the staff, Nick Witt, suggested that the company use the regression approach. Witt has already done the analysis on a home computer and reports the "correct" cost equation as:

$$\text{Monthly overhead} = \$26{,}501 + \$10.70 \text{ per delivery}$$

When asked for the data used to generate the regression, Witt produces the following list:

Month	Overhead Costs	Number of Deliveries
1	$142,860	11,430
2	151,890	12,180
3	192,600	15,660
4	141,030	11,250
5	203,490	12,780
6	180,630	14,730
7	159,630	12,510
8	183,990	15,060
9	194,430	15,450
10	150,120	11,970
11	154,080	12,630
12	184,800	15,300
13	183,120	14,580

The company controller is somewhat surprised that the cost estimates are so different. You have therefore been assigned to check Witt's equation.

Required

Build your own spreadsheet. Analyze Witt's results and state your reasons for supporting or rejecting his cost equation.

Problem 11.49
Interpretation of
Regression Results
(LO 3)

Lerner, Inc., is accumulating data to prepare its annual profit plan for the coming year. The behavior pattern of the maintenance costs must be determined. The accounting staff has suggested using regression to derive an equation in the form of $y = a + bx$ for maintenance costs. Monthly data regarding maintenance hours and costs for the preceding year were entered into the regression analysis.

Total hours of maintenance for the year:	4,800
Total costs for the year:	$43,200
Regression results:	
Intercept:	$684.65
b coefficient:	$7.2884
R²:	.79724

Required

a. In a regression equation expressed as $y = a + bx$, what is the letter b best described as?

b. What is the letter y in the regression equation best described as?

c. What is the letter x in the regression equation best described as?

d. Based on the data derived from the regression analysis, what are the estimated costs for 360 maintenance hours in a month?

e. What is the percent of the total variance that can be explained by the regression equation?

[CMA adapted]

Problem 11.50
Multiple Regression,
Activity-Based Costing
(LO 3)

The accounting department of Insecurity Protection Services, a company that provides security services for rich, famous, and insecure people (and anyone else who can afford them) is analyzing the costs of its accounting services. Analysts have selected the following cost drivers: number of paychecks processed, customer accounts maintained, and special analyses.

The cost data and level of cost-driver activity for the past 16 months follow:

Month	Special Analyses	Customer Accounts	Paychecks Processed	Accounting Service Costs
1	2	325	1,029	$ 63,800
2	4	310	993	68,900
3	2	302	1,268	64,000
4	1	213	1,028	61,300
5	2	222	984	61,600
6	0	214	712	50,800
7	1	131	762	51,020
8	1	123	739	54,300
9	0	115	708	50,500
10	2	296	1,232	64,800
11	2	213	978	58,000
12	1	222	929	57,500
13	2	217	1,059	62,200
14	2	132	942	54,900
15	4	300	1,299	71,530
16	4	315	1,283	64,800
Totals	30	3,650	15,945	$959,950

Required

a. *Build your own spreadsheet.* Using regression analysis, find the best cost-estimation equation.

b. Assuming the following levels of cost-driver volume for a month, what is the accounting department's estimated costs of doing business based on the multiple regression results?

> 1,000 paychecks processed
> 200 customer accounts maintained
> 3 special analyses

c. Insecurity Protection Services is considering outsourcing the processing of all paychecks. Compared to your answer in requirement (b), how much would the accounting department save per month by outsourcing all paycheck processing (before considering the cost of outsourcing)?

Refer to problem 11.50.

Problem 11.51
Account Analysis
(LO 4)

Required

a. Before proceeding to requirement (b) of this problem, indicate the information required to perform account analysis for Insecurity Protection Services' accounting department cost estimation that is not in problem 11.50.

b. Now assume that Insecurity Protection Services' accounting department had the following total costs for each cost driver for the 16 months reported in Problem 11.50.

> Total cost of paychecks processed $180,000
> Total cost of maintaining customer accounts.......................... 110,000
> Total cost of performing special analyses 60,000
> Total facilities-level costs (total for 16 months)....................... 610,000
> Total costs $960,000

What are the cost-driver rates for (1) paychecks processed, (2) customer accounts maintained, and (3) special analyses performed?

c. Assuming the following level of cost-driver volumes for a month, what is the accounting department's estimated costs of doing business using the account analysis approach?

> 1,000 paychecks processed
> 200 customer accounts maintained
> 3 special analyses

d. Insecurity Protection Services is considering outsourcing the processing of all paychecks. Compared to your answer in requirement (c), how much would the accounting department save by outsourcing payroll (before considering the cost of outsourcing)?

Problem 11.52
Engineering Estimates
(LO 5)

Refer to Problems 11.50 and 11.51. Insecurity Protection Services hired an engineering consulting firm to perform an engineering estimate of the accounting department's costs. The firm identified the following cost estimates based on information for the current period:

Facilities costs (per month)	$40,000	
Paycheck processing	5.00	per paycheck
Customer account maintenance	50.00	per account
Special analyses	2,500	per analysis

Required

a. Assuming the following level of cost-driver volume for a month, what is the accounting department's estimated costs of doing business?

> 1,000 paychecks processed
> 200 customer accounts maintained
> 3 special analyses

b. Insecurity Protection Services is considering outsourcing the processing of all paychecks. Compared to your answer in requirement (a), how much would the accounting department save by outsourcing payroll (before considering the cost of outsourcing)?

Problem 11.53
Multiple Regression,
Activity-Based Costing
(LO 3)

Analysts for Sun Black, maker of fashionable sunglasses, have selected the following cost drivers: number of units produced, batches of sunglasses, customer orders processed, and new products designed to explain operating costs.

The cost data and levels of cost-driver activity for the past 18 months follows.

Month	Units	Batches	Customer Orders	New Products	Costs
1	35,100	693	252	4	$ 1,730,890
2	28,900	670	240	2	1,753,860
3	37,200	550	185	1	1,562,890
4	26,800	535	116	1	1,389,940
5	31,800	535	120	0	1,200,300
6	29,000	577	105	0	1,245,660
7	32,500	610	110	2	1,514,900
8	31,400	660	126	2	1,555,200
9	42,500	737	160	3	1,706,130
10	38,000	631	185	4	1,781,060
11	51,200	756	233	4	2,101,610
12	46,900	729	245	5	2,162,230
13	41,500	780	260	5	2,087,270
14	49,700	726	235	4	2,017,920
15	44,000	645	255	3	1,991,870
16	49,300	710	169	2	1,839,080
17	30,100	600	172	3	1,738,730
18	39,850	589	170	3	1,575,150
Total	685,750	11,733	3,337	48	$30,954,690

Required

a. *Build your own spreadsheet.* Using regression analysis, find the best cost-estimation equation.

b. Assuming the following level of cost-driver volume for a new plant for one month, what is the estimated cost using the multiple regression results?

> 30,000 units produced
> 500 batches
> 150 customer orders
> 3 new products

c. Sun Black is considering a plan to reduce the number of batches by 100 per factory per month. Compared to your answer in requirement (b), how much would *each factory save per month* by reducing the number of batches by 100 per month?

Refer to Problem 11.53.

Problem 11.54
Account Analysis
(LO 4)

Required

a. Before proceeding to requirement (b) of this problem, indicate the information in addition to that provided in Problem 11.53 required to perform account analysis.

b. Now assume that Sun Black had the following breakdown of costs:

Facilities cost	$ 7,200,000
Unit-level cost	6,900,000
Batch-level cost	8,000,000
Customer-order cost	6,200,000
New-product cost	2,600,000
Total costs	$30,900,000

What are the cost-driver rates using account analysis?

c. What are the estimated costs for a month assuming the following level of cost-driver volumes using the account analysis approach?

> 30,000 units produced
> 500 batches
> 150 customer orders
> 3 new products

Refer to Problems 11.53 and 11.54. Sun Black hired an engineering consulting firm to perform an engineering estimate of sunglass production costs. The consulting firm identified the following monthly cost estimates based on information for the current period:

Problem 11.55
Engineering Estimates
(LO 5)

Facilities costs	$400,000	
Unit-level costs	9	per unit produced
Batch-level costs	500	per batch
Customer order costs	1,500	per customer order
New-product costs	60,000	per new product

Required

Assuming the following level of cost-driver volume for a month, what is the estimated cost using the engineering estimates?

> 30,000 units produced
> 500 batches
> 150 customer orders
> 3 new products

Jammin' Corporation plans to manufacture Inexcess, a product that requires a substantial amount of direct labor on each unit. Based on the company's experience with other products that required similar amounts of direct labor, management believes that a learning factor exists in the production process used to manufacture Inexcess.

Problem 11.56
Learning Curves
(Appendix B)
(LO 7)

Each unit of Inexcess requires 50 square feet of direct material at a cost of $30 per square foot, for a total material cost of $1,500. The standard direct-labor rate is $25 per direct-labor hour. Variable manufacturing overhead is assigned to products at a rate of $40 per direct-labor hour. In determining an initial bid price for all products, the company marks up variable manufacturing costs (= direct materials + direct labor + variable overhead) 30 percent. (That is, the bid = 130 percent of variable manufacturing costs.)

Data on the production of the first two lots (16 units) of Inexcess follow:

1. The first lot of eight units required a total of 3,200 direct-labor hours.

2. The second lot of eight units required a total of 2,240 direct-labor hours.

Based on prior production experience, Jammin' estimates that production time will show no significant improvement after the first 32 units. Therefore, a standard (for planning purposes) for direct-labor hours will be established based on the average number of hours per unit for units 17 through 32.

Required

a. What is the basic premise of the learning curve?

b. Based on the data presented for the first 16 units, what learning rate appears to be applicable to the direct labor required to produce Inexcess? Support your answer with appropriate calculations.

c. Calculate the standard for direct-labor hours that Jammin' should establish for each unit of Inexcess.

d. After the first 32 units have been manufactured, Jammin' was asked to submit a bid on an additional 96 units. What price should Jammin' bid on this order of 96 units? Explain your answer.

e. Knowledge of the learning curve can be a valuable management tool. Explain how management can apply this tool in planning and controlling business operations.

[CMA adapted]

Problem 11.57
Learning Curves
(Appendix B)
(LO 7)

Krylon Company has purchased 800 pressure gauges annually from CO_2, Inc. The price of these gauges has increased each year, reaching $1,000 per unit last year. Because the purchase price has increased significantly, Krylon management has asked for a cost estimate of manufacturing gauges in its own facilities.

A team of employees from the engineering, manufacturing, and accounting departments have prepared a report for management that includes the following estimate for an assembly run of 100 units. Additional production employees will be hired to manufacture the pressure gauges. However, no additional equipment or space is needed.

The report states that total costs for 100 units are estimated at $240,000 as shown here, or $2,400 per unit.

Materials	$10,000
Direct labor consisting entirely of hourly production workers (varies with production volume)	25,000
Labor-related overhead that varies closely with direct labor (varies with production volume)	50,000
Overhead not related to labor (e.g., building rent)	75,000
General and administrative costs to support the production	80,000
Total costs	$240,000

The current purchase price is $1,000 a unit, so the report recommends a continued purchase of the product.

Required

a. Before considering the learning curve effects, was the recommendation to continue purchasing the gauges correct? Explain your answer and include any supportive calculations you consider necessary.

b. Assume that Krylon could experience labor-cost improvements on the pressure gauge assembly consistent with an 80 percent learning curve. An assembly run of 100 units represents the initial lot or batch for measurement purposes. Should Krylon produce or purchase 800 pressure gauges in this situation? Explain your answer.

[CMA adapted]

Cases

Case 11.58
Regressions Run from
Published Data
(LO 1, 3)

Obtain 11 years of data from the published financial statements of a company. Using the first 10 years of data, perform a regression analysis in which the dependent variable is cost of goods sold and the independent variable is revenue (some companies call it *sales*). Now use the results from the regression on the first 10 years of data to estimate the cost of goods sold for the year 11. How far off were you in estimating cost of goods sold for the year 11? Estimate the cost of goods sold for year 5. How far off were you in estimating cost of goods sold for year 5?

Required

Prepare a report that describes your work and discusses reasons that your estimate of cost of goods sold is different than the actual cost of goods sold for year 11. You will be able to find the data on the Internet. Also, Moody's, Standard & Poor's and Value-Line are good sources of financial data.

Case 11.59
Data correction and
regression analysis
(LO 3)

Optical Storage Technology, Inc. (OST) manufactures CD and DVD drives for personal and business computers in 18 locations in North America. Several years ago OST implemented quality and time-based management practices throughout its manufacturing divisions (see Chapter 7 for discussions of quality and time management), and by now few differences in performance should remain. Divisions report key operational and financial measures directly to OST headquarters, whose financial staff each month review the data and look for unusual activity or costs. The analysts also provide forecasting information for budgeting and evaluation purposes. The following table contains several key performance measures for the 18 divisions for last month.

| | Operating Performance Measures | | | Financial Performance |
Division	Defects per month	First-time pass rate, %	Average cycle time per unit (minutes)	Manufacturing Overhead Cost
1	149	71.10	80.60	$78,300
2	141	65.80	83.13	81,300
3	124	67.20	76.83	70,700
4	143	61.90	81.67	78,900
5	124	63.50	77.75	72,800
6	158	80.00	79.10	79,300
7	170	86.20	81.08	83,000
8	142	60.80	82.20	84,700
9	183	77.40	86.88	92,200
10	151	68.10	84.80	8,120
11	152	65.80	82.20	84,700
12	131	71.10	78.90	76,000
13	164	65.70	82.20	84,800
14	146	62.40	84.08	83,000
15	160	64.20	86.10	84,400
16	158	72.20	84.63	87,400
17	149	82.30	77.92	76,500
18	172	69.70	81.60	82,600

Required

a. Review the preceding data and consider making any needed corrections using one of the following common data-correction practices:

 (1) Obtain the correct figure(s) from the divisions.

 (2) If data in part (1) cannot be obtained, delete entire division(s) that have errors, which is conservative, but costly when data are scarce.

 (3) Replace the incorrect figure(s) with the average value of the variable (without the error), which saves data but has no other justification.

b. In your opinion, how did performance across divisions compare last month? What assumptions are necessary to make cross-divisional comparisons? What additional data would you like to have? Explain.

c. Use regression analysis to find the best simple or multiple regression equation that explains manufacturing overhead costs across divisions. Describe how you performed the analysis and how you selected the best model.

d. Analysts have collected performance data for six divisions from the month just ended. Use these data to test the predictive ability of three of your models, including the best model by following the following steps:

 (1) Use each regression equation and the operating performance data to estimate manufacturing overhead costs.

 (2) Subtract estimated overhead costs from actual overhead costs; call this difference the *estimation error*.

 (3) Across models, compare either the average (mean) of the absolute value of estimation errors or the square root of the mean squared errors for each model.* Which model has the lowest average estimation error? Does this result surprise you? Why or why not?

Division	Average Defects per Month	First-Time Pass Rate, %	Average Cycle Time per Unit (minutes)	Actual Manufacturing Overhead Cost
1	146	73.00	81.00	$78,580
2	150	68.00	79.00	78,350
3	118	80.60	75.00	70,350
4	134	63.00	80.00	77,330
5	131	78.20	76.00	72,150
6	149	68.90	82.00	81,060

* Both are common measures of estimation accuracy. Absolute values can be computed with Excel's ABS() function; then compute the mean. The root mean squared error (RMSE) for each model can be computed by squaring the prediction errors, computing the mean squared error, and computing the square root. Clearly, this is spreadsheet-friendly work.

Chapter 12

Financial and Cost-Volume-Profit Models

After completing this chapter, you should be able to:

1. Design financial models to match strategic and operational decisions, such as profit planning or optimal use of a scarce resource.

2. Build a basic cost-volume-profit (CVP) financial model.

3. Build a computerized financial planning model.

4. Build a financial model that reflects the effects of taxes, multiple products, and multiple cost drivers.

5. Apply scenario and sensitivity analyses to model the risk of decisions.

6. Manage scarce resources.

7. Apply the Theory of Constraints to manage scarce resources (Appendix A).

8. Use linear programming to model decisions about the use of multiple scarce resources (Appendix B).

Cost-*Management* Challenges

(Solutions are on page 489.)

1. **What** does a cost-management analyst need to know to build useful financial planning models?

2. **Can** financial models help define future risks so that managers at least know what the uncertainties are?

3. **Should** organizations always try to maximize revenues or even the sales of products and services with the most throughput, contribution margin, or profit per unit? Are resource constraints an issue?

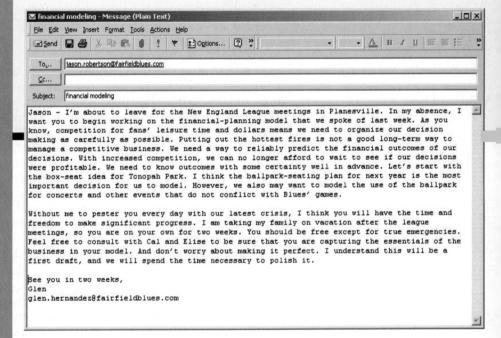

To... Jason.robertson@fairfieldblues.com
Cc...
Subject: financial modeling

Jason - I'm about to leave for the New England League meetings in Planesville. In my absence, I want you to begin working on the financial-planning model that we spoke of last week. As you know, competition for fans' leisure time and dollars means we need to organize our decision making as carefully as possible. Putting out the hottest fires is not a good long-term way to manage a competitive business. We need a way to reliably predict the financial outcomes of our decisions. With increased competition, we can no longer afford to wait to see if our decisions were profitable. We need to know outcomes with some certainty well in advance. Let's start with the box-seat idea for Tonopah Park. I think the ballpark-seating plan for next year is the most important decision for us to model. However, we also may want to model the use of the ballpark for concerts and other events that do not conflict with Blues' games.

Without me to pester you every day with our latest crisis, I think you will have the time and freedom to make significant progress. I am taking my family on vacation after the league meetings, so you are on your own for two weeks. You should be free except for true emergencies. Feel free to consult with Cal and Elise to be sure that you are capturing the essentials of the business in your model. And don't worry about making it perfect. I understand this will be a first draft, and we will spend the time necessary to polish it.

See you in two weeks,
Glen
glen.hernandez@fairfieldblues.com

Introducing Financial Modeling

Fairfield Blues, Inc., based in Fairfield, Massachusetts, owns a minor league baseball team of the same name and a ballpark, Tonopah Park. The team belongs to the independent New England League, which means that the 12 member teams are not affiliated with any major league team. The league's salary cap for a 24-person team is approximately $130,000 for the six-month season; players and coaches earn from $600 to $1,200 per month. The Fairfield Blues play all home games at Tonopah Park, which opened in 1919. The ballpark retains an old-time, family atmosphere and charm that continues to draw large crowds (4,000-seat capacity) regardless of the Blues' record. The Town of Fairfield runs a small concession stand outside the ballpark, which has always allowed ticket holders to bring in their own food and nonalcoholic drinks (no bottles or cans, however). The metropolitan area around Fairfield is experiencing significant growth as some Boston-area high-technology firms relocate seeking lower-cost housing and a more relaxed lifestyle. The growing population of people accustomed to many entertainment options also has created an opportunity for the company to promote outdoor concerts and other events at the ballpark on days or evenings without baseball games.

Four retired major-league players formed Fairfield Blues, Inc., and purchased Tonopah Park several years ago with funding from their retirement accounts, friends, family, a regional airline, and a local bank. In a short time, they have built the team and ballpark into a strong regional company. However, a neighboring city recently built a large amusement park and concert complex that threatens to drain attendance from Tonopah Park. Prior to leaving for two weeks for New England League meetings and a vacation, Fairfield Blues' chief operating officer and co-founder, Glen Hernandez, emailed his assistant, Jason Robertson, about several pressing issues that needed attention.

Hernandez's email raises several interesting issues in addition to the specific decisions facing the company. Many young firms, Fairfield Blues included, normally first devote efforts to developing an accounting system that concentrates on preparing financial reports. External parties such as stockholders, banks, and government agencies require financial reporting, and financial reports can be excellent for reviews of past operations. Young, successful companies typically outgrow their informal management styles and methods. As operations become larger and more complex, decisions become more difficult. Most firms develop financial *models* to help them organize and scrutinize their decision-making processes and options.

Recall that a model is a representation of reality. You likely have had interactions with models over the years through role-playing computer games, architects' scale models of proposed real estate developments, and simulators used by driver education and pilot-training programs. These models represent realistic conditions and simulate actual outcomes, for example, of a pilot's decision to turn, land, or ascend to avoid a storm. Using models, gamers, architects, drivers, pilots, and managers can learn from their decisions quickly and without the possible adverse consequences of learning from mistakes made under actual conditions. Furthermore, these people can identify opportunities for success that they might not have seen otherwise.

Definition of Financial Models

LO I Design financial models to match strategic and operational decisions, such as profit planning or optimal use of a scarce resource.

A **financial model** is an accurate, reliable simulation of relations among relevant costs, benefits, value, and risk that is useful for supporting business decisions. A good financial model works in much the same way as a flight simulator, allowing an organization to test the interactions of decisions and economic variables in a variety of settings. These models require analysts to develop a set of relations that represent a company's operating and financial activities, such as the ratio of variable costs to sales, inventory turnover ratios, and the relative proportions of various products sold. The financial model should allow a user to explore the effect of different situations on the business. For example, Fairfield Blues' managers might want to know the impact of a proposed ticket price increase on sales, cash flow, and profitability. For example, the following financial model predicts profits for three different levels of sales, which in this simple model is the only driver of benefits and costs.

Sales Levels

Sales units	100	200	300
Sales revenue at $10 per unit...............................	$1,000	$2,000	$3,000
Variable costs at $5 per unit	500	1,000	1,500
Contribution margin	$ 500	$1,000	$1,500
Fixed costs	800	800	800
Operating income...	($ 300)	$ 200	$ 700

Financial models offer several benefits to users. Once the model has been developed, users can spend significant time on business analysis without being overwhelmed by the related number crunching. In addition, like the simulators just discussed, many of these models allow an organization to study the impact of a possible business action by reviewing the potential results before that action occurs. In other words, it is possible to identify a good or bad project or decision prior to committing the organization's resources to a course of action. Furthermore, valid financial models can help train inexperienced employees and increase their understanding of how their actions affect financial outcomes.

The primary goal of this chapter is to explain and demonstrate methods of building, using, and interpreting financial models. To accomplish this goal, it presents specific decision contexts faced regularly by many organizations. These decision contexts include profit planning and the optimal use of scarce resources. Common examples of financial models used by organizations of all types and sizes include these:

■ *Models of relations among an organization's costs, revenues, and income.* For example, a financial model of this type can compute product profitability given assumptions about quantity sold, sales price, activities, and variable and fixed costs. This model also estimates the effects of adding or dropping a product or outsourcing a service or the effects of adding more scarce resources. Chapter 13 and a number of the earlier chapters of this text use this very broad class of financial model focused on financial planning. The present chapter also uses this model type to illustrate methods of building, using, and interpreting financial models.

■ *Models of relations between current investments and long-term profitability or value.* Various types of investment models (e.g., discounted cash flow and payback models) are the focus of Chapter 14.

■ *Models of pro forma (or budgeted) financial statements.* This type of model shows how a firm's financial position evolves from a beginning balance sheet, to a cash flow statement, to an income statement, and finally to an ending balance sheet. This important type of financial model is the topic of Chapter 15.

■ *Specialized financial models for sophisticated decision making.* These include but certainly are not restricted to examples such as the following:

   ■ Xcel Energy's models of consumer and industry demand for energy that contains hundreds of variables and many equations.

   ■ Econometric models of the economy that the Federal Reserve Board uses to estimate economic impacts of a possible change in interest rates.

   ■ Merck's R&D–impact model that incorporates the valuation of its R&D projects.

Objectives of Financial Modeling

Although financial models vary in complexity and purpose, they should be designed to have the following three common characteristics and objectives.

Usefulness for decision making.   Decision makers must make better decisions using these models than they can without them, and the benefits of better decisions must exceed the costs of developing and using the models. Otherwise, the financial model is nothing but an elaborate (and probably expensive) toy. Unfortunately, anecdotes about resources wasted on complex, unused financial models or financial decision-support systems abound. The most common reasons for the failure of these models are (1) user lack of understanding of factors that are relevant to decisions and (2) excessive complexity.

Accurate and reliable simulation of relevant factors and relations.   Decisions often hinge on the accuracy of measurements and the realism of the simulated relations among factors. The model should simulate the essential elements of business decisions, processes, and the environment. Clearly, models cannot capture all of the realism of the world (or the model would be the world!). However, a useful model must reflect the essential, relevant factors that drive decisions and relations among the factors. Furthermore, reliability requires that outcomes predicted by the model should closely approximate what is observed in the real world. If a model's predictions are not reliable, managers will not and should not use the model. The model builder must be able to demonstrate that decision makers can rely on a new model to be more reliable than earlier ones, past practice, or "gut feelings."

Flexible and responsive analyses.   Financial models can be "back of the envelope" figures or more elaborate manual calculations. For example, your checkbook is a relatively simple, manual financial model of your cash position. Simple or not, an arithmetic error can cause you extensive grief and anxiety until you find and correct it. Think of the effort required to manually correct an arithmetic error or change a key factor in one of the Federal Reserve Board's complex economic models.

Complex financial modeling is not feasible today without taking advantage of the power of computer software (e.g., spreadsheets or specially designed modeling programs). Well-designed financial models allow decision makers to *easily* explore the predicted outcomes from varied decisions and assumptions about key factors. If the model is difficult to use or does not clearly show the effects of changes in decisions and key factors, decision makers probably will not use it. Before we explore building computer models, however, we first discuss some general principles of financial modeling in the context of manual profit-planning models.

Using Cost-Volume-Profit (CVP) Planning Models

LO 2 Build a basic cost-volume-profit (CVP) financial model.

The most basic financial model, the **cost-volume-profit (CVP) model,** reflects the effects of changes in an organization's activities, such as sales volume, and of its prices and costs on profit or income. The simplest CVP model assumes that the only activity that drives profits is sales volume. The name of this basic model predates the popularity of activity-based costing, which recognizes many more potential drivers of profits than only sales volume. Nonetheless, the CVP name has stuck.[1] The basic model is worth learning and understanding because it can be extended to model the more complex profit impacts of changes in other revenue and cost drivers, demand, activity-based costs, taxation, and product or service mix. For example, basic or extended CVP models can help companies such as the following make decisions whether:

- Federal Express should add another cargo flight between San Francisco and Memphis.
- News Corp's profit will change if viewer ratings decline for *The Simpsons* program.
- Kansas City Public Library can cover its costs for the year if it expands its current circulation capacity and replaces some librarians with computerized "help" and check-out functions.

---

[1] A more general name for these financial planning models is CRD (cost and revenue driver) models, but CVP is widely used at this time. Besides, pronouncing this acronym might reduce confidence in the model.

■ Boulder Community Hospital should enlarge its current laboratory or outsource some testing to independent laboratories.

■ Fairfield Blues, this chapter's focus company, should convert some of its general admission seating to reserved box seating.

Each of these decisions concerns the effects of changing cost drivers or activities on costs, revenues, and profits. These decisions are candidates for CVP modeling.

Many nonprofit organizations also use forms of CVP modeling. Although legally they do not seek to generate profits, managers of nonprofit organizations must plan the effects of changing cost drivers and activities on their revenue and costs. For instance, commissioners of one of the fastest-growing counties in the United States, Douglas County, Colorado, must model the effects of rapid population growth on tax revenues and the cost of providing and maintaining infrastructure such as water, sewer system, schools, roads, and police protection. Pride Industries, a nonprofit employer of handicapped individuals in Sacramento, California, also uses financial modeling to determine whether revenues from its services and manufacturing operations will cover its costs.

Basic Cost-Volume-Profit Model

We apply the basic CVP model to the Fairfield Blues' seating plans for Tonopah Park.[2] Based on a review of past seasons' accounting records, Jason Robertson performed statistical analyses to estimate average fixed facility costs per season, ticket prices, and unit-level variable costs per ticket sold.[3] He found that other cost and revenue drivers either might not be important factors for profitability or can be incorporated later into a more complex model.

Robertson then updated the historical amounts to reflect expected price and cost changes and developed the following cost and price estimates for the ballpark during the six-month baseball season:

Facility cost per season (mortgage, salaries, utilities, etc.) $450,000

Variable cost per ticket sold (programs, custodians, etc.) $2

Price per ticket $7

He believed that these price and cost estimates are appropriate for typical seasonal operations for the coming year. He can easily adjust facility costs for more or fewer salaries or variable costs for more or less costly programs. Although he also can adjust ticket prices, doing so might not reflect the team's newly competitive situation. Robertson suspects that next year's attendance might be sensitive (i.e., elastic) to changes in ticket prices. Let's next discuss how he can use these factors in a simple, manual financial planning model. Later, we will transform this manual model into a more powerful computer model.

Cost-Volume-Profit Model and the Break-Even Point

Suppose that the Fairfield Blues plans to sell 90,000 tickets during a season. The following income statement for the season shows that its estimated operating income is zero:

Volume, Revenues, and Costs	Estimated Amounts
Seasonal ticket volume	90,000 tickets
Sales revenue (90,000 × $7)	$630,000
Less variable costs (90,000 × $2)	180,000
Total contribution margin	$450,000
Less facility costs	450,000
Operating income	$ 0

[2] Later in the chapter we also will model plans to promote concerts and other events at the ballpark.

[3] Chapter 11 presents detailed discussions of cost estimation.

Notice that the income statement (1) is a financial model of the key revenue and cost driver (ticket sales), (2) highlights the distinction between variable costs and committed facility costs, and (3) shows the outcome of the plan to sell 90,000 tickets, which is a profit of zero. The organization has no profit or loss at this activity level; it therefore *breaks even.* This ticket volume is the organization's **break-even point,** the volume of activity that produces equal revenues and costs. If no other activities except ticket sales drive costs and revenues, the team's break-even point is 90,000 tickets per season.[4]

How can Robertson compute the Blues' break-even point if we did not already know that it is 90,000 tickets per month? He can use either a *contribution-margin* or an *equation* approach to the basic CVP model to find the break-even point.

Contribution-margin approach.   Each ticket sells for $7, but $2 of this amount is used to cover variable costs. Thus, $5 per ticket is the *contribution margin* per ticket that in total covers the facility cost of $450,000. When enough tickets have been sold so that these $5 contributions add up to $450,000, the organization will break even. We can therefore compute the 90,000-ticket, break-even sales volume as follows:

$$\text{Break-even sales volume} = \text{Fixed costs per period}$$
$$\div \text{Contribution margin per unit of volume}$$
$$\text{Fairfield Blues' break-even volume} = \$450,000 \text{ per month} \div \$5 \text{ per ticket}$$
$$= 90,000 \text{ tickets per month}$$

Equation approach.   An equivalent approach to finding the break-even point is based on this equation:

$$\text{Operating income (or profit)} = \text{Sales revenue} - \text{Costs}$$

If costs are separated into variable and fixed components, the income calculation is captured by the following expression:

$$\text{Operating income} = \text{Sales revenue} - \text{Variable costs} - \text{Fixed costs}$$

This is also expressed as

$$\text{Operating income} = (\text{Selling price} \times \text{Sales volume}) - (\text{Variable cost per unit} \times \text{Sales volume}) - \text{Fixed costs}$$

This also is equivalent to

$$\text{Operating income} = [(\text{Selling price} - \text{Variable cost per unit}) \times \text{Sales volume}] - \text{Fixed costs}$$

Setting operating income equal to *zero* because we seek the break-even point, this becomes

$$[(\text{Selling price} - \text{Variable cost per unit}) \times \text{Break-even sales volume}] - \text{Fixed costs} = 0$$

Moving fixed costs to the other side of the equal sign, the equation becomes

$$[(\text{Selling price} - \text{Variable cost per unit}) \times \text{Break-even sales volume}] = \text{Fixed costs}$$

Now solving for sales volume, we have

$$\text{Break-even sales volume} = \text{Fixed costs} \div (\text{Selling price} - \text{Variable cost per unit})$$

---

[4] Recall from Chapter 4 that many organizations have a hierarchy of cost-driving activities. Our early examples consider only variable and facility-level activities. For convenience, some refer to all nonvariable costs as "fixed" costs, although this can be a dangerous practice because it can incorrectly imply to decision makers that these costs cannot be changed or do not change with respect to other activities. We address this in later sections.

For Fairfield Blues this is

$$\text{Break-even sales volume} = \$450,000 \div (\$7 - \$2)$$
$$= \$450,000 \div \$5$$
$$= 90,000 \text{ tickets}$$

Note that both the equation and contribution-margin approaches take us to the same place: dividing facility or fixed costs by the contribution margin per unit.

Basic CVP Model in Graphical Format

The contribution-margin and equation approaches are two equivalent techniques for finding the break-even point. Both methods reach the same conclusion, so personal preference dictates the approach to be used. The resulting figures for Fairfield Blues are graphed in Exhibit 12–1. Panel A shows a CVP graph, and panel B shows an alternative profit-volume graph, which condenses the revenue and cost information to a single line.

The graphs, which also are financial models, disclose more information than the break-even calculation and can be useful in presentations to illustrate the effects of changes in volume on profit. The vertical distance between the lines on the graph in panel A or the distance from the X-axis and the line in panel B reflects the profit or loss at a particular sales volume. If Fairfield Blues sells fewer than 90,000 tickets in a month, it will suffer a loss. The size of the loss increases as ticket sales decline. Conversely, the team enjoys a profit if sales exceed 90,000 tickets. For example, if the team sells 170,000 tickets in a season, its profit will be $400,000.

CVP and Target Income

The founders and other stockholders of the Fairfield Blues, like the owners of any other business, desire to earn a competitive return on their investment. The founders have invested some of their retirement funds in the team and ballpark, and other stockholders have contributed capital that they could invest elsewhere. In this case, the stockholders estimate that the value of the company is $4,000,000 and that they should receive a 10 percent return on that investment value. Therefore, they believe that the company should generate a target income of $400,000, which is a 10 percent return on their investment. The rationale is that the stockholders can sell the company, reinvest the proceeds, and earn a comparable return. To be a viable investment, the Fairfield Blues must meet stockholders' opportunity costs.

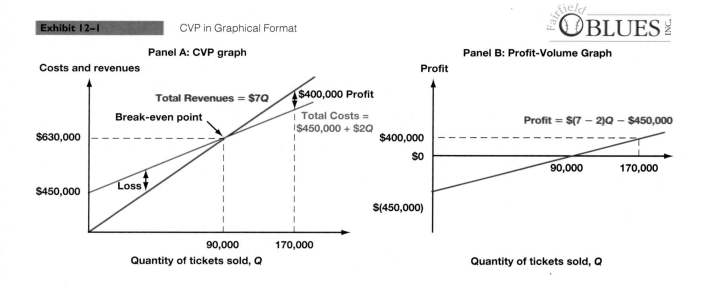

Exhibit 12–1   CVP in Graphical Format

Integrating the target income into the CVP model is straightforward. In the previous case, the company had to sell 90,000 tickets to cover the fixed costs and break even. Now it must go one step further: Cover the fixed costs *and* earn $400,000 income. With each ticket continuing to contribute $5, the necessary calculation using either the contribution margin or equation method becomes

Target sales volume = (Fixed costs + Target income) ÷ Contribution margin per ticket
= ($450,000 + $400,000) ÷ $5
= $850,000 ÷ $5
= 170,000 tickets

Note that Exhibit 12–1 also shows the target sales volume, the quantity 170,000 that achieves the target income, to the right of the break-even point in both panels.

Operating Leverage

Most organizations, including the Fairfield Blues, commit to spending for resources such as salaries, rents, licenses, interest, and taxes, which can be very difficult to restructure in the short term. Large amounts of these facility costs expose an organization to the adverse effects of fluctuating sales because contribution margins are relatively small compared to committed costs. **Operating leverage** reflects the risk of missing sales targets and is measured by the ratio of the contribution margin to operating income. High levels of operating leverage reflect the risk that an organization faces from missing sales targets because facility costs are relatively high and small changes in sales can easily push the organization into a loss.[5] Conversely, low levels of operating leverage mean that facility costs are relatively low compared to the contribution margins. Consider the following example that contrasts the Fairfield Blues with a competitor that has relatively higher operating leverage.

	Fairfield Blues	Maxwell Espressos
Sales price per unit	$7.00	$9.00
Variable cost per unit	$2.00	$2.00
Contribution margin per unit	$5.00	$7.00
Expected sales quantity	170,000	170,000
Expected profitability:		
Sales revenue	$1,190,000	$1,530,000
Variable costs	340,000	340,000
Contribution margin	$ 850,000	$1,190,000
Facility costs	450,000	790,000
Operating income	$ 400,000	$ 400,000
Operating leverage	$850,000 ÷ $400,000 = 2.13	$1,190,000 ÷ $400,000 = 2.98

These two companies have the same levels of expected sales and equal operating incomes; at this sales level, their difference in facility costs ($790,000 − $450,000) is covered by their difference in contribution margin ($1,190,000 − $850,000). Although one might be indifferent to the two companies at this level of sales, their exposure to changes in sales is different. Fairfield Blues' operating leverage, 2.13, is lower than that of Maxwell Espressos, which is 2.98. This reflects Espressos' higher exposure to the effects of lower than expected sales. What if each company's actual sales level declined by 10,000 units to 160,000? Which company's income is hurt

---

[5] Historically, one of the rationales behind the rate regulation of public utilities was to guarantee them an adequate return on very large committed costs in exchange for reliable public service. Guaranteed rates of return were compensation for assuming the risk associated with high operating leverage in the public interest.

more? Consider the following, which shows the effects of lower sales volume for both companies:

	Fairfield Blues	Maxwell Espressos
Sales price per unit	$7.00	$9.00
Variable cost per unit	$2.00	$2.00
Contribution margin per unit	$5.00	$7.00
Actual sales quantity	160,000	160,000
Actual profitability:		
Sales revenue	$1,120,000	$1,440,000
Variable costs	320,000	320,000
Contribution margin	$ 800,000	$1,120,000
Facility costs	450,000	790,000
Operating income	$ 350,000	$ 330,000
Operating leverage	2.29	3.39

Because sales are lower, both companies' operating incomes naturally are lower than expected, but Espressos has taken the larger hit because its facility costs are higher than those of the Blues. Note also that unless Espressos reduces facility costs, its situation becomes riskier as reflected by its still higher operating leverage. In contrast, if its sales were expected to be consistently above the indifference point of 170,000 tickets per season, the Espressos' higher contribution margin per ticket makes it more profitable than the Fairfield Blues. Many aspects of financial models reflect this type of impact on profits. We later cover more general approaches to modeling variability and risk.

Identifying Elements of a Financial Model

Relations among Revenues and Costs

Revenue and cost drivers are the building blocks of financial models, and relations among them are the mortar that holds them together. A fundamental lesson of cost management is that many decisions drive costs; *costs do not just happen*. Decisions also drive revenues, but not all of them are at the discretion of managers. The previous example reflected an environment in which only unit-level activity (ticket sales) appeared to drive revenues and costs because the model builder considered all other driving activities to be fixed or committed. For now, we continue to model profits with a single, unit-level revenue and cost-driving activity, but we model the more general case later in the chapter.

Manual versus Computer Models

In concept, financial modeling does not require a computer. After all, organizations used manual financial models similar to our previous examples before computers were available. However, it is a fact of modern business that virtually all financial modeling is performed with computer spreadsheets or specialized modeling software. This software enables quicker, more flexible, and more complex modeling than was possible before. It is inconceivable that we should extend our discussion of financial modeling without recognizing the impact and value of computer software.

LO 3 Build a computerized financial planning model.

Set Up of Computer Spreadsheet Models

Computer spreadsheets such as Microsoft® Excel and Lotus 1-2-3® are among the most powerful and most commonly used business tools. Mastery of the fundamentals of spreadsheets is essential for anyone who undertakes any cost-management analysis, particularly financial modeling. This discussion is not meant to substitute for either formal courses or diligent self-study, either of which can lead to mastery of spreadsheets. The purpose is to convey some fundamentals of building a flexible financial model.

Spreadsheets are ideally suited for financial modeling. One important key to unlocking the power of these spreadsheets is to use the spreadsheet *not* merely as a calculator but as a *model* of relations among financial and nonfinancial factors. Let's transform Fairfield Blues' manual profit-planning model into the computer model shown in Exhibit 12–2. The steps we perform can be extended to a more complex spreadsheet model and are outlined in the following sections.

Gathering information.   First, gather all facts, assumptions, and estimates that underlie the model. These include estimates of sales prices, profit targets, and so forth. Some analysts call these the model's input data or *parameters*. They are the model's cost- and revenue-driver building blocks. Fairfield Blues' profit-planning parameters include the ticket price, variable cost per ticket sold, facility costs per season, profit target, and percentage of seating capacity sold per game. Note that profit targets can be expressed as absolute dollar amounts or as returns on either sales or invested capital. To facilitate analysis with the model, these parameters should be located and clearly identified in a defined parameter or input-data area of the spreadsheet. Exhibit 12–2 clearly identifies the model's input-data cells. This is the only place that the parameters are located as numbers, but the analysis section of the model can use them throughout.

Modeling relations among parameters.   Second, understand and describe the relations of the model's parameters. Changing a model's parameters should change its outcomes. This usually involves modeling how one parameter affects another with an algebraic relation or *formula*. For Fairfield Blues' profit-planning model, these formulas are the equations underlying the income statement and are located apart from the input data section. The model in Exhibit 12–2 has three types of CVP analyses below the data input section: break-even (cells A7 to B10), target profit (A11 to B16), and planned profit (C7 to D13). The last analysis shows expected profits at a planned level of ticket sales (183,600 tickets = 4,000-seat capacity × 54 games × 85 percent seats sold, in this example) that might differ from either break-even volume or target volume.

Separate parameters and formulas.   Third, to facilitate the analysis of the model, the formulas in the analysis sections should *never* contain the actual numerical values of the parameters. Instead, use the parameters' cell locations in all formulas where they occur. Exhibit 12–2 models the financial relationships in column B, rows 8 to 16 and column D, rows 8 to 13. Placing the cursor on any of these cells shows that *none con-*

Exhibit 12–2

Computerized Profit-Planning Model

Microsoft Excel - Fairfield Blues

File   Edit   View   Insert   Format   Tools   Data   Window   Help

Arial   ▾ 10 ▾   **B** U D ≡ $ % , .°   ▦ ▾ ◇ ▾ ▾ ▷ ▷ ◁ ◁ ▾ 🖆 🖫 🖻 🖺 ∽ ▾

B10   ▾   = =B8/B9

	A	B	C	D
1	**Profit-planning model**			
2	**Input data**		Sales price per ticket	$ 7.00
3	Ballpark seating capacity per game	4,000	Variable cost per ticket	$ 2.00
4	Home games per season	54	Fixed facility costs per season	$ 450,000
5	Average percentage seats sold per game	85%	Target profit	$ 400,000
6				
7	**Break-even analysis**		**Planned-profit analysis**	
8	Fixed costs (D4)	$ 450,000	Planned sales volume in units (B3*B4*B5)	183,600
9	Divided by contribution margin per ticket (D2-D3)	$ 5.00	Sales revenues (D2*D8)	$ 1,285,200
10	Break-even volume in units (B8/B9)	90,000	Less variable costs (D3*D8)	367,200
11	**Target-profit analysis**		Contribution margin (D9-D10)	918,000
12	Fixed costs (D4)	$ 450,000	Less fixed costs (D4)	450,000
13	Plus target profit (D5)	400,000	Operating profit (loss) (D11-D12)	$ 468,000
14	Target total contribution margin (B12+B13)	$ 850,000		
15	Divided by contribution margin per unit (D2-D3)	$ 5.00		
16	Target volume in units (B14/B15)	170,000		
17				

◄ ◄ ► ►\ **Exhibit 12-2** / Exhibit 12-3 / Exhibit 12-4 / Exhibit 12-5 / Exhibit 12-4 | ◄ |

Ready

tain numbers. Instead, the amounts displayed in the cells are the *computed effects of formulas* that combine the model's parameters and preceding calculations, as appropriate. For this exposition, columns A and C also show these formulas, although this usually is not done because some formulas are very complex. If you highlight the cell B10, you see in the formula bar at the top of the spreadsheet that it contains the formula "=B8/B9," which models the break-even relation. Likewise, cell B16 contains the formula, "=B14/B15," which computes the target unit volume. D13 contains the formula, "=D11 − D12," which completes the calculation of the operating profit or loss at the planned sales volume.

Building models often is a group effort, requiring input from many perspectives and functions.

The major benefit to separating the model's parameters and relations follows:

> **Making a change to a parameter in the one highly visible place where it occurs as a number causes the model to recalculate outcomes by incorporating the new parameter value everywhere it is used in formulas.**

Otherwise, changing a parameter requires changing every formula that uses the parameter. For large models, this can be very difficult and wastes valuable analysis time. Furthermore, someone other than the model's creator who wishes to use it might not know where to find every occurrence of the parameter and might use the model to generate inaccurate information.

Following these guidelines for constructing financial models creates powerful and flexible decision-making aids. Analysts can extend simple models to include complications of taxes, multiple products, multiple revenue and cost drivers, scarce resources, and risk. You should consider replicating the model in Exhibit 12–2 on a computer so that you can better appreciate this and following sections of the chapter.

Modeling Taxes

Profit-seeking firms pay taxes on their periodic profits, meaning that target income figures should be set high enough to meet profit requirements and cover the firm's tax obligations. The relationship between an organization's pretax income and after-tax income can be expressed in the following formula:

LO 4 Build a financial model that reflects the effects of taxes, multiple products, and multiple cost drivers.

$$\text{After-tax income} = \text{Before-tax income} - \text{Income taxes}$$
$$= \text{Before-tax income} - (\text{Before-tax income} \times t)$$
$$= \text{Before-tax income} \times (1 - t)$$

where t is the average or *effective* income tax rate.

Dividing both sides by $(1 - t)$ gives

$$\text{After-tax income}/(1 - t) = \text{Before-tax income}$$

Now we can find the desired before-tax income that will generate the desired after-tax income, given the company's effective tax rate, which will meet the profit target and cover the tax obligation.

To illustrate, we continue the previous Fairfield Blues example to show how the team can earn the desired $400,000 profit target *after tax.* Assume that the company

Exhibit 12–3

Profit-Planning Model with an Average, Effective Tax Rate

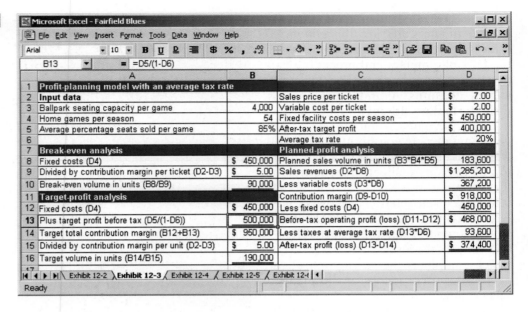

Microsoft Excel - Fairfield Blues

B13   = =D5/(1-D6)

	A	B	C	D
1	Profit-planning model with an average tax rate			
2	Input data		Sales price per ticket	$ 7.00
3	Ballpark seating capacity per game	4,000	Variable cost per ticket	$ 2.00
4	Home games per season	54	Fixed facility costs per season	$ 450,000
5	Average percentage seats sold per game	85%	After-tax target profit	$ 400,000
6			Average tax rate	20%
7	Break-even analysis		Planned-profit analysis	
8	Fixed costs (D4)	$ 450,000	Planned sales volume in units (B3*B4*B5)	183,600
9	Divided by contribution margin per ticket (D2-D3)	$ 5.00	Sales revenues (D2*D8)	$1,285,200
10	Break-even volume in units (B8/B9)	90,000	Less variable costs (D3*D8)	367,200
11	Target-profit analysis		Contribution margin (D9-D10)	$ 918,000
12	Fixed costs (D4)	$ 450,000	Less fixed costs (D4)	450,000
13	Plus target profit before tax (D5/(1-D6))	500,000	Before-tax operating profit (loss) (D11-D12)	$ 468,000
14	Target total contribution margin (B12+B13)	$ 950,000	Less taxes at average tax rate (D13*D6)	93,600
15	Divided by contribution margin per unit (D2-D3)	$ 5.00	After-tax profit (loss) (D13-D14)	$ 374,400
16	Target volume in units (B14/B15)	190,000		
17				

Exhibit 12-2 \ **Exhibit 12-3** / Exhibit 12-4 / Exhibit 12-5 / Exhibit 12-6

Ready

is subject to a 20 percent average or effective income tax rate. We first convert the after-tax target profit to a before-tax amount, as follows:

$$\text{Before-tax income} = \text{After-tax income} \div (1 - t)$$
$$= \$400,000 \div (1 - .20)$$
$$= \$500,000$$

The before-tax income of $500,000 is inserted as the target income in the following calculation, now requiring Fairfield Blues to sell 190,000 tickets to generate its after-tax profit target of $500,000:

$$\text{Target sales volume} = (\text{Fixed cost} + \text{Target before-tax income})$$
$$\div \text{Contribution margin per ticket}$$
$$= (\$450,000 + \$500,000) \div \$5 = \underline{190,000 \text{ tickets}}$$

Exhibit 12–3 shows Fairfield Blues' profit-planning model that Robertson modified to include the tax obligation, modeled as the average tax rate in D6. Note that the break-even analysis in Exhibit 12–3 (A7 to B10) is unchanged because at zero profit, Fairfield Blues pays no taxes. Subsequent analyses differ because of the inclusion of the tax rate. The target-profit analysis (A11 to B16) uses the before-tax profit target, B13 = D5/(1-D6), to calculate the target volume of 190,000 tickets (B16). The planned profit analysis in cells C7 to D15 has been changed in this exhibit to reflect the effect of taxes. Note that because the average tax rate is included as an input parameter and in volume and profit analyses, Robertson also can model the company's operations given changes to its average tax rate that result from different tax-planning actions. More complexities of tax planning require a more complex profit-planning model.[6] Note also that this analysis shows that expected ticket sales will not meet the company's after-tax target (see the planned profit in D15). This shortfall is a motivation for modeling the possible impacts of altering the ballpark's seating.

Modeling Multiple Products

The previous Fairfield Blues' models assume that the company has only one product: a "general admission" seat. Most firms produce more than one product at their facilities, which adds some complexity to their profit-planning analyses.

---

[6] The complexity of tax planning is beyond the scope of this text.

Recall that Fairfield Blues' seasonal facility costs total $450,000 and the variable cost per ticket is $2. Suppose that the company has decided to replace some of its 4,000 general admission seats with 800 reserved box seats. These 800 seats will be more comfortable and afford a better view of the field than the ballpark's remaining general admission seating, which will now have 3,200 seats. Management has decided to reduce its general admission price to $6 per ticket and charge $15 per ticket for box seats. The construction project will result in an increase in seasonal fixed costs of $100,000 because of added depreciation.[7] Variable costs per ticket are unchanged.

Notice that 80 percent of the available seats are general admission seats (3,200 ÷ 4,000) and 20 percent are box seats. Assume that ticket sales for each type of seat will be in the same proportion as the number of different seats available. Therefore, if it sells 100,000 tickets per season, for example, sales should be as follows:

General admission seat tickets.......................... 100,000 × .8 = 80,000 tickets
Box-seat tickets .... 100,000 × .2 = 20,000 tickets

For any organization that sells multiple products, the relative proportion of each type of product planned or actually sold is called the **sales mix** or **product mix.** It is an important assumption in multiproduct profit planning because it is used to compute a **weighted-average unit contribution margin (WAUCM),** a tool for finding the break-even point and performing other profit-planning exercises. WAUCM is the average of the various products' unit contribution margins *weighted* by the relative proportion of each product sold. Contribution margin for general admission seats is $4 per ticket ($4 = $6 − $2) and for box seats is $13 per ticket ($13 = $15 − $2). Fairfield Blues' weighted-average unit contribution margin for the sale of regular and box seats is:

Weighted-average unit contribution margin (WAUCM) = ($4 × .8) + ($13 × .2) = $5.80

The team's new break-even point in tickets is computed by replacing a single-product contribution margin with the multiproduct WAUCM in the break-even formula introduced earlier, namely:

$$\textbf{Break-even sales volume} = \textbf{Fixed cost per period} \div \textbf{WAUCM per unit}$$
$$= \textbf{\$550,000} \div \textbf{\$5.80}$$
$$= \underline{\textbf{94,828 tickets}} \text{ (rounded)}$$

(Recall that the construction of box seats increases fixed costs from $450,000 to $550,000.) This number of tickets, however, is a combination of regular and box seats and must be interpreted considering the sales mix. The team will break even for the month if it sells the following tickets:

General admission seat tickets.......................... 94,828 × .8 = 75,862 tickets
Box-seat tickets .... 94,828 × .2 = 18,966 tickets
Break-even sales volume .... 94,828 tickets

One may convert these sales volume figures to sales dollar figures by multiplying each product sales volume by its sales price, as follows

Break-even sales dollars = ($6 × 75,862) + ($15 × 18,966) = $739,662

Observe that the break-even point of 94,828 tickets or $739,662 is valid only for the 80:20 sales mix assumed in computing the weighted-average unit contribution margin. A shift in sales mix generally results in a different WAUCM, which changes the break-even or target income figure. Thus, the sales mix is an important input parameter for the many organizations that provide multiple products or services from common facilities.

---

[7] Many organizations build financial models to reflect accounting accruals such as depreciation. However, financial models also can reflect cash flows, excluding depreciation and similar accruals.

Cost Management in Practice 12.1

Sales Mix Concept in Action

You have no doubt seen the sales-mix concept in action by observing recent trends in gasoline sales. The old-fashioned gas station has rapidly given way to the convenience store that also sells gasoline. Or, in some cases, gas stations might be a partner with, say, Subway, BurgerKing, or McDonald's. In still other instances, the convenience store might also sell fresh produce and flowers, as well as provide services such as a post office, pharmacy, and laundry.

What's the reason behind the change? Although gas stations usually require expensive sites, gasoline retailing is a low-margin business—10 percent. Convenience-store items, on the other hand, have margins of around 30 percent. These latter goods now account for at least half of sales, and overall profitability has increased. The next step might be for the marketers to purposely take a loss on the gas just to attract customers who might also purchase food. This practice is already happening in some European markets. *Source: R. L. Sullivan,* "Exxonsafeway." (Full citations to references are in the Bibliography.)

Multiproduct Profit-Planning Model

Exhibit 12–4 shows Fairfield Blues' profit-planning model with the modification of two types of seating (A6 to B8) and the sales mix assumption (A9 to B11). The other addition to the model is the computation of the weighted-average unit contribution margin (WAUCM in cell B14), which is computed as explained earlier. Using the WAUCM value of $5.80 allows Robertson to compute the break-even volume of 94,828 tickets in cell B18. Why is the break-even ticket volume higher than before (recall that with only general admission seating, the breakeven was 90,000 tickets)? The break-even volume is higher now because, although Fairfield Blues has added a new product (box seating) with a higher unit contribution margin, it also has increased fixed costs per season by $100,000. Thus, the company must sell more tickets to break even. Notice, however, that the target sales to reach the desired after-tax profit is 181,034 tickets (B24). This is a lower ticket volume than before because the

Exhibit 12–4

Profit-Planning Model with Taxes and Multiple Products

	A	B	C	D
1	Profit-planning model with multiple products			
2	**Sales input data**		**Cost input data**	
3	Ballpark seating capacity per game	4,000	Variable cost per ticket	$ 2.00
4	Home games per season	54	Fixed facility costs per season	550,000
5	Average percentage seats sold per game	85%	After-tax target profit	400,000
6	Sales price per ticket		Average tax rate	20%
7	Box seating	$ 15.00		
8	General admission seating	6.00		
9	Sales mix assumption			
10	Box seating	20.0%		
11	General admission seating	80.0%		
12				
13	Weighted average unit contribution margin		Planned-profit analysis	
14	WAUCM (B10*(B7-D3) + B11*(B8-D3))	$ 5.80	Planned sales volume in units (B3*B4*B5)	183,600
15	Break-even analysis		Sales revenues	
16	Fixed costs (D4)	$ 550,000	Box seating (D14*B10*B7)	$ 550,800
17	Divided by WAUCM (B14)	5.80	General admission seating (D14*B11*B8)	881,280
18	Break-even volume in units (B16/B17)	94,828	Total revenues	$ 1,432,080
19	Target-profit analysis		Less variable costs (D14*D3)	367,200
20	Fixed costs (D4)	$ 550,000	Contribution margin (D18-D19)	$ 1,064,880
21	Before-tax target profit (D5/(1-D6))	500,000	Less fixed costs (D4)	550,000
22	Target contribution margin	$1,050,000	Before-tax profit (loss) (D20-D21)	$ 514,880
23	Divided by WAUCM (B14)	$ 5.80	Less taxes at average tax rate (D6*D22)	102,976
24	Target volume in units (B22/B23)	181,034	After-tax profit (loss) (D22-D23)	$ 411,904

Cell B14 formula: =B10*(B7-D3) + B11*(B8-D3)

Sheet tabs: Exhibit 12-2 / Exhibit 12-3 / **Exhibit 12-4** / Exhibit 12-5 / Exhibit 12-6

Effect of Sales Mix on Financial Performance

You're the Decision Maker 12.1

The sales mix is relevant not only for multiproduct profit planning but also for assessing an organization's actual sales and profit performance. Suppose that Fairfield Blues plans to sell 183,600 tickets next season (85 percent of seats sold) with the assumed 80:20 sales mix and expects to exceed its after-tax income target. Suppose also that during the next season, all ticket prices and costs occurred as planned. However, the team actually sold 185,760 tickets (86 percent of seats sold). One might expect that actual, after-tax profit should exceed the target even more because ticket volume exceeded the planned and target volumes. However, during this season when 185,760 tickets were sold, the actual sales mix was 84 percent general admission and 16 percent box seats, which is a departure from the 80:20 sales mix assumption.

a. What is the effect on break-even and target volumes and profit from the changes in sales volume and sales mix?

b. Explain how the changes in outcomes were caused by the actual inputs.

(Solutions begin on p. 489.)

higher WAUCM ($5.80 versus $5.00) requires fewer tickets to be sold above the breakeven (after fixed costs are covered) to meet the same after-tax profit target.

Lower break-even and target volumes usually are desirable because they mean that fixed costs are relatively low and the operation is less vulnerable to the effects of lower sales (recall the earlier discussion of operating leverage). Does this mean that the baseball team *will* be more profitable? It does only if customers are willing to pay the higher prices for box seats *and* if they purchase tickets in accordance with the planned sales mix. Achieving the planned sales volume (D14) of 183,600 tickets *and* the assumed sales mix should result in exceeding the after-tax profit target of $400,000 by $11,904 (see D24).

Modeling Multiple Cost Drivers

Drivers of Profits

A critique of the profit-planning model in Exhibit 12–4 reveals several limitations despite the addition of taxes and multiple products. As we just showed, for example, the sales mix must remain as predicted, or a change might influence the organization's profitability. Similarly, a company's technology, efficiency, and management must remain constant because these cost and revenue drivers also affect profit-planning relations. The model also is based on straight-line, linear relations among revenues and costs, thus ignoring basic factors such as quantity discounts. Perhaps most troubling is the model's use of a single cost-driver activity, sales volume. Most organizations have multiple cost and revenue drivers that affect profits.

LO 4 Build a financial model that reflects the effects of taxes, multiple products, and multiple cost drivers.

Cost-driver activities. Activity-based costing (Chapter 4) directs us to investigate decisions about activities performed at the unit, batch, product, customer, and facility levels to identify significant cost drivers. If these activities are relevant to profit planning, financial models should include them. Models should reflect the effects of all major cost-driving activities, some of which occur at other than the unit level. For example, the number of tickets sold drives some unit-level costs of the Fairfield Blues, but decisions about seating capacity, staffing, maintenance, and grounds keeping also drive the team's costs.

Revenue-driver activities. Revenues are the result of sales prices and sales volumes. Managers can set prices, but customers decide whether to pay them. In perfectly competitive markets, organizations are price takers, not price setters,[8] so modeling

---

[8] In a perfectly competitive market (an ideal situation), no single participant can affect prices, supply, or demand. Entry to the market has no restrictions, and prices reflect all relevant market knowledge.

The number of skier days drives revenues and costs at ski resorts.

revenues is straightforward by multiplying the market price by the expected sales quantity, which is limited only by the organization's capacity. But if markets are less than perfect—and they often are—other factors also drive revenues. Ticket prices surely drive the team's revenues, but advertising, the quality (and cost) of the team and its competitors, and external competition for leisure time and dollars probably drive revenues, too. Because many factors driving revenues are external to the organization and because even internal ones are complex (e.g., the relation of advertising to revenues), many organizations understand revenue drivers less than they do their cost drivers. Because they represent half of the profit equation, understanding revenue drivers surely is as important as understanding cost drivers. However, an exploration of revenue drivers, except under conditions of perfect competition, is beyond the scope of this text.

Profit-Planning Models with Multiple Cost Drivers

Before we show the integration of multiple cost drivers into profit-planning models, we quickly review the nature of unit-, batch-, product-, customer-, and facility-level activities and costs. Recall the following:

- *Unit-level activities* are performed for each individual unit of product or service.
- *Batch-level activities* are performed to benefit multiple units of similar output equally and simultaneously (i.e., in batches). Batch-level activities include setting up machines to run a particular batch of units. Related costs are traced easily to specific batches but not to individual output units.
- *Product-level activities* are needed to support a specific product or service, that is, an entire product line. Such activities include new product designs, improved existing product quality and product function, product advertising, and production process monitoring.
- *Customer-level activities* are performed to meet the needs of specific customers. Examples of related costs include those attributable to unique packaging, shipping, and distribution needs, and to personnel assigned to handle specific customer accounts. (Chapter 6 discusses customer-level analysis in detail.)
- *Facility-level activities* are required for an organization to have the capacity to produce goods and services. These activities are at the highest level of the activity hierarchy and tend to support all organizational processes. Typical examples include physical plant operations and top management activities.

Including these cost-driving activities changes the nature of profit-planning models. The basic CVP model assumes that revenues and variable costs vary with sales activity while other costs remain constant. However, costs can vary because of drivers other than sales activity. The following is an example of a total cost expression reflecting multiple relevant activities (recall that we will model revenues assuming competitive markets):

Total cost = (Unit variable cost × Number of units) + (Batch cost × Batch activity)
+ (Product cost × Product activity) + (Customer cost × Customer activity)
+ (Facility cost × Facility activity)

Observe that this calculation no longer relies only on sales activity (e.g., the number of tickets sold) as the cost driver but introduces the impacts of multiple activities. As a result, some costs viewed as fixed under a traditional analysis are now considered variable with respect to appropriate cost-driving activities (batches, products, etc.).

Use of ABC in Financial Modeling

Using various statistical analyses and his own knowledge of cost behavior, Jason Robertson developed the following set of activities and costs to extend his previous financial model, now shown in Exhibit 12–5. In this more complex model, Robertson also has included costs and revenues related to offering another product at Tonopah Park: six summer concerts.

■ *Unit-level activities and costs.* Robertson assumed that the ballpark can sell 85 percent of its seats for baseball games and concerts (total tickets computed in E3 = 204,000 = 4,000 × (54 + 6) × 85 percent). The only unit-level costs related to games or concerts are for printing tickets and preparing game or concert programs, which Robertson estimated per ticket to be $1 (in cell D3). He decided

Exhibit 12–5   Profit-Planning Model with Multiple Cost Drivers

	A	B	C	D	E
	Microsoft Excel - Fairfield Blues				
	File Edit View Insert Format Tools Data Window Help Acrobat				
	B17	= =D4*E4+(D4+D5)*E5			
1	Profit-planning model with multiple products and cost activities				
2	Sales input data		Cost input data	Activity cost	Activity
3	Ballpark seating capacity per game	4,000	Unit-level cost per ticket	$ 1.00	204,000
4	Home games per season	54	Batch-level cost - Baseball game	2,400	54
5	Concerts per summer season	6	- Concert (additional)	20,000	6
6	Average percentage seats sold per event	85%	Product-level costs - Baseball	200,000	
7	Sales price per ticket		- Concerts	10,000	
8	Box seating	$ 15.00	Customer-level cost	800	20
9	General admission seating	6.00	Facility costs per season - Tonopah Park	150,000	
10	Sales mix assumption		- Administration	79,500	
11	Box seating	20.0%	After-tax target profit per season	400,000	
12	General admission seating	80.0%	Average tax rate	20%	
13					
14	Weighted-average unit contribution margin		Planned-profit analysis		
15	WAUCM (B11*(B8-D3) + B12*(B9-D3))	$ 6.80	Sales revenues		
16	Annual break-even analysis		Box seating (B3*(B4+B5)*B6*B8*B11)	$ 612,000	
17	Batch-level costs (D4*E4+(D4+D5)*E5)	$ 264,000	Regular seating (B3*(B4+B5)*B6*B9*B12)	979,200	
18	Product-level costs (D6+D7)	210,000	Total ticket revenues	$ 1,591,200	
19	Customer-level costs (D8*E8)	16,000	Less unit-level costs (D3*E3)	204,000	
20	Facility-level costs (D9+D10)	229,500	Batch-level costs (D4*E4+(D4+D5)*E5)	264,000	
21	Total non-unit-level costs	$ 719,500	Product-level costs (D6+D7)	210,000	
22	Divided by WAUCM (B15)	$ 6.80	Customer-level costs (D8*E8)	16,000	
23	Break-even volume in units (B21/B22)	105,809	Facility-level costs (D9+D10)	229,500	
24	Target profit analysis		Total operating costs	$ 923,500	
25	Total non-unit-level costs costs (B21)	$ 719,500	Before-tax profit (loss) (D18-D24)	$ 667,700	
26	Target profit before-tax (D11/(1-D12))	500,000	Less taxes at average tax rate (D12*D25)	133,540	
27	Target contribution margin	$ 1,219,500	Profit (loss) after tax (D25-D26)	$ 534,160	
28	Divided by WAUCM (B15)	$ 6.80	Target profit after tax (D11)	400,000	
29	Target volume in units (B27/B28)	179,338	Excess (deficiency) of profit (D27-D28)	$ 134,160	
30					

Exhibit 12-2 / Exhibit 12-3 / Exhibit 12-4 \ **Exhibit 12-5** / Exhibit 12-6 / YTD

Ready

that the previously included variable custodial costs *used* were not supplied on a unit-level basis but were a game-level cost (see the next bullet point). Note that this lower per-unit cost increases the WAUCM of baseball games from $5.80 to $6.80 per average ticket (B15). This higher WAUCM does not magically make the team more profitable. Robertson's analysis has more accurately separated the costs that follow, which the simpler models had treated improperly as unit-level variable or committed facility costs.

- *Batch-level activities and costs.* Each game or concert is like a batch of production. For example, if Fairfield Blues sells a total of 3,900 tickets for a Saturday game, this is a "batch" of 3,900 units. Robertson estimated the cost per game, or concert, to be $2,400 (D4), which includes wages paid to security, parking attendants, custodians, ticket takers, and ushers. This batch cost is the same even if the company sold only 3,000 tickets for a game or concert. The league schedule showed that the team will have 54 games per season next year (B4 and copied in E4). Robertson began the concert planning by assuming six summer concerts next year (B5 and E5). For top regional performers, the company additionally must pay approximately $20,000 per concert, which is another batch cost (D5).

- *Product-level activities and costs.* The baseball team and concert series hosted by the ballpark are separate product lines. Robertson identified the product-level costs to be the cost of acquiring the rights to the team, advertising, hiring the players and coaches, transporting the team to away games, and purchasing baseball equipment and uniforms. He estimated this cost to be $200,000 per season (D6). He estimated that managing the inaugural concert series costs an additional $10,000 for part-time personnel and advertising (D7).

- *Customer-level activities and costs.* As a community service, Fairfield Blues rents vans and hires drivers once per week to pick up customers who are unable to drive. The drivers bring these customers to games, usually on Saturday or Sunday afternoons, and then take them home after the games. Robertson estimated the cost of this service to be $800 (D8) every time the service is performed, about 20 games per season (E8).

- *Facility-level activities and costs.* Robertson identified facility-level activities and estimated their costs in two parts, the ballpark and administration.
  - *Tonopah Park.* Robertson estimated the ballpark, including depreciation, utilities, and maintenance, to cost $150,000 per season (D9).
  - *Administration.* Robertson estimated administrative activities, including payroll and marketing, to cost $79,500 per season (D10).

The results of Robertson's model and input parameters show estimated operating income to be $534,160 per season after taxes (cell D27). He was pleased to see that the initial plan exceeded the profit target by $134,160 (D29). By building this financial planning model, Robertson was able to anticipate this favorable outcome. He knew, however, that this outcome depended on the validity of the assumptions that formed the input data. Numerous alternative actual inputs must be considered. Possible variation in these parameters indicates the risk of decisions considered by the company. By focusing on the various cost-driving activities, Robertson now can identify different inputs that might be more likely to occur, producing different profit outcomes. We next cover several types of risk analysis, sensitivity and scenario analyses, and show the additional decision-making power of using financial planning models.

Using Sensitivity and Scenario Analyses

LO 5 Apply scenario and sensitivity analyses to model the risk of decisions.

All decisions about the future are made without knowing actual outcomes. Decisions might not translate into perfectly executed actions, and external factors might be different than those expected. This is the natural condition of risky decision making, which characterizes all business management. Financial planning models by themselves cannot reduce risks, but they can help managers understand the causes and extent of risk. They then can take actions that are most likely to result in favorable outcomes, for example by ruling out actions that are too risky or by hedging their bets.[9] In addition to operating leverage, discussed earlier, we consider two related sources of risk that can be modeled: parameter variability and alternative combinations of parameters. We present two common methods for modeling these risks more precisely: sensitivity analysis and scenario analysis.[10]

Sensitivity Analysis: What If?

Previous analyses tentatively concluded that Fairfield Blues can exceed its monthly target profit. However, numerous assumptions about its financial variables formed this conclusion. Review the data input section of Exhibit 12–5. Any of these 19 data inputs (ticket prices, activity costs, activity levels, and so on) could be wrong. That is, actual values might be different from planned ones, and actual profits, therefore, also might differ. Jason Robertson and Fairfield Blues' management could wait to find out what will actually happen: whether they actually will have sufficient profit. Alternatively, they can use several methods to assess the risk of their decision-making problem and then take actions to manage their risks.

One of the most common methods of assessing risk is *sensitivity analysis.* It tests a financial planning model for changes in outcomes (e.g., profits) caused by changes in each of the model's parameters (e.g., ticket sales). Sensitivity analysis answers the question, What if this parameter is changed? The more sensitive the outcome is to a parameter change, the more risk the changes in that parameter pose. Obviously, manual sensitivity analysis is a tedious, error-prone task, and few organizations undertake it unless they use computerized financial models. This is where the power and ease of using a computerized model becomes apparent.

Robertson first determined the most likely value of each of the parameters ("base" values). Next, he determined the likely range of each parameter. An analyst can determine these values and ranges by considering historical data, or, in the case of new operations, similar experiences, test cases, or analysts' best estimates. Robertson then introduced a change to one of the parameters in Exhibit 12–5, first changing the parameter to the upper and then to the lower end of the range while keeping all other parameters in the exhibit at their most likely values. He then recorded the resulting profit caused by each change and repeated the analysis for all relevant parameters. Do analysts and managers always have the most reliable information they need to perform this detailed analysis? Unfortunately, no, but using informed estimates in most cases is better than performing no analysis at all. Exhibit 12–6 presents a summary of Robertson's sensitivity analysis of Fairfield Blues' financial model, which we now interpret.

Column A of Exhibit 12–6 identifies all parameters, and column B has the most likely or base parameter values. Robertson's estimates of the highest feasible parameter values are in column C, and the lowest feasible values are in column D. Using relations from Exhibit 12–5, column E computes the estimated base profit,[11] which is the same for all parameters because all are set at their most likely or base levels. Column F computes the estimated profit if each parameter in turn is set to its *highest* value while keeping all others at base levels. Similarly, Column G computes the estimated profit if each parameter is set in turn to its *lowest* value, again keeping all others at base levels.

---

[9] A *hedging action* seeks to neutralize risks, for example, by simultaneously contracting to buy and sell a desired quantity of inputs at a fixed price; gains or losses on the two contracts may offset. The company's only cost could be the cost of the contract, which is similar to buying insurance. For example, General Mills might contract both to buy and sell grain for its cereals at a fixed price. If the eventual market price is higher (or lower) than the contract price, General Mills' gain on the "buy" contract matches the loss on the "sell" contract (or vice versa).

[10] *Monte Carlo simulation analysis* is another method used when sufficient data exist to estimate parameters' probability distributions.

[11] The formula in each cell of column E contains the revenue and cost relations from Exhibit 12–5 and the base parameters.

Exhibit 12–6   Summary of Sensitivity Analysis

	A	B	C	D	E	F	G	H
			Range			Profit		
2	**Input data**	Base	High	Low	Base	High	Low	Elasticity
3	Ballpark seating capacity per game	4,000	4,100	3,900	$ 534,160	$ 561,904	$ 506,416	2.08
4	Home games per season	54	60	50	$ 534,160	633,616	467,856	1.68
5	Concerts per summer season	6	8	-	534,160	571,152	423,184	0.21
6	Average percentage seats sold per event	85%	90%	75%	534,160	599,440	403,600	2.08
7	Sales price per ticket - Box seats	$ 15.00	$18.00	$14.00	534,160	632,080	501,520	0.92
8	General admission seats	$ 6.00	$ 7.00	$ 5.00	534,160	664,720	403,600	1.47
9	Sales mix assumption - Box seats	20%	25%	10%	534,160	607,600	387,280	0.55
10	General admission seats	80%	90%	75%	534,160	607,600	387,280	1.10
11	Unit-level cost per ticket	$ 1	$ 2.00	$ 0.80	534,160	370,960	566,800	0.31
12	Batch-level cost - Baseball game	$ 2,400	3,000	2,000	534,160	508,240	551,440	0.19
13	- Concert (additional)	$ 20,000	25,000	10,000	534,160	510,160	582,160	0.18
14	Product-level costs - Baseball	$ 200,000	220,000	175,000	534,160	518,160	554,160	0.30
15	- Concerts	$ 10,000	12,000	8,000	534,160	532,560	535,760	0.01
16	Customer level cost	$ 800	500	1,000	534,160	538,960	530,960	0.02
17	Customer level activity	20	25	-	534,160	530,960	546,960	0.02
18	Facility costs per season - Tonopah Park	$ 150,000	175,000	130,000	534,160	514,160	550,160	0.22
19	- Administration	$ 79,500	90000	70000	534,160	525,760	541,760	0.12
20	Average tax rate	20%	30%	18%	534,160	467,390	547,514	0.25

Formula bar: H3 = =ABS(((F3-$E3)/$E3)/((C3-$B3)/$B3))

Sheet tabs: Exhibit 12-5 | **Exhibit 12-6** | YTDM 12.1 | YTDM 12.2 | Exhibit12-9 | operating levera

Monthly profits range between a high of $664,720 (F8), which reflects the highest price of general admission tickets, and a low of $370,960, which reflects the highest unit-level cost (F11). Clearly, profits are sensitive to ticket prices and unit-level costs, but sorting through the mass of numbers in this summary and comparing changes in profits with respect to such different changes in inputs can be difficult. We need a way to directly compare all of these profit and parameter changes.

We can compare outcome effects by computing the **model elasticity,** the ratio of the percentage change in profit divided by the percentage change in an input parameter. This calculation is analogous to the elasticity of demand, which economists use to compare reactions of demand to changes in prices of different goods. Because elasticity is a ratio of pure percentage numbers, it is independent of the units of measurement. Thus, elasticities of profit to changes in the numbers of tickets or games are comparable. Column H shows the model elasticity for each of the parameters.

Model elasticity = Percentage change of profit ÷ Percentage change of input

For example, the model elasticity to general admission seat prices (H8) is computed as

General admission seat price elasticity = Percentage change of profit
÷ Percentage change of general admission
seat price
$$H8 = [(F8 - E8) \div E8] \div [(C8 - B8) \div B8]$$
$$1.47 = [(664,720 - 534,160) \div 534,160] \div [(7 - 6) \div 6]$$

You may interpret this elasticity to indicate that a 1 percent change in general admission ticket price should cause a 1.47 percent change in profit.[12] An elasticity greater than 1.0 identifies a parameter with a disproportionate effect on profits (this column heading is highlighted in Exhibit 12–6). Actions to change parameters with the highest elasticity should have the greatest impacts on profits. The parameters with the greatest potential to affect profits, according to this model, are the ballpark seating capacity (row 3) and the average percentage of seats sold (row 6). With model elas-

---

[12] Because the profit calculation contains only linear relations among the variables, using either the highest or lowest parameter value and corresponding profit results in the same estimated elasticity. This is not the general economic situation, and one could compute elasticities to both high and low parameter values.

ticities of 2.08, the way to affect profits the most is to change either the seating capacity (temporarily or permanently) or the percentage of seats sold. Conversely, changes in parameters with low elasticity will have relatively small effects on profits. As informative as this analysis can be, it assumes that each parameter affects profits independently of the others. This is not the general case, but analysts should monitor and measure these elastic parameters carefully.

Scenario Analysis (Best, Worst, and Most Likely Cases)

Robertson reasoned that some parameters should not be changed independently of others. His financial model makes it easy to change any combination of variables together, but the number of possible combinations of parameter changes is very large. Many managers assess the risk of their decision making by **scenario analysis,** which creates *realistic* combinations of changed parameters. Of all the many possible combinations, only a few are realistic; that is, they very well can happen or actually have happened in the past. By using the model to compute each scenario's profit, managers can see the different outcomes from a number of realistic sets of conditions. For example, an increase in ticket prices might be accompanied by a decrease in ticket volume. Analysts commonly prepare the *best-case, worst-case,* and *most likely case* for review by managers. The most likely case usually, but not necessarily, sets all parameters to their most likely or base values. The best-case scenario is the *realistic* combination of the highest prices, highest unit-volumes, and lowest costs and cost-driving activities. Conversely, the worst-case scenario is the realistic combination of lowest prices, lowest unit volumes, and highest costs and cost-driving activities. Describing these cases often requires the collective judgment of a cross-functional team because so many business interactions are involved. The range of outcomes resulting from the various cases shows how good or bad things might be, and the range of outcomes indicates the actual risks of the decision the manager faces.

Suppose that Robertson, without the help of other employees, identified best- and worst-case scenarios as shown in Exhibit 12–7 and set the model parameters to each case's values. The resulting profits are at the bottom of the exhibit. A careful look at the combinations might lead you to label them as "wildly optimistic" and "hopelessly catastrophic" cases! If these are realistic scenarios, one might characterize this company's management as "very risky." The best case seems extremely good, and the worst case seems just as extremely bad. If Robertson were to present these scenarios to Fairfield Blues' top management, he might receive many questions about their realism. Indeed, before he considers presenting these scenarios, he should be confident that each tells a plausible story and that he can communicate this story to top management. He would be wise to consult others to develop realistic scenarios.

Scenario Analysis

Research Insight 12.1

Researchers in many fields use scenario analysis to understand the dimensions of risky decision making. For example, weather researchers use complex computer models to predict the landfall of a hurricane several days in advance, given different ocean current, air, and water temperature scenarios. Research continues to improve the models' ability to predict hurricane intensity. Biologists use population dynamics models to predict the future of endangered species given alternative decisions to modify their environment. Recent modeling of Orca whales in Washington's Puget Sound examined seven likely scenarios including changes in (1) toxic chemicals, such as PCBs, (2) salmon populations, which are in decline, forcing Orcas to eat contaminated bottom fish, (3) stress from whale-watching boats, and (4) effects of capturing young whales for marine parks 20 years ago. The results indicated that "even best-case scenarios do not look very good." *Sources:* "Computer's View of a Hurricane," *USA Today;* C. Dunagan, "Report: Washington Orcas Endangered," Scripps Howard News Service. November 18, 2000.

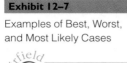

Input Data	Best Case	Worst Case	Most Likely
Ballpark seating capacity per game	4,100	3,900	4,000
Home games per season	60	50	54
Concerts per summer season	8	—	6
Average percentage seats sold per event	90%	75%	85%
Sales price per ticket—Box seats	$18.00	$14.00	$15.00
General admission seats	$7.00	$5.00	$6.00
Sales mix assumption—Box seats	25%	10%	20%
General admission seats	75%	90%	80%
Unit-level cost per ticket	$0.80	$2.00	$1.00
Batch-level cost—Baseball game	$2,000	$3,000	$2,400
—Concert (additional)	$10,000	$25,000	$20,000
Product-level costs—Baseball game	$175,000	$220,000	$200,000
—Concerts	$8,000	$12,000	$10,000
Customer-level cost	$500	$1,000	$800
Customer-level activity (chdufferred games)	—	25	20
Facility costs per season—Tonopah Park	$130,000	$175,000	$150,000
—Administration	$70,000	$90,000	$79,500
Average tax rate	18%	30%	20%
Scenario profit	$1,350,322	$(71,138)	$534,160

Modeling Scarce Resources

LO 6 Manage scarce resources.

Choosing which goods and services to produce and sell is a basic managerial decision. For all organizations, the possible volume and mix of products is limited by available capacity (i.e., scarce resources). For instance, consider the following:

■ A campus bookstore might decide to use its limited space to sell general merchandise or to increase textbook sales.

■ Because of a personnel shortage, a small consulting firm must choose between working for client A or client B.

■ A nonprofit health clinic must choose which patients it can serve and which it must turn away.

■ Sales representatives, in their limited time, must call on customers that provide the greatest profit potential.

A manager must understand and analyze the factors that limit the organization's ability to achieve its objectives. Surprisingly, the solution to improvement usually is not to make each part of the operation as efficient as possible.

Profit from a Single Scarce Resource Maximization

As an introduction to modeling scarce resources, let's observe decision making in the television commercial division of Fairfield's Channel 2, which produces TV commercials for the Fairfield Blues and other regional companies. Manager Cerise Hamilton has built the division's reputation so that it has no shortage of work. The problem is deciding which jobs to accept. Demand exceeds the available time of her two skilled editors, which she has identified is the scarcest resource for completing commercials. To maintain quality (and to retain her skilled editors), she limits maximum editing time to 100 hours per week. The issue facing Hamilton is which jobs to accept to maximize weekly profits.[13]

When an organization has a scarce resource, it wants to make the best possible use of that resource. *In the short run, Hamilton can maximize her division's profit by processing jobs that generate the most contribution margin per unit of scarce resource,* in this case, editing hours.

In a typical week, Hamilton chooses among three types of jobs: short commercial advertising, long commercial advertising, and short public service announcements. The following job data are available:

	Short Commercials	Long Commercials	Short Public Service Announcements
Contribution margin value of each job	$2,500	$5,500	$1,800
Estimated editing hours per job	4	11	3

The following figures show that short commercial jobs have the highest contribution margin per editing hour, allowing Channel 2 to generate the highest profit for its scarce editing time.

$$\text{Short commercial: } \$2,500 \div 4 \text{ hours } = \$625 \text{ contribution margin per hour}$$
$$\text{Long commercials: } \$5,500 \div 11 \text{ hours } = \$500 \text{ contribution margin per hour}$$
$$\text{Short public service announcements: } \$1,800 \div 3 \text{ hours } = \$600 \text{ contribution margin per hour}$$

Based on these figures, choosing to work on the short commercial jobs is the best use of the scarce editing time. Every hour spent on another job has an opportunity cost of the difference in contribution margin per hour compared to short commercials. For example, an editing hour spent on long commercials forgoes at least $125 in profit ($625 − $500). The total results for the week in the following table confirm the desirability of directing the use of scarce editing time to short commercials.

	Short Commercials	Long Commercials	Short Public Service Announcements
Contribution margin value of each job	$ 2,500	$ 5,500	$ 1,800
Estimated editing hours per job	4	11	3
Editing-hours capacity	100	100	100
Weekly jobs completed and sold	25	9	33
Weekly throughput	$62,500	$49,500	$59,400

Appendix A to this chapter extends the discussion of managing scarce resources to more complex situations using the Theory of Constraints.

Chapter Summary

This chapter presents an overview of financial modeling and the management of scarce resources. An understanding of financial planning or cost-volume-profit (CVP) relationships is necessary for the successful management of any enterprise. Financial modeling provides a reliable overview of the effects on profit of changes in quantities, activity costs, sales mix, sales prices, and changes in bottlenecks (Appendix A). The basic CVP model is subject to several limitations, with one of the most troubling being the use of a single cost driver. The model can be expanded using activity-based costing to yield more realistic results. Spreadsheets used in conjunction with sensitivity and scenario analyses greatly facilitate risky decision making. Any attempts to improve an organization's profitability must consider the effects of constrained resources. The Theory of Constraints offers an effective method for the short-term management of constraints (Appendix A). Modeling multiple constraints is possible with linear programming (Appendix B).

---

[13] Hamilton could have other objectives, including diversity of creative work or maintaining a broad market presence, which might cause her to trade off some profit.

Appendix A to Chapter Twelve

Theory of Constraints

LO 7 Apply the Theory of Constraints to manage scarce resources.

In the 1980s, Dr. Eliyahu Goldratt formalized an approach to management called the **Theory of Constraints (TOC),**[14] which seeks to improve productive processes by focusing on constrained resources. Theory of Constraints is a management method to improve productive processes in manufacturing and service organizations by measuring process capacity, identifying process constraints, using process constraints effectively, and coordinating other processes to the needs of bottlenecks. It argues that improving the use of constrained resources involves six steps. We next summarize these steps, and then we apply them to the Fairfield Blues.

1. *Identify the appropriate measure of value created.* In the short run, throughput is the measure appropriate for most profit-seeking firms. Other types of organizations should adopt measures of value appropriate for their goals; for example, the IRS might value the number of tax returns processed correctly the first time.

2. *Identify the organization's bottleneck.* A **bottleneck** is the *constraint* or constraining factor limiting production *or* sales. A **constraint** is a process or resource in a system that limits the capacity or throughput of the system. All productive processes have limited capacities, but most organizations have one or a few processes that limit throughput. Bottlenecks often are apparent because a backlog of parts, assemblies, casework, or paperwork builds up just before the bottleneck process.

3. *Use the bottleneck properly by using it to produce or sell only the most highly valued or profitable products or services.* With a single bottleneck, the most value can be generated by producing the product or service that creates the most value (e.g., throughput) per unit of constrained capacity. This is the simple case illustrated earlier. Multiple constraints require more complex tools, such as linear programming, which is described in Appendix B to this chapter.

4. *Synchronize all other processes to the bottleneck by producing no more of other intermediate outputs than the bottleneck can reasonably process.* Allowing all processes to produce up to their capacity wastes resources by creating unused parts, assemblies, or partially completed services, which only add to inventory but do not create throughput. These excess inventories can become obsolete and usually obscure quality problems, as discussed in Chapter 7. Furthermore, some excess inventories might be defective inputs, which will waste the bottleneck capacity when processed.

5. *Increase the bottleneck's capacity or outsource the production of its output.* The only way to increase throughput is to relieve the bottleneck. In the long run, the organization can add capacity, but in the short run, outsourcing can be more profitable than forgone sales.

6. *Avoid inertia and return to step 1.* Relieving one bottleneck probably will create another one as production and sales grow. Managing by the Theory of Constraints involves always looking for ways to increase throughput. The Theory of Constraints can be applied to any productive process; it is by no means limited to manufacturing processes.

---

[14] Many books and articles discuss the Theory of Constraints. The most accessible and popular source is E. Goldratt and J. Cox, *The Goal;* it is highly recommended reading. A concise review that probably should be read after *The Goal* is J. Ruhl, "An Introduction to the Theory of Constraints." (Full citations to references are in the Bibliography.)

Application of the Theory of Constraints

Let's return to the management of Fairfield Blues to illustrate how Robertson can help management increase the company's profitability by modeling and interpreting its constrained resources. By following the steps outlined earlier for the Theory of Constraints, Robertson can identify the company's bottleneck(s) and help develop strategies to improve profits.

Identify the appropriate measure of value created. From a seasonal perspective, ticket sales, baseball games, and concerts can be part of throughput. The spending for capacity to play baseball games, promote concerts, and provide facilities, however, appears to be committed for the longer term and, therefore, is not part of throughput, which is sales less spending for resources used (see Chapter 2). Ticket costs probably are directly related to the number of tickets sold, so ticket costs at $1 per ticket are part of throughput. If the team played one more game per season, however, do batch costs increase by $2,400 (the estimated batch cost per game), or is some part of that cost committed salary or depreciation that does not increase? Likewise, if Fairfield Blues decided to pick up nondriving customers for one additional game, do customer costs increase by $800, or is some of this cost committed too?

After investigating the differences between resource spending and usage, and after subtracting portions of committed costs, Robertson measured the elements of monthly throughput as follows:

Throughput Element	Unit of Activity	Throughput Price or Cost per Unit of Activity	Capacity	Planned Usage
Box-seat price	Tickets sold, Q_B	$15	800 per event	680 per event
General admission price	Tickets sold, Q_{GA}	$6	3,200 per event	2,720 per event
Ticket cost	Tickets sold ($Q_B + Q_{GA}$)	$1	4,000 per event	3,400 per event
Game cost	Games, G	$2,400	54 per season	54 per season
Concert cost	Concerts, C	$22,400	6 per season	6 per season
Customer pickup	Pick-up games, G_P	$500	20 per season	20 per season

Total *periodic* throughput is the throughput per event multiplied by the number of events less other periodic throughput costs. The Fairfield Blues' seasonal throughput is measured by the following equation:

$$\text{Seasonal throughput} = (\$15 \times Q_B) + (\$6 \times Q_{GA}) - [\$1 \times (Q_B + Q_{GA})] \times (G + C)$$
$$- [\$2,400 \times G] - [\$22,400 \times C] - [500 \times G_P]$$

Identify the organization's bottleneck(s). Unlike a manufacturing plant or a bank, Fairfield Blues has no stacks of excess inventory or stacks of loan applications to identify bottlenecks. What really limits the company's monthly throughput? The place to look is the company's capacity to perform major activities: ticket sales, number of events, customer pickups, and facilities.

The preceding table shows that the only *apparent* bottlenecks are the number of events, which the league has set at 54 home games per season and the company management has set at six concerts per season. By management policy, event capacity equals event usage. Other activities appear to have some excess capacity. Well, then, why not add to the number of seasonal events? First, if the number of concerts, for example, can be increased, what is the increase in throughput? The simplest answer is that each concert adds throughput equal to the following:

$$\text{Throughput from each concert} = (\$15 \times Q_B) + (\$6 \times Q_{GA}) - [\$1 \times (Q_B + Q_{GA})] \times 1 - \$22,400$$
$$= (\$15 \times 680) + (\$6 \times 2,720) - [\$1 \times (680 + 2,720)] - \$22,400$$
$$= \underline{\$720}$$

Second, is this the correct answer? If Fairfield Blues added another concert (or 10) each season, does each really add $720 each in throughput? If not, why not? The difficulty is that the number of concerts may not be the true bottleneck but only a visible symptom. If the number of concerts is not the constraining factor, what is? Perhaps we can understand the problem by looking at current operations a bit closer. Ticket sales do generate seasonal revenues and throughput for the company, but why is every event not a sellout? If the company does not sell out now, will adding events increase the number of tickets sold or merely cannibalize current performances?

The true bottleneck might be a marketing problem. Perhaps the events do not match the tastes of the majority of potential ticket buyers. Perhaps the local market is not large enough to support more baseball or concert fans. Perhaps the quality of the events is not sufficient to draw more customers at current prices. After applying the logic and analysis of the Theory of Constraints, many organizations are surprised to learn that their most significant bottleneck is not a production constraint but a marketing constraint—a failure to understand and meet market needs better.

Use the bottleneck(s) properly.   By working with other members of the company's management team, Robertson began focusing on the company's marketing and learned the following about each marketing activity:

1. Improvements to facilities (ballpark and general management activities) and the quality of the team either were not feasible in the short run or would not increase ticket sales appreciably.
2. Advertising placed in community, club, and company newsletters at a cost of $1,200 per season could increase box-seat sales by approximately 10 per event.
3. Advertising placed in neighborhood weekly papers at a cost of $600 per season might increase general admission seat sales by 10 per event.
4. Exhibition games between the Fairfield Blues and the four local high school teams would sell 50 percent of available seats, with net proceeds divided equally between the Fairfield Blues and the high school teams.
5. Increasing the number of concerts would not add appreciably to overall ticket sales. Six per summer season seems to be about the right number for the community.
6. Increasing the number of times that nondriving customers are picked up would not increase ticket sales appreciably at this time. Perhaps in 10 years when the population has aged, this might increase ticket sales or be necessary to maintain ticket sales.

Synchronize all other processes to the bottleneck(s).   Once company management decides on a course of action to manage a bottleneck, it must ensure the coordination of all activities; that is, no excess activity should exist in other areas. This might not be difficult for the Fairfield Blues, but it can be for manufacturing facilities. Historically, firms have evaluated their manufacturing departments on measures such as percentage of capacity used, unallocated overhead, percentage of downtime, or idle time. All of these measures provide the incentive to fully use productive capacity without regard to bottleneck constraints. Thus, before a firm can coordinate its manufacturing departments to bottleneck throughput, it should change its measures of manufacturing performance. Chapters 7 and 20 discuss this important issue in more detail from quality or time, lead indicator, and compensation perspectives.

Increase the bottleneck's capacity or outsource the production of its output.   In the short term, the Fairfield Blues can add a few more games and try to increase attendance at each performance. If the market can be developed to support even more ticket sales, Fairfield Blues might consider whether to increase its overall seating capacity. This is a longer-term decision that has investment implications. This type of strategic decision is covered in Chapter 14.

Avoid inertia and return to step 1.   The Theory of Constraints warns that the elimination of a bottleneck causes another to pop up elsewhere, so managers must be vigilant to continue to increase value created and throughput efficiently.

Appendix B to Chapter Twelve

Linear Programming

Many firms face the problem of how best to use multiple scarce resources. An example presented in the body of this chapter showed that when a single resource is constrained, management should produce the good or service that has the highest payoff per unit of scarce resource. However, the situation becomes more complicated if the organization faces decisions among multiple products with two or more scarce resources. Recall that we previously modeled multiproduct decision making by *assuming* a product mix. A quantitative tool called "linear programming" is designed to help find the product mix that maximizes profits when multiple constraints exist. Linear programming, as its name implies, assumes that all model relations are linear. Nonlinear methods are available when this assumption is not met. This appendix assumes some prior exposure to linear programming.

LO 8 Use linear programming to model decisions about the use of multiple scarce resources.

Introduction to Linear Programming Models

Linear programming shows how best to allocate multiple scarce resources among alternative courses of action in the short run when capacity cannot be increased. Linear programming finds the combination of products or services that maximizes throughput or contribution margin or minimizes cost within the limits of constrained resources. To illustrate how linear programming works, it is necessary first to describe its elements.

Objective function is a mathematical relation of inputs and outputs to be maximized or minimized. For example, the objective of the linear programming problem might be to maximize monthly throughput, revenues less throughput costs. The objective function is the equation that models throughput, for example. *Constraints* represent capacity limits of the various processes and resources. Linear programming constraints state algebraically that resources used must not exceed the resources available.

Feasible solution space is the combination of input and output values that satisfy the constraints. When more than one constraint is binding (i.e., acting as a bottleneck), maximizing the throughput per unit of constrained resource is not sufficient. Linear programming investigates the possibly numerous feasible combinations of inputs and outputs that satisfy the constraints to find the optimum point.

Optimum point is the set of inputs and outputs in the feasible solution space that maximizes or minimizes the objective function. In rare cases, multiple points are optimal.

For this discussion, we assume that linear programming problems are modeled on the computer. Our focus is on setting up the problems so they can be entered into the computer and on interpreting the output, not on the mathematical procedures used to derive the solutions. Of course, this means that the user must know enough about linear programming and the decision context to recognize an improbable solution that is the result of improperly constructing the model.

Assume that a Fairfield company called Creative Constructs, Inc., makes the sets for television and theater productions that can be staged at Tonopah Park. Over time it has developed an expertise in producing three standardized wood products from high-quality, recycled lumber (usually taken from demolished old houses and old farm buildings): armchairs (A), bookshelves (B), and cabinets (C). The demand for its products is so high that it now markets these three products commercially.

Each product must be processed through two departments (1) cutting and (2) assembly and finishing before it is sold. Exhibit 12–8 presents data about product selling prices, costs, and the rate at which each product uses scarce resources. In addition to the information provided in Exhibit 12–8, we learn that the company can obtain only 2,000 board feet of high-quality, recycled lumber per week. The cutting

Exhibit 12–8   Creative Constructs' Model Parameters

	Armchairs (A) per Unit	Bookshelves (B) per Unit	Cabinets (C) per Unit
Selling price	$14.00	$18.00	$24.00
Unit-level material cost (lumber)	6.00	7.20	10.80
Unit-level conversion cost (labor and overhead)	2.32	3.40	4.96
Contribution margins (also throughput)	5.68	7.40	8.24
Material requirements in board feet	4.00	7.00	6.00
Labor requirements in hours—Cutting department	0.30	0.30	0.40
Labor requirement in hours—Assembly and finishing department	0.50	0.20	0.50
Demand	At least 100 per week	No more than 100	No constraint

department has a maximum of 180 hours of labor available each week, and the assembly and finishing department has a maximum of 240 hours of labor available each week. No overtime is allowed.

Only variable or unit-level costs, which primarily are the costs of materials and hourly labor, are affected by the choice of which product to make. Higher-level costs, such as batch-, product-, and facility-level costs, are the same regardless of which product Creative Constructs produces and sells. The production decision is to determine which product mix maximizes weekly profit.

Linear programming model formulation.   Creative Construct's product mix decision can be solved using linear programming models. Building a linear programming model for it requires transforming the data (in this example, in Exhibit 12–8) into equation form. Maximize total contribution margin (higher-level costs are unaffected by short-run product mix):

$$\$5.68A + \$7.40B + \$8.24C$$

Subject to the following constraints:

Direct materials	$4A + 7B + 6C$	$\leq 2{,}000$ board feet
Cutting	$.30A + .30B + .40C$	≤ 180 labor hours
Assembly and finishing	$.50A + .20B + .50C$	≤ 240 labor hours
Armchair sales	A	≥ 100 units sold
Bookcase sales	B	≤ 100 units sold

The direct materials constraint means that the number of board feet of lumber required for each armchair (product A) is 4, for each bookcase (product B) is 7, and for each cabinet (product C) is 6. The total of all the wood required cannot exceed the maximum of 2,000 board feet available per week. The cutting constraint similarly means that the total of all labor hours used to make A at .30 per unit, B at .30 per unit, and C at .40 per unit cannot exceed the maximum of 180 labor hours available per week. The assembly and finishing constraint likewise states that the total assembly and finishing labor hours used to complete products A, B, and C cannot exceed the 240 labor hours available per week. The sales constraints mean that the total units of A produced and sold must be at least 100 per week; sales and production of B cannot exceed 100 per week. Product C has no sales constraint.

Exhibit 12–9 displays the input of these parameters and relations into a spreadsheet model. Data inputs are in cells A1 to F9 and correspond to the preceding descriptions of the sales and production activities. An additional input is in row 10. This input, "initial guess at sales levels," is a beginning point for the model solution.

Exhibit 12–9

Spreadsheet Linear
Programming Model

	Microsoft Excel - Fairfield Blues					

B14   =B4*B12

	A	B	C	D	E	F
1	Data input	Armchairs	Bookcases	Cabinets		Constraint
2	Contribution margin per unit	$ 5.68	$ 7.40	$ 8.24		
3	Resource constraints					
4	Direct materials, board feet per unit	4.00	7.00	6.00	less than	2,000
5	Cutting, hours per unit	0.30	0.30	0.40	less than	180
6	Assembly and finishing, hours per unit	0.50	0.20	0.50	less than	240
7	Demand constraints					
8	Armchair sales, units				at least	100
9	Bookcase sales, units				no more than	100
10	Initial guess at sales levels	10	10	10		
11	Linear Program Model	Armchairs	Bookcases	Cabinets	Total	Constraint
12	Units sold (replaced by the optimal solution)	10	10	10	30	
13	Contribution margin (B2*B12,C2*C12,D2*D12)	$ 57	$ 74	$ 82	$ 213	
14	Board feet of material used (B4*B12, etc.)	40	70	60	170	2,000
15	Cutting hours used (B5*B12, etc.)	3	3	4	10	180
16	Assembly and finishing hours used (B6*B12, etc.)	5	2	5	12	240
17	Sales of Armchairs (B12)	10			10	100
18	Sales of Bookcases (C12)		10		10	100
19						

Exhibit 12-5 / Exhibit 12-6 / YTDM 12.1 / YTDM 12.2 \ Exhibit 12-9 /

Ready

To begin the solution, you can enter any feasible number of units, even zeros, into
cells B10 to D10. We entered positive numbers so that the spreadsheet displays
nonzero figures computed in the other cells.

Using the Excel spreadsheet, the model (rows 12 to 18) is entered in roughly the
same format as our earlier financial planning models; each cell of the model is a formula of inputs and outputs. The number of units sold (row 12) initially is set equal to
the number of guesses in row 10; these numbers can vary to create a more profitable
solution. Contribution margins (CMs) in row 13 are computed by multiplying the
CMs per unit in row 2 by the units sold in row 12. The sum of the product CMs is the
current value of the objective function and is shown in E13.

Rows 4 through 9 display the data for the five constraints described previously.
Row 14 computes the amount of lumber used for the number of units sold. Note that
at the initial sales levels, the total amount of lumber used, 170 board feet (E14), is
less than the constrained amount of 2,000 board feet, shown in F14. Cells E15 to E18
similarly compute the amounts of other scarce resources and of sales that are constrained for comparison with the constrained amounts in column F.

The Excel "Tools" menu has an option called "Solver," which is a powerful mathematical programming module (you might need to "add in" this module). Clicking on
"Solver" generates the following window where you enter the linear programming
elements as represented by the model. The "target cell" or objective function is E13,

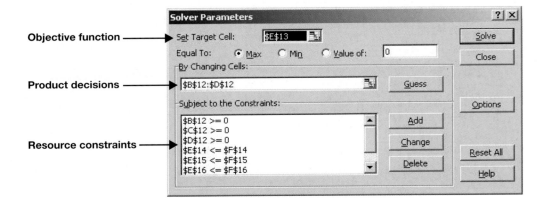

the sum of product contribution margins. Next you specify whether to maximize or minimize the value in this cell or to force it to meet a specific value. Then you show which cells to vary to find alternative solutions, the unit sales in row 12. By clicking on the "Add" button you can enter each of the constraints in equation form. Note the first three constraints (e.g., B12 > = 0). These equations state that each unit of sales cannot be negative, which makes eminent sense, but the program must be told this explicitly. Finally, clicking on the "Solve" button generates the optimal solution.

Linear programming model solution.   Exhibit 12–10 is the revision of the model in Exhibit 12–9 after Solver has found the optimal solution and replaced the initial guesses in row 12 with the optimal sales levels. Note that you can produce other, more detailed reports on the properties of the solution (e.g., limits and sensitivity analyses) by clicking appropriate buttons after obtaining this solution. You should consult an appropriate linear programming text for the use of this additional information.

The linear programming model has replaced the initial guesses in row 12 with the optimal solution to produce and sell 440 armchairs (B12), no bookcases (C12), and 40 cabinets (D12). The weekly contribution margin generated by this solution is $2,829 (E13). Compare the total resources used by this solution (cells E14 to E18) to the corresponding constrained amounts (F14 to F18). This solution uses all lumber available (2,000 board feet, E14 = F14), and all assembly and finishing hours available (240 hours, E16 = F16). These appear to be the bottlenecks (or "binding" constraints) at this solution. We can compare the benefit of relaxing each of these constraints by some feasible amounts (i.e., change the constraint values by some feasible amounts and observe the increase in CM) to the costs of acquiring more capacity. Note, however, that the cutting department has excess capacity (or "slack") (E15 < F15) of 32 hours, nearly one full-time, hourly employee. Thus, the available cutting time is not a binding constraint. Maintaining this level or increasing capacity in this department might be a waste of resources in the long run if this solution represents future optimal operations. Creative Constructs also can consider dropping the bookcase product line if it appears that this solution will persist. The sales constraints also appear to have no effect on this solution because armchair sales easily exceed the minimum of 100 (E17 > F17) and bookcase sales are zero (shown by dashes in C12 to C18), well below the maximum (E18 < F18).

Exhibit 12–10

Linear Programming Solution

Microsoft Excel – Fairfield Blues					
File Edit View Insert Format Tools Data Window Help					
E13 ▼ = =SUM(B13:D13)					
A	B	C	D	E	F
1 Data input	Armchairs	Bookcases	Cabinets		Constraint
2 Contribution margin per unit	$ 5.68	$ 7.40	$ 8.24		
3 Resource constraints					
4 Direct materials, board feet per unit	4.00	7.00	6.00	less than	2,000
5 Cutting, hours per unit	0.30	0.30	0.40	less than	180
6 Assembly and finishing, hours per unit	0.50	0.20	0.50	less than	240
7 Demand constraints					
8 Armchair sales, units				at least	100
9 Bookcase sales, units				no more than	100
10 Initial guess at sales levels	10	10	10		
11 Linear Program Model	Armchairs	Bookcases	Cabinets	Total	Constraint
12 Units sold (replaced by the optimal solution)	440	-	40	480	
13 Contribution margin (B2*B12,C2*C12,D2*D12)	$ 2,499	$ -	$ 330	$ 2,829	
14 Board feet of material used (B4*B12, etc.)	1,760	-	240	2,000	2,000
15 Cutting hours used (B5*B12, etc.)	132	-	16	148	180
16 Assembly and finishing hours used (B6*B12, etc.)	220	-	20	240	240
17 Sales of Armchairs (B12)	440			440	100
18 Sales of Bookcases (C12)		-		-	100
19					

Exhibit 12-5 / Exhibit 12-6 / YTDM 12.1 / YTDM 12.2 \ Exhibit 12-9 /

Ready

Key Terms

For each term's definition, refer to the indicated page or turn to the glossary at the end of the text.

bottleneck,* 482

break-even point, 464

constraint,* 482

cost-volume-profit (CVP) model, 462

feasible solution space,† 485

financial model, 460

linear programming,† 485

model elasticity, 478

objective function,† 485

operating leverage, 466

optimum point,† 485

product mix, 471

sales mix, 471

scenario analysis, 479

Theory of Constraints (TOC),* 482

weighted-average unit contribution margin (WAUCM), 471

*Term appears in the chapter Appendix A.

†Term appears in the chapter Appendix B.

Meeting the Cost Management Challenges

1. What does a cost-management analyst need to know to build useful financial planning models?

Managers make decisions all the time that affect future operations. Sometimes it is better to be lucky than good, but by nature, luck is random. A run of good luck is just as likely to be followed by one of bad luck unless managers take actions to make systematically good decisions. There might be intuitively brilliant managers who always make the right decisions. If they really exist, we can only envy them. Obviously, we believe that most of us can benefit from organizing decisions and building useful financial planning models. As the chapter explains, to build useful financial models, a cost-management analyst needs to know the following:

a. What is the manager trying to manage (i.e., optimize)?

b. What are the parameters and the relations among the parameters that are relevant to managers' decisions?

c. What are feasible ranges of parameters and realistic scenarios of combinations of parameters?

d. How do constrained resources affect managers' ability to optimize operations? Can those constraints be relaxed? For example, can the organization obtain more capacity?

2. Can financial models help define future risks so that managers at least know what the uncertainties are?

Financial models can help define future risks and uncertainties. Unfortunately, some managers view the output of financial planning models as either gospel truth or fanciful dreaming. The key to building and using financial planning models successfully is to understand that as built, they represent only one of many tools available and that the numbers do not speak for themselves. In the hands of a questioning, skeptical user, a flexible financial planning model can be a wondrous time saver and realistic simulation of the organization's internal and external environments. The user can spin unlimited scenarios and try unlimited "what-if" analyses. If there is a method to this madness and a plan for testing the scenarios, the user can develop a good sense for where both opportunities and dangers exist.

3. Should organizations always try to maximize revenues or even the sales of products and services with the most throughput, contribution margin, or profit per unit? Are resource constraints an issue?

They should not. Focusing on the cost or revenues of products and services at the unit level can improve sales and production incentives, but that might not be enough to improve revenues. Some organizations do reward for maximizing sales growth, which can be an effective way to build market share but also can lead to suboptimal profits. Resource constraints are always an issue in some manner. The Theory of Constraints provides a good framework for managing constrained resources in any environment.

Solutions to You're the Decision Maker

12.1 Effect of Sales Mix on Financial Performance p. 473

a. Consider the following spreadsheet, which is identical to Exhibit 12–4 except for the changed and highlighted inputs of average percentage of seats sold (B5), which affects sales volume (D14), and sales mix (cells B10 and B11). This

revised model shows that the change in actual sales mix has an adverse effect on after-tax profits despite a higher-than-planned ticket volume.

b. Actual sales emphasized lower contribution-margin general admission tickets at the expense of higher contribution-margin box-seat tickets. The sales-mix change lowered the

WAUCM from $5.80 to $5.44 (B13) and consequently increased both the break-even volume (B18) and target volume (B24). Because the actual ticket volume was lower than the target volume required at the actual, lower WAUCM, Fairfield Blues did not reach its after-tax target of $400,000 (see D24). This type of adverse effect can occur whenever managers increase sales or market share without regard to the contribution margins of products. Motivating managers to increase sales or market share can be counterproductive to meeting an organization's goal of profitability. Designing incentive systems is the topic of Chapter 20.

Microsoft Excel - Fairfield Blues

File Edit View Insert Format Tools Data Window Help Acrobat

B14   = =B10*(B7-D3) + B11*(B8-D3)

	A	B	C	D
1	**Profit-planning model with multiple products**			
2	**Sales input data**		**Cost input data**	
3	Ballpark seating capacity per game	4,000	Unit-level variable cost per ticket	$ 2.00
4	Home games per season	54	Fixed facility costs per season	550,000
5	Average percentage seats sold per game	86%	After-tax target profit	400,000
6	Sales price per ticket		Average tax rate	20%
7	Box seating	$ 15.00		
8	General admission seating	6.00		
9	Sales mix assumption			
10	Box seating	16.0%		
11	General admission seating	84.0%		
12				
13	**Weighted-average unit contribution margin**		**Planned-profit analysis**	
14	WAUCM (B10*(B7-D3) + B11*(B8-D3))	$ 5.44	Planned sales volume in units (B3*B4*B5)	185,760
15	**Break-even analysis**		Sales revenues	
16	Fixed costs (D4)	$ 550,000	Box seating (D14*B10*B7)	$ 445,824
17	Divided by WAUCM (B14)	5.44	General admission seating (D14*B11*B8)	936,230
18	Break-even volume in units (B16/B17)	101,103	Total revenues	$ 1,382,054
19	**Target-profit analysis**		Less variable costs (D14*D3)	371,520
20	Fixed costs (D4)	$ 550,000	Contribution margin (D18-D19)	$ 1,010,534
21	Before-tax parget profit (D5/(1-D6))	500,000	Less fixed costs (D4)	550,000
22	Target contribution margin	$1,050,000	Before-tax profit (loss) (D20-D21)	$ 460,534
23	Divided by WAUCM (B14)	$ 5.44	Less taxes at average tax rate (D6*D22)	92,107
24	Target volume in units (B22/B23)	193,015	After-tax profit (loss) (D22-D23)	$ 368,428
25				

YTDM 12.1 / YTDM 12.2 / Exhibit12-9 / operating leverage /

Ready

Review Questions

12.1   Review the chapter's key terms and define them.

12.2   What are the characteristics of a good financial planning model?

12.3   What benefits do financial models provide to users?

12.4   What are the objectives of financial modeling?

12.5   What are the elements of a cost-volume-profit (CVP) model? Is this the best name for this type of model?

12.6   Explain the difference between break-even point and target break-even point.

12.7   Explain how a cost-volume-profit (CVP) graph is also a financial model.

12.8   What are the advantages of computerized financial models compared to manual financial models?

12.9   Why should a financial model's parameters be located as numbers in only one place?

12.10   When is using the average tax rate desirable in modeling the effects of taxes in a financial model?

12.11   Explain the sales mix assumption in financial planning analysis. Why is this assumption made?

12.12   What is the meaning of the term "weighted-average unit contribution margin?" What does this amount contribute toward covering?

12.13   What is the difference between using throughput or contribution margin as the contribution toward profit in financial planning models?

12.14   Briefly explain how financial planning models benefit from activity-based costing (ABC).

12.15   What is sensitivity analysis? Scenario analysis? What are their purposes?

12.16   Briefly describe the proper approach to making a production decision when a single limited resource is involved.

12.17   (Appendix A) How is the Theory of Constraints as much a cost-management attitude as a modeling method?

Critical Analysis

12.18 In a strategy meeting, a manufacturing company's president said, "If we raise the price of our product, the company's break-even point will be lower." The financial vice president responded by saying, "Then we should raise our price. The company will be less likely to incur a loss." With whom do you agree and disagree? Why?

12.19 A company recently constructed a financial planning model to predict monthly cash inflows and outflows. The model is based on various financial relationships including collection patterns of receivables, inventory outflows, expense payments, and so forth, all obtained by analyzing monthly data of the past three years. Before the spreadsheet model is put into use, management insists that employees perform some validity testing to ensure that the model is working properly. Suggest how the model might be tested to ensure that it is, in fact, valid.

12.20 "Cost-volume-profit (CVP) analysis is an oversimplification of the real world. For this reason, it has little to offer a decision maker." Comment.

12.21 Picture the cost-volume-profit (CVP) model. Explain how the model can be used to evaluate the performance of an organization's (1) divisions and (2) divisional managers. The managers are evaluated annually for purposes of pay raises and promotions. What are the inherent dangers in using this model for evaluation purposes?

12.22 Management notes that the contribution from one product is higher than the contribution from a second product. Hence, management concludes that the company should concentrate on manufacturing the first product. Under what, if any, conditions will this approach result in maximum profits?

12.23 A sporting goods retailer is running a monthly special that prices tennis balls and golf balls to yield a negative contribution margin. What causes a negative contribution margin? What is the likely motive behind the retailer's actions?

12.24 You have built a fairly complex financial planning model for your organization. It contains many parameters and assumptions about how the parameters are related. When you presented the base-case results of the model to your planning committee, the general response was, "Well, I guess we need to drop product X from the product line and that probably will mean closing the manufacturing plant in Omaha." You were shocked by this reaction even though the model did show product X to be unprofitable. How should you have presented your model and the results?

12.25 You and your cost-management team spent months building and testing a financial planning model of your organization's operations. When you previewed the model to a long-time manager, her reaction was, "I don't trust computer models any more than I trust manual election counts. Garbage in equals garbage out, as far as I am concerned." How should you use this reaction to prepare for presenting your model to the organization's chief executive?

12.26 (Appendix A) Proponents of the Theory of Constraints approach to managing processes argue that managers should review every task or operation performed in an organization and ask, Does completing this task help the organization achieve its goal? If the answer is no, managers should find a way to eliminate the effort. Do you believe this test can be applied to every task in an organization? Should every task that fails the test be eliminated? Explain.

12.27 Respond to this comment: "We are unable to meet demand for our product, yet you refuse to let us operate all our processes at least at practical capacity. I think that is a waste of equipment and personnel. What am I supposed to do, have them sweep the floors and let this expensive equipment sit idle?"

12.28 One of your company's top salespersons approaches you and says, "I just heard that I am not allowed in the production area anymore because you have outlawed our efforts to push customers' orders through the process. Listen, my sales performance is the best in the company because my customers know that I will fight to get their orders through this labyrinth of a plant. You are threatening my ability to work effectively for this company. There is no way that you are going to keep me off the production floor without a huge fight. I'll see you at the executive committee meeting on Wednesday." Prepare your arguments to justify your decision to outlaw the expediting of customers' orders by sales personnel.

12.29 (Appendix A) Provide possible reactions to recommendations to implement the Theory of Constraints from the perspective of an employee in a:
  a. Bottleneck process.
  b. Nonbottleneck process.
  c. Sales organization.
  d. Customer service organization.

Exercises

Canyon Escape sells individual tickets for $75 for walking tours of the Grand Canyon. Unit-level costs, including lunch, are $15 per ticket; fixed costs total $200,000 per year.

Exercise 12.30
Cost-Volume-Profit
(LO 2, 3)

Required

a. How many tickets must be sold to break even?

b. What level of revenue is needed to earn a target income of $42,000?

c. If unit-level costs increase to $20 per ticket, what decrease in annual fixed costs must be achieved to keep the same break-even point as calculated in requirement (a)?

d. *Build your own spreadsheet.* Prepare a computer spreadsheet to complete requirements (a)–(c) of this exercise.

Exercise 12.31
Cost-Volume-Profit
(LO 2, 3)

Delta Safety Systems manufactures a component used in aircraft radar systems. The firm's fixed costs are $3,000,000 per year. Delta's variable cost of each component is $3,000, and it sells the components for $5,000 each. The company sold 2,000 components during the prior year.

Required

a. Compute the break-even point in units.

b. Suggest several possible actions that management can take if it wants to decrease the break-even point.

c. The sales manager believes that a reduction in sales price to $4,500 will result in orders for 1,000 more components each year. In comparison with last year's results, will the company benefit if it changes the price? Show calculations to support your answer.

d. *Build your own spreadsheet.* Prepare a computer spreadsheet to complete requirements (a)–(c) of this exercise.

Exercise 12.32
Cost-Volume-Profit and
Capacity
(LO 2, 3)

Superior Manufacturing produced and sold 50,000 temperature gauges last year at $42 each. This level of activity amounted to 80 percent of the firm's total productive capacity. The costs related to this level of activity follow:

	Manufacturing	Selling	Administrative	Total
Unit level	$600,000	$150,000	$ 0	$750,000
Facility level	200,000	180,000	600,000	980,000

Required

a. How many gauges must it sell to break even?

b. Compute last year's income or loss from sales of temperature gauges.

c. Considering your answer in requirement (a), at what percentage of total productive capacity must Superior operate to achieve a break-even operation?

d. *Build your own spreadsheet.* Prepare a computer spreadsheet to complete requirements (a)–(c) of this exercise. What if the sales price drops to $32 per unit?

Exercise 12.33
Cost-Volume-Profit
(LO 2)

Choose the best answer for each of the following:

1. A firm has a negative contribution margin. To reach break-even, it must:
   a. Increase unit-selling price.
   b. Increase sales volume.
   c. Decrease sales volume.
   d. Decrease fixed cost.
   e. Increase fixed cost.

2. If the firm decreases total contribution margin by a given amount, operating profit:
   a. Remains unchanged.
   b. Decreases by the same amount.
   c. Decreases by more than the given amount.
   d. Increases by the same amount.
   e. Does none of the above.

3. The break-even point is increased by:
   a. A decrease in variable costs.
   b. A decrease in fixed costs.
   c. An increase in selling price.
   d. An increase in variable costs.
   e. None of the above.

[CPA adapted]

Exercise 12.34
Cost-Volume-Profit and
Taxes
(LO 3, 4)

Aqua Systems Engineering provides consulting services to city water authorities. A recent income statement revealed variable costs of $740,000 on a sales level of $1,000,000. Annual fixed expenses are $200,000, and the firm's income tax rate is 35 percent.

Required

a. Calculate the firm's break-even volume of service revenue.

b. How much before-tax income must the firm earn to make an after-tax net income of $100,000?

c. What level of revenue must the firm generate to earn an after-tax net income of $100,000?

d. Suppose the firm's income tax rate rises to 40 percent. What will happen to the break-even level of consulting revenue?

e. *Build your own spreadsheet.* Prepare a computer spreadsheet to complete requirements (a)–(d) of this exercise. What if variable costs increase to $840,000?

Ken's Bicycle Shop sells mountain bikes. For purposes of a cost-volume-profit analysis, the shop owner has divided sales into two categories, as follows:

Exercise 12.35
Cost-Volume-Profit and Multiple Products
(LO 3, 4)

Product Category	Sales Price	Invoice Cost	Sales Commissions
High quality	$700	$375	20% of sales
Medium quality	500	235	20% of sales

The shop anticipates selling 500 bicycles, 300 of which will be medium quality. Annual fixed costs are $80,000. Ignore taxes.

Required

a. What is the shop's sales mix?

b. What is the shop's break-even sales volume in dollars? (*Hint:* Find the break-even sales volume first.)

c. How many bicycles of each type must the firm sell to earn a target net income of $50,000?

d. *Build your own spreadsheet.* Prepare a computer spreadsheet to complete requirements (a)–(c) of this exercise. What if the market for high quality bikes drops 20 percent and Ken maintains market share?

Concord Manufacturing, which uses an activity-based costing system, sells 20,000 units per year of Glaxo containers at $40 each. Unit-level activities cost $25 per unit; facilities costs total $125,000 per year. Additional data follow:

Exercise 12.36
Cost-Volume-Profit and ABC
(LO 3, 4)

▨ Batch size is 1,000 units at a cost of $2,000 per batch.

▨ Product-level activities consist of 500 engineering hours per year at $80 per hour.

Required

a. From an activity-based costing perspective, identify one problem associated with the basic cost-volume-profit (CVP) model.

b. What is Concord's annual break-even point?

c. Compute Concord's expected operating income before tax, including the costs in the preceding bulleted list.

d. *Build your own spreadsheet.* Prepare a computer spreadsheet to complete requirements (a)–(c) of this exercise. What is Concord's break-even quantity? (*Hint:* Batch size is 1,000 units. Use trial and error or Excel's Solver wizard and round up to the nearest 1,000.)

Chicago Consulting Group, which uses an activity-based costing (ABC) system, offers a software-training seminar to companies for $12,000 per seminar for 100 students; unit-level activities cost $30 per student; and facility costs total $180,000 per year. Additional data follow:

Exercise 12.37
Cost-Volume-Profit and Activity-Based Costing
(LO 3, 4)

▨ Batch-level activities are $2,500 per seminar (travel, etc.).

▨ Product-level activities consist of 1,000 product maintenance hours per year to keep the seminar up to date at $75 per hour.

Required

In small groups, complete the following:

a. From an ABC perspective, identify one problem associated with the basic cost-volume-profit model.

b. Compute Chicago Consulting Group's operating income before tax considering the costs in the preceding bulleted list, and an expected 100 seminars per year.

c.   *Build your own spreadsheet.* Prepare a computer spreadsheet to complete requirements (a) and (b) of this exercise. Be prepared to demonstrate this spreadsheet model to the class. What is Chicago's break-even seminar quantity? (*Hint:* Use trial and error or Excel's Solver wizard and round up to the nearest whole seminar.

Exercise 12.38
Cost-Volume-Profit
(LO 4)

Review the information in rows 1–5 of Exhibit 12–3. Assume that Fairfield Blues takes actions to decrease its average tax rate to 18 percent by outsourcing its tax planning. This increases facility-level costs by an average of $10,000 per season.

Required

a.   Compute the new break-even volume.

b.   Compute the new target profit volume.

c.   Explain the changes in these volumes.

d.   Compute the new profit (loss) after tax.

e.   *Build your own spreadsheet.* Prepare a computer spreadsheet to complete requirements (a)–(d) of this exercise.

Exercise 12.39
Scarce Resource
(LO 6)

Quicksilver's management has been reviewing company profitability and is attempting to improve performance through better planning. The company manufactures three products in its jewelry line: necklaces, bracelets, and rings. Selected data follow.

	Necklaces	Bracelets	Rings
Selling price	$50.00	$37.50	$25.00
Contribution margin	$20.00	$15.00	$10.00
Machine time required	.5 hours	.25 hours	.30 hours

Machine time is limited to 120 hours per month, and demand for each product far exceeds the company's ability to produce. At the present time, Quicksilver manufactures an equal number of each product. The sales manager has urged the company to concentrate on necklace production because of its high selling price relative to bracelets and rings. Quicksilver will produce no bracelets or rings if it accepts this recommendation. Ignore taxes.

Required

a.   If fixed costs are $2,500 per month, what profit will the company obtain by following the sales manager's recommendation?

b.   What is the maximum profit obtainable and what product or product combination must be sold to obtain that maximum? (*Hint:* Compute the contribution margin of each product per unit of constrained resource.)

Exercise 12.40
Scarce Resource
(LO 6)

Manufacturing cost and other data for two components, 543 and 789, used by Baltimore Electronics follow.

	Component	
	543	789
Direct materials	$0.40	$8.00
Direct conversion cost	2.60	5.50
Sales price	5.00	15.00
Yearly demand (units)	6,000	8,000
Machine hours per unit	4	2

In past years, Baltimore has manufactured all of its components. However, during the coming year, the firm will have only 30,000 hours of machine time available. Ignore taxes.

Required

a.   Can Baltimore fully satisfy demand? Show calculations to support your answer.

b.   Determine the number of units of each component that Baltimore should make during the coming year.

[CPA adapted]

Classic Corporation manufactures two models, small and large. The weekly time available for processing the two models is 100 hours in machining and 90 hours in polishing. The contribution margin is $3 for the small model and $4 for the large model. Each model is processed as follows:

	Machining	Polishing
Small	1 hour	2 hours
Large	4 hours	3 hours

Required

In small groups, complete the following:

a. Formulate the objective function and constraint equations necessary to solve for the optimum product mix.
b. Prepare a short memo explaining how the linear programming approach differs from profit planning with an assumed product mix.

[CPA adapted]

Exercise 12.41
Linear Programming
(Appendix B)
(LO 8)

Identify which of the following insurance claim processes are most likely to be current and future bottleneck processes.

Exercise 12.42
Bottleneck identification
(Appendix A)
(LO 7) eXcel
mhhe.com/hilton3e

A Process	B Available Hours per Week	C Value-Adding Time (hours per claim)	D Theoretical Capacity (claims per week) (D = B ÷ C)	E Practical Capacity (85%) (E = 0.85 × D)	F Average Demand	G Excess Capacity (G = E − F)
Receive claim	40	.08 hr	?	?	400	?
Route claim to adjuster	80	.16 hr	?	?	400	?
Investigate and settle claim	400	1.20 hr	?	?	400	?
Issue payment and close claim	50	.12 hr	?	?	400	?

Identify which of the following business processes for a small (two-person) independent telephone company are most likely to be current and future bottleneck processes.

Exercise 12.43
Bottleneck Identification
(Appendix A)
(LO 7) eXcel
mhhe.com/hilton3e

A Process	B Available Hours per Week	C Value-Adding Time (hours per claim)	D Theoretical Capacity (activity per week) (D = B ÷ C)	E Practical Capacity (80%) (E = 0.80 × D)	F Average Demand	G Excess Capacity (G = E − F)
Advertising (ads)	5	.50 hr	?	?	5	?
Bill collecting (bills)	10	.20 hr	?	?	40	?
Service installations	60	.25 hr	?	?	150	?
Credit analyses	10	.25 hr	?	?	150	?
Purchases of phone service from Southwestern Bell	5	.15 hr	?	?	150	?
Invoicing and billing (bills)	10	.02 hr	?	?	1,000	?
Business planning and analysis (plans)	5	5.00 hr	?	?	2	?

Search the periodicals in your library or on the Internet for an article about or description of an organization that applied the principles of the Theory of Constraints to improve its productive processes. Prepare either a two-page written description or analysis of that organization's experience or a five-minute oral presentation (instructor's choice). You should cover the following points:

1. Description of the organization.
2. Description of the production problem.

Exercise 12.44
Theory of Constraints
(Appendix A)
(LO 7)

3.   Steps taken by the organization.
4.   Results of the steps taken.
5.   Credibility of the article or description.

Exercise 12.45
Theory of Constraints
(LO 7)

Prepare a group response either in favor of or against the following comment: "The greatest obstacle to improving the overall efficiency of an organization is the cost-accounting mentality that seeks to make each individual process as efficient as possible." Be prepared to debate your position.

Problems

Problem 12.46
Cost-Volume-Profit
Analysis
(LO 2, 3)

PhotoKing transfers old home movies (primarily super-8 film and VHS tape) to DVD. The current year's projected sales volume is 2,000 units. The company has been selling the service for an average of $200 per recorded DVD; variable costs consist of the $2 purchase price of the blank DVD and a $2 handling and packaging cost. PhotoKing's annual committed costs for this process (equipment and labor) are $400,000.

Required

a.   Calculate PhotoKing's break-even point for the current year in units.

b.   Management is planning for the coming year when it expects unit sales volume to increase by 10 percent, the unit purchase price of the disks to drop by 30 percent, and committed costs to increase by 10 percent. What is the new break-even volume in units? What volume of units and dollar sales must PhotoKing achieve in the coming year to make a profit of $40,000 if its average selling price remains at $200?

c.   *Build your own spreadsheet.* Prepare a spreadsheet model of PhotoKing's retailing operation that is flexible to changes in parameters.

[CMA adapted]

Problem 12.47
Multiple Products and
Scenario Analysis
(LO 3, 4, 5)

Refer to the information for Fairfield Blues presented in Exhibit 12–5, rows 1 to 12. Assume that you have some new information about costs and activities for next year. Namely, you learn that the cost per game should be $3,000 instead of $2,400, the cost per ticket should be $1.50 instead of $1.00, and the estimated number of tickets sold should be 200,000 instead of 204,000. Assume that all other information in rows 1–12 of Exhibit 12–5 is valid.

Required

a.   Compute the new weighted-average unit contribution margin (WAUCM) considering this new information.

b.   Compute the new break-even volume.

c.   Compute the new target profit volume.

d.   Compute the estimated operating income for next year for Fairfield Blues.

e.   *Build your own spreadsheet.* Duplicate the spreadsheet model in Exhibit 12–5 to complete requirements (a)–(d) of this problem.

Problem 12.48
Cost-Volume-Profit
(LO 2, 3)

A financial analyst is studying two packaging systems, basic and deluxe. The basic system has variable operating costs of $6 per unit and annual committed costs of $600,000; in contrast, the deluxe system has variable costs of $3 and committed costs of $800,000. The company sells its products for $40 per unit, subject to a 10 percent sales commission. Ignore taxes.

Required

a.   Which of the two systems will be more profitable for the firm if sales are expected to average 120,000 units per year?

b.   How many units must the company sell to break even if it selects the deluxe system?

c.   At what volume level will management be indifferent to the basic system and the deluxe system?

d.   *Build your own spreadsheet.* Prepare a spreadsheet model to analyze the choice between the two packaging systems. How do changes in unit variable costs affect the indifference volume?

A financial analyst is studying the feasibility of two alternative assembly methods, manual and automated. The automated method has variable operating costs of $2.10 per unit and annual committed costs of $130,000; in contrast, the manual method has variable costs of $4.20 and committed costs of $60,000. The company sells its products for $23 per unit.

Problem 12.49
Cost-Volume-Profit
(LO 2, 3)

Required

a. What is the break-even point of each method?

b. Above what volume level will management prefer the automated method to the manual method?

c. *Build your own spreadsheet.* Prepare a spreadsheet model to analyze this choice of assembly methods. How do changes in committed costs affect the preference for a method?

Kalifo Company manufactures a line of electric garden tools that hardware stores sell. The company's controller, Will Fulton, has just received the upcoming year's sales forecast for the firm's three products: weeders, hedge clippers, and leaf blowers. Kalifo has experienced considerable variations in sales volumes and variable costs over the past two years, and Fulton believes that the forecast should be carefully evaluated from a cost-volume-profit viewpoint. The preliminary budget information for next year follows.

Problem 12.50
Multiple Products
(LO 3, 4)

	Weeders	**Clippers**	**Blowers**
Unit sales	40,000	40,000	80,000
Unit selling price	$80	$110	$135
Variable manufacturing cost per unit	$53	$69	$77
Variable selling cost per unit	$5	$4	$6

The committed manufacturing overhead is budgeted at $3,200,000, and the company's committed selling and administrative expenses are forecast to be $1,600,000. Kalifo has a tax rate of 40 percent.

Required

a. Estimate Kalifo Company's budgeted net income for next year.

b. Assuming that the sales mix remains as budgeted, determine how many units of each product Kalifo must sell to break even.

c. *Build your own spreadsheet.* Prepare a spreadsheet model similar to Exhibit 12–5 to analyze the requirements of this problem. Make the model flexible to accommodate part (d), which follows.

d. After preparing the original estimates, management determined that the variable manufacturing cost of leaf blowers will increase by 20 percent and the variable selling cost of hedge clippers will increase by 40 percent. However, management has decided not to change the selling price of either product. In addition, management recently learned that the firm's leaf blower has been rated as the best value on the market, and the company now expects to sell three times as many leaf blowers as each of the other products. Under these circumstances, determine how many units of each product Kalifo must sell to break even.

[CMA adapted]

HiSpeed Pumps, Inc., manufactures small, highly efficient pumps for marine application. Last year the firm sold 30,000 pumps at an average of $329 each. An ABC study recently revealed that HiSpeed's activities had the following costs:

Problem 12.51
Financial Planning and
Activity-Based Costing
(LO 3, 4)

Unit, Batch, and Facility-Level Activity

Unit-level manufacturing	30,000 units at $162 per unit
Setup	300 setups at $400 per setup
Engineering	3,500 hours at $125 per hour
Inspection	1,000 inspections at $350 per inspection
Factory overhead (rent, utilities, supervision, depreciation)	$2,610,500
Fixed selling and administrative costs	1,300,000

Management is considering both the installation of automated manufacturing equipment and the implementation of just-in-time (JIT) inventory and production management. If the new equipment is installed, setups will be twice as frequent but quicker and less expensive by 80 percent per setup. Because a total quality program will accompany JIT implementation, HiSpeed anticipates only 10 percent as many inspections at $350 each. After installation of the new equipment and system, engineering hours will increase by 15 percent, at $125 per hour. Factory overhead increases by 30 percent; however, the automated equipment allows HiSpeed to cut its unit variable cost by 15 percent. The overall improvement in product quality supports a selling price increase of 10 percent. HiSpeed's effective tax rate is 40 percent.

Required

a.   *Build your own spreadsheet.* Prepare a spreadsheet model of HiSpeed's operations to complete this requirement and (b). Compute HiSpeed's old and new break-even volumes before and after the proposed automated equipment is installed. What is the implication of the new break-even amount?

b.   How many units must HiSpeed sell to show an after-tax profit of $200,000, assuming that the new technology is adopted?

c.   What will be the impact if the engineers' professional union negotiates a 15 percent pay increase because of the increased qualifications of engineers required by the new process?

Problem 12.52
Financial Planning and Activity-Based Costing
(LO 3, 4)

mhhe.com/hilton3e

Boing, Inc., operates a commuter airline. Last year the airline flew 10,000 flights and sold 400,000 one-way tickets at $59 per ticket. Total costs amounted to $21,600,000. An activity-based costing study recently revealed that Boing's costs include the following components:

Activity Cost Driver	Activity Cost
Miles flown (2,000,000 miles at $2 per mile)	$ 4,000,000
Number of passengers (400,000 passengers at $4 per passenger)	1,600,000
Number of flights (10,000 flights at $840 per flight)	8,400,000
Number of television advertisements (20 at $60,000 each)	1,200,000
Airplane lease	4,200,000
Physical plant	1,600,000
Marketing and administrative	600,000
Total	$21,600,000

Required
Complete the following requirements.

a.   Assume that the projections for next year include 10 percent increases in miles flown, passengers, and flights. Advertisements will double. All cost-driver rates are projected to increase by 5 percent over the amounts listed. Costs for airplane leases, ground facilities, and sales and administrative costs will increase 7 percent. With those projections, prepare a computerized financial model that has a ticket price increase of $5 per one-way ticket.

b.   Management wants to consider a new ticket-pricing method. Assume that it believes it can sell 300,000 tickets for reserved seating at $75 per ticket. In addition, it proposes to sell discount tickets on less popular flights for $40 per ticket. Using the same cost and activity data in requirement (a), how many discount tickets must Boing sell to generate the same operating income as it did when it sold 440,000 tickets for $64 each?

c.   What happens if the number of $75 tickets Boing can sell in requirement (b) is 10 to 20 percent less than expected? Do you recommend that Boing add the new service in requirement (b)?

Problem 12.53
Managing Scarce Resources
(LO 6)

Cerise Hamilton was having a conversation with her neighbor, a production supervisor for Avco Corporation, a metal products company. Avco's metal turning department has 90,000 machine hours to manufacture two products: S109 and T678. The following data are available:

	S109	T678
Unit contribution margin	$8	$6
Machine hours per unit	5 hours	3 hours
Maximum monthly sales	15,000 units	10,000 units

Required
Assume Cerise Hamilton's role in discussing the following issues with her neighbor.

a.   Does Avco have sufficient machine time to fill all sales orders?

b.   Should Avco focus on the manufacture of S109 or T678?

c.   Set a production schedule for Avco that makes the most profitable use of its manufacturing time.

Refer to the data for Fairfield Blues in rows 1 to 12 of Exhibit 12–5. Assume that it is considering these alternative scenarios:

1. Increase the number of concerts to 10 per year. Average attendance at concerts will decline 10 percent per performance from the level planned, but all other data are the same as in rows 1 to 12 of Exhibit 12–5.

2. Decrease the number of concerts to four per year. Average concert attendance will increase 25 percent, but all other data are the same as in rows 1 to 12 of Exhibit 12–5.

3. Increase the box seating by 25 percent, maintain average attendance in each category of seating, and increase the number of concerts to 10 per year. All other data are the same as in rows 1 to 12 of Exhibit 12–5.

Problem 12.54
Scenario Analysis
(LO 3, 5)

Required

a. Using a spreadsheet, duplicate the financial model in Exhibit 12–5 to project the operating income for each of the three scenarios.

b. Prepare a memo to management to recommend the best scenario to choose from the three listed and the base-case scenario.

University Bookstore is a nonprofit retail outlet for textbooks, computers, and general merchandise (including trade books, supplies, and university-licensed apparel and gifts). It is located near the main campus of State University and controls the majority of the local market share for new and used textbooks. Other retail outlets, such as Barnes & Noble, University Drugstore (a private company), and CompUSA, have larger shares of the local market for other items. Tammy Waialua is a full-time accounting student and part-time employee of University Bookstore who recently studied the current chapter on managing constrained resources. She observed that the bookstore's primary constraints are floor and shelf space for fast-selling items such as textbooks and market share for slow-selling items such as general merchandise.

Average inventory levels and the most recent year's cost of goods sold in the three departments follow.

Problem 12.55
Theory of Constraints in a Nonprofit Organization
(Appendix A)
(LO 7)

Department	Average Inventory	Annual Cost of Goods Sold
New and used textbooks	$1,000,000	$4,000,000
Computers	400,000	1,500,000
General merchandise	1,200,000	1,400,000

Tammy approached her boss, the bookstore's general manager, and suggested that they try to improve its efficiency by managing its constraints more effectively. The general manager thanked Tammy for her concern but assured her that this manufacturing technique was neither needed by nor applicable to the nonprofit bookstore.

Required

In small groups, complete the following:

a. Explain how University Bookstore's constraints can be both floor space (internal) and market share (external).

b. Is Tammy or her boss correct about the relevance of the Theory of Constraints to the bookstore's operations? Explain.

c. Prepare a short report with recommendations for managing the bookstore more efficiently.

Many commercial companies offer computer software packages to build financial planning models. Managing complex operations can be very difficult without effective computer software. Selecting among the various available packages can be quite difficult, and many organizations rely on the advice and assistance of consultants to select and install the software. Nonetheless, anyone contemplating the purchase of such software is advised to become an informed consumer. The primary question is whether a software package generates the analysis and information needed to manage constrained resources. Beyond that general consideration are others:

Problem 12.56
Financial Planning
Software
(LO 1)

1. *Design features.* How flexible or adaptable is the software?

2. *Thoroughness of analysis.* Does the software model all of the important processes? Does it allow tests of changes to conditions (what-if analysis)?

3. *Thoroughness of reports.* Does the software provide detailed but understandable effects of alternative process changes?

4. *Integration capability.* Does the software accept input from existing information systems or common software? Does it provide output that is compatible with existing systems and software?

5. *Technical elements.* Is the software compatible with existing hardware and operating systems?

6.   *Customer service.* Is the supplier reputable? Does it provide full support for the software before and after the sale?

7.   *Cost.* Is the cost of the software acceptable?

Required

a.   Search the Internet for at least two commercial financial planning software packages. (*Hint:* Search for the key words, "financial model software.")

b.   To the extent possible, contrast the two packages according to the preceding seven considerations.

c.   Be prepared to present your analysis.

Problem 12.57
Spreadsheet Model
(LO 2, 3)

Marie, your housemate and art student, plans to start a small T-shirt printing business to partially finance her education. A generous art teacher has donated old but serviceable equipment and the use of a heated garage. Marie will produce original and custom designs per customer requests. Relevant facts about the T-shirt printing operation follow:

▨   Jobs will be marked up 100 percent over the cost of materials to cover the cost of design and printing time.

▨   Plain, high-quality T-shirts cost $4.50 each.

▨   T-shirts can be printed with one or two colors, front and/or back, resulting from one to four different elements per shirt design.

▨   Each design element requires a separate silk screen, which costs $35, and a developing film, which costs $15.

▨   Each color application (i.e., up to four per shirt, one for each design element) uses heat-sensitive paint costing $0.30 per application.

▨   Orders must be placed in increments of 10 between a minimum of 30 and a maximum of 50.

Required

Build your own spreadsheet. Marie has asked you to help build a spreadsheet model that will allow her to price jobs of different sizes and complexity. Do so.

Problem 12.58
Linear Programming
(Appendix B)
(LO 8)

A computer spreadsheet solution of a linear programming model follows:

E226 =SUM(B226:D226)

	A	B	C	D	E	F
213	12.60					
214	**Data input** Products	Whos	Whats	Wheres		Constraint
215	**Contribution margin per unit**	$ 8.00	$ 7.00	$ 9.00		
216	**Resource constraints**					
217	Direct materials, per unit	12.00	3.00	6.00	less than	500
218	Design hours per unit	1.00	2.00	3.00	less than	80
219	Machining, hours per unit	2.00	1.00	1.00	less than	80
220	**Demand constraints**					
221	Whos sales, units				no more than	20
222	Wheres sales, units				at least	30
223	**Initial guess at sales levels**	10	10	10		
224	**Linear Program Model** Products	Whos	Whats	Wheres	Total	Constraint
225	**Units sold (replaced by the optimal solutio**	30	11	9	50	
226	**Contribution margin**	$ 240	$ 77	$ 81	$ 398	
227	**Material used**	360	33	54	447	500
228	**Design hours used**	30	22	27	79	80
229	**Machining hours used**	60	11	9	80	80
230	**Sales of Whos**		11		11	20
231	**Sales of Wheres**			9	9	30
232						

Required

a.   Write the linear programming objective function and constraints in equation form.

b.   Explain the meaning of each cell in the linear program model section of the spreadsheet.

You are about to interview with Fairfield Blues for a staff accountant's position. Upon arriving at the interview, a human resources specialist hands you a short examination that covers cost-volume-profit analysis.

Problem 12.59
CVP
(LO 1)

Required

Briefly respond to the following questions.

a.   Assume that Fairfield Blues has three full-time salaried employees. It is considering a proposal to reduce all salaries and replace them with a commission based on ticket revenue. What will be the effect of the new compensation plan on the company's facility costs and variable costs? What might happen to total revenue if management compensation is based, in part, on a percentage of ticket revenue?

b.   If the company experiences an increase in property taxes, will the firm's break-even point rise or fall?

c.   If the costs for each ticket increase, what will be the effect on the company's unit contribution margin?

A computer spreadsheet solution of a linear programming model follows:

Problem 12.60
Linear Programming
(Appendix B)
(LO 8)

	A	B	C	D	E	F
	Microsoft Excel					_ □ ×
	File Edit View Insert Format Tools Data Window Help					_ ♂ ×
	E13 ▼ = =SUM(B13:D13)					
	A	B	C	D	E	F
1	Data input Products	Baubles	Bangles	Beads		Constraint
2	Contribution margin per unit	$ 12.00	$ 8.00	$ 14.00		
3	Resource constraints					
4	Direct materials, per unit	22.00	8.00	13.00	less than	800
5	Design hours per unit	4.00	1.00	5.00	less than	120
6	Machining, hours per unit	2.00	1.00	2.00	less than	80
7	Demand constraints					
8	Bangles sales, units				no more than	30
9	Beads sales, units				at least	10
10	Initial guess at sales levels	10	10	10		
11	Linear Program Model Products	Baubles	Bangles	Beads	Total	Constraint
12	Units sold (replaced by the optimal solution)	10	30	10	50	
13	Contribution margin (B2*B12,C2*C12,D2*D12)	$ 120	$ 240	$ 140	$ 500	
14	Material used (B4*B12, etc.)	220	240	130	590	800
15	Design hours used (B5*B12, etc.)	40	30	50	120	120
16	Machining hours used (B6*B12, etc.)	20	30	20	70	80
17	Sales of Bangles (C12)		30		30	30
18	Sales of Beads (D12)			10	10	10
19						
	◄ ◄ ► ►◄ \12-62 / 12.60 / Sheet3 /		◄			► ◄
	Ready					

Required

a.   Write the linear programming objective function and constraints in equation form.

b.   Explain the meaning of each cell in the linear program model section of the spreadsheet.

Cases

Virtually no organization publicizes its break-even point to external parties. Airlines are a notable exception, but only a handful disclose this key operating statistic. Access the homepages of Continental Airlines and Comair Holdings, Inc. Continental is a global carrier and one of the largest in the industry. COMAIR, on the other hand, is a much smaller entity, operating regional jets and playing a major role in Delta Connection's program at its Cincinnati and Orlando hubs.

Case 12.61
Cost-Volume-Profit
(LO 1, 2)

Required

In small groups, complete the following:

a.   Learn more about these two firms by exploring their Web sites.

b.   By reviewing key financial and operating statistics disclosed by the carriers, find the break-even load factor— the percentage of seats that must be occupied by paying passengers for the airline to break even. What break-even load factors have these carriers disclosed in recent periods?

c.   Explain several underlying factors/characteristics of these carriers that likely cause their break-even points to differ.

Case 12.62
Managing Constraints
(Appendix A)
(LO 7)

The Tooling Business Unit (TBU) of the Huge Company manufactures tools, setup jigs, fixtures, and prototypes used throughout the company's operations. The market value of products produced at TBU is estimated to be $1 billion annually. These products are machined and/or welded from metal stock or are made from advanced composite materials. These products are used in turn to produce the company's ultimate products and must be manufactured to exceptionally close tolerances. TBU employs approximately 1,000 highly skilled machinists, operators, and toolmakers that take great pride in their skills and the high quality of their products (i.e., conformance to required tolerances).

For example, one of TBU's products is a jig that the aerospace division uses to manufacture aircraft wings. The jig has gross dimensions of 75 feet × 20 feet × 8 feet, which has elements (subassemblies) that are machined on a computer-numerically-controlled (CNC) machine to tolerances of one-thousandth of an inch. These are extremely close tolerances for such large fixtures.

Another critical feature of TBU's products is that they are made in very small numbers (e.g., almost never more than one or two of a kind). Because of the uniqueness of manufacturing at TBU, numerous manual and computer (i.e., software) setups are required during any month, and large production runs virtually are nonexistent.

The production of TBU's tools and fixtures precede the production of Huge's products. Any delays in delivering them to the manufacturing divisions set back delivery dates to customers. Furthermore, because of the complexities of manufacturing, any delays are often compounded with delays from other suppliers. An added complication for TBU is that tooling designs often arrive behind schedule from internal customers, who are the product divisions, and TBU is expected to make up as much lost time as possible.

Thus, TBU's objectives are to:

1.   Manufacture complex parts to exacting tolerances.

2.   Meet or improve scheduled delivery dates.

Dave Winfield, a young industrial engineer and recent MBA graduate, and his new management team inherited a chaotic manufacturing situation at TBU. Thousands of orders from dozens of manufacturing divisions were being shepherded through TBU by an extensive expediting system. Each customer division placed at least one expediter at TBU. This expediter's primary objective was to see that the division's jobs moved through TBU's machining or fabricating workstations as quickly as possible. It was common for a workstation operator to halt work on one order to begin work on another at the request of a favored or especially persuasive expediter. It also was common to find a behind-schedule order languishing at a workstation while the operator worked on another order that was not due for weeks. Because of the exacting tolerances required for most of TBU's products, these problems were most critical at its CNC workstations. The results were a large backlog of orders, many idle workstations, some overwhelmed workstations, and many unhappy customers who blamed TBU for their inability to meet their (external) customers' delivery dates.

Required

a.   As Dave Winfield you have been charged with bringing order to TBU and improving the business unit's on-schedule performance. How do you proceed?

b.   What do you recommend for managing TBU capacity?

Predicting the profitability of a ski resort's winter operations can be as difficult as forecasting the weather and the world political situation, as events of the 2001–2002 season confirmed. Nonetheless, modeling aspects of the operations, which can be quantified and related, can prove useful to ski resort managers as they plan for next year's activities and assess the impacts of different planning scenarios. This case relies on publicly available information to identify potentially important factors that could be included in a financial model of Vail Resorts winter ski resort operations.[15]

Vail Mountain opened for skiing in 1962 with two chairlifts, one gondola, and a $5 lift ticket. During the inaugural 1962–1963 season, the mountain recorded 55,000 skier days. By 1968 Vail had installed its first snow-making systems and achieved 1 million cumulative skier days. By 2003, Vail Resorts had expanded its ownership to five major mountain resorts in Colorado, Nevada, and Wyoming and had large interests in several others. In the 2000–2001 season, Vail Mountain alone recorded more than 1.6 million skier visits, and its other Colorado resorts achieved nearly 3.3 million.

The 2001–2002 season, however, was plagued by below-normal snowfall in Colorado and a general fall-off of tourism related to a weakening economy, terrorism, and war. These events might have conspired to create a worst-case planning scenario than managers could have expected. Having a flexible financial planning model of resort operations would help managers assess future risks and respond quickly to events as they unfold.

Elements of Ski Resort Operations

Until recently, managers of North American ski resorts could rely on estimates of skier-visit days as the primary driver of resort revenues and variable costs. Furthermore, in Colorado, gross margin percentages at one time reliably averaged approximately 56 percent of revenue on an average stay of seven days per skier. The average stay at a single resort, however, has declined over the years from seven days to barely four days; the decline reflects the combined effects of an aging population, reduced vacation time, increased vacation costs, and stays at multiple resorts during a single vacation.[16]

In recent years, ski resorts have consolidated into large corporate entities, such as American Skiing (i.e., Kilington and Sugarbush), Intrawest (i.e., Whistler/Blackcomb, Copper, and Mammoth), and Vail Resorts (Vail, Beaver Creek, Breckenridge, Keystone, and Hevenly Valley). This consolidation created management, marketing, and operational efficiencies that have greatly increased competition for overall declining skier-visit days.

Increased competition has led to improved marketing analysis and differential pricing for destination (e.g., nonlocals who stay overnight) and local (e.g., daily drive-in) skiers. Ticket prices paid by destination skiers for individual days have climbed steadily by approximately 10 percent annually ($65 per day), but season passes for local individuals ($300 per season) and families ($500 per season) have declined dramatically as resorts compete for the steady cash flow from local skiers. Although destination skiers represent approximately 55 percent of its total skier visits, Vail Resorts earns approximately 75 percent of its operating income before tax, depreciation, and amortization (EBITDA) from destination skiers. In contrast, one of its major competitors, Intrawest, earns approximately 70 percent of its EBITDA from destination skiers, who represent only 20 percent of its skier visits.

Resorts earn revenues from ticket sales, meals, lodging, rentals, retail sales, and real estate sales. Most revenue growth has been from increases in nonticket sales revenue. Vail's average revenue per skier visit was $99 for 2003, down from the previous year's $106. Destination skiers contribute roughly $195 per day, compared to $31 for local skiers. Additional operating data for Vail Resorts are in the following table which was extracted from Vail Resorts 10-K reports (dollar values are in millions).

[15] Many large ski resort companies, such as Vail Resorts in Colorado, have made significant investments in golf courses, tennis facilities, and so on to make the summer and fall seasons important sources of income (see, for example, www.vailresorts.com). This case considers only winter operations. This case makes further simplifying assumptions by ignoring long-term investment decisions and assuming that assets in place do not change. This is almost never the case for large resorts that vie for scarce tourism dollars.

[16] G. Rudowsky, "Staying on Top of Aspen."

Case 12.63
Modeling Ski Resort
Operations
(LO 4)

Ski Resort Risk Factors

Skiing is an expensive, time-consuming, weather-dependent recreational activity. Skier visits, particularly destination visits, are affected by early season snowfall, the health of the economy, airline service, promotions, and competition among resorts. Poor snowfall, an economic downturn, and political conditions adversely affected Vail Resorts' 2001–2002 operations, compared to the 2000–2001 season. Therefore, the financial planning model should reflect the effects of sources of risk.

	Revenues		Operating Expenses			Statistics		Balance Sheet Information		
Fiscal Year	Mountain/ Resort	Lodging	Mountain	Lodging	Depreciation and Amortization	Skier Visits	Resort Revenue per Skier Visit	Total Assets	Long-term Debt (including current maturities)	Stock-holders' Equity
2003[a]	$ 470,148	$159,849	$370,779	$150,624	$82,242	5,730	$ 99.18	$1,455,442	$584,151	$496,246
2002	400,478	150,928	308,896	137,259	68,480	4,732	106.53	1,449,026	602,786	504,004
2001	391,373	124,207	299,414	109,664	65,580	4,975	97.67	1,188,546	388,380	494,000
2000[b]	373,786	116,610	284,136	103,570	61,748	4,595	100.96	1,135,596	394,235	475,791
1999	424,647		346,936		53,569	4,606	90.25	1,094,548	398,186	464,300
1998[c]	350,803		242,009		45,432	4,717	74.37	958,167	318,520	449,848
1997[d]	259,038		172,715		34,044	4,273	60.62	855,949	265,062	405,666
1996	140,288		89,890		18,148	2,228	62.97	422,612	144,750	123,907
1995	126,349		82,305		17,968	2,136	59.15	429,628	191,313	167,694

Notes: a. Vail Resorts purchased Heavenly Valley in 2003.

b. Vail began reporting mountain and lodging operations separately in 2000. Prior years reported them jointly as Resort Operations.

c. Vail changed its calendar year end to July 31 in 1998. 10-month data for 1997 and 1998 follow:

1998	$336,547		$217,764		$36,838	4,717	$71.35	$912,122	$284,014	$462,624
1997	248,511		155,412		27,604	4,273	58.16	814,816	236,347	417,187

1998 (12-month) data are 10-month data scaled up by the same percentage increase as experienced in 1997.

d. Vail purchased Keystone and Breckinridge in 1997.

Requirements

a. Transform the information from (1) this case, (2) any other relevant sources, such as Vail Resorts' recent 10-K reports (be sure to properly identify them), and (3) additional assumptions you believe are necessary (explain them) into data input that form parameters for a financial planning model of Vail Resorts ski resort operations. For this case ignore nonwinter, nonresort operations and any long-term investments.

b. Using the parameters from requirement (a), create a computerized financial planning model that forecasts the profitability of next season's ski resort operations.

c. Conduct sensitivity and scenario analyses that identify and illustrate financial planning risks within this model.

d. Identify qualitative factors that managers of Vail Resorts should consider in their planning along with the outcomes of using your financial planning model.

Case 12.64
Financial Modeling of Credit Card Operations
(LO 1, 2, 3)

A newspaper article reported that GE Capital Corp. planned to charge a $25 fee to cardholders who pay off their monthly credit card bills in full.[17] Too many of its credit card customers paid in full each month and did not incur any finance charges, which averaged 17.1 percent of the unpaid monthly balance. GE Capital did obtain payments from merchants at rates of 3 to 5 percent of purchases, but those payments were insufficient to meet GE Capital's profit objectives.

[17] Patricia Lamiell, "Credit Card Firms Look for New Penalties: GE Capital to Charge $25 if Cardholder Pays Off Full Balance."

About 20 percent of GE Capital's 5 million cardholders keep the cards only for emergency use. The company informed them and those who do not carry a balance (about 36 percent) that it would begin charging them $25 per year if they do not begin to carry a balance (and pay finance charges).

Credit-card research companies predicted that most credit-card issuers would charge such a penalty for little or nonuse and, furthermore, would find additional opportunities to charge fees. This comes after an era when issuers gave out cards to poor credit risks, shunned annual fees, and gave cash rebates to encourage the use of their cards. Cash rebates have been as high as $140 per year for customers who charge $10,000 per year. The problem is that issuers need interest income to generate profits and pay for all the incentives. GE Capital loses $65 a year for every customer who earns the maximum rebate but pays no finance charges.

Thus, firms are bringing back annual fees, calling them penalties for nonuse. GE Capital also plans to reduce interest rates to 11.9 percent for those who currently pay off their balances, hoping to motivate them to spend more and carry a balance.

Required

In small groups, take the perspective of GE Capital Corp and prepare responses and a presentation that cover the following questions.

a.   What are GE Capital's goals and tangible objectives? Do you consider them fair? Explain.

b.   From the article, identify the likely drivers of revenue and costs.

c.   Develop a spreadsheet model that allows GE Capital's managers to see the financial effects of alternative courses of action. Be prepared to demonstrate this model to the class.

Chapter 13

Cost Management and Decision Making

After completing this chapter, you should be able to:

1. Structure business decision-making problems into objectives, alternative actions, and expected outcomes.

2. Identify both quantitative and qualitative relevant costs and benefits of decision alternatives.

3. Use decision trees to describe business decisions.

4. Use a benefit-cost approach for common decisions such as obtaining new technology or capability; outsourcing (make versus buy); or modifying, adding, or dropping a product, service, or business unit; and pricing, including special orders and lifecycle costs.

(Solutions are on page 533.)

Cost-*Management* Challenges

1. **What** are the risks if Bootstrap Industries always values job creation more than covering its costs?

2. **Should** Bootstrap set its prices to increase employment or to generate funds for internal investment?

Bootstrap Industries' mission is simple and unchanging: **to create jobs for people with disabilities.** We measure our success by the number of jobs created, the quality of those jobs, the environment we create within our organization, the service we deliver to our customers, and our impact in the community. We ended last year with 3,000 employees working in Washington and Oregon. Disabilities typically would have excluded more than half of them from employment. Our annual revenue grew 30% to almost $70 million as we continued to experience tremendous success in our businesses. That 99% of our total revenue last year came from service and product sales confirms Bootstrap's self-sufficiency. We are successful because of our commitment to core values:

Bootstrap's Core Values Are the Foundation of Our Success

Bootstrap Industries, based in Portland, Oregon, is a nonprofit organization that relies on careful business decision making to succeed in a competitive market. Note that its primary goal is to seek good jobs for otherwise unemployable people. It is able to do so on a long-term basis because it follows many of the decision-making practices of successful profit-seeking companies.

Bootstrap Industries provides outsourced services to customers such as federal and state governments, Intel Corporation, Boeing, Hewlett-Packard, NEC Electronics, Packard Bell, Wells Fargo Bank, Target, Blue Shield, The Oregonian, Kaiser Permanente, and Pasco Scientific. Bootstrap offers employment ranging from high-tech to low-tech jobs. It offers specialized services such as electronic circuit board assembly and clean room maintenance. It manages food-service operations at two major military bases in the State of Washington, preparing and serving more than 100,000 meals monthly. Additionally, Bootstrap Industries owns and operates Sasquatch Snowshoes, which manufactures snowshoes for recreational snowshoers and competitive racers. We use examples from this division of Bootstrap Industries to illustrate cost management and decision making.

Bootstrap's mission statement raises difficult trade-offs among possibly conflicting goals. Should managers make a decision that increases profits but requires the use of fewer disabled employees? Should managers decide to forgo an unprofitable opportunity that offers high-quality jobs? Should prices for services and products seek to generate profits or growth of sales and employment? Making these trade-offs is challenging but is easier when managers have good information about alternatives, their impacts, and the uses of resources.

The focus of this chapter is how cost-management information can support and improve the evaluation of trade-offs and alternatives. We begin with a discussion of the decision-making process, which leads us to consider important types and qualities of useful information for decision making. We also describe the use of several useful cost-management tools for evaluating profit-planning and cost-reduction decisions. The primary purpose of this chapter is to show how to evaluate decisions within a consistent benefit-cost framework.

Decision-Making Process

LO I Structure business decision-making problems into objectives, alternative actions, and expected outcomes.

Understanding and making recommendations for decision making have occupied philosophers and scientists for hundreds, if not thousands, of years. The literature is vast, and even a brief excursion into this field of human behavior can be both fascinating and confusing.[1] It is safe to say that great diversity of opinion exists about how humans *do* and *should* make decisions. We cannot hope to resolve all the unknowns and controversies here, but we can provide some guidance about systematic decision making. What follows is a benefit-cost framework of decision making with five stages within which we consider the role of cost management.[2] One objective of this framework is to reinforce that cost management is a purposeful activity—more value creation at lower cost—and a proactive attitude—decisions drive costs; costs do not just happen.

Exhibit 13–1 presents the decision-making framework formally. In this chapter we will briefly discuss stage I: setting goals. This chapter focuses more, however, on the role of cost management in stage II: gathering information and stage III: evaluating alternatives. Note that as shown in Exhibit 13–1, other parts of the text also consider types of information that support all five stages in more detail. One of the most important parts of this framework is the feedback to all other parts of the process.

---

[1] A modern coverage of decision making is found in P. Kleindorfer, H. Kunreuther, and P. Schoemaker, *Decision Sciences: An Integrative Approach.* (Full citations to references are in the Bibliography.)

[2] This framework is adapted from Kleindorfer et al.; H. Simon, "Strategy and Organizational Evolution"; and J. Shank, "Strategic Cost Management: New Wine or Just New Bottles?"

Feedback is critical to managers' and workers' sustained learning and retraining; it is the essence of a "learning organization" to learn from its successes and failures and to improve future decisions.

Stage I: Setting Goals and Objectives

Alice: Would you tell me, please, which way I ought to go from here?
Cheshire Cat: That depends a good deal on where you want to get to.
Alice: I don't much care where. . . .
Cheshire Cat: Then it doesn't matter which way you go.
Alice: . . . so long as I get somewhere.
Cheshire Cat: Oh, you're sure to do that, if you only walk long enough.[3]

Do individuals or organizations succeed by luck alone? A critical assumption of professional management is that consistent organizational success is not the result of pure luck or random actions. Rather, long-term success is the result of carefully pursuing specific, attainable goals. Although Alice's adventures might have been dreams, she eventually navigated them by clarifying her goals and making the best decisions possible with available information. Organizations should do no less.

Selecting Goals

Organizations exist to achieve specific goals, such as generating superior returns to stockholders, offering the best customer service, providing meaningful employment, or eradicating hunger or disease. Without a clear set of goals, an organization's members have no clear guidance for their actions and decisions. Many organizational problems can be traced to the lack of either clear goals or clearly communicated goals. Bootstrap Industries, the focus organization of this chapter, clearly directs its activities and decisions to achieve the goal of meaningful employment for disabled persons.

As a nonprofit organization, generating an excess of revenues (profit) from operations means that Bootstrap can:

- Invest more in its programs and employees.
- Continue to improve the capabilities of its employees to deliver quality services.
- Continue to meet its specific employment goals.

Specifying Tangible Objectives

Most organizational goals are abstract in nature (achieving the "best customer service," for example). Although these goals provide essential guidance, successful organizations also provide tangible objectives or benchmarks by which to measure progress toward their goals. That is, **tangible objectives** are benchmarks capable of being measured in some manner. As shown in Exhibit 13–2, Bootstrap Industries provides specific guidance to its employees by translating its goal of meaningful employment for disabled persons into tangible objectives of annual increases in employment and acquisition of high-quality customers. For example, when making business decisions, Bootstrap managers ask themselves, Will this action lead to employment growth and improvement in the quality of jobs for our employees? Without tangible objectives, direction and progress toward goals is unclear.

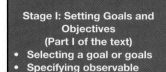

Exhibit 13–1

Decision-Making Framework (and links to the parts of this text)

Stage I: Setting Goals and Objectives
(Part I of the text)
- Selecting a goal or goals
- Specifying observable objectives

Stage II: Gathering Information
(Parts II and III of the text)
- Creating useful information
- Generating feasible alternative actions

Stage III: Evaluating Alternatives
(Parts III and IV of the text)
- Anticipating the future outcome(s) of each action
- Choosing the best alternative(s)

Stage IV: Planning and Implementation
(Part IV of the text)
- Planning resources and activities
- Implementing the best alternative rapidly and efficiently

Stage V: Obtaining Feedback
(Part V of the text)
- Evaluating actual outcomes
- Improving future decisions and implementations

---

[3] L. Carroll, *Alice's Adventures in Wonderland.*

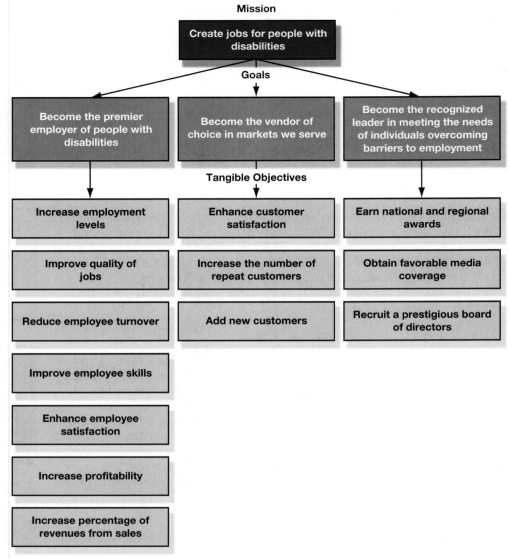

We now consider two common types of tangible objectives: target profit and target cost. We also will use target cost objectives as motivation for gathering additional information and generating alternatives.

Setting Tangible Objectives

Target profit.   Nearly every organization that sells products or services has a tangible objective of generating a **target profit,** which is the desired excess of periodic or project sales revenues over costs. Nonprofit and most government organizations that sell products or provide services have a target of zero profit overall, which means that they seek to recover the costs of operations from their activities. Profit-seeking organizations, including private companies and governmental enterprises, such as the postal service or railroads in some countries, seek a target profit sufficient to ensure survival or growth. These target profits might be the result of competitive market or governmental pressures and can be computed, for example, by applying a profit percentage to sales prices or invested assets. Target profits in turn generate plans for managing sales and costs.[4]

---

[4] Target costing is presented in detail in Chapter 5. Planning for sales and costs is the topic of Chapter 15.

Bootstrap Industries computes a target profit for its Sasquatch Snowshoes division by multiplying a target profit percentage, 20 percent, by the market price, $100.[5]

$$\text{Target profit per unit} = \text{Target profit percentage} \times \text{Market price per unit}$$
$$= .20 \times \$100 = \$20 \text{ per unit}$$

Target cost. The *target cost* is the most that a good or service can cost and still meet both customer needs (e.g., quality and function) and company profit targets. The target cost is a tangible objective that can be very difficult to meet without changes in organizations, processes, or designs. Bootstrap Industries' Sasquatch Snowshoe division competes with other manufacturers, such as Yuba, Tubbs, and Red Feather, and must meet market expectations for price and value. Bootstrap uses the process of target costing to manage the development of new snowshoe models to meet target costs. Target costing is not the only approach to setting goals, but its popularity is increasing because it focuses on a systematic process for creating products and services with features customers want at prices they are willing to pay.

Bootstrap's target price for the Rambler snowshoe is the market price of $100 for similar products offered by competitors. Bootstrap does not believe that it can demand a higher price and still maintain the 5,000 unit sales volume necessary to meet its employment goals. It could charge a lower price than competitors, but then it would sacrifice revenues necessary to cover costs and fund important activities. Bootstrap managers believe that its commercial products should earn a 20 percent return on sales to cover other activities, such as training and counseling new employees. Therefore, the target profit on the Rambler snowshoe is $100 \times 0.20 = $20. Subtracting the target profit from the target price, $100 - $20 = $80, yields the average target cost per pair (unit) of Rambler snowshoes.

$$\text{Target cost} = \$100 - (\$100 \times 0.20) = \$80 \text{ per unit.}$$

With the current production process, can Bootstrap sell the Rambler snowshoe at $100 per pair and earn its target return? If not, Bootstrap must scrap the product idea or improve either the product design or the production process. Bootstrap's analysts estimate that the existing product design and current processes will use resources as follows to meet the 5,000 unit sales volume (Chapter 11 discusses cost estimation).

Unit sales volume	5,000
Variable cost per unit	$45
Committed fixed costs	$235,000

Committed costs are set by company policies, such as Bootstrap's commitment to employee training. Using these estimates, analysts estimate current total costs as follows:

$$\text{Current total costs} = \$235,000 + \$45 \times 5,000 = \$460,000$$

This compares unfavorably, however, to the total target cost required if Bootstrap is to meet its required return of 20 percent because the total target cost is $80 \times 5,000 = $400,000. Therefore, Bootstrap must reduce total costs by $60,000 ($460,000 - $400,000) to meet its goals of creating employment and funding for activities.

This cost reduction target of at least $60,000 is a tangible objective that proceeds from the company's goals. The next task is to find additional reliable information to support decisions about how to accomplish that objective.

Stage II: Gathering Information

Cost-management information that supports management decision making often incorporates measures with varying **information quality,** the dimensions of which are decision usefulness, subjectivity, objectivity, accuracy, timeliness, cost,

---

[5] Many companies compute target profit as a percentage of the market price because other bases, such as invested assets, are too difficult to measure for individual products.

and relevance for current decisions. The overriding criterion of cost management information is **decision usefulness.** Does it help managers make sufficiently better decisions to justify the cost of the information?

Objectivity versus Subjectivity

Cost management relies heavily on measurements of various kinds. All measurement inherently involves subjectivity and objectivity. **Subjectivity** describes the degree of disagreement about what to measure, how to measure it, what the observed measure is, or whether the measurement is important. **Objectivity,** the degree of consensus about measurement, is the mirror image of subjectivity. Clearly, some measures are more subjective or objective than others; that is, all measures conceptually reside somewhere on a continuum from subjective to objective. For example, the numbers in the financial statements of Bootstrap Industries (and other companies) are considered to be *objective* measurements prepared with great care. Nonetheless, considerable judgment about financial statement measures and disclosures still exists. Closer to the subjectivity end of the spectrum is the measurement of Bootstrap's product or service quality perceptions, which reside in and vary among individuals. Even subjective measures can be useful, however. For example, perceptions of the quality of food or services can vary among Bootstrap's customers, but Bootstrap management believes that gathering these more subjective measures is essential because they can presage potential opportunities or problems. Similarly, many find value in the number of stars or "thumbs up" awarded to restaurants and movies.

Accuracy

Information pertinent to a decision problem must also be accurate or it will be of little use. **Accuracy** is precision in measurement. For example, the estimated cost Bootstrap incurred if it were to buy and maintain facilities for its snowshoe division, Sasquatch Snowshoes, is useful for decisions about whether to continue to rent or buy its own facilities. However, if the cost figures are inaccurate because of erroneous calculations or incomplete records, the usefulness of the figures is greatly diminished.

Timeliness

Information is useful if it is timely; that is, **timeliness** means that information is available in time to fully consider it when making a decision. For example, information about alternative production processes is not very useful if it cannot be prepared before a deadline to decide which process Bootstrap should use.

Relevance

The **relevance** of information refers to whether it is pertinent to a decision; that is, knowing the information or different values of the information can influence choice. Because different decisions typically require different information, an important issue is deciding what information is relevant to the specific situation. The most timely, accurate, objective information is useless if it is irrelevant to the decision. **Relevant costs and benefits** occur in the future *and* differ for feasible alternatives. Costs that differ for alternatives also are called **differential costs.** Some highly accurate information might not be useful to a decision maker. Suppose that Bootstrap will continue to operate manufacturing facilities in Oregon but is considering expanding the size of its rented facilities. Precise data about future rents in Colorado, where the company does not plan to locate, are irrelevant to the decision of whether to rent expanded facilities in Oregon. We elaborate on this important characteristic of cost-management information in the next section of the chapter.

Identification of Relevant Costs and Benefits

A particular cost might or might not be relevant to the decision at hand. Some decisions involve many types of relevant, differential costs. For example, consider the problem of reducing the costs to produce Rambler snowshoes to meet the profit target. Suppose that the two alternatives to improving costs are to use either a robotic or an improved manual assembly process. All unit-, batch-, product-, customer-, and facility-level costs might differ for the robotic and manual assembly alternatives.[6] Therefore, this decision should consider all of these affected costs. However, if adding or replacing robotic machinery does not affect the manufacturing building itself, the decision process can ignore facility-related costs.

Now consider Exhibit 13–3, a preliminary analysis of costs and benefits of the two snowshoe production process alternatives considered by Bootstrap's managers: (1) installing robotic equipment or (2) improving the current manual process. Which benefits and costs are *relevant* to the choice in the alternatives to attempt the cost-reduction target?

The target price, sales, and production volume[7] are the same as discussed previously. Analysts have refined estimates of alternative production costs to include unit-level costs per unit, product-level equipment and supervision costs, training, and

---

[6] Recall that the activity cost hierarchy is discussed in Chapters 2 and 4.

[7] Sasquatch Snowshoes does not build products for inventory; thus, production equals sales. See Chapter 7 for a discussion of just-in-time production.

Panel A

Quantitative Data	Alternative 1: Robotic Assembly	Alternative 2: Improved Manual Assembly
Target (market) price	$ 100	$ 100
Sales and production in units	5,000	5,000
Unit-level cost per unit	$ 20	$ 40
Product-level costs:		
Equipment	$110,000	$ 40,000
Supervision	10,000	10,000
Training	5,000	20,000
Facility-level (building) costs	150,000	150,000

Panel B

Quantified Annual Benefit or Cost	Alternative 1: Robotic Assembly	Alternative 2: Improved Manual Assembly	Difference in Alternatives
Sales revenue	$500,000	$500,000	$ 0
Unit-level costs	$100,000	$200,000	$(100,000)
Product-level costs:			
Equipment	110,000	40,000	70,000
Supervision	10,000	10,000	0
Training	5,000	20,000	(15,000)
Facility-level (building) costs	150,000	150,000	0
Total costs	375,000	420,000	(45,000)
Profit	$125,000	$ 80,000	$ 45,000
Return on sales	25%	16%	

Exhibit 13–3

Data Used for Preliminary Analysis of Two Snowshoe Production Process Alternatives

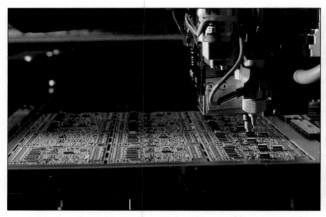

Choosing between automated and manual processes trades off costs, quality, and employment.

facility-level or building costs. The analysis in panel B of Exhibit 13–3 uses these revenue and cost drivers to estimate the profitability of each alternative. Does the choice between the alternatives hinge on all of (or only) these factors?

Let's examine panel B of Exhibit 13–3. Observe that sales revenues of $500,000 are expected to be the same for each alternative. Therefore, although revenues are surely important to Bootstrap, they do not differ and, therefore, are not relevant to choosing one of the alternatives. Similarly, product-related supervision costs, $10,000, and facility-related building costs, $150,000, are irrelevant because they are the same for both alternatives. The decision hinges on other information.

Unit-level costs, product-level equipment, and training costs of the alternatives do differ, however, and therefore are relevant. Although it is important to list all benefits and costs (otherwise some might be omitted inadvertently), the decision clearly hinges on the three costs that differ for each alternative: the annual unit-level cost and the product-level equipment and training costs. You can trace the total difference in cost and profit for the two alternatives, $45,000, to the net of the unit-level costs ($100,000 lower for robotic assembly), equipment costs ($70,000 higher for robotic assembly), and training costs ($15,000 lower for robotic assembly). In nearly all cases, you can make a choice between alternatives by identifying and comparing only their differential costs and benefits.

$$\text{Cost difference for alternatives} = \$100,000 - 70,000 + 15,000$$
$$= \underline{\$45,000} \text{ in favor of alternative 1}$$

Observe that only alternative 1 meets the company's requirement for return on sales of at least 20 percent. Note also that this analysis considers only quantitative information.

Impact on the Future

What time period is affected when a manager makes a decision? Possible answers to this question include tomorrow, next week, the next quarter, or the next two years. Notice that the past is not included in the response. Benefits and costs that have already occurred cannot be changed because they are history.

To be relevant to a decision, the cost or benefit must occur in the future. For example, Bootstrap Industries advertised last year's Rambler snowshoe for sale at prices below cost; you might wonder how the company can stay in business. Of course, its Sasquatch Snowshoe division cannot continue as an ongoing entity if it consistently follows this practice. Bootstrap recognizes that the original cost of last year's snowshoes is a *sunk cost,* which is a past payment for resources that cannot be changed by any current or future decision. For example, the purchase price paid in the past for equipment or merchandise or the past production cost of inventory is irrelevant to decisions about what to do with these assets in the future.

To illustrate, suppose that Sasquatch has 100 pairs of last year's Rambler snow-shoes, which cost $92 per pair to manufacture.[8] This year's much improved model is now available, but competitive pressures are keeping sales prices constant. Bootstrap's management does not believe that it now can sell the old snowshoes at the current $100 price. Given the current market, management believes that the snowshoes must sell at a reduced price of $60. In this decision, Bootstrap's management disregards the original $92 cost; it is sunk, history. A number of future marketing and inventory control issues might arise, but the historical manufacturing cost is irrelevant to the decision of how to best dispose of the old-model snowshoes. Their cost might as well be considered to be zero when deciding how to dispose of them.

Managers are sometimes tempted to keep merchandise such as last year's snowshoes (or other assets, such as machines) rather than to sell them below cost. Losses have a negative connotation and depress a firm's financial performance for the period. In many cases, however, keeping the assets is the wrong decision. For example, if Bootstrap does not dispose of the old snowshoes immediately, even at an accounting loss, the company might have to sell them at a greater loss later or to write the inventory off entirely, with nothing to show in return. Under the circumstances, unless a higher price is likely in the future, the decision to sell now at a reduced price is probably preferred. The problem is that the old inventory already is devalued below production cost, but management just does not want to recognize this. Consider the following likely outcomes:

Alternative Decisions	Sell 100 Pairs Old Snowshoes Now	Write Off 100 Pairs Snowshoes Later	Difference
Revenue	100 × $60 = $ 6,000	$ 0	$6,000
Production (inventory) cost	100 × $92 = 9,200	100 × $92 = 9,200	0
Loss	$(3,200)	$(9,200)	$6,000

Clearly, Bootstrap is better off by $6,000 if it swallows a mild loss now to avoid a greater loss later. Sometimes managers want to avoid the loss now and hope that their successors will have to face the problem, but the company is better off if it ignores the sunk costs.

Trade-Off between Information Cost and Quality

In an ideal world, perhaps, the information of the highest quality possesses high levels of the characteristics of relevance, accuracy, and timeliness—all obtained at low cost. However, the most relevant, accurate, and timely information might be excessively expensive to create and maintain on an ongoing basis. Thus, cost management analysts often must make trade-offs between the cost and quality of information. At some point, managers should be unwilling to seek increased quality of information because its cost would exceed its benefit for making better decisions.

Feasible, alternative actions. Where do decision alternatives come from? (*Hint:* They do not magically appear like the Cheshire Cat.) One alternative, however, is always available: the status quo, which also is the "do nothing" or "do nothing differently" alternative. Organizations always should consider the status quo seriously, but its inertia should not be a deciding factor. Organizations often identify other alternatives by thoroughly seeking information from, among others:

- *Employees,* who know their work best and often have excellent suggestions for improvement.
- *Customers,* who can articulate their unmet needs and visions of the future.
- *Competitors,* which are seeking the same competitive edge and already have made changes that this organization can imitate or improve.
- *Noncompetitors,* which use "best practices" that might be transferrable to this organization.

---

[8] Chapters 2 and 4 discuss measurements of production and service costs in more detail.

- ▪ *Universities,* which seek to push beyond the boundaries of scientific, engineering, and social practices and exist to create and disseminate knowledge.
- ▪ *Consultants,* who observe best practices and can help adapt them to this organization.
- ▪ The *Internet,* which is a continually evolving repository of vast and growing knowledge.

Of course, managers could spend all of their time searching for and evaluating alternatives, which is a form of "analysis paralysis" and ignores the fact that information about decisions in a competitive world must be timely to be useful. Knowing when to cut off the search for more alternatives usually is a matter of management judgment, weighing the trade-off of the value of possibly finding a better alternative against the cost of delaying decisions.

Stage III: Evaluating Alternatives

Once alternatives have been identified, the next stage of decision making is to evaluate the quantitative and qualitative factors related to each alternative. **Qualitative factors** are the characteristics of a decision that cannot easily or should not be expressed in numerical terms. These can include such things as employee morale, customers' perceptions of style of products or customization of services, control given up if certain processes currently performed internally are outsourced to external contractors, reputation that an organization develops if a manager emphasizes his or her own goals rather than those of the entire organization, and so on. Although we can never know for certain what all benefits and costs will be, the objective of careful evaluation is to significantly improve on the random choice of an alternative. Otherwise, why not just roll a die or flip a coin? If that were all there is to decision making, there would be far fewer interesting (and high-paying) management jobs.

The Decision Tree: A Helpful Decision Aid

LO 3 Use decision trees to describe business decisions.

Since most decisions consider several alternatives or many alternatives with complex options, evaluating the alternatives systematically is advisable. A useful decision aid is a **decision tree,** which diagrams decisions and alternative outcomes expected from those decisions in a "tree, branch, and limb" format. The choice of the most desirable alternative is made after considering the benefits and costs of each "limb." Exhibit 13–4 is a decision tree of the two alternative choices for producing snowshoes that were discussed earlier. Although it might not be necessary for simple decisions, a decision tree can help identify and communicate the dimensions of complex decisions that managers face. Making complex decisions without such a decision aid can be confusing and prone to errors, particularly the omission of relevant factors.

To build the decision tree of Bootstrap's decision problem shown in Exhibit 13–4, follow these steps:

1. *Display the decision alternatives in the order the decisions must be made.* Bootstrap's cost-reduction alternatives shown in diamond shapes are *the status quo* or *change.* If the decision is to change, two alternatives exist: *automate the process* or *improve the manual process.* Complex situations can have multiple layers of decisions, and decision trees can be complicated.

2. *Trace the path of each decision to its ultimate outcomes and identify the set of outcomes that result from each decision path.* Exhibit 13–4 expresses outcomes in terms of Bootstrap's tangible objectives of the elements of profit, product quality, and employment.

3. *Measure the benefits and costs of each set of outcomes.* In this exhibit, we express the outcomes in qualitative terms, but we will quantify many of them in the next section.

Anticipation of the Future Outcome(s) of Each Action

Predicting the future might be the most difficult aspect of decision making as well as the most important one. Managers choose among alternatives based on predicted

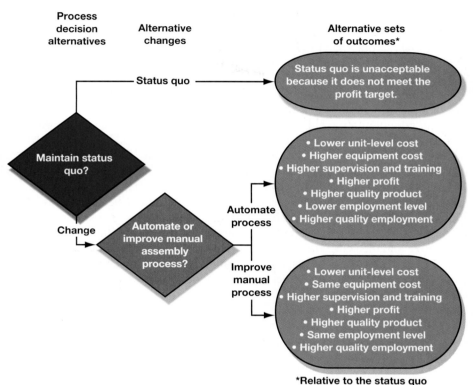

Exhibit 13–4

Bootstrap Industries
Decision Tree: Rambler
Model

costs and benefits, and the more reliable these estimates are, the more useful they are to support decisions. The first task of anticipating future outcomes is to identify the types of relevant outcomes (costs and benefits). The second task is to estimate them quantitatively or qualitatively, as appropriate.

Considering the past.   Relevant decision information must involve costs and benefits that will take place in the future. Although sunk costs are not directly relevant to a decision situation, a study of the past can prove beneficial for predicting the future. In our framework, the decision-making process requires various predictions—revenues, costs, cash flows, and the like—before making a decision. When making these predictions, the analyst considers past experience and historical data. Although this might seem contradictory to the earlier recommendation to ignore sunk costs, understanding the past can contribute reliable information about what the future will hold. Although it is a subtle difference, sunk costs themselves are irrelevant to decisions, but analysts can use them to help estimate or predict future costs, which are relevant.

Predicting benefits and costs of completely new products.   In new-product situations, the past might be of limited use to predicting benefits and costs. Before deciding to launch new products, many organizations produce prototype products or experiment with processes to learn what related future costs might be. After estimating the effects of learning to operate processes more efficiently, these prototype costs should be the bases for reliable estimates of future costs.[9]

Organizations also can use the services of consultants who have experience in other organizations with similar products or services. Sometimes organizations hire employees from these organizations to acquire their knowledge of products, services, processes, and estimated costs and benefits.

Choice of the Best Alternative: Estimated Benefits and Costs

This section discusses the preparation of quantitative data that reflects the decision tree in Exhibit 13–4. This analysis using these data should faithfully represent the

---

[9] Chapter 11 covers the issue of cost estimation in detail.

decision alternatives and each set of outcomes to clearly identify what can or cannot be measured quantitatively. The analysis also should clearly note any nonobvious assumptions so that managers can question and modify the analysis to reflect alternative assumptions. It should identify the net benefits (usually profits or cost reductions achieved) of each alternative.

Exhibit 13–5 shows an analysis of qualitative and quantitative benefits and costs of the alternatives shown graphically in Exhibit 13–4. Cost-management analysts have added quantitative and qualitative data relevant to Bootstrap's employment and quality goals (panel A) and costs related to the status quo. The quantitative data in panel B of Exhibit 13–5 are the same as those in Exhibit 13–3. Note that current costs ($460,000) are the sum of status-quo unit-level costs ($51 × 5,000) plus product- and facility-level costs ($40,000 + 10,000 + 5,000 + 150,000).

Each column shows a different alternative, including the status quo. Panel C of Exhibit 13–5 shows data regarding quantitative benefits and costs that differ for the alternatives. It is possible to create columns that show line-by-line differences for each alternative and the status quo. However, that creates a cluttered table that is difficult to read. Generally, keeping the presentation simple and directing attention to important outcomes is preferable. Because a desired cost reduction drove the decision-making problem, Exhibit 13–5 directs attention to the last two rows, which show that (1) the status quo achieves no cost reduction (of course), (2) the improved manual process does not achieve the desired cost-reduction, and (3) the robotic process does achieve the cost-reduction target with a cushion or *margin of safety* of $25,000. The **margin of safety**

Exhibit 13–5

Data Regarding the Benefits and Costs of Process Alternatives: Bootstrap Industries' Rambler Model

	1 Status Quo: Manual Assembly	2 Alternative 1: Robotic Assembly	3 Alternative 2: Improved Manual Assembly
Panel A: Qualitative Data			
Skill level	Medium	Higher	Higher
Product quality	Medium	Higher	Higher
Panel B: Quantitative Data			
Nonsupervisory employment level	50	20	50
Target (market) price	$ 100	$ 100	$ 100
Sales and production volume	5,000	5,000	5,000
Unit-level cost per unit	$ 51	$ 20	$ 40
Product-level costs:			
Equipment	40,000	110,000	40,000
Supervision	10,000	10,000	10,000
Training	5,000	5,000	20,000
Facility-level (building) costs	150,000	150,000	150,000
Currently feasible costs	460,000	—	—
Cost reduction target	60,000	—	—
Panel C: Quantified Annual Benefit or Cost			
Sales revenue	$500,000	$500,000	$500,000
Unit-level costs	$255,000	$100,000	$200,000
Product-level costs:			
Equipment	40,000	110,000	40,000
Supervision	10,000	10,000	10,000
Training	5,000	5,000	20,000
Facility-level (building) costs	150,000	150,000	150,000
Total costs	$460,000	$375,000	$420,000
Profit	$ 40,000	$125,000	$ 80,000
Return on sales	8.0%	25.0%	16.0%
Cost reduction achieved	$ —	$ 85,000	$ 40,000
Margin of safety	$ (60,000)	$ 25,000	$ (20,000)

which is the amount by which a quantitative objective is exceeded. A quantitative margin of safety is not a sufficient guide to choose among alternatives if the qualitative factors also are important.

Choice of the Best Alternative Using Both Quantitative and Qualitative Information

A comparison of quantified factors that reduce to a single profit or cost-reduction number might not make the best alternative obvious. Other factors can be just as (or more) important to decision making. To clarify the importance of qualitative analyses, consider how quantitative analysis can allow managers to put a value on the sum total of the qualitative factors. For example, suppose that a cost-management analyst gives Bootstrap managers the numerical analysis of the Rambler-model process, provided in Exhibit 13–5. This analysis shows that robotics (alternative 1) will reduce annual costs by $25,000 more than the target and $45,000 more than improving the manual process by additional employee training (alternative 2). This seems to clearly favor the robotic process, but panel A shows it conflicts with the organization's objectives of (1) employing persons with disabilities and (2) improving their skills, which favor alternative 2, improving the manual process through more training. How important are these qualitative factors to Bootstrap managers? If they decide to improve the manual process with more training, the qualitative considerations must be more important than the cost-reduction target and worth at least $45,000 to the organization and its stakeholders. The $45,000 given up by not selecting the robotic assembly process is the opportunity cost of the decision, or the amount forgone by choosing one mutually exclusive alternative or opportunity over another.[10]

Weighing trade-offs between quantitative and qualitative costs and benefits and considering opportunity costs in making decisions are hallmarks of management decision making. Managers' skill, experience, judgment, and ethical standards are crucial in making such difficult choices. Although the improved manual process does not achieve the required cost reduction and provides high-quality employment, we would not be surprised if Bootstrap chooses alternative 2.

Examples of Common Decisions: Outsource, or Add or Drop a Product, or Service, or Business Unit

The decision-making framework and use of relevant information are applicable to many types of business decisions that involve identifying alternative courses of action and comparing alternative sets of relevant benefits and costs. Cost-management analysts can apply the framework in Exhibit 13–1 to virtually any business decision. We now consider several common business decisions.

LO 4 Use a benefit-cost approach for common decisions such as obtaining new technology or capability; outsourcing (make versus buy); or modifying, adding, or dropping a product, service, or business unit; and pricing including special orders and lifecycle costs.

Outsourcing or Make-or-Buy Decision

An **outsourcing** or make-or-buy decision is any decision an organization makes about acquiring goods or services internally or externally. A restaurant that uses its own ingredients to prepare meals from scratch has chosen the "make" alternative; one that serves meals from frozen entrees acquired from suppliers has chosen the "buy" alternative. An electronics firm that assembles its own circuit boards "makes," whereas one that contracts with Bootstrap Industries for the assembly of circuit boards "buys."

The outsourcing or make-or-buy decision is part of a company's value-chain strategy. Some companies meet their goals by performing all processes of the value chain to control all activities that lead to the final product or service. Others prefer to rely on outsiders for some inputs and specialize in only certain steps of the total process. Outsourcing is one of the fastest-growing business activities because many firms are choosing to concentrate on their core activities, leaving other peripheral tasks to

---

[10] Sometimes organizations hedge their bets by adopting enough of an alternative to retain the *option* to fully adopt it in the future (see Chapter 14 for details on evaluating options).

organizations with expertise in performing them. An equipment manufacturer, for example, might outsource all printing activities to a Kinko's-type operation. Whether to rely on outsiders for a substantial amount of goods and services depends on relevant cost comparisons and other factors that are not so easily quantified, such as suppliers' dependability and quality.

Bootstrap Industries' outsourcing.   To analyze the outsourcing decision with our decision-making framework, let's look at Bootstrap Industries from the perspective of one of its customers, Hewlett-Packard (HP), which designs and manufactures computers, computer peripherals, and other electronics products. We focus on the part of HP's circuit-board function that it has outsourced to Bootstrap. HP certainly has the expertise to assemble (make) its own circuit boards, but this process is not how HP adds the most value to its products. HP has therefore outsourced much of the circuit-board assembly work to other organizations, such as Bootstrap, that have developed expertise in this area and that provide reliable, high-quality service. Outsourcing allows HP to partner with Bootstrap in creating jobs for disabled persons and then to reassign its resources to higher-valued work elsewhere in the firm.

HP received a $176,000 bid from Bootstrap to perform the contracted assembly of circuit boards for a normal month of operations. The analysis in Exhibit 13–6 indicates why HP was inclined to outsource the work to Bootstrap.

The estimated total assembly cost savings of $36,000 per month was enough to get HP's attention, but Bootstrap's reputation for quality, reliability, and just-in-time delivery convinced HP that it could safely outsource these assemblies to Bootstrap.[11]

Let's examine whether each part of the analysis appears to be relevant to the decision. (*Note:* Some people believe that the numbers "speak for themselves," but that is almost *never* true; judgment and analysis almost always are necessary.) Looking at the first row, outsourcing the assembly to Bootstrap increases HP's unit-level costs by $141,000. It saves $35,000 in-house (materials, testing, etc.) but spends $176,000 for the expected number of circuit boards it needs to support product manufacturing. This increase in unit-level costs must be made up in other cost areas. In return for the contract price, Bootstrap guarantees to provide defect-free cir-

---

[11] Achieving ISO 9002 quality certification clearly has helped Bootstrap attract and retain demanding customers such as HP. ISO quality certification and just-in-time methods are discussed in Chapter 7.

Exhibit 13–6

Data Regarding Circuit-Board Assembly Outsourcing

Monthly Costs Incurred by HP	1 Alternative 1: Status Quo: In-House Assembly Costs	2 Alternative 2: Outsource Assembly to Bootstrap	3 Difference by Outsourcing
Unit-level costs	$ 35,000	$176,000	**$ 141,000** higher
Product-level costs	197,000	40,000	**$(157,000)** lower
Facility-level costs	38,000	18,000	**$ (20,000)** lower
Total assembly costs	**$270,000**	**$234,000**	**$ (36,000) lower**

cuit boards just in time to install in HP's products. Because Bootstrap is a certified supplier and regards certification seriously, HP can rely on this guarantee.

The second row of Exhibit 13–6 shows that outsourcing reduces HP's product-level costs by $157,000. Most of that cost reduction is the result of HP's sale of assembly equipment no longer needed to Bootstrap, which benefited both parties. HP still will incur some employee-related product-level costs because it prefers to not lay off its employees but will assign them to other work, so outsourcing will not cause HP's total product-level costs to decline to zero. HP will reduce facility-level costs by $20,000 by selling other unused equipment, for which neither HP nor Bootstrap has a use. Facility-level costs will not decline to zero because HP has created a new administrative function to administer, manage, and monitor its outsourcing contracts and activities, costing $18,000 per month to manage the Bootstrap contract. The net cost savings of $36,000 per month plus the virtual guarantee of high-quality service makes this outsourcing contract desirable; savings without the quality guarantee might not be sufficient.

Pitfalls of outsourcing.   Although many organizations reduce operating costs by outsourcing processes, they often find that other factors can affect the decision to retain, outsource, or bring back important processes. Analysts assume that freed-up resources will be either saved or applied to higher valued activities, but does this happen? If not, the organization now pays for the outsourced activities and for resources that are idle or assigned to less valued activities—with no substantial improvements. Another assumption is that outsourced activities are of at least as high quality as the replaced activities. If not, the organization might save operating costs in the short run but end up paying more to correct quality shortfalls. Outsourcing often is sold on the promise of access to better knowledge and technology from an external provider who specializes in certain activities. If in fact the external provider is not more advanced, the organization might pay the provider to learn how to provide better services to others or might not experience the promised improvements.

Outsourcing activities that interact with customers poses special risks. Customers might be alienated when they realize they are not dealing with the company that sold them the products. Companies that have outsourced processes such as billing and postsales service also might find that they have lost valuable customer contacts and timely information about their changing needs. Finally, organizations need to ensure that the outsourcing contracts and incentives are compatible with control of sensitive information and value-adding processes. Outsourcing companies claim that they have "firewalls" between the information provided by different customers, but a company would have little satisfaction in winning a lawsuit for breach of privacy if the outsourcing company leaked key customer or product information to a competitor. The damage could be so great that legal fees and lost opportunities would overwhelm any monetary settlement. Organizations also must be able to ensure that the outsource provider is meeting contractual obligations; therefore, outsourcing performance must be auditable, and the company must have recourse if obligations are not met.

Decision to Add or Drop a Product, Service, or Business Unit

One of the most difficult decisions managers make concerns adding or dropping a product, service, or business unit. These are difficult decisions because they usually have major effects on the organization's strategy and on its stakeholders. Consequently, managers do not make them lightly.

The term "business unit" can refer to a product, a market territory, a department, a warehouse, or just about any other business segment imaginable (for example, HP's outsourced circuit-board assembly process). Products that were formerly profitable might be losing market share to newer goods and no longer adequately cover costs. On the other hand, a company can add a business unit to serve new product markets or geographic regions. In nearly all of these cases, managers must make difficult trade-offs among quantitative and qualitative costs and benefits.

Making these decisions is not easy, but managers can feel comfortable that they have made them correctly by following the decision-making framework. Note that no analysis of whether to drop or add a business unit is complete without considering the status quo: the current net benefits from the resources being used by the potentially added or dropped unit. For example, computing how much can be saved by dropping an unprofitable business unit is not sufficient, managers also must consider whether the recovered resources can be used more profitably. At a minimum, for example, Bootstrap could sell its resources and invest the proceeds in low-risk, marketable securities, but this would not meet its organizational goals.

To illustrate the proper handling of these strategic decisions, let's analyze how Bootstrap decided whether to close a landscaping facility. The data considered in the initial analysis is shown in Exhibit 13–7. The status quo of this operation will generate an annual loss of $52,000, which indicates that, although the operation does employ 21 people, it does not meet the tangible objective of operating at a profit. A relevant issue is whether Bootstrap can improve overall profitability (eliminate the loss) by closing the operation.

The third column presents the benefits and costs that change by closing the facility but doing nothing else. Let's look at these items carefully because they are key to understanding what Bootstrap must do to improve its profitability.

Relevant benefits.   The revenues in panel C of Exhibit 13–7 shows that for now Bootstrap does not have an alternative business use for the resources that can be recovered by closing the landscaping operation. Thus, it shows no revenues to

Exhibit 13–7

Data Regarding Dropping a Business Unit by Bootstrap Industries

	Status Quo: Operate Landscaping Facility	Close Landscaping Facility	
Panel A: Qualitative Data			
Skill level	Low	Low	
Product quality	Low	NA	
Panel B: Quantitative Data			
Supervisory employment	1	1	
Nonsupervisory employment	20	20	
Service revenues per year	$300,000	$ 0	
Unit-level costs	30,000	0	
Service-level costs:			
Equipment	32,000	0	
Building rental	36,000	0	
Facility-level costs:			
Wages	200,000	200,000	
Supervision	24,000	24,000	
Central office services	20,000	20,000	
Training	10,000	10,000	
Panel C: Quantified Annual Benefit or Cost			**Difference if Closed**
Sales revenue	$300,000	$ 0	($300,000)
Unit-level costs	$ 30,000	$ 0	$ 30,000
Service-level costs:			
Equipment	32,000	0	32,000
Building rental	36,000	0	36,000
Facility-level costs:			
Wages	200,000	200,000	0
Supervision	24,000	24,000	0
Central office services	20,000	20,000	0
Training	10,000	10,000	0
Total costs	352,000	254,000	98,000
Profit (loss)	**($ 52,000)**	**($254,000)**	**($202,000)**

replace the forgone $300,000 in sales that the operation generates. Let's leave this for now, but clearly we need to revisit this item.

Relevant costs. Unit-level costs will decline to zero by closing the landscaping facility, saving $30,000 annually because the landscaping materials and supplies will no longer be necessary. Service-level costs, the costs directly attributable to operating the service, also will decline to zero. Neither the landscaping equipment, which we assume will be sold, nor the building, whose rental agreement either has expired or can be canceled without penalty, will be necessary after closing the operation. This will save another $68,000 ($32,000 + $36,000) in service-level costs per year.

Perhaps surprisingly, Bootstrap expects no facility-level cost reductions attributable to closing the landscaping operation. The closed operation does not incur those costs, but Bootstrap's goals and commitments mean that the rest of the organization must bear them. It will not lay off the supervisor and 20 employees of the landscaping operation but will reassign them to other work. Many organizations, profit-seeking firms included, have similar employment commitments and lay off employees only as a last resort. Thus, employee wages and salaries of the operation are committed facility-level costs to the organization and closing often will not result in these employee-related cost reductions. Similarly, although the closed operation will not use central office services, such as payroll or insurance services, closing it will not reduce Bootstrap's capability (e.g., administrative personnel) to provide those services. The rest of the organization will bear these costs which also will not be saved. Because of Bootstrap's goals and objectives to increase the skills of its employees, the organization similarly does not expect to reduce annual training costs by closing the landscaping operation.

Unfinished business. Clearly, Exhibit 13–7 shows that the analysis of the decision to close the remote operation is not finished. Simply closing it (doing nothing else) would save $98,000 in annual costs but also would forgo $300,000 in revenues for a net reduction in profits of $202,000. Surely this do-nothing alternative does not advance Bootstrap's progress in meeting its goals of high-quality employment and profitable operations. What must Bootstrap's managers do, and what is the magnitude of the problem?

To complete the data needed for the analysis, Bootstrap must identify and analyze alternative uses of its recovered employee resources in a manner similar to that shown previously in Exhibit 13–5. The objective of this analysis is to find the best alternative that generates quality employment and operates profitably. In fact, Bootstrap did find such an alternative (see You're the Decision Maker 13.1).

It is important to note that the presentation *format* of these data can be applied to any organization's decision making about adding or dropping a business unit, but the specifics of which benefits and costs might or might not be saved or avoided will differ across organizations.

Relevant Costs of Replacing Equipment

As you can tell by now, all of these short-term decisions are similar because they can be based on relevant revenues and costs. Irrelevant (nondifferential) revenues and costs can be ignored for decision making (although perhaps not for reporting or performance measurement purposes). We now consider the common decision whether to replace

---

You're the Decision Maker 13.1

Further Analysis of Dropping a Business

Complete the analysis in Exhibit 13–7 by considering the changes predicted for the following two alternatives for fully employing the resources freed-up by closing the remote landscaping operation.

a. Increase in skill level to medium and product quality to high; realize service revenues of $400,000, unit-level costs of $40,000, equipment costs of $50,000, building rental of $40,000; and training costs of $40,000.

b. Increase product quality to medium; realize service revenues of $300,000, unit-level costs of $14,000, equipment costs of $20,000, building rental of $10,000.

(Solutions begin on page 534.)

equipment before the end of its useful life. Sometimes new, more efficient equipment becomes available before the existing equipment must be replaced, and managers can decide to replace the old equipment early. What are the relevant revenues and costs? If the new equipment has a greater capacity (and if additional product can be sold), revenues might be higher than with the existing equipment. If the new equipment is more efficient, its operating costs should be lower (per unit and perhaps in total). If so, what's to prevent replacing the existing equipment early? Several factors can work against an early replacement. First, the company could take a loss on the disposal of the old equipment; that is, its disposal value might be less than its book value (purchase price less accumulated depreciation). Managers might be unwilling to add that loss to periodic income even though the historical purchase price and book value are irrelevant, sunk costs. Second, the new equipment might be more expensive to purchase and might result in higher periodic depreciation cost, fixed costs, operating leverage, and break-even point (see Chapter 12). This effect can increase the risk of making profit targets, which can affect managers' evaluations and compensation.

The organization will benefit most if managers consider only the relevant revenues and costs associated with an equipment replacement (note that Chapter 14 incorporates several more important factors: the time value of money and taxes). Consider the following decision faced by the manager of Bootstrap's outsourcing operations, discussed earlier. The manager considered whether to replace an existing assembly machine two years before the end of its useful life because a new, improved model is now available. The installed cost of the new machine is $55,000, and it has a two-year expected life. Both the old and new machines will have no disposal value after two years, but the existing machine could be sold for $10,000 now. The new machine has lower annual operating costs ($22,000 versus $45,000) and has a 10 percent greater capacity, which should increase revenues and labor costs proportionately. Review the following income analysis.

Although the new machine generates a surplus (income) of $13,600 more than the old machine (highlighted in green), the manager might not want to either admit that the purchase of the old machine just a year before was a mistake and should be written off or report a loss of $26,000 on its disposal (highlighted in yellow). These adverse effects have persuaded some managers to forgo replacing equipment even when the replacement is beneficial.

Input Data	Old Machine	New Machine	
Purchase cost	$ 54,000	$ 55,000	
Useful life	3	2 years	
Remaining useful life	2	2 years	
Current disposal value	$ 10,000	$ —	
Future disposal value (in two years)	—	—	
Annual machine operating costs	$ 45,000	$ 22,000	
Capacity increase over existing equipment		10%	

Income Analysis of 2 Years of Operations	Old Machine	New Machine	Difference
Revenues	$176,000	× 1.10 = $193,600	$17,600
Costs			
Direct labor	50,000	× 1.10 = 55,000	5,000
Machine operating costs	90,000	44,000	(46,000)
Depreciation	36,000	55,000	19,000
Loss on disposal of old machine*	—	26,000	26,000
Total operating costs	176,000	180,000	4,000
Surplus funds (Net income)	$ —	$ 13,600	$13,600

*Disposal of old machine

Purchase cost	$54,000
Accumulated depreciation	18,000
Book value	36,000
Current disposal value	10,000
Loss on disposal of old machine	$26,000

Now review the following relevant cost analysis, which totally ignores the sunk cost of the old machine and depreciation costs (allocations of sunk costs) of both machines. The loss on sale in the previous analysis might have tax implications for profit-seeking firms but not for Bootstrap Industries. The other differences are that the disposal value of the old machine is a relevant benefit, and the purchase cost of the new machine is treated as a relevant cost of the decision (both are highlighted in yellow).

Relevant Cost Analysis of 2 Years of Operations	Old Machine	New Machine	Difference
Relevant benefits			
Revenues	$176,000	× 1.10 = $193,600	$17,600
Disposal of old equipment		10,000	10,000
Relevant costs			
Purchase of new machine		55,000	55,000
Direct labor	50,000	× 1.10 = 55,000	5,000
Machine operating costs	90,000	44,000	(46,000)
Net benefit (cost)	$ 36,000	$ 49,600	$13,600

Notice that the net benefit difference is exactly the same, $13,600 in favor of the new machine. This is not a coincidence because the analysis covers the full life of the new machine. Therefore, focusing only on relevant benefits and costs avoids displaying the apparent adverse consequences, which could deter an economically sound decision. Bootstrap can use the $13,600 surplus to fund activities such as training that will enhance employee capabilities. An additional benefit of this decision is the expansion of opportunities for Bootstrap employees in the outsourcing business. If the added capacity of the new machine can result in increased sales of outsourced services, Bootstrap probably will replace the equipment.

Pricing Decisions

We conclude our overview of decision making with the topic of pricing. This is a troublesome area for many organizations; determining the "right" price for a good or service is important and can be very difficult. A company that sets its prices too high does not generate sales, resulting in total profitability below target. On the other hand, prices set too low might lead to an increase in sales activity, but the revenues might fail to cover costs. Both results miss the target profits.

Influences on Prices

Generally speaking, organizations consider several factors when determining prices: markets, customers, competitors, costs, life cycles, timing, and a variety of legal, political, and image-related issues.

Markets. Many products and services are offered in highly competitive markets (e.g., agricultural products, automobiles, personal desktop computers, cellular phones and service, small appliances) in which prices are readily observable. Deviating from market prices means either losing sales with prices that are too high or losing profits with prices that are too low. Setting prices in these markets requires understanding competitors' offerings and whether a product's or service's deviation from market norms (e.g., adding a higher or lower quality component) can support either higher or lower prices. In competitive markets, all producers must meet the market price. To make a profit, they must produce at a cost sufficiently below market price to survive.

Customers. An organization should consider pricing decisions for new products from the perspective of its customers. Prices that are too high will not generate the sales levels necessary to recover costs and target profits because customers will seek a less expensive or substitute product or service. They might wait for a competitor's offering. Conversely, setting prices too low could underestimate customers' willingness to pay for what might be a valuable innovation. Understanding customers' willingness to pay for the attributes and functions of a product or service is key to setting prices successfully.

Competitors. Competitors' actions also influence pricing decisions. A competitor's aggressive pricing policy can force a business to lower its prices. On the other hand, a business without a competitor has some discretion and can set higher prices to take advantage of the lack of competition. Setting high prices for items that are unprotected by patents or copyrights will generate abnormally high profits and invite competition.

International borders frequently mean little to competitive firms. Firms with overcapacity in their domestic markets (i.e., domestic supply exceeds demand at desired prices) can price aggressively in export markets. For instance, software companies such as Microsoft with high development costs and low unit-level costs can seek foreign markets as an outlet for their goods. In a foreign market, a firm can exploit the high development costs that it has already incurred at home and therefore charge lower prices than local competition, which must incur these costs before introducing their own new products. Managers increasingly consider both their domestic and international competition when making pricing decisions. International firms that price aggressively in foreign markets must be careful to avoid charges of "dumping" their products at artificially low prices that discourage foreign competition. US manufacturers, for example, often complain that open markets allow foreign competitors to dump their products in the United States. Supporting those charges has been difficult because of the complexity of measuring costs and the values of other product features, such as postsale services, which might not be offered in all locations.[12]

Costs. The role of costs in price setting varies widely among organizations and industries. Managers of organizations that operate in less competitive markets might set prices at least partially on the basis of costs by adding a *markup* to production costs. While companies can price below cost as a promotion or "loss leader," no profit-seeking organization can price its goods and services on average below cost for an extended period.

Managers have some latitude in determining the markup, but market forces usually are influential here as well. No company's management can set prices blindly at cost plus a markup without considering the market. If, for example, a company has a markup policy of 40 percent and defines cost as $200, the target-selling price is $280 [$200 + $200 × .40]. Managers judge the marked-up $280 target price in light of what competitors are charging and the amount that customers are willing to pay.

Charging an excessive markup can increase profits in the short term, but it also invites competition to enter the market or customers to seek substitutes. If the price is deemed too high, management can lower its desired markup or redesign the product or service to achieve its target price. However, as Peter Drucker pointed out, cost-based pricing can be a dangerously expensive approach:

> Most American and practically all European companies arrive at their prices by adding up costs and then putting a profit margin on top. And then, as soon as they have introduced the product, they have to start cutting the price, have to redesign the product at enormous expense, have to take losses—and often have to drop a perfectly good product because it is priced incorrectly.[13]

Drucker argues that target or price-led costing is a much more effective approach to pricing for almost all companies because it requires up-front knowledge of the market and customers that is incorporated into products. Although market research is costly, Drucker argues cost-based pricing often requires much more costly fixing of pricing and product problems that never should have occurred. The analogy to managing quality is clear (see Chapter 7).

Some organizations, however, such as cable television or intrastate telecommunication in the United States, legally must base prices on costs. Managers propose prices

---

[12] An interesting twist to the practice of "dumping" is the domestic backlash that prescription drug companies received recently. Under pressure from the United Nations, they agreed to sell AIDS drugs in Africa at 10 percent or less of the domestic price only to receive scorn from domestic consumers who recoiled at the apparently high profits earned on domestic sales. See "AIDS Gaffes in Africa Come Back to Haunt Drug Industry in the United States."

[13] P. Drucker, "The Five Deadly Business Sins."

based on marked-up costs that generally must be approved by a regulatory agency of the state or local government. Many government contracts are based on the recovery of costs, so measuring costs are of prime importance in pricing these contracts.

Many organizations consider only current production costs in production or pricing decisions when they should consider full life cycle costs. A **product's life cycle** is the time from its initial research and development to the point at which customer support is withdrawn. The specific phases of the cycle often include the following:

1. Idea generation (early research and development).
2. Concept feasibility.
3. Product design and planning.
4. Prototype or working model.
5. Product launch or rollout.
6. Product manufacturing, delivery, and service to customers.
7. Product termination.

The cycle's duration varies considerably among industries, services, and products. For example, the life cycle of automobile models is 5 to 10 years; in contrast, it can be less than 1 year for fad toys and fashion clothing. The realization that the great majority of a product's cost is determined well before it is produced for customers is important. Thus, many organizations can use target costing to simultaneously manage both the development and cost of the product.

Life cycle costing tracks costs attributable to each product or service from start to finish, from cradle to grave. It provides important information for cost management and pricing. Many organizations traditionally consider only future production, sales, and customer-service costs in pricing decisions. However, early activities such as research and development, product planning, and concept design for new products can consume significant resources, and sales prices must cover these costs if the firm is to operate profitably. In other words, sales revenues and, thus, prices must consider and eventually cover all life cycle costs, indeed, all value-chain costs, for the organization to meet target profits in the long term. Note that target costing explicitly considers life cycle costs in computing target costs.

Bootstrap Industries measures life cycle costs when pricing many of its services. For example, the equipment costs of its landscaping services reflect the life cycle costs of ownership and operation over the life of the equipment. Consider the life cycle costs of pickup trucks, trailers, and lawn mowers in Exhibit 13–8. Note that hourly costs are rounded to two decimal points.

The landscaping equipment life cycle costs include the major categories of ownership and operating costs. While the elements of these major categories will vary according to the organization and its activities, Exhibit 13–8 is similar to the analyses performed by many organizations that use life cycle costing. Costs are measured on an hour-of-use basis because Bootstrap Industries prices and bills its landscaping jobs based on hours of work performed. Bootstrap Industries has divided ownership costs into purchase, opportunity, insurance, and property tax and license costs and has divided each by the normal hourly use per year to obtain hourly rates and the total hourly ownership cost (row 21). To the cost of ownership, Bootstrap adds the hourly operating costs for fuel, scheduled maintenance, and repairs. The total operating costs are summed in row 33, and the total cost of ownership and operating are computed in row 34.

Bootstrap Industries used the hourly life cycle costs to measure the equipment costs of the landscaping facility it considered dropping in Exhibit 13–7, as follows:

Estimation of Landscaping Equipment Costs

Equipment	Pickup Trucks	Trailers	Lawn Mowers	Total
Hourly ownership and operating cost rounded to two decimal places (Exhibit 13–8)..........	$ 14.70	$ 1.45	$ 7.80	
Landscaping hours	× 1,400	× 1,400	× 1,205	
Landscaping cost (rounded)	$20,580	$2,025	$9,395	$32,000

Exhibit 13–8

Life Cycle Costs of
Landscaping Equipment

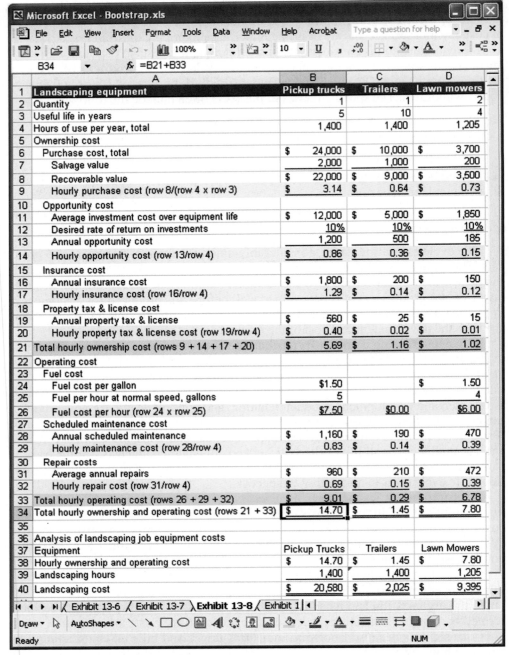

Landscaping equipment	Pickup trucks	Trailers	Lawn mowers
1 Landscaping equipment	Pickup trucks	Trailers	Lawn mowers
2 Quantity	1	1	2
3 Useful life in years	5	10	4
4 Hours of use per year, total	1,400	1,400	1,205
5 Ownership cost			
6 Purchase cost, total	$ 24,000	$ 10,000	$ 3,700
7 Salvage value	2,000	1,000	200
8 Recoverable value	$ 22,000	$ 9,000	$ 3,500
9 Hourly purchase cost (row 8/(row 4 x row 3)	$ 3.14	$ 0.64	$ 0.73
10 Opportunity cost			
11 Average investment cost over equipment life	$ 12,000	$ 5,000	$ 1,850
12 Desired rate of return on investments	10%	10%	10%
13 Annual opportunity cost	1,200	500	185
14 Hourly opportunity cost (row 13/row 4)	$ 0.86	$ 0.36	$ 0.15
15 Insurance cost			
16 Annual insurance cost	$ 1,800	$ 200	$ 150
17 Hourly insurance cost (row 16/row 4)	$ 1.29	$ 0.14	$ 0.12
18 Property tax & license cost			
19 Annual property tax & license	$ 560	$ 25	$ 15
20 Hourly property tax & license cost (row 19/row 4)	$ 0.40	$ 0.02	$ 0.01
21 Total hourly ownership cost (rows 9 + 14 + 17 + 20)	$ 5.69	$ 1.16	$ 1.02
22 Operating cost			
23 Fuel cost			
24 Fuel cost per gallon	$1.50		$ 1.50
25 Fuel per hour at normal speed, gallons	5		4
26 Fuel cost per hour (row 24 x row 25)	$7.50	$0.00	$6.00
27 Scheduled maintenance cost			
28 Annual scheduled maintenance	$ 1,160	$ 190	$ 470
29 Hourly maintenance cost (row 28/row 4)	$ 0.83	$ 0.14	$ 0.39
30 Repair costs			
31 Average annual repairs	$ 960	$ 210	$ 472
32 Hourly repair cost (row 31/row 4)	$ 0.69	$ 0.15	$ 0.39
33 Total hourly operating cost (rows 26 + 29 + 32)	$ 9.01	$ 0.29	$ 6.78
34 Total hourly ownership and operating cost (rows 21 + 33)	$ 14.70	$ 1.45	$ 7.80
35			
36 Analysis of landscaping job equipment costs			
37 Equipment	Pickup Trucks	Trailers	Lawn Mowers
38 Hourly ownership and operating cost	$ 14.70	$ 1.45	$ 7.80
39 Landscaping hours	1,400	1,400	1,205
40 Landscaping cost	$ 20,580	$ 2,025	$ 9,395

Additionally, the company can use these estimated life cycle costs to cost and price future landscaping jobs if it decides to retain this work capability.

Pricing law in the United States.   Organizations do not have complete freedom when they set prices for products and services. Legally, managers must adhere to laws that prohibit organizations from unfairly discriminating among their customers in setting prices. Law also prohibits collusion, the agreement of all major firms in an industry to set their prices at the same levels.

US antitrust laws, including the Robinson–Patman Act, the Clayton Act, and the Sherman Act, restrict certain types of pricing behaviors that often focus on deliberate attempts to reduce competition and ultimately charge higher prices. The Robinson–Patman Act in particular prohibits price discrimination, which refers to quoting different prices to different customers for the same products with the intent to

Pricing and the Internet

How does the Internet affect pricing? John Chambers of Cisco believes that because customers can quickly compare prices from many suppliers, "Everything gets cheaper forever." So the only survival techniques are to continuously manage costs and innovate to create new customer value. This access to multiple suppliers and lower costs is not restricted to large companies. Individuals increasingly turn to Internet-based retail outlets whose prices are constantly available to the market.

How do companies set prices on the Internet where the balance of pricing power is shifting to customers? The answer appears to be that companies are "price takers" when the products or services are commodities (similar, widely available products), and they must be very conscious of their costs to survive. On the other hand, innovative products and services can command premium prices until they, too, become commodities, which the Internet can cause to happen quickly. So companies charge high prices while they can, but they should have innovative replacements in process. Cisco itself is not immune to the power of the market to discipline a lack of innovation. The company has been criticized for outsourcing its new-product development and recently laid off thousands of employees and wrote off billions of dollars in restructuring and obsolete inventory in response to the bursting of the Internet bubble in 2001. *Sources:* "Letting the Masses Name Their Price", *Business Week,* September 18, 2000; "Cisco Revenue to Fall Well Short of Estimates amid Business Slowdown," *The Wall Street Journal,* April 12, 2001.

harm competitors and consumers.[14] Such price differences are unlawful unless they can be clearly justified by variations in the costs incurred to produce, sell, or deliver goods. Managers must keep careful records justifying these cost differences when they exist because the records can be vital to a legal defense in court challenges.

Law also prohibits **predatory pricing,** which involves temporarily setting a price below cost to injure competitors that cannot sustain losses and consequently must leave the market. Predatory pricing drives out competitors and allows the "predator" to earn abnormally high profits by charging higher prices after competitors have left the market. Note that the occasional sale or special price in a retail setting is not unlawful because the intent is to stimulate store traffic, not to drive out the competition. In determining whether a price is predatory, courts examine an organization's cost records.

Cost determination is a troublesome area, especially for manufacturers, because cost can be calculated in a variety of ways, as covered in detail in Chapters 2 and 4. Cost determination also is a problem for warehouse-type retailers such as Wal-Mart, Home Depot, and Office Max, but in a different way. These large retailers have such significant influence on the market that they commonly are able to obtain price concessions from their suppliers. Low costs from suppliers coupled with their low overhead means that these large businesses can sell products to the public below the cost paid by, say, the local family-owned camera shop or hardware store and still earn a sizable profit margin. These large firms must be able to demonstrate that their low prices are justified by low costs that are themselves not the result of unfair business practices. This is one area in which a decision maker is well advised to have an accountant on the left and a lawyer on the right before setting very low prices that might be considered harmful to competition.[15]

Pricing politics and image.   Political considerations can be relevant to price setting. For example, if consumers perceive that an industry reaps unfairly large profits, they might exert political pressure on legislators to tax those profits differentially or to intervene in some way to regulate prices.[16] For example, because it periodically raises retail prices, the oil and gas industry regularly attracts this type of attention.

---

[14] The Robinson–Patman Act covers goods but not services.

[15] For recent case law, see the "Legal Developments" section of the *Journal of Marketing.* Also see T. Barton and J. MacArthur, "Activity-Based Costing and Predatory Pricing: The Case of the Petroleum Retail Industry."

[16] See, for example, S. Cahan and W. H. Kaempfer. "Industry Income and Congressional Regulatory Legislation: Interest Groups vs. Median Voter."

Companies also consider their public image in the price-setting process. A firm with a reputation for top-quality goods usually sets the price of a new product high to be consistent with its image. As many have discovered, however, the same brand-name product might be available on the Internet or at a discount store or outlet mall at a fraction of the price charged by a more exclusive retailer. The wide availability of discounted merchandise prices is causing some high-end retailers, such as Nordstrom, to justify higher prices by offering ambience and services not offered elsewhere.

Special-Order Price Decisions

Occasionally companies receive requests from customers for either unexpected quantities of a product or service or one-time customized products or services. Because these are unusual occurrences, usual prices might not be appropriate. The decisions to accept these *special orders* and to price them obviously are tied together. One-time, **special orders** by definition are irregular and do not have lasting implications for other products or customers. For example, an athletic team's emergency order for replacement New Balance shoes that were lost enroute to a postseason tournament might occasion a short-term pricing decision by New Balance that would not affect the normal pricing of its shoes. We emphasize that deviations from normal pricing practices can have lasting effects if customers begin to expect the deviations to indicate changes in normal pricing.

Relevant costs of special orders.   Special orders often affect only unit-level costs. Occasionally, however, a decision to accept a special order causes product-level or facility-level costs to change. For example, if to complete a one-time special order a company must purchase new equipment, secure additional supervisors, or lease more space, these costs should be considered as relevant parts of the order's total cost. The importance of identifying relevant, differential costs can be more important in pricing special orders than in regular pricing situations in which market forces provide a stronger guide to pricing.

The relevant costs required for producing and selling a good or service combine to form a firm's minimum selling price. In some cases, relevant costs might be very low, such as selling one additional seat on an already scheduled airline flight or allowing one more student to enroll in an already scheduled college course. The relevant costs in these cases are *only the differential costs incurred in the short term to fill the seat or enroll the student.* Prices often reflect this differential cost awareness (although college tuition does not, as far as we are aware). For example, a person making travel arrangements at the last minute can find steeply discounted airfares and hotel rooms on the Internet because airlines and hotels are eager to generate additional revenues that at least cover differential costs (fuel, food, cleaning, etc.) when they (1) have no prospects for charging normally higher prices and (2) can charge normal prices for most services. Obviously, they cannot afford to offer discounted prices to all customers all the time.

Bootstrap Industries normally prices its facility-support services to cover all costs plus a target profit but departs from that pricing practice in some special-order situations. For example, if it temporarily has unused resources (e.g., the employees from the closed landscaping operation discussed earlier), the opportunity cost at the moment is low. Bootstrap might try to obtain special-order business initially at a loss to impress the customer with the quality of its work in hopes of winning future, regular business. Bootstrap uses a target-costing approach to price special orders.

Exhibit 13–9 presents data for use in the analysis of a special-order request received by Bootstrap to clean up a state government building damaged by a severe storm. The first column of numbers in panels A, B, and C shows the normal elements of Bootstrap's service costs. Because of the nature of the special order,

	Normal Services	Adjustment for Special Order	Adjusted for Special Order
Panel A: Qualitative Data			
Employee skill level...	Low	0	Low
Service quality..	High	0	High
Panel B: Quantitative Data			
Number of employees...	NA	NA	12
Number of days...	NA	NA	8
Crew size..	6	0	6
Supervision cost (per 6-person crew per day)	$ 84.00	$ 0.00	$84.00
Panel C: Costs per Employee per Day			
Wages and benefits	$ 60.00	$ 0.00	$60.00
Supplies and equipment...	11.00	2.00	13.00
Supervision	14.00	0.00	14.00
Transportation (within city)	5.00	(5.00)	0.00
Central office services..	9.00	(9.00)	0.00
Total cost per employee per day	$ 99.00	(12.00)	$87.00
Profit as a percent of sales	20%	(15.00)%	5%
Bid price per employee per day..............................	$123.75	$(32.17)	$91.58*
Panel D: Special-Order Benefit or Cost			
Total bid price	$ 8,792		
Service costs:			
Wages and benefits...	$ 5,760		
Supplies and equipment	1,248		
Supervision	1,344		
Transportation	0		
Facility costs:			
Central office services	0		
Total costs	8,352		
Profit..	$ 440		
Return on bid..	**5.00%**		

*$91.58 = $87.00 ÷ (1 − .05)

Exhibit 13–9

Analysis of a Special Order

B⊕otstrap
I N D U S T R I E S

Bootstrap decided to make a few changes to its normal pricing (shown in italics in the following list). The elements of the decision, which are part of the input data of Exhibit 13–9, follow:

- Maximum crew size (6) and supervision cost ($84 per crew per day) are unchanged, and 12 employees are needed to do the work.
- Wage and benefit cost for employees is unchanged at $60 per day.
- Supplies and equipment cost is *increased by $2 per day* to reflect increased cleaning needs.
- Transportation cost is *zero* because the state will provide daily transportation.
- Central office services cost is *zero,* reflecting the facility-cost nature of this cost, which does not change as a result of this special order.
- Target profit as a percentage of sales is *reduced to 5 percent* from the normal 20 percent to increase chances of winning the bid in hopes of earning repeat business.

Exhibit 13–9 computes the special-order cost per unit, in this case the cost per employee, in the column Adjusted for Special Order.

Because Bootstrap will have a cost savings and will disregard irrelevant central office costs, the cost per employee per day is $12 lower than normal (the Adjustment for Special Order Column), which might justify a lower bid price than normal. Reducing the target profit from 20 percent to 5 percent also indicates that Bootstrap can charge a lower special-order price than normal. Bootstrap has an incentive to lower its price for this job because it could open opportunities for more government jobs and increased employment—a key consideration when jobs of any kind are scarce.

Note that the formula for the target price in panel D of Exhibit 13–9 is a variation of the target-cost formula presented earlier in the chapter. Bootstrap computes its target price for a special order as a target profit percentage markup over special-order costs. As in target costing, the percentage return defines the relation between price and cost, but, in the reverse of target costing, the cost now is given and the special order per unit price is solved for.

$$\text{Special-order price} = \text{Special-order cost (\$87)} + \textit{Target profit}$$

The required percentage return on the order price replaces the target profit per unit, as follows:

$$\text{Special-order price} = \text{Special-order cost (\$87)} + \textit{Target profit percentage} (0.05) \\ \times \textit{Special-order price}$$

Rearranging terms in three more steps yields:

$$\text{Special-order cost (\$87)} = \text{Special-order price} - \text{Target profit percentage (0.05)} \\ \times \text{Special-order price} \\ = \text{Special-order price} \times (1 - \text{Target profit percentage 0.05}) \\ \text{Special-order price} = \text{Special-order cost (\$87)} \div (1 - \text{Target profit percentage 0.05})$$

Substituting the special-order cost ($87.00) and the target profit percentage (5 percent) into the last equation yields a special-order price of $91.58 per employee per day, which is $32.17 lower than normal.

$$\text{Special-order price} = \$87.00 \div (1 - .05) = \$91.58 \text{ per employee per day}$$

Exhibit 13–9 computes the total bid price, $8,792, by multiplying the bid price per employee per day by 12 employees and 8 days. In a similar manner, service and facility costs of the total costs for the special order are shown. The expected profit from the special order, $440, is 5 percent of the total bid price, as expected.

If special orders indicate new, long-term business with the state, the relevant costs also should include costs to increase service or administrative capacity. Furthermore, long-term business should generate normal profits. Consider an airline example to add an additional base to serve growing demand; long-term differential costs include the costs to buy and maintain additional aircraft, pay salaries, and operate ground facilities, among others. These costs must be recovered by prices over the years that the airline will operate flights through this new base. Because of the need to consider the effects of interest costs, the decision-making framework varies slightly for long-term decision making.[17]

You're the Decision Maker 13.2

Alternative Analysis of Special Order

Consider that Bootstrap Industries did not have unemployed resources when the state made the special clean-up order.

a.   Does this situation affect the pricing of the special order?

b.   What bid price do you recommend in this situation?

(Solutions begin on page 534.)

---

[17] Long-term decision making is the topic of Chapter 14.

Chapter Summary

This chapter provides a framework for decision making that explicitly describes the types of information necessary to make good business decisions. The decision-making framework was defined as follows:

Stage I.   Setting goals and objectives.
Stage II.   Gathering information.
Stage III. Evaluating alternatives.
Stage IV.   Planning and implementing.
Stage V.   Obtaining feedback.

This framework can be applied to nearly every type of business decision, as illustrated in this chapter by decisions involving target costing, cost reduction, process alternatives, make or buy, outsourcing, adding or dropping business, pricing, and special orders. In every case, managers should consider how alternative decisions affect estimated quantitative and qualitative benefits and costs.

In applying this framework, managers must consider the trade-offs involved between the cost and the quality of information, which is described by dimensions of subjectivity, accuracy, timeliness, and relevance. In many cases, qualitative information also is critical to making the best decisions.

This chapter examines planning and decision making in the context of a company that has difficult and potentially conflicting goals. Not all companies are this conflicted, but most organizations make decisions that involve trade-offs among its goals. Achieving the maximum levels of conflicting goals is rarely possible, but managers should be aware of the trade-offs that must be made and should strive to make their decisions "optimal"; that is, they should ensure that their decisions achieve the highest goal performance that is feasible given constrained resources and inevitable trade-offs among goals.

Outsourcing is a particularly difficult decision because it often involves trading off profitability for currently performed activities and jobs. On the other hand, oursourcing provides opportunities for jobs and profits by others.

Life cycle costing is becoming common in industries that either use long-lived equipment or have long product-development cycles. Although most approaches to life cycle costing in practice do not consider the time value of money (see Chapter 14), life cycle costs do account for the costs of ownership and operation over the life of a piece of equipment or a process. Ignoring the full life cycle costs can lead to undercosting, incorrect decisions, and loss of profits over the life of a product or process.

Key Terms

For each term's definition, refer to the indicated page or turn to the glossary at the end of the text.

accuracy, 512	life cycle costing, 527	product life cycle, 527	special orders, 530
decision tree, 516	margin of safety, 518	qualitative factors, 516	subjectivity, 512
decision usefulness, 512	objectivity, 512	relevance, 512	tangible objectives, 509
differential costs, 512	outsourcing, 519	relevant costs and	target profit, 510
information quality, 511	predatory pricing, 529	benefits, 512	timeliness, 512

Meeting the Cost Management Challenges

1.   What are the risks if Bootstrap Industries always values job creation more than covering its costs?

Bootstrap Industries' primary mission is to create good jobs for disabled persons while operating profitably. This sets up an inherent conflict of goals because some jobs might offer good training and meaningful employment, especially to the most disabled employees, but the revenue earned from those jobs might not cover current and long-term costs of operations. The company cannot expect its customers to charitably pay more than the work is worth, but the company also tries to expand employment opportunities. This could mean that Bootstrap must place limits on the level of disabilities it can accommodate. On the other hand, Bootstrap must be careful that it is not just pursuing profitable jobs

that do not offer meaningful employment. This would be contrary to its basic mission. Bootstrap's managers must always ask, Is this new employment opportunity a good and profitable one? If it's not profitable now, can it be? Or is the quality of the work sufficient for some employees to override the lack of profits? Can other jobs make up the loss from this opportunity? What else do we give up if we trade off either job quality or profit?

2.   Should Bootstrap set its prices to increase employment or to generate funds for internal investment?

Bootstrap Industries has been successful because it charges prices that *overall* increase employment and generate internal investment funds. As discussed previously, Bootstrap might choose some unprofitable jobs that offer exceptional opportunities for employment, now or in the future. Bootstrap might allow more profitable jobs to subsidize less profitable jobs, but job (or product) mix must be managed very carefully (see Chapter 12). If Bootstrap cuts the difference between revenue and costs (e.g., the average contribution margin) too closely, it will not generate the surplus funds (which others might call profits) that it needs to cover invest-

ments in training, equipment, outreach, and other activities that are necessary to meet its mission of creating future employment opportunities *and* operating profitably. Accepting some unprofitable jobs requires a careful balancing act to ensure that the company overall generates sufficient internal funds for future operations.

Solutions to You're the Decision Maker

13.1 Further Analysis of Dropping a Business
p. 523

Both alternatives promise improved profitability over the status quo, with alternative B showing the higher improvement of $54,000 compared to the status quo. However, several qualitative features of both alternatives are worth additional scrutiny.

Alternative A appears to generate a loss (although much less than the status quo) but also promises improvements in both employee skill level and product quality. Are these qualitative improvements worth forgoing the increased profit ($16,000) of alternative B? Perhaps. Looking closer at alternative B reveals some possible additional risk. The work must achieve improved product quality with no additional training investment and the

Microsoft Excel - Bootstrap.xls

File Edit View Insert Format Tools Data Window Help Acrobat

D30 = D18-D29

	A	B	C	D
		Status quo: Operate remote facility		
1	**Input Data**	**facility**	**Alternative A**	**Alternative B**
2	Supervisory employment	1	1	1
3	Nonsupervisory employment	20	20	20
4	Skill level	low	medium	low
5	Product quality	low	high	medium
6	Service revenues per year	$300,000	$400,000	$300,000
7	Unit-level costs	$30,000	$40,000	$14,000
8	Service-level costs			
9	Equipment	$32,000	$50,000	$20,000
10	Building rental	$36,000	$40,000	$10,000
11	Facility-level costs			
12	Wages	$200,000	$200,000	$200,000
13	Supervision	$24,000	$24,000	$24,000
14	Central office services	$20,000	$20,000	$20,000
15	Period costs			
16	Training	$10,000	$40,000	$10,000
17	**Annual Benefit or Cost**	**Status quo: Operate remote facility**	**Alternative A**	**Alternative B**
18	Sales revenue	$300,000	$400,000	$300,000
19	Unit-level costs	30,000	40,000	14,000
20	Service-level costs			
21	Equipment	32,000	50,000	20,000
22	Building rental	36,000	40,000	10,000
23	Facility-level costs			
24	Wages	200,000	200,000	200,000
25	Supervision	24,000	24,000	24,000
26	Central office services	20,000	20,000	20,000
27	Period costs			
28	Training	10,000	40,000	10,000
29	Total costs	352,000	414,000	298,000
30	Profit	($52,000)	($14,000)	$2,000

Exhibit 13-8 / Exhibit 13-9 / Equip \ YTDM 13-1 /

Draw ▾ AutoShapes ▾

Ready   NUM

status quo skill level. Is that possible? Is the risk of failing to meet quality expectations warranted by possibly higher profits? Perhaps not. In either case, managers need to evaluate these trade-offs.

13.2 Alternative Analysis of Special Order p. 532

a. If Bootstrap did not have unemployed resources, pricing the special order might be affected. Accepting the special order requires either additional capacity (hiring and training new employees) or deferring or canceling other work. The first alternative incurs additional costs that should be considered in pricing.

b. Bootstrap probably will price the special order to reflect at least normal cost levels, $123.75 per employee per day. Adding trained employees quickly might not be feasible in time to meet the special-order demands but can be attractive. If additional work with the state is likely, Bootstrap can discount its target profit as a way to win the work in the short run. If Bootstrap defers or cancels other work, it loses the net benefits of that other work and might harm its reputation. Bootstrap is unlikely to take actions that would harm its good reputation, but it requires covering at least normal costs and target profits (perhaps more to cushion losses from reduced reputation effects).

Review Questions

13.1 Review the chapter's key terms and define them.

13.2 List and briefly describe each of the five stages of the decision-making framework.

13.3 Distinguish between an organization's goals and tangible objectives.

13.4 Distinguish between *target costing* and *target pricing*.

13.5 Describe a conflict that might occur between accuracy, timeliness, relevance, and cost of information.

13.6 What criteria must be satisfied for information to be relevant?

13.7 "A quantitative analysis allows a decision maker to put a price on the total value of qualitative characteristics in a decision situation." Explain this statement and give an example.

13.8 Give two examples of sunk costs and explain why these amounts might be both useful to and irrelevant in decision making.

13.9 Why might a manager inappropriately consider sunk costs when making a decision?

13.10 What considerations other than costs are relevant to outsourcing decisions?

13.11 Traditional accounting systems record only actual transactions. How can opportunity costs, which usually are not actual transactions, be important in decision making?

13.12 Explain several legal influences on pricing decisions.

13.13 Explain the following assertion: "Price setting generally requires a balance between market forces and cost considerations."

13.14 Explain how a company develops its target price and target cost.

13.15 Explain the relationship, if any, between life cycle costs and the pricing of goods and services.

13.16 Distinguish between *price discrimination* and *predatory pricing*.

Critical Analysis

13.17 Respond to the following statement: "Benefit-cost analysis is completely different in nonprofits such as Bootstrap because they have no profit to measure the value of alternatives."

13.18 Peter Drucker argues that one of the seven deadly business sins is to base prices on costs, which means first measuring the current cost of a product or service and then "marking it up" by adding a profit margin. He blames the disappearance of the US consumer-electronics industry in part on its practice of basing prices on costs. Can a domestic industry disappear because of its pricing practice? What is an alternative to basing prices on costs? What does this alternative require that is different from basing prices on costs?

13.19 The manager of a telecommunications company once commented, "Not all future costs are relevant to business decisions, but costs are not relevant unless they occur in the future." Is the manager correct? Explain.

13.20 "In the long run, we need to achieve superior quantitative financial performance. But in the short run we need to achieve superior qualitative, nonfinancial performance." Is this correct? Explain.

13.21 CEO: "It's all well and good for you to say that I should disregard sunk costs when I consider whether to sell this unprofitable operation. After we report lower-than-expected profits, you won't have to answer the angry questions from stockholders and analysts because our

share price has dropped or from employees who say this is just a way to keep from paying bonuses." Explain the CEO's rationale for not selling an unprofitable business unit. Do you agree? Why or why not?

13.22 Some skeptics suspect that continually upgrading an organization's information system has more to do with keeping up with appearances than with improving the accuracy, timeliness, relevance, and cost of information for decision making. How do you determine the accuracy of this suspicion?

13.23 Where to place the city's new shelter for homeless people has resulted in overwhelming recognition that a new shelter is needed but "not in my neighborhood." As winter approaches, the director of the shelter and the publisher of the local newspaper have accused the city of "analysis paralysis" as it continues meetings and hearings to find a suitable location. Can you suggest a feasible approach to making this difficult decision? Be as specific as you can.

13.24 "With our high fixed costs, high variable costs, and competitive markets, there really is little we can do to increase our profits." Should you accept this argument without question? Explain.

13.25 A medium-size retailer of upscale retail goods is considering outsourcing its data-processing, human resources, billing, and legal activities. Prepare a list of the benefits and costs of these considerations.

13.26 A manager in your organization has just received a special order at a price that is below cost. The manager points to the document and says, "These are the kinds of orders that will get you in trouble. Every sale must bear its share of the full costs of running the company. If we sell below our cost, we'll be out of business in no time." Comment on the manager's remark.

13.27   To go from Dallas to Los Angeles for a business meeting, Nancy Wilkinson booked a flight for $950 with a depar- ture on Wednesday and a return on Friday of the same week. The reservation agent told Nancy that if she were to return on Sunday, the ticket price would fall to $288. What factor(s) did the airline appear to focus on when setting its ticket prices? Is it likely that the airline could have been accused of price discrimination and violating the Robinson–Patman Act? Explain.

Exercises

Exercise 13.28
Decision Making
(LO 1)

Consider the following decision-making problem and structure it using the framework presented in this chapter.

"I don't know where to begin. Right now, I feel that throwing a dart at a dartboard will give me just as much insight into how to make this decision as any other method. Can you help? I am paying my way through college using savings from my summer job. I get a small allowance from my parents, but they can't afford to send much. I find that I don't have enough money to pay my bills and have any left over for entertainment or new clothes. I am afraid that I will be broke before the year is over and have to drop out of school. I don't mind having to budget, but do I have to abandon any hope for a life, too?"

Exercise 13.29
Decision Making
(LO 1)

Consider the following decision-making problem and structure it using the framework presented in this chapter.

"We employ 20 full-time internal auditors who review internal operations for quality and efficiency and do much of the compliance work prior to our annual audit by a Big 4 firm. The auditors report directly to me as the CFO. I know that many similar firms have outsourced the internal audit function to Big 4 firms or others that specialize in internal auditing. They do so primarily for cost savings, but I am concerned about loss of control, quality, and sensitive information that might be leaked to competitors. We also use internal auditing as a management-training program, where fast-track managers get wide exposure to all parts of the company. How do we get that training if we outsource internal auditing?"

Exercise 13.30
Decision Making
(LO 1)

Consider the following decision-making problem and structure it using the framework presented in this chapter.

"We have a full-time staff who maintain and clean our buildings and facilities, but we are consider- ing outsourcing that work to Bootstrap Industries. I think our own staff does a good job, but they really are not critical to the company's success. On the other hand, they are good people and have families to support. I also know that Bootstrap will do a good job, and, if we outsource, it will be cheaper and we won't have any paperwork or employment hassles. I'm having a hard time making this decision."

Exercise 13.31
Pricing methods
(LO 2, 4)

Customers, costs, competitors, cost-plus formulas, and target-costing procedures all play a role in the pricing of goods and services. Sometimes the pricing process is relatively straightforward; on other occasions it is more complex. The preceding factors and the procedures followed often vary from one business to the next.

Required

Form a team with three other students in your class and visit the manager or sales manager of a business: big, small, retailer, wholesaler, manufacturer, service business. Determine the relative significance of customers, costs, competitors, cost-plus formulas, and target costing in the firm's pricing methods. What approach does the manager use when (1) the good or service is new, unique, and untested in the market- place and (2) the manager has little knowledge on which to base a decision? What has been the man- ager's biggest success and failure in pricing? Submit your findings to your instructor in a memo or email with an attached table or diagram that summarizes your findings.

Exercise 13.32
Information dimensions
(LO 2)

Give an example of an information item at each extreme level for the following information dimensions.

	Example of Information at	
Information Dimensions	**Very High Level**	**Very Low Level**
Subjectivity	?	?
Accuracy	?	?
Timeliness	?	?
Cost	?	?
Relevance	?	?

In recent years, the number of new cars leased by individuals has increased significantly. Many consumers, dealers, and manufacturers find the leasing alternative preferable to bank financing or an outright purchase, especially when prices are high and vehicle sales are slow.

Exercise 13.33
Decision between leasing and buying
(LO 2, 4)

Required
Form small groups to visit a local automobile dealership. Talk to an employee in the financing area about the relative merits of leasing versus purchasing a new automobile. Obtain dollar amounts comparing leasing to purchasing. List the relevant costs and benefits associated with the two alternatives. Include any qualitative considerations as well. Summarize your findings in a decision-tree outline submitted to your instructor. (Do not lease or purchase an automobile as part of your assignment.)

Match the cost(s) most likely to be relevant to each listed decision.

Exercise 13.34
Relevant Costs
(LO 2)

Decision	**Cost**
Accept a special order _____	a. Internal unit-level manufacturing cost
Close a plant _____	b. Cost to buy externally
Launch a new product _____	c. Opportunity cost of alternative use
Make or buy a product component _____	d. Cost paid for parts on hand
Outsource a business activity _____	e. Lease cost for facility
	f. Loss of quality reputation
	g. Loss of control
	h. Loss of employee trust

Match the cost(s) most likely to be relevant to each listed decision.

Exercise 13.35
Relevant Costs
(LO 2)

Decision	**Cost**
Accept a special order _____	a. $15 internal unit-level manufacturing cost
Close a plant _____	b. Increased employee turnover
Launch a new product _____	c. $20,000 opportunity cost of alternative use
Make or buy a product component _____	d. $20 cost paid for parts on hand
Outsource a business activity _____	e. Reduced ability to guarantee deliveries
	f. Increased warranty and repair expense
	g. $25 cost to buy externally
	h. $50,000 penalty to break annual lease for facility

Prepare a decision tree to reflect the choice of living and eating on campus versus renting an apartment five miles from campus. The student living off campus can buy a meal ticket, but living off campus requires transportation costs (bicycle, walk, bus, or car). Identify quantitative and qualitative costs and benefits.

Exercise 13.36
Decision Tree
(LO 3)

Prepare a decision tree to reflect the choice between repairing an old car or buying a new or used car. Identify quantitative and qualitative costs and benefits.

Exercise 13.37
Decision Tree
(LO 3)

Consider the quantitative costs and benefits of two alternatives. What must be the value of the qualitative factors if the less profitable alternative is chosen?

Exercise 13.38
Quantitative and Qualitative Factors
(LO 2)

Cost or Benefit	**Status Quo**	**Alternative**
Revenues	$50,000	$50,000
Costs	$30,000	$40,000
Quality	Medium	Very high
Meets production schedules	Medium	High

Consider the quantitative costs and benefits of two alternatives. What must be the value of the qualitative factors if the less profitable alternative is chosen?

Exercise 13.39
Quantitative and Qualitative Factors
(LO 2)

Cost or Benefit	**Alternative 1**	**Alternative 2**
Cost savings	$20,000	$30,000
Flexibility	High	Medium
Quality	Very high	Medium
Meets delivery schedules	High	Medium

Exercise 13.40
Outsourcing
(LO 2, 4)

Locate a recent article on outsourcing practices. Complete the following requirements based on the article.

Required

a.   What are the major reasons for the decision to outsource?

b.   What are the major concerns about outsourcing?

c.   Which business functions are outsourced?

Exercise 13.41
Pricing
(LO 4)

Replace the question marks with information based on markup over cost for A–E.

	A	B	C	D	E
Unit-level cost	$12	$20	$32	$8	$60
Product-level cost per unit	$ 6	$22	$12	?	$24
Facility-level cost per unit	$15	$16	?	$3	$16
Mark-up percentage	25%	?	40%	100%	75%
Price per unit	?	$87.00	$71.40	$54.00	?

Exercise 13.42
Relevant Cost
(LO 2)

San Diego Construction (SDC) builds custom luxury homes along the coast of the Pacific Ocean. The company was nearing the completion of a home for Jan and Bill Kennedy when the couple suddenly declared bankruptcy. At that time, SDC had invested $1,525,000 in the project.

The firm can sell the uncompleted residence "as is" to a new buyer for $1,400,000, or it can invest another $160,000 to finish the project and sell it on the open market for $1,600,000.

Required

a.   What is true about the original $1,525,000 investment from a decision-making perspective?

b.   Which of the following options—do nothing, sell "as is" at $1,400,000, or sell "finished" at $1,540,000—should SDC pursue? Why?

Exercise 13.43
Relevant Cost
(LO 2)

Chavez Digital Machining's performance for the first 11 months of the year has been a surprise with sales and profits somewhat above expectations. On December 20, just prior to the holiday break, Patrick Olmec faced the decision of scrapping some old equipment and replacing it. The old equipment had a book value of $400,000 but could be sold for only $250,000. The new machinery had a cost of $1,500,000 and was expected to produce net annual savings in cash operating costs of $180,000 over a 10-year life. The investment predicts returns higher than the minimum required by the company. Olmec's year-end bonus is computed on the basis of company profitability.

Required

a.   Discuss the conflict that sometimes arises in business between decision making and performance evaluation.

b.   Should Olmec acquire the new machinery? Why? Show computations to support your answer. Ignore taxes and the time value of money.

Problems

Problem 13.44
Cost Reduction
(LO 4)

MicroStorage Technology (MST) is developing a high-speed modem to connect hand-held computers with a satellite-based data network.

Required

a.   Given the following information, compute MST's cost-reduction target.

Expected market price	$175
Required return on sales	25%
Product life	3 years
Currently feasible cost	$45,000,000
Expected average annual sales, units	90,000

b.   If MST believes it can reduce the cost of the modem by no more than 18 percent, is this a feasible product for MST? Why or why not?

Mercy Hospital is a private hospital that serves an aging population. The hospital administrator, Donna Morgan, believes that insurance companies and Medicare will move to fixed payments for specific procedures, which will put increasing pressure on hospitals to control costs. A common procedure performed at Mercy Hospital is hip-replacement surgery. Morgan has asked the hospital's CFO to prepare information on the current costs of hip replacements at Mercy so that they can explore the financial viability of this (and other) procedures. Consider the following information gathered by the CFO:

Problem 13.45
Cost Reduction
(LO 4)

mhhe.com/hilton3e

> Expected charge reimbursement (sales price) $25,000
> Required return on charges (return on sales)* 30%
> Current average cost per hip replacement $22,000
>
> *To cover profit goals and other support service costs.

Required

a. Are hip-replacement surgeries financially viable?

b. A cross-functional team of administrators, surgeons, nurses, and support personnel analyzed the hospital's hip-replacement procedure and estimated that, through better scheduling and postoperative care, Mercy could reduce hospital stays from an average of nine days to five days with no loss of quality of care. In fact, because elderly patients would be hospitalized for shorter periods, they would be less likely to contract respiratory infections. Improvements in the procedure can result in a reduction of the average cost of a hip replacement by $8,000. If this were accomplished, what is the expected return on charges for a hip replacement?

[Adapted from J. H. Evans III, Y. C. Hwang, and N. Nagarajan, "Cost Reduction and Process Reengineering in Hospitals."]

Black Diamond, Inc., has been manufacturing 5,000 units of part 10541 per month. At this level of production, the company's costs (expressed on a per-unit basis) follow.

Problem 13.46
Outsourcing
(LO 2, 4)

> Unit-level cost $40
> Facility-level cost 15
> Total cost per unit.............................. $55

Black Diamond can outsource the manufacture of 5,000 units of part 10541 to Mogul Company at a cost of $48 per unit to Black Diamond. If Black Diamond does outsource the part, it has determined that it can sell some facilities it presently uses to produce part 10541 and use the remaining facilities to manufacture a new product, RAC. Black Diamond also has determined that facility costs can drop by one-third if it outsources part 10541 to Mogul.

Required

a. Should Black Diamond make or buy this part?

b. How much profit must the new product RAC generate to justify the decision to outsource part 10541?

c. What other considerations are important to this outsourcing decision?

[CPA adapted]

Chapman & Tracy is a regional firm that offers audit, tax, and consulting services. The partners are concerned about the profitability of their audit business, and a closure decision might be forthcoming. If the firm drops the audit activities, it might do more tax work. Only 30 percent of the facility costs associated with auditing disappears by dropping the auditing function. More tax work can increase tax revenues by 40 percent, but tax service–level costs also increase by 40 percent. Total facility cost is unchanged whether or not tax work is increased. Segmented income statements for these three product lines follow.

Problem 13.47
Add/Drop Business Unit
(LO 2, 4)

mhhe.com/hilton3e

	Auditing	**Tax**	**Consulting**
Sales	$300,000	$500,000	$600,000
Service-level cost	250,000	300,000	350,000
Shared facility cost	50,000	60,000	80,000
Operating income (loss)	$ 0	$140,000	$170,000

Required

a.   Determine which alternative Chapman & Tracy should choose: (1) drop the auditing line without increasing tax work or (2) drop auditing and increase tax work.

b.   What other considerations are important to the decision to drop auditing?

Problem 13.48
Add/Drop Business Unit
(LO 3, 5)

Buy-U Deli's owner is disturbed by the poor profit performance of her ice cream counter. She has prepared the following profit analysis for the year just ended:

Sales	$45,000
Less: Cost of food	20,000
Gross profit	$25,000
Less: Operating expenses:	
Wages of counter personnel	$12,000
Paper products (e.g., napkins)	4,000
Utilities (based on percent of sales)	2,900
Depreciation of counter equipment and furnishings	3,000
Depreciation of building (based on percentage of sales)	5,000
Deli manager's salary (based on percentage of time spent on ice cream)	6,000
Total operating expenses	32,900
Income (loss) on ice cream counter	$ (7,900)

Required

a.   Critique and revise the owner's analysis as you think appropriate. Justify your changes.

b.   Should the owner close the counter? What other factors should she consider before closing it?

Problem 13.49
Opportunity Cost
(LO 2, 4)

Marlene Judd is a 55-year-old science teacher at Lamar Tech. She is considering leaving the teaching profession next year and going to graduate school to earn a master's degree in business administration (MBA). Judd plans to attend a prestigious university as a full-time student. The MBA takes two full years to complete with annual tuition of $25,000 and living costs of $10,000 (comparable to her current living costs).

Judd's annual salary upon graduation is anticipated to be $80,000 and likely will increase at 5 percent per year. This year she will earn $48,000 at Lamar Tech; expected pay raises in teaching are 2 percent annually.

Required

a.   Is there an opportunity cost in this situation? If so, how much?

b.   Calculate the real cost of attending school for two years and attaining the degree.

c.   What options might Judd consider to reduce the degree's real cost?

d.   What other factors should Judd consider in her decision to attend graduate school?

Problem 13.50
Special Order
(LO 4)

Intermountain Products Company is presently operating at 75 percent of capacity, producing 120,000 units of an electronic component. The firm recently received a special order from Scott Corporation for 40,000 components with reduced function at $6 per unit. Unit-level costs for the modified component will decrease by 20 percent, and the order will require a one-time setup cost of $80,000. Planned production costs for 120,000 units of output follow.

Units	120,000
Unit-level costs	$360,000
Facility costs	600,000
Total costs	$960,000
Cost per unit	$ 8.00

The sales manager believes that the firm should accept the order even if it results in a loss because the sale might build future markets. The production manager does not want it to be accepted primarily because it shows a loss of $1.10 per unit when computed on the new average unit cost.

Required

a.   Explain the production manager's calculation of the loss per unit. Show supporting computations.

b.   Is the special order profitable? Show supporting computations.

c.   What other factors should be considered before accepting this special order?

[CPA adapted]

Obtain a copy of the article "The Environmental Impacts of Genetically Modified Plants: Challenges to Decision Making," by Sandra Batie, *American Journal of Agricultural Economics* 85, no. 5(2003):1107–1111. Work in small groups to develop a 15-minute presentation that completes the following requirements.

Problem 13.51
Group Decision Making
(LO 1, 2)

Required

a. Using the decision-making framework presented in Exhibit 13–1, describe decision making about the management of genetically modified plants.

b. Describe the major risk factors that create uncertainty about decision making with regard to genetically modified plants.

c. (Optional) Provide an update of decision making about genetically modified plants incorporating more recent developments.

Maytag Corp. recently purchased rival Amana Appliances and is consolidating its manufacturing and assembly processes. Maytag now wants to reduce costs for the combined businesses by moving some labor-intensive assembly operations to Mexico. The new assembly plant, with an estimated initial investment of $2 million, will receive plastic and metal parts from Maytag's manufacturing plants and will return subassemblies to Maytag's US operations for final assembly. The new operation will employ about 230 people and will be similar to Maytag's Hoover floor-care plant that it has operated for more than 17 years. Amana has operated assembly operations in Amana, Iowa, Florence, South Carolina, and Searcy, Arkansas.

Problem 13.52
Decision Tree and
Benefit-Cost Analysis
(LO 1, 2, 3)

Required

a. Use the decision-making framework in Exhibit 13–1 (and your imagination) to describe Maytag Corp.'s decision making about whether to locate a new assembly plant in Mexico.

b. Prepare a decision tree that describes Maytag Corp.'s assembly plant decision making and includes qualitative and quantitative benefits and costs.

[Adapted from Michael Lauzon, "Maytag Moving Some Assembly to Mexico."]

TGIF Financial Corp. has been one of Visa U.S.A.'s largest bank debit-card issuers. Visa U.S.A. recently settled a lawsuit brought by retailers who protested Visa's excessive fees for accepting payments via debit cards, which have a lower risk than credit cards. Visa paid the $2 billion settlement to retailers and sought to recover it from debit-card issuers like TGIF as "membership fees." Visa argued that banks like TGIF had prospered under the old higher debit-card fees and now must share the settlement. TGIF's pro rata share as one of the largest debit-card issuers was $70,000,000. Visa encouraged early payment by offering a 6 percent discount. Many banks, including TGIF, balked at the membership fees, which were not part of any original agreements with Visa. TGIF was about to renew its 10-year contract with Visa but considered switching its debit cards to MasterCard. Visa countered by imposing a "transfer fee" on any bank that switched its business to rival MasterCard before paying its share of the settlement. The transfer fee was set at 3 percent of the bank's annual Visa cardholder charges.

Problem 13.53
Benefit-Cost Analysis
(LO 1, 2)

TGIF normally earned 2 percent on cardholder charges, which translates into annual revenues of $60 million. If TGIF transferred its debit-card business to MasterCard, it would earn 1.8 percent from the same level of charges and avoid paying the settlement but would incur the transfer fee, which the bank did not want to fight in the courts, fearing bad publicity. Visa- and MasterCard-related operating expenses were approximately equal.

Required

a. What quantitative and qualitative factors should TGIF Financial consider before deciding whether to renew its contract with Visa, pay its share of the settlement early, or switch to MasterCard?

b. Should TGIF Financial renew its contract with Visa or switch to MasterCard? Explain and show relevant calculations.

c. *Build your own spreadsheet.* Prepare a spreadsheet to analyze this decision. What is the MasterCard earnings rate that equalizes the financial considerations of this decision? (Hint: Use Excel's Solver wizard.)

[Adapted from David Breitkopf, "Muted Response After New Visa Charge Revelation."]

Obtain a copy of the article "Unlocking the Benefits of World Trade" by Jeffrey Schott, *The Economist,* November 1, 2003. Work in small groups to develop a 15-minute presentation that completes the following requirements.

Problem 13.54
Decision Making
(LO 1, 2)

Required

a. Use the decision-making framework presented in Exhibit 13–1 to describe the reported decision making at the global trade talks in Cancun, Mexico, in September 2003.

b. Describe the major factors that impeded decision making at the Cancun talks.

c. Describe how you wold measure costs and benefits of alternative decisions, such as elimination of agricultural subsidies or tariffs on manufactured clothing.

d. Summarize the status of decision making at the end of the Cancun talks.

e. (Optional) Provide an update of decision making for global trade, incorporating more recent developments.

Problem 13.55
Cost Reduction
(LO 4)

Sayre Sewing Machine Company has been in operation for over 25 years. During this time, it has shown consistent growth and has developed a strong following of satisfied customers. Merlene Sayre, company president, states that her business philosophy is "a quality product at a competitive price." Until recently, this philosophy has carried the company to its current position. The company is planning for next year's operations, and Sayre is concerned about the projected increased foreign competition.

For the last three years, Sayre has been manufacturing as its only product a machine that has the characteristics of both a serger and a zigzag machine, called the Sergzig. During the current year, the company expects to sell 200,000 machines at an average price of $700. To remain competitive and continue to sell 200,000 machines, Sayre believes that the company will have to reduce the selling price to $580 for the next year.

At the current level of sales and production, Sayre earns 15 percent return on sales, as shown:

Sales price per unit		$700
Product costs per unit:		
Materials		
Computer chip	$77	
Motor..	60	
Housing unit	50	
Mechanical parts	86	
Miscellaneous parts	22	
Assembly labor......................................	90	
Testing labor	60	$445
Product-level equipment		70
General administrative cost		80
Total product costs		$595
Profit per unit		$105
Return on sales		15%

In planning for next year, even at the reduced sales price the company wants to maintain the 15 percent return on sales by reducing costs as follows:

- Sayre can purchase the computer chip at $48 per unit by committing to a long-term purchase agreement for the year's needs with the supplier. The long-term agreement calls for the supplier to certify that all chips are defect-free.

- Sayre can reduce the number of housing units and miscellaneous parts by 18 percent by substituting equivalent but less expensive parts and by redesigning the housing to eliminate multiple parts.

- Because of these changes, the company can reduce assembly and testing labor and equipment and facility costs specific to the Sergzig by 20 percent (net of redesign costs).

- All other product costs will remain the same.

Required

a. List the advantages and disadvantages of Sayre's proposed changes. Explain the risks involved with the proposed changes.

b. Based on the new data for next year, can Sayre meet or exceed its target of 15 percent return on sales? Show calculations.

c. Assume that competition during the next year is stronger than Sayre anticipates and that the average selling price is only $540 per unit. Calculate the cost reduction necessary to achieve the 15 percent return on sales. Show calculations.

[CMA adapted]

Review Exhibit 13–3.

Required

Build your own spreadsheet. Set up exhibit 13–3 as a spreadsheet and make individual changes, again except for requirement (e), and indicate how each affects the choice between methods. Make each of the following changes independently of the others, except for requirement (e).

a.   Expected market price is raised to $120.

b.   Unit-level costs: alternative 1 = $25, alternative 2 = $45.

c.   Equipment costs: alternative 1 = $150,000, alternative 2 = $30,000.

d.   Expected sales volume is increased by 20 percent.

e.   Combine the conditions of (a)–(d) and compute the alternatives' returns on sales.

f.   *Team Focus:* Assume that you are the cost-management member of the target-costing team. Your natural tendency is to be skeptical of expected increases in sales prices and reductions in costs, and the marketing member of the team has jokingly referred to you as the "grim reaper." (Accountants call this tendency "conservatism.") Learning how to temper marketing and engineering team members' natural optimism with "financial reality" without losing credibility and influence is an important lesson for cost-management analysts. What questions should you ask about the preceding alternatives for the analysis?

SciFi Paperback Books is an internet retailer of science fiction paperback books. Based on a sales volume of 200,000 units, the projected net income for the current year is $700,000. The company has been selling the books for an average of $15 each; unit-level costs consist of the $8 purchase cost and a $1 handling cost. SciFi's annual committed facility and period costs are $500,000. SciFi's books generally have a one-year product life.

Required

a.   If SciFi desires a 20 percent return on sales, what cost reduction is required at the current year's prices and costs?

b.   What cost reduction is required if there are the following changes in next year's costs and prices that result from taking no management actions; that is, maintaining the status quo:

    ▓   5 percent decrease in sales price

    ▓   20 percent increase in purchase cost

    ▓   60 percent increase in handling cost

    ▓   15 percent increase in committed costs

    ▓   12 percent decrease in sales quantity

c.   Explain why maintaining the status quo often is a prescription for declining profitability.

[CMA adapted]

A financial analyst is studying two new distribution systems, basic and deluxe. The basic system has unit-level shipping costs of $8 per unit and annual facility costs of $500,000; in contrast, the deluxe system has unit-level shipping costs of $4 per unit and annual facility costs of $780,000. The deluxe system promises greater customer service. The company sells its products for $30 per unit, less a 5 percent sales commission.

Required

a.   Which of the two systems will be more profitable for the firm if sales are expected to average 50,000 units per year?

b.   At what unit-volume level will management be indifferent as to the profit for the basic system and the deluxe system?

c.   In requirement (a) by how much does the company value the promised greater customer service if it selects the deluxe system? How can the company verify this level of value?

Problem 13.59
Make or Buy
(LO 3, 5)

Xyon Company purchases 10,000 pumps annually from Kobec, Inc. Because the price keeps increasing and reached $88 per unit last year, Xyon's management has asked for a cost estimate to manufacture the pump internally. Xyon makes stampings and castings and has little experience with products that require assembly.

　　The engineering, manufacturing, and accounting departments have prepared a report for management that includes the following estimate for an assembly run of 10,000 pumps. To manufacture the pumps Xyon will hire additional production employees but will need no additional equipment, space, or supervision. The report estimates that total costs for 10,000 units are estimated at $1,200,000, or $120 a unit. The current purchase price is $88 a unit, so the report recommends the continued purchase of the product. If the pumps are purchased, the currently unused space could be leased for $150,000 annually.

Components	$ 270,000
Assembly labor*	290,000
Share of existing facility costs based on labor	640,000
Total costs	$1,200,000

*Assembly labor consists of hourly production workers.

Required

a. Was the analysis prepared by Xyon Company's engineering, manufacturing, and accounting departments and their recommendation to continue purchasing the pumps correct? Explain your answer and include any supporting calculations that you consider necessary.

b. Present several benefits and problems of dealing with outside suppliers such as Kobec, Inc.

[CMA adapted]

Problem 13.60
Drop a Service
(LO 2, 4)

Melville College is a small liberal arts school located in Massachusetts. It is evaluating its botany program because the program's tuition revenues and costs recently produced an $80,000 loss, which is typical of performance in the past few years. Tuition revenues earned totaled $320,000; operating expenses were faculty salaries, $215,000; supplies, $10,000; and other facility costs, $175,000. If the program is dropped, the following are expected:

　▪　Some students will change majors, but overall college enrollment will decline as other students transfer to other universities. Total lost tuition revenue is estimated at $195,000.

　▪　Untenured faculty members with combined salaries of $170,000 can be dismissed. The tenured faculty will transfer to the biology department. In addition, 75 percent of the program's supplies cost can be saved.

　▪　Other facility costs include $98,000 of general college overhead costs that are assigned to the program and $77,000 of salaries earned by office and support personnel. One of these employees (annual salary, $22,000) will be transferred to the music school; other employees can be laid off.

　▪　Equipment will be removed and transferred to the fine arts school at a cost of $1,100. The vacated space can be converted to a weight and physical conditioning facility for student athletes. This new facility likely will help attract better athletes and make the college's athletic programs more competitive.

The director of development reports that Florence Ficus, an alumna and supporter of the botany program, is now sole owner of the highly successful Ficus Scientific Corporation. Ficus has designated the college as a major beneficiary of her estate.

Required

a. Should Melville drop the botany program? Show calculations.

b. What other factors should be considered if the decision is made to drop the program?

c. What options might be open to Melville if it continues the program and the college's president mandates that "program losses must be eliminated within three years"?

Problem 13.61
Equipment Replacement
(LO 4)

Review the equipment replacement decision described on page 524. The outsourcing services manager is concerned about the assumptions regarding increased sales and lowered operating costs with the new equipment.

Required

a. *Build your own spreadsheet.* The spreadsheet financial model should reproduce the analysis of the equipment replacement decision.

b. What is (1) the percentage capacity increase or (2) the amount of new operating costs that equate the net benefits of the two types of equipment? (*Hint:* Use Excel's Solver wizard.)

c. Why might a manager in this situation not replace the old equipment? Should Bootstrap Industries replace the equipment? Explain.

The radiology department of Community Hospital two years ago purchased an imaging device that cost $750,000. Its expected useful life was five years; however, this year an improved version of the imaging device is available. The improved version costs $900,000 but has a shorter operating life of three years. The improvements to the device are lower annual operating costs (down from $650,000 to $360,000) and 8 percent increased throughput. The increased throughput should boost current annual revenues of $1,000,000 proportionately but not affect other operations or costs. The present imaging device could be disposed of and sold now for $350,000, but both the present and replacement device will have zero disposal values in three years.

Problem 13.62
Equipment Replacement
(LO 4)

Required

a. *Build your own spreadsheet.* The spreadsheet financial model should analyze the device replacement decision.

b. What is (1) the percentage throughput or (2) the amount of new operating costs that equate the net benefits of the two imaging devices? (*Hint:* Use Excel's Solver wizard.)

c. Why might a manager in this situation not replace the old equipment? Should Community Hospital replace the imaging device? Explain.

Cosmos Corporation manufactures collectible toy cars in a plant that has theoretical capacity to produce 3,000 cars each month. Current monthly production is 80 percent of practical capacity. The normal selling price is $36; unit-level costs and facility costs for the current activity level are as follows:

Problem 13.63
Special Order
(LO 2, 4)

Unit-level costs	$ 28,560
Facility-level costs:	
Manufacturing	96,000
Marketing.................................	78,000
Total costs	$202,560

Cosmos has just received a special order from a Japanese company for 1,100 cars at $31 each, with a target completion date in three months. Cosmos has never competed in the global marketplace. The company has hired a consultant for $5,500 each month of the contract to obtain advice on conducting business in Japan.

Required

a. Does Cosmos have sufficient productive capacity to accept the order? Explain.

b. Is the order attractive from a financial perspective? Show computations to support your answer.

c. Discuss any other considerations that Cosmos should include in analyzing the order.

d. Is it beneficial for Cosmos to take a loss on this order if it desires to enter the Japanese market? Discuss briefly.

Framar, Inc., manufactures automation machinery according to customer specifications. The company operated at 75 percent of practical capacity during the year just ended with the following results:

Problem 13.64
Special Order
(LO 2, 4)

Sales revenue	$25,000,000
Less: Sales commissions (10%)	2,500,000
Net sales	$22,500,000
Expenses:	
Unit-level costs...	$15,750,000
Facility-level costs	2,250,000
Total costs	$18,000,000
Income before taxes	4,500,000
Income taxes (40%)......................................	$ 1,800,000
Net income..	$ 2,700,000

Framar, which expects continued operations at 75 percent of capacity, recently submitted a bid of $135,238 on some custom-designed machinery to APA, Inc. To derive the bid amount, Framar used a pricing formula based on last year's operating results:

Estimated materials (unit level)	$ 29,200
Estimated labor (unit level)	56,000
Facility costs at 14.29% of unit-level costs	12,171
Estimated total costs excluding sales commissions	$ 97,371
Add 25% markup for profits and taxes	24,343
Suggested price (with profits) before sales commissions.............................	$121,714
Suggested total price: $121,714 ÷ .9 to adjust for 10% commission	$135,238

Required

a.   Calculate the impact the order will have on Framar's net income if APA accepts the $135,238 bid.

b.   Assume that APA has rejected Framar's bid but has stated that it is willing to pay $127,000 for the machinery. Should Framar manufacture the machinery for the counteroffer of $127,000? Explain your answer, and show calculations.

c.   At what bid price will Framar break even on the order?

d.   Explain how the profit performance in the coming year is affected if Framar accepted all of its work at prices similar to APA's $127,000 counteroffer described in requirement (b).

[CMA adapted]

Problem 13.65
Special Order
(LO 2, 3, 4)

Hamilton Industries manufactures standard and custom-designed bottling equipment. Early in December, Lyan Company asked Hamilton to quote a price for a custom bottling machine to be delivered the following April. Lyan intends to make a decision on the purchase by January 1, so Hamilton has the entire first quarter of the year for construction if its bid is accepted.

Hamilton's pricing policy for custom-designed equipment is 50 percent markup on full manufacturing cost. Cost-management analysts have derived the following estimates for normal costs caused by the decision to accept the machine order:

Materials	$56,000
Labor (3,000 hours at $20 per hour)	60,000

No new facilities are required, but because existing facility costs must be covered by work performed and delivered to customers, facility costs normally are added to cost estimates in direct proportion to labor hours used in the manufacturing effort. Hamilton typically employs 90 manufacturing workers equivalent to 180,000 labor hours per year (40 hours per week × 50 weeks = 2,000 per employee). Dividing the $2,448,000 expected facility cost for the year by the typical employment level of 180,000 hours provides the facility cost per labor hour rate of $13.60. Thus, an additional cost of $40,800 (= $13.60 per hour × 3,000 hours) normally would be added to the cost of the Lyan job.

Hamilton's current production schedule calls for the full use of its available direct-labor hours per month during the first quarter. If it is awarded the contract for the Lyan equipment, Hamilton must reduce production of one of its standard products or its employees must work overtime at 150 percent of their normal hourly rate. Because many workers have holiday bills to pay, enough employees might work overtime to complete both the Lyan order and Hamilton's standard products.

Should employees not work enough overtime hours, the company will lose sales of the standard product equal to the reduced production. Hamilton has maintained good relations with its normal customers. If Hamilton gives its normal customers sufficient notice, it is not likely to lose them permanently. The standard product that can be reduced has a unit sales price of $15,000 and the following costs:

Materials	$ 2,500
Labor (250 hours at $20)	5,000
Facility cost	3,400
Total	$10,900

Required

a. Construct a decision tree that represents Hamilton's business decision. For each alternative, identify both quantitative and qualitative benefits and costs.

b. Calculate the alternative bids that Hamilton would submit using its pricing policy for custom-designed equipment.

c. Calculate the minimum bids that Hamilton should be willing to submit on the equipment if management desired to generate the same total profit as currently planned for the year's first quarter.

d. Assume that Hamilton is prepared to submit a bid slightly above a minimum calculated in requirement (c). Prior to submitting a bid, one of Hamilton's design engineers got a call from an acquaintance at Tygar Corporation, one of Hamilton's chief competitors: "Hey, Joe, we've just prepared a bid for Lyan Company for some customized equipment. I want to come by the house this evening and show you our bid. You know I have always wanted to work for Hamilton." Should Joe accept his acquaintance's offer? Explain.

e. Contrast Hamilton's approach to pricing with the features of target costing.

[CMA adapted]

Greenacres Construction Company wants to compute the life cycle costs of equipment used in its projects. Greenacres will use these life cycle costs to bid and cost its construction jobs. Although no rules govern life cycle costing by private companies, Greenacres wants to account for as much of its operating and ownership costs as possible to be sure that it bids and costs its jobs fully. Analysts have obtained the following information for a backhoe.

Problem 13.66
Life Cycle Costs
(LO 4)

Purchase cost	$135,000
Resale cost at replacement	47,250
Useful life, years	7
Operating hours per year	1,200
Opportunity cost of capital	16%
Annual insurance cost	$768
Annual property tax	$1,145
Fuel consumption per hour, gallons	5
Fuel cost per gallon	$1.25
Annual scheduled maintenance cost	$7,344
Annual repair cost	$5,400
Hourly operator cost (wage + benefits)	$20.00

Required

a. Compute the life cycle ownership, operating, and total costs per hour for the backhoe.

b. Prepare a bid price on a job that has the following characteristics:

Direct labor hours	600
Direct labor hourly rate (wage + benefits)	$18.40
Equipment (backhoe) hours	120
Construction materials	$5,500
Overhead rate per direct labor hour	$9.80
Overhead rate per equipment hour	$7.75
Target rate of return on sales	25%

c. The general manager of Greenacres Construction expects that the bidding on the job in requirement (b) will be very competitive, and the winner will have opportunities for more work with the customer. The economy has not fully recovered in the region, and construction work is scarce. The general manager suggests eliminating the opportunity cost of equipment and the overhead rates and reducing the return on sales to 10 percent. Recompute the bid price and comment on the wisdom of these cuts.

[Adapted from Larry Stewart, "Master Fleet Decisions by Estimating Life Costs"]

Problem 13.67
Life Cycle Costs
(LO 4)

Quantorus Data Storage Company (QDS) wants to compute the life cycle costs of equipment used in its manufacturing process. QDS will use these life cycle costs to cost its data storage products. Although no rules govern life cycle costing by private companies, QDS wants to account for as much of its operating and ownership costs as possible to be sure that it costs its products accurately. Analysts have obtained the following information for a piece of robotic assembly equipment.

Purchase cost	$250,000
Resale cost at replacement	$ 40,000
Useful life, years	3
Operating hours per year...	4,000
Opportunity cost of capital	12%
Annual insurance cost	$1,500
Annual property tax	$445
Energy consumption per hour, kilowatt-hours (kwh)	50
Energy cost per kwh	$.0125
Annual scheduled maintenance cost	$10,440
Annual repair cost	$24,110
Hourly operator cost (wage + benefits).................................	$35

Required

a.   Compute the life cycle ownership, operating, and total costs per hour for the robotic assembly equipment.

b.   Prepare the cost of a batch of product that has the following characteristics:

Units of product per batch....................................	400
Direct labor hours	200
Direct labor hourly rate (wage + benefits)	$28.40
Assembly equipment hours...................................	80
Direct materials	$45,500
Overhead rate per direct labor hour	$19.80
Overhead rate per equipment hour	$72.75
Target rate of return on sales	20%

c.   The vice president of manufacturing at QDS expects that the market price for the product in requirement (b) will be very competitive, about $150 per unit, and the low-cost producer will have opportunities to gain market share. The vice president suggests eliminating the opportunity cost of equipment and the overhead rates, which represent allocations of committed costs. Recompute the cost per unit and comment on the wisdom of these cuts.

Cases

Case 13.68
Benefit-Cost Analysis
(LO 1, 2, 4)

Grand Coulee Dam on the Columbia River was completed in 1941 with the objectives of providing employment, inexpensive electrical power, and agricultural irrigation. Since then, additional project objectives have included recreation, flood control, and wildlife conservation. Beneficiaries of Grand Coulee Dam include:

▪   Farmers, who lobbied effectively for the project and receive water and power at subsidized prices.

▪   Power users, who also lobbied effectively for the project and enjoy below-market rates for electric power.

▪   Downstream residents, who are protected from floods.

▪   Recreationists, who have access to boating, lake fishing, and hunting.

▪   Pacific Northwest residents, who have benefited from the extensive regional economic development resulting from the availability of inexpensive electric power.

Others have borne the costs of Grand Coulee Dam. These cost bearers include:

- US taxpayers, who financed the project but will not see significant repayments until and beginning in 2009.

- Native Americans and Canadian First Nation members, who lost traditional fishing rights and culture because the dam halted annual salmon and steelhead migrations in the Columbia River above the dam and lost reservation lands because Lake Roosevelt, created by the dam, flooded occupied and hunting lands, mostly without compensation or consultation.

- Commercial and sports fishers, who lost livelihoods and recreation because the dam halted annual salmon and steelhead migrations above the dam, without compensation or consultation.

- White settlers, who were displaced from lands flooded by the lake and who received little or no relocation assistance or adequate compensation and were not consulted.

- Farmers, who live outside the power and irrigation district and who must pay unsubsidized prices for power and water.

Granted, this information is available with 70 years of hindsight. Nonetheless, many of the benefits and costs were disputed prior to the project, but only the benefits (along with political maneuvering) were considered in the decision making. Furthermore, the project had no considerations of irreversible effects or provisions for reevaluations and possible modifications.

Required

You have been hired by the World Bank to set up a process for identifying and evaluating the benefits and costs of a major hydroelectric and irrigation project in an undeveloped country.

a. What are the major categories of benefits and costs you should expect from this project? Will quantifying and comparing these benefits and costs be problematic? Explain.

b. How would you structure the decision-making process about whether to proceed with this project?

c. How would you propose to reevaluate the success of the project after completion?

[Adapted from Leonard Ortolano and Katherine Kao Cushing, "Grand Coulee Dam 70 Years Later: What Can We Learn?"]

The supply of electrical power is a critical issue in the Amazon region of Brazil where small population centers are geographically isolated. Brazilian law mandates a reliable 24-hour supply of electricity to populations in designated development areas, and the government desires the lowest cost method. Wind-powered generators are unreliable except on the Atlantic coast. Hydropower plants are unreliable because of continuing droughts.

Case 13.69
Benefit-Cost Analysis: Diesel vs. Solar Power in Brazil
(LO 1, 2 4)

Diesel-powered generators are the most reliable, but fuel is expensive, costly to transport, and the cause of extensive environmental damage to water and air. Diesel systems can use batteries to store unused electricity for backup power or other uses. Diesel systems also can be supplemented by photovoltaic (PV) arrays or operated without batteries to avoid environmental damage from discarded batteries.

Pure PV systems can convert sunlight directly into electrical energy without environmental damage, transport or storage of fuel, and use of batteries (and consequent environmental damages). Equatorial regions such as the Amazon have abundant solar energy where PV systems can be highly efficient. Diesel plants are manufactured in Brazil; PV systems are manufactured in the United States and Europe.

A pilot project sought to investigate the relative benefits and costs of PV arrays with backup diesel generators as village-level sources of electrical energy. The project examined the operations of 86 hybrid plants that ranged from small (5–12 kilowatts), which served approximately 50 people each, to large (50–100 kilowatts), which served approximately 750 people each. The pilot project generated the following data (costs are in Brazil reias, 3 R$ = $1 US).

	Plant Power Range, Kilowatts (kW)				
	5–12	**12–25**	**25–50**	**50–100**	**Total**
Number of PV-diesel hybrid plants	10	19	20	37	86
Saved diesel fuel (liters per year)	179,495	763,417	1,610,140	5,875,510	8,428,562
Energy produced (kilowatt hours per year)	478,296	3,057,415	8,968,050	26,770,560	39,274,321
Total investment, R$	3,012,910	12,896,675	27,555,585	103,110,431	146,575,601
Population served, total people	499	3,185	9,342	27,886	40,912
Energy costs, R$/MWH, at diesel cost of R$1.95/liter*					
Only diesel power generation, no batteries	R$ 2,270	R$ 1,135	R$ 946	R$ 800	
Only diesel power generation, with batteries	2,376	1,240	1,058	920	
Diesel power with 25% PV, with batteries	1,911	1,061	924	821	
Diesel power with 50% PV, with batteries	1,559	992	901	832	
Diesel power with 75% PV, with batteries	1,208	924	878	844	
PV-diesel hybrid system, no batteries...........................	2,154	1,186	1,025	904	
Only PV power generation, with batteries	2,362	2,350	2,353	2,341	

*Energy costs are life cycle costs divided by the energy generated in megawatt hours.

Required

You have been hired by the Brazilian government to evaluate the PV-diesel hybrid pilot project by answering the following questions about the village-level systems.

a.   What qualitative and quantitative considerations are important for choosing among the possible systems? What information beyond that presented might be important to the choice?

b.   Should stand-alone diesel generators be abandoned? Should they be supplemented with PV arrays? Do PV systems alone make sense?

c.   Are PV-diesel hybrid systems attractive for any or all village sizes?

d.   Which system(s) do you recommend? Why?

[A. Schmid and C. Hoffman, "Replacing Diesel by Solar in the Amazon: Short-Term Economic Feasibility of the PV-Diesel Hybrid Systems."]

Case 13.70
Benefit-Cost Analysis:
Social Benefits and
the CPI
(LO 1, 2, 4)

The consumer price index (CPI) is used to annually adjust Social Security payments and the personal tax exemption (a subtraction from taxable income). The intent is to prevent inflation (a general increase in prices) from eroding benefits paid to retired workers and from inflating taxes paid. For example, assume the CPI increased 3 percent this year. This year's annual Social Security payment of $15,000 would be adjusted by 3 percent to $15,450 for next year. Likewise, this year's personal tax exemption would be increased by 3 percent from $2,500 to $2,575. Some economists believe that the CPI overestimates the annual rate of inflation by as much as 1.5 percentage points and results in overpayments of Social Security and undercollection of taxes. They have argued that the social security payment and the personal exemption should be adjusted by the CPI less the amount of the measurement error.

The CPI measures average aggregate prices of the typical "market basket" of goods and services purchased by consumers each month. It is based on about 80,000 prices monthly in a $7+ trillion economy that constantly changes. Thus, the CPI must be an imperfect index, but it is probably the best available measure of changes in consumers' purchasing power. The total impact of the CPI (and any adjustments to it) on social security payments and taxes can be huge. The Congressional Budget Office estimates the CPI error to range between 0.2 and 0.8 percentage points; the Federal Reserve Bank sees an error range of 0.5 to 1.5 points; and a congressional committee estimates the range to be between 0.7 and 1.5 points. Some observers believe the most likely measurement error is 0.5 percentage points.

For simplicity, assume the following statistics:

		Base Annual Growth (percent)
Annual increase in the CPI		3.0%
Current working population 150,000,000		1.0
Current Social Security beneficiaries.................................. 30,000,000		2.0
Average annual Social Security benefit $15,000		
Personal exemption (reduction in taxable income) $2,500		
Average tax rate... 20%		

Required

a. Find a recent article on the political, social, or economic issues related to problems of paying for Social Security benefits in the United States or Europe. Summarize the major conclusions of this article.

b. *Build your own spreadsheet.* Using the provided statistics (and a spreadsheet), project the amounts of Social Security payments and reductions in tax collected because of the personal exemption for the next 10 years and in total. (*Note:* These statistics are simplifications, but the requested analysis can generate results that are similar to very complex analyses.)

c. Re-estimate the projected payments and reductions in tax collections using the most likely, smallest, and largest CPI measurement errors. Ignoring the time value of money, compute the government's 10-year total "savings" from reduced Social Security payments and increased tax collections compared to the amounts using the base annual increase in the CPI.

d. Social Security payments and personal exemptions affect some pension costs and the take-home pay of workers. The board of directors of your company has asked you to draft a letter for their signature to your state senators and representatives outlining how and why you think the CPI should be used to adjust Social Security benefits and personal exemptions. Prepare that letter.

[Adapted from Robert J. Samuelson, "What's in a Number?"]

Chapter 14

Strategic Issues in Making Investment Decisions

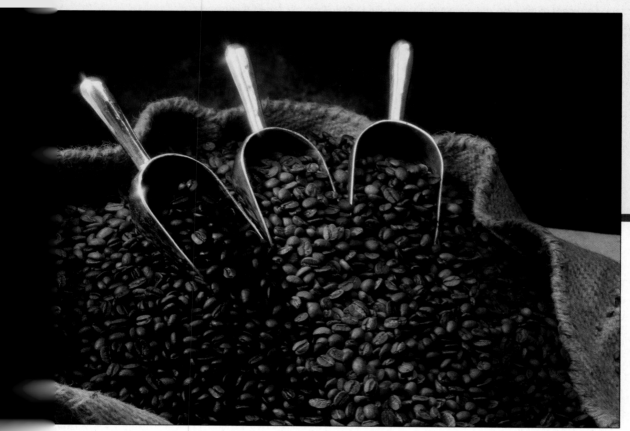

After completing this chapter, you should be able to:

1. Understand the nature of strategic investment decisions.

2. Identify external and internal information for strategic investments.

3. Learn to use forecasts of quantitative and qualitative effects of strategic investments in net present value analysis.

4. Model the impacts of competitors' actions.

5. Know when and how to apply real option analysis to evaluate strategic investments.

6. Identify and evaluate ethical issues in strategic investment decisions.

Cost-Management Challenges

(Solutions are on page 581.)

1. **How** does the proposed investment by ShadeTree Roasters influence the types of information the company should obtain and the analyses it should perform?

2. **What** do net present value and real option value analyses imply for the success of ShadeTree Roasters' long-term decision?

3. **How** do ethical considerations appear to hurt ShadeTree Roasters' investment opportunities in the short run but help in the long run?

EMAIL MEMORANDUM

From: James Paige, President and CEO

To: Judy Collins, Chief Financial Officer

Subject: Priority strategic investment analysis

Judy—Please put our two best analysts on the central Europe project that we discussed with the board of directors. If the project makes good sense, I would like to get approval at the next board meeting. That doesn't give us a lot of time, but I think we need to move quickly. So please put the analysts to work full-time on the project. You have most of the data, but the analysts may contact me or any of the staff for more information or clarification. I do want you to closely supervise the analysis. This might be a big move for us, and we want to do it right, as usual.

Unless you see serious problems with the investment earlier, I would like to see the following deliverables and a rehearsal two weeks before the board meeting:

1. External and internal analyses

2. Competitor analysis

3. Discounted cash flow analysis of the project, to include net present value and real option value analyses.

4. Qualitative factors that might affect the success of the project

Thanks in advance. I look forward to the analyses.

James

ShadeTree Roasters, Inc., started as the entrepreneurial effort by two coffee-loving college classmates in Toronto, Canada. Today it is a successful, growing international company. The company sold its first bag of fresh-roasted, organic coffee to a small college shop in Toronto and now, 15 years later, sells organic coffees, teas, and related specialty items in 200 of its own stores located in North America and western Europe. ShadeTree Roasters competes directly with larger companies such as Starbucks and is seeking future growth opportunities that have been overlooked by its larger competitors. In particular, ShadeTree is investigating the launch of a major effort in central Europe, where most coffee and tea sales are currently to restaurants and grocery markets. This chapter describes the methods that ShadeTree Roasters and other companies use and the issues they confront when considering major decisions, such as the development of a new business venture.

Investment Decisions

Investments are major decisions that have long-term consequences beyond current consumption. For example, buying a coffee business is an investment, but buying a cup of coffee is not. Investments also include the decision by an airline to replace aging aircraft with new planes or to expand ground facilities at an existing airport. Investments also include the decision by a real estate developer to buy agricultural land and convert it to a new housing development, or the decision of a student to forgo current income to attend college full-time. All of these decisions have important long-term effects for the individuals or organizations who give up something now to obtain something better in the future.

Two effects of time on a decision and its outcomes distinguish an investment decision from the decisions considered in earlier chapters. First, making a decision commits resources for a lengthy period of time, and that commitment usually prevents taking other future opportunities. Thus, investments have an opportunity cost, which usually is represented by forgone interest or income from the precluded alternatives. Second, modeling management flexibility to modify an investment as time and information unfold can affect the desirability of alternative decisions. We will model both of these investment characteristics in this chapter.

Financial accounting, economics, and finance textbooks cover the basics of making investment decisions, also called *capital budgeting decisions,* using various techniques, such as discounted cash flow (DCF) methods. DCF methods model an investment's opportunity cost as the effect of the forgone rate of interest available from the next-best alternative investment. Appendix A to this chapter provides a basic overview of the mechanics of one DCF method, net present value (NPV) analysis, which is the DCF approach used in this chapter. Please refer to Appendix A if you want to review this material that we assume has been covered in other courses of study.

The purpose of this chapter is to describe how to model strategic investment decisions. We combine NPV analysis with options of changing decisions when possible. Applying the previous chapters' lessons of (1) building financial models and (2) making decisions using relevant information creates an approach that can be applied generally to most strategic decisions.

Strategic Investments

LO I Understand the nature of strategic investment decisions.

A **strategic investment** is a choice among alternative courses of action and the allocation of resources to those alternatives most likely to succeed after anticipating (1) changes in *natural, social, and economic conditions* and (2) *actions of competitors.* In contrast, routine decisions are choices made under continuing conditions and are unrelated to competitors' actions. ShadeTree Roasters' proposed expansion of operations to central Europe is a strategic investment because the company must consider *both changes in the emerging economy of the region* and *actions that its competitors*

Strategic Investments around the Globe

RealNetworks, Time Warner, and Benetton are examples of global companies making strategic investments to distinguish themselves from competitors. RealNetworks had invested in MusicNet, an Internet music subscription service, with Warner Music Group, EMI Recorded Music, and BMG Entertainment. However, RealNetworks also made a strategic investment in Listen.com, which is an innovative competitor that uses RealNetworks' technology. Soon RealNetworks declared MusicNet—a business in which it had been a leading investor—to be outmoded business-to-business strategy and Listen.com to be the best direct approach to consumers. RealNetworks expanded its strategic investment into the purchase of Listen.com, leaving its former partners with what it believes to be an obsolete approach to distributing music to consumers.

Media giant Time Warner led the international expansion into the Chinese cinema market by investing in a luxurious multiplex cinema in Shanghai. Time Warner's entry into the China market is a strategic investment to establish the standard for new Chinese cinemas and itself as the chief provider of international movies. Time Warner intended to leave behind other competitors such as 20th Century Fox Corp., Columbia Studios, and MGM (Metro-Goldwyn-Mayer) that had not yet expanded to this potentially huge market.

Benetton, the Italian clothier, launched a communication campaign, called "Food for Life," with the UN's World Food Program to fight global hunger. Benetton realized that investing in resources to fight a serious world problem also was a strategic investment to improve its brand image. *Sources: B. Garrity and M. Benz,* "Real's Listen Purchase Could Affect MusicNet"; *XINHUA,* "Time Warner Spearheads China's Potentially Huge Cinema Market"; *and A. Hargrave-Silk,* "Benetton Uses Ad Budget on UN Humanitarian Campaign." (Full citations to references are in the Bibliography.)

Cost Management in Practice 14.1

might take to serve the same market. On the other hand, we would not consider ShadeTree's investment in a new delivery truck used for continuing operations as a strategic investment.

If an organization has kept good records on past investment decisions, analysts might learn why some alternative investments were chosen but others were not. These lessons about the effects of uncontrollable events and past actions can be applied to future investment decisions.

ShadeTree Roasters must consider relevant future uncontrollable factors and competitors' actions because they can influence the future growth of the central European coffee and tea market and ShadeTree's market share. These factors in turn will affect ShadeTree's sales, costs, and profits. We assume that ShadeTree cannot control the total market size and market growth, but its and competitors' actions do affect ShadeTree's market share.

Uncontrollable External Factors

Making a successful investment decision depends on anticipating such factors as changes in climate, business cycles, consumers' income, tastes, and preferences, and changes in political/legal conditions. Furthermore, choosing investments includes planning for actions if these external factors turn out to be much better or worse than expected. These factors cannot be controlled by individuals, but planning allows identifying them, assessing their impacts, and developing contingency plans. Farmers, for example, decide to plant specific commodity crops such as corn or coffee after predicting favorable weather and market conditions. Many also purchase crop insurance as protection against unfavorable environmental events. They might have contingency plans, such as leasing their land or water rights to others if the weather turns unexpectedly bad. Ski resorts that invest in improvements during the summer off-season make similar decisions. Health care companies that invest in

LO 2 Identify external and internal information for strategic investments.

assisted-living care and nursing homes anticipate growing demand for these services from an aging population. ShadeTree Roasters, Inc., anticipates that demand for coffee and tea will grow in the emerging economies of central Europe. Furthermore, ShadeTree believes that its services and products will add value beyond what is currently available while still respecting local culture and traditions.[1]

Whether an individual or organization makes the right investment decisions can reflect some element of chance or luck, but consistent success usually reflects careful gathering and evaluation of relevant information. Consistent success is also often the result of preparing for unexpected external events that could be much better or worse than expected. Developing thorough and relevant information for investment decisions is also known as conducting a *due diligence* investigation. Investigating an investment with **due diligence** is exercising all reasonable care to identify potential problems and opportunities of a proposed investment. The most common sources of problems are legal and environmental liabilities that an organization might inherit unknowingly when purchasing an existing business or property. Operating in a different legal environment might affect the nature of contracts, environmental responsibilities, and employee obligations in unforeseen ways. Likewise, a proposed investment might offer unexpected benefits by complementing current operations or opening unexpected opportunities.

We now consider the types of external information that ShadeTree Roasters has gathered and evaluated to support its decision whether to expand its operations to central Europe.

Information about External Events

Decisions have to be made, but no organization or individual has a crystal ball to forecast the future business environment. The premise of cost management, indeed of all business study, is that well-planned and modeled decisions are consistently better than random choices or choices based on hunches. As discussed in earlier chapters, decisions should be based on relevant information, which is information about future costs and benefits that differ among alternatives. Broadly speaking, relevant external information includes alternative, uncontrollable, and uncertain future events and the likelihood or odds that future events will occur.[2] Cost management analysts at ShadeTree Roasters identified the sources and potential usefulness of these sources shown in Exhibit 14–1. These sources generate information about the range of possible uncontrollable events and how likely they are to occur.

Identification of Uncontrollable Future Events

Identifying possible future events, such as changes in weather or social conditions, depends on learning from past experience, understanding current trends, and anticipating future changes that depart from the past. Unless an organization is very large and operating in diverse conditions, most organizations' past financial records generally are of little use in identifying future events. Usually a company's financial records reflect one set of decisions made and only one set of uncontrollable events that occurred. If an organization has kept careful records of past expectations of possible events, the list of possibilities might be a useful starting point to generate a new list. However, analysts might rely too much on the old list and might not consider future possibilities that are more relevant. Therefore, generating a new list can be beneficial.

Organizations often use formal, group brainstorming methods (anonymous or face to face), decision-support software, or lower-tech meetings to identify the range of future events. Using a group to combine individual knowledge and critical think-

---

[1] ShadeTree Roasters also plans for competitors' actions, which is discussed later in this chapter.

[2] The formal study of making decisions with this type of information is called *statistical decision theory*. This chapter uses a simple but realistic approach to making investment decisions under uncertainty.

External Information	Organization's Financial Records	Interviews with Knowledgeable Individuals (company personnel and consultants)	Publicly Available Information
Uncontrollable future events	Past financial records have limited usefulness for predicting future events if the organization has never operated in a similar environment.	Company personnel who can think creatively might identify future events. Experienced consultants also can be excellent sources of future events.	News, government, foundation, and industry analyses can be excellent sources of future events.
Likelihood of future events' occurrence	Past financial records have limited usefulness for predicting future odds if the organization has never operated in a similar environment.	Experienced consultants and company personnel can estimate odds, but individuals are notoriously weak at this task.	News, government, foundation, and industry analyses can be excellent sources of the likeliness of future events.

Exhibit 14–1

Sources and Usefulness of External Information

ing can be even more effective than relying on a very knowledgeable individual. Organizations sometimes use skilled consultants to manage the brainstorming efforts or to augment the knowledge necessary to identify future events.

Government agencies, foundations, industry associations, and news organizations also can be valuable sources of analyses of past and possible future events. An added benefit of these analyses is that they often are free of charge and can be objective. Evaluating the accuracy and objectivity of these analyses and applying their findings, however, requires expertise that the organization might not have and might justify the use of knowledgeable consultants.

ShadeTree Roasters' managers used consulting services, external reports, and consultant-managed brainstorming sessions that identified the following possible future events relevant to the decision to invest in central European operations.

■ *Natural events.* Because ShadeTree's primary products and services are based on agricultural products, natural events, such as climate change or plant diseases, can affect the company's future operations and profitability. However, these factors affect all of the company's operations but do not affect the proposed investment relative to alternative investments in the coffee and tea business. ShadeTree is well aware of environmental change and supports research to improve the biological diversity of coffee and tea plants that might protect its future supplies. However, major climatic or biological changes could cause the company to rethink its entire business. Indeed, this chapter's approach to investment decision making could be used to completely reorient the business, but that is beyond the scope of our discussion. We assume that future natural events affect all of ShadeTree's global business equally and that the chance of a general catastrophe is small.

■ *Economic events.* Per capita income in central Europe is expected to grow at an above average rate, generating more leisure time and disposable income, which should create above average growth in demand for premium coffees and teas. The social aspects of coffee and tea drinking will continue to be important in the region. Both expected developments support ShadeTree Roasters' plan to open stores in central Europe. Coffee and tea prices fluctuate, but ShadeTree has made long-term purchase commitments with growers' cooperatives to lock in current prices. ShadeTree operates in foreign countries, and the company has made currency investments, which are a form of insurance to protect against currency fluctuations.[3] Because many central European countries have joined or soon will join the European Union, ShadeTree will conduct the new regional business in euros (€).

- *Social, political, and legal events.* Population, which drives demand, is expected to mirror the rest of Europe's relatively low rate of growth. Analysts expect the influences of western European and North American culture to grow, but strong preferences for regional drinks and ambiance also are expected. The region's political climate is expected to improve for private businesses that invest regionally and hire local employees through attractive tax incentives. Most coffees and teas are grown in developing countries with histories of political, economic, and legal instability. Instability could affect the company's supply source of green coffee and tea. To protect its sources and to meet its social responsibility goals, ShadeTree's long-term purchase agreements are with local cooperatives that foster environmentally and socially conscious agricultural and business practices (also known as *fair trade* practices). These agreements result in somewhat higher costs than those of competitors such as Starbucks, but ShadeTree expects that its business practices will resonate with Europeans' environmental and social concerns and will be a major competitive advantage for the company.

ShadeTree Roasters' analysts used the current measure of the central European nongrocery coffee and tea market size (total annual sales) of €50 million from industry and governmental analyses. The analysts applied all of the environmental information to estimate the annual sales growth of coffee and tea. Although each environmental event can have an independent effect on demand and could be considered separately, for simplicity we consider only the aggregate impact of future events on estimates of central Europe's annual market growth. ShadeTree Roasters' analysts provided three estimates of future coffee and tea market annual growth as follows:

Central Europe Coffee and Tea Estimates	Possible Annual Market Growth Estimates (percent)
High estimate	8%
Medium estimate	4
Low estimate	2

Likelihood of the Occurrence of Future Events

A central question confronting investment decision makers is: How likely are the relevant future events? Although decision making should focus on the most likely events, decisions also should consider less likely but catastrophic events. The key to using this type of information is not to overweight unlikely events. For example, some people fear commercial flying and drive instead, although the odds of being in an auto accident far exceed the odds of being in a commercial airplane crash. Good reasons might exist to drive rather than fly in certain cases, but fear of flying commercially is not justified by experience.

Three approaches to modeling the effects of likely future events include sensitivity analysis, scenario analysis, and expected value analysis.

- *Sensitivity analysis* forecasts the effects of a likely change in *each* future, relevant event on investment outcomes. Factors that have the most potential impact on outcomes deserve the most attention. If one or more uncontrollable factors seem likely to cause disastrous outcomes, managers might reject the investment.
- *Scenario analysis* forecasts the effects of likely *combinations* of future events on investment outcomes. Commonly considered scenarios include the most likely, best-, and worst-case scenarios. If the most likely case scenario is favorable and

---

[3] These investments are called *hedges*.

if the worst-case scenario is neither a disaster nor judged to be very likely, managers probably would approve the investment.

■ **Expected value analysis** summarizes the combined effects of relevant future events on decision outcomes, weighted by the probabilities or odds that the events will occur. Both sensitivity and scenario analyses are very popular approaches to modeling future events for investment decisions, particularly when explicit odds of future events cannot be estimated.

Because Chapter 12 covers sensitivity and scenario analyses in detail, this chapter explains and applies only expected value analysis to modeling future events relevant to strategic investment decisions. All three analyses can be applied to these decisions.

Expected Value Analysis

Expected value analysis depends on measures of the probability or odds of the actual occurrence of each relevant future event. Two general approaches exist to measure probabilities or odds: (1) assess the degree of belief (or confidence) about future events and (2) count the historical frequency (or distribution) of occurrence of similar past events.[4] Measuring probabilities or odds by assessing degree of belief is difficult and subjective if future events are unrelated to past events. For example, a stockbroker might believe that the S&P 500 index will rise tomorrow, and if asked, she might say that she is 80 percent certain that the index will rise. However, another stockbroker might be 80 percent certain that the index will drop tomorrow. You might rely on one stockbroker's degree of belief if you are confident that he or she has unique information or analysis skills; otherwise, their assessments are highly subjective.

If the occurrence of past events is relevant, one could feel comfortable using historical frequencies to predict future events. For example, the weather forecast of a 70 percent chance of rain tomorrow means that, when today's weather conditions have been observed in the past, rain occurred 70 percent of the time the next day. Although rain is not certain tomorrow, that forecast might justifiably cause a farmer to wait a few days before cutting a hayfield and risk a ruined crop by cutting just before a rainstorm.

ShadeTree Roasters' analysts believe that the probabilities of future annual market growth can be predicted from past experience in the region. The analysts have used government, industry, and their own analyses to estimate the probabilities of market growth as follows:

Relevant Future Event	Probability of Occurrence
Annual market growth = 8%	30%
Annual market growth = 4	40
Annual market growth = 2	30
Total probability	100%

Observe that the probabilities associated with the annual market growth estimates sum to 100 percent because with certainty some rate of growth will occur and because for simplicity these are assumed to be the only possible outcomes.[5]

The **expected value** of a future event is the measure of each possible outcome weighted or multiplied by its probability of occurrence. The expected value of annual market growth is computed as:

$$\text{Expected market growth} = 8\% \times .30 + 4\% \times .40 + 2\% \times .30$$
$$\text{E[market growth]} = 2.4\% + 1.6\% + .6\% = \underline{4.6\%}$$

---

[4] Degree of belief can be related to historical frequency, as in the application of Bayes' Theorem. See a statistics text for an explanation of Bayes' Theorem.

[5] Certainly, more future events are relevant to the decision, but the complication of modeling additional events is not necessary to demonstrate the lessons of the chapter. Modeling more events means the investment models must be expanded. More complicated methods also might use probability distributions or Monte Carlo simulations of possible market growth outcomes.

You're the Decision Maker 14.1

Sensitivity of Expected Value Analysis

The expected market growth of 4.6 percent is a critical assumption or parameter of ShadeTree's expansion decision.

a. Compute the expected market growth rate with the following sets of possible growth rates and probabilities.

    1. Possible growth rates = 10%, 5%, −2%; probabilities = .4, .3, .3

    2. Possible growth rates = 8%, 4%, 2%; probabilities = .2, .6, .2

    3. Possible growth rates = 10%, 5%, −2%; probabilities = .2, .2, .6

b. Explain how the different expected market growth rates might affect the investment decision.

(Solutions begin on page 581.)

It is possible but not likely that the actual value of the future annual growth will be precisely 4.6 percent. However, the expected value of market growth summarizes what is known about possible values and their likelihood of occurrence. ShadeTree Roasters can use the expected value of 4.6 percent market growth with other internal information to compute the NPV of the proposed investment in central Europe, as we demonstrate after discussing the gathering of internal information.

Internal Information

A major stage of information gathering is to predict the effects of each uncontrollable future event on planned operations and activities and on expected costs and benefits. Exhibit 14–2 displays common sources of internal investment information. An organization's internal financial records can be sources of relevant operating activities, costs, and cost savings that might be applied to the proposed investment. For example, the results of statistical analyses of past costs might be "engineered" for differences expected with the proposed investment activities (see Chapter 11). Activity-based costing information (see Chapters 4 and 5) can be particularly useful for planning activities and costs. If the proposed investment is unlike past operations, an organization can use consultants and publicly available information to identify operating activities and activity costs. Consultants can be quite useful if they have experience with other organizations that have operated under similar conditions. Public information about a region's economy and infrastructure also can be useful for forecasting activities and costs. Company personnel might be able to apply tools of engineering analysis (see Chapter 11) to create new processes, activities, and costs required by the proposed investment.

Evaluating an investment involves generating the following internal information forecasts:

- The resources and activities necessary to operate the investment for all levels of uncertain future events over the life of the investment: Generally the people, working capital, equipment, and facilities vary with different event outcomes. Expected annual and total sales activities often indicate the scale and breadth of operations that must be planned for the life of the investment.

- The resources necessary to acquire the investment: generally the purchase price and subsequent installment payments, if any.

- The revenues, expenses, and net cash flows associated with annual sales and related production activities.

- The expected NPV of the investment.

We now illustrate these uses of internal information by examining ShadeTree's analysis of its proposed investment in new operations in central Europe.

Exhibit 14–2

Sources and Usefulness of
Internal Information

Internal Information	Organization's Financial Records	Interviews with Knowledgeable Individuals (company personnel and consultants)	Publicly Available Information
Future events affect investment costs and benefits.	Account or regression analysis of financial records might be useful to predict costs or benefits if expected future activities are similar to recent experience.	Consultants can bring knowledge of other organizations' experiences with similar events. Company personnel can apply others' experiences and perform engineering analysis to predict costs and benefits.	Descriptions of other organizations' experiences with similar events can be helpful for predicting future costs and benefits.

Bundling Assets

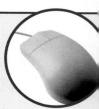

Research Insight 14.1

The well-known producer of construction equipment, Caterpillar, Inc., found that it needed to change its investment analysis procedures when it changed to high-technology manufacturing methods. Historically, the company made incremental investments in its old mass production processes. However, Caterpillar invested in high-technology production more efficiently when it made "bundles" of related investments simultaneously instead of one at a time.

Investing in bundles of assets allowed managers to think about how assets created synergies. Sometimes, an investment that appeared only marginally profitable made better sense as part of a bundle of assets. For example, a machine that reduced labor cost might have a negative net present value when examined by itself as a labor-saving device. When combined with other assets that together sped up the production process, however, the whole bundle had a higher positive net present value than without the labor-saving asset.

This approach of investing in bundles of assets is consistent with economic theory, which argues that the entire set of complementary assets is necessary to achieve economic efficiency. Lower efficiency results if an organization leaves out one or more apparently inefficient assets from the bundle. All are needed for efficient operations. This might explain why reports of widespread adoptions of manufacturing innovations, such as JIT (see Chapter 7), have not been matched by increases in profitability. Perhaps a set of investments is required, but some firms have attempted to economize by leaving out one or more of the set. *Sources: P. Miller and T. O'Leary, "Capital Budgeting Practices and Complementarity Relations in the Transition to Modern Manufacturing: A Field-Based Analysis"; and P. Milgrom and J. Roberts, "Complementarities and Fit: Strategies, Structure and Organizational Change in Manufacturing."*

Forecasts of ShadeTree's Investment Information

The information needed to evaluate ShadeTree's proposed investment is shown in Exhibit 14–3. The information is divided into internal and external information categories. Most internal information items, such as the gross margin ratio of 65 percent in cell C8, are represented by only one estimate. This does not mean that ShadeTree's analysts know these items with certainty, which, of course, they cannot. Analysts can use expected values or sensitivity and scenario analyses (see Chapter 12) to measure the sensitivity of the predicted outcomes to changes in these figures. The information in Exhibit 14–3 is a simple set of internal data, but it is sufficient to generate the analyses of this chapter. Undoubtedly, ShadeTree's analysts would have prepared detailed estimates of the components and likely values of all of the information items, which could change over the investment's five-year horizon. They could include all of these details in the financial model of the investment decision, but this is unnecessarily complex for our purposes.

One information item deserves more discussion. The expected market share of 20 percent in cell C11 of Exhibit 14–3 is, of course, an estimate like the others and might turn out to be different than expected. The specific point we want to make now

LO 3 Learn to use forecasts of quantitative and qualitative effects of strategic investments in net present value analysis.

Exhibit 14–3   ShadeTree Roasters' Investment Information

	A	B	C	D	E	F	G	H
4		**Internal Information**			**External Information**			
5		Tax rate	40%		Annual market growth	Possible values	Probability	Expected value
6		Required rate of return	8%		Market growth - high	8%	30%	
7		Decision horizon	5	years	Market growth - middle	4%	40%	4.6%
8		Gross margin ratio	65%		Market growth - low	2%	30%	
9		SG&A costs - cash (000)	€ 5,000	per year			100%	
10		Initial investment - cash (000)	€ 5,500		Initial market size (annual sales)	€ 50,000	,000	
11		Market share - with no major competitor	20%		Market share - with major competitor	10%		
12					Probability of a major competitor	40%		

Input / Now-No Comp / Now-Comp / Wait-No Comp / Wait-C

is that this is an estimate of market share *without a major competitor.* What if a major competitor, such as Starbucks, also decides to enter this new market? ShadeTree's analysts expect that this would cause a large reduction in ShadeTree's market share (see cell F11). We will consider the impacts of this possibility on both expected cash flows and decision making after illustrating the basic investment decision model, which is shown in Exhibit 14–4.

If DCF methods are new to you or are not fresh in your mind, this would be a good time to turn to Appendix A to this chapter. Mark this place and return to it after your study and review of basic DCF methods.

The analysis in Exhibit 14–4 combines the information in Exhibit 14–3 to produce the project's estimated annual cash flows, which are shown in row 15, for each year of the investment's life.[6] For example, multiplying 1 plus the expected rate of market growth (1.046) by the market size for year 0 in B2 (€50 million in the year before operations begin) yields a new estimate of market size for year 1 in the amount of €52.3 million (C2). The model computes each succeeding year's market size similarly from the preceding year. Multiplying each year's market size in row 2 by ShadeTree's expected market share (20 percent, row 3) generates that year's estimate of sales revenues in row 4. Multiplying sales revenue by 1 minus the gross margin ratio (1 − .65 = .35) yields the cost of goods sold (row 5), and subtraction gives annual gross margin (row 6). Committed costs (beginning in row 7) include the investment outlay in year 0 of €5.5 million (B8), which ShadeTree will pay in cash before operations begin. This investment cost, which includes costs of leases, fixtures, and related store facilities, will be amortized, straight-line, over the investment life (row 8). Also subtracting sales, general, and administrative costs (SG&A in row 9) generates operating income before tax (row 11). Subtracting taxes at 40 percent (row 12) results in operating income after tax (row 13).

DCF methods use estimates of cash flow, not accounting income, because cash flow can be used for consumption or reinvestment in other projects, but accounting income itself cannot.[7] The analysis in Exhibit 14–4 assumes that all but one income

---

[6] Note that Exhibit 14–4 shows euro amounts in thousands for clarity of presentation. Be sure to work through and understand this exhibit because all of this chapter's investment models are similar.

[7] Recall that accounting income is a measure of financial performance that often deviates from cash flow.

Exhibit 14–4   Forecasted Investment Cash Flows and Net Present Value—No Major Competitor

Microsoft Excel - ShadeTree.xls

File Edit View Insert Format Tools Data Window Help Acrobat

B16 ▼ ƒx =NPV(Input!C6,C15:G15)+B15

	A	B	C	D	E	F	G
1	ShadeTree Roasters Expansion - no competitior, invest now	Year 0	Year 1	Year 2	Year 3	Year 4	Year 5
2	Expected market size (thousands)	€ 50,000	€ 52,300	€ 54,706	€ 57,222	€ 59,854	€ 62,608
3	Market share		20%	20%	20%	20%	20%
4	Sales		€ 10,460	€ 10,941	€ 11,444	€ 11,971	€ 12,522
5	Cost of goods sold		3,661	3,829	4,006	4,190	4,383
6	Gross margin		6,799	7,112	7,439	7,781	8,139
7	Committed costs						
8	Investment (cash/non-cash)	(5,500)	1,100	1,100	1,100	1,100	1,100
9	SG&A - cash		5,000	5,000	5,000	5,000	5,000
10	Total committed costs		6,100	6,100	6,100	6,100	6,100
11	Operating income before tax		699	1,012	1,339	1,681	2,039
12	Tax (savings)		280	405	536	672	816
13	Operating income after tax		419	607	803	1,009	1,223
14	Add-back non-cash expenses		1,100	1,100	1,100	1,100	1,100
15	Annual cash flows	(€ 5,500)	€ 1,519	€ 1,707	€ 1,903	€ 2,109	€ 2,323
16	Expected NPV - yrs 1-5, no competitor	€ 2,012					

⏮ ◀ ▶ ⏭ \ Input \ **Now-No Comp** / Now-Comp / Wait-No Comp / Wait-Comp / blank /

Ready   NUM

item is a cash flow in each year. The noncash item is the amortization expense of the investment cost €1.1 million per year (row 8). This expense has understated annual cash flow and is added back to operating income after tax (row 14) to measure expected annual cash flows (row 15). The model's final step is to discount the future cash flows and compute the investment's expected net present value (NPV), which is calculated in cell B16.[8] The positive NPV of €2,012,000 indicates that the proposed investment is expected to be more profitable than required by ShadeTree's required rate of return of 8 percent.

Sensitivity and Scenario Analyses

Quite a number of assumptions or model parameters determine the positive NPV of €2,012,000 in Exhibit 14–4. Among these parameters are the size of the market in year 0, the market growth rate, and ShadeTree's market share.

a. Explain how these parameters affect expected revenues (change each separately and put others at the base levels from the text).

b. Compute year 1's gross margin if the market size is €60 million or €40 million.

c. Compute year 1's gross margin if the market growth rate is 2 percent or 6 percent.

d. Compute year 1's gross margin if ShadeTree's market share is 30 percent or 15 percent.

e. The most likely scenario uses the parameters in Exhibit 14–3. Compute year 1's gross margin under best-case and worst-case scenarios using the parameters in requirements (b)–(d).

(Solutions begin on page 581.)

You're the Decision Maker 14.2

---

[8] The spreadsheet model uses the NPV function, which assumes that cash flows occur at the end of each period. The best way to learn about functions is to use the "insert-function" from the menu bar, select the function, and follow the function wizard. See Appendix A to this chapter to review the manual calculation of net present value.

Cost Management in Practice 14.2

Nonfinancial Benefits of Investing in Improved Technology at Ford

Analyses of investments in improved technology frequently do not show positive net values. Technological innovations usually have high initial cost and a long time period before they generate sizable cash inflows. We observed this phenomenon during interviews at Ford Motor Company.

For example, Ford was considering investing in flexible, computerized equipment that would revolutionize one plant's production processes. The new equipment would allow the company to change quickly from making one part to another, reduce batch-level costs, reduce inventory levels, reduce production downtime, and free capacity for expansion. In addition to these explicit benefits, the engineers and production managers who supported the project saw it as a way to learn more about flexible manufacturing, which could provide major benefits to the rest of the company in the future. These benefits were not quantifiable, however, so some analysts in the company argued against giving them explicit weight in the DCF analysis.

Ford initially rejected the project based on the DCF analysis. The CEO of the company was convinced, however, that the project would have additional benefits beyond currently measurable cash flows. He believed that the project was justified because it would help the company improve its production methods. Consequently, Ford made the investment despite its measured negative NPV. All reports indicate that the investment has delivered both the explicit cash flows and improvements to other production processes. *Source:* An author's interview with executives and staff at Ford Motor Company.

If qualitative aspects of the investment and competitors' actions were not concerns, ShadeTree's managers probably would approve the investment. Chapter 13 explained how qualitative aspects of decisions can outweigh the quantitative or financial aspects if, for example, the investment was expected to have adverse impacts on the organization's employees, customers, reputation, nonfinancial goals, or ability to operate in a legal or socially responsible way. Alternatively, beneficial qualitative outcomes might weigh in favor of an investment that does not meet strict DCF criteria.

Future Actions of Competitors

LO 4 Model the impacts of competitors' actions.

How would major competitors' decisions affect the expected values of investments? Few decisions depend only on unknown future uncontrollable events, such as weather or political change. The decisions of competitors in the local or global economy also can affect many investment decisions and outcomes. ShadeTree Roasters is hoping that major competitors either will not identify the same market opportunity in central Europe or will not meet emerging market demand effectively. We now add the complexity of a major competitor to the effects of previously discussed internal and external information.

The investment information in Exhibit 14–3 includes an estimate of ShadeTree's market share (10 percent, cell F11) should a major competitor, such as Starbucks, enter the market effectively. Because success attracts competition, ShadeTree analysts estimate a 40 percent probability (cell F12 of Exhibit 14–3) that a major competitor will enter the market after observing ShadeTree's start-up operations in year 0. The impacts of the competitive entry could be felt as soon as year 2, and ShadeTree's analysts expect its market share to drop from 20 to 10 percent. ShadeTree's analysts modified the investment model to reflect the impacts of a major competitor. The modified model is shown in Exhibit 14–5.

The only data input difference between the models in Exhibit 14–4 (without a major competitor) and Exhibit 14–5 (with a major competitor) is ShadeTree's expected market share, which is the 10 percent figure repeated in cells D3–G3. This drop in market share dramatically changes the company's expected sales revenues, operating income, and cash flows. The summary measure of the investment's value, the NPV in cell B16, is now a large negative number (€4,966,000). This negative NPV indicates that the expansion would be a financial disaster for ShadeTree if a major competitor enters the market a year later and has the expected effect on market share. If it proceeded and a major competitor entered, the company would waste most of its €5.5 million investment.

Exhibit 14–5   Forecasted Investment Cash Flows and Net Present Value with a Major Competitor

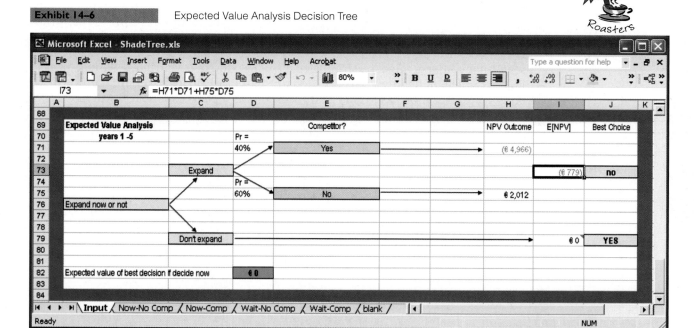

Microsoft Excel - ShadeTree.xls

B16   =NPV(Input!C6,C15:G15)+B15

	A	B	C	D	E	F	G
1	ShadeTree Roasters Expansion - with competitior, invest now	Year 0	Year 1	Year 2	Year 3	Year 4	Year 5
2	Expected market size (thousands)	€ 50,000	€ 52,300	€ 54,706	€ 57,222	€ 59,854	€ 62,608
3	Market share		20%	10%	10%	10%	10%
4	Sales		€ 10,460	€ 5,471	€ 5,722	€ 5,985	€ 6,261
5	Cost of goods sold		3,661	1,915	2,003	2,095	2,191
6	Gross margin		6,799	3,556	3,719	3,891	4,070
7	Committed costs						
8	Investment (cash/non-cash)	(5,500)	1,100	1,100	1,100	1,100	1,100
9	SG&A - cash		5,000	5,000	5,000	5,000	5,000
10	Total committed costs		6,100	6,100	6,100	6,100	6,100
11	Operating income before tax		699	(2,544)	(2,381)	(2,209)	(2,030)
12	Tax (savings)		280	(1,018)	(952)	(884)	(812)
13	Operating income after tax		419	(1,526)	(1,428)	(1,326)	(1,218)
14	Add-back non-cash expenses		1,100	1,100	1,100	1,100	1,100
15	Annual cash flows	(€ 5,500)	€ 1,519	(€ 426)	(€ 328)	(€ 226)	(€ 118)
16	NPV - yrs 1-5, with competitor	(€ 4,966)					

Input / Now-No Comp \ **Now-Comp** / Wait-No Comp / Wait-Comp / blank /

Exhibit 14–6   Expected Value Analysis Decision Tree

Microsoft Excel - ShadeTree.xls

I73   =H71*D71+H75*D75

	B	C	D	E	F	G	H	I	J
68									
69	**Expected Value Analysis**			Competitor?			NPV Outcome	E[NPV]	Best Choice
70	years 1 -5		Pr =						
71			40%	Yes			(€ 4,966)		
72									
73		Expand						(€ 779)	no
74			Pr =						
75			60%	No			€ 2,012		
76	Expand now or not								
77									
78									
79		Don't expand						€ 0	YES
80									
81									
82	Expected value of best decision if decide now		€ 0						
83									
84									

Input / Now-No Comp / Now-Comp / Wait-No Comp / Wait-Comp / blank /

However, this financial disaster is not a certainty. ShadeTree's analysts estimate a 40 percent chance that this outcome will occur. Expected value analysis weighs each expected outcome by its probability of occurrence to obtain the expected NPV of the proposed investment. Exhibit 14–6 presents the expected value analysis decision tree (see Chapter 13). The expected NPV or E[NPV] of the expansion decision is negative (€779,000) as shown in cell I73 and here:

$$E[NPV] = .4 \times (4,996,000) + .6 \times 2,012,000 = (€779,000)$$

Expected value analysis shows emphatically that the best decision is not to expand to central Europe because the odds are that it will be a losing venture. This analysis shows that a better decision is to invest the company's capital in other projects that earn at least the required rate of return (and earn a NPV of €0; see cell D82). But is this the right decision?

Real Option Value Analysis

LO 5 Know when and how to apply real option analysis to evaluate strategic investments.

Under common investment conditions, the preceding NPV analysis is incorrect. First, even if ShadeTree cannot recover its investment (a sunk cost), terminating the project after one year would be less costly than continuing to operate with the next four years of negative cash flows. In other words, if ShadeTree has the option of quitting at no cost after a competitor enters, the expected NPV of the project is larger because the company can avoid four years of negative cash flows. The calculation of the revised NPV, which uses only the year 0 and year 1 cash flows from Exhibit 14–5 (cells B15 and C15), is as follows:

Investment Event	NPV	Probability	Weighted Value
Expand without a major competitor	= €2,012,000	.60	€ 1,207,200
Expand with a competitor, but terminate after 1 year *(.9259 is the one-year present value factor for a rate of 8%)*	= (€5,500,000) + €1,519,000 × .9259 = (€4,093,558)	.40	€(1,637,423)
Total expected NPV			€ (430,223)

Although we will show that even this analysis is simplified, the new analysis begins to incorporate management's flexibility to terminate the project. This is an important, relatively new way of describing investments that can completely reverse this type of decision. The negative NPV apparently signals to reject the investment, but ShadeTree should make no decision until it includes more information about the company's flexibility. This flexible approach to investment analysis is called **real option value (ROV) analysis.** It combines analyses of decision trees, expected values, and NPV to describe investments as a series of options to change investments. As we have seen, an investment might be terminated, but it also might be expanded, shrunk, phased in, redesigned, or deferred. The decision tree part of ROV analysis describes the flexibility an organization has to change its decisions as it gains experience with the invest-

Research Insight 14.2

Investing in High Technology

Academics and consultants have criticized traditional expected NPV analysis for high-technology investments for years because analysts tend to use:

- Discount rates that are too high and overstate the risk of the investment.
- Time horizons that are too short to capture long-term benefits of the technology.
- Only easily quantified costs and benefits that ignore the impacts on other operations and customers from improvements in quality, cycle time, and flexibility to meet customers' needs.
- NPV models that do not reflect management flexibility as well as ROV analysis does.

Researchers recommend using ROV analysis for investments in such diverse fields as biotechnology, information technology, and manufacturing flexibility. For example, Jens Bengtsson has classified numerous applications of ROV analysis to flexibility of machines, processes, internal logistics, plants, and products themselves. Because technology changes rapidly and is highly uncertain, traditional NPV analysis might lead to rejection of many technology investments. However, ROV analysis forces analysts to model how the organization might respond to changes. Modeling this flexibility can lead to the adoption of more technology investments, but perhaps in different forms rather than the "all-or-nothing" investments characterized by NPV analysis. Merck/Schering-Plough and Matsushita Electronics are among the many firms that use real option value analysis of investments. *Sources: R. Kaplan and A. Atkinson, Advanced Management Accounting, Chapter 12; and J. Bengtsson, "Manufacturing Flexibility and Real Options: A Review"; N. Nichols, "Scientific Management at Merck: An Interview with CFO Judy Lewent"; and N. Takezawa, "A Real Option Valuation of Delivery Time Uncertainty".*

ment. ROV analysis investigates impacts of decisions to go one way or another on a decision tree. If ShadeTree could terminate the expansion once it learned that Starbucks had entered the market and cut its market share in half, shouldn't ShadeTree build that flexibility into its analysis? We now turn to modeling that flexibility.

Value of Deferring Irreversible Decisions

We now turn to modeling the flexibility to defer a decision, a condition that can make the usual expected NPV analysis incorrect. Sometimes acting quickly can prevent competitors from dominating a market. However, waiting to gather more information about the investment or uncontrollable events might identify new opportunities to take or problems to avoid. For example, assume that by waiting a year, ShadeTree Roasters could learn whether its nemesis, Starbucks, will or will not decide to serve the central European market.

The first step of ROV analysis is to describe the proposed investment alternatives with decision trees. We consider two alternatives: (1) defer expansion for one year or (2) expand now. Exhibit 14–7 displays the decision tree for alternative 1: wait one year. As shown in column C, the first decision is to defer the expansion decision. ShadeTree Roasters will wait a year to learn whether Starbucks will enter the central European market. If Starbucks does not enter the market then, ShadeTree analysts believe that it will not do so in the foreseeable future.

By waiting a year, ShadeTree can convert the 40 percent probability that Starbucks will enter the market into a 100 percent probability of having a major competitor or not. Although we know from the previous analysis that expansion facing a major competitor likely would be a disaster, the decision tree includes space for the NPV outcome of such an expansion (cell H6) because in general analysts want to compute all relevant outcomes. Cells H8 and H12 have zero NPV values to show that analysts assume the decision not to expand will result in earning the required rate of return.

Completion of this part of the ROV analysis entails estimating the NPV values of the decision to invest with or without a major competitor (cells H8 and H12). Column I is set up to choose the best decision from each set of outcomes, with or without a major competitor. Finally, cell E14 computes the expected value of the decision to wait one year, as will be shown. Exhibits 14–8 (with a competitor) and 14–9 (without a competitor) present the NPV computations that will be placed in

Exhibit 14–7	Real Option Value Decision Tree—Defer Decision One Year

Microsoft Excel - ShadeTree.xls

File   Edit   View   Insert   Format   Tools   Data   Window   Help   Acrobat

J17

	A	B	C	D	E	F	G	H	I	J	K
2											
3											
4		**Real Option Analysis**	Outcome			Competitor?		Expand?	NPV Outcome	Best Choice	
5		**Wait one year**									
6				Pr =				Expand	?	?	
7				40%		Yes					
8								Don't expand	€ 0	?	
9			Defer decision								
10				Pr =				Expand	?	?	
11				60%		No					
12								Don't expand	€ 0	?	
13											
14		Expected value of best decision if wait one year			?						
15											
16											

Input / Now-No Comp / Now-Comp / Wait-No Comp / Wait-Comp \ blank /

Ready

Exhibit 14–8 Real Option Value Analysis—Wait One Year, with a Major Competitor

Microsoft Excel - ShadeTree.xls

File Edit View Insert Format Tools Data Window Help Acrobat

B16   =NPV(Input!C6,C15:H15)

	A	B	C	D	E	F	G	H
1	ShadeTree Roasters Expansion – with competitor, wait one year	Year 0	Year 1	Year 2	Year 3	Year 4	Year 5	Year 6
2	Market size (thousands)	€ 50,000	€ 52,300	€ 54,706	€ 57,222	€ 59,854	€ 62,608	€ 65,488
3	Market share			20%	10%	10%	10%	10%
4	Sales			€ 10,941	€ 5,722	€ 5,985	€ 6,261	€ 6,549
5	Cost of goods sold			3,829	2,003	2,095	2,191	2,292
6	Gross margin			7,112	3,719	3,891	4,070	4,257
7	Committed costs							
8	Investment (cash/non-cash)		(5,500)	1,100	1,100	1,100	1,100	1,100
9	SG&A - cash			5,000	5,000	5,000	5,000	5,000
10	Total committed costs			6,100	6,100	6,100	6,100	6,100
11	Operating income before tax			1,012	(2,381)	(2,209)	(2,030)	(1,843)
12	Tax (savings)			405	(952)	(884)	(812)	(737)
13	Operating income after tax			607	(1,428)	(1,326)	(1,218)	(1,106)
14	Add-back non-cash expenses			1,100	1,100	1,100	1,100	1,100
15	Annual cash flows		(€ 5,500)	€ 1,707	(€ 328)	(€ 226)	(€ 118)	(€ 6)
16	NPV - yrs 1-6, competitor, wait	(€ 4,140)						

Input / Now-No Comp / Now-Comp / Wait-No Comp / **Wait-Comp** / blank /

Ready   NUM

Exhibit 14–9 Real Option Value Analysis—Wait One Year, without a Major Competitor

Microsoft Excel - ShadeTree.xls

File Edit View Insert Format Tools Data Window Help Acrobat

B16   =NPV(Input!C6,C15:H15)

	A	B	C	D	E	F	G	H
1	ShadeTree Roasters Expansion – no competitor, wait one year	Year 0	Year 1	Year 2	Year 3	Year 4	Year 5	Year 6
2	Expected market size (thousands)	€ 50,000	€ 52,300	€ 54,706	€ 57,222	€ 59,854	€ 62,608	€ 65,488
3	Market share			20%	20%	20%	20%	20%
4	Sales			€ 10,941	€ 11,444	€ 11,971	€ 12,522	€ 13,098
5	Cost of goods sold			3,829	4,006	4,190	4,383	4,584
6	Gross margin			7,112	7,439	7,781	8,139	8,513
7	Committed costs							
8	Investment (cash/non-cash)		(5,500)	1,100	1,100	1,100	1,100	1,100
9	SG&A - cash			5,000	5,000	5,000	5,000	5,000
10	Total committed costs			6,100	6,100	6,100	6,100	6,100
11	Operating income before tax			1,012	1,339	1,681	2,039	2,413
12	Tax (savings)			405	536	672	816	965
13	Operating income after tax			607	803	1,009	1,223	1,448
14	Add-back non-cash expenses			1,100	1,100	1,100	1,100	1,100
15	Annual cash flows		(€ 5,500)	€ 1,707	€ 1,903	€ 2,109	€ 2,323	€ 2,548
16	NPV - yrs 1-6, no competitor, wait	€ 2,619						

Input / Now-No Comp / Now-Comp / **Wait-No Comp** / Wait-Comp / blank /

Ready   NUM

Exhibit 14–7's decision tree. There is one difference between these computations and the NPV calculation in Exhibits 14–4 and 14–5. The timing of the investment and operations has been deferred one year to years 2 to 6. Note that the analyses assume that the market will grow as expected from year 0, as before.

ShadeTree would not expand after learning of a major competitor because the NPV of expansion would be negative (€4,140,000) (see cell B16 of Exhibit 14–8) if that event occurs. The company will reinvest elsewhere and earn at least the required rate of return, which generates €0 NPV. On the other hand, ShadeTree will expand without a major competitor because the NPV would be positive, €2,619,000 (see cell B16 of Exhibit 14–9).

Exhibit 14–10 presents the completed decision tree for this part of the analysis. The decision tree shows that the best choices are not to expand if a major competitor enters the market (NPV = €0, cell H22) and to expand if a major competitor does not enter (NPV = €2,619,000, cell H24). The probability of a major competitor is 40 percent and that no major competitor will materialize is 60 percent. The expected NPV of the decision to wait one year (cell D28) is computed as follows from the best option choices:

$$\text{E[NPV, defer decision]} = €0 \times .40 + 2{,}619{,}000 \times .60 = \underline{€1{,}571{,}000}$$

The expected NPV of deferring the decision for one year cannot be compared directly with the previous analysis of investing now because both sets of analyses should cover the same time period, years 1 to 6. This is particularly important in this situation because the assumption of continued market growth drives the expected profitability of the investment. It is a simple matter to extend the previous analyses to a sixth year (see Appendix B of this chapter for the spreadsheets for the decision to invest now over six years). Exhibit 14–11 presents the decision tree for the alternative of investing now with the results of extending operations and the analysis to a sixth year. This analysis assumes that ShadeTree could extend its operations for an additional year for an additional annual committed cost as in previous years. However, this committed cost in the sixth year is treated as a cash outlay and is not added back to operating income after tax. The company could and perhaps should model other possibilities for year 6.

The NPV outcomes in cells H34 and H36 of Exhibit 14–11 show that the entry of a competitor would be a financial disaster (as before) even if the company can terminate the operations after a year. If a competitor entered, ShadeTree's best decision would be to terminate the operation with a negative expected NPV of (€4,093,000) (cell H36). Without a major competitor, ShadeTree expects a positive NPV of €2,925,000 (cell H38) from continuing operations and would not consider terminating the project (cell H40). Extending the analysis to six years makes the investment favorable, with an overall expected NPV of €118,000 (cell D45). The expected NPV

Exhibit 14–10	Real Option Value Decision Tree—Defer Decision One Year, with Calculations

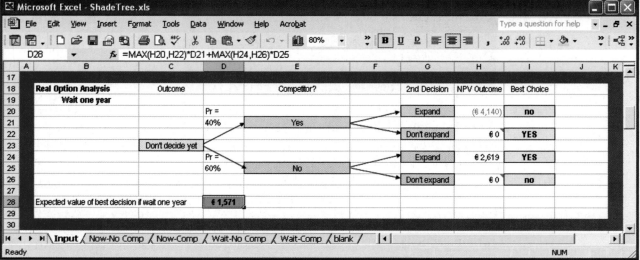

Exhibit 14–11   Real Option Value Decision Tree—Decide Now, Years 1–6

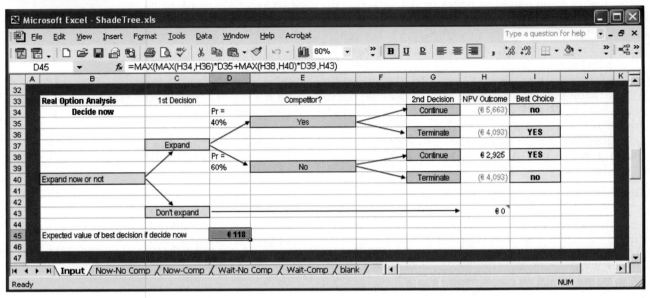

of the decision to expand now is computed as follows from the best option choices of this alternative:

$$\text{E[NPV, expand now]} = (€4{,}093{,}000) \times .40 + 2{,}925{,}000 \times .60 = \underline{€118{,}000}$$

This improvement in expected NPV from the first analysis in Exhibit 14–6 is the direct result of the assumed continued market growth through year 6, which makes the effects of competition less severe and the effects of lack of competition more favorable. This analysis indicates that the company could invest now profitably, but that would be wrong because the better option is to wait and gather more information.

Value of the Option to Wait

The option to develop real estate can have significant value.

The **real option value** of an investment is the difference between the expected NPV of one option form of the investment and the next best option. In this investment situation and others, when the investment is irreversible and relevant information can be obtained over time, deferring a decision can be more valuable than acting immediately. As the previous analyses have shown, ShadeTree's investment is more valuable if it can wait for a year rather than investing now. The real option value of waiting can be computed by comparing the NPV values of the decisions to defer or invest now.

$$\text{E[value of waiting]} = \text{E[NPV, wait from Exhibit 14–10]} - \text{E[NPV, invest now, from Exhibit 14–11]}$$
$$\text{E[value of waiting]} = €1{,}571{,}000 - €118{,}000 = \underline{€1{,}454{,}000}$$

In other words, if ShadeTree Roasters can be assured that it will learn about its competitors' actions in the next year, the company should defer its investment decision.

Apply Real Option Value Analysis

You're the Decision Maker 14.3

a. Why did ShadeTree's analysts extend the ROV analysis without a major competitor to six years? Is this a reasonable approach to the analysis? Why or why not?

b. Compute expected NPV values with the following alternative investment model outcomes. (*Hint:* Draw decision trees similar to those in Exhibits 14–10 and 14–11).

    1. Defer the decision to invest one year: NPV[with competitor] = (€3,000,000) ; NPV[no competitor] = €6,000,000

    2. Invest now: NPV[with competitor, continue] = (€2,800,000); NPV[with competitor, terminate after one year] = (€500,000); NPV[no competitor] = €6,500,000

    3. Compute the real option value of waiting.

    4. What does the computation in part (3) indicate is the best investment strategy?

(Solutions begin on page 582.)

The decisions to reject the investment or invest now with a six-year horizon are incorrect. ROV analysis shows in this case that the best decision is to defer the decision and learn more about its competitors' future actions.

Legal and Ethical Issues in Strategic Investment Analysis

One meaning of the real option value computation is that ShadeTree Roasters would be willing to pay up to the amount of €1,454,000 to secure its option to invest in the central European market one year later. By waiting a year, ShadeTree can learn about its competitors' actions and avoid head-to-head competition, which the company expects to lose. Perhaps ShadeTree might consider spending up to this amount to guarantee its right to 20 percent of the market. This could be done legally by setting up a joint venture with an existing company or illegally by paying bribes. Alternatively, the company could purchase additional market and industry analyses that might predict its competitors' future actions more precisely, or it could conduct questionable or illegal industrial espionage. With large money amounts at risk and the possibility of financial (or personal career) disaster, some individuals can be tempted to commit illegal or unethical acts to improve the chances of a favorable investment.

LO 6 Identify and evaluate ethical issues in strategic investment decisions.

World Demands Ethical Investment Practice, but What Is It?

Trade unions, regulators, investors, nongovernment organizations, and some business executives have succeeding in influencing US laws and recent *Organisation for Economic Cooperation and Development* guidelines that prohibit bribery and other corrupt practices by multinational companies. However, no uniform definitions of these unethical practices exist. What is one country's bribe can be another's "business facilitation" cost; one company's bribed official might be another's "business intermediary" who is essential to finding new markets. Furthermore, although some European countries have stricter laws against corrupt practices than the United States has, prosecution has been rare in these countries. Worldwide enforcement of anticorruption laws may be too weak to cause improved practices.

An added complication arises when regulators attempt to prosecute executives who knew or should have known about illegal practices. US firms are required by law to have effective internal control systems, but recent events have proved that these can be subverted. Even if prosecutors cannot prove that executives ordered bribes or fraudulent investment reports, for instance, executives could be prosecuted for failing to properly supervise those who actually carried out the unethical or illegal acts. However, establishing that an executive should have known that a subordinate, who is layers away in the hierarchy, was misbehaving can be almost impossible without evidence of relevant communications between them.

Even if governments cannot define or prosecute illegal investment activities, socially conscious investors might affect business practices by using their own social investment criteria to:

- Screen for positive and negative issues such as bribery or environmental performance.
- Generate shareholder advocacy on social issues.
- Invest directly in their community.
- Provide the financial foundation for new, socially responsible companies.

Whether these investor-driven approaches can affect ethical investment practices in a material way remains to be seen.[9]

Internal Ethical Pressures

Individuals can be pressured to misstate information or results regarding strategic investments because of:

- *Bias from personal commitment to an investment project.* This bias can begin as myopia, or not wanting to look sufficiently far ahead, or to admit that a favorite project might be a failure. After an investment is approved, this bias can continue as "escalation to commitment," which results in throwing good money after bad rather than facing the fact that an investment should be terminated and written off.

- *Fear of loss of prestige, position, or compensation from a failed investment.* The pressures to succeed and not to admit failure can be very strong in any type of organization. Some organizations have an "up-or-out" advancement policy, and only those that continue to succeed financially are rewarded. While the best result of this pressure is that managers invest in good projects and manage them well, sometimes projects perform below expectations. A manager might give in to the temptation to misstate investment success or might force analysts to do so. This can lead to continued misstatements that ultimately cannot be sustained. The predictable results include wasted resources, lost time, and ruined reputations.

- *Greed and intentional behavior to defraud an organization or its stakeholders.* Some people, unfortunately, are ethically challenged and seek opportunities to defraud others. Trust is very important in business, but trust has been and will be abused. The best defenses are to invest with people who have earned trust and to use an effective system of controls.

Anyone who has followed corporate misbehavior in the United States over the past several years knows that greed is a powerful motivator. The combination of greed and initial financial success can lead to a sense of invincibility and entitlement to greater wealth. When markets inevitably turn down or when predicted events do not occur, powerful managers have pressured analysts to misstate investment success and outlook in order to sustain their image and income. Wealthy criminals might be able to hide their assets and escape prosecution, but analysts who connive with them likely cannot and will be ruined financially and personally.

Roles of Internal Controls and Audits

Internal controls that can counter pressures to invest unethically include hiring practices, formal investment reporting and reviews, codes of ethics, and internal audits of ongoing and past investments. Under the Sarbanes-Oxley Act of 2002, publicly owned firms are required to have effective internal control systems.

Hiring practices.   Perhaps one of the most effective ways to ensure ethical investment practices is to hire ethical people. Few believe that screening for ethical orientation

---

[9] See the following articles for interesting discussions related to this section: M. Kaminski, "Global Vice Squad"; M. McNamee, N. Byrnes, and E. Thornton, "Banking's Bigwigs May Be Beyond the Law's Reach"; and C. Harrington, "Socially Responsible Investing."

(not the same as religious beliefs) is enough to prevent all unethical acts, but experience has proven the value of at least performing background and reference checks.

Investment reporting and reviews.   Many organizations have formal reporting and periodic reviews of investment projects, before and after acceptance. Reporting and review elements include financial analyses to demonstrate that projects will meet or are meeting required rates of return and qualitative analyses to verify that projects meet the goals and objectives of the organization and to verify that investment managers are adhering to investment guidelines, including ethical requirements.

Codes of ethics.   Many organizations have ethical codes that describe approved and prohibited practices. These ethical codes educate and support employees who want to behave ethically but either would not know what to do or might be pressured to act unethically. They also form grounds for termination of employees who violate the codes. For example, many ethical codes prohibit employees from soliciting or accepting gifts from potential suppliers or outsourced service providers. This is to help ensure that evaluations of investments and other projects will not be biased by favoritism or obligations induced by gifts and the expectations of future gifts. Likewise, employees usually are forbidden to offer gifts or other inducements to external persons who have influence over the organization's investment projects and who might relax regulations or tax requirements in return. This usually is illegal and can backfire if a competitor offers a larger gift. Codes of ethics are little more than the paper they are written on unless all employees from top to bottom follow them or are fired if they do not.

Internal audits.   **Internal audits** are examinations of operations, programs, and financial results performed by independent investigators. Effective internal audits can be powerful reinforcements of ethical investment policies and deterrents to those tempted to violate those policies for new and existing investments. The threat and consequences of being caught at unethical investment practices might be enough to dissuade those who might be tempted to misbehave. Furthermore, internal audits of the investment process and ongoing investments also can be valuable sources of information about what worked and what did not. This information can be used to revise investment practices and improve investment decisions in the future.

Chapter Summary

This chapter focuses on strategic investment decisions. Investment decisions are long-term commitments of capital and effort that preclude other opportunities. Thus, these decisions have opportunity costs over time, which are measured by forgone interest. Analysts use discounted cash flow (DCF) methods to evaluate alternative investments. Appendix A reviews net present value (NPV) analysis, which is a common DCF method. Strategic investment analysis accounts for uncertain future events and competitors' actions. Strategic analysis also considers management flexibility to change investments as relevant information is gathered.

Real option value (ROV) analysis combines decision-tree representations of management flexibility, NPV analysis, and expected value analysis to analyze strategic investments. ROV analysis can lead to materially different investment decisions when, for example, investments are irreversible and deferred decisions can benefit from additional information that becomes available over time.

The large monetary amounts of strategic investments can provide temptations for unethical and illegal practices that most organizations forbid. Organizations use multiple internal controls to encourage ethical and legal behavior, including hiring policies, training, reporting and reviews, ethical codes, and internal audits.

Appendix A   to Chapter Fourteen

Discounted Cash Flow Analysis

The purpose of this appendix is to present the basic concepts and method of the discounted cash flow (DCF) method of net present value (NPV) analysis. The appendix will serve as a review for readers who have learned NPV analysis but are rusty on the concepts or as an introduction for those who are unfamiliar with the topic. Most organizations use DCF methods to analyze alternative investments. However, some organizations also use non-DCF methods, such as the **payback period,** which is the time necessary to recover the investment cost from nondiscounted cash flows. DCF analysis combines estimates of current and future cash flows associated with an investment and discounts the cash flows to account for the opportunity costs of committing funds to the investment. The internal rate of return (IRR) method is another common DCF technique that uses the same cash flow information. Finance and economics textbooks provide more extensive discussions of both NPV and IRR methods.

We first discuss estimating current and future cash flows and then demonstrate how the NPV method discounts those flows.

Estimating Cash Flows for DCF Analysis

DCF methods are based on the current and future cash flows expected from a particular investment opportunity. The amounts and timing of the cash flows determine the economic value of the investment, so accurately predicting future cash flows is a key to effective investment analysis using DCF methods.

Investment projects can have three types of cash flows that are estimated separately. These are:

- *Investment cash flows,* which are of three types:
  1. Asset acquisition, which might include
     a. New equipment costs, including installation and start-up costs
     b. Future reinvestment or refurbishing costs
     c. Proceeds of replaced existing assets
  2. Tax effects arising from a loss or gain on the sale of replaced assets (if any)
  3. Tax credits (if any)
- *Periodic operating cash flows,* which are incremental cash inflows and outflows from normal operating activities. Normally, these are revenues and expenses, but not all revenues and expenses are cash flows in the period in which they are recognized for income. For example, depreciation is an expense, but it is not a cash flow in the period recognized. Periodic operating cash flows can contribute to operating income and can be subject to taxation.
- *Disinvestment (or termination) cash flows,* which are the costs of shutting down or terminating an investment. These cash flows might include proceeds from the sale of assets, tax effects of loss or gain on the sale, severance and outplacement costs, and restoration costs.

To illustrate NPV analysis, assume that ShadeTree Roasters is planning to replace some of its coffee roasting equipment for higher capacity equipment that is also more energy efficient. The proposed investment information is provided in Exhibit 14–12.

The new equipment cost of $180,000 (B4 of Exhibit 14–12) is a cash outflow, by convention at the end of the current year (year 0). The equipment cost [net of salvage value (B8)] will be depreciated on a straight-line basis over its useful life of five years (B6). The installation and training cost, $20,000 (B5) is a cash outflow that is deductible in year 0. The old equipment that will be replaced can be sold for $10,000 (B7); its tax basis of zero (B12) means that the company will be taxed on the gain of $10,000 (B7 − B12) from the sale. Analysts estimate that the company will sell the new equipment after five years for $15,000 (B8), which will be a cash inflow at the end of year 5, but not a taxable gain if the company uses straight-line depreciation (other depreciation methods can result in expected taxable gains).

The annual increase in revenues, $30,000 (B9), from the larger capacity of the new roasting equipment will improve operating income by that amount. The increase in operating costs of the new equipment, $16,000 (B10), will decrease operating income, but the energy cost savings, $40,000 (B11), will increase operating income. These combined with the depreciation of the new equipment, $33,000 ((B4 − B8) ÷

B6), will change operating income. Subtracting taxes at 40 percent (B14), which is assumed to cover federal, state, and local taxes, generates operating income after tax.

Operating income after tax understates operating cash flows because depreciation is deducted although it is not a cash flow. Adding back depreciation restates operating income after tax to operating net cash flow. The final step is to add or subtract any nonoperating cash flows. Putting all this information together over the five-year life of the investment generates estimates of annual net cash flows that are the heart of DCF analysis. Mistakes or misstatements in these estimates can result in wrong investment decisions that can be quite harmful. On the other hand, careful estimates can identify promising investment alternatives that can generate valuable cash flows and competitive advantages.

The five-year estimates of the investment's cash flows are shown in Exhibit 14–13. Work carefully through this exhibit to row 35 to verify how net cash flows are computed from the input data.

Exhibit 14–12

Example Input Data

	A	B
3	**Data input**	
4	New equipment cost	$ 180,000
5	Installation and training cost	20,000
6	Equipment useful life	5
7	Salvage value of old equipment	10,000
8	Salvage value of new equipment	15,000
9	Annual increase in revenues	30,000
10	Annual increase in operating costs	16,000
11	Annual energy cost savings	$ 40,000
12	Tax basis of old equipment	-
13	Tax credit on energy efficient equipment	5%
14	Income and capital gains tax rate	40%
15	Discount rate	8%

(B17 fx 0)

Exhibit 14–13

Example Investment Net Cash Flows

C35 fx =C33+C34

	A	B	C	D	E	F	G
16	**Investment analysis**			**End of Year**			
17	Initial cash flows	0	1	2	3	4	5
18	Investment cost	$ (180,000)					
19	Installation and training cost	(20,000)					
20	Proceeds from old equipment	10,000					
21	Tax savings from deductible training	8,000					
22	Tax on gain from sale of old equip.	(4,000)					
23	Tax credit on purchase	9,000					
24	Annual operating income items						
25	Increase in revenues		$ 30,000	$ 30,000	$ 30,000	$ 30,000	$ 30,000
26	Energy cost savings		40,000	40,000	40,000	40,000	40,000
27	Increase in operating costs		(16,000)	(16,000)	(16,000)	(16,000)	(16,000)
28	Depreciation		(33,000)	(33,000)	(33,000)	(33,000)	(33,000)
29	Change in operating income		21,000	21,000	21,000	21,000	21,000
30	Tax on changes		(8,400)	(8,400)	(8,400)	(8,400)	(8,400)
31	After tax change in operating income		12,600	12,600	12,600	12,600	12,600
32	Add back non-cash expenses		33,000	33,000	33,000	33,000	33,000
33	After tax operating cash flow		45,600	45,600	45,600	45,600	45,600
34	Salvage of new equipment						15,000
35	Net cash flow	(177,000)	45,600	45,600	45,600	45,600	60,600

The payback period for this investment is approximately 3.9 years, computed as follows:

$$\text{Initial investment cost} = \$177{,}000$$
$$\text{Annual (equal) net cash flow} = 45{,}600 \text{ a year}$$
$$\text{Payback period} = \text{Initial investment cost} \div \text{Annual (equal) net cash flow}$$
$$\text{Payback period} = \$177{,}000 \div \$45{,}600 \text{ a year} = \underline{3.9 \text{ years}}$$

Note that the payback period implies that NCFs are received uniformly throughout a year, which might not be the case. If the annual net cash flows are unequal, the payback period is computed by sequentially adding the cumulative NCF to the initial investment cost until the investment cost is fully recovered. Consider the following example with uneven annual NCFs.

Year	Annual NCF	Cumulative NCF	Unrecovered Initial Investment Cost
0			$(10,000)
1	$3,600	$ 3,600	(6,400)
2	4,000	7,600	(2,400)
3	6,000	13,600	3,600

The cumulative NCF recovers the initial investment cost sometime in the third year. By the end of the second year, only $2,400 is needed to recover the initial investment cost. By the end of the third year, the cumulative NCF is greater than the initial investment cost by $3,600. We can approximate the payback period as two years' NCF plus a proportion of the third year's $6,000 NCF, as follows:

$$\text{Payback period} = (2 + \$2{,}400 \div \$6{,}000) \text{ years} = 2 + 0.4 \text{ years} = \underline{2.4 \text{ years}}$$

NPV analysis of the investment in Exhibit 14–13 will continue after discussions of the discount rate and discounting cash flows.

Importance of the Discount Rate

The one piece of input data that we have not discussed is the discount rate of 8 percent (Exhibit 14–12, cell B15). This is crucial information because the **discount rate** measures the opportunity cost of investing. Organizations should use a discount rate, so called because we will use it to discount future cash flows, that measures the rate of return the company would forgo by choosing a particular investment. Choosing a rate that is too high might cause the company to reject quite profitable investments. Choosing a rate that is too low might cause the company to accept subpar investments and forgo better returns that it could earn elsewhere. The debate continues in finance and economics about how to choose the proper discount rate, or opportunity cost of capital. For publicly held companies, some experts argue that the discount rate should be the long-term return on equity investments (about 8 percent) because that is the general opportunity for stockholders. Others argue that firms should use the "risk-free" rate, adjusted for the expected risk of the particular project, although there is no general agreement about how to properly adjust for risk.[10]

Public or governmental organizations also have difficulty choosing the proper discount rate. Because the federal government is so large and diversified, some economists argue that the proper discount rate is the risk-free rate (about 3 to 4 percent). However, others argue that because public investment displaces private investment (by taking taxes that private parties otherwise would invest), government agencies should use a higher rate comparable to private investment rates of return. The stakes can be quite high, depending on how these disputes are decided, but this interesting topic is beyond the scope of this text.

---

[10] Analysts who build discount rates this way usually estimate the risk-free rate as the rate of return of long-term government bonds.

Effects of inflation.   Inflation reflects general price increases in an economy. The expected inflation rate also can be a component of the discount rate and future cash flows. Market rates of return (e.g., the opportunity rate of a similar investment) contain an expectation of inflation. For example, a market-based opportunity rate of 8 percent might be composed of an expectation of a 3 percent inflation rate and a 5 percent rate of return on a comparable investment without inflation.[11] Adjusting DCF analysis for inflation involves adjusting the discount rate for the expected inflation rate and adjusting future cash flows for expected inflation. Therefore, if one uses a market or opportunity rate, which already includes expected inflation, as the discount rate, future cash flows also should reflect expected inflation. The effects of inflation are multiplied or "compounded" over time: Each year's inflation builds on the previous year's inflation. For example, assume that the expected inflation rate is 3 percent each year, and future cash inflows without inflation are expected to be $12,000 per year (in current dollars). If the analysis takes place in Year 0, future cash inflows should be inflated as follows:

Year 0	Year I	Year 2	Year 3 ...	Year N
NCF in current (noninflated) dollars	$12,000	$12,000	$12,000	$12,000
Cumulative inflation at 3 percent	$(1.03)^1$	$(1.03)^2$	$(1.03)^3$	$(1.03)^N$
	= 1.03	= 1.0609	= 1.0927	
Inflation-adjusted NCF (rounded)	= $12,360	= $12,731	= $13,113	

For simplicity, the examples and analyses in this chapter ignore the effects of inflation.

Discounting future cash flows.   To account for the opportunity cost of investing, DCF methods discount future cash flows to the amounts that would have to be invested now at the discount rate to yield the expected future cash flows. For example, if the discount rate is 10 percent and the expected cash flow in one year is $110, one would have to invest $100 now at 10 percent to generate a total of $110 one year from now. The $100 figure is the *present value* of the future $110 at a 10 percent discount rate. In general, the **present value** of a future cash flow is the equivalent amount that would have to be invested today to generate that amount at a given discount or opportunity rate.

   When one expects a series of future cash flows, compute the total present value by summing the present values of each period's cash flows. Most investments have a purchase price or investment cost that is payable now. The **net present value (NPV)** of an investment is the present value of its future cash flows less its purchase price. If the NPV is positive, it promises returns in excess of the discount or opportunity rate, and vice versa.

Computing Net Present Value

NPV analysis discounts each future period's net cash flow separately to reflect the effect of compound interest. For example, if the expected future net cash flow in *two* years is $130, one would have to invest a present value amount for two years and forgo the first year's interest on the amount and the second year's interest on both the present value amount and its first year's interest. If the discount rate is 10 percent, we can solve for the present value, P, as follows:

$$[P \times (1 + .10)](1 + .10) = \$130$$
$$P \times (1 + .10) \times (1 + .10) = \$130$$
$$P \times (1 + .10)^2 = \$130$$
$$P = \$130 \div (1 + .10)^2$$
$$P = \$130 \times [1 \div (1 + .10)^2]$$
$$P = \$130 \times (.826) = \$107$$

---

[11] Technically, the inflation rate and the inflation-free opportunity rate interact, but at low rates of interest, the interaction is negligible.

Thus, $107 invested today at 10 percent would grow to $130 in two years. The figure .826 is the 10 percent *present value factor* for an amount to be received two years from now. These present value factors have been tabulated for many discount rates and time periods (see examples in Exhibit 14–14) and are internally calculated by business calculators and spreadsheet programs to compute present values.

To compute the NPV of an investment manually, follow these steps:

1. Estimate current and future net cash flows (similar to Exhibit 14–13) and the relevant discount rate.

2. Multiply each period's future net cash flow by the appropriate present value factor for the time period and discount rate to compute the discounted cash flows. Note that current cash flows in year 0 are multiplied by 1 plus the discount rate, raised to the 0 power, which is 1. Note also that computing present values manually can generate rounding errors, but these are almost never critical to investment decisions.

3. Sum the current and discounted future net cash flows to obtain the NPV.

Exhibit 14–15 extends Exhibit 14–13 to present the NPV analysis of ShadeTree Roasters' equipment replacement decision. Cash flows are the same as in Exhibit 14–13. Present value factors for the discount rate of 8 percent are in row 36. The present values, or discounted cash flows, are the net cash flows multiplied by the present value factors and appear in row 37. As shown in cell B38, the investment has

---

Exhibit 14–14   Selected Present Value Factors

	Present value of $1								
				Discount Rate					
Year	2%	3%	4%	5%	6%	7%	8%	9%	10%
1	0.980	0.971	0.962	0.952	0.943	0.935	0.926	0.917	0.909
2	0.961	0.943	0.925	0.907	0.890	0.873	0.857	0.842	0.826
3	0.942	0.915	0.889	0.864	0.840	0.816	0.794	0.772	0.751
4	0.924	0.888	0.855	0.823	0.792	0.763	0.735	0.708	0.683
5	0.906	0.863	0.822	0.784	0.747	0.713	0.681	0.650	0.621
6	0.888	0.837	0.790	0.746	0.705	0.666	0.630	0.596	0.564
7	0.871	0.813	0.760	0.711	0.665	0.623	0.583	0.547	0.513
8	0.853	0.789	0.731	0.677	0.627	0.582	0.540	0.502	0.467
9	0.837	0.766	0.703	0.645	0.592	0.544	0.500	0.460	0.424
10	0.820	0.744	0.676	0.614	0.558	0.508	0.463	0.422	0.386

				Discount Rate					
Year	11%	12%	13%	14%	15%	16%	17%	18%	19%
1	0.901	0.893	0.885	0.877	0.870	0.862	0.855	0.847	0.840
2	0.812	0.797	0.783	0.769	0.756	0.743	0.731	0.718	0.706
3	0.731	0.712	0.693	0.675	0.658	0.641	0.624	0.609	0.593
4	0.659	0.636	0.613	0.592	0.572	0.552	0.534	0.516	0.499
5	0.593	0.567	0.543	0.519	0.497	0.476	0.456	0.437	0.419
6	0.535	0.507	0.480	0.456	0.432	0.410	0.390	0.370	0.352
7	0.482	0.452	0.425	0.400	0.376	0.354	0.333	0.314	0.296
8	0.434	0.404	0.376	0.351	0.327	0.305	0.285	0.266	0.249
9	0.391	0.361	0.333	0.308	0.284	0.263	0.243	0.225	0.209
10	0.352	0.322	0.295	0.270	0.247	0.227	0.208	0.191	0.176

Exhibit 14–15   Example of NPV Analysis

	B	C	D	E	F	G
16 Investment analysis			**End of Year**			
17 Initial cash flows	0	1	2	3	4	5
18 Investment cost	$ (180,000)					
19 Installation and training cost	(20,000)					
20 Proceeds from old equipment	10,000					
21 Tax savings from deductible training	8,000					
22 Tax on gain from sale of old equip.	(4,000)					
23 Tax credit on purchase	9,000					
24 Annual operating income items						
25 Increase in revenues		$ 30,000	$ 30,000	$ 30,000	$ 30,000	$ 30,000
26 Energy cost savings		40,000	40,000	40,000	40,000	40,000
27 Increase in operating costs		(16,000)	(16,000)	(16,000)	(16,000)	(16,000)
28 Depreciation		(33,000)	(33,000)	(33,000)	(33,000)	(33,000)
29 Change in operating income		21,000	21,000	21,000	21,000	21,000
30 Tax on changes		(8,400)	(8,400)	(8,400)	(8,400)	(8,400)
31 After tax change in operating income		12,600	12,600	12,600	12,600	12,600
32 Add back non-cash expenses		33,000	33,000	33,000	33,000	33,000
33 After tax operating cash flow		45,600	45,600	45,600	45,600	45,600
34 Salvage of new equipment						15,000
35 Net cash flow	(177,000)	45,600	45,600	45,600	45,600	60,600
36 Present value factors	1.000	0.926	0.857	0.794	0.735	0.681
37 Present values of cash flows	(177,000)	$ 42,222	$ 39,095	$ 36,199	$ 33,517	$ 41,243
38 Net present value	$ 15,276					

Cell B38 selected: =SUM(B37:G37)

Sheet tabs: **Example** / PV factors / Sheet3

a positive NPV of $15,276 and probably will be accepted, as long as no serious quali-
tative factors are uncovered.

   Most NPV analyses are completed using spreadsheet software and the software's
NPV function, but it is important that you know how the arithmetic is done. Don't
forget that the difficult parts of NPV analysis are estimating future cash flows and the
proper discount rate. Spreadsheets are important NPV tools because they simplify the
arithmetic and facilitate sensitivity analysis.

Appendix B to Chapter Fourteen

Analysis of ShadeTree Roasters' Decision to Invest Now, Years 1–6

Analyses such as the ones in Exhibit 14–16 and 14–17 are easily extended to additional time periods if Chapter 12's modeling guidelines have been followed. If every
cell in the exhibits is a formula that refers to either data input (e.g., the "Input" worksheet shown in the bottom bar of this screen shot) or other results on this worksheet,
one can simply copy and paste year 5's cells to any number of subsequent years. One
must be careful, however, to ensure that the assumptions that govern the earlier years
also apply to the later years. For example, analysts should question whether the company would be able to extend operations for a sixth year for a cash outlay at the same
level of committed costs, €1,100,000, as before. If the economic life of the investment really is five years, additional cash investment beyond the previous annual
committed costs might be necessary for a sixth year.

Exhibit 14–16   Forecasted Cash Flows and Net Present Value—No Major Competitor, Years 1–6

Microsoft Excel - ShadeTree.xls

File Edit View Insert Format Tools Data Window Help Acrobat

B17 =NPV(Input!C6,C15:H15)+B15

A	B	C	D	E	F	G	H
1 ShadeTree Roasters Expansion - no competitior, invest now	Year 0	Year 1	Year 2	Year 3	Year 4	Year 5	Year 6
2 Expected market size (thousands)	€ 50,000	€ 52,300	€ 54,706	€ 57,222	€ 59,854	€ 62,608	€ 65,488
3 Market share		20%	20%	20%	20%	20%	20%
4 Sales		€ 10,460	€ 10,941	€ 11,444	€ 11,971	€ 12,522	€ 13,098
5 Cost of goods sold		3,661	3,829	4,006	4,190	4,383	4,584
6 Gross margin		6,799	7,112	7,439	7,781	8,139	8,513
7 Committed costs							
8 Investment (cash/non-cash)	(5,500)	1,100	1,100	1,100	1,100	1,100	**1,100**
9 SG&A - cash		5,000	5,000	5,000	5,000	5,000	5,000
10 Total committed costs		6,100	6,100	6,100	6,100	6,100	6,100
11 Operating income before tax		699	1,012	1,339	1,681	2,039	2,413
12 Tax (savings)		280	405	536	672	816	965
13 Operating income after tax		419	607	803	1,009	1,223	1,448
14 Add-back non-cash expenses		1,100	1,100	1,100	1,100	1,100	-
15 Annual cash flows	(€ 5,500)	€ 1,519	€ 1,707	€ 1,903	€ 2,109	€ 2,323	€ 1,448
16 Expected NPV - yrs 1-5, no competitor	€ 2,012						
17 Expected NPV - yrs 1-6, no competitor	€ 2,925						

Input \ **Now-No Comp** \ Now-Comp \ Wait-No Comp \ Wait-Comp \ blank

Ready   NUM

Exhibit 14–17   Forecasted Cash Flows and Net Present Value—with a Major Competitor, Years 1–6

Microsoft Excel - ShadeTree.xls

File Edit View Insert Format Tools Data Window Help Acrobat

B18 =NPV(Input!C6,C15:H15)+B15

A	B	C	D	E	F	G	H
1 ShadeTree Roasters Expansion - with competitior, invest now	Year 0	Year 1	Year 2	Year 3	Year 4	Year 5	Year 6
2 Expected market size (thousands)	€ 50,000	€ 52,300	€ 54,706	€ 57,222	€ 59,854	€ 62,608	€ 65,488
3 Market share		20%	10%	10%	10%	10%	10%
4 Sales		€ 10,460	€ 5,471	€ 5,722	€ 5,985	€ 6,261	€ 6,549
5 Cost of goods sold		3,661	1,915	2,003	2,095	2,191	2,292
6 Gross margin		6,799	3,556	3,719	3,891	4,070	4,257
7 Committed costs							
8 Investment (cash/non-cash)	(5,500)	1,100	1,100	1,100	1,100	1,100	**1,100**
9 SG&A - cash		5,000	5,000	5,000	5,000	5,000	5,000
10 Total committed costs		6,100	6,100	6,100	6,100	6,100	6,100
11 Operating income before tax		699	(2,544)	(2,381)	(2,209)	(2,030)	(1,843)
12 Tax (savings)		280	(1,018)	(952)	(884)	(812)	(737)
13 Operating income after tax		419	(1,526)	(1,428)	(1,326)	(1,218)	(1,106)
14 Add-back non-cash expenses		1,100	1,100	1,100	1,100	1,100	-
15 Annual cash flows	(€ 5,500)	€ 1,519	(€ 426)	(€ 328)	(€ 226)	(€ 118)	(€ 1,106)
16 NPV - yrs 1-5, with competitor	(€ 4,966)						
17 NPV if terminate after 1 year	(€ 4,093)						
18 NPV - yrs 1-6, with competitor, now	(€ 5,663)						

Input \ Now-No Comp \ **Now-Comp** \ Wait-No Comp \ Wait-Comp \ blank

Ready   NUM

Key Terms

For each term's definition, refer to the indicated page or turn to the glossary at the end of the text.

*Term appears in Appendix A of this chapter.

Meeting the Cost Management Challenges

1. How does the proposed investment by ShadeTree Roasters influence the types of information the company should obtain and the analyses it should perform?

The proposed investment to expand to a new market where a major competitor also can enter is a risky venture and could be financially disastrous. The company must gather information about relevant external factors that it cannot control and internal factors that it can partially control. External factors include current and expected market size, growth, and expected market share. Perhaps the most important external factors are the company's opportunity rate and the probability of whether a major competitor will enter the market. Internal factors include expected investment and operating costs, changes in costs (assumed to be zero in this chapter), effective tax rate, and flexibility of investment. Because the investment is considered to be irreversible (a sunk cost) and because the company has some flexibility (the ability to defer the decision in this chapter), ShadeTree should use real option value (ROV) analysis for financial analysis of the investment. On the qualitative side, ShadeTree also expects to benefit in central Europe from marketing its social and environmental policies, which differ from those of major competitors. The company also expects to benefit from being sensitive to local cultures and by hiring and sourcing locally.

2. What do net present value and real option value analyses imply for the success of ShadeTree Roasters' long-term decision?

Traditional expected net present value analysis indicates the company should reject the investment. However, expected NPV analysis does not model the company's flexibility to terminate or defer the investment (among many possible types of investment flexibility). Real option value analysis does model that flexibility. Although terminating the project as soon as a major competitor enters the market is better than continuing, the best decision is to defer or wait for a year and try to learn about major competitors' plans.

3. How do ethical considerations appear to hurt ShadeTree Roasters' investment opportunities in the short run but help in the long run?

The large real option value of waiting to learn about a competitor's likely action presents a temptation perhaps to bribe government officials who can influence the decision of who can enter the market or to conduct industrial espionage to find out competitors' plans. In one sense, these could be financially effective actions—in the short run. These and other similar actions are probably unethical and illegal. Getting caught could mean criminal and civil penalties, lost opportunities, and ruined reputations. Even getting away with these improper activities this time is no guarantee that they will be harmless because they might instill an unethical climate in the company and could lead to complete collapse of the company's (and any manager's) reputation and future business opportunities. In the long run, unethical behavior is more costly because customers or business partners will expect the worst behavior and do business with an unethical company only if they can be protected by either charging higher prices or by requiring costly bonding and insurance. More likely, they will refuse to do business, and the unethical company might itself fail.

Solutions to You're the Decision Maker

14.1   Sensitivity of Expected Value Analysis, p. 560

a.   The computations follow directly:

1.   Expected market growth = $10\% \times .40 + 5\% \times .30 - 2\% \times .30$

E[market growth] = $4.0\% + 1.5\% - .6\% = \underline{\underline{4.9\%}}$

2.   Expected market growth = $8\% \times .20 + 4\% \times .60 + 2\% \times .20$

E[market growth] = $1.6\% + 2.4\% + .4\% = \underline{\underline{4.4\%}}$

3.   Expected market growth = $10\% \times .20 + 5\% \times .20 - 2\% \times .60$

E[market growth] = $2.0\% + 1.0\% - 1.2\% = \underline{\underline{1.8\%}}$

b.   The changes in parts (1) and (2) do not appear to change the expected growth rate dramatically. However, a small change in a growth rate can have a large absolute effect on a large market over time. If these growth rates are likely, the company should apply them to the investment model(s) to gauge their effects on expected NPV. The last expected growth rate in part (1c) could result in a failed project if it actually happened. This small rate of growth probably would not justify the investment, but analysts should "plug" it into the models to measure the effects. Another consideration not discussed in the chapter is that the range or variation in possible growth rates can be a source of risk because they could lead to more extreme cash flow outcomes. All of these sets of growth rates have wider ranges and variances. Thus, if any of these were the growth rates used instead, the project might be considered riskier than before.

14.2   Sensitivity and Scenario Analyses,   p. 563

a.   These parameters directly drive the company's expected revenues. The original market size is multiplied by the expected growth rate, which in turn is multiplied by the expected market share. The result is the estimated annual revenue. This linkage is perhaps the most crucial part of the investment models because they drive cash inflows. Cash outflows, as modeled, are more predictable.

b.

	Market Size = €60 Million		Market Size = €40 Million	
	Year 0	Year I	Year 0	Year I
Expected market size (thousands)	€60,000	€62,760	€40,000	€41,840
Market share		20%		20%
Sales		€12,552		€ 8,368
Cost of goods sold		4,393		2,929
Gross margin		€ 8,159		€ 5,439

c.

	Market Growth Rate = 2%		Market Growth Rate = 6%	
	Year 0	Year I	Year 0	Year I
Expected market size (thousands)	€50,000	€51,000	€50,000	€53,000
Market share		20%		20%
Sales		€10,200		€10,600
Cost of goods sold		3,570		3,710
Gross margin		€ 6,630		€ 6,890

d.

	Market Share = 30%		Market Share = 15%	
	Year 0	Year I	Year 0	Year I
Expected market size (thousands)	€50,000	€52,300	€50,000	€52,300
Market share		30%		15%
Sales		€15,690		€ 7,845
Cost of goods sold		5,492		2,746
Gross margin		€10,199		€ 5,099

e. Many alternative scenarios are possible, but consider that the best-case scenario can be:

> Market size = €60 million; market growth rate = 6 percent; market share = 30 percent

The worst case scenario can be:

> Market size = €40 million; market growth rate = 2 percent; market share = 15 percent

	Best-Case Scenario		Worst-Case Scenario	
	Year 0	Year I	Year 0	Year I
Expected market size (thousands)	€60,000	€63,600	€40,000	€40,800
Market share		30%		15%
Sales		€19,080		€ 6,120
Cost of goods sold		6,678		2,142
Gross margin		€12,402		€ 3,978

14.3   Apply Real Option Value Analysis,   p. 571

a. The analysts extended the "no competitor" option to six years because investment alternatives must be of comparable time periods. If analysts had not included a sixth year, they are explicitly assuming that the company will generate zero net cash flow from its investment funds. At a minimum, the company should earn its required rate of return. In the chapter's case, analysts are assuming that the company could extend operations for a sixth year at the same committed cost. That might be overly optimistic, and they perhaps should model other possibilities.

b. 1. The decision tree of the alternative to defer investment one year follows:

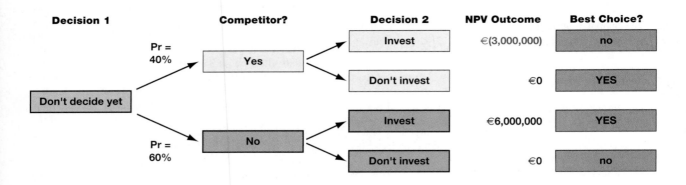

If a competitor enters, the company would not invest and would earn a zero NPV.

The expected NPV of deferring the decision is

$$€0 \times .40 + 6,000,000 \times .60 = €3,600,000$$

2.   The decision tree of the alternative to invest now follows:

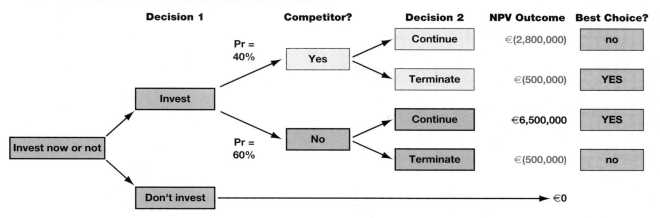

If a competitor enters, the company would terminate the project after one year.

The expected NPV of the decision to invest now is

$$(€500,000) × .40 + 6,500,000 × .60 = \underline{€3,700,000}$$

3.   The real option value of the decision to wait is

$$€3,600,000 − €3,700,000 = \underline{(€100,000)}$$

4.   These calculations indicate that the best strategy is to invest now rather than wait. The primary reason for this outcome is the relatively low cost of terminating the investment after one year. This means that the investment is mostly reversible. Under this condition (unlike the situation in the chapter), waiting is not beneficial. Investing now and starting the cash flows in the first year is better than deferring them a year.

Review Questions

14.1   What is different between a consumption decision and an investment decision?

14.2   How do discounted cash flow (DCF) methods analyze investment decisions?

14.3   What two types of factors affect strategic investment decisions?

14.4   Describe the strategic nature of the investments by RealNetworks, Time Warner, and Benetton described in Cost Management in Practice 14.1.

14.5   How can organizations anticipate and plan for uncontrollable external events, such as weather?

14.6   What are the most common problems that can be discovered during due diligence investigations of investment opportunities?

14.7   When might an organization's financial records be useful for anticipating uncontrollable future events and their likelihood of occurrence?

14.8   Why might creative employees and experienced consultants be good sources of information about uncontrollable future events and their likelihood of occurrence?

14.9   What are the advantages of using news, government, foundation, and industry analyses of uncontrollable future events and their likelihood of occurrence?

14.10   What are three approaches to modeling the effects of uncontrollable future events and their likelihood of occurrence?

14.11   How does expected value analysis summarize what is known about uncontrollable future events and their likelihood of occurrence?

14.12   If expected market growth can be either 10 percent or 2 percent with probabilities of occurrence of 30 percent and 70 percent, respectively, what is the expected value of market growth?

14.13   Describe the meaning of the amount calculated in review question 14.12 for planning and for actual future market growth.

14.14   Why might a company, such as Caterpillar, find advantages to evaluating "bundles" of investment simultaneously rather than singly, as described in Cost Management in Practice 14.2?

14.15   Describe how ShadeTree analysts forecasted gross margin in Exhibit 14–4.

14.16   Explain why analysts added back depreciation expense to compute operating cash flow in Exhibit 14–4.

14.17   Explain why Ford Motor Co. decided that qualitative factors overrode NPV analysis of investing in flexible, computerized equipment (Cost Management in Practice 14.2).

14.18   Why should organizations try to anticipate competitors' actions as part of analyzing strategic investments? Give an example.

14.19   What is different about real option value (ROV) analysis compared to traditional net present value (NPV) analysis?

14.20   How might ROV analysis lead to accepting an investment that traditional NPV analysis says to reject?

14.21   Why did ShadeTree analysts extend the decision time frame from five to six years in Exhibit 14–11 (and Appendix B)?

14.22   Explain how the real option value of an investment is derived from ROV analysis.

14.23   Describe three problems that external parties, such as regulatory agencies, have with enforcing ethical investment practices by organizations.

14.24   Why might individuals misstate information or results regarding strategic investments?

14.25   Describe how internal controls and audits can support ethical investment practices.

Critical Analysis

14.26 Respond to this comment: "Net present value analysis is too narrow and excludes important factors in decision making."

14.27 "If an investment does not fit with an organization's strategic plan, it is probably not a good idea, even if the NPV is positive." Do you agree or disagree? Explain.

14.28 Where would real option value analysis be more useful, replacing a machine with a new model that has a five-year life or replacing a mass-production method with a flexible, JIT production method? Explain.

14.29 Respond to this observation in the context of investment decisions: "Estimating future cash flows is a nightmare compared to measuring the cost of capital."

14.30 The strategic planning group of a large forest products company started with 400 possible strategic investments and then slashed that number to 40 before doing NPV analysis. Other than NPVs, what criteria do you think this group might have used to narrow the list from 400 to 40?

14.31 Due diligence investigations include studying the environmental impacts of investment decisions. Name two industries in which environmental impact studies are likely to be very important and two industries in which they are likely to be relatively unimportant.

14.32 Sometimes investments with a positive NPV have a negative impact on earnings. For example, investing in certain types of research and development could result in a large expense at the time of investment with the benefits coming years later. Suppose an executive rejects all investments that decrease current earnings, citing qualitative factors and the belief that lower earnings will depress stock prices to the detriment of stockholders. What other, unspoken factors might be behind this behavior?

14.33 The chapter describes how the Italian clothier Benneton and ShadeTree Roasters have included social causes in their strategic plans. Do you think this is a good business practice? Explain.

14.34 Contrast the strategic investments by RealNetworks and Time Warner that are described in Cost Management in Practice 14.1. Are you comfortable with both decisions as described? Explain.

14.35 ShadeTree Roasters is planning an expansion to central Europe, but the chapter does not discuss contingency plans beyond terminating the investment if a major competitor enters the market. Individually or with a small group, develop a plan C that ShadeTree Roasters might implement if market growth is much lower than expected.

14.36 Expected NPV analysis does not model the risk of investments directly. Discuss how sensitivity and scenario analyses model investment risk. Some experts argue that these analyses are better for modeling risk than adding a higher risk premium to the discount rate for riskier projects. Explain why that might be the case.

14.37 Explain how ABC and NPV analyses can be used together to evaluate an investment.

14.38 A manufacturer of computer data storage devices wants to replace its mass production method by investing in a flexible, JIT production method. The company plans to spend millions of dollars on new equipment, remodeled facilities, and relations with suppliers to implement the new method. To economize, the company plans to keep its current management structure by which line workers who build the products report performance and problems to middle managers, who then consult with higher management and the engineering department to resolve any difficulties. Can you predict any problems with the efficiency of the new production process?

14.39 "Of course depreciation is a source of cash flow. There it is right on your NPV analysis." Explain.

14.40 Consider both sides of this argument. *Side 1:* "Portraying all the possible combinations of different future external events can become hopelessly complex. Imagine the size of a decision tree that has 15 future events with three different levels each. Because reality can be even more complex than that, ROV analysis can never be truly useful and one might as well just use NPV analysis." *Side 2:* "You are right, reality is complex, but using a simplistic approach to investment analysis does not make the world simpler; it just makes the world look that way. ROV analysis can be useful even in a very complex environment because it forces analysts to understand complexity and model its implications for investments." State and explain your side of this argument.

14.41 You are a member of a strategic planning team that is considering a decision, the success of which depends on your major competitor's actions. Your colleague suggests that the best legal way to learn about a competitor's future actions is to hire away one of the competitor's key employees. What do you think of this approach?

Exercises

Exercise 14.42
Strategic Investments
(LO 1)

Required
Give at least one reason for classifying each of the following investment decisions as either routine or strategic.

a. The University of Minnesota's decision to replace existing personal computers after three years.

b. Microsoft's decision to purchase a small, innovative company that is developing new technology.

c. Southwest Airlines' decision to base its airplane maintenance facilities in Mexico to take advantage of lower labor costs.

d. General Electric's decision to expand its in-house "college."

Required

Give at least one reason for classifying each of the following decisions as either routine or strategic.

a.   Storage Technology's decision to build a central, computerized warehouse to serve its JIT manufacturing operations in Puerto Rico.

b.   Procter & Gamble's decision to design and conduct activity-based management studies to improve its internal support service operations.

c.   IBM's decision to approve and fund a new product proposal.

d.   Whole Food's decision to open a large store in the home city of its chief rival, Wild Oats Markets.

Exercise 14.43
Strategic Investments
(LO 1)

Required

Identify two relevant, uncontrollable external events and two possible competitors' actions that might affect each of the following investment decisions:

a.   Level3's decision to install thousands of miles of fiber-optic cable between major cities to support worldwide internet-based communications.

b.   DaimlerChrysler's decision to develop hydrogen fuel–cell powered vehicles.

c.   Motorola's decision to develop *Iridium,* a satellite-based telecommunication system.

d.   Merck/Schering-Plough's investment in *Zetia,* a drug to block absorption of cholesterol.

Exercise 14.44
Uncontrollable External
Events
(LO 2)

Required

Identify two relevant, uncontrollable external events and two possible competitors' actions for each of the following investment decisions:

a.   A decision by the State of Texas to replace a state-run prison with one operated by a private corporation.

b.   A decision by Community Hospital to build a new hospital campus in a growing community on donated land in a flood plain.

c.   A decision by the State of California to raise in-state college tuition by 25 percent.

d.   A decision by Qwest to outsource its computer programming and customer call operations to a separate company located in India.

Exercise 14.45
Uncontrollable External
Events
(LO 2)

The City of Aurora is considering an investment that would expand a community center. City analysts forecast the following net cash flows over the next 10 years, after which a major reinvestment is expected.

End of Year	Net Cash Flow
0	$ (400,000)
1	40,000
2	50,000
3	60,000
4	70,000
5	70,000
6	80,000
7	80,000
8	80,000
9	70,000
10	70,000

Exercise 14.46
Using Forecasts in NPV
Analysis
(LO 3)

mhhe.com/hilton3e

Required

a.   What is the net present value of the project if the appropriate discount rate is 10 percent?

b.   What is the net present value of the project if the appropriate discount rate is 8 percent?

Consider the investment decision in Exercise 14.46. What qualitative factors might be critical to evaluating this decision? If the discount rate is 10 percent, what monetary value of the qualitative factors would make the project financially viable?

Exercise 14.47
Evaluating Qualitative
Factors
(LO 3)

Exercise 14.48
Using Forecasts in NPV Analysis
(LO 3)

Tax-exempt Community Health Center is considering opening a new branch office to reduce travel costs incurred by patients and staff. Because the center depends on community support and donations and has no budget excess, it must make wise investment decisions. A financial executive who volunteers at the center made the following estimates of cost savings related to the new center over the next five years.

End of Year	Cost Savings
1	$10,000
2	12,000
3	14,000
4	16,000
5	18,000

Required

a. What is the most the center should commit for a five-year lease on a building, fixtures, and other start-up costs if the appropriate discount rate is 8 percent?

b. What is the most the center should commit for a five-year lease on a building, fixtures, and other start-up costs if the appropriate discount rate is 4 percent?

Exercise 14.49
Evaluating Qualitative Factors
(LO 3)

Consider the investment decision in Exercise 14.48. What qualitative factors might be critical to evaluating this decision? If the lowest-cost alternative is $70,000 and if the discount rate is 8 percent, what monetary value of the qualitative factors would make the project financially viable?

Exercise 14.50
Modeling Competitors' Actions
(LO 4)

Fish Taco Company (FTC) is planning to open a taco store near new university campus housing. FTC estimates that the current neighborhood's fast-food market is $200,000 per year, which will double when the new housing is occupied next year. FTC expects to capture 25 percent of the total neighborhood market unless MacBurger also opens a new store in the area. In that case, FTC expects to gain only 10 percent of the market. FTC's gross margin ratio is 30 percent.

Required

a. Compute FTC's forecasted gross margin for next year *without* a major competitor.

b. Compute FTC's forecasted gross margin for next year *with* a major competitor.

Exercise 14.51
Modeling Competitors' Actions
(LO 4)

Mid-sized Reunion City plans to completely renovate its aging shopping mall. The city depends on sales tax revenues of 3 percent of sales at the mall to fund many city services, but sales at the mall have declined to a current $80 million. Reunion City's plans call for 20 percent annual growth in sales at the mall after renovation, which will take one year unless the neighboring city of Pleasantville attracts a WalMart Superstore. In that case Reunion City's mall might experience only 5 percent annual growth. The mall's sales tax revenues will decline 25 percent from its current level during the renovation period.

Required

a. Compute Reunion City's sales tax revenues after the renovation *without* competition from Pleasantville.

b. Compute Reunion City's sales tax revenues after the renovation *with* competition from Pleasantville.

Exercise 14.52
Decision Tree and Expected NPV
(LO 5)

Fish Taco Company (Exercise 14.50) is planning to open a new store that might be affected by the entry of MacBurger into the same market area. FTC could invest in the new store now by buying and improving property. FTC analysts believe there is a 40 percent chance that MacBurger will enter the market. They have prepared the following NPV estimates:

Decision and Competitor's Action	NPV Estimate
Invest now, without a major competitor	$ 15,063
Invest now, with a major competitor	(28,058)
Invest now, with a major competitor, terminate after one year	(15,556)

Required

a. Prepare a decision tree of this investment alternative similar to this one in Exhibit 14–11.

b. Compute the expected NPV of the decision to invest now.

Exercise 14.53
Decision Tree and Expected NPV
(LO 5)

Fish Taco Company (Exercises 14.50 & 14.52) is planning to open a new store that might be affected by the entry of MacBurger into the same market area. FTC could defer its decision to invest by one year to learn whether MacBurger will enter the market. FTC analysts believe there is a 40 percent chance that MacBurger will enter the market. They have prepared the following NPV estimates:

Decision and Competitor's Action	NPV Estimate
Defer the decision, without a major competitor	$ 15,712
Defer the decision, with a major competitor	(17,410)

Required

a.   Prepare a decision tree of this investment alternative similar to the one in Exhibit 14–10.

b.   Compute the expected NPV of the decision to defer the decision one year.

Fish Taco Company (Exercises 14.50, 14.52, and 14.53) is planning to open a new store that might be affected by the entry of MacBurger into the same market area. Assume the expected NPV of investing in the new store now is $3,000 and the expected NPV of deferring the decision one year is $9,000.

Required

a.   What is the real option value of waiting for one year?

b.   Explain the economic meaning of this amount.

Exercise 14.54
Real Option Value
(LO 5)

Required

Give at least one reason that each of the following investment activities might be unethical or illegal and one reason that each of the following investment activities might *not* be unethical or illegal.

a.   Paying a fee to a third party who understands local market conditions and can streamline interactions with government regulators.

b.   Restating the expected salvage value of an investment.

c.   Obtaining information about a competitor's planned actions.

d.   Not giving close supervision to subordinates who make investment plans or decisions.

e.   Not modeling an adverse scenario of future events.

Exercise 14.55
Ethical Investment
Practices
(LO 6)

Required

Perform an Internet search for a company that describes how an ethical code guides its investment practices. Prepare a short memorandum to your instructor that describes the company, its ethical code, and how the code affects investment practices.

Exercise 14.56
Codes of Ethical
Investment Practices
(LO 6)

Find an article in a business periodical that discusses internal controls and investment practices. Prepare a short memorandum to your instructor that describes how internal controls affect investment activities.

Exercise 14.57
Internal Controls and
Investment Practices
(LO 6)

Problems

Furlong Manufacturing is considering investing in a robotics manufacturing process. Purchase and installation of the process will cost an estimated $2,900,000. This amount must be paid immediately. The company expects to dismantle this production process at the end of its seven-year life and salvage the equipment for $100,000. Furlong will depreciate the process equipment at $400,000 per year. Starting in year 4, the company expects significant quality improvements valued at $2.1 million until the end of the process in year 7. Because this investment is risky, the company believes it should use an 18 percent discount rate. The company's effective tax rate is 35 percent.

Required

a.   Compute the net present value of this investment.

b.   Is this a routine or strategic investment? Explain.

c.   What is your evaluation of the way this company models risk?

[CMA adapted]

Problem 14.58
Use Forecasts in Net
Present Value Analysis
(LO 3)

mhhe.com/hilton3e

Problem 14.59
Use Forecasts in Net
Present Value Analysis
(LO 3)

Octopus Garden, Inc., manufactures innovative, trendy toys and gifts. Successful gifts provide a very high rate of return, averaging 16 percent, and the company's development department has a very good success rate. Marketing research indicates that the latest new toy can be sold for three years but not after that. To meet expected demand for the new toy, Octopus Garden needs to buy additional equipment and obtain 25,000 square feet of space. The company has 12,500 square feet of unused space, which it controls under a lease with three more years at $3 per square foot per year. Octopus Garden can rent an additional 12,500 square feet for three years at $4 per square foot per year. The equipment will be purchased for $900,000, depreciated at $300,000 per year, and salvaged for $50,000. Sales, general, and administrative (SG&A) costs are allocated to all products, although these costs are not traced to specific products. Octopus Garden analysts have made the following income forecasts:

End of	Year I	Year 2	Year 3
Sales	$ 900,000	$1,400,000	$ 600,000
Unit, batch & product costs	750,000	400,000	350,000
SG&A (allocated)	40,000	75,000	35,000
Rent of existing space	37,500	37,500	37,500
Rent of new space	50,000	50,000	50,000
Depreciation	300,000	300,000	300,000
Income before tax	$(277,500)	$ 537,500	(172,500)
Tax (savings) @ 35%	(97,125)	188,125	(60,375)
Income after tax	$(180,375)	$ 349,375	$(112,125)

Required

a.   Compute after-tax net cash flows for this investment.

b.   Compute the net present value of this investment. Is this a desirable project? Explain why or why not.

[CMA adapted]

Problem 14.60
Assess the Effects of the
Discount Rate in Net
Present Value Analysis
(LO 3)

The financial staff of North American Motors used a 30 percent discount rate to analyze a technological improvement that promised to save the company millions in quality-related costs. The financial staff recommended that top management reject the project. Production managers responded by email that they believed the new process and equipment were necessary to improve product quality, which had fallen behind that of competitors. They argued that, although quality improvements were a strategic goal of the company, the direct reduction in quality costs was only a small part of the benefits of this project. The company's reputation and sales would improve as the quality of its products improved.

Martha Flowers, chief financial analyst, replied to the production managers' arguments by stating, "You have not quantified these so-called benefits from improved company reputation, and we don't believe it is possible to do so. Therefore, we have to evaluate this project by the numbers, and the net present value is negative. So, our recommendation is 'no.'"

The production managers complained that the use of a 30 percent discount rate was far too high. Lead production manager Art High said, "I don't know what thin air you have been breathing, but we almost never get a 30 percent return on investments."

Flowers responded, "We have audited your past technology investments and found that they almost never performed as well as you said they will. Because of your unrealistic projections, we bumped up the discount rate."

After seeing these emails and a flurry of subsequent ones that became progressively more heated, the division president took two aspirin and called you in for advice. "Make sense of this," he said. "Write a short report that communicates what's really going on here, and advise me what to do with this project."

Required
Write the report requested by the division president.

Problem 14.61
Model Effects of
Competitors' Actions in
Net Present Value
Analysis
(LO 4)

Healthy Noodles, Inc., is planning to open a noodles restaurant near a new housing development and office park. Healthy Noodles estimates that the neighborhood's fast-food market will be $400,000 per year when the new housing and offices are occupied next year. Noodles expects to capture 25 percent of the total neighborhood market unless MacBurger also opens a new store in the area. In that case, Noodles expects to gain only 15 percent of the market. Noodles' gross margin ratio is 40 percent. Its analysts believe there is a 50 percent chance that MacBurger will enter the market. They have prepared the following estimates that they believe are valid for the first four years of the investment.

First year's market	$ 400,000
Annual market growth	10%
Market share without MacBurger	25%
Market share with MacBurger	15%
Gross margin ratio	40%
Opportunity (discount) rate	8%
Investment cost	$ (80,000)
Tax rate	35%
Depreciation	20,000
SG&A	8,000
Probability of MacBurger entry	50%

Required

a. *Build your own spreadsheet.* Prepare spreadsheet models similar to those in Exhibits 14–8 and 14–9, assuming that Healthy Noodles can defer its investment decision one year to resolve uncertainty about MacBurger's intentions.

b. What does this analysis indicate about the possible effects of MacBurger's entry into this market?

c. On the basis of this analysis, would you recommend that Healthy Noodles defer its decision? Explain.

This is a continuation of Problem 14.61.

Required

a. *Build your own spreadsheet.* Prepare spreadsheet models similar to Exhibits 14–16 and 14–17 (Appendix B) that permit comparisons with the models in Problem 14.61. Assume that Healthy Noodles makes its investment decision now without resolving the uncertainty about MacBurger's intentions. Also assume that Healthy Noodles can terminate its investment after one year and sell its assets for $60,000. It also can extend its operations through year 5 by spending an additional $30,000 at the end of year 4, which is deductible from income in year 5.

b. What does this analysis indicate about what Healthy Noodles should do if MacBurger does enter the market in a year?

c. On the basis of this analysis, would you recommend that Healthy Noodles invest in the new restaurant now? Explain.

Problem 14.62
Model Effects of
Competitors' Actions in
Net Present Value
Analysis
(LO 4)

This is a continuation of Problems 14.61 and 14.62.

Required

a. Prepare decision trees similar to those in Exhibits 14–10 and 14–11 that contain expected net present values of Healthy Noodles' investment options.

b. Does this analysis indicate that it is better for Healthy Noodles to invest now or wait a year to find more information about MacBurger's plans? Explain.

c. Compute the real option value of waiting one year on this investment decision.

d. What is the economic meaning of the amount calculated in requirement (c)?

Problem 14.63
Apply Real Option Value
Analysis
(LO 5)

Unreal Networks, Inc., participated with several large music industry firms in a joint venture to distribute music electronically to third parties, such as Internet service providers and computer manufacturers, who would then sell the rights to download music to consumers. Unreal Networks is considering an investment in a start-up company that uses Unreal's Internet-based audio and video technology to deliver music directly to consumers. However, the start-up company's technology was unproven and consumer enthusiasm for paying to download music was unclear. Unreal Networks has identified two investment options: (1) buy a controlling share of the start-up company now or (2) invest a smaller amount now both to support the technology and secure a relationship with the start-up with an option to buy the company later. If Unreal buys the start-up, it will terminate participation in the current joint venture.

Unreal's analysts identified two major external events that could affect consumers' willingness to pay for downloaded music. First, Apple Computer was beginning a service to sell downloaded music at $.99 per song. The success of that business could signal consumers' willingness to pay for selected music. Second, music recording companies were planning a legal strategy to discourage unlicensed music sharing and downloading. If successful, these approaches could enlarge the market for paid downloads. Either of these events could improve the prospects for significant returns from a purchase of the start-up company; success of both would be a stronger signal.

Problem 14.64
Apply Real Option Value
Analysis
(LO 5)

Required

a.   Draw decision trees that describe the investment options that Unreal Networks was considering. Indicate the amounts that it must measure to complete the decision trees.

b.   Describe the methods you would use to measure each of the amounts identified in requirement (a).

c.   How would you recommend assessing the risks of the investment options?

d.   What qualitative factors might be important to this decision?

Problem 14.65
Evaluate Ethical Issues in Strategic Investment Analysis
(LO 6)

One-Day Shades Corp. is considering expanding its Las Vegas manufacturing operations. It can either convert a warehouse that it owns in the suburbs, or it can expand its current plant downtown. After the board of directors approved the expansion, George Wilson, the controller, set about to determine which proposal had the higher net present value. He assigned this task to Helen Guerning, the assistant controller. She completed her task, which indicated that the warehouse proposal had a negative net present value, but the downtown expansion proposal had a slightly positive one.

Wilson was displeased with Guerning's report on the suburban warehouse proposal. He returned it to her, stating, "You must have made an error. This proposal should look better." She suspected that Wilson wanted the suburban warehouse proposal to succeed so that he could avoid his lengthy commute to the city on the days he worked at the expansion site.

She checked her figures and found nothing wrong, although she believed that estimates of property sales values at the end of the investment lives provided by the real estate department were particularly uncertain. She made minor changes to the wording of the report to that effect but left the substance of the report unchanged. Wilson was still angry and demanded a second revision. He told Guerning to double the estimate of the suburban warehouse's salvage value because he believes that the real estate department is being too conservative and that suburban land values will increase dramatically as the region continues to grow. This change would make the suburban warehouse proposal's net present value positive and higher than that of the downtown expansion.

Required

a.   Was Guerning's first revision on the proposal for the warehouse proposal unethical? Explain.

b.   Was Wilson's conduct unethical when he gave Guerning specific instructions on preparing the second revision? Explain.

c.   How should Guerning attempt to resolve this issue? Should she discuss this issue with anyone outside the organization?

[CMA adapted]

Problem 14.66
Evaluate Ethical Issues in Strategic Investment Analysis
(LO 6)

Barbara Ciruli joined Toscana Corporation of Florence, Italy as a financial analyst three months ago. She is about to make her first presentation to the management committee responsible for selecting strategic investments. Ciruli has two proposals that require the same investment cost and have the same project life. Both involve an investment in new products. Project Alta would generate a net present value of €750,000; project Bassa would generate a net present value of €600,000.

The management committee decided that both analyses and projects were acceptable but that taking on both at the same time would stretch managers' capabilities beyond reasonable limits. The committee proposed going ahead with one project now and then starting the second project after the first one is going smoothly. The committee asked Ciruli which project she thinks would be less risky to start first.

Ciruli's cousin Roberto is the most highly qualified engineer in the company and was responsible for much of the design of product Bassa. She has the highest admiration for him and plans to recommend project Bassa despite its lower net present value.

Required

a.   Should investment projects be selected solely on a net present value basis? Why or why not?

b.   Is Ciruli's bias toward her cousin's project unethical? Why or why not?

c.   How would you recommend that Barbara Ciruli proceed to evaluate the risk of each project and make a recommendation to the management committee?

Cases

Case 14.67
Expected Net Present Value Analysis
(LO 1–4)

Liquid Chemical Co.—Part 1.[12] Liquid Chemical Company manufactures chemical products that require careful packing. The company has been profitable for the past decade and expects continued, future profitability. The company operates a department that maintains its containers in good condition and makes new ones as needed using a special patented container lining made from a material known as GHL.

---

[12] Adapted from a case by Professor David Solomons, Wharton School of the University of Pennsylvania.

Matt Walsh, the general manager, believed the firm might save money and get equal service by buying its containers and maintenance services from an outside source. He approached Packages, Inc., and asked for a quotation for making and maintaining the containers. He also asked Carol Dyer, his chief financial analyst, for a statement of the cost of operating the container department.

Packages, Inc.'s quotation specified that it can supply 3,000 new containers for $1,250,000 a year and can perform routine maintenance on containers for $375,000 a year, the contract to run for a guaranteed term of five years and renewable from year to year thereafter. If the required quantity increases, the contract price is increased proportionally. If the required quantity decreases below 3,000 containers, however, Liquid Chemical must pay the contracted amount.

Walsh compared these figures with Dyer's cost figures for last year's container department operations. Those figures are as follows:

Materials		$ 700,000
Labor		
Supervisor		50,000
Workers		450,000
Department overheads		
Manager's salary (Duffy)	$ 80,000	
Rent on container department	45,000	
Depreciation on machinery	150,000	
Maintenance of machinery	36,000	
Other expenses	157,500	468,500
Total department costs		$1,668,500
Proportion of general administrative overhead		225,000
Total cost of container department for year		$1,893,500

Walsh concluded that closing the department and entering into the contract offered by Packages, Inc., was optimal. However, he gave the manager of the container department, Les Duffy, an opportunity to question this conclusion before he acted on it. Even if his department were closed, Duffy's own position was not in jeopardy. There are no net cash consequences for the firm of transferring Duffy to another position because he can fill a position that would otherwise be filled by a newly hired manager paid $80,000 per year.

Duffy thought the matter over. The next morning, he spoke to Walsh and said he thought there were several factors to consider before his department was closed. "For instance," he said, "what will you do with the machinery? It cost $1,200,000 four years ago, but you'd be lucky if you got $200,000 for it now, even though it's good for another five or six years.

"Another matter," Duffy said, "is the expected quantity of containers we will need. The contract prices can be negotiated upward but not downward. The odds are 25 percent that in any given year we will need only 2,000 containers, but we could just as easily need 4,000. We can save costs internally if demand drops, but we would have to eat the extra contract costs if we outsource containers and maintenance and demand drops."

Walsh called Dyer in and reported Duffy's points. Dyer said, "I think my figures are pretty conclusive for 3,000 containers per year. At 2,000 or 4,000 containers per year, materials and machine maintenance costs would shift proportionately, but most likely we would not save or incur additional other costs at those levels. We're also paying $85,000 a year in rent for a warehouse for other corporate purposes. If we closed Duffy's department, we'd have all the warehouse space we need without renting."

"That's a good point," said Walsh. "Moreover, I don't think we can find room easily for the supervisor or any of the workers elsewhere in the firm. We are bound to spend something on outplacement and retraining. Allow $30,000 a year for five years. We also should budget an additional $20,000 for severance pay to be paid in a lump sum when or if we close the department."

Duffy added, "What about this $225,000 for general administrative overhead? You surely don't expect to sack anyone in the general office if I'm closed, do you?"

"Probably not," said Dyer, "but someone has to pay for these costs. We can't ignore them when we look at an individual department because if we do that with each department in turn, we'll finish up by convincing ourselves that word processing, accounting, administration and the like don't have to be paid for."

"Well, I've told the people at Packages, Inc. that I'd let them know my decision within a week," said Walsh. "I'll let you know what I decide to do before I contact them."

Assume the company has an after-tax cost of capital of 10 percent per year and uses an income tax rate of 40 percent for decisions like these. Depreciation for book and tax purposes is straight-line over eight years. The machinery has a tax basis of $600,000. Any gain or loss on sale of machinery is taxed at 40 percent. For ease of analysis, assume that all cash flows occur at the end of each year. Input data are available here or from your instructor electronically.

Data Input

Tax rate	40%
Hurdle (discount) rate	10%
Decision horizon	5 years
Materials	
Total materials (make containers, do maintenance)	$700,000 per year
Machinery	
Machinery purchase cost	$1,200,000
Machinery salvage value at year 0	200,000
Age of machinery	4 years
Machinery depreciation, assuming zero salvage value	$150,000 per year
Depreciable life of machinery...	8 years
Opportunity cost of facility rental	$85,000 per year
Labor costs	
Labor	$450,000 per year
Supervisor	$50,000 per year
Manager	$80,000 per year
Severance costs..	$20,000 year 0
Training & outplacement costs	$30,000 per year
Machinery maintenance...	$36,000 per year
Other expenses	$157,500 per year
Maintenance contract for containers	$375,000 per year
Container contract ....$1,250,000 per year	
Container demand, units per year, probability now	2,000 25%
Container demand, units per year, probability now	3,000 50%
Container demand, units per year, probability now	4,000 25%

Required

Individually or with a small group, answer the following questions.

a.   Describe Walsh's two alternative choices and the major uncontrollable, external event identified in the case.

b.   *Build your own spreadsheet.* Prepare a financial model of the alternative choices. Which action should be taken? Support your conclusion with a net present value analysis of the alternative costs.

c.   How sensitive is your conclusion in requirement (b) to changes in the discount rate? Demonstrate and explain using sensitivity analysis.

Case 14.68
Real Option Value
Analysis
(LO 5)

Liquid Chemical Company—Part 2. Use the information and analyses from Case 14.67 to continue the case. Liquid Chemical's chief competitor is being investigated by the Environmental Protection Agency (EPA). The competitor is facing punitive action for repeated violations. The most serious sanction against the competitor will require it to close its plant for at least three years for cleanup and retooling. Liquid Chemical's legal staff estimates the probability of this sanction to be 40 percent. Lesser sanctions will increase the competitor's costs but will not lead to a shutdown. The EPA outcome will be known in one year. During a shutdown, total regional demand for containers will drop, and Walsh believes that Liquid Chemical should be able to negotiate 30 percent lower costs for the five-year outsourcing contracts for maintenance and containers. Additionally, if the competitor shuts down, Dyer estimates that the probability of Liquid Chemical's demand for only 2,000 containers per year drops to zero and the probabilities of demand for either 3,000 or 4,000 containers per year are equal. Duffy has convinced Walsh that if Liquid Chemical decides to not outsource containers and maintenance, the company should commit to continuing internal operations for the foreseeable future. Assume the following:

▪   Internal operations will continue for at least one year if the decision is delayed.

▪   The company could elect to outsource containers and maintenance after learning the competitor's status.

▪   Neither demand probabilities nor outsourcing costs revert to original values after a competitor shutdown.

Ms. Dyer has prepared the following additional analyses.

Decide Now?	Decision 1: Internal or Outsource?	Competitor Shutdown?	Decision 2: Internal or Outsource?	Expected NPV
Yes	Internal	Yes	Internal	$4,136,050
Yes	Internal	Yes	Outsource	3,329,610
Yes	Internal	No	Internal	3,882,412

Decide Now?	Decision 1: Internal or Outsource?	Competitor Shutdown?	Decision 2: Internal or Outsource?	Expected NPV
Yes	Internal	No	Outsource	$4,225,615
Yes	Outsource	Yes	Outsource	4,470,259
Yes	Outsource	No	Outsource	4,212,848
No	Internal	Yes	Internal	4,136,050
No	Internal	Yes	Outsource	3,329,610
No	Internal	No	Internal	3,882,412
No	Internal	No	Outsource	4,225,615

Required

Individually or with a small group, address the following:

a. Prepare a decision tree of the decisions to decide now or wait a year.

b. Does waiting a year for the EPA ruling before making this decision have value? Demonstrate and support your answer using real option value analysis. What is your recommendation?

Reunion City plans to remodel its aging shopping mall.[13] The city owns the property and depends on sales tax revenue of 3 percent of sales at the mall to fund many city services, but annual sales at the mall have declined 5 percent to a current $80 million. Reunion City's plans call for 20 percent annual growth in sales at the mall after remodeling, which will take one year, unless the neighboring city of Pleasantville attracts a WalMart Superstore. In that case, Reunion City's mall might experience only 10 percent annual growth. The city manager believes that if the city acts quickly, the probability that WalMart will move to Pleasantville is 20 percent, but if the city delays as much as a year, the probability rises to 75 percent.

Case 14.69
Real Option Value
Analysis
(LO 1–5)

The mall's sales tax revenues will decline 25 percent during the remodeling period. Because merchants and customers alike are fleeing the aging mall, the city believes it must either remodel the mall or demolish it now and sell the land to private developers. The city's current remodeling costs will be $10 million. However, the city's district federal representative is certain that she can obtain an urban renewal grant for 40 percent of the cost, but congressional approval will take one year. The city's current budget crisis makes the federal grant very attractive. Is it worth waiting for?

Reunion City's director of finance, Rich Lopez, has consulted private developers and the city's planning and urban renewal boards to assemble the following estimates relevant to the mall remodeling.

Data Input	Amount (thousands)
Remodeling cost—now	$(10,000)
Remodeling cost—defer one year	$(6,000)
Current mall sales	$80,000 per year
Administrative costs	$1,000 per year
Net proceeds of demolition	$5,000
Discount rate	6%
Sales tax rate	3%
Current rate of sales decline	−5% per year
Sales growth without WalMart	20% per year
Sales growth with WalMart	10% per year
Sales decline during remodeling	−25% per year
Probability of WalMart if delay	75%
Probability of WalMart if act now	20%
Remodel life	10 years

Required

a. From the perspective of Reunion City, prepare a real option value (ROV) analysis of the decision either to remodel the mall now or defer a year. (*Hint:* Deferring the decision one year means you should give all alternatives equal lives.) What is your recommendation?

b. Demonstrate the sensitivity of the ROV analysis to estimates of the probabilities of WalMart's actions now or later.

c. What qualitative factors might be important to the decision?

d. Make a presentation of your analysis suitable for discussion at a meeting of Reunion City's mayor, director of finance, planning board, and urban renewal board.

---

[13] This case is based on and extends Exercise 14.51.

Chapter 15

Budgeting and Financial Planning

After completing this chapter, you should be able to:

1. Describe the key role that budgeting plays in the strategic planning process.

2. Explain five purposes of budgeting systems.

3. Describe and prepare a master budget, including each of its components.

4. Describe and evaluate a typical organization's process of budget administration.

5. Understand the behavioral implications of budgetary slack and participative budgeting.

6. Describe contemporary trends in the budgeting process as an element of a cost-management system.

7. Use the economic-order-quantity model to make inventory-ordering decisions and discuss the implications of the JIT approach for inventory management (Appendix).

Cost-*Management* Challenges

(Solutions are on page 626.)

1. **Why** does Collegiate Apparel need an annual budget? Specifically, what purposes would the budgeting process serve?

2. **How** could Collegiate Apparel's budget facilitate communication and coordination among the company's president, sales manager, and production supervisor?

3. **What** is a master budget? What are its main components for a manufacturer such as Collegiate Apparel?

4. **How** could Collegiate Apparel's president or a company's board of directors use the budget to influence the firm's future direction?

5. **Would** participative budgeting be effective for Collegiate Apparel Company?

Collegiate Apparel Company
2150 Boundary Bay Road
Vancouver, British Columbia
Canada

Memorandum

To: Timothy Williams
         President
From: Meg Johnston
         Sales Manager
cc: Bradley Roaldsson
         Production Supervisor
Subject: Sales forecast for the next four quarters

I have completed the sales forecast for the next four quarters for inclusion in the annual budget and anticipate unit sales as follows:

1st quarter	15,000 units
2nd quarter	5,000 units
3rd quarter	10,000 units
4th quarter	20,000 units
Total	50,000 units

As usual, the heaviest volume is expected to be in the first and fourth quarters. The first quarter sales reflect the return of students to campus for the spring semester (or winter quarter). The fourth quarter sales reflect not only heavy sales during the fall semester (or quarter) but also sales during the December holiday period. As you will notice, the forecast shows a slight increase over the current year's projected sales. (Next year's sales forecast of 50,000 units represents a 4.2 percent increase over the current year's projection of 48,000 units.) Interestingly, it appears that our volume at large universities will increase by about 5,000 units, but this is offset by an anticipated decline of 3,000 sales units at medium and small institutions. The reasons for this are not immediately clear, and I intend to explore this issue further. More targeted advertising at the small and medium school markets might be worth considering.

The assumptions on which the sales forecast is based include very little change in general economic conditions, a continued low rate of inflation, little change in the student populations at the institutions we serve, and no anticipated change in students' affinity for college logo apparel.

To support this forecast, I conducted telephone interviews with buyers from the campus book stores from a representative sample of institutions in the small, medium, and large college categories.

Please let me know if I can provide any further information at this time.

As the memo on the preceding page indicates, Collegiate Apparel Company is about to begin its annual budgeting, or financial planning, process. Developing a budget is a critical step in planning any economic activity. This is true for businesses, governmental agencies, and individuals. We all must budget our money to meet day-to-day expenses and to plan for major expenditures, such as buying a car or paying for college tuition. Similarly, businesses of all types and governmental units at every level must make financial plans to conduct routine operations, to plan for major expenditures, and to help make financing decisions.

Before exploring Collegiate Apparel Company's budgeting process in detail, let's step back and take a broader view of organizational planning and the role of budgeting in cost-management systems.

Auto manufacturers rely on district sales budgets in delivering new vehicles to their dealerships.

Class sizes and other activities in colleges are determined in part by budgetary considerations.

Strategic Planning: Achieving and Maintaining a Competitive Advantage

LO I Describe the key role that budgeting plays in the strategic planning process.

Every enterprise has a set of goals, such as profitability, growth, or public service. To achieve those goals, an organization's top management periodically (or even continuously) engages in strategic planning. Achieving and maintaining a competitive advantage usually are primary goals of this strategic-planning exercise. Management often outlines the organization's **critical success factors,** the key strengths that are most responsible for making the organization successful. Critical success factors enable a company to outperform its competitors. By identifying these factors and ensuring that they are incorporated into the strategic plan, companies are able to maintain an edge over competitors. In addition, important critical success factors can be exploited to improve the company's overall competitiveness.

For example, Southwest Airlines (www.southwestair.com) has relied on several factors to maintain its competitive edge. It keeps its prices consistently low and its routes in the short to medium range, and Southwest uses only one type of plane (keeping costs to a minimum). The company's management knows that these are among Southwest's critical success factors and has continued to increase the airline's competitiveness by building these factors into the strategic planning process.

Can you think of some critical success factors for a small manufacturer, such as Collegiate Apparel Company, whose target market consists of college students?

What Is a Strategic Long-Range Plan?

Although a statement of goals is necessary to guide an organization, it is important to detail the specific steps required to achieve them. A **strategic long-range plan** expresses the specific steps required to achieve an organization's goals. Because the long-range plan considers the intermediate and distant future, it is usually stated in rather broad terms. Strategic plans discuss the major capital investments required to maintain present facilities, increase capacity, diversify products or processes, and develop particular markets. For example, a paper company's strategies included the following:[1]

- *Cost control.* Optimize the contribution from existing product lines by holding product cost increases to less than the general rate of inflation. This will involve acquiring new machinery proposed in the capital budget as well as replacing our five least efficient plants over the next five years.
- *Market share.* Maintain our market share by providing a level of service and quality comparable to our top competitors. This requires improving our quality control to reduce customer complaints and returned merchandise from a current level of 4 percent to 1 percent within two years.

Each strategy statement was supported by projected activity levels (sales volumes, aggregate costs, and cash flow projections) for each of the next five years. At this stage, management had not stated the plans in much detail, but the plans had been well thought out and provided a general framework for guiding management's operating decisions.

Long-range plans are achieved in year-by-year steps. The guidance is more specific for the coming year than it is for more distant years. The plan for the coming year is called the *master budget,* which we will explore in detail later in the chapter. First, however, let's look more closely at the purposes of budgeting systems and the various types of budgets.

What Are the Key Purposes of Budgeting Systems?

A **budget** is a detailed plan, expressed in quantitative terms, that specifies how an organization will acquire and use resources during a particular period of time. A **budgeting system** comprises the procedures used to develop a budget. Budgeting systems have five primary purposes: planning, facilitating communication and coordination, allocating resources, managing financial and operational performance, and evaluating performance and providing incentives.

LO 2 Explain five purposes of budgeting systems.

Planning

The most obvious purpose of a budget is to quantify a plan of action. The budgeting process forces the individuals who constitute an organization to plan ahead. The development of a quarterly budget for a Westin Hotel, for example, forces the hotel manager, the reservation manager, and the food and beverage manager to plan for the staffing and supplies needed to meet anticipated demand for the hotel's services.

Facilitating Communication and Coordination

For any organization to be effective, each manager throughout the organization must be aware of the plans made by other managers. To plan reservations and ticket sales effectively, the reservations manager for American Airlines must know the flight schedules developed by the airline's route manager. The budgeting process pulls together the plans of each manager in an organization.

Allocating Resources

Generally, an organization's resources are limited, and budgets provide one means to allocate resources among competing uses. The City of San Francisco, for example, must allocate its revenue among basic safety services (such as police and fire protection),

---

[1] The source of these strategy statements was the company's internal documents, which the company provided to the authors.

maintenance of property and equipment (such as city streets, parks, and vehicles), and other community services (such as child care services and programs to prevent alcohol and drug abuse).

Managing Financial and Operational Performance

A budget is a plan, and plans are subject to change. Nevertheless, a budget serves as a useful benchmark with which actual results can be compared. For example, Allstate Insurance Company can compare its actual sales of insurance policies for a year against its budgeted sales. Such a comparison can help managers evaluate the firm's effectiveness in selling insurance. (The next chapter examines the control purpose of a budget in more depth.)

Evaluating Performance and Providing Incentives

Comparing actual results with budgeted results also helps managers to evaluate the performance of individuals, departments, divisions, or entire companies. Since budgets are used to evaluate performance, they also can be used to provide incentives for people to perform well. For example, IBM Corporation, like many other companies, provides incentives for managers to improve profits by awarding bonuses to managers who meet or exceed their budgeted profit goals.

How would each of these five purposes of budgeting systems be relevant in managing a small manufacturing company such as Collegiate Apparel Company?

Organizations Use Many Types of Budgets

Different types of budgets serve different purposes. A **master budget,** or **profit plan,** is a comprehensive set of budgets covering all phases of an organization's operations for a specified period of time. We examine a master budget in detail later in this chapter.

Budgeted financial statements, often called **pro forma financial statements,** show how the organization's financial statements will appear at a specified time if operations proceed according to plan. Budgeted financial statements include a *budgeted income statement,* a *budgeted balance sheet,* and a *budgeted statement of cash flows.*

A **capital budget** is a plan for buying and selling capital assets, such as buildings and equipment. We cover capital budgeting in Chapter 14. A **financial budget** is a plan that shows how the organization will acquire its financial resources, such as issuing stock or incurring debt.

Budgets are developed for specific time periods. *Short-range budgets* cover a year, a quarter, or a month, whereas *long-range budgets* cover periods longer than a year. **Rolling** (or **revolving** or **continuous**) **budgets** are continually updated by periodically adding a new incremental time period, such as a quarter, and dropping the period just completed.

Master Budget as a Planning Tool

LO 3 Describe and prepare a master budget, including each of its components.

The master budget, the principal output of a budgeting system, is a comprehensive profit plan that ties together all phases of an organization's operations. The master budget comprises many separate budgets, or schedules, that are interdependent. Exhibit 15–1 portrays these interrelationships in a flowchart, which shows the components of a master budget for a manufacturing firm. (Later in the chapter, we explore Collegiate Apparel Company's master budget in detail.)

Sales Budget: The Starting Point

The starting point for any master budget is a sales revenue budget based on forecasted sales of goods or services. Airlines forecast the number of passengers on each of their routes. Banks forecast the number and dollar amount of consumer loans and home mortgages to be provided. Hotels forecast the number of rooms that will be occupied during various seasons. Manufacturing and merchandising companies fore-

Exhibit 15–1   Components of a Master Budget for a Manufacturing Firm

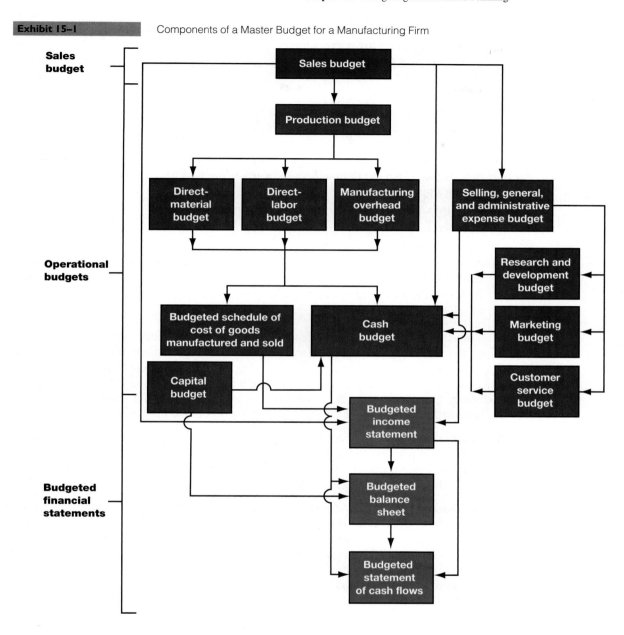

cast sales of their goods. Some companies sell both goods and services. For example, Kmart is a large merchandising company, but its automotive-service branch provides the firm with substantial service revenue.

Sales forecasting.   All companies have two things in common when it comes to forecasting sales of services or goods: Sales forecasting is a critical step in the budgeting process, and it is very difficult to do accurately. **Sales forecasting** is the process of predicting sales of services or goods. Various procedures are used in sales forecasting, and the final forecast usually combines information from many different sources. Many firms have a top-management-level market research staff whose job is to coordinate the company's sales forecasting efforts. Typically, everyone from key executives to the firm's sales personnel is asked to contribute sales projections. These are among the major factors considered when forecasting sales:

1. *Past sales levels and trends.*
   a.   For the firm developing the forecast (for example, Exxon).
   b.   For the entire industry (for example, the petroleum industry).

2. *General economic trends.* (Is the economy growing? How fast? Is a recession or an economic slowdown expected?)

3. *Economic trends in the company's industry.* (In the petroleum industry, for example, is personal travel likely to increase, thereby implying increased demand for gasoline?)

4. *Other factors expected to affect sales in the industry.* (Is an unusually cold winter expected, which would result in increased demand for home heating oil in northern climates?)

5. *Political and legal events.* (For example, is any legislation pending in Congress that would affect the demand for petroleum, such as tax incentives to use alternative energy sources?)

6. *The intended pricing policy of the company.*

7. *Planned advertising and product promotion.*

8. *Expected actions of competitors.*

9. *New products contemplated by the company or other firms.* (For example, has an automobile firm announced the development of a vehicle that runs on hydrogen fuel, thereby reducing the demand for gasoline?)

10. *Market research studies.*

The starting point in the sales forecasting process is generally the sales level of the prior year. Then the market research staff considers the information just discussed along with input from key executives and sales personnel. A great deal of effort generally goes into the sales forecast since it is such a critical step in the budgeting process. A slightly inaccurate sales forecast, coming at the very beginning of the budgeting process, will throw off all of the other schedules that make up the master budget.

Sales staff.   Sales personnel are in the unique position of being close to the customers, and they might possess the best information in the company about customers' immediate and near-term needs. However, they might be tempted to bias their sales forecasts if such forecasts are used as the norm for performance evaluation.

Market researchers.   To provide a check on forecasts from local sales personnel, management often turns to market researchers. This group probably does not have the same incentives that sales personnel have to bias the budget. Furthermore, researchers have a different perspective on the market. They might know little about customers' immediate needs, but they can predict long-term trends in attitudes and the effects of social and economic changes on the company's sales, potential markets, and products.

Delphi technique.   The Delphi technique is another sales forecasting method used to enhance forecast accuracy and reduce bias in estimates. With this method, members of the forecasting group prepare individual forecasts and submit them anonymously. Each group member obtains a copy of all forecasts but is unaware of their sources. The group then discusses the results. In this way, group members address and reconcile differences among individual forecasts without involving the personality or position of individual forecasters. After discussing the differences, each group member prepares a new forecast and distributes it anonymously to the others. These forecasts are then discussed in the same manner as before. The process is repeated until the forecasts converge on a single best estimate of the coming year's sales level.

Econometric models.   Another forecasting approach is to enter past sales data into a regression model to obtain a statistical estimate of factors affecting sales. For example, the predicted sales for the coming period could be related to factors such as economic indicators, consumer-confidence indexes, back-order volume, and other internal and external factors that the company deems relevant. Advocates of these econometric models contend that they can include many relevant predictors and manipulate the assumed values of the predictors to examine a variety of hypothetical conditions and then relate them to the sales forecast.

Sophisticated analytical models for forecasting are now widely available. Most companies' computers have software packages that allow economical use of these models. Nonetheless, it is important to remember that no model removes the uncertainty surrounding sales forecasts. Management often finds that the intuition of local sales personnel is a better predictor than sophisticated analysis and models. As in any decision, management should use cost–benefit tests to determine which methods are most appropriate.

Operational Budgets: Meeting the Demand for Goods and Services

Based on the sales budget, a company develops a set of **operational budgets,** which specify how its operations will be carried out to meet the demand for its goods or services. The budgets constituting this operational portion of the master budget are depicted in the middle portion of Exhibit 15–1, which portrays the master budget for a manufacturing firm.

Manufacturing firms. A manufacturing company develops a production budget, which shows the number of product units to be manufactured. From the production budget, a manufacturer develops budgets for the direct materials, direct labor, and overhead required in the production process. These budgets provide the basis for a budgeted schedule of cost of goods manufactured and sold. A budget for selling, general, and administrative (SG&A) expenses is also prepared. The SG&A budget includes budgets for research and development (R&D), design, marketing, distribution, and customer service.

Merchandising firms. The operational portion of a merchandising firm's master budget is similar to that of a manufacturer, but instead of a production budget for goods, a merchandiser develops a budget for merchandise purchases. A merchandiser does not have a budget for direct materials because it does not engage in production. However, the merchandiser develops budgets for labor (or personnel), overhead, and selling and administrative expenses.

Service-industry firms. Based on the sales budget for its services, a service-industry firm develops a set of budgets that show how it will meet the demand for those services. An airline, for example, prepares the following operational budgets: a budget of planned air miles to be flown; materials budgets for spare aircraft parts, aircraft fuel, and in-flight food; labor budgets for flight crews and maintenance personnel; and an overhead budget.

Cash budget. Every business prepares a cash budget. This budget shows expected cash receipts as a result of selling goods or services and planned cash disbursements to pay the bills incurred by the firm.

Capital budget. The capital budget, which is prepared in all types of organizations, details plans for major acquisitions and disposals of assets, such as plant and equipment, vehicles, and land.

Summary of operational budgets. Although operational budgets differ according to the operations of individual companies in various industries, they are also similar in important ways. In each firm, operational budgets encompass a detailed plan for using the basic factors of production (materials, labor, and overhead) to produce a product or provide a service.

Budgeted Financial Statements: Completing the Master Budget

The final portion of the master budget, depicted in Exhibit 15–1, includes a budgeted income statement, a budgeted balance sheet, and a budgeted statement of cash flows. These budgeted financial statements show the overall financial results of the organization's planned operations for the budget period.

Master Budget for Nonprofit Organizations

The master budget for a nonprofit organization includes many of the components shown in Exhibit 15–1. However, there are some important differences. Many nonprofit organizations provide services free of charge. Hence, they have no sales budget as shown in Exhibit 15–1. However, such organizations do begin their budgeting process with a budget that shows the level of services to be provided. For example, the budget for the City of Dallas would show the planned levels of various public services. Nonprofit organizations also prepare budgets showing their anticipated funding. The City of Dallas budgets for revenue sources such as city taxes, state and federal revenue sharing, and sale of municipal bonds.

In summary, all organizations begin the budgeting process with plans for (1) the goods or services to be provided and (2) the revenue to be available, whether from sales or from other funding sources.

International Aspects of Budgeting

As the economies and cultures of countries throughout the world become intertwined, more and more companies are becoming multinational in their operations. Firms with international operations face a variety of additional challenges in preparing their budgets. First, a US multinational firm's budget must reflect the translation of foreign currencies into US dollars. Since almost all the world's currencies fluctuate in their values relative to the dollar, this makes budgeting for those translations difficult. Although multinationals have sophisticated financial ways to hedge against such currency fluctuations, the budgeting task for these firms is still more challenging. Second, budget preparation is difficult when inflation (or deflation) is high or unpredictable. While the United States has experienced periods of high inflation, some foreign countries have experienced hyperinflation, sometimes with annual

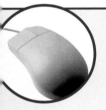

Research Insight 15.1

Practice-Based and Theoretical Approaches to Budgeting Research

Budgeting has drawn the interest of researchers for many years, both from a practice-based and a theoretical perspective. A recent example of practice-based research by Hansen, et al. focused on approaches currently being employed by practitioners to address shortcomings in traditional budgeting practices.[a] One such approach "advocates *improving* the budgeting process and primarily focuses on the planning problems with budgeting." The foremost example of this approach is *activity-based budgeting* (ABB), which "focuses on generating a budget from an activity-based model of the organization." The ABB approach "contends that budgeting serves primarily a planning role, and that budgeting suffers because the financial-oriented, higher-level budgeting process is not adequately connected to the underlying operational model of the organization."

In recent years, the Consortium for Advanced Manufacturing International (CAM-I) has promoted the concept of *beyond budgeting*, which seeks to replace annual budgeting with continuous, real-time budgeting. This effort has evolved into the Beyond Budgeting Round Table (www.bbrt.org). The BBRT has identified six budgeting principles and six organizational principles that support *beyond budgeting*. These principles include using autonomous teams and flexible goals, such as outperforming top competitors rather than meeting a fixed sales target, and then evaluating team performance similarly (e.g., did the team outperform the competition?). Together these 12 principles describe a flexible ("lean") organization that might be freer to adapt to changing conditions than one characterized by traditional, centrally controlled, annual budgeting. Proponents claim it is the wave of the future, but, while we are more cautious, we do believe that *beyond budgeting* is an exciting development that bears watching and deserves objective research.

Theoretical approaches to budgeting have employed one of three perspectives:[b] (1) *economics,* which asks what is the economic value [and effect] of budgeting practices; (2) *psychology,* which asks what are the effects of budgeting practices on individuals' behavior and performance; and (3) *sociology,* which asks how budgeting influences decision making and bargaining among the plurality of interests in an organization. A recent example of economics-based, theoretical research "experimentally investigated the effects of budget-based contracts and budget levels (performance targets) on group performance." A variety of budget-based contracts was compared to see which types of contracts result in the best overall group performance. *Sources:* [a]*S. Hansen, D. Otley, and W. A. Van der Stede, "Practice Developments in Budgeting: An Overview and Research Perspective"; and [b]J. G. Fisher, S. A. Peffer, and G. Z. Sprinkle, "Budget-Based Contracts, Budget Levels, and Group Performance." See also F. W. Rankin, S. T. Schwartz and R. A. Young, "Management Control Using Nonbinding Budgetary Announcements." (Full citations to references are in the Bibliography.)*

inflation rates well over 100 percent. Predicting such high inflation rates is difficult and further complicates a multinational's budgeting process. Finally, the economies of all countries fluctuate in terms of consumer demand, availability of skilled labor, laws affecting commerce, and so forth. Companies with offshore operations face the task of anticipating such changing conditions in their budgeting processes.

Activity-Based Budgeting

The process of constructing a master budget can be significantly enhanced if the concepts of activity-based costing are applied.[2] Activity-based costing uses a two-stage cost-assignment process. In stage I, overhead costs are assigned to cost pools that represent the most significant activities constituting the production process. The activities identified vary across manufacturers, but such activities as engineering design, materials handling, machine setup, production scheduling, inspection, quality control, and purchasing provide examples.

After assigning costs to the activity cost pools in stage I, cost drivers are identified that are appropriate for each cost pool. Then in stage II the overhead costs are allocated from each activity cost pool to cost objects (e.g., manufactured goods, services, and customers) in proportion to the amount of activity consumed.

Applying ABC concepts to the budgeting process yields **activity-based budgeting (ABB),**[3] which is the process of developing a master budget using information obtained from an activity-based costing (ABC) analysis. Under ABB, the first step is to specify the products or services to produce and the customers to serve. Then the activities that are necessary to produce these products and services are determined. Finally, the resources necessary to perform the specified activities are quantified. Conceptually, ABB takes the ABC model and reverses the flow of the analysis, as depicted in Exhibit 15–2. As portrayed in the diagram, ABC assigns resource costs to activities and then assigns activity costs to products and services produced and customers served. ABB, on the other hand, begins by forecasting the demand for products and services as well as the customers to serve. These forecasts then are used to plan the activities for the budget period and budget the resources necessary to carry out the activities.

In the next section of the chapter, we illustrate the process of constructing a master budget. Notice how the conceptual ABB model is employed in the budgeting process. After completing the master-budget illustration, we explore the benefits and implications of the ABB approach.

---

[2] Activity-based costing (ABC) is covered in Chapter 4.

[3] This section is based on the following references: J. A. Brimson and J. Antos, *Driving Value Using Activity-Based Budgeting;* S. Borjesson, "A Case Study on Activity-Based Budgeting"; and R. S. Kaplan and R. Cooper, *Cost and Effect.* (Full citations to references are in the Bibliography.)

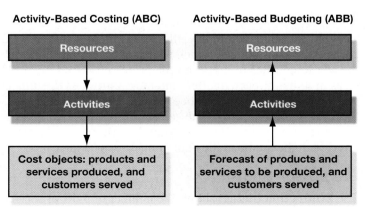

Exhibit 15–2

Activity-Based Costing versus Activity-Based Budgeting*

*Source: R. S. Kaplan and R. Cooper, *Cost and Effect.*

Cost Management in Practice 15.1

Benefits of ABB

American Express has successfully used ABB for its travel-related services in its New York operations. This relatively new system has been used to identify and implement cost reduction and process improvement initiatives. Then, an activity-by-activity analysis of each department has allowed process improvement savings to be factored into the forecasted costs for each department in the next budget cycle.

AT&T Paradyne designs and produces medium- and high-speed data communications equipment, which provides an interface between telephone networks and computers. The company's activity-based costing project ultimately led to activity-based budgeting. As ABM and ABB matured at AT&T Paradyne, the company began to experience a culture change. A key lesson learned in this case was that linking activity-based costing to the budgeting process and performance evaluation led to the integration of ABC into the management of the company. *Source: D. M. Aldea and D. E. Bullinger, "Using ABC for Shared Services, Charge-Outs, Activity-Based Budgeting, and Benchmarking"; and J. Collins, "Advanced Use of ABM: Using ABC for Target Costing, Activity-Based Budgeting, and Benchmarking."*

Illustrating the Master Budget

LO 3 Describe and prepare a master budget, including each of its components.

To illustrate the steps involved in developing a master budget, we focus on Collegiate Apparel Company, a small manufacturer of T-shirts bearing the names and logos of several major universities in Canada and the United States. Located in Vancouver, British Columbia, the company is wholly owned and managed by Timothy Williams, who started the firm four years ago. The entire business is operated in a single building. The manufacturing process is highly automated, using three machines to cut out pieces of fabric, stitch them together, and imprint the name and logo of one of several universities. The entire production cycle for a T-shirt requires just 12 minutes.

Collegiate Apparel Company's master budget for the year 20x1 has just been completed. It contains the following schedules, which are displayed and explained in the following pages.

Schedule	Title of Schedule
1	Sales Budget
2	Production Budget
3	Direct-Material Budget
4	Direct-Labor Budget
5	Manufacturing Overhead Budget
6	Selling, General, and Administrative Expense Budget
7	Cash Receipts Budget
8	Cash Disbursements Budget
9	Cash Budget
10	Budgeted Schedule of Cost of Goods Manufactured and Sold
11	Budgeted Income Statement
12	Budgeted Balance Sheet

Sales Budget

The first step in developing Collegiate Apparel Company's 20x1 master budget is to prepare the sales budget, which is displayed in schedule 1. The **sales budget** displays the projected sales in units and the projected sales revenue. It displays the projected sales in units for each quarter, and then multiplies the unit sales by the sales price to determine sales revenue. Notice that there is a significant seasonal pattern in the sales forecast, with the bulk of the sales coming in the fall and winter. (This is the sales forecast to which Collegiate Apparel Company's sales manager, Meg Johnston, referred in the memo at the beginning of this chapter.)

Production Budget

The **production budget** shows the number of units of services or goods that are to be produced during a budget period. Collegiate Apparel's production budget, displayed

Revised Production Budget

You're the Decision Maker 15.1

Suppose you are in charge of Collegiate Apparel's budgeting process. The sales manager has just informed you that the sales forecast has been increased by 20 percent during each quarter of 20x1 and the first quarter of 20x2.

a. Revise Collegiate's production budget for 20x1. Assume that the expected finished-goods inventory on January 1, 20x1, is still 1,500 units.

b. Now put yourself in the position of Collegiate's production supervisor. If the sales manager said she was only somewhat confident in the increased sales forecast, would you recommend increasing production to the levels in your revised budget? Why?

(Solutions begin on page 626.)

Schedule 1

COLLEGIATE APPAREL COMPANY
Sales Budget
For the Year Ending December 31, 20x1

	Quarter				
	1st	2nd	3rd	4th	Year
Sales in units	15,000	5,000	10,000	20,000	50,000
Unit sales price	× $12	× $12	× $12	× $12	× $12
Total sales revenue............................	$180,000	$60,000	$120,000	$240,000	$600,000

in schedule 2, determines the number of T-shirts to be produced each quarter based on the quarterly sales projections in the sales budget (see schedule 2). Schedule 2 is based on the following formula.

$$
\begin{array}{ccccc}
\text{Sales in} & + & \text{Desired ending} & = & \text{Total} \\
\text{units} & & \text{inventory of} & & \text{units} \\
& & \text{finished goods} & & \text{required}
\end{array}
$$

$$
\begin{array}{ccccc}
\text{Total} & & \text{Expected beginning} & & \text{Units} \\
\text{units} & - & \text{inventory of finished} & = & \text{to be} \\
\text{required} & & \text{goods} & & \text{produced}
\end{array}
$$

Focus on the second-quarter column in schedule 2, which is shaded. Expected sales are 5,000 T-shirts, and management desires to have 1,000 finished units on hand at the end of the quarter. This is 10 percent of the expected sales for the third quarter. However, 500 T-shirts are expected to be in inventory at the beginning of the second quarter. Thus, only 5,500 T-shirts need to be produced.

Schedule 2

COLLEGIATE APPAREL COMPANY
Production Budget
For the Year Ending December 31, 20x1

	Quarter				
	1st	2nd	3rd	4th	Year
Sales in units.. (from schedule 1)	15,000	5,000	10,000	20,000	50,000
Add desired ending inventory of finished goods*	500	1,000	2,000	1,500†	1,500
Total units required	15,500	6,000	12,000	21,500	51,500
Less expected beginning inventory of finished goods......................	1,500	500	1,000	2,000	1,500
Units to be produced	14,000	5,500	11,000	19,500	50,000

*10 percent of the next quarter's expected sales.

†10 percent of the expected sales for the first quarter of the next year, 20x2, which is assumed to be 15,000 units.

Direct-Material Budget

The **direct-material budget** shows the number of units and the cost of material to be purchased and used during a budget period. As is true for almost all manufacturers, Collegiate Apparel's direct-material cost is a unit-level cost. Each shirt requires 1.5 yards of fabric. Collegiate Apparel's direct-material budget, displayed in schedule 3, shows the total amount of material needed to make T-shirts during each quarter. The shaded portion of schedule 3, which computes the amount of fabric to be purchased each quarter, is based on the following formula.

Raw material required for production	+	Desired ending inventory of raw material	=	Total raw material required

		Total raw material required	−	Expected beginning inventory of raw material	=	Raw material to be purchased

The lower, unshaded portion of schedule 3 computes the cost of each quarter's raw-materials purchases. (This information also will be needed later in the budgeting process in schedule 10.)

Production and purchasing: An important link.   Notice the important link between planned production and purchases of raw material. This link is apparent in schedule 3, and it is also emphasized in the formula preceding the schedule. Let's focus on the second quarter. Since 5,500 T-shirts are to be produced, 8,250 yards of material will be needed (5,500 units times 1.5 yards per unit). In addition, management desires to have 1,650 yards of material in inventory at the end of the quarter.[4] Thus, total needs are 9,900 yards. Does Collegiate Apparel Company need to purchase this much raw material? No, it does not, because 825 yards will be in inventory at the beginning of the quarter. Therefore, the firm needs to purchase only 9,075 yards of material during the quarter (9,900 yards less 825 yards in the beginning inventory).

Schedule 3

COLLEGIATE APPAREL COMPANY
Direct-Material Budget
For the Year Ending December 31, 20x1

	Quarter				
	1st	2nd	3rd	4th	Year
Units to be produced (from schedule 2)	14,000	5,500	11,000	19,500	50,000
Raw material required per unit (yards of fabric)	× 1.5	× 1.5	× 1.5	× 1.5	× 1.5
Raw material required for production (yards)	21,000	8,250	16,500	29,250	75,000
Add desired ending inventory of raw material (yards)*	825	1,650	2,925	2,100†	2,100
Total raw material required	21,825	9,900	19,425	31,350	77,100
Less expected beginning inventory of raw material (yards)	2,100	825	1,650	2,925	2,100
Raw material to be purchased (yards)	19,725	9,075	17,775	28,425	75,000
Cost per yard	× $2	× $2	× $2	× $2	× $2
Total cost of raw material purchases	$39,450	$18,150	$35,550	$56,850	$150,000

* 10 percent of the next quarter's expected raw material requirements.

† 10 percent of the expected raw material requirements for the first quarter of the next year, 20x2, which is assumed to be 21,000 yards.

---

[4] It often is desirable to have a buffer inventory just before a bottleneck operation.

Inventory management. Planned production and raw-material purchases is a particularly critical linkage in manufacturing firms. Thus, considerable effort is devoted to careful inventory planning and management. How did management decide how much raw material to have in inventory at the end of each quarter? Examination of schedule 3 reveals that each quarter's desired ending inventory of raw material is 10 percent of the *material needed for production* in the next quarter. For example, 1,650 yards of raw material (.10 × 16,500) will be in inventory at the end of the second quarter because 16,500 yards will be needed for production in the third quarter. The effect of this approach is to have a larger ending inventory when the next quarter's planned production is greater. Inventories are drawn down when the subsequent quarter's planned production is lower.

The appendix to this chapter explores various other tools used in inventory management.

Direct-Labor Budget

The **direct-labor budget** shows the number of hours and the cost of the direct labor to be used during a budget period. Collegiate Apparel Company's direct-labor budget is displayed in schedule 4. Based on each quarter's planned production, this schedule computes the amount of direct-labor needed each quarter and the cost of the required labor. Collegiate Apparel is a small company, and owner Timothy Williams hires all of his direct-labor production employees from the Vancouver area collegiate community. College students are employed, on a part-time basis only, to meet the labor demands of a given time period. Thus, Collegiate Apparel's direct labor may be adjusted up or down to meet short-term needs. As a result, direct labor for this company is a unit-level cost. As schedule 4 shows, each T-shirt manufactured requires .2 hours (12 minutes) of direct labor.

A note on direct labor and the cost hierarchy. It is important to note that the position of direct labor in the cost hierarchy depends on management's ability to adjust the organization's labor force to match short-term requirements, as well as management's attitude about making such adjustments. For either strategic business reasons or ethical concerns, many companies strive to maintain a relatively stable labor force. If production employees are retained when production declines, direct labor will not be a unit-level cost. In the extreme case when employees are virtually never laid off, direct labor becomes a facility- or general-operations-level cost.

Collegiate Apparel's ability to easily adjust the total hours of its part-time workforce results in a unit-level designation for direct-labor cost in this situation.

Schedule 4

COLLEGIATE APPAREL COMPANY
Direct-Labor Budget
For the Year Ending December 31, 20x1

	Quarter				
	1st	2nd	3rd	4th	Year
Units to be produced (from schedule 2)	14,000	5,500	11,000	19,500	50,000
Direct labor required per unit (hours)	× .2	× .2	× .2	× .2	× .2
Total direct-labor hours required	2,800	1,100	2,200	3,900	10,000
Direct-labor cost per hour	× $10	× $10	× $10	× $10	× $10
Total direct-labor cost	$28,000	$11,000	$22,000	$39,000	$100,000

Manufacturing-Overhead Budget

The **manufacturing-overhead budget** shows the cost of overhead expected to be incurred in the production process during the budget period. Collegiate Apparel's manufacturing-overhead budget, displayed in schedule 5, lists the expected cost of each overhead item by quarter. At the bottom of the schedule, the total budgeted overhead for each quarter is shown. Then each quarter's depreciation is subtracted to determine the total cash disbursements to be expected for overhead during each quarter.

Schedule 5

COLLEGIATE APPAREL COMPANY
Manufacturing-Overhead Budget
For the Year Ending December 31, 20x1

	Quarter				
	1st	2nd	3rd	4th	Year
Unit-Level Costs					
Units	*14,000*	*5,500*	*11,000*	*19,500*	*50,000*
Indirect material ($.25 per unit)	$ 3,500	$ 1,375	$ 2,750	$ 4,875	$ 12,500
Electricity (for machinery) ($.15 per unit)	2,100	825	1,650	2,925	7,500
Total unit-level costs	$ 5,600	$ 2,200	$ 4,400	$ 7,800	$ 20,000
Batch-Level Costs					
Production runs	*28*	*11*	*22*	*39*	*100*
Setup ($100 per run)	$ 2,800	$ 1,100	$ 2,200	$ 3,900	$ 10,000
Purchasing and material handling ($120 per run)	3,360	1,320	2,640	4,680	12,000
Inspection ($80 per run)	2,240	880	1,760	3,120	8,000
Total batch-level costs	$ 8,400	$ 3,300	$ 6,600	$11,700	$ 30,000
Product-Level Costs					
New style designs	*2*	*2*	*2*	*2*	*8*
Design ($500 per design)	$ 1,000	$ 1,000	$ 1,000	$ 1,000	$ 4,000
Total product-level costs	$ 1,000	$ 1,000	$ 1,000	$ 1,000	$ 4,000
Facility- and General-Operations-Level Costs					
Supervisory salaries	$14,000	$14,000	$14,000	$14,000	$ 56,000
Insurance and property taxes	2,400	2,400	2,400	2,400	9,600
Maintenance	2,600	2,600	2,600	2,600	10,400
Utilities	2,500	2,500	2,500	2,500	10,000
Depreciation	15,000	15,000	15,000	15,000	60,000
Total facility- and general-operations-level costs	$36,500	$36,500	$36,500	$36,500	$146,000
Total overhead	$51,500	$43,000	$48,500	$57,000	$200,000
Less depreciation	15,000	15,000	15,000	15,000	60,000
Total cash disbursements for overhead	$36,500	$28,000	$33,500	$42,000	$140,000

This cash-disbursement information will be needed later in the budgeting process when the cash disbursements budget is constructed (schedule 8).

Activity-based budgeting and the cost hierarchy.   Collegiate Apparel's unit-level costs include indirect material and electricity used to run the production machinery. Batch-level costs include machine setup, purchasing and material handling, and inspection. The cost driver for these costs is the number of production runs. A run typically produces 500 T-shirts. Collegiate Apparel's only product-level cost is design. The company typically commissions two new style designs each quarter from a local freelance textile designer. Each new design costs $500. The remaining overhead costs in schedule 5 include all costs at the facility or general-operations level.

Benefits of ABB.   Proponents of ABB believe that real, sustainable payoffs from activity-based costing and activity-based management will not be forthcoming until an organization's budgeting process embraces the ABM approach. Utilizing ABC information in the budgeting process provides solid reasoning for budgeting costs at particular levels since the underlying ABC information is based explicitly on the relationships among cost drivers, activities, and resources consumed. Moreover, the resulting budget is more useful to management because it reveals how cost levels will change if the predicted quantities of the cost drivers change. For example, what will happen to Collegiate Apparel's setup costs in the first quarter if the quantity produced is 14,000 units as reflected in the budget (see schedule 5), but 35 production runs are used to produce these 14,000 units instead of 28 runs as specified in the budget? According to schedule 5, setup cost is $100

Revision of Manufacturing Overhead Budget

Suppose it is September 15, 20x1, and the production plan has been revised for the fourth quarter so that 24,000 units will be manufactured. The fourth quarter production runs will be 600 units each. Moreover, three new design styles will be commissioned instead of two.

a. Revise the *fourth quarter* manufacturing overhead budget to reflect the changed production plan.

b. Suppose a special adjustment will need to be made on the cutting machine at the midpoint of each production run at a cost of $150. Where will this cost appear in the overhead budget?

(Solutions begin on page 626.)

You're the Decision Maker 15.2

per production run ($2,800 ÷ 28 runs). Therefore, 35 runs would result in $3,500 of setup cost in the first quarter instead of $2,800 as forecast in the budget. This is true even if 14,000 units are produced as forecast in the budget.

Traditional budgeting processes, which do not embrace the ABB approach, often classify costs such as setup, purchasing and materials handling, quality control and inspection, or design engineering as *fixed costs* since they do not vary with the number of units produced. The ABB approach, however, recognizes that these costs are really *variable* if the budget analyst is careful to identify the appropriate cost driver with which each of these costs varies.

Selling, General, and Administrative (SG&A) Expense Budget

The **selling, general, and administrative (SG&A) expense budget** shows the planned amounts of expenditures for selling, general, and administrative expenses during the budget period. Collegiate Apparel Company's selling, general, and administrative expense budget is displayed in schedule 6. This budget lists the expenses of administering the firm and selling its product.

Activity-based budgeting and the cost hierarchy. Sales commissions and freight-out (i.e., shipping) are unit-level expenses. The cost driver for these unit-level expenses is the number of units *sold* (not the number of units *produced*). Licensing fees paid to universities for permission to use their names and logos on Collegiate Apparel's T-shirts are customer-level costs. Each university typically charges a licensing fee, which is fixed within broad ranges of unit sales. As a small company, however,

Schedule 6

COLLEGIATE APPAREL COMPANY
Selling, General, and Administrative Expense Budget
For the Year Ending December 31, 20x1

	1st	2nd	3rd	4th	Year
Unit-Level Expenses					
Units	15,000	5,000	10,000	20,000	50,000
Sales commissions	$ 9,000	$ 3,000	$ 6,000	$12,000	$30,000
Freight-out	6,000	2,000	4,000	8,000	20,000
Total unit-level expenses	$15,000	$ 5,000	$10,000	$20,000	$50,000
Customer-Level Expenses					
Licensing fees for use of universities' names and logos	$ 1,500	$ 1,500	$ 1,500	$ 1,500	$ 6,000
Total customer-level expenses	$ 1,500	$ 1,500	$ 1,500	$ 1,500	$ 6,000
Facility- and General-Operations-Level Expenses					
Sales salaries	$ 2,000	$ 2,000	$ 2,000	$ 2,000	$ 8,000
Advertising	250	250	250	250	1,000
Clerical wages	2,500	2,500	2,500	2,500	10,000
Total facility- and general-operations-level expenses	$ 4,750	$ 4,750	$ 4,750	$ 4,750	$19,000
Total expenses	$21,250	$11,250	$16,250	$26,250	$75,000

Collegiate generally pays the minimum fee at each university, since it sells a relatively small number of shirts at each college. Since Collegiate plans to sell to the same colleges during each quarter of 20x1, the licensing fees are the same each quarter. Collegiate sells its products to university bookstores.

The remainder of Collegiate Apparel's selling, general, and administrative expenses are incurred at the facility or general-operations level.

Cash Receipts Budget

The **cash receipts budget** details the expected cash collections during a budget period. Collegiate Apparel Company's cash receipts budget is displayed in schedule 7. The firm collects 80 percent of its billings during the same quarter in which the sale is made and another 18 percent in the following quarter. Two percent of each quarter's sales are expected to be uncollectible accounts.

Schedule 7

| | **COLLEGIATE APPAREL COMPANY**
 Cash Receipts Budget
 For the Year Ending December 31, 20x1 | | | | |

		Quarter			
	1st	**2nd**	**3rd**	**4th**	**Year**
Sales revenue (from schedule 1)	$180,000	$60,000	$120,000	$240,000	$600,000
Collections in quarter of sale (80% of revenue)	$144,000	$48,000	$ 96,000	$192,000	$480,000
Collections in quarter following sale (18% of prior quarter's revenue)*	43,200†	32,400	10,800	21,600	108,000
Total cash receipts	$187,200	$80,400	$106,800	$213,600	$588,000

*Two percent of each quarter's sales are expected to be uncollectible, as follows:

		Quarter			
	1st	**2nd**	**3rd**	**4th**	**Year**
Uncollectible accounts	$3,600	$1,200	$2,400	$4,800	$12,000

†The revenue in the prior quarter (i.e., the 4th quarter of 20x0) is assumed to be $240,000. Therefore, the $43,200 is 18% × $240,000.

How to budget cash receipts.   To understand how the cash receipts budget is prepared, let's focus again on the second quarter column, which is shaded. The $60,000 of total revenue comes directly from schedule 1, the sales budget (second column, last row). Since most of Collegiate Apparel Company's sales are on account, not all of the second quarter's revenue will be collected during the second quarter. The cash that the firm will collect during the second quarter includes two components, as depicted in the following diagram.

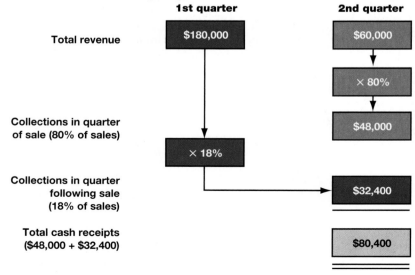

The second quarter's total cash receipts are the sum of $48,000 (which relates to second quarter sales) and $32,400 (which relates to first quarter sales).

One final point to notice is that 2 percent of each quarter's sales are not expected to be collected. Thus, the $1,200 of second quarter uncollectible accounts amounts to 2 percent of the second quarter's revenue (2% × $60,000).

Cash Disbursements Budget

The **cash disbursements budget** details the expected cash payments during a budget period. Schedule 8 displays Collegiate Apparel Company's cash disbursements budget. The shaded top portion shows the schedule of cash payments for raw material purchases, which are made on account. The company pays for 60 percent of its purchases on account during the quarter in which the purchase is made. The remaining 40 percent of each quarter's purchases are paid for during the quarter following the purchase.

The unshaded portion of schedule 8 shows all of the company's direct-labor, manufacturing overhead, and selling, general, and administrative expenditures.

Schedule 8

	COLLEGIATE APPAREL COMPANY Cash Disbursement Budget For the Year Ending December 31, 20x1				

	Quarter				
	1st	**2nd**	**3rd**	**4th**	**Year**
Cost of raw material purchases (from schedule 3)	$ 39,450	$18,150	$ 35,550	$ 56,850	$150,000
Cash payments for purchases made during the quarter (60% of current quarter's purchases)	$ 23,670	$10,890	$ 21,330	$ 34,110	$ 90,000
Cash payments for prior quarter's purchases (40% of prior quarter's purchases)	22,740*	15,780	7,260	14,220	60,000
Total cash payments for direct-material purchases	$ 46,410	$26,670	$ 28,590	$ 48,330	$150,000
Other cash disbursements:					
Direct labor (schedule 4)	$ 28,000	$11,000	$ 22,000	$ 39,000	$100,000
Indirect material (schedule 5)	3,500	1,375	2,750	4,875	12,500
Electricity (schedule 5)	2,100	825	1,650	2,925	7,500
Setup (schedule 5)	2,800	1,100	2,200	3,900	10,000
Purchasing and material handling (schedule 5)	3,360	1,320	2,640	4,680	12,000
Inspection (schedule 5)	2,240	880	1,760	3,120	8,000
Design (schedule 5)	1,000	1,000	1,000	1,000	4,000
Supervisory salaries (schedule 5)	14,000	14,000	14,000	14,000	56,000
Insurance and property taxes (schedule 5)	2,400	2,400	2,400	2,400	9,600
Maintenance (schedule 5)	2,600	2,600	2,600	2,600	10,400
Utilities (schedule 5)	2,500	2,500	2,500	2,500	10,000
Sales commissions (schedule 6)	9,000	3,000	6,000	12,000	30,000
Freight-out (schedule 6)	6,000	2,000	4,000	8,000	20,000
Licensing fees (schedule 6)	1,500	1,500	1,500	1,500	6,000
Sales salaries (schedule 6)	2,000	2,000	2,000	2,000	8,000
Advertising (schedule 6)	250	250	250	250	1,000
Clerical wages (schedule 6)	2,500	2,500	2,500	2,500	10,000
Total of other cash disbursements	$ 85,750	$50,250	$ 71,750	$107,250	$315,000
Total cash disbursements	$132,160	$76,920	$100,340	$155,580	$465,000

*40% of the purchases in the 4th quarter of the prior year, 20x0, which is assumed to be $56,850.

How to budget cash disbursements.   Collegiate Apparel Company purchases raw material, direct labor, and various services. The raw material purchases are made on account, which means payment is not made in cash at the time of the purchase. The shaded top portion of schedule 8 shows the purchases on account. Let's focus on the second quarter column. The second quarter's raw material purchases on account amount to $18,150. Does the company pay for all of the $18,150 purchases on account during the same quarter? No, it does not. As the following diagram shows, the second quarter's actual cash payment for purchases made on account includes two components.

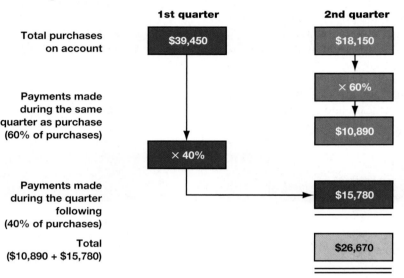

The second quarter's total cash payments *for purchases made on account* are the sum of $10,890 (which relates to second quarter purchases on account) and $15,780 (which relates to first quarter purchases on account).

We are not finished with the second quarter's cash disbursements yet, because Collegiate Apparel Company *also pays for some of its purchases in cash at the time of purchase.* These cash expenditures are detailed in the unshaded lower portion of schedule 8. The amounts are drawn from schedules 5 and 6, which detail expenditures for manufacturing overhead and selling, general, and administrative expenses, respectively. For example, schedule 5 lists $28,000 for cash expenditures on manufacturing overhead costs in the second quarter, and schedule 6 lists $11,250 for selling, general, and administrative expenditures.

Finally, the last row in the cash disbursements budget (schedule 8) shows the total cash disbursements during each quarter. Thus, the $76,920 total payment in the second quarter is the sum of $26,670 (for raw material purchases on account) and $50,250 for other purchases made in cash.

Cash Budget: Combining Receipts and Disbursements

The **cash budget** details the expected cash receipts and disbursements during a budget period. Collegiate Apparel's completed cash budget is displayed in schedule 9. The shaded top portion pulls together the cash receipts and cash disbursements detailed in schedules 7 and 8. The lower portion of schedule 9 discloses the company's plans to take out a short-term bank loan on January 2, 20x1, for the purpose of building an addition on to its production facility. The pattern of construction payments reflects high outlays early in the year as the major construction takes place. The high payment in the fourth quarter is due to the costs of reconfiguring the production line after the addition is finished. The company will repay the loan (with interest) in four installments on the last day of each quarter in 20x1. The funds for repayment will come from excess cash generated from operations during 20x1.

Also shown in schedule 9 are the interest payments on the short-term bank loan.

Schedule 9

	COLLEGIATE APPAREL COMPANY **Cash Budget** **For the Year Ending December 31, 20x1**				

	Quarter				
	1st	**2nd**	**3rd**	**4th**	**Year**
Cash receipts (from schedule 7)	$ 187,200	$ 80,400	$ 106,800	$ 213,600	$ 588,000
Less cash disbursements (from schedule 8).................................	(132,160)	(76,920)	(100,340)	(155,580)	(465,000)
Change in cash balance during quarter due to operations	$ 55,040	$ 3,480	$ 6,460	$ 58,020	$ 123,000
Proceeds from bank loan (1/2/x1)	100,000				100,000
Payments for construction of plant addition	(45,000)	(15,000)	(5,000)	(35,000)	(100,000)
Repayment of principal on bank loan (at the end of each quarter)	(25,000)	(25,000)	(25,000)	(25,000)	(100,000)
Interest on bank loan (at 10% per year)*	(2,500)	(1,875)	(1,250)	(625)	(6,250)
Change in cash balance during the period	$ 82,540	$(38,395)	$ (24,790)	$ (2,605)	$ 16,750
Cash balance, beginning of period	10,000	92,540	54,145	29,355	10,000
Cash balance, end of period	$ 92,540	$ 54,145	$ 29,355	$ 26,750	$ 26,750

*Interest computations:

Quarter	**Unpaid Principal During the Quarter**	**Annual Interest Rate**	**Portion of Year**	**Interest Payment†**
1st	$100,000	10%	1/4	$2,500‡
2nd	75,000	10	1/4	1,875
3rd	50,000	10	1/4	1,250
4th	25,000	10	1/4	625

†Unpaid principal × Annual interest rate × 1/4
‡$100,000 × .10 × 1/4 = $2,500

Budgeted Schedule of Cost of Goods Manufactured and Sold

The **budgeted schedule of cost of goods manufactured and sold** details the direct-material, direct-labor, and manufacturing overhead costs to be incurred and shows the cost of the goods to be sold during a budget period. Schedule 10 shows Collegiate Apparel's budgeted schedule of cost of goods manufactured and sold. The following Excel spreadsheet shows how the cost of the beginning and ending inventories of finished goods in schedule 10 are determined. From schedule 2, we see that the expected beginning and ending inventories of finished goods for 20x1 consist of 1,500 units. The absorption manufacturing cost for one unit of product is $9. The direct-material cost per unit is $3 (schedule 3), and the unit direct-labor cost is $2 (schedule 4). Recall that the *absorption* cost includes the direct-materials and direct-labor costs and an allocation of *all* manufacturing overhead costs (i.e., overhead at

	Microsoft Excel - Calculation of absorption unit cost						
	File Edit View Insert Format Tools Data Window Help						
G8		= =SUM(G1:G6)					
	A	B	C	D	E	F	G
1	Direct material (1.5 yards x $2 per yard)						$ 3.00
2	Direct labor (.2 hour x $10 per hour)						2.00
3	Unit-level manufacturing overhead ($20,000/50,000 units)						0.40
4	Batch-level manufacturing overhead ($30,000/50,000 units)						0.60
5	Product-level manufacturing overhead ($4,000/50,000 units)						0.08
6	Facility and general operations level manufacturing overhead ($146,000/50,000 units)						2.92
7							
8	Total absorption unit cost						$ 9.00

Sheet1 (2) / Sheet1 / Sheet2 / Sheet3 /

Ready

Schedule 10

COLLEGIATE APPAREL COMPANY Budgeted Schedule of Cost of Goods Manufactured and Sold For the Year Ending December 31, 20x1		
Direct material (see schedule 3 for details):		
Raw-material inventory, January 1	$ 4,200*	
Add: Purchases of raw material	150,000	
Raw material available from use	$154,200	
Deduct: Raw-material inventory, December 31	4,200*	
Direct material used..		$150,000
Direct labor (see schedule 4 for details)		100,000
Manufacturing overhead (see schedule 5 for details)............................		200,000
Total manufacturing costs		$450,000
Add: Work-in-process inventory, January 1....................................		0†
Subtotal		$450,000
Deduct: Work-in-process inventory, December 31		0†
Cost of goods manufactured..		$450,000
Add: Finished-goods inventory, January 1		13,500‡
Cost of goods available for sale		$463,500
Deduct: Finished-goods inventory, December 31.................................		13,500‡
Cost of goods sold..		$450,000

* From Schedule 3: 2,100 yards × $2 per yard.

† The company's production cycle is short enough that it has no work-in-process inventory at any time.

‡ From Schedule 2: 1,500 units × $9 per unit, which is the absorption manufacturing cost per unit.

the unit, batch, product, and facility or general operations levels). The overhead cost information comes from schedule 5.

Budgeted Income Statement

The **budgeted income statement** shows the expected revenue and expenses for a budget period, assuming that planned operations are carried out. Collegiate Apparel Company's budgeted income statement is displayed in schedule 11.

Budgeted Balance Sheet

The **budgeted balance sheet** shows the expected end-of-period balances for the company's assets, liabilities, and owners' equity, assuming that planned operations are carried out. Collegiate Apparel Company's budgeted balance sheet for December 31, 20x1, is displayed in schedule 12. To construct this budgeted balance sheet, we start with the firm's balance sheet projected for the *beginning* of the budget year (Exhibit 15–3) and adjust each account balance for the changes expected during 20x1. These expected changes are reflected in the various 20x1 budget schedules.

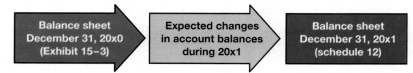

Explanations for the account balances on the budgeted balance sheet for December 31, 20x1, are given in the second half of schedule 12. Examine these explanations carefully. Notice how the budgeted balance sheet pulls together information from most of the schedules constituting the master budget.

Assumptions and Predictions Underlying the Master Budget

A master budget is based on many assumptions and estimates of unknown parameters. What are some of the assumptions and estimates used in Collegiate Apparel Company's master budget? The professional sales budget was built on an assumption

Schedule 11

COLLEGIATE APPAREL COMPANY Budgeted Income Statement For the Year Ending December 31, 20x1		
Sales revenue (from schedule 1)		$600,000
Less: Cost of goods sold (from schedule 10)		450,000
Gross margin		$150,000
Other expenses:		
Selling, general, and administrative expenses (from schedule 6)	$75,000	
Uncollectible accounts expense (from schedule 7: 2% × $600,000)*	12,000	
Interest expense (from schedule 9)*	6,250	
Total other expenses		93,250
Net income		$ 56,750

*Usually these two expenses are included in selling, general, and administrative expenses. They are listed separately in our illustration because they were determined after the selling, general, and administrative expense budget had already been explained.

Schedule 12

COLLEGIATE APPAREL COMPANY Budgeted Balance Sheet As of December 31, 20x1		
Assets		
Current assets:		
Cash (from schedule 9)		$ 26,750
Accounts receivable (net of allowance for uncollectible accounts)		43,200*
Inventory		
Raw material (from schedule 10)	$ 4,200	
Finished goods (from schedule 10)	13,500	
Supplies	2,000	
Total inventory		19,700
Total current assets		$ 89,650
Long-lived assets:		
Building	$ 500,000†	
Equipment	320,000	
Less accumulated depreciation	(300,000)‡	
Building and equipment (net of accumulated depreciation)		520,000
Total assets		$609,650
Liabilities and Owner's Equity		
Current liabilities:		
Accounts payable		$ 22,740§
Total current liabilities		$ 22,740
Long-term liabilities:		
Note payable (noninterest bearing; due on December 31, 20x3)		200,000
Total liabilities		$222,740
Owner's equity		386,910#
Total liabilities and owner's equity		$609,650

Explanatory notes for schedule 12:

* From schedule 7: 4th quarter sales of $240,000 times 18% amounts to $43,200.

† Balance in the building account on the December 31, 20x0, balance sheet, plus the $100,000 cost of the building construction project in 20x1 (schedule 9).

‡ Balance in the Accumulated Depreciation account on the December 31, 20x0, balance sheet, plus the $60,000 in depreciation during 20x1 (schedule 5).

§ From schedule 8: 4th quarter raw material purchases of $56,850 times 40% amounts to $22,740.

Balance in owner's equity on the December 31, 20x0, balance sheet, plus the 20x1 budgeted net income of $56,750 (schedule 11).

COLLEGIATE APPAREL COMPANY
Balance Sheet
December 31, 20x0

Assets

Current assets:		
Cash		$ 10,000
Accounts receivable (net of allowance for uncollectible accounts)		43,200
Inventory		
Raw material	$ 4,200	
Finished goods	13,500	
Supplies	2,000	
Total inventory		19,700
Total current assets		$ 72,900
Long-lived assets:		
Building	$ 400,000	
Equipment	320,000	
Less accumulated depreciation	(240,000)	
Building and equipment (net of accumulated depreciation)		480,000
Total assets		$552,900

Liabilities and Owner's Equity

Current liabilities:	
Accounts payable	$ 22,740
Total current liabilities	$ 22,740
Long-term liabilities:	
Note payable (noninterest bearing; due on December 31, 20x3)	200,000
Total liabilities	$222,740
Owner's equity	330,160
Total liabilities and owner's equity	$552,900

about the seasonal nature of demand for college T-shirts. The direct-material budget uses an estimate of the direct-material price, $2 per yard, and the quantity of material required per T-shirt, 1.5 yards. An estimate of the direct labor required to make a T-shirt was used in the direct-labor budget.

These are only a few of the many assumptions and estimates used in Collegiate's master budget. Some of these estimates are much more likely to be accurate than others. For example, the amount of material required to make a T-shirt is not likely to differ from past experience unless the type of material or production process is changed. In contrast, estimates such as the price of material, the cost of utilities, and sales demand are much more difficult to predict.

Financial Planning Models

Managers must make assumptions and predictions in preparing budgets because organizations operate in a world of uncertainty. One way to cope with that uncertainty is to supplement the budgeting process with a *financial planning model*. A **financial planning model** is a set of mathematical relationships that express the interactions among the various operational, financial, and environmental events that determine the overall results of an organization's activities. A financial planning model is a mathematical expression of all the relationships expressed in the flowchart of Exhibit 15–1.

To illustrate this concept, focus on the following equation, which was used to budget uncollectible accounts expense in schedule 7.

$$\left(\begin{array}{c}\text{Uncollectible} \\ \text{accounts expense}\end{array}\right) = .02 \text{ (Sales revenue)}$$

Financial Planning Model: Uncollectible Accounts Expense

Refer again to Collegiate's cash receipts budget in schedule 7. Apply the financial planning concept to perform sensitivity analysis on the implications of different estimates of the rate of uncollectible accounts expense.

a. Prepare a table with a row for each of the following estimates of the rate of uncollectible accounts: 1, 2, 3, and 4 percent. Also include a row for the budgeted sales revenue. Your table should have five columns, one for each quarter and one for the entire year. The entries in the table will be the budgeted uncollectible accounts expense. (If you have access to spreadsheet software, prepare the table as a spreadsheet.)

b. How could this financial planning model help Collegiate Apparel to manage its uncollectible accounts expense?

(Solutions begin on page 626.)

Suppose that Collegiate Apparel's management is uncertain about this 2 percent estimate. A financial planning model might include the following equation instead.

$$\left(\begin{array}{c}\textbf{Uncollectible}\\\textbf{accounts expense}\end{array}\right) = p\ (\textbf{Sales revenue})$$

where

$$0 \le p \le 1.0$$

The budget staff can run the financial planning model as many times as desired on a computer, using a different value for p each time. Perhaps the following values would be tried: .04, .045, .05, .055, and .06. Now management can answer the question, What if 4 percent of sales prove to be uncollectible? In a fully developed financial planning model, the key estimates and assumptions are expressed as general mathematical relationships. Then the model is run on a computer many times to determine the impact of different combinations of these unknown variables. "What-if" questions can be answered about unknown variables such as inflation, interest rates, the value of the dollar, demand, competitors' actions, production efficiency, union demands in forthcoming wage negotiations, and a host of other factors. The widespread availability of personal computers and electronic spreadsheet software has made financial planning models a more and more common management tool.

Chapter 12 includes a more thorough discussion of financial planning models.

Responsibility for Budget Administration

The procedures that small organizations use to gather information and construct a master budget are usually informal. At Collegiate Apparel Company, for example, the firm's owner, Tim Williams, coordinates the budgeting process. In contrast, larger organizations usually designate a **budget director** or **chief budget officer** who specifies the process by which budget data are gathered, collects the information, and prepares the master budget. This is often the organization's controller. To communicate budget procedures and deadlines to employees throughout the organization, the budget director often develops and disseminates a budget manual. The **budget manual** indicates who is responsible for providing various types of information, when the information is required, and what form the information is to take. For example, the budget manual for a large manufacturing firm might specify that each regional sales director is to send an estimate of the following year's sales, by product line, to the budget director by September 1. The budget manual also states who should receive each schedule when the master budget is complete.

A **budget committee,** consisting of key senior executives, advises the budget director during the preparation of the budget. The authority to give final approval to the master budget usually belongs to the board of directors, or the board of trustees in

LO 4 Describe and evaluate a typical organization's process of budget administration.

Cost Management in Practice 15.2

E-Budgeting

E-budgeting is an increasingly popular, Web-based tool that can help streamline a company's budgeting process. The *E* in E-budgeting stands for both *electronic* and *enterprisewide*. Employees throughout an organization, at all levels and around the globe, can submit and retrieve budget-related information electronically via the World Wide Web. Among the organizations using E-budgeting is Toronto-Dominion Bank (www.tdbank.com). When the bank's executives were searching for a new solution capable of handling the bank's enterprisewide budgeting and planning function, they turned to the Internet. "In the past, we have compiled our business plan using hundreds of spreadsheets, and our analysts have spent a disproportionate amount of time compiling and verifying data from multiple sources," according to Toronto-Dominion's controller. "Implementing a Web-based, enterprisewide budgeting solution will help us develop business plans and allow our analysts to be proactive in monitoring quarterly results." *Source: S. Hornyak, "Budgeting Made Easy."*

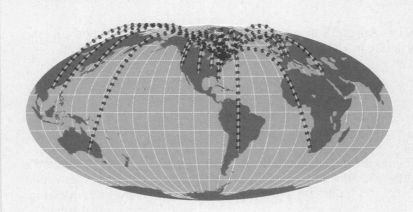

many nonprofit organizations. Usually the board has a subcommittee whose task is to examine the proposed budget carefully and recommend approval or any changes deemed necessary. By exercising its authority to make changes in the budget and grant final approval, the board of directors, or trustees, can wield considerable influence on the overall direction the organization takes.

Behavioral Implications of Budgets

LO 5 Understand the behavioral implications of budgetary slack and participative budgeting.

In perhaps no other area of management are behavioral implications more important than in budgeting. A budget affects virtually everyone in an organization: those who prepare the budget, those who use the budget to facilitate decision making, and those who are evaluated using the budget. The human reactions to the budgeting process can have considerable influence on an organization's overall effectiveness. A great deal of study has been devoted to the behavioral effects of budgets. This discussion barely scratches the surface by briefly considering two issues: budgetary slack and participative budgeting.

Budgetary Slack: Padding the Budget

The information on which a budget is based comes largely from people throughout an organization. For example, the sales forecast relies on market research and analysis by a market research staff but also incorporates the projections of sales personnel. If a territorial sales manager's performance is evaluated on the basis of whether the sales budget for the territory is exceeded, what is the incentive for the sales manager in projecting sales? The incentive is to give a conservative, or cautiously low, sales estimate. The sales manager's performance will look much better in the eyes of top management when a conservative estimate is exceeded than when an ambitious estimate is not met. At least that is the *perception* of many sales managers, and in the behavioral area, perceptions are what count most.

When a supervisor provides a departmental cost projection for budgetary purposes, there is an incentive to overestimate costs. When the actual cost incurred in the department proves to be less than the inflated cost projection, the supervisor appears to have managed in a cost-effective way.

These illustrations are examples of **padding the budget,** which means intentionally underestimating revenue or overestimating costs. The difference between the revenue or cost projection that a person provides and a realistic estimate of the revenue or cost is called **budgetary slack.** For example, if a plant manager believes the annual utilities cost will be $23,000 but gives a budgetary projection of $25,000, the manager has built $2,000 of slack into the budget.

Why do people pad budgets with budgetary slack? There are three primary reasons. First, people often *perceive* that their performance will look better in their superiors' eyes if they can "beat the budget." Second, budgetary slack is often used to cope with uncertainty. A departmental supervisor might feel confident in the cost projections for 10 cost items. However, the supervisor also might believe that some unforeseen event during the budgetary period could result in unanticipated costs. For example, an unexpected machine breakdown could occur. One way to deal with that unforeseen event is to pad the budget. If nothing goes wrong, the supervisor can beat the cost budget. If some negative event does occur, the supervisor can use the budgetary slack to absorb the impact of the event and still meet the cost budget.

The third reason that people pad cost budgets is that budgetary cost projections are often cut in the resource-allocation process. Thus, a vicious circle exists. Budgetary projections are padded because they will likely be cut, and they are cut because they are likely to have been padded.

How does an organization solve the problem of budgetary slack? First, it can avoid relying on the budget as a negative evaluative tool. If a departmental supervisor is harassed by the budget director or some other top manager every time a budgetary cost projection is exceeded, the likely behavioral response will be to pad the budget. In contrast, if the supervisor is allowed some managerial discretion to exceed the budget when necessary, the tendency toward budgetary padding will decrease. Second, managers can be given incentives not only to achieve budgetary projections but also to *provide accurate projections.* This can be accomplished by asking managers to justify all or some of their projections and by rewarding managers who consistently provide accurate estimates.

Most managers and accountants consider intentional padding of a budget to be unethical. Unfortunately, though, it is a fact of budgetary life.

Participative Budgeting

Most people will perform better and make greater attempts to achieve a goal if they have been consulted in setting that goal. **Participative budgeting** involves employees throughout an organization in the budgetary process. Such participation can give employees the feeling that "this is our budget" rather than the all-too-common feeling that "this is the budget you imposed on us."[5]

Although participative budgeting can be very effective, it can also have shortcomings. Too much participation and discussion can lead to vacillation and delay. Also, when those involved in the budgeting process disagree in significant and irreconcilable ways, the process of participation can accentuate those differences. Finally, the problem of budget padding can be severe unless incentives for accurate projections are provided.

Ethical Issues in Budgeting

A departmental or divisional budget often is the basis for evaluating a manager's performance. Actual results are compared with budgeted performance levels, and those who outperform the budget often are rewarded with promotions or salary increases.

---

[5] Recent economic modeling research demonstrates the value of cooperation in a budgeting process. See Qi Chen, "Cooperation in the Budgeting Process."

In many cases, bonuses are tied explicitly to performance relative to a budget. For example, the top-management personnel of a division might receive a bonus if divisional profit exceeds budgeted profit by a certain percentage.

Serious ethical issues can arise in situations when a budget is the basis for rewarding managers. For example, suppose a division's top-management personnel will split a bonus equal to 10 percent of the amount by which actual divisional profit exceeds the budget. This might create an incentive for the divisional budget officer, or other managers supplying data, to pad the divisional profit budget. Such padding would make the budget easier to achieve, thus increasing the chance of a bonus. Alternatively, there might be an incentive to manipulate the actual divisional results to maximize management's bonus. For example, year-end sales could be shifted between years to increase reported revenue in a particular year.

Budget personnel could have such incentives for either of two reasons: (1) they might share in the bonus or (2) they might feel pressure from the managers who would share in the bonus. Padding the budget or manipulating reported results to maximize one's personal gain or that of others is a serious ethical violation.

Zero-Base Budgeting for Discretionary Costs

Many organizations have attempted to measure discretionary costs through a budgeting method called zero-base budgeting. Numerous companies (e.g., Texas Instruments, Xerox, and Control Data) and governmental units (e.g., the State of Georgia) have implemented zero-base budgeting at one time or another. **Zero-base budgeting** initially sets the budget for virtually every activity in the organization to zero. To receive funding during the budgeting process, each activity must be justified in terms of its continued usefulness. The zero-base-budgeting approach forces management to rethink each phase of an organization's operations before allocating resources.

Base Budgeting

Some organizations use a base-budgeting approach without going to the extreme of zero-base budgeting. **Base budgeting** sets the initial budget for each of the organization's departments in accordance with a **base package,** which includes the minimal resources required for the subunit to exist at an absolute minimal level. Below this level of funding, the subunit would not be a viable entity. Any increases above the base package would result from a decision to fund an **incremental package,** which describes the resources needed to add various activities to the base package. The decision to approve such an incremental budget package would have to be justified on the basis of the costs and benefits of the activities included. Base budgeting has been effective in many organizations because it forces managers to take an evaluative, questioning attitude toward each of the organization's programs.

Contemporary Trends in Budgeting and Financial Planning

LO 6 Describe contemporary trends in the budgeting process as an element of a cost-management system.

As with all aspects of the field of cost management, the area of budgeting is in transition. "When it comes to benchmarking and best practices, nothing is more in vogue than reengineering the financial planning process. 'This really is the number one topic in business right now,'" according to a partner with KPMG's World-Class Finance consulting division. "The emerging concept of financial planning is gradually replacing the traditional budgeting process, enabling controllers to become true business partners by focusing on value-added tasks."[6]

---

[6] I. McLemore, "Reinventing the Budget."

The whole concept of *cost management,* in which costs "don't just happen" but are actively managed, is key to the emerging philosophy of contemporary budgeting and financial planning. The use of activity-based costing concepts to construct a meaningful budget, coupled with the activity-based management objective of eliminating non-value-added costs, is key for improving the budgeting process.

In Collegiate Apparel's budgeting process, for example, a variety of cost drivers was recognized and costs were classified according to their level in the ABC cost hierarchy. By constructing the budget using ABC concepts, managers are better able to understand why costs are incurred, how to manage costs, and how to improve profitability.

Research Insight 15.2

Best Practices in Budgeting

According to research performed by The Hacket Group, an Ohio-based consulting firm, best practices in budgeting and financial planning include the following:

- Link the financial planning process to strategic planning through operational targets derived from strategic objectives.
- Integrate the forecasting process with the planning process.
- Make sure that users at all levels can retrieve and submit data electronically.
- Ensure that software and other financial modeling tools use multiple "what-if" scenarios.
- Focus budget reiterations on ways to meet operational targets not to process financials.
- Base line-item detail on materiality (substantially less detail than in the chart of accounts).
  Source: I. McLemore, "Reinventing the Budget."

Chapter Summary

The *budget* is a key tool for planning, control, and decision making in virtually every organization. Budgeting systems are used to force planning, to facilitate communication and coordination, to allocate resources, to control profit and operations, and to evaluate performance and provide incentives. Various types of budgets are used to accomplish these objectives.

The comprehensive set of budgets that covers all phases of an organization's operations is called a "master budget." The first step in preparing a master budget is to forecast sales of the organization's services or goods. Based on the sales forecast, operational budgets are prepared to plan production of services or goods and to outline the acquisition and use of materials, labor, and other resources. Finally, a set of budgeted financial statements is prepared to show what the organization's overall financial condition will be if the organization carries out its planned operations.

Since budgets affect almost everyone in an organization, they can have significant behavioral implications. One common problem in budgeting is the tendency of people to *pad* budgets. The resulting *budgetary slack* makes the budget less useful because the padded budget does not present an accurate picture of expected revenue and expenses. Participative budgeting is the process of allowing employees throughout the organization to have a significant role in developing the budget. Participative budgeting can result in greater commitment to meet the budget by those who participated in the process.

Appendix to Chapter Fifteen

Inventory Management

A key decision in manufacturing, retail, and some service industry firms is how much inventory to keep on hand. Once inventory levels have been established, they become an important input to the budgeting system. Inventory decisions involve a delicate balance between three classes of costs: ordering costs, holding costs, and shortage costs. Examples of costs in each of these categories are given in Exhibit 15–4.

LO 7 Use the economic-order-quantity model to make inventory-ordering decisions and discuss the implications of the JIT approach for inventory management.

Exhibit 15–4

Inventory Ordering,
Holding, and Shortage
Costs

Ordering Costs
  Time spent in finding suppliers and expediting orders
  Clerical costs of preparing purchase orders
  Transportation costs
  Receiving costs (e.g., unloading and inspection)
Holding Costs
  Costs of storage space (e.g., warehouse depreciation)
  Security
  Insurance
  Forgone interest on working capital tied up in inventory
  Deterioration, theft, spoilage, or obsolescence
Shortage Costs
  Lost sales and dissatisfied customers
  Loss of quantity discounts on purchases
  Disrupted production when raw materials are unavailable
    Idle workers
    Extra machinery setups

Economic Order Quantity

It is now 20x3 and Collegiate Apparel has expanded its production capability. Owner and president, Tim Williams, has signed a contract with a large US university to supply all its athletic T-shirts for use in its physical education program. Unlike the T-shirts in Collegiate's regular product line, which are 100 percent cotton, the athletic shirts for the contract are to be a cotton/polyester blend. The contract calls for 24,000 shirts to be delivered each year.

Collegiate Apparel's production supervisor, Brad Roaldsson, has decided to use an economic order quantity (EOQ) decision model to determine the size and frequency with which the fabric should be ordered. The **EOQ model** is a mathematical tool for determining the order quantity that minimizes the cost of ordering and holding inventory, which is called the **economic order quantity, or EOQ.**

Roaldsson has determined that Collegiate will need 1,200 bolts of cotton/polyester fabric per year to produce the shirts for the contract. Each bolt costs $110. He estimates that it costs $50 to place and receive a typical order, and that the annual cost of carrying fabric in inventory is $12 per bolt.

Tabular approach. Suppose that Roaldsson orders 150 bolts of fabric in each order placed during the year. The total annual cost of ordering and holding fabric in inventory is calculated as follows:

$$\frac{\textbf{Annual requirement}}{\textbf{Quantity per order}} = \frac{\textbf{1,200}}{\textbf{150}} = \textbf{8} = \textbf{Number of orders}$$

$$\textbf{Annual ordering cost} = \textbf{8 orders} \times \textbf{\$50 per order} = \textbf{\$400}$$

$$\textbf{Average quantity in inventory} = \textbf{Quantity per order} \div \textbf{2} = \textbf{150} \div \textbf{2} = \textbf{75 bolts}$$

$$\textbf{Annual holding cost} = \left(\begin{matrix}\textbf{Average quantity}\\\textbf{in inventory}\end{matrix}\right) \times \left(\begin{matrix}\textbf{Average carrying}\\\textbf{cost per bolt}\end{matrix}\right)$$

$$= \textbf{75} \times \textbf{\$12} = \textbf{\$900}$$

$$\begin{matrix}\textbf{Total annual cost}\\\textbf{of inventory policy}\end{matrix} = \begin{matrix}\textbf{Ordering}\\\textbf{cost}\end{matrix} + \begin{matrix}\textbf{Holding}\\\textbf{cost}\end{matrix} = \textbf{\$400} + \textbf{\$900} = \textbf{\$1,300}$$

Notice that the $1,300 cost does *not* include the purchase cost of the fabric at $110 per bolt. We are focusing only on the costs of *ordering* and *holding* fabric inventory.

Can Roaldsson do any better than $1,300 for the annual cost of the fabric inventory policy? Exhibit 15–5, which tabulates the inventory costs for various order quantities, indicates that Roaldsson can lower the costs of ordering and holding fabric inventory. Of the five order quantities listed, the 100-bolt order quantity yields the lowest total annual cost. Unfortunately, this tabular method for finding the least-cost order quantity is cumbersome. Moreover, it does not necessarily result in the optimal order quantity. It is possible that some order quantity other than those listed in Exhibit 15–5 is the least-cost order quantity.

Equation approach. The total annual cost of ordering and holding inventory is given by the following equation:

$$\text{Total annual cost} = \left(\frac{\text{Annual requirement}}{\text{Order quantity}}\right)\left(\frac{\text{Cost per}}{\text{order}}\right) + \left(\frac{\text{Order quantity}}{2}\right)\left(\frac{\text{Annual holding}}{\text{cost per unit}}\right)$$

The following formula for the least-cost order quantity, called the *economic order quantity* (or *EOQ*), has been developed using calculus:

$$\text{Economic order quantity} = \sqrt{\frac{(2)(\text{Annual requirement})(\text{Cost per order})}{\text{Annual holding cost per unit}}}$$

Applying the EOQ formula in Collegiate Apparel's problem yields the following EOQ for fabric:

$$\text{EOQ} = \sqrt{\frac{(2)(1,200)(50)}{12}} = 100$$

Graphical approach. Another method for solving the EOQ problem is the graphical method, which is presented in Exhibit 15–6. Notice that the ordering-cost line slants down to the right. This indicates a decline in these costs as the order size increases and the order frequency decreases. However, as the order size increases, so does the average inventory on hand. This results in increased holding costs as indicated by the positive slope of the holding-cost line. The EOQ falls at 100 units, where the best balance is struck between these two costs. Total costs are minimized at $1,200.

	50	80	100	120	150
Order size	50	80	100	120	150
Number of orders (1,200 ÷ order size)	24	15	12	10	8
Ordering costs ($50 × number of orders)............	$1,200	$ 750	$ 600	$ 500	$ 400
Average inventory (order size ÷ 2)	25	40	50	60	75
Holding costs ($12 × average inventory)	$ 300	$ 480	$ 600	$ 720	$ 900
Total annual cost (ordering cost + holding cost)	$1,500	$1,230	$1,200	$1,220	$1,300

Minimum

Exhibit 15–5

Tabulation of Inventory-Ordering and Holding Costs: Collegiate Apparel Company

COLLEGIATE APPAREL COMPANY

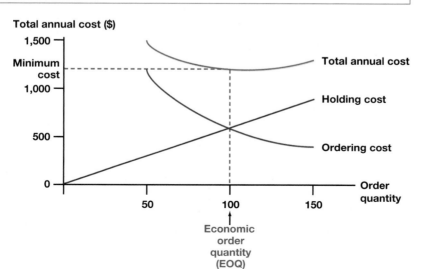

Exhibit 15–6

Graphical Solution to Economic Order Quantity Decision: Collegiate Apparel Company

COLLEGIATE APPAREL COMPANY

Timing of Orders

The EOQ model helps management decide how much each order will include. Another important decision is when to order. This decision depends on the **lead time,** which is the length of time it takes for the materials to be received after an order has been placed. Suppose that the lead time for fabric is 15 days (approximately one-half month). Collegiate Apparel's use of 1,200 bolts of fabric per year, with a constant production rate throughout the year, implies that it uses 100 bolts each month. Production manager Roaldsson should order fabric in the economic order quantity of 100 bolts when the inventory falls to 50 bolts. By the time the new order arrives one-half month later, the 50 bolts in inventory will have been used in production. Exhibit 15–7 depicts this pattern of ordering and using inventory. By placing an order early enough to avoid a stockout, management considers the potential costs of shortages.

Safety stock.   Our example assumed that fabric usage is constant at 100 bolts per month. Suppose instead that monthly usage fluctuates between 80 and 120 bolts. Although average monthly usage still is 100 bolts, there is the potential for an excess usage of 20 bolts in any particular month. This means that the usage during the half-month lead time required to receive an order fluctuates between 40 and 60 bolts, so there is the potential for excess usage of 10 bolts during the half-month lead time. In light of this uncertainty, management might wish to keep a safety stock of fabric equal to the potential excess usage of 10 bolts during the half-month lead time. A **safety stock** is the potential excess usage of material when material usage fluctuates during the lead time. With a safety stock of 10 bolts, the reorder point is 60 bolts. Thus, Roaldsson should order the EOQ of 100 bolts when fabric inventory falls to 60 bolts. During the half-month lead time, another 40 to 60 bolts of fabric will be consumed in production. Although a safety stock increases inventory holding costs, it minimizes the potential costs caused by shortages.

Inventory Management under JIT: Implications for EOQ

The EOQ model minimizes the total cost of ordering and holding purchased inventory. Thus, this inventory management approach seeks to balance the cost of ordering against the cost of storing inventory. Under the JIT philosophy, the goal is to keep *all* inventories as low as possible. *Any* inventory-holding costs are seen as inefficient and wasteful. Moreover, JIT purchasing minimizes ordering costs by reducing the number of vendors, negotiating long-term supply agreements, making less frequent payments, and eliminating inspections. The implication of the JIT philosophy is that inventories should be minimized by more frequent deliveries in smaller quantities.

Exhibit 15–7

Ordering, Lead Time, and Usage of Inventory: Collegiate Apparel Company

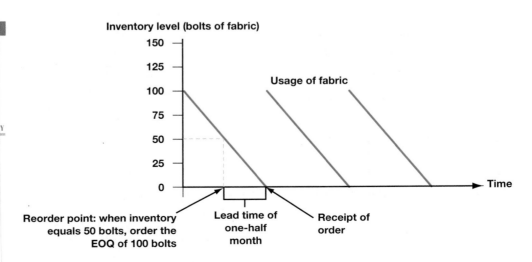

Holding Costs per Unit	Ordering Costs per Order				
	$50	$40	$30	$20	
$12	100	89	77	63	EOQ declines
13	96	86	74	61	
14	93	83	72	59	
15	89	80	69	57	
	EOQ declines				

Note: The annual requirement is assumed to be 1,200 units for each case in this table. This was the annual requirement for bolts of fabric in the Collegiate Apparel illustration. (Several of the EOQs in the table are rounded.)

Exhibit 15–8

Economic Order Quantity with Different Ordering and Holding Costs

COLLEGIATE APPAREL COMPANY

This result can be demonstrated using the EOQ formula, as shown in Exhibit 15–8. As the cost of holding inventory increases, the EOQ decreases. Moreover, as the cost of placing an order declines, the EOQ decreases.

The economics underlying the EOQ model supports the JIT viewpoint that inventory should be purchased or produced in small quantities and should be kept to the absolute minimum. However, the basic philosophies of JIT and EOQ are quite different. The EOQ approach takes the view that some inventory is necessary and the goal is to optimize the order quantity to balance the cost of ordering against the cost of holding inventory. Also implicit in this approach is the need to hold some buffer stock of inventory prior to bottleneck operations. (Review our discussion of this issue in Chapter 4.) In contrast, the JIT philosophy argues that holding costs tend to be higher than might be apparent because of the inefficiency and waste of storing inventory. Thus, inventory should be minimized, or even eliminated completely if possible. Moreover, under the JIT approach, orders typically vary in size, depending on needs. The EOQ model, in contrast, results in a constant order quantity.

The JIT approach to production and inventory management is much more than "just an inventory system." It has implications for many other issues in cost management. See Chapter 7 for additional discussion.

Key Terms

For each term's definition, refer to the indicated page or turn to the glossary at the end of the text.

activity-based budgeting (ABB), 603

base budgeting, 620

base package, 620

budget, 597

budget committee, 617

budget director (or chief budget officer), 617

budget manual, 617

budgetary slack, 619

budgeted balance sheet, 614

budgeted (or pro forma) financial statements, 598

budgeted income statement, 614

budgeted schedule of cost of goods manufactured and sold, 613

budgeting system, 597

capital budget, 598

cash budget, 612

cash disbursements budget, 611

cash receipts budget, 610

critical success factors, 596

direct-labor budget, 607

direct-material budget, 606

EOQ model,* 622

economic order quantity (EOQ),* 622

financial budget, 598

financial planning model, 616

incremental package, 620

lead time,* 624

manufacturing-overhead budget, 607

master budget (or profit plan), 598

operational budgets, 601

padding the budget, 619

participative budgeting, 619

production budget, 604

profit plan (or master budget), 598

rolling budget (revolving or continuous budget), 598

safety stock,* 624

sales budget, 604

sales forecasting, 599

selling, general, and administrative (SG&A) expense budget, 609

strategic long-range plan, 596

zero-base budgeting, 620

*Terms appear in the Appendix.

Meeting the Cost Management Challenges

1. Why does Collegiate Apparel need an annual budget? Specifically, what purposes would the budgeting process serve?

All organizations, including Collegiate Apparel Company, need to plan their operations. Budgeting is a crucial part of the planning process. The purposes of the budgeting process are planning, facilitating communication and coordination, allocating resources, managing financial and operational performance, and evaluating performance and providing incentives.

2. How could Collegiate Apparel's budget facilitate communication and coordination among the company's president, sales manager, and production supervisor?

A budget facilitates communication and coordination by making each manager throughout the organization aware of the plans made by other managers. The budgeting process pulls together the plans of each manager in the organization.

3. What is a master budget? What are its main components for a manufacturer such as Collegiate Apparel?

A master budget, or financial plan, is a comprehensive set of budgets covering all phases of an organization's operations for a specified period of time. A manufacturer's master budget includes the following main components: sales budget, operational budgets (including a production budget, inventory budgets, a labor budget, an overhead budget, a selling and administrative

expense budget, and a cash budget), and budgeted financial statements (including a budgeted income statement, budgeted balance sheet, and budgeted statement of cash flows).

4. How could Collegiate Apparel's president or a company's board of directors use the budget to influence the future direction of the firm?

A corporation's board of directors generally has final approval over the master budget. By exercising its authority to make changes in the budget and grant final approval, the board of directors can wield considerable influence on the overall direction the organization takes. Since the budget is used as a resource-allocation mechanism, the board of directors can emphasize some programs and curtail or eliminate others by allocating funds through the budgeting process.

In Collegiate Apparel's case, the company is wholly owned and managed by its president, who also has final approval over the firm's master budget.

5. Would participative budgeting be effective for Collegiate Apparel Company?

The idea of participative budgeting is to involve employees throughout an organization in the budgetary process. Such participation can give employees the feeling that "this is our budget," rather than the feeling that "this is the budget you imposed on us." When employees feel that they were part of the budgeting process, they are more likely to strive to achieve the budget. As in most organizations, participative budgeting would likely increase the effectiveness of Collegiate Apparel's budgeting process.

Solutions to You're the Decision Maker

15.1   Revised Production Budget for 20x1   p. 605

a. Revised budget:

	Quarter				
	1st	2nd	3rd	4th	Year
Sales in units (revised upward by 20%)......................................	18,000	6,000	12,000	24,000	60,000
Add desired ending inventory of finished goods*......................	600	1,200	2,400	1,800†	1,800
Total units required...	18,600	7,200	14,400	25,800	61,800
Less expected beginning inventory of finished goods	1,500	600	1,200	2,400	1,500
Units to be produced	17,100	6,600	13,200	23,400	60,300

*10 percent of the next quarter's expected sales

†10 percent of the expected sales for the 1st quarter of the next year, 20x2, which is now revised upward by 20% to 18,000 units

b. This is where the art of management comes into play. If the increase in sales is not very certain, management has a tough decision to make. One possible strategy is to increase production as indicated in the preceding table for the first quarter or two and to see whether the increased demand materializes and then cut back production if it does not. Another possibility is to produce quantities between those specified in the original and revised budgets.

15.2   Revision of Manufacturing Overhead Budget
     p. 609

a. Revised fourth quarter budget:

Unit-Level Costs

Units..	***24,000***
Indirect material	$ 6,000
Electricity...	3,600
Total unit-level costs	$ 9,600

Batch-Level Costs

Production runs (24,000 units ÷ 600 units)	**40**
Setup	$ 4,000
Purchasing and material handling	4,800
Inspection	3,200
Total batch-level costs	$12,000

Product-Level Costs

New design styles	**3**
Design	$ 1,500
Total product-level costs	$ 1,500

Facility and General Operations-Level Costs

Supervisory salaries	$14,000
Insurance and property taxes............................	2,400
Maintenance...	2,600
Utilities	2,500
Depreciation	15,000
Total facility and general-operations-level costs......	$36,500
Total overhead	$59,600
Less depreciation...	15,000
Total cash disbursements for overhead	$44,600

b. The special adjustment on the cutting machine will be a batch-level cost. The appropriate cost driver is production runs.

15.3 Financial Planning Model: Uncollectible Accounts Expense p. 617

a. This table shows the budgeted uncollectible accounts expense for different rates of uncollectible accounts.

b. Predictive information such as this is crucial for the management of uncollectible accounts expense. Management might decide, for example, to implement more restrictive credit and collection policies if the uncollectible accounts rate exceeds 2 percent.

X Microsoft Excel - Uncollectible Accounts Expense

File Edit View Insert Format Tools Data Window Help

F5 = =+F1*A5

	A	B	C	D	E	F
1	Sales revenue	$180,000	$60,000	$120,000	$240,000	$600,000
2	0.01	1,800	600	1,200	2,400	6,000
3	0.02	3,600	1,200	2,400	4,800	12,000
4	0.03	5,400	1,800	3,600	7,200	18,000
5	0.04	7,200	2,400	4,800	9,600	24,000

Sheet1 / Sheet2 / Sheet3 /

Ready

Review Questions

15.1 What are the relationships among organization goals, strategic plans, and a master budget for the coming period?

15.2 What is meant by the term *operational budgets?* List three operational budgets that a hospital would prepare.

15.3 Use an example to explain how a budget could be used to allocate resources in a university.

15.4 Give an example of the effect of general economic trends on sales forecasting in the airline industry.

15.5 What is the danger of relying entirely on middle-management estimates of sales, costs, and other data used in budget planning?

15.6 What is the purpose of a *budget manual?*

15.7 Describe the role of a *budget director.*

15.8 Discuss the importance of predictions and assumptions in the budgeting process.

15.9 What is the purpose of a financial planning model? Briefly describe how such a model is constructed.

15.10 Define the term *budgetary slack* and briefly describe a problem it can cause.

15.11 How can an organization help to reduce the problems caused by budgetary slack?

15.12 Explain the concept of *zero-base budgeting.*

15.13 (Appendix) Explain the differences in the basic philosophies underlying the JIT and EOQ approaches to inventory management.

Critical Analysis

15.14 Draw a flowchart similar to the one in Exhibit 15–1 for a service station. The service station provides automotive maintenance services in addition to selling gasoline and related products.

15.15 The chief executive officer of Home Workout Equipment Corporation remarked to a colleague, "I don't understand why other companies waste so much time in the budget-

ing process. I set our company goals, and everyone strives to meet them. What's wrong with that approach?" Comment on the executive's remarks.

15.16 Give three examples of how the City of San Diego could use a budget for planning purposes.

15.17 A budget is also a legal limitation on expenditures of governmental agencies. If governmental employees are asked about their agencies' needs for the coming fiscal period, what types of biases are they likely to incorporate in their estimates? Why?

15.18 If a company prepares budgeted income statements and balance sheets, why is a cash budget necessary?

15.19 List the steps you would go through in developing a budget to meet your college expenses.

15.20 Surveying the accounts payable records, a clerk in the controller's office noted that expenses appeared to rise significantly within a month of the close of the budget period. The organization did not have a seasonal product or service to explain this behavior. Can you suggest an explanation?

15.21 Briefly describe three issues that create special challenges for multinational firms in preparing their budgets.

15.22 Borealis Corporation has established a bonus plan for its employees. An employee receives a bonus if his or her subunit meets the cost levels specified in the annual budget plan. If the subunit's costs exceed the budget, its employees earn no bonus. What problems might arise with this bonus plan?

15.23 How would the use of a just-in-time inventory system affect a company's budget plans?

Exercises

Exercise 15.24
Estimate of Sales
Revenue
(LO 2, 3)

Marlin County Bank (MCB) has $30 million in commercial loans with an average interest rate of 6 percent. The bank also has $24 million in consumer loans with an average interest rate of 8 percent. Finally, the bank owns $4.5 million in government securities with an average rate of 7 percent.

MCB estimates that next year its commercial loan portfolio will fall to $29 million, and the interest rate will fall to 5 percent. Its consumer loans will expand to $25 million with an average interest rate of 8.5 percent, and its government securities portfolio will increase to $6 million with an average rate of 6.5 percent.

Required
Estimate MCB's revenues for the coming year.

Exercise 15.25
Estimate of Production
(LO 3)

Pawtucket Pillow Corporation has just made its sales forecasts for the coming period. Its marketing department estimates that the company will sell 630,000 units during the coming year. In the past, management maintained inventories of finished goods at approximately two months' sales. The inventory at the start of the budget period is 50,000 units. Sales occur evenly throughout the year.

Required
Estimate the production level required for the coming year to meet these objectives.

Exercise 15.26
Estimate of Sales
Revenue
(LO 2, 3)

Zimmermann and Company, Ltd. is a large securities dealer in Frankfurt, Germany. Last year, the company made 45,000 trades with an average commission of 220 euros. Small investors are abandoning the market, whose volume is expected to decline by 15 percent for the coming year. The firm's volume generally changes with the market. However, in addition to market factors, the firm expects an additional 10 percent decline in the number of trades due to unfavorable publicity.

Offsetting these factors is the observation that the average commission per trade is likely to increase by 20 percent because trades are expected to be large in the coming year.

Required
Estimate Zimmermann's commission revenue for the coming year. (Remember to express your answer in terms of euros. On the day this exercise was written, the euro was equivalent in value to .8981 US dollars.)

Exercise 15.27
City or State Budget; Use
of Internet
(LO 1, 2)

Choose a city or state in the United States (or a Canadian city or province), and use the Internet to explore the annual budget of the governmental unit you selected. For example, you could check out the budget for Los Angeles at www.losangeles.com. Alternatively, take a look at the US federal budget at www.fms.treas.gov/annualreport/index.html.

Required
List three items in the budget that you found surprising or particularly interesting, and explain why.

Exercise 15.28
Estimate of Production
and Materials
Requirements
(LO 3)

PlasTech Company makes a line of specialized plastic tubing items. During each of the next two years, it expects to sell 320,000 units. The beginning finished-goods inventory is 80,000 units. However, the target ending finished-goods inventory for each year is 40,000 units.

Each unit requires 5 feet of plastic tubing. At the beginning of the year, 200,000 feet of plastic tubing are in inventory. Management has set a target to have tubing materials on hand equal to three months of production requirements. Sales and production occur evenly throughout the year.

Required

Compute the total targeted production of the finished product for the coming year. Compute the required purchases of tubing materials for the coming year. (Note that production in the following year should be 320,000 units of finished product.)

Lehighton Products' management wishes to purchase goods in one month for sale in the next. On January 31, the company has 8,000 digital music players in stock, although sales for the next month (February) are estimated to total 8,600 players. Sales for March are expected to equal 7,000 players, and April sales are expected to total 7,400 players.

    Tape players are purchased at a wholesale price of $290. The supplier has a financing arrangement by which Lehighton pays 60 percent of the purchase price in the month when the players are delivered and 40 percent in the following month. Interlaken purchased 10,000 players in January.

Exercise 15.29
Estimate of Purchases and Cash Disbursements
(LO 3)

Required

a.   Estimate purchases (in units) for February and March.

b.   Estimate the cash required in February and March to pay for the company's first-quarter purchases.

Read "At Disney, String of Weak Cartoons Leads to Cost Cuts: Disney Puts *Lilo and Stitch* on a Tight Budget," *The Wall Street Journal,* June 18, 2002, A1, A6, by Bruce Orwall.

Exercise 15.30
Budgeting in the Film Industry
(LO 1, 2)

Required

How did Disney change its approach with the production of *Lilo and Stitch?*

Good Times, Inc., buys plain mylar balloons and prints different designs on them for various occasions. It imports the balloons from Taiwan, so at all times it keeps on hand a stock equal to the balloons needed for two months' sales. The balloons cost $ .70 each and must be paid for in cash. The company has 14,000 balloons in stock. Sales estimates, based on contracts received, are as follows for the next six months:

Exercise 15.31
Estimate of Purchases and Cash Disbursements
(LO 3)

mhhe.com/hilton3e

June	6,200
July	8,900
August	6,600
September	7,100
October	4,800
November	3,600

Required

a.   Estimate purchases (in units) for June, July, and August.

b.   Estimate the cash required to make purchases in June, July, and August.

San Joaquin Produce Company is preparing its cash budget for July. The following information is available concerning its accounts receivable:

Exercise 15.32
Estimate of Cash Collections
(LO 3)

Estimated credit sales for July	$380,000
Actual credit sales for June	250,000
Estimated collections in July for credit sales in July	25%
Estimated collections in July for credit sales in June	70%
Estimated collections in July for credit sales prior to June	$ 29,000
Estimated write-offs in July for uncollectible credit sales	16,000
Estimated provision for bad debts in July for credit sales in July	14,000

Required

What are the estimated cash receipts from accounts receivable collections in July?

[CPA adapted]

Sounds Fine, Inc., is a large retailer of stereo equipment. The controller is about to prepare the budget for the first quarter of 20x1. Past experience has indicated that 75 percent of the store's sales are cash sales. The collection experience for the sales on account is as follows:

Exercise 15.33
Use of Budgets for Financial Planning
(LO 2, 3)

> 80 percent during month of sale
> 15 percent during month following sale
> 5 percent uncollectible

    The total sales for December 20x0 are expected to be $380,000. The controller believes that sales in January 20x1 could range from $200,000 to $320,000.

Required

a. Demonstrate how financial planning can be used to project cash receipts in January 20x1 for three different levels of January sales. Use the following columnar format.

	Total Sales in January 20x1		
	$200,000	**$260,000**	**$320,000**
Cash receipts in January 20x1			
From December sales on account	$	$	$
From January cash sales			
From January sales on account			
Total cash receipts	$	$	$

b. How could the controller of Sounds Fine, Inc., use this financial planning approach to help in planning operations for January?

Exercise 15.34
Estimate of Cash Receipts
(LO 3)

The Wedding Place specializes in custom wedding attire. The average price of each of bride's wedding ensembles is $3,200. For each wedding, The Wedding Place receives a 20 percent deposit two months before the wedding, 50 percent the month before, and the remainder on the day the goods are delivered. Based on information at hand, The Wedding Place expects to prepare outfits for the following number of weddings during the coming months:

January	5
February	3
March	2
April.......................................	4
May	5
June	11

Required

a. What are the expected revenues for The Wedding Place for each month, January through June? Revenues are recorded in the month of the wedding.

b. What are the expected cash receipts for each month, January through April?

Exercise 15.35
Estimate of Cash Receipts
(LO 3)

Oceanside Pools, Inc., manages neighborhood pools in Oceanside, Florida. The company attempts to make service calls at least once a month to all homes that subscribe to its service. More frequent calls are made during the summer. The number of subscribers also varies with the season. The number of subscribers and the average number of calls to each subscriber for the months of interest follow:

	Subscribers	Service Calls
March	100	0.5
April	120	1.0
May	260	1.8
June	300	2.2
July...............................	300	2.0
August	280	1.7

The average price charged for a service call is $50. Of the service calls, 20 percent are paid in the month the service is rendered, 60 percent in the month after the service is rendered, and 18 percent in the second month after. The remaining 2 percent is uncollectible.

Required

a. What are Ocean Pools' expected cash receipts for May, June, July, and August?

b. *Build your own spreadsheet.* Build an Excel spreadsheet to solve requirement (a). Use your spreadsheet to determine the new values for expected cash receipts in May, June, July, and August if each of the following input parameters changes by the amount indicated. (Unless otherwise indicated, treat each parameter change independently.)

1. The price per service call is $55.
2. Collections are 15 percent in the month of sale and 65 percent in the following month.
3. There were 110 subscribers in March.
4. All of the changes listed in parts (1) through (3) occur simultaneously.

Refer to the original data in the preceding exercise. Oceanside Pools estimates that the number of subscribers in September should fall 10 percent below August levels, and the number of service calls should decrease by an estimated 20 percent. The following information is available for costs incurred in August. All costs except depreciation are paid in cash.

Service costs	
Variable costs	$ 4,720
Maintenance and repair	4,200
Depreciation (fixed)	2,200
Total	$11,120
Marketing and administrative costs:	
Marketing (variable)	$ 2,500
Administrative (fixed)	2,300
Total	$ 4,800
Total costs	$15,920

Variable cash and marketing costs change with volume. Fixed depreciation will remain the same, but fixed administrative costs will increase by 5 percent beginning September 1. Maintenance and repair are provided by contract, which calls for a 1 percent increase in September.

Required

a. Prepare a budgeted income statement for September.

b. *Build your own spreadsheet.* Build an Excel spreadsheet to solve requirement (a). Use your spreadsheet to determine the new values for total revenue, total expenses, and operating income for September if each of the following input parameters changes by the amount indicated. (Unless otherwise indicated, treat each parameter change independently.) Assume the original data from the preceding exercise.

1. There were 300 subscribers in August.

2. Depreciation costs for service equipment were $3,000 instead of $2,200.

3. The number of September subscribers will be 15 percent below the August level.

4. All of the changes listed in parts (1) through (3) occur simultaneously.

a. The following information relates to Madison Industries:

Units required per year	240,000
Cost of placing an order	$300
Unit carrying cost per year	$400

Assuming that the units will be required evenly throughout the year, what is the EOQ?

b. Ewing Company requires 160,000 units of product Q for the year. The units will be required evenly throughout the year. The cost to place an order is $54, and the cost to carry a unit in inventory for the year is $12. What is the EOQ?

[CPA adapted]

Zodiac Company uses 810 tankloads a year of a specific input material. The tankloads are delivered by rail to a siding on the company property. The supplier is offering a special discount for buyers of large quantities. The schedule is as follows:

Quantity Ordered (tankloads)	Percentage Discount
1–19	0
20–79	2
80–149	5
150 and more	6

Ordering costs amount to $500, and carrying costs are $450 per tankload and are not affected by the discounts. Each tankload costs $1,500.

Required

Compute the optimal order quantity. (Round to the nearest whole number.)

Exercise 15.39
Impact of Constraints on
Optimal Order
(Appendix)
(LO 7)

Considering the situation in the preceding exercise, suppose that the maximum storage capacity for the company is 50 tankloads.

Required
What is the optimal order? Demonstrate why.

Problems

Problem 15.40
Budgeted Purchases
and Cash Flows
(LO 3)

Kaleidoscope Cutlery seeks your assistance in developing cash and other budget information for September, October, and November. On August 30, the company had cash of $5,500, accounts receivable of $437,000, inventories of $309,400, and accounts payable of $133,055. The budget is to be based on the following assumptions.

Sales

▨ Each month's sales are billed on the last day of the month.

▨ Customers are allowed a 3 percent discount if payment is made within 10 days after the billing date. Receivables are recorded in the accounts at their gross amounts (not net of discounts).

▨ The billings are collected as follows: 60 percent within the discount period, 25 percent by the end of the month, 9 percent by the end of the second month, and 6 percent are uncollectible.

Purchases

▨ Of all purchases of merchandise and selling, general, and administrative expenses, 54 percent is paid in the month purchased and the remainder in the following month.

▨ The number of units in each month's ending inventory equals 130 percent of the next month's units of sales.

▨ The cost of each unit of inventory is $20.

▨ Selling, general, and administrative expenses, of which $2,000 is depreciation, equal 15 percent of the current month's sales.

Actual and projected sales follow:

	Dollars	Units
July	$354,000	11,800
August	363,000	12,100
September	357,000	11,900
October	342,000	11,400
November	360,000	12,000
December	366,000	12,200

Required
Using the preceding information, compute the following amounts:

a. Budgeted purchases in dollars for September.
b. Budgeted purchases in dollars for October.
c. Budgeted cash collections during September.
d. Budgeted cash disbursements during October.
e. Budgeted number of units of inventory to be purchased during November.

[CPA adapted]

Problem 15.41
Preparation of a
Production Budget
(LO 3)

EarthWare, Inc., manufactures floral containers. The controller is preparing a budget for the coming year and asks for your assistance. The following costs and other data apply to container production:

Direct material per container:
1 pound Z-A styrene at $.40 per pound
2 pounds Vasa finish at $.80 per pound

Direct labor per container:
¼ hour at $8.60 per hour

Overhead per container:

Indirect labor	$ .11
Indirect material..	.04
Power	.07
Equipment costs	.34
Building occupancy	.21
Total overhead per unit	$ .77

You learn that equipment costs and building occupancy are facility-level (fixed) costs and are based on a normal production of 20,000 units per year. Other overhead costs are unit-level (variable) costs. Plant capacity is sufficient to produce 25,000 units per year.

Labor costs per hour are not expected to change during the year. However, the Vasa finish supplier has informed EarthWare's management that it will impose a 10 percent price increase at the start of the coming budget period. No other costs are expected to change.

During the coming budget period, management expects to sell 18,000 units. Finished-goods inventory is targeted to increase from 4,000 units to 7,000 units to prepare for an expected sales increase the year after next. Production will occur evenly throughout the year. Inventory levels for Vasa finish and Z-A styrene are expected to remain unchanged throughout the year. There is no work-in-process inventory.

Required

Prepare a production budget and estimate the material, labor, and overhead costs for the coming year.

The following information is available for 20x5 for Panhandle Products:

Revenue (100,000 units)	$725,000
Manufacturing costs:	
Materials (unit level)	42,000
Unit-level (variable) overhead cash costs	35,600
Facility-level (fixed) overhead cash costs..........................	81,900
Depreciation (facility level)..	249,750
Marketing and administrative costs:	
Marketing (unit level, cash)...	105,600
Marketing depreciation..	37,400
Administrative (facility level, cash)	127,300
Administrative depreciation	18,700
Total costs	$698,250
Operating profit..	$ 26,750

Problem 15.42
Preparation of Budgeted Financial Statements; Estimation of Cash Receipts
(LO 1, 2, 3)

All depreciation charges are facility-level costs and are expected to remain the same for 20x6. Sales volume is expected to increase by 18 percent, but prices are expected to fall by 5 percent. Material costs are expected to decrease by 8 percent. Unit-level (variable) manufacturing overhead costs are expected to decrease by 2 percent per unit. Facility-level (fixed) manufacturing overhead costs are expected to increase by 5 percent.

Unit-level (variable) marketing costs change with volume. Administrative cash costs are expected to increase by 10 percent. Inventories are kept at zero.

Required

a. Prepare a budgeted income statement for 20x6.
b. Estimate the cash from operations expected in 20x6.

Technomatics, Inc., based in Singapore, manufactures two different types of housings used for electric motors. In the fall of the current year, James Li, the controller, compiled the following data. (All monetary amounts are given in terms of the national currency of Singapore, the Singaporean *dollar*.) On the day this problem was written, the Singaporean dollar was equivalent in value to 0.5548 US dollars.

Problem 15.43
Activity-Based Overhead Budget; Sales, Production, and Purchases Budgets
(LO 3)

■   Raw-material prices and inventory levels:

Raw Material	Expected Inventories January 1, 20x0	Desired Inventories, December 31, 20x0	Anticipated Purchase Price
Sheet metal	32,000 lb.	36,000 lb.	$8
Bar stock	29,000 lb.	32,000 lb.	5
Base	6,000 units	7,000 units	3

■   Use of raw material:

	Amount Used per Unit	
Raw Material	Small Housing	Large Housing
Sheet metal	4 lb.	5 lb.
Bar stock	2 lb.	3 lb.
Base		1 unit

■   Direct-labor requirements and rates:

Product	Hours per Unit	Rate per Hour
Small housing	2	$15
Large housing	3	20

■   Finished-goods inventories (in units):

Product	Expected January 1, 20x0	Desired December 31, 20x0
Small housing	20,000	25,000
Large housing	8,000	9,000

■   Manufacturing overhead:

Overhead Cost Item	Activity-Based Budget Rate
Purchasing and material handling	$.25 per pound of sheet metal and bar stock purchased
Depreciation, utilities, and inspection	$4.00 per housing produced (either type)
Shipping	$1.00 per housing shipped (either type)
General manufacturing overhead	$3.00 per direct-labor hour

■   Sales forecast for 20x0:

Product	Units	Price
Small housing	60,000	$65
Large housing	40,000	95

Required

Prepare the following budgets for 20x0:

a.   Sales budget (in dollars).
b.   Production budget (in units).
c.   Raw-material purchases budget (in quantities).
d.   Raw-material purchases budget (in dollars).
e.   Direct-labor budget (in dollars).
f.   Manufacturing overhead budget (in dollars).

[CPA adapted]

Problem 15.44
Sales Expense Budget
(LO 3)

Venus Software Company has just received its sales expense report for January, which follows:

Item	Amount
Sales commissions	$139,000
Sales staff salaries	31,000
Telephone and mailing	16,200
Building lease payment	20,000
Heat, light, and water	4,100
Packaging and delivery	27,400
Depreciation	12,500
Marketing consultants	19,700

You have been asked to develop budgeted costs for the coming year. Since this month is typical, you decide to prepare an estimated budget for a typical month in the coming year, and you uncover the following additional data:

- Sales volume is expected to increase by 5 percent.
- Sales prices are expected to increase by 10 percent.
- Commissions are based on a percentage of selling price.
- Sales staff salaries will increase 4 percent next year regardless of sales volume.
- Building rent is based on a five-year lease that expires in three years.
- Telephone and mailing expenses are scheduled to increase by 8 percent even with no change in sales volume. However, these costs are variable with the number of units sold, as are packaging and delivery costs.
- Heat, light, and water are scheduled to increase by 12 percent regardless of sales volume.
- Depreciation includes furniture and fixtures used by the sales staff. The company has just acquired an additional $19,000 in furniture that will be received at the start of next year and will be depreciated over a 10-year life using the straight-line method.
- Marketing consultant expenses were for a special advertising campaign that runs from time to time. During the coming year, the costs are expected to average $35,000 per month.

Required

Prepare the company's budget for sales expenses for a typical month in the coming year.

Atlantico produces and distributes industrial chemicals in its Delmarva Division, which is located in Wilmington, Delaware. Delmarva's earnings increased sharply in 20x0, and bonuses were paid to the management staff for the first time in several years. Bonuses are based in part on the amount by which reported income exceeds budgeted income.

Problem 15.45
Ethics; Budgetary
Pressure; Management
Bonuses; Budgetary
Constraints
(LO 4, 5)

Jim Kern, vice president of finance, was pleased with Delmarva's 20x0 earnings and thought that the pressure to show financial results would ease. However, Ellen North, Delmarva's division manager, told Kern that she saw no reason why the 20x1 bonuses should not be double those of 20x0. As a result, Kern felt pressure to increase reported income to exceed budgeted income by an even greater amount. This would ensure increased bonuses.

Kern met with Bill Keller of Pristeel, Inc., a primary vendor of Delmarva manufacturing supplies and equipment. Kern and Keller have been close business contacts for many years. Kern asked Keller to identify all of Delmarva's purchases of perishable supplies as equipment on Pristeel's sales invoices. The reason Kern gave for his request was that Delmarva's division manager had imposed stringent budget constraints on operating expenses but not on capital expenditures. Kern planned to capitalize the purchase of perishable supplies and include them with the Equipment account on the balance sheet. In this way Kern could defer the expense recognition for these items to a later year. This procedure would increase reported earnings, leading to increased bonuses. Keller agreed to do as Kern had asked.

While analyzing the second quarter financial statements, Gary Wood, Delmarva's director of cost management, noticed a large decrease in supplies expense from one year ago. Wood reviewed the Supplies Expense account and noticed that only equipment but no supplies had been purchased from Pristeel, a major source for supplies. Wood, who reports to Kern, immediately brought this to Kern's attention.

Kern told Wood of North's high expectations and of the arrangement made with Keller of Pristeel. Wood told Kern that his action was an improper accounting treatment for the supplies purchased from Pristeel. Wood requested that he be allowed to correct the accounts and urged that the arrangement with Pristeel be discontinued. Kern refused the request and told Wood not to become involved in the arrangement with Pristeel.

After clarifying the situation in a confidential discussion with an objective and qualified peer within Delmarva, Wood arranged to meet with North, Delmarva's division manager. At the meeting, Wood disclosed the arrangement Kern had made with Pristeel.

Required

Prepare a presentation to the class covering the following issues:

a. Explain why the use of alternative accounting methods to manipulate reported earnings is unethical.

b. Is Gary Wood, Delmarva's director of cost management, correct in saying that the supplies purchased from Pristeel, Inc., were accounted for improperly? Explain your answer.

c.   Assuming that Jim Kern's arrangement with Pristeel, Inc., was in violation of the Standards of Ethical Conduct for Management Accountants, discuss whether Wood's actions were appropriate or inappropriate. (The standards are given in the Appendix to Chapter 1).

[CMA adapted]

Problem 15.46
Comprehensive Budget
Plan
(LO 1, 3)

CoffeeBreak, Inc., a manufacturer of coffee mugs, decided in October 20x0 that it needed cash to continue operations. It began negotiating for a one-month bank loan of $100,000 starting November 1, 20x0. The bank would charge interest at the rate of 1 percent per month and require the company to repay interest and principal on November 30, 20x0. In considering the loan, the bank requested a projected income statement and cash budget for November. The following information is available:

▢   The company budgeted sales at 120,000 units per month in October 20x0, December 20x0, and January 20x1, and at 90,000 units in November 20x0. The selling price is $2 per unit.

▢   The inventory of finished goods on October 1 was 24,000 units. The finished-goods inventory at the end of each month equals 20 percent of sales anticipated for the following month. There is no work-in-process inventory.

▢   The inventory of raw material on October 1 was 22,800 pounds. At the end of each month, the raw-material inventory equals no less than 40 percent of production requirements for the following month. The company purchases materials as needed in minimum quantities of 25,000 pounds per shipment.

▢   Selling expenses are 10 percent of gross sales. Administrative expenses, which include depreciation of $500 per month on office furniture and fixtures, total $33,000 per month.

▢   The manufacturing budget for coffee cups, based on normal production of 100,000 units per month, follows:

Material (½ pound per cup, 50,000 pounds, $1 per pound)	$ 50,000
Labor	40,000
Variable overhead	20,000
Fixed overhead (includes depreciation of $4,000)	10,000
Total	$120,000

▢   CoffeeBreak's customers are allowed a 1 percent discount if payment is made within 10 days, and these discounts are always taken. Bad debts are projected at ½ percent of gross sales.

Required

a.   Prepare schedules computing inventory budgets by months for the following:

(1)   Production in units for October, November, and December.

(2)   Raw-material purchases in pounds for October and November.

b.   Prepare a projected income statement for November. Cost of goods sold should equal the variable manufacturing cost per unit times the number of units sold plus the total fixed manufacturing cost budgeted for the period.

[CPA adapted]

Problem 15.47
Preparation of Budgeted
Financial Statements;
Estimation of Cash
Receipts
(LO 1, 3)

Meridian, Inc., has the following data from 20x5 operations, which are to be used for developing 20x6 budget estimates:

Revenue (100,000)	$790,000
Manufacturing costs:	
Material (unit level)	133,000
Unit-level (variable) overhead cash costs	180,900
Facility-level (fixed) overhead cash costs	72,000
Depreciation (facility level)	89,000

Marketing and administrative costs:

Marketing (unit level, cash)...	95,000
Marketing depreciation...	22,600
Administrative (facility level, cash)	90,110
Administrative depreciation	8,400
Total costs	691,010
Operating profits..	$ 98,990

All depreciation charges are facility-level costs. Old manufacturing equipment with an annual depreciation charge of $9,700 will be replaced in 20x6 with new equipment that will incur an annual deprecia-
tion charge of $14,000. Sales volume and prices are expected to increase by 12 percent and 6 percent,
respectively. On a per-unit basis, expectations are that material costs will increase by 10 percent and
unit-level (variable) manufacturing overhead costs will decrease by 4 percent. Facility-level (fixed)
overhead costs are expected to decrease by 7 percent.

   Unit-level (variable) marketing costs will change with volume. Administrative cash costs are
expected to increase by 8 percent. Inventories are kept near zero.

Required

a.   Prepare Meridian's budgeted income statement for 20x6.

b.   Estimate the cash from operations expected in 20x6.

The San Angelo Division of Lone Star Corporation produces an intricate component used in the company's product line. The division manager has been concerned recently by a lack of coordination
between purchasing and production personnel and believes that a monthly budgeting system would be
better than the present system.

   The San Angelo division manager has decided to develop budget information for the third quarter
of the current year as an experiment before the budget system is implemented for an entire year. In
response to the division manager's request, the divisional controller accumulated the following data.

Problem 15.48
Production, Materials,
Labor, and Overhead
Budgets
(LO 3)

▨   San Angelo Division expects to sell 60,000 units during the current year. Sales through June 30,
   the first six months of the current year, are 24,000 units. Actual sales in units for May and June and
   estimated unit sales for the next four months are as follows:

May (actual)	4,000
June (actual)	4,000
July (estimated)	5,000
August (estimated)	6,000
September (estimated)	7,000
October (estimated).......................................	7,000

▨   The desired monthly ending inventory of completed components is 80 percent of the next month's
   estimated sales. There are 5,000 finished units in inventory on June 30.

▨   Data regarding the materials used in the component are shown in the following schedule. The
   desired monthly ending inventory for all raw materials is an amount sufficient to produce the next
   month's estimated sales.

Raw Material	Units of Raw Material per Finished Component	Cost per Unit	Inventory Level June 30
B42	6	$2.40	35,000 units
F68	4	3.60	30,000 units
M03	2	1.20	14,000 units

▨   Each component must pass through three different processes to be completed. Data regarding
   direct labor follow:

Process	Direct-Labor Hours per Finished Component	Cost per Direct-Labor Hour
Forming	.400	$16.00
Assembly	1.000	11.00
Finishing	.125	12.00

■ The division produced 27,000 components during the six-month period ending June 30. The actual unit-level (variable) overhead costs incurred during this six-month period are given in the following schedule. The divisional controller believes the unit-level (variable) overhead costs will be incurred at the same rate during the last six months of the current year.

Supplies	$ 59,400
Electricity	27,000
Indirect labor	54,000
Other	8,100
Total variable overhead	$148,500

The facility-level (fixed) overhead costs *actually incurred* during the first six months of the year amounted to $93,500. These facility-level overhead costs are *budgeted* for the full year as follows:

Supervision	$ 60,000
Taxes	7,200
Depreciation	86,400
Other	32,400
Total fixed overhead	$186,000

Required

a. Prepare a production budget in units for San Angelo for the third quarter of the current year, ending September 30.

b. Independent of your answer to requirement (a), assume that San Angelo Division plans to produce 18,000 units during the third quarter ending September 30 and 60,000 units for the entire year ending December 31.

   (1) Prepare a raw-material purchases budget, in units and dollars, for the third quarter, ending September 30.

   (2) Prepare a direct-labor budget, in hours and dollars, for the third quarter, ending September 30.

   (3) Prepare a manufacturing-overhead budget for the six-month period ending December 31 of the current year.

[CMA adapted]

Problem 15.49
Production and Direct-Labor Budgets; Activity-Based Overhead Budget
(LO 2, 3, 4)

Nassau Company manufactures stereo headphones in Princeton, New Jersey. Brent Dean, director of cost management, is responsible for preparing the company's master budget. In compiling the budget data for 20x1, Dean has learned that new automated production equipment will be installed on March 1. This will reduce the direct labor per set of headphones from 1 hour to .75 hours.

Labor-related costs include pension contributions of $.50 per hour, workers' compensation insurance of $.20 per hour, employee medical insurance of $.80 per hour, and employer contributions to Social Security equal to 7 percent of direct-labor wages. The cost of employee benefits paid by the company on its employees is treated as a direct-labor cost. Nassau Company has a labor contract that calls for a wage increase to $18.00 per hour on April 1, 20x1. Management expects to have 16,000 headphone sets on hand at December 31, 20x0, and has a policy of carrying an end-of-month inventory of 100 percent of the following month's sales plus 50 percent of the second following month's sales.

These and other data compiled by Dean are summarized in the following table.

	January	February	March	April	May
Estimated unit sales	10,000	12,000	8,000	9,000	9,000
Sales price per unit	$50.00	$47.50	$47.50	$47.50	$47.50
Direct-labor hours per unit	1.0	1.0	.75	.75	.75
Wage per direct-labor hour	$16.00	$16.00	$16.00	$18.00	$18.00
Manufacturing overhead					
Purchasing, material handling, and inspection (per unit produced)	$3.00	$3.00	$3.00	$3.00	$3.00
Shipping and handling (per unit sold)	$2.00	$2.00	$2.00	$2.00	$2.00
Other manufacturing overhead (per direct-labor hour)	$7.00	$7.00	$7.00	$7.00	$7.00

Required

a. Prepare a production budget and a direct-labor budget for Nassau Company by month and for the first quarter of 20x1. Both budgets can be combined in one schedule. The direct-labor budget should include direct-labor hours and show the detail for each direct-labor cost category.

b. For each item used in the firm's production budget and direct-labor budget, identify the other components of the master budget that also would use these data.

c. Prepare a manufacturing overhead budget for each month and for the first quarter.

[CMA adapted]

Arrow Space, Inc., manufactures specialized ceramic components used in the aerospace industry. The company's materials and parts manager is currently revising the inventory policy for XL-20, one of the chemicals used in the production process. The chemical is purchased in 10-pound canisters for $95 each. The firm uses 4,800 canisters per year. The controller estimates that to place and receive a typical order of XL-20 costs $150. The annual cost of storing XL-20 is $4 per canister.

Problem 15.50
Economic Order
Quantity; Equation
Approach; JIT
Purchasing (Appendix)
(LO 7)

Required

a. Write the formula for the total annual cost of ordering and storing XL-20.

b. Use the EOQ formula to determine the optimal order quantity.

c. What is the total annual cost of ordering and storing XL-20 at the economic order quantity?

d. How many orders will be placed per year?

e. Arrow Space's controller, Jane Turnbull, recently attended a seminar on JIT purchasing. Afterwards she analyzed the cost of storing XL-20, including the costs of wasted space and inefficiency. She was shocked when she concluded that the real annual holding cost was $19.20 per canister. Turnbull then met with Doug Kaplan, Arrow Space's purchasing manager. Together they contacted Reno Industries, the supplier of XL-20, about a JIT purchasing arrangement. After some discussion and negotiation, Kaplan concluded that the cost of placing an order for XL-20 could be reduced to just $20. Using these new cost estimates, Turnbull computed the new EOQ for XL-20.

  (1) Use the equation approach to compute the new EOQ.

  (2) How many orders will be placed per year?

Refer to the *original* data given in the preceding problem for Arrow Space, Inc.

Problem 15.51
Economic Order
Quantity; Tabular
Approach (Appendix)
(LO 7)

Required

a. Prepare a table showing the total annual cost of ordering and storing XL-20 for each of the following order quantities: 400, 600, and 800 canisters.

b. What are the weaknesses in the tabular approach?

Refer to the *original* data given in problem 15.50 for Arrow Space, Inc.

Problem 15.52
Economic Order
Quantity; Graphical
Approach (Appendix)
(LO 7)

Required

Prepare a graphical analysis of the economic order quantity decision for XL-20.

Refer to the *original* data given in problem 15.50 for Arrow Space, Inc. The lead time required to receive an order of XL-20 is one month.

Problem 15.53
Economic Order
Quantity; Lead Time and
Safety Stock (Appendix)
(LO7)

Required

a. Assuming stable usage of XL-20 each month, determine the reorder point for XL-20.

b. Suppose that the monthly usage of XL-20 fluctuates between 300 and 500 canisters, although annual demand remains constant at 4,800 canisters. What level of safety stock should the materials and parts manager keep on hand for XL-20? What is the new reorder point for the chemical?

Cases

Case 15.54*
Comprehensive Master
Budget; Acquisition of
Automated Materials-
Handling System
(LO 1, 2, 3)

mhhe.com/hilton3e

Pacifico, Inc., is a small, rapidly growing wholesaler of consumer electronic products. The firm's main product lines are small kitchen appliances and power tools. Malinda Alexander, Pacifico's general manager of marketing, recently completed a sales forecast. She believes the company's sales during the first quarter of 20x1 will increase by 10 percent each month over the previous month's sales. Then Alexander expects sales to remain constant for several months. Pacifico's projected balance sheet as of December 31, 20x0, is as follows:

Cash	$ 29,000
Accounts receivable	276,000
Marketable securities	15,000
Inventory	154,000
Buildings and equipment (net of accumulated depreciation)	626,000
Total assets	$1,100,000
Accounts payable	$ 176,400
Bond interest payable	12,500
Property taxes payable	3,600
Bonds payable (10%; due in 20x6)	300,000
Common stock	500,000
Retained earnings	107,500
Total liabilities and stockholders' equity	$1,100,000

Shawn Garrity, the assistant controller, is now preparing a monthly budget for the first quarter of 20x1. In the process, the following information has been accumulated:

1.   Projected sales for December 20x0 are $400,000. Credit sales typically are 75 percent of total sales. Atlantico's credit experience indicates that 10 percent of the credit sales is collected during the month of sale, and the remainder is collected during the following month.

2.   Pacifico's cost of goods sold generally is 70 percent of sales. Inventory is purchased on account, and 40 percent of each month's purchases are paid during the month of purchase. The remainder is paid during the following month. To have adequate stocks of inventory on hand, the firm attempts to have inventory at the end of each month equal to half of the next month's projected cost of goods sold.

3.   Garrity has estimated that Pacifico's other monthly expenses will be as follows:

Sales salaries	$21,000
Advertising and promotion	16,000
Administrative salaries	21,000
Depreciation	25,000
Interest on bonds	2,500
Property taxes	900

In addition, sales commissions run at the rate of 1 percent of sales.

Note: Case 18.48 (River Beverages) in Chapter 18 includes significant managerial issues related to the budgeting process and may be assigned at this time.

4. Pacifico's president, Carrie Howland, has indicated that the firm should invest $125,000 in an auto-mated inventory-handling system to control the movement of inventory in the firm's warehouse just after the new year begins. This equipment purchase will be financed primarily from the firm's cash and marketable securities. However, Howland believes that Pacifico needs to keep a minimum cash balance of $19,000. If necessary, the remainder of the equipment purchases will be financed using short-term credit from a local bank. The minimum period for such a loan is three months. Garrity believes that short-term interest rates will be 10 percent per year at the time of the equipment purchases. If a loan is necessary, Howland has decided it should be paid off by the end of the first quarter if possible.

5. Pacifico's board of directors has indicated its intention to declare and pay dividends of $50,000 on the last day of each quarter.

6. The interest on any short-term borrowing will be paid when the loan is repaid. Interest on Pacifico's bonds is paid semiannually on January 31 and July 31 for the preceding six-month period.

7. Property taxes are paid semiannually on February 28 and August 31 for the preceding six-month period.

Required

Work as a group to prepare Pacifico's master budget for the first quarter of 20x1 by completing the fol-lowing schedules and statements.

a. Sales budget:

	20x0	20x1			
	December	January	February	March	1st Quarter
Total sales					
Cash sales					
Sales on account......................					

b. Cash receipts budget:

	20x1			
	January	February	March	1st Quarter
Cash sales				
Cash collections from credit sales .... made during current month				
Cash collections from credit sales made during preceding month............................				
Total cash receipts				

c. Purchases budget:

	20x0	20x1			
	December	January	February	March	1st Quarter
Budgeted cost of goods sold					
Add: Desired ending inventory					
Total goods needed					
Less: Expected beginning inventory					
Purchases					

d.   Cash disbursements budget:

	20x1			
	January	**February**	**March**	**1st Quarter**
Inventory purchases:				
Cash payments for purchases during the current month*				
Cash payments for purchases during the preceding month†				
Total cash payments for inventory purchases				
Other expenses:				
Sales salaries				
Advertising and promotion				
Administrative salaries				
Interest on bonds‡...				
Property taxes‡				
Sales commissions				
Total cash payments for other expenses				
Total cash disbursements....................................				

*40% of the month's purchases (schedule c).

†60% of the prior month's purchases (schedule c).

‡Bond interest is paid every six months, on January 31 and July 31. Property taxes also are paid every six months, on February 28 and August 31.

e.   Complete the first three lines of the summary cash budget. Then do the analysis of short-term financing needs in requirement (f). Then finish requirement (e).

Summary cash budget:

	20x1			
	January	**February**	**March**	**1st Quarter**
Cash receipts (from schedule b)				
Less: Cash disbursements (from schedule d)				
Change in cash balance during period due to operations				
Sale of marketable securities (1/2/x1)				
Proceeds from bank loan (1/2/x1)				
Purchase of equipment				
Repayment of bank loan (3/31/x1)				
Interest on bank loan				
Payment of dividends...				
Change in cash balance during first quarter				
Cash balance, 1/1/x1				
Cash balance, 3/31/x1				

f.   Analysis of short-term financing needs:

Projected cash balance as of December 31, 20x0	$
Less: Minimum cash balance...	_____
Cash available for equipment purchases..	$
Projected proceeds from sale of marketable securities	_____
Cash available	$
Less: Cost of investment in equipment	_____
Required short-term borrowing...	$_____

g. Prepare Pacifico's budgeted income statement for the first quarter of 20x1. (Ignore income taxes.)

h. Prepare Pacifico's budgeted statement of retained earnings for the first quarter of 20x1.

i. Prepare Pacifico's budgeted balance sheet as of March 31, 20x1. (*Hint:* On March 31, 20x1, Bond Interest Payable is $5,000 and Property Taxes Payable is $900.)

Triple-F Health Club (Family, Fitness, and Fun) is a nonprofit health club. Its board of directors is developing plans to acquire more equipment and expand club facilities. The board plans to purchase about $25,000 of new equipment each year and wants to begin a fund to purchase an adjoining property in four or five years when the expansion will need the space. The adjoining property has a market value of about $300,000.

The club manager is concerned that the board has unrealistic goals in light of its recent financial performance. She sought the help of a club member with an accounting background to assist her in preparing the club's records, including the cash-basis income statements that follow. The review and discussions with the manager disclosed the additional information that follows the statement.

Case 15.55
Preparation and Interpretation of Cash Budget for Service Organization
(LO 1, 2, 3)

TRIPLE-F HEALTH CLUB Statement of Income (Cash Basis) For the Year Ended October 31 (in thousands)		
	20x7	**20x6**
Cash revenue:		
Annual membership fees	$355.0	$300.0
Lesson and class fees	234.0	180.0
Miscellaneous	2.0	1.5
Total cash received	$591.0	$481.5
Cash costs:		
Manager's salary and benefits	$ 36.0	$ 36.0
Regular employees' wages and benefits	190.0	190.0
Lesson and class employee wages		
and benefits	195.0	150.0
Towels and supplies	16.0	15.5
Utilities (heat and light)	22.0	15.0
Mortgage interest	35.1	37.8
Miscellaneous	2.0	1.5
Total cash costs	$496.1	$445.8
Cash income	$ 94.9	$ 35.7

Additional information follows:

1. Other financial information as of October 31, 20x7:

    a. Cash in checking account, $7,000.

    b. Petty cash, $300.

    c. Outstanding mortgage balance, $360,000.

    d. Accounts payable for supplies and utilities unpaid as of October 31, 20x7, and due in November 20x7, $2,500.

2. The club purchased $25,000 worth of exercise equipment during the current fiscal year. Cash of $10,000 was paid on delivery, with the balance due on October 1, which had not been paid as of October 31, 20x7.

3. The club began operations in 20x1 in rental quarters. In October 20x3, it purchased its current property (land and building) for $600,000, paying $120,000 down and agreeing to pay $30,000 plus 9 percent interest annually on the unpaid loan balance each November 1, starting November 1, 20x4.

4. Membership rose 3 percent during 20x7, approximately the same annual rate of increase the club has experienced since it opened and that is expected to continue in the future.

5. Membership fees were increased by 15 percent in 20x7. The board has tentative plans to increase them by 10 percent in 20x8.

6. Lesson and class fees have not been increased for three years. The number of classes and lessons has grown significantly each year, and the percentage growth experienced in 20x7 is expected to be repeated in 20x8.

7. Miscellaneous revenues are expected to grow in 20x8 (over 20x7) at the same percentage as experienced in 20x7 (over 20x6).

8. Lesson and class employees' wages and benefits will increase to $291,525. The wages and benefits of regular employees and the manager will increase 15 percent. Towels and supplies, utilities, and miscellaneous expenses are expected to increase 25 percent.

Required

a. Construct a cash budget for 20x8 for the Triple-F Health Club.

b. Write a memo to the health club's board of directors to accompany the budget. In the memo, identify any operating problem(s) that this budget discloses for the Triple-F Health Club.

c. Is the manager's concern that the board's goals are unrealistic justified? Explain your answer.

[CMA adapted]

PART FIVE

Evaluating and Managing Performance

Creating and Managing Value-Added Effort

◀ **A Look Back**

The preceding part covered financial and operational budgeting, cost estimation, and decision making.

▼ **A Look at This Part**

The first two chapters in Part Five explore standard-costing systems and cost-variance analysis as a cost-management tool. The third chapter in this part covers organizational design issues, responsibility accounting, and various measures of investment center performance. The fourth chapter in Part V covers transfer pricing. The final chapter in this part explores the use of lead and lag measures to motivate, communicate, and evaluate, and includes a discussion of the balanced scorecard.

Chapter 16

Standard Costing, Variance Analysis, and Kaizen Costing

After completing this chapter, you should be able to:

1. Discuss how companies use standard-costing systems to manage costs, and describe two ways to set standards.

2. Distinguish between perfection and practical standards.

3. Compute and interpret the direct-material price and quantity variances and the direct-labor rate and efficiency variances.

4. Describe several methods used to determine the significance of cost variances.

5. Discuss some behavioral effects of standard costing and the controllability of variances.

6. Explain how companies use standard costs in product costing.

7. Summarize some advantages attributed to standard costing.

8. Describe the changing role of standard-costing systems in today's manufacturing environment.

9. Explain the concept of kaizen costing and its potential benefits.

10. Compute and interpret mix and yield variances (Appendix).

1. **How** could Koala Camp Gear's controller set standards for the production of tents using the company's standard-costing system?

2. **What** is the appropriate interpretation of each variance detailed in Koala Camp Gear Company's cost-variance report?

3. **Who** is in the best position in the organization to influence each of these variances?

4. **What** criticisms are made of standard-costing systems as they are used in today's business environment?

Koala Camp Gear Company

EMAIL MEMORANDUM

2145 Yarra Drive
Melbourne, Victoria
Australia

To: Geoff Weatherby
Production Manager

From: Marc Wesley
Controller

cc: Margo Hastings
President and CEO

Subject: June cost-variance report

The cost-variance report for direct material and direct labor for the month of June appears below. I suggest that we add a discussion of the report to tomorrow morning's staff meeting. This report is based on June output of 3,000 Tree Line tents.

The unfavorable direct-material variances (both price and quantity), while cause for concern, are not nearly as high in percentage terms as the direct-labor rate variance. We need to get to the bottom of these variations from standard costs, and we can begin with tomorrow morning's meeting. Before then I will analyze the direct-labor costs in greater detail to see whether I can provide any insights into our June performance.

Cost Variance Report for June: Direct Material and Direct Labor

	Amount	Percentage of Standard Cost
Direct material:		
Standard cost, given actual output	$288,000	
Direct-material price variance	6,000 U*	2.08%
Direct-material quantity variance	3,200 U*	1.11%
Direct labor:		
Standard cost, given actual output	$108,000	
Direct-labor rate variance	5,900 U*	5.46%
Direct-labor efficiency variance	1,800 F*	(1.67)%

*U denotes unfavorable; F denotes favorable

Koala Camp Gear
Company

The memorandum on the preceding page includes a cost-variance report intended to help the management of Koala Camp Gear Company manage the company's production costs. How do small manufacturing companies such as Koala, or large companies such as Dell Computer or Daimler/Chrysler, manage and control the many costs they incur in their production process? As the preceding chapter explained, a budget provides a plan for managers to follow in making decisions and directing an organization's activities. At the end of a budget period, the budget serves another useful purpose. At that time, managers use it as a benchmark against which to compare the results of actual operations. Did the company make as much profit as anticipated in the budget? Were costs higher or lower than expected?

In addition to budgets, many companies use *standards* to help manage costs and profits. A *standard* is a benchmark performance level. For example, many manufacturing firms set standards for the amount and price of direct materials and for the amount and rate paid for direct labor used to produce their products. At the end of the period, management compares the standards with actual results. These comparisons help management gain insight into what went right and what went wrong in the production process.

Use of Standard-Costing Systems for Control

LO I Discuss how companies use standard-costing systems to manage costs, and describe two ways to set standards.

Any control system has three basic parts: a predetermined or *standard* performance level, a measure of *actual* performance, and a *comparison* of standard and actual performances. A thermostat, a control system with which we are all familiar, has three parts. First, it has a predetermined or standard temperature, which you can set at any desired level. If you want the temperature in a room to be 70 degrees, you set the thermostat at the *standard* of 70 degrees. Second, the thermostat has a thermometer, which measures the *actual* temperature in the room. Third, the thermostat *compares* the preset or standard temperature with the actual room temperature. If the actual temperature differs from the preset or standard temperature, the thermostat activates a heating or cooling device.

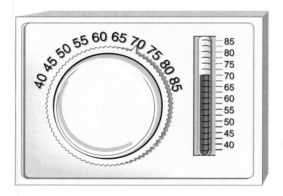

A cost manager's budgetary-control system works like a thermostat. First, a predetermined, or *standard cost* is set. In essence, a **standard cost** is a budget for the production of one unit of product or service. It is the cost chosen by the cost-management analyst to serve as the benchmark in the budgetary-control system. When the firm produces many units, the cost-management analyst uses the standard unit cost to determine the total standard or budgeted cost of production. For example, suppose that the standard direct-material cost for one of Koala Camp Gear's tent models is $96, and the firm manufactures 1,000 units. The total standard or budgeted direct-material cost, given actual output of 1,000 units, is $96,000 ($96 × 1,000).

Second, the cost-management analyst measures the actual cost incurred in the production process.

Third, the cost-management analyst compares the actual cost with the budgeted, or standard, cost. Any difference between the actual cost and the standard cost is called a **cost variance.** Cost-management analysts then use these cost variances to control costs.

Management by Exception

Although managers do not have time to explore the causes of every variance between actual and standard costs, they do take the time to investigate the causes of significant cost variances. This process of following up only on significant cost variances is called **management by exception.** When operations are going along as planned, actual costs and profit are typically close to the budgeted amounts. However, significant departures from planned operations appear as significant cost variances. Managers investigate these variances to determine their cause, if possible, and take corrective action when indicated.

What constitutes a significant variance? This question has no precise answer, since it depends on the size and type of the organization and its production process. We consider this issue later in the chapter when we discuss common methods for determining the significance of cost variances. First, however, we turn our attention to the process of setting standards.

Setting Standards

Cost-management analysts typically use two methods to set cost standards: analysis of historical data and task analysis.

Analysis of historical data. One indicator of future costs is historical cost data. In a mature production process, when the firm has considerable production experience, historical costs can provide a reliable basis for predicting future costs. The methods for analyzing cost behavior that we studied in Chapter 12 are used in making cost predictions. The cost analyst often needs to adjust these predictions to reflect movements in price levels or technological changes in the production process. For example, the amount of leather required to manufacture a pair of Dr. Martens shoes is likely the same this year as last year unless a significant change in the process used to manufacture shoes has occurred. However, the price of leather is likely to be different this year than last, and this fact must be reflected in the new standard cost of a pair of shoes.

Despite the relevance of historical cost data in setting cost standards, cost-management analysts must guard against relying on these data excessively. Even a seemingly minor change in the way a product is manufactured could make historical data almost totally irrelevant. Moreover, new products also require new cost standards. For new products, such as genetically engineered vaccines, no historical cost data exist on which to base standards. In such cases, the cost analyst must turn to another approach.

Task analysis. Another way to set cost standards, called **task analysis,** is the technique of analyzing the process of manufacturing a product to determine what it *should* cost. The emphasis shifts from what the product *did* cost in the past to what it *should* cost in the future. In using this approach, the cost-management analyst typically works with engineers who are intimately familiar with the production process. Together they conduct studies to determine exactly the amount of direct material that should be required and the way that machinery should be used in the production process. Time-and-motion studies sometimes are conducted to determine how long each step performed by direct laborers should take. Storyboarding sessions sometimes are used to develop a detailed process map of all the activities in a work center.

A combined approach. Cost-management analysts often apply both historical cost analysis and task analysis in setting cost standards. It might be, for example, that the technology has changed for only one step in the production process. In such a case, the cost analyst works with engineers to set cost standards for the technologically changed part of the production process. However, the accountant likely relies on the less expensive method of analyzing historical cost data to update the cost standards for the remaining steps in the production process.

Participation in setting standards. Standards should not be determined by accounting staff alone. People generally are more committed to meeting standards if they are allowed to participate in setting them. For example, production supervisors should have a role in setting production cost standards, and sales managers should be involved in setting targets for sales prices and volume. In addition, knowledgeable staff personnel should participate in the standard-setting process—a team consisting

Cost Management in Practice 16.1

This Toyota–General Motors plant in Fremont, California, succeeded in letting employees set their own standards.

Employees Set Standards

The Toyota-General Motors joint venture in Fremont, California, known as New United Motor Manufacturing, Inc. (NUMMI), allows employees to set their own work standards. The NUMMI plant had been a General Motors plant notorious for poor quality, low productivity, and morale problems.

At the old Fremont GM plant, industrial engineers who had little, if any, work experience making cars would shut themselves in a room and ponder how to set standards, ignoring the workers, who in turn ignored the standards. Now, at NUMMI, workers themselves hold the stopwatches and set the standards. Worker team members time each other, looking for the most efficient and safest way to do the work.

The workers standardize each task so that everyone in the team will do it the same way. They compare the standards across shifts and for different tasks and prepare detailed written specifications for each task. The workers are more informed about how to do the work right than industrial engineers are, and they are more motivated to meet the standards they set than those set by industrial engineers working in an ivory tower.

Involving the workers has had benefits in addition to improved motivation and standards. These include improved safety, higher quality, easier job rotation because tasks are standardized, and more flexibility because workers are both assembly line workers and industrial engineers. *Source: P. Adler, "Time-and-Motion Regained."* (Full citations to references are in the Bibliography.)

of production engineers, production supervisors, and cost-management analysts should perform task analysis.

Employee reluctance to reveal cost-saving ideas: an ethical issue. In some cases, employees may be reluctant to reveal cost-saving ideas that they have discovered to management or to the standard-setting team. The reason for this is that when such cost-saving ideas are communicated to management, the standards are then reset to a tighter (i.e., more difficult to achieve) level. Thus, employees may believe that they have no incentive to be forthcoming about such matters if the end result will be to make their standards more difficult to meet. One way to mitigate this behavior is to reward employees for submitting cost-saving ideas that are implemented and result in more efficient processes. (See Exercise 17.31 in Chapter 17 for more on this ethical issue.)

Perfection versus Practical Standards: A Behavioral Issue

LO 2 Distinguish between perfection and practical standards.

How difficult should it be to attain standard costs? Should cost-management analysts set standards so that actual costs rarely exceed standard costs? Or, should standards be so difficult to attain that actual costs frequently exceed them? The answers to these questions depend on the purpose for which standards are used and the way standards affect behavior.

Perfection standards.   A **perfection** (or **ideal**) **standard** is one that can be attained only under nearly perfect operating conditions. Such standards assume peak efficiency, the lowest possible input prices, the best-quality materials obtainable, and no disruptions in production due to causes such as machine breakdowns or power failures. Some managers believe that a perfection standard motivates employees to achieve the lowest cost possible. They claim that since the standard is theoretically attainable, employees have an incentive to come as close as possible to achieving it.

Other managers and many behavioral scientists disagree. They believe that perfection standards discourage employees, since such high standards are so unlikely to be attained. Moreover, setting unrealistically difficult standards could encourage employees to sacrifice product quality to achieve lower costs. By skimping on the quality of raw materials or the attention to manual production tasks, employees might be able to lower the production cost. However, this lower cost could come at the expense of a higher rate of defective units. Thus, the firm ultimately might incur higher costs than necessary if defective products are returned by customers or scrapped upon inspection.

Practical standards.   Standards that are as tight as practical but still are expected to be attained are called **practical** (or **attainable**) **standards.** Such standards assume a production process that is as efficient as practical under normal operating conditions. Practical standards allow for events such as occasional machine breakdowns and normal amounts of raw-material waste. Attaining a practical standard keeps employees on their toes without demanding miracles. Most behavioral theorists believe that practical standards encourage more positive and productive employee attitudes than do perfection standards.

Use of Standards by Nonmanufacturing Organizations

Service-industry firms, nonprofit organizations, and governmental units also use standard costs. For example, airlines set standards for fuel and maintenance costs. A county motor-vehicle office might have a standard for the number of days required to process and return an application for vehicle registration. American Express (www.americanexpress.com) used standards to speed and improve service. According to *BusinessWeek,* the company's financial service operations were broken into basic tasks. For each of these tasks, performance standards were set, and means were devised for achieving the standards.[1] Dutch Pantry, a restaurant chain in the eastern United States, established a standard-costing system in its centralized food-processing facility.[2] According to an article in *The Wall Street Journal,* the United Parcel Service (UPS) (www.ups.com) set standards for various delivery tasks. For example, a standard of 3 feet per second was established as the standard pace at which drivers should walk to a customer's door.[3] These and similar organizations use standards in budgeting and cost management in much the same way that manufacturers use standards.

---

[1] "Boosting Productivity at American Express," *BusinessWeek.* (Full citations to references are in the Bibliography.)

[2] D. Boll, "How Dutch Pantry Accounts for Standard Costs."

[3] "Up to Speed: United Parcel Service Gets Deliveries Done by Driving Its Workers," *The Wall Street Journal.*

American Express used standards to help management speed up and improve its customer service operations.

If you were managing a Hertz car-rental agency, for what kinds of costs would you set standards?

Costs and Benefits of Standard-Costing Systems

Standard-costing systems provide information that can help managers control costs. However, implementing and maintaining cost standards is itself a costly endeavor. Establishing standards can be a time-consuming, labor-intensive, and expensive process. Moreover, standards must be updated periodically to reflect changes in the cost structure of a production process. As with any management-information system, each finer level of detail in a standard-costing system entails higher costs to generate and use the information. Deciding the appropriate level of standard-cost detail and the frequency with which reports should be generated is part of the cost analyst's information-system design problem. Ultimately, the benefits of the information, in terms of improved production cost control and decision making, must be weighed against the cost of generating the information.

Cost Variance Analysis

To illustrate the use of standards in controlling costs, we focus on Koala Camp Gear Company, a manufacturer of camping tents based in Melbourne, Australia. Although relatively small, Koala Camp Gear has established a reputation for excellence throughout Australia, Europe, and the United States. Most of the company's sales are domestic, but exports have been increasing to the United Kingdom, Germany, Switzerland, Italy, and the United States. Koala recently introduced its newest product, a lightweight but durable backpacking tent trade-named the Tree Line tent. Margo Hastings, Koala's founder and CEO, plans to market the Tree Line tent aggressively in Europe and the United States.

Koala Camp Gear plans to manufacture only the Tree Line tent itself. The company will purchase aluminum tent poles as finished components and package them with the tent. As detailed in the memorandum at the beginning of this chapter, Koala's controller, Marc Wesley, recently set standards for the direct materials and direct labor required to manufacture the Tree Line tent as follows.

Direct-Material Standards

The fabric in a tent is considered a direct material. The thread is inexpensive and is considered an indirect material, part of manufacturing overhead. The standard quantity and price of fabric for the production of one Tree Line tent are as follows:

Standard quantity:	
Fabric in finished product	11 sq. meters
Allowance for normal waste..	1 sq. meter
Total standard quantity required per tent.....................	12 sq. meters
Standard price:	
Purchase price per sq. meter of	
fabric (net of purchase discounts)............................	$7.75
Transportation cost per sq. meter	.25
Total standard price per sq. meter of fabric	$8.00

The standard quantity of fabric needed to manufacture one Tree Line tent is 12 square meters, even though only 11 square meters actually remain in the finished product. One square meter of fabric is wasted as a normal result of the cutting and trimming that are part of the production process. Therefore, the entire amount of fabric needed to manufacture a tent is included in the standard quantity of material.

The standard price of fabric reflects all costs incurred to acquire the material and transport it to the plant. Notice that the cost of transportation is added to the purchase price. Any purchase discounts are subtracted out from the purchase price to obtain a net price.

To summarize, the **standard direct-material quantity** is the total amount of materials normally required to produce a finished product, including allowances for normal waste or inefficiency. The **standard direct-material price** is the total delivered cost after subtracting any purchase discounts.

Direct-Labor Standards

The standard quantity and rate for direct labor for the production of one Tree Line tent are as follows:

Standard quantity:	
Direct labor required per tent	2 hours
Standard rate:	
Hourly wage rate..	$15
Fringe benefits (20% of wages)	3
Total standard rate per hour	$18

The **standard direct-labor quantity** is the number of labor hours normally needed to manufacture one unit of product. The **standard direct-labor rate** is the total hourly cost of compensation, including fringe benefits.

Standard Costs Given Actual Output

During June, Koala manufactured 3,000 Tree Line tents. The total standard or budgeted costs for direct material and direct labor are computed as follows:

Direct material:	
Standard direct-material cost per tent	
(12 sq. meters × $8 per sq. meter)	$ 96
Actual output...	× 3,000
Total standard direct-material cost	$288,000
Direct labor:	
Direct labor cost per tent (2 hours × $18 per hour)	$ 36
Actual output...	× 3,000
Total standard direct-labor cost	$108,000

Notice that the total standard cost for the direct-material and direct-labor inputs is based on Koala's *actual output.* The division should incur costs of $396,000 ($288,000 + $108,000) for direct material and direct labor, *given that it produced 3,000 tents.* The total standard costs for direct material and direct labor serve as the cost-management analyst's benchmarks against which to compare actual costs. This comparison then serves as the basis for controlling direct-material and direct-labor costs.

A note about manufacturing overhead. We focus in this chapter on the use of standard-costing systems to control direct-materials and direct-labor costs. In the next chapter, we extend our analysis to the control of overhead costs using a tool called *flexible budgeting.*

Analysis of Cost Variances

During June, Koala incurred the following actual costs for direct material and direct labor.

Direct-material purchases: actual cost	
40,000 sq. meters at $8.15 per sq. meter	$326,000
Direct material used: actual cost	
36,400 sq. meters at $8.15 per sq. meter	$296,660
Direct labor: actual cost	
5,900 hours at $19 per hour	$112,100

Compare these actual expenditures with the total standard costs for the production of 3,000 tents. Koala spent more than the budgeted amount for both direct material and direct labor. But why were these excess costs incurred? Could the cost-management analyst provide any other analysis to help answer this question?

Exhibit 16–1

Direct-Material Price and
Quantity Variances

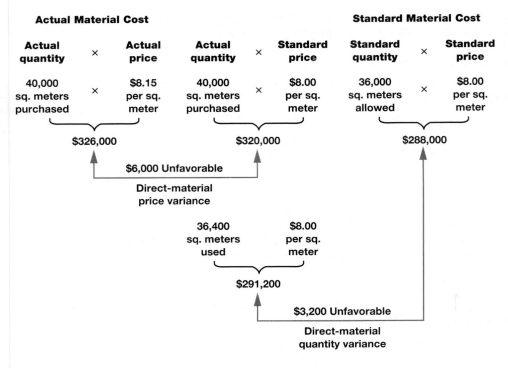

Direct-Material Variances

LO 3 Compute and interpret the direct-material
price and quantity
variances and the direct-
labor rate and efficiency
variances.

What caused Koala to spend more than the anticipated amount on direct material? First, the company purchased fabric at a higher price ($8.15 per square meter) than the standard price ($8.00 per square meter). Second, the company used more fabric than the standard amount. The amount actually used was 36,400 square meters instead of the standard amount of 36,000 square meters, which is based on actual output of 3,000 tents. The cost-management analyst can show both of these deviations from standards by computing a direct-material price variance (or purchase price variance) and a direct-material quantity variance. The **direct-material price variance (or purchase price variance)** is the difference between the actual and standard price multiplied by the actual quantity of material purchased. The **direct-material quantity variance** is the difference between the actual quantity and the standard quantity of material allowed, given actual output, multiplied by the standard price. The computations for these variances are displayed in Exhibit 16–1.

The formula for the direct-material price variance is as follows:

$$\text{Direct-material price variance} = (PQ \times AP) - (PQ \times SP)$$
$$= PQ(AP - SP)$$

where

$$PQ = \text{quantity purchased}$$
$$AP = \text{actual price}$$
$$SP = \text{standard price}$$

Koala's direct-material price variance for June is computed as follows:

$$\text{Direct-material price variance} = PQ(AP - SP)$$
$$= 40,000\ (\$8.15 - \$8.00)$$
$$= \$6,000\ \text{Unfavorable}$$

This variance is unfavorable because the actual purchase price exceeded the standard price. Notice that the price variance is based on the quantity of material *purchased* (*PQ*), not the quantity actually used in production.

As Exhibit 16–1 shows, the following formula defines the direct-materials quantity variance.

$$\text{Direct-material quantity variance} = (AQ \times SP) - (SQ \times SP)$$
$$= SP(AQ - SQ)$$

where

$$AQ = \text{actual quantity used}$$
$$SQ = \text{standard quantity allowed}$$

Koala's direct-material quantity variance for June is computed as follows:

$$\text{Direct-material quantity variance} = SP(AQ - SQ)$$
$$= \$8.00\,(36,400 - 36,000)$$
$$= \$3,200\ \text{Unfavorable}$$

This variance is unfavorable because the actual quantity of direct material used in June exceeded the standard quantity allowed, given actual June output of 3,000 tents. The quantity variance is based on the quantity of material actually *used* in production (AQ).

Identifying the quantity purchased versus quantity used. The direct-material price variance is based on the quantity purchased (PQ). This makes sense because deviations between the actual and standard price, which are highlighted by the price variance, relate to the *purchasing* function in the firm. Timely action to follow up a significant price variance will be facilitated by calculating this variance as soon as possible after the material is *purchased.*

In contrast, the direct-material quantity variance is based on the amount of material *used* in production (AQ). The quantity variance highlights the deviations between the quantity of material actually used (AQ) and the standard quantity allowed (SQ). Thus, it makes sense to compute this variance when the material is *used* in production.

Basing the quantity variance on actual output. Notice that the standard quantity of material must be based on the actual production output for the quantity variance to be meaningful. It makes no sense to compare standard or budgeted material usage at one level of output (say, 2,000 tents) with the actual material usage at a *different* level of output (say, 3,000 tents). Everyone would expect more direct material to be used in the production of 3,000 tents than of 2,000 tents. For the direct-material quantity variance to provide helpful information for management, the standard, or budgeted, quantity must be based on *actual output.* Then the quantity variance compares the following two quantities:

When we extend our analysis to the control of manufacturing overhead costs in the next chapter, you will see that a similar comment can apply to overhead cost control. Using a tool called *flexible budgeting,* we compare the overhead cost allowed, *given actual output,* with the actual overhead cost incurred.

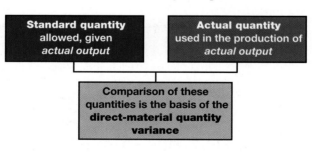

Direct-Labor Variances

Why did Koala Camp Gear spend more than the anticipated amount on direct labor during June? First, the company incurred a cost of $19 per hour for direct labor instead of the standard amount of $18 per hour. Second, Koala used only 5,900 hours of direct labor, which is less than the standard quantity of 6,000 hours, given actual output of 3,000 tents. The cost-management analysts study direct-labor costs by computing a direct-labor rate variance and a direct-labor efficiency variance. The **direct-labor rate variance** is the difference between the actual and standard hourly labor rate

Exhibit 16–2

Direct-Labor Rate and
Efficiency Variances

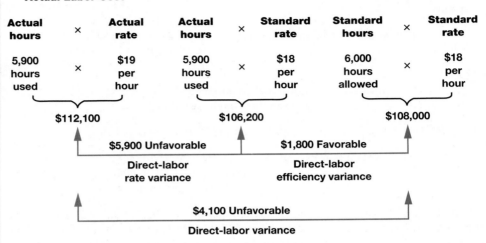

multiplied by the actual quantity of direct labor used. The **direct-labor efficiency variance** is the difference between the actual hours and the standard hours of direct labor allowed, given actual output, multiplied by the standard hourly labor rate. Exhibit 16–2 displays the computations for these variances.

The formula for the direct-labor rate variance is as follows:

$$\text{Direct-labor rate variance} = (AH \times AR) - (AH \times SR)$$
$$= AH(AR - SR)$$

where

$$AH = \text{actual hours used}$$
$$AR = \text{actual rate per hour}$$
$$SR = \text{standard rate per hour}$$

Koala's direct-labor rate variance for June is computed as follows:

$$\text{Direct-labor rate variance} = AH(AR - SR)$$
$$= 5{,}900\ (\$19 - \$18)$$
$$= \$5{,}900 \text{ Unfavorable}$$

This variance is unfavorable because the actual rate exceeded the standard rate during June.

As Exhibit 16–2 shows, the formula for the direct-labor efficiency variance is as follows:

$$\text{Direct-labor efficiency variance} = (AH \times SR) - (SH \times SR)$$
$$= SR(AH - SH)$$

where

$$SH = \text{standard hours allowed}$$

Koala's direct-labor efficiency variance for June is computed as follows:

$$\text{Direct-labor efficiency variance} = SR(AH - SH)$$
$$= \$18\ (5{,}900 - 6{,}000)$$
$$= \$1{,}800 \text{ Favorable}$$

This variance is favorable because the actual number of direct-labor hours used in June were less than the number of standard hours allowed, *given actual June output* of 3,000 tents.

Notice that the direct-labor rate and efficiency variances add up to the total direct-labor variance. However, the rate and efficiency variances have opposite signs since one variance is unfavorable and the other is favorable.

Direct-labor rate variance	$5,900 Unfavorable	Favorable and unfavorable variance designations cancel just as plus and minus signs cancel in arithmetic.
Direct-labor efficiency variance	1,800 Favorable	
Direct-labor variance	$4,100 Unfavorable	

Basing the efficiency variance on actual output.   The number of standard hours of direct labor allowed is based on the *actual* production output. It is not meaningful to compare standard or budgeted labor usage at one level of output with the actual hours used at a different level of output.

Multiple Types of Direct Material and Direct Labor

Manufacturing processes usually involve several types of direct material. In such cases, direct-materials price and quantity variances are computed for each type of material. Then these variances are added to obtain a total price variance and a total quantity variance, as follows:

Direct material X	$1,500 F*	$1,900 U*
Direct material Y	2,400 U	300 U
Direct material Z	900 U	400 F
Total variance	$1,800 U	$1,800 U

*F denotes a favorable variance; U denotes an unfavorable variance.

Similarly, if a production process involves several types of direct labor, rate and efficiency variances are computed for each labor type. Then they are added to obtain a total rate variance and a total efficiency variance.

When a manufacturing process involves multiple types of direct material or direct labor, additional variance analysis can be conducted to analyze the proportions with which the multiple inputs are used. This analysis is covered in the Appendix to this chapter.

Allowance for Defects or Spoilage

In some manufacturing processes, a certain amount of defective production or spoilage is normal. This must be considered when the standard quantity of material is computed. To illustrate, suppose that 1,000 liters of chemicals are normally required in a chemical process to obtain 800 liters of good output. If total good output in February is 5,000 liters, what is the standard allowed quantity of input?

$$\text{Good output quantity} = 80\% \times \text{Input quantity}$$

Dividing both sides of the equation by 80%

$$\frac{\text{Good output quantity}}{80\%} = \text{Input quantity allowed}$$

Using the numbers in the illustration

$$\frac{5,000 \text{ liters of good output}}{80\%} = 6,250 \text{ liters of input allowed}$$

The total standard allowed input is 6,250 liters, given 5,000 liters of good output.

Global Use of Standard-Costing Systems

Standard-costing systems are common throughout the world. Research has shown, for example, that standard costing is widely used in Japan, the United Kingdom, and Germany, as well as in the United States. In Germany, *grenzplankostenrechnung,* which means "flexible standard costing," is used for cost planning and control. "Reporting systems based on *grenzplankosten-rechnung* consist of monthly statements of each cost center's actual and planned demand for resources, actual costs, standard costs, and different types of variances." *Sources: P. Sharman,* "German Cost Accounting"; *and B. Gaiser,* "German Cost Management Systems."

Research Insight 16.1

Significance of Cost Variances: When to Follow Up

LO 4 Describe several methods used to determine the significance of cost variances.

Managers are busy people. They do not have time to investigate the causes of every cost variance. *Management by exception* enables managers explore the causes of only significant variances. But what constitutes an exception? How does the manager know when to follow up on a cost variance and when to ignore it?

These questions are difficult to answer because to some extent the answers are part of the art of management. A manager applies judgment and experience in making guesses, pursuing hunches, and relying on intuition to determine when to investigate a variance. Nevertheless, there are guidelines and rules of thumb that managers often apply.

Size of Variances

The absolute size of a variance is one consideration. Managers are more likely to follow up on large variances than on small ones. The relative size of the variance is probably even more important. A manager is more likely to investigate a $40,000 material quantity variance that is 20 percent of the standard direct-material cost of $200,000 than a $60,000 labor efficiency variance that is only 2 percent of the standard direct-labor cost of $3,000,000. The *relative* magnitude of the $40,000 material quantity variance (20 percent) is greater than the *relative* magnitude of the $60,000 labor efficiency variance (2 percent). For this reason, cost-management analysts often show the relative magnitude of variances in their cost-variance reports. For example, Koala's June cost-variance report is shown in the spreadsheet in Exhibit 16–3.

Managers often apply a rule of thumb that considers both the absolute and the relative magnitude of a variance. An example of such a rule is the following: Investigate variances that are either more than $10,000 or more than 10 percent of standard cost.

Recurring Variances

Another consideration in deciding when to investigate a variance is whether the variance occurs repeatedly or only infrequently. Suppose that a manager uses the rule of thumb just stated and the following direct-materials quantity variances occur.

Exhibit 16–3

Cost-Variance Report for June. Koala Camp Gear

Company

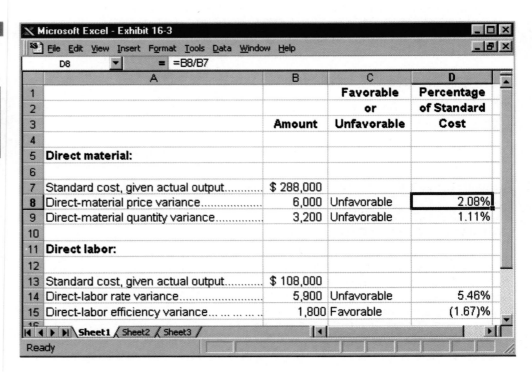

	A	B	C	D
1			**Favorable**	**Percentage**
2			**or**	**of Standard**
3		**Amount**	**Unfavorable**	**Cost**
4				
5	**Direct material:**			
6				
7	Standard cost, given actual output............	$ 288,000		
8	Direct-material price variance..................	6,000	Unfavorable	2.08%
9	Direct-material quantity variance..............	3,200	Unfavorable	1.11%
10				
11	**Direct labor:**			
12				
13	Standard cost, given actual output............	$ 108,000		
14	Direct-labor rate variance.........................	5,900	Unfavorable	5.46%
15	Direct-labor efficiency variance...............	1,800	Favorable	(1.67)%

Month	Variance	Percentage of Standard Cost*
September	$6,000 F	6.0%
October	6,400 F	6.4%
November	3,200 F	3.2%
December	6,200 F	6.2%

*The standard direct-material cost is $100,000.

Strict adherence to the rule of thumb indicates no investigation since none of the monthly variances is more than $10,000 or 10 percent of standard cost. Nevertheless, the manager might investigate this variance in December, since it has *recurred* at a reasonably high level for several consecutive months. In this case, the consistency of the variance triggers an investigation, not its absolute or relative magnitude.

Trends

A trend in a variance also might call for investigation. Suppose that a manager observes the following direct-labor efficiency variances.

Month	Variance	Percentage of Standard Cost*
September	$ 250 U	.25%
October	840 U	.84%
November	4,000 U	4.00%
December	9,300 U	9.30%

*The standard direct-labor cost is $100,000.

None of these variances is large enough to trigger an investigation if the manager uses the "$10,000 or 10 percent" rule of thumb. However, the four-month *trend* is worrisome. An alert manager will likely follow up on this unfavorable trend to determine its causes before costs get out of hand.

Controllability

Another important consideration in deciding when to investigate the causes of a variance is the manager's view of the controllability of the cost item. A manager is more likely to investigate a variance for a cost that someone in the organization can control than a variance for a cost that cannot be controlled. For example, there might be little point to investigating a materials-price variance if the organization has no control over the price. This could happen, for example, if the firm has a long-term contract with a supplier of the material at a price determined on the international market. In contrast, the manager is likely to follow up on a variance that should be controllable, such as a direct-labor efficiency variance or a direct-materials quantity variance.

Favorable Variances

Investigation of significant favorable variances is just as important as of significant unfavorable variances. For example, a favorable direct-labor efficiency variance could indicate that employees have developed a more efficient way to perform a production task. By investigating the variance, management can learn about the improved method. A similar approach might be used elsewhere in the organization.

Costs and Benefits of Investigation

The decision to investigate a cost variance is a cost–benefit decision. The costs of investigation include the time spent by the investigating manager and the employees in the department where the investigation occurs. Other potential costs include the disruption of the production process to conduct the investigation and to take corrective actions to eliminate the cause of a variance. The benefits of a variance investigation include reduced future production costs if the cause of an unfavorable variance can be eliminated. Another potential benefit is the cost savings associated with lowering the

Computerized databases of cost information facilitate statistical analysis of cost performance.

cost standards when the cause of a favorable variance is discovered. Weighing these considerations takes the judgment of skillful and experienced managers. Key to this judgment is an intimate understanding of the organization's production process and day-to-day contact with its operations.

Statistical Analysis

Cost variances are caused by many factors. For example, a direct-labor efficiency variance could be caused by inexperienced employees, employee inefficiency, poor-quality raw materials, poorly maintained machinery, or an intentional work slowdown due to employee grievances. In addition to these substantive reasons, there are purely random causes of variances. People are not robots, and they are not perfectly consistent in their work habits. Random fluctuations in direct-labor efficiency variances can be caused by factors such as employee illnesses, sleep deprivation, workers experimenting with different production methods, or simply random fatigue. Ideally, managers are able to sort out the randomly caused variances from those with substantive and controllable underlying causes. Although accomplishing this with 100 percent accuracy is impossible, a *statistical control chart* can help.

A **statistical control chart** plots cost variances across time and compares them with a statistically determined *critical value* that triggers an investigation. Determination of this critical value usually involves assuming that cost variances have a normal probability distribution with a mean of zero. The critical value is set at some multiple of the distribution's standard deviation. Variances greater than the critical value are investigated. (Chapter 7 discusses the use of statistical control charts for quality control.)

Exhibit 16–4 shows a statistical control chart with a critical value of 1 standard deviation. The manager would investigate the variance observed in April since it falls

Exhibit 16–4
Statistical Control Chart

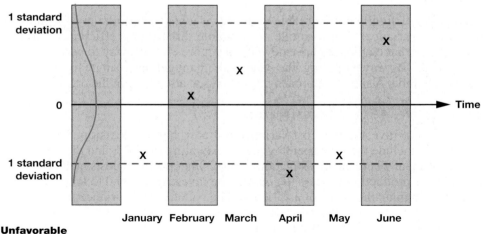

further than 1 standard deviation from the mean (zero). The variances for the remaining five months would not be investigated. The presumption is that these minor variances are due to random causes and are not worth the cost of investigating.

Direct-Material and Direct-Labor Variances

In December, Koala Camp Gear Company produced 2,000 Tree Line tents and incurred the following actual costs for direct material and direct labor:

    Purchased 25,000 sq. meters of tent fabric at $8.25 per sq. meter.

    Used 24,500 sq. meters at $8.25 per sq. meter.

    Used 4,200 hours of direct labor at $16.75 per hour.

The standard costs for tent production were the same in December as those given earlier in the chapter for June.

a. Compute Koala's direct-material and direct-labor variances for December using the format shown in Exhibits 16–1 and 16–2.

b. Suppose that Koala's management uses a statistical control chart to plot cost variances and help management decide which variances to investigate. Let's assume that the cost-management team has estimated that all of Koala's variances exhibit a normal probability distribution with a mean of zero and a standard deviation of $4,800. The critical value is 1 standard deviation. Which of Koala's December cost variances would you investigate? Explain.

(Solutions begin on page 676.)

You're the Decision Maker 16.1

Behavioral Effects of Standard Costing

Standard costs and variance analysis help managers discern "the story behind the story"—the details of operations that underlie reported cost and profit numbers. Standard costs, budgets, and variances also are used to evaluate the performance of individuals and departments. The performance of individuals, relative to standards or budgets, often is used to help determine salary increases, bonuses, and promotions. When standards and variances affect employee reward structures, they can profoundly influence behavior.

LO 5 Discuss some behavioral effects of standard costing and the controllability of variances.

For example, suppose that the manager of a hotel's Food and Beverage Department earns a bonus when food and beverage costs are below the budgeted amount, given actual sales. This reward structure will provide a concrete incentive for the manager to control food and beverage costs. But such an incentive can have either positive or negative effects. The bonus might induce the manager to seek the most economical food suppliers and to watch more carefully for employee theft and waste. However, the bonus also might persuade the manager to buy cheaper but less tender steaks for the restaurant. This could ultimately result in lost patronage for the restaurant and the hotel.

Ethical issues also might arise when employees' performance relative to standards affects their reward system. Assume, for example, that a manufacturer's purchasing manager earns a bonus when a significant favorable material-price variance is recorded. Suppose that the purchasing manager has an opportunity to purchase below-standard material at a significant reduction in price. Let's assume that the inferior quality of the material is not readily apparent and that the negative implications will not be realized until long after the products are manufactured and sold. It is a serious violation of ethical standards for the purchasing manager to buy the off-standard material.

One aspect of skillful management is knowing how to use standards, budgets, and variances to get the most out of an organization's employees. Unfortunately, there are no simple answers or formulas for success in this area.

Controllability of Variances

Cost management is accomplished through the efforts of individual managers in an organization. By determining which managers are in the best position to influence each cost variance, the managerial accountant can assist managers in deriving the greatest benefit from cost variance analysis.

Which Managers Influence Cost Variances?

Who is responsible for the direct-materials price and quantity variances? The direct-labor rate and efficiency variances? Answering these questions is often difficult because any one person rarely has complete control of any event. Nevertheless, it often is possible to identify the manager who is *most able to influence* a particular variance even if he or she does not exercise complete control over the outcome.

Direct-material price variance. The purchasing manager generally is in the best position to influence material price variances. Through skillful purchasing practices, an expert purchasing manager can get the best prices available for purchased goods and services. To achieve this goal, the purchasing manager uses practices such as buying in quantity, negotiating purchase contracts, comparing prices among vendors, and global sourcing.

Despite these purchasing skills, the purchasing manager is not in complete control of prices. The need to purchase component parts with precise engineering specifications, the all-too-frequent rush requests from the production department, and worldwide shortages of critical materials all contribute to the challenges that the purchasing manager faces.

Direct-material quantity variance. The production supervisor is usually in the best position to influence material quantity variances. Skillful supervision and motivation of production employees, coupled with the careful use and handling of materials, contribute to minimal waste. Production engineers also are partially responsible for material quantity variances since they determine the grade and technical specifications of materials and component parts. In some cases, using a low-grade material results in more waste than using a high-grade material.

Direct-labor rate variance. Direct-labor rate variances generally result from using a different mix of employees than that anticipated when the standards were set. Wage rates differ among employees due to their skill levels and their seniority with the organization. Using a higher proportion of more senior or more highly skilled employees than a task requires can result in unfavorable direct-labor rate variances. The production supervisor is generally in the best position to influence the employee work schedules.

Direct-labor efficiency variance. The production supervisor is usually most responsible for the efficient use of employee time. Through motivation toward production goals and effective work schedules, employee efficiency can be maximized.

Interaction among Variances

Interactions among variances often occur, making the determination of the responsibility for a particular variance even more difficult. To illustrate, consider the following incident, which occurred at Koala Camp Gear Company during March. The purchasing manager obtained a special price on tent fabric from a new supplier. When the material was placed into production, it turned out to be a lower grade of material than the production employees were used to. The fabric was of a slightly different composition, which made the material tear easily during cutting. Koala could have returned the material to the supplier, but doing so would have interrupted production and kept the company from filling its orders on time. Since using the off-standard material would not affect the quality of the company's finished products, the production manager decided to keep the material and make the best of the situation.

The ultimate result was that Koala incurred four interrelated variances during March. The material was less expensive than normal, so the direct-material price variance was favorable. However, the employees had difficulty using the material, which resulted in more waste than expected. Hence, the division incurred an unfavorable direct-material quantity variance.

What were the labor implications of the off-standard material? Due to the difficulty in working with the fabric, the employees required more than the standard amount of time. This resulted in an unfavorable direct-labor efficiency variance. Finally, the production supervisor had to use his most senior employees to work with the off-standard material. Since these people earn relatively high wages, the direct-labor rate variance was also unfavorable.

To summarize, the purchase of off-standard material resulted in the following interrelated variances:

Purchase of off-standard material ⇒ {
Favorable direct-material price variance
Unfavorable direct-material quantity variance
Unfavorable direct-labor rate variance
Unfavorable direct-labor efficiency variance
}

Such interactions of variances make the assignment of responsibility more difficult for any particular variance.

Trade-offs among variances.   Does the preceding incident mean that the decision to buy and use the off-standard material was a poor one? Not necessarily. Perhaps these variances were anticipated, and a conscious decision was made to buy the material anyway. How could this be a wise decision? Suppose the amounts of the variances were as follows:

$(7,900)	Favorable direct-material price variance
1,100	Unfavorable direct-material quantity variance
1,900	Unfavorable direct-labor rate variance
2,100	Unfavorable direct-labor efficiency variance
$(2,800)	Favorable net overall variance

Koala saved money overall on the decision to use a different grade of fabric. Given that the quality of the final product was not affected, the company's management acted wisely.

A value-chain perspective.   Think back to our discussions of the value chain in earlier chapters. Recall that the *value chain* is the set of linked operations or processes that begins by obtaining resources and ends with providing products or services that customers value. Exhibit 16–5 depicts Koala Camp Gear Company's value chain.

The preceding discussion regarding interactions and trade-offs among variances emphasizes that variances in one part of the value chain can result from root causes in another part of the chain. For example, when Koala Camp Gear's purchasing manager bought tent fabric at a special price, and the material turned out to be below standard, several direct-material and direct-labor variances resulted in the production process. Thus, an incident in the supply component of Koala's value chain resulted in cost variances in the production component of the chain.

Think about other possible interactions in Koala's value chain. Could production cost variances be caused by events in Koala's design process? How about its downstream processes, such as marketing or distribution?

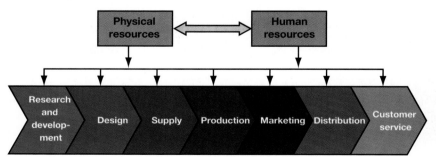

Exhibit 16–5

Koala Camp Gear Company's Value Chain

Use of Standard Costs for Product Costing

LO 6 Explain how companies use standard costs in product costing.

Our discussion of standard costing has focused on its use in controlling costs. Firms that employ standard-costing systems also use standards for product costing. As production takes place, product costs are added to the Work-in-Process Inventory account. The flow of product costs through a firm's manufacturing accounts is depicted in Exhibit 16–6. In a **standard-costing system** the *standard* costs of direct material and direct labor are entered into Work-in-Process Inventory.

Journal Entries under Standard Costing

Direct material.   During June, Koala purchased 40,000 square meters of direct material for $326,000. It actually used 36,400 square meters in production. However, the standard cost of direct material, given June's actual output of 3,000 Tree Line tents, was only $288,000. The following journal entries record these facts and isolate the direct-material price and quantity variances.

Raw-Material Inventory	320,000	
Direct-Material Price Variance	6,000	
Accounts Payable		326,000

To record the purchase of raw material and the incurrence of an unfavorable price variance.

Work-in-Process Inventory	288,000	
Direct-Material Quantity Variance	3,200	
Raw-Material Inventory		291,200

To record the use of direct material in production and the incurrence of an unfavorable quantity variance.

Notice that the material purchase recorded in the Raw-Material Inventory account appears at its standard price ($320,000 = 40,000 square meters purchased × $8 per square meter). The $288,000 debit entry to Work-in-Process Inventory adds only the standard cost of the material to Work-in-Process Inventory as a product cost ($288,000 = 36,000 square meters allowed × $8 per square meter). The two variances are isolated in their own variance accounts. Since both are unfavorable, they are represented by debit entries.

Exhibit 16–6

Flow of Product Costs through Manufacturing Accounts

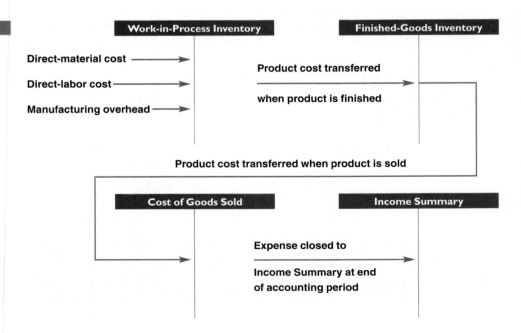

Direct labor.   The following journal entry records the actual June cost of direct labor as an addition to Wages Payable. The entry also adds the standard cost of direct labor to Work-in-Process Inventory and isolates the direct-labor variances.

Work-in-Process Inventory	108,000	
Direct-Labor Rate Variance	5,900	
Direct-Labor Efficiency Variance		1,800
Wages Payable		112,100

To record the usage of direct labor and the direct-labor variances for June.

Since the direct-labor efficiency variance is favorable, it is recorded as a credit entry.

Disposition of variances.   Variance accounts are temporary accounts as are revenue and expense accounts, and they are closed at the end of each accounting period. Most companies close their variance accounts directly into Cost of Goods Sold. The journal entry required to close Koala's June variance accounts follows:

Cost of Goods Sold	13,300	
Direct-Labor Efficiency Variance	1,800	
Direct-Labor Rate Variance		5,900
Direct-Material Price Variance		6,000
Direct-Material Quantity Variance		3,200

The increase of $13,300 in Cost of Goods Sold is explained as follows:

	Unfavorable Variances Increase Cost of Goods Sold	Favorable Variance Decreases Cost of Goods Sold	Net Increase in Cost of Goods Sold
Direct-labor efficiency variance		$1,800	
Direct-labor rate variance	$ 5,900		
Direct-material price variance	6,000		
Direct-material quantity variance	3,200		
Total	$15,100	− $1,800	= $13,300

The unfavorable variances represent costs of operating inefficiently, relative to the standards, and thus cause Cost of Goods Sold to be higher. The opposite is true for favorable variances.

   An alternative method of variance disposition is to apportion all variances among Work-in-Process Inventory, Finished-Goods Inventory, and Cost of Goods Sold. This accounting treatment reflects the effects of unusual inefficiency or efficiency in all accounts through which the manufacturing costs flow. This method, called *variance proration,* is covered in Appendix A to Chapter 17.

Cost Flows under Standard Costing

In a standard-costing system, standard costs are entered in Work-in-Process Inventory and flow through all manufacturing accounts. Thus, in Exhibit 16–6, all product costs flowing through the accounts are standard costs. To illustrate, suppose that Koala finished 3,000 Tree Line tents in June and sold 2,500 of them. The journal entries to record the flow of standard direct-material and direct-labor costs are as follows:

Finished-Goods Inventory	396,000*	
Work-in-Process Inventory		396,000

*Total standard cost of direct material and direct labor: $396,000 = $288,000 + $108,000.

Cost of Goods Sold	330,000*	
Finished-Goods Inventory		330,000

*2,500 of 3,000 tents sold; five-sixths of $396,000 is $330,000.

Our Koala Camp Gear illustration is not really complete yet because we have not discussed manufacturing overhead costs. This topic is covered in the next chapter. The important point at this juncture is that in a standard-costing system, *standard costs flow through the manufacturing accounts rather than actual costs.*

Impact of Information Technology on Standard Costing

Standard-costing systems can facilitate the use of information technology to link together several business processes. When a manufacturer uses standard costing for product costing and cost management, the standard costs of materials and labor are loaded into the computer. When raw materials or purchased components are requisitioned for production, the standard cost of the materials or components used is automatically recorded by accessing the computer database where the standard quantities and prices of the materials are stored. Similarly, when production employees work on a production job, their time on the job is recorded and the standard labor cost is automatically determined by accessing the standard labor times and rates in the computer database.

Use of Bar Codes

Bar codes are now widely used to capture important events in manufacturing processes. In *real-time shop floor data-collection systems,* production employees can record the time they begin working on a particular job order by scanning the bar code on their employee ID badge and a bar code assigned to the production job order. The standard direct-labor cost is assigned to the production job.

When raw materials arrive at the production facility, their bar code is scanned and the event is recorded. Inventory records are updated automatically. Raw materials and partially completed components are assigned bar codes, and their movement through the production process is efficiently recorded. For example, raw materials might be requisitioned by a production employee simply by scanning the bar code assigned to the needed raw materials. When the materials are sent from the warehouse to the requisitioning production department, the bar code is scanned again. Inventory records are updated instantly, and the standard cost of the materials is recorded as a product cost.

Computer-Aided Design

Standard-costing systems also can be integrated with a computer-aided design (CAD) system to assist design engineers in the product design process. The standard costs of material and labor are stored in the computer database where the product design team

Many companies use computer-aided design (CAD) systems, which make standard cost information available to the design engineers.

can access them easily. This information enables a product design engineer to get a quick answer to the question, What will be the new product cost if certain design changes are made to the product? If, for example, the engineer wants to know the cost of changing the exterior case on a particular computer model, this information is easily determined by accessing the cost database.[4]

---

[4] S. W. Anderson and K. Sedatole, "Designing Quality into Products: The Use of Accounting Data in New Product Development." J. M. Patell, "Cost Accounting, Process Control, and Product Design: A Case Study of the Hewlett-Packard Personal Office Computer Division."

In other applications, cost data from target-costing or value engineering approaches are used in new product design. At Boeing, for example, "firm-specific cost and productivity data are used to improve traditional engineering cost estimates in the early, system design stage of product development."

Standard Costing: Its Traditional Advantages

Standard costing has been a widely used accounting system in manufacturing companies for both cost control and product-costing purposes for several decades. This remains true today, and the use of standard costing is spreading to nonmanufacturing firms as well. The widespread use of standard costing over such a long time period suggests that it has traditionally been perceived as advantageous. However, today's manufacturing environment is changing dramatically. Some managers are calling into question the usefulness of the traditional standard-costing approach. They argue that the role of standard-costing systems must change.

In this section, we will list some advantages traditionally attributed to standard-costing systems. In the next section, we will discuss some of the contemporary criticisms of the standard-costing approach and suggest several ways in which the role of standard costing is beginning to change.

Some advantages traditionally attributed to standard costing include these:

- Computation of standard costs and cost variances enables managers to employ *management by exception.* This approach conserves valuable management time.
- Standard costs provide a basis for *sensible cost comparisons.* As we discussed earlier, comparing budgeted costs at one (planned) activity level with actual costs incurred at a different (actual) activity level makes no sense. Standard costs enable the cost manager to compute the standard allowed cost, given actual output, which then serves as a sensible benchmark to compare with the actual cost.
- Variances provide a means of *performance evaluation* and rewards for employees.
- Since the variances are used in performance evaluation, they provide *motivation* for employees to adhere to standards.
- Use of standard costs in product costing results in *more stable product costs* than the use of actual production costs. Actual costs often fluctuate erratically, whereas standard costs change only periodically.
- A standard-costing system is usually *less expensive* than an actual or normal costing system. (In actual and normal costing systems, the actual cost of direct material and direct labor is accumulated as product costs. See Chapter 3 for further discussion.)

Like any tool, a standard-costing system can be misused. When employees are criticized for every cost variance, the positive motivational effects will quickly vanish. Moreover, if standards are not revised often enough, they will become outdated. Then the benefits of cost benchmarks and product costing will disappear.

Changing Role of Standard-Costing Systems in Today's Manufacturing Environment

The rise of global competition, the introduction of JIT production methods and flexible manufacturing systems, the goal of continuous process improvement, and the emphasis on product quality are dramatically changing the manufacturing environment. What are the implications of these changes for the role of standard-costing systems? We begin by listing some contemporary criticisms of standard costing.

LO 7 Summarize some advantages attributed to standard costing.

LO 8 Describe the changing role of standard-costing systems in today's manufacturing environment.

Criticisms of Standard Costing in Today's Manufacturing Environment

Listed here are several drawbacks attributed to standard costing in an advanced manufacturing setting.[5]

- The variances calculated under standard costing are too aggregated and come too late to be useful. Some accountants argue that traditional standard costing is out of step with the philosophy of *cost-management systems* and *activity-based management*. A production process comprises many activities, and these activities result in costs. By focusing on the activities that incur costs, by eliminating non-value-added activities, and by continually improving performance in value-added activities, an organization can minimize costs and maximize profit. What is needed are performance measures that focus directly on performance issues that management wants to improve. For example, such issues could include product quality, processing time, and delivery performance.

- Traditional cost variances also are too aggregated in the sense that they are not tied to specific product lines, production batches, or flexible-manufacturing-system (FMS) cells. The aggregate nature of the variances makes determining their cause difficult.

- Traditional standard-costing systems focus too much on the cost and efficiency of direct labor, which is rapidly becoming a relatively unimportant factor of production.

- One of the most important conditions for the successful use of standard costing is a stable production process. However, the introduction of flexible manufacturing systems has reduced this stability, with frequent switching among a variety of products on the same production line.

- Shorter product life cycles mean that standards are relevant for only a short time. When new products are introduced, new standards must be developed.

- Traditional standard-costing systems tend to focus too much on cost minimization, rather than increasing product quality or customer service. Indeed, standard-costing systems can cause dysfunctional behavior in a JIT/FMS environment. For example, buying the least expensive materials of a given quality to avoid a material price variance could result in using a vendor whose delivery capabilities are not consistent with JIT requirements.

- Automated manufacturing processes tend to be more consistent in meeting production specifications. As a result, variances from standards tend to be very small or nonexistent.

- Traditional standard costs are not defined broadly enough to capture various important aspects of performance. For example, the standard direct-materials price does not capture all *costs of ownership*. In addition to the purchase price and transportation costs, the *total cost of ownership (TCO)* includes the costs of ordering, paying bills, scheduling delivery, receiving, inspecting, handling, and storing, as well as any production-line disruptions resulting from untimely or incorrect delivery.[6]

Adaptation of Standard-Costing Systems

As a result of these criticisms of standard-costing systems, some highly automated manufacturers have deemphasized standard costing in their control systems. Most manufacturing firms continue to use standard costing to some extent, however, even after adopting advanced manufacturing methods.[7] Such firms make changes in their use of standard costing to reflect various features of advanced manufacturing technology.

---

[5] The sources for this material are R. S. Kaplan, "Limitations of Cost Accounting in Advanced Manufacturing Environments"; H. T. Johnson, "Performance Measurement for Competitive Excellence"; R. A. Bonsack, "Does Activity-Based Costing Replace Standard Costing?"; and M. Sukurai, "The Influence of Factory Automation on Management Accounting Practices: A Study of Japanese Companies."

[6] Some companies are developing cost-of-ownership reporting systems. Among them are Northrop Aircraft Division, McDonnell Douglas, Texas Instruments, and Black & Decker. See L. Carr and C. Ittner, "Measuring the Cost of Ownership"; and L. M. Ellram, "Activity-Based Costing and Total Cost of Ownership: A Critical Linkage."

Cost Management in Practice 16.2

Cost of Ownership

Northrop Aircraft Division (www.northgrum.com) tracks various elements of the total cost of ownership (TCO)* through its cost-based Supplier Performance Rating System (SPRS). Among the cost factors that SPRS measures are the costs Northrop incurs due to suppliers' hardware, paperwork, or delivery deficiencies. Any "nonconformance event is assigned a standard cost based on industrial engineering studies of the hours required to resolve the problem."

Texas Instruments (www.ti.com) has developed a supplier rating system called CETRAQ, which stands for cost, environmental responsibility, technology, responsiveness, assurance of supply, and quality. The company's vendors are regularly measured on these six criteria.

At a Spennymore, England, plant owned by Black & Decker (www.blackanddecker.com), the company "has integrated the cost-of-ownership concept into its activity-based costing system." Among the TCO issues included are quality, delivery, flexibility, and customer service. Also considered is a suppliers' billing reliability. "As one Spennymore manager noted, 'You can be dealing with the best company in the world in terms of quality, but if they can't get their invoices right, you're going to have trouble doing business with them.'" *Source: L. Carr and C. Ittner, "Measuring the Cost of Ownership." The information about Texas Instruments is based on an author's research in 2003.*

*The *total cost of ownership* includes all costs incurred to have materials in place and ready for use in production, including the purchase price; the transportation cost; and the costs of ordering, receiving, inspecting, and storing the materials.

Reduced importance of labor standards and variances.   As direct labor has come to occupy an ever-diminishing role in the manufacturing environment, the standards and variances used to control labor costs also have declined in importance. The heavy emphasis of traditional standard-costing systems on labor efficiency variances is giving way to variances that focus on the more critical inputs to the production process. Machine hours, materials and support-department costs, product quality, and manufacturing cycle times have assumed greater importance as the objects of managerial control.

Emphasis on material and overhead costs.   As labor continues to diminish in importance, materials and support-department costs also have assumed greater significance. Controlling the costs of materials and quality and controlling non-unit-level costs through cost-driver analysis become key aspects of the cost-management system.

Cost drivers.   Identification of the factors that drive production costs becomes more important in the cost-management system. Cost drivers such as machine hours, number of parts, engineering change orders, and production runs become the focus of the cost-management system.

Shifting cost structures.   Advanced manufacturing systems require large outlays for production equipment, which entail a shift in the cost structure from unit-level costs toward non-unit-level costs. Overhead cost control becomes especially critical. The next chapter explores the role of standard-costing systems in controlling overhead costs.

High quality and zero defects.   Total quality management (TQM) programs that typically accompany a JIT approach strive for very high quality levels for both raw materials and finished products. One result should be very low materials price and quantity variances and low costs of rework.

Non-value-added costs.   A key objective of a cost-management system is to eliminate non-value-added costs. As these costs are reduced or eliminated, standards must be revised frequently to provide accurate benchmarks for cost control.

Shorter product life cycles.   As product life cycles shorten, developing standards and revising them more frequently become necessary.

Nonfinancial measures for operational control.   Managerial accountants traditionally have focused on financial measures of performance such as deviations from budgeted

---

[7] For example, see J. M. Patell, "Cost Accounting, Process Control, and Product Design: A Case Study of the Hewlett-Packard Personal Office Computer Division"; J. B. Schiff, "ABC at Lederle"; and R. A. Bonsack, "Does Activity-Based Costing Replace Standard Costing?"

costs. Financial measures still are very important, but to an ever-greater extent, financial performance criteria are being augmented by nonfinancial measures. In today's advanced manufacturing environment, operational measures are being developed to control key aspects of the production process.

Benchmarking.   One widely used method to control costs and improve operational efficiency is *benchmarking*—the continual search for the most effective method of accomplishing a task by comparing existing methods and performance levels with those of other organizations or other subunits within the same organization. For example, hospitals routinely benchmark their costs of patient care by diagnostic-related groups (such as circulatory disorders) with the costs of other hospitals.

Real-time information systems.   A computer-integrated manufacturing (CIM) system enables the cost-management analyst to collect operating data as production occurs and to report relevant performance measures to management on a real-time basis. This enables managers to eliminate the causes of unfavorable variances more quickly.

Kaizen Costing

LO 9 Explain the concept of kaizen costing and its potential benefits.

In today's global business environment, for some companies to survive, they must continually seek to reduce production costs. If a standard-costing system is used in such a competitive environment, the standards must be reduced every year or even every month. **Kaizen costing** is the process of cost reduction during the manufacturing phase of a product.[8] The Japanese word *kaizen* refers to continual and gradual improvement through small betterment activities rather than large or radical improvement made through innovation or large investments in technology. The idea is simple. Improvement is the goal and responsibility of every worker, from the CEO to the manual laborers, in every activity, every day, all the time! Through the small but continual efforts of everyone, significant reductions in costs can be attained over time.

To help achieve the continuous cost reduction implied by the kaizen costing concept, an annual (or monthly) *kaizen cost goal* is established. Then actual costs are tracked over time and compared to the kaizen goal. Depending on the nature of the production process and the competitive environment, a company could focus its kaizen costing efforts on a particular segment of its cost structure. For example, Sumitomo Electric Industries (www.sei.com.jp), a Japanese company that is the world's third largest manufacturer of electrical wire and cable, concentrates its kaizen cost-reduction program on material costs.[9] In contrast, "at the Kyoto brewery of Kirin beer (www.kirin.com), cost-reduction programs typically identified four or five targets for improvement each year. This continuous change of focus helped keep the programs active."[10]

Citizen Watch Company (www.citizenwatch.com) focuses its kaizen costing efforts on direct labor. "The major way to reduce labor is to alter the time required to operate or support the production machines. Alterations can be achieved in two ways. First, the running speed of the machines can be increased so that more parts per hour can be produced. Second, a single employee can be used to operate more machines."[11]

We present a typical kaizen costing chart in Exhibit 16–7.[12] Notice that the cost base, or reference point, is the actual cost performance at the end of the prior year. A kaizen goal is established for the cost-reduction rate and amount during the current year. Actual cost performance throughout the year is compared with the kaizen goal. At the end of the current year, the current actual cost becomes the cost base, or reference point, for the next year. Then, a new (lower) kaizen goal is established, and the cost-reduction effort continues.

---

[8] Y. Monden and K. Hamada, "Target Costing and Kaizen Costing in Japanese Automobile Companies."

[9] R. Cooper, *When Lean Enterprises Collide.*

[10] Ibid., p. 251.

[11] Ibid., pp. 240, 241.

[12] The kaizen costing chart depicted is based on one used at Daihatsu, a Japanese auto manufacturer owned in part by Toyota. See Y. Monden and J. Lee, "How a Japanese Auto Maker Reduced Costs."

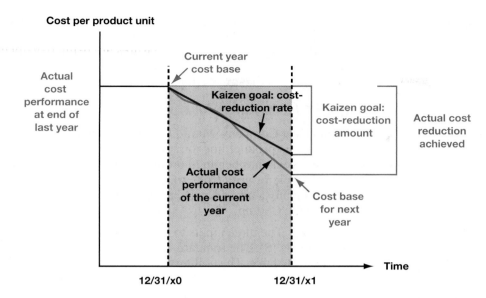

Exhibit 16–7

Typical Kaizen Costing Chart

How are kaizen costing goals met? The continual and relentless reduction of non-value-added activities and costs, the elimination of waste, and improvements in manufacturing cycle time all contribute to the effort. In addition, management takes seriously the improvement suggestions and kaizen efforts of all employees and implements them when appropriate. The result is a continually more efficient and cost-effective production process.

Chapter Summary

A standard-costing system is a traditional cost-management technique with two purposes: cost control and product costing. Accountants work with others in the organization to set standard costs for direct material, direct labor, and manufacturing overhead through either historical cost analysis or task analysis. The cost-management analyst uses the standard cost as a benchmark against which to compare actual costs incurred. Managers then use management by exception to determine the causes of significant cost variances. This cost-management purpose of the standard-costing system is accomplished by computing a direct-materials price variance, a direct-materials quantity variance, a direct-labor rate variance, and a direct-labor efficiency variance.

Managers determine the significance of cost variances through judgment and rules of thumb. The absolute and relative size of variances, recurrence of variances, variance trends, and controllability of variances are all considered in deciding whether variances warrant investigation. The product-costing purpose of the standard-costing system is achieved by entering the standard cost of production in Work-in-Process Inventory as a product cost. Standard-costing systems offer an organization many benefits, but these benefits will be obtained only if the standard-costing system is used properly.

Today's manufacturing environment is changing rapidly due to the influences of worldwide competition, JIT, flexible manufacturing systems, and an emphasis on product quality and customer service. As a result, many manufacturers are adapting their standard-costing systems to reflect these aspects of the contemporary manufacturing environment.

Kaizen costing is the process of cost reduction during the manufacturing phase of a product. *Kaizen* refers to continual and gradual improvement through small betterment activities. Many companies facing global competition find that continual cost reduction is crucial to their survival.

Appendix to Chapter Sixteen

Production Mix and Yield Variances

Manufacturing processes typically involve multiple direct-material inputs. Food, chemical, steel, fabric, plastic, and many other products require a mix of direct materials, some of which can be substituted for each other without greatly affecting product

LO 10 Compute and interpret mix and yield variances.

quality. Moreover, multiple types of direct labor often are required (e.g., machinists and assembly employees). When a manufacturing process involves multiple types of direct material or direct labor, additional variance analysis can be conducted to analyze the proportions with which the multiple inputs are used. Such an analysis assumes that some degree of substitutability exists among the inputs to the production process.

Production Mix and Yield Variances Illustrated

Koala
Camp
Gear
Company

Let's return to Koala Camp Gear Company. Margo Hastings's nephew has convinced her that Koala should expand its product line to include certain camp foods. For its initial entry into this market, Koala has begun to produce trail mix. Variously known to outdoor enthusiasts as trail mix or gorp (for "good ole' raisins and peanuts"), this venerable food has sustained many a hiker. Koala has introduced its trail mix product under the brand name Crocodile Chomp.

Multiple direct-material inputs.   The three inputs to Crocodile Chomp are raisins (R), peanuts (P), and sunflower seeds (S). The standard costs and quantities for Crocodile Chomp are given in the following table. The trail mix is produced in 10-kilogram units; subsequently, each unit is divided into 20 half-kilo packages (a little over a pound).

(a) Direct Material	(b) Standard Price per Kilogram	(c) Standard Number of Kilograms per Unit of Finished Product	(d) Standard Proportion (Col c ÷ 10)
R	$2.00	4	.4
P	1.60	4	.4
S	1.50	2	.2
Total		10	

During September, Koala produced 1,000 units of Crocodile Chomp (i.e., 10,000 kilograms of trail mix). However, it purchased and consumed 10,800 kilograms of inputs, as the following table shows.

(a) Direct Material	(b) Actual Price	(c) Actual Amount Used	(d) Actual Proportion Used (Col. c ÷ 10,800)
R	$2.00	3,780 kilograms	.35
P	1.80	5,400 kilograms	.50
S	1.45	1,620 kilograms	.15
Total		10,800 kilograms	

First, let's compute the direct-material price and quantity variances for September. Notice that the quantity purchased (*PQ*) and the actual quantity used (*AQ*) are the same, due to the perishability of the inputs.

Direct Material	PQ (AP − SP)	Price Variance	SP (AQ − SQ*)	Quantity Variance
R	3,780 ($2.00 − $2.00)	0	$2.00 (3,780 − 4,000)	$ 440 F
P	5,400 ($1.80 − $1.60)	$1,080 U	$1.60 (5,400 − 4,000)	2,240 U
S	1,620 ($1.45 − $1.50)	81 F	$1.50 (1,620 − 2,000)	570 F
Total		$ 999 U		$1,230 U

*SQ, the standard quantity allowed given actual output, is equal to the standard input proportion multiplied by 10,000 kilograms (the actual output produced).

As the variance analysis shows, the total price variance is $999 unfavorable, and the total quantity variance is $1,230 unfavorable. Now we divide the quantity variance into a *direct-material mix variance* and a *direct-materials yield variance*. The **direct-material mix variance** for a particular direct material is the difference between the actual and standard input proportions for that direct material multiplied by that material's standard price and multiplied by the actual total quantity of all direct materials used. The direct-material mix variance is computed as follows. Notice that the total direct-material mix variance is defined as the sum of the direct-material mix variances for each input.

$$\begin{array}{c}\text{Direct-material}\\\text{mix variance}\end{array} = \begin{array}{c}\text{Sum of direct material mix variances}\\\text{for each direct material used}\end{array}$$

$$\begin{array}{c}\text{Direct-}\\\text{material mix}\\\text{variance for}\\\text{direct}\\\text{material } i\end{array} = \left(\begin{array}{c}\text{Standard}\\\text{price of}\\\text{direct}\\\text{material } i\end{array}\right) \times \left(\begin{array}{c}\text{Actual}\\\text{input}\\\text{proportion}\\\text{for direct}\\\text{material } i\end{array} - \begin{array}{c}\text{Standard}\\\text{input}\\\text{proportion}\\\text{for direct}\\\text{material } i\end{array}\right) \times \left(\begin{array}{c}\text{Actual total}\\\text{quantity of}\\\text{all direct}\\\text{materials}\\\text{used}\end{array}\right)$$

Using this formula, Koala's September direct-material mix variances are computed as follows:

R mix variance = \$2.00 × (.35 − .40) × 10,800 =	\$1,080 F	
P mix variance = \$1.60 × (.50 − .40) × 10,800 =	1,728 U	
S mix variance = \$1.50 × (.15 − .20) × 10,800 =	810 F	
Total mix variance	\$ 162 F	

Koala's September direct-material mix variance is \$162 favorable, which means that the mix of inputs was altered in such a way that it had a favorable impact on the total production cost. Notice that signs (F or U) are assigned to the individual input components of the mix variance in accordance with this rule: F if the actual input proportion is lower than the standard input proportion and U otherwise. During September, the actual input proportions for raisins and sunflower seeds were lower than their standard input proportions; the actual proportion for peanuts was higher than its standard. It is important to note, however, that *it is the total direct-material mix variance of \$162 F that is a meaningful measure for management's analysis, not the individual mix variance components.*

The **direct-material yield variance** for a particular direct material is the difference between the actual quantity of all direct materials used and the standard quantity of all direct materials, given actual output, multiplied by that particular direct material's standard price and multiplied by that direct material's standard input proportion. Again, the total direct-material yield variance is defined as the sum of the individual yield variance components for the several inputs.

$$\begin{array}{c}\text{Direct-material}\\\text{yield variance}\end{array} = \begin{array}{c}\text{Sum of direct material yield variances}\\\text{for each direct material used}\end{array}$$

$$\begin{array}{c}\text{Direct-}\\\text{material yield}\\\text{variance for}\\\text{direct}\\\text{material } i\end{array} = \left(\begin{array}{c}\text{Standard}\\\text{price of}\\\text{direct}\\\text{material } i\end{array}\right) \times \left(\begin{array}{c}\text{Actual}\\\text{quantity of}\\\text{all direct}\\\text{materials}\\\text{used}\end{array} - \begin{array}{c}\text{Standard}\\\text{allowed total}\\\text{quantity of}\\\text{all direct}\\\text{materials}\\\text{given actual}\\\text{output}\end{array}\right) \times \left(\begin{array}{c}\text{Standard}\\\text{input}\\\text{proportion}\\\text{for direct}\\\text{material } i\end{array}\right)$$

Using this formula, Koala's September direct-material yield variances are computed as follows:

R yield variance = \$2.00 × (10,800 − 10,000) × .40 =	\$ 640 U	
P yield variance = \$1.60 × (10,800 − 10,000) × .40 =	512 U	
S yield variance = \$1.50 × (10,800 − 10,000) × .20 =	240 U	
Total yield variance	\$1,392 U	

Koala's September direct-material yield variance is \$1,392 unfavorable. The interpretation is that the total inputs used (10,800 kilograms) exceeded the standard quantity allowed given actual output (10,000 kilograms of input allowed for 10,000 kilograms of output). As with the mix variance, the most meaningful interpretation applies to the *total yield variance* rather than its individual components.

Notice that Koala's direct-material mix variance (\$162 F) and yield variance (\$1,392 U) add up to the direct-material quantity variance (\$1,230 U). Koala's September direct-material variances in the production of Crocodile Chomp are summarized in Exhibit 16–8.

Exhibit 16–8

September Direct-Material
Variances in the
Production of Crocodile
Chomp Trail Mix

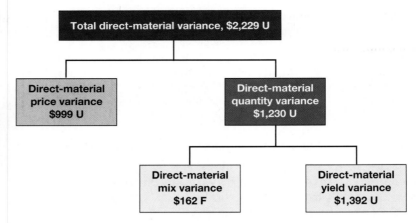

Multiple direct-labor inputs. The same analysis for direct material can be applied to direct labor if a company has multiple types of direct-labor input. Suppose, for example, that Koala's direct-labor employees in the Crocodile Mix line include inspectors, mixers, and packers, each with a different standard pay rate. Moreover, assume that there is a standard or expected input proportion for each type of direct labor. Then we can apply the same analysis to direct labor as we used for direct material. Just substitute the words "direct labor" for "direct material" in all of the formulas given in the preceding section. Now the total direct-labor variance consists of the direct-labor rate and efficiency variances, and the direct-labor efficiency variance is decomposed into a *direct-labor mix variance* and a *direct-labor yield variance*. The **direct-labor-mix variance** for a particular type of direct labor is the difference between the actual and standard input proportions for that type of direct labor multiplied by that labor type's standard rate and multiplied by the actual total quantity of all direct labor used. The **direct-labor yield variance** for a particular type of direct labor is the difference between the actual quantity of all direct labor used and the standard quantity of all direct labor, given actual output, multiplied by the standard rate for that particular type of direct labor and multiplied by the standard input proportion for that type of direct labor. As with direct materials, this analysis makes sense only if some degree of substitutability exists among the various types of direct labor.

Mix and Yield Variances in Service Organizations

The concepts underlying production mix and yield variances can be applied to service organizations also. Service organizations often make substitutions among different types of labor. Ernst & Young, for example, might substitute partner time for staff time on a particular audit job.

Consider the well-known consulting firm of Kirk, Spock and McCoy, which has bid a job for 1,000 hours: 300 hours of partner time at a cost of $60 per hour and 700 hours of staff time at a cost of $20 per hour. Due to scheduling problems, the partner spends 500 hours, and the staff member spends 500 hours. If the actual costs are $60 for partner time and $20 for staff time, no labor rate variance exists. However, even though the 1,000 hours required were exactly what was bid, the job cost is $8,000 over budget, as shown here:

$$\text{Actual cost} = (500 \text{ hours} \times \$60) + (500 \text{ hours} \times \$20)$$
$$= \$30,000 + \$10,000$$
$$= \$40,000$$
$$\text{Budgeted cost} = (300 \text{ hours} \times \$60) + (700 \text{ hours} \times \$20)$$
$$= \$18,000 + \$14,000$$
$$= \$32,000$$
$$\text{Cost overrun} = \$8,000$$

We can apply the mix and yield variance analysis to help us understand this cost overrun. First, there is no yield variance because the total number of actual hours and total budgeted hours are the same. (Review the formula for the yield variance.) However, there is an unfavorable mix variance of $8,000, which is calculated as follows by applying the mix variance formula given earlier in the appendix.

Partner labor mix variance = $60 × (.5* − .3†) × 1,000 =	$12,000 U	
Staff labor mix variance = $20 × (.5* − .7†) × 1,000 =	4,000 F	
Total mix variance	$ 8,000 U	

* The actual input proportions were .5 for both partner and staff time (500 ÷ 1,000).

† The budgeted (standard) input proportions were .3 for partner time (300 ÷ 1,000) and .7 for staff time (700 ÷ 1,000).

Thus, the entire budget overrun of $8,000 is due to the unfavorable mix effect of substituting expensive partner time for less expensive staff time. This scenario had no rate (price) or yield effects at all.

Key Terms

For each term's definition refer to the indicated page, or turn to the glossary at the end of the text.

cost variance, 648

direct-labor efficiency
   variance, 656

direct-labor mix
   variance,* 674

direct-labor rate variance, 655

direct-labor yield
   variance,* 674

direct-material mix
   variance,* 672

direct-material price
   variance (or purchase
   price variance), 654

direct-material quantity
   variance, 654

direct-material yield
   variance,* 673

kaizen costing, 670

management by
   exception, 649

perfection (or ideal
   standard), 650

practical (or attainable)
   standard, 651

standard cost, 648

standard-costing system, 664

standard direct-labor
   quantity, 653

standard direct-labor rate, 653

standard direct-material
   price, 653

standard direct-material
   quantity, 652

statistical control chart, 660

task analysis, 649

Meeting the Cost-Management Challenges

1. **How** could Koala Camp Gear's controller set standards for the production of tents using the company's standard-costing system?

Koala Camp Gear's controller could use several approaches to set standards. One method of setting standards is the analysis of historical cost data, which provide an indicator of future costs. The methods for analyzing cost behavior described in Chapter 11 are used to predict future costs on the basis of historical costs. These predictions then form the basis for setting standards. Another standard-setting method is task analysis, which analyzes a production process to determine what the cost to produce a product or service should be. The emphasis shifts from what the product did cost in the past to what it should cost in the future.

A perfection (or ideal) standard is the cost expected under perfect or ideal operating conditions. A practical (or attainable) standard is the cost expected under normal operating conditions.

2. **What** is the appropriate interpretation of each variance detailed in Koala Camp Gear Company's cost-variance report?

Koala Camp Gear's unfavorable direct-material price variance means that it paid a higher price for the material than was expected when the standard was set. (A favorable variance has the opposite interpretation.)

Koala's unfavorable direct-material quantity variance means that a larger amount of material was used in the pro-

duction process than should have been used in accordance with the standard. (A favorable variance has the opposite interpretation.)

The unfavorable direct-labor rate variance experienced by Koala Camp Gear Company means that it paid a higher labor rate than was anticipated when the standard was set. One possible cause is that labor rate raises granted were higher than those anticipated in setting the standards. Another possibility is that more highly skilled workers were used to perform tasks than were required or anticipated when the standards were set. (A favorable variance has the opposite interpretation.)

Koala Camp Gear's favorable direct-labor efficiency variance means that it used less labor to accomplish a given task than was required in accordance with the standards. (An unfavorable variance has the opposite interpretation.)

3. **Who** is in the best position in the organization to influence each of these variances?

The purchasing manager is in the best position to influence the direct-material price variance.

The production manager is usually in the best position to influence the direct-material quantity variance.

In some cases, the production manager is in the best position to influence the direct-labor rate variance. In other cases, the personnel manager or union negotiator has more influence.

The production manager is usually in the best position to influence the direct-labor efficiency variance.

4. **What** criticisms are made of standard-costing systems as they are used in today's business environment?

Eight criticisms of standard costing in an advanced manufacturing setting are the following:

▨ Variances are too aggregate and too late to be useful.
▨ Variances are not tied to specific product lines, production batches, or flexible manufacturing system (FMS) cells.
▨ Standard-costing systems focus too much on direct labor.
▨ Frequent switching among products in an FMS cell makes cost standards less appropriate.

▨ Shorter product life cycles mean that individual standards are soon outmoded.
▨ Traditional standard-costing systems tend to focus too much on cost minimization rather than on increasing product quality or customer service.
▨ Automated manufacturing processes are highly reliable in meeting production specifications. As a result, variances from standards tend to be very small or nonexistent.
▨ Traditional standard costs are not defined broadly enough to include important costs, such as the total cost of ownership.

Solution to You're the Decision Maker

16.1   Direct-Material and Direct-Labor Variances
       p. 661

a. The direct-material and direct-labor variances are computed in Exhibits 16–9 and 16–10, respectively.

b. The direct-material price variance and the direct-labor rate variance should be investigated since they exceed 1 standard deviation. The direct-material price variance is $6,250 unfavorable, and the direct-labor rate variance is $5,250 favorable.

Exhibit 16–9

Direct-Material Price and Quantity Variances: You're the Decision Maker

Direct-Material Price and Quantity Variances

Actual Material Cost   **Standard Material Cost**

Actual quantity	×	**Actual price**	**Actual quantity**	×	**Standard price**	**Standard quantity**	×	**Standard price**
25,000 sq. meters purchased	×	$8.25 per sq. meter	25,000 sq. meters purchased	×	$8.00 per sq. meter	24,000 sq. meters allowed	×	$8.00 per sq. meter

$206,250 $200,000 $192,000

$6,250 Unfavorable

Direct-material price variance

24,500 sq. meters used $8.00 per sq. meter

$196,000

$4,000 Unfavorable

Direct-material quantity variance

Using Formulas

Direct-material price variance $= PQ(AP - SP)$
$$= 25,000 \ (\$8.25 - \$8.00) = \$6,250 \text{ Unfavorable}$$
Direct-material quantity variance $= SP(AQ - SQ)$
$$= \$8.00 \ (24,500 - 24,000) = \$4,000 \text{ Unfavorable}$$

Direct-Labor Rate and Efficiency Variances

Actual Labor Cost

Actual hours	×	Actual rate		Actual hours	×	Standard rate		Standard hours	×	Standard rate

4,200 hours used	×	$16.75 per hour		4,200 hours used	×	$18.00 per hour		4,000 hours allowed	×	$18.00 per hour

Standard Labor Cost

$70,350 $75,600 $72,000

$5,250 Favorable $3,600 Unfavorable

Direct-labor   Direct-labor
rate variance   efficiency variance

Exhibit 16–10

Direct-Labor Rate and
Efficiency Variances:
You're the Decision Maker

Koala Camp Gear
Company

Using Formulas

Direct-labor rate variance = $AH(AR - SR)$
$$= 4,200\ (\$16.75 - \$18.00) = \$5,250 \text{ Favorable}$$
Direct-labor efficiency variance = $SR(AH - SH)$
$$= \$18.00\ (4,200 - 4,000) = \$3,600 \text{ Unfavorable}$$

Review Questions

16.1 One of the principles espoused by management is that one should manage by exception. How can responsibility reporting systems and/or analysis of variances assist in that process?

16.2 Explain how standard material prices and quantities are set.

16.3 What is the interpretation of the *direct-material price variance?*

16.4 What manager usually is in the best position to influence the direct-material price variance?

16.5 What is the interpretation of the *direct-material quantity variance?*

16.6 What manager usually is in the best position to influence the direct-material quantity variance?

16.7 Describe the factors that managers often consider when determining the significance of a variance.

16.8 What is the interpretation of the *direct-labor rate variance?* What are some possible causes?

16.9 What manager generally is in the best position to influence the direct-labor rate variance?

16.10 What is the interpretation of the *direct-labor efficiency variance?*

16.11 What manager generally is in the best position to influence the direct-labor efficiency variance?

16.12 Describe how standard costs are used for product costing.

16.13 What is meant by the term *kaizen* costing?

16.14 (Appendix) List four companies that probably use direct-material mix and yield variances.

Critical Analysis

16.15 Distinguish between *perfection* and *practical* standards. Which type of standard is likely to produce the best motivational effects?

16.16 In a service environment with no inventories, is variance analysis useful? Why or why not?

16.17 Why should management want to divide production cost variances into price and efficiency variances?

16.18 Explain why the quantity purchased (*PQ*) is used in computing the direct-material price variance, but the actual quantity consumed (*AQ*) is used in computing the direct-material quantity variance.

16.19 Refer to question 16.18. Why does an analogous question *not* arise in the context of the direct-labor variances?

16.20 Many companies set wage rates through union negotiations. Under these circumstances, how could a labor price variance arise that is the responsibility of a line manager?

16.21 Discuss several ways in which standard-costing systems should be adapted in today's advanced manufacturing environment.

16.22 Which of the following terms is most consistent with the old saying, "Slow and steady wins the race": advanced manufacturing system, product innovation, kaizen costing, or investment in high technology? Explain.

Exercises

Exercise 16.23
Direct-Material Variances:
Material Purchased and
Material Used Are Not
Equal
(LO 3)

Hasegawa Company manufactures laboratory glassware in its plant near Kyoto, Japan. The controller recently reported the following information concerning direct-material requirements in department 8.

Standard direct-material cost per unit produced	1.31 *yen*
Direct material purchased (actual)..	58,158 *yen*
Standard cost of material purchased	57,510 *yen*
Standard price times actual amount of material used	38,340 *yen*
Actual production...	28,000 units

Required

Compute the direct-material cost variances for department 8. Prepare an analysis for management like the one in Exhibit 16–1. (Remember to express your analysis in terms of *yen,* the Japanese national currency.)

Exercise 16.24
Direct-Labor Variances
(LO 3)

The standard direct-labor cost per unit for Reimal Housewares, Inc. was $10 ($5 per hour times 2 hours per unit). During the period, actual direct-labor costs amounted to $18,800, 3,900 direct-labor hours were worked, and 1,900 units were produced.

Required

Compute the direct-labor rate and efficiency variances for the period. (Refer to Exhibit 16–2 for the format.)

Exercise 16.25
Direct-Labor Variances
(LO 3)

The standard direct-labor cost per reservation for Adventure Air Charters is $ .65 ($6.50 per hour divided by 10 reservations per hour). During the period, actual direct-labor costs totaled $44,500, 6,800 direct-labor hours were worked, and 72,000 reservations were made.

Required

Compute the direct-labor rate and efficiency variances for the period. (Refer to Exhibit 16–2 for the format.)

Exercise 16.26
Standard Costs; Ethics
(LO 1, 5)

Agrico, Inc. produces items made from local farm products that it distributes to supermarkets. Because price competition has become increasingly important over the years, Abby Tyler, the company's controller, is planning to implement a standard-costing system. She asked her cost-management analyst, Larry Madison, to gather cost information on the production of strawberry jam (Agrico's most popular product). Madison reported that strawberries cost $ .90 per quart, the price he intends to pay to his good friend who has been operating a strawberry farm in the red for the last few years. Due to an oversupply in the market, the prices for strawberries have dropped to $ .65 per quart. Madison is sure that the $ .90 price will be enough to pull his friend's strawberry farm out of the red and into the black.

Required

Is Madison's behavior regarding the cost information he provided to Tyler unethical? Explain your answer.

[CMA adapted]

Exercise 16.27
Standards for a New
High-Tech Product
(LO 1, 2)

Read "When Hybrid Cars Collide," *The Wall Street Journal,* February 6, 2003, p. B1, by Norohiku Shirouzu.

Required

As a group, discuss how companies developing new high-tech products would set standard costs for them. What special challenge does the "format" issue present in standard setting for the new hybrid automobiles?

Exercise 16.28
Straightforward
Computation of
Variances
(LO 3)

Columbus Container Company manufactures recyclable soft-drink cans. A unit of production is a case of 12 dozen cans.

Actual material purchases amounted to 240,000 kilograms at $ .81 per kilogram. Actual costs incurred in the production of 50,000 units follow:

Direct labor	$211,900 for 13,000 hours
Direct material..........................	$170,100 for 210,000 kilograms

The following standards have been set by the production-engineering staff and the controller.

Direct material:	Direct labor:
Quantity, 4 kilograms	Quantity, .25 hour
Price, $ .79 per kilogram	Rate, $16 per hour

Required

Use the variance formulas to compute the direct-material price and quantity variances and the direct-labor rate and efficiency variances. Indicate whether each variance is favorable or unfavorable.

Refer to the data in the preceding exercise.

Required

Use diagrams similar to those in Exhibits 16–1 and 16–2 to determine the direct material and direct-labor variances. Indicate whether each variance is favorable or unfavorable.

Exercise 16.29
Determination of Variances Using Diagrams
(LO 3)

Refer to the data in Exercise 16.28 for Columbus Container Company.

Required

a. Prepare journal entries to:

(1) Record the purchase of direct material on account.

(2) Add direct-material and direct-labor cost to Work-in-Process Inventory.

(3) Record the direct-material and direct-labor variances.

(4) Close these variances to Cost of Goods Sold.

b. Set up T-accounts, and post the journal entries to the general ledger.

Exercise 16.30
Preparation of Journal Entries under Standard Costing; Posting Journal Entries for Variances
(LO 6)

Choose one of the following manufacturers (or any manufacturer of your choosing), and use the Internet to gather information about any new products the company has recently introduced or plans to introduce.

Boeing (www.boeing.com)   Kodak (www.kodak.com)

Caterpillar (www.caterpillar.com)   Pfizer (www.pfizer.com)

Ford (www.ford.com/us)   Xerox (www.xerox.com)

Required

Discuss the steps you think the company took in establishing standard costs for its new product.

Exercise 16.31
Development of Standards for New Products; Internet Use
(LO 1, 2, 8)

Due to evaporation during production, Piscataway Plastics Company requires 8 pounds of material input for every 7 pounds of good plastic sheets manufactured. During May, the company produced 4,725 pounds of good sheets.

Required

Compute the total standard allowed input quantity given the good output produced.

Exercise 16.32
Standard Allowed Input
(LO 1)

Kalamazoo Chemical Company manufactures industrial chemicals. The company plans to introduce a new chemical solution and needs to develop a standard product cost. The new chemical solution is made by combining a chemical compound (lotrel) and a solution (salex), heating the mixture, adding a second compound (protet), and bottling the resulting solution in 10-liter containers. The initial mix, which is 11 liters in volume, consists of 12 kilograms of lotrel and 9.6 liters of salex. A 1-liter reduction in volume occurs during the boiling process. The solution is cooled slightly before 5 kilograms of protet are added. The addition of protet does not affect the total liquid volume.

The purchase price of the direct materials used in the manufacture of this new chemical solution follow:

Exercise 16.33
Determination of Standard Material Cost
(LO 1)

Lotrel	$1.58 per kilogram
Salex	1.80 per liter
Protet	2.40 per kilogram

Required

Determine the standard direct-material cost of a 10-liter container of the new product.

[CMA adapted]

Exercise 16.34
Cost Variance
Investigation
(LO 4)

The controller for Tribecca Caterers', Inc., uses a statistical control chart to help management determine when to investigate variances. The critical value is 1 standard deviation. The company incurred the following direct-labor efficiency variances during the first six months of the current year.

January..............................	$250 F	April	$ 900 U
February...........................	800 U	May...............................	1,050 U
March	700 U	June	1,200 U

The standard direct-labor cost during each of these months was $19,000. The controller has estimated that the firm's monthly direct-labor variances have a standard deviation of $950.

Required

a. Draw a statistical control chart and plot the preceding variance data. Which variances should be investigated?

b. Suppose that the controller's rule of thumb is to investigate all variances equal to or greater than 6 percent of standard cost. Which variances will be investigated?

c. Would you investigate any of the variances listed other than those indicated by the rules discussed in requirements (a) and (b)? Why?

Exercise 16.35
Labor Mix and Yield
Variances (Appendix)
(LO 10)

Boca Raton Burrito has two categories of direct labor, unskilled, which costs $6.50 per hour, and skilled, which costs $10.30 per hour. Management has established standards per "equivalent meal," which has been defined as a typical meal consisting of a burrito, a drink, and a side order. Standards have been set as follows:

Unskilled labor	10 minutes per equivalent meal
Skilled labor	4 minutes per equivalent meal

During May, Boca Raton Burrito sold 30,000 equivalent meals and incurred the following labor costs:

Unskilled labor	4,600 hours	....	33,000
Skilled labor....................................	1,800 hours	....	$17,500

Required

a. Compute the direct-labor rate and efficiency variances.

b. Compute the direct-labor mix and yield variances.

Exercise 16.36
Direct-Material Mix and
Yield Variances
(Appendix)
(LO 10)

mhhe.com/hilton3e

Caltex, Inc. has set the following direct-material standards for its product, the universal gismo.

Standard costs for one unit of output:
Material I, 10 units of input at $100 per unit
Material II, 20 units of input at $150 per unit

During August, the company had the following results:

Universal gismos produced	2,000 units
Materials purchased and used:	
Material I	22,000 units at $94
Material II	38,000 units at $152

Required

a. Compute the direct-material price and quantity variances.

b. Compute the direct-material mix and yield variances.

Problems

Orion Corporation has established the following standards for the prime costs of one unit of its chief product, dartboards.

	Standard Quantity	**Standard Price or Rate**	**Standard Cost**
Direct material	8.5 pounds	$1.80 per pound	$15.30
Direct labor	.25 hour	$8.00 per hour	2.00
Total...			$17.30

Problem 16.37
Direct-Material and Direct-Labor Variances
(LO 3)

During May, Orion purchased 160,000 pounds of direct material at a total cost of $315,200. The total wages for May were $42,000, 90 percent of which were for direct labor. Orion manufactured 19,000 dartboards during May, using 142,500 pounds of direct material and 5,000 direct-labor hours.

Required
Compute the following variances for May, and indicate whether each is favorable or unfavorable.

a. Direct-material price variance.
b. Direct-material quantity variance.
c. Direct-labor rate variance.
d. Direct-labor efficiency variance.

[CMA adapted]

Analyze each of the following scenarios independently.

a. Information about Maxey Corporation's direct-material cost follows:

Standard price per direct-material ounce	$ 345
Actual quantity purchased and used	420 ounces
Standard quantity allowed for production	435 ounces
Price variance	$2,950 F

Problem 16.38
Direct-Material and Direct-Labor Variances; Missing Data
(LO 3)

What was the actual purchase price per ounce, rounded to the nearest cent?

b. Yankay Company reports the following direct-labor information for its primary product for October:

Standard rate	$ 7.00 per hour
Actual rate paid..	$ 7.20 per hour
Standard hours allowed for actual production	1,400 hours
Direct-labor efficiency variance	$ 500 U

What were the actual hours worked, and what was the direct-labor rate variance?

Texarkana Textiles, Inc. manufactured 500 units of a special multilayer fabric with the trade name Stylex during July.

The standard prime costs for one unit of Stylex are:

Direct material: 20 yards at $1.35 per yard...	$27
Direct labor: 4 hours at $9.00 per hour	36
Total standard prime cost per unit of output	$63

Problem 16.39
Direct-Material and Direct-Labor Variances
(LO 3)

The following information from the Stylex production department pertains to July:

Direct material purchased: 18,000 yards at $1.38 per yard..................	$24,840
Direct material used: 9,500 yards at $1.38 per yard	13,110
Direct labor used: 2,100 hours at $9.15 per hour..................................	19,215

Required
Compute the following variances for the month of July, indicating whether each variance is favorable or unfavorable.

a. Direct-material price variance.
b. Direct-material quantity variance.

    c.   Direct-labor rate variance.

    d.   Direct-labor efficiency variance.

    e.   *Build your own spreadsheet.* **Build** an Excel spreadsheet to solve requirements (a) through (d). Use your spreadsheet to determine the new values for each of the variances listed in requirements (a) through (d) if each of the following input parameters changes by the amount indicated. (Unless otherwise indicated, treat each parameter change independently.)

        (1)   The actual direct-material price is $1.40 per yard.

        (2)   The standard direct material quantity per unit of Stylex is 21 yards.

        (3)   The standard direct-labor rate is $9.10 per hour.

        (4)   All of the changes in parts (1) through (3) occur simultaneously.

    [CPA adapted]

Problem 16.40

Behavioral Impact of Implementing a Standard-Costing System

(LO 1, 5)

PrimeCare, Inc., a manufacturer of custom-designed home health care equipment, has been in business for 15 years. Last year, to better control the costs of its products, the controller implemented a standard-costing system. Reports for tracking performance are issued monthly, and any unfavorable variances are investigated further.

    The production manager complained that the standards are unrealistic, stifle motivation by concentrating only on unfavorable variances, and are out of date too quickly. He noted that his recent switch to titanium for the wheelchairs has resulted in higher material costs but decreased labor hours. The net result was no increase in the total cost to produce the wheelchair. The monthly reports continue to show an unfavorable material variance and a favorable labor variance despite indications that the workers are slowing down.

Required

    a.   Describe several ways that a standard-costing system strengthens management cost control.

    b.   Give at least two reasons to explain why a standard-costing system could negatively impact the motivation of production employees.

    [CMA adapted]

Problem 16.41

Development of Standard Costs; Causes of Variances; Ethics

(LO 1, 5, 7)

TasteeFruit Company is a small producer of fruit-flavored frozen desserts. For many years, its products have had strong regional sales on the basis of brand recognition. However, other companies have begun marketing similar products in the area, and price competition has become increasingly important. John Wakefield, the company's controller, is planning to implement a standard-costing system and has gathered considerable information on production and materials requirements for TasteeFruit's products. He believes that the use of standard costing will allow the company to make better pricing decisions.

    TasteeFruit's most popular product is raspberry sherbet. The sherbet is produced in 10-gallon batches, and each batch requires six quarts of good raspberries. The fresh raspberries are sorted by hand before entering the production process. Because of imperfections in the raspberries and normal spoilage, one quart of berries is discarded for every four quarts accepted. Three minutes is the standard direct-labor time for the sorting required to obtain one quart of acceptable raspberries. The acceptable raspberries are then blended with the other ingredients; blending requires 12 minutes of direct-labor time per batch. After blending, the sherbet is packaged in quart containers. Wakefield has gathered the following information from Teresa Adams, TasteeFruit's cost accountant.

    ▨   TasteeFruit purchases raspberries at a cost of $ .80 per quart. All other ingredients cost a total of $ .45 per gallon.

    ▨   Direct labor is paid at the rate of $9 per hour.

    ▨   The total cost of material and labor required to package the sherbet is $.41 per quart.

    Adams has a friend who owns a berry farm that has been losing money in recent years. Because of good crops, an oversupply of raspberries has been available, and prices have dropped to $ .50 per quart. Adams has arranged for TasteeFruit to purchase raspberries from her friend and hopes that $ .80 per quart will help her friend's farm become profitable again.

Required

    a.   Develop the standard cost of direct material, direct labor, and packaging for a 10-gallon batch of raspberry sherbet.

    b.   As part of the implementation of a standard-costing system, Wakefield plans to train those responsible for maintaining the standards in the use of variance analysis. He is particularly concerned with the causes of unfavorable variances. As his assistant, prepare a page for a company training document that discusses the following:

(1)   The possible causes of unfavorable material price variances and identifies the individual(s) who should be held responsible for these variances.

(2)   The possible causes of unfavorable labor efficiency variances and identifies the individual(s) who should be held responsible for these variances.

c.   Citing the specific ethical standards of competence, confidentiality, integrity, and objectivity for management accountants, explain why Adams's behavior regarding the cost information provided to Wakefield is unethical. (See the Appendix to Chapter 1 for these ethical standards.)

d.   *Build your own spreadsheet.* Build an Excel spreadsheet to solve requirement (a). Use your spreadsheet to determine the new values for all of the amounts calculated in requirement (a) if each of the following input parameters changes by the amount indicated. (Unless otherwise indicated, treat each parameter change independently.)

(1)   The standard cost of raspberries is $.90 per quart.

(2)   The standard cost of direct labor for sorting and blending is $9.50 per hour.

(3)   The total standard cost of material and labor for packaging is $.45 per quart of sherbet.

(4)   All of the changes in parts (1) through (3) occur simultaneously.

[CMA adapted]

Surf's Up, Inc. manufactures fiberglass boards used for riding the waves at the beach. The products are sold under the brand name Crazy Board. The standard cost for material and labor is $89.20 per board. This includes 8 kilograms of direct material at a standard cost of $5.00 per kilogram and 6 hours of direct labor at $8.20 per hour. The following data pertain to November:

Problem 16.42
Variances; Journal Entries; Missing Data
(LO 3, 6)

- Units completed: 5,600 units.
- Purchases of material: 50,000 kilograms for $249,250.
- Total actual labor costs: $300,760.
- Actual hours of labor: 36,500 hours.
- Direct-material quantity variance: $1,500 unfavorable.
- Work-in-process inventory on November 1: none.
- Work-in-process inventory on November 30: 800 units (75 percent complete as to labor; material is issued at the beginning of processing).

Required

a.   Compute the following amounts. Indicate whether each variance is favorable or unfavorable.

(1)   Direct-labor rate variance for November.

(2)   Direct-labor efficiency variance for November.

(3)   Actual kilograms of material used in the production process during November.

(4)   Actual price paid per kilogram of direct material in November.

(5)   Total amounts of direct-material and direct-labor cost transferred to Finished-Goods Inventory during November.

(6)   Total amount of direct-material and direct-labor cost in the balance of Work-in-Process Inventory at the end of November.

b.   Prepare journal entries to record the following:

- Purchasing raw material.
- Adding direct material to Work-in-Process Inventory.
- Adding direct labor to Work-in-Process Inventory.
- Recording variances.

[CMA adapted]

United Kingdom Agribusiness, Ltd. (UKA), manufactures agricultural machinery in Manchester, England. At a recent staff meeting the controller presented the following direct-labor variance report for the year just ended.

Problem 16.43
Cost-Variance Investigation
(LO 4)

UNITED KINGDOM AGRIBUSINESS, LTD. Direct-Labor Variance Report (all variances in British pounds sterling)				
	Direct-Labor **Rate Variance**		**Direct-Labor** **Efficiency Variance**	
	Amount	**Standard Cost, %**	**Amount**	**Standard Cost, %**
January	£ 800 F	.16%	£ 5,000 U	1.00%
February	4,900 F	.98	7,500 U	1.50
March	100 U	.02	9,700 U	1.94
April	2,000 U	.40	12,800 U	2.56
May	3,800 F	.76	20,100 U	4.02
June	3,900 F	.78	17,000 U	3.40
July	4,200 F	.84	28,500 U	5.70
August	5,100 F	1.02	38,000 U	7.60
September	4,800 F	.96	37,000 U	7.40
October	5,700 F	1.14	42,000 U	8.40
November	4,200 F	.84	60,000 U	12.00
December	4,300 F	.86	52,000 U	10.40

UKA's controller uses the following rule of thumb: Investigate all variances equal to or greater than £30,000, which is 6 percent of standard cost.

Required

a.   Which variances would have been investigated during the year? (Indicate month and type of variance.)

b.   What characteristics of the variance pattern shown in the report should draw the controller's attention regardless of the usual investigation rule? Explain. Given these considerations, which variances would you have investigated? Why?

c.   Is it important to follow up on favorable variances, such as those shown in the report? Why?

d.   The controller believes that the firm's direct-labor rate variance has a normal probability distribution with a mean of zero and a standard deviation of £5,000. Prepare a statistical control chart and plot the company's direct-labor rate variances for each month. The critical value is 1 standard deviation. Which variances would have been investigated under this approach?

Problem 16.44

Kaizen Costing Chart

(LO 8, 9)

Melbourne Electronics Corporation manufactures TV sets in Australia, largely for the domestic market. The company recently implemented a kaizen costing program with the goal of reducing the manufacturing cost per television set by 10 percent during 20x1, the first year of the kaizen effort. The cost per TV set at the end of 20x0 was $500. The following table shows the average cost per television set estimated during each month of 20x1. (On the day this problem was written, the Australian dollar was equivalent in value to .5153 US dollars.)

Month	Cost per Set	Month	Cost per Set
January	$500	July	$485
February	500	August	470
March	495	September	460
April	492	October	460
May	490	November	450
June	485	December	440

Required

Prepare a kaizen costing chart for 20x1 to show the results of Melbourne Electronics Corporation's first year of kaizen costing. In developing the chart, use the following steps:

a.   Draw and label the axes of the kaizen costing chart.

b.   Indicate the current year cost base and the kaizen goal (cost-reduction rate) on the chart.

c.   Label the horizontal axis with the months of 20x1. Label the vertical axis with dollar amounts in the appropriate range.

d.   Plot the 12 monthly estimates of the average cost per TV set. Then draw a line connecting the cost points that were plotted.

e. Complete the chart with any other labels necessary.

f. Briefly explain the purpose of kaizen costing. How could a continuous quality-improvement program, coupled with the kaizen costing effort implemented by Melbourne Electronics Corporation, help the firm begin competing in the worldwide market?

Gibraltar Insurance Company compares actual results with standard costs. The standard direct-labor rates are established each year when the annual plan is formulated and held constant for the entire year. The standard direct-labor rates in effect for the current fiscal year and the standard hours allowed for the actual output of insurance claims for April in the claims department are shown in the following schedule:

Problem 16.45
Direct-Labor Mix and Yield Variances (Appendix)
(LO 10)

	Standard Direct-Labor Rate per hour	Standard Direct-Labor Hours Allowed for Actual Output
Labor class III	$8	500
Labor class II	7	500
Labor class I	5	500

The wage rates for each labor class increased under the terms of a new contract. The standard wage rates were not revised to reflect the new contract.

The actual direct-labor hours worked and the actual direct-labor rates per hour experienced for the month of April were as follows:

	Actual Direct-Labor Rate per Hour	Actual Direct-Labor Hours
Labor class III	$8.50	550
Labor class II	7.50	650
Labor class I	5.40	375

Required

a. Calculate the dollar amount of the total direct-labor variance for April for Gibraltar Insurance Company, and break the total variance into the following components:
 (1) Direct-labor rate and efficiency variances.
 (2) Direct-labor mix and yield variances.

b. Prepare a variance chart similar to Exhibit 16–8.

[CMA adapted]

Oakland Chemical Corporation manufactures a wide variety of chemical compounds and liquids for industrial uses. The standard mix for producing a single batch of 500 gallons of doroxaline follows:

Problem 16.46
Direct-Material Mix and Yield Variances (Appendix)
(LO 10)

Input Chemical	Quantity (in gallons)	Cost (per gallon)	Total Cost
Kalite	100	$2.00	$200
Salex	300	.75	225
Cralyn	225	1.00	225
Total	625		$650

A 20 percent loss in the doroxaline's liquid volume occurs during processing due to evaporation. The finished liquid is sold in 10-gallon bottles. Thus, the standard material cost for a 10-gallon bottle is $13.

The actual quantities and the cost of direct materials placed in production during November were as follows. (All materials purchased are immediately placed into production during the same period.)

Input Chemical	Quantity (in gallons)	Total Cost
Kalite	8,480	$17,384
Salex	25,200	17,640
Cralyn	18,540	16,686
Total	52,220	$51,710

A total of 4,000 bottles (40,000 gallons) of doroxaline were produced during November.

Required

a. Calculate the total direct-material variance for doroxaline for the month of November, and then further analyze the total variance by computing these variances:

   (1) Direct-material price and quantity variances.

   (2) Direct-material mix and yield variances.

b. Prepare a variance chart similar to Exhibit 16–8.

Cases

Case 16.47*
Direct-Material and
Direct-Labor Variances;
Job-Order Costing;
Journal Entries
(LO 3, 6)

Manhattan Fashions, Inc., manufactures inexpensive men's dress shirts, which are produced in lots to fill each special order. Its customers are department stores in various cities. Manhattan Fashions sews the particular store's labels on the shirts. During November the company worked on three orders, for which the month's job-cost records disclose the following data.

Lot Number	Boxes in Lot	Material Used (yards)	Hours Worked
A43	1,000	24,100	2,980
A44	1,700	40,440	5,130
A45	1,200	28,825	2,890

The following additional information is available:

1. The firm purchased 95,000 yards of material during November at a cost of $106,400.

2. Direct labor during November amounted to $165,000. According to payroll records, production employees were paid $15 per hour.

3. There was no work in process on November 1. During November, lots A43 and A44 were completed. All material was issued for lot A45, which was 80 percent completed as to labor.

4. The standard costs for a box of six shirts are as follows:

Direct material	24 yards at $1.10	$ 26.40
Direct labor	3 hours at $14.70	44.10
Manufacturing overhead	3 hours at $12.00	36.00
Standard cost per box		$106.50

Required

a. Prepare a schedule computing the standard cost of lots A43, A44, and A45 for November.

b. For each lot produced during November, prepare a schedule showing the following:

   (1) Direct-material price variance.

   (2) Direct-material quantity variance.

   (3) Direct-labor efficiency variance.

   (4) Direct-labor rate variance.

   Indicate whether each variance is favorable or unfavorable.

c. Prepare journal entries to record each of the following events for Manhattan Fashions.

   ▣   Purchase of material.

   ▣   Incurrence of direct-labor cost.

   ▣   Addition of direct-material and direct-labor cost to Work-in-Process Inventory.

   ▣   Recording of direct-material and direct-labor variances.

[CPA adapted]

---

*Note: Cases 17.67 and 17.68 in Chapter 17 include more integrative cost-variance analyses as well as more significant managerial implications.

Clapton Guitar Company manufactures acoustic guitars. The company uses a standard, job-order cost-accounting system in two production departments. Highly skilled artisans build the wooden guitars in the construction department and coat them with several layers of lacquer. Then the units are transferred to the finishing department, where the bridge of the guitar is attached and the strings are installed. The guitars also are tuned and inspected in the finishing department. The following diagram depicts the production process:

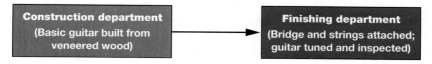

Each finished guitar contains seven pounds of veneered wood. In addition, one pound of wood is typically wasted in the production process. The veneered wood used in the guitars has a standard price of $12 per pound. The other parts needed to complete each guitar, such as the bridge and strings, cost $16 per guitar. The labor standards for Clapton's two production departments follow:

> Construction department: 6 hours of direct labor at $20 per hour
>
> Finishing department: 3 hours of direct labor at $15 per hour

The following additional information pertains to the month of July:

1. Neither production department had any beginning or ending work-in-process inventories.
2. The company had no beginning finished-goods inventory.
3. The company actually produced 500 guitars and sold 300 guitars on account for $400 each.
4. The company purchased 6,000 pounds of veneered wood at a price of $12.50 per pound.
5. Actual usage of veneered wood was 4,500 pounds.
6. Enough parts (bridges and strings) to finish 600 guitars were purchased at a cost of $9,600.
7. The construction department used 2,850 direct-labor hours. The total direct-labor cost in the construction department was $54,150.
8. The finishing department used 1,570 direct-labor hours. The total direct-labor cost in that department was $25,120.
9. The finishing department had no direct-material variances.

Required

a. Prepare a schedule that computes the standard costs of direct material and direct labor in each production department.

b. Prepare three exhibits that compute the July direct-material and direct-labor variances in the construction department and the July direct-labor variances in the finishing department. (Refer to Exhibits 16–1 and 16–2 for guidance.)

c. Prepare a cost variance report for July similar to that shown in Exhibit 16–3.

Refer to the preceding case.

Required

a. Prepare journal entries to record all events listed for Clapton Guitar Company during July. Specifically, the journal entries should reflect the following events.
   (1) Purchase of direct material.
   (2) Use of direct material.
   (3) Incurrence of direct-labor costs.
   (4) Addition of production costs to the Work-in-Process Inventory account for each department.
   (5) Incurrence of all variances.
   (6) Completion of 500 guitars.
   (7) Sale of 300 guitars.
   (8) Closing all variance accounts to Cost of Goods Sold.

b. Draw T-accounts and post the journal entries prepared in requirement (a). Assume that the beginning balance in all accounts is zero.

Case 16.48
Comprehensive Problem
on Variance Analysis
(LO 3, 5, 7)

Case 16.49
Journal Entries under
Standard Costing;
Continuation of Case
16.48
(LO 6)

Chapter 17

Flexible Budgets, Overhead Cost Management, and Activity-Based Budgeting

After completing this chapter, you should be able to:

1. Explain how cost-management analysts use flexible budgets to control overhead costs.

2. Prepare and interpret a flexible-overhead budget using formula and columnar formats.

3. Explain how overhead is applied to Work-in-Process Inventory under standard costing.

4. Discuss some important issues in choosing an activity measure for budgeting overhead.

5. Compute and interpret the variable-overhead spending and efficiency variances and the fixed-overhead budget and volume variances.

6. Prepare and interpret an overhead cost performance report.

7. Record manufacturing overhead under standard costing by preparing journal entries.

8. Explain why an activity-based flexible budget can provide more useful cost-management information than a conventional flexible budget.

9. Prorate variances among the relevant accounts (Appendix A).

10. Explain and illustrate backflush costing in a just-in-time environment (Appendix B).

11. Compute and interpret sales variances (Appendix C).

(Solutions are on page 721.)

Cost-*Management* Challenges

(Solutions are on page 721.)

1. **How** can Koala Camp Gear's management use a flexible budget to manage overhead costs?

2. **How** would you respond to the concerns raised by Koala Camp Gear's production manager in his memo to the controller?

3. **How** could Koala's managers improve the management of overhead costs?

Koala
Camp
Gear
Company

EMAIL MEMORANDUM

2145 Yarra Drive
Melbourne, Victoria
Australia

To: Marc Wesley
            Controller
From: Geoff Weatherby
            Production Manager
Subject: Flexible budget and overhead-variance report for June

   Since joining Koala Camp Gear Company in May, I have appreciated the information provided by your department in support of production operations. I was a bit surprised, however, upon receiving the overhead-variance report for June. Having carefully examined the flexible budget and the June overhead-variance report, and having followed up on several of the more significant variances, several questions remain.

   First, the $1,680 variable-overhead spending variance is of concern. Does this mean that the company is paying excessive prices for overhead items, such as electrical power or heat?

   Second, the $1,800 variable-overhead efficiency variance seems out of line. In the production area, we have paid particular attention lately to controlling our usage of overhead types of items, such as the various indirect materials and indirect labor. I do not believe we have been inefficient in their usage.

   Third, the $7,500 fixed-overhead volume variance seems to be totally beyond our control. How is this variance computed, and what does it mean?

   I would appreciate an opportunity to discuss these issues at your earliest convenience.

Geoff Weatherby's questions, expressed in the memo to Marc Wesley, Koala Camp Gear's controller, reflect concern about how Weatherby and his department are performing in their management of overhead costs. Also apparent in the memo is some uncertainty about how the variances on which he and his department are evaluated in part are determined and interpreted. This Koala Camp Gear Company memo raises the issue as to how companies manage and control overhead costs.

How do manufacturing firms, such as Nike and General Electric, control the many overhead costs incurred in their production processes? Unlike direct material and direct labor, manufacturing-overhead costs are not traceable to individual products. Moreover, manufacturing overhead is a pool of many different types of costs. Indirect material, indirect labor, and other indirect production costs often exhibit different relationships to productive activity. Moreover, different individuals in an organization are responsible for different types of overhead costs. Considering all of these issues together, controlling manufacturing overhead presents a challenge for cost-management analysts. This chapter presents a traditional cost-management system that is widely used to control overhead costs. We begin with flexible budgets.

Definition of Flexible-Overhead Budgets

LO 1 Explain how cost-management analysts use flexible budgets to control overhead costs.

Direct material and direct labor are traceable to products, and the determination of standard costs for these inputs is straightforward. If a surfboard requires 9.1 kilograms of fiberglass at $10 per kilogram, the standard direct-material cost for the surfboard is $91. But how much electricity does it take to produce a surfboard? How much supervisory time, equipment depreciation, or machinery repair services does the board require? Since all of these overhead costs are indirect costs of production, we cannot set overhead cost standards for the surfboard. If this approach does not provide the answer to managing overhead costs, what does?

The cost-management tool that most companies use to control overhead costs is called a **flexible budget,** which is defined as a budget that is valid for a range of activity. Thus, a flexible budget resembles the budgets we studied in Chapter 15, with one important difference: A *flexible budget is not based on only one level of activity.* Instead, a flexible budget covers a range of activity within which the firm operates. The **relevant range** is the range of activity levels within which management expects the organization to operate and within which cost behavior patterns remain relatively stable. The flexible budget, then, is a detailed plan for controlling overhead costs that is valid in the firm's *relevant range* of activity.[1] In contrast, a **static budget** is based on a particular planned level of activity.

Flexible budgets and the overhead-control techniques based on them traditionally are based on a simplified view of a firm's overhead cost structure. Overhead costs are classified as variable or fixed. Variable costs change in total in proportion to changes in the company's activity, as expressed in terms of a single, volume-based measure such as machine hours, labor hours, or throughput. Fixed costs do not change in total as the organization's activity changes. Chapter 11, which covers cost estimation, presents various methods for classifying costs as variable or fixed.

To illustrate, suppose that the cost-management analyst for Koala Camp Gear Company determines that electricity is a variable cost, incurred at the rate of $ .20 per machine hour. Examine the two different budgets for electricity costs in Exhibit 17–1. The static budget is based on management's predicted level of activity for June, 6,000 machine hours. This estimate is based on *planned* production of 4,000 Tree Line tents, each of which requires 1.5 machine hours. The flexible budget includes three different production activity levels within the relevant range: 4,500, 6,000, and 7,500 machine hours.

---

[1] See Chapter 11, which covers cost estimation, for a discussion of the relevant range concept.

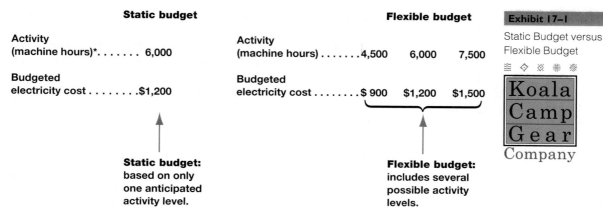

Static budget

Activity
(machine hours)*. 6,000

Budgeted
electricity cost $1,200

Static budget:
based on only
one anticipated
activity level.

Flexible budget

Activity
(machine hours) 4,500   6,000   7,500

Budgeted
electricity cost . . . .$ 900 $1,200 $1,500

Flexible budget:
includes several
possible activity
levels.

Exhibit 17–1

Static Budget versus
Flexible Budget

Koala
Camp
Gear
Company

*Based on *planned* June production of 4,000 tents, at 1.5 machine hours per tent.

Advantages of Flexible Budgets

Why is the distinction between static and flexible budgets so important? Suppose that Koala produced 3,000 Tree Line tents during June, used 4,500 machine hours, and incurred electricity costs of $1,050. Does this constitute effective or ineffective control of electricity costs? Which budget in Exhibit 17–1 is more useful in answering this question?

A manager using the static budget makes the following comparison:

Actual Electricity Cost	Budgeted Electricity Cost (static budget)	Cost Variance
$1,050	$1,200	$150 Favorable

This comparison suggests that operating personnel maintained excellent control over electricity costs during June, generating a favorable variance of $150. Is this a valid analysis and conclusion?

The fault with this analysis is that the manager is comparing the electricity cost incurred at the *actual* activity level, 3,000 tents, with the budgeted electricity cost at the *planned* activity level, 4,000 tents. Since these activity levels are different, we should expect the electricity cost to be different.

A more sensible approach is to compare the actual electricity cost incurred with the cost that should be incurred when 3,000 tents are manufactured. At this production level, 4,500 machine hours should be used (1.5 per tent). The flexible budget in Exhibit 17–1 shows that the manager should expect $900 of electricity cost at the 4,500 machine-hour level of activity. Therefore, an analysis based on the flexible budget gives the following comparison:

Actual ElectricityCost	Budgeted Electricity Cost (flexible budget)	CostVariance
$1,050	$900	$150 Unfavorable

Now the manager's conclusion is different; the revised analysis indicates an unfavorable variance. Electricity cost was higher than it should have been, given the actual level of output. The flexible budget provides the correct basis for comparison between actual and expected costs, given actual activity.

Activity Measure: Based on Input or Output?

Notice that the flexible budget for electricity cost in Exhibit 17–1 is based on machine hours, which is an *input* in the production process. The machine-hour activity levels shown in the flexible budget are the standard allowed machine hours given various levels of output. If 3,000 tents are produced, and the standard allowance per tent is 1.5 machine hours, the standard allowed number of machine hours is 4,500.

Why are the activity levels in the flexible budget based on machine hours, an *input* measure, instead of the number of tents produced, an *output* measure? When only a single product is manufactured, it makes no difference whether the flexible budget was based on input or output. In our illustration, either of the flexible budgets shown in Exhibit 17–2 could be used.

Now suppose that during July, Koala Camp Gear Company manufactured three different tent model products: 1,000 Tree Line, 1,500 River's Edge, and 600 Valley. The controller has assigned the following standards to these products.

Product Model	Standard Machine Hours per Unit
Tree Line	1.5
River's Edge	1.8
Valley	2.0

During July, Koala's production output was 2,800 tents. Is 2,800 tents a meaningful output measure? Adding numbers of Tree Line, River's Edge, and Valley model tents, which require different amounts of productive inputs, is like adding apples and oranges. It is not sensible to base a flexible budget for electricity cost on units of output when the output consists of different products with different electricity requirements. In this case, the flexible budget must be based on an *input* measure. The standard allowed number of machine hours for the July production is computed as follows:

Product Model	Units Produced	Standard Machine Hours per Unit	Total Standard Allowed Machine Hours
Tree Line	1,200	1.5	1,800
River's Edge	900	1.8	1,620
Valley	700	2.0	1,400
Total			4,820

Recall that Koala's cost-management analyst estimates electricity cost at $ .20 per machine hour. Thus, the flexible budget cost of electricity during July is computed as follows:

Standard allowed machine hours given July output	4,820
Electricity cost per machine hour	×$ .20
Flexible budget for electricity cost	$ 964

The important point here is that the number of *units of output* usually is not a meaningful measure in a multiproduct firm because it requires the addition of numbers of dissimilar products. To avoid this problem, output is measured in terms of the standard input allowed *given actual output*. Then it is possible to base the flexible overhead budget on this standard input measure.

Exhibit 17–2

Flexible Budgets: Input versus Output

Koala Camp Gear Company

1.5 standard machine hours allowed per tent

Flexible budget (based on input)

Activity: Standard machine hours allowed	4,500	6,000	7,500
Budgeted electricity cost	$900	$1,200	$1,500

Flexible budget (based on output)

Activity: Tents manufactured	3,000	4,000	5,000
Budgeted electricity cost	$900	$1,200	$1,500

In a multiproduct company, flexible budgets usually are based on standard inputs allowed (such as machine hours) rather than outputs (such as the number of tents manufactured).

Flexible-Overhead Budget Illustrated

Koala's monthly flexible-overhead budget appears in Exhibit 17–3. The overhead costs in the flexible budget are divided into variable and fixed costs. The total budgeted variable cost increases proportionately with increases in the activity. Thus, when the number of machine hours increases by 25 percent, from 6,000 hours to 7,500 hours, the total budgeted variable-overhead cost also increases by 25 percent, from $36,000 to $45,000. In contrast, the total budgeted fixed overhead does not change with increases in activity; it remains constant at $30,000 per month.

LO 2 Prepare and interpret a flexible overhead budget using formula and columnar formats.

Formula flexible budget.   When overhead costs can be divided into variable and fixed categories, we can express the flexible overhead budget differently. The format used in Exhibit 17–3 is called a *columnar flexible budget*. The budgeted overhead cost for each overhead item is listed in a column under a particular activity level. Notice that the columnar format allows for only a limited number of activity levels. Koala's flexible budget shows only three.

A more general format for expressing a flexible budget is called a *formula flexible budget*. In this format, the cost-management analyst expresses the relationship between activity and total budgeted overhead cost with the following formula.

$$\begin{array}{c}\text{Total budgeted}\\\text{monthly overhead}\\\text{cost}\end{array} = \left(\begin{array}{c}\text{Budgeted variable-}\\\text{overhead cost per}\\\text{activity unit}\end{array} \times \begin{array}{c}\text{Total}\\\text{activity}\\\text{units}\end{array}\right) + \begin{array}{c}\text{Budgeted fixed-}\\\text{overhead cost}\\\text{per month}\end{array}$$

To use this formula for Koala, we first compute the budgeted variable-overhead cost per machine hour. Dividing total budgeted variable-overhead cost by the associated activity level yields a budgeted variable-overhead rate of $6 per machine hour. Notice that we can use any activity level in Exhibit 17–3 to compute this rate.

$$\frac{\$27,000}{4,500} = \frac{\$36,000}{6,000} = \frac{\$45,000}{7,500} = \$6 \text{ per machine hour}$$

Koala's formula flexible-overhead budget is as follows:

$$\begin{array}{c}\text{Total budgeted}\\\text{monthly overhead}\\\text{cost}\end{array} = (\$6 \times \text{Total machine hours}) + \$30,000$$

To check the accuracy of the formula, compute the total budgeted overhead cost at each activity level shown in Exhibit 17–3.

Activity (machine hours)	Formula Flexible Overhead Budget	Budgeted Monthly Overhead Cost
4,500	$6 × 4,500 + $30,000 =	$57,000
6,000	$6 × 6,000 + $30,000 =	$66,000
7,500	$6 × 7,500 + $30,000 =	$75,000

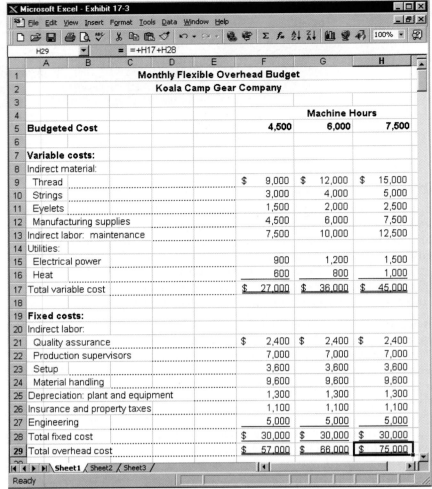

The budgeted monthly overhead cost computed here is the same as that shown in Exhibit 17–3 for each activity level.

    The formula flexible budget is more general than the columnar flexible budget because the formula allows the cost-management analyst to compute budgeted overhead costs at any activity level. Then the flexible-budgeted overhead cost can be used at the end of the period as a benchmark against which to compare the actual overhead costs incurred.

Overhead Application in a Standard-Costing System

Recall that *overhead application* refers to the addition of overhead cost to the Work-in-Process Inventory account as a product cost. In a normal-costing system, as described in Chapter 3, overhead is applied as shown in panel A of Exhibit 17–4. Overhead application is based on *actual* hours. In a standard-costing system, overhead application is based on *standard* hours allowed given actual output (panel B of Exhibit 17–4). Notice that the difference between normal costing and standard costing, insofar as overhead is concerned, lies in the quantity of hours used.

    Both normal-costing and standard-costing systems use a predetermined overhead rate (i.e., an overhead rate computed at the beginning of the accounting period). In a standard-costing system, the predetermined overhead rate is also referred to as the *standard overhead rate*. Koala Camp Gear Company calculates its predetermined or standard overhead rate annually. The rate for the current year, computed in Exhibit

A. Normal costing

Exhibit 17–4

Overhead Application

Manufacturing Overhead*	
Actual overhead	Applied overhead: *Actual hours* × Predetermined overhead rate

Work-in-Process Inventory
Applied overhead: *Actual hours* × Predetermined overhead rate

Difference lies in the quantity of hours used.

B. Standard costing

Manufacturing Overhead*	
Acutal overhead	Applied overhead: *Standard allowed hours* × Predetermined (or standard) overhead rate

Work-in-Process Inventory
Applied overhead: *Standard allowed hours* × Predetermined (or standard) overhead rate

*Many companies have only one Manufacturing Overhead account. Actual overhead is accumulated on the left-hand (debit) side of the account. Applied overhead is accumulated on the right-hand (credit) side of the account.

17–5, is based on *planned* activity of 6,000 machine hours per month. Notice that Koala breaks its predetermined overhead rate into a variable rate and a fixed rate.

We continue the discussion of the use of standard costs for product costing later in this chapter.

Choice of Activity Measure

Koala Camp Gear Company bases its flexible overhead budget on machine hours. Different companies use a variety of activity measures in practice. Machine hours, direct-labor hours, direct-labor cost, total process time, and direct-materials cost are among the most common measures.

LO 4 Discuss some important issues in choosing an activity measure for budgeting overhead.

Criteria for choosing the activity measure.   How should the cost-management analyst select the activity measure for the flexible budget? The activity measure should be one that varies in a similar pattern to the way that variable overhead varies. As productive activity increases, both variable-overhead cost and the activity measure should increase in roughly the same proportion. As productive activity declines, both variable-overhead cost and the activity measure should decline in roughly the same

Exhibit 17–5

Predetermined Overhead Rate: Koala Camp Gear Company

	Budgeted Overhead	Planned Monthly Activity	Predetermined Overhead Rate
Variable	$36,000*	6,000 machine hours	$ 6.00 per machine hour
Fixed	30,000*	6,000 machine hours	5.00 per machine hour
Total	$66,000	6,000 machine hours	$11.00 per machine hour

*From the flexible budget (Exhibit 17–3) for planned monthly activity of 6,000 machine hours.

Koala Camp Gear
Company

Increasing automation in manufacturing has resulted in direct labor becoming a less appropriate activity measure in flexible budgeting. Advanced manufacturing environments, such as flexible manufacturing systems (FMS) and computer-integrated manufacturing (CIM), have caused a shift in many companies' cost structures away from direct-labor cost and toward overhead costs. Pictured here are a labor-intensive shoe factory, and a high-tech circuit-board manufacturing robot in Seoul, South Korea.

proportion. In short, variable-overhead cost and the activity measure should *move together* as overall productive activity changes.

Impact of changing manufacturing technology.   Direct-labor time has traditionally been the most popular activity measure for manufacturing firms. However, as automation increases, more and more firms are switching to measures such as machine hours or process time for their flexible overhead budgets. Machine hours and process time are linked more closely than direct-labor hours to the robotic technology and computer-integrated manufacturing (CIM) systems common in today's manufacturing environment.

Dollar measures can be misleading.   Companies sometimes use dollar measures, such as direct-labor or raw-materials costs, as the basis for flexible-overhead budgeting. However, such measures have significant drawbacks. Dollar measures are subject to price-level changes and fluctuate more than physical measures. For example, the direct-labor *hours* required to manufacture a tent are relatively stable over time. However, the direct-labor *cost* varies as wage levels and fringe-benefit costs change with price-level changes in the economy.

The choice of an activity measure on which to base the flexible budget for variable overhead is really a problem in cost estimation, which Chapter 11 addresses.

Impact of Information Technology

Spreadsheet programs such as Excel® make flexible budgeting easier than traditional computing methods.[2] Once the variable cost rates have been determined, generating a flexible budget for any activity level is a simple exercise. (Refer to the Excel spreadsheet in Exhibit 17–3, which displays Koala Camp Gear's columnar flexible budget.)

Many businesses are adopting integrated business software packages that handle a broad range of computing needs such as customer and supplier databases, personnel and payroll functions, production scheduling and management, inventory records, financial accounting, and cost-management functions. Flexible budgeting typically is included in such software packages. Among the integrated software packages in wide use are PeopleSoft (www.peoplesoft.com) and the German product SAP, which stands for Systems Applications and Products in Data Processing (www.sap.com).

---

[2] Excel® is a registered trademark of Microsoft Corporation (www.microsoft.com).

Overhead Cost Variances

The flexible-overhead budget is the cost-management analyst's primary tool for controlling manufacturing-overhead costs using this traditional cost-management technique. At the end of each accounting period, the cost-management analyst uses the flexible-overhead budget to determine the level of overhead cost that should have been incurred, given the actual level of activity. Then the cost-management analyst compares the overhead cost in the flexible budget with the actual overhead cost incurred. The analyst then computes four separate overhead variances, each of which conveys information useful in managing overhead costs.

To illustrate overhead variance analysis, we continue our illustration of Koala Camp Gear Company.

LO 5 Compute and interpret the variable-overhead spending and efficiency variances and the fixed-overhead budget and volume variances.

Flexible Budget: Basis for Management of Overhead Cost

Koala's monthly flexible-overhead budget, displayed in Exhibit 17–3, shows budgeted variable and fixed manufacturing-overhead costs at three levels of production activity. During June, Koala manufactured 3,000 Tree Line tents. Since production standards allow 1.5 machine hours per tent, the total standard number of machine hours allowed is 4,500 hours, computed as follows.

Actual production output	3,000 Tree Line tents
Standard machine hours allowed per tent	$\times$ 1.5
Total standard machine hours allowed	4,500 machine hours

From the 4,500 machine-hours column in Exhibit 17–3, the budgeted overhead cost for June follows:

	Budgeted Overhead Cost for June
Variable overhead	$27,000
Fixed overhead	30,000

From the cost-accounting records, the controller determined that the following overhead costs were actually incurred during June:

	Actual Cost for June
Variable overhead	$30,480
Fixed overhead	32,500
Total overhead	$62,980

The production supervisor's records indicate that actual machine usage in June was:

Actual machine hours for June	4,800

Notice that the actual number of machine hours used (4,800) exceeds the standard number of machine hours allowed given actual production output (4,500).

We now have assembled all of the information necessary to compute Koala's overhead variances for June.

Variable-Overhead Variances

Koala's total variable-overhead variance for June is computed as follows:

Actual variable overhead	$30,480
Budgeted variable overhead	27,000
Total variable-overhead variance	$ 3,480 Unfavorable

What caused the company to spend $3,480 more than the budgeted amount on variable overhead? To discover the reasons behind this performance, the cost-management analyst computes a *variable-overhead spending variance* and a *variable-overhead efficiency variance.* The **variable-overhead spending variance** is the difference between the actual variable-overhead cost and the product of the standard variable-overhead rate and the actual quantity of an activity base (or cost driver). The **variable-overhead efficiency variance** is the difference between the actual and standard quantity of an activity base (or cost driver) multiplied by the standard variable-overhead rate. Exhibit 17–6 depicts the computation of these variances.

Two equivalent formulas for the variable-overhead spending variance follow.

1. **Variable-overhead**
    spending variance = Actual variable overhead − (AH × SVR)

or

2. **Variable-overhead**
    spending variance = (AH × AVR) − (AH × SVR)

where

> *AH* = **Actual machine hours**
> *AVR* = **Actual variable-overhead rate (actual variable overhead ÷ AH)**
> *SVR* = **Standard variable-overhead rate**

These two formulas are equivalent because actual variable overhead is equal to actual hours times the actual variable-overhead rate ($AH \times AVR$). Formula 2 can be simplified:

3. **Variable-overhead spending variance = AH(AVR − SVR)**

Koala's variable-overhead spending variance for June is computed as follows (using formula 1):

$$
\begin{aligned}
\text{Variable-overhead} \\
\text{spending variance} &= \text{Actual variable overhead} - (AH \times SVR) \\
&= \$30{,}480 - (4{,}800 \times \$6.00) \\
&= \$1{,}680 \text{ Unfavorable}
\end{aligned}
$$

Exhibit 17–6

Variable-Overhead Spending and Efficiency Variances

(1)	(2)	(3)	(4)*
Actual variable overhead	**Actual machine hours times the standard rate**	**Flexible budget: variable overhead**	**Variable overhead applied to work in process**
Actual machine hours × **Actual rate** **(AH)** × **(AVR)**	**Actual machine hours** × **Standard rate** **(AH)** × **(SVR)**	**Standard machine hours allowed** × **Standard rate** **(SH)** × **(SVR)**	**Standard machine hours allowed** × **Standard rate** **(SH)** × **(SVR)**
4,800 machine hours × \$6.35 per machine hour†	4,800 machine hours × \$6.00 per machine hour	4,500 machine hours × \$6.00 per machine hour	4,500 machine hours × \$6.00 per machine hour
\$30,480	\$28,800	\$27,000	\$27,000

\$1,680 Unfavorable	\$1,800 Unfavorable	No difference
Variable-overhead spending variance	**Variable-overhead efficiency variance**	

*Column (4) is not used to compute the variances. It is included to point out that the flexible-budget amount for variable overhead, $27,000, is the amount that will be applied to Work-in-Process Inventory for product-costing purposes.

† Actual variable-overhead rate $(AVR) = \dfrac{\text{Actual variable-overhead cost}}{\text{Actual machine hours}} = \dfrac{\$30{,}480}{4{,}800} = \$6.35$

This variance is unfavorable because the actual variable-overhead cost exceeded the expected amount after adjusting that expectation for the actual number of machine hours used.

As Exhibit 17–6 shows, the following formula defines the variable-overhead efficiency variance.

$$\text{Variable-overhead efficiency variance} = (AH \times SVR) - (SH \times SVR)$$

where

$$SH = \text{Standard machine hours}$$

Writing this formula more simply, we have the following expression:

$$\text{Variable-overhead efficiency variance} = SVR(AH - SH)$$

Koala's variable-overhead efficiency variance for June is computed as follows:

$$
\begin{aligned}
\text{Variable-overhead efficiency variance} &= SVR(AH - SH) \\
&= \$6.00\,(4{,}800 - 4{,}500) \\
&= \$1{,}800 \text{ Unfavorable}
\end{aligned}
$$

This variance is unfavorable because actual machine hours exceeded the standard machine hours allowed given actual output.

Cost-management versus product costing. Columns (1), (2), and (3) in Exhibit 17–6 are used to compute the variances for *cost-management purposes*. Column (4) is not needed to compute the variances, but it is included in the exhibit to show the variable overhead applied to work in process for the *product-costing purpose*. Notice that the variable-overhead cost on the flexible budget, $27,000, is the same as the amount applied to work-in-process.

Graph of variable-overhead variances. Exhibit 17–7 provides a graphical analysis of Koala's variable-overhead variances for June. The graph shows the variable-overhead rate per machine hour on the vertical axis. The standard rate is $6.00 per machine hour; the actual rate is $6.35 per machine hour (actual variable-overhead cost of $30,480 divided by 4,800 actual machine hours). Machine hours are shown on the horizontal axis.

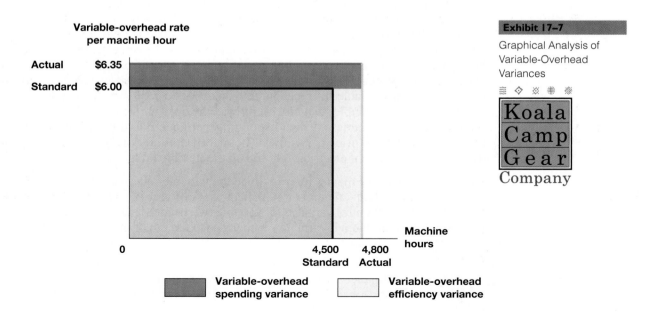

Exhibit 17–7

Graphical Analysis of Variable-Overhead Variances

Koala Camp Gear Company

The medium-shaded blue area on the graph represents the flexible-budget amount for variable overhead given actual June output of 3,000 Tree Line tents. The large area on the graph enclosed by colored lines on the top and right sides represents actual variable-overhead cost. The colored area between, representing the total variable-overhead variance, is divided into the spending and efficiency variances.

Managerial interpretation of variable-overhead variances. What do the variable-overhead variances mean? What information do they convey to management? The formulas for computing the variable-overhead variances resemble those used to compute the direct-labor variances. To see this, compare Exhibit 17–6 (variable overhead) with Exhibit 16–2 (direct labor).

Despite the similar formulas, the interpretation of the variable-overhead variances is quite different from that of the direct-labor variances.

How to interpret the efficiency variance. Recall that an unfavorable direct-labor efficiency variance results when more direct labor is used than the standard allowed quantity. Thus, direct labor has been used inefficiently relative to the standard. However, that is not the proper interpretation of an unfavorable variable-overhead efficiency variance. Koala's variable-overhead efficiency variance did *not* result from using more of the variable-overhead items, such as electricity and indirect materials, than the standard allowed amount. Instead, this variance resulted when Koala used *more machine hours* than the standard quantity given actual output. Recall that the cost-management analyst had found that variable-overhead cost varies in a pattern similar to the way machine hours vary. Since 300 more machine hours were used than the standard quantity allowed, the division's management should expect that variable-overhead costs will be higher. Thus, the variable-overhead efficiency variance has nothing to do with efficient or inefficient usage of electricity, indirect material, and other variable-overhead items. This variance simply reflects an adjustment in the cost-management analyst's expectation about total variable-overhead cost because the company used more than the standard quantity of machine hours.

What is the important difference between direct labor and variable overhead that causes this different interpretation of the efficiency variance? Direct labor is a traceable cost and is budgeted on the basis of direct-labor hours. Variable overhead, on the other hand, is a pool of *indirect* costs that are budgeted on the basis of *machine hours*. The indirect nature of variable-overhead costs causes the different interpretation.

What does the spending variance reveal? An unfavorable direct-labor rate variance is straightforward to interpret; the actual labor rate *per hour* exceeds the standard rate. Although the formula for computing the variable-overhead spending variance is similar to that for the direct-labor rate variance, its interpretation is quite different.

An unfavorable spending variance simply means that the total actual cost of variable overhead is higher than expected after adjusting for the actual quantity of machine hours used. An unfavorable spending variance could result from paying a higher than expected price per unit for variable-overhead items. The variance also could result from using more of the variable-overhead items than expected based on the flexible budget.

Suppose, for example, that electricity was the only variable-overhead cost item. An unfavorable variable-overhead spending variance could result from paying a higher than expected price per kilowatt-hour for electricity or from using more than the expected amount of electricity (based on the flexible budget), or both.

Variable-overhead cost management. Since the variable-overhead efficiency variance indicates nothing about efficient or inefficient usage of variable overhead, the spending variance is the real control variance for variable overhead. Managers can use the spending variance to alert them if variable-overhead costs are out of line with expectations.

Fixed-Overhead Variances

To analyze performance with regard to fixed overhead, the cost-management analyst calculates two fixed-overhead variances: the fixed-overhead budget variance and the fixed-overhead volume variance.

Fixed-overhead budget variance.   The variance that managers use to control fixed overhead is called the *fixed-overhead budget variance.* The **fixed-overhead budget variance** is the difference between actual fixed overhead and budgeted fixed overhead. It is computed as follows:

$$\begin{array}{l}\text{Fixed-overhead} \\ \text{budget variance} = \text{Actual fixed overhead} - \text{Budgeted fixed overhead}\end{array}$$

Koala's fixed-overhead budget variance for June is computed as follows:

$$\begin{array}{ll}\text{Fixed-overhead} \\ \text{budget variance} = \text{Actual fixed overhead} &- \text{Budgeted fixed overhead} \\ \quad\quad\quad\quad = \$32,500 &- \$30,000^* \\ \quad\quad\quad\quad = \$2,500 \text{ Unfavorable}\end{array}$$

*From the flexible budget (Exhibit 17–3).

The fixed-overhead budget variance is unfavorable because Koala spent more than the budgeted amount on fixed overhead. Notice that we need not specify an activity level to determine budgeted fixed overhead. All three columns in the flexible budget (Exhibit 17–3) specify $30,000 as budgeted fixed overhead.

Fixed-overhead volume variance.   The **fixed-overhead volume variance** is the difference between budgeted fixed overhead and applied fixed overhead. It is computed as follows:

$$\begin{array}{l}\text{Fixed-overhead} \\ \text{volume variance} = \text{Budgeted fixed overhead} - \text{Applied fixed overhead}\end{array}$$

Koala's applied fixed overhead for June is $22,500, which is computed as follows:

$$\begin{array}{lll}\text{Applied fixed overhead} = \text{Predetermined fixed-} &\times \text{Standard hours} \\ \quad\quad\quad\quad\quad\quad\quad\quad \text{overhead rate} &\quad\text{allowed} \\ \quad\quad \$22,500 \quad = \$5 \text{ per machine hour} &\times \ 4,500 \text{ machine} \\ &\quad\quad\quad\quad\quad \text{hours}\end{array}$$

The $5 predetermined fixed-overhead rate was calculated in Exhibit 17–5. The 4,500 standard machine hours allowed is based on actual June production of 3,000 tents, each with a standard allowance of 1.5 machine hours.

Koala's fixed-overhead volume variance is calculated as follows:

$$\begin{array}{ll}\text{Fixed-overhead} \\ \text{volume variance} = \text{Budgeted fixed overhead} &- \text{Applied fixed overhead} \\ \quad\quad\quad\quad = \$30,000 &- \$22,500 \\ \quad\quad\quad\quad = \$7,500 \text{ Unfavorable}\end{array}$$

Managerial interpretation of fixed-overhead variances.   Exhibit 17–8 shows Koala's two fixed-overhead variances for June. The budget variance is the real control variance for fixed overhead because it compares actual expenditures with budgeted fixed-overhead costs.

The volume variance provides a way to reconcile two different purposes of the cost-accounting system. For the *cost-management purpose,* the cost-accounting system recognizes that fixed overhead does not change as production activity varies. Hence, budgeted fixed overhead is the same at all activity levels in the flexible budget. (Review Exhibit 17–3 to verify this.) Budgeted fixed overhead is the basis for controlling fixed overhead because it provides the benchmark against which actual expenditures are compared.

For the *product-costing purpose* of the cost-accounting system, budgeted fixed overhead is divided by planned activity to obtain a predetermined (or standard) fixed-overhead rate. For Koala, this rate is $5 per machine hour (budgeted fixed overhead of $30,000 divided by *planned* activity of 6,000 machine hours). This predetermined rate is then used to apply fixed overhead to Work-in-Process Inventory. During any

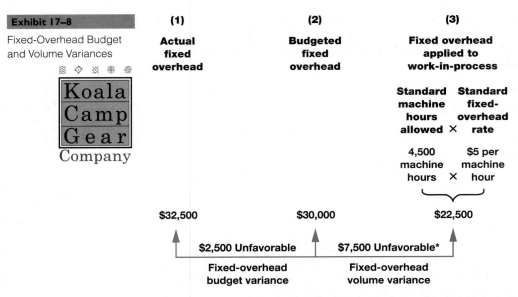

Exhibit 17–8

Fixed-Overhead Budget and Volume Variances

Koala Camp Gear Company

*Consistent with our discussion of the fixed-overhead volume variance, some accountants would designate a positive variance as unfavorable.

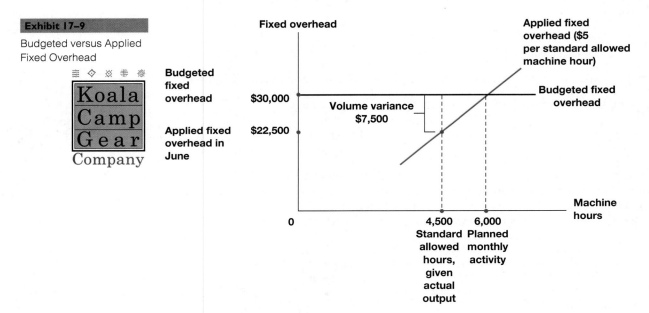

Exhibit 17–9

Budgeted versus Applied Fixed Overhead

Koala Camp Gear Company

period in which the standard number of machine hours allowed, given actual output, differs from the planned level of machine hours, budgeted fixed overhead will differ from applied fixed overhead.

Exhibit 17–9 illustrates this point graphically. Budgeted fixed overhead is constant at $30,000 for all levels of activity. However, applied fixed overhead increases with activity since fixed overhead is applied to Work-in-Process Inventory at the rate of $5 per standard machine hour allowed. Notice that budgeted and applied fixed overhead are equal *only* if the number of standard hours allowed equals the planned activity level of 6,000 machine hours. When this happens, no fixed-overhead volume variance exists. Koala has a $7,500 volume variance in June because the standard hours allowed and planned hours are different.

Capacity utilization.   A common, but faulty, interpretation of a positive volume variance is that it measures the cost of underutilizing productive capacity. The reasoning behind this view is that the planned activity level used to compute the predetermined fixed-overhead rate is a measure of normal capacity utilization. Moreover, fixed-overhead

International Use of Flexible Budgeting to Control Costs

Flexible budgeting as a means of controlling overhead costs is found in cost-management systems worldwide. In Germany, for example, *grenzplankostenrechnung* (or "flexible standard costing") exhibits many of the features illustrated in this chapter. Under the German approach "each cost center distinguishes between variable costs (e.g., energy) and fixed costs (e.g., a manager's salary)." The number of machine hours is a common activity measure. "For purposes of cost planning and control, companies budget each cost center's expenses and then distribute the expenses to each month of the budgeted year. The budgeted costs are standards for efficient resource consumption. . . ." The cost and performance information "allows for effective discussions about productivity improvement" among department managers, management accountants, and plant managers. (Refer to Research Insight 16.1 for more information on *grenzplankostenrechnung*.) *Source: P. Sharman,* "German Cost Accounting," *and B. Gaiser,* "German Cost Management Systems." (Full citations to references are in the Bibliography.)

Research Insight 17.1

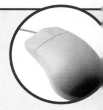

costs such as depreciation and property taxes are costs incurred to create productive capacity. Therefore, the predetermined fixed-overhead rate measures the cost to provide an hour of productive capacity. If 6,000 machine hours are planned, but output is such that only 4,500 standard machine hours are allowed, capacity has been underutilized by 1,500 hours. Since each hour costs $5 (Koala's predetermined fixed-overhead rate), the cost of underutilization is $7,500 (1,500 × $5), which is Koala's volume variance.

The fault with this interpretation of the volume variance is that it ignores the real cost of underutilizing productive capacity. The real cost results from the lost contribution margins of the products *not* produced when capacity is underutilized. Moreover, this interpretation fails to recognize that underutilizing capacity and reducing inventory could be a wise managerial response to slackening demand.

For this reason, we interpret the volume variance merely as a way to reconcile the two purposes of the cost-accounting system. Some accountants designate a positive volume variance as *unfavorable*. Their reasoning is that when the volume variance is closed to Cost of Goods Sold expense at the end of the accounting period (as explained later in the chapter), the effect is to increase cost of goods sold, which in turn has an unfavorable effect on income. In contrast, other accountants argue that no sign (favorable or unfavorable) should be assigned to the volume variance.

What Do Four-Way, Three-Way, and Two-Way Variance Analyses Tell the Cost Manager?

Four variances were discussed in the preceding two sections: the variable-overhead spending and efficiency variances and the fixed-overhead budget and volume variances. Some managers prefer to combine the variable-overhead spending and fixed-overhead budget variances into a single *combined spending variance*. Since this presentation leaves only three separate variances, it is called a *three-way analysis*. Other managers prefer to combine the variable-overhead spending, variable-overhead efficiency, and

Overhead Variances

In December, Koala Camp Gear Company produced 3,600 Tree Line tents, used 5,700 machine hours, and incurred the following manufacturing-overhead costs:

Variable overhead	$37,050
Fixed overhead	29,000

Koala's monthly flexible overhead budget for December is the same as that given in Exhibit 17–3.

a. Compute Koala's variable-overhead variances using the format shown in Exhibit 17–6. Compute the company's fixed-overhead variances using the format shown in Exhibit 17–8.

b. How should Koala's management interpret the fixed-overhead budget variance?

c. Under what circumstances would there have been no fixed-overhead volume variance for Koala Camp Gear's December operations?

(Solutions begin on page 722.)

You're the Decision Maker 17.1

Exhibit 17–10

Four-Way, Three-Way, and Two-Way Variance Analyses: Koala Camp Gear Company

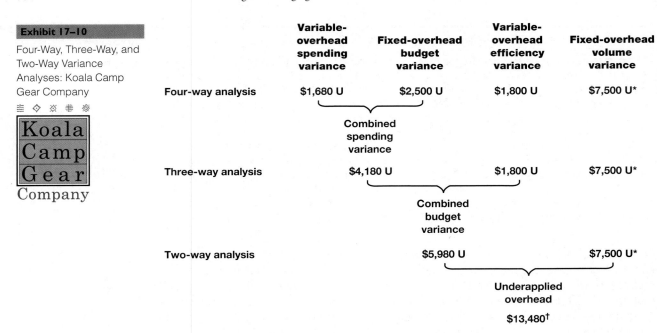

	Variable-overhead spending variance	Fixed-overhead budget variance	Variable-overhead efficiency variance	Fixed-overhead volume variance
Four-way analysis	$1,680 U	$2,500 U	$1,800 U	$7,500 U*
		Combined spending variance		
Three-way analysis	$4,180 U		$1,800 U	$7,500 U*
			Combined budget variance	
Two-way analysis		$5,980 U		$7,500 U*
			Underapplied overhead $13,480†	

*The volume variance is positive since budgeted fixed overhead is higher than applied fixed overhead. Consistent with the discussion in the preceding section, some accountants would designate it as unfavorable.

†The underapplied overhead, $13,480, is the difference between actual overhead, $62,980, and overhead applied to Work-in-Process Inventory, $49,500 ($27,000 variable + $22,500 fixed).

fixed-overhead budget variances into a single *combined budget variance*. Since this presentation leaves only two separate variances, it is called a *two-way analysis*. Exhibit 17–10 displays the four-way, three-way, and two-way variance analyses for Koala's June performance.

Using the Overhead Cost Performance Report in Cost Management

LO 6 Prepare and interpret an overhead cost performance report.

The variable-overhead spending and efficiency variances and the fixed-overhead budget variance can be computed for each overhead cost item in the flexible budget. When these itemized variances are presented along with actual and budgeted costs for each overhead item, the result is an *overhead cost performance report*. An **overhead cost performance report** shows the actual and flexible-budget cost levels for each overhead item, together with the variable-overhead spending and efficiency variances and the fixed-overhead budget variance. Koala's performance report is displayed in Exhibit 17–11. Management would use this report to exercise control over each of the division's overhead costs.

Notice that the performance report includes only spending and efficiency variances for the variable items and only a budget variance for the fixed items. Upon receiving this report, a manager might investigate the relatively large variances for indirect material (thread), indirect labor (maintenance), and engineering.

Research Insight 17.2

Performance Reports

A recent survey of US manufacturers found that 96 percent of the responding companies' prepare periodic performance reports including variances from standard costs for management. However, 62 percent of the respondents believed that the reports contained too much detail, and only 41 percent of the responding production managers believed their reports to be timely. Just 37 percent of the survey respondents believed that their performance reports enabled them to assign responsibility for the variances. A need for improvement in the performance reporting system was suggested by 71 percent of the surveyed managers. *Source: S. A. Moscove,* "Enhancing Detective Controls through Performance Reporting."

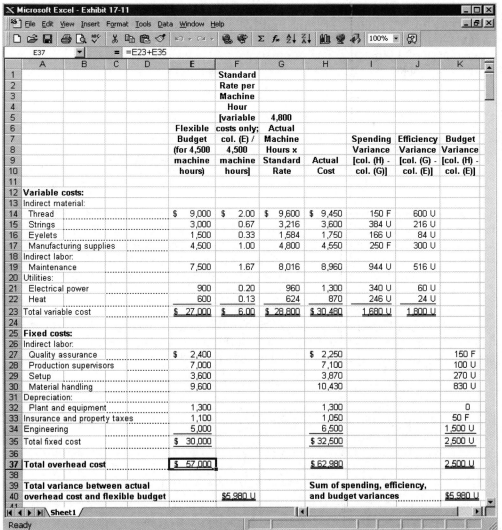

Exhibit 17–11

Overhead Cost
Performance Report:
Koala Camp Gear
Company

The spreadsheet shows:

	Flexible Budget (for 4,500 machine hours)	Standard Rate per Machine Hour [variable costs only; col. (E) / 4,500 machine hours]	4,800 Actual Machine Hours x Standard Rate	Actual Cost	Spending Variance [col. (H) - col. (G)]	Efficiency Variance [col. (G) - col. (E)]	Budget Variance [col. (H) - col. (E)]
Variable costs:							
Indirect material:							
Thread	$ 9,000	$ 2.00	$ 9,600	$ 9,450	150 F	600 U	
Strings	3,000	0.67	3,216	3,600	384 U	216 U	
Eyelets	1,500	0.33	1,584	1,750	166 U	84 U	
Manufacturing supplies	4,500	1.00	4,800	4,550	250 F	300 U	
Indirect labor:							
Maintenance	7,500	1.67	8,016	8,960	944 U	516 U	
Utilities:							
Electrical power	900	0.20	960	1,300	340 U	60 U	
Heat	600	0.13	624	870	246 U	24 U	
Total variable cost	$ 27,000	$ 6.00	$ 28,800	$ 30,480	1,680 U	1,800 U	
Fixed costs:							
Indirect labor:							
Quality assurance	$ 2,400			$ 2,250			150 F
Production supervisors	7,000			7,100			100 U
Setup	3,600			3,870			270 U
Material handling	9,600			10,430			830 U
Depreciation:							
Plant and equipment	1,300			1,300			0
Insurance and property taxes	1,100			1,050			50 F
Engineering	5,000			6,500			1,500 U
Total fixed cost	$ 30,000			$ 32,500			2,500 U
Total overhead cost	$ 57,000			$ 62,980			2,500 U
Total variance between actual overhead cost and flexible budget		$5,980 U		**Sum of spending, efficiency, and budget variances**			$5,980 U

Cell reference: E37 =E23+E35

Using Standard Costs in Product Costing

A standard-costing system uses the standard costs for product costing as well as for cost control. The costs of direct material, direct labor, and manufacturing overhead are all entered into Work-in-Process Inventory at their standard costs. (Review Exhibit 17–4.)

LO 7 Record manufacturing overhead under standard costing by preparing journal entries.

Journal Entries under Standard Costing

During June, Koala incurred actual manufacturing-overhead costs of $62,980, which include $30,480 of variable overhead and $32,500 of fixed overhead. A summary journal entry to record these actual expenditures follows:

Manufacturing Overhead	62,980	
Indirect-Material Inventory		19,350*
Wages Payable		32,610*
Utilities Payable		2,170
Accumulated Depreciation		1,300
Prepaid Insurance and Property Taxes		1,050
Engineering Salaries Payable		6,500

*The credit amounts can be verified in column H of Exhibit 17–11. For example, indirect-material costs amounted to $19,350 ($9,450 + $3,600 + $1,750 + $4,550). The credit to Wages Payable is for indirect-labor costs, which amounted to $32,610 ($8,960 + $2,250 + $7,100 + $3,870 + $10,430).

The application of manufacturing overhead to Work-in-Process Inventory is based on a predetermined overhead rate of $11 per machine hour (the total of the variable and the fixed rates) and 4,500 standard machine hours allowed given an actual output of 3,000 tents. The summary journal entry is:

Work-in-Process Inventory	49,500	
Manufacturing Overhead		49,500*

*Applied overhead = $11.00 × 4,500 = $49,500.

Now the Manufacturing Overhead account appears as follows:

Manufacturing Overhead			
Actual	62,980	49,500	Applied

The *underapplied overhead* for June is $13,480 ($62,980 − $49,500). This means that the overhead applied to Work-in-Process Inventory in June was $13,480 less than the actual overhead cost incurred. Notice that the underapplied overhead equals the sum of the four overhead variances for June. The total of the four overhead variances always equals the overapplied or underapplied overhead for the accounting period.

Disposition of Variances

As explained in Chapter 16, variances are temporary accounts, and most companies close them directly to Cost of Goods Sold at the end of each accounting period. The journal entry required to close out Koala's underapplied overhead for June is:

Cost of Goods Sold	13,480	
Manufacturing Overhead		13,480

The journal entry to close underapplied or overapplied overhead typically is made annually rather than monthly.

An alternative accounting treatment is to prorate (or allocate) underapplied or overapplied overhead among Work-in-Process Inventory, Finished-Goods Inventory, and Cost of Goods Sold, as explained in Appendix A to this chapter.

Activity-Based Flexible Budget

LO 8 Explain why an activity-based flexible budget can provide more useful cost-management information than a conventional flexible budget.

The flexible budget shown in Exhibit 17–3, which underlies our variance analysis for Koala Camp Gear Company, is based on a single cost driver. Overhead costs that vary with respect to *machine hours* are categorized as variable; all other overhead costs are treated as fixed. This approach is consistent with traditional, volume-based product-costing systems.

Under the more accurate product-costing method called *activity-based costing* (ABC), several cost drivers are identified.[3] Costs that could appear fixed with respect to a single volume-based cost driver, such as machine hours, can be variable with respect to other appropriate cost drivers. The activity-based costing approach also can be used as the basis for a flexible budget for planning and cost-management purposes. Exhibit 17–12 displays an *activity-based flexible budget* for Koala, using the same data as Exhibit 17–3. An **activity-based flexible budget** is based on several cost drivers rather than a single, volume-based cost driver.

Compare the conventional flexible budget (Exhibit 17–3) and the activity-based flexible budget (Exhibit 17–12). The key difference lies in the costs that were categorized as fixed on the conventional flexible budget. These costs *are* fixed with respect to machine hours but are *not* fixed with respect to other more appropriate cost drivers. For example, cost pool II includes quality assurance and setup costs, which vary with respect to the number of production runs.

---

[3] Activity-based costing is covered in Chapter 4.

Exhibit 17–12

Activity-Based Flexible
Budget

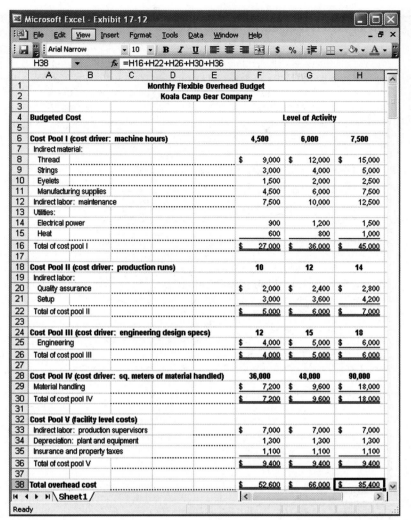

Microsoft Excel - Exhibit 17-12

H38 =H16+H22+H26+H30+H36

		Level of Activity		
Monthly Flexible Overhead Budget				
Koala Camp Gear Company				
Budgeted Cost				
Cost Pool I (cost driver: machine hours)	4,500	6,000	7,500
Indirect material:				
Thread	$ 9,000	$ 12,000	$ 15,000
Strings	3,000	4,000	5,000
Eyelets	1,500	2,000	2,500
Manufacturing supplies	4,500	6,000	7,500
Indirect labor: maintenance	7,500	10,000	12,500
Utilities:				
Electrical power	900	1,200	1,500
Heat	600	800	1,000
Total of cost pool I	$ 27,000	$ 36,000	$ 45,000
Cost Pool II (cost driver: production runs)	10	12	14
Indirect labor:				
Quality assurance	$ 2,000	$ 2,400	$ 2,800
Setup	3,000	3,600	4,200
Total of cost pool II	$ 5,000	$ 6,000	$ 7,000
Cost Pool III (cost driver: engineering design specs)	12	15	18
Engineering	$ 4,000	$ 5,000	$ 6,000
Total of cost pool III	$ 4,000	$ 5,000	$ 6,000
Cost Pool IV (cost driver: sq. meters of material handled)	36,000	48,000	90,000
Material handling	$ 7,200	$ 9,600	$ 18,000
Total of cost pool IV	$ 7,200	$ 9,600	$ 18,000
Cost Pool V (facility level costs)				
Indirect labor: production supervisors	$ 7,000	$ 7,000	$ 7,000
Depreciation: plant and equipment	1,300	1,300	1,300
Insurance and property taxes	1,100	1,100	1,100
Total of cost pool V	$ 9,400	$ 9,400	$ 9,400
Total overhead cost	$ 52,600	$ 66,000	$ 85,400

How Does ABC Affect Performance Reporting?

The activity-based flexible budget provides a more accurate prediction (and benchmark) of overhead costs. For example, suppose that activity in August is as follows:

Machine hours	7,500
Production runs	14
Engineering design specs	12
Direct material handled (sq. meters)	90,000

The following table compares the budgeted cost levels for several overhead items on the conventional and activity-based flexible budgets.

Overhead Cost Item	Conventional Flexible Budget (Exhibit 17–3)	Activity-Based Flexible Budget (Exhibit 17–12)
Electrical power	$1,500	$ 1,500
Quality assurance	2,400	2,800
Setup	3,600	4,200
Material handling	9,600	18,000
Engineering	5,000	4,000
Insurance and property taxes	1,100	1,100

The budgeted electrical power is the same on both budgets because both use the same cost driver (machine hours). Insurance and property taxes are also the same because both budgets recognize them as facility-level fixed costs. However, the other overhead

Cost Management in Practice 17.1

Activity-Based Budgeting at Whirlpool

When managers at Whirlpool Corporation's (www.whirlpool.com) Evansville, Indiana, plant developed their activity-based costing system, more accurate information for budgeting was high on the list of priorities. The Evansville plant's product lines included 333 different refrigerator and vertical freezer models. These products exhibited a wide range of complexity, and the annual production volume ranged from a single unit to 12,000 units. The ABC cost hierarchy in Whirlpool's system designated costs at the following five levels: unit, batch, product, process, and plant. Among the cost drivers used were the following:

- Setups
- Purchase orders
- Assembly complexity
- Engineering change orders
- Receipts

- Design complexity
- Machine hours
- Inspections
- Scrap dollars
- Direct-labor hours

One of the main objectives of a flexible budgeting system is to enable management to predict cost incurrence at different levels of production for each type of product. At Whirlpool, management found that its traditional accounting system significantly distorted product costs. The traditional system, which budgeted overhead costs on the basis of either machine hours or direct-labor hours, undercosted low-volume products and overcosted high-volume products. "An interesting but extreme example of this phenomenon involved the overhead comparison for a product with an annual production rate of one unit. Under the traditional system, this product carried an overhead burden of $64.48, whereas the overhead assigned by the ABC system was a whopping $25,447.11." More typical of the results, though, is the following comparison among three of Whirlpool's product lines.

Production Volume Class	Annual Production Volume	Traditional Overhead Assigned	ABC Overhead Assigned	Percentage Change in Assigned Overhead
Low	292	$66.23	$132.55	100.1%
Medium	2,959	67.91	56.46	(16.9)
High	12,000	64.17	42.92	(33.1)

The main cause of such cost distortion is that many of Whirlpool's production costs are not unit-level costs. Thus, the traditional system, which budgets overhead on the basis of a unit-level cost driver (either machine hours or direct-labor hours), cannot possibly capture the consumption of (support department) overhead costs by product lines with widely differing production volumes. An ABC system enables management to budget production costs much more accurately by accounting for the many overhead costs that are batch-, product-, process-, or plant-level costs. "In the past decade, Whirlpool has faced increasing competition, higher overhead, and greater product diversity. Managers initiated and supported the ABC pilot program to obtain accurate information for dealing with these challenges." *Source: C. B. Greeson and M. C. Kocakulah, "Implementing an ABC Pilot at Whirlpool."*

costs are budgeted at different levels because the conventional and activity-based flexible budgets use *different cost drivers* for these items. The conventional budget treats quality assurance, setup, materials-handling, and engineering costs as fixed, but the activity-based flexible budget shows that they are all variable with respect to the appropriate cost driver.

These differences are important for performance reporting. The activity-based flexible budget provides a more accurate benchmark against which to compare actual costs. Suppose that the actual quality assurance cost in August is $2,700. Using the conventional flexible budget would result in an unfavorable variance of $300 ($2,700 − $2,400). However, the activity-based flexible budget yields a favorable variance of $100 ($2,800 − $2,700).[4]

---

[4] For further reading on this topic, see R. E. Malcolm, "Overhead Control Implications of Activity Costing"; Y. T. Mak and M. L. Roush, "Flexible Budgeting and Variance Analysis in an Activity-Based Costing Environment"; and R. S. Kaplan, "Flexible Budgeting in an Activity-Based Costing Framework." (Full citations to references are in the Bibliography.)

Other Issues in Variance Analysis

We conclude the chapter with a brief mention of two other issues in variance analysis, which we explore in detail in Appendices B and C.

Standard Costing in a Just-in-Time Environment

A just-in-time manufacturing setting, with demand-pull of products through the manufacturing process, minimizes inventories. As a result, some companies have simplified their accounting system by charging all manufacturing costs directly to Cost of Goods Sold. This method of accounting, known as *backflush costing,* is explained in detail in Appendix B to this chapter. [Also, see Chapter 7 for a discussion of just-in-time (JIT) production and inventory management systems.]

Sales-Variance Analysis

We have concentrated in this chapter on *cost* variance analysis as a tool for cost management. Equally important in affecting a company's bottom line, though, is its *sales* performance. The sales price and the sales volume of each product have a significant impact on a company's revenue, contribution margin, and profit. Appendix C to this chapter covers *sales variance analysis,* a technique used to help management understand and manage the effects of the company's sales performance on its profitability.

Chapter Summary

Overhead is a heterogeneous pool of indirect costs. Since it is not easy to trace overhead costs to products or services, a flexible budget specifies budgeted overhead costs at various levels of activity. A columnar flexible budget is based on several distinct activity levels, and a formula flexible budget is valid for a continuous range of activity. A conventional flexible overhead budget is based on some activity measure, or cost driver, that varies in a pattern similar to that of variable overhead. Machine hours, process time, and direct-labor hours are common cost drivers.

In a standard-costing system, the flexible budget is used to manage overhead costs. The cost-management analyst uses the amount of overhead cost specified by the flexible budget as a benchmark against which to compare actual overhead costs. The analyst computes four overhead variances: the variable-overhead spending and efficiency variances and the fixed-overhead budget and volume variances. These variances help management to control overhead costs.

The standard or predetermined overhead rate also is used as the basis for product costing in a standard-costing system. The amount of overhead cost entered into Work-in-Process Inventory equals the standard overhead rate multiplied by the standard amount of the cost driver allowed, or activity base, given actual output.

With an activity-based costing system, the development of an activity-based flexible budget is possible. Such a flexible budget is more accurate than conventional flexible budgets because multiple cost drivers are identified to explain the behavior of overhead costs.

Appendix A to Chapter Seventeen

Proration of Cost Variances

The direct-materials, direct-labor, and manufacturing overhead variances computed in this and the preceding chapter are *temporary accounts.* They are computed as a cost-management tool to direct management's attention to situations that could require their intervention. At the end of an accounting period, most companies close all of the variances to Cost of Goods Sold. This approach was demonstrated in the Koala Camp Gear illustration.

Some companies use a more accurate procedure to dispose of variances. This approach recognizes that underestimation or overestimation of the production costs affects not only Cost of Goods Sold but also Work-in-Process Inventory and Finished-Goods Inventory. As the following display shows, direct materials, direct

LO 9 Prorate variances among the relevant accounts.

labor, and applied overhead pass through all three of these accounts. Therefore, all three accounts are affected by any deviation from the standards.

Proration is the process of allocating cost variances to Work-in-Process Inventory, Finished-Goods Inventory, and Cost of Goods Sold. The amount of the current period's standard cost remaining in each account is the basis for the proration procedure.

Among the companies that prorate cost variances are those required to do so under the rules specified by the *Cost Accounting Standards Board (CASB)*. The **Cost Accounting Standards Board (CASB)** is a federal agency chartered by Congress in 1970 to develop cost-accounting standards for large government contractors. Congress discontinued the agency in 1980 but recreated it in 1990. The standards set forth by the agency apply to significant government contracts and have the force of federal law in the United States.

Illustration of Variance Proration

Koala Camp Gear Company recently added a second product to its Camp Foods product line. In addition to trail mix, sold under the name Crocodile Chomp, Koala now produces an instant-drink powder brand-named Kiwi Boost. The instant drink is a mix of dried fruit powders, sugar, and vitamins designed to provide quick energy and essential nutrients on the trail.

During September, Koala purchased 5,000 kilograms of the raw materials used to make Kiwi Boost. The following table shows what happened to the purchased materials during the month. As the table indicates, 1,500 kilograms of the materials remained in raw-materials inventory on September 30, and the remaining 3,500 kilograms were consumed in production.

Remaining in Raw-Material Inventory on 9/30	1,500 kilograms
Standard quantity allowed in Work-in-Process Inventory on 9/30	500 kilograms
Standard quantity allowed in Finished-Goods Inventory on 9/30	750 kilograms
Standard quantity allowed in Cost of Goods Sold for September	1,250 kilograms
Amount consumed in production in excess of standard quantity allowed during September	1,000 kilograms
Total quantity purchased in September	5,000 kilograms

The standard costs to produce Kiwi Boost are given in Exhibit 17–13. The exhibit also includes the variances computed for September. Notice that 1,000 of the 5,000 kilograms of raw materials purchased were consumed by inefficiency and are reflected in the unfavorable direct-materials quantity variance. Therefore, we can account for the 5,000 kilograms of material purchased as follows:

Remaining in Raw-Material Inventory (1,500 kilograms)	30%
In the unfavorable quantity variance (1,000 kilograms)	20
In Work-in-Process Inventory (500 kilograms)	10
In Finished-Goods Inventory (750 kilograms)	15
In Cost of Goods Sold (1,250 kilograms)	25
Total purchased amount accounted for (5,000 kilograms)	100%

An analysis of the labor records shows that 20 percent of the standard direct-labor hours allowed for September were related to the units remaining in Work-in-Process Inventory

	Standard Cost	Variance
Direct material:		
Purchases (added to Raw-Material Inventory at standard price):		
5,000 kilograms × $1.00 per kilogram	$ 5,000	
Standard cost: 2,500 kilograms × $1.00 per kilogram	2,500	
(1) Price variance: $PQ(AP - SP)$ = 5,000($1.30 − $1.00)		1,500 U
(2) Quantity variance: $SP(AQ - SQ)$ = $1.00(3,500 − 2,500)		1,000 U
Direct labor:		
Standard cost: 500 hours × $25.00 per hour	12,500	
(3) Rate variance: $AH(AR - SR)$ = 600($25.50 − $25.00)		300 U
(4) Efficiency variance: $SR(AH - SH)$ = $25.00(600 − 500)		2,500 U
Variable overhead (applied based on direct-labor hours):		
Standard cost: 500 hours × $10.00 per hour	5,000	
(5) Spending variance: Actual variable overhead − $(AH)(SVR)$		
= $5,400 − (600)($10.00)		600 F
(6) Efficiency variance: $SVR(AH - SH)$ = $10.00(600 − 500)		1,000 U
Fixed overhead (applied based on direct-labor hours):		
Budgeted cost: 700 hours × $20.00 per hour	14,000	
(7) Budget variance: Actual fixed overhead − Budgeted fixed overhead		
= $12,800 − $14,000		1,200 F
(8) Volume variance: Budgeted fixed overhead − Applied fixed overhead		
= $14,000 − (500 hours) ($20.00 per hour)		4,000 U
Total of all variances		$8,500 U

Exhibit 17–13

Standard Costs and September Variances in the Production of Kiwi Boost

Koala Camp Gear Company

on September 30; 30 percent of the standard direct-labor hours allowed were related to Finished-Goods Inventory; and 50 percent of the hours were related to Cost of Goods Sold.

The proration of variances is illustrated in Exhibit 17–14. The eight variances are prorated to each manufacturing account in proportion to the standard amount of the period's inputs remaining in that account at the end of the period. For example, 30 percent of the 5,000 kilograms of materials purchased remained in the Raw-Materials Inventory account. Therefore, 30 percent of the unfavorable direct-materials price variance is prorated to the Raw-Materials Inventory account. The balance in the account will be increased by $450 (.30 × $1,500). Since the direct-materials quantity variance is calculated using the standard price, the quantity variance is adjusted to reflect the actual price of the materials before the quantity variance is prorated. Thus, the actual cost of inefficiently consuming 1,000 kilograms of material is not $1,000 but is $1,300 (1,000 kilograms consumed inefficiently × $1.30 per kilogram). The adjusted quantity variance then is prorated to the accounts affected by efficiency (i.e., the Work-in-Process Inventory, Finished-Goods Inventory, and Cost of Goods Sold accounts). The adjusted quantity variance is not prorated to the Raw-Material Inventory account because efficiency is a concept that applies only to the production process, not to materials that remain in raw-materials inventory.

The following journal entry is required to prorate the variances, as computed in Exhibit 17–14.

Raw-Material Inventory	450	
Work-in-Process Inventory	1,610	
Finished-Goods Inventory	2,415	
Cost of Goods Sold	4,025	
Variable-Overhead Spending Variance	600	
Fixed-Overhead Budget Variance	1,200	
Direct-Material Price Variance		1,500
Direct-Material Quantity Variance		1,000
Direct-Labor Rate Variance		300
Direct-Labor Efficiency Variance		2,500
Variable-Overhead Efficiency Variance		1,000
Fixed-Overhead Volume Variance		4,000

Exhibit 17–14

Proration of September
Variances in the
Production of Kiwi Boost

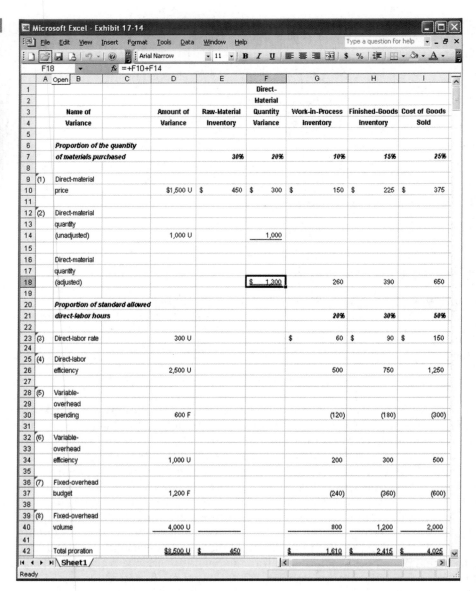

Exhibit 17–14

Proration of September Variances in the Production of Kiwi Boost

Koala Camp Gear Company

	Name of Variance	Amount of Variance	Raw-Material Inventory	Direct-Material Quantity Variance	Work-in-Process Inventory	Finished-Goods Inventory	Cost of Goods Sold
	Proportion of the quantity of materials purchased		30%	20%	10%	15%	25%
(1)	Direct-material price	$1,500 U	$ 450	$ 300	$ 150	$ 225	$ 375
(2)	Direct-material quantity (unadjusted)	1,000 U		1,000			
	Direct-material quantity (adjusted)			$ 1,300	260	390	650
	Proportion of standard allowed direct-labor hours				20%	30%	50%
(3)	Direct-labor rate	300 U			$ 60	$ 90	$ 150
(4)	Direct-labor efficiency	2,500 U			500	750	1,250
(5)	Variable-overhead spending	600 F			(120)	(180)	(300)
(6)	Variable-overhead efficiency	1,000 U			200	300	500
(7)	Fixed-overhead budget	1,200 F			(240)	(360)	(600)
(8)	Fixed-overhead volume	4,000 U			800	1,200	2,000
	Total proration	$8,500 U	$ 450		$ 1,610	$ 2,415	$ 4,025

Now all of the variance accounts have been closed out to zero to begin the next period. The inventory and cost of goods sold accounts have been adjusted to reflect the deviations from standard costs as reflected in the variances.

Appendix B to Chapter Seventeen

Standard Costing in a Just-in-Time Environment

LO 10 Explain and illustrate backflush costing in a just-in-time environment.

Just-in-time manufacturing settings with a demand-pull of products through manufacturing minimize inventories. As a result, the accounting system can be simplified by charging all costs directly to Cost of Goods Sold (CGS). If inventories exist at the end of the period, a portion of the current period costs originally charged to Cost of Goods Sold is credited to Cost of Goods Sold and debited back to the respective inventory account as an end-of-period adjustment. This method, called **backflush costing,** is a simplified system in which all manufacturing costs are charged to CGS, and then end-of-period adjustments are made to credit CGS and debit the inventory accounts.

Using backflush standard costing, costs are charged to Cost of Goods Sold at standard. Variances are charged to a separate account. If there are no inventories at the end of the period, the variance account is expensed or combined with Cost of Goods Sold at standard. The latter result is Cost of Goods Sold *at actual.*

If inventories exist at the end of the period, and if the difference between the standard cost of inventories and actual cost is immaterial, the inventories can be stated at standard cost. In this situation, variances need not be prorated. (Appendix A covers proration.)

If prorating variances makes a material difference in the financial statements or is required by contract, the variance is prorated from the variance account to the respective inventory accounts based on the proportions of the current period costs in each of the inventory accounts and Cost of Goods Sold, as described in Appendix A. The results should be the same as if the variances had been accounted for in the traditional manner discussed earlier in this chapter.

To illustrate, suppose that during the next year, Koala Camp Gear Company switched to demand-pull accounting. Assume that the Cost of Goods Sold and related variance account appear as follows before adjustment:

Cost of Goods Sold (at Standard Cost)	
Direct material	60,000
Direct labor	30,000
Manufacturing overhead	70,000

Cost Variances		
Direct-material price	3,500	
Direct-material quantity	2,500	
	6,600	Direct-labor and manufacturing overhead

The debits to Cost of Goods Sold are at standard price (SP) multiplied by the standard quantity of input per unit of output (SQ) multiplied by the actual units produced. If inventories are minimal, the balance in the variance account is expensed.

If the company has substantial ending inventories, the costs in Cost of Goods Sold are transferred to the inventory accounts. Assume that no beginning inventories exist and that $42,000 of the $60,000 standard cost of materials is traced to the inventory accounts:

Direct-Material Inventory	$35,000
Work-in-Process Inventory	5,000
Finished-Goods Inventory	2,000
Total	$42,000

The total amount is credited to Cost of Goods Sold with debits to each inventory account, as shown in Exhibit 17–15.

A similar adjustment is made for direct labor and manufacturing overhead. Suppose that 20 percent of the labor and overhead amounts are still in Work-in-Process Inventory and 8 percent are in Finished-Goods Inventory. The dollar amounts to be transferred from Cost of Goods Sold to the inventory accounts are as follows:

	Direct Labor	Manufacturing Overhead
Work-in-Process Inventory	$6,000	$14,000
Finished-Goods Inventory	2,400	5,600
Total	$8,400	$19,600

The resulting inventory and Cost of Goods Sold accounts appear in Exhibit 17–15 after the adjustments.

Exhibit 17–15

Backflush Standard
Costing

Koala
Camp
Gear
Company

Direct-Material Inventory	
0	
35,000	

Work-in-Process Inventory	
	0
Direct material	5,000
Direct labor	6,000
Manufacturing overhead	14,000
Balance	25,000

Finished-Goods Inventory	
	0
Direct material	2,000
Direct labor	2,400
Manufacturing overhead	5,600
Balance	10,000

Cost of Goods Sold (at Standard Cost)		
Direct material	60,000	42,000
Direct labor	30,000	8,400
Manufacturing overhead	70,000	19,600

Variances		
Direct-material price	3,500	
Direct-material quantity	2,500	
	6,600	Direct labor and manufacturing overhead

Appendix C to Chapter Seventeen

Sales Variance Analysis

LO 11 Compute, and interpret sales variances.

In this and the preceding chapter, we explored cost-variance analysis as a tool for cost management. In this appendix we turn our attention to assessing a company's overall sales performance. One common method for analyzing sales performance is *sales variance analysis*. This approach examines the difference (variance) between actual sales performance and budgeted sales performance by computing a set of variances, with each variance focusing on some underlying aspect of sales performance. Sales variance analysis can be carried out in either of two alternative ways:

1. *Focus on sales revenue.* The first approach to sales variance analysis analyzes the difference (variance) between actual and budgeted *sales revenue*.
2. *Focus on contribution margin.* The second approach to sales-variance analysis analyzes the difference (variance) between actual and budgeted *contribution margin.* Under this approach we are implicitly assuming that the organization's cost structure can be represented by the traditional (and relatively simple) cost-behavior pattern that includes only variable costs and fixed costs. *Variable costs* are those that vary in proportion to the level of a single, unit-level cost driver. A product's *unit contribution margin,* then, is the product's sales price minus its

variable cost (including both variable manufacturing costs and variable selling costs). (See Chapter 2 for further discussion of fixed and variable costs.)

The next section discusses the revenue approach to sales variance analysis in more detail. After computing and interpreting all of the revenue sales variances, we conclude the section with a general discussion of the contribution-margin approach to sales-variance analysis.

Illustration of Sales-Variance Analysis

To illustrate sales variance analysis, let's focus again on Koala Camp Gear Company, the small Australian manufacturer of camping equipment. To keep the illustration rel-  atively simple, we focus on the company's early years when it manufactured only tents. This occurred before Koala added other product lines, such as camp foods and other camping equipment. During these early years, Koala Camp Gear Company manufactured three models of camping tents: the Tree Line (T), the River's Edge (R), and the Valley (V). Data from the year on which our illustration is based appear in Exhibit 17–16. The exhibit presents both budget data and actual data for the year of the analysis. Notice that the budgeted total sales revenue for the year was $9,950,000, but the actual total sales revenue achieved was $11,110,000. What was behind this difference (variance) of $1,160,000 in sales revenue?

Notice also that Koala's budgeted total contribution margin for the year was $1,750,000, but the company's actual total contribution margin was $2,227,500. This actual total contribution-margin result was $477,500 higher than expected. How did this come about?

To help Koala's management gain insight into the answers to these questions, we now consider the sales-variance analysis for the year summarized in Exhibit 17–16.

Focus on revenue. First we present Koala's sales-variance analysis from a sales-revenue perspective. The analysis to be conducted is summarized in Exhibit 17–17. Notice that the terms *revenue* or *sales price* preface the name of each variance to make it clear that these variances focus on *sales revenue*.

The **revenue budget variance** is the difference between the actual total sales revenue and the budgeted total sales revenue. It is defined by the following formula.[5] This variance is simply the difference between the actual total sales revenue and the budgeted total sales revenue.

$$\begin{array}{c} \text{Revenue budget} \\ \text{variance} \end{array} = \begin{array}{c} \text{Sum of revenue budget variances} \\ \text{for each product} \end{array}$$

$$\begin{array}{c} \text{Revenue} \\ \text{budget variance} = \\ \text{for product } i \end{array} \left(\begin{array}{c} \text{Actual} \\ \text{sales revenue} \\ \text{for product } i \end{array} - \begin{array}{c} \text{Budgeted} \\ \text{sales revenue} \\ \text{for product } i \end{array} \right)$$

Applying the formula yields the following results for Koala Camp Gear Company.

T revenue budget variance = ($190) (30,250) − ($180) (30,000) = $ 347,500 F
R revenue budget variance = ($215) (22,000) − ($220) (15,000) =   1,430,000 F
V revenue budget variance = ($230) (2,750) − ($250) (5,000) =   617,500 U
    Revenue budget variance .... $1,160,000 F

An individual component of the revenue budget variance is favorable if the product's actual revenue exceeds its budgeted revenue but is unfavorable if it is less than the budgeted amount. Although Koala's revenue budget variance for Valley model tents is unfavorable, the company's revenue budget variance is favorable overall, $1,160,000 F. This result also is apparent from the information given in Exhibit

[5] Some accountants refer to this variance as a *static-budget variance in revenues*.

Exhibit 17–16

Data for Illustration of
Sales Variance Analysis:
Koala Camp Gear
Company

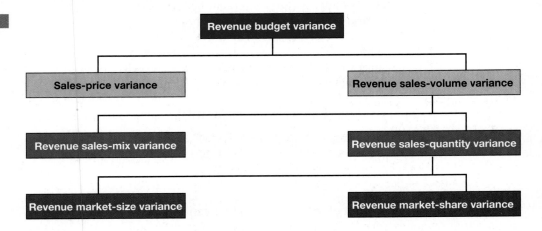

Microsoft Excel - Exhibit 17-16

H28 ▼ ＝SUM(H25:H27)

BUDGET DATA:

	Tent Model	Budgeted Price	Budgeted Unit Variable Cost	Budgeted Unit Contribution Margin	Budgeted Unit Sales Volume	Budgeted Sales Proportion*	Budgeted Total Sales Revenue	Budgeted Total Contribution Margin
	T	$ 180	$ 150	$ 30	30,000	0.60	$ 5,400,000	$ 900,000
	R	220	180	40	15,000	0.30	3,300,000	600,000
	V	250	200	50	5,000	0.10	1,250,000	250,000
Total					50,000		$ 9,950,000	$ 1,750,000

*Budgeted sales proportion = product's budgeted sales volume/50,000.

Budgeted industry volume　　1,000,000 units
Budgeted market share　　.05 (50,000/1,000,000)

ACTUAL DATA:

	Tent Model	Actual Price	Actual Unit Variable Cost	Actual Unit Contribution Margin	Actual Unit Sales Volume	Actual Sales Proportion*	Actual Total Sales Revenue	Actual Total Contribution Margin
	T	$ 190	$ 155	$ 35	30,250	0.55	$ 5,747,500	$ 1,058,750
	R	215	165	50	22,000	0.40	4,730,000	1,100,000
	V	230	205	25	2,750	0.05	632,500	68,750
Total					55,000		$ 11,110,000	$ 2,227,500

*Actual sales proportion = product's actual sales volume/55,000.

Actual industry volume　　1,375,000 units
Actual market share　　.04 (55,000/1,375,000)

Sheet1 / Sheet2 / Sheet3 /
Ready

Exhibit 17–17

Revenue Sales-Variance
Analysis

- Revenue budget variance
  - Sales-price variance
  - Revenue sales-volume variance
    - Revenue sales-mix variance
    - Revenue sales-quantity variance
      - Revenue market-size variance
      - Revenue market-share variance

17–16, since it reveals that Koala's actual total sales revenue of $11,110,000
exceeded budgeted sales revenue of $9,950,000.

What additional insight can management learn about Koala's sales-revenue performance? As Exhibit 17–17 shows, the revenue budget variance can be broken
down into two variances: *the sales-price variance* and the *revenue sales-volume variance*. We next turn our attention to these variances and their interpretations.

The **sales price variance** focuses on the differences between actual and budgeted sales prices while holding constant the sales volume at its actual level. The sales-price variance is defined in the following formula.[6]

$$\begin{array}{c} \text{Sales-price} \\ \text{variance} \end{array} = \begin{array}{c} \text{Sum of sales-price variances} \\ \text{for each product} \end{array}$$

$$\begin{array}{c} \text{Sales-price} \\ \text{variance} \\ \text{for product } i \end{array} = \left(\begin{array}{c} \text{Actual} \\ \text{sales price} \\ \text{for product } i \end{array} - \begin{array}{c} \text{Budgeted} \\ \text{sales price} \\ \text{for product } i \end{array} \right) \times \begin{array}{c} \text{Actual} \\ \text{sales volume} \\ \text{for product } i \end{array}$$

Using this formula, Koala's sales price variance is computed as follows:

T	sales price variance = ($190 − $180) × 30,250 =	$302,500 F
R	sales price variance = ($215 − $220) × 22,000 =	110,000 U
V	sales price variance = ($230 − $250) × 2,750 =	55,000 U
	Sales price variance	$137,500 F

Each individual component of the sales-price variance is favorable if the product's actual sales price exceeds its budgeted sales price (and unfavorable otherwise). Koala's overall sales-price variance is favorable, because of the Tree Line tent's higher than expected sales price, even though the sales price of the other two tent models was lower than expected.

The **revenue sales-volume variance** holds constant the products' sales prices at their budgeted levels and focuses on deviations between actual and budgeted sales volumes. The revenue sales-volume variance is computed as shown in the following formula.[7]

$$\begin{array}{c} \text{Revenue} \\ \text{sales-volume} \\ \text{variance} \end{array} = \begin{array}{c} \text{Sum of revenue sales-volume variances} \\ \text{for each product} \end{array}$$

$$\begin{array}{c} \text{Revenue} \\ \text{sales-volume} \\ \text{variance} \\ \text{for product } i \end{array} = \left(\begin{array}{c} \text{Actual unit} \\ \text{sales volume} \\ \text{for product } i \end{array} - \begin{array}{c} \text{Budgeted unit} \\ \text{sales volume} \\ \text{for product } i \end{array} \right) \times \begin{array}{c} \text{Budgeted} \\ \text{sales price} \\ \text{for product } i \end{array}$$

Applying the formula yields the following results for Koala Camp Gear Company.

T	revenue sales-volume variance = (30,250 − 30,000) × $180 =	$ 45,000 F
R	revenue sales-volume variance = (22,000 − 15,000) × $220 =	1,540,000 F
V	revenue sales-volume variance = (2,750 − 5,000) × $250 =	562,500 U
	Revenue sales-volume variance	$1,022,500 F

Each individual component of the revenue sales-volume variance is favorable if the product's actual sales volume exceeds its budgeted sales volume but unfavorable if it is lower than the budgeted amount. Notice that the higher than expected sales volume for Tree Line tents and River's Edge tents were sufficient to make Koala's overall revenue sales-volume variance favorable ($1,022,500 F) even though the Valley model tent experienced disappointing sales-volume results.

We can derive more insight into the revenue implications of the sales-volume results by breaking down the revenue sales-volume variance into two variances: the *revenue sales-mix variance* and the *revenue sales-quantity variance*.[8] Let's now turn our attention to those variances and their interpretation.

---

[6] Some accountants refer to this variance as a *flexible-budget variance in revenues.*

[7] Some accountants refer to this variance as a *revenue sales-activity variance.*

[8] Review Exhibit 17–17.

The **revenue sales-mix variance** focuses on the effects of changes in the sales mix while holding constant the effects of the products' sales prices and the total sales volume. The revenue sales-mix variance is computed as shown in the following formula.

$$
\begin{array}{c}
\text{Revenue} \\
\text{sales-mix} \\
\text{variance}
\end{array}
=
\begin{array}{c}
\text{Sum of revenue sales-mix variances} \\
\text{for each product}
\end{array}
$$

$$
\begin{array}{c}
\text{Revenue} \\
\text{sales-mix} \\
\text{variance} \\
\text{for product } i
\end{array}
=
\begin{array}{c}
\text{Budgeted} \\
\text{sales price} \\
\text{for product } i
\end{array}
\times
\left(
\begin{array}{c}
\text{Actual sales} \\
\text{proportion} \\
\text{for product } i
\end{array}
-
\begin{array}{c}
\text{Budgeted} \\
\text{sales} \\
\text{proportion} \\
\text{for product } i
\end{array}
\right)
\times
\begin{array}{c}
\text{Actual total} \\
\text{unit sales} \\
\text{volume for} \\
\text{all products}
\end{array}
$$

Using this formula, Koala's revenue sales-mix variance is computed as follows:

T revenue sales-mix variance = $180 × (.55 − .60) × 55,000 =	$ 495,000	U
R revenue sales-mix variance = $220 × (.40 − .30) × 55,000 =	1,210,000	F
V revenue sales-mix variance = $250 × (.05 − .10) × 55,000 =	687,500	U
Revenue sales-mix variance	$ 27,500	F

Each individual component of the revenue sales-mix variance is favorable if the product's actual sales proportion exceeds its budgeted sales proportion but unfavorable if it is lower than the budgeted proportion. Koala's overall favorable revenue sales-mix variance ($27,500 F) tells us that Koala's actual sales mix differed from its budgeted sales mix in such a way that the effect on overall sales revenue was positive. The higher than expected proportion of sales for the River's Edge tent was sufficiently favorable to overcome the lower proportions of sales for the other two tent models. Note that *it is the overall revenue sales-mix variance that conveys a meaningful interpretation for management's analysis, not the individual products' mix-variance components.*[9]

The **revenue sales-quantity variance** holds constant the sales-price and sales-mix effects and focuses on the effect of the overall unit sales volume. The revenue sales-quantity variance is computed as shown in the following formula.

$$
\begin{array}{c}
\text{Revenue} \\
\text{sales-quantity} \\
\text{variance}
\end{array}
=
\begin{array}{c}
\text{Sum of revenue sales-quantity variances} \\
\text{for each product}
\end{array}
$$

$$
\begin{array}{c}
\text{Revenue} \\
\text{sales-quantity} \\
\text{variance} \\
\text{for product } i
\end{array}
=
\begin{array}{c}
\text{Budgeted} \\
\text{sales price} \\
\text{for product } i
\end{array}
\times
\left(
\begin{array}{c}
\text{Actual total} \\
\text{unit sales} \\
\text{volume for} \\
\text{all products}
\end{array}
-
\begin{array}{c}
\text{Budgeted} \\
\text{total unit} \\
\text{sales volume} \\
\text{for all products}
\end{array}
\right)
\times
\begin{array}{c}
\text{Budgeted sales} \\
\text{proportion for} \\
\text{product } i
\end{array}
$$

The formula yields the following calculation of Koala's revenue sales-quantity variance:

T revenue sales-quantity variance = $180 × (55,000 − 50,000) × .60 =	$540,000	F
R revenue sales-quantity variance = $220 × (55,000 − 50,000) × .30 =	330,000	F
V revenue sales-quantity variance = $250 × (55,000 − 50,000) × .10 =	125,000	F
Revenue sales-quantity variance	$995,000	F

The revenue sales-quantity variance is favorable if actual total sales volume exceeds budgeted total sales volume but is unfavorable if it is lower. Since Koala's actual sales volume, 55,000 units, exceeded the budgeted level of 50,000 units, the company's revenue sales-quantity variance is favorable.[10]

---

[9] Students who completed the Appendix to Chapter 16, which covers production mix and yield variances, might notice a conceptual and computational similarity between the revenue sales-mix variance and the production mix variance.

[10] Students who completed the Appendix to Chapter 16 might notice a conceptual and computational similarity between the revenue sales-quantity variance and the production yield variance.

Although Koala's actual total sales volume exceeded the budget, did the company maintain its market share? Was the increase in Koala's sales volume due to an industry wide increase in sales, or did Koala increase its share of a constant or declining market? We can address these questions by decomposing the revenue sales-quantity variance into two variances: the *revenue market-size variance* and the *revenue market-share variance*.[11]

The **revenue market-size variance** holds constant the company's market share at its budgeted level and focuses on changes in total industry volume. The revenue market-size variance is computed as shown in the following formula, holds constant the company's market share at its budgeted level and focuses on changes in total industry volume (i.e., market size).[12]

$$
\begin{array}{c}
\text{Revenue} \\
\text{market-} \\
\text{size} \\
\text{variance}
\end{array}
=
\begin{array}{c}
\text{Budgeted} \\
\text{weighted-} \\
\text{average unit} \\
\text{sales price}
\end{array}
\times
\left(
\begin{array}{c}
\text{Actual total} \\
\text{market-} \\
\text{unit sales} \\
\text{volume}
\end{array}
-
\begin{array}{c}
\text{Budgeted} \\
\text{total market-} \\
\text{unit sales} \\
\text{volume}
\end{array}
\right)
\times
\begin{array}{c}
\text{Budgeted} \\
\text{market-share} \\
\text{proportion}
\end{array}
$$

To apply the formula, we first need to compute Koala's budgeted weighted-average unit sales price.

T	($180) (30,000) =	$5,400,000
R	($220) (15,000) =	3,300,000
V	($250) (5,000) =	1,250,000
	Total budgeted revenue	$9,950,000

$$\text{Budgeted weighted-average unit sales price} = \$9{,}950{,}000 \div 50{,}000 \text{ units}$$
$$= \$199$$

Another way to compute the budgeted weighted-average unit sales price is to weight the three products' budgeted sales prices by their budgeted sales proportions as follows:

$$(\$180)\,(.60) + (\$220)\,(.30) + (\$250)\,(.10) = \$199$$

Applying the formula yields the following result for Koala Camp Gear Company.

$$\text{Revenue market-size variance} = \$199 \times (1{,}375{,}000 - 1{,}000{,}000) \times .05$$
$$= \$3{,}731{,}250 \text{ F}$$

Koala's revenue market-size variance is favorable simply because the actual total industry sales volume of 1,375,000 units exceeded the expected total industry volume of 1,000,000 units (see Exhibit 17–16). However, did Koala maintain its expected market share in the face of this overall industry expansion?

The **revenue market-share variance** holds constant the total industry volume at its actual sales level and focuses on the company's market share. The revenue market-share variance is computed as shown in the following formula, holds constant the total industry volume at the actual sales level and focuses on the company's market share.

$$
\begin{array}{c}
\text{Revenue} \\
\text{market-} \\
\text{share} \\
\text{variance}
\end{array}
=
\begin{array}{c}
\text{Budgeted} \\
\text{weighted-} \\
\text{average unit} \\
\text{sales price}
\end{array}
\times
\left(
\begin{array}{c}
\text{Actual} \\
\text{market-} \\
\text{share} \\
\text{proportion}
\end{array}
-
\begin{array}{c}
\text{Budgeted} \\
\text{market-share} \\
\text{proportion}
\end{array}
\right)
\times
\begin{array}{c}
\text{Actual total} \\
\text{market-} \\
\text{unit sales} \\
\text{volume}
\end{array}
$$

Using this formula, Koala's revenue market-share variance is computed as follows:

$$\text{Revenue market-share variance} = \$199 \times (.04 - .05) \times 1{,}375{,}000$$
$$= \$2{,}736{,}250 \text{ U}$$

---

[11] Review Exhibit 17–17.

[12] Some accountants refer to this variance as a *revenue industry-volume variance*.

Although the total industry sales volume was higher than expected, Koala Camp Gear Company's share of the market was lower than expected. Koala garnered only 4 percent of overall industry volume instead of the anticipated 5 percent share. This decline in market share is likely of considerable concern to Koala's management.

We have completed the revenue sales-variance analysis for Koala Camp Gear Company, and our results are summarized in Exhibit 17–18. The exhibit highlights the hierarchical design of the sales-variance analysis for which some variances are decomposed into others to gain additional insight into the phenomena underlying Koala's overall sales revenue performance.

Focus on contribution margin.   Now we will briefly discuss Koala's sales variance analysis from the contribution-margin perspective. The analysis is summarized in Exhibit 17–19 (using the data from Exhibit 17–16, as in the preceding section). Notice that the name of each variance is prefaced by the term *contribution margin* to make clear that the analysis has a contribution-margin focus rather than a sales-revenue focus. Each variance is analogous to its counterpart in the revenue sales variance analysis. For example, the contribution-margin budget variance is calculated in exactly the same way as the revenue budget variance except for the fact that the prod-

Exhibit 17–18

Revenue Sales-Variance
Analysis: Koala Camp
Gear Company

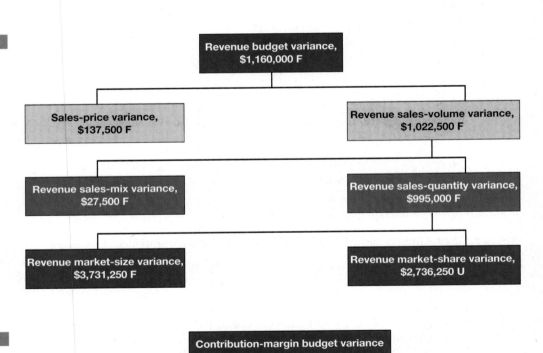

Exhibit 17–19

Contribution-Margin-Sales
Variance Analysis

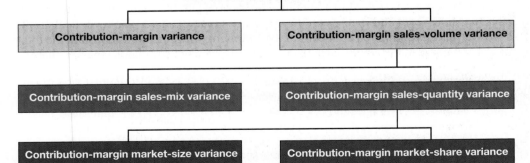

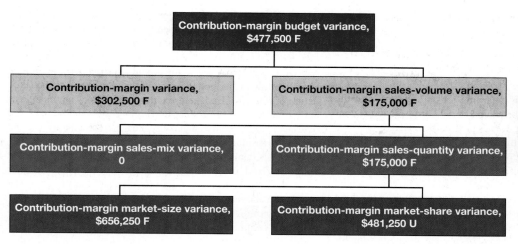

Exhibit 17–20

Contribution-Margin Sales
Variance Analysis: Koala
Camp Gear Company

ucts' contribution margins are used instead of their sales prices. Moreover, the interpretations of the contribution-margin budget variance and the revenue budget variance are analogous. It simply comes down to whether management wants to focus its analysis on sales revenue or contribution margin.

The results of Koala Camp Gear's contribution-margin sales-variance analysis is shown in Exhibit 17–20. Once again, the exhibit highlights the hierarchical nature of the variance analysis for which certain variances comprise other variances to gain insight into the phenomena underlying a company's sales performance.

Key Terms

For each term's definition, refer to the indicated page or turn to the glossary at the end of the text.

activity-based flexible budget, 706

backflush costing,[†] 712

Cost Accounting Standards Board (CASB),[*] 710

fixed-overhead budget variance, 701

fixed-overhead volume variance, 701

flexible budget, 690

overhead cost performance report, 704

proration[*], 710

relevant range, 690

revenue budget variance,[‡] 715

revenue market-share variance,[‡] 719

revenue market-size variance,[‡] 719

revenue sales-mix variance,[‡] 718

revenue sales-quantity variance,[‡] 718

revenue sales-volume variance,[‡] 717

sales-price variance,[‡] 717

static budget, 690

variable-overhead efficiency variance, 698

variable-overhead spending variance, 698

———————

[*] Appears in Appendix A.

[†] Appears in Appendix B.

[‡] Appears in Appendix C.

Meeting the Cost-Management Challenges

1. How can Koala Camp Gear's management use a flexible budget to manage overhead costs?

A static budget is based on only one level of activity. In contrast, Koala Camp Gear's flexible budget allows for several different levels of activity. The advantage of a flexible budget is that it responds to changes in the activity level. It enables a comparison between actual costs incurred at the actual level of activity and the standard costs allowed that should have been incurred at the actual level of activity. Flexible-overhead budgets are based on an input activity measure, such as machine hours or direct-labor hours, to provide a meaningful measure of production activity. An output measure, such as the number of units produced, could be used effectively only in a single-product enterprise. If multiple, heterogeneous products are produced, basing the flexible budget on an output measure aggregated across highly different types of products would not be meaningful.

2. How would you respond to the concerns raised by Koala Camp Gear's production manager in his memo to the controller?

The following explanation regarding the interpretation of the overhead variances would be an appropriate response to the concerns raised by Koala Camp Gear's production manager.

The interpretation of the variable-overhead spending variance is that a different total amount was spent on variable overhead than should have been spent in accordance with the variable-overhead rate, given the actual level of the cost driver on which the variable-overhead budget is based. For example, if machine hours are used to budget variable overhead, an unfavorable spending variance means that a higher total amount was spent on variable overhead than should have been spent, after adjusting for the actual machine time used. The spending variance is the control variance for variable overhead.

Suppose, for example, that electricity is the only variable-overhead cost item. An unfavorable variable-overhead spending variance does not imply that the company paid more than the anticipated rate per kilowatt-hour for electricity. An unfavorable spending variance could result from spending more per kilowatt-hour for electricity or from using more electricity than anticipated, or some combination of these two causes.

The interpretation of the variable-overhead efficiency variance is related to the efficiency of activity use on which variable overhead is budgeted. For example, if the basis for the variable-overhead budget is machine hours, an unfavorable variable-overhead efficiency variance results when the actual machine hours exceed the standard machine hours allowed. Thus, the variable-overhead efficiency variance will disclose no information about the efficiency with which variable-overhead items are used. Rather, it results from inefficiency or efficiency, relative to the standards, in the usage of the cost driver (such as machine hours).

The interpretations of the direct-labor and variable-overhead efficiency variances are very different. The direct-labor efficiency variance conveys information about the efficiency with which direct labor was used, relative to the standards. In contrast, the variable-overhead efficiency variance conveys no information about the efficiency with which variable-overhead items were used.

The fixed-overhead volume variance is the difference between budgeted fixed overhead and applied fixed overhead. The best interpretation for this variance is that it is a means of reconciling two disparate purposes of the standard-costing system: the control purpose and the product-costing purpose. For the control purpose, budgeted fixed overhead recognizes the fixed nature of this cost. Budgeted fixed overhead does not change as activity changes. For product-costing purposes, budgeted fixed overhead is divided by an activity measure (or cost driver) and applied to products on the basis of a fixed-overhead rate. The result of this dual purpose for the standard-costing system is that budgeted fixed overhead and applied fixed overhead will differ when the actual production activity differs from the budgeted production activity.

A common but misleading interpretation of the fixed-overhead volume variance is that it is a measure of the cost of underutilizing or overutilizing production capacity. For example, when budgeted fixed overhead exceeds applied fixed overhead, the fixed-overhead volume variance is positive. (Some accountants designate a positive fixed-overhead volume variance as unfavorable.) Some people claim that it is a measure of the cost of not having utilized production capacity to the anticipated level. However, this interpretation is misleading because the real cost of underutilizing capacity lies in the forgone contribution margins from the products that were not produced and sold.

3. How could Koala's managers improve the management of overhead costs?

An activity-based flexible budget would give Koala Camp Gear's management team a richer, more detailed perspective on the behavior and control of the company's overhead costs.

Conventional flexible budgets typically are based on a single cost driver, such as direct-labor hours or machine hours. Costs are categorized as variable or fixed. The fixed costs do not vary with respect to the single cost driver on which the flexible budget is based. An activity-based flexible budget is based on multiple cost drivers. Cost drivers are selected on the basis of how well they explain the behavior of the costs in the flexible budget. Costs that are treated as fixed in a conventional flexible budget can vary with respect to an appropriate cost driver in an activity-based flexible budget.

Solution to You're the Decision Maker

17.1 Overhead Variances p. 703

a. The solution is given in Exhibits 17–21 and 17–22.

b. The fixed-overhead budget variance is the difference between actual fixed overhead and budgeted fixed overhead. During December, Koala Camp Gear simply spent less for these cost items than anticipated in the budget.

c. There will be no fixed-overhead volume variance during a period in which budgeted and applied fixed overhead are equal. This will happen only if the number of standard allowed hours equals the planned monthly activity level of 6,000 machine hours.

Exhibit 17–21

Variable-Overhead Spending and Efficiency Variations: You're the Decision Maker

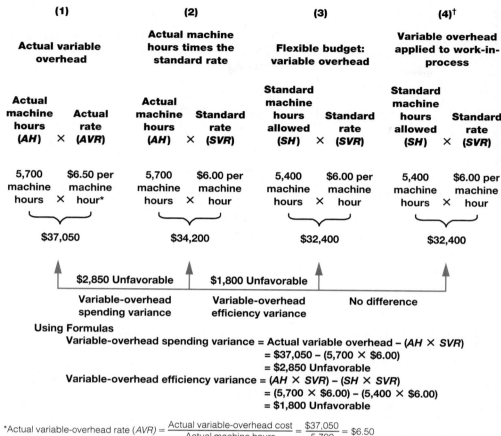

(1)	**(2)**	**(3)**	**(4)**†
Actual variable overhead	**Actual machine hours times the standard rate**	**Flexible budget: variable overhead**	**Variable overhead applied to work-in-process**

Actual machine hours (AH) ×	**Actual rate (AVR)**	**Actual machine hours (AH)** ×	**Standard rate (SVR)**	**Standard machine hours allowed (SH)** ×	**Standard rate (SVR)**	**Standard machine hours allowed (SH)** ×	**Standard rate (SVR)**
5,700 machine hours ×	$6.50 per machine hour*	5,700 machine hours ×	$6.00 per machine hour	5,400 machine hours ×	$6.00 per machine hour	5,400 machine hours ×	$6.00 per machine hour
$37,050		$34,200		$32,400		$32,400	

$2,850 Unfavorable $1,800 Unfavorable   No difference

Variable-overhead spending variance   Variable-overhead efficiency variance

Using Formulas

Variable-overhead spending variance = Actual variable overhead – (AH × SVR)
= $37,050 – (5,700 × $6.00)
= $2,850 Unfavorable

Variable-overhead efficiency variance = (AH × SVR) – (SH × SVR)
= (5,700 × $6.00) – (5,400 × $6.00)
= $1,800 Unfavorable

*Actual variable-overhead rate $(AVR) = \dfrac{\text{Actual variable-overhead cost}}{\text{Actual machine hours}} = \dfrac{\$37,050}{5,700} = \$6.50$

†Column (4) is not used to compute the variances. It is included to point out that the flexible-budget amount for variable overhead, $32,400, is the amount that will be applied to Work-in-Process Inventory for product-costing purposes.

Exhibit 17–22

Fixed-Overhead Budget and Volume Variations: You're the Decision Maker

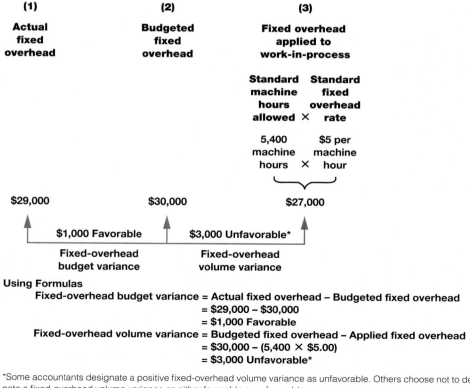

(1)	**(2)**	**(3)**
Actual fixed overhead	**Budgeted fixed overhead**	**Fixed overhead applied to work-in-process**

		Standard machine hours allowed ×	**Standard fixed overhead rate**
		5,400 machine hours ×	$5 per machine hour
$29,000	$30,000		$27,000

$1,000 Favorable $3,000 Unfavorable*

Fixed-overhead budget variance   Fixed-overhead volume variance

Using Formulas

Fixed-overhead budget variance = Actual fixed overhead – Budgeted fixed overhead
= $29,000 – $30,000
= $1,000 Favorable

Fixed-overhead volume variance = Budgeted fixed overhead – Applied fixed overhead
= $30,000 – (5,400 × $5.00)
= $3,000 Unfavorable*

*Some accountants designate a positive fixed-overhead volume variance as unfavorable. Others choose not to designate a fixed-overhead volume variance as either favorable or unfavorable.

Review Questions

17.1   What types of organizations use flexible budgets?

17.2   Distinguish between a columnar and a formula flexible budget.

17.3   What is the interpretation of the variable-overhead spending variance?

17.4   What is the interpretation of the variable-overhead efficiency variance?

17.5   Distinguish between the interpretations of the direct-labor and variable-overhead efficiency variances.

17.6   What is the fixed-overhead budget variance?

17.7   Why are fixed-overhead costs sometimes called *capacity-producing costs?*

17.8   Draw a graph showing budgeted and applied fixed overhead with a positive (or *unfavorable*) volume variance.

17.9   Distinguish between the control purpose and the product-costing purpose of standard costing and flexible budgeting.

17.10   Show, using T-accounts, how manufacturing overhead is added to Work-in-Process Inventory when standard costing is used.

17.11   (Appendix A) Explain two ways to dispose of variances at the end of the year.

17.12   (Appendix B) Briefly describe the procedure known as *backflush costing.*

17.13   (Appendix C) Into what two variances is a revenue sales-volume variance decomposed? What is the purpose of computing these two variances?

17.14   (Appendix C) Why is there no efficiency variance for revenue?

17.15   (Appendix C) What information does the computation of a market-size variance provide?

17.16   (Appendix C) If the sales-volume variance is zero, is there any reason to compute a sales mix variance?

Critical Analysis

17.17   "I don't understand why you accountants want to prepare a budget for a period that is already over. We know the actual results by then—all that flexible budgeting does is increase the controller's staff and add to our overhead." Comment on this remark.

17.18   Why are flexible overhead budgets based on an activity measure such as machine hours or direct-labor hours?

17.19   How does the concept of flexible budgeting reinforce the notion that employees should be held responsible only for what they can control or heavily influence?

17.20   How has computer-integrated-manufacturing (CIM) technology affected overhead application?

17.21   Give one example of a plausible activity base to use in flexible budgeting for each of the following organizations: an insurance company, an express delivery service, a restaurant, and a state tax-collection agency.

17.22   Budgets for government units are usually prepared one year in advance of the budget period. Expenditures are limited to the budgeted amount. At the end of the period, performance is evaluated by comparing budget authorizations with actual receipts and outlays. What management-control problems are likely to arise from such a system?

17.23   Bodin Company's only variable-overhead cost is electricity. Does an unfavorable variable-overhead spending variance imply that the company paid more than the anticipated rate per kilowatt hour?

17.24   Describe a common but misleading interpretation of the fixed-overhead volume variance. Why is this interpretation misleading?

17.25   Does the fixed-overhead volume variance represent a difference in the cash outflows for the company when compared to budgeted cash outflows?

17.26   What is the conceptual problem of applying fixed-manufacturing overhead as a product cost?

17.27   (Appendix C) The marketing manager of a company noted, "We had a favorable revenue budget variance of $391,000, yet company profit went up by only $98,000. Some part of the organization has dropped the ball; let's find out where the problem is and straighten it out." Comment on this remark.

17.28   (Appendix C) A company sells three products that must be purchased in a single package. Does computing a sales-mix variance provide any benefit under these circumstances?

17.29   (Appendix C) How could a CPA firm use a sales-mix variance to analyze its revenue?

Exercises

Exercise 17.30
Construction of a Flexible-Overhead Budget; Hospital
(LO 1, 2)

Adirondack Community Hospital's controller estimates that the hospital uses 30 kilowatt-hours of electricity per patient-day, and that the electric rate will be $ .10 per kilowatt-hour. The hospital also pays a fixed monthly charge of $950 to the electric utility to rent emergency backup electric generators.

Required
Construct a flexible budget for the hospital's electricity costs using each of the following techniques.

a.   Formula flexible budget.

b.   Columnar flexible budget for 30,000, 40,000, and 50,000 patient-days of activity. List variable and fixed electricity costs separately.

Read "On Factory Floors, Top Workers Hide Secrets to Success," *The Wall Street Journal*, July 1, 2002, pp. A1, A10, by Timothy Aeppel.

Exercise 17.31
Sharing Cost-Saving Ideas
(LO 1)

Required

As a group, discuss the phenomenon described in the article. Why does it occur? What can be done to mitigate against this behavior? Is this behavior ethical?

Neptune Glassware Company had the following actual results for April:

Exercise 17.32
Straightforward Computation of Overhead Variances
(LO 5)

Actual variable overhead	$320,000
Actual fixed overhead	$97,000
Actual direct labor	50,000 hours
Actual output	20,000 units

The company has the following standards and flexible-budget data.

Standard variable-overhead rate	$6.00 per direct-labor hour
Standard quantity of direct labor	2 hours per unit of output
Budgeted fixed overhead	$100,000
Budgeted output	25,000 units

Required

Use the variance formulas to compute the following variances. Indicate whether each variance is favorable or unfavorable where appropriate.

a.   Variable-overhead spending variance.
b.   Variable-overhead efficiency variance.
c.   Fixed-overhead budget variance.
d.   Fixed-overhead volume variance.

Refer to the data in the preceding exercise for Neptune Glassware Company.

Exercise 17.33
Diagram of Overhead Variances
(LO 5)

Required

Use diagrams similar to those in Exhibits 17–6 and 17–8 to compute the variable-overhead spending and efficiency variances and the fixed-overhead budget and volume variances.

Refer to the data in Exercise 17.32 for Neptune Glassware Company.

Exercise 17.34
Graph of Overhead Variances
(LO 5)

Required

Draw graphs similar to those in Exhibit 17–7 (variable overhead) and Exhibit 17–9 (fixed overhead) to depict the overhead variances.

You recently received the following note from the production supervisor of the company where you serve as controller. "I don't understand these crazy variable-overhead efficiency variances. My employees are very careful in their use of electricity and manufacturing supplies, and we use very little indirect labor. What are we supposed to do?"

Exercise 17.35
Variable-Overhead Efficiency Variance
(LO 1, 5)

Required

Write a brief memo responding to the production supervisor's concern.

Fayetteville Financial originates mortgage loans for residential housing. The company charges a service fee for processing loan applications that is set twice a year based on the cost of processing a loan application. For the first half of this year, Fayetteville Financial estimated that it would process 75 loans. Correspondence, credit reports, supplies, and other materials that vary with each loan are estimated to cost $45 per loan. The company hires a loan processor at an estimated cost of $27,000 per year and an assistant at an estimated cost of $20,000 per year. The cost to lease office space and pay utilities and other related costs are estimated at $58,000 per year.

Exercise 17.36
Nonmanufacturing Cost Variances
(LO 4, 5)

During the first six months of this year, Fayetteville Financial processed 79 loans. Cost of materials, credit reports, and other items related to loan processing were 8 percent higher than expected for the volume of loans processed.

The loan processor and her assistant cost $23,800 for the six months. Leasing and related office costs were $28,100.

Required

Analyze the variances for Fayetteville Financial. (*Hint:* Loans are the output.)

Exercise 17.37
Activity-Based Flexible Budget; Ethics
(LO 8)

Refer to Koala Camp Gear's activity-based flexible budget in Exhibit 17–12. Suppose that the company's activity in February is described as follows:

Machine hours	7,500
Production runs..	16
Engineering design specs	12
Direct material (sq. meters)..................................	40,000

Required

a. Determine the flexible budgeted cost for each of the following:
   (1) Indirect material (thread)
   (2) Utilities (heat)
   (3) Quality assurance
   (4) Engineering
   (5) Material handling
   (6) Insurance and property taxes

b. Compute the variance for setup cost during the month assuming that the actual setup cost was $4,540.
   (1) Using the activity-based flexible budget.
   (2) Using Koala's conventional flexible budget (Exhibit 17–3).

c. Compute the variance for engineering cost during the month assuming the actual engineering cost was $4,750.
   (1) Using the activity-based flexible budget.
   (2) Using Koala's conventional flexible budget (Exhibit 17–3).

d. Comment on the ethical issues in the following scenario: When Koala's director of engineering, John Margrove, was shown a preliminary copy of the February cost-variance report, which was based on the activity-based flexible budget, he was dismayed at the unfavorable variance. Refer to your answer to requirement (c).

   The next day, during an afternoon golf outing with his friend Marc Wesley, Koala's controller, Margrove learned that the reported unfavorable engineering cost variance would have been favorable if the report had been based on the traditional flexible budget instead of the activity-based flexible budget. Margrove was quite annoyed about this, and he began to pressure his friend to use the traditional flexible budget as the basis for the variance report. "What's the big deal?" pressed Margrove. "Who's going to know anyway? Just bury that ABC stuff, and use the tried and true method. Nobody will question your methods, and my report will look better."
   (1) Comment on John Margrove's behavior.
   (2) How should Marc Wesley respond? What standards of ethical behavior for management accountants are involved here? (See the Appendix to Chapter 1.)

Exercise 17.38
City or State Budget; Activity-Based Flexible Budget; Cost Drivers
(LO 4, 8)

Choose a city or state in the United States (or a Canadian city or province), and use the Internet to explore the annual budget for the governmental unit you selected. For example, you could check out the annual budget for Los Angeles at www.losangeles.com.

Required

a. Select three items in the budget and explain how these items would be treated if the budget were converted to an activity-based flexible budget.

b. What would be appropriate cost drivers for the budgetary items you selected?

Exercise 17.39
Standard Material Costs; Proration of Variances
(Appendix A)
(LO 9)

Lackawanna Ladder Company acquired 50,000 units of direct material for $70,000 last year. The standard price paid for the material was $1.30 per unit. During last year, 45,000 units of material were used in the production process. Materials are entered into production at the beginning of the process. The standard allowed quantity for the amount of output that was actually produced is 48,000 units. Eighty percent of the units that used these materials were completed and transferred to Finished-Goods

Inventory. Sixty percent of these units that had been transferred to Finished-Goods Inventory were sold this period. There were no beginning inventories.

Required

a. Prepare journal entries, and show the flow of costs through T-accounts.

b. Prorate the direct-materials price variance to the appropriate accounts.

Refer to the data for Lackawanna Ladder Company in the preceding exercise. If the company were operating in a just-in-time environment and charging its standard costs directly to Cost of Goods Sold (at standard cost), show the flow of costs through the T-accounts required to adjust Cost of Goods Sold (at standard cost), to reflect end-of-period inventories. Variances are expensed.

Exercise 17.40
Standard Costing in a
Just-in-Time Environment
(Appendix B)
(LO 10)

During the current period, Plattsburg Pipe Company paid $38,000 for 30,000 units of material, all of which was immediately put into process. During the period, 14,800 units of output were produced, and 14,500 units were sold. Three hundred units remain in finished-goods inventory. Each unit of output requires two units of material, which has a standard cost of $1.35 per unit of material. Standard variable overhead is $69,600 for 15,000 units of production. The variable-overhead efficiency variance was $1,800 U, and actual variable overhead was $69,341.

Fixed overhead, which includes all labor costs, is budgeted at $146,000. Actual fixed overhead for the period was $143,200. Fixed overhead is applied to production at $10 per unit of output. All variances are expensed.

Exercise 17.41
Standard Costing in a
Just-in-Time Environment
(Appendix B)
(LO 10)

Required

a. Show the flow of these costs if the company initially charges all manufacturing costs to Cost of Goods Sold (at standard cost), that is, using backflush standard costing.

b. Show the adjustment that would be made to reflect the ending inventory balances.

Sand 'n Surf Beach Wear, Inc., manufactures and sells beach T-shirts. The business is very competitive. The budget for last year called for sales of 200,000 units at $9 each. However, as the summer season approached, management realized that the company could not sell 200,000 units at the $9 price but would have to offer price concessions. Budgeted variable cost is $3.65 per unit. Actual results showed sales of 190,000 units at an average price of $8.50 each. The actual variable cost was $3.65 per unit.

Exercise 17.42
Sales Variances
(Appendix C)
(LO 11)

Required

Compute the following variances for Sand 'n Surf Beach Wear: revenue budget variance, sales-price variance, and revenue sales-volume variance.

Woods Corporation sells two models of golf gloves. The budgeted per-unit price is $10.95 for Standard and $24.95 for Ultra. The budget called for sales of 400,000 Standards and 180,000 Ultras during the current year. Actual results showed sales of 300,000 Standards, with a price of $11.29 per unit, and 200,000 Ultras, with a price of $25.39 per unit. The standard variable cost is $5 per unit for a Standard and $10 per unit for Ultras.

Exercise 17.43
Sales-Mix and Sales-
Quantity Variances
(Appendix C)
(LO 11)

mhhe.com/hilton3e

Required

Compute each of the following variances from a contribution-margin perspective: (*Hint:* Use the formulas given in Appendix C but substitute each product's contribution margin for its sales price.)

a. Sales-volume variance.

b. Sales-mix and sales-quantity variances.

Cerritos Company manufactures valves in its plant outside Rio de Janeiro, Brazil. For the most recent year, the company budgeted sales of 20,000 units of its sole product, assuming that the company would have 20 percent of 100,000 units sold in a particular market. The actual results were 18,000 units, based on a 15 percent share of a total market of 120,000 units. The budgeted contribution margin is 3 *real* per unit. (The *real* is Brazil's national monetary unit.)

Exercise 17.44
Market-Size and Market-
Share Variances
(Appendix C)
(LO 11)

Required

Compute the sales-quantity variance and break it down into the market-size and market-share variances. Cerritos' cost-management team takes a contribution-margin perspective when doing sales variance analysis. (*Hint:* Use the same formulas given in Appendix C but substitute the contribution margin for the sales price. Remember to express your analysis in terms of the *real,* Brazil's national currency.)

Exercise 17.45
Market-Share Analysis;
Use of Internet
(Appendix C)
(LO 11)

One aspect of sales-variance analysis involves helping management gain insight into the company's market share. Select one of the following companies (or any company you choose) and use the Internet to gather information about that company's share of a particular market. You also might need to use the Internet to access economic data about the overall industry volume for the type of product you selected (e.g., www.ia-online.com/stats/index.htm).

DaimlerChrysler (www.daimlerchrysler.com)

Ford (www.ford.com/us)

General Motors (www.gm.com)

Toyota (www.toyota.com)

Required
Estimate the market share in a particular product area (e.g., minivans or sport utility vehicles) for the company you selected.

Exercise 17.46
Sales-Price, Sales-
Volume, Market-Size,
and Market-Share
Variances (Appendix C)
(LO 11)

Piedmont Condiments, Inc., makes bulk artificial seasonings for use in processed foods. A seasoning was budgeted to sell in 21-liter drums at a price of $48 per drum. The company expected to sell 150,000 drums. Budgeted variable costs are $10 per drum. During the year, Piedmont Condiments sold 125,000 drums at a price of $47.

Required
Piedmont Condiments' cost-management staff computes sales variances from a revenue perspective.

a.   Compute the sales-price and sales-volume variances.

b.   Assume that the budgeted sales volume was based on an expected 10 percent share of a total market volume of 1.5 million drums, but the actual results were based on a 12.5 percent share of a total market of 1 million drums. Compute the market-size and market-share variances.

Problems

Problem 17.47
Overhead Cost and
Variance Relationships
(LO 5)

Heartstrings Greeting Cards, Inc., reported a $50 unfavorable spending variance for variable overhead and a $500 unfavorable budget variance for fixed overhead. The flexible budget had $32,100 variable overhead based on 10,700 direct-labor hours; only 10,600 hours were worked. Total actual overhead was $54,350. Estimated number of hours for computing the fixed-overhead application rate was 11,000.

Required
a.   Prepare a variable-overhead variance analysis.

b.   Prepare a fixed-overhead variance analysis.

Problem 17.48
Manufacturing Variances
for Variable Costs;
Review of Chapters 16
and 17
(LO 5)

Churchill and Blair, Ltd., manufactures a special type of brass fitting in its plant in London, England. The company prepares its budgets on the basis of standard costs. A monthly responsibility report shows the differences between budgeted and actual costs. Variances are analyzed and reported separately. Material price variances are computed at the time of purchase.

The following information relates to the current period. [All monetary amounts are given in British pounds (£) sterling.]

Standard costs (per unit of output)
    Direct material, 1 kilogram @ £1 per kilogram .... £ 1
    Direct labor, 2 hours @ £4 per hour.. 8
    Variable manufacturing overhead (25% of direct-labor cost)........ _2_
    Total standard cost per unit £11

Actual costs for the month follow:

Material purchased .... 3,000 kilograms at £.9 per kilogram
Output .... 1,900 units using 2,100 kilograms of material
Actual direct-labor cost.................................. 3,200 hours at £5 per hour
Actual variable overhead £4,500

Required

Prepare a cost-variance analysis for the variable costs (i.e., direct material, direct labor, and variable overhead). Remember to express your analysis in terms of the British monetary unit, pounds.

Alberta Apparel Company, located in Calgary, uses a standard-costing system. The firm estimates that it will operate its manufacturing facilities at 800,000 machine hours for the year. The estimate for total budgeted overhead is $2,000,000. The standard variable-overhead rate is estimated to be $2 per machine hour or $6 per unit. The actual data for the year follow.

Actual finished units	250,000
Actual machine hours	764,000
Actual variable overhead	$1,690,000
Actual fixed overhead	$ 391,000

Problem 17.49
Overhead Variances;
Journal Entries
(LO 3, 5, 7)

Required

a.   Compute the following variances. Indicate whether each is favorable or unfavorable where appropriate.

   (1)   Variable-overhead spending variance.

   (2)   Variable-overhead efficiency variance.

   (3)   Fixed-overhead budget variance.

   (4)   Fixed-overhead volume variance.

b.   Prepare journal entries to do the following:

   ▨   Record the incurrence of actual variable overhead and actual fixed overhead.

   ▨   Add variable and fixed overhead to Work-in-Process Inventory.

   ▨   Close underapplied or overapplied overhead to Cost of Goods Sold.

[CMA adapted]

Lake Huron Metal Stamping, Inc., shows the following overhead information for the current period:

Standard variable-overhead rate per direct-labor hour	$3
Standard direct-labor hours allowed for actual production	3,500 hours
Actual direct-labor hours used	3,300 hours
Actual overhead incurred	$14,700, of which $9,800 is variable
Budgeted fixed overhead	$4,320

Problem 17.50
Overhead Variances
(LO 5)

Required

a.   Compute the variable-overhead spending and efficiency variances and the fixed-overhead budget variance.

b.   Interpret each variance.

Four Corners Insurance Company insures clients in Colorado, New Mexico, Arizona, and Utah. The company uses a flexible overhead budget for its application-processing department. The firm offers five types of policies. The company processed the following number of insurance applications during July:

Automobile	250
Renter's	200
Homeowner's	100
Health	400
Life	200

Problem 17.51
Standard Hours Allowed
Flexible Budget; Multiple
Products; Insurance
Company
(LO 1, 2, 4)

The following number of standard hours are allowed for clerical processing.

Automobile	1.5 hour
Renter's	1.0 hour
Homeowner's	2.0 hours
Health	2.0 hours
Life	5.0 hours

Four Corners' controller estimates that the variable-overhead rate in the application-processing department is $4 per hour and that fixed-overhead costs will amount to $1,900 per month.

Required

a.   How many standard clerical hours are allowed in July given actual application activity?
b.   Why is it not sensible to base the company's flexible budget on the number of applications processed instead of the number of clerical hours allowed?
c.   Construct a formula flexible overhead budget for the company.
d.   What is the flexible budget for total overhead cost in July?

Problem 17.52
Graph of Budgeted and
Applied Overhead;
Recording Studio
(LO 1, 2, 3)

Countrytime Studios is a recording studio in Nashville. The studio budgets and applies overhead costs on the basis of production time. Its controller anticipates 10,000 hours of production time to be available during the year. The following overhead amounts have been budgeted for the year.

Variable overhead	$80,000
Fixed overhead	90,000

Required

a.   Draw two graphs, one for variable overhead and one for fixed overhead. The variable on the horizontal axis of each graph should be production time, in hours, ranging from 5,000 to 15,000 hours. The variable on the vertical axis of each graph should be overhead cost (variable or fixed). Each graph should include two lines, one for the flexible-budget amount of overhead and one for applied overhead.
b.   Write a brief memo to Countrytime Studio's general manager explaining the graphs so that she will understand the concepts of budgeted and applied overhead.

Problem 17.53
Variance Computations
with Missing Data;
Review of Chapters 16
and 17
(LO 5, 6)

The following information is provided to assist you in evaluating the performance of the production operations of Ulysses Company:

Standard costs per unit:	
Direct material	$ 1.65 × 5 pounds per unit of output
Direct labor..	14.00 per hour × 1/2 hour per unit
Variable overhead	11.90 per direct-labor hour
Master production budget:	
Direct material	$165,000
Direct labor..	140,000
Manufacturing overhead	199,000
Actual costs:	
Direct material purchased and used	$188,700 (102,000 pounds)
Direct labor..	140,000 (10,700 hours)
Manufacturing overhead	204,000 (61% is variable)

Variable overhead is applied on the basis of direct-labor hours. The company's actual production was 21,000 units.

Required

a.   As a group, prepare a complete cost-variance report suitable for presentation to the class. Include the following in your report:
   ▪   Direct-materials price and quantity variances.
   ▪   Direct-labor rate and efficiency variances.
   ▪   Variable-overhead spending and efficiency variances.
   ▪   Fixed-overhead budget and volume variances.
b.   *Build your own spreadsheet.* Build an Excel spreadsheet to solve requirement (a). Use your spreadsheet to determine the new values for all of the variances calculated in requirement (a) if each of the following input parameters changes by the amount indicated. (Unless otherwise indicated, treat each parameter change independently.)
   (1)   Actual production is 22,000 units.
   (2)   Standard direct-material cost is $1.70 per pound of input.
   (3)   Standard direct-labor rate is $13 per hour.
   (4)   Actual manufacturing overhead cost is $210,000 (61 percent variable).
   (5)   All of the changes listed in parts (1) through (4) occur simultaneously.

Bo Vonderweidt is the production manager of the Cincinnati Plant, a division of the large corporation, Plantimum, Inc. He has complained several times to the corporate office that the cost reports used to evaluate his plant are misleading. Vonderweidt states, "I know how to get good quality product out. Over a number of years, I've even cut materials used to do it. The cost reports don't show any of this; they're always negative, no matter what I do. There's no way I can win with accounting or the people at headquarters who use these reports."

A copy of the latest report is shown here.

Problem 17.54
Analysis of Cost Reports
(LO 6)

CINCINNATI PLANT
Cost Report
For the Month of October
(in thousands)

	Budgeted Cost	Actual Cost	Excess Cost
Direct material	$ 405	$ 440	$ 35
Direct labor	570	540	(30)
Overhead	105	134	29
Total	$1,080	$1,114	$ 34

Required

Write a brief report to management that identifies and explains at least three changes to the report that would make the cost information more meaningful and less threatening to the production manager.

[CMA adapted]

Scholastic Software, Inc., distributes educational software packages used in the public schools nationwide. Mark Fletcher, president of Scholastic Software, was looking forward to seeing the performance reports for November because he knew the company's sales for the month had exceeded budget by a considerable margin. The company had been growing steadily for approximately two years. Fletcher's biggest challenge at this point was to ensure that the company did not lose control of expenses during this growth period. When Fletcher received the November reports, he was dismayed to see the large unfavorable variance in the company's Monthly Selling Expense Report that follows.

Problem 17.55
Flexible Budget;
Performance Report
(LO 1, 2, 6)

SCHOLASTIC SOFTWARE, INC.
Monthly Selling Expense Report
For the Month of November

	Annual Budget	November Budget	November Actual	November Variance
Unit sales	2,000,000	280,000	310,000	30,000
Dollar sales	$80,000,000	$11,200,000	$12,400,000	$1,200,000
Orders processed	54,000	6,500	5,800	(700)
Sales personnel per month	90	90	96	(6)
Advertising	$19,800,000	$ 1,650,000	$ 1,660,000	$ 10,000 U
Staff salaries	1,500,000	125,000	125,000	—
Sales salaries	1,296,000	108,000	115,400	7,400 U
Commissions	3,200,000	448,000	496,000	48,000 U
Per-diem expense	1,782,000	148,500	162,600	14,100 U
Office expenses	4,080,000	340,000	358,400	18,400 U
Shipping expenses	6,750,000	902,500	976,500	74,000 U
Total expenses	$38,408,000	$ 3,722,000	$ 3,893,900	$ 171,900 U

Fletcher called in the company's new controller, Susan Porter, to discuss the implications of the variances reported for November and to plan a strategy for improving performance. Porter suggested that the company's reporting format might not be giving Fletcher a true picture of the company's operations. She proposed that Scholastic Software implement flexible budgeting. Porter offered to redo the Monthly Selling Expense Report for November using flexible budgeting so that Fletcher could compare the two reports and see the advantages of flexible budgeting.

Porter discovered the following information about the behavior of Scholastic Software's selling expenses:

▪ The total compensation paid to the sales force consists of a monthly base salary and a commission, which varies with sales dollars.

▪ Sales office expense is a semivariable cost with the variable portion related to the number of orders processed. The fixed portion of office expense is $3,000,000 annually and is incurred uniformly throughout the year.

▪ Subsequent to the adoption of the annual budget for the current year, Scholastic Software decided to open a new sales territory. As a consequence, the company hired six additional salespeople effective November 1. Porter decided that these additional six people should be recognized in her revised report.

▪ Per-diem reimbursement to the sales force, while a fixed amount per day, is variable with the number of sales personnel and the number of days spent traveling. Scholastic Software's original budget was based on an average sales force of 90 people throughout the year with each salesperson traveling 15 days per month.

▪ The company's shipping expense is a semivariable cost with the variable portion, $3 per unit, dependent on the number of units sold. The fixed portion is incurred uniformly throughout the year.

Required

a. As Porter's assistant, draft a memo for her to send to Fletcher citing the benefits of flexible budgeting. Explain why Scholastic Software should use flexible budgeting in this situation.

b. Prepare a revised Monthly Selling Expense Report for November that would permit Fletcher to more clearly evaluate Scholastic Software's control over selling expenses. The report should have a line for each selling expense item showing the appropriate budgeted amount, the actual selling expense, and the monthly dollar variance.

[CMA adapted]

Problem 17.56
Comprehensive Variance
Problem; Review of
Chapters 16 and 17
(LO 5)

Corona, Inc., manufactures a special fabric used in space suits. Corona's actual activity for the past month follows:

Material purchased	18,000 meters at $ .92 per meter
Material used	9,500 meters
Direct labor	2,100 hours at $6.10 per hour
Total manufacturing overhead	$11,100
Production	500 units

The company's standard costs are detailed as follows:

Direct material, 20 meters at $ .90 per meter	$18
Direct labor, 4 hours at $6 per hour..	24
Manufacturing overhead applied at five-sixths of direct-labor cost	
(variable costs = $15; fixed costs = $5)...	20
Variable selling and administrative cost	12
Fixed selling and administrative cost	7
Total unit cost...	$81

Standards have been computed based on a budgeted activity level of 2,400 direct-labor hours per month.

Required
Prepare variance analyses for the variable and fixed costs. Indicate which variances, if any, cannot be computed.

Problem 17.57
Overhead Variances
(LO 5)

Redwood Company developed its overhead application rate from the annual budget, which is based on an expected total output of 720,000 units requiring 3,600,000 machine hours. The company is able to schedule production uniformly throughout the year.

A total of 66,000 units requiring 315,000 machine hours were produced during May. Actual overhead costs for May amounted to $375,000. The actual costs, as compared to the annual budget and to one-twelfth of the annual budget, are as follows:

REDWOOD COMPANY
Annual Budget

	Total Amount	Per Unit	Per Machine Hour	Monthly Budget	Actual Costs for May
Variable overhead:					
Indirect material	$1,224,000	$1.70	$ .34	$102,000	$111,000
Indirect labor.....................................	900,000	1.25	.25	75,000	75,000
Fixed overhead:					
Supervision	648,000	.90	.18	54,000	49,000
Utilities	540,000	.75	.15	45,000	55,000
Depreciation	1,008,000	1.40	.28	84,000	85,000
Total	$4,320,000	$6.00	$1.20	$360,000	$375,000

Required

a. Prepare a schedule showing the following amounts for Redwood Company for May.

   (1) Applied overhead costs.

   (2) Variable-overhead spending variance.

   (3) Fixed-overhead budget variance.

   (4) Variable-overhead efficiency variance.

   (5) Fixed-overhead volume variance.

   Where appropriate, be sure to indicate whether each variance is favorable or unfavorable.

b. Draw a graph similar to Exhibit 17–7 to depict the variable-overhead variances.

c. Why does your graph differ from Exhibit 17–7 other than the fact that the numbers differ?

[CMA adapted]

Scrooge & Zilch is a law firm with partners and staff members. Each billable hour of partner time has a $275 budgeted price and $130 budgeted variable cost. Each billable hour of staff time has a budgeted price of $65 and budgeted variable cost of $35. This month, the partnership budget called for 8,500 billable partner hours and 34,650 staff hours. Actual results follow:

Problem 17.58
Sales-Price, Sales-
Volume, Sales-Mix, and
Sales-Quantity Variances
(Appendix C)
(LO 11)

	Revenue	Billable Hours	Variable Cost
Partner	$2,150,000	8,000 hours	$1,040,000
Staff	2,225,000	34,000 hours	1,190,000

Required

Compute the following variances from a revenue perspective:

a. Sales-price and sales-volume variances.

b. Sales-mix and sales-quantity variances.

The following information has been prepared by Alexis Wells, a member of the cost-management staff of Conundrum Corporation, a manufacturer of puzzles.

Problem 17.59
Contribution-Margin,
Sales-Mix, and Sales-
Quantity Variances
(Appendix C)
(LO 11)

CONUNDRUM CORPORATION
Income Statement
For the Year Ended December 31, 20x0
(dollar amounts in thousands)

	Product CF-11		Product MT-8		Total	
	Budget	Actual	Budget	Actual	Budget	Actual
Unit sales	2,000	2,800	6,000	5,600	8,000	8,400
Sales..	$6,000	$7,560	$12,000	$11,760	$18,000	$19,320
Variable costs	$2,400	$2,800	$ 6,000	$ 5,880	$ 8,400	$ 8,680
Fixed costs	1,800	1,900	2,400	2,400	4,200	4,300
Total costs	$4,200	$4,700	$ 8,400	$ 8,280	$12,600	$12,980
Operating profit	$1,800	$2,860	$ 3,600	$ 3,480	$ 5,400	$ 6,340

Required

Analyze the preceding data to show the impact of sales volume, contribution margin, sales quantity, and sales mix on operating profit. Conundrum Corporation's cost-management staff analyzes sales variances from a contribution-margin perspective. (*Hint:* Use the formulas given in Appendix C, but substitute each product's contribution margin for its sales price.)

[CMA adapted]

Problem 17.60
Contribution-Margin
Sales-Variance Analysis
(Appendix C)
(LO 11)

Catskill Airlines plans its budget and subsequently evaluates sales performance based on passenger miles. A passenger mile is one paying passenger flying one mile. For this month, the company estimated that its contribution margin would amount to 20 cents per passenger mile and that 40 million passenger miles would be flown.

As a result of improvement in the economy, 43 million passenger miles were flown this month. The price per passenger mile averaged 32 cents. The budgeted variable cost per mile was 10 cents. Management's subsequent analysis indicated that the industry flew 107 million passenger miles this month, which was 7 percent more passenger miles than expected. The actual variable cost per passenger mile was 10 cents.

Required

Taking a contribution-margin perspective, do as complete a sales variance analysis as possible. (*Hint:* Use the formulas given in Appendix C, but substitute the contribution margin for the sales price.)

Problem 17.61
Revenue Sales-Variance
Analysis Using Industry
Data and Multiple
Product Lines
(Appendix C)
(LO 11)

Calumet Carpet Company makes three grades of indoor-outdoor carpets. Sales volume for the annual budget is determined by estimating the total market volume for indoor-outdoor carpet and then applying the company's prior year market share, adjusted for planned changes due to company programs for the coming year. Volume is apportioned for the three grades based on the prior year's product mix, again adjusted for planned changes due to company programs for the coming year.

The following are the actual and the budgeted results of operations for March (dollar amounts in thousands).

Actual	Grade 1	Grade 2	Grade 3	Total
Sales, units	800 rolls	1,000 rolls	2,100 rolls	3,900 rolls
Sales, dollars	$ 810	$2,000	$3,000	$5,810
Variable costs	560	1,610	2,320	4,490
Contribution margin	$ 250	$ 390	$ 680	$1,320
Manufacturing fixed cost	210	220	315	745
Product margin	$ 40	$ 170	$ 365	$ 575
Marketing and administrative costs (all fixed)				275
Operating profit				$ 300

Budget	Grade 1	Grade 2	Grade 3	Total
Sales, units	1,000 rolls	1,000 rolls	2,000 rolls	4,000 rolls
Sales, dollars	$1,000	$2,000	$3,000	$6,000
Variable costs	700	1,600	2,300	4,600
Contribution margin	$ 300	$ 400	$ 700	$1,400
Manufacturing fixed cost	200	200	300	700
Product margin	$ 100	$ 200	$ 400	$ 700
Marketing and administrative costs (all fixed)				250
Operating profit				$ 450

Industry volume was estimated at 40,000 rolls for budgeting purposes. Actual industry volume for March was 38,000 rolls.

Required

From a revenue perspective:

a. Prepare an analysis to disaggregate the revenue budget variance into the sales price and sales-volume variances.

b. Break down the sales-volume variance into the parts caused by sales mix and sales quantity.

c. Break down the sales-quantity variance into its market-size and market-share components.

[CMA adapted]

Refer to your solution to the preceding problem for Calumet Carpet Company.

Required

Write a memo to the company president that summarizes and comments on the sales variance analysis.

Problem 17.62
Commentary on Sales-Variance Analysis; Continuation of Problem 17.61 (Appendix C)
(LO 11)

Refer to your solution for Problem 17.61 regarding Calumet Carpet Company.

Required

Prepare a sales variance-chart similar to Exhibit 17–18 to summarize the sales variance analysis for Calumet Carpet Company.

Problem 17.63
Sales-Variance Analysis; Continuation of Problem 17.61 (Appendix C)
(LO 11)

South Bend Chemical Company manufactures two products, Florimene and Glyoxide, used in the plastics industry. The company prepares its budget on the basis of standard costs. The following data are for August:

Problem 17.64
Comprehensive Variance Analysis; Review of Chapters 16 and 17
(LO 5)

	Florimene	**Glyoxide**
Actual results:		
Direct material	3,100 kilograms at $ .90 per kilogram	4,700 kilograms at $1.15 per kilogram
Direct labor	4,900 hours at $14.05 per hour	7,400 hours at $15.10 per hour
Variable overhead	$16,170	$25,234
Fixed overhead	$20,930	$26,400
Units produced	1,000 units	1,200 units
Standards:		
Direct material	3 kilograms at $1 per kilogram	4 kilograms at $1.10 per kilogram
Direct labor	5 hours at $14 per hour	6 hours at $15 per hour
Variable overhead (per direct-labor hour)	$3.20	$3.50
Fixed overhead (per month)	$22,356	$26,520
Expected activity (direct-labor hours)	5,750	7,800

Required

a. Prepare a complete variance analysis for each variable cost for each product.
b. Prepare a complete fixed-overhead variance analysis for each product.
c. Now assume that the fixed-overhead costs are applied to units produced using the following standard rate per direct-labor hour:

$$\text{Florimene: } \$3.888 \text{ per hour} = \frac{\$22,356}{5,750 \text{ expected direct-labor hours}}$$

$$\text{Glyoxide: } \$3.40 \text{ per hour} = \frac{\$26,520}{7,800 \text{ expected direct-labor hours}}$$

Prepare two-way, three-way, and four-way analyses of overhead variances for each product.

Savannah Machine Tool Company has an automated production process, and production activity is quantified in terms of machine hours. It uses a standard-costing system. The annual static budget for 20x6 called for 6,000 units to be produced, requiring 30,000 machine hours. The standard-overhead rate for the year was computed using this planned level of production. The 20x6 manufacturing cost report follows.

Problem 17.65
Use of a Flexible Budget; Review of Chapters 16 and 17
(LO 1, 2, 5)

SAVANNAH MACHINE TOOL COMPANY
Manufacturing Cost Report
For the Year 20x6
(in thousands of dollars)

	Static Budget	Flexible Budget		
Cost Item	30,000 Machine Hours	31,000 Machine Hours	32,000 Machine Hours	Actual Cost
Direct material:				
G27 aluminum	$ 252.0	$ 260.4	$ 268.8	$ 270.0
M14 steel alloy	78.0	80.6	83.2	83.0
Direct labor:				
Assembler	273.0	282.1	291.2	287.0
Grinder	234.0	241.8	249.6	250.0
Manufacturing overhead:				
Maintenance	24.0	24.8	25.6	25.0
Supplies	129.0	133.3	137.6	130.0
Supervision	80.0	82.0	84.0	81.0
Inspection	144.0	147.0	150.0	147.0
Insurance	50.0	50.0	50.0	50.0
Depreciation	200.0	200.0	200.0	200.0
Total cost	$1,464.0	$1,502.0	$1,540.0	$1,523.0

Savannah Machine Tool Company develops flexible budgets for different levels of activity for use in evaluating performance. It produced a total of 6,200 units during 20x6, requiring 32,000 machine hours. The preceding manufacturing cost report compares the company's actual cost for the year with the static budget and the flexible budget for two different activity levels.

Required

Compute the following amounts. For variances, indicate favorable or unfavorable where appropriate. Answers should be rounded to two decimal places when necessary.

a.   The standard number of machine hours allowed to produce one unit of product.

b.   The actual cost of direct material used in one unit of product.

c.   The cost of material that should be processed per machine hour.

d.   The standard direct-labor cost for each unit produced.

e.   The variable-overhead rate per machine hour in a flexible-budget formula. (*Hint:* Use the high-low method to estimate cost behavior. In the high-low method of cost estimation, the difference between the cost levels at the high and low *activity* levels is divided by the difference between the high and low *activity* levels. This quotient provides a simple estimate of the *variable* cost rate per unit of activity.)

f.   The standard fixed-overhead rate per machine hour used for product costing.

g.   The variable-overhead spending variance. (Assume that management has determined that the actual fixed overhead cost in 20x6 amounted to $324,000.)

h.   The variable-overhead efficiency variance.

i.   The fixed-overhead budget variance.

j.   The fixed-overhead volume variance. [Make the same assumption as in requirement (g).]

k.   The total budgeted manufacturing cost (in thousands of dollars) for an output of 6,050 units. (*Hint:* Use the flexible-budget formula.)

[CMA adapted]

Problem 17.66
Comprehensive Sales-
Variance Analysis;
Revenue Perspective
and Contribution Margin
Perspective (Appendix C)
(LO 11)

The Lexington plant of AccuTime, Inc. manufactures three styles of clock radio. The basic model (B) targets the teenage market. The standard model (S) is popular with college students. AccuTime's newest product, the deluxe model (D), is designed for home and office use.

For the most recent year, AccuTime's sales manager predicted a total annual industry volume for clock radios of 200,000 units, and the following budget data were compiled by the controller for AccuTime's three products.

Model	Budgeted Price	Budgeted Unit Variable Cost	Budgeted Unit Sales Volume
Basic	$30	$20	4,000
Standard	50	30	5,000
Deluxe	90	50	1,000

When actual results for the year were recorded, the actual industry volume for clock radios was much higher than anticipated, 250,000 units. AccuTime's actual results for the year follow:

Model	Actual Price	Actual Unit Variable Cost	Actual Unit Sales Volume
Basic	$32	$17	6,000
Standard	55	30	5,400
Deluxe	85	50	600

To help top management understand the year's sales results, AccuTime's controller has asked you, his assistant, to prepare a complete sales-variable analysis.

Required

a.   Summarize the preceding information for AccuTime by preparing a table similar to Exhibit 17–16.

b.   Prepare a complete sales-variance analysis from a revenue perspective.

c.   Prepare a complete sales-variance analysis from a contribution-margin perspective.

Cases

Techno Arcade, Inc. manufactures video game machines. Market saturation and technological innovations have caused pricing pressures that have resulted in declining profits. To stem the slide in profits until new products can be introduced, top management has turned its attention to both manufacturing economies and increased production. To realize these objectives, an incentive program has been developed to reward production managers who contribute to an increase in the number of units produced and achieve cost reductions. In addition, a just-in-time purchasing program has been implemented, and raw materials are purchased on an as-needed basis.

Case 17.67
Comprehensive Review of Variances; Behavioral Effects (Appendix C)
(LO 5, 11)*

The production managers have responded to the pressure to improve manufacturing performance in several ways that have resulted in an increased number of completed units over normal production levels. The video game machines put together by the Assembly Group require parts from both the Printed Circuit Boards (PCB) and the Reading Heads (RH) groups. To attain increased production levels, the PCB and RH groups started rejecting parts that previously would have been tested and modified to meet manufacturing standards. Preventive maintenance on machines used in the production of these parts has been postponed with only emergency repair work being performed to keep production lines moving. The Maintenance Department is concerned that there will be serious breakdowns and unsafe operating conditions.

The more aggressive Assembly Group production supervisors have pressured maintenance personnel to attend to their machines at the expense of other groups. This has resulted in machine downtime in the PCB and RH groups which, when coupled with demands for accelerated parts delivery by the Assembly Group, has led to more frequent part rejections and increased friction among departments. Techno Arcade operates under a standard-costing system. The standard costs are as follows:

	Standard Cost per Unit		
	Quantity	Cost	Total
Direct material:			
Housing unit	1 unit	$20	$ 20
Printed circuit boards	2 boards	15	30
Reading heads	4 heads	10	40
Direct labor:			
Assembly group	2.0 hours	8	16

(Table continues on next page.)

---

*This case integrates material from Chapters 15, 16, and 17 and relates to learning objectives from all three chapters.

PCB group	1.0 hour	9	9
RH group	1.5 hours	10	15
Total	4.5 hours		
Variable overhead*		2	9
Total standard cost per unit			$139

*Applied on the basis of direct labor: 4.5 direct-labor hours at $2 per hour.

Techno Arcade prepares monthly performance reports based on standard costs. The following table shows the contribution report for May, when production and sales both reached 2,200 units. The budgeted and actual unit sales price in May were the same at $200.

TECHNO ARCADE, INC.
Contribution Report
For the Month of May

	Actual	Budgeted	Variance
Units	2,200	2,000	200 F
Revenue	$440,000	$400,000	$40,000 F
Variable costs:			
Direct material	$220,400	$180,000	$40,400 U
Direct labor	93,460	80,000	13,460 U
Variable overhead	18,800	18,000	800 U
Total variable costs	$332,660	$278,000	$54,660 U
Contribution margin	$107,340	$122,000	$14,660 U

Techno Arcade's top management was surprised by the unfavorable contribution-margin variance in spite of the increased sales in May. Jack Rath, director of cost management, was assigned to report on the reasons for the unfavorable contribution results as well as the individuals or groups responsible. After a thorough review of the data, Rath prepared the following usage report.

TECHNO ARCADE, INC.
Usage Report
For the Month of May

Cost Item	Actual Quantity	Actual Cost
Direct material:		
Housing units	2,200 units	$ 44,000
Printed circuit boards	4,700 boards	75,200
Reading heads	9,200 heads	101,200
Direct labor:		
Assembly	3,900 hours	31,200
Printed circuit boards	2,400 hours	23,760
Reading heads	3,500 hours	38,500
Total	9,800 hours	
Variable overhead		18,800
Total variable cost		$332,660

Rath reported that the PCB and RH groups supported the increased production levels but experienced abnormal machine downtime, causing idle personnel. This required the use of overtime to keep up with the accelerated demand for parts. The idle time was charged to direct labor. Rath also reported that the production managers of these two groups resorted to parts rejections as opposed to testing and modifying procedures formerly applied. Rath determined that the Assembly Group met management's objectives by increasing production while utilizing lower than standard hours.

Required

As a group, prepare a presentation to the class addressing the following requirements.

a. Calculate the following variances, and explain the $14,660 unfavorable variance between the budgeted and actual contribution margin during May. Assume that all raw material purchased during May was placed into production.

(1) Direct-labor rate variance.

(2) Direct-labor efficiency variance.

(3) Direct-material price variance.

(4) Direct-material quantity variance.

(5) Variable-overhead spending variance.

(6) Variable-overhead efficiency variance.

(7) Sales-price variance.

(8) Contribution-margin sales-volume variance.

b. **(1)** Identify and briefly explain the behavioral factors that could promote friction among the production managers and between the production managers and the maintenance manager.

     (2) Evaluate Rath's analysis of the unfavorable contribution results in terms of its completeness and its effect on the behavior of the production groups.

[CMA adapted]

"I just don't understand these financial statements at all!" exclaimed Elmo Knapp. Knapp explained that he had turned over management of Racketeer, Inc., a division of American Recreation Equipment, Inc., to his son, Otto, the previous month. Racketeer, Inc., manufactures tennis rackets.

    "I was really proud of Otto," he beamed. "He was showing us all the tricks he learned in business school, and if I say so myself, I think he was doing a rather good job for us. For example, he put together this budget for Racketeer, which makes it very easy to see how much profit we'll make at any sales volume. (See Exhibit A.) As best as I can figure it, in March we expected to have a volume of 8,000 units and a profit of $14,500 on our rackets. But we did much better than that! We sold 10,000 rackets, so we should have made almost $21,000 on them."

Case 17.68
Comprehensive
Overview of Budgets and
Variance Analysis*†
(LO 5)

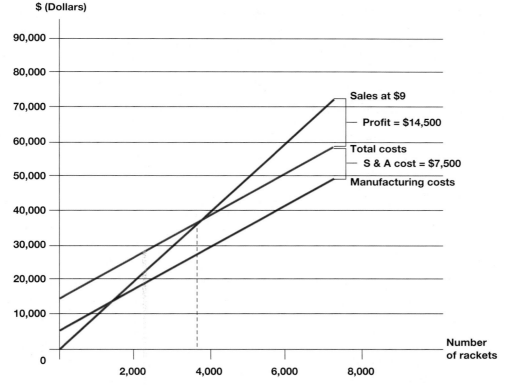

Exhibit A

Profit Graph,
Racketeer, Inc.

---

    * © Michael W. Maher.

    † This case integrates material from Chapters 15, 16, and 17 and relates to learning objectives from all three chapters. Students might wish to review the discussion in Chapter 2 on absorption and variable costing before beginning this case.

"Another one of Otto's innovations is this standard-costing system," said Knapp proudly. "He sat down with our production people and came up with a standard production cost per unit. (See Exhibit B.) He tells me this will let us know how well our production people are performing. Also, he claims it will cut down on our clerical work."

Knapp continued, "But one thing puzzles me. My calculations show that we should have earned profit of nearly $21,000 in March. However, our accountants came up with less than $19,000 in the monthly income statement. (See Exhibit C.) This bothers me a great deal. Now, I'm sure our accountants are doing their job properly. But still, it appears to me that they're about $2,200 short."

"As you can probably guess," Knapp concluded, "we are one big happy family around here. I just wish I knew what those accountants are up to . . . coming in with a low net income like that."

Required

Prepare a report for Elmo Knapp and Otto Knapp that reconciles the profit graph with the actual results for March. (See Exhibit D.) Show the source of each variance from the original plan (8,000 rackets) in as much detail as you can, and evaluate Racketeer's performance in March. Recommend improvements in Racketeer's profit-planning and control methods.

Exhibit B

Standard Costs, Racketeer, Inc.*

	Per Racket
Raw material:	
Frame (one frame per racket)	$3.15
Stringing materials: 20 feet at $.03 per foot	.60
Direct labor:	
Skilled: ⅛ hour at $9.60 per hour	1.20
Unskilled: ⅛ hour at $5.60 per hour	.70
Manufacturing overhead:	
Indirect labor	.10
Power	.03
Supervision†	.12
Depreciation†	.20
Other†	.15
Total standard cost per frame	$6.25

*Standard costs are calculated for an estimated production volume of 8,000 units each month.
† Fixed costs.

Exhibit C

Income Statement for March, Racketeer, Inc.

RACKETEER, INC.
Income Statement for March
Actual

Sales:		
10,000 rackets at $9		$90,000
Standard cost of goods sold:		
10,000 rackets at $6.25		62,500
Gross profit after standard costs		$27,500
Variances:		
Material variance		(490)
Labor variance		(392)
Overhead variance		(660)
Gross profit		$25,958
Selling and administrative expense		$ 7,200
Operating profit		$18,758

Direct material purchased and used:

Stringing materials .... 175,000 feet at $.025 per foot

Frames (Note: some frames were ruined

   during production) .... 7,100 at $3.15 per frame

Direct labor:

Skilled ($9.80 per hour) .... 900 hours

Unskilled ($5.80 per hour) .... 840 hours

Overhead:

Indirect labor .... $ 800

Power 250

Depreciation... 1,600

Supervision... 960

Other 1,250

Production .... 7,000 rackets

Exhibit D

Actual Production Data for
March, Racketeer, Inc.

Chapter 18

Organizational Design, Responsibility Accounting, and Evaluation of Divisional Performance

After completing this chapter, you should be able to:

1. Understand the role of responsibility accounting in fostering goal or behavioral congruence.

2. List several benefits and costs of decentralization.

3. Describe the distinguishing characteristics of a cost center, a discretionary cost center, a revenue center, a profit center, and an investment center.

4. Prepare a performance report and explain the relationships between the reports for various responsibility centers.

5. Compute an investment center's return on investment, residual income, and economic value added.

6. Explain how a manager can improve return on investment by increasing either the sales margin or capital turnover.

7. Describe some advantages and disadvantages of return on investment and residual income as performance measures.

8. Explain various approaches for measuring a division's income and invested capital.

Cost-*Management* Challenges

(Solutions are on page 771.)

1. **When** companies grow larger, as typified by the acquisition described in Outback Outfitters' press release, how should they manage operations? What are some benefits and costs of decentralization?

2. **How** could a responsibility accounting system foster goal or behavioral congruence for Outback Outfitters?

3. **What** are the major types of responsibility accounting centers?

4. **What** is the key feature of activity-based responsibility accounting?

5. **How** is investment center performance typically measured?

EMAIL MEMORANDUM

Outback Outfitters, Ltd.
10 Woolloomooloo Place
Sydney, New South Wales
AUSTRALIA

PRESS RELEASE   For immediate release; no restrictions.
Contact: Talia Demarest, Media Relations

Outback Outfitters, Ltd., announces its acquisition of Koala Camp Gear Company. One of Australia's largest retailers of camping equipment and outdoor apparel, Outback Outfitters operates retail outlets throughout Australia, New Zealand, and the United Kingdom. Outback also operates a mail-order business from its headquarters in Sydney. Outback's president and CEO, Jack Darwin, made this comment on the acquisition: "For some time we have been looking to acquire a manufacturing company that could supply us with our own private-label merchandise. In Koala Camp Gear Company, we have found just the right firm. Koala has achieved a reputation around the world for the quality of its products. The Koala Camp Gear and Wallaby Wear product lines are well known from Melbourne to San Francisco to London. With this acquisition, Outback Outfitters will be poised to extend its reach throughout Europe and the United States. We couldn't ask for a better fit between Koala Camp Gear Company and Outback Outfitters. We welcome the folks from Koala into our corporate family, and we look forward to a very prosperous future."

When an organization begins its operations, it is usually small, and its decision making generally is centralized. It is relatively easy in a small organization for managers to keep in touch with routine operations through face-to-face contact with employees. A manager's task is increasingly difficult as an organization becomes larger and more complex. For example, as Outback Outfitters grows through the acquisition of Koala Camp Gear Company, as described in the press release on the preceding page, the new company's operations will be more complicated. Managers must make more decisions and manage more employees. A common rule of thumb is that one supervisor usually can manage about 10 subordinates. Consequently, all but very small organizations delegate managerial duties.

Decentralized Organizations and Responsibility Accounting

LO 1 Understand the role of responsibility accounting in fostering goal or behavioral congruence.

Most large organizations are divided into smaller units, each of which is assigned particular responsibilities. These units are called by various names, including *divisions, segments, business units, work centers, and departments.* Each department comprises individuals who are responsible for particular tasks or managerial functions. The managers of an organization should ensure that the people in each department are striving toward the same overall goals. **Goal congruence** results when the managers of subunits throughout an organization have a common set of objectives. This occurs when the group acts as a team in pursuit of a mutually agreed upon goal. Individual goal congruence occurs when an individual's personal goals are consistent with organizational goals.

Although complete congruence is rare, in some cases, a strong team spirit suppresses individual desires to act differently. Examples include some military units and some athletic teams. Many companies attempt to achieve this esprit de corps. Japanese companies have worked particularly hard to create a strong team orientation among workers that has resulted in considerable goal congruence.

In most business settings, however, personal goals and organization goals differ. Performance evaluation and incentive systems are designed to encourage employees to behave as if their goals were congruent with organization goals. This results in **behavioral congruence;** that is, an individual behaves in the best interests of the organization regardless of his or her own goals.

How can an organization's cost-management system promote goal, or at least behavioral, congruence? **Responsibility accounting** refers to the various concepts and tools used to measure the performance of people and departments in order to foster goal or behavioral congruence.

Centralization versus Decentralization

Some organizations are very **centralized,** where decisions are handed down from the top echelon of management and subordinates carry them out. The military is a good example of centralized authority. At the other extreme are highly **decentralized** companies in which decisions are made at divisional and departmental levels. In many conglomerates, operating decisions are made in the field; corporate headquarters is, in effect, a holding company. The majority of companies fall between these two extremes. At General Motors, for example, operating units are decentralized, and the research and development and finance functions are centralized.

Many companies begin with a centralized structure but become more and more decentralized as they grow. Consider the following example of a fast-food franchise that started with one hamburger stand.

Benefits and Costs of a Decentralized Organization Structure

LO 2 List several benefits and costs of decentralization.

Most large organizations are decentralized. To better understand the purpose of a responsibility accounting system, it is helpful first to consider the benefits and costs associated with decentralization.

Cost Management in Practice 18.1

Benefits of Decentralization

We had a counter and 10 stools when we started. When winter came, we had to take out two stools to put in a heating furnace and almost went broke from the loss of revenue! But during the following year, I obtained the statewide franchise for a nationally known barbecue chain, and I expanded my menu.

At first, I did a little of everything—cooking, serving, bookkeeping, and advertising. I hired one full-time employee. There was little need for any formal management control system—I made all important decisions, and they were carried out. Soon we had eight outlets. I was still trying to manage everything personally. Decisions were delayed. A particular outlet would receive food shipments, but no one was authorized to accept delivery. If an outlet ran out of supplies or change, its employees had to wait until I arrived to authorize whatever needed to be done. With only one outlet, I was able to spend a reasonable amount of time on what I call high-level decision making—planning for expansion, arranging financing, developing new marketing strategies, and so forth. But with eight outlets, all of my time was consumed with day-to-day operating decisions.

Finally, I realized that the company had grown too big for me to manage alone. So I decentralized, setting up each outlet just like it was an independent operation. Now each outlet manager takes care of day-to-day operating decisions. This not only frees my time for more high-level decision making but also provides a better opportunity for the managers to learn about management, and it gives me a chance to evaluate their performance for promotion to higher management positions, which I intend to create soon. *Source:* This example, based on the actual experience of a small company, came to light during an author's research.

Benefits of decentralization.   Decentralization has several positive effects:

- Managers of the organization's subunits are specialists. They have *specialized information and skills* that enable them to manage their departments most effectively.

- Allowing managers some autonomy in decision making provides *managerial training* for future higher-level managers. For example, the manager of a company-owned McDonald's restaurant might eventually be promoted to regional supervisor in the company.

- Managers with some decision-making authority usually exhibit more positive *motivation* than those who merely execute the decisions of others.

- Delegating some decisions to lower-level managers provides *time relief to upper-level managers,* enabling them to devote time to strategic planning.

- *Empowering* employees to make decisions draws on the knowledge and expertise of those closest to day-to-day operations.

- Delegating decision making to the lowest level possible enables an organization to give a *timely response* to opportunities and problems as they arise.

Costs of decentralization.   Decentralization also has potential negative consequences:

- Managers in a decentralized organization sometimes have a *narrow focus* on their own subunit's performance rather than on the attainment of their organization's overall goals.

- As a result of this narrow focus, managers might tend to *ignore the consequences of their actions on the organization's other subunits.*

- In a decentralized organization, some tasks or *services might be duplicated* unnecessarily. For example, two departments in a decentralized university might both have a computer system (e.g., server and networked personal computers), when one might serve both departments at a lower cost.

The fundamental purpose of a responsibility accounting system is to help an organization reap the benefits of decentralization, while minimizing the costs. To this end, responsibility accounting systems are designed to foster goal or behavioral congruence throughout an organization.

Responsibility Accounting

LO 3 Describe the distinguishing characteristics of a cost center, a discretionary cost center, a revenue center, a profit center, and an investment center.

The purpose of a responsibility accounting system is to ensure that each manager and employee in an organization is striving to meet the overall goals set by top management. The basis of a responsibility accounting system is the designation of each subunit in the organization as a particular type of *responsibility center*. A **responsibility center** is a subunit in an organization whose manager is held accountable for specified financial (and nonfinancial) results of the subunit's activities. Five common types of responsibility centers are (1) cost, (2) discretionary cost, (3) revenue, (4) profit, and (5) investment.

Cost Center

A **cost center** is an organizational subunit, such as a work center or department, whose manager is responsible for the cost of an activity for which a well-defined relationship exists between inputs and outputs. Cost centers often are found in manufacturing operations where inputs, such as direct materials and direct labor, can be specified for each output. The production departments of manufacturing plants are usually cost centers. The concept has been applied in nonmanufacturing settings as well. In banks, for example, standards can be established for check processing, so check-processing departments might be cost centers. In hospitals, food-service departments, laundries, and laboratories often are set up as cost centers.

Discretionary Cost Center

The cost centers just described require a well-specified relationship between inputs and outputs for performance evaluation. A **discretionary cost center** is an organizational subunit whose manager is held accountable for costs, but the subunit's input-output relationship is not well specified. Examples of discretionary cost centers include legal, accounting, research and development, advertising, marketing, and numerous other administrative departments. Discretionary cost centers also are common in government and other nonprofit organizations whose budgets are used as a ceiling on expenditures. Managers typically are evaluated on bases other than costs. However, there usually are penalties for exceeding the budget ceiling.

Revenue Center

The manager of a **revenue center** is held accountable for the revenue attributed to the subunit. For example, the reservations department of an airline and the sales department of a manufacturer are revenue centers.

Profit Center

A **profit center** is an organizational subunit whose manager is held accountable for profit. Since profit is equal to revenue minus expenses, profit-center managers are held accountable for both the revenue and expenses attributed to their subunits. An example of a profit center is a company-owned restaurant in a fast-food chain.

American Airlines' reservations center in Tucson, Arizona, is a revenue center.

Fast-food businesses, such as this McDonald's restaurant, are profit centers.

This airplane assembly plant is an investment center.

Investment Center

The manager of an **investment center** is held accountable for the subunit's profit *and the invested capital* used by the subunit to generate its profit. A division of a large corporation is typically designed as an investment center.[1]

Illustration of Responsibility Accounting

To illustrate the concepts used in responsibility accounting, we refer again to Koala Camp Gear Company. Margo Hastings' company prospered through its first decade. Hastings added additional products, and the firm grew rapidly. Then Hastings sold her company to Outback Outfitters, Ltd., a large Australian retailer specializing in outdoor apparel, camping gear, and other outdoor equipment. Hastings retired and now is basking in the sun in Fiji.

Outback Outfitters is a household name throughout Australia, New Zealand, and the United Kingdom. The retailer is known for its high-quality outdoor apparel and equipment and its experienced and helpful sales personnel. Outback Outfitters owns retail stores in all the major cities in Australia and New Zealand, as well as in London and Manchester in England, and Glasgow in Scotland. In addition to its retail outlets throughout the world, Outback operates a large mail-order sales operation based in Sydney. Outback's mail-order operation was modeled after the operation of L. L. Bean, the highly successful U.S. mail-order company based in Freeport, Maine.

Jack Darwin, Outback's founder and CEO, had long thought that Outback should acquire a high-quality manufacturing company to provide Outback with its own private-label line of outdoor merchandise. Darwin had kept an eye on Koala Camp Gear Company for several years and, when the time seemed right, entered into negotiations with Hastings for the acquisition of the company she founded.

Outback Outfitters is now organized into three divisions. The Retail Division operates the company's sales outlets in Australia, New Zealand, and the United Kingdom. The Mail-Order Division, based in Sydney, is responsible for Outback's mail-order sales operation. The Koala Camp Gear Division manufactures a wide variety of camping gear and outdoor apparel. The camping gear retains the successful trade name Koala Camp Gear, and the division's outdoor apparel carries the trade name Wallaby Wear.

The Koala Camp Gear Division operates three manufacturing plants, and each plant has a sales department and a production department. The production department in each plant is organized into several work centers.

Exhibit 18–1 shows Outback Outfitter's organization chart, and Exhibit 18–2 depicts the firm's responsibility accounting system. As depicted in Exhibit 18–1, Outback has five levels in its organization chart: corporate, division, plant, department, and work center.

Corporate Level

The chief executive officer of Outback Outfitters, Ltd., is the company's president. The president, who is responsible to the company's stockholders, is accountable for corporate profit in relation to the capital (assets) invested in the company. Therefore, the entire company is an *investment center*. The president has the autonomy to make significant decisions that affect the company's profit and invested capital. For example, the president would make the final decision to build a new plant for the Koala Camp Gear Division.

---

[1] Although an important conceptual difference exists between profit centers and investment centers, the latter term is not always used in practice. Some managers use the term "profit center" to refer to both types of responsibility centers. Hence, when businesspeople use the term "profit center," they may be referring to a true profit center (as defined in this chapter) or to an investment center.

Exhibit 18–1

Organization Chart:
Outback Outfitters, Ltd.

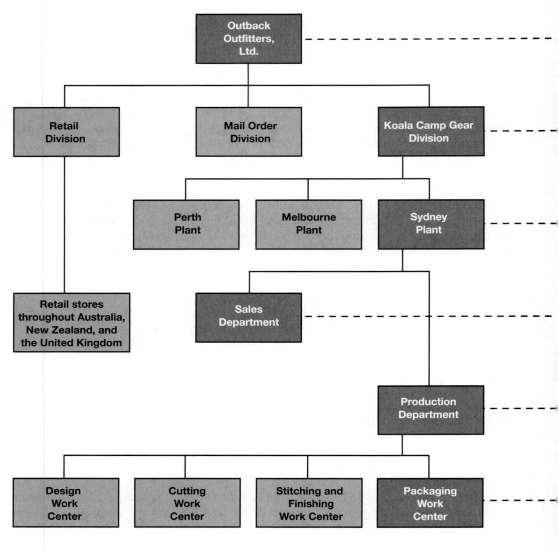

Division Level

The vice president of Koala Camp Gear Division is accountable for the profit it earns in relation to the capital invested in this division. Hence, the Koala Division is an *investment center.* Its vice president has the authority to make significant investment decisions regarding the division, up to a monetary limit specified by Outback Outfitters' CEO. For example, the vice president could decide to buy new production equipment but could not buy a new plant.

All three division managers enjoy a great deal of autonomy in managing their business units. Outback's CEO, Jack Darwin, has said on more than one occasion, "I hired good people to manage Outback's three divisions, and I'm going to stay out of their way and let them do it." In keeping with Darwin's philosophy of decentralization for Outback Outfitters, the Retail Division and the Mail-Order Division are free to buy merchandise not only from the Koala Camp Gear Division but also from other manufacturers. Similarly, the Koala Division's goods are marketed not only through Outback Outfitter's retail sales operations but also to retailers throughout the world. Of course, the highly prized brand names of Koala Camp Gear and Wallaby Wear are imprinted only on the merchandise sold through Outback Outfitters.

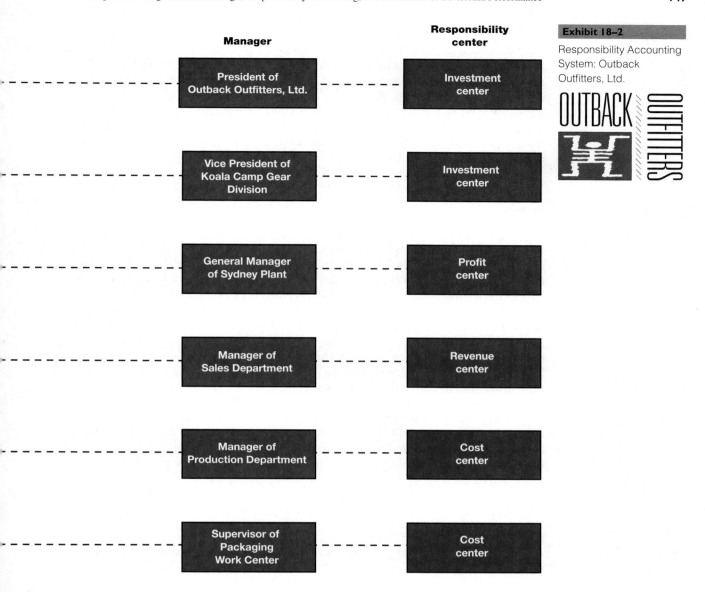

Manager	Responsibility center
President of Outback Outfitters, Ltd.	Investment center
Vice President of Koala Camp Gear Division	Investment center
General Manager of Sydney Plant	Profit center
Manager of Sales Department	Revenue center
Manager of Production Department	Cost center
Supervisor of Packaging Work Center	Cost center

Exhibit 18–2

Responsibility Accounting System: Outback Outfitters, Ltd.

Plant Level

The general manager of the Sydney plant in the Koala Camp Gear Division is accountable for the profit the plant earns. The general manager does not have the authority to make major investment decisions but is responsible for operational decisions. For example, the general manager hires the managers and supervisors in the plant, approves salary increases, and generally oversees the plant's operation. Since the plant's general manager has no authority to make major investment decisions, she is held accountable only for the plant's profit, not for the capital invested. Thus, the Sydney plant is a *profit center.*

Department Level

The Sales Department manager is held accountable for the sales made from the Sydney plant. He has the authority to set sales prices, hire sales personnel, and make other sales-related decisions. Thus, the sales department is a *revenue center.*

The Production Department is a *cost center,* whose manager is held accountable for the costs incurred in manufacturing the Sydney plant's products. He has the authority to make decisions about purchasing raw materials, hiring production employees, and so forth.

Work Center Level

Each work center supervisor is held accountable for the costs incurred in that particular work center. For example, the supervisor of the Packaging Work Center has the authority to make decisions about the choice of packaging materials, the scheduling of employees involved in packaging, and the packaging process itself. Hence, the Packaging Work Center is a *cost center.* The Cutting and Stitching and Finishing Work Centers are also cost centers. The Design Work Center, however, is a *discretionary cost center.* In the Design Work Center, the relationship between inputs and outputs is less definitive than in the other two work centers.

Performance Reports

Each responsibility center's performance is summarized periodically on a **performance report,** which shows the budgeted and actual amounts of key financial results appropriate for the type of responsibility center involved. For example, a cost center's performance report concentrates on budgeted and actual amounts for various cost items attributable to the cost center. Performance reports also typically show the variance between budgeted and actual amounts for the financial results conveyed in the report. The data in a performance report help managers use *management by exception* to control an organization's operations effectively. **Management by exception** means that managers follow up on only the most significant variances between budgeted and actual results. This allows the managers to use their limited time most effectively.[2] The performance report for the Sydney plant's Cutting Work Center is displayed as the spreadsheet in Exhibit 18–3.

As the organization chart in Exhibit 18–1 shows, Outback Outfitters, Ltd., is a *hierarchy.* This means that each subunit manager reports to one higher-level manager, from the work center supervisor all the way up to the president and chief executive officer. Such an organization also has a hierarchy of performance reports since the performance of each subunit constitutes part of the performance of the next higher-level subunit. For example, the cost performance in the Sydney plant's Cutting Work Center constitutes part of the cost performance of the plant's production department.

---

[2]See the preceding two chapters for discussion of cost-management systems designed to facilitate management by exception.

Exhibit 18–3

Performance Report for
Second Quarter: Cutting
Work Center, Sydney Plant

	Budget 2nd Quarter	Budget Year to Date	Actual 2nd Quarter	Actual Year to Date	Variance* 2nd Quarter		Variance* Year to Date	
Wages	$ 79,000	$ 167,000	$ 77,000	$ 168,000	$ 2,000	F	$ 1,000	U
Fabric	795,000	1,670,000	793,000	1,669,000	2,000	F	1,000	F
Manufacturing overhead:								
Unit level	60,000	140,000	61,000	144,000	1,000	U	4,000	U
Batch level	65,000	104,000	59,000	120,000	6,000	F	16,000	U
Product-sustaining level	31,000	87,000	35,000	72,000	4,000	U	15,000	F
Total expense	$ 1,030,000	$ 2,168,000	$ 1,025,000	$ 2,173,000	$ 5,000	F	$ 5,000	U

*F denotes favorable variance; U denotes unfavorable variance.

Exhibit 18–4   Performance Reports for Second Quarter: Selected Subunits of Outback Outfitters, Ltd. (all numbers in thousands)

	Budget*		Actual*		Variance†	
	Second Quarter	Year to Date	Second Quarter	Year to Date	Second Quarter	Year to Date
Company	$29,655	$63,562	$29,711	$63,565	$ 56 F	$ 3 F
Retail Division	$12,395	$26,415	$12,365	$26,325	$ 30 U	$ 90 U
Mail Order Division	5,000	11,200	5,100	11,300	100 F	100 F
Koala Camp Gear Division	12,260	25,947	12,246	25,940	14 U	7 U
Total profit	$29,655	$63,562	$29,711	$63,565	$ 56 F	$ 3 F
Koala Camp Gear Division						
Perth Plant	$ 6,050	$12,700	$ 6,060	$12,740	$ 10 F	$ 40 F
Melbourne Plant	2,100	4,500	2,050	4,430	50 U	70 U
Sydney Plant	4,110	8,747	4,136	8,770	26 F	23 F
Total profit	$12,260	$25,947	$12,246	$25,940	$ 14 U	$ 7 U
Sydney Plant						
Sales Department	$ 5,570	$11,780	$ 5,590	$11,815	20 F	35 F
Production Department	(1,460)	(3,033)	(1,454)	(3,045)	6 F	12 U
Total profit	$ 4,110	$ 8,747	$ 4,136	$ 8,770	$ 26 F	$ 23 F
Production Department						
Design Work Center	$ (20)	$ (40)	$ (22)	$ (39)	$ 2 U	$ 1 F
Cutting Work Center	(1,030)	(2,168)	(1,025)	(2,173)	5 F	5 U
Stitching and Finishing Work Center	(300)	(600)	(295)	(603)	5 F	3 U
Packaging Work Center	(110)	(225)	(112)	(230)	2 U	5 U
Total cost	$ (1,460)	$ (3,033)	$ (1,454)	$ (3,045)	$ 6 F	$ 12 U
Cutting Work Center						
Wages	$ (79)	$ (167)	$ (77)	$ (168)	$ 2 F	$ 1 U
Fabric	(795)	(1,670)	(793)	(1,669)	2 F	1 F
Manufacturing overhead:						
Unit level	(60)	(140)	(61)	(144)	1 U	4 U
Batch level	(65)	(104)	(59)	(120)	6 F	16 U
Product-sustaining level	(31)	(87)	(35)	(72)	4 U	15 F
Total cost	$ (1,030)	$ (2,168)	$ (1,025)	$ (2,173)	$ 5 F	$ 5 U

*Numbers without parentheses denote profit; numbers with parentheses denote expenses.

†F denotes favorable variance; U denotes unfavorable variance. For comparisons between budgeted and actual *profit* amounts, a favorable variance results when actual profit exceeds budgeted profit. For comparisons between budgeted and actual cost amounts, a favorable variance results when the actual cost is *lower than* the budgeted amount.

Exhibit 18–4 shows the relationships between the March performance reports for several subunits of Outback Outfitters. The Cutting Work Center is the lowest-level subunit shown, and its performance report is the same as that displayed in Exhibit 18–3. The *total cost* line from the Cutting Work Center's performance report is included as one line in the performance report of the Production Department. Also included are the total cost figures for the department's other work centers. How is the *total cost* line for the Production Department used in the performance report for the Sydney plant? Follow the relationships in Exhibit 18–4, which are emphasized with arrows.

The hierarchy of performance reports starts at the bottom and builds toward the top, just as the organization structure depicted in Exhibit 18–1 builds from the bottom upward. Each manager in the organization receives the performance report for his or her own subunit in addition to the performance reports for the major subunits

in the next lower level. For example, the general manager of the Sydney plant receives the reports for each of its departments, sales and production. With these reports, the plant's general manager can evaluate her subordinates as well as her own performance. This will help the general manager to improve the plant's performance, motivate employees, and plan future operations.

In addition to the financial information in the performance reports, managers at all levels in the organization make significant use of nonfinancial performance data. See Chapters 1 and 20 for discussions of such nonfinancial information and the balanced scorecard perspective on performance evaluation.

Budgets, Variance Analysis, and Responsibility Accounting

Notice that the performance reports in Exhibit 18–4 make significant use of budgets and variance analysis. Thus, the topics of budgeting, variance analysis, and responsibility accounting are closely interrelated. The flexible budget provides the benchmark against which actual revenues, expenses, and profits are compared. As you learned in the preceding chapters, the use of a flexible budget is important so that appropriate comparisons can be made. Comparing the actual costs incurred in the Sydney plant's Cutting Department, for example, with the budgeted costs established for a different level of activity makes no sense.

The performance reports in Exhibit 18–4 also show variances between budgeted and actual performance. These variances often are broken down into smaller components to help management pinpoint responsibility and diagnose performance. Variance analysis, which was discussed in detail in the preceding two chapters, is an important tool in a responsibility accounting system.

Activity-Based Responsibility Accounting

Traditional responsibility accounting systems tend to focus on the financial performance measures of cost, revenue, and profit for the *subunits* of an organization. Contemporary cost-management systems, however, are beginning to focus more and more on *activities*. Costs are incurred in organizations and their subunits because of activities. *Activity-based costing* (ABC) systems associate costs with the activities that drive those costs. The database created by an ABC system, coupled with nonfinancial measures of operational performance for each activity, enables management to employ *activity-based responsibility accounting.*[3]

Activity-based responsibility accounting is a system for measuring the performance of an organization's employees and subunits, which focuses not only on the cost of performing activities but on the activities themselves. Is a particular activity necessary? Does it add value to the organization's product or service? Can the activity be improved? By seeking answers to these questions, managers can eliminate non-value-added activities and increase the cost effectiveness of the activities that do add value.

How Responsibility Accounting Affects Behavior

Responsibility accounting systems can influence employee behavior significantly. Whether the behavioral effects are positive or negative, however, depends on how an organization implements responsibility accounting.

---

[3] See C. J. McNair, "Interdependence and Control: Traditional vs. Activity-Based Responsibility Accounting." See also K. L. Towry, "Control in a Teamwork Environment," for research addressing the role of various factors on the effectiveness of mutual monitoring in a team setting. (Full citations to references are in the Bibliography.)

Does It Provide Information or Place Blame?

The proper focus of a responsibility accounting system is *information*. The system should identify the individual in the organization who is in the best position to explain each particular event or financial result. The emphasis should be on providing that individual and higher-level managers with information to help them understand the reasons behind the organization's performance. When properly used, a responsibility accounting system *does not emphasize blame*. If managers believe they are beaten over the head with criticism and rebukes when unfavorable variances occur, they are unlikely to respond in a positive way. Instead, they will tend to undermine the system and view it with skepticism. But when the responsibility accounting system emphasizes its informational role, managers tend to react constructively and strive for improved performance.

Is There Really Cost or Revenue Controllability?

Some organizations use performance reports that distinguish between controllable and uncontrollable costs or revenues. For example, the supervisor of the Cutting Work Center influences the hours and efficiency of the work center employees, but this manager probably cannot change the wage rates. A performance report that distinguishes between the financial results influenced by the supervisor and those the supervisor does not influence has the advantage of providing complete information to the supervisor, but the report recognizes that certain results are beyond his or her control.

Identifying costs as controllable or uncontrollable is not always easy. Many cost items are influenced by more than one person. The time frame also can be important in determining controllability. Some costs are controllable over a long time frame, but not within a short time period. To illustrate, suppose that the Cutting Work Center supervisor has signed a one-year contract with a local fabric supplier. The supervisor can influence the cost of fabric if the time period is a year or more but cannot control the cost on a weekly basis.

How Can Desired Behavior Be Motivated?

Organizations often use the responsibility accounting system to motivate actions that upper-level management considers desirable. Sometimes the responsibility accounting system can solve behavioral problems and promote teamwork. Consider the following scenario, originally reported by Professor R. R. Villers, in which the production scheduler in a manufacturing firm was frequently asked to interrupt production of one product with a rush order for another product. Rush orders typically resulted in higher costs because more production setups were required. Since the production scheduler was evaluated on the basis of costs, he was reluctant to accept rush orders. The sales manager, on the other hand, was evaluated on the basis of sales revenue. By agreeing to customers' demands for rush orders, the sales manager satisfied his customers. This resulted in more future sales and favorable performance ratings for the sales manager.

As the rush orders became more and more frequent, the production manager began to object. The sales manager responded by asking whether the production scheduler wanted to take the responsibility for losing a customer by refusing a rush order. The production scheduler did not want to be blamed for lost sales, so he grudgingly accepted the rush orders. However, considerable ill will developed between the sales manager and production scheduler.

The company's managerial accountants came to the rescue by redesigning the responsibility accounting system. The system was modified to accumulate the extra costs associated with rush orders and charge them to the sales manager's responsibility center rather than the production scheduler's center. The ultimate result was that the sales manager chose more carefully which rush-order requests to make, and the production manager accepted them gracefully.

Acceptance or rejection of a rush order is a cost–benefit decision.

Potential Costs of Accepting Rush Order	**Potential Benefits of Accepting Rush Order**
Disrupted production	Satisfied customers
More setups	Increased future sales
Higher costs	
Need to outsource*	

*See Chapter 7 for a discussion of issues pertaining to the effects of binding capacity constraints.

The problem described in this scenario developed because two different managers were considering the costs and benefits of the rush-order decision. The production manager was looking only at the costs while the sales manager was looking only at the benefits. The modified responsibility accounting system made the sales manager look at *both the costs and the benefits* associated with each rush order. Then the sales manager could make the necessary trade-off between costs and benefits in considering each rush order. Some rush orders were rejected because the sales manager decided that the costs exceeded the benefits. Other rush orders were accepted when the importance of the customer and potential future sales justified it.[4] This example illustrates how a well-designed responsibility accounting system can make an organization run more smoothly and achieve higher performance.

Performance Measurement in Investment Centers

LO 5 Compute an investment center's return on investment, residual income, and economic value added.

How do the top managers of large companies such as Microsoft and Exxon evaluate their divisions and other major subunits? The largest subunits within these and similar organizations usually are designated as *investment centers*. The manager of this type of *responsibility center* is held accountable not only for the investment center's *profit* but also for the *capital invested* to earn that profit. Invested capital refers to assets, such as buildings and equipment, used in a subunit's operations. In this section, we study the methods used to evaluate investment centers and the performance of their managers.[5]

Refer again to Outback Outfitters' organization chart (Exhibit 18–1). The Mail-Order Division, Koala Camp Gear Division, and the Retail Division are investment centers. This responsibility center designation is appropriate because each division manager has the authority to make decisions that affect both profit and invested capital. For example, the Retail Division manager approves the overall pricing policies in the Retail Division's stores and has the autonomy to sign contracts to buy merchandise for resale. These actions influence the division's profit. In addition, the Retail Division manager has the authority to build new Outback Outfitters stores, rent space in shopping centers, or close existing stores. These decisions affect the amount of capital invested in the division.

The primary goals of any profit-making enterprise include maximizing its profitability and using its invested capital as effectively as possible. Cost managers use three different measures to evaluate the performance of investment centers: return on

---

[4] Customer profitability analysis, which was covered in Chapter 6, can help in making a rush-order acceptance decision when key customers are involved. Also critical to the decision about accepting a rush order are considerations of the impact of accepting the order on production capacity. If accepting the rush order does not affect bottleneck processes, the organization will not incur an opportunity cost by producing the order.

[5] Recall that in practice the term *profit center* sometimes is used interchangeably with the term *investment center*. To be precise, however, the term *profit center* should be reserved for a subunit whose manager is held accountable for profit but not for invested capital.

investment, residual income, and economic value added (EVA®, a registered trademark of Stern Stewart.) We illustrate each of these measures for Outback Outfitters, Ltd., using the following data from the most recent year.

	Mail-Order Division	Koala Camp Gear Division	Retail Division
Sales revenue	$350,000,000	$405,000,000	$960,000,000
Income	14,000,000	45,000,000	48,000,000
Invested capital	70,000,000	300,000,000	480,000,000

Return on Investment as a Performance Measure

Traditionally, the most common investment-center performance measure is **return on investment (ROI),** which is defined as the investment center's income divided by its invested capital.

$$\text{Return on investment (ROI)} = \frac{\text{Income}}{\text{Invested capital}}$$

The ROI calculations for Outback Outfitters' three divisions for the most recent year are:

	$\dfrac{\text{Income}}{\text{Invested Capital}}$	=	Return on Investment (ROI)
Mail-Order Division	$\dfrac{\$14,000,000}{\$70,000,000}$	=	20%
Koala Camp Gear Division	$\dfrac{\$45,000,000}{\$300,000,000}$	=	15%
Retail Division	$\dfrac{\$48,000,000}{\$480,000,000}$	=	10%

Note that the ROI calculation for each division considers *both divisional income and the capital invested* in the division. Why is this important? Suppose that each division were evaluated only on the basis of its divisional profit. The Retail Division reported a higher divisional profit than the Mail-Order Division. Does this mean that the Retail Division performed better than the Mail-Order Division? The answer is no; although the retail division's profit exceeded the Mail-Order Division's profit, the Retail Division used much more invested capital to earn its profit. The Retail Division's assets are almost seven times the assets of the Mail-Order Division.

Considering the relative size of the two divisions, we would expect the Retail Division to earn a higher profit than the Mail-Order Division. The important question is not how much profit each division earned but how effectively each division used its invested capital to earn a profit.

Factors underlying ROI.   We can rewrite the ROI formula as follows:

$$\text{Return on investment} = \frac{\text{Income}}{\text{Invested capital}} = \frac{\text{Income}}{\text{Sales revenue}} \times \frac{\text{Sales revenue}}{\text{Invested capital}}$$

Notice that the *sales revenue* term cancels out in the denominator and numerator when the two right-hand fractions are multiplied.

Writing the ROI formula in this way highlights the factors that determine a division's return on investment. Income divided by sales revenue is called the **sales margin,** a measure of the percentage of each sales dollar that remains as profit after all expenses are covered. Sales revenue divided by invested capital is called the **capital turnover;** it focuses on the number of sales dollars generated by every dollar of invested capital. The sales margin and capital turnover for Outback Outfitters' three divisions are calculated as follows:

	Sales margin	×	Capital turnover	= ROI
	$\dfrac{\text{Income}}{\text{Sales revenue}}$	×	$\dfrac{\text{Sales revenue}}{\text{Invested Capital}}$	= ROI
Mail-Order Division	$\dfrac{\$14,000,000}{\$350,000,000}$	×	$\dfrac{\$350,000,000}{\$70,000,000}$	= 20%
Koala Camp Gear Division	$\dfrac{\$45,000,000}{\$405,000,000}$	×	$\dfrac{\$405,000,000}{\$300,000,000}$	= 15%
Retail Division	$\dfrac{\$48,000,000}{\$960,000,000}$	×	$\dfrac{\$960,000,000}{\$480,000,000}$	= $10%

The Retail Division's sales margin is 5 percent ($48,000,000 profit ÷ $960,000,000 sales revenue). Thus, each dollar of divisional sales resulted in a 5 cent profit. The division's capital turnover was 2 ($960,000,000 sales revenue ÷ $480,000,000 invested capital). Thus, each dollar of capital invested in the division's assets, such as store buildings, display shelves, checkout equipment, and inventory, generated $2 of sales revenue.

LO 6 Explain how a manager can improve return on investment by increasing either the sales margin or capital turnover.

Improving a division's ROI. How could the Retail Division manager improve the division's return on investment? Since ROI is the product of the sales margin and the capital turnover, ROI can be improved by increasing either or both of its components. For example, if the Retail Division manager increases the division's sales margin to 7 percent while holding the capital turnover constant at 2, the division's ROI would climb from 10 percent to 14 percent, as follows:

$$\underset{\text{improved ROI}}{\text{Retail Division's}} = \underset{\text{sales margin}}{\text{Improved}} \times \underset{\text{capital turnover}}{\text{Same}}$$

$$14\% \quad = \quad 7\% \quad \times \quad 2$$

To bring about the improved sales margin, the Retail Division manager would need to increase divisional profit to $67,200,000 on sales of $960,000,000 ($67,200,000 ÷ $960,000,000 = .07). How could profit be increased without changing total sales revenue? There are two possibilities: (a) increase sales prices while selling less quantity, and thereby incurring lower cost of goods sold expense, or (b) decrease operating expenses. Neither of these is necessarily easy to do. In increasing sales prices, the division manager must be careful not to lose sales to the extent that total sales revenue declines. Similarly, reducing the expenses must not diminish product quality, customer service, or overall store atmosphere. Any of these changes could also result in lost sales revenue.

An alternative way to increase the Retail Division's ROI is to increase its capital turnover. Suppose that the Retail Division manager increased the division's capital turnover to 3 while holding the sales margin constant at 5 percent. The division's ROI would climb from 10 percent to 15 percent:

$$\underset{\text{improved ROI}}{\text{Retail Division's}} = \underset{\text{sales margin}}{\text{Same}} \times \underset{\text{capital turnover}}{\text{Improved}}$$

$$15\% \quad = \quad 5\% \quad \times \quad 3$$

To obtain the improved capital turnover, the Retail Division manager would need to either increase sales revenue or reduce the division's invested capital. For example, the improved ROI could be achieved by reducing invested capital to $320,000,000 while maintaining sales revenue of $960,000,000—a very tall order. The division manager can lower invested capital somewhat by reducing inventories and can increase sales revenue by using store space more effectively. Reducing inventories might lead, however, to stockouts and lost sales, and crowded aisles could drive customers away.

Improving ROI is a difficult challenge, and it requires the expertise and constant attention of a skilled management team.

Residual Income as a Performance Measure

Although ROI has traditionally been the most popular investment-center performance measure, it has one major drawback. To illustrate, suppose that Outback's Koala Camp Gear Division manager is considering a major investment in computer-integrated manufacturing (CIM) equipment for all three of Koala's plants. The equipment will cost $50 million. The investment in the CIM system is expected to result in annual operating savings of $5.5 million and will therefore increase divisional income by $5.5 million. Thus, the return on this new investment is 11 percent:

$$\frac{\text{Return on investment}}{\text{in new equipment}} = \frac{\text{Increase in divisional profit}}{\text{Increase in invested capital}} = \frac{\$5,500,000}{\$50,000,000} = 11\%$$

Now suppose that it costs Outback Outfitters 10 cents for each dollar of capital to invest in operational assets. What is the optimal decision for the Koala Camp Gear Division manager to make, *viewed from the perspective of the company as a whole?* Since it costs Outback Outfitters 10 percent for every dollar of capital, and the return on the investment in new equipment is 11 percent, an autonomous division manager should decide to buy the new equipment.

Now consider what is likely to happen. The Koala Camp Gear Division manager's performance is evaluated on the basis of his division's ROI. Without the new equipment, the divisional ROI is 15 percent ($45,000,000 divisional profit ÷ $300,000,000 invested capital). If he purchases the new equipment, his divisional ROI will decline:

Koala Camp Gear Division's Return on Investment

Without Investment in New CIM Equipment	With Investment in New CIM Equipment
$\frac{\$45,000,000}{\$300,000,000} = 15\%$	$\frac{\$45,000,000 + \$5,500,000}{\$300,000,000 + \$50,000,000} < 15\%$

Why did this happen? Although the investment in new equipment earns a return of 11 percent, which is higher than the company's cost of raising capital (10 percent), the return is less than the division's ROI without the equipment (15 percent). Averaging the new investment with that already in place in the Koala Camp Gear Division merely reduces the division's ROI. Since the division manager is evaluated using ROI, he will be reluctant to decide to acquire the new equipment.

The problem is that the ROI measure omits an important piece of information: It ignores the firm's cost of raising investment capital. For this reason, many managers prefer to use a different investment-center performance measure called *residual income* instead of ROI. Before turning our attention to residual income, however, let's consider the ethical issues involved in the scenario just described.

Ethical considerations. The Koala Camp Gear Division manager faces a tough decision regarding the purchase of the new equipment. The equipment will earn a return greater than Outback Outfitters' cost of acquiring investment capital. Thus, the purchase is in the best interest of the company as a whole. However, purchasing the equipment will lower Koala Camp Gear Division's ROI, and the division manager is evaluated on the basis of divisional ROI. Perhaps his promotion potential, salary increases, and bonuses are affected by the division's ROI, to say nothing of similar opportunities for his fellow managers in the Koala Camp Gear Division.

What should the division manager do? Ethical considerations suggest that the division manager should go ahead and purchase the CIM equipment, even though this decision could potentially jeopardize his prospects with the company, along with those of his divisional colleagues. The division manager, like all managers and employees, is supposed to be looking out for the best interests of the company and its owners. Nevertheless, anecdotal evidence, along with considerations of basic human nature, suggest that it might be unrealistic to expect such a manager to put the interests of corporate shareholders ahead of his own perceived interests, those of his family, and those of his colleagues and their families. What would you do?

Regardless of how you answer this rhetorical question, a very important point for our study of cost-management systems is just this: To the extent possible, it is best for all concerned if the performance evaluation system results in goal or (at least behavioral) congruence so that managers have an incentive to make decisions consistent with corporate goals.

Computing residual income.   The **residual income (RI)** of an investment center is its profit minus its invested capital times an imputed interest rate.

$$\begin{array}{c}\text{Residual} \\ \text{income}\end{array} = \begin{array}{c}\text{Investment} \\ \text{center's} \\ \text{profit}\end{array} - \left(\begin{array}{c}\text{Investment} \\ \text{center's} \\ \text{invested capital}\end{array} \times \begin{array}{c}\text{Imputed} \\ \text{interest} \\ \text{rate}\end{array}\right)$$

where the imputed interest rate is the firm's cost of acquiring investment capital.

Residual income is a dollar amount, not a ratio like ROI. It is the amount of an investment center's profit that remains (as a residual) after subtracting an imputed interest charge. The imputed interest charge is estimated and reflects the organization's minimum required rate of return on invested capital. The imputed interest rate should be the rate of return on investments of similar risk that is being forgone by Outback Outfitters, Ltd., as a result of tying up invested capital in the investment center being evaluated. In some firms, the imputed interest rate depends on the risk of the investment for which the funds will be used. Thus, divisions that have different levels of risk sometimes are assigned different imputed interest rates.

The residual income of Outback's Koala Camp Gear Division is computed here, both with and without the investment in the new CIM system. The imputed interest rate is 10 percent.

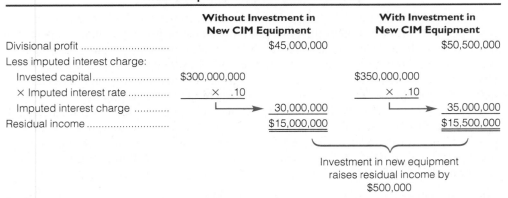

Koala Camp Gear Division's Residual Income

	Without Investment in New CIM Equipment		With Investment in New CIM Equipment	
Divisional profit		$45,000,000		$50,500,000
Less imputed interest charge:				
Invested capital..........................	$300,000,000		$350,000,000	
× Imputed interest rate	× .10		× .10	
Imputed interest charge		30,000,000		35,000,000
Residual income		$15,000,000		$15,500,000

Investment in new equipment
raises residual income by
$500,000

Notice that the Koala Camp Gear Division's residual income will *increase* if the new equipment is purchased. What will be the division manager's incentive if he is evaluated on the basis of residual income instead of ROI? He will want to make the investment because that decision will increase his division's residual income. Thus, goal congruence is achieved when divisional performance is evaluated using residual income.

Why does residual income facilitate goal congruence while ROI does not? Because the residual-income formula incorporates an important piece of data that is excluded from the ROI formula: the firm's minimum required rate of return on invested capital. To summarize, ROI and RI are compared as follows:

LO 7 Describe some advantages and disadvantages of return on investment and residual income as performance measures.

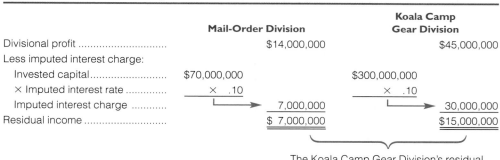

$$\text{ROI} = \frac{\text{Investment center's profit}}{\text{Investment center's invested capital}} \quad \longleftarrow \quad \text{Two pieces of data}$$

$$\text{Residual income} = \text{Investment center's profit} - \left(\text{Investment center's invested capital} \times \text{Imputed interest rate} \right)$$

Three pieces of data

Unfortunately, residual income also has a serious drawback: It should not be used to compare the performance of different-sized investment centers because it incorporates a bias in favor of the larger investment center. To illustrate, the following table compares the residual income of Outback's Mail-Order and Koala Camp Gear Divisions. Notice that the Koala Camp Gear Division's RI is considerably higher than that of the Mail-Order Division. This is entirely due to the much larger size of the Koala Division, as evidenced by its far higher invested capital amount.

Comparison of Residual Income: Two Divisions

	Mail-Order Division		Koala Camp Gear Division	
Divisional profit		$14,000,000		$45,000,000
Less imputed interest charge:				
Invested capital.........................	$70,000,000		$300,000,000	
× Imputed interest rate	× .10		× .10	
Imputed interest charge		7,000,000		30,000,000
Residual income		$ 7,000,000		$15,000,000

The Koala Camp Gear Division's residual income is much higher simply because it is larger than the Mail-Order Division.

In short, neither ROI nor RI provides a perfect measure of investment-center performance. ROI can undermine goal congruence. Residual income distorts comparisons between investment centers of different sizes. As a result, some companies routinely use both measures for divisional performance evaluation.

Evaluating the Success of a Division

One of Koala Camp Gear Division's suppliers, Queensland Fabrics Company, has two divisions, which reported the following results for the most recent year:

You're the Decision Maker 18.1

	Brisbane Division	Cairns Division
Income...	$ 900,000	$ 200,000
Invested capital	6,000,000	1,000,000
ROI...	15%	20%

Which was the most successful division for the year? Think carefully about this and back up your answer with a quantitative analysis.

(Solutions begin on page 772.)

Economic Value Added (EVA) as a Performance Measure

The most contemporary measure of investment center performance is *economic value added (EVA)*. The **economic value added (EVA)** is an investment center's after-tax operating income minus its total assets (net of its current liabilities) times the company's weighted-average cost of capital.

$$\begin{matrix}\text{Economic} \\ \text{value} \\ \text{added}\end{matrix} = \begin{matrix}\text{Investment} \\ \text{center's after-} \\ \text{tax operating} \\ \text{profit}\end{matrix} - \left[\left(\begin{matrix}\text{Investment} \\ \text{center's} \\ \text{total assets}\end{matrix} - \begin{matrix}\text{Investment} \\ \text{center's} \\ \text{current} \\ \text{liabilities}\end{matrix}\right) \times \begin{matrix}\text{Weighted} \\ \text{average} \\ \text{cost of} \\ \text{capital}\end{matrix}\right]$$

Like residual income, the economic value added is a dollar amount. It differs from residual income in two important ways. First, an investment center's current liabilities are subtracted from its total assets. Second, the weighted-average cost of capital is used in the calculation.

Weighted-average cost of capital.   Outback Outfitters, Ltd., has two sources of long-term capital: debt and equity. The cost of issuing debt to Outback Outfitters is the after-tax cost of the interest payments on the debt, considering the fact that the interest payments are tax deductible. The cost of Outback's equity capital is the investment opportunity rate of its investors, that is, the rate they could earn on investments of similar risk to that of investing in Outback Outfitters. The **weighted-average cost of capital (WACC)** is the average of the after-tax cost of debt capital and the cost of equity capital, weighted by the relative proportions of the firm's capital provided by debt and equity.

$$\begin{matrix}\text{Weighted-} \\ \text{average} \\ \text{cost of} \\ \text{capital}\end{matrix} = \frac{\left(\begin{matrix}\text{After-tax} \\ \text{cost of} \\ \text{debt} \\ \text{capital}\end{matrix}\right)\left(\begin{matrix}\text{Market} \\ \text{value} \\ \text{of debt}\end{matrix}\right) + \left(\begin{matrix}\text{Cost of} \\ \text{equity} \\ \text{capital}\end{matrix}\right)\left(\begin{matrix}\text{Market} \\ \text{value of} \\ \text{equity}\end{matrix}\right)}{\begin{matrix}\text{Market} \\ \text{value} \\ \text{of debt}\end{matrix} + \begin{matrix}\text{Market} \\ \text{value of} \\ \text{equity}\end{matrix}}$$

The interest rate on Outback Outfitters' $400 million debt is 9 percent, and the company's tax rate is 30 percent. Therefore, Outback's after-tax cost of debt is 6.3 percent [9% × (1−30%)]. Let's assume that the cost of Outback's equity capital is 12 percent. Moreover, the market value of the company's equity is $600 million.[6] The following calculation shows that Outback Outfitters' WACC is 9.72 percent.

$$\begin{matrix}\text{Weighted-average} \\ \text{cost of capital}\end{matrix} = \frac{(.063)(\$400,000,000) + (.12)(\$600,000,000)}{\$400,000,000 + \$600,000,000} = .0972$$

Finally, Outback Outfitters has $20 million in current liabilities, distributed as follows:

Division	Current Liabilities
Mail Order	$6,000,000
Koala Camp Gear	5,000,000
Retail	9,000,000

---

[6] The *book value* of Outback Outfitters' equity is $430 million, but that amount does not reflect the current value of the company's assets or the value of intangible assets such as the Koala Camp Gear and Wallaby Wear brand names.

Now we can compute the economic value added (or EVA) for each of Outback's three divisions.

Division	After-Tax Operating Income (in millions)	−	[(Total Assets (in millions)	−	Current Liabilities (in millions))	×	WACC]	=	Economic Value Added
Mail-Order	$14 × (1 − .30)	−	[($ 70	−	$6)	×	.0972]	=	$ 3,579,200
Koala Camp Gear	$45 × (1 − .30)	−	[($300	−	$5)	×	.0972]	=	$ 2,826,000
Retail	$48 × (1 − .30)	−	[($480	−	$9)	×	.0972]	=	$(12,181,200)

The EVA analysis reveals that Outback's Retail Division is in trouble. Its substantial negative EVA merits the immediate attention of the management team. It could be that Outback should focus more of its resources on the mail-order and manufacturing businesses.

We return to the EVA measure later in this chapter when we explore its relationship to managerial incentives.

Measuring Invested Capital and Income

The return-on-investment, residual-income, and economic-value-added (EVA) measures of investment-center performance all use profit and invested capital in their formulas. This raises the question of how to measure divisional profit and invested capital. This section illustrates various approaches resolving these measurement issues.

LO 8 Explain various approaches for measuring a division's income and invested capital.

Measuring Invested Capital

We focus on Outback's Koala Camp Gear Division to illustrate several alternative approaches to measuring an investment center's capital. Exhibit 18–5 lists the assets and liabilities associated with the Koala Camp Gear Division. Notice that Exhibit 18–5 does not constitute a complete balance sheet. First, there are no long-term liabilities, such as bonds payable, associated with the Koala Camp Gear Division. Although Outback Outfitters has long-term debt, assigning portions of that debt to the company's individual divisions is not meaningful. Second, it has no stockholders' equity associated with the Koala Camp Gear Division. The owners of the company own stock in Outback Outfitters, not in its individual divisions.

Average balances. ROI, residual income, and EVA are computed for a period of time, such as a year or a month. Asset balances, on the other hand, are measured at a point in time, such as December 31. Since divisional asset balances generally change over

Assets*		
Current assets (cash, accounts receivable, inventories, etc.)		$ 34,000,000
Long-lived assets (land, buildings, equipment, vehicles, etc.):		
Gross book value (acquisition cost)	$304,000,000	
Less: Accumulated depreciation	64,000,000	
Net book value		240,000,000
Plant under construction		26,000,000
Total assets		$300,000,000
Liabilities*		
Current liabilities (accounts payable, salaries payable, etc.)		$ 5,000,000

*This is not a balance sheet, but a list of the average balances of certain assets and liabilities associated with the Koala Camp Gear Division during the year.

Exhibit 18–5

Assets and Liabilities Associated with Koala Camp Gear Division

OUTBACK OUTFITTERS

time, we use average balances in calculating ROI, residual income, and EVA. For example, if the Koala Camp Gear Division's balance in invested capital was $290 million on January 1, and $310 million on December 31, we would use the average invested capital of $300 million in the ROI, residual income, and EVA calculations.

Should total assets be used?   Exhibit 18–5 shows that during the most recent year the Koala Camp Gear Division had *average balances* of $34 million in current assets, $240 million in net long-lived assets, and $26 million tied up in a plant under construction. (Outback Outfitters is building a new high-tech plant in Brisbane to manufacture its new line of diving equipment.) In addition, Exhibit 18–5 discloses that the Koala Camp Gear Division's average balance of current liabilities was $5 million.

What is the division's invested capital? Consider several possibilities here:

- *Total assets.* The management of Outback Outfitters has decided to use *average total assets* for the year in measuring each division's invested capital. Thus, $300 million is the amount used in the ROI, residual income, and EVA calculations discussed earlier in this chapter. This measure of invested capital is appropriate if the division manager has considerable authority in making decisions about *all* of the division's assets, *including nonproductive assets.* In this case, the Koala Division's partially completed plant is a nonproductive asset. Since the division manager had considerable influence in deciding to build the new plant and is responsible for overseeing the project, average total assets provides an appropriate measure.

- *Total productive assets.* In other companies, top management direct division managers to keep nonproductive assets, such as vacant land or construction in progress. In such cases, the exclusion of nonproductive assets from the measure of invested capital is appropriate. Then *average total productive assets* are used to measure invested capital. If Outback Outfitters had chosen this alternative, $274 million would have been used in the ROI, residual income, and EVA calculations (total assets of $300 million less $26 million for the plant under construction).

- *Total assets less current liabilities.* Some companies allow division managers to secure short-term bank loans and other short-term credit. In such cases, invested capital often is measured by *average total assets less average current liabilities.* This approach encourages investment-center managers to minimize resources tied up in assets and maximize the use of short-term credit to finance operations. If Outback Outfitters had used this approach, the Koala Camp Gear Division's invested capital would have been $295 million, total assets of $300 million less current liabilities of $5 million. (*Note:* Current liabilities are always subtracted from total assets for the measure of invested capital used in the EVA measure.)

Gross or net book value.   Another decision to make in choosing a measure of invested capital is whether to use the *gross book value (acquisition cost)* or the *net book value* of long-lived assets. (Net book value is the acquisition cost less accumulated depreciation.) Outback Outfitters' management has decided to use the average net book value of $240 million to value the Koala Camp Gear Division's long-lived assets. If gross book value had been used instead, the division's measure of invested capital would have been $364 million, as the following calculation shows.

Current assets	$ 34,000,000
Long-lived assets (at gross book value)	304,000,000
Plant under construction	26,000,000
Total assets (at gross book value)	$364,000,000

Advantages are associated with both gross and net book value as a measure of invested capital.

Advantages of Net Book Value

- Using net book value maintains consistency with the balance sheet prepared for external reporting purposes. This allows for more meaningful comparisons of ROI measures across different companies.
- Using net book value to measure invested capital is also more consistent with the definition of income, which is the numerator in ROI calculations. In computing income, the current period depreciation on long-lived assets is deducted as an expense.

Advantages of Gross Book Value

- The usual methods of computing depreciation, such as the straight-line and the declining-balance methods, are arbitrary. Hence, they should not be allowed to affect ROI, residual-income, or EVA calculations.
- When long-lived assets are depreciated, their net book value declines over time. This results in a misleading increase in ROI, residual income, and EVA across time. The spreadsheet in Exhibit 18–6 illustrates this phenomenon for the ROI calculated on an equipment purchase under consideration by the Koala Camp Gear Division manager. Notice that the ROI rises steadily across the five-year horizon if invested capital is measured by net book value. However, using gross book value eliminates this problem. The use of an accelerated depreciation method instead of the straight-line method is even more pronounced in the increasing trend in ROI.

Dysfunctional behavioral effects.   The tendency for net book value to produce a misleading increase in ROI over time can seriously affect the incentives of investment-center managers. Investment centers with old assets show much higher ROIs than

Acquisition cost of equipment $10,000,000

Useful life .... 5 years

Salvage value at end of useful life 0

Annual straight-line depreciation $2,000,000

Annual income generated by asset (before deducting depreciation) $3,000,000

Exhibit 18–6

Increase in ROI over time (when net book value is used)

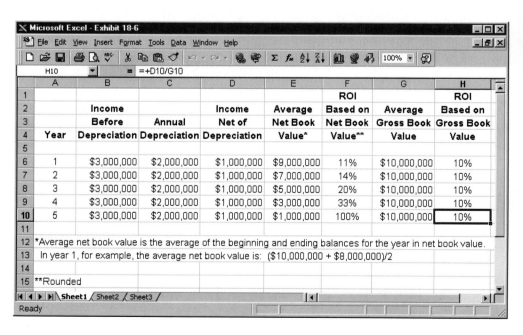

Microsoft Excel - Exhibit 18-6

File   Edit   View   Insert   Format   Tools   Data   Window   Help

H10   = =+D10/G10

	A	B	C	D	E	F	G	H
1						**ROI**		**ROI**
2		**Income**		**Income**	**Average**	**Based on**	**Average**	**Based on**
3		**Before**	**Annual**	**Net of**	**Net Book**	**Net Book**	**Gross Book**	**Gross Book**
4	**Year**	**Depreciation**	**Depreciation**	**Depreciation**	**Value***	**Value****	**Value**	**Value**
5								
6	1	$3,000,000	$2,000,000	$1,000,000	$9,000,000	11%	$10,000,000	10%
7	2	$3,000,000	$2,000,000	$1,000,000	$7,000,000	14%	$10,000,000	10%
8	3	$3,000,000	$2,000,000	$1,000,000	$5,000,000	20%	$10,000,000	10%
9	4	$3,000,000	$2,000,000	$1,000,000	$3,000,000	33%	$10,000,000	10%
10	5	$3,000,000	$2,000,000	$1,000,000	$1,000,000	100%	$10,000,000	10%
11								
12	*Average net book value is the average of the beginning and ending balances for the year in net book value.							
13	In year 1, for example, the average net book value is: ($10,000,000 + $8,000,000)/2							
14								
15	**Rounded							

Sheet1 / Sheet2 / Sheet3 /

Ready

investment centers with relatively new assets. This can discourage investment-center managers from investing in new equipment. If this behavioral tendency persists, a division's assets can become obsolete, making the division uncompetitive.

Allocating assets to investment centers.   Some companies control certain assets centrally, although these assets are needed to operate the divisions. Common examples are cash and accounts receivable. Divisions need cash to operate, but many companies control cash balances centrally to minimize their total cash holdings. Some large retail firms manage accounts receivable centrally. A credit customer of Outback Outfitters, for example, can make a payment at the local store, mail the payment to corporate headquarters, or use a credit card.

When certain assets are controlled centrally, some basis generally is chosen to allocate these asset balances to investment centers for measuring invested capital. For example, cash could be allocated based on the budgeted cash needs in each division or on the basis of divisional sales. Accounts receivable usually are allocated on the basis of divisional sales. Divisions with less stringent credit terms are allocated proportionately larger balances of accounts receivable.

Measuring Investment-Center Income

In addition to choosing a measure of investment-center capital, management must also decide how to measure an investment center's income. The key issue is controllability; the choice involves the extent to which uncontrollable items are allowed to influence the income measure. Exhibit 18–7 illustrates six different possibilities for measuring the income of Outback's Koala Camp Gear Division, using the division's revenue and expense data for the most recent year. All of the information in Exhibit 18–7 is derived from data collected by the division's cost-accounting system, but notice that some of the numbers require making judgments about controllability, which would be made by the corporate-level cost-management staff. For example, the corporate cost-management staff makes a judgment regarding how much of the division's general and facility-level expenses is controllable by the division manager and how much of these expenses is controllable by others.

Outback Outfitters' top management uses the *profit margin controllable by division manager*, $45 million, to evaluate the Koala Camp Gear Division manager. This profit measure is used in calculating ROI, residual income, and EVA. Some fixed costs traceable to the division have not been deducted from this $45 million amount, but the division manager cannot control or significantly influence these costs. Hence, they are excluded from the ROI calculation in evaluating the division manager. In calculating economic value added (EVA), the $45 million profit-margin amount is converted to an after-tax basis by multiplying by 1 minus the tax rate of 30 percent.

Exhibit 18–7

Divisional Income Statement: Koala Camp Gear Division

	Sales revenue	$405,000,000
	Unit-level, batch-level, product-line-level, and customer-level expenses	273,000,000
(1)	Divisional contribution margin	$132,000,000
	General and facility-level expenses controllable by division manager	87,000,000
(2)	Profit margin controllable by division manager	$ 45,000,000
	General and facility-level expenses traceable to division but controlled by others	15,000,000
(3)	Profit margin traceable to division	$ 30,000,000
	Common general and facility-level expenses, allocated from company headquarters	5,000,000
(4)	Divisional income before interest and taxes	$ 25,000,000
	Interest expense allocated from company headquarters	13,000,000
(5)	Divisional income before taxes	$ 12,000,000
	Income taxes allocated from company headquarters	3,600,000
(6)	Divisional net income	$ 8,400,000

Managers versus investment centers. A distinction between an investment center and its manager is important. In evaluating the *manager's* performance, only revenues and costs that the manager can control or significantly influence should be included in the profit measure. The performance measure's overall objective is to provide incentives for goal-congruent behavior. No performance measure can motivate a manager to make decisions about the costs he or she cannot control. This explains the reliance of Outback Outfitters' top management on the profit margin controllable by the division manager to compute the manager's performance measure.

Evaluating the Koala Camp Gear Division as a viable economic investment is a different matter altogether. In this evaluation, traceability of costs rather than controllability is the issue. For this purpose, Outback's top management uses the profit margin traceable to the division to compute the divisional ROI, residual income, or EVA. As Exhibit 18–7 shows, this amount is $30 million.

Other profit measures. Some companies also use the other measures of divisional profit shown in Exhibit 18–7 (lines 4, 5, and 6). The rationale behind these divisional income measures is that all corporate costs must be covered by the operations of the divisions. Allocating corporate costs, interest, and income taxes to the divisions makes division managers aware of these costs.

Determining the Impact of Inflation and Deflation: Current Value versus Historical-Cost Accounting

Whether measuring investment-center income or invested capital, the impact of price-level changes should not be forgotten. During periods of inflation, historical-cost asset values soon cease to reflect the cost of replacing those assets. Therefore, some managers argue that investment-center performance measures based on historical-cost

---

Deciding between Alternative Merchandise Inventory Plans

You're the Decision Maker 18.2

The manager of the Outback Outfitters store in Adelaide is evaluated using ROI. Corporate headquarters requires an ROI of 10 percent of assets. The manager estimates that for the coming year revenue will be $260,000, and cost of goods sold will be $163,000. Operating expenses for this level of sales will be $26,000. Investment in the store assets throughout the year is $187,500 before considering the following proposal.

A representative of Tasmania Trading Company approached the Outback Outfitters manager about carrying its line of camp cookware. This line is expected to generate $75,000 in sales in the coming year at the Adelaide store with a cost of merchandise sold of $57,000. Annual operating expenses for this additional merchandise line are $8,500. To carry the line of goods, an inventory investment of $55,000 throughout the year is required.

As an alternative, Tasmania is willing to "floor plan" the merchandise so that the Adelaide store will not have to invest in any additional inventory. Tasmania's charge for floor planning would be $6,750 per year. The floor-planning arrangement with Tasmania would offer two advantages to Outback's Adelaide store. First, Tasmania rather than Outback Outfitters would maintain the $55,000 investment in the inventory. Outback would still incur the $57,000 annual cost-of-merchandise-sold expense and the $8,500 in additional operating expenses, plus the $6,750 charge for floor planning. Second, Tasmania would take charge of maintaining floor displays for its merchandise in the Adelaide store, as well as giving Outback's management advice on optimal merchandise placement within the store.

Assume that Outback's cost of capital is 10 percent.

a. What is the Adelaide store's expected ROI for the coming year if it does not carry Tasmania's cookware in the store?

b. What is the store's expected ROI if the manager invests in the Tasmania inventory and carries the cookware line?

c. What is the store's expected ROI if the manager elects to take the floor-plan option?

d. Would the manager prefer (a), (b), or (c)? Why?

(Solutions begin on page 772.)

accounting are misleading. Yet surveys of corporate managers indicate that an accounting system based on current values would not alter their decisions. Most managers believe that measures based on historical-cost accounting are adequate when used in conjunction with budgets and performance targets. As managers prepare those budgets, they build their expectations about inflation (or deflation) into the budgets and performance targets.

Another reason for using historical-cost accounting for internal purposes is that it is required for external reporting. Thus, historical-cost data already are available, while installing current-value accounting would add substantial incremental costs to the organization's information system.

Measuring Income and Invested Capital: Summary

To summarize, the primary objective in choosing measures for the evaluation of investment centers and their managers is goal (or at least behavioral) congruence. Cost managers should design investment-center performance measures that reward managers for pursuing the goals of the overall organization.

Use of Investment Center Performance Measures to Provide Managerial Incentives

Most financial performance measures are based on periodic earnings (quarterly or annual), components of earnings, or a variation of earnings. Remember that although components of earnings used in external reports must comply with GAAP, those in incentive compensation plans need not. Designers of incentive plans should match incentives from earnings numbers to desired behavior. For example, some incentive plans in the United States omit or capitalize R&D expenses from earnings to counter any disincentives to conduct research caused by required expensing of R&D for GAAP.

Financial performance measures commonly include levels or *changes* of the following:

- Revenues.
- Costs.
- Cash flow.
- Operating income (before or after extraordinary items, taxes).
- Return on investment (total assets, net assets, or equity).
- Residual income or EVA.
- Stock price.

All of these measures except stock price are explicitly based on earnings-related numbers. The last three items are most commonly used to evaluate business-unit performance and provide interesting opportunities for the discussion of incentives and motivation. Let's briefly discuss them in this context.[7]

Return on Investment (ROI)

Allowing for the many possible variations of its components (i.e., alternative measures of return and investment), ROI is the most commonly used measure of business-unit performance for several reasons. First, measuring the components of ROI causes no additional costs because they are part of periodic financial reporting. Second, ROI components are among the most reliable, verifiable, and objective numbers the company prepares, and using them leads to few disputes. Third, as a percentage return,

---

[7] Chapter 20 provides further discussion of managerial incentive issues.

ROI is easy to understand and compare across similar business units. These benefits, in fact, have caused some companies that jumped on the EVA "bandwagon" to return to using ROI as the predominant financial performance measure.[8]

Residual Income or Economic Value Added

Residual income (and its more recent variation EVA) has been recommended as a measure of business-unit performance since at least the 1920s when General Motors adopted it.[9] Residual income (RI) is a desirable performance measure in corporate incentive plans because it increases when investments generate earnings in excess of the cost of capital. RI also increases when companies eliminate investments that earn less than the cost of capital. Thus, residual income should reflect changes in the firm's value.[10]

One of the selling points for EVA is that it permits multiple adjustments to reported earnings to adjust for "accounting distortions," but adjusting earnings to align incentives with desired behavior is not new. For many years, companies have adjusted reported earnings in the following ways:

- Capitalize expenditures on research and development (in the United States).
- Capitalize expenditures on customer development, advertising, and promotion if these expenditures will benefit future years.
- Capitalize expenditures on employee training that will benefit future years.
- Make price-level adjustments so assets, revenues, and expenses are stated in current year currency values.
- Use gross book values or restated net book values to reflect the assets' actual economic value.
- Restate inventories to replacement cost.
- Do not amortize goodwill.

Note that this list is neither a recommended guideline nor a complete list of adjustments (one consulting company advertises more than 160 adjustments to reported earnings). Each situation is unique and could require its own set of adjustments (or none at all).

Another selling point of EVA is that allegedly it more closely reflects (e.g., is a lead indicator of) stock price performance than do reported earnings.[11] Thus, using EVA, as the performance measure for incentive plans should more closely align managers' and stockholders' interest. Recent research partially supports this claim, but at this time the superiority of EVA or RI over reported earnings is open to question (see Research Insight 18.1 for a discussion). This might be another reason that some companies continue to use or are returning to more conventional financial measures of performance, such as ROI. Residual income, in some form, however, is unlikely to be only a passing fad because it is based on a fundamental concept of economic profit generated after considering all costs, including the opportunity cost of capital. The notion that companies earning an economic profit will add wealth to their owners is well grounded in economic theory and in practice.

---

[8] See C. Ittner and D. Larcker, "Innovations in Performance Measurement: Trends and Research Implications" for an extensive discussion.

[9] General Electric apparently coined the actual term "residual income" in the 1950s. See M. Bromwich and M. Walker, "Residual Income Past and Future."

[10] A number of technical issues must be met to guarantee this relation (e.g., NPV-based depreciation), but most RI and EVA users appear to treat these as minor issues.

[11] Both TIAA-CREF, the teacher's retirement system and CALPERS, the public employees retirement system in California have used EVA to evaluate how well corporate managers are using resources. In some cases, these giant retirement systems have taken corporate managers to task for failing to create sufficient value for shareholders.

Research Insight 18.1

Does EVA Pay?

Residual income (RI) and economic value added (EVA) have a long history as prescriptions for better performance evaluations. Economic researchers have been interested in finding the conditions when RI or EVA will reflect changes in firm value: If RI or EVA go up, stock prices should go up, and vice versa (yes, these conditions might exist). Current accounting and finance research indicates that division managers evaluated using residual income make investing, financing, and operating decisions that should increase stock prices. Thus, residual income/EVA might be an effective incentive device. However, the stock market does not appear to increase prices of shares of companies when they *adopt* EVA-based incentive plans, but if managers make better decisions, stock prices should increase. Perhaps the value of EVA-based plans does not exceed their cost. Furthermore, some research indicates that stock-price returns are more closely correlated with net income than with EVA. Perhaps net income is a better reflection of changes in firm value than EVA. At this time, we cannot establish a clear link between EVA-based incentives and increased stockholder value. More research is needed in this area. *Sources: M. Bromwick and M. Walker,* "Residual Income Past and Future," *G. Biddle, R. Bowen, and J. Wallace,* "Economic Value Added: Some Emperical EVAdence"; *J. S. Wallace,* "Adopting Residual Income-Based Compensation Plans: Do You Get What You Pay For?"; *G. C. Biddle, R. M. Bowen, and J. S. Wallace,* "Does EVA® Beat Earnings? Evidence on Associations with Stock Returns and Firm Values." *For alternative points of view, see P.A. Dierks and A. Patel,* "What Is EVA® and How Can It Help Your Company?"; *and J. Freedman,* "New Research Red Flags EVA® for Stock Picks." (Full citations to references are in the Bibliography.)

Stock-Price Performance

If an objective is to align managers' interests to those of stockholders, why not use stock-price performance as the performance evaluation measure? When stock price rises, both managers and stockholders are better off and vice versa. However, business-unit managers in large companies might see little connection between their actions and the performance of the company's stock. Furthermore, a company's stock can fluctuate widely based on factors over which the manager has no control, including economic and industry trends, interest rates, politics, technology, and customer tastes and preferences.

Therefore, tying managers' compensation to stock-price performance places a good deal of risk on them. Furthermore, this type of risk is not easy for managers to diversify because the performance measure is based on just one stock—that of their company.

Despite these problems with stock price as a measure of performance, many companies generally provide at least some incentive for managers to be concerned about stock performance by rewarding with stock awards. Some companies go beyond stock awards. Polaroid, for example, requires its executives to own stock valued at a multiple of their base pay (one, three, or five times, depending on the position). Extensive stock ownership gives executives an interest in how well their company's stock is doing even if stock price is not an explicit performance measure.

Nonfinancial Performance Measures

Evidence indicates that the use of nonfinancial measures of performance in incentive plans is increasing. Of course, organizations have used nonfinancial measures for managing operations for many years,[12] but including them in incentive plans is an important development.[13] Perhaps the greatest advantages of adding nonfinancial

---

[12] See Chapter 7 of this text for examples of commonly used quality, time, and productivity measures and Chapter 20 for examples of nonfinancial performance measures included in performance measurement.

[13] See R. Banker, G. Potter, and D. Srinivasan, "An Empirical Investigation of an Incentive Plan That Includes Nonfinancial Performance Measures," for an example.

Cost Management in Practice 18.2

Use of Nonfinancial Measures of Performance

Professors Ittner and Larcker of the Wharton School of Business have reviewed the findings of many surveys, cases, and field studies investigating firms' uses of nonfinancial measures of performance for both management and incentive compensation. They report that as many as 36 percent of firms explicitly include nonfinancial measures in executive incentive plans. On average, 37 percent of the total evaluation was based on these nonfinancial measures. Firms that use nonfinancial measures in their incentive plans tend to be more innovative, to have adopted TQM, to have long product-development cycles, to have been more subject to regulation, and to have had "noisier" financial performance. Thus, factors, such as innovativeness and adoption of TQM, apparently affect the use of nonfinancial measures of performance in incentive plans.

Nonfinancial measures of performance used most commonly in incentive plans include customer satisfaction, productivity, employee performance, community/environmental performance, and innovation. But Ittner and Larcker point out that very little objective research reflects whether using these measures in incentive plans results in better *long-term* financial performance. At this point, firms might be reluctant to disclose that they have found successful packages of measures alternatively, they might include these measures based on the logic of linkages among lead and lag indicators of performance rather than hard evidence.

Ittner and Larcker found in a different study, that perceived subjectivity of nonfinancial performance measures led to the abandonment of the balanced scorecard as the basis for incentive compensation in a large bank. The bank's incentive system returned its primary focus to financial performance despite the validity of nonfinancial measures as lead indicators of financial performance. As mentioned earlier, perceived subjectivity of some measures could impair their usefulness as incentive devices. *Sources: C. Ittner and D. Larcker,* "Innovations in Performance Measurement: Trends and Research Implications" *and* "The Use of Subjectivity in Multi-Criteria Bonus Plans."

measures to the incentive system are (1) focus on the drivers of profit and (2) recognition of the time lags betwen nonfinancial and financial performance.

As with all aspects of incentive plans, however, nonfinancial performance measures have costs as well as benefits. Difficulties of including nonfinancial measures in incentive plans include these:

- Increased cost of performance measurement and supporting information systems.
- Increased cost of reporting and verifying the validity of performance measures.
- Difficulty in determining the proper balance between financial and nonfinancial measures.
- Danger of "information overload" from too many measures causing lack of focus on overall performance.
- Increased opportunities for disputes over the validity of performance measures.
- Increased opportunities for manipulating formula-based incentive plans that include multiple measures.

If adding nonfinancial measures adds problems, why not use financial performance over a period of time long enough to capture the effects of nonfinancial performance?[14] One answer might be that nonfinancial measures can add value in excess of their costs. Another might be that although competition for managerial talent requires frequent evaluation and payment of compensation, financial performance cannot be matched to efforts in a timely manner. These answers might explain why many organizations have added problematic nonfinancial performance measures to their incentive systems. The measures to use and how to include them in performance-based incentive plans are some of the greatest challenges of incentive plan design, and more research is needed in this area.

---

[14] A. Rappaport articulates this question in his book *Creating Shareholder Value.*

Viewing an Investment Center as a Collection of Investments

ROI, residual income, and EVA are short-run performance measures. They focus on only one period of time, yet an investment center is really a collection of assets (investments), each of which has a multiperiod life. To evaluate any one of these individual investments correctly requires a multiperiod viewpoint, which considers the timing of the cash flows from the investment. For example, an investment could start out slowly in its early years but could be economically justified by its expected high performance in later years. Any evaluation of the investment center in one particular year that ignores the long-term performance of its various investments can result in a misleading conclusion. Thus, single-period performance measures suffer from myopia; they focus on only a short time segment that slices across the division's collection of investments.

To avoid this short-term focus, some organizations downplay such measures as ROI, residual income, and EVA in favor of an alternative approach. Instead of relating profit to invested capital in a single measure, these characteristics of investment-center performance are evaluated separately. Actual divisional profit for a time period is compared to a flexible budget, and variances are used to analyze performance. The division's major investments are evaluated through a *postaudit* of the investment decisions.[15] For example, a particular investment could have been undertaken because of expected high performance several years into the future. When that time comes, a review will determine whether the project lived up to expectations.

Evaluating periodic profit through flexible budgeting and variance analysis, coupled with postaudits of major investment decisions, is a more complicated approach to evaluating investment centers. However, it does help management avoid the myopia of single-period measures such as ROI, RI, and EVA.

Performance Measurement in Nonprofit Organizations

Management control in a nonprofit organization presents a special challenge. These organizations are often managed by professionals, such as physicians in a hospital. Moreover, many people participate in a nonprofit organization at some personal sacrifice, motivated by humanitarian or public service ideals. Often, such people are less receptive to formal control procedures than their counterparts in business.

The goals of nonprofit organizations often are less clear-cut than those of businesses. Public service objectives can be difficult to specify with precision and even more difficult to measure in terms of achievement. For example, one community health center was established in an economically depressed area with three stated goals:

1. To reduce costs in a nearby hospital by providing a clinic for people to use instead of the hospital emergency room.
2. To provide preventive as well as therapeutic care and establish outreach programs in the community.
3. To become financially self-sufficient.

These objectives conflict somewhat since goal 2 does not provide revenue to the center but goals 1 and 3 focus on financial efficiency. Moreover, the health center was staffed with physicians who could have achieved much higher incomes in private practice. The management control tools described in this and the preceding two chapters can be used in nonprofit organizations. However, the challenges in doing so effectively often are greater.

---

[15] The evaluation of long-term investment decisions is covered in Chapter 14.

Chapter Summary

Responsibility accounting systems are designed to foster *goal* or *behavioral congruence* among the managers in decentralized organizations. Each subunit in an organization is designated as a cost center, discretionary cost center, revenue center, profit center, or investment center. The cost-management team prepares a performance report for each responsibility center. These reports show the performance of the responsibility center and its manager for a specified time period. The most effective performance reports include both financial and nonfinancial information pertaining to performance.

To use responsibility accounting effectively, the emphasis must be on information rather than blame. The intent should be to provide managers with information to help them better manage their sub-units. Responsibility accounting systems can bring about desired behavior, such as reducing the number of rush orders in a manufacturing company.

The three most common measures of investment-center performance are return on investment (ROI), residual income (RI), and economic value added (EVA). Each of these performance measures relates an investment center's income to the capital invested to earn it. Residual income and EVA have the additional advantage of incorporating the organization's cost of acquiring capital in the performance measure. An investment center's ROI may be improved by increasing either the sales margin or capital turnover. ROI, residual income, and EVA all require the measurement of a division's income and invested capital, and the methods for making these measurements vary in practice.

The primary criterion for judging the effectiveness of performance measures for responsibility-center managers is the extent to which the measures promote goal or behavioral congruence.

Key Terms

For each term's definition, refer to the indicated page or turn to the glossary at the end of the text.

activity-based responsibility
  accounting, 752

behavioral congruence, 744

capital turnover, 755

centralization, 744

cost center, 746

decentralization, 744

discretionary cost center, 746

economic value added
  (EVA), 760

goal congruence, 744

investment center, 747

management by
  exception, 750

performance report, 750

profit center, 746

residual income (RI), 758

responsibility accounting, 744

responsibility center, 746

return on investment
  (ROI), 755

revenue center, 746

sales margin, 755

weighted-average cost of
  capital (WACC), 760

Meeting the Cost Management Challenges

1. When companies grow larger, as typified by the acquisition described in Outback Outfitters' press release, how should they manage operations? What are the benefits and costs of decentralization?

Several benefits of decentralization follow:

- The managers of an organization's subunits have specialized information and skills that enable them to manage their departments most effectively.

- Allowing managers autonomy in decision making provides managerial training for future higher-level managers.

- Managers with some decision-making authority usually exhibit more positive motivation than those who merely execute the decisions of others.

- Delegating some decisions to lower-level managers provides time relief to upper-level managers.

- Delegating decision making to the lowest level possible enables an organization to give a timely response to opportunities and problems.

Several costs of decentralization are as follows:

- Managers in a decentralized organization might have a narrow focus on their own unit's performance.

- Managers might tend to ignore the consequences of their actions on the organization's other subunits.

- In a decentralized organization, some tasks or services might be duplicated unnecessarily.

2. How could a responsibility accounting system foster goal or behavioral congruence for Outback Outfitters?

A responsibility accounting system fosters goal or behavioral congruence by establishing the performance criteria by which to evaluate each manager. Development of performance measures and standards for those measures can help to ensure that managers are striving to meet goals that support the organization's overall objectives.

3. What are the major types of responsibility accounting centers?

The major types of responsibility accounting centers are cost centers, discretionary cost centers, revenue centers, profit centers, and investment centers.

4. What is the key feature of activity-based responsibility accounting?

Under activity-based responsibility accounting, management's attention is directed to activities rather than focused primarily on cost, revenue, and profit measures of subunit performance. Activity-based responsibility accounting uses the database generated by an activity-based costing system coupled with nonfinancial measures of operational performance for key activities. This approach can help management eliminate non-value-added activities and improve the cost effectiveness of activities that do add value to the organization's product or service.

5.   How is investment center performance typically measured?

The three commonly used measures of investment center performance are return on investment (ROI), residual income (RI), and economic value added (EVA).

Solutions to You're the Decision Maker

18.1   Evaluating the Success of a Division   p. 759

The answer to the question as to which division is the most successful depends on the firm's cost of capital. To see this relationship, compute the residual income (RI) for each division using various imputed interest rates.

a.   Imputed interest rate of 10%:

	Brisbane Division	Cairns Division
Divisional profit......................................	$900,000	$200,000
Less: Imputed interest charge:		
$6,000,000 × 10%	600,000	
$1,000,000 × 10%		100,000
Residual income..................................	$300,000	$100,000

b.   Imputed interest rate of 14%:

	Brisbane Division	Cairns Division
Divisional profit......................................	$900,000	$200,000
Less: Imputed interest charge:		
$6,000,000 × 14%	840,000	
$1,000,000 × 14%		140,000
Residual income..................................	$ 60,000	$ 60,000

c.   Imputed interest rate of 15%:

	Brisbane Division	Cairns Division
Divisional profit......................................	$900,000	$200,000
Less: Imputed interest charge:		
$6,000,000 × 15%	900,000	
$1,000,000 × 15%		150,000
Residual income..................................	$ 0	$ 50,000

If the firm's cost of capital is 10 percent, the Brisbane division has a higher residual income than the Cairns division. With a cost of capital of 15 percent, the Cairns division has a higher residual income. At a 14 percent cost of capital, the divisions have the same residual income. This scenario illustrates one of the advantages of RI over ROI. Since the RI calculation includes an imputed interest charge reflecting the firm's cost of capital, it gives a more complete picture of divisional performance.

18.2   Deciding between Alternative Merchandise Inventory Plans   p. 765

a. and b.   Income statements summarizing the alternatives are as follows:

	Regular Merchandise	Camp Cookware	Total
Revenue	$260,000	$75,000	$335,000
Cost of goods sold	163,000	57,000	220,000
Gross margin..................	$ 97,000	$18,000	$115,000
Operating expenses	26,000	8,500	34,500
Operating profit..............	$ 71,000	$ 9,500	$ 80,500
Investment.....................	$187,500	$55,000	$242,500
ROI	37.87%	17.27%	33.20%

Although the camp cookware provides a higher return than the cost of capital, it lowers the status quo ROI.

c.   If the floor plan is used, the investment base will remain at $187,500 because Outback will not have to carry the additional $55,000 inventory investment for the Tasmania product line. Operating profits will equal $80,500 minus the floor-plan charge of $6,750 for a net profit of $73,750. The ROI will be 39.33 percent ($73,750 ÷ $187,500).

d.   The manager would prefer the floor plan because it would raise the store's ROI above the current ROI of 37.87 percent.

Review Questions

18.1   Why is goal congruence important to an organization's success?

18.2   Could the type of budget items for which some responsibility centers are accountable differ? That is, might some responsibility centers be responsible only for costs, some only for revenues, and some for both? Give examples.

18.3   Accounting is supposed to provide a neutral, relevant, and objective measure of performance. Why would problems arise when applying accounting measures in the context of performance evaluation?

18.4   Suppose you overheard this comment, "This whole problem of measuring performance for segment managers using accounting numbers is so much hogwash. We pay our managers a good salary and expect them to do the best possible job. At least with our system, there is no incentive to play with the accounting data." Does the comment make sense?

18.5   Define and give examples of the following terms: *cost center, discretionary cost center, revenue center, profit center,* and *investment center.*

18.6 What are the advantages of using an ROI-type measure rather than a division's profit as a performance evaluation technique?

18.7 The production department manager has just received a responsibility report showing a substantial unfavorable variance for overtime premium. The manager objects to the inclusion of this variance because the acceptance of a large rush order by the sales department caused the overtime. To whom should this variance be charged?

18.8 Under what conditions does the use of ROI measures inhibit a division manager's goal-congruent decision making?

18.9 Create an example showing the calculation of residual income. What information is used in computing residual income that is not used in computing ROI?

18.10 Why do some companies use gross book value instead of net book value to measure a division's invested capital?

18.11 Define the term *economic value added (EVA)*. How does it differ from residual income?

18.12 Describe an alternative to using ROI, residual income, or EVA to measure investment-center performance.

Critical Analysis

18.13 Under what circumstances is it appropriate to change Outback Outfitters' Sydney plant from a profit center to an investment center?

18.14 "Performance reports based on controllability are impossible. Nobody really *controls* anything in an organization!" Do you agree or disagree? Explain your answer.

18.15 Central management of Adler, Inc., evaluated divisional performance using residual income (RI) measures. The division managers were ranked according to the RI in each division. All division managers with residual income in the upper half of the ranking received a bonus. The bonus amount was in proportion to the RI amount. No bonus was paid to managers in the lower half of the ranking. What biases might arise in this system?

18.16 Explain why distinguishing between investment centers and their managers is important in performance evaluation.

18.17 Explain how the manager of the automobile division of an insurance company could improve her division's ROI.

18.18 Management of division A is evaluated based on residual income measures. The division can either rent or buy a certain asset. Might the performance evaluation tech-

nique have an impact on the rent-or-buy decision? Why or why not?

18.19 What is the chief disadvantage of ROI as an investment-center performance measure? How does the residual-income measure eliminate this disadvantage?

18.20 Distinguish between the following measures of invested capital and briefly explain when each should be used: (1) total assets, (2) total productive assets, and (3) total assets less current liabilities.

18.21 Bleak Prospects, Inc., found that its market share was slipping. Bleak encouraged division managers to maximize ROI and make decisions consistent with that goal. Nonetheless, frequent customer complaints resulted in lost business. Moreover, Bleak depended on an established product line and was unable to find new products for expansion while its competitors seemed to be able to generate new products almost yearly. What would you suggest Bleak Products' management do to improve its situation?

18.22 Why does ROI or residual income typically rise across time in a division? What undesirable behavioral implications could this phenomenon have?

Exercises

For each of the following organizational subunits, indicate the type of responsibility center that is most appropriate.

a. A movie theater in a company that operates a chain of theaters.

b. A radio station owned by a large broadcasting network.

c. The claims department in an insurance company.

d. The ticket sales division of a major airline.

e. A bottling plant of a soft-drink company.

f. An orange juice factory operated by a large orange grower.

g. The College of Engineering at a large state university.

h. The European Division of a multinational manufacturing company.

i. The outpatient clinic in a profit-oriented hospital.

j. The Mayor's Office in a large city.

Exercise 18.23
Designing Responsibility Center
(LO 1, 3)

Read "7-Eleven, Amid Pressures, Makes Big Bets," *The Wall Street Journal,* April 25, 2002, by Ann Zimmerman.

Required
How will 7-Eleven's investment likely impact the company's ROI? Explain.

Exercise 18.24
Return on Investment
(LO 7, 8)

Exercise 18.25
Performance Report;
Hotel
(LO 4)

The following data pertain to the Cape Cod Inn for the month of August. The inn's organization chart shows that the food and beverage department has the following subunits: banquets and catering, restaurants, and kitchen.

	Flexible Budget: August (in thousands)*	Actual Results: August (in thousands)*
Banquets and catering	$ 655	$ 663
Restaurants	1,795	1,789
Kitchen staff wages	(85)	(86)
Food	(690)	(690)
Paper products	(125)	(122)
Unit-level (variable) overhead in kitchen	(75)	(78)
Facility-level (fixed) overhead in kitchen	(90)	(93)

*Numbers without parentheses denote profit; numbers with parentheses denote expenses.

Required

Prepare an August performance report for Cape Cod Inn's food and beverage department similar to the lower portion of Exhibit 18–4, which relates to Koala's Production Department and Cutting Work Center. The report should have three numerical columns instead of six with headings analogous to those in Exhibit 18–4. (Your report will not have any year-to-date columns.) Your performance report should cover only the food and beverage department and the kitchen. Draw arrows to show the relationships among the numbers in the report. Refer to Exhibit 18–4 for guidance.

Exercise 18.26
Responsibility
Accounting; Equipment
Breakdown
(LO 1)

As a group, prepare a report to the class regarding how a responsibility accounting system should handle each of the following scenarios:

a. Department A manufactures a component, which Department B then uses. Department A recently experienced a machine breakdown that held up production of the component. As a result, Department B was forced to curtail its own production, thereby incurring large costs of idle time. An investigation revealed that Department A's machinery had not been properly maintained.

b. Refer to the scenario in requirement (a), but suppose that the investigation revealed that the machinery in Department A had been properly maintained.

Exercise 18.27
ROI versus Residual
Income
(LO 5, 7)

eXcel
mhhe.com/hilton3e

Rosito Company manufactures clothing in Buenos Aires, Argentina. The company's outerwear division is considering the acquisition of a new asset that will cost 360,000 pesos and have a cash flow of 140,000 pesos per year for each of the five years of its life. Depreciation is computed on a straight-line basis with no salvage value.*

*Several countries call their currency the *peso*. On the day this exercise was written, Argentina's peso was worth 1.0002 U.S. dollars.

Required

a. What is the ROI for each year of the asset's life if the division uses beginning-of-year asset balances and net book value for the computation?

b. What is the residual income each year if the imputed interest rate is 25 percent?

Exercise 18.28
Impact of New Project on
Performance Measures
(LO 5)

Midwest Company's Cleveland Division manager is considering the acquisition of a new asset that will increase the division's profit. The division already earns $390,000 on assets of $1.3 million. The company's cost of capital is 20 percent. The new investment has a cost of $225,000 and will have a yearly cash flow of $84,000. The asset will be depreciated using the straight-line method over a six-year life and is expected to have no salvage value. Division performance is measured using ROI with beginning-of-year net book values in the denominator.

Required

a. What is the division ROI before acquisition of the new asset?

b. What is the division ROI in the first year after acquisition of the new asset?

The Cleveland Division manager in the preceding exercise has the option to lease the asset on a year-to-year lease for $74,000 per year. All depreciation and other tax benefits would accrue to the lessor.

Exercise 18.29
Impact of Purchasing versus Leasing on Performance Measures
(LO 5, 7)

Required

a. What is the division ROI if it leases the asset?

b. What is the division's residual income before considering the project?

c. What is the division's residual income if the asset is purchased?

d. What is the division's residual income if the asset is leased?

The following data are available for the two divisions of North American Products, Inc.

Exercise 18.30
Alternative Measures of Division Performance
(LO 5, 7)

	East Division	West Division
Division operating profit	$ 35,000	$195,000
Division investment	100,000	750,000

The cost of capital for the company is 20 percent.

Required

a. As a group, determine which division had the better performance. Explain your answer.

b. Would your evaluation change if the company's cost of capital were 25 percent? Why?

Select one of the following companies (or any company of your choosing), and use the Internet to explore its most recent annual report.

Exercise 18.31
ROI and Residual Income; Annual Reports; Use of Internet
(LO 5, 7)

American Airlines (**www.americanair.com**)   Pizza Hut (**www.pizzahut.com**)

Deere and Company (**www.deere.com**)   Ramada Inn (**www.ramada.com**)

Firestone Tire & Rubber (**www.firestone.com**)   Wal-Mart (**www.wal-mart.com**)

IBM (**www.ibm.com**)

Required

a. Calculate the company's overall return on investment (ROI). Also, calculate the company's overall residual income. (Assume an imputed interest rate of 10 percent.) List and explain any assumptions you make.

b. Does the company include a calculation of ROI in its on-line annual report? If it does, do your calculations agree with those of the company? If not, what are some possible explanations?

Alameda Division of California Metals Corporation just started operations. It purchased depreciable assets costing $2 million and having an expected life of four years, after which the assets can be salvaged for $400,000. In addition, the division has $2 million in assets that are not depreciable. After four years, the division will have $2 million available from these nondepreciable assets. In short, the division has invested $4 million in assets that will last four years, after which it will salvage $2.4 million, so annual depreciation is $400,000. Annual cash-operating flows are $1,000,000. In computing ROI, this division uses end-of-year asset values in the denominator. Depreciation is computed on a straight-line basis, recognizing the salvage values noted.

Exercise 18.32
Compare ROI Using Historical Cost Net Book Value versus Gross Book Value
(LO 5, 8)

Required

a. Compute ROI using net book value for each year.

b. Compute ROI using gross book value for each year.

c. Assume the same data except that the division uses beginning-of-year asset values in the denominator for computing ROI.

(1) Compute ROI using net book value.

(2) Compute ROI using gross book value.

(3) How different is the ROI computed using end-of-year asset values from the ROI using beginning-of-year values?

Exercise 18.33
Calculation of Weighted-
Average Cost of Capital
for EVA
(LO 5)

Tribeca Construction Associates, a real estate developer and building contractor in Manhattan, has two sources of long-term capital: debt and equity. Tribeca's cost of issuing debt is the after-tax cost of the interest payments on the debt, considering the fact that the interest payments are tax deductible. Tribeca's cost of equity capital is the investment opportunity rate of Tribeca's investors, that is, the rate they could earn on investments of similar risk to that of investing in Tribeca Construction Associates. The interest rate on Tribeca's $60 million of long-term debt is 10 percent, and the company's tax rate is 40 percent. Tribeca's cost of equity capital is 15 percent. Moreover, its market value (and book value) of equity is $90 million.

Required
Calculate Tribeca Construction Associates' weighted-average cost of capital.

Exercise 18.34
Economic Value Added;
Continuation of
Preceding Exercise
(LO 5)

Refer to the data in the preceding exercise for Tribeca Construction Associates. The company has two divisions, real estate and construction. The divisions' total assets, current liabilities, and before-tax operating income for the most recent year follow:

Division	Total Assets	Current Liabilities	Before-Tax Operating Income
Real estate	$100,000,000	$6,000,000	$20,000,000
Construction	60,000,000	4,000,000	18,000,000

Required
Calculate the economic value added for each of Tribeca Construction Associates' divisions. (You will need to use the weighted-average cost of capital, which was computed in the preceding exercise.)

Problems

Problem 18.35
Responsibility Centers
Designation; Hotel
(LO 1, 2, 3)

The following partial organization chart pertains to the Nantucket Hotel and Resort, a division of Seaside Resorts, Inc. Top management has specified that the hotel is a profit center, because the hotel's managmement does not have the authority to make significant investment decisions.

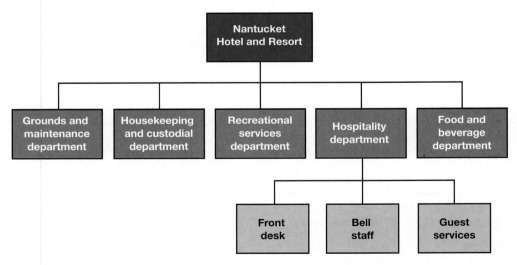

Each of the hotel's main departments is managed by a director (e.g., director of hospitality). The front desk subunit, which is supervised by the front desk manager, handles the hotel's reservations, room assignments, guest payments, and key control. The bell staff, managed by the bell captain, is responsible for greeting guests, front-door service, assisting guests with their luggage, and delivering room-service orders. The guest services subunit, supervised by the manager of guest services, is responsible for assisting guests with local transportation arrangements, advising guests on tourist attractions, and conveniences such as valet and floral services.

Required

As an outside consultant, write a memo to the hotel's general manager suggesting a responsibility-center designation for each of the subunits shown in the organization chart. Justify your choices.

Phoenix Medical Equipment Company manufactures a variety of equipment used in hospitals. The company operates in a very price-competitive industry, so it has little control over the price of its products. It *must* meet the market price. To do so, the firm must keep production costs in check by operating as efficiently as possible. Sandra Jefferson, the company's president, has stated that to be successful, the company must provide a very high-quality product and meet its delivery commitments to customers on time. Phoenix Medical Equipment Company is organized as shown below.

Problem 18.36
Design of a
Responsibility
Accounting System
(LO 1, 2, 3)

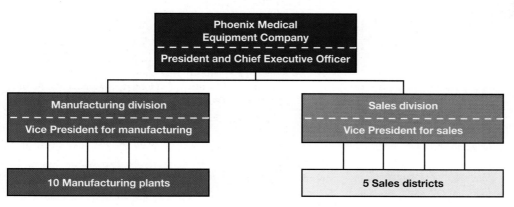

The company's two vice presidents currently disagree regarding the responsibility-accounting system. The vice president for manufacturing claims that the 10 plants should be cost centers. He recently expressed the following sentiment: "The plants should be cost centers because the plant managers do not control the sales of our products. Designating the plants as profit centers would result in holding the plant managers responsible for something they can't control." The vice president for marketing holds a contrary view. He recently made the following remarks: "The plants should be profit centers. The plant managers are in the best position to affect the company's overall profit."

Required

As the company's new controller, you have been asked to make a recommendation to Sandra Jefferson regarding the responsibility-center issue. Write a memo to her making a recommendation and explaining the reasoning behind it. In your memo address the following points.

a. Assuming that Phoenix Medical Equipment Company's overall goal is profitability, what are the company's critical success factors? A *critical success factor* is a variable that meets these two criteria: It is largely under the company's control, and the company must succeed in this area to reach its overall goal of profitability.

b. Which responsibility-accounting arrangement for the plants is most consistent with achieving success on the company's critical success factors?

c. What responsibility-center designation is most appropriate for the company's sales districts?

d. As a specific example, consider the rush-order problem illustrated in the chapter. Suppose that Phoenix Medical Equipment Company often receives rush orders from its customers. Which of the two proposed responsibility-accounting arrangements is best suited to making good decisions about accepting or rejecting rush orders? Specifically, should the plants be cost centers or profit centers?

American Traditions, Inc., manufactures antique reproduction furniture. The need for a widely based manufacturing and distribution system has led to a highly decentralized management structure. Each division manager is responsible for producing and distributing corporate products in one of eight geographical areas of the country.

Residual income is used to evaluate division managers. The residual income for each division equals its contribution to corporate profits before taxes less a 20 percent investment charge on a division's

Problem 18.37
Performance Report
Analysis for a
Decentralized
Organization
(LO 1, 4)

investment base. Each division's investment is the sum of its year-end balances of accounts receivable, inventories, and net plant fixed assets (cost less accumulated depreciation). Corporate policies dictate that divisions minimize their investments in receivables and inventories. Investments in plant fixed assets are a joint division/corporate decision based on proposals made by division managers, available corporate funds, and general corporate policy.

Patrick Anderson, division manager for the southeastern sector, prepared the year 2 and preliminary year 3 budgets for his division late in year 1. Final approval of the year 3 budget took place in late year 2 after adjustments for trends and other information developed during year 2. Preliminary work on the year 4 budget also took place at that time. In early October of year 3, Anderson asked the division controller to prepare the following report, which presents performance for the first nine months of year 3.

AMERICAN TRADITIONS, INC.
Southeastern Sector
(in thousands)

	Year 3			Year 2	
	Annual Budget	Nine-Month Budget*	Nine-Month Actual	Annual Budget	Actual Results
Sales revenue	$2,800	$2,100	$2,200	$2,500	$2,430
Divisional costs and expenses:					
Direct material and labor	$1,064	$ 798	$ 995	$ 900	$ 890
Supplies	44	33	35	35	43
Maintenance and repairs	200	150	60	175	160
Plant depreciation	120	90	90	110	110
Administration	120	90	90	90	100
Total divisional costs: and expenses	$1,548	$1,161	$1,270	$1,310	$1,303
Divisional margin	$1,252	$ 939	$ 930	$1,190	$1,127
Allocated corporate fixed costs	360	270	240	340	320
Divisional profit	$ 892	$ 669	$ 690	$ 850	$ 807

	Budgeted Balance 12/31/Year 3	Budgeted Balance 9/30/Year 3	Actual Balance 9/30/Year 3	Budgeted Balance 12/31/Year 2	Actual Balance 12/31/Year 2
Divisional investment:					
Accounts receivable	$ 280	$ 290	$ 250	$ 250	$ 250
Inventories	500	500	650	450	475
Plant fixed assets (net)	1,320	1,350	1,100	1,150	1,100
Total	$2,100	$2,140	$2,000	$1,850	$1,825

*American Traditions' sales occur uniformly throughout the year.

Required

a. Evaluate Patrick Anderson's performance for the nine months ending September 30 of year 3. Support your evaluation with pertinent facts from the problem.

b. Identify the features of American Traditions' division performance-measurement reporting and evaluation system that need to be revised if it is to be effective.

[CMA adapted]

Problem 18.38
Preparation of
Performance Reports;
Hospital
(LO 1, 4)

Potomac General Hospital serves the metropolitan Washington, D.C., area. The hospital is a nonprofit organization supported by patient billings, county and state funds, and private donations. An organization chart and cost information for August follow.

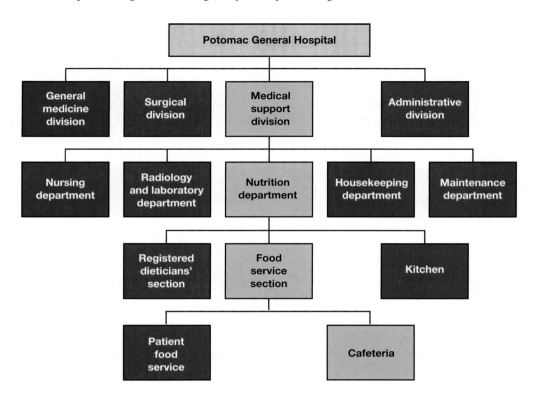

	Actual		Budget	
	August	**Year to Date**	**August**	**Year to Date**
Cafeteria:				
Food servers' wages	$ 9,000	$ 72,000	$ 8,000	$ 64,000
Paper products	4,400	36,200	4,500	36,000
Utilities	1,050	8,100	1,000	8,000
Maintenance	100	1,100	400	3,200
Custodial	1,100	8,600	1,100	8,800
Supplies	900	9,600	1,200	9,600
Patient food service	18,500	137,000	17,000	136,000
Registered dieticians' section	7,500	60,000	7,500	60,000
Kitchen	29,400	246,000	31,000	248,000
Nursing department	75,000	580,000	70,000	560,000
Radiology and laboratory department	18,100	144,000	18,000	144,000
Housekeeping department	11,600	86,000	10,000	80,000
Maintenance department	6,000	77,000	13,000	104,000
General medicine division	204,000	1,670,900	210,000	1,680,000
Surgical division	141,000	1,115,800	140,000	1,120,000
Administrative division	53,500	406,000	50,000	400,000

Required

a. Prepare a set of cost-performance reports similar to Exhibit 18–4 with six columns. The first four columns will have the same headings as those in the preceding table. The last two columns will have the following headings: Variance—August, and Variance—Year to Date.

Since all information in the performance reports for Potomac General Hospital is cost information, you do not need to show these data in parentheses. Use F or U to denote whether each variance in the reports is favorable or unfavorable.

b. Using arrows, show the relationships between the numbers in your performance reports for Potomac General Hospital. Refer to Exhibit 18–4 for guidance.

c. As the hospital's administrator, which variances in the performance reports would you want to investigate further? Why?

Problem 18.39
ROI and Residual
Income; Missing Data;
Improving ROI
(LO 5, 6)

Michigan Pipe Fitting Corporation has two divisions to which the following data pertain. The company's required rate of return on invested capital is 8 percent.

	Detroit Division	Flint Division
Sales revenue	$10,000,000	?
Income	$ 2,000,000	$400,000
Average investment	$ 2,500,000	?
Sales margin	?	20%
Capital turnover	?	1
ROI	?	?
Residual income	?	?

Required

a. Fill in the blanks in the preceding table.

b. Explain three ways the Detroit Division manager could improve her division's ROI. Use numbers to illustrate these possibilities.

c. Suppose the Flint Division's sales margin increased to 25 percent while its capital turnover remained constant. Compute the division's new ROI.

Problem 18.40
Equipment Replacement
and Performance
Measures; Ethics
(LO 5, 7)

CompuTech, Inc., a manufacturer of products using the latest microprocessor technology, has appointed you the manager of its Micro Technology Division. Your division has $800,000 in assets and manufactures a special chip assembly. On January 2 of the current year, you invested $1 million in automated equipment for chip assembly. At that time, your expected income statement was as follows:

Sales revenue	$3,200,000
Operating costs:	
Unit level (variable)	400,000
Facility level (fixed, all cash)	1,500,000
Depreciation:	
New equipment	300,000
Other	250,000
Division operating profit	$ 750,000

On October 25 a sales representative from Klondike Machine Company approached you. For $1.3 million, Klondike offers a new assembly machine with significant improvements over the equipment you bought on January 2. The new equipment would expand department output by 10 percent while reducing cash fixed costs by 5 percent. The new equipment would be depreciated for accounting purposes over a three-year life. Depreciation would be net of the new machine's $100,000 salvage value. The new equipment meets your company's 20 percent cost of capital criterion. If you purchase the new machine, it must be installed prior to the end of the year. For practical purposes, though, you can ignore depreciation on the new machine because it will not go into operation until the start of the next year.

The old machine, which has no salvage value, must be disposed of to make room for the new machine.

Your company has a performance evaluation and bonus plan based on ROI. The return includes any losses on disposals of equipment. Investment is computed based on the average balance of assets for the year, net book value.

Required

a. What is your division's ROI this year if it does not acquire the new machine?

b. What is your division's ROI this year if it does acquire the new machine?

c. If the new machine is acquired and operates according to specifications, what ROI is expected for next year?

d. Is it ethical to decline to purchase the new machine? Explain.

e. *Build your own spreadsheet.* Build an Excel spreadsheet to solve requirements (a) through (c). Use your spreadsheet to determine the new values for the ROI calculated in requirements (a), (b), and (c) if each of the following input parameters changes by the amount indicated. (Unless otherwise indicated, treat each parameter change independently.)

(1) This year's sales revenue is $3,400,000.

(2) This year's unit-level operating costs are $350,000.

(3) This year's facility-level (fixed) operating costs are $1,400,000.

(4) All of the changes listed in (1) through (3) occur simultaneously.

Refer to the information given in the preceding problem. As the Micro Technology Division manager, you are still assessing the problem of whether to acquire Klondike Machine Company's machine. You learn that the new machine could be acquired next year, but it will cost 15 percent more then. Its salvage value would still be $100,000. Other costs or revenue estimates would be apportioned on a month-by-month basis for the time each machine is in use. (Ignore fractions of months.)

Problem 18.41
Evaluation of Trade-Offs in Return Measurement; Continuation of Preceding Problem
(LO 5, 7)

Required

a. When would you want to purchase the new machine if you wait until next year?

b. What are the costs that must be considered in making this decision?

Refer to Exhibit 18–6. Prepare a similar table of the changing ROI assuming the following accelerated depreciation schedule. Assume income before depreciation of $150,000 per year. (If there is a loss, leave the ROI column blank.)

Problem 18.42
ROI Increases over Time; Accelerated Depreciation; Increasing Residual Income Over Time
(LO 5, 7)

Year	Depreciation
1	$200,000
2	120,000
3	72,000
4	54,000
5	54,000
Total	$500,000

Required

a. How does your table differ from the one in Exhibit 18–6? Why?

b. What are the implications of the ROI pattern in your table?

c. Prepare a table similar to Exhibit 18–6, which focuses on residual income. Use a 10 percent rate to compute the imputed interest charge. The table should show the residual income on the investment during each year in its five-year life. Assume income before depreciation of $150,000 per year and straight-line depreciation with no salvage value.

Glasgow Drilling Company is an oil and gas exploration and drilling company operating off the coast of Scotland. Oil and gas companies inevitably incur costs on unsuccessful exploration ventures called *dry holes*. A debate continues over whether those costs should be written off as period expenses or capitalized as part of the full cost of finding profitable oil and gas ventures. Glasgow has been writing these costs off to expense as incurred. However, this year a new management team was hired to improve the profit picture of the firm's Oil and Gas Exploration Division with the provision that it would receive a bonus equal to 10 percent of any profits in excess of the division's base-year profits. However, no bonus would be paid if profits were less than 20 percent of end-of-year investment. The following information was included in the division's performance report.

Problem 18.43
Impact of Decisions to Capitalize or Expense on Performance Measurement
(LO 5, 7)

	Base Year	This Year	Increase over Base Year
Sales revenue	$4,000,000	$4,100,000	
Costs incurred:			
Dry holes	800,000	0	
Depreciation and other amortization	750,000	780,000	
Other costs	1,550,000	1,600,000	
Division profit	$ 900,000	$1,720,000	$820,000
End-of-year investment	$6,900,000	$8,100,000*	

*Includes other investments not at issue here.

During the year, the new team spent $1 million on exploratory activities, of which $900,000 was for unsuccessful ventures. The new management team has included the $900,000 in the current end-of-year investment base because, it states, "You can't find the good ones without hitting a few bad ones."

Required

a.   What is the ROI for the base year and the current year?

b.   What is the amount of the bonus that the new management team is likely to claim?

c.   If you were on Glasgow's board of directors, how would you respond to the new management's claim for the bonus?

Problem 18.44
Divisional Performance
Measurement;
Behavioral Issues
(LO 1, 5, 7)

Gigantic Corporation's division managers have been expressing growing dissatisfaction with the methods Gigantic uses to measure division performance. Division operations are evaluated every quarter by comparison with the master budget prepared during the prior year. Division managers claim that many factors are completely out of their control but are included in this comparison, resulting in an unfair and misleading performance evaluation.

The managers have been particularly critical of the process used to establish standards and budgets. The annual budget, stated by quarters, is prepared six months prior to the beginning of the operating year. Pressure by top management to reflect increased earnings has often caused divisional managers to overstate revenues and/or understate expenses. In addition, once the budget is established, divisions must "live with the budget." Frequently, external factors such as the state of the economy, changes in consumer preferences, and actions of competitors have not been recognized in the budgets that top management supplied to the divisions. The credibility of the performance review is curtailed when the budget cannot be adjusted to incorporate these changes.

Recognizing these problems, top management agreed to establish a committee to review the situation and to make recommendations for a new performance evaluation system. The committee consists of each division manager, the corporate controller, and the executive vice president. At the first meeting, one division manager outlined an achievement of objectives system (AOS). In this performance evaluation system, division managers are evaluated according to three criteria:

■   *Doing better than last year.* Various measures are compared to the same measures of the prior year.

■   *Planning realistically.* Actual performance for the current year is compared to realistic plans and/or goals.

■   *Managing current assets.* Various measures are used to evaluate division management's achievements and reactions to changing business and economic conditions.

One division manager believed that this system would overcome many of the current system's inconsistencies because divisions could be evaluated from three different viewpoints. In addition, managers would have the opportunity to show how they would react and account for changes in uncontrollable external factors.

Another manager cautioned that the success of a new performance evaluation system would be limited unless it had the complete support of top management.

Required

a.   Explain whether the proposed AOS would improve Gigantic Corporation's evaluation of division performance.

b.   Develop specific performance measures for each of the three criteria in the proposed AOS that could be used to evaluate division managers.

c.   Discuss the motivational and behavioral aspects of the proposed performance measurement system. Also recommend specific programs that could be instituted to promote morale and give incentives to divisional management.

[CMA adapted]

Problem 18.45
ROI and Management
Behavior
(LO 1, 5, 7)

Toronto Machine Tool Company (TMTC) is a highly diversified and decentralized company. Each division is responsible for its own sales, pricing, production, and costs of operations; management of accounts receivable, inventories, and accounts payable; and use of existing facilities. Corporate headquarters manages cash.

Division executives present investment proposals to corporate management, who analyze and document them as well as make the final decision to commit funds for investment purposes.

The corporation evaluates divisional executive performance using the ROI measure. The asset base is composed of fixed assets employed plus working capital, exclusive of cash. The ROI performance of a division executive is the most important appraisal factor for salary changes. In addition, each executive's annual performance bonus is based on ROI results, with increases in ROI having a significant impact on the amount of the bonus.

TMTC adopted the ROI performance measure and related compensation procedures about 10 years ago and seems to have benefited from the program. The corporation's ROI increased during the first years of the program. Although each division's ROI continued to grow, corporate ROI declined in recent years. The corporation has accumulated a sizable amount of short-term marketable securities in the past three years.

Corporate management is concerned about the increase in the short-term marketable securities. A recent article in a financial publication suggested that some companies had overemphasized the use of ROI with results similar to those experienced by TMTC.

Required

a.   Describe the specific actions that division managers might have taken to cause the ROI to increase in each division but decline for the corporation. Illustrate your explanation with appropriate examples.

b.   Using the concepts of goal congruence and motivation of division executives, explain how TMTC's overemphasis on the use of the ROI measure might result in the recent decline in the corporation's ROI and the increase in cash and short-term marketable securities.

c.   What changes could be made in TMTC's compensation policy to avoid this problem? Explain your answer.

[CMA adapted]

Louisiana Shrimp Boats, Inc. (LSB), is a seafood restaurant chain operating throughout the south. The company has two sources of long-term capital: debt and equity. LSB's cost of issuing debt is the after-tax cost of the interest payments on the debt, considering the fact that the interest payments are tax deductible. LSB's cost of equity capital is the investment opportunity rate of LSB's investors, that is, the rate they could earn on investments of risk similar to that of investing in Louisiana Shrimp Boats, Inc. The interest rate on LSB's $80 million of long-term debt is 9 percent, and the company's tax rate is 40 percent. LSB's cost of equity capital is 14 percent. Moreover, the market value (and book value) of LSB's equity is $120 million.

Louisiana Shrimp Boats, Inc., consists of two divisions: properties division and food service division. The divisions' total assets, current liabilities, and before-tax operating income for the most recent year are as follows:

Division	Before-Tax Operating Income	Total Assets	Current Liabilities
Properties	$29,000,000	$145,000,000	$3,000,000
Food Service	15,000,000	64,000,000	6,000,000

Required

a.   Calculate the weighted-average cost of capital for Louisiana Shrimp Boats, Inc.

b.   Calculate the economic value added (EVA) for each of LSB's divisions.

Problem 18.46
Weighted-Average Cost of Capital; Economic Value Added
(LO 5)

mhhe.com/hilton3e

Cases

Drawem Company purchased Bildem Company three years ago. Prior to the acquisition, Bildem manufactured and sold electronic products to third-party customers. Since becoming a division of Drawem, Bildem now manufactures electronic components only for products made by Drawem's Macon Division.

Drawem's corporate management gives the Bildem Division management considerable latitude in running the division's operations. However, corporate management retains authority for decisions regarding capital investments, product pricing, and production quantities.

Drawem has a formal performance evaluation program for all divisional management teams that relies substantially on each division's ROI. Bildem Division's income statement provides the basis for the evaluation of its divisional management. (See the following income statement.)

The corporate accounting staff prepares the division's financial statements. Corporate general services costs are allocated on the basis of sales dollars, and the computer department's actual costs are

Case 18.47
Evaluation of Performance Evaluation System; Behavioral Issues
(LO 1, 5, 8)

apportioned among the divisions on the basis of use. The net division investment includes division fixed assets at net book value (cost less depreciation), division inventory, and corporate working capital apportioned to the divisions on the basis of sales dollars.

DRAWEM COMPANY
Bildem Division
Income Statement
For the Year Ended June 30
(in thousands)

Sales revenue		$8,000
Costs and expenses:		
Product costs:		
Direct material	$1,000	
Direct labor	2,200	
Manufacturing overhead	2,600	
Total	$5,800	
Less: Increase in inventory	700	5,100
Engineering and research		240
Shipping and receiving		480
Division administration:		
Manager's office	$ 420	
Cost management	80	
Human services	164	664
Corporate cost:		
General services	$ 460	
Computer	96	556
Total costs and expenses		$7,040
Divisional operating profit		$960
Net plant investment		$3,200
Return on investment		30%

Required

a. As a group, discuss Drawem Company's financial reporting and performance evaluation program as it relates to the responsibilities of Bildem Division.

b. Based on your response to requirement (a), write a memo to management recommending appropriate revisions of the financial information and reports used to evaluate the performance of Bildem's divisional management. If revisions are not necessary, explain why.

[CMA adapted]

Case 18.48
Budgeting and
Responsibility
Accounting
(LO 1, 2, 3)*†

Overview

River Beverages is a food and soft-drink company with worldwide operations. The company is organized into five regional divisions with each vice president reporting directly to the CEO, Cindy Wilkins. Each vice president has an R&D department, controller, and three divisions; carbonated drinks, juices and water, and food products. Management believes that the structure works well for River Beverages because different regions have different tastes and the division's products complement each other. River Beverages' companywide and divisional organization charts are shown here.

Industry

The US beverage industry has become mature with its growth matching population growth. In one recent year alone, consumers drank about 50 billion gallons of fluids. Most of the industry growth has come from the nonalcoholic beverage market, which is growing by about 1.1 percent annually. In the nonalcoholic arena, soft drinks are the largest segment, accounting for 53.4 percent of the beverages consumed. Americans consume about 26 billion gallons of soft drinks, ringing up retail sales of $50 bil-

---

*© Michael W. Maher.

† This integrative case relates to issues from Chapters 15 and 18, and it relates to learning objectives from both chapters.

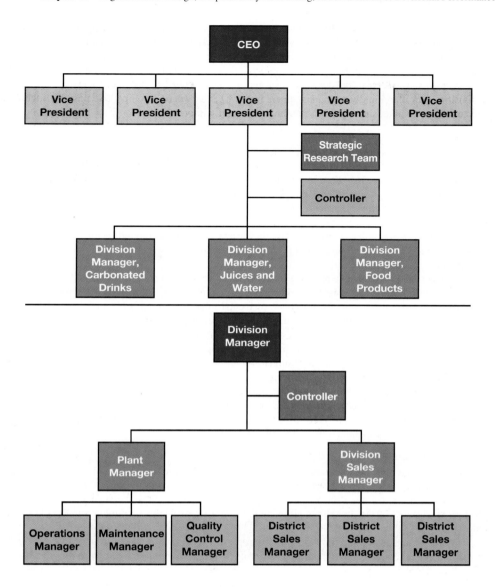

lion every year. Water (bottled and tap) is the next largest segment, representing 23.7 percent of the market. Juices represent about 12 percent of the beverages consumed. The smallest but fastest-growing segment is ready-to-drink teas, which is growing by more than 91 percent in volume but accounts for less than 1 percent of the beverages consumed.

Sales Budgets

Susan Johnson, plant manager at River Beverages' noncarbonated drink plant in St. Louis, recently completed the annual budgeting process. According to Johnson, division managers have decision-making authority in their business units except for capital financing activities. Budgets keep the division managers focused on corporate goals.

At the beginning of December, division managers submit a report to the vice president for the region summarizing capital, sales, and income forecasts for the upcoming fiscal year beginning July 1. Although the initial report is not prepared with much detail, it is prepared carefully because it is used in the strategic planning process.

Next, the strategic research team begins a formal assessment of each market segment in its region. The team develops sales forecasts for each division and compiles them into a company forecast. The team considers economic conditions and current market share in each region. Management believes the strategic research team is effective because it is able to integrate division products and more accurately forecast demand for complementary products. In addition, the team ensures continuity of assumptions and achievable sales goals.

Once the corporate forecast has been completed, the district sales managers estimate sales for the upcoming budget year. The district sales managers are ultimately responsible for the forecasts they prepare. The district sales forecasts are then compiled and returned to the division manager. The division manager reviews the forecast but cannot make any revisions without discussing the changes with the district sales managers. Next, the district sales forecasts are reviewed by the strategic research team and the division controller. Finally, top management reviews each division's competitive position, including plans to increase market share, capital spending, and quality improvement plans.

Plant Budgets

After top management approves the sales budget, it is separated into a sales budget for each plant. Plant location is determined by product type and where the product needs to be distributed. The budget is broken down further by price, volume, and product type. Plant managers budget contribution margins, fixed costs, and pretax income using information from the plant sales budget.

The plants are designated as profit centers. Each plant's budgeted profit is determined by subtracting budgeted variable costs and budgeted fixed costs from the sales forecast. If actual sales fall below forecasts, the plant manager is still responsible for achieving the budgeted profit. One of the most important aspects of the plant budgeting process is that plant managers break the plant budget down into various plant departments.

Operations and maintenance managers work together to develop cost standards and cost-reduction targets for all departments. Budgeted cost reductions from productivity improvements, unfavorable variances, and facility-level costs are developed for each department, operation, and cost center in the plant.

Before plant managers submit their budgets, a member of the strategy team and the regional controller visit the plant to keep corporate management in touch with what is happening at the plant level and to help corporate management understand how plant managers determine their budgets. The visits also allow corporate management to provide budget preparation guidance if necessary. The visits are especially important because they force plant management to keep in touch with corporate-level managers.

The final budgets are submitted and consolidated by April 1. The vice president reviews them to ensure that they are in line with corporate objectives. After all changes have been made by the vice presidents and the chief executive officer (CEO), the budgets are submitted to the board of directors for approval. The board votes on the final budget in early June.

Performance Measurement

The corporate office generates variance reports monthly. River Beverages has a sophisticated information system that automatically generates reports based on input downloaded daily from each plant. Managers in the organization also can manually generate the reports. Most managers generate variance reports several times during the month, allowing them to solve problems before the problems get out of control.

Corporate management reviews the variance reports, looking closely at overbudget variance problems. Plant managers are questioned only about overbudget items. Management believes that this ensures that the plant managers are staying on top of problem areas, and that this keeps the plants operating as efficiently as possible. One week after the variance reports are generated, plant managers are required to submit a response outlining the causes of any variances and how they plan to prevent the problems in the future. If a plant manager has repeated problems, corporate management might send a specialist to the plant to work with the plant manager to solve the problems.

Sales and Manufacturing Relations

"We are expected to meet our approved budget," remarked Kevin Greely, a division controller at River Beverages. "A couple years ago, one of our major restaurant customers switched to another brand. Even though the restaurant sold over one million cases of our product annually, we were not allowed to make revisions to our budget."

Budgets are rarely adjusted after approval. However, if sales decline early in the year, plant managers might file an appeal to revise the budgeted profit for the year. If sales decline late in the year, management usually does not revise the budgeted amounts but asks plant managers to cut costs wherever possible and delay any unnecessary expenditures until the following year. Remember that River Beverages sets budgets so it is able to see where to make cuts or where it can find any operating inefficiencies. Plant managers are not forced to meet their goals, but they are encouraged to cut costs below budget.

The sales department is primarily responsible for product price, sales volume, and delivery timing while plant managers are responsible for plant operations. As you might imagine, problems occur between plant and regional sales managers from time to time. For example, rush orders could cause production costs to be higher than normal for some production runs. Another problem could occur when a sales manager runs a promotional campaign that causes margins to shrink. In both instances, a plant manager's profit will be affected negatively while a sales manager's sales will be affected positively. Such situations are often passed up to the division level for resolution; however, the customer is always the primary concern.

Incentives

River Beverages' management has devised what it thinks is an effective system to motivate plant managers. First, plant managers are promoted only when they have displayed outstanding performance in their current position. Second, monetary incentives reward plant managers for reaching profit goals. Finally, charts produced monthly display budgeted items versus actual results. Although not required to do so, most plant managers publicize the charts and use them as a motivational tool. The charts allow department supervisors and staff to compare activities in their department to similar activities in other plants around the world.

CEO's Message

Cindy Wilkins, CEO of River Beverages, looks to the future and comments, "Planning is an important aspect of budget preparation for every level of our organization. I would like to decrease the time spent on preparing the budget, but I believe that it keeps people thinking about the future. The negative aspect of the budgeting process is that sometimes it overcontrols our managers. We need to stay nimble enough to react to customer demands while staying structured enough to achieve corporate objectives. For the most part, our budget process keeps our managers aware of sales goals and alerts them when sales or expenses are off track."

Required

a. Discuss each step in River Beverages' budgeting process. Begin with the division manager's initial reports and end with the board of directors' approval. Is each step necessary? Explain.

b. Evaluate River Beverages' responsibility-accounting system. Specifically, should the plant managers be held responsible for costs or profits? Why?

c. Write a report to River Beverages' management stating the advantages and disadvantages of the company's budgeting process. Start your report by stating your assumption(s) about what River Beverages' management wants the budgeting process to accomplish.

Chapter 19

Transfer Pricing

After completing this chapter, you should be able to:

1. Explain the purpose and role of transfer pricing.

2. Use the general economic rule to set an optimal transfer price.

3. Explain how to base a transfer price on market prices, costs, or negotiations.

4. Discuss the implications of transfer pricing in a multinational company.

5. Discuss the effects of transfer pricing on segment reporting.

Cost-*Management* Challenges

(Solutions are on page 803.)

1. **What** is the primary objective of Outback Outfitters' cost-management team in determining a transfer-pricing policy?

2. **Describe** four methods by which Outback Outfitters can set transfer prices.

3. **Explain** the significance of excess capacity in the transferring division.

4. **Why** might income tax laws affect the transfer-pricing policies of multinational companies?

EMAIL MEMORANDUM

Outback Outfitters, Ltd.
Retail Division
212 Rushcutters Bay Road
Sydney, New South Wales
AUSTRALIA

Memorandum

To: Eric Devon
           Vice President, Koala Camp Gear Division
From: Marie Waters
           Vice President, Retail Division
Subject: Transfer price for 'RooPacks

    I have received an inquiry from a local civic organization regarding the purchase of 800 'RooPacks to be distributed in conjunction with the Australia Day celebration coming up on January 26. My contact has offered the Retail Division a price of $55 per backpack. This price is substantially below our usual retail price of $70, so I am requesting a transfer price from the Koala Camp Gear Division to enable each of our divisions to make a profit on the transfer.

    Please advise me at your earliest convenience as to the transfer price that Koala would need in this special situation. I have promised a response to our potential customer by the end of business on Tuesday next.

The memo from Marie Waters of Outback Outfitters' Retail Division to Eric Devon of Koala Camp Gear Division (Koala Division) indicates that in this company, as in many others, divisions often exchange products. Internal transfers of products create the need for some pricing mechanism between divisions to accurately reflect the costs and revenues of doing business. The pricing mechanism commonly used to reflect transfers, called a **transfer price,** is the amount charged when one division of an organization sells goods or services to another division. In this example, Outback Outfitters' Retail Division is requesting a transfer price from the company's Koala Division for a special order of 'RooPacks, one of Outback's most popular items.

Although transfer prices commonly are used in today's organizations, they present some challenges for cost-management analysts. For example, when a division of General Electric Corporation buys parts for the kitchen appliances it manufactures from another GE division, how does GE record this exchange in its accounting records for the two divisions? When an engineering student at Cornell University takes an accounting course in the school of management, how does the university record this event? Both of these situations require the transfer of goods or services from one subunit of the organization to another.

Let's explore some of the challenges that cost-management analysts face in determining how to establish transfer prices to represent the substance of the transactions that occur between divisions.

Impact of Transfer Pricing on Organizations

LO I Explain the purpose and role of transfer pricing.

The transfer price charged when one division of an organization sells goods or services to another division does not affect the overall organization's total profit, *assuming that a transfer is made.* However, the transfer price does affect the profit measurement for both the selling and buying divisions because, in effect, the divisions are completing sales transactions with each other. A high transfer price results in high profit for the selling division but low profit for the buying division. A low transfer price has the opposite effect. Consequently, the transfer-pricing policy *can* affect the *incentives* of autonomous division managers as they decide whether to make the transfer. Exhibit 19–1 depicts this scenario.

Companies such as Sega of America and Nintendo, which buy video games from their Japanese parent companies, and Honda, which buys motorcycles from its Japanese parent company, make international transfers of goods and, therefore, require transfer prices to reflect these transactions. The transfer price becomes a cost to the

Exhibit 19–1   The Transfer-Pricing Scenario

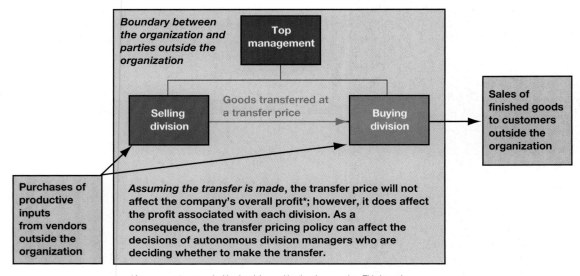

*Assumes no tax complexities involving multinational companies. This issue is addressed later in the chapter.

buying division and revenue to the selling division, which has important implications for both divisions.

This automobile assembly division buys parts from several other divisions.

If the divisions are evaluated using some investment-center performance measure, such as return on investment (ROI), residual income (RI), or economic value added (EVA), the transfer price can affect each division's reported performance. The higher the transfer price, the more favorable is the performance measure for the selling division and the less favorable is the comparable performance measure for the buying division, all other things being equal.

Goal and Behavioral Congruence

What should be management's goal in setting transfer prices for internally transferred goods or services? In a decentralized organization, the managers of profit centers and investment centers often have considerable autonomy in deciding whether to accept or reject orders and whether to buy from inside or outside the organization. For example, a large manufacturer of farm equipment allows its assembly division managers to buy parts either from another division of the company or from independent manufacturers. The goal in setting transfer prices is to establish incentives for autonomous division managers to make decisions that support the organization's overall goals.

Suppose that it is in the best interests of Outback Outfitters for the camping equipment manufactured by the Koala Camp Gear Division to be transferred to the Retail Division's stores throughout Australia and the United Kingdom, as well as to Outback's Mail-Order Division. In other words, if Outback Outfitters were centralized, manufactured products would be transferred from the Koala Camp Gear Division to the Retail and Mail-Order Divisions. However, Outback is a decentralized company, and the Retail and Mail-Order Division managers are free to buy goods from either the Koala Camp Gear Division or an outside company. Similarly, the Koala Camp Gear Division manager is free to accept or reject an order for products, at any given price, from the Retail or Mail-Order Divisions. The goal in setting the transfer price is to provide incentives for each of these division managers to act in the company's best interests. The transfer price should be chosen so that each division manager, when striving to maximize his or her own division's profit, makes the decision that maximizes the company's profit.

General Transfer-Pricing Rule

Management's objective in setting a transfer price is to encourage goal, or at least behavioral, congruence among the division managers involved in the transfer. A general rule to ensure goal congruence follows.

LO 2 Use the general economic rule to set an optimal transfer price.

$$\text{Transfer price} = \begin{array}{c}\text{Additional } \textit{outlay} \\ \textit{cost} \textbf{ per unit} \\ \text{incurred because} \\ \text{goods are transferred}\end{array} + \begin{array}{c}\textit{Opportunity cost} \\ \textbf{per unit to the} \\ \text{organization} \\ \text{because of the transfer}\end{array}$$

The general rule specifies the transfer price as the sum of two cost components. The first component is the *outlay cost* incurred by the division that produces the goods or services to be transferred. Outlay costs include the direct unit-level costs of the product or service and any other outlay costs incurred as a result of the transfer. The second component in the general transfer-pricing rule is the opportunity cost incurred by the organization as a whole because of the transfer. Recall that an *opportunity cost* is a benefit that is forgone as a result of taking a particular action.

We illustrate the general transfer-pricing rule for Outback Outfitters. Its Koala Camp Gear Division manufactures backpacks in its Melbourne plant. The division transfers some of its products to the company's Retail and Mail-Order Divisions. These backpacks carry the brand name 'RooPack and are imprinted with the Koala Camp Gear label. The Koala Camp Gear Division also sells some of its backpacks to other companies in the *external market* under different labels.

The Melbourne plant incurs the following costs to manufacture a backpack and transport it to a buyer.

Production:
Standard unit-level cost (including packaging) $39
Transportation:
Standard unit-level transportation cost 1

In applying the general transfer-pricing rule, we distinguish between two different scenarios.

Scenario 1: No excess capacity.   Suppose that the Koala Camp Gear Division can sell all backpacks it can produce to outside buyers at a market price of $60 each. Since the division can sell all of its production, it has *no excess capacity. Excess capacity* exists only when more goods can be produced than the producer is able to sell because of low demand for the product.

What transfer price does the general rule yield under this scenario of no excess capacity? The transfer price is determined as follows:

Outlay cost per backpack:
Standard unit-level cost of production $39
Standard unit-level cost of transportation... 1
Total outlay cost $40
Opportunity cost per backpack:
Wholesale selling price in external market $60
Unit-level cost of production and transportation 40
Opportunity cost (forgone contribution margin)... $20

The general transfer-pricing rule yields the following transfer price.

$$\text{Transfer price} = \text{Outlay cost} + \text{Opportunity cost}$$
$$\$60 \quad = \quad \$40 \quad + \quad \$20$$

The *outlay cost* that the Koala Camp Gear Division incurs to transfer a backpack includes the standard unit-level production cost of $39 and the standard unit-level transportation cost of $1. The *opportunity cost* incurred by Outback Outfitters when its Koala Division transfers a backpack to the Retail or Mail-Order Division *instead of* selling it in the external market is the forgone contribution margin from the lost sale, equal to $20. The company loses a sale in the external market for every backpack transferred to the Retail or Mail-Order Division because the Koala Camp Gear Division has *no excess capacity.* Every backpack transferred to another company division results in one less backpack sold in the external market.

Goal or behavioral congruence.   How does the general transfer-pricing rule promote goal or behavioral congruence? Suppose the Retail Division's stores can sell a 'RooPack for $70. What is the best way for Outback Outfitters to use the limited production capacity in the Koala Camp Gear Division's Melbourne plant? The answer is determined as follows:

Contribution to Outback Outfitters from Sale in External Market		**Contribution to Outback Outfitters from Transfer to Retail Division**	
Wholesale selling price per backpack................	$60	Retail selling price per backpack	$70
Standard unit-level cost	40	Standard unit-level cost	40
Contribution margin	$20	Contribution margin...............................	$30

The best use of the Melbourne plant's limited production capacity is to produce 'RooPacks for transfer to the Retail Division. If the transfer price is set at $60, as the general rule specifies, goal congruence is maintained. The Koala Camp Gear Division manager is willing to transfer 'RooPacks to the Retail Division because the transfer price of $60 equals the external wholesale market price. The Retail Division manager is willing to buy the 'RooPacks because her division will have a contribution margin of $10 on each 'RooPack transferred ($70 retail sales price minus the $60 transfer price).

Now consider a different situation. A local organization has made a special offer to the Retail Division manager to buy several hundred 'RooPacks to sell in a promotional campaign associated with the annual Australia Day celebration. The organization has offered to pay $55 per backpack. What will the Retail Division manager do? She must pay a transfer price of $60 per backpack, so the Retail Division would lose $5 per unit if the special offer were accepted ($60 − $55). The Retail Division manager will decline the special offer. Is this decision in the best interests of Outback Outfitters as a whole? If she accepts the offer, the positive contribution to the company as a whole would be $15 per backpack as shown in the following table:

**Contribution to Outback Outfitters
If Special Offer Is Accepted**

Special price per backpack	$55
Standard unit-level cost to company	40
Contribution to company per backpack	$15

However, the company can make even more if its Koala Camp Gear Division sells 'RooPacks directly in its external market. Then the contribution to the company is $20, as we have just seen. (The external market price of $60 per backpack minus a standard unit-level cost of $40 per backpack equals $20 per unit.) Thus, Outback Outfitters is better off, as a whole, if the Retail Division's special offer is rejected. Once again, the general transfer-pricing rule results in goal-congruent decision making.

Scenario II: Excess capacity. Now let's change our basic assumption and suppose that the Koala Division's Melbourne plant has excess production capacity. This means that the total demand for its products from all sources, including the Retail and Mail-Order Divisions and the external market, is less than the plant's production capacity. Under this scenario of excess capacity, what does the general rule specify for a transfer price?

$$\text{Transfer price} = \text{Outlay cost} + \text{Opportunity cost}$$
$$\$40 \quad = \quad \$40 \quad + \quad 0$$

The *outlay cost* in the Koala Camp Gear Division's Melbourne plant is still $40, since it does not depend on whether there is idle capacity or not. The *opportunity cost,* however, is now zero. There is no opportunity cost to the company when a backpack is transferred to the Retail Division because the Koala Camp Gear Division can still satisfy all of its external demand for backpacks. Thus, the general rule specifies a transfer price of $40, the total standard unit-level cost of production and transportation.

Goal or behavioral congruence. Let's reconsider what will happen when the Retail Division manager receives the local organization's special offer to buy backpacks at $55 per unit. The Retail Division will now show a positive contribution of $15 per backpack on the special order:

Special price per backpack	$55
Transfer price paid by Retail Division	40
Contribution to Retail Division	$15

The Retail Division manager will accept the special offer. This decision is also in the best interests of Outback Outfitters. The contribution to the company, as a whole, will be $15 per unit on every backpack transferred to the Retail Division to satisfy the special order. Once again, the general transfer-pricing rule maintains goal-congruent decision-making behavior.

Notice that the general rule yields a transfer price that leaves the Koala Camp Gear Division manager indifferent to making the transfer. At a transfer price of $40, the contribution to the Koala Camp Gear Division is zero (transfer price of $40 less outlay cost of $40). To avoid this problem, we can view the general rule as providing a lower bound on the transfer price. Some companies allow the producing division to add a markup to this lower bound in order to provide a positive contribution margin. This in turn provides a positive incentive to make the transfer.

Difficulty in implementing the general rule.   The general transfer-pricing rule always promotes goal-congruent decision making *if the rule can be implemented.* However, the rule is often difficult or impossible to implement due to the difficulty of measuring opportunity costs. Such a cost-measurement problem can arise for a number of reasons. One reason is that the external market might not be perfectly competitive. Under **perfect competition,** the market price does not depend on the quantity sold by any one producer. Under **imperfect competition,** a single producer can affect the market price by varying the amount of product available in the market. In such cases, the external market price depends on the producer's production decisions. This in turn means that the opportunity cost the company incurs as a result of internal transfers depends on the quantity sold externally. These interactions could make accurately measuring the opportunity cost caused by a product transfer impossible.

Transfer pricing can be quite complex when selling and buying divisions cannot sell and buy all they want in perfectly competitive markets. In some cases, no outside market exists at all. Companies often find that not all transactions between divisions occur as top management prefers. In extreme cases, the transfer-pricing problem is so complex that top management reorganizes the company so that buying and selling divisions report to one manager who oversees the transfers.

Other reasons for difficulty in measuring the opportunity cost associated with a product transfer include uniqueness of the transferred goods or services, a need for the producing division to invest in special equipment to produce the transferred goods, and interdependencies among several transferred products or services. For example, the producing division might provide design services as well as production of the goods for a buying division. What is the opportunity cost associated with each of these related outputs of the producing division? In many such cases, sorting out the opportunity costs is difficult.

The general transfer-pricing rule provides a good conceptual model to use in setting transfer prices. Moreover, in many cases it can be implemented. When the general rule cannot be implemented, organizations turn to other transfer-pricing methods, as we shall see next.

Transfers Based on the External Market Price

LO 3 Explain how to base a transfer price on market prices, costs, or negotiations.

A common approach is to set the transfer price equal to the price in the external market. In the Outback Outfitters illustration, the Koala Camp Gear Division would set the transfer price for a 'RooPack at $60 per unit since that is the price the division can obtain in its external market. When the producing division has no excess capacity and perfect competition prevails, when no single producer can affect the market price, the general transfer-pricing rule and the external market price yield the same transfer price. This fact is illustrated for Outback Outfitters as follows:

General Transfer-Pricing Rule

$$
\begin{aligned}
\text{Transfer price} &= \begin{array}{c}\text{Outlay cost}\end{array} + \begin{array}{c}\text{Opportunity cost}\end{array} \\
&= \begin{array}{c}\text{Unit-level cost of}\\ \text{production and}\\ \text{transportation}\end{array} + \begin{array}{c}\text{Forgone}\\ \text{contribution margin}\\ \text{on an external sale}\end{array} \\
&= \qquad\quad \$40 \qquad\quad + \qquad (\$60 - \$40) \qquad = \$60
\end{aligned}
$$

Market Price

$$\text{Transfer price} = \text{External market price} = \$60$$

In more complicated situations in which the producing division has excess capacity or the external market is imperfectly competitive, the general rule and the external market price do not yield the same transfer price.

If the transfer price is set at the market price, the producing division should have the option to either produce goods for internal transfer or sell them in the external market. The buying division should be required to purchase goods from inside its organization if the producing division's goods meet the product specifications. Otherwise, the buying division should have the autonomy to buy from a supplier outside its own organization. The company should establish an arbitration process to handle pricing disputes that may arise.

Transfer prices based on market prices are consistent with the responsibility-accounting concepts of profit centers and investment centers. In addition to encouraging division managers to focus on divisional profitability, market-based transfer prices help to show each division's contribution to the company's overall profit. Suppose that the Koala Camp Gear Division of Outback Outfitters transfers backpacks to the Retail Division at a market-based transfer price of $60 per unit. The following contribution margins will be earned by the two divisions and the company as a whole.

Koala Camp Gear Division		**Retail Division**	
Transfer price	$60	Retail sales price	$70
Standard unit-level cost	40	Transfer price	60
Contribution margin	$20	Contribution margin	$10

Outback Outfitters	
Retail sales price	$70
Standard unit-level cost	40
Contribution margin	$30

When aggregate divisional profits are determined for the year, and ROI, residual income, and EVA are computed, the use of a market-based transfer price helps to assess each division's contributions to overall corporate profits.

Distress market prices.   Occasionally an industry experiences a period of significant excess capacity and extremely low prices. For example, when gasoline prices soared due to a foreign oil embargo, the market prices for recreational vehicles and power boats fell temporarily to very low levels.

Under such extreme conditions, basing transfer prices on market prices can lead to decisions that are not in the best interests of the overall company. Basing transfer prices on artificially low *distress market prices* could lead the producing division to sell or close the productive resources devoted to producing the product for transfer. Under distress market prices, the producing division manager might prefer to move the division into a more profitable product line. Although such a decision might improve the division's profit in the short run, it could be contrary to the best interests of the company overall. It might be better for the company as a whole to avoid divesting itself of any productive resources and to ride out the period of market distress. To encourage an autonomous division manager to act in this fashion, some companies set the transfer price equal to the long-run *average external market price* rather than the current (possibly depressed) market price.

Negotiated Transfer Prices

Many companies use negotiated transfer prices. Division managers or their representatives actually negotiate the price at which transfers will be made. Sometimes they start with the external market price and then make adjustments for various reasons. For example, the producing division could enjoy some cost savings on internal

LO 3 Explain how to base a transfer price on market prices, costs, or negotiations.

You're the Decision Maker 19.1

Setting a Transfer Price

Fast Track Shoe Company has two divisions, production and marketing. Production manufactures Fast Track shoes, which it sells to both the marketing division and to other retailers (the latter under a different brand name). Marketing operates several small shoe stores in shopping centers that sell both Fast Track and other brands.

Relevant facts for production, which is operating far below its capacity, follow:

Sales price to outsiders	$28.50 per pair
Unit-level cost to produce	$18.00 per pair
Facility-level costs	$100,000 per month

The following data pertain to the sale of Fast Track shoes by marketing, which is operating far below its capacity:

Sales price	$40 per pair
Unit-level marketing costs	$1 per pair

The company's unit-level manufacturing and marketing costs are differential costs in this decision, but the facility-level manufacturing and marketing costs are not.

a. What is the minimum price that the marketing division can charge for the shoes and still cover the company's differential manufacturing and marketing costs?

b. What is the appropriate transfer price for this situation?

c. What effect would a transfer price set at $28.50 have on the minimum price set by the marketing manager?

d. How would your answer to (b) change if the production division were operating at full capacity?

(Solutions begin on page 804.)

transfers that are not obtained on external sales. Commissions might not have to be paid to sales personnel on internally transferred products. In such cases, a negotiated transfer price could split the cost savings between the producing and buying divisions. In other instances, a negotiated transfer price could be used because no external market exists for the transferred product.

Two drawbacks sometimes characterize negotiated transfer prices. First, negotiations can lead to divisiveness and competition between participating division managers. This can undermine the spirit of cooperation and unity that is desirable throughout an organization. Second, although negotiating skill is a valuable managerial talent, it should not be the sole or dominant factor in evaluating a division manager. If, for example, the producing division's manager is a better negotiator than the buying division's manager, the producing division's profit might look better than it should simply because of its manager's superior negotiating ability.

Cost-Based Transfer Prices

Organizations that do not base transfer prices on market prices or negotiations often turn to **cost-based transfer-pricing,** which sets the transfer price on the basis of the cost of the product or service transferred.

Unit-level cost. One cost-based approach is to set the transfer price equal to the standard unit-level cost. The problem with this approach is that even when the producing division has excess capacity, it is not allowed to show any contribution margin on the transferred products or services. To illustrate, suppose that the Koala Camp Gear Division has excess capacity and the transfer price is set at the standard unit-level cost of $40 per backpack. The division has no positive incentive to produce and transfer backpacks to the Retail Division. The Koala Division's contribution margin from a transfer will be zero (transfer price of $40 minus unit-level costs of $40 equals zero). Some companies avoid this problem by setting the transfer price at standard unit-level cost plus a markup to allow the producing division a positive contribution margin.

Absorption or full cost. An alternative cost-based approach is to set the transfer price equal to the absorption, *or* full, cost of the transferred product or service. *Absorption* (or *full*) *cost* equals the product's unit-level cost plus an assigned portion of the higher-level costs (batch-level, product-line-level, customer-level, and general or facility-level costs).

Suppose that for the current year, the Koala Camp Gear Division's Melbourne plant has budgeted higher-level costs totaling $1.8 million and production of 100,000 backpacks. The full cost per backpack is calculated as follows:

$$\text{Full cost} = \begin{array}{c}\text{Standard}\\ \text{unit-level}\\ \text{cost}\end{array} + \text{Assigned higher-level costs}$$

$$= \$40 \quad + \quad \frac{\$1{,}800{,}000 \text{ budgeted higher-level costs}}{100{,}000 \text{ budgeted units of production}}$$

$$= \$40 \quad + \quad \$18$$

$$= \$58$$

Under this full-cost-based approach, the transfer price is set at $58 per backpack.

Possible dysfunctional decision-making behavior. Basing transfer prices on full cost entails a serious risk of causing dysfunctional decision-making behavior. Full-cost-based transfer prices lead the buying division to view those costs that are non-unit-level costs for the entire company as unit-level costs to the buying division. This can cause faulty decision making.

To illustrate, suppose that the Koala Camp Gear Division has excess capacity, and the transfer price of backpacks equals the full cost of $58 per pack. What happens if the Retail Division receives the special offer discussed previously, to sell backpacks to a local organization at a special price of $55 per unit? The Retail Division manager will reject the special order since her division would incur a loss of $3 per backpack.

Special price per backpack	$55
Transfer price based on full cost	58
Loss	$ 3

What is in the best interests of the company as a whole? Outback Outfitters would realize a positive contribution of $15 per backpack on those sold in the special order:

Special price per backpack	$55
Standard unit-level cost in Koala Camp Gear Division	40
Contribution to company as a whole	$15

What has happened here? Setting the transfer price equal to the full cost of $58 has turned a non-unit-level cost in the Koala Camp Gear Division and, hence, a non-unit-level cost for the company as a whole into a unit-level cost from the viewpoint of the Retail Division manager. The manager would tend to reject the special offer, even though accepting it would benefit the company as a whole.

Although the practice is common, transfer prices should not be based on full cost. The risk is too high that the cost behavior in the producing division will be obscured. This can all too easily result in dysfunctional decisions in the buying division.

A note on ethics. What are the ethical implications in the situation just discussed? If the retail division manager realizes that buying the backpacks from the Koala Division is in the best interests of Outback Outfitters, shouldn't she buy from Koala, even if it hurts her division's performance? Strict adherence to ethical standards suggest that she should. Realistically, however, human nature suggests that we cannot always count on such behavior to take place. Moreover, most transfer-pricing scenarios are much more complicated than the Outback Outfitters situation. More often than not, a buying division manager does not have enough information to clearly conclude what is in the overall company's best interests. It is important, therefore, to strive to set transfer pricing policies so that goal or behavioral congruence will be maintained.

Standard versus Actual Costs

Throughout our discussion of transfer prices, we have used *standard costs* rather than *actual costs.* This was true in our discussion of the general transfer-pricing rule as well as for cost-based transfer prices. Transfer prices should not be based on actual costs because such a practice would allow an inefficient producing division to pass its excess production costs on to the buying division via the transfer price. When standard costs are used in transfer-pricing formulas, the selling division is not forced to pick up the tab for the producer's inefficiency. Moreover, the producing division is given an incentive to control its costs since any costs of inefficiency cannot be passed on.

Deere and Co. was one of the pioneers in developing activity-based costing. One of the company's objectives for the ABC system was more accurate transfer prices.

Activity-Based Costing

Many companies are implementing activity-based costing to improve the accuracy of costs in cost-based transfer pricing. One of the primary motives for Deere and Co. to develop its activity-based costing system, for example, was to improve the accuracy of cost numbers in its internal transfers of parts.

Remedy for Motivational Problems of Transfer-Pricing Policies

When the transfer-pricing policy does not give a supplier a profit on the transaction, motivational problems can arise. For example, if transfers are made at differential unit-level costs, the supplier earns no contribution toward profit on the transferred goods. Then the transfer-pricing policy does not motivate the supplier to transfer internally because internal transfers have no likely profit. This situation can be remedied in several ways.

A supplier whose transfers are almost all internal usually is organized as a cost center. The cost center manager is normally held responsible for costs, not for revenues. Hence, the transfer price does not affect the manager's performance measures. In companies in which such a supplier is a profit center, the artificial nature of the transfer price should be considered when evaluating the results of that profit center's operations.

A supplying center that does business with both internal and external customers could be set up as a profit center for external business when the manager has price-setting power and as a cost center for internal transfers when the manager does not have such power. Performance on external business could be measured as if the responsibility center were a profit center; performance on internal business could be measured as if the responsibility center were a cost center.

Undermining of Divisional Autonomy

Suppose the manager of Outback's Koala Camp Gear Division has excess capacity but insists on a transfer price of $58 based on full cost. The Retail Division manager is faced with the special offer for backpacks at $55 per unit. She regrets that she must decline the offer because it would cause her division's profit to decline although the company's interests would be best served by accepting it. The Retail Division manager calls the company president and explains the situation. She asks the president to intervene and force the Koala Camp Gear Division manager to lower his transfer price.

As the company president, what would you do? If you stay out of the controversy, your company will lose the contribution on the special order. If you intervene, you will run the risk of undermining the autonomy of your division managers. You established a decentralized organization structure for Outback Outfitters and hired competent managers because you believed in the benefits of decentralized decision making.[1]

There is no obvious answer to this dilemma. In practice, central managers are reluctant to intervene in such disputes unless the negative financial consequences to the organization are quite large. Most managers believe that decentralized decision making has benefits that are important to protect even if it results in an occasional dysfunctional decision.

You're the Decision Maker 19.2

Dysfunctional Decisions and Transfer-Pricing Policy

Meridian Electronics Company's production division was operating below capacity. Its assembly division received a contract to assemble 10,000 units of a final product, XX-1. Each unit of XX-1 required one part, A-16, which the production division makes. Both divisions are decentralized, autonomous investment centers and are evaluated based on operating profits and ROI.

The vice president of the assembly division called the vice president of the production division and made a proposal:

Megan (Assembly VP): Look, Joe, I know you're running below capacity out there in your division. I'd like to buy 10,000 units of A-16 at $30 per unit. That will enable you to keep your production lines busy.

Joe (Production VP): Are you kidding, Megan? I happen to know that it would cost you a lot more if you had to buy A-16s from an outside supplier. We refuse to accept less than $40 per unit, which gives us our usual markup and covers our costs.

Megan: Joe, we both know that your unit-level costs for each unit of A-16 are only $22. I realize I'd be getting a good deal at $30, but so would you. You should treat this as a special order. Anything over your differential costs on the order is pure profit. Look, Joe, if you can't do better than $40, I'll have to go elsewhere. I have to keep my costs down, too, you know.

Joe: The $40 per unit is firm. Take it or leave it!

The assembly division subsequently sought bids on the part and was able to obtain its requirements from an outside supplier for $40 per unit. The production division continued to operate below capacity. The actions of the two divisions cost the company $180,000.

a. Show how the $180,000 cost to Meridian Electronics Company was calculated.

b. Put yourself in the place of Meridian's CEO. If you were approached by the assembly division VP to intervene in this situation, what would you do? Explain.

(Solutions begin on page 804.)

Dual Transfer Prices

A *dual transfer-pricing system* could be installed to provide the selling division a profit but charge the buying division with costs only. A **dual transfer-pricing system** charges the buying division for the cost of the transferred product, however the cost might be determined, and credits the selling division with the cost plus some profit allowance. The difference is accounted for in a special centralized account. This system would preserve cost data for subsequent buyer divisions and would encourage internal transfers by providing a profit on such transfers for the selling divisions.

Some companies use dual transfer prices to encourage internal transfers; however, other methods can also encourage internal transfers. For example, many companies recognize internal transfers and incorporate them explicitly in their reward systems. Other companies base part of a supplying manager's bonus on the purchasing center's profits.

---

[1] See the discussion of the costs and benefits of decentralization at the beginning of the preceding chapter.

Research Insight 19.1

Transfer Pricing Based on Actual Cost

Recent theoretical research on transfer pricing investigated how to optimally set a transfer price, given that the price is set using a cost-plus approach based on actual cost. This research compared two approaches to setting a transfer price based on the actual product cost: (1) the *multiplicative method*, by which the transfer price is a fixed percentage (e.g., the transfer price equals 125 percent of the actual product cost) and (2) the *additive method*, by which the transfer price is a fixed dollar amount above the actual product cost (e.g., the transfer price equals the actual product cost plus $X).

Under the specific assumptions of the model employed in this research, the investigator found that "the additive method is optimal among the class of cost-plus methods. In particular, its performance is superior to that of the multiplicative method." The research found that the manager in the selling division has a greater incentive to control (or reduce) the actual product cost of the transferred product under the additive approach to transfer pricing. *Source: S. A. Sahay, "Transfer Pricing Based on Actual Cost."*

Global Transfer-Pricing Practices

Surveys of corporate practices report that nearly half of the US companies surveyed used a cost-based transfer-pricing system: 33 percent used a market-price-based system, and 20 percent used a negotiated system. Similar results have been found for companies in Canada and Japan. Generally, we find that when negotiated prices are used, the prices negotiated are between the market price at the upper limit and some measure of cost at the lower limit.[2]

No optimal transfer-pricing policy dominates all others. An established policy most likely is imperfect in the sense that it does not always lead to the economically optimal outcome. As with other management decisions, however, the cost of any system must be weighed against its benefits. Improving a transfer-pricing policy beyond some point (for example, to obtain better measures of unit-level costs and market prices) results in the system's costs exceeding its benefits. As a result, management tends to settle for a system that seems to work reasonably well rather than to devise a "textbook-perfect" system.

Multinational Transfer Pricing

LO 4 Discuss the implications of transfer pricing in a multinational company.

In international transactions, transfer prices could affect tax liabilities, royalties, and other payments because laws vary in different countries (or states). Because tax rates vary among countries, companies have incentives to set transfer prices that will increase revenues (and profits) in low-tax countries and increase costs (thereby reducing profits) in high-tax countries.

Tax avoidance by foreign companies using inflated transfer prices has been a controversial issue in recent years. Foreign companies that sell goods to their US subsidiaries at inflated transfer prices artificially reduce the profit of the US subsidiaries. According to some reports, the United States could collect billions per year in additional taxes if transfer pricing was calculated according to US tax laws. (Many foreign companies dispute this claim.)

Transfer prices and tax effects: An illustration.   To understand the effects of transfer pricing on taxes, consider the case of Nehru Jacket Corporation. Its facility in Country B imports materials from the company's Country S facility.[3] The tax rate in Country B is 70 percent and in Country S is 40 percent.

---

[2] *S. Borkowski,* "Environmental and Organizational Factors Affecting Transfer Pricing: A Survey"; *R. Tang,* "Canadian Transfer Pricing Practices"; *R. Tang, C. Walter, and R. Raymond,* "Transfer Pricing—Japanese vs. American Style"; R. Benke and J. Edwards, *Transfer Pricing: Techniques and Uses.*

[3] B denotes country with buying division; S denotes country with selling division.

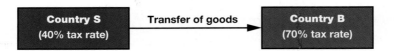

Country S	Transfer of goods	Country B
(40% tax rate)		(70% tax rate)

During the current year, Nehru incurred production costs of $2 million in Country S. Costs incurred in Country B, aside from the cost of the jackets, amounted to $6 million. (We call these "third-party costs.") Sales revenues in Country B were $24 million. Similar goods imported by other companies in Country B would have cost an equivalent of $3 million. However, Nehru points out that because of its special control over its operations in Country S and the special approach it uses to manufacture its goods, the appropriate transfer price is $10 million. What would Nehru's total tax liability in both jurisdictions be if it used the $3 million transfer price? What would the liability be if it used the $10 million transfer price?

Assuming that the $3 million transfer price is used, the tax liability is computed in Exhibit 19–2. In contrast, Exhibit 19–3 computes the tax liability assuming the $10 million transfer price. Nehru Jacket Corporation can save $2,100,000 in taxes simply by changing its transfer price!

To say the least, international taxing authorities look closely at transfer prices when they examine the tax returns of companies engaged in related-party transactions that cross national boundaries. Companies frequently must provide adequate support for the use of the transfer price that they have chosen for such a situation. Transfer-pricing disputes also occur at the state and province levels because of different tax rates.

Import duties.   Another international issue that can affect a firm's transfer-pricing policy is the imposition of import duties, or tariffs. These are fees a government charges an importer, generally on the basis of the reported value of the goods being imported. Consider as an example a firm with divisions in Europe and Asia. If the Asian country imposes an import duty on goods transferred in from the European division, the company has an incentive to set a relatively low transfer price on the transferred goods. This minimizes the duty to be paid and maximizes the overall profit for the company as a whole. As in the case of taxation, countries sometimes pass laws to limit a multinational firm's flexibility in setting transfer prices for the purpose of minimizing import duties.

	Country S	Country B
Revenue	$ 3,000,000	$24,000,000
Third-party costs	(2,000,000)	(6,000,000)
Transferred goods costs		(3,000,000)
Taxable income	$ 1,000,000	$15,000,000
Tax rate	× .40	× .70
Tax liability	$ 400,000	$10,500,000
Total tax liability	$10,900,000	

Exhibit 19–2

Tax Liability for Corporation Assuming a $3 Million Transfer Price

---

Transfer Pricing for Multinational Companies

Refer to the preceding information for Nehru Jacket Corporation. Assume that the tax rate for both countries is 40 percent.

What would be the tax liability for Nehru if the transfer were set at $3 million? At $10 million? (Solutions begin on page 804.)

You're the Decision Maker

19.3

Cost Management in Practice 19.1

International Implications of Transfer Pricing

A Japanese motorcycle manufacturer uses just-in-time production for its manufacturing facility in Japan. Its US subsidiary is a distribution company that sells to dealers in the United States. Both the Japanese manufacturing facility and the US distribution subsidiary were profitable as long as demand for the product in the United States remained high.

Eventually, demand in the United States for motorcycles declined. The US subsidiary found itself with lots of inventory, so much that it had more than a year's supply of the product on hand. Meanwhile, the Japanese manufacturing plant was reluctant to reduce production below its efficient operating level and, because it followed the just-in-time philosophy, did not stockpile finished-goods inventory in Japan.

As inventories increased at the US subsidiary, so did expenses to store and sell them. The US subsidiary showed declining profits and eventually incurred losses. The US Internal Revenue Service claimed that the low profits and losses were the result of the transfer price set by the Japanese manufacturer (which was based on full-absorption manufacturing costs) and the fact that the Japanese manufacturer continued to ship products that the US subsidiary had difficulty selling. Consequently, according to the IRS, the Japanese manufacturer should bear some of the costs of the US subsidiary's high inventory levels. *Source: Based on an author's research.*

Exhibit 19–3		**Country S**	**Country B**
Tax Liability for Corporation Assuming a $10 Million Transfer Price	Revenue	$10,000,000	$24,000,000
	Third-party costs	(2,000,000)	(6,000,000)
	Transferred goods costs		(10,000,000)
	Taxable income	$ 8,000,000	$ 8,000,000
	Tax rate	× .40	× .70
	Tax liability	$ 3,200,000	$ 5,600,000
	Total tax liability	$8,800,000	

Segment Reporting and Transfer Pricing

LO 5 Discuss the effects of transfer pricing on segment reporting.

The Financial Accounting Standards Board (FASB) requires companies engaged in different lines of business to report certain information about their segments that meet its technical requirements.[4] This reporting requirement is intended to provide a measure of the performance of those segments of a business that are significant to the company as a whole.

The following are the principal items that must be disclosed about each segment:

- Revenue
- Operating profits or loss
- Identifiable assets
- Depreciation and amortization
- Capital expenditures
- Certain specialized items

In addition, if a company has significant foreign operations, it must disclose revenues, operating profits or losses, and identifiable assets by geographic region.

Negotiated transfer prices, which could be useful for internal purposes, are not generally acceptable for external segment reporting. In general, the accounting profession has indicated a preference for market-based transfer prices.[5] This preference arises because the purpose of the segment disclosure is to enable an investor to eval-

---

[4] The requirements, which are too detailed to cover here, are specified in FASB, *Statement of Financial Accounting Standards No. 14,* "Financial Reporting for Segments of a Business Enterprise."

[5] See, for example, FASB, *Statement of Financial Accounting Standards No. 69,* which specifies the use of market-based transfer prices when calculating the results of operations for an oil and gas exploration and production operation.

uate a company's divisions as though they were free-standing enterprises. Presumably, sales would be based on market transactions, not on managers' ability to negotiate prices.

Although the conceptual basis for market-based transfer prices is sound in this setting, the practical application can be difficult. Frequently, the segments are really interdependent, so market prices might not really reflect the same risk in an intracompany sale that they do in third-party sales.

In addition, in many situations, market prices either are not readily available or might exist for only some products. When these problems arise, management usually attempts to estimate the market price by obtaining market prices for similar goods and adjusting the price to reflect the characteristics of the goods transferred within the company. An alternative is to take the cost of the item transferred and add an allowance to represent the normal profit for the item.

Transfer Pricing in the Service Industry

Service industry firms and nonprofit organizations also use transfer pricing when services are transferred between responsibility centers. For example, the interest rate at which banks transfer depositors' funds to the loan department is a form of transfer price. At Cornell University, if a student in the law school takes a course in the school of management, a transfer price is charged to the law school for the credit hours of instruction provided to the law student. At Cornell, the transfer price is called an *accessory instruction fee.* Since the transfer price is based on tuition charges, it is a market-price-based transfer price.

Chapter Summary

When products or services are transferred between divisions in the same organization, divisional performance is affected by the *transfer price.* A general rule states that the transfer price should equal the outlay cost incurred to make the transfer plus the organization's opportunity cost associated with the transfer. Due to difficulties in implementing the rule, most companies base transfer prices on external market prices, costs, or negotiations. In some cases, these practical transfer-pricing methods could result in dysfunctional decisions. Top management then must weigh the benefits of intervening to prevent suboptimal decisions against the costs of undermining divisional autonomy.

Since tax rates vary in different countries, companies have incentives to set transfer prices to increase revenues (and profits) in low-tax countries and increase costs (thereby reducing profits) in high-tax countries.

Companies with significant segments are required to report on those segments separately in the financial statements. The accounting profession has indicated a preference for market-based transfer prices when reporting on a segment of a business.

Key Terms

For each term's definition, refer to the indicated page or turn to the glossary at the end of the text.

cost-based transfer pricing, 796

dual transfer pricing, 799
imperfect competition, 794

perfect competition, 794
transfer price, 790

Meeting the Cost-Management Challenges

I. **What** is the primary objective of Outback Outfitters' cost-management team in determining a transfer-pricing policy?

The goal of Outback Outfitters' cost-management team in setting transfer prices is to establish incentives for autonomous division

managers to make decisions that support the organization's overall goals. Transfer prices should be chosen so that each division manager, when striving to maximize his or her own division's profit, makes the decision that maximizes the company's profit.

2. **Describe** four methods by which Outback Outfitters can set transfer prices.

Outback Outfitters could set transfer prices using four methods as follows:

1. Transfer price is equal to additional outlay costs because goods are transferred plus opportunity costs to the organization because of the transfer.

2. Transfer price is the external market price.

3. Transfer prices can be set on the basis of negotiations among the division managers.

4. Transfer prices can be based on the cost of producing the goods or services to be transferred.

3. **Explain** the significance of excess capacity in the transferring division.

When the transferring division has excess capacity, the opportunity cost to produce a unit for transfer is zero.

4. **Why** might income tax laws affect the transfer-pricing policies of multinational companies?

The management of a multinational company has an incentive to set transfer prices to minimize the income reported for divisions in countries with relatively high income tax rates and to shift this income to divisions in countries with relatively low income tax rates. Some countries' tax laws prohibit this practice; other countries' laws permit it.

Solutions to You're the Decision Maker

19.1   Setting a Transfer Price   p. 796

a. From a company's perspective, the minimum price is the unit-level cost to produce and market the goods, $19. If the company were centralized, we would expect this information to be conveyed to the marketing manager, who would be instructed not to set a price below $19.

b. The transfer price per pair that correctly informs the marketing manager about the differential costs of manufacturing is $18.

c. If the production manager set the price at $28.50, the marketing manager would set the minimum price at $29.50 ($28.50 + $1.00). So the marketing manager sets the price in excess of $29.50 per pair. In fact, prices of $28, $25, or anything higher than $19 would have generated a positive contribution margin from the production and sale of shoes.

d. If the production division had been operating at capacity, an implicit opportunity cost of internal transfers to the company is the lost contribution margin ($28.50 − $19.00 = $9.50) from not selling in the wholesale market.

The transfer price should have been as follows:

$$
\begin{array}{l}
\text{Outlay cost of} \ + \ \text{Opportunity cost to} \\
\text{production} \qquad \quad \text{company if goods are} \\
\qquad \qquad \qquad \quad \text{transferred internally} \\
= \ \$19.00 + \$9.50 \\
= \ \$28.50
\end{array}
$$

Marketing would have appropriately treated the $28.50 as part of its differential cost to buy and sell the shoes.

19.2   Dysfunctional Decisions and Transfer-Pricing Policies   p. 799

a. The two divisions' actions cost Meridian $180,000. This amount is the difference between the price paid for part A-16 from the outside supplier ($40) and the differential unit-level cost to produce one unit of A-16 in the production division ($22) times the 10,000 units in the order.

b. This is a tough call with no clearly correct answer. If the CEO does not intervene, it will cost Meridian $180,000. The cost of intervention, however, is undermining the autonomy of the production and assembly division managers.

19.3   Transfer Pricing for Multinational Companies   p. 801

For the $3 million transfer, the total tax is (.40 × $1,000,000) + (.40 × $15,000,000) = $6,400,000

For $10 million, the total tax is (.40 × $8,000,000) + (.40 × $8,000,000) = $6,400,000.

With equal tax rates, inflating the transfer price has no advantage.

Review Questions

19.1 Why do transfer prices exist even in highly centralized organizations?

19.2 Describe four methods by which transfer prices can be set.

19.3 Why are market-based transfer prices considered optimal under many circumstances?

19.4 What are the limitations to market-based transfer prices?

19.5 What are the advantages and disadvantages of top management's direct intervention in a transfer-pricing dispute?

19.6 Why do companies often use prices other than market prices for interdivisional transfers?

19.7 What is the basis for choosing between actual and standard costs for cost-based transfer pricing?

19.8 Some have suggested that managers should negotiate transfer prices. What are the disadvantages of a negotiated transfer-pricing system?

19.9 What is the general transfer-pricing rule?

19.10 Explain the effect of import duties, or tariffs, on the transfer-pricing policies of multinational companies.

Critical Analysis

19.11 How does the choice of a transfer price affect the operating profits of both segments involved in an intracompany transfer?

19.12 What are some goals of a transfer-pricing system in a decentralized organization?

19.13 Division A has no external markets. It produces monofilament used by division B, which cannot purchase this particular type of monofilament from any other source. What transfer-pricing system would you recommend for the interdivisional sales of monofilament? Why?

19.14 Refer to Cost Management in Practice 19.1 on page 802. Why did the Internal Revenue Service dispute the US subsidiary's reported profits and losses?

19.15 When setting a transfer price for goods sold across international boundaries, what factors should management consider?

19.16 "Setting transfer prices by negotiation is detrimental to the company." Do you agree or disagree with this statement by the CEO of a midsize manufacturing company? Why?

19.17 "Basing transfer prices on full absorption costs can really screw up decision making in a company!" Explain this remark by a manufacturing vice president, and construct a simple numerical example to make the point.

19.18 "In setting transfer prices for multinationals, tax considerations can be the tail that wags the dog." Explain.

Exercises

Seneca Associates is a real estate company operating in the Finger Lakes region of central New York. Its leasing division rents and manages properties for others, and its maintenance division performs services such as carpentry, painting, plumbing, and electrical work. The maintenance division, which has an estimated variable cost of $34 per labor hour, works for both Seneca and other companies. It could spend 100 percent of its time working for outsiders. Maintenance division charges $68 per hour for labor performed for outsiders, the same rate that other maintenance companies charge. The leasing division complained that it could hire its own maintenance staff at an estimated variable cost of $39 per hour.

Exercise 19.19
Application of Transfer
Pricing Rules
(LO 1, 2)

Required

a. What is the minimum transfer price that the maintenance division should obtain for its services, assuming that it is operating at capacity?

b. What is the maximum price that the leasing division should pay?

c. Would your answers in requirements (a) or (b) change if the maintenance division had idle capacity? If so, which answer would change, and what would the new amount be?

Intercoastal Company's Western Division has an opportunity to transfer component Z50 to the company's Eastern Division. The Western Division, which offers its Z50 product to outside markets for $150, incurs variable costs of $55 per unit and fixed costs of $37,500 per month based on monthly production of 1,000 units.

The Eastern Division can acquire the Z50 product from an alternate supplier for $157.50 per unit or from the Western Division for $150 plus $10 per unit in transportation costs.

Exercise 19.20
Transfer-Pricing System
Evaluation
(LO 1, 2)

Required

a. What are the costs and benefits of the alternatives available to the Western and Eastern Divisions with respect to the transfer of the Western Division's Z50 product? Assume that the Western Division can market all that it can produce.

b. How would your answer change if the selling division had idle capacity sufficient to cover all of the buying division's needs?

Peninsula Metals, Inc., has two divisions. The fabrication division transfers partially completed components to the assembly division at a predetermined transfer price. The fabrication division, which has a standard variable production cost per unit of $300, has no excess capacity and could sell all of its components to outside buyers at $380 per unit in a perfectly competitive market.

Exercise 19.21
General Transfer-Pricing
Rule
(LO 1, 2)

Required

a. Determine a transfer price using the general rule.

b. How would the transfer price change if the fabrication division had excess capacity?

Refer to the preceding exercise. The fabrication division's full (absorption) cost of a component is $340, which includes $40 of applied fixed-overhead costs. The transfer price has been set at $374, which is the fabrication division's full cost plus a 10 percent markup.

Exercise 19.22
Cost-Based Transfer
Pricing; Ethics
(LO 1, 3)

The assembly division has a special offer of $465 for its product. The assembly division incurs variable costs of $100 in addition to the transfer price for the fabrication division's components. Both divisions currently have excess production capacity.

Required

a.   Is the assembly division's manager likely to accept or reject the special offer? Why?

b.   Is this decision in the best interests of Peninsula Metals as a whole? Why?

c.   Suppose that the assembly division manager decides to reject the special offer. Is the manager acting ethically? Explain.

d.   How could the situation be remedied using the transfer price?

Exercise 19.23
Transfer-Pricing System
Evaluation
(LO 1, 2, 3)

Edgeworth Box Company has two decentralized divisions, X and Y. Division X always has purchased certain units from division Y at $150 per unit. Because division Y plans to raise the price to $200 per unit, division X desires to purchase these units from outside suppliers for $150 per unit. Division Y's costs follow:

Variable costs per unit	$140
Annual fixed costs	$30,000
Annual production of these units for division X..................	1,000 units

Required

If division X buys from an outside supplier, the facilities that division Y uses to manufacture these units would remain idle. What would be the result if Edgeworth Box Company enforces a transfer price of $200 per unit between divisions X and Y?

[CPA adapted]

Exercise 19.24
International Transfer-
Pricing Policy: Use of
Internet
(LO 4)

Use the Internet to explore international transfer-pricing policies by going to the Web site for the OECD (Organization for Economic Cooperation and Development) at www.oecd.org. Use the *Search OECD Online* function and enter *transfer pricing* when prompted for a word or phrase for which to search.

Required

Peruse the OECD transfer-pricing guidelines. Choose an issue that interests you and report on it to the class.

Exercise 19.25
Transfer-Pricing System
Evaluation
(LO 1, 2, 3)

Sacramento Transit, Ltd., operates a local mass transit system. The transit authority is a governmental agency related to the state government. It has an agreement with the state government to provide rides to senior citizens for 10 cents per trip. The government reimburses Sacramento Transit for the "cost" of each trip taken by a senior citizen.

The regular fare is 80 cents per trip. After analyzing its costs, Sacramento Transit figured that with its operating deficit, the full cost of each ride on the transit system is $2.00. The number of senior citizens on any route does not affect routes, capacity, or operating costs.

Required

a.   What alternative prices could be used to determine the governmental reimbursement to Sacramento Transit?

b.   Which price would Sacramento Transit prefer? Why?

c.   Which price would the state government prefer? Why?

Exercise 19.26
Transfer-Pricing System
Evaluation
(LO 1, 2, 3)

Universal Electronics, Inc., permits its decentralized units to "lease" space to one another. Division X has leased some idle warehouse space to division Y for $1.50 per square foot per month. Recently, division X obtained a new five-year contract, which will increase its production sufficiently so that the warehouse space is more valuable to it. Division X has notified division Y that it will increase the rental price to $5.30 per square foot per month. Division Y can lease space at $2.90 per square foot in another warehouse from an outside company but prefers to stay in the shared facilities. Division Y's management states that it prefers not to move. If division X cannot use the space now being leased to division Y, it will have to rent other space for $4.45 per square foot per month. (The difference in rental prices occurs because division X requires a more substantial warehouse building than division Y.)

Required

As a group, recommend a transfer price and explain your reasons for choosing that price.

Read "Is Wolverine Human? A Judge Answers No; Fans Howl in Protest," *The Wall Street Journal,* January 20, 2003, pp. A1, A5, by Neil King, Jr.

Required

What implications does this seemingly innocuous question have for tariffs and cost management at Toy Biz, Inc.? What are the implications for cost-based transfer pricing?

Outdoor Greenery, owned 60 percent by Kwasi Peterson and 40 percent by Maya Jefferies, grows specimen plants for landscape contractors. The wholesale price of each plant is $15. During the past year, Outdoor sold 5,000 specimen plants.

Of the plants sold last year, 1,000 were sold to Lively Landscape Co. Peterson has a 20 percent interest in Lively Landscape Co., and Jefferies has a 60 percent interest in Lively Landscape Co. At the end of the year, Jefferies noted that Lively was the largest buyer of Outdoor Greenery's plants. She suggested that the plant company give Lively Landscape a 10 percent reduction in prices for the coming year in recognition of its position as a preferred customer.

Required

Assuming that Lively Landscape purchases the same number of plants at the same prices in the coming year, what effect would the price reduction have on the operating profits that accrue to Peterson and to Jefferies for the coming year?

Piedmont Homes, Inc., has two divisions, building and financing. The building division oversees construction of single-family homes in "economically efficient" subdivisions. The financing division takes loan applications and packages mortgages into pools and sells them in the loan markets. It also services the mortgages. Both divisions meet the requirements for segment disclosures under accounting rules.

The building division had $68 million in sales last year. Costs, other than those charged by the financing division, totaled $52 million. The financing division obtained revenues of $16 million from servicing mortgages and incurred outside costs of $14 million. In addition, the financing division charged the building division $8 million for loan-related fees. The building division's manager complained to Piedmont's CEO that the financing division was charging twice the commercial rate for loan-related fees and that the building division would be better off sending its buyers to an outside lender.

The financing division's manager stated that although commercial rates might be lower, it was more difficult to service Piedmont mortgages, and therefore, the higher fees were justified.

Required

a. What are the reported segment operating profits for each division, ignoring income taxes and using the $8 million transfer price for the loan-related fees?

b. What are the reported segment operating profits for each division, ignoring income taxes and using a $4 million commercial rate as the transfer price for the loan-related fees?

Continental Lumber Corporation has two operating divisions. Its logging operation in Canada mills and ships logs to the United States where the company's building supplies division uses them. Operating expenses amount to $2 million in Canada and $6 million in the United States exclusive of the costs of any goods transferred from Canada. Revenues in the United States are $15 million.

If the lumber were purchased from one of the company's US lumber divisions, the costs would be $3 million. However, if the lumber had been purchased from an independent Canadian supplier, the cost would be $4 million. Assume that the marginal income tax rate is 60 percent in Canada and 40 percent in the United States.

Required

What is the company's total tax liability to both jurisdictions for each of the two alternative transfer-pricing scenarios ($3 million and $4 million)? Explain.

Down Under Corporation, based in Melbourne, Australia, has two operating divisions, an amusement park in Sydney and a hotel in Brisbane. The two divisions meet the Australian requirements for segment disclosures. Before transactions between the two divisions are considered, revenues and costs were as follows (in thousands of *Australian dollars*):

	Hotel	Amusement Park
Revenue	$11,200	$7,400
Costs	6,200	5,000

The amusement park and the hotel had a joint marketing arrangement by which the hotel gave free passes to the amusement park and the amusement park gave discount coupons good for stays at the hotel. The value of the free passes to the amusement park redeemed during the past year totaled $1,600,000. The discount coupons redeemed at the hotel resulted in a $600,000 decrease in hotel revenues. As of the end of the year, all current year coupons have expired.

Required

a.   Is there a transfer-pricing issue in this exercise? Explain.

b.   What are the operating profits for each division, considering the effects of the costs arising from the joint marketing agreement?

Problems

Problem 19.32
Basic Transfer Pricing
(LO 1, 2, 3)

Carlyle Corporation's Northwest Division produces electric motors, 20 percent of which Northwest Division sells to Carlyle's Redstone Division. It sells the remainder to outside customers. Carlyle treats its divisions as profit centers and allows division managers to choose their sources of sale and supply. Corporate policy requires that all interdivisional sales and purchases be recorded at variable cost as a transfer price. Northwest Division's budgeted sales and standard-cost data for the current year, based on capacity of 100,000 units, are as follows:

	Redstone Division	Outside Companies
Sales	$ 900,000	$8,000,000
Unit-level (variable) costs	(900,000)	(3,600,000)
Facility-level (fixed) costs	(300,000)	(1,200,000)
Gross margin	$(300,000)	$3,200,000
Unit sales	20,000	80,000

Northwest Division has an opportunity to sell the 20,000 units shown in the table to an outside customer at a price of $75 per unit. Redstone can purchase its requirements from an outside supplier for $85 per unit.

Required

As a group, make a presentation to your class addressing the following questions.

a.   Assuming that Northwest Division desires to maximize its gross margin, should it sell to the new customer and drop its sales to Redstone during the current year? Why?

b.   Assume, instead, that Carlyle permits division managers to negotiate the transfer price. The managers agree on a tentative transfer price of $75 per unit, to be reduced based on an equal sharing of the additional gross margin to Northwest Division resulting from the sale of 20,000 motors to Redstone at $75 per unit. What is the actual transfer price?

c.   Assume now that Northwest Division has an opportunity to sell the 20,000 motors that Redstone division would buy to the same customers that are buying the other 80,000 motors produced by Northwest. Northwest could sell all 100,000 motors to outside customers for $100. What actions by each division manager are in the best interests of Carlyle Corporation?

d.   Under the scenario described in requirement (c), use the general transfer-pricing rule to compute the transfer price that Northwest Division should charge Redstone for motors.

e.   Will the transfer price computed in requirement (d) result in the most desirable outcome from the standpoint of Carlyle Corporation? Explain your answer.

[CPA adapted]

Problem 19.33
Analysis of Transfer-Pricing Data
(LO 1, 2, 3)

mhhe.com/hilton3e

Universal Machine Tool, Inc. is a decentralized organization that evaluates division management based on measures of division contribution margin. Divisions L and N operate in similar product markets. Division L produces a sophisticated electronic assembly that it can sell up to 140,000 units to the outside market for $16 per unit per year. These units require 2 direct-labor hours each.

If L modifies the units with an additional one-half hour of labor time, it can sell them for $18 per unit to N, which will accept up to 120,000 of these units per year.

If N does not obtain 120,000 units from L, it purchases them for $18.50 each from the outside. Division N incurs $8 of additional labor and other out-of-pocket costs to convert the assemblies into a home digital electronic radio, calculator, telephone monitor, and clock unit. The units can be sold to the outside market for $45 each.

Division L estimates that its total costs are $925,000 for fixed costs and $6 per direct-labor hour. Its capacity is limited to 400,000 direct-labor hours per year.

Required

Determine the following:

a. Total contribution margin to L if it sells 140,000 units to the outside.

b. Total contribution margin to L if it sells 120,000 units to N.

c. The costs to be considered in determining the optimal company policy for sales by division L.

d. The annual contributions and costs for L and N under the optimal policy.

Eclipse Company's division S has an investment base of $600,000. The division produces and sells 90,000 units of a product at a market price of $10 per unit. Its variable costs total $3 per unit. The division also charges each unit with a share of fixed costs. The fixed cost is computed as $5 per unit, based on planned production of 100,000 units. The budgeted and actual fixed overhead are equal, and any volume variances are closed to Cost of Goods Sold.

Division T wants to purchase 20,000 units from division S but is willing to pay only $6.20 per unit because it has an opportunity to accept a special order at a reduced price. The order is economically justifiable only if division T can acquire the division S output at a reduced price.

Problem 19.34
Transfer Pricing with Imperfect Markets; ROI Evaluation; Normal Costing
(LO 1, 2, 3)

mhhe.com/hilton3e

Required

a. What is the ROI for division S without the transfer to division T?

b. What is division S's ROI if it transfers 20,000 units to division T at $6.20 each?

c. What is the minimum transfer price for the 20,000-unit order that S would accept if it were willing to maintain the same ROI with the transfer as it would accept by selling its 90,000 units to the outside market?

The Topeka Division (TD) of Great Plains Corporation, operating at capacity, has been asked by Jaydee division to supply it with electrical fitting no. 1726. TD sells this part to its regular customers for $7.50 each. Jaydee, which is operating at 50 percent capacity, is willing to pay $5 each for the fitting. It will put the fitting into a brake unit that it is manufacturing on a cost-plus basis for a commercial airplane manufacturer.

TD has a $4.25 variable cost of producing fitting no. 1726. The cost of the brake unit as built by Jaydee follows:

Problem 19.35
Transfer Pricing: Performance Evaluation Issues
(LO 1, 2, 3)

Purchased parts—outside vendors	$22.50
KC fitting no. 1726	5.00
Other variable costs	14.00
Fixed overhead and administration	8.00
Total	$49.50

Jaydee believes that the price concession is necessary to get the job. The company uses ROI and dollar profits to measure divisional and division manager performance.

Required

a. If you were TD's division controller, would you recommend that it supply fitting no. 1726 to Jaydee? Why or why not? (Ignore any income tax issues.)

b. Is it to the short-run economic advantage of Great Plains Corporation for TD to supply Jaydee with fitting no. 1726 at $5 each? Explain your answer. (Ignore any income tax issues.)

c. Discuss the organizational and managerial behavior difficulties, if any, inherent in this situation. As Great Plains Corporation's controller, what would you advise the corporation's president to do in this situation?

[CMA adapted]

New England Window Corporation manufactures windows for the home-building industry. The frame division produces the window frames. It then transfers the frames to the glass division, which installs the glass and hardware. The company's best-selling product is a three-by-four-foot, double-paned operable window.

The frame division also can sell frames directly to custom home builders, which install the glass and hardware. The sales price for a frame is $80. The glass division sells its finished windows for $190. The markets for both frames and finished windows exhibit perfect competition.

Problem 19.36
Comprehensive Transfer-Pricing Problem
(LO 1, 2, 3)

The standard cost of the window is detailed as follows:

	Frame Division	Glass Division
Direct material	$15	$30*
Direct labor	20	15
Variable overhead	30	30
Total	$65	$75

*Not including the transfer price for the frame.

Required

a.   Assume that the frame division has no excess capacity.

    (1)   Use the general rule to compute the transfer price for window frames.

    (2)   Calculate the transfer price if it is based on standard variable cost with a 10 percent markup.

b.   Assume that the frame division has excess capacity.

    (1)   Use the general rule to compute the transfer price for window frames.

    (2)   Explain why your answers to requirements (a1) and (b1) differ.

    (3)   Suppose that the predetermined fixed-overhead rate in the frame division is 125 percent of direct-labor cost. Calculate the transfer price if it is based on standard full cost plus a 10 percent markup.

    (4)   Assume that the transfer price established in requirement (b3) is used. The glass division has been approached by the US Army with a special order for 1,000 windows at $155. From the perspective of New England Window as a whole, should the glass division accept or reject the special order? Why?

    (5)   Assume the same facts as in requirement (b4). Will an autonomous glass division manager accept or reject the special order? Why?

c.   Comment on the use of full cost as the basis for setting transfer prices.

Problem 19.37
International Transfer Prices
(LO 1, 4)

Worldwide Merchants Co-op (WMC) operates a fleet of container ships in international trade between Great Britain and Thailand. All of the shipping income (that is, that related to WMC's ships) is deemed as earned in Great Britain. WMC also owns a dock facility in Thailand that services WMC's fleet. Income from the dock facility is deemed earned in Thailand, however. WMC's income attributable to Great Britain is taxed at a 75 percent rate. Its income attributable to Thailand is taxed at a 20 percent rate. Last year, the dock facility had operating revenues of $4 million, excluding services performed for WMC's ships. WMC's shipping revenues for last year were $26 million.

Costs to operate the dock facility were $5 million last year; costs to operate the shipping operation, before deduction of dock facility costs, were $17 million. No similar dock facilities in Thailand are available to WMC.

However, a facility in Malaysia would have charged WMC an estimated $3 million for the services that WMC's Thailand dock provided its ships. WMC management noted that if the services had been provided in Great Britain, the costs for the year would have totaled $8 million. WMC argued to the British tax officials that the appropriate transfer price is the price that would have been charged in Great Britain. British tax officials suggest that the Malaysian price is the appropriate one.

Required

What is the difference in tax costs to WMC for the alternate transfer prices for dock services, that is, its price in Great Britain versus that in Malaysia?

Problem 19.38
Transfer Prices and Tax Regulations
(LO 1, 4)

Global Corporation has two operating divisions in a semiautonomous organization structure. Division X, located in the United States, produces part XZ-1, which is an input to division Y, located in the south of France. Division X uses idle capacity to produce XZ-1, which has a domestic market price of $60. Its variable costs are $25 per unit. The company's US tax rate is 40 percent of income.

In addition to the transfer price for each XZ-1 received from division X, division Y pays a $15 shipping fee per unit. Part XZ-1 becomes a part of division Y's output product. The output product costs an additional $10 to produce and sells for an equivalent $115. Division Y could purchase part XZ-1 for $50 per unit from a Paris supplier. The company's French tax rate is 70 percent of income. Assume that French tax laws permit transferring at either variable cost or market price.

Required

What transfer price is economically optimal for Global Corporation? Support your answer with an appropriate analysis.

Eastern Safety Systems, Inc. (ESSI) consists of three subsidiary divisions—Boston Corporation, Raleigh Company, and Memphis Company—that operate as if they were independent companies. Each division has its own sales force and production facilities. Each division management is responsible for sales, cost of operations, acquiring and financing divisional assets, and working capital management. ESSI corporate management evaluates the performance of the divisions and division managements on the basis of ROI.

Problem 19.39
Transfer-Pricing System
Evaluation
(LO 1, 2, 3)

Memphis Company has just been awarded a contract for a product that uses a component manufactured by outside suppliers and by Raleigh Company, which is operating well below capacity. Memphis used a cost figure of $3.80 for the component in preparing its bid for the new product. Raleigh supplied this cost figure in response to Memphis's request for the average variable cost of the component; it represents the standard variable manufacturing cost and variable marketing costs.

Raleigh's regular selling price for the component that Memphis needs is $6.50. Raleigh management indicated that it could supply Memphis the required quantities of the component at the regular selling price less variable selling and distribution expenses. Memphis management responded by offering to pay standard variable manufacturing cost plus 20 percent.

The two divisions have been unable to agree on a transfer price. Corporate management has never established a transfer price policy. The corporate vice president of finance suggested a price equal to the standard full manufacturing cost (that is, no selling and distribution expenses) plus a 15 percent markup. The two division managers rejected this price because each considered it grossly unfair.

The unit cost structure for the Raleigh component and the suggested prices follow.

Costs:

Standard variable manufacturing cost..	$3.20
Standard fixed manufacturing cost	1.20
Variable selling and distribution expenses	.60
Total	$5.00

Prices:

Regular selling price	$6.50
Regular selling price less variable selling and distribution expenses ($6.50 − $ .60)	$5.90
Variable manufacturing plus 20% ($3.20 × 1.20)	$3.84
Standard full manufacturing cost plus 15% ($4.40 × 1.15).................	$5.06

Required

a. Discuss the effect that each proposed price might have on the attitude of Raleigh's management toward intracompany business.

b. Is the negotiation of a price between the Memphis and Raleigh divisions a satisfactory method to solve the transfer price problem? Explain your answer.

c. As an outside consultant, write a letter to ESSI's corporate management recommending whether it should become involved in this transfer-pricing controversy.

[CMA adapted]

Gulliver's Travel, Ltd., has four operating divisions: airline, hotel, auto rental, and travel services. Each division is a separate segment for financial reporting purposes. Revenues and costs for the past year related to outside transactions were as follows (dollars in millions):

Problem 19.40
Segment Reporting and
Transfer Pricing
(LO 1, 5)

	Airline	Hotel	Auto Rental	Travel Services
Revenue	$245	$106	$89	$32
Costs	157	71	66	30

The airline participated in a frequent stayer program with the hotel chain. The airline reported that it had traded hotel award coupons during the past year for travel that had a $26 million retail value, assuming that the travel was redeemed at full airline fares. Auto rental division offered 20 percent discounts to Gulliver's Travel's airline passengers and hotel guests. These discounts to airline passengers were estimated to have a $7 million retail value. Gulliver's Travels hotel guests redeemed $3 million in auto rental discount coupons. Gullivers' Travels hotels also provided rooms for flight crews of the airline division, a $13 million value for the year.

Travel services division booked flights on Gulliver's Travels' airline valued at $4 million for the year. This service for intracompany hotel bookings was valued at $2 million and for intracompany auto rentals at $1 million.

While preparing these data for financial statement presentation, the hotel division's controller stated that the value of the airline coupons should be based on the differential and opportunity costs of the travel awards, not on the full fare for the tickets issued. The fact that a travel award is usually allocated to seats that would otherwise be empty or that are restricted similar to those on discount tickets supported this argument. If the differential and opportunity costs were used for this transfer price, the value would be $5 million instead of $26 million. The airline controller made a similar argument concerning the auto rental discount coupons. If the differential cost basis were used for the auto rental coupons, the transfer price would be $1 million instead of the $7 million.

Gulliver's Travels, Ltd., reports assets in each segment as follows:

Airline	$955 million
Hotel	385 million
Auto rental	321 million
Travel services	65 million

Required

a. Using the retail values for transfer pricing for segment-reporting purposes, what are the operating profits for each of Gulliver's Travels' divisions?

b. What are the operating profits for each division using the differential cost basis for pricing transfers?

c. Rank each division by ROI using the transfer pricing method in (a), as well as using the transfer pricing method in (b). What effect does the transfer-pricing system have on the rankings?

Problem 19.41
Evaluation of the Profit
Impact of Alternative
Transfer Decisions
(LO 1, 2, 3)

Oneida Company manufactures a line of fingernail polish. The manufacturing process entails adding and mixing coloring ingredients; the finished product is packaged in a company-produced glass bottle and packed in cases containing six bottles each. Because the appearance of the bottle highly influences sales volume, the company developed an unusual bottle production process.

The polish manufacturing plant uses all of the company's bottle production. Each division is considered a separate profit center and is evaluated as such. As the new corporate controller, you are responsible for determining the proper transfer price to use for the bottles produced for the polish division.

Bottle division's cost analysis indicates that it can produce bottles at these costs:

Volume (cases)	Total Cost	Cost per Case
2,000,000	$3,200,000	$1.60
4,000,000	5,200,000	1.30
6,000,000	7,200,000	1.20

These costs include fixed costs of $1.2 million and variable costs of $1 per equivalent case. These data have caused considerable corporate discussion as to the proper price to use in the transfer of bottles to the polish division. This interest is heightened because a significant portion of a division manager's income is an incentive bonus based on profit center results.

The polish division has the following costs in addition to the bottle costs:

Volume (cases)	Total Cost	Cost per Case
2,000,000	$16,400,000	$8.20
4,000,000	32,400,000	8.10
6,000,000	48,400,000	8.07

At your request, bottle division's general manager asked other bottle manufacturers to quote a price for the number and sizes that the polish division demands. These competitive prices follow:

Volume (equivalent cases)	Total Price	Price per Case
2,000,000	$ 4,000,000	$2.00
4,000,000	7,000,000	1.75
6,000,000	10,000,000	1.67

The marketing department provided the following price-demand relationship for the finished product:

Sales Volume (cases)	Total Sales Revenue	Sales Price per Case
2,000,000	$25,000,000	$12.50
4,000,000	45,600,000	11.40
6,000,000	63,900,000	10.65

Required

a. Oneida Company has used market-price transfer prices in the past. Using the current market prices and costs and assuming a volume of 6 million cases, calculate operating profits for the:

 (1) Bottle division.

 (2) Polish division.

 (3) Corporation.

b. Is this production and sales level the most profitable volume for the:

 (1) Bottle division?

 (2) Polish division?

 (3) Corporation?

[CMA adapted]

Stein Company, located in Sweden, manufactures telecommunications products in Sweden and has marketing divisions located throughout Europe, Asia, and North America. The North American marketing division, located in the United States, imports manufactured products from Sweden. Suppose that Swedish and US tax authorities allow transfer prices between full manufacturing costs and market prices based on comparable imports into the United States. Any US import duty paid in the United States is deductible from US income taxes. The following data have been collected by the cost management team.

Problem 19.42
International Transfer Price and Tax
(LO 3, 4, 5)

Units sold	1,000,000
Sweden's income tax rate on Swedish operating income	50%
US income tax rate on US division's operating income	35%
US import duty based on transfer price	10%
Variable manufacturing cost of product A4	$32.00 USD* per unit
Full absorption manufacturing cost of product A4	50.00 USD per unit
Net selling price in the United States	75.00 USD per unit
Comparable imported product sales price in the United States	65.00 USD per unit
Sales price in Sweden	60.00 USD per unit

*USD = US dollars.

a. Calculate the after-tax profits of the Swedish and US divisions from a transfer of 1,000,000 units of product model A4 at either full manufacturing cost or the comparable import selling price.

b. What transfer price should Stein Company select to minimize its total import duties and tax liabilities from this transfer? Explain.

   c. Suppose that Stein's manufacturing division could sell all of its production of product A4 for $60 USD per unit in Sweden and was free to do so. Suppose also that division managers are paid a bonus based on their division's operating profit after tax. What are the pros and cons of Stein Company's bonus and transfer-pricing policies? What is your recommendation?

   d. *Build your own spreadsheet.* Build an Excel spreadsheet to solve requirements (a) through (c). Use your spreadsheet to determine new values for the amounts calculated in requirements (a), (b), and (c) if each of the following input parameters changes by the amount indicated. (Unless otherwise indicated, treat each parameter change independently.)

   (1) The Swedish income tax rate is 60 percent.

   (2) The US income tax rate is 40 percent.

   (3) The US import duty on the transfer price is 12 percent.

   (4) The full absorption manufacturing cost of product A4 is $45 per unit.

   (5) The net selling price in the United States is $70.

   (6) All of the changes listed in (1) through (5) occur simultaneously.

Cases

Case 19.43
Transfer Pricing;
Incentive Issues*
(LO 1, 2, 3)

"We can't drop our prices below $210 per hundred pounds," exclaimed Greg Berman, manager of Forwarders, a division of Custom Freight Systems. "Our margins are already razor thin. Our costs just won't allow us to go any lower. Corporate rewards our division based on our profitability, and I won't lower my prices below $210."

   Custom Freight Systems is organized into three divisions: Air Cargo provides air cargo services; Logistics Services operates distribution centers and provides truck cargo services; and Forwarders provides international freight-forwarding services. Freight forwarders typically buy space on planes from international air cargo companies. This is analogous to a charter company that books seats on passenger planes and resells them to passengers. In many cases, freight forwarders hire trucking companies to transport the cargo from the plane to the domestic destination. The following diagram depicts Custom Freight Systems' operations.

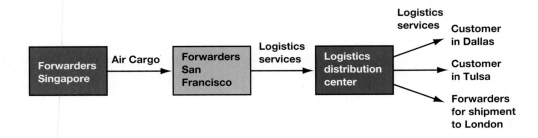

   Management believes that the three divisions integrate together well and are able to provide one-stop transportation services to customers. For example, a Forwarders branch in Singapore receives cargo from a shipper, prepares the necessary documentation, and then ships the cargo on Air Cargo to a domestic Forwarders station. The domestic Forwarders station ensures that the cargo passes through customs and ships it to the final destination with Logistics Services as shown in the preceding diagram.

   Management evaluates each division separately and rewards division managers based on profit and return on investment. Responsibility and decision-making authority are decentralized. Similarly, each division has a sales and marketing organization. Division salespeople report to the vice president of sales for Custom Freight Systems as well as a division sales manager as depicted in the following organization chart. Custom Freight Systems believes that it has successfully motivated division managers by paying bonuses for high division profits.

---

* Prepared by Thomas B. Rumzie under the direction of Michael W. Maher. © Copyright Michael W. Maher.

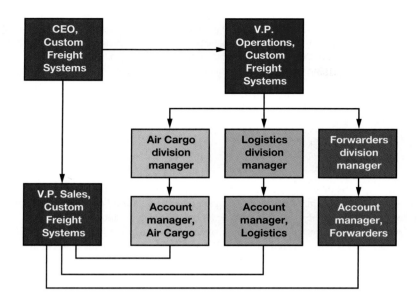

Recently, Logistics Services was preparing a bid for a customer. The customer had freight to import from an overseas supplier and wanted Logistics Services to submit a bid for a distribution package that included providing air freight from the supplier, receiving the freight and providing customs clearance services at the airport, warehousing the shipment, and distributing it to customers.

Because this was a contract for international shipping, Logistics Services needed to contact different freight forwarders for shipping quotes. Logistics Services requested quotes from the Forwarders division and United Systems, a competing freight forwarder. Divisions of Custom Freight Systems are free to use the most appropriate and cost-effective suppliers.

Logistics Services received bids of $210 per hundred pounds from Forwarders and $185 per hundred pounds from United Systems. Forwarders specified in its bid that it will use Air Cargo, a division of Custom Freight Systems. Forwarder's variable costs were $175 per hundred pounds, which included the cost of subcontracting air transportation. Air Cargo, which was experiencing a period of excess capacity, quoted Forwarders the market rate of $155; its variable costs typically are 60 percent of the market rate.

The price difference between the two different bids alarmed Susan Burns, a contract manager at Logistics Services. Burns knows this is a competitive business and is concerned because the difference between the high and low bids was at least $1,000,000 (current projections for the contract estimated 4,160,000 pounds during the first year). Burns contacted Greg Berman, the manager of Forwarders, and discussed the quote. "Don't you think full markup is unwarranted due to the fact that you and the airlines have so much excess capacity?" Burns complained.

She soon realized that Berman was not going to drop the price quote. "You know how small margins are in this business. Why should I cut my margins even smaller just to make you look good?" Berman asked.

Burns went to Bennie Espinosa, vice president of Custom Freight Systems and chairperson for the corporate strategy committee. "That does sound strange," said Espinosa, "I need to examine the overall cost structure and talk to Berman. I'll get back to you by noon Monday."

Required

a. Which bid should Logistics Services accept: the internal bid from Forwarders or the external bid from United Systems?

b. What should the transfer price be on this transaction?

c. What should Bennie Espinosa do?

d. Do the reward systems for the division managers support the best interests of Forwarders and of Custom Freight Systems? Give examples that support your conclusion.

e. Assume the same information as given in the case, but instead of receiving one outside bid, Logistics Services receives two. The new bid is from World Services for $195 per hundred pounds. It offered to use Air Cargo for air cargo. Air Cargo will charge World $155 per hundred pounds. The bids from Forwarders and United Systems remain the same as before (i.e., $210 and $185, respectively). Which bid should the Logistics Services take? Explain.

Case 19.44
Minimum and Maximum
Acceptable Transfer
Prices*†
(LO 1, 2)

Memphis Instrumentation, Inc., manufactures small gauges for use in household appliances and industrial machinery. The firm has two divisions: appliance and industrial. The company is decentralized, and each division is completely autonomous in its decision making.

The appliance division produces two instruments, A and B. Cost information about these products follows.

Appliance Division	Instrument A	Instrument B
Direct material	$ 5.00	$ 4.00
Direct labor	10.00	20.00
Fixed overhead	20.00	40.00
Full cost	$35.00	$64.00

The appliance division has no variable overhead. Its direct-labor rate is $10 per hour, and a maximum of 10,000 hours is available per year. Fixed overhead is $200,000 per year and is applied on the basis of direct-labor hours. The planned activity level is 10,000 direct-labor hours per year.

The demand in the external market for instrument A at a price of $45 per unit is unlimited. Anywhere from zero to 3,000 units of instrument B can be sold annually in the external market at a price of $94 per unit. The external market has demand for no more than 3,000 units of instrument B per year.

The industrial division also has two products, type Y gauges and type Z gauges. Cost information about these products follows.

Industrial Division	Type Y Gauges	Type Z Gauges
Direct material	$12.00	$ 7.00
Direct labor	10.00	20.00
Fixed overhead	10.00	20.00
Full cost	$32.00	$47.00

In addition to the costs listed in the preceding table, each type Z gauge unit uses one unit of instrument B, which is produced in the appliance division and transferred to the industrial division. The costs in the preceding table for type Z gauge are the *only* costs incurred in the industrial division to transform a B instrument into a type Z gauge. They do *not* include the transfer price of instrument B or the costs of manufacturing instrument B.

The industrial division has no variable overhead. The direct-labor rate is $10 per hour, and a maximum of 10,000 hours is available per year. Fixed overhead of $100,000 per year is applied on the basis of direct-labor hours. The planned activity level is 10,000 hours per year.

The demand for type Z gauges at a fixed price of $257 is unlimited. Anywhere from zero to 6,000 units of type Y gauges can be sold annually at a fixed price of $92 per unit. Demand for type Y gauges is no more than 6,000 per year.

The labor used in the two divisions is different and is *not* transferable between them. The situation is summarized in the following diagram.

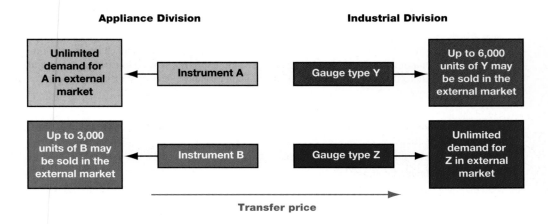

---

* This is a very challenging case.

† © Copyright Ronald W. Hilton.

Required

The first four questions refer to the transfer price *per unit of instrument B* for units transferred. Show calculations. Ignore any long-term or qualitative factors.

a. What is the minimum unit transfer price acceptable to the appliance division for any number of units of instrument B transferred in the range zero to 2,000 units?

b. What is the minimum unit transfer price acceptable to the appliance division for any number of B units transferred in the range 2,001 to 5,000 units?

c. What is the maximum unit transfer price acceptable to the industrial division for any number of B units transferred in the range zero to 2,000 units?

d. What is the maximum unit transfer price acceptable to the industrial division for any number of B units transferred in the range 2,001 to 5,000 units?

e. Suppose that appliance division sets the transfer price at its minimum acceptable level in each of the ranges zero to 2,000 units, and 2,001 to 5,000 units. How many units will be transferred? Remember that each division manager has the authority to accept or reject a transfer between the two divisions.

Chapter 20

Strategy, Balanced Scorecards, and Incentive Systems

After completing this chapter, you should be able to:

1. Explain the importance of using leading and lagging indicators to build a balanced scorecard for communication, motivation, and evaluation.

2. Understand how an organization selects related measures for a balanced scorecard.

3. Evaluate the benefits and costs of a balanced scorecard.

4. Explain how an organization implements a balanced scorecard.

5. Understand the key principles of performance-based incentive systems.

6. Evaluate the advantages and disadvantages of alternative features of incentive systems.

7. Discuss ethical issues of incentive systems.

8. Understand three theories of motivation and incentives (Appendix).

Cost-*Management* Challenges

(Solutions are on page 856.)

1. **How** does a balanced scorecard differ from the measures of organizational cost and performance, which have been used for as long as organized companies have existed? What does it add that previous measures did not?

2. **Should** Valley Commercial Bank design its incentive system to increase customer satisfaction? Is it possible to overstress customer satisfaction?

3. **How** can Valley Commercial Bank or any organization weigh the trade-offs of various incentives for improving financial performance?

Valley Commercial Bank IPO Exceeds Expectations

By Dissociated Press financial reporter, Graham Crystal

BOSTON: Valley Commercial Bank (VCB) President and CEO William Grom announced an initial public offering (IPO) of shares that generated $25 million, which was more than the bank and its underwriters had expected.

Speaking to the state's financial press online from bank headquarters, Grom remarked, "This shows that the market values a successful track record and a bright future. There is abundant capital for good business plans and capable management, and ours are second to none. Valley Commercial Bank has served an important market niche by providing financial services for fast-growing, well-managed, high-technology firms. They see us as valuable partners, and it definitely helps that we have experienced and overcome the same growing pains that they face."

Twenty-three investors founded VCB 10 years ago to serve the hot local economy. The founders, some of whom are officers of the bank, now have gained expansion capital and many new stockholders.

The independent five-branch bank specializes in banking with high-technology businesses and professionals such as public accountants, architects, and dentists. VCB has dominated its niche based on personal relations and customer service.

VCB's prospectus shows that its balanced scorecard and incentive system resemble those found at many of its high-tech customers. CEO Grom emphasized that although unusual for a bank, this performance-based incentive plan is necessary to attract, motivate, and retain its highly competent and sought-after employees.

The bank's design of its balanced scorecard and incentive system to align bank employees' fortunes with those of its new stockholders might be another reason for the success of its initial public offering.

The financial services market has become increasingly competitive as banks, insurance companies, stock brokerages, and hybrids compete to manage retirement funds, provide access to securities markets, and meet the banking needs of individuals and growing entrepreneurial businesses. The need to provide these services quickly, inexpensively, accurately, and innovatively has transformed the once stodgy, conservative financial services industry. Banks, in particular, have become more aggressive in designing and marketing innovative services in response to other organizations that now are able to offer competitive services, in some cases without the same level of regulatory requirements that banks face.

Valley Commercial Bank: Ahead of the Competition

Since its founding 10 years ago, Valley Commercial Bank (VCB) has managed to stay ahead of its competition by consistently creating and designing innovative, reliable services that are first to market. VCB offers commercial-customer services in traditional branch banks and, to a greater extent, via its e-banking website and round-the-clock customer service available by telephone or the Internet.

The news report of its initial public offering (IPO) of company stock followed intensive efforts by Valley Commercial Bank's board of directors, officers, and key executives and was the occasion of a well-deserved celebration.

The bank had positioned itself for the successful IPO of shares in part by building a **balanced scorecard**, which is a performance measurement system or business model that ties together knowledge of strategy, processes, activities, and operational and strategic performance measures. Balanced scorecard models offer great opportunities and challenges to improve value and performance through better communication, knowledge, and incentives. The bank also created consistent employee incentives that (1) communicate its strategy to employees, (2) attract, motivate, and retain excellent employees, and (3) align their interests with the the bank's strategy and long-term interests of external stakeholders. In general, an effective **incentive system** communicates strategy, motivates employees, and reinforces achievement of organizational goals.

This final chapter presents the design of balanced scorecards and incentive systems as "capstone" topics of cost management because they bring together concerns about costs, revenues, value, and their drivers to devise systems that guide and motivate individuals to create long-term value at lowest cost.

Using Leading and Lagging Indicators in Balanced Scorecards to Communicate, Motivate, and Evaluate

LO 1 Explain the importance of using leading and lagging indicators for a balanced scorecard for communication, motivation, and evaluation.

Valley Commercial Bank identifies and uses its balanced scorecard to communicate plans and results to employees, motivate and evaluate its employees, and evaluate its success at meeting its financial goals. Many of the measures in this balanced scorecard are *leading indicators* of future performance.

Leading and Lagging Indicators

Leading indicators are measures that identify future nonfinancial and financial outcomes to guide management decision making. Combining relevant leading indicators into a balanced scorecard also makes it a business model of logically linked or cause-and-effect performance measures that reflect key operational and strategic relations. Identifying and measuring reliable leading indicators of performance is an important part of modern cost management because these measures allow employees to plan or gauge their progress toward meeting performance objectives. Employees know, for example, that certain levels of these leading indicators signal desired future cost or profit performance. If, as plans are implemented, the measured leading indicators show that the organization is likely to miss its performance target, employees can take corrective actions in time to get back on course.

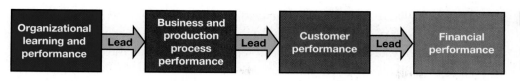

Exhibit 20–1

Lead and Lag Relations
among Indicators of
Performance

Many leading indicators of performance are nonfinancial in nature and include the following categories of measures:

- *Organizational learning and growth measures,* which describe the way employees and organizations increase their capabilities to develop new products and provide existing products more efficiently.
- *Business and production process efficiency measures,* which describe how efficiently the organization actually transforms resources into products. (*Note:* This can include outsourced processes and processes in the extended value chain.)
- *Customer value measures,* which describe how the organization creates customer satisfaction and loyalty.

In contrast to using leading indicators, when analysts at Valley Commercial Bank and other companies report the profits from the products that they have sold in the market, they are reporting **lagging indicators,** which are measures of the final outcomes of earlier management plans and their execution. Most financial performance measures are lagging indicators and in many cases measure results too late to significantly affect future performance.

Building leading and lagging indicators into a balanced scorecard illustrates relations among performance measures at different stages of an organization's value chain. Therefore, a leading indicator at one stage could be a lagging indicator of a preceding stage, as shown in Exhibit 20–1. Process efficiency can lag organizational learning and growth; customer satisfaction and loyalty can lag changes in process efficiency; and financial outcomes of profit and cash flow can lag changes in the preceding measures. Organizations that monitor and effectively communicate these leading and lagging indicators are more likely to (a) consistently and efficiently create valued services and products and (b) generate competitive profit and cash flow.

Communicating Strategy to Employees

Many employees of an organization do not understand the impacts of their activities on customer value and profitability because their jobs are narrow or they do not interact directly with customers. Communicating leading indicators in a balanced scorecard can make the effects of employees more visible. Once they realize how they affect customer value and financial performance, all employees are more likely to find and support ways to improve activities and processes. A comprehensive and reliable model of leading indicators should tell employees a credible story about how the organization can meet its strategic goals. The story told by a balanced scorecard can be a powerful communication device to overcome the natural skepticism many people have about why certain measures are gathered, reported, and monitored.

Motivating Employees and Evaluating Performance

Visible leading indicators can contribute to employees' improved motivation and commitment. Simply posting weekly sales or quality charts on the team bulletin board, as many companies do, probably is not enough. Even awarding bonuses for improving leading indicators can backfire if this practice reduces cooperation among individuals or teams in competition for the bonuses. Unless employees know that their efforts to improve processes actually result in improved organizational performance—better customer satisfaction, for example—charts and reports of these leading indicators can recede into background noise. A balanced scorecard can be an effective motivator and trusted evaluation tool because it helps employees understand how their efforts affect performance up and down the value chain.

Modern Origin and Use of Balanced Scorecards

Robert Kaplan and David Norton combined multiple leading indicators of performance into what they have called a *balanced scorecard*.[1] Although the concept of using leading and lagging indicators is not new, a balanced scorecard is a new way to package and present them that appears to be more successful than previous, less organized methods. A balanced scorecard's structure and intuitive appeal appear to add value to strategic management.

This approach represents a fundamental change in management style for most companies that previously focused on achieving the financial objectives that lag the activities of most of the organization's employees. For example, Valley Commercial Bank's balanced scorecard should tell all employees from janitor to teller to branch manager how their work leads to VCB's financial success. Exhibit 20–2 shows example links from (1) increased employee training to (2) the improved loan approval process to (3) increased customer value to (4) better financial results. The rationale is that if VCB improves customer satisfaction, it is more likely to retain a loyal customer base. A loyal customer base will provide word-of-mouth promotion that will lead to a larger customer base. A larger base of the right customers (see Chapter 6) means more revenue, which should lead to better financial performance. The opposite also is true, but by the time top managers observe poor financial performance, a problem already has occurred and caused damage. Managing drivers of profits can be better for all concerned than correcting problems later.

Balanced Scorecard's Strategic Performance Measures

A balanced scorecard expresses an organization's mission and strategy in the major areas of leading and lagging performance. Kaplan and Norton recommend using the four areas in Exhibit 20–3. This exhibit shows that all four areas of performance can interact and reflect the organization's strategy in a more complex way than previously shown in Exhibits 20–1 and 20–2. Each area can be a source of competitive advantage and can affect every other area. A successful balanced scorecard is not a random selection of readily available measures of performance. These carefully

Exhibit 20–2

Sequence of Performance from Employee Training to Financial Results

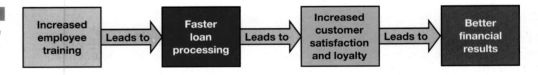

Increased employee training → Leads to → Faster loan processing → Leads to → Increased customer satisfaction and loyalty → Leads to → Better financial results

Research Insight 20.1

Small Companies and a Balanced Scorecard

Many large, international firms, including Bank of Montreal, KPMG, Tenneco, Allstate, AT&T, and Elf Atochem, are adopting a balanced scorecard approach. It is less well known, however, that many small companies, government, and nonprofit organizations also are adopting it. This is not a trivial undertaking for any company, and small companies often do not have sufficient staff to develop a balanced scorecard on their own. Many companies rely on experienced consultants to guide the development of a balanced scorecard. *Sources: C. Chow et al.,* "Applying a balanced scorecard to Smaller Companies." *For a description of a European model that predates a balanced scorecard by nearly 50 years, see M. Epstein and J.-F. Manzoni,* "A Balanced Scorecard and Tableau de Bord: Translating Strategy into Action." *See also C. Ittner and D. Larcker,* "Are Non-Financial Measures Leading Indicators of Financial Performance?" *for an investigation of statistical relations among leading and lagging indicators of performance.* (Full citations to references are in the Bibliography.

---

[1]See Kaplan and Norton's books, *A Balanced Scorecard* and *The Strategy-Focused Organization.* (Full citations to references are in the Bibliography.)

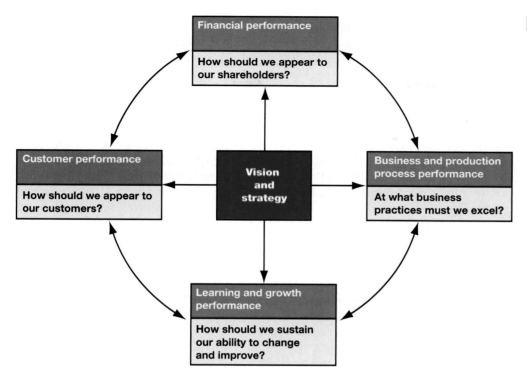

Exhibit 20–3

The Balanced Scorecard: Four Areas of Strategic Action (adapted from R. Kaplan and D. Norton, *The Balanced Scorecard*)

designed and selected measures reflect the tangible objectives that are consistent with meeting the organization's goals.

The learning and growth area indicates how employee capabilities and the infrastructure for innovation and long-term growth should contribute to strategic goals. In many ways, this is the most exciting area because it is the prime source of the organization's future value. The business and production process area indicates how processes should work to add value to customers. The customer area indicates how the company's customer-oriented strategy and operations add financial value. Finally, the financial area measures the company's success in adding value to shareholders (or other stakeholders). For organizations that do not have shareholders, the financial area indicates how well the strategy and operations contribute to improving the organization's financial health.

Designing a Balanced Scorecard

Consider the following independent questions.

a. Virtually all companies use financial performance measures to evaluate division and department managers. What are the advantages of focusing also on nonfinancial performance?

b. You are interviewing for a job. The interviewer says, "Historically, we have relied just on financial performance measures to evaluate division managers. We know the limitations of relying solely on financial performance measures, but we see a balanced scorecard as being too costly to implement. What do you think we should do?"

c. *Team Focus:* You work for an internationally known consulting firm that has been asked by Singapore Airways to design and install a balanced scorecard system. You are starting to assemble a team of airline consultants and employees to work on the project. What characteristics should team members have? What airline departments or segments do you want on the team?

(Solutions begin on page 856.)

You're the Decision Maker 20.1

Implementation of a Balanced Scorecard

LO 2 Understand how an organization selects related measures for a balanced scorecard.

We now examine how to implement the four typical strategic areas of a balanced scorecard.

Organizational Learning and Growth

Improvements in operating performance result largely from enhancing the capabilities of the organization's employees and motivating them to use those capabilities so that the organization can learn and improve its processes and products. **Employee capabilities** are employees' knowledge and skills that create the organization's ability to meet future customer needs and generate new sales. Organizational learning involves the use of employees' capabilities to create new or improved business and production processes, procedures, products, customer databases, and proprietary, copyrighted, or patented intellectual property. Knowledge developed by key individuals to benefit the organization is of no lasting benefit unless it is shared. Furthermore, a key individual can leave the organization and take his or her knowledge, which can be doubly costly if the employee joins a competitor. Like many other companies, VCB uses teams to manage nearly every decision and process. Teamwork encourages employees to share their capabilities and thus transform individual knowledge into organizational knowledge.

Different organizations might require different levels of some employee capabilities, such as education, to prosper. However, all organizations can expect better operating results when employees are well trained, motivated, committed, and encouraged to improve processes. Valley Commercial Bank sets objectives for a number of measures of employee capabilities, and it regularly monitors employees to encourage improvement. The areas of performance include the following:

- Employee training and education.
- Employee satisfaction.
- Employee turnover.
- Innovativeness.
- Opportunities for improvement.

These are shown in the following expansion of Exhibit 20–1 to reflect simplified effects of investments in organizational learning and growth.

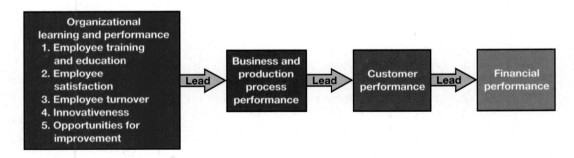

Employee training and education.   VCB pays for employee education programs to motivate employees to improve their individual and team capabilities. Hiring and promotions also depend, in part, on the educational levels achieved by potential or current employees. One top manager at VCB stated the rationale for measuring employee training, "Yes, we want long-term, loyal employees, but we don't want people who have become uncreative or who lack the drive for constant improvement. By giving managers incentives to send their people to training programs, the bank should have people who are really up-to-date with the latest ideas. And, frankly, I don't care whether they take classes in virtual banking or foreign language or communications skills, as long as it's expanding their minds and keeping them creative."

Educating employees is a major determinant of the success of new strategies and performance measurement. Here General Electric conducts its successful Workout program.

Employee satisfaction.   Managing employee satisfaction recognizes that employee morale is important for improving retention, productivity, quality, customer satisfaction, and responsiveness to situations. Managers can measure employee satisfaction by taking surveys, interviewing employees, or observing employees at work. VCB employs an external consultant to measure employee satisfaction twice a year.

Employee turnover.   Managing employee turnover recognizes that employees develop organization-specific knowledge and are a valuable nonfinancial asset to the company. Finding and hiring good talent to replace people who leave are costly. A common measure of employee turnover is the percentage of people who leave voluntarily each year because generally these are people the organizations would like to keep.

Innovativeness.   Competition in Valley Commercial Bank's industry requires continuous innovation and attention to customer needs. New products or improvements to current offerings depend on the ability of an organization's employees to be innovative and translate innovations into new offerings. VCB measures its innovativeness by the percentage of sales generated by new products.

Opportunities for improvement.   Organizations can encounter new opportunities to improve processes, products, and services. Proactive organizations, however, work to create these opportunities. VCB encourages all employees to make suggestions for innovations and improvements. The bank estimates the value of employee suggestions from cost savings or revenue enhancements. A top manager who proposed the measure stated, "We'd prefer to have employees come up with one excellent idea a year that had a large impact rather than a hundred trivial ideas that did not amount to much in the end."

Evaluation of measures of organizational learning and growth.   Do investments in organizational learning and growth pay off? Most organizations intuitively believe that they do; however, predicting and measuring the impacts of these investments is particularly difficult. As noted earlier, one complication is that investments in employees can walk out the door if these personnel leave. Another complication is that investments in employees might not result in tangible outcomes for years, and, by then, many other events could have occurred to obscure the impacts of training and education.

In concept, evaluation of these investments can use concepts presented in previous chapters: modeling of Chapter 12, decision making of Chapter 13, and discounted cash flow techniques of Chapter 14. Consider the following example of VCB's decision to spend $80,000 annually for the next three years on training focusing on customer service for its branch-bank employees. If the effects of each year's training are expected to lag one year and persist for three years, what annual benefit (X) can justify this training investment?

First, ignore the time value of money (Chapter 14), and then consider the following pattern of expenditures and benefits:

Investments in Learning and Growth	Year 0	Year I	Year 2	Year 3	Year 4	Year 5	Total
Training cost	$(80,000)	$(80,000)	$(80,000)				$(240,000)
First year's training benefits		X	X	X			
Second year's training benefits			X	X	X		
Third year's training benefits				X	X	X	
Total training benefits		X	2X	3X	2X	X	9X

The break-even benefit level equates the total benefits to total costs as follows:

$$\text{Incremental profit} = \text{Total benefits} - \text{Total costs}$$
$$\text{Break-even profit} = 0 = 9X - \$\,240{,}000$$
$$9X = \$\,240{,}000$$
$$\text{Break-even benefit level, } X = \$\,26{,}667 \text{ per year}$$

The preceding analysis ignores the time value of money. Now assume that VCB's cost of capital is 10 percent. The break-even analysis becomes a bit more complex because of the need to discount each of the future expenditures and unknown annual benefits by the appropriate factors.

Investments in Learning and Growth	Year 0	Year I	Year 2	Year 3	Year 4	Year 5
Training cost	$(80,000)	$(80,000)	$(80,000)			
First year's training benefits		X	X	X		
Second year's training benefits			X	X	X	
Third year's training benefits				X	X	X
Total benefits		X	2X	3X	2X	X
10% discount factors	1.000	0.909	0.826	0.751	0.683	0.621

$$\text{Break-even profit} = .909X + .826(2X) + .751(3X) + .683(2X) + .621(X) -$$
$$1.000(80{,}000) - .909(80{,}000) - .826(80{,}000)$$
$$0 = 6.803X - 2.736(80{,}000)$$
$$\text{Break-even benefit level, } X = \$\,32{,}170 \text{ per year (rounded)}$$

Should VCB invest in this customer-satisfaction training program? It should if the bank believes that the benefits occur in the expected pattern and (including the effects of the time value of money) equal at least $32,170 annually. This analysis contains many assumptions about an uncertain future, which can be modeled using sensitivity and scenario analyses (see Chapter 12). Perhaps the biggest assumption of this analysis is that the benefits of investments in learning and growth can be observed in future profits, independently of other improvement actions. Top management probably would look at this analysis and determine subjectively whether the needed benefits are likely before making the decision.

Business and Production Process Performance

Logically, a cause-and-effect relation exists between improvements in organizational learning and growth and improvements in internal business and production processes. Ideally, a well-trained workforce has the capability to improve internal business processes. Valley Commercial Bank has learned that the most important areas of process performance are:

- New service development.
- Employee productivity and error rates.
- Service costs.
- Process improvements.
- Supplier relations.

The following diagram extends Exhibit 20–1 to show effects of these measures.

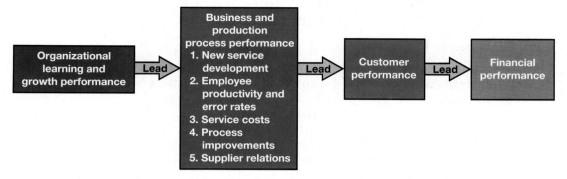

New product development. One of Valley Commercial Bank's most important leading indicators of the capability to beat the competition is the average time to develop a new service (from the first team meeting to the delivery of the first service). In part because of innovative suggestions from employees, VCB has reduced the average new-service development time by more than 50 percent in the past five years. This allows the bank to consistently be early to the market with innovative services. It also has led to VCB's reputation and stature as the premiere supplier of financial services to emerging high-technology businesses.

Employee productivity and error rates. Managing productivity recognizes the importance of output from scarce resources (see Chapter 7). Output can be measured in terms of a physical measure, such as miles driven, pages produced, or lawns mowed, or as a financial measure, such as revenue per employee or profits per employee. One simple measure of productivity at VCB is the number of loans processed without error per loan officer each month. The bank has similar productivity measures for the other major parts of its business.

Service costs. Similar to many manufacturing and service organizations, VCB regularly computes costs per loan, checking account, and other services. The bank uses ABC information to effect continuous improvements in these costs without losses in quality or customer service (see Chapters 4 and 5).

Process improvements. Valley Commercial Bank once had a problem with the cycle time (see Chapter 7) for processing many loans. Customers complained, and the bank believed that it was about to lose existing and future customers. To remedy this situation, the bank increased the importance of cycle-time management. Performance measures were average cycle time (from application to provision of funds) and percentage of loans completed within one month. As a result of the focus on loan-cycle time, the bank's employees developed permanent loan application files on the bank's secure website for repeat customers. With a few keystrokes, customers can update their files and usually complete their self-correcting loan applications within a few minutes. These innovations in service were possible because bank employees were trained, experienced, and sufficiently motivated that they wanted to help their company.

Supplier relations. Supplier relations are becoming increasingly important as companies outsource more business or production activities that the companies once performed internally. Obviously, even though a company has outsourced an internal process, it still must ensure the quality of that process. Valley Commercial Bank outsourced its statement preparation for bank accounts and billing for loan payments. Any errors made by the companies performing those services reflected badly on the bank, as if its own employees had performed the services themselves. Therefore, the bank appointed a manager for each outsourced service. The outsourcing contract required the supplier to provide auditable performance statistics, including cycle times and internal error rates, which the bank's manager reviewed daily.

Evaluation of measures of business and production process efficiency. VCB can evaluate investments in its process efficiency in much the same way as it evaluates learning and growth improvements: Estimate future relevant costs and benefits, and evaluate process-efficiency decisions as break-even or investment decisions using the methods discussed in Chapters 12, 13, and 14.

Customer Performance

Successful organizations consistently satisfy customers' expectations. **Customer value** reflects the degree to which products satisfy customers' expectations about price, function, and quality. To meet strategic goals of improving customer value, an organization must first define its customers and second identify its customers' expectations (see Chapter 6).

Valley Commercial Bank knows that its customers are business owners and professionals who want considerable personal attention and 24-hour service, and they are willing to pay higher fees to get that service. The bank knows that it cannot compete with large interstate banks on price and breadth of services, but it can compete on the basis of the personal attention and availability of service to its customers. The bank uses the following performance measures, among others, to manage customer value:

- Customer satisfaction.
- Customer retention and loyalty.
- Market share.
- Customer risk.

The following figure illustrates how these measures can affect financial performance.

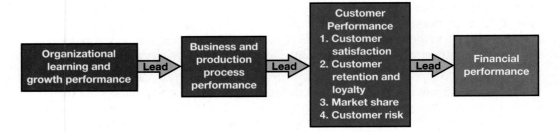

Customer satisfaction.   Customer-satisfaction measures indicate whether the company is meeting customers' expectations or even delighting them. Customer satisfaction with current products is a leading indicator of future sales. If a company knows that customers are becoming dissatisfied, its alert and well-trained employees are able to take corrective actions in time to prevent loss of future sales. Improvements in customer satisfaction usually lag organizational capabilities and process efficiency. In addition, customer measures can give advance notice about changing customer perceptions and needs, which influence future sales. Some companies wait to see whether customers buy their products. Others, like VCB, are more aggressive and obtain leading indicators of customer satisfaction to help them keep ahead of the competition.

VCB regularly surveys customers randomly to measure their satisfaction with current services. In addition, the bank regularly meets with groups of customers to discuss their future needs. At these meetings, customers also express what they value about the bank's services relative to those provided by competitors. This is valuable information that can help the bank position its current services and design future ones to gain a competitive advantage over its competitors from achieving customer satisfaction measures.

Customer retention.   **Customer retention** or **loyalty** measures how well a company keeps its customers. Once a firm has a customer, keeping that customer should be much easier than capturing a new one. Satisfied customers, whose needs are met, tend to be loyal or repeat customers and continue to buy existing and probably new products from reliable providers. Valley Commercial Bank believes that its high

Innovative Leading Indicators of Customer Value

Many organizations benefit from timely information about how customers' needs are being met. For example, the CFO of 20th Century Fox measures daily box-office ticket sales to monitor the success of new movie releases. If ticket sales are much less than the expected pattern over time, managers can decide whether to pull the movie from theaters or immediately begin advertising and promotion campaigns to boost sales. Every morning the CFO of Current, Inc., a mail-order greeting card company, measures the day's volume of mail (actually, the linear feet of mail) to estimate the day's cash receipts and sales orders and to gauge the success of recent catalog mailings. He is confident that the number of feet of mail is a reliable leading indicator because of his careful observations over a number of years. He can begin financial planning and provide feedback to catalog sales managers even before the mail is opened and analyzed. *Source: Interview by one of the authors.*

Cost Management in Practice 20.1

average customer retention rate can be counted as a key leading indicator of future sales from new products.

Market share. *Market share* measures a company's proportion of the total business in a particular market. Companies typically measure market share as the proportion of dollar sales, unit volume, or number of customers. For example, VCB management determined that it served 12 percent of the small businesses and the professionals in the region. Its goal was to become the dominant bank in that market segment, with "dominant" defined as securing more than 20 percent of the small business and professional accounts and loans. Having the largest share of this market would indicate that VCB is the bank of choice for new business and professional customers moving into the region, which should ensure continued sales growth.

Customer risk. Many organizations implicitly loan money to customers by allowing them to buy products on credit. Banks such as Valley Commercial do this explicitly and are exposed to more risk (i.e., loan default) because the amounts are larger and terms of the loans usually are longer than the typical 30- or 60-day-credit sales terms. Because customers might default on their loan obligations, the bank also must evaluate risk of default. To moderate the incentives created by desires for sales growth and market share, VCB also monitors the risk profiles of its customers using information in new loan applications. Risk information is a leading indicator of future default rates. Although a default rate of zero is undesirable because it implies taking no risks and missing sales opportunities, the bank cannot let the default rate increase to an excessive level without affecting its profitability and its regulatory status. Monitoring the default rate, however, is an important source of feedback on the effectiveness of screening its customers' risk profiles.

Evaluation of measures of customer value. Ideally, improvements in measures of customer value are leading indicators of improvements in financial performance. VCB and other organizations can apply the decision-making and modeling methods described in earlier chapters. Certainly, this application requires valid customer-related measures, which can be difficult to obtain at reasonable cost. Many organizations use customer-satisfaction surveys, which—if administered carefully—can illuminate customer problems and opportunities. Consider the following survey results from 100 VCB customers (1 = a very unfavorable evaluation and 5 = a highly favorable evaluation).

VCB Customer Satisfaction Variable	Number of Customer Responses						
	1	2	3	4	5	Total	Ave.
Automated bank services meet customer needs	32	25	22	16	5	100	2.37
Automated services are superior to competitors' services	17	22	20	21	20	100	3.05
Employees can and do respond to special requests	12	20	20	22	26	100	3.30
Employees give prompt service	6	14	22	17	41	100	3.73
Employees are superior to competitors' employees	5	12	20	23	40	100	3.81

What can you infer from these data? If the survey respondents are representative of VCB's preferred customers, the survey data in Exhibit 20–4 reveal both inferior and superior services. Review the charts in Exhibit 20–4. Panel A shows that customers on average have low regard for the bank's automated services but consider them to be comparable to its competitors' automated services. This seems to be an opportunity for VCB to improve its automated bank services and, perhaps, create a competitive advantage. Conversely, the bank appears to have a competitive advantage because of customers' high regard for its employees. The bank should exploit this advantage, perhaps by advertising that features them. Panel B, which shows the frequency of responses, reinforces these conclusions. Note that the unfavorable pattern of responses on the first question regarding VCB's automated services is nearly a mirror image of employee-related responses. VCB should consider the costs and benefits of improving its automated services and exploiting the favorable view of its employees.

Financial Performance

The relations among the leading indicators in the areas of organizational learning and growth, business and production process efficiency, and customer value logically result in financial outcomes. This is the compelling "story" of a balanced scorecard. When organizations use a balanced scorecard as an overall picture of themselves, for example, financial performance might mean customer profitability, net income, return on investment, EVA, or stock price gains—all of these and others are commonly used. Because this text covers these financial performance measures in detail in Chapters 6 and 18, we do not explore them here.

A key point of a balanced scorecard is that financial performance measures are important but are not sufficient guides for organizations to meet their goals. Nor are the lead-indicator measures a replacement for the bottom-line score of financial performance. A balanced scorecard, as the name implies, looks for a *balance* among multiple performance measures, both leading and lagging indicators of performance, to guide organizational performance toward success. Leading indicators point the way to financial success, and lagging indicators, including actual financial performance, provide opportunities for learning about what worked, what did not, and what should be improved.

Exhibit 20–4   Valley Commercial Bank's Customer Satisfaction

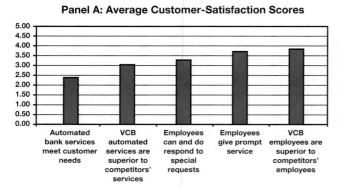

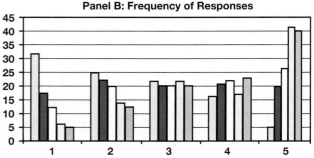

☐ **Automated bank services meet customer needs**

■ **VCB automated services are superior to competitors' services**

☐ **Employees can and do respond to special requests**

☐ **Employees give prompt service**

▨ **VCB employees are superior to competitors' employees**

Valley Commercial uses four financial performance measures:

1. *Net interest margin,* the difference between the bank's cost of funds and its average earnings from the use of those funds.
2. *Sales revenue growth,* the percentage change in revenue from one period to the next.
3. *Customer profitability* (see Chapter 6).
4. *Overall return on assets* (see Chapter 18).

Managers had difficulty explaining financial performance, good or bad, with only these measures because they did not fully understand their causes. However, they now understand that financial success follows good performance on the leading indicators. Poor financial performance can be traced to lapses in leading indicator performance; importantly, managing those leading indicators can prevent poor financial performance. Explaining financial performance provides important feedback, but bank employees know that monitoring and correcting leading indicator performance is an effective way to ensure future financial success—and to avoid unpleasant explanations of financial shortfalls.

The following figure illustrates how other areas of performance affect financial performance.

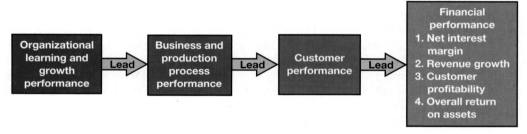

Evaluation of measures of financial performance.   Financial measures of performance tend to be the most objective measures because most organizations (and society) have dedicated significant resources (e.g., regulation, auditing, and internal controls) to ensure the validity of their financial performance measures. Even so, incidents of financial fraud or earnings manipulation are not rare, necessitating continual reliance on monitoring activities (see the appendix to this chapter). Although an organization can rate or rank performance fairly objectively, the less objective leading indicators of financial performance are important for evaluating future success.

Benefits and Costs of a Balanced Scorecard

We have presented four areas of performance and have discussed VCB's related performance measures. There is nothing magic about having four areas of performance; companies have used more or fewer. Organizations should use the areas and performance measures that reflect their critical processes and the links between them. Linking these performance measures distinguishes a balanced scorecard from a list of important or key performance indicators, also known as *critical success factors.*

LO 3 Evaluate the benefits and costs of a balanced scorecard.

Benefits of a Balanced Scorecard

A balanced scorecard's greatest value is that it encourages all employees to consider the impacts of their decisions on profitability. A balanced scorecard can be a reliable guide because of its modeled cause-and-effect relationships. An example of a cause-and-effect relationship included in a balanced scorecard is this: "Reducing the number of defective products decreases the average production cycle time because there are fewer products to rework." This clearly demonstrates the importance of controlling the number of defects. A reasonable question is whether the label, format, and

Cost Management in Practice 20.2

Sears' Employee-Customer-Profit Chain

Managers at Sears, one of the largest US retailers, credit its return to profitability to the development and use of its own balanced scorecard, which it calls the "employee-customer-profit chain." This scorecard, which took nearly three years to develop, enables Sears to measure and manage the drivers of employee and customer satisfaction. Equally important was Sears' ability to integrate its scorecard into its incentive system and communicate its underlying strategy to all employees. The best set of measures does little to improve the interaction of employees and customers unless the employees believe the scorecard's "story" of successful retailing. Key to telling the story was Sears' ability to demonstrate the causal links among its scorecard measures; the story sounded plausible, and hard data supported it.

The Sears scorecard has three areas of performance, which the company labels as (1) a compelling place to work (corresponds to organizational learning and growth), (2) a compelling place to shop (corresponds to business and production process efficiency and customer value), and (3) a compelling place to invest (corresponds to financial performance). Exhibit 20–5 illustrates the cause-and-effect relations among Sears' measures of performance, which the retailer claims are statistically valid. This is one of the few published accounts of the causal properties of a balanced scorecard. *Source: A. Rucci, S. Kirn, and R. Quinn, "The Employee-Customer-Profit Chain at Sears."*

method of a balanced scorecard are essential to achieving the benefits of modeling cause-and-effect relations among key performance indicators. Can other formulations of cause and effect achieve these benefits? Probably, but little objective research currently exists in this area. Early studies attribute some effects to a balanced scorecard, both favorable and unfavorable. This is an important area of research that will receive increased attention in coming years.[2]

Another important value of a balanced scorecard is that it appears to work in various types of organizations. Cost Management in Practice 20.2 describes the process and result at Sears, the large retailing organization. Other types of organizations, including small companies, government, universities, and nonprofit hospitals also report successful applications (see cases 20.76, 20.77, and 20.78 at the end of the chapter).

Costs of a Balanced Scorecard

The value of a balanced scorecard comes with costs. Presently, no studies of the costs to design and implement a balanced scorecard have been published, but these costs surely exist. They include the costs of consultants (if used), measurement, education, and use. Some reported and unreported balanced scorecard failures might be attributed to the failure to anticipate these costs. We do know that developing and implementing a balanced scorecard is not an overnight endeavor. Many organizations have spent several years on the process from concept to general use. Furthermore, a balanced scorecard is never completed; it continuously evolves as the organization learns and evolves, so many costs are ongoing.

Measurement costs.   Because of the urgency of creating a balanced scorecard, some organizations decide to reuse existing measures and piece together a balanced scorecard. Picking and choosing from an inventory of existing measures can be a first step, but new measures inevitably are necessary. Organizations should resist the temptation to economize by using only currently available measures because some areas of performance probably have no suitable measures available. Each new performance measure has a cost of design, validation, data collection, maintenance, and revision, which can be significant. Establishing credible links between measures or areas of performance also is no trivial task. Anticipating the full costs of additional performance measures is more an art than an exact science, but that does not justify ignoring these costs.

---

[2] For example, see M. Lipe and S. Salterio, "The Balanced Scorecard: Judgmental Effects of Information Organization and Diversity"; M. Malina and F. Selto, "Communicating and Controlling Strategy: An Empirical Study of the Effectiveness of a Balanced Scorecard"; and C. D. Ittner, D. F. Larcker, and M. W. Meyer, "The Use of Subjectivity in Multi-Criteria Bonus Plans."

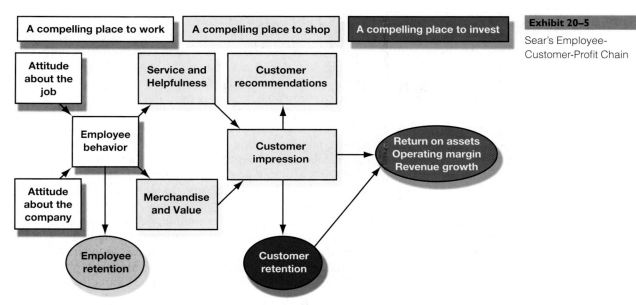

Exhibit 20–5

Sear's Employee-
Customer-Profit Chain

Source: A. Rucci, S. Kirn, and R. Quinn, "The Employee-Customer-Profit Chain at Sears."

Education costs.   Just as numbers almost never speak for themselves, creating a balanced scorecard does not ensure that members of the organization understand it or how to use it. Organizations should plan for and not underestimate the education, training, coaching, and interpretation activities needed to integrate a balanced scorecard.

Use costs.   The costs of using a balanced scorecard also might be significant. Although early studies indicate that information overload is not a problem, assuming that individuals can manage many performance measures simultaneously is unwise, particularly if some measures conflict and require trade-offs. Organizations are learning to assign responsibility or "ownership" to balanced scorecard measures just as they had for responsibility accounting in the past (see Chapter 18).

Unanswered Balanced Scorecard Questions

Balanced scorecards present many opportunities for improved strategy formulation, communication, and evaluation. However, many unanswered questions surround using balanced scorecards. Questions related to using a balanced scorecard include these:

- Is strategy formulation more effective and efficient?
- Is strategy communication more effective and efficient?
- Is motivation improved?
- Is the evaluation process improved?
- Is performance improved?
- Are causal relations among measures reliable and demonstrable?

Answers to these and other questions will stimulate improvements to scorecard models.

Balanced Scorecard Implementation at Valley Commercial Bank

Some organizations develop a balanced scorecard at top levels of management and impose it. This approach can be successful, just as top-down management succeeds in some situations, but most observers believe that a participative, bottom-up approach to designing a balanced scorecard improves its acceptance and use by the organization's members. After all, the foundation of a balanced scorecard is learning and growth, reflecting employee capabilities to gain, transfer, and apply knowledge. It makes sense to involve them in a balanced scorecard design.

LO 4 Explain how an organization implements a balanced scorecard.

Valley Commercial Bank's cost-management team sketched the initial balanced scorecard based on its understanding of the bank's strategy and processes and input from key employees. The team then spent more than a year working with employees representing all levels, functions, and major activities of the bank to design the scorecard. After more than a year of interaction with other employees, the team unveiled a balanced scorecard using the performance measures previously discussed. Exhibit 20–6 displays VCB's scorecard areas and measures.

Exhibit 20–7 is a graphical representation of part of VCB's balanced scorecard model. The cost-management team used this simplified chart to explain several cause-and-effect relationships among the four areas of performance. In this simplified model, profitability—VCB's ultimate goal—is achieved, in part, by retaining existing customers through improving loan processing. These links tell the story of VCB's success in its competitive market for banking services. This graphical representation of the bank's strategy was an effective communication and education tool. You should "walk through" this model carefully, beginning with the hours of job-related training, following the direction of the arrows from one box to the next.

Along with the extensive effort to develop its balanced scorecard, VCB's top management also examined its incentive system for consistency and effectiveness. We now turn to the related topic of incentive systems.

| Exhibit 20–6 | Valley Commercial Bank's Balanced Scorecard Areas and Measures |

Scorecard Areas	Scorecard Performance	Scorecard Measures	Performance Targets
Organizational learning and growth	Employee training and education	Percentage of employees involved in approved training and education	100 percent
	Employee satisfaction	Employee satisfaction index	Maintain current level
	Employee turnover	Voluntary turnover percentage	Below industry average
	Innovativeness	Percentage of sales from new services	50 percent
	Opportunities for improvement	Employee suggestions	Estimated value of employee suggestions
Business and production process efficency	New service development	Average new service development time	Continuous improvement
	Productivity (loans)	Error-free loans processed per employee	Continuous improvement
	Defective service (loans)	Errors per loan officer	Zero
	Service costs	Cost per loan, checking account, and other services	Continuous improvement
	Process improvements	Average process (e.g., loan) cycle time	One week
	Supplier relations	Supplier cycle time, error rates	Below industry averages
Customer value	Customer satisfaction	Customer satisfaction index	Above competitors' average
	Customer retention and loyalty	Customer retention rate	Above industry average
	Sales growth	Account and revenue growth	10 percent per year
	Market share	Professional and business market share	30 percent
	Customer risk	Customer risk profiles and loan default rate	Maintain current levels
Financial performance	Service profitability	Net interest margin	5 percent
	Growth	Revenue growth	Above industry average
	Customer profitability	Percentage of loss customers	Zero
	Competitive return	Return on assets	Above industry average

Exhibit 20–7   Portion of Valley Commercial Bank's Balanced Scorecard

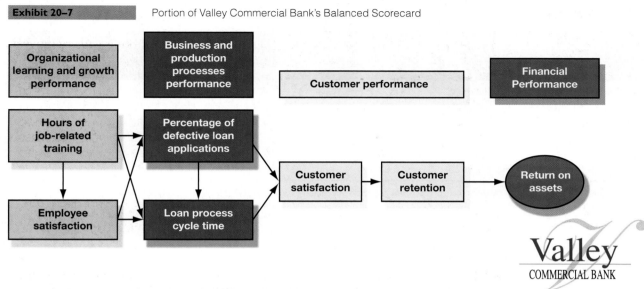

Fundamental Principles of Incentive Systems

Alfred Sloan, famous chief executive officer of General Motors, instituted one of the first incentive systems. A strong advocate of using incentives, he started a bonus plan in 1918 at General Motors to better motivate division managers to act in the best interests of the company and its shareholders. This bonus plan stressed *pay for performance* based on the achievement of desired levels of performance. **Pay for performance** bases at least some portion of a manager's income on measure(s) of organizational performance rather than a guaranteed amount. Although modern incentive systems can be complex, all are similar to Sloan's original because they stress pay for performance. Thus, two key principles of an incentive system are:

LO 5 Understand the key principles of performance-based incentive systems.

1. Measurement of performance.
2. Compensation based on measured performance.

Today, virtually all large companies, many small ones, and an increasing number of nonprofit organizations use incentive plans for executives, managers, and, to a lesser degree, employees at all levels. You could easily find yourself eligible for incentive compensation soon after completing your studies. For example, employment with a business assurance or consulting firm might offer you mostly salary with a long-term opportunity of a partnership and profit sharing. A high-technology company, on the other hand, might offer a relatively low initial salary with an early opportunity for stock ownership. Similarly, once you are with an organization, you must decide how to attract and retain good employees with different incentives. The structure of incentive systems can matter greatly to employees and employers.

These plans can have a substantial impact on annual pay. For example, CEOs of major US firms are paid millions of dollars per year on average, and often much of this pay is based on incentives related to performance. The components of CEO pay vary across firms and are changing because of the financial bubble that burst in 2000 and, in the United States, because of the Sarbanes-Oxley Act of 2002, which was a reaction to CEO misdeeds and compensation-related, financial disclosure failures that accompanied the bubble.[3] Exhibit 20–8 illustrates representative variety in CEO compensation for a recent, postbubble year.

It is interesting to speculate how the different incentive systems might affect CEO behavior. For example, would Tecumseh Products' all-salary system motivate its CEO differently than Medtronic's mostly unrealized long-term compensation system? We will discuss these issues later, but, apart from the money, is the "real world"

---

[3] See a summary at www.aicpa.org/info/sarbanes/index.asp.

Exhibit 20–8   Examples of Recent CEO Compensation ($000)

Company	CEO Salary	Bonus	Realized Long-Term Compensation*	Unrealized Long-Term Compensation*	Total
Tecumseh Products	$ 475.00	$ 0	$ 0	$ 0	$ 475.00
Disney	1,000.00	6,250.00	0	0	7,250.00
McGraw-Hill	1,063.00	1,002.40	0	12,465.80	14,531.20
Boeing	109.60	152.60	0	32,814.10	33,076.30
Medtronic	1,025.00	1,368.70	1,575.90	37,075.20	41,044.80
Lehman Brothers	750.00	6,650.00	37,539.60	65,874.70	110,814.30

* Long-term compensation typically consists of stock grants, stock appreciation rights, and stock-option grants. Unrealized compensation usually is from stock appreciation rights and stock option grants that had not been exercised. These terms are explained later in the chapter. Data were obtained from the *Wall Street Journal*/Mercer 2003 CEO Compensation Survey, May 2004, which is available online at http://online.wsj.com/documents/Execpay_ceocomp04.pdf.

different from school? If you are currently a student, you already work within a performance-based incentive system; grades in courses can be based on multiple measures of performance. You can easily imagine how differences in the rewards or incentives might alter your motivation and behavior. Do you study as hard for a course that you take pass-fail as for one you take for a grade? Do you concentrate on the same parts of the course if the grade is based on a comprehensive paper versus problem-oriented exams? Variations in incentives and rewards affect student behavior as they do CEOs and other employees who work for rewards. The key to designing incentive systems is to understand as well as possible which behaviors are desired and how incentives and rewards are likely to influence behaviors. In nearly every case, you get what you measure and reward—even if it is not what you intended.

Unintended Consequences of Incentive Systems

A classic article titled "On the Folly of Rewarding A While Hoping for B" speaks to fundamental problems with many incentive systems.[4] The title of the article reveals that designers of incentive plans can be surprised to find that these systems motivate unintended behavior or create disincentives to desired behavior. Here is an example that affects most of us: Most US states regulate the rates that energy-producing companies can charge. The stated objectives of the regulation are to offer the utility a fair profit while protecting consumers. Traditionally, rates have been based on the costs incurred to produce energy. However, at the same time most utilities operate with "fuel-adjustment clauses" that allow them to separately recover all costs of fuel used to produce power. These clauses create disincentives to invest in improvements that reduce fuel costs because the investments increase the utility's costs but only consumers would realize the cost savings from lower fuel consumption. Rate regulation and fuel adjustment clauses clearly tell utilities that investments to reduce fuel consumption are a waste of money, an unintended consequence of the regulatory system.

Early on, Valley Commercial Bank had a problem of rewarding A when top management really wanted B. As a small service-oriented bank, VCB realized the importance of customer relations and relied on satisfying its customers to keep them coming back for more loans and services. The original incentive system, however, emphasized short-term profits and cost minimization, which gave branch managers the incentive to reduce staff. This narrow focus resulted in fewer employees spending less time with customers and lower customer satisfaction. As a result, the bank began to lose some of its key customers because of its incentive system, which it soon revised.

---

[4] S. Kerr, "On the Folly of Rewarding A While Hoping for B."

Desired Behavior—It's Where to Begin

The starting point of designing an effective incentive system is knowing the behavior that the organization wants to motivate. Managers cannot motivate people to "do the right thing" if no one knows what the right thing is. An effective incentive system should motivate employees to achieve the organization's goals and objectives and reward them if they do.

Reality Intrudes

Unfortunately, translating goals into effective incentive systems is not always as easy as it might seem because sometimes the desired outcome is not easily observed. Here is a seemingly easy question: What is the "right thing" for a profit-seeking corporation? The standard answer in a market economy is a long-term competitive return for stockholders. In reality, translating even this standard statement into an incentive plan can be a challenge.

What's so hard about creating an incentive system that promotes a "long-term competitive return for stockholders"? For one thing, the "long-term" might be 5 or 10 years from now. A company may wait that long to reward or penalize managers, but what if it needs to reward good managers now or risk losing them to competitors? What is the "competitive" benchmark? What is the proper measure of "return"? Are "stockholders" the only *stakeholders* in the company (that is, those who have an interest in its actions)? We now turn to the important issue of tying desired behavior to desired performance in the chapter.

Role for Theories of Incentives and Behavior

A company could develop incentive plans by trial and error, trying alternatives until a plan appears to generate the desired behavior. Although it might succeed eventually, using trial and error is not the most efficient way to proceed. Fortunately, a number of theories are well grounded in observations of individuals and organizations and can provide reliable advice. Not surprisingly, because incentives are so important, researchers have studied the psychology and economics of incentives for many years. Relying on the guidance from this research is an efficient way to begin to design an incentive plan. The most commonly used theories of incentives are expectancy theory, goal-setting theory, and agency theory. See the appendix to this chapter for an overview of these important theories that we synthesize here. Our interpretation of these theories and observations of successful practice generate the following guidelines for designing effective incentive plans.

Theory and Practice	Guideline
Most individuals are motivated by self-interest	Performance-based rewards must be greater than alternative rewards from nonperformance.
Organizations get the behavior they reward	Performance measures and related rewards must reflect organizational goals.
Effort follows rewards	Employees must believe that their efforts influence performance and will be rewarded.
Difficult but attainable goals motivate best	Impossible goals are demotivators and so are easy goals. Make goals difficult but not impossible.
Fairness is a basis for sustained motivation	Rewards must be linked to desired performance in a fair and consistent manner.
Manipulation undermines fairness and effort	Performance measures must be observable and verifiable.
Different rewards can motivate effort	Rewards must meet market conditions, and rewards must be available.
Incentive systems involve trade-offs	Minimizing the overall costs of aligning goals and monitoring behavior is a goal of incentive system design.

Features of Performance-Based Incentive Systems

LO 6 Evaluate the advantages and disadvantages of alternative features of incentive systems.

Incentive systems can include many alternative features. We now turn to a number of specific choices that designers of incentive systems must make. Identifying the required trade-offs between effective rewards, goal alignment, monitoring, and cost necessitates choosing among many alternative incentive-system configurations and reviewing systems in place to be sure they are still effective.[5]

Exhibit 20–9 displays the many choices that accumulate to create the elements of an effective performance-based incentive system. Designers of incentive systems should consider all of these choices because ignoring any of them can lead to a less-effective system. All of the elements in Exhibit 20–9 speak to this question: *Given the goal(s) of the organization, which alternative incentive(s) will motivate the desired behavior most effectively?* The answer to that question must be placed in context: *The situation faced by each company determines the answer.* There are no universally right or wrong answers, but there are better or worse answers in a particular situation. Furthermore, many equally effective combinations of incentive plan elements might exist in similar situations. Our aim is to provide an overview of the choices, not to suggest the correct choices for any situation. We discuss each of the boxed alternatives in Exhibit 20–9 in turn.

Absolute or Relative Performance

One may evaluate performance against absolute objectives or relative to others' performance. **Absolute performance evaluation** compares individual performance to set objectives or expectations. For example, in classes that use absolute performance evaluation, the instructor grades on an absolute scale, and how well others perform does not affect your grade. For example, panel A of Exhibit 20–10 illustrates a grade distribution that uses absolute cutoffs (100 percent < A < 90 percent; 90 percent ≤ B < 80 percent, etc.). **Relative performance evaluation** compares an individual's performance to that of others. In classes that use relative performance evaluation, the instructor grades on the curve; that is, your grade depends on how you perform relative to everyone else. For example, panel B of Exhibit 20–10 reflects a grade distribution relative to an instructor's desired curve of 12.5 percent As, 50 percent Bs, 25 percent Cs, and 12.5 percent Ds and Fs. Both approaches can be effective, but the situation determines the effectiveness. For example, grading on an absolute basis, when exams are extremely difficult, can reduce one's belief that studying can lead to

---

[5] Personal and corporate income tax regulations also can have major effects on the design of incentive systems. These issues are beyond the scope of this text.

Exhibit 20–9

Performance-Based Incentive System Choices

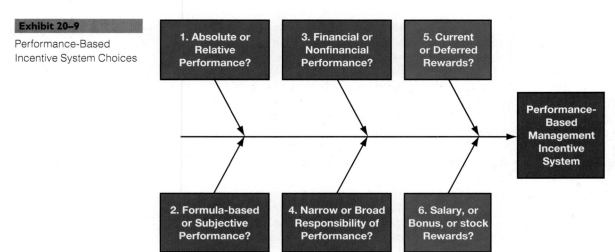

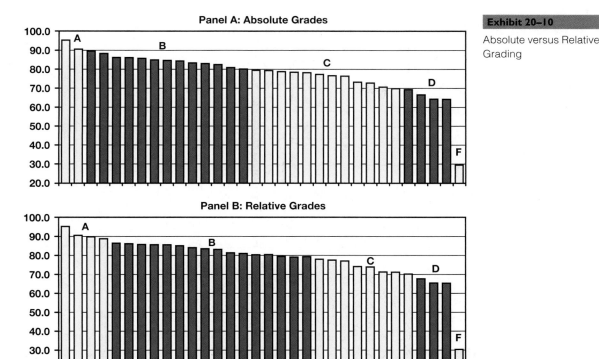

Exhibit 20–10

Absolute versus Relative Grading

a high grade. Thus, studying effort might be less in this situation than if the instructor graded on a relative basis, where final grades reflect relative performance on difficult exams.

Like other companies that use a relative performance evaluation, VCB *benchmarks* branch-bank performance with that of other banks in the same industry.[6] Thus, a branch that generated 3 percent revenue growth in a market where the average revenue growth was 4.5 percent might receive a lower evaluation than a VCB branch that earned 3 percent in a market with 2 percent average revenue growth. Just as grading on the curve shields students from the risk of an extremely difficult test, relative performance evaluation shields a manager from the risk of managing a division in a market that performs poorly. Relative performance evaluation also motivates high performance if the manager's division is in a market that performs well.

A disadvantage of relative performance evaluation is that it does not provide incentives for managers to move out of poorly performing markets into those that perform well. Why would successful managers in a poor market move to a more competitive market where relative performance evaluation makes the likelihood of rewards low? Furthermore, if good managers decide to move, they might have to work much harder for the same relative performance.

At VCB, top management believes that relative performance evaluation of some aspects of performance is effective. Using relative performance evaluation, top management assesses each branch bank's revenue growth performance relative to each other and to similar banks in the same market. The bank rewards the managers of branches with the highest relative revenue growth. This controls for unforeseen changes in business conditions that might affect all banks' revenue growth. Consider the relative evaluations in Exhibit 20–11. Using a set of comparative banks, VCB branches F, E, and B achieved below-average revenue growth, but VCB branches G,

---

[6] For a field study of companies using relative performance evaluation, see M. Maher, "The Use of Relative Performance Evaluation in Organizations."

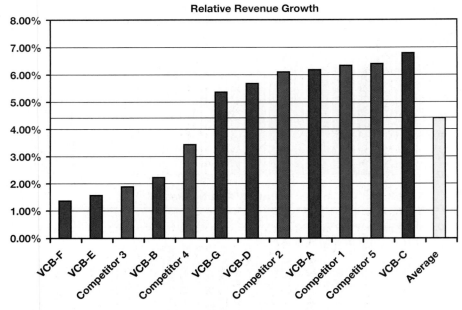

D, A, and C had above-average revenue growth. Thus, under the same conditions that all faced, branches G, D, A, and C outperformed the average.

Using relative performance evaluation allows VCB to avoid the difficult task of setting appropriate revenue growth objectives necessary for absolute performance evaluation. Unless the objectives are sufficiently difficult and accurately reflect future business conditions, the absolute objectives might be ineffective motivators. If they are set too high or business conditions deteriorate, managers perceive little chance of earning rewards. Conversely, if objectives are set too low or the business climate improves, managers can easily earn their rewards. In the first case, VCB misses opportunities for growth because managers do not try, and in the second case, it pays too much for less than best efforts.

Formula-Based or Subjective Performance

Some companies base rewards on a **performance evaluation formula,** which computes rewards earned for specific achievements. For example, VCB rewards revenue growth by paying branch managers a bonus based on the following explicit formula: For each percentage point by which revenue growth exceeds the market average, say 5 percent, the manager receives a bonus of 4 percent of his or her base salary. Thus, a manager knows, for example, that if her branch's revenue growth was 8 percent for a particular year (that is, three percentage points above the 5 percent threshold percent) and her base salary is $100,000 per year, her bonus is $12,000 (three percentage points times 4 percent per point times $100,000). A manager who did not meet the market average revenue growth rate receives no bonus.

> Target revenue growth for bonus = 5 percent per year
> Actual branch revenue growth = 8 percent per year
> Branch manager base salary = $100,000 per year
> Branch manager bonus = (8 − 5) growth points × (.04) × $100,000 = $12,000

This bonus is in addition to the manager's base salary. VCB included this incentive as part of its formula but rejected a formula-*only* approach to performance evaluation for branch managers as too restrictive to its culture and business climate. One consideration was that using only a formula penalizes managers assigned to problem branches, which VCB management believed is demoralizing and leads to unwanted loss of talented managers. Another factor that limited VCB's enthusiasm for using only an incentive formula was concern about setting the right formula parameters (e.g., average market growth and bonus percentage). Different parameters generate different incentives and might lead to different actions. Having diverse sources of compensation minimizes the risk of incentive-formula mistakes and allows for some experimentation with different formula parameters.

Formula-based evaluations importantly require measures that are accurate, reliable, and verifiable. Inaccurate, unreliable, or manipulated measures can create the opportunity for conflict over measured performance and incentives to cheat. Conflict and cheating might encourage eventual measurement improvements but can seriously impair the organization's performance while the inadequate measures are in place. Sometimes taking actions that improve the evaluation numbers but that are detrimental to the organization in the long run is possible (e.g., branch managers can add riskier customers to increase recorded revenues without adjusting for expected future losses). Organizations also can measure some areas of formula-based nonfinancial performance as reliably as financial performance, but most organizations historically have had more ability and need to measure and verify financial performance because of financial and tax reporting requirements.

Companies also may use **subjective performance evaluation** by using non-quantified criteria. The advantage of subjective evaluation is that it considers factors that a formula does not explicitly capture. For example, suppose that the sales growth of one of VCB's branches was below target because it serves a declining market. The bank wants to maintain a presence there, however, because the market area will be the focus of economic redevelopment activities by local and federal governments. Matching the future benefits and opportunity costs of this management decision in an explicit formula can be difficult. Subjective performance evaluation also can eliminate opportunities for "gaming" formula-based evaluations. Subjective evaluation can counter the tendency to manipulate the numbers in the formula. Recent financial reporting scandals have shown that these gaming motivations can be strong.

The advantage of a formula-based plan is that managers know precisely what is expected of them and what reward they will receive relative to expectations. The subjective approach is a less certain form of incentive plan and can be susceptible to favoritism, political maneuvering, and even a "good-old-boys" approach to incentive compensation. Incentive compensation might become a function more of how well superiors like managers than of performance, thus reducing the link between effort and reward. Employees often are comfortable with a subjective approach when they believe in upper management's ability, are willing to take some risks, and trust upper management. Otherwise, employees tend to prefer a formula approach.

An increasing number of organizations use elements of both subjective and formula-based incentives. For example, VCB rewards branch managers based on a formula that includes revenue growth, net interest margin, and return on net assets as well as subjective evaluation based on industry norms, a manager's level of responsibility, and the judged value of a manager's contributions.

Financial or Nonfinancial Performance

Financial performance reflects the achievement of financial goals, such as cost control, revenue growth, earnings, and residual income. Chapter 18 of this text provides extensive discussion of these performance measures, which we do not repeat here. Organizations that ostensibly measure performance with only financial or only nonfinancial performance measures could be found. Some profit-seeking firms apparently base rewards only on "bottom-line" financial performance. Some nonprofit organizations overtly reward only on the basis of meeting nonfinancial goals. However, nearly every organization really uses both financial and nonfinancial measures of performance. For example, in the most bottom-line-oriented corporation, an executive who exceeds financial goals will not last long after being convicted of a serious crime. Furthermore, the most altruistic, nonfinancial, nonprofit organization cannot tolerate an executive who repeatedly fails to operate within the organization's financial means or diverts the organization's funds for personal use. Financial and nonfinancial performance measurement is not an either-or issue but involves identifying which measures and what balance to use. We next briefly review financial performance measures.

Financial performance: Accounting measures or stock price?   Financial performance measures commonly include levels or growth of the following:[7]

- Revenues.
- Costs.
- Cash flow.
- Operating income (before or after extraordinary items, taxes).
- Return on investment (total assets, net assets, or equity).
- Residual income or EVA .
- Stock price.

All of these measures except stock price are explicitly based on accounting earnings-related numbers. The last three items are most commonly used to evaluate business-unit performance. VCB uses a mix of financial performance measures in its performance evaluations. Executives are evaluated on residual income, and branch managers are evaluated on net interest margin, return on assets, and revenue growth. VCB does not evaluate or provide incentives based on the bank's stock price because the bank feels that (1) the stock price normally is not directly controllable by managers and (2) basing incentives on stock price might cause undesirable consequences if managers tried to manipulate the stock price. VCB believes that stock price performance will follow financial performance.

Nonfinancial performance: operational, organizational, social and environmental factors. Evidence indicates that the use of nonfinancial measures of performance in incentive plans is increasing. Of course, organizations have used nonfinancial measures for managing operations for many years, but including them in incentive plans is an important development.[8]

Perhaps the greatest advantages of adding nonfinancial measures to the incentive system are (1) focus on the leading indicators of profit and (2) recognition of the time lags between nonfinancial and financial performance. Incentives based on nonfinancial performance direct employees' attention to leading activities more effectively than do indirect incentives based on lagging financial performance alone. Although employees might know that poor quality can surface later as lower profits, for example, the time lag and lack of direct effect can lower the belief that their quality-related actions affect performance. Value Commercial Bank evaluates nonfinancial performance for compensation, although it does so subjectively.

As with all aspects of incentive plans, however, nonfinancial performance measures have costs as well as benefits. Costs of including nonfinancial measures in incentive plans include these:

- Increased cost of performance measurement and supporting information systems.
- Increased cost of reporting and verifying the validity of performance measures.
- Difficulty in determining the proper balance between financial and nonfinancial measures.
- Danger of "information overload" from too many measures causing lack of focus on overall performance.
- Increased opportunities for disputes over the validity of performance measures.
- Increased opportunities for manipulating formula-based incentive plans that include multiple measures.

---

[7] Typically, growth is computed as follows, using annual revenue as an example: Revenue growth = (This year's revenue − Last year's revenue) ÷ Last year's revenue.

[8] See the beginning of this chapter and Chapter 7 for examples of commonly used measures.

Cost Management in Practice 20.3

Use of Nonfinancial Measures of Performance

Professors Ittner and Larcker of the Wharton School of Business have reviewed the findings of many surveys, cases, and field studies investigating firms' uses of nonfinancial measures of performance for both management activities and incentive compensation. They report that as many as 36 percent of firms explicitly include nonfinancial measures in executive incentive plans. On average, 37 percent of the total evaluation was based on these nonfinancial measures. Firms that use nonfinancial measures in their incentive plans tend to be more innovative, to have adopted TQM, to have long product-development cycles, to have been more subject to regulation, and to have had "noisier" financial performance. Thus, factors, such as innovativeness and adoption of TQM, apparently affect the use of nonfinancial measures of performance in incentive plans.

Nonfinancial measures of performance used most commonly in incentive plans include customer satisfaction, productivity, employee performance, community/environmental performance, and innovation. But Ittner and Larcker point out that very little objective research reflects whether using these measures in incentive plans results in better *long-term* financial performance. At this point, firms might be reluctant to disclose that they have found successful packages of measures; alternatively, they might include these measures based on the logic of linkages among leading and lagging indicators of performance rather than hard evidence. *Source: C. Ittner and D. Larcker, "Innovations in Performance Measurement: Trends and Research Implications." See also R. Banker, G. Potter, and D. Srinivasan, "An Empirical Investigation of an Incentive Plan That Includes Nonfinancial Performance Measures."*

If adding nonfinancial measures adds problems, why not use financial performance observed over a period of time long enough to capture the effects of nonfinancial performance?[9] One answer might be that nonfinancial measures can add value in excess of their costs. Another might be that although competition for managerial talent requires frequent evaluation and payment of compensation, financial performance cannot be matched to efforts in a timely manner. These answers might explain why many organizations have added nonfinancial performance measures to their incentive systems. For example, McDonald's evaluates and compensates many managers on nonfinancial performance, such as customer and employee satisfaction, social responsibility, and adoption of technology. The measures to use and the ways to include them in performance-based incentive plans are some of the greatest challenges of incentive system design, and more research is needed in this area.

Narrow or Broad Responsibility of Performance

An organization can define performance narrowly or broadly. Should a manager's rewards depend on the performance of that individual, of the manager's division, or of the company as a whole? For example, should VCB evaluate its branch managers based their performance on a set of personal goals, the performance of the manager's branch bank, or the performance of the bank as a whole? Basing compensation on only the performance of the company as a whole gives managers incentives to cooperate, share information, and consider the impact of their actions on the entire organization. This is especially important in large companies whose managers might not see much relationship between their actions and the company's performance.

Incentives work best, however, when individuals see a strong link between their actions and performance results (see the appendix to this chapter). Moving from incentives based on individual performance to companywide performance lessens an individual's influence on the performance measure. Many companies reward division managers for both business-unit and companywide performance, seeking a balance that is appropriate for their situations. VCB rewards *executives* based on overall bank performance. The bank strives to create incentives for cooperation among *branch managers* by linking some of their rewards to the bank's overall economic performance.

---

[9]A. Rappaport articulates this question in his book *Creating Shareholder Value.*

Microsoft Excel - VCB

File Edit View Insert Format Tools Data Window Help Acrobat

D12   = =IF(D8-D2>0,(D8-D2)*100,0)*D3*D6

	A	B	C	D
1	Financial Performance Bonus Parameters	VCB Residual Income	Branch Return on Investment	Branch Revenue Growth
2	Bonus target	$0	8%	4.4%
3	Bonus weight	0.002	0.03	0.04
4	VCB residual income	$800,000		
5		Branch A	Branch B	Branch C
6	Manager salary	$100,000	$100,000	$100,000
7	Return on investment	9%	10%	12%
8	Revenue growth	6.2%	2.2%	6.7%
9	Branch manager bonus			
10	VCB residual income, B3*IF(B4-B2>0,B4-B2,0)	$ 1,600	$ 1,600	$ 1,600
11	Return on investment, IF(B7-C2>0,(B7-C2)*100,0)*C3*B6	3,000	6,000	12,000
12	Revenue growth, IF(B8-D2>0,(B8-D2)*100,0)*D3*B6	7,200	-	9,200
13	Total bonus	$ 11,800	$ 7,600	$ 22,800
14				

Exhibit 21-4 / Exhibit 21-5 \ Exhibit 21-6 / YTDM 21.1 /

Ready

Consider the partial bonuses based on individual branch and overall bank financial performance shown in Exhibit 20–12. Note that each branch manager receives a $1,600 bonus based on VCB's overall residual income performance (row 10) computed as follows:[10]

$$\text{Residual income bonus} = \text{Residual income bonus weight} \times \text{VCB}$$
$$\text{residual income in excess of target}$$
$$= B3 * \text{IF}(B4 - B2 > 0, B4 - B2, 0)$$
$$= .002 \times (\$800,000 - \$0) = \$1,600$$

Current or Deferred Rewards

Employees prefer rewards sooner than later, but the organization often could benefit from waiting. Rewards for performance can be given now based on current performance or later on sustained performance. Current compensation rewards can be in the form of cash or stock that can be cashed immediately or soon after the award. For example, a manager might be rewarded quickly with a cash bonus if the residual income increases 10 percent by the end of the year or later on a deferred basis if the residual income increases by an average of 10 percent per year over the next three years. Thus, the company defers any rewards for the first and second years' performance until after the third year. An alternative is to grant the rewards now but restrict their payment until a future date. These deferred rewards can be cash or stock as well as stock options. We defer coverage of stock and option rewards to the next section.

Current rewards.   Current rewards have the obvious advantage of being closely linked to current performance. Because uncertainty related to current rewards is low, current rewards should provide strong motivation to improve current performance. The disadvantage of current rewards is that they can induce employees to manipulate the performance measures without concern for future performance or with the expectation of "cashing out" and leaving the organization before undesirable consequences occur.

Deferred rewards.   Advantages of deferred rewards based on sustained performance are that (1) good managers might have incentives to stay with the company (e.g., "golden handcuffs") and (2) managers have incentives to focus attention on long-term performance. Many commentators argue that managers, particularly in the United States, are too short-term oriented. They take actions now that look good in the short term but are detrimental in the long term. A good example is the failure of some companies to invest in new technology. This "myopic" view of performance keeps earnings high in the short term by avoiding write-offs or high depreciation expenses but can be detrimental in the long term. Switching to deferred rewards

---

[10] Note that the use of the "IF" function ensures a bonus *only if* residual income (B4) exceeds the target (B2). Other formulas compute bonuses based on branch performance in excess of targets in similar ways.

based on sustained financial performance can capture the lagged effects of good or poor nonfinancial performance and create incentives to make needed improvements.

A disadvantage of a deferred reward is that managers might view it as coming too far in the future to be motivational. Giving a manager a reward in stock to be paid five years from now is less attractive than giving a payment at the end of the current year.

VCB uses a combination of current and deferred awards for top managers but primarily pays current awards for lower-level managers and their subordinates. When making deferred awards to executives, the bank defers the award for three years. This time period appears to be sufficiently long (1) to capture lagged effects of actions and (2) to motivate the managers to think about the future but (3) is not so far in the future that incentive effects of the managers themselves are lost.

Salary, Bonus, or Stock Rewards

Most management incentive plans include multiple forms of reward, including salary, bonus, stock, stock appreciation rights, and stock options. Organizations design the reward package to address the motivational issues raised earlier in the chapter, within stockholder and taxation guidelines, and many have found that a combination of rewards is more effective than a single form of reward. Most large organizations have compensation committees that design the mix of rewards to reflect the company's compensation philosophy. Some organizations stress salary; others stress performance-based compensation to provide more motivation. For example, VCB states the following:

> One of the essential elements of the Bank's compensation policy is to align the interests of the CEO, executive officers, and key employees with the interests of stockholders. . . . The total compensation package is designed to provide a significant percentage of executive compensation from programs such as the bonus plan and stock-based long-term incentive programs, which link executive rewards to long-term shareholder rewards.

Salary.   Nearly all management employees work in exchange for some salary that is more or less guaranteed. Occasionally, an executive works without salary, but this usually is in exchange for stock or other deferred rewards or as a charitable contribution to a nonprofit organization. The typical salary issues are (1) the level of salary and (2) the proportion of compensation that is salary versus performance-based reward. Salary levels often are benchmarked with the organization's industry and the level of responsibility within the organization. At extremes, a manager receives 100 percent of his compensation from salary, or another manager receives 100 percent of her compensation based on performance. What difference does the proportion of salary make?

At 100 percent of compensation, a salary insulates an employee from most risks, so one might think that the employee will be inclined to make risky decisions. In reality, however, such compensation is more likely to attract employees who are not inclined to take risks. Furthermore, fixed compensation can turn away employees who recognize that their compensation has no upside potential regardless of their effort or ability to manage. Because most stockholders can diversify their investments, they prefer that managers take some risks, but they must compensate them for doing so.

One way to motivate risk taking is to shift some compensation from salary and make it depend on performance that is affected by managers' risky decisions. Making all compensation based on performance might not be desirable, however, because, as mentioned earlier, this places all of the risk on managers. The organization might attract only extreme risk takers or those who demand a large stake in the organization in exchange for the risk they must bear. Most organizations find a balance between guaranteed salary and performance-based compensation that attracts, retains, and motivates employees to make good decisions.

Cash bonuses.   Cash bonus awards have the advantage of being liquid and highly attractive because the reward is immediate and unconstrained. Companies usually make cash bonus awards based on the achievement of performance objectives. Often these bonuses have a floor or lower threshold of performance (e.g., a minimum return on investment) before the employee earns any bonus. Many cash bonus incentives also have a ceiling or an upper threshold beyond which no more bonuses can be earned. Much interesting research has focused on the motivational properties of these awards and the incentives they generate to manipulate financial measures of performance.[11]

Tying managers' incentive compensation to the company's stock performance has the obvious benefit of aligning managers' incentives with those of shareholders.

Stock awards.   Stock awards, in contrast to cash bonuses, might not be redeemable for cash until some time in the future. Some companies have an unwritten rule that managers cannot sell company stock until they leave the firm or retire. Stock awards that cannot be immediately sold, while perhaps not as attractive as an equivalent amount of cash, can align the interests of managers with those of shareholders better than cash awards can. For this reason, top-executive compensation often is composed more heavily of stock than of cash bonus or salary. (See Exhibit 20–8.)

Stock appreciation rights.   **Stock appreciation rights (SARs)** confer bonuses to employees based on increases in stock prices for a predetermined number of shares. For example, suppose you have been granted 10 SARs and the stock price increased $25. Your bonus would be equal to $10 \times \$25 = \$250$. This incentive combines the immediacy of a cash bonus with the long-term benefit to owners of increases in stock prices.

Stock options.   **Stock options** give an individual the right to purchase a certain number of shares at a specified price over a specified time period and provide strong incentives for managers to increase stock value over the long run.[12] A stock option has a lower monetary value than a share of stock, so a company might create more incentive to increase share prices by awarding stock options than simply awarding the same value and fewer shares of stock. Managers who receive large awards of stock options have much to gain from increases in share prices. This does not mean that managers lose nothing if the stock price declines, however, because the value of the options decline and managers suffer the opportunity cost of not increasing stock value (or earning an alternative cash bonus). Awards of stock options, therefore, have the motivational impact of stock grants but at a lower cost to the company. Despite the benefits of stock options, their use has declined in the years after the financial bubble burst in 2000.

In addition, sufficient concern now exists that stock-option awards give managers too much incentive to manipulate stock prices in the short run rather than build the company for the long term. A number of top US executives have tried recently to illegally manipulate stock prices but have found that getting caught means losing their reputation, wealth, and, in some cases, freedom. Perhaps when a climate of trust has been earned and then returns, firms will again base more compensation on stock

---

[11] A classic article is by Paul Healy, "The Effect of Bonus Schemes on Accounting procedures and Accrual Decisions."

[12] A readable article on stock options is "What You Need to Know About Stock Options" by B. Hall.

options. Until then, we should expect more stock awards and bonuses based on accounting and operating performance.

VCB rewards its branch managers with cash bonuses for meeting revenue growth, net interest margin, and return on net asset objectives. Executives also earn stock based on meeting overall residual income objectives. The proportions of executive compensation value have averaged 40 percent salary, 30 percent cash bonus, and 30 percent stock. At present, VCB does not extend significant long-term compensation to lower-level managers. Most of their compensation is salary and bonus based.

Ethical Aspects of Incentives and Compensation

Few people object to the concept and practice of pay for performance. Most people, however, object when pay is inconsistent with performance. For decades compensation experts have observed that executive pay often rises even in companies whose operating or stock price performance has dropped. Add extensive downsizing to this mismatch of pay and performance, and many see high executive pay as unethical and unfair to both stockholders and employees whose returns and pay have decreased. The mismatch of executive pay and firm performance has been widely observed in diverse organizations such as energy firms, telecommunications, charities, investment funds, and health care.

LO 7 Discuss ethical issues of incentive systems.

How can a mismatch between pay and performance persist? In some cases, the mismatch is the result of poorly designed incentive systems that generate high rewards even when stockholders lose money.[13] In other cases, critics blame rampant CEO greed and lack of oversight by stockholders' representatives on boards of directors.[14] Others like Graef Crystal cite lack of required disclosures and widespread corporate structures that leave compensation decisions in the hands of the CEOs themselves, who cannot be trusted to report performance fairly or be objective critics of their own performance and value to the firm.[15]

If managers really cannot be trusted, one might predict that many stockholders believe the worst and either do not purchase stock or discount the value of the stock for the amount of excessive pay. In fact, stockholders' fear of untamed executive behavior might explain why so many pulled their billions of dollars (or what was left) out of the stock market following the bubble burst in 2000. Concern for the integrity of the stock market and the well-being of the entire economy partly explains the origin of the Sarbanes-Oxley Act of 2002, which among other things places the responsibility for reported performance squarely on CEOs. The intent is that they can never again say, "I'm just the CEO. I don't understand the complexity of accounting."

In fairness, many organizations have restructured their incentive systems to better match pay and performance. For example, in a recent year, McDonald's did not reach its operating goals, and executives received no bonus compensation. Some firms restructured their systems voluntarily, but many others did so in response to increased disclosures required by 1992 SEC regulations and more recently the Sarbanes-Oxley Act of 2002.[16]

It is likely that these regulatory actions will more closely align executive pay and performance, but in the end it is difficult to mandate integrity or ethical behavior. The least costly economic system would be based on trust and integrity; however, that ideal state is contrary to human nature. The costs of aligning incentives and monitoring behavior are high, but the opportunity cost of allowing unethical behavior is higher. Unethical behavior will be a continuing problem, but the return of investors to the stock market might be a sign of increasing trust in improved pay for performance incentive systems.

---

[13] For example, see N. Mathiason, "Failing Fund Men Pile on the Pounds."

[14] V. Galloro and L. Benko, "Are They Worth It?"

[15] G. Crystal, "Why CEO Compensation Is so High"; M. Jensen and K. Murphy, "CEO Incentives—It's Not How Much You Pay, but How."

[16] See K. Lo, "Economic Consequences of Regulated Changes in Disclosure: The Case of Executive Compensation." Interestingly, Lo found that managers of firms whose stockholders had the most to gain from improved incentive systems were most likely in 1991 to lobby against increased disclosures of their pay.

Incentive Plans in Nonprofit Organizations

Nonprofit organizations range from small, informal organizations such as sports clubs, student organizations, and parent groups supporting sports and music activities to large, well-established organizations such as the United Way, the American Red Cross, most universities, and government departments and agencies, such as the US Postal Service, the Department of Transportation, and the Environmental Protection Agency. By definition, a *nonprofit organization* has something other than earning a profit as its primary goal. Thus, effective nonprofit incentive systems primarily should create incentives for managers to perform well on nonfinancial dimensions.[17]

Although nonprofits do not try to maximize profits, they must provide services in a cost-effective manner. Nonprofits compete for scarce funds and nonmonetary support and must be able to show donors and supporters that their contributions are being used effectively. *Smart Money* magazine, for example, annually analyzes the efficiency of charitable organizations. Thus, a nonprofit's concern for creating value at lowest cost can be similar to that of a profit-seeking firm. Nonprofit organizations also must demonstrate proper accountability for the use of funds and manage their operations and revenues to ensure that they break even.

Despite differences between for-profit and nonprofit organizations, nonprofits increasingly use features of executive incentive plans developed in the private sector. These organizations also compete for top management talent and must align executives' interests with those of the organizations. Many nonprofit organizations award performance bonuses up to 10 percent of salary. Some nonprofit hospitals offer performance bonuses based on cost savings, health care improvements, and other factors. Many organizations, however, decline to develop incentives to retain management talent only to find that they must pay much more to replace talent lost to the private sector or more aggressive nonprofits.

Incentive plans also can create difficulties for nonprofits. For example, Harrisburg Hospital in Pennsylvania lost its nonprofit, tax-exempt status in part because the state's courts ruled that its executive compensation plan, which gave cash bonuses for return on equity and revenue performance, clearly was designed to promote the hospital's bottom line. The court observed that, although incentive plans were not contrary to the notion of a nonprofit organization, this incentive plan aligned managers' interests more with earning profits than providing charitable health care services. The incentive plan was convincing evidence that the hospital had a strong profit motive.[18]

You're the Decision Maker 20.2

Designing Incentive Systems

You are a consultant advising Valley Commercial Bank about its incentive systems for lower-level managers and employees. Your interviews with branch and department managers inform you that they are satisfied with the new balanced scorecard performance measurement system (see Exhibit 20–6) but believe that they are not rewarded for performing well. Nonmanagement employees likewise enjoy their jobs but do not believe that they have real incentives to work harder or better. At the end of each year, most branch and department managers and employees receive annual salary increases between 4 percent and 6 percent. Branch managers also earn bonuses up to 10 percent of their salary for meeting sales growth and return on asset objectives. Promotions appear to be based on seniority; the longer a person is in a job, the better the person's chances for promotion. Do the interview responses signal a potential problem? If so, what do you think that VCB should do?

(Solution begins on page 857.)

---

[17] For a comprehensive treatment of management control in nonprofit organizations, see R. N. Anthony and D. W. Young, *Management Control in Nonprofit Organizations.*

[18] *Harrisburg Hospital v. Dauphin County Board of Assessment Appeals*

Summary of Valley Commercial Bank's Incentive System

Incentive system designers should consider each element of Exhibit 20–9 to ensure that the plan addresses all alternative choices. To sum, VCB seeks to attract, motivate, and retain competent employees and to align their interests with shareholders' long-term interests. The bank's incentive system has the following features:

- *Absolute or relative performance.* VCB uses both forms of performance: Residual income and environmental performance are compared to absolute objectives; evaluations of revenue growth, net interest margin, and return on assets are based on relative performance of similar business units.
- *Formula-based or subjective performance.* VCB also uses both formula and subjective evaluations. Residual income, net interest margin, and return-on-asset incentives for branch managers are formula based, but the bank subjectively evaluates other areas of performance that are measured less reliably (e.g., the value of employee suggestions).
- *Financial or nonfinancial performance.* As mentioned, VCB uses only financial performance measures in its formula-based incentive plans. The bank understands the value of its nonfinancial performance for long-term success, but quality of measurement is an issue. If the bank could reliably measure key nonfinancial performance from its balanced scorecard, it would formally include some of them in its formula-based incentives. Until then, VCB will continue to evaluate nonfinancial performance subjectively. Top candidates for inclusion in the incentive formula include employee satisfaction, productivity, and customer satisfaction because they are based on reliable instruments and can be audited.
- *Narrow or broad responsibility of performance.* VCB evaluates its executives on bankwide performance but its branch managers primarily on branch performance, with a relatively small emphasis on bankwide performance.
- *Current or deferred rewards.* VCB executives receive both current and deferred rewards; lower-level managers receive mostly current rewards.
- *Salary or bonus rewards.* All VCB employees receive a salary, but executives receive most of their compensation from bonus or stock rewards. Currently, lower-level managers receive most compensation from salaries, and lower-level employees receive all compensation from salaries.

Although VCB has put much effort into designing its incentive plans, every plan can be improved. The bank's board of directors annually reviews it in light of recent developments and changes in competitive pressures and recommends improvement. Current recommendations include refining some nonfinancial performance measures for inclusion in the bank's incentive formulas. The bank's president and CEO also serves on the boards of directors of several charitable, nonprofit organizations and has been urging their boards to adopt features of the incentive plans of VCB and other successful companies.

Balanced Scorecard–Based Incentives

If the performance measures in Exhibit 20–6 are important to VCB's success, employees should take actions to improve each of them and they should be in the scorecard. The issue is whether employees will do that without explicit incentives attached to each measure. Perhaps, if employees believe the story that a balanced scorecard tells, as discussed earlier, they will manage their activities to improve the measures with or without explicit incentives.

Without explicit incentives, an organization must be sure that employees understand how performance on these measures affects the financial results and that rewards and penalties will result from successful financial performance. Removing rewards one or more levels of activity away from an individual's actions can reduce the rewards' effectiveness, however. As a result, the success story told by a balanced scorecard's measures must be repeated again and again until it is part of the organization's culture. In some organizations this can be as effective as creating explicit incentives. However, organizational culture is difficult to change, so an organization might find it difficult to revise the story of success if needed.

Extending a balanced scorecard to an evaluation and incentive system involves two additional steps:

- Weighting the performance measures.
- Tying explicit incentives to measures (individually or in total).

Performance on each measure in the system should have rewards. It does seem likely that no one person or management level should be evaluated on all of the measures, however. That can lead to information overload and unreasonable expectations for the influence one person can have on overall performance. A more reasonable approach is to assign responsibility and incentives for the various measures to persons who can best affect or control outcomes. Some organizations also assign overall scorecard incentives to managers at higher levels to reinforce the goal to ensure that subordinates are working to improve the measures they directly control. The nature of the incentive system (measures and rewards) will differ according to the organization.

Effective incentive systems usually require reliable, objective, and verifiable performance measures and clear guidance for evaluating trade-offs. Because the primary purpose of a balanced scorecard is to communicate and implement strategy, many organizations have not resolved these incentive issues. Partly as a result, some companies experienced significant internal conflict when they began to use a balanced scorecard as an incentive device. In a few cases, these companies have dispensed with a balanced scorecard altogether, but in others the conflict has led to compromises and improvements in performance measures and internal auditing procedures.

Because VCB's balanced scorecard had no major surprises and most employees can see the rationale behind each scorecard area and its measures, almost no debate about the scorecard itself occurred. Employees at all levels understand that the scorecard is a balanced set of measures that reflects the bank's strategy to grow and prosper. Bank employees report that they understand why and how their efforts can improve the bank's financial performance. This was a major improvement in the communication of the bank's strategy and led employees to focus on improving the measures that they can influence.

Although none of the performance measures was perfect, top management believed that using them for performance evaluation reinforces the desired behavior and generates superior profitability. However, many employees express concern about the use of the scorecard as a fomula-based evaluation and incentive system because they believe that some measures are too subjective or capable of manipulation. They wonder how they should act when faced with trade-offs between measures that might conflict (e.g., reducing costs or improving customer satisfaction) and whether they will be penalized for making trade-offs. Because VCB's employees trust top management and are comfortable with some subjective evaluations, the bank has been able to coordinate its formula-based and subjective evaluations (as discussed earlier) with the use of a balanced scorecard for communication, motivation, and evaluation. As in nearly all organizations, VCB's balanced scorecard and incentive system continue to evolve and improve.

Chapter Summary

Leading indicators of performance are early measures of outcomes of activities that allow organizations to predict problems, identify opportunities, and prevent mistakes. Leading indicators predict organizational outcomes such as customer satisfaction and future sales. Employees use leading indicators to manage activities and processes to ensure favorable final outcomes. Employees act to make improvements based on signals from leading indicators rather than wait to see whether final outcomes are favorable or unfavorable before making improvements or corrections.

Organizations use performance measures of (1) organizational learning and growth, (2) business and production processes, and (3) customers as leading indicators of (4) financial performance.

A balanced scorecard is a model of cause-and-effect relations among leading and lagging indicators of performance. It is useful for measuring and communicating the effects of activities on organizational performance. A balanced scorecard shows the cause and effect among these four areas of performance. One can think logically of performing well on learning and growth as leading to improved business processes and improved customer satisfaction and loyalty, which leads to improved financial performance. Various linkages exist among the four areas, but the point is that performing well on the three leading (usually nonfinancial) areas should lead to improved financial performance and that financial performance lags nonfinancial performance. If it is possible to quantify these cause-and-effect relationships, a balanced scorecard can be a valuable financial planning model.

The two key elements of an incentive system are the *measure(s) of performance* and the *method(s) of compensation.* Managers make many choices regarding incentive systems. These choices regarding performance evaluation include whether to rely on measures of current or future performance, whether to use division or companywide performance measures, whether to base performance on accounting results or stock performance, and whether to use absolute or relative performance evaluation. Furthermore, these choices include whether to base rewards on a subjective evaluation or a fixed formula and whether to reward good performance with cash, stock, or prizes. The objective of designing incentive plans is to select a package of performance measures and rewards that will attract, motivate, and retain good employees and align their interests with those of the organization.

Appendix to Chapter Twenty

Theories of Incentives and Behavior

We discuss two views of incentives and human behavior that address key parts of incentive systems, expectancy and agency theories of motivation and incentives. These are not opposing views, but they stress different aspects of motivation and behavior. Together, they provide a relatively complete picture of the nature of incentives that motivate behavior.

LO 8 Understand three theories of motivation and incentives.

Expectancy Theory of Motivation and Incentives

Expectancy theory explains that people are motivated by monetary or nonmonetary incentives to act in ways that they expect to provide them the rewards that they desire and to prevent the penalties that they wish to avoid.[19] This theory's roots are in organizational psychology. To motivate people to behave in a particular way, incentive plans must do two things:

1. Provide desirable rewards or undesirable penalties.
2. Provide a high probability that behaving as the organization desires will lead to those rewards or penalties.

That is, the incentive plan provides *expectancy* that desired behavior leads to desired rewards. For example, the goal of a course of study is to disseminate or acquire knowledge. The incentive system to motivate achievement of that goal is a system of grades awarded for examination performance. It is fair to assume that high grades are desirable, so the reward itself is in place. What if the instructor's exams—the measures of performance—are so unrelated to the material being studied that there is a low probability that studying will improve exam scores? Expectancy theory predicts that students will not be motivated to study by this incentive system because they believe that studying has a low probability of improving test scores. Thus, neither the instructor nor the students will achieve the goal of learning—acquiring knowledge through study—because the incentive plan does not provide sufficient expectancy that rewards will be related to studying.

---

[19] T. B. Green, *Performance and Motivation Strategies for Today's Workforce: A Guide to Expectancy Theory Applications.*

Exhibit 20–13   Expectancy Theory, Incentives, and Motivation

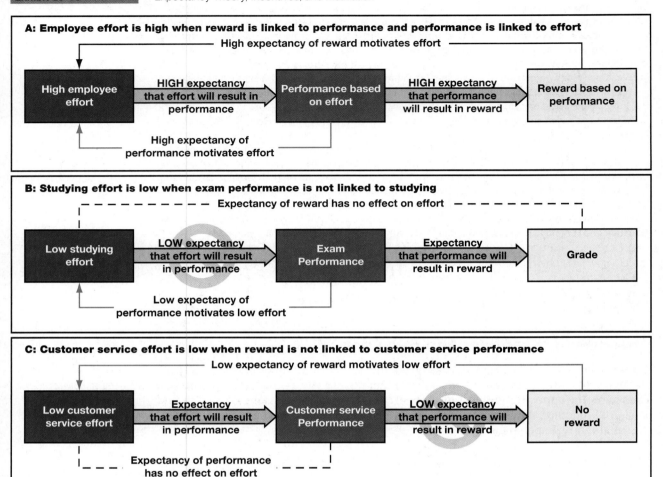

A: Employee effort is high when reward is linked to performance and performance is linked to effort

High expectancy of reward motivates effort

| High employee effort | → HIGH expectancy that effort will result in performance → | Performance based on effort | → HIGH expectancy that performance will result in reward → | Reward based on performance |

High expectancy of performance motivates effort

B: Studying effort is low when exam performance is not linked to studying

Expectancy of reward has no effect on effort

| Low studying effort | → LOW expectancy that effort will result in performance → | Exam Performance | → Expectancy that performance will result in reward → | Grade |

Low expectancy of performance motivates low effort

C: Customer service effort is low when reward is not linked to customer service performance

Low expectancy of reward motivates low effort

| Low customer service effort | → Expectancy that effort will result in performance → | Customer service Performance | → LOW expectancy that performance will result in reward → | No reward |

Expectancy of performance has no effect on effort

Valley
COMMERCIAL BANK

Expectancy success and failure.   Exhibit 20–13 reflects the basic elements of expectancy theory. Panel A shows the ideal incentive system: Effort is high when employees have a high expectancy that their efforts affect performance *and* that the performance will be rewarded appropriately. The feedback arrows in panel A reflect that both of the high expectancies reinforce the motivation to exert effort. Panel B, however, shows a breakdown in the incentive system. This is the situation describing students exerting low study effort if they have a low expectancy that studying will affect exam performance. The promise of a high grade based on high performance has no effect because the link in the expectancy chain between studying and exam performance has broken. Some incentive systems' expectancy chains are broken at the link between performance and reward; still others are broken at both links.

Expectancy theory and VCB's old incentives.   Panel C of Exhibit 20–13 applies expectancy theory to customer service activities at VCB before improving the incentive system. Top management wants to improve customer relations and for several years has gathered measures of customer satisfaction using customer-satisfaction questionnaires about the bank's services. (You might have completed these in assessing restaurant or hotel quality and service and in evaluating your instructors.) At one time the bank provided no rewards to employees for efforts that build customer satisfaction. As shown in panel C of Exhibit 20–13, expectancy theory explains why VCB's employees were not motivated to build customer satisfaction: They were not rewarded for it. (This does not consider personal rewards that might have come from employees' interactions with the customers.) Consequently, VCB probably did not have as many satisfied customers as it might have had with a better incentive plan.

Recently, to promote customer satisfaction, the bank began to reward employees if customers are satisfied with the services they receive. This makes the incentive system more like panel A of Exhibit 20–13. Because VCB management and employees believe that good service is likely to build customer satisfaction and customer satisfaction predictably leads to rewards, this incentive system promotes the desired behavior.

Extrinsic and intrinsic rewards.   **Extrinsic rewards** come from outside the individual from teachers, parents, organizations, or partners and include grades, money, praise, and prizes. **Intrinsic rewards,** on the other hand, come from within the individual, such as the satisfaction from studying hard, the feeling of well-being from physical exercise, the pleasure from helping someone in need, or the satisfaction of doing a good job. Getting an A on an exam is an extrinsic reward; satisfaction with your performance is an intrinsic reward.

Although VCB originally did not reward its employees for building customer satisfaction, the employees might have received an intrinsic reward, such as internal satisfaction from providing good service. They also might have been rewarded with thanks and affection from loyal customers, which are also extrinsic rewards, but not from the bank. By adding extrinsic rewards to the incentive plan, VCB reinforced existing rewards and increased the likelihood that employees would work to improve customer satisfaction by increasing the expectancy of rewards from desired behavior.

People receive many intrinsic and extrinsic rewards. Teachers and caregivers, such as nurses, often work for wages less than their ability and effort can command because they receive intrinsic rewards from the work. In addition, many people volunteer their services not only because of the intrinsic rewards but also for the extrinsic rewards—praise and gratitude—they receive. These are factors to consider in designing incentive systems. Some jobs inherently have more rewards than others do, and what people consider to be rewards differs. Some are motivated mostly by money; others are more motivated by public praise.

One size does *not* fit all. Creating incentives tailored to each individual is difficult for most organizations. However, improving everyone's opportunities for intrinsic rewards from desired behavior by making work interesting might be possible. Ensuring that extrinsic rewards are distributed fairly and based on the terms of the incentive plan is also important. To augment rewards from the job, many organizations encourage employees to seek intrinsic (satisfaction) and extrinsic ("volunteer of the month") rewards by donating their time to charitable work; some companies even allow employees to take some time from their jobs for charitable work.

An effective incentive plan considers opportunities for both intrinsic and extrinsic rewards and penalties and allows opportunities for variations, particularly of intrinsic rewards. Effective motivation usually requires a balance between extrinsic and intrinsic rewards, but the balance point varies with the organization and the people it attracts and retains.

Goal-setting theory.   Related to incentives is *goal-setting theory,* which is perhaps the most thoroughly tested incentive theory.[20] Goal-setting theory has established the following conclusions:

- Impossible goals all but eliminate motivation because people realize that the desired performance and rewards cannot be achieved, regardless of effort.
- Easy goals reduce motivation to the minimum necessary to achieve them. Easy goals create lost opportunities to create more value at lower cost.
- Difficult but attainable goals consistently create the most motivation, effort, and lead to the highest level of performance compared to either impossible or easy goals.

---

[20] E. A Locke. and G. P. Latham. 1990. *A Theory of Goal Setting and Task Performance.*

Agency Theory of Incentives and Behavior

Agency theory is an economic concept of incentives and behavior based on the relationship between a principal (e.g., employer) who offers an incentive plan (or contract) and an agent (e.g., employee) who accepts the contract to work on behalf of the principal. In agency theory, incentive plans serve four purposes: they (1) improve organizational success by (2) motivating the employee to work, (3) by aligning the employee's goals with the employer's goals, and (4) allocating decision authority. A corporation such as VCB, for example, exhibits multiple principal–agent relationships, which include the following:

Principals	Contract	Agents
VCB shareholders	Rewards ↔ Oversight of management	VCB board of directors
VCB board of directors	Rewards ↔ Strategic management of VCB	VCB top management
VCB top management	Rewards ↔ Operational management of branch banks	VCB branch managers
VCB branch managers	Rewards ↔ Performance of branch-bank activities	VCB branch employees

VCB employees are agents of branch managers, who are agents of top managers at bank headquarters, who are agents of the board of directors and shareholders who own the company. Note that most employees have both a principal role and an agent role. What binds them together is an enforceable incentive plan or contract; principals offer rewards in exchange for making specific decisions.

The focus of expectancy theory and agency theory differs, but they complement each other. *Expectancy theory* focuses on the characteristics of the incentive plans that motivate people whereas *agency theory* focuses on the contracting behavior between principal and agent. In a sense, they are two sides of the same coin. Applied to organizational settings, expectancy theory seeks to understand the types of performance measures and rewards that motivate employees. Agency theory, on the other hand, assumes that both principals and agents want to maximize their rewards at minimum cost, but they need each other.

The principal provides the work and the rewards, which the agent does not, but the agent has the ability to do the work, which the principal does not. However, each has an opportunity cost in most cases: The agent can work elsewhere, and the principal can put her money in the bank and earn interest. The principal wants to maximize her profits, which includes minimizing incentive costs, and the agent wants to minimize his effort to earn a market wage. The incentive plan needed to bring them together at least meets both parties' opportunity costs, aligns both parties' goals, and clearly describes the decisions to be made.

Improper incentives can cause misbehavior.   Agency theory is complicated by the reality that once employed, employees do not necessarily behave in the ways that their employers desire. Furthermore, because any measure of performance is imperfect, neither party can regard the incentive system as entirely fair. Employers might suspect undetected manipulation of performance measures, and employees might resent the risk imposed on them by imperfect measures. The employer could respond with other constraints on or monitoring of behavior at work. Employees might believe that working at a more leisurely pace, surfing the Web instead of working on company projects, or loafing with their friends at work are fair. Some employees even have incentives to steal more than time from the company. Furthermore, some employees might not have the skills or knowledge that they professed when they were hired or that they should maintain to stay employable at their current pay. All of these result in costs—lost opportunities to create value—for the employer and the employee. The incentive system not only must motivate employees to work but also must be designed so that employees' rewards are fair and contingent on the organization's meeting its goals.

Minimizing agency costs with incentives and monitoring.   The principal seeks to minimize total **agency costs,** which are the sum of opportunity costs of misbehavior and out-

of-pocket costs for incentives
and monitoring performance.
The incentive plan must
attract and motivate qualified
employees to behave according to the organization's
goals, but doing this costs
money for paying employees
and for monitoring to ensure
that performance measures
are valid. These payments
reduce the value left for principals, so they seek to minimize them. A company might
spend so much money on
incentives and reporting
(e.g., bonuses, accounting
reports, internal audits) that
no employee will ever do

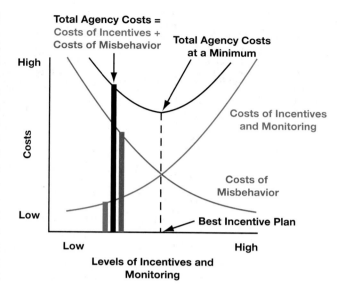

Exhibit 20–14

Best Incentive Plans
Minimize Total Agency
Costs

something that is not in shareholders' interests—and no qualified employee will submit to these working conditions. However, such actions are unlikely to be economical given the high costs of the incentives and reporting compared to the opportunity
costs of misbehavior. As Exhibit 20–14 shows, the best incentive plan trades off the
costs of administering alternative incentive plans against the costs of misbehavior. The
best incentive plan is not the one that drives the costs of misbehavior to zero (far right),
nor is it the one that spends the least on incentives and reporting (far left). The best plan
is located between these extremes, reflected by a "level" of incentives and monitoring on
the X-axis. In theory, this is the mix of incentives and monitoring mechanisms that minimizes total agency costs. Agency theory shows that the "perfect" incentive system is too
expensive and that some level of employee misbehavior is desirable; the overall best
system is a result of evaluating trade-offs.

Changes to reduce agency costs.   All organizations experience some agency costs.
According to agency theory, organizations change their incentive plans when they
perceive an opportunity to reduce total agency costs. For example, VCB's board of
directors realized that the bank's incentive system motivated managers to minimize
current spending and cut staff rather than to build customer satisfaction. Bank managers were "playing by the rules," but the incentive plan directed them to act in a way
that was not in the long-term interests of the bank's shareholders. One agency cost
identified was a loss of profits because the bank was losing dissatisfied customers.
Note that this also hurt employees because the bank was less profitable. As described
in the body of the chapter, VCB changed the incentive system to include rewards for
improved customer satisfaction because the bank believed the cost of the new incentive system was less than the lost profit from losing dissatisfied customers.

Key Terms

For each term's definition, refer to the indicated page or turn to the glossary at the end of the text.

absolute performance evaluation, 838	customer value, 828	lagging indicator, 821	relative performance evaluation, 838
agency costs,* 854	employee capabilities, 824	leading indicator, 820	stock appreciation rights (SARs), 846
agency theory,* 854	expectancy theory,* 851	pay for performance, 835	
balanced scorecard, 820	extrinsic rewards,* 853	performance evaluation formula, 840	stock options, 846
customer retention or loyalty, 828	Incentive system, 820		subjective performance evaluation, 841
	intrinsic rewards,* 853		

*Term appears in the Appendix.

Meeting the Cost Management Challenges

1. **How** does a balanced scorecard differ from the measures of organizational cost and performance, which have been used for as long as organized companies have existed? What does it add that previous measures did not?

A balanced scorecard is a cost-management tool that is gaining in popularity. Its validity as a guide for managers' strategic choices and operating actions depends on the validity of the leading and lagging relationships that are built into this tool. A valid balanced scorecard predicts the financial outcomes of actions taken to improve performance in organizational capabilities and learning, business and production process efficiency, and customer value. Previously, managers and employees understood intuitively that all activities affect bottom-line profitability, but a balanced scorecard can both display and measure cause-and-effect relations among important activities. This creates a credible "story" about the way that the organization can succeed that perhaps only top managers understood before. Use of a balanced scorecard can help all employees appreciate how their activities affect the bottom line.

2. **Should** Valley Commercial Bank design its incentive system to increase customer satisfaction? Is it possible to overstress customer satisfaction?

VCB should measure customer satisfaction and reward employees who enhance it. There is a saying that "what gets measured gets noticed." Measurement by itself is a strong motivator. Having customers complete satisfaction surveys and tracking complaints are ways to measure customer satisfaction. It is important for bank employees to see how effort leads to performance and how performance leads to rewards. The bank should reward performance that leads to customer satisfaction, including the performance of employees who do not have direct contact with customers. For example, maintenance employees keep the place clean, which enhances customer satisfaction. Bank management should note that rewards are not necessarily limited to pay and promotions. Praise is an excellent reward.

It is possible to overstress customer satisfaction by losing sight of the costs to provide it. Therefore, any incentive plan should include incentives for customer satisfaction and other drivers of bank profits. The trick is to balance these incentives so that the overall result is improved long-term profitability.

3. **How** can Valley Commercial Bank or any organization weigh the trade-offs of various incentives for improving financial performance?

This obviously is a key issue. Why develop a performance-based incentive plan unless it is going to improve financial performance (assuming a profit-seeking firm)? Otherwise, this is just another non-value-added activity that should be eliminated. Managers can never know in advance whether a package of incentives will be worthwhile, but several sources of information can help. First, a manager's own knowledge of the organization and the drivers of its success can lead her to identify the most important measures of performance. Second, benchmarking current incentive plans against those of the competition or "world-class" organizations might show opportunities for adopting new measures and rewards that will be successful. Reputable consultants also have a wealth of knowledge about the determinants of successful incentive plans their clients use and might be able to predict how different features are likely to work with or against each other to affect financial performance in your situation. Many organizations treat new incentive plans, such as new products or services, and test them on subunits as prototypes for the rest of the organization. That way, management can learn how the measures and rewards work, what trade-offs they require, and how they affect financial performance without risking mistakes that affect the whole organization.

Solutions to You're the Decision Maker

20.1   Designing a Balanced Scorecard   p. 823

a. Financial measures indicate how well the organization has done in the past whereas nonfinancial measures indicate future success. Organizations that perform well on the nonfinancial performance measures should have financial success in the future. Therefore, directing employee attention to nonfinancial areas, such as improving business efficiency, should result in future financial success. In addition to these advantages, most employees can relate better to nonfinancial performance measures. For example, it is easier for a supervisor to think about training employees well and reducing employee turnover than to think about increasing return on investment.

b. The company will incur considerable costs to design and implement a balanced scorecard. The company should specify its vision and strategy (if it has not done so), develop nonfinancial performance measures, design an information system to collect the nonfinancial performance data, collect data, use the data to evaluate performance, and provide rewards and penalties based on such performance evaluation. The benefits are improved organizational performance, which might be difficult to measure. Management will have to decide whether the benefits outweigh the costs, which are easier to measure. Note that there is a high start-up cost; the benefits generally come later.

c. You want somebody on the team who is well respected by top management because their buy-in is important. This would be someone who has "the ear of top management," so to speak. The team should include someone who understands each of the four areas; someone with financial expertise; someone who knows what is needed to generate customer satisfaction; someone who understands the operations of the airline who can improve business processes; and someone who knows how to link learning and growth to the other areas. That team should presumably include people who know both marketing and operations very well. Inclusion of someone who knows the industry to help benchmark Singapore Airways with competitors will be helpful. The team should include employees who are respected by their peers and who are creative and willing to take risks.

20.2 Designing Incentive systems, p. 848

This incentive system appears to have a problem. The bank seems to have convinced these employees that a balanced scorecard's measures are appropriate for their activities. This is an important step in instituting any performance-measurement system. The bank appears not to do well, however, in linking rewards to performance at all levels. Executives can be motivated by overall bank performance and the attendant bonus and stock awards, but lower-level employees do not have the same reward system or motivation; the expectancy chain is broken at the link between performance and reward. This can create a problem causing lower-level employees to seek their own rewards in ways that are detrimental to the bank. For example, they might spend excessive time on personal business or surfing the Web when they should be working to improve their knowledge, internal processes, or customer satisfaction. They might understand that their actions are detrimental, but they also might believe that out of a sense of fairness, they have a right to steal time and effort from the bank. As long as they do not shirk so much that they get fired, their salaries and annual raises appear to be secure.

You might recommend setting up an incentive plan that provides bonuses for performance on each of a balanced scorecard's measures for lower-level employees who can affect those measures (if appropriate). The bonuses can be cash, prizes, or stock (depending on the management level of the individual and the interests of the particular employees). Lower-level employees might be more motivated by prizes; branch and department managers might be more motivated by cash and stock. The bank should include incentives to focus on the future, especially for managers, so at least some of the rewards should be deferred and based on future performance. Overall performance should combine individual and organizational performance so employees see the payoff of their own individual actions as well as take actions that benefit the organization as a whole.

Review Questions

20.1 Review and define each of the chapter's key terms.

20.2 What is the difference between a *leading* and a *lagging* indicator of performance?

20.3 How can employee capabilities be measured? Why is this important for improving efficiency, identifying opportunities, and preventing mistakes?

20.4 How can improvements in employee capabilities affect process efficiency.

20.5 How can improvements in process efficiency affect customer value.

20.6 How can improvements in customer value affect financial performance.

20.7 Is financial performance important to all types of organizations, even nonprofits? Explain.

20.8 What is the difference between a set of leading and lagging indicators and a balanced scorecard?

20.9 Explain differences in balanced scorecards for profit-seeking and nonprofit organizations.

20.10 Explain how an increase in employee capabilities can flow through an organization and how the effects are reflected in a balanced scorecard.

20.11 Why is "pay for performance" the foundation of incentive systems?

20.12 What are the key elements of an incentive system?

20.13 Explain how an incentive system's design might create disincentives to desired behavior.

20.14 What is the starting point in designing an effective incentive system?

20.15 Contrast absolute and relative performance evaluations.

20.16 What are the advantages and disadvantages of formula-based versus subjective performance evaluations?

20.17 What is the possible relation between a balanced scorecard and the use of financial and nonfinancial measures of performance?

20.18 What are the advantages and disadvantages of narrowly defining performance for evaluations? Of broadly defining performance?

20.19 What are the advantages and disadvantages of making all rewards immediate and of deferring them?

20.20 What are the different incentive effects of salary, cash bonus, stock, and stock options?

20.21 (Appendix) What are the two ingredients of a successful incentive system according to expectancy theory?

20.22 (Appendix) Explain how the expectancy chain can be broken, which reduces the effectiveness of an incentive system.

20.23 (Appendix) What is an intrinsic reward? How is an intrinsic reward different than an extrinsic reward? Are both necessary?

20.24 (Appendix) What are the roles of an incentive system according to agency theory?

20.25 (Appendix) According to agency theory, what is the best incentive system?

Critical Analysis

20.26 The chief operating officer of a nonprofit organization states, "It's all very well for a company like Sears to implement a balanced scorecard. It has measures in all four areas of the scorecard and has to satisfy stockholders. Without a profit measure or motive in the last area of the scorecard, I just don't see how or why we should expend the effort to build a partial balanced scorecard." How do you answer this observation?

20.27 A business executive says, "The financial area of a balanced scorecard indicates how the organization adds value to shareholders. I am involved with two organizations; a small business that is a partnership with no shareholders, and a church that has no shareholders. A balanced scorecard makes a lot of sense to me, but the financial area is clearly irrelevant for these two organizations." How do you respond to this statement?

20.28 Respond to the following statement: "Most measures of performance, such as profits and product costs, are useless for management decision making because they measure what has happened, not what will happen."

20.29 Until recently the CEO of Xerox Corporation prominently stated in his letter to the company's annual reports that Xerox always strives to improve customer satisfaction. Xerox no longer makes this claim so prominently. Is it possible to create too much customer satisfaction? Explain.

20.30 Customers' perceptions of value can differ across cultures. Many people believe that US–based companies are ignorant or arrogant when it comes to appreciating other cultures. Do you think this is true? What are the possible costs of lack of appreciation of other cultures? How can you prepare yourself to contribute value to an organization by appreciating other cultures?

20.31 Westinghouse Corporation formerly advertised that its employees are its most important assets. If that is true for Westinghouse (and presumably for other organizations, too), why does its balance sheet (and presumably those of other organizations) not have a category of assets for employees?

20.32 "It is a bigger mistake to develop an unreliable balanced scorecard than never to build one at all." Do you agree with this statement? Why or why not?

20.33 (Appendix) The manager of an organization is having trouble getting employees to perform adequate work for the organization's benefit. "I pay them a good salary," says the manager, "and I give them big pay increases when I feel generous. I just can't figure out why they won't work harder. Maybe it's this generation of people. You know, when I was a young worker . . ." At this point, your brain shuts down. Using the principles of expectancy and agency theories, explain why the employees might not be working as desired.

20.34 (Appendix) Shauna Dormino is taking a job in a non-profit organization, Freedom from Hunger. Anisa Morenez is taking a job at IBM. The women are equally qualified, each will do the same type of work, and each will put in the same number of hours each week, yet Dormino's job pays $20,000 less than Morenez's job, has fewer benefits, and offers less opportunity for advancement. Why might Dormino take such a job?

20.35 You are offered an executive position at a small high-technology company. The salary is considerably lower than your current salary, but after one year, you will be eligible for many stock options. Your only performance measure will be the company's stock price. What are the advantages and disadvantages of this incentive plan to you and to the company?

20.36 You are offered the general manager position at a large, mostly autonomous division of a very large company. The company is market driven and has 20 similar divisions in different industries. The division you are offered has performed poorly in the past, but it is in an industry with high profit potential. Describe elements of an incentive plan that induces you to take this job and that the company might accept.

20.37 You are the chair of the board of directors of a large regional charitable organization that has been recognized nationally for outstanding public service. It has just lost its CEO to a profit-seeking firm poised for its initial public offering of shares. You must convene the board to recruit a new CEO and are concerned about attracting, motivating, and retaining a highly competent executive. What major factors should you consider when designing an incentive plan for this executive?

Exercises

Exercise 20.38
Classify Balanced Scorecard Measures
(LO 2)

Match each of the following performance measures to one or more of the four areas of a balanced scorecard. Note that a performance measure can relate to more than one area.

Performance Measures

Employee productivity

Employee satisfaction

Return on assets

Customer satisfaction

Employee turnover

On-time delivery performance from suppliers

Percent of customers who are repeat customers

On-time delivery performance to customers

Product quality

Balanced Scorecard Areas

Organizational learning and growth

Business and production process efficiency

Customer value

Financial performance

Exercise 20.39
Classify Balanced Scorecard Measures
(LO 2)

Match each of the following performance measures to one or more of the four areas of a balanced scorecard. Note that a performance measure can relate to more than one area.

Performance Measures

Throughput time

Return on sales

Customer satisfaction

Percent of sales dollars invested in employee training

Ratings of supplier performance

Increase in market share

Employee retention

On-time delivery performance to customers

Product quality

Balanced Scorecard Areas

Organizational learning and growth

Business and production process efficiency

Customer performance

Financial performance

Arrange the following measures in an order that reflects their possible use as leading or lagging indicators of performance. Note that a measure of performance can itself be a leading indicator of later performance.

Customer satisfaction	Anticipation of customer needs
Acquisition of new customers	Product quality
On-time deliveries	Process efficiency
Customer retention	Employee satisfaction
Customer profitability	Employee skills
Product innovations	Compliance with environmental regulations
Market share	Supplier reliability and quality
Overall profitability	

Exercise 20.40
Match Leading and Lagging Indicators
(LO 1)

Perform an Internet search for a comprehensive article on a real organization's management of organizational learning and growth. Prepare a five-minute presentation (with transparencies or PowerPoint slides) of your findings and how they relate to the chapter's coverage of this topic.

Exercise 20.41
Describe Measures of Organizational Learning and Growth
(LO 2)

Review the Forms 10-K or annual reports for the following companies (*Hint:* Use the SEC's EDGAR database.) Summarize how each of the following organizations manages customer satisfaction: Goodyear Tire & Rubber, a tire manufacturer; Abercrombie & Fitch, an apparel retailer; and Southwest Airlines, an airline company.

Exercise 20.42
Management of Customer Satisfaction
(LO 2)

Review the Forms 10-K or annual reports for one company from each of the following industries: auto manufacturing, coffee and tea, and life insurance. (*Hint:* Use the SEC's EDGAR database.) Summarize how each of these organizations manages customer satisfaction.

Exercise 20.43
Management of Customer Satisfaction
(LO 2)

Perform an Internet search for a comprehensive article on an actual organization's management of customer satisfaction or cultural differences. Prepare a five-minute presentation (with transparencies or PowerPoint slides) of your findings and how they relate to the chapter's coverage of this topic.

Exercise 20.44
Describe Balanced Scorecard Measures
(LO 2)

Trust Bank conducts regular customer surveys to assess its customer satisfaction, which is measured by averaging responses (from 1 = highly unfavorable to 5 = highly favorable) on five variables that measure customers' satisfaction with the bank's services. Quantify Trust Bank's recent customer satisfaction from the following information. Do you see a pattern in the scores? If so, what does it tell Trust Bank about its customer satisfaction?

Exercise 20.45
Prepare Customer Satisfaction Measure
(LO 2)

Customer Satisfaction Variable Response	Number of Customer Responses				
	1	2	3	4	5
Automated bank services meet customer needs	16	25	22	22	15
Trust Bank services are superior to competitors' services	8	17	24	36	15
Employees give prompt service	6	14	22	41	17
Employees are courteous and friendly	7	12	20	38	23
Employees can and do respond to special requests	12	26	20	21	21

Exercise 20.46
Prepare Customer
Satisfaction Measure
(LO 2)

Montpelier Co. conducts regular customer surveys to assess customer satisfaction with its products and postsale services, which is measured by averaging responses (from 1 = highly unfavorable to 5 = highly favorable) on five variables that measure customer satisfaction with the company's products. Quantify Montpelier's recent customer satisfaction from the following information. Do you see a pattern in the scores? If so, what does it tell Montpelier about its customer satisfaction?

Customer Satisfaction Variable Response	Number of Customer Responses				
	1	2	3	4	5
Montpelier's products are defect free	20	21	22	22	15
Montpelier's products are superior to competitors' products	8	17	24	36	15
Montpelier's products perform reliably	6	14	22	41	17
Montpelier's repair services are prompt	7	12	20	38	23
Montpelier's warranty is superior to competitors' warranty	12	21	20	26	21

Exercise 20.47
Implementation of
Balanced Scorecards
(LO 4)

In a small group, conduct an Internet search for an article published in the past three years that describes how a real organization successfully designed and implemented its balanced scorecard. Prepare a five-minute presentation (with transparencies or PowerPoint slides) of your findings and how they relate to the chapter's coverage of this topic.

Exercise 20.48
Implementation of
Balanced Scorecards
(LO 4)

In a small group, conduct an Internet search for an article published in the past three years that describes how an organization *unsuccessfully* designed or implemented its balanced scorecard. Prepare a five-minute presentation (with transparencies or PowerPoint slides) of your findings and how they relate to the chapter's coverage of this topic.

Exercise 20.49
Effects of Performance-
Based Incentive Plans
(LO 5)

Wannabe University (WU) is a medium-size public university with 15,000 students and 1,000 faculty members. The university built its national reputation on the excellence of its teaching and interactions with undergraduate students. Because government support of the university has dropped dramatically, the administration has decided that it must now build the university's reputation on research, which will require obtaining research grants to replace the lost government funding. The university proposes to reward each faculty member with a salary increase that is primarily based on the annual number of articles they publish in high-quality journals. Most faculty members and students were attracted to WU, however, because of its focus on teaching and faculty/student interaction.

Required
In a small group, prepare a brief report or visual presentation to WU's central administration that explains the advantages and disadvantages of its incentive plan proposal.

Exercise 20.50
Alternative Features of
Incentive Plans
(LO 6)

Magnum Manufacturing rewards its key executives exclusively on return on investment (ROI). The vice president of administration suggests to the CEO that Magnum can increase its ROI by outsourcing most of its manufacturing and logistics activities to business partners and suppliers, thereby greatly reducing its asset base. The CFO/treasurer cautions that although this would reduce the company's asset base, such extensive outsourcing would reduce the company's earnings, cash flow, and flexibility. The vice president of manufacturing also warns that the company might outsource its competitive advantage as well.

Required

In a small group, prepare a brief report or visual presentation to Magnum Manufacturing's CEO that evaluates the impact of the company's incentive plan on the recommendation to outsource most activities. What trade-offs should the company's executives consider?

Problems

eToys, Inc., had been one of the leading Internet-based retailers of children's toys. However, in 2001 it generated a large loss, its stock price plummeted, and it declared bankruptcy. KB Toys purchased the company's website, a warehouse, and its customer list for $15 million. The following table summarizes some of the causes of the eToys financial disaster.

Problem 20.51
Balanced Scorecard Measures
(LO 2)

Problem	Solution	Lesson
Loss of control over shipping and late shipments resulting from outsourcing some order fulfillment	Opened two additional warehouses, staffed entirely by eToys employees	Provide the best service to customers by keeping the work in-house
Severe seasonal peaks and drops in revenue	Expanded into baby supplies, party goods, and hobbies	Diversify while staying true to the target market
Serious doubts on Wall Street that the company can turn a profit and survive	Held first-ever analysts' conference, committed to profitability by a specific target date	Communicate with the people who hold the purse strings even when the news is not positive

Required

a.   In your opinion, what types of employees and what specific skills should KB Toys develop and maintain if it is to avoid the fate of eToys?

b.   Write a memo outlining the steps you think KB Toys should take, including the development of leading indicators of employee capabilities.

[Adapted from A. Weintraub, "For Creditors, the Toy Chest is Empty" *Business Week*, September 23, 2002.]

As prices for many items have stabilized because of competition, some Internet-based retailers now are competing on the basis of real-time customer service provided by live company representatives. These e-tailers report improved customer satisfaction, traffic, and sales growth that they attribute to real-time customer service. Whether this improved customer satisfaction and sales growth has led to improved profitability is unclear. Consider the following actual and predicted data for HomeMarket.com, which is contemplating adding real-time customer service, through online chat technology

Problem 20.52
Benefits and Costs of Balanced Scorecard Measures
(LO 3)

Current data:

Annual sales	$11,000,000
Average cost of sales as percent of sales	60%
Sales growth percent	3%
Predictions related to new customer service:	
Increase in customer satisfaction	5%
Software and training costs for new customer service	$300,000
Ongoing operating costs for new customer service	$2,500,000
Cost savings from reduction of email response service	$100,000
Additional sales growth	20%

Required

a.   Identify the costs and benefits of HomeMarket.com's proposed customer service operation. (Ignore taxes.)

b.   *Build your own spreadsheet.* Use a spreadsheet to thoroughly analyze the profitability of the proposed customer service operation. Be prepared to present your analysis.

[Adapted from T. Mullaney, "Needed: The Human Touch."]

Paragon Sports, a major sporting goods retailer, is considering upgrading its customer-support activities by improving online databases and training of customer-service personnel. Consider the following data:

Problem 20.53
Benefits and Costs of Balanced Scorecard Measures
(LO 3)

Current data:

Annual sales $15,000,000

Average cost of sales as percent of sales... 60%

Sales growth 4%

Predictions related to new-customer service:

Increase in customer satisfaction 10%

Software and training costs for new customer service $300,000

Ongoing operating costs for new customer service $400,000

Cost savings from reduction of email response service $100,000

Additional sales growth.. 6%

Required

a. Prepare an analysis of the costs and benefits of Paragon Sports' proposed customer-service improvements. (Ignore taxes.)

b. *Build your own spreadsheet.* Use a spreadsheet to thoroughly analyze the profitability of the proposed customer-service operation. Be prepared to present your analysis.

Problem 20.54
Costs and Benefits of
Balanced Scorecard
Measures
(LO 3)

mhhe.com/hilton3e

Bonanza Real Estate is considering enrolling in Rush Corp's Customer Value Seminar, a $2,000 per person, week-long intensive seminar that teaches sales staff to build customer satisfaction and loyalty and to sell products more effectively by understanding customers' needs. Rush Corp advertises a money-back guarantee if its sales seminars do not pay for themselves in increased profits so long as new employees also are trained. Bonanza will send its entire sales force of 100 to the seminar in the current year and its new employees each year thereafter for five years. The company normally experiences annual turnover in sales personnel of 20 percent; its annual cost of capital is 10 percent.

Required

What equal, annual net benefit must Bonanza Real Estate experience to validate Rush Corp's money-back guarantee over this six-year period? (Ignore taxes.) Prepare a spreadsheet analysis of the costs and benefits of Bonanza's proposed customer service improvements. Be prepared to present your analysis.

Problem 20.55
Costs and Benefits of
Balanced Scorecard
Measures
(LO 3)

Quattro Drive is considering improvements to its warehousing and distribution operations including a $400,000 purchase of robotic machinery with a useful life of five years. Other improvements entail the installation of new computing equipment and software at a start-up cost of $250,000 and $75,000 per year for the next five years. Employee training costs will increase by $40,000 this year and remain at that level for the next five years. The firm's annual cost of capital is 8 percent.

Required

What equal, annual net benefit must Quattro Drive experience over the current and next five years to justify the process improvements? (Ignore taxes.) Prepare a spreadsheet analysis of the costs and benefits of Quattro's proposed process improvements. Be prepared to present your analysis.

Problem 20.56
Measuring Leading and
Lagging Performance
(LO 1, 2)

Ruth Chambers, an executive in a large bank, recently attended a conference on management in the banking industry. At the conference, a Citibank manager presented a diagram similar to the one in Exhibit 20–2. Chambers is intrigued by the performance measurement problems posed by the diagram. She asks, "How do you measure the performance of each step in the sequence from increased employee training to better financial results?"

Required

Using a balanced scorecard as a reference point, write a report to Chambers that explains how to measure performance for each step in the sequence from increased employee training to better financial results.

Problem 20.57
Implementation of
Balanced Scorecards
(LO 4)

Branford San Miguel, the managing partner of the Melbourne office of the consulting firm of PriceCoopersErnst (PCE) developed a diagram similar to the one in Exhibit 20–2 for a client who owns a small manufacturing company. The diagram had the following links:

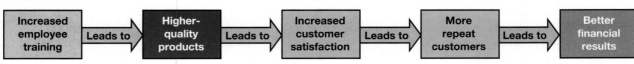

Afterward, San Miguel commented to his fellow consultants, "I wish I could apply this model to our consulting business. But what we produce is advice, which is not very tangible."

Required

In a small group and using a balanced scorecard as a reference point, write a report to San Miguel that explains how to implement the model shown in the problem to the consulting business. Be specific in stating how to measure the performance of each step in the sequence from increased employee training to better financial results.

Sheila Mack, an owner of 42 fast-food franchises, has come to you for advice. She wants to try a balanced scorecard in her stores. She is concerned because some attempts to implement improvements in the past have not been successful. "I've heard store managers say, 'Somebody must have gone to a conference or read some book, because here comes another crackpot idea for us to implement. If we just play along for a while, this too will pass. Then we can get back to business as usual.' I don't want store managers to think a balanced scorecard is just another fad. I want them to take it seriously. I want them to give it a fair trial."

Problem 20.58
Implementation of Balanced Scorecards
(LO 4)

Required

Write a short report to Mack advising her how to implement a balanced scorecard so that her store managers will give it a fair trial.

In a small group, select a real organization of any type for study. Review the organization's website and/or annual report. For each of the four balanced scorecard areas of performance, identify no more than four performance measures. Write a report that states specifically how you plan to measure performance. How might you validate these measures? If possible, you might find it useful to interview a manager in the company that you pick.

Problem 20.59
Identify Balanced Scorecard Measures
(LO 2)

One of your suppliers comes to your next meeting in a new Cadillac Escalade, mentions new membership to an exclusive country club, and has started to build a lake house.

Problem 20.60
Leading Indicators of Fraud
(LO 3)

Required

a. Obtain and read the article by Strand et al., "Are Your Vendors Stealing from You?" *Strategic Finance,* Oct. 2000.

b. Write a memo that explains how the information in the article can be used to develop leading indicators of problematic supplier relations.

Obtain and read the classic article by S. Kerr, "On the Folly of Rewarding A While Hoping for B." *Academy of Management Executive,* 1995, Vol 9. No 1.

Problem 20.61
Unintended Consequences of Incentive Systems
(LO 5)

Required

a. Explain the apparent reasons that the phenomenon of "Rewarding A While Hoping for B" is so prevalent in incentive systems.

b. Describe an example of "Rewarding A While Hoping for B" from your own experience.

Despite conflicting evidence and opinions about the causes of global warming, it is happening. Furthermore, institutional investors and insurers are getting nervous about the environmental disasters that might follow.

Problem 20.62
Leading and Lagging Indicators of Casualty Losses
(LO 1)

Required

a. Obtain and read the article by Sarah Murray "Investors and Insurers Face Up to the Impact of Climate Change and Subsequent Environmental Disasters," in the *Financial Times,* October 16, 2003.

b. Explain how large investors and insurance companies might use leading indicators of global warming to improve investing and managing risks.

Problem 20.63
Analyze Alternative
Incentive System
Features
(LO 6)

Valley Commercial Bank wants to reward its branch bank managers for exceeding revenue growth targets and is considering alternative incentive formulas that award bonuses as a percentage of salary for each percentage point that actual revenue growth exceeds the target as follows.

Formula Parameter	Alternative 1	Alternative 2
Revenue growth target	5%	10%
Bonus percentage	4 percentage points	8 percentage points

Required

a. Compute and then contrast the bonus earned by a branch bank manager with an average salary of $65,000 per year and branch revenue growth of 8 percent with each of the *four* combinations of formula parameters.

b. What are the motivational advantages and disadvantages of each of the four incentive formulas?

c. What are the advantages and disadvantages of the incentive formula approach to motivating revenue growth?

Problem 20.64
Analyze Alternative
Incentive System Factors
(LO 6)

PMI wants to reward its operations managers for reducing the number of defects below target rates. It is considering alternative incentive formulas that award bonuses as a percentage of salary for each percentage point that actual defect rates are under the target as follows.

Formula Parameter	Alternative 1	Alternative 2
Defect rate target	1%	4%
Bonus percentage	5 percentage points	8 percentage points

Required

a. Compute and contrast the bonus earned by a manager with an average salary of $87,000 per year and a defect rate of 2 percent with each of the four combinations of formula parameters.

b. What are the motivational advantages and disadvantages of each of the *four* incentive formulas?

c. What are the advantages and disadvantages of the incentive formula approach to motivating reduction of defects?

Problem 20.65
Using Performance
Measures as Leading
Indicators
(LO 1, 2, 6)

mhhe.com/hilton3e

Valley Commercial Bank has a criterion to loan only to companies that have an economic value added greater than zero for the past year and for the past three years, on average. Answer the following questions.

a. The bank is considering loaning money to a small company that has the following economic characteristics. Does this company meet the bank's criterion for a positive economic value added?

   ■ Average operating income before tax for the last three years equals $1,500,000 per year.

   ■ The tax rate equals 35 percent for all three years.

   ■ The appropriate weighted-average cost of capital equals 15 percent, which is applicable to all three years.

   ■ The average total assets over the past three years equal $7,000,000.

   ■ The average current liabilities over the past three years equal $1,000,000.

b. You work as a loan officer for VCB. A prospective borrower who just graduated from college has come to you for advice. Because her father had been seriously injured in an automobile accident, she is now running the family business, which is a small winery. She wants to borrow money from VCB to buy some wine-processing equipment that will make the company more efficient. The winery had been profitable in the past, but at this point, its economic value added, according to VCB's calculations, is $(120,000) for a company that has revenue of $6,000,000 and total assets of $4,000,000. Ordinarily, the bank will not loan her the money to buy the new equipment. Assume the same cost of capital and tax rates as in part (a). What do you advise?

Problem 20.66
Ethical Impacts of
Alternative Incentives
(LO 6, 7)

Division managers of Atlantis, Ltd., have expressed dissatisfaction with the company's division performance measurement system. Division operations are evaluated every quarter by comparing their EVA with the expected EVA identified in the prior year. Division managers claim that many factors are completely out of their control but are included in this comparison, which they say results in an unfair and misleading performance evaluation.

Pressure by top management to reflect increased earnings has often caused division managers to overstate operating income before taxes. In addition, once the EVA target has been set, divisions must live with it; no adjustments for unforeseen events are possible. Frequently, external factors (the economy, competitors' actions, and changes in consumer tastes) have not been recognized in the EVA targets that top management supplied to the divisions.

Recognizing these problems, top management agreed to review its procedures. Based on this review, it proposed to change its procedures so division managers have the opportunity to show how they deal with unforeseen events. Top management also agreed to use relative performance evaluation by comparing each division's performance to the performance of other divisions in the same industry and to the performance of outside companies in the same industry.

Required

Write a report to Atlantis top management that explains whether the proposed changes are an improvement over the evaluation of division performance that it now uses. Be sure to address how the company proposes to implement relative performance evaluation.

[CMA adapted]

Many critics of business executives complain that they focus on short-term financial results at the expense of investing in the long-term success of their companies. Executives themselves comment that they are constantly pressured to meet annual or even quarterly earnings targets. One executive said, "If I don't perform well in the short term, I won't be around in the long term." The critics argue that focusing on the short term means that companies do not invest enough in research and development or new technology, things that might have a negative short-term impact on earnings but might benefit the company in the long run. For purposes of answering these questions, assume that the short term is one year or less, the middle term is one to five years, and the long term is more than five years.

Problem 20.67
Ethical Impacts of
Alternative Incentives
(LO 6, 7)

Required

Prepare a written report that addresses the following:

a. Based on library and/or Internet research, indicate whether these organizations appear to be focusing on the short, middle, or the long term: Toys "R" Us (toys), Cisco (Internet hardware and software), and United Way (charitable nonprofit).

b. What is your recommendation for the design of an incentive plan that helps the top executives in requirement (a) to make long-term decisions?

Leslie Fay, the dressmaker, had a compensation plan that offered the chief operating officer and the chief financial officer bonuses if the company's net income reached $16 million (approximately 2 percent of sales). The company reported a net income of $23 million, and the two executives received bonuses. However, much of the net income was fraudulent, resulting from recording sales that had not occurred. The fraud occurred away from corporate headquarters in New York at the company's Wilkes-Barre, Pennsylvania, office where the company's finances were handled. Leslie Fay's chief financial officer set up an autocratic rule in Wilkes-Barre. The chairman and chief executive officer of the company, who was paid $3.6 million, mostly in the form of a bonus, said he was bewildered by the accounting scandal.

Problem 20.68
Ethical Impacts of
Alternative Incentives
(LO 6, 7)

Required

a. What effect might the bonus plan for the chief operating officer and chief financial officer have had on the fraud, if any?

b. How might the location of financial operations in Wilkes-Barre, Pennsylvania, instead of at corporate headquarters in New York have made it easier for someone to commit fraud?

[Adapted from "Loose Threads: Dressmaker Leslie Fay Is an Old-Style Firm That's in a Modern Fix," *The Wall Street Journal*, February 23, 1993: A1, A20.]

Perform an Internet search to investigate the goals, objectives, and incentive systems used by Patagonia, CitySoft, Working Assets, and Pride Industries.

Problem 20.69
Ethical Impacts of
Alternative Incentives
(LO 6, 7)

Required

Write a short report that list the organizational goals, objectives, and any disclosed information on incentive systems for each.

Problem 20.70
Ethical Impacts of
Alternative Incentives
(LO 6, 7)

Obtain a copy of the article, "Whistle-Blower Woes," *CFO Magazine,* October 2003, by Alix Nyberg. Prepare a short report that discusses the interactions of executive compensation plans, financial fraud, whistle-blowing, and the Sarbanes-Oxley Act of 2002.

Problem 20.71
Ethical Impacts of
Alternative Incentives
(LO 6, 7)

Obtain copies of the articles, "Blind Ambition," *BusinessWeek,* October 23, 1995, and "Judgment Day at Bausch & Lomb," *BusinessWeek,* December 25, 1995. Write a short report that outlines allegations of financial fraud caused by financial performance pressures at Bausch & Lomb, Inc.[21]

Problem 20.72
Ethical Impacts of
Alternative Incentives
(LO 6, 7)

M. Payne reports that employee theft costs US businesses billions of dollars per year and is growing at 2 percent per year.[22] Obtain a copy of the articles "Are You Teaching Your Employees to Steal?" *Strategic Finance,* August 2000: 34–39 by Gary Zeune, and "A Radio Chip in Every Consumer Product" by C. Deutsch and B. Feder, *The New York Times,* February 25, 2003: C1.

Required

Prepare a short report that identifies common organizational practices that either deter or encourage employee theft.

Problem 20.73
Analyze Alternative
Incentives
(LO 6)

Nantucket Market wants to reward revenue growth by paying its 50 store managers a bonus based on an explicit formula: For each percentage point by which revenue growth exceeds target growth, the manager receives a bonus of 1 percent of his or her base salary. Nantucket Market's corporate annual revenue growth target is 30 percent, but half of that is expected from acquiring or opening new stores. Store managers' salaries average $40,000 per year but range from $30,000 to $60,000. In the prior year, existing stores' revenue growth averaged 12 percent but ranged from 22 percent to 118 percent.

Required

a.   At the average store manager salary and average store revenue growth levels, what are the expected individual and total bonuses earned with a 10 percent growth target and a 6 percent bonus percentage?

b.   If Nantucket Market's average gross margin percentage is 20 percent, by how much must corporate sales increase to at least pay for the revenue growth bonus incentive computed in requirement (a)?

c.   Compute the individual and total bonus earned and required revenue increase for each of the 16 combinations of incentive formula parameters: 10 or 15 percent growth targets, 12 or 18 percent actual store growth, 2 or 6 percent bonus, and $30,000 or $60,000 salary. Note that the number of possible parameters and combinations is nearly unlimited. (*Hint:* Use a spreadsheet to compute these bonuses.)

d.   Make a recommendation to Nantucket Market about how to design its revenue growth incentive formula. How should the company create incentives for managers whose stores do not qualify for the revenue growth bonus?

Problem 20.74
Analyze Alternative
Incentive System
Features
(LO 6)

Contaminant Measuring Devices (CMD) wants to reward on-time deliveries to customers by paying its 10 department managers a bonus based on an explicit formula: For each percentage point by which on-time deliveries exceed the target, the manager receives a bonus of 1 percent of his or her base salary. CMD's corporate annual on-time delivery target is 85 percent. Store managers' salaries average $60,000 per year but range from $50,000 to $80,000. In the prior year, the company's on-time delivery rate averaged 90 percent but ranged from 75 percent to 98 percent across departments.

---

[21] Bausch & Lomb's troubles also are the focus of Harvard Business School case 9-198-009.

[22] M. Payne, "Employee Theft a Rising Concern," *Sacramento Bee,* December 3, 2000.

Required

a. At the average store manager salary and average department on-time delivery rate, what is the expected individual and total bonus earned with an 85 percent on-time delivery rate target and a 10 percent bonus percentage?

b. CMD's average gross margin percentage is 65 percent. If a 1 percent annual increase in on-time deliveries is expected to increase revenues by $100,000, by how much must the corporate on-time delivery rate increase to at least pay for the on-time delivery rate bonus incentive computed in requirement (a)?

c. Compute the individual and total bonus earned and required on-time delivery rate increase for each of the 16 combinations of incentive formula parameters: 85 or 95 percent on-time delivery rate targets, 92 or 98 percent actual on-time deliveries, 5 or 10 percent bonus, and $50,000 or $80,000 salary. Note that the number of possible parameters and combinations is nearly unlimited. (*Hint:* Use a spreadsheet to compute these bonuses.)

d. Make a recommendation to CMD about how to design its on-time delivery rate incentive formula. Include in your recommendation how the company should create incentives for managers whose stores do not qualify for the revenue growth bonus. Approximately 3 percent of late deliveries have been attributed to failures by the delivery company used by CMD.

Cases

"All this talk about developing leading indicators of our process performance and customer needs is really missing the mark," argued Ronald Melcher, the executive vice president of marketing for Industrial Foods, Inc. (IFI), which provides food items for airline kitchens. "What we need most are leading indicators of what Fulsome Foods, our chief competitor, will do. I know a very capable corporate intelligence [CI] firm that will find out pretty much everything we need to know and do it very discreetly."

Harold Baum, IFI's CEO, agreed, "I don't ever want to be in a fair fight. I want an edge everyplace I go. What type of information do you have in mind?"

"Well, how about how Fulsome makes decisions on pricing? I'm thinking that if we knew who has to approve price cuts and how long it takes them to make those approvals, we can find the right time, say when those people are out of town, and ambush them by offering serious discounts to their customers. We can have the price cuts in place before they can respond. We can snare some serious market share."

"Wait just a minute, fellows," cautioned Kerry Kahaner, IFI's chief financial officer. "I assume you know that industrial espionage is now a federal crime, and we can land in jail for 15 years and pay $10 million in fines for spying on our competitors."

"Calm down, Kerry, nobody's talking about doing anything illegal here, and besides, we won't be doing it. That's what consultants are for," explained Melcher. "The CI firm I am talking about, New World Intelligence, assures me that what they do is legal, although some of their tactics stray into gray areas. But it's their necks on the line, not ours. We just tell them what we want to know, and they generate the report."

"And send us a hefty bill for their efforts," retorted Kahaner. "Still, I want a better idea of their methods and possible results before I sign on. Do you have any examples, Ron?"

"As a matter of fact, I read about one recent example in *BusinessWeek*. New World Intelligence (NWI) saved Monsanto over $80 million in advertising planned to combat sucralose, Johnson & Johnson's new competitor to Monsanto's artificial sweetener, Nutrasweet. NWI got information from inside the US Food & Drug Administration (FDA) that, even though Canada approved sucralose, it was unlikely that the FDA ever would. And you know what? The FDA still hasn't approved sucralose. Monsanto would have wasted $80 million without NWI. Wouldn't you buy information that can save $80 million? That's what I call a useful leading indicator."

Required

a. Search your library or the Internet to find information on the practice, ethics, and legality of corporate intelligence.

b. Based on your research, how do you advise the management team of Industrial Foods regarding its plans to use corporate intelligence? In particular, what is your opinion of Ronald Melcher's plan?

c. Some argue that the use of corporate intelligence is common practice in Asia and Europe and that US firms are foolish not to use it and use it as thoroughly as their international competitors. Others, including E. A. Kampouris, CEO of $5.2 billion American Standard, Inc., disagree. He stated, "This is not warfare. I don't consider our competitors as communists or Hitler." Prepare a memo to IFI management explaining your stand on the use of corporate intelligence.

[Adapted from "They Snoop to Conquer," *BusinessWeek*, October 28, 1996.]

Case 20.75
Corporate Intelligence and Leading Indicators of Performance
(LO 1, 7)

Case 20.76
Implementation of
Balanced Scorecard
Measures
(LO 2, 3, 4)

"I am really confused," sighed Brian Allen, the CFO of a newly formed biotechnology firm. "I think we need to build a balanced scorecard to guide our decision making and to help us see whether we are meeting our goals, but everything I have read about balanced scorecards makes me wonder whether we, as a small company, can really build one. I don't think we can afford to waste the time if we can't do it.

"Here's an article in *Fortune* that implies that a balanced scorecard is essential, but professors and businesses using scorecards can't agree whether the relationships must be quantified or not. Professor Shank said great companies 'don't talk profits, they talk key drivers [leading indicators].' He seems to be saying that managing the lead indicators will leading to improved profits but that you don't necessarily need a quantified relationship to know that. On the other hand, Professor Selden says in the article that you have to begin with financial measurements; otherwise, how can you be sure that doing more of something really will add value? And the example companies are all large and well established, like Shell Oil, Motorola, and Analog Devices. If everything has to be quantified, we won't be able to build a useful balanced scorecard. After all, we have existed as a company for only two years, and how much data can we have?"

You reply, "I've just seen another article by Professor Chow that indicates even small companies can use a balanced scorecard. From the examples in this article, I'm not sure that you have to be able to quantify scorecard relationships to build a useful scorecard. Look at this scorecard for another biotechnology company. I imagine that its information needs must be similar to yours, Brian."

Refer to the goals and objectives in the following example scorecard.

Example Scorecard

Objectives	Measures
Goal: Increase Customer Value	
New products	Percent of sales from new products
Early purchase of seasonal products	Percent of sales that are early purchases
Accurate invoices	Percent of error-free invoices
Early payment	Percent of customers that pay early
Product quality	Product performance vs. industry standards
Customer satisfaction	Customer-satisfaction surveys
Goal: Improve Business and Production Process Efficiency	
Low-cost producer	Product cost vs. competitors' product cost
Inventory reduction	Inventory as a percent of sales
New products	Number of new product introductions
Goal: Leading by Innovation	
New active ingredients	Number of new ingredients
Proprietary products and processes	Number of patents
Goal: Financial Performance	
Growth	Percent increase in revenue
Profitability	Return on equity; earnings per share
Industry leadership	Market share

Required

Write a report in which you do the following:

a. Expand on "your" comment; do balanced scorecard relationships need to be quantified to be useful? Explain.

b. Comment on the completeness of the example scorecard. Can you suggest additions and/or deletions from the objectives and measures? If possible, review websites or annual reports of several biotechnology companies (e.g., Amgen, Genentech, or other companies that you might find from an Internet search of the keyword "biotechnology"), and read the letter from the president or the management discussion and analysis to help you. Annual reports or 10-K reports are available for publicly traded US companies on the Security and Exchange Commission's EDGAR database.

c. Explain how a balanced scorecard similar to the preceding one can help Allen and his management team to achieve the following objectives:

   (1) Develop cost-management information to help meet strategic goals.

   (2) Analyze and evaluate organizational change.

   (3) Evaluate the effects of alternative uses of resources on performance.

   (4) Implement and manage change.

[Adapted from C. W. Chow et al. "Applying the Balanced Scorecard to Small Companies." *Management Accounting,* August 1997.]

Obtain and read the article "The Employee-Customer-Profit Chain at Sears," by A. Rucci, S. Kirn, and R. Quinn. *Harvard Business Review,* Jan-Feb, 1998.

Case 20.77
Impacts of a Balanced Scorecard
(LO 1, 2, 3, 4)

Required

In a small group, prepare a written or visual report that addresses the following questions.

a.   Is this article an objective report of a design and an implementation of a balanced scorecard performance-measurement system? Explain.

b.   What additional information do you want about Sears' employee-customer-profit chain? How can you use that information to guide the design and implementation of a similar system in another organization?

c.   How has Sears performed financially over time and relative to its competitors since its reported use of the employee-customer-profit chain? Can you attribute any differences to its employee-customer-profit chain? Why or why not?

Following several years of budget cuts, administrators at the University of California, Davis, sought ways to make the university more efficient, "to do more with less." Janet Hamilton, vice chancellor of administration, searched books and articles, contacted consulting firms, and talked to her counterparts at universities across the United States looking for new management methods that could change the university from a bureaucratic to a customer-oriented organization. After reading about reengineering, total quality initiatives, and a variety of other management techniques, she came across a balanced scorecard. She believed that it was the right tool for the campus and set about implementing it.

Case 20.78
Impacts of a Balanced Scorecard
(LO 1, 2, 3, 4)

At first, she did not call a balanced scorecard by name, fearing that employees would think of it as just another management fad to endure until the administration tired of it and went on to something new. Instead, Hamilton pilot tested balanced scorecard ideas in one support department, environmental health and safety (EHS), until it worked. With the success at EHS behind her, she moved to implement it across the board in other support departments, such as police, fire, and printing services.

Each department developed its own particular performance measures to achieve the following objectives (the list has been shortened to save space):

Organizational Learning and Growth

▨   Create a workplace that fosters teamwork, pride, and integrity.

▨   Attract and retain a highly skilled workforce.

▨   Encourage and reward enterprising behaviors.

Business and Production Process Efficiency

▨   Develop clear policies, simple procedures, and efficient work processes.

▨   Anticipate the future, and design programs and services to ensure future success.

Customer Value

▨   Consistently satisfy customers.

Financial Performance

▨   Ensure financial integrity for capital and financial assets throughout the campus.

▨   Deliver services in a cost-effective manner.

Required

a.   Was the vice chancellor overly cautious in not calling this a "balanced scorecard"?

b.   Comment on the wisdom of beginning a balanced scorecard with a pilot project. How can you extrapolate the experience of a support-service department, such as environmental health and safety, to an academic unit, such as a college of business?

c.   What opportunities and difficulties do you see in applying a balanced scorecard to a university setting?

[Adapted from interviews with university administrative staff.]

Part 1. SecondData Corporation provides outsourced data-processing services for large banks, insurance companies, and credit-card companies. The president and CEO of SecondData, Christine Howard, recently attended a conference at which Professor Robert Kaplan of the Harvard Business School delivered the keynote address. His speech covered recent innovations in management techniques that, in his opinion, are revolutionizing modern organizations. He spent most of his time explaining the concept of a balanced scorecard, but he also analyzed several successful applications of a balanced scorecard for which he had first-hand knowledge.

Case 20.79
Analyze Impacts of a Balanced Scorecard
(LO 1, 2, 3, 4)

Howard came away from the conference convinced that the balance scorecard is a powerful concept, but she was skeptical that organizations really can build models of its uses of resources and important outcomes. She wondered whether other respected management "gurus" were as enthusiastic about a balanced scorecard.

Requirement I

Write a memorandum (two pages, double-spaced maximum) to Howard describing the concept of a balanced scorecard as explained by Kaplan and Norton and several other authors. Provide references.

Part 2. Howard invited you to attend her next executive committee meeting (attended by senior officers in the firm) to discuss the concept of a balanced scorecard and to generate discussion about whether SecondData Corporation should consider implementing the concept. Following is a partial transcript of that meeting.

Howard:	I'm pleased to welcome one of our bright young staff members, who is going to briefly explain the balanced scorecard I told you about last week. I want us to begin discussions about the concept and move toward deciding whether to implement it.
You:	I'm delighted to be here, and I'm eager to present this exciting concept to you. I hope you will ask lots of questions and all contribute answers. If you think there is more information I should develop, I'll be happy to do so and report back to you as soon as possible.
Marketing VP:	I've heard of this so-called balanced scorecard, and I must say that it sounds like nothing more than the latest management fad. Of course, we should pay attention to our critical variables, inputs and outputs, but do you really think it is possible to build these models? I remember a little of my college statistics, and I particularly remember that statistical modeling is very complex. I suspect that by the time you collected enough data to analyze, it would be obsolete.
CFO:	I'm not sure that statistical analysis is what is called for anyway. Aren't these balanced scorecards just someone's best guess about what variables are important and how they might be connected? I think it's meant to be a way to communicate strategy, not actually manage it. Even then, I worry about whose "guesses" we will use.
Human Resources Director:	I know that whatever we choose to measure will be the focus of all our division managers' attention. We have 18 divisions that are directly responsible for generating our profits. We had better be careful about what we measure and how we get everyone to buy in. Any suggestions?

Requirement 2

Compose a brief reply (two pages, double-spaced maximum) to these executives' concerns about a balanced scorecard.

Part 3. You decide to talk to several division managers and their key staff members to get their beliefs about key scorecard variables and possible linkages. A transcript of several of these interviews that you believe are representative follows.

Division Manager 1:	I'm glad you are taking the time to talk to me and other managers out here on the front lines. I think there has been too much "top-down" management lately, and I hate to see the executive committee impose a balanced scorecard on us. It doesn't always know what is happening out here. Fire away with your questions; I'll help as much as I can.
You:	Can you tell me what you pay most attention to as you manage this division?
DM 1:	Well, as one of the oldest and largest divisions in SecondData, I'm very concerned about labor costs and a market that seems more competitive. We also have one of the oldest labor forces, so I am concerned about their skills and education level. I think there is a strong relation between the quality of employees and errors and the time it takes to complete orders. I want to hire some younger employees with more current skills, but I have to wait for attrition.
You:	What do you think your customers most want from you?
DM 1:	Obviously, they want our service at the lowest price, but they are willing to pay for high quality and orders completed on time. The marketing department developed a customer-satisfaction survey that I have never understood.

SECOND DATA CORPORATION
Various Statistics Collected for Domestic Business Units

Division	Age of Division (years)	Number of Employees	Voluntary Turnover Rate	Average Grade Level Completed	Average Hourly Wage	Average Defects per Month	Cycle Time per Order (hours)	Percentage On-Time Deliveries	Customer Satisfaction Score	Regional Population (thousands)	Throughput ($ millions)	Operating Expense ($ millions)	Assets Employed ($ millions)
1	10.1	1,709	4.5%	10.71	$11.11	149.24	61.11	80.6%	78.3	973.0	$3,081	$3,197	$6,690
2	7.4	1,220	5.1	11.93	9.49	140.71	55.84	84.5	89.9	872.0	3,073	2,340	11,856
3	7.2	1,169	6.2	11.95	10.11	123.94	57.22	82.1	68.5	556.0	2,952	2,043	8,236
4	11.0	1,726	6.4	10.15	10.13	143.49	51.92	85.2	83.4	760.0	3,140	2,435	7,158
5	7.1	1,567	5.4	11.62	9.89	123.70	53.53	81.6	82.7	676.0	3,259	2,971	5,126
6	6.1	1,314	5.6	10.31	9.59	158.26	69.98	79.1	71.0	862.0	2,920	2,485	10,315
7	10.2	1,136	8.6	11.14	7.59	169.65	76.23	78.9	83.0	618.0	2,778	1,873	8,034
8	8.4	1,108	4.3	11.97	8.35	141.68	50.83	82.2	84.7	593.0	3,383	2,335	10,945
9	7.9	1,815	5.1	10.47	8.02	183.40	67.36	78.3	73.0	539.0	2,762	2,291	7,274
10	9.9	1,655	4.9	11.02	8.65	151.12	58.15	84.8	81.2	946.0	3,108	2,492	3,991
11	10.0	1,076	4.4	10.65	8.66	151.87	55.79	82.2	86.6	731.0	3,409	1,677	4,623
12	9.6	1,248	6.2	10.96	6.42	131.04	61.12	78.9	79.1	814.0	3,291	1,783	9,445
13	8.4	1,563	8.3	10.14	10.13	164.41	55.67	82.2	84.8	831.0	3,392	2,703	5,676
14	10.4	1,210	8.0	10.73	8.71	143.53	52.36	84.9	92.4	517.0	2,647	1,718	4,382
15	8.0	1,133	6.0	10.75	8.09	160.04	54.21	86.1	84.4	598.0	2,431	1,823	7,524
16	11.1	1,954	8.9	10.36	5.72	157.51	62.19	83.8	87.4	948.0	3,215	2,115	4,520
17	6.6	1,401	4.5	11.34	10.59	148.51	72.26	77.0	72.7	515.0	2,825	2,816	12,030
18	10.8	1,141	5.1	10.65	10.31	171.69	59.69	81.6	82.6	507.0	2,427	2,240	8,854

I suppose it is trying to measure something related to our ability to meet customers' needs.

Division Controller 11:	You can talk all you want about fancy new concepts of measurement, but the only measurement that really counts at SecondData is return on assets. (I've learned this the hard way!) I understand that there is talk about using economic value added rather than ROA, but I'm not sure what that will add. It's just a variation on the same theme.
You:	Are there process measures that you worry about, too?
DC 11:	Yes, we do monitor the number of defects, you know, incorrect billings and such. They really drive up our cycle time, and I am sure our customers are not happy if some of those errors slip by. I also monitor our employee voluntary turnover rate, which is one of the lowest in the company. I think that this reflects good management and our ability to control the quality of our processes.
Division Manager 17:	Unfortunately, we have the special difficulty of being in one of the regions with the smallest population. We have to pay higher wages for employees, and we don't have the revenue potential of some of the other divisions. I tell you, it's difficult to meet corporate's profit goals under these conditions. I'll tell you another thing: I think there is a lot of randomness in our environment. I don't think we understand how factors affect each other. Sorting that out will be quite a challenge. Good luck.

Requirement 3

From this interview and your own reasoning, develop a possible balanced scorecard model. Explain how the interviews have influenced your model. Describe each of the measures you have included in your model and explain how they should be causally linked. Prepare a graphical representation of your scorecard model.

Part 4. You have collected a table of data on each of the 18 business units of SecondData Corporation.

Requirement 4

To the extent possible, use the methods of cost estimation presented in Chapter 11 and these data to test the validity of your proposed balanced scorecard model. Describe which aspects of the model that the analysis supports and which it refutes. Briefly discuss the advantages and disadvantages of using these data to verify the model. What additional data would you like to have? Make recommendations to Howard and the executive committee about whether they should proceed to develop and implement a balanced scorecard. What opportunities and difficulties do you foresee?

Case 20.80
Alternative Incentives
(LO 6)

Using information from a recent proxy statement, prepare a short presentation that describes the evaluation and compensation criteria for top executives at a large publicly held corporation. Choose a firm that evaluates and rewards on both financial and nonfinancial criteria.

Case 20.81
Alternative Incentives
(LO 6)

Megaloid Corporation has hired you to develop a pay-for-performance incentive system based on its four key areas of performance. Megaloid's CEO ultimately wants each of the company's 20 divisions to perform at the 90th percentile level of the industry for each goal. The company reliably measures performance against each of these goals as follows.

Performance Area	Performance Measure	Current Megaloid Divisions' Average Performance	Current Industry 90th Percentile Performance
1. Employee productivity	Sales per employee	$175,000	$200,000
2. Product quality	Customer-found defect rate	2.0%	0.02%
3. Customer satisfaction	Customer satisfaction score (1 to 100)	72	89
4. Profitability	Return on investment	10.3%	30%

Although each of the 20 divisions performs at different levels, for simplicity assume that three types of divisions exist: high performers, medium performers, and low performers with the following average frequency and performances:

Performance Measure	Low Performers	Medium Performers	High Performers
Number of divisions	6	10	4
Sales per employee	$158,333	$175,000	$200,000
Customer-found defect rate	3.33%	2.00%	0.01%
Customer satisfaction score (1 to 100)	59	72	92
Return on investment	−9.50%	10.30%	40%

Required

a. Assume that each division manager is paid an annual salary of $75,000. If you were to propose an incentive plan that paid a 1 percent of salary bonus for exceeding the industry's 90th percentile performance, what would be the average and total amounts of bonus compensation paid for the current levels of performance?

b. What would be the average and total amounts of bonus compensation paid if two low performers improved to the medium category and two medium performers improved to the high category? What if all divisions were high performers?

c. Do you think the incentive plan in requirements (a) and (b) is a good plan or not? Would an incentive plan that paid bonus compensation for *improvements* in performance be a good idea? Explain.

d. Propose an alternative incentive plan that rewards absolute performance and relative improvement.

CMP Media is a leading high-technology business-to-business multimedia company that provides information and integrated marketing services to technology and health care professionals worldwide. CMP Media offers marketers and advertisers comprehensive media solutions tailored to meet their individual needs. CMP's diverse products and services include newspapers, magazines, Internet products, research, education and training, trade shows and conferences, direct marketing services, and custom publishing. CMP Media was purchased from the Leeds family in 1999 by the U.K. firm, United Business Media.

Case 20.82
Ethical Impacts of Alternative Incentive System Features: Performance and Measurement at CMP Media
(LO 6, 7)

Company Principles

CMP Media has operated with a set of socially responsible principles for more than 30 years. The company credits these principles with its ability to hire and retain excellent employees, innovate its processes and products, provide exceptional customer value, and (until recently) generate consistent financial success.

Financial Results at CMP Media

In 2002, the company continued to suffer the effects of the technology market downturn in which CMP's major customers were cautious in committing their marketing and advertising budgets. Turnover (sales revenues) in this business fell 31.9 percent to £252.4 million while profits were down 112.5 percent to an operating loss of £9.9 million. CMP has improved its market leading position. It now has a 29 percent share of the market for the period, ahead of last year's 25 percent, and still maintains well over twice the market share of its nearest competitors.

CMP MEDIA
Comparative Operating Results
2001 and 2002
Millions of GBP (£)

	Turnover	Operating Profit
2002	£ 252.4	£ (9.9)
2001	£ 370.4	£ (8.8)
Percent change	(31.9)%	(12.5)%

1 GBP (£) ≃ 1.5 USD ($)

Performance Measurement at CMP Media

CMP Media had been a family owned business for most of its existence. Most officers and key managers were family members or long-term employees who fully embraced the company's operating principles. Therefore, executives felt no need to formalize the operating principles into the company's incentive system. The company ran smoothly by consensus. Since the purchase of the company by United

Business Media and the nearly simultaneous economic downturn in the high-tech sector, the company has felt increased pressure to improve its financial results. Indeed, its two consecutive operating loss years were unprecedented in company history. The company is unwilling, however, to discard any of its operating principles, and the parent company so far agrees.

You (and up to two others) have been retained by CMP Media to design a performance-based incentive system for CMP Media that is consistent with all of its operating principles.

Required

a.   Review information about theories of motivation and the elements of performance-based incentive plans (Appendix).

b.   Prepare a report that describes your input to the following table and explains how your choices will effectively motivate employees to achieve the company's goals.

c.   Would you recommend any trade-offs among operating principles? Explain.

d.   Combine your performance measures into a cause-and-effect, balanced scorecard–type model. Explain how you would establish the validity and usefulness of this performance model.

CMP Media's Five Operating Principles	Two Objectives for Each Goal	One Performance Measure for Each Objective	Incentives Plans for 5 Executives, 20 Managers, and 400 Workers
1. Be a great company to do business with for customers and suppliers.			
2. Be an excellent company to work for—able to hire, motivate, and develop outstanding, diverse people who work together harmoniously toward a common objective.			
3. Provide only superior products and services.			
4. Contribute actively to a better social and physical environment.			
5. Be profitable to provide the resources for future growth, quality, and financial stability.			

[Information regarding CMP Media was taken from its website (www.cmp.com—now removed) and that of its parent, United Business Media (www.unm.com).]

Glossary

A

ABC full costing assigns as many costs to products as possible

ABC unit costing assigns only the costs of unit-level resources to products

abnormal spoilage is due to reasons other than the usual course of operations of a process

absolute performance evaluation compares individual performance to set standards or expectations

absorption or **full costing** applies all manufacturing-overhead costs to (or absorbs) manufactured goods

account analysis estimates costs by measuring fixed and variable costs for each activity account

accuracy is precision in measurement

activity is any discrete task that an organization undertakes to make or deliver a good or service

activity-based budgeting (ABB) is the process of developing a master budget using information obtained from an activity-based (ABC) analysis

activity-based costing (ABC) is a costing method that first assigns costs to activities and then to goods and services based on how much each good or service uses the activities

activity-based flexible budget is based on several cost drivers rather than a single, volume-based cost driver

activity-based management (ABM) is used by management to evaluate the costs and values of process activities to identify opportunities for improved efficiency

activity-based responsibility accounting is a system for measuring the performance of an organization's employees and subunits, which focuses not only on the cost of performing activities but also on the activities themselves

activity dictionary lists activities performed by an organization to produce its products

actual costing assigns only actual costs of both direct and indirect resources (i.e., direct materials, direct labor, and manufacturing overhead) to products

actual overhead is the amount of manufacturing overhead actually incurred during an accounting period

adjusted *R*-square serves the same purpose as the *R-square* but applies a statistical penalty for each added independent variable

administrative costs are incurred to manage the organization and provide staff support

agency costs are the sum of opportunity costs of misbehavior and out-of-pocket costs for incentives and monitoring performance

agency theory is an economic theory of incentives and behavior based on the relationship between a principal who offers an incentive plan and an agent who accepts the plan to work on behalf of the principal

applied overhead is the amount of manufacturing overhead assigned to Work-in-Process Inventory as a product cost. It is calculated by multiplying the predetermined overhead rate by the actual *cost driver* volume.

appraisal activities (also called *detection* or *inspection activities*) inspect inputs and attributes of individual units of product or service to detect whether they conform to specifications or customer expectations

attributes of a product or service are its tangible and intangible features

average cycle time equals total processing time for all units divided by good units produced

B

backflush costing is a simplified cost-accounting system in which all manufacturing costs are charged directly to Cost of Goods Sold, and then end-of-period adjustments are made to credit Cost of Goods Sold and debit the respective inventory accounts

balanced scorecard is a performance measurement system or business model that ties together knowledge of strategy, processes, activities, and operational and strategic performance measures

bar-coding systems create a unique bar code for each order and allow companies to mark and track all orders electronically

base budgeting is a budgeting system wherein the initial budget for each organizational department is set in accordance with a *base package,* which includes the minimal resources required for the subunit to exist at an absolute minimal level

base package includes the minimal resources required for the subunit to exist at an absolute minimal level

batch-level costs are incurred for every batch of product or service produced

batch-level resources and activities are acquired and performed to make a group, or batch, of similar products

behavioral congruence occurs when an individual behaves in the best interests of the organization regardless of his or her own goals

benchmarking is a technique for determining an organization's competitive advantage by learning about its own products, services, and operations and comparing them against the best performers

benchmarks are important competitive features that form the bases of comparison and exist either inside or outside one's own organization, or in other industries

benefit-cost analysis see *cost-benefit analysis*

bottleneck is the *constraint* or constraining factor limiting production or sales

break-even point is the volume of activity that produces equal revenues and costs for the organization

budget is a detailed plan, expressed in quantitative terms, that specifies how an organization will acquire and use resources during a particular period of time

budget committee advises the *budget director* during the preparation of the budget

budget director (or **chief budget officer**) specifies the process by which budget data are gathered, collects the information, and prepares the master budget

budget manual indicates who is responsible for providing various types of budget information, when the information is required, and what form the information is to take

budgetary slack is the difference between the revenue or cost projection that a person provides and a realistic estimate of the revenue or cost

budgeted balance sheet shows the expected end-of-period balances for the company's assets, liabilities, and owners' equity

budgeted (or **pro forma**) **financial statements** show how the organization's financial statements will appear at a specified time if operations proceed according to plan

budgeted income statement shows the expected revenue and expenses for a budget period, assuming that planned operations are carried out

budgeted schedule of cost of goods manufactured and sold details the direct-materials, direct-labor, and manufacturing overhead costs to be incurred, and shows the cost of the goods to be sold during a budget period

budgeting system comprises the procedures used to develop a budget

business processes support or enable production processes

by-product is the output from a joint-production process that is minor in quantity and/or economic value when compared to the main products

C

capacity is a measure of a process's ability to transform resources into valued products and services

capital budget is a plan for buying and selling capital assets

capital turnover is sales revenue divided by invested capital

cash budget details the expected cash receipts and disbursements during a budget period

cash disbursements budget details the expected cash payments during a budget period

cash receipts budget details the expected cash collections during a budget period

cause-and-effect analysis involves formulating diagnostic signals that identify potential causes of product or service defects

centralization places the responsibility for decisions with the top echelon of management

committed cost is a cost for which management has taken actions that result in some level of commitment to incur it

common-size statements express items as percentages of revenue

competitive advantage is a resource, process or value chain that enables an organization to provide more value, perhaps at lower cost, than its competitors

constant gross margin percentage method allocates joint costs to products in a way that the gross margin as a percentage of revenue is the same for each product

constraint is a process or resource in a system that limits the throughput of the system

contribution margin is the amount of sales revenue remaining, after covering all variable costs, to contribute to covering fixed cost and profit

control chart describes variation in product or service attributes over time by measuring important quality features but additionally compares them to maximum- and minimum-desired levels

conversion costs include direct labor and manufacturing overhead

cost is the sacrifice made, usually measured by the resources given up, to achieve a particular purpose

cost-accounting systems measure the use of resources in production

Cost Accounting Standards Board (CASB) is a federal agency chartered by Congress in 1970 to develop cost-accounting standards for large government contractors

cost allocation assigns indirect costs to products or organizational units (e.g., departments)

cost allocation bases are factors used to assign indirect costs to cost objects

cost center is an organizational subunit whose manager is responsible for the cost of an activity for which a well-defined relationship exists between inputs and outputs

cost driver is a characteristic of an activity or event that causes that activity or event to incur costs

cost estimation is the process of estimating the relationship between costs and the cost drivers that cause those costs

cost object is any end to which a cost is assigned, such as a product unit or a department

cost of goods sold is the expense measured by the cost of the units sold during a specific period of time

cost of quality (COQ) is the cost of activities to control quality and costs of activities to correct failure to control quality

cost management is a philosophy, an attitude, and a set of techniques to create more value at lower cost

cost pools are groups or categories of individual cost items

cost variance is the difference between the actual cost and the standard cost

cost-based transfer pricing sets the transfer price on the basis of the cost of the product or service transferred

cost-benefit analysis is a method to measure the effects of plans by comparing costs and benefits, which can be either quantitative or qualitative

cost-driver base is the base used to trace or assign costs to activities

cost-driver rate is the estimated cost of resource consumption per unit of cost-driver base for each activity

cost-management systems represent a set of cost-management techniques that function together to support the organization's goals and activities

cost-reduction target is the difference between the total target cost and the currently feasible total cost

cost-volume-profit (CVP) model is a profit-planning model that reflects the effects of changes in an organization's sales volume, revenue, and costs on profit or income

critical success factors are the key strengths that are most responsible for making the organization successful

currently feasible cost is the cost of all current operations necessary to produce and deliver a product

customer costing analyzes the costs of activities to serve specific customers

customer-level costs are incurred for specific customers

customer-level resources and activities are acquired and performed to serve specific customers

customer profile categorizes individual or types of customers according to the major activities that drive revenues and costs

customer profitability analysis identifies the costs and benefits of serving specific customers or customer types to improve an organization's overall profitability

customer retention or **loyalty** measures indicate how well a company is doing in keeping its customers

customer satisfaction is the degree to which expectations of attributes, customer service, and price have been or are expected to be met

customer value reflects the degree to which products and services satisfy customers' expectations about price, function, and quality

customer-focused quality is a broad focus on meeting or exceeding customer expectations

customer-response time is the amount of time between a customer's placing an order for a product or requesting service and the delivery of the product or service to the customer

D

decentralization places decision-making responsibility at divisional and departmental levels

decision tree is a diagram of decisions and alternative outcomes expected from those decisions in a "tree, branch, and limb" format

decision usefulness of information is whether managers make sufficiently better decisions to justify the cost of the information

defect is an attribute (tangible or intangible) that falls short of customer expectations

Deming Prize, created in Japan by the Japanese Union of Scientists and Engineers, is awarded to companies around the world that excel in quality improvement

dependent variables are caused by, or at least correlated with, independent variables

differential costs are costs that differ between decision alternatives

direct costs are costs traceable to a particular cost object

direct labor is the cost of compensating employees whose work creates the organization's products

direct materials are resources such as raw materials, parts, and components that one can feasibly observe being used to make a specific product

direct method of cost allocation charges the costs of support-service departments to internal customers without making allocations among support-service departments

direct-labor budget shows the number of hours and the cost of direct labor to be used during a budget period

direct-labor efficiency variance is the difference between the actual hours and the standard hours of direct labor allowed, given actual output, multiplied by the standard hourly labor rate

direct-labor mix variance for a particular type of direct labor, is the difference between the actual and standard input proportions for that type of direct labor multiplied by that labor type's standard rate and multiplied by the actual total quantity of all direct labor used

direct-labor rate variance is the difference between the actual and standard hourly labor rate multiplied by the actual quantity of direct labor used

direct-labor yield variance for a particular type of direct labor, is the difference between the actual quantity of all direct labor used and the standard quantity of all direct labor, given actual output, multiplied by the standard rate for that particular type of direct labor and multiplied by the standard input proportion for that type of direct labor

direct-material budget shows the number of units and the cost of materials to be purchased and used during a budget period

direct-material mix variance for a particular direct material is the difference between the actual and standard input proportions for that direct material multiplied by that material's standard price and multiplied by the actual total quantity of all direct materials used

direct-material price variance (or **purchase price variance**) is the difference between the actual and standard price multiplied by the actual quantity of material purchased

direct-material quantity variance is the difference between the actual quantity and the standard quantity of material allowed, given actual output, multiplied by the standard price

direct-material yield variance for a particular direct material is the difference between the actual quantity of all direct materials used and the standard quantity of all direct materials, given actual output, multiplied by that particular direct material's standard price and multiplied by that direct material's standard input proportion

direct-service (or **line**) **departments** provide services directly to external customers

discount rate is an interest rate used to discount future cash flows to their net present values

discretionary cost center is an organizational subunit whose manager is held accountable for costs, but the subunit's input-output relationship is not well specified

distribution costs include the costs of packing, shipping, and delivering products or services to customers

dual transfer pricing charges the buying division for the cost of the transferred product and credits the selling division with the cost plus some profit allowance

due diligence is exercising all reasonable care to identify potential problems and opportunities of a proposed investment

E

economic order quantity (or **EOQ**) is the order quantity that minimizes the cost of ordering and holding inventory

economic value added (EVA®) is an investment center's after-tax operating income minus its total assets (net of its current liabilities) times the company's weighted-average cost of capital

employee capabilities are employees' knowledge and skills that indicate the organization's ability to meet future customer needs and generate new sales

engineering estimates measure the work involved in the activities that go into a product then assign a cost to each of those activities

EOQ model is a mathematical tool for determining the order quantity that minimizes the cost of ordering and holding inventory

equivalent units represent the amount of work actually performed on products not yet complete translated to the work required to complete an equal number of whole units

excess (or unused) capacity is the amount (if any) by which practical capacity exceeds the demand for the output of the process

expectancy theory explains that people are motivated to act in ways that they expect to provide them the rewards that they desire and to prevent the penalties that they wish to avoid

expected value is the value of each possible measure weighted or multiplied by its probability of occurrence

expected value analysis summarizes the combined effects of relevant future events on decision outcomes, weighted by the probabilities or odds that the events will occur

expense is defined as the cost incurred when an asset is used up or sold for the purpose of generating revenue

extended value chain encompasses the ways companies obtain their resources and distribute their products and services, possibly using the services of other organizations

external failure requires activities when defective products or services are detected after being delivered to customers

extrinsic rewards including grades, money, praise, and prizes that come from outside the individual

F

facility (or general-operations) level costs are incurred to maintain the overall facility and infrastructure of the organization

facility-level resources and activities are acquired and performed to provide the general capacity to produce goods and services

feasible solution space is the combination of input and output values that satisfy the constraints

final product is one that is ready for sale without further processing

financial budget shows how the organization will acquire its financial resources

financial model is an accurate, reliable simulation of relations among relevant costs, benefits, value, and risk that is useful for supporting business decisions

financial planning model is a set of mathematical relationships that expresses the interactions among the various operational, financial, and environmental events that determine the overall results of an organization's activities

finished goods are products ready for sale

first-in, first-out (FIFO) costing is an inventory method that identifies the first units completed as the first ones sold or transferred out

fixed costs remain unchanged in total as the volume of activity changes

fixed-overhead budget variance is the difference between actual fixed overhead and budgeted fixed overhead

fixed-overhead volume variance is the difference between budgeted fixed overhead and applied fixed overhead

flexible budget is a budget that is valid for a range of activity

flowchart reflects cause-and-effect and sequential linkages among process activities

G

Gantt chart depicts the stages required to complete a project and the sequence in which the stages are to be performed

goal congruence results when managers of subunits throughout an organization have a common set of objectives

H

high-low method estimates a cost function using only the costs and the level of cost-driver activity from the highest and lowest levels of cost-driver activity

histogram is a chart that displays the frequency distribution of an attribute's measures—its range and degree of concentration around an average attribute value

I

idle time is time not spent productively by an employee

imperfect competition describes the situation when a single producer can affect the market price by varying the amount of product available in the market

incentive system communicates strategy, motivates employees, and reinforces achievement of organizational goals

incremental package describes the resources needed to add various activities to the base package

independent variables are the cost drivers that the analyst believes cause, or at least are correlated with, the dependent variable costs

indirect costs are costs not feasibly traceable to a particular cost object

indirect labor cost consists of the wages of production employees who do not work directly on the product but are required for the manufacturing facility to operate

indirect materials relates to materials that either (1) are not a part of the finished product but are necessary to manufacture it or (2) are part of the finished product but are insignificant in cost

information quality has dimensions of usefulness, subjectivity, accuracy, timeliness, cost, and relevance

input a material or activity that is required to produce a product or service

intermediate product is a product that might require further processing before it is salable to the ultimate consumer

internal audit is an examination of operations, programs, and financial results performed by independent investigators

internal failure requires activities to correct defective processes, products, and services that are detected before delivering them to customers

internal rate of return (IRR) is the interest rate that equates the present value of inflows and outflows from an investment project

intrinsic rewards come from within the individual including the satisfaction from studying hard, the feeling of well-being from physical exercise, the pleasure from helping someone in need, or the satisfaction of doing a good job

inventoriable cost is another term for *product cost*

inventory carrying costs are costs of receiving, handling, storing, and insuring inventory

investment center is an organizational subunit whose manager is held accountable for the subunit's profit and the invested capital used by the subunit to generate its profit

ISO 9000 is a set of international standards for quality management

J

job-cost record (or **file, card** or **sheet**) reports the costs of all production-related resources used on the job to date

job-order costing treats each individual job as the unit of output and assigns costs to each job as resources are used

joint products are the products that jointly result from processing a common input

joint costs are costs to operate joint processes, including the disposal of waste

joint process simultaneously converts a common input into several outputs

just-in-time (JIT) processes purchase, make, and deliver services and products just when needed

K

kaizen costing is the process of cost reduction during the manufacturing phase of a product

L

lagging indicator is the measure of the final outcomes of earlier management plans and their execution

leading indicator is the measure that identifies future nonfinancial and financial outcomes to guide management decision making

lead time is the time required for the material to be received after an order is placed

learning curve is the mathematical or graphic representation of the systematic relationship between the amount of experience in performing a task and the time required to perform it

learning phenomenon is a systematic relationship between the amount of experience in performing a task and the time required to perform it

life cycle costing tracks costs attributable to each product or service from start to finish

linear programming shows how best to allocate multiple scarce resources among alternative courses of action in the short run when capacity cannot be increased

lost units are goods that evaporate or otherwise disappear during a production process

lower control limit is the minimum-desired level of product or service feature

M

main product is a joint output that generates a significant portion of the net realizable value from the process

Malcolm Baldrige Quality Award created by the US Congress in 1987, recognizes US firms with outstanding records of quality improvement and quality management

management by exception is the process of following up only on significant cost variances

manufacturing overhead includes all costs of transforming material into a finished product other than direct material and direct labor

manufacturing-overhead budget shows the cost of overhead expected to be incurred in the production process during the budget period

margin of safety is the amount by which a quantitative objective is exceeded

marketing costs include the costs of personnel, databases, equipment, and facilities dedicated to providing market research, marketing strategy, and marketing plans

master budget, or **profit plan** is a comprehensive set of budgets covering all phases of an organization's operations for a specified period of time

material requisition form is the source document for the transfer of raw material from Raw-Material Inventory to Work-in-Process Inventory and to the job-cost record for the production job

maximum quality level is total delight of the customer or zero defects, depending on one's definition of quality

mixed costs have both a fixed and a variable component

model is a representation of reality

model elasticity is the ratio of the percentage change in profit divided by the percentage change of an input parameter

multicollinearity is the correlation between two or more independent variables in a multiple regression equation

multiple regression is a regression equation with more than one independent variable

N

net present value (NPV) is the present value of a project's future cash flows less its purchase price. It is the economic value of a project at a point in time

net realizable value (NRV) is the measure of a product's contribution to profit after the *split-off point* and is computed as sales revenue minus additional processing costs

net realizable value (NRV) method allocates joint costs based on the NRV of each *main product* at the *split-off point*

new product (or **service**) **development time** is the period between the first consideration of a product and its initial sale to the customer

non-value-added activities do not contribute to customer-perceived value

normal costing assigns to production jobs the cost of actual direct materials, actual direct labor, and applied manufacturing overhead, which are calculated by multiplying the predetermined overhead rate by the actual amount of the cost driver

normal spoilage   is spoiled product that results from the regular operation of the production process

O

objective function   is a mathematical relation of inputs and outputs to be maximized or minimized

objectivity   describes the degree of consensus about what to measure, how to measure it, what the observed measure is, or whether the measurement is important

operating leverage   reflects the risk of missing sales targets and is measured by the ratio of contribution margin to operating income

operation   is a standardized method of making a product that is repeatedly performed

operation costing   is a hybrid of *job-order* and *process costing,* which is used when companies produce batches of similar products with significantly different types of material

operational budgets   specify how an organization's operations will be carried out to meet its demand for goods or services

operational performance analysis   measures whether the performance of current operations is consistent with expectations

opportunity cost   is the forgone benefit of the best alternative use of a resource

optimum point   is the set of inputs and outputs in the feasible solution space that maximizes or minimizes the objective function

outsourcing   is acquiring goods or services from an outside provider

overapplied overhead   refers to actual overhead that is less than applied overhead

overhead cost performance report   shows the actual and flexible-budget cost levels for each overhead item, together with the variable-overhead spending and efficiency variances and the fixed-overhead budget variance

overhead variance   is the difference between the actual and the applied manufacturing overhead amounts

overtime premium   is the extra hourly compensation paid to an employee who works beyond the time normally allowed by regulation or labor contracts

P

padding the budget   means intentionally underestimating revenue or overestimating costs

Pareto chart   prioritizes the causes of problems or defects as bars of varying height, in order of frequency or size

participative budgeting   involves employees throughout an organization in the budgeting process

payback period   is the time necessary to recover the investment cost from nondiscounted cash flows

pay for performance   bases at least a portion of a manager's income on measure(s) of organizational performance rather than a guaranteed amount

perfect competition   describes the situation when the market price does not depend on the quantity sold by any one producer

perfection (or **ideal**) **standard**   is one that can be attained only under nearly perfect operating conditions

performance evaluation formula   describes rewards earned for specific achievements

performance measure   is an indicator that allows a person to determine the level of performance according to some critical attribute and to compare performance to expectations

performance report   shows the budgeted and actual amounts of key financial (or nonfinancial) results appropriate for the type of *responsibility center* involved

period costs   are identified with the time period in which they are incurred rather than with units of purchased or produced goods

physical-measures (or **quantities**) **method**   is a joint-cost allocation based on the relative volume, weight, energy content, or other physical measure of each joint product at the *split-off point*

pilot project   is a limited-scope project intended to be a small-scale model of a larger, possibly systemwide, project

practical (or **attainable**) **standards**   are challenging, but possible, to achieve

practical capacity   of a process is its *theoretical capacity* less planned downtime for scheduled maintenance or improvements

predatory pricing   involves temporarily setting a price below cost to broaden demand for a product and injure competitors

predetermined overhead rate   is the budgeted manufacturing overhead divided by the budgeted level of the cost driver

present value   is the equivalent amount that would have to be invested today to generate a future cash flow at a given discount or opportunity rate

prevention   refers to activities that seek to prevent defects in the products or services being produced

price discrimination   is the quoting of different prices to different customers for the same products, with an intent to harm competitors

prime costs   are the primary costs of producing a good or service that includes *direct materials* and *direct labor,* but not overhead

prior department costs   are manufacturing costs incurred in another department and transferred to a subsequent department in the manufacturing process

process   is a related set of tasks, manual or automated, that transforms inputs into identifiable outputs

process capacity   is a measure of a process's ability to transform recourses into valued products and services

process costing   treats all units processed during a time period as the output to be costed and does not separate and record costs for each unit produced

process efficiency   is the ability to transform inputs into outputs at lowest cost

product cost   is a cost assigned to goods that were either purchased or manufactured for resale

product-costing system   is a system that accumulates the costs of a production process and assigns them to the products that constitute the organization's output

product life cycle   is the time that elapses from its initial research and development to the point at which customer support is withdrawn

product mix   is the relative proportion of each type of product planned or actually sold

production budget   shows the number of units of services or goods that are to be produced during a budget period

production cost reports summarize production and cost results for a period

production cycle time is the time between starting and finishing a production process, including time to correct mistakes

production (or line) departments provide goods and services directly to external customers

production processes directly result in the production of products or services provided to external customers

productivity is the ratio of outcomes of a process divided by the amount of resources necessary to complete the process

product-level costs are incurred for each line of product or service

product-level resources and activities are acquired and performed to produce and sell a specific good or service

profit center is an organizational subunit whose manager is held accountable for profit

profit plan (or master budget) is a comprehensive set of budgets covering all phases of an organization's operations for a specified period of time

prorated overhead variance assigns proportionate amounts of it to Work-in-Process Inventory, Finished-Goods Inventory, and Cost of Goods Sold

proration is the process of allocating cost variances to Work-in-Process Inventory, Finished-Goods Inventory, and Cost of Goods Sold

Q

qualitative factors are the characteristics of a decision that cannot easily or should not be expressed in numerical terms

qualitative information is descriptive and based on characteristics or perceptions, such as relative desirability, rather than quantities

quantitative information is expressed in dollars or other quantities relating to size, frequency, and so on

R

raw material is material that has not yet been entered into production

real option value (ROV) is the difference between the expected NPV of one option form of the investment and the next best option

real option value (ROV) analysis combines analyses of decision trees, expected values, and NPV to describe investments as a series of options to change investments

reciprocal method recognizes and allocates costs of all services provided by any support-service department, including those provided to other support-service departments

reciprocal services are services provided among multiple support-service departments

regression analysis is a statistical method used to create an equation relating independent (or X) variables to dependent (or Y) variables

relative performance evaluation is based on comparing an individual's performance to that of others

relative sales value at split-off method allocates joint costs based on the relative sales values of the joint products at their *split-off point*

relevance refers to whether information is pertinent to a decision

relevant costs and benefits occur in the future and differ among feasible decision alternatives

relevant range is the range of activity within which the organization expects to operate and over which assumed cost patterns are reasonably accurate

residual income of an *investment center* is its profit minus its invested capital times an inputted interest rate

resources supplied refer to the capacity that the organization makes available for use

resources used refer to the resources actually used for productive purposes

responsibility accounting refers to the various concepts and tools used to measure the performance of people and departments in order to foster goal or behavioral congruence

responsibility center is a subunit in an organization whose manager is held accountable for specified results of the subunit's activities

return on investment (ROI) for an investment center is its income divided by its invested capital

return on quality (ROQ) is the view that assumes there is a trade-off between the costs and benefits of improving quality

revenue budget variance is the difference between the actual total sales revenue and the budgeted total sales revenue

revenue center is an organizational subunit whose manager is held accountable for the revenue attributed to the subunit

revenue market-share variance holds constant the total industry volume at its actual sales level and focuses on the company's market share

revenue market-size variance holds constant the company's market share at its budgeted level and focuses on changes in total industry volume

revenue sales-mix variance focuses on the effects of changes in the sales mix while holding constant the effects of the products' sales prices and the total sales volume

revenue sales-quantity variance holds constant the sales-price and sales-mix effects and focuses on the effect of the overall unit sales volume

revenue sales-volume variance holds constant the products' sales prices at their budgeted levels and focuses on deviations between actual and budgeted sales volumes

revolving (or continuous) budget is another name for a *rolling budget*

rolling (or revolving or continuous) budget is continually updated by periodically adding a new incremental time period

R-square (R^2) is the proportion of the variation in the dependent variable explained by the X, or independent, variables

run refers to sequential values above or below the mean or values sequentially increasing or decreasing

run chart shows trends in variation in product or service attributes over time by reflecting measures of important quality features taken at defined points in time

S

safety stock is the potential excess usage of material when material usage fluctuates during the *lead time*

sales budget displays the projected sales in units and the projected sales revenue

sales forecasting   is the process of predicting sales of services or goods

sales margin   is income divided by sales revenue

sales mix   is the relative proportion of each type of product planned or actually sold

sales-price variance   focuses on the differences between actual and budgeted sales prices while holding constant the sales volume at its actual level

scatter diagram   is a plot of two measures that could be related

scattergraph   plots costs against activity levels

scenario analysis   creates realistic combinations of changed parameters

scenarios   are realistic combinations of changed parameters

selling costs   are the costs of sales personnel, databases, equipment, and facilities devoted to sales activities

selling, general, and administrative (SG&A) expense budget shows the planned amounts of expenditures for selling, general, and administrative expenses during a budget period

semivariable costs   have both a fixed and a variable component

sensitivity analysis   is the study of how the outcome of a decision-making process changes as one or more of the assumptions change

simple regression   is a type of statistical analysis in which the regression equation has only one independent variable

special orders   are irregular and do not have lasting implications for other products or customers

split-off point   is the point at which joint products separate in the production process

spoilage   represents goods that are damaged, do not meet specifications, or are otherwise not suitable for further processing or sale as good output

standard cost   is a budget for the production of one unit of product or service

standard costing   uses a predetermined (or standard) rate for both direct and indirect costs (i.e., direct material, direct labor, and manufacturing overhead) to assign manufacturing costs to products

standard direct-labor quantity   is the number of labor hours normally needed to manufacture one unit of product

standard direct-labor rate   is the total hourly cost of compensation, including fringe benefits

standard direct-material price   is the total delivered cost after subtracting any purchase discounts

standard direct-material quantity   is the total amount of materials normally required to produce a finished product, including allowances for normal waste or inefficiency

standard-costing system   enters the *standard costs* of direct material, direct labor, and manufacturing overhead into the Work-in-Process Inventory account

static budget   is valid for only one planned activity level

statistical control chart   plots *cost variances* across time and compares them with a statistically determined critical value that triggers an investigation

step (semifixed) costs   increase in steps as the amount of the cost-driver volume increases

step method   of cost allocation allocates costs first from the support-service department with the largest proportion of its total allocation base in other support-service departments to other support-services or support- and direct-service or production departments, then allocates costs from less general support-service departments

stock appreciation rights (SARs)   confer bonuses on employees based on increases in stock prices for a predetermined number of shares

stock options   give an individual the right to purchase a certain number of shares at a specified price over a specified time period

strategic decision making   is the process of choosing and implementing actions that will affect an organization's future abilities to achieve its goals

strategic investment   is a choice among alternative courses of action and the allocation of resources to those alternatives most likely to succeed after anticipating (1) changes in natural, social, and economic conditions and (2) actions of competitors

strategic long-range plan   expresses the specific steps required to achieve an organization's goals

strategic performance analysis   measures whether a strategic decision has met expectations

strategic planning   is the process of deciding on an organization's major programs and the approximate resources to be devoted to them

strategy   is an organization's overall plan or policy to achieve its goals

subjective performance evaluation   is based on nonquantified criteria

subjectivity   describes the degree of disagreement about what to measure, how to measure it, what the observed measure is, or whether the measurement is important

sunk costs   are past payments for resources that cannot be changed by any current or future decision

support (or **service**) **departments**   do not work directly on a product but are necessary for the production process to operate

support-service costs   are the costs of resources supplied by an organization to provide the support services

support-service (or **indirect**) **departments**   provide support services to each other and to the production departments

T

tangible objectives   are benchmarks capable of being measured in some manner

target cost   is the highest cost of a good or service that meets both customer needs and company profit goals

target costing   is a decision-making method that seeks to achieve products and services with specific features at *target costs* based on expected market prices and *target profits*

target profit   is the desired excess of periodic or project sales revenues over costs

task analysis   is the technique of setting standards by analyzing the production process

tax credit   is a reduction in state and/or federal income taxes

theoretical capacity of a process is the maximum possible rate of transformation of inputs into outputs if the process were fully used, with no downtime or unused capacity

theory of constraints seeks to improve productive processes by focusing on constrained resources

throughput costing assigns only the unit-level spending for direct costs as the cost of products or services

throughput efficiency is the relation of throughput achieved to resources used

throughput (cycle) time is the average time required to convert raw material into finished goods

throughput time ratio is the ratio of the time spent adding customer value to products and services divided by total cycle time (also known as the "ratio of work content to lead time")

time value of money is the concept that cash received earlier is worth more than cash received later

timeliness means that information is available in time to fully consider it when making a decision

total delight occurs when a customer receives a product or service that far exceeds his or her expectations of quality

total factor productivity is the value of goods and services divided by the total cost of providing them

total quality management (TQM) is the view that improvements in quality, as defined by customers, will always result in improved organizational performance because improving quality will improve efficiency as problems are identified and eliminated

transfer price is the amount charged when one division of an organization sells goods or services to another division

***t*-statistic,** t, is the value of b, the coefficient, divided by its standard error, SE_b

U

underapplied overhead refers to actual overhead that exceeds applied overhead

unit-level costs are incurred for every unit of product manufactured or service produced

unit-level resources and activities are acquired and performed specifically for individual units of product or service

unused capacity is the difference between the resources supplied and the resources used. Unused capacity is the amount of capacity that the organization has supplied that is not being used for productive purposes

upper control limit is a maximum-desired level of product or service feature

V

value chain is the relationship of an organization's processes that links ideas, resources, suppliers, and customers

value-added activities enhance the value of products and services in the eyes of the organization's customer while meeting its own goals

variable (or direct) costing applies only variable manufacturing overhead to manufactured goods as a product cost along with direct materials and direct labor

variable costs change in total in direct proportion with a change in the activity volume

variable-overhead efficiency variance is the difference between the actual and standard hours of an activity base (or cost driver) multiplied by the standard variable-overhead rate

variable-overhead spending variance is the difference between the actual variable-overhead cost and the product of the standard variable-overhead rate and the actual hours of an activity base (or cost driver)

variances are the differences between a plan's actual and expected quantities

virtual organizations maintain only the most important operations of the value chain and outsource everything else

W

weighted-average cost of capital (WACC) is the average of the after-tax cost of debt capital and the cost of equity capital, weighted by the relative proportions of the firm's capital provided by debt and equity

weighted-average costing is an inventory method that for product-costing purposes combines costs and equivalent units of a period with the costs and the equivalent units in beginning inventory

weighted-average unit contribution margin (WAUCM) is the average of the various products' unit contribution margins weighted by the relative proportion of each product sold

work in process refers to partially completed products

Z

zero-base budgeting initially sets the budget for virtually every activity in the organization to zero

Photo Credits

Chapter 1

p. 2, © Roger Tully/Getty Images/Stone; p. 6, Ryan McVay/Getty Images; p. 14 Photo courtesy of Hewlett-Packard Company.

Chapter 2

p. 34, © Chuck Savage/CORBIS; p. 41, Photolink/Getty Images; p. 41, Photolink/Getty Images; p. 41, Kim Steele/Getty Images; p. 53, Photolink/Getty Images; p. 53 © Royalty-Free/CORBIS; p. 53, © Maximilian Stock Ltd./Photo Researchers, Inc.; p. 53, ©William Taufic/CORBIS; p. 53, © 2001 PhotoDisc, Inc.

Chapter 3

p. 86, © Peter Aprahamian/CORBIS; p. 97, © Annie Griffiths Belt/CORBIS; p. 110, © Michael L. Abramson/Woodfin Camp & Associates; p. 110, PhotoDisc/Getty Images.

Chapter 4

p. 136, AP/ Wide World Photos; p. 138, © Vittoriano Rastelli/Corbis. All Rights Reserved; p. 143, © Royalty Free/CORBIS.

Chapter 5

p. 178, © Jim Sulley/WirePix./The Image Works; p. 185, © Spencer Grant/PhotoEdit; p. 189 © 2001 PhotoDisc, Inc.

Chapter 6

p. 212, © Allan H Shoemake/Getty Images/Taxi; p. 216, © Joe Sohm/The Image Works;p. 220, © Royalty-Free/CORBIS.

Chapter 7

p. 244, Photolink/Getty Images; p. 246, AP/Wide World Photos; p. 258, Courtesy TRW; p. 268, Courtesy of Dell Inc.

Chapter 8

p. 292, AP/Wide World Photos; p. 307, © Richard T. Nowitz/CORBIS; p. 310, © 2001 PhotoDisc, Inc.

Chapter 9

p. 332, © Royalty Free/CORBIS; p. 341, © Royalty-Free/CORBIS; p. 346, © D. Cavagnaro/Visuals Unlimited.

Chapter 10

p. 362, Getty Images; p. 364, © Royalty-Free/CORBIS; p. 369, © Sherwin Crasto/Reuters/CORBIS

Chapter 11

p. 408, © Great American Stock/Index Stock Imagery; p. 414, John A. Rizzo/Getty Images; p. 420 Photolink/Getty Images.

Chapter 12

p. 458, ©Jim West/The Image Works; p. 469, © 2001 PhotoDisc, Inc.; p. 474, Corbis. All Rights Reserved.

Chapter 13

p. 506, © Billy Hustace/Getty Images/Stone; p. 514, © Matthew Borkoski/Stock, Boston LLC.; p. 514, © Jeffrey Muir Hamilton/Stock, Boston LLC.

Chapter 14

p. 552, © Greg Kuchik/Getty Images; p. 555, ©2003 Benetton Group SpA, Ph James Mollison, In collaboration with the World Food Programme; p. 570, Emma Lee/Life File/Getty Images.

Chapter 15

p. 594, ©Norbert Schwerin/The Image Works; p. 596, ©Craig Nelson/Index Stock Imagery; p. 596, Digital Imagery ©2001 PhotoDisc, Inc./Scott T. Baxter.

Chapter 16

p. 646, © Cheyenne Rouse/Index Stock Imagery; p. 650 © Spencer Grant/PhotoEdit; p. 651, © Susan Van Etten/PhotoEdit; p. 651, ©2004 Hertz System, Inc. Hertz is a registered service mark and trademark of Hertz System, Inc.; p. 660, ©Royalty Free/CORBIS; p. 666, ©Michael Rosenfeld/Stone.

Chapter 17

p. 688, © C. Moore/CORBIS; p. 696, © Steve Raymer/CORBIS; p. 696, © Bruce Ando/Index Stock Imagery.

Chapter 18

p. 742, © David Young-Wolff /PhotoEdit; p. 746, © Royalty-Free/CORBIS; p. 746, © Mary Kate Denny/PhotoEdit; p. 746, © Jeffrey Muir Hamilton.

Chapter 19

p. 788, © David Samuel Robbins/CORBIS; p. 791, Digital Vision/Getty Images; p. 798, © David Young-Wolff/PhotoEdit.

Chapter 20

p. 818, © William Taufic/CORBIS; p. 825, Photo courtesy of GE; p. 846, © Royalty-Free/CORBIS.

Bibliography

Chapter 1

Brown, S. L. and K. M. Eisenhardt. 1998. *Competing on the Edge: Strategy as Structured Chaos.* Boston: Harvard Business School Press.

Drucker, P. *Managing in a Time of Great Change.* New York: Dutton, 1995.

Edwards, J. B., editor. *Emerging Practices in Cost Management.* Boston: Warren Gorham & Lamont: 1997.

Eisenhardt, Kathleen M. 1999. "Strategy as Strategic Decision Making." *Sloan Management Review;* Spring, Vol. 40 Issue 3, p65, 8p

Hendry, John, 2000. "Strategic Decision Making, Discourse, and Strategy as Social Practice." *Journal of Management Studies,* Nov, Vol. 37, Issue 7.

Kotter, J. P. "Why Transformation Efforts Fail." *Harvard Business Review* (March–April 1995): 61.

National Association of Accountants. *Standard No. 1B.* "Statement on Management Accounting: Objectives of Management Accounting." New York: MAA; 1982, *www.imanet.org.*

Spicer, B., et al. *Transforming Government Enterprises.* St. Leonards, Australia: The Centre for Independent Studies, 1996.

Walther, T., H. Johansson, J. Dunleavy, and E. Hjelm. *Reinventing the CFO: Moving from Financial Management to Strategic Management.* New York: McGraw-Hill, 1997.

Widener, S., and F. Selto. "Management Control Systems and Boundaries of the Firm." *Journal of Management Accounting Research,* 1999: 45–74.

Chapter 2

Ansberry, C. "In the New Workplace, Jobs Morph to Suit Rapid Change of Pace," *The Wall Street Journal,* March 3, 2002, pp. A1, A7.

Conlin, M. "The Big Squeeze on Workers," *BusinessWeek,* May 13, 2002, pp. 96–98; and M. Conlin, "The Software Says You're Just Average," *BusinessWeek,* February 25, 2002, p. 126.

Eig, J. "Do Part-Time Workers Hold Key to When the Recession Breaks?" *The Wall Street Journal,* January 3, 2002, p. A1.

Chapter 3

Drucker, P. "The Next Information Revolution." Forbes ASAP (*www.forbes.com/asap*), August 24, 1998.

Pfeiffer, G., R. Capettini, and G. Whittenburg. "Gump, Forest—Accountant: A Study of Accounting in the Motion Picture Industry," *Journal of Accounting Education* v15, no. 3: 319–344.

Barsky, N.P., and A.E. Ellinger, "Unleashing the Value in the Supply Chain," *Strategic Finance* 82, no. 7 (January 2001), pp. 33–37.

Chapter 4

Boyd, L. "Cost Information: The Use of Cost Information for Making Operating Decisions." *Journal of Cost Management,* May/June 1997: 42–47.

Campbell, R., P. Brewer, and T. Mills. "Designing an Information System Using Activity-Based Costing and the Theory of Constraints." *Journal of Cost Management,* January/February 1997: 16–25.

Carlson, D., and S. M. Young. "Activity-Based Total Quality Management at American Express." *Journal of Cost Management,* Spring 1993: 48–58.

Gurowka, J. "ABC, ABM, and the Volkswagen Saga." *CMA Magazine,* May 1996: 30–33.

Johnson, H. T. "It's Time to Stop Overselling Activity-Based Concepts: Start Focusing on Total Customer Satisfaction Instead." *Management Accounting,* September 1992: 26–35.

Innes, J., F. Mitchell, and D. Sinclair. "Activity-Based Costing in the U.K.'s Largest Companies: A Comparison of 1994 and 1999 Survey Results." *Management Accounting Research* 11: 349–62.

Kee, R. "Integrating Activity-Based Costing with the Theory of Constraints to Enhance Production-Related Decision Making." *Accounting Horizons,* December 1995: 48–61.

Kennedy, T., and J. Affleck-Graves, "The Impact of Activity-Based Costing Techniques on Firm Performance," *Journal of Management Accounting Research* 13: 19–45.

Porter, M. *Competitive Advantage.* New York: Free Press, 1985.

Selto, F. "Implementing Activity-Based Management," *Journal of Cost Management,* Summer 1995: 36–49.

Chapter 5

Anderson, S. W., and S. M. Young. *Implementing Management Innovations: Lessons Learned from Activity-Based Costing in the U.S. Automobile Industry.* Boston: Kluwer Academic Publishers, 2001.

Bala Krishnan, R., and N. S. Soderstrom. "The Cost of System Congestion: Evidence from the Health Care Sector." *Journal of Management Accounting Research* 12: 97–114.

Brewer, P. "National Culture and Activity-Based Costing Systems: A Note." *Management Accounting Research,* June 1998: 241–60.

"Call It Dumbsizing: Why Some Companies Regret Cost-Cutting." *The Wall Street Journal,* May 14, 1996: A1.

Compton, T., L. Hoshower, and W. Draeger. "Reengineering Transaction Processing Systems at Cummins Engine." *Journal of Cost Management,* May/June 1998: 6–12.

Convey, S. "Eliminating Unproductive Activities and Processes." *CMA Magazine,* 1991: 20–24.

Maher, M., and M. L. Marais. "A Field Study on the Limitations of Activity-Based Costing When Resources Are Provided on a Joint and Indivisible Basis." *Journal of Accounting Research* 36, no. 1: 129–42.

Noreen, E. "Conditions under Which Activity-Based Costing Systems Provide Relevant Costs." *Journal of Management Accounting Research,* 3: 159–68.

Palmer, C. "Dial Tones for Deadbeats." *Forbes,* November 3, 1997: 81–82.

Pederson, R. B. "Weyerhaeuser: Streamlining Payroll." *Management Accounting* (US), October 1991: 38–41.

Selto, F. "Implementing Activity-Based Management." *Journal of Cost Management,* Summer 1995: 36–49.

Shields, M., and M. McEwen. "Implementing Activity-Based Costing Systems Successfully." *Journal of Cost Management,* Winter 1996: 13–22.

Silver & Gold Record, University of Colorado at Boulder, March 12, 1998.

Stiles, R., and S. Mick. "What Is the Cost of Controlling Quality? Activity-Based Accounting Offers an Answer." *Hospital & Health Services Administration,* Summer 1997: 193.

Turney, P. "Activity-Based Management." *Management Accounting,* January 1992: 20–25.

Chapter 6

Anderson, E. W., C. Fornell, and D. R. Lehmann. "Customer Satisfaction, Market Share and Profitability: Findings from Sweden." *Journal of Marketing* 58, no. 3: 53–66.

Banker, R. D., G. Potter, and D. Srinivasan. "An Empirical Investigation of an Incentive Plan That Includes Nonfinancial Performance Measures." *The Accounting Review* 75, no. 1: 65–92.

Bose, G., and E. Haskell. "Keeping the Ones with the 'Right Stuff.'" *Journal of Lending & Credit Risk Management,* April 1999: 59–62.

Boston Consulting Group. "Naturix-Bowen Case Study-MEL-Training-1st Yr Finance-1999." Melbourne, Australia.

Brady, D. "Why Service Stinks." *BusinessWeek,* October 23, 2000.

Burrows, P. "Sun's Bid to Rule the Web." *BusinessWeek,* July 24, 2000.

Carroll, P., and M. Tadikonda. "Customer Profitability: Irrelevant for Decisions?" *Banking Strategies,* November/December 1997: 76–82.

Green, C. "Profitability Measurement for Small-Business Banking: A Strategic View." *Commercial Lending Review,* Fall 1997.

Ittner, C. D., and D. F. Larcker. "Are Non-Financial Measures Leading Indicators of Financial Performance? An Analysis of Customer Satisfaction." *Journal of Accounting Research,* 36 (supplement): 1–35.

Johnson, H. T. "It's Time to Stop Overselling Activity-Based Concepts." *Management Accounting,* September 1992: 26–35.

Judge, P. C. "Do You Know Who Your Most Profitable Customers Are?" *BusinessWeek,* September 14, 1998.

Kaplan, R. S. "In Defense of Activity-Based Cost Management." *Management Accounting,* November 1992: 58–63.

Parry, C. "Hotels Plan Sector-Wide ABC Model." *Financial Management,* (London) September 2003: 7.

Rust, R. T., and A. J. Zahorik. "Customer Satisfaction, Customer Retention, and Market Share." *Journal of Retailing* 69, no. 2: 193–215.

Chapter 7

Balakrishnan, R., T. Linsmeier, and M. Venkatachalam. "Financial Benefits from JIT Adoption: Effects of Customer Concentration and Cost Structure." *The Accounting Review,* April 1996: 183–205.

Barker, R. C. "Production Systems without MRP: A Lean Time-Based Design." *Omega International Journal of Management Science* 22, no. 4: 394–60.

Billesbach, T., and R. Hayen. "Long-Term Impact of Just-in-Time on Inventory Performance Measures." *Production and Inventory Management Journal,* 1st Quarter 1994: 62–67.

Brinkman, S., and M. Appelbaum. "The Quality Cost Report: It's Alive and Well at Gilroy Foods." *Management Accounting* (U.S.), September 1994: 61–65.

Carr, L. "Quality: Cost of Quality—Making It Work." *Journal of Cost Management,* Spring 1995: 61–65.

Coy, P. "Researching the Nitty-Gritty of Quality Control," *BusinessWeek.* May 29, 1995.

Deming, W. E. "A Seminal Thinker Takes a Detailed Look at the Quality of Quality." *Automobile Magazine,* October 1991: 106–11.

Dugan, I. J. "If They Can Make It There . . ." *BusinessWeek,* September 16, 1996.

Hof, R. D. "The Sad Saga of Silicon Graphics." *BusinessWeek,* August 4, 1997.

Ittner, C., and D. Larcker. "Total Quality Managment and the Choice of Information and Reward Systems." *Journal of Accounting Research* 33 (supplement): 1–34.

Ittner, C., and D. Larcker. "Quality Strategy, Strategic Control Systems, and Organizational Performance." *Accounting, Organizations and Society* 22, no. 3/4: 293–314.

Kalagnanam, S., and E. M. Matsumura. "Quality: Costs of Quality in an Order Entry Department." *Journal of Cost Management,* Fall 1995: 68–74.

Procter, S. "The Extent of JIT Manufacturing in the UK: Evidence from Aggregate Economic Data." *Integrated Manufacturing Systems* 6, no. 4: 16–25.

Rust, R., A. Zahorik, and T. Keiningham. "Return on Quality (ROQ): Making Service Financially Accountable." *Journal of Marketing,* April 1995: 58–70.

Selto, F., C. Renner, and S. M. Young. "Assessing the Organizational Fit of a JIT Manufacturing System." *Accounting, Organizations and Society* 20: 665–84.

Simpson, P. "As Workers Turn Into Risk-Takers . . . One Plant Really Turns on the Steam." *BusinessWeek,* December 15, 1997 (international edition).

"Two-faced Capitalism." *The Economist,* January 24, 2004.

White, R. "An Empirical Assessment of JIT in U.S. Manufacturers." *Production and Inventory Management Journal* 34, no. 2: 38–42.

Youssef, M. "Measuring the Intensity Level of JIT Activities and Its Impact on Quality." *International Journal of Quality & Reliability Management,* 1995: 59–80.

Chapter 8

Joshi, S., R. Krishnan, and L. Lave. "Estimating the Hidden Costs of Environmental Regulation." *The Accounting Review,* vol. 76, no. 2: 171–198.

Kunes, T. "A Green and Lean Workplace?" *Strategic Finance,* February 2001, p. 71–83; reprinted in Edwards, J., ed., *Emerging Practices in Cost Management.* 2001. Women, Gorham & Lamont, Valhalla, NY.

"Splinters Everywhere." *BusinessWeek,* January 10, 1994.

"Targeting Costs in Process and Service Industries." *Harvard Business Review,* January–February 1996: 93.

Timian, K. A., and M. Fleming. "Toward Diversified Cost Accounting Systems." *National Public Accountant,* vol. 45, no. 1: 24–26.

Chapter 9

"The First Report and Order Re Local Competition." FCC Common Carrier Docket 96–98, Part Two. Deposition by Mr. Dennis L. Rica (MCI, Inc.) for the Ohio Public Utilities Commission. United States Court of Appeals for the Eighth Circuit Opinion No. 96-3321.

"A Power Pinching Way to Recycle Rust-Proof Steel." *BusinessWeek,* November 11, 1991.

Slater, K., and C. Wootton. *A Study of Joint and By-Product Costing in the U.K.* London: The Chartered Institute of Management Accountants, U.K., 1988.

Chapter 10

Dean, G. W., M. P. Moye, and P. J. Blayney. *Overhead Cost Allocation and Performance Evaluation Practices of Australian Manufacturers.* Sydney, Australia: The Accounting and Finance Foundation, 1991.

Fremgren, J. M., and S. S. Liao. *The Allocation of Corporate Indirect Costs.* New York: National Association of Accountants, 1981.

Johnson, H. T., and D. Loewe. "How Weyerhaeuser Manages Corporate Overhead Costs." *Management Accounting,* August 1987: 20–26.

Spicer, B., D. Emmanuel, and M. Powell. *Transforming Government Enterprises.* St. Leonards, Australia: Centre for Independent Studies, 1996.

Wolfson, M. "Empirical Evidence of Incentive Problems and Their Mitigation in Oil and Gas Tax Shelter Programs." In *Principals and Agents,* J. Pratt and R. Zeckhauser, eds. Boston: Harvard Business School Press, 1985.

Zimmerman, J. L. "The Costs and Benefits of Cost Allocations." *The Accounting Review* 54, no. 3: 510–11.

Chapter 11

Anderson, M., R. Banker, and S. Janikiraman. 2003. Are selling, general, and administrative costs "sticky"? *Journal of Accounting Research.*

Anderson, S.W. "Measuring the Impact of Product Mix Heterogeneity on Manufacturing Overhead Cost." *The Accounting Review* 70, no. 3: 363–387.

Balakrishnan, R., M. Peterson, and N. Soderstrom. 2003. Does capacity utilization affect the "stickiness" of cost? University of Iowa working paper.

Banker R.J., G. Potter, and R.G. Schroeder. "An Empirical Analysis of Manufacturing Overhead Cost Drivers." *Journal of Accounting and Economics* 19, no. 1: 115–37.

Ittner, C., D.F. Larcker, and T. Randall. "The Activity-Based Cost Hierarchy, Production Policies and Firm Profitability." *Journal of Management Accounting Research* 9: 143–62.

Maher, M.W., and M.L. Marais. "A Field Study on the Limitations of Activity-Based Costing When Resources Are Provided on a Joint and Indivisible Basis." *Journal of Accounting Research* 36, no. 1: 129–42.

Noreen, E., and N. Soderstrom. "Are Overhead Costs Strictly Proportional to Activity? Evidence from Hospital Service Departments." *Journal of Accounting and Economics* 17, no. 1/2: 255–78.

Subramanium, C., and M. Weidenmeir, 2003. Additional evidence on the stickiness of costs. Texas Christian University working paper.

Chapter 12

"Computer's View of a Hurricane." *USA Today* (*www.usatoday.com/weather/whurl15.htm*).

Dunagan, C. "Report: Washington Orcas Endangered." Scripps Howard News Service, November 18, 2000.

Goldratt, E., and J. Cox. *The Goal.* Great Barrington, MA: North River Press, 1984.

Lamiell, P. "Credit Card Firms Look for New Penalties: G. E. Capital to Charge $25 Fee if Cardholder Pays Off Full Balance." *Boulder Daily Camera,* September 11, 1996.

Rocky Mountain News, June 23, 2001: 11C.

Ruhl, J. "An Introduction to the Theory of Constraints." *Journal of Cost Management,* Summer 1996: 43–48.

Sullivan, R. L. "Exxonsafeway." *Forbes* 157, no. 5: 106.

Chapter 13

"AIDS Gaffes in Africa Come Back to Haunt Drug Industry in the US." *The Wall Street Journal,* April 22, 2001.

Batie, Sandra. "The Environmental Impacts of Genetically Modified Plants: Challenges to Decision Making." *American Journal of Agricultural Economics* 85 168, no. 5 (2003): 1107–1111.

Breitkopf, David. Muted Response After New Visa Charge Revelation. *American Banker.*

Cahan, S., and W.H. Kaempfer, "Industry Income and Congressional Regulatory Legislation: Interest Groups vs. Median Voter." *Economic Inquiry* 3, no. 1 (1992): 47–56.

Carroll, L. *Alice's Adventures in Wonderland,* Chapter 6.

"Cisco Revenue to Fall Well Short of Estimates Amid Business Slowdown." *The Wall Street Journal,* April 12, 2001.

Drucker, P. "The Five Deadly Business Sins." *The Wall Street Journal,* October 21, 1993: A1.

Evans, J. III, Y.C. Hwang, and N. Nagarajan, "Cost Reduction and Process Reengineering in Hospitals." *Journal of Cost Management,* May–June 1997: 20–27.

Kleindorfer, P., H. Kunreuther, and P. Schoemaker. *Decision Sciences: An Integrative Approach.* Cambridge University Press, 1993.

Lauzon, Michael. "Maytag Moving Some Assembly to Mexico." *Plastics News,* September 10, 2001: 5.

"Letting the Masses Name Their Price." *BusinessWeek,* September 18, 2000.

Ortolano, Leonard, and Katherine Kao Cushing. "Grand Coulee Dam 70 Years Later: What Can We Learn?" *Water Resources Development,* 18, no. 3 (2002): 373–390.

Ozanne, M. "Outsourcing: Managing Strategic Partnerships for the Virtual Enterprise." *Fortune* 72, no. 3: S21–22.

Samuelson, Robert J. "What's in a Number?" *Newsweek,* October 23, 1995: 52.

Schmid, A., and C. Hoffman. "Replacing Diesel by Solar in the Amazon: Short-Term Economic Feasibility of the PV-Diesel Hybrid Systems." *Energy Policy* 32 (2004): 881–898.

Schott, Jeffrey. "Unlocking the Benefits of World Trade." *The Economist,* November 1, 2003.

Shank, J. "Strategic Cost Management: New Wine or Just New Bottles?" *Journal of Management Accounting Research,* Fall 1989: 47–65.

Simon, H. "Strategy and Organizational Evolution." *Strategic Management Journal,* 14: (1993) 131–42.

Stewart, Larry. "Master Fleet Decisions by Estimating Life Costs." *Construction Equipment,* April 2001: 47–54.

Chapter 14

Bengtsson, J. "Manufacturing Flexibility and Real Options: A Review." *International Journal of Production Economics* 74 (2001): 213–24.

Garrity, B. and M. Benz. "Real's Listen Purchase Could Affect MusicNet." *Billboard,* May 3, 2003.

Hargrave-Silk, A. "Benetton Uses Ad Budget on UN Humanitarian Campaign." *Media Asia,* April 4, 2003.

Harrington, C. "Socially Responsible Investing," *Journal of Accountancy,* January 2003.

Kaminski, M. "Global Vice Squad." *Wall Street Journal,* June 30, 2003.

Kaplan, R. and A. Atkinson. *Advanced Management Accounting,* 3rd ed. Upper Saddle River, NJ: Prentice Hall, 1998.

McNamee, M., N. Byrnes, and E. Thornton. "Banking's Bigwigs May Be Beyond the Law's Reach," *BusinessWeek,* May 19, 2003.

Milgrom, P., and J. Roberts. "Complementarities and Fit: Strategies, Structure and Organizational Change in Manufacturing." *Journal of Accounting and Economics,* 19, no. 2–3, 179–208.

Miller, P., and T. O'Leary, "Capital Budgeting Practices and Complementarity Relations in the Transition to Modern Manufacture: A Field-Based Analysis." *Journal of Accounting Research,* 35, no. 2, 257–71.

Nichols, N. "Scientific Management at Merck: An Interview with CFO Judy Lewent." *Harvard Business Review,* January–February 1994.

Takezawa, N. "A Real Option Valuation of Delivery Time Uncertainty." Working paper, International University of Japan, June 2003.

XINHUA. "Time Warner Spearheads China's Potentially Huge Cinema Market." EBSCO Publishing, June 19, 2003.

Chapter 15

Aldea, D. M., and D. E. Bullinger, "Using ABC for Shared Services, Charge-Outs, Activity-Based Budgeting, and Benchmarking." In *Activity-Based Management: Arthur Andersen's Lessons from the ABM Battlefield.* S. Player and D. E. Keys, eds. New York: John Wiley & Sons, 1999: 152–58.

Borjesson, S. "A Case Study on Activity-Based Budgeting," *Journal of Cost Management* 10, no. 4: 7–18.

Brimson, J., and J. Antos. *Driving Value Using Activity Based Budgeting.* New York: John Wiley & Sons, 1999.

Chen, Q. "Cooperation in the Budgeting Process," *Journal of Accounting Research,* December, 2003: 775–96.

Collins, J. "Advanced Use of ABM: Using ABC for Target Costing, Activity-Based Budgeting, and Benchmarking." In *Activity-Based Management: Arthur Andersen's Lessons from the ABM Battlefield.* S. Player and D. E. Keys, eds. New York: John Wiley & Sons, 1999: 152–58.

Covaleski, M. A., J. H. Evans III, J. L. Luft, and M. D. Shields. "Budgeting Research: Three Theoretical Perspectives and Criteria for Selective Integration." *Journal of Cost Management,* 2003:3.

Fisher, J. G., S. A. Peffer, and G. B. Sprinkle. "Budget-Based Contracts, Budget Levels, and Group Performance." *Journal of Cost Management,* 2003:51.

Hansen, S. C., D. T. Otley, and W. A. Van der Stede. "Practice Developments in Budgeting: An Overview and Research Perspective." *Journal of Cost Management,* 2003:95.

Hornyak, S. "Budgeting Made Easy." *Management Accounting,* October 1998: 18–23.

Kaplan, R. S., and R. Cooper. *Cost and Effect.* Boston: Harvard Business School Press, 1998: 301–15.

McLemore, I. "Reinventing the Budget." *Controller,* August 1998: 87–90.

Rankin, F. W., S. T. Schwartz, and R. A. Young. *Journal of Cost Management,* 2003:75.

Chapter 16

Adler, P. "Time and Motion Regained." *Harvard Business Review,* January/February 1993: 97–108.

Anderson, S. W., and K. Sedatole. "Designing Quality into Products: "The Use of Accounting Data in New Product Development." *Accounting Horizons,* September 1998: 213–233.

Boll, D. "How Dutch Pantry Accounts for Standard Costs." *Management Accounting,* October 1982: 32.

Bonsack, R. A. "Does Activity-Based Costing Replace Standard Costing?" *Journal of Cost Management,* Winter 1990: 46–47.

"Boosting Productivity at American Express." *BusinessWeek,* October 5, 1981.

Carr, L., and C. Ittner. "Measuring the Cost of Ownership." *Journal of Cost Management,* Fall 1992: 42–51.

Cooper, R. *When Lean Enterprises Collide.* Boston: Harvard Business School Press, 1995: 241–42.

Ellram, L. M. "Activity-Based Costing and Total Cost of Ownership: A Critical Linkage." *Journal of Cost Management,* Winter 1994: 22–30.

Gaiser, B. "German Cost Management Systems." *Journal of Cost Management,* September/October 1997: 35–41.

Johnson, H. T. "Performance Measurement for Competitive Excellence." In *Measures for Manufacturing Excellence.* R. S. Kaplan, ed. Boston: Harvard Business School Press, 1990: 63–90.

Kaplan, R. S. "Limitations of Cost Accounting in Advanced Manufacturing Environments." In *Measures for Manufacturing Excellence.* Robert S. Kaplan, ed. Boston: Harvard Business School Press, 1990: 1–14.

Monden, Y., and K. Hamada. "Target Costing and Kaizen Costing in Japanese Automobile Companies." *Journal of Management Accounting Research* 3 (1991): 16–17.

Monden, Y., and J. Lee. "How a Japanese Auto Maker Reduces Costs." *Management Accounting,* August 1993: 24.

Patell, J. M. "Cost Accounting, Process Control, and Product Design: A Case Study of the Hewlett-Packard Personal Office Computer Division." *The Accounting Review,* October 1987: 808–37.

Schiff, J. B. "ABC at Lederle." *Management Accounting,* August 1993: 58.

Sharman, P. "German Cost Accounting." *Strategic Finance,* December 2003: 31–38.

Shirouzu, N. "When Hybrid Cars Collide." *The Wall Street Journal,* February 6, 2003: B1.

Sukurai, M. "The Influence of Factory Automation on Management Accounting Practices: A Study of Japanese Companies." In *Measures for Manufacturing Excellence,* Robert S. Kaplan, ed. Boston: Harvard Business School Press, 1990: 39–62.

"Up to Speed: United Parcel Service Gets Deliveries Done by Driving Its Workers." *The Wall Street Journal,* April 22, 1986.

Chapter 17

Aeppel, T. "On Factory Floors, Top Workers Hide Secrets for Success." *The Wall Street Journal,* July 1, 2002: A1, A10.

Gaiser, B. "German Cost Management Systems." *Journal of Cost Management,* September/October 1997: 35–41.

Greeson, C.B., and M.C. Kocakulah. "Implementing an ABC Pilot at Whirlpool." *Journal of Cost Management,* March/April 1997:16–21.

Kaplan, R. S. "Flexible Budgeting in an Activity-Based Costing Framework." *Accounting Horizons,* June 1994: 104–9.

Mak, Y. T., and M. L. Roush. "Flexible Budgeting and Variance Analysis in an Activity-Based Costing Environment." *Accounting Horizons,* June 1994: 93–103.

Malcolm, R.E. "Overhead Control Implications of Activity Costing." *Accounting Horizons,* December 1991: 69–78.

Moscove, S.A. "Enhancing Detective Controls through Performance Reporting," *Journal of Cost Management,* March/April 1998: 28.

Sharman, P. "German Cost Accounting." *Strategic Finance,* December 2003: 30–38.

Chapter 18

Banker, R., G. Potter, and D. Drinivasan. "An Empirical Investigation of an Incentive Plan that Includes Nonfinancial Performance Measures." *The Accounting Review,* 75: 65–92.

Biddle, G., R. Bowen, and J. Wallace. "Economic Value Added: Some Empirical EVAdence."

Biddle, G. C., R. M. Bowen, and J. S. Wallace. "Does EVA® Beat Earnings? Evidence on Associations with Stock Returns and Firm Values." *Journal of Accounting and Economics,* 24, no. 3, December 1997, pp. 301–36.

Bromwich, M., and M. Walker. "Residual Income Past and Future." *Management Accounting Research,* 5, no. 9: 391–419.

Butler, S., and M. Maher. *Management Incentive Compensation Plans.* Montvale, NJ: Institute of Management Accountants, 1986.

Dierks, P. A., and A. Patel. "What Is EVA® and How Can It Help Your Company?" *Management Accounting,* 79, no. 5, November 1997, pp. 52–58.

Freedman, J. "New Research Red Flags EVA® for Stock Picks," *Management Accounting,* 79, no. 7, January 1998, pp. 62–63.

Ittner, C., and D. Larcker. "Innovation in Performance Measurement: Trends and Research Implications." *Journal of Management Accounting Research,* 1998: 205–38.

Ittner, C., and D. Larcker. "The Use of Subjectivity in Multi-Criteria Bonus Plans." Working paper, The Wharton School, 1999.

McNair, C. J. "Interdependence and Control: Traditional vs. Activity-Based Responsibility Accounting." *Journal of Cost Management,* Summer 1990: 15–23.

Rappaport, A. *Creating Shareholder Value: A Guide for Managers and Investors.* Free Press, 1997.

Towry, K. L. "Control in a Teamwork Environment—The Impact of Social Ties on the Effectiveness of Mutual Monitoring Contracts." *The Accounting Review,* October 2003, pp. 1069–1096.

Wallace, J. S. "Adopting Residual Income-Based Compensation Plans: Do You Get What You Pay For?" *Journal of Accounting and Economics,* 24, no. 3, pp. 275–300.

Zimmerman, A. "7-Eleven, Amid Pressures, Makes Big Bets." *The Wall Street Journal,* April 25, 2002.

Chapter 19

Benke, R., and J. Edwards. *Transfer Pricing: Techniques and Uses.* New York: National Association of Accountants, 1980.

Borkowski, S. "Environmental and Organizational Factors Affecting Transfer Pricing: A Survey." *Journal of Management Accounting Research,* 2 (1990): 1–15.

FASB. *Statement of Financial Accounting Standards No. 14.* "Financial Reporting for Segments of a Business Enterprise." Stamford, CT: FASB, 1976.

FASB. *Statement of Financial Accounting Standards No. 69.* "Disclosures About Oil and Gas Producing Activities." Stamford, CT: FASB, 1982.

King, N. Jr. "Is Wolverine Human? A Judge Answers No; Fans Howl in Protest." *The Wall Street Journal,* January 20, 2003: A1, A5.

Sahay, S. A. "Transfer Pricing Based on Actual Cost." *Journal of Cost Management,* (2003): 177–192.

Tang, R. "Canadian Transfer Pricing Practices." *CA Magazine,* March 1980.

Tang, R. "Transfer Pricing in the 1990s." *Management Accounting,* February 1991: 25.

Tang, R., C. Walter, and R. Raymond. "Transfer Pricing—Japanese vs. American Style." *Management Accounting,* January 1978.

Chapter 20

Anthony, R. N., and D. W. Young. 1988. *Management Control in Nonprofit Organizaions*. 4th ed., Homewood, IL: R. D. Irwin.

Banker, R., G. Potter, and D. Srinivasan. "An Empirical Investigation of an Incentive Plan that Includes Nonfinancial Performance Measures." *The Accouning Review*, 75: 65–92.

Chow, C., K. Haddad, and J. Williamson. 1997. "Applying the Balanced Scorecard to Small Companies." *Management Accounting* (U.S.), August v. 79(2): 21–7.

Crock, S., and G. Smith. 1996. "They Snoop to Conquer." *BusinessWeek,* October 28, (3499):172–5 .

Crystal, G. 1991. "Why CEO Compensation is so High." *California Management Review,* Fall: 9–29.

Deutsch, C., and B. Feder. 2003. "A Radio Chip in Every Consumer Product." *The New York Times,* February 25: C1.

Epstein, M., and J. F. Manzoni. "The Balanced Scorecard and Tableau de Bord: Translating Strategy into Action." *Management Accounting,* August 1997: 28–36.

Galloro, V., and L. Benko. 2003. "Are They Worth It?" *Modern Healthcare,* 33(31): 6–8.

Green, T. B. 1992. *Performance and Motivation Strategies for Today's Workforce: A Guide to Expectancy Theory Applications.* Westport, CT: Greenwood Publishing Group.

Hall, B. 2000. "What You Need to Know About Stock Options." *Harvard Business Review,* March-April: 121–200.

"Harrisburg Hospital v. Dauphin County Board of Assessment Appeals." Commonwealth Court of Pennsylvania 708 A.2d 1284 (1998).

Healy, P. 1985. "The Effect of Bonus Schemes on Accounting Procedures and Accrual Decisions." *Journal of Accounting and Economics,* v 7 (1/3): 85–107.

Ittner, C., and D. Larcker. 2003. "The Use of Subjectivity in Multi-Criteria Bonus Plans." *The Accounting Review,* v. 78 (3): 725–68.

Ittner, C., and D. Larcker. 1998. "Are Non-Financial Measures Leading Indicators of Financial Performance?" *Journal of Accounting Research,* v. 36 (supplement): 1–35.

Ittner, C. D., and D. F. Larcker. 1998. "Innovations in Performance Measurement: Trends and Research Implications." *Journal of Management Accounting Research,* v10(1): 205–238.

Jensen, M., and K. Murphy. 1990. "CEO Incentives—It's No How Much You Pay, But How." *Harvard Business Review,* v68(3): 138–153.

Kaplan, R. S., and D. P. Norton. 1996. *The Balanced Scorecard.* Boston, MA: Harvard Business School Press.

Kaplan, R. S., and D. P. Norton. 2000. *The Strategy-Focused Organization.* Boston, MA: Harvard Business School Press.

Kerr, S. 1995. "On the Folly of Rewarding A, While Hoping for B." *Academy of Management Executive*, v. 9 (1): 7–14.

Lipe, M. G., and S. Salterio. 2000. "The Balanced Scorecard: Judgmental Effects of Information Organization and Diversity." *The Accounting Review,* v. 75 (3), July: 283–98.

Lo, K. 2003. "Economic Consequences of Regulated Changes in Disclosure: The Case of Executive Compensaion." *Journal of Accounting and Economics,* v. 35: 285–314.

Locke, E. A., and G. P Latham. 1990. *A Theory of Goal Setting and Task Performance.* Englewood Cliffs, NJ: Prentice Hall.

Malina, M., and F. Selto. 2001. "Communicating and Controlling Strategy: An Empirical Study of the Effectiveness of the Balanced Scorecard." *Journal of Management Accounting Research,* v. 13: 47–90.

Maher, M. 1987. "The Use of Relative Performance Evaluation in Organizations." In *Accounting and Management Field Study Perspectives,* edited by W. Bruns and R. Kaplan. Boston, MA: Harvard Business School Press: 295–315.

Maremont, M., and J. Barnathan. 1995. "Blind Ambition." *BusinessWeek*, October 23, n. 3447: 18–87.

Maremont, M. 1995. "Judgment Day at Bausch & Lomb." *BusinessWeek*, December 25, n. 3456: 39.

Mathiason, N. 2003. "Failing Fund Men Pile on the Pounds." *The Observer,* May 4, business pages: 8.

Murray, S. 2003. "Investors and Insurers Face Up to the Impact of Climate Change and Subsequent Environmental Disasters." *Financial Times,* October 16: 6.

Nyberg, A. 2003. "Whistle-Blower Woes." *CFO Magazine,* October 23, v. 19 (13): 50–7.

Payne, M. "Employee Theft a Rising Concern." *Sacramento Bee,* December 3, 2000.

Rappaport, A. *Creating Shareholder Value: A Guide for Managers and Investors.* Free Press, 1997.

Rucci, A., S. Kirn, and R. Quinn. 1998. "The Employee-Customer-Profit Chain at Sears." *Harvard Business Review,* Jan–Feb: 83–97.

Strand, C. A., S. T. Welch, S. A. Holmes, and R. H. Strawser. "Are Your Vendors Stealing from You?" *Strategic Finance,* v. 82 (4): 66–71.

The Wall Street Journal. 1993. "Loose Threads: Dressmaker Leslie Fay is an Old-Style Firm That's in a Modern Fix." February 23: A1, A20.

Weintraub, A. 2002. "For Creditors, the Toy Chest is Empty." *BusinessWeek,* September 23.

Zuene, G. 2000. "Are You Teaching Your Employees to Steal?" *Strategic Finance,* August: 34–39.

Financial services industry, absorption vs.
variable costing, 63
Financial statements, 38; *see also* Income
statement
budgeted financial statements, 461, 598, 601
common-size profit statements, 228–229
costs reported in, 38–44
manufacturing companies, 41–44
retail companies, 40–41
service firms, 40
users of, 38
Finished goods, 44, 47
Finished-goods inventory, 44, 47, 58, 93–94,
102–103
Firewalls, 521
First-in, first-out (FIFO) costing, 298, 311–317
advantages/disadvantages of, 315–317
beginning/ending WIP inventory, 311–317
cost of goods transferred out to WIP
inventory, 314–315
costs per equivalent unit, 313–314
equivalent number of units produced,
312–313
flow of physical units, 311–312
prior department costs, 317
T-accounts, 314–315
total costs to be accounted, 313
"Fishbone" (Ishikawa) cause-and-effect
diagram, 253
Fisher, J. G., 602, 890
Fixed cost behavior, 50
Fixed costs, 49, 54, 58n, 63, 464, 609
variable costs vs., 49–51
Fixed manufacturing overhead, 58
Fixed-overhead budget variance, 701
Fixed-overhead costs, 64
Fixed-overhead variances, 700–703
Fixed-overhead volume variance, 701
Fleming, M., 331, 889
Flexible budget, 690
Flexible-budget variance in revenues, 717n
Flexible budgeting, 653, 655
Flexible capacity, 269
Flexible (lean) organization, 602
Flexible-overhead budgets
activity measure choice, 695–696
activity measure, input or output, 691–692
advantages of, 691
definition of, 690–696
illustration of, 693–694
information technology impact, 696
international use of, 703.
management of overhead costs by, 697
manufacturing technology and, 696
standard-costing system, 694–695
Flexible standard costing, 657, 703
Flowchart, 254–255
Forecasting, 433–435
Formula (in financial model), 468–469
Formula-based evaluations, 840–841
Formula flexible budget, 693–694

Fornell, C., 218, 888
Freedman, J., 768, 891
Fremgren, J. M., 369, 889
Frequency distribution, 250
Full costing; *see* Absorption costing
Full-time equivalents, 296, 369
Functional roles, 13–14
Future events, 556–558
likelihood of occurrence of, 558–559
scenario analysis, 558–559
sensitivity analysis forecast, 558

G

Gaiser, B., 657, 703, 891
Galloro, V., 847, 892
Gantt, Henry, 113
Gantt chart, 113
Garrity, B., 555, 890
General and administrative costs, 220, 224–226
General-operations-level costs, 52
Global transfer-pricing practices, 800–802
Goal congruence, 744
Goal-setting theory, 853
Goals, selection of, 509
Golden handcuffs, 844
Goldratt, E., 482, 889
Goodness of fit, 431
Green, C., 242, 888
Green, T. B., 851, 892
Greeson, C. B., 708, 891
Gross book value, 762–763
Gross margin, 41, 343–344
Guaranteed rates of return, 466n
Gurowka, J., 162, 887

H

Haddad, K., 892
Hall, B., 846, 892
Hamada, K., 670, 891
Hansen, S. C., 602, 890
Hargrave-Silk, A., 555, 890
Harrington, C., 572, 890
*Harrisburg Hospital v. Dauphin County Board
of Assessment Appeals*, 848n
Harvest strategy, 8–9, 12
Haskell, E., 242, 888
Hayen, R., 270, 888
Health care organization, resource use and
resource supply, 193
Healy, P., 846, 892
Hedges, 558n
Hedging action, 477n
Hendry, J., 8, 887
Heteroscedasticity, 439
Hidden costs, 300
High-low method, 421–422
High technology investment, 566

High-volume goods and services, 157
Higher-level resources, 158
Hilton, R. W., 816
Hiring practices, 572–573
Histogram, 250
Historical-cost accounting, 765–766
Historical data analysis
decision-making and, 517
for setting standards, 649
Hjelm, E., 4, 887
Hof, R. D., 246, 888
Hoffman, C., 550, 890
Hold strategy, 8–9, 12
Holding costs, 622
Holmes, S. A., 892
Homoscedasticity, 439
Hornyak, S., 618, 890
Hoshower, L., 208, 887
Human resources, 142, 253
support-service costs, 376, 379
Hwang, Y. C., 539, 889
Hybrid cost-estimation model, 432–433

I

Ideal standard, 650
Idle time, 43
Image, pricing decisions and, 529–530
Imperfect competition, 794
Import duties, 801
Incentive systems, 598, 790, 820; *see also*
Performance-based incentive systems
agency theory of incentives and behavior,
854–855
behavioral theory and, 851–855
CEO compensation (example), 836, 847
desired behavior, 837
ethical aspects of, 847–850
expectancy theory of motivation, 851–853
extrinsic and intrinsic rewards, 853
fundamental principles of, 835–837
goal-setting theory and, 853
nonfinancial performance measures,
768–769
in nonprofit organizations, 848
role for theories of incentives and
behaviors, 837
unintended consequences of, 836, 854
Income, measurement of, 761–766
Income statement
absorption-costing, 59–60
alternative product-costing systems effects,
58–66
cost of goods, 108
manufacturing companies, 41–45
overproduction of inventory, 65–66
reconciliation under absorption and variable
costing, 61–62
retail companies, 40
retailer (example), 40
schedule of cost of goods manufactured and
sold, 45–47